About the author

JAMES HALLIDAY is Australia's most respected wine writer. Over the past thirty-plus years he has worn many hats: lawyer, winemaker and grape grower, wine judge, wine consultant, journalist and author. He has discarded his legal hat, but actively continues in his other roles, incessantly travelling, researching and tasting wines in all the major wine-producing countries. He judges regularly at wine shows in Australia, the UK, the US, South Africa and New Zealand.

James Halliday has written or contributed to more than 50 books on wine since he began writing in 1979 (notable contributions include those to the *Oxford Companion to Wine* and the *Larousse Encyclopedia of Wine*). His books have been translated into Japanese, French, German, Danish and Icelandic, and have been published in the UK and US as well as Australia.

His works include *Classic Wines of Australia and New Zealand* (third edition), *Wine Odyssey: A Year of Wine, Food and Travel* and *Varietal Wines*.

JAMES HALLIDAY
AUSTRALIAN
WINE
COMPANION

JAMES HALLIDAY

WINE
COMPANION

2005
EDITION

Collins

Collins

An imprint of HarperCollins*Publishers*

First published as *Australia and New Zealand Wine Companion* in Australia in 1997
This edition published in Australia in 2004
by HarperCollins*Publishers* Pty Limited
ABN 36 009 913 517
A member of HarperCollins*Publishers* (Australia) Pty Limited Group
www.harpercollins.com.au

Published in the United Kingdom in 2004
by Collins
Collins is a registered trademark of HarperCollins*Publishers* Ltd
The Collins website address is www.collins.co.uk

HarperCollins*Publishers*
25 Ryde Road, Pymble, Sydney, NSW 2073, Australia
31 View Road, Glenfield, Auckland 10, New Zealand
77–85 Fulham Palace Road, London W6 8JB, United Kingdom
2 Bloor Street East, 20th floor, Toronto, Ontario M4W 1A8, Canada
10 East 53rd Street, New York NY 10022, USA

ISBN 0 7322 8023 0 (Australia)
ISBN 0 00 719 783 7 (UK)
ISSN 1448-3564

A catalogue record for this book is available from the British Library.

Cover and internal design by de Luxe & Associates
Cover photography by Karl Schwerdtfeger
Typeset by HarperCollins in Miller Text 9/10
Printed and bound in Australia by Griffin Press on 60gsm Bulky Paperback White

5 4 3 2 1   04 05 06 07

Contents

INTRODUCTION by James Halliday —————————————————— viii

HOW TO USE THIS BOOK ————————————————————————— x

WINE REGIONS OF AUSTRALIA —————————————————————— xiv

AUSTRALIAN VINTAGE CHART ————————————————————— xvi

BEST OF THE BEST OF AUSTRALIAN WINE 2005 —————————— xix

   Best of the best by variety ———————————————————————— xx

   Special value wines ———————————————————————————— xxix

   Ten of the best new wineries ————————————————————— xxxi

   Best wineries of the regions ————————————————————— xxxiii

AUSTRALIA'S GEOGRAPHICAL INDICATIONS ————————————— xxxv

AUSTRALIAN VINTAGE 2004: A SNAPSHOT ———————————— xxxviii

WINE AND FOOD OR FOOD AND WINE? ——————————————— xlii

GRAPE VARIETY PLANTINGS ————————————————————————— xlv

AUSTRALIAN WINERIES AND WINES 2005 ——————————————— 1

INDEX OF WINERIES (by region) ——————————————————— 603

Introduction

The inclusion of 377 new winery entries (compared to 240 last year, and 188 the year before that) might suggest the helter-skelter rate of growth in the Australian wine industry is continuing to accelerate rather than abate. Indeed, I have tasting notes of wines from another 75 wineries which have entered wine shows I have judged, but which for arcane reasons have declined to furnish the details necessary for an entry in this book.

Thus I have no doubt there will be another substantial increase in the number of new wineries in next year's edition; vineyards planted between 2000 and 2002 will come into production, leading to yet more planned or unplanned ('oh dear, we can't sell our grapes') winery births. If you are one of these new wineries, please send an email to me at jpaulag@ozemail.com.au.

But the 2003 viticultural statistics (see page *xlvii* for further comment) from the Australian Bureau of Statistics (published in late February 2004) came up with an ominous bottom line: plantings as at 2003 barely changed from those of 2002. The figures (in hectares) since 1996 show just how remarkable the near-halt is given the year-on-year growth prior to 2003.

1996	1997	1998	1999	2000	2001	2002	2003
77,682	88,474	98,439	122,915	146,177	148,275	158,549	160,100

However, the small yields of the 2002 and 2003 vintages have been followed by a large yield in 2004, resulting in a massive increase in tonnage (up from 1 329 595 tonnes in 2003 to an estimated 1 730 000 tonnes in 2004) and causing much alarm about overproduction. There is little doubt that there will be significant short-term pain for small and large producers alike, but even greater problems will surface three to five years down the track if new plantings of not less than 10 000 hectares a year fail to materialise.

The point made by analysts from within and without the industry is that Australia will be unable to protect its share in its export markets if production doesn't increase. Our new world competitors are all lifting production (with no pause in plantings) and will be only too happy to take up the slack.

There has also been short-term pain for the *Australian Wine Companion* as I have grappled with the ever-increasing competition for space in a book which (for practical reasons) simply cannot go past 600-plus pages. For the past few years I have been increasingly concerned about the distortion of the individual wine ratings: only the best wines have made it into the book, with all the lesser wines disappearing onto the cutting room floor.

So there has been a radical restructure: instead of providing ratings for just over 50 per cent of the wines I tasted in the 12-month period, I have rated 95 per cent of the wines tasted (not counting multiple tastings of single wines). The only way I could achieve this was to significantly shorten the length of each tasting note, and to only reproduce notes for wines scoring 87 points or above – and in a minority of instances, 86 points. (For details of the points system, see How to Use This Book on the following page.)

With some exceptions, therefore, wines scoring 84 to 86 are given a drinking span, price and points; those between 80 and 83 (everyday wines) are given a price and points; and those below 80 are simply given points.

For similar space constraint reasons, best vintages have been dropped (after all, this is a book about recent releases), and the drinking span simplified by adopting a single year up to which the wine should live and develop. The individual food matches have also been dropped, however, a new section on wine and food matching has been included on page *xlii.*

Overall, the industry remains as dynamic as ever despite the iniquitous tax regime imposed on it by the Federal Government, with its own unique and very special GST (in addition to the standard 10 per cent) of 29 per cent, euphemistically known as WET, or Wine Equalisation Tax. But that is the subject for another book. In the meantime, drink a couple of glasses of fine Australian wine each day, for the overwhelming body of medical research proves you will live longer if you do. You will also be much happier.

– JAMES HALLIDAY

How to use this book

The *Australian Wine Companion* is arranged with wineries in alphabetical order. The entries should be self-explanatory, but here I will briefly take you through the information for each entry.

The major difference between this 2005 edition and those which preceded it is the entirely new approach to tasting notes. Rather than give a restricted number of moderately lengthy tasting notes for the best wines from each winery, and giving no clue about the lesser wines, I have given a rating to all of the thousands of wines tasted for this book, and, as a trade-off, shortened the tasting notes for those wines scoring 87 points or above. Thus last year there were tasting notes for 2700 wines; this year there are tasting notes for 3113 wines, and ratings for the remaining wines.

As mentioned in the introduction, space has also dictated the removal of best vintages, and likewise the individual food match recommendation. Instead of the latter, there is a new section on wine and food matching on page *xlii*.

Winery entries

Cullen Wines ★★★★★

Caves Road, Cowaramup, WA 6284 **REGION** Margaret River
T (08) 9755 5277 **F** (08) 9755 5550
OPEN 7 days 10–4 **WINEMAKER** Vanya Cullen, Trevor Kent **EST.** 1971 **CASES** 20 000

PRODUCT RANGE ($18–82 CD) Flagship wines: Semillon Sauvignon Blanc, Chardonnay, Pinot Noir, Mangan Malbec Petit Verdot Merlot, Diana Madeline Cabernet Sauvignon Merlot; premium wines: Robinson's Riesling, Classic Dry White, Velvet Red, Autumn Harvest; Ellen Bussell White and Red.

SUMMARY One of the pioneers of Margaret River, and has always produced long-lived wines of highly individual style from the substantial and mature estate vineyards. Since the 2003 vintage the vineyard has received A grade certification from the Biological Farmers Association, and received the award as best runner-up for best organic producer (all crops) with less than 5 years' certification ...

WINERY NAME Cullen Wines

Although it might seem that stating the winery name is straightforward, this is not necessarily so. To avoid confusion, wherever possible I use the name that appears most prominently on the wine label, and do not refer to any associated trading name.

RATINGS ★ ★ ★ ★ ★

The winery star system may be interpreted as follows:

★ ★ ★ ★ ★ Outstanding winery regularly producing exemplary wines.
★ ★ ★ ★ ☆ Extremely good; virtually on a par with a five-star winery.
★ ★ ★ ★ Consistently produces high-quality wines.
★ ★ ★ ☆ A solid, reliable producer of good wines.
★ ★ ★ Typically good, but may have a few lesser wines.
★ ★ ☆ Adequate.
NR Normally ascribed where I have not tasted wines from the producer in the past 12 months.

If the ratings seem generous, so be it. The fact is that Australia is blessed with a marvellous climate for growing grapes, a high degree of technological skill, and a remarkable degree of enthusiasm and dedication on the part of its winemakers. Across the price spectrum, Australian wines stand tall in the markets of the world. I see no reason, therefore, to shrink from recognising excellence.

CONTACT DETAILS Caves Road, Cowaramup, WA 6284 T (08) 9755 5277 F (08) 9755 5550

The details are usually those of the winery and cellar door but in a few instances may simply be of the winery; this occurs when the wine is made at another winery under contract and is sold only through retail.

REGION Margaret River

The mapping of Australia into Zones and Regions with legally defined boundaries is now well underway. This edition sees radical changes (and additions) to the regional names and boundaries. Wherever possible the official 'Geographic Indication' name has been adopted, and where the registration process is incomplete, I have used the most likely name. Occasionally you will see 'Warehouse' as the region. This means the wine is made from purchased grapes, in someone else's winery. In other words, it does not have a vineyard or winery in the ordinary way.

OPEN 7 days 10–4

Although a winery might be listed as not open or only open on weekends, some may in fact be prepared to open by appointment. Many will, some won't; a telephone call will establish whether it is possible or not. Also, virtually every winery that is shown as being open only for weekends is in fact open on public holidays as well. Once again, a telephone call will confirm this.

WINEMAKER Vanya Cullen, Trevor Kent

In the large companies the winemaker is simply the head of a team; there may be many executive winemakers actually responsible for specific wines.

EST. 1971

A more or less self-explanatory item, but keep in mind that some makers consider the year in which they purchased the land to be the year of establishment, others the year in which they first planted grapes, others the year they first made wine, others the year they first offered wine for sale, and so on. There may also be minor complications where there has been a change of ownership or a break in production.

CASES 20 000

This figure (representing the number of cases produced each year) is merely an indication of the size of the operation. Some winery entries do not feature a production figure; this is either because the winery (principally but not exclusively the large companies) regard this information as confidential or the information was not available at the time of going to press.

PRODUCT RANGE ($18–82 CD) Flagship wines: Semillon Sauvignon Blanc, Chardonnay, Pinot Noir, Mangan Malbec Petit Verdot Merlot ...

The **price range** (featured at the beginning of the product range) covers the least expensive through to the most expensive wines usually made by the winery in question (where the information was available). Hence there may be a significant spread. That spread, however, may not fully cover fluctuations that occur in retail pricing, particularly with the larger companies. Erratic and often savage discounting remains a feature of the wine industry, and prices must therefore be seen as approximate.

For Australia, this spread has been compounded by the introduction on 1 July 2000 of the Goods and Services Tax (GST) of 10 per cent and the special and uniquely discriminatory Wine Equalisation Tax (WET) of 29 per cent imposed on top of one another in a tax-on-tax pyramid.

I have indicated whether the price is cellar door (CD), mailing list (ML) or retail (R). By and large, the choice has been determined by which of the three methods of sale is most important to the winery. The price of Australian wines in other countries is affected by a number of factors, including excise and customs duty, distribution mark-up and currency fluctuations. Contact the winery for details.

In regard to the **product range**, it is not possible to give a complete list of the wines, particularly for the larger companies. The saving grace is that these days most of the wines are simply identified on their label by their varietal composition.

SUMMARY One of the pioneers of Margaret River, and has always produced long-lived wines of highly individual style from the substantial and mature estate vineyards. Since the 2003 vintage the vineyard has received A grade certification from the Biological Farmers Association, and received the award as best runner-up for best organic producer (all crops) with less than 5 years' certification ...

My summary of the winery. Little needs to be said, except that I have tried to vary the subjects I discuss in this part of the winery entry.

 The vine leaf symbol indicates the 377 wineries that are new entries in this year's listing.

Tasting notes

RATINGS

94–100 ▼▼▼▼▼ Outstanding. Wines of the highest quality, usually with a distinguished pedigree.

90–93 ▼▼▼▼▽ Highly recommended. Wines of great quality, style and character, worthy of a place in any cellar.

87–89 ▼▼▼▼ Recommended. Wines of above average quality, fault-free, and with clear varietal expression.

84–86 ▼▼▼▽ Fair to good. Wines with plenty of flavour (usually varietal) and good balance; free of technical faults.

80–83 ▼▼▼ Everyday wines: price is particularly relevant; under $10 will represent good value.

75–79 ▼▼▽ Also tasted: usually wines with some deficiency, technical or otherwise.

I should emphasise that the ratings are for the vintage(s) specified in the notes. Thus in outstanding vintages such as 2002 many of the red wines in particular have higher points than normal. I also freely acknowledge that the 100-point scale is effectively a 20-point scale, with 0.1 increments if viewed as being out of 20. In international usage the same holds true.

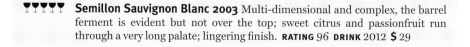

▼▼▼▼▼ **Semillon Sauvignon Blanc 2003** Multi-dimensional and complex, the barrel ferment is evident but not over the top; sweet citrus and passionfruit run through a very long palate; lingering finish. **RATING** 96 **DRINK** 2012 $ 29

The tasting note opens with the vintage of the wine tasted. With the exception of a very occasional classic wine, this tasting note will have been made within the 12 months prior to publication. Even that is a long time, and during the life of this book the wine will almost certainly change. More than this, remember that tasting is a highly subjective and imperfect art. NV = non-vintage. The price of the wine is listed where information is available.

DRINK 2012

Rather than give a span of drinking years, I have simply provided a (conservative) 'best by' date. Modern winemaking is such that, even if a wine has 10 or 20 years' future during which it will gain much greater complexity, it can be enjoyed at any time over the intervening months and years.

Wine regions of Australia

Key to regions

1 Lower Hunter Valley
2 Upper Hunter Valley
3 Hastings River
4 Mudgee
5 Orange
6 Cowra
7 Swan Hill
8 Murray Darling
9 Riverina
10 Perricoota
11 Hilltops
12 Canberra District
12A Gundagai
13 Tumbarumba
14 Shoalhaven
15 Henty
16 Grampians
17 Pyrenees
18 Ballarat
19 Bendigo
19A Heathcote
20 Goulburn Valley
21 Upper Goulburn
22 Rutherglen and Glenrowan
23 King Valley
24 Alpine Valleys and Beechworth
25 Gippsland
26 Mornington Peninsula
27 Yarra Valley
28 Geelong
29 Sunbury
30 Macedon Ranges
31 Northern Tasmania
32 Southern Tasmania
33 Mount Gambier
34 Coonawarra
35 Wrattonbully
36 Mount Benson
37 Padthaway
38 Langhorne Creek
39 McLaren Vale
39A Kangaroo Island
39B Southern Fleurieu Peninsula
40 Adelaide Hills
41 Eden Valley
42 Adelaide Plains
43 Barossa Valley
44 Riverland
45 Clare Valley
46 Southern Eyre Peninsula
47 Great Southern
48 Pemberton and Manjimup
49 Blackwood Valley
50 Margaret River
51 Geographe
52 Peel
53 Perth Hills
54 Swan District
55 South Burnett
55A Queensland Coastal
56 Granite Belt

WA

54 **Perth**
• 53
52
51 49
50 48 47

Australian vintage chart

Each number represents a mark out of ten for the quality of vintages in each region. '-' denotes no rating.

■ RED   ▨ WHITE

NSW

	2000	2001	2002	2003
ORANGE RED	5	6	9	10
WHITE	6	5	9	9
GUNDAGAI RED	-	6	7	6
WHITE	-	6	7	7
LOWER HUNTER VALLEY RED	9	4	8	8
WHITE	9	8	7	7
RIVERINA/GRIFFITH RED	5	5	10	7
WHITE	6	4	8	7
HILLTOPS RED	-	9	9	5
WHITE	-	9	8	6
UPPER HUNTER VALLEY RED	8	5	7	8
WHITE	9	8	7	8
CANBERRA DISTRICT RED	5	8	9	8
WHITE	6	8	8	7
TUMBARUMBA RED	-	7	8	5
WHITE	-	6	6	4
MUDGEE RED	4	5	9	6
WHITE	5	6	7	6
SOUTHERN HIGHLANDS RED	-	-	5	5
WHITE	-	-	5	6
HASTINGS RIVER RED	8	5	9	6
WHITE	9	7	9	6
COWRA RED	6	7	9	8
WHITE	8	7	5	9
PERRICOOTA RED	-	7	9	6
WHITE	-	6	8	6
SHOALHAVEN RED	-	4	7	6
WHITE	-	5	5	7

VIC

	2000	2001	2002	2003
MORNINGTON PENINSULA RED	9	8	8	9
WHITE	8	8	9	8
MACEDON RED	8	7	9	10
WHITE	8	7	8	9
YARRA VALLEY RED	9	7	10	9
WHITE	9	6	9	9
GEELONG RED	9	6	9	8
WHITE	8	6	9	9
SUNBURY RED	8	8	9	9
WHITE	8	9	8	7

Australian Wine Companion 2005 | xvii

	2000	2001	2002	2003
GRAMPIANS	8	8	7	9
	9	7	7	8
PYRENEES	8	9	8	8
	8	7	8	6
HENTY	10	6	8	7
	9	5	8	10
BENDIGO	8	9	9	7
	6	6	7	6
HEATHCOTE	-	8	9	8
	-	7	8	6

	2000	2001	2002	2003
GOULBURN VALLEY	8	8	9	8
	7	7	8	6
UPPER GOULBURN	-	7	9	7
	-	7	7	6
STRATHBOGIE RANGES	-	-	8	8
	-	-	8	7
GLENROWAN & RUTHERGLEN	7	7	10	9
	6	6	9	7
KING VALLEY	8	6	10	7
	8	7	9	8

	2000	2001	2002	2003
ALPINE VALLEYS	8	6	9	4
	7	8	8	4
BEECHWORTH	-	-	8	8
	-	-	7	6
GIPPSLAND	8	8	5	7
	8	7	5	6
MURRAY DARLING	-	5	9	7
	-	5	8	6

SA

	2000	2001	2002	2003
CLARE VALLEY	6	7	10	8
	7	9	10	10
BAROSSA VALLEY	4	8	10	7
	6	5	8	7
EDEN VALLEY	6	9	9	7
	6	8	10	9

	2000	2001	2002	2003
ADELAIDE HILLS	5	8	9	8
	6	8	9	8
ADELAIDE PLAINS	7	8	9	6
	6	7	8	7

	2000	2001	2002	2003
COONAWARRA	6	8	9	9
	7	7	8	8
PADTHAWAY	7	8	9	8
	9	7	9	9
MOUNT BENSON & ROBE	-	5	9	8
	-	7	9	9

	2000	2001	2002	2003		2000	2001	2002	2003		2000	2001	2002	2003
WRATTONBULLY					**SOUTHERN FLEURIEU**					**KANGAROO ISLAND**				
	9	6	8	7		-	7	8	7		-	7	7	7
	8	6	7	8		-	6	8	7		-	6	6	7
McLAREN VALE					**LANGHORNE CREEK**					**RIVERLAND**				
	8	7	9	8		7	7	9	8		7	5	10	8
	8	5	8	7		8	8	7	7		8	6	9	9

WA

	2000	2001	2002	2003		2000	2001	2002	2003
MANJIMUP					**SWAN DISTRICT**				
	-	9	7	6		7	9	10	7
	-	8	8	6		6	6	9	6
MARGARET RIVER					**PEMBERTON**				**PEEL**				

	2000	2001	2002	2003		2000	2001	2002	2003		2000	2001	2002	2003
MARGARET RIVER					**PEMBERTON**					**PEEL**				
	9	10	8	8		8	8	7	6		-	-	8	8
	8	9	8	8		8	8	8	7		-	-	9	8
GREAT SOUTHERN					**GEOGRAPHE**					**PERTH HILLS**				
	7	10	8	7		8	6	7	8		6	6	9	7
	6	8	8	6		9	9	9	8		8	8	8	8

QLD

	2000	2001	2002	2003		2000	2001	2002	2003
GRANITE BELT					**SOUTH BURNETT**				
	10	8	9	8		8	7	7	8
	9	7	8	7		7	6	7	8

TAS

	2000	2001	2002	2003		2000	2001	2002	2003
NORTHERN TASMANIA					**SOUTHERN TASMANIA**				
	9	8	9	7		10	8	9	8
	9	8	9	7		9	8	9	7

Best of the best of Australian wine 2005

As always, I have resisted the temptation to rewrite history, and have left the points where they fell. Single tastings are fallible, and I am sure that there have been omissions (as well as acts of generosity).

Nonetheless, considering the principal vintages – 2003 and 2002 for the whites, 2002 and 2001 for the reds – I am confident that these wines are representative of the best of their variety, and do reflect the vintage conditions.

I have discontinued the 'Dark Horse' listing, but substituted a far larger one: a region-by-region listing of all the five-star wineries. In the majority of instances the ratings are based on the wines currently available, but with some recognition of prior track record.

Best of the best by variety

Riesling

The 2003 vintage in Australia was very good for Riesling, but not quite in the class of 2002: last year's list of 38 wines has dropped to 24 this time around. Perhaps the most notable feature is the number of other cool climate regions – Tasmania, Great Southern and Henty – which have wines in the list.

97	2003 Grosset Polish Hill Riesling
97	2003 Seppelt Drumborg Riesling
96	2003 Elsewhere Vineyard Riesling
96	1999 Pewsey Vale Museum Release The Contours Riesling
96	1998 Pewsey Vale The Contours Eden Valley Riesling
95	2003 Glen Eldon Riesling
95	2003 Granite Hills Knight Riesling
95	1998 Peter Lehmann Eden Valley Reserve Riesling
95	2003 Wellington Riesling
95	2003 Wilson Vineyard DJW Riesling
94	2002 Abbey Creek Vineyard Riesling
94	2003 Crawford River Riesling
94	2003 Ferngrove Vineyards Cossack Riesling
94	2003 Freycinet Riesling
94	2003 Geoff Weaver Lenswood Riesling
94	2003 Goundrey Reserve Riesling
94	2003 Grosset Watervale Riesling
94	2003 Hungerford Hill Clare Valley Riesling
94	2003 Moorilla Estate Riesling
94	2003 Nepenthe Vineyards Adelaide Hills Riesling
94	2003 O'Leary Walker Watervale Riesling
94	2003 Sandalford Riesling
94	2002 Wine & Truffle Company Riesling
94	2003 Wolf Blass Gold Label Riesling

Semillon

Twenty wines, the same as there were in the 2003 *Australian Wine Companion*. While the Hunter Valley dominates, there is (as with Riesling) a significant contribution from other regions and hence other styles.

96   2003 Keith Tulloch Semillon
96   1998 McWilliam's Mount Pleasant Lovedale Semillon
96   2002 Wills Domain Semillon
95   2003 Ferngrove Vineyards Estate Leaping Lizard Semillon
95   1996 McWilliam's Mount Pleasant Museum Elizabeth Semillon
95   1997 Tyrrell's Belford Semillon
94   2001 Alkoomi Wandoo
94   1998 Brokenwood ILR Reserve Semillon
94   2002 Colvin Semillon
94   2002 Juniper Estate Semillon
94   2003 Margan Family Beltree Semillon
94   1995 McWilliam's Mount Pleasant Museum Elizabeth Semillon
94   2003 Merum Semillon
94   2002 Mount Horrocks Semillon
94   2003 Nightingale Semillon
94   2003 Pothana Belford Semillon
94   2002 Pothana Belford Semillon
94   2001 Tintagel Semillon
94   1998 Tyrrell's Stevens Reserve Semillon
94   2003 Tyrrell's Vat 1 Semillon

Sauvignon Blanc and blends – and a few others

An odd assembly of spotted dogs, albeit with exactly 50 per cent contributed by Semillon Sauvignon Blanc blends and another 20 per cent plus by Sauvignon Blanc. But I never expected to find two Verdelhos in such august company.

96   2003 Cullen Semillon Sauvignon Blanc
95   2003 Grosset Semillon Sauvignon Blanc
95   2002 Rosabrook Estate Semillon Sauvignon Blanc
94   2003 Craigow Gewurztraminer
94   2003 Ferngrove Vineyards Semillon Sauvignon Blanc
94   2003 Robert Channon Verdelho
94   2003 Shaw & Smith Sauvignon Blanc
94   2003 Stella Bella Sauvignon Blanc
94   2002 Suckfizzle Sauvignon Blanc Semillon
94   2003 West Cape Howe Sauvignon Blanc
94   2003 Wise Single Vineyard Verdelho
94   2003 Xanadu Sauvignon Blanc Semillon
94   2003 Xanadu Semillon Sauvignon Blanc
94   2002 Yalumba The Virgilius

Chardonnay

This is getting out of control: 67 wines compared to 47 last year, and 36 the year before. But I believe it reflects a concerted push by Australia's winemakers towards more subtlety, finesse and elegance. (Those on 94 points are listed in abbreviated form in alphabetical running text format.)

97	2001 Leeuwin Estate Art Series Chardonnay
96	2002 Bindi Chardonnay
96	2002 Bindi Quartz Chardonnay
96	2002 Cullen Chardonnay
96	2001 Devil's Lair Chardonnay
96	2000 Penfolds Yattarna Chardonnay
96	2002 Tarrington Vineyards Chardonnay
95	2001 Caledonia Australis Chardonnay
95	2002 Carlei Estate Yarra Valley Chardonnay
95	2000 Cope-Williams Chardonnay
95	2002 Domaine Chandon Green Point Reserve Chardonnay
95	2001 Geoff Weaver Lenswood Chardonnay
95	2002 Houghton Pemberton Chardonnay
95	2000 Leeuwin Estate Art Series Chardonnay
95	2001 Leura Park Estate Chardonnay
95	2000 Metier Tarraford Vineyard Chardonnay
95	2002 Montalto Vineyards Chardonnay
95	2001 Petaluma Piccadilly Vineyard Chardonnay
95	2001 Petaluma Tiers Chardonnay
95	2002 Shaw & Smith M3 Vineyard Chardonnay
95	2002 Toolangi Vineyards Reserve Chardonnay
95	1999 Yarra Burn Bastard Hill Chardonnay
95	2002 Yering Station Reserve Chardonnay
94	2002 Ashton Hills, 2002 Balnaves, 2002 Bannockburn Vineyards, 2002 Barratt, 2002 Barringwood Park, 2002 by Farr, 2002 Cape Mentelle, 2002 Cassegrain Fromenteau Reserve, 2002 Chalkers Crossing Tumbarumba, 2002 Clyde Park Vineyard Reserve, 2002 Curlewis, 2003 Deep Woods Estate Boneyard, 2002 Diamond Valley Yarra Valley, 2002 Eagle Vale, 2002 Eldridge Estate, 2001 Farawell, 2002 Farr Rising Geelong, 2001 Goundrey Reserve, 2002 Grosset Piccadilly, 2001 Hardys Eileen Hardy, 2002 Henschke Lenswood Croft, 2002 Howard Park, 2003 Jamiesons Run Limestone Coast, 2002 MadFish, 2002 Main Ridge Estate, 2000 Mantons Creek Vineyard, 2002 Montgomery's Hill, 2002 Montrose Stony Creek, 2002 Moorooduc Estate, 2002 Narkoojee Reserve, 2002 Pierro, 2000 Pipers Brook Vineyard The Summit, 2000 Providence Vineyards

Miguet Reserve, 1998 Providence Vineyards Monet Reserve, 2001 Red Hill Estate Classic Release, 2001 Reynolds Vineyards Moon Shadow, 2002 Scotchmans Hill, 2002 Shadowfax, 2002 Starvedog Lane, 2002 Tamar Ridge Friends, 2002 Vale Vineyard, 2002 Voyager Estate, 2002 Wedgetail Estate, 2001 Wellington.

Sparkling and Sweet

A marriage of convenience, purely to save space in an increasingly congested section of the book. However, the wines deserve their place.

96	1999 Jansz
96	1999 Yarrabank Cuvee
95	1997 Brown Brothers Patricia Pinot Noir Chardonnay Brut
95	1999 Clover Hill
95	2001 Domaine Chandon Vintage Brut
95	1998 Pipers Brook Pirie Cuvee
95	1999 Yellowglen Vintage Cuvee Victoria
94	1998 Delamere Cuvee
94	1999 Domaine Chandon Brut Rose
94	1997 Domaine Chandon Yarra Valley Brut
94	1999 Hardys Sir James Vintage
94	1996 Jansz Late Disgorged
94	2000 Lillypilly Estate Noble Blend
94	1999 Mount William Blanc de Blanc
95	1999 Brown Brothers Patricia Noble Riesling
95	2001 Craigow Botrytis Riesling
94	2002 De Bortoli Noble One
94	2001 De Bortoli Noble One
94	NV Wild Broke Idlewild Succo del Sol
94	2001 Tamar Ridge Josef Chromy Botrytis
94	2003 Westend Estate 3 Bridges Golden Mist Botrytis Semillon

Pinot Noir

Exactly the same number (38) as there were last year, driven by the cool 2002 vintage which favoured the southern regions of mainland Australia, and which answered the challenge of Tasmania's 2001 wines. (Those on 94 points are listed in abbreviated form in alphabetical running text format.)

96	2002 Barratt The Reserve Pinot Noir
96	2002 Curlewis Reserve Pinot Noir
96	2002 Diamond Valley Vineyards Close Planted Pinot Noir
96	2002 Frogmore Creek Reserve Pinot Noir
96	2002 Tarrington Vineyards Pinot Noir
95	2002 Bannockburn Vineyards Pinot Noir
95	2000 Bannockburn Vineyards Serre Pinot Noir
95	2002 Barratt The Bonython Pinot Noir
95	2002 Bindi Original Vineyard Pinot Noir
95	2002 Diamond Valley Estate Pinot Noir
95	2001 Domaine Chandon Green Point Reserve Pinot Noir
95	2002 Eldridge Estate Pinot Noir
95	2002 Farr Rising Mornington Pinot Noir
95	2002 Freycinet Pinot Noir
95	2002 Morning Star Estate Pinot Noir
95	2002 Phillip Island Vineyard Gippsland Pinot Noir
95	2001 Port Phillip Estate Pinot Noir
94	2002 Ashton Hills, 2000 Candlebark Hill Reserve, 2002 Charlotte's Vineyard, 2002 Chatto Tamar Valley, 2001 Curly Flat, 2002 De Bortoli Yarra Valley, 2001 De Bortoli Yarra Valley, 2002 del Rios Reserve Bendigo, 2001 Diamond Valley Close Planted, 2002 ese Vineyards, 2001 Meure's Wines d'Meure, 2002 Paringa Estate Peninsula, 2002 Patrick's Vineyard, 2002 Port Phillip Estate, 2002 Providence Vineyards Miguet Reserve, 2002 Rochford's Eyton E Yarra Valley, 2002 Scorpo, 2002 Tamar Ridge, 2001 Tarrington Vineyards Cuvee Emilie, 2002 Yarra Ridge, 2002 Yering Station Reserve.

Shiraz

Thirty-four Shirazs on 95 points or more, compared to 32 last year. The huge group of 77 wines on 94 points precludes even a running list. The majority of those 77 wines are from 2002, and in turn from south-eastern Australia. In the following list, 2002 and 2001 are the dominant players; I suspect that next year 2002 will be even stronger as the most expensive (and best) wines are progressively released.

97	2000 McWilliam's Mount Pleasant Maurice O'Shea Shiraz
96	2002 Bannockburn Vineyards Shiraz
96	2001 Best's Thomson Family Shiraz
96	2002 Clyde Park Vineyard Shiraz
96	2001 Flinders Bay Shiraz
96	1999 Henschke Hill Of Grace

96	2000 Houghton Frankland Shiraz
96	2002 Journeys End Vineyards Beginning Shiraz
96	2002 Kalleske Greenock Shiraz
96	1999 Saltram No. 1 Reserve Shiraz
96	2002 Schubert Estate Goose Yard Block Shiraz
96	2002 Torbreck The Descendant
95	2000 Annie's Lane Copper Trail Shiraz
95	2001 Balnaves of Coonawarra Shiraz
95	2001 Bannockburn Shiraz
95	2002 Bidgeebong Gundagai Shiraz
95	2001 Bremerton Old Adam Shiraz
95	2001 Brokenwood Graveyard Shiraz
95	2002 Shiraz by Farr
95	1999 Grant Burge Meshach Shiraz
95	2002 Hanging Rock Heathcote Shiraz
95	2000 Hardys Tintara Limited Release Shiraz
95	1993 Huntington Estate Special Reserve Shiraz
95	2001 Kingston Estate Echelon Shiraz
95	2002 Mitolo Reiver Barossa Shiraz
95	2002 Mr Riggs Shiraz
95	1999 Penfolds Grange
95	2001 Plantagenet Mount Barker Shiraz
95	2000 Rosemount Estate Balmoral Syrah
95	1999 Seppelt St Peters Shiraz
95	2002 Shadowfax Werribee Shiraz
95	2001 Wirra Wirra RSW Shiraz
95	2002 WJ Walker Lake Grace Shiraz
95	2001 Wolf Blass Platinum Label Adelaide Hills Shiraz

Shiraz blends and other varieties

A marked increase on last year's seven wines; these blends are full of interest and character, and we will see more and more Shiraz Viognier blends at the top.

96	2002 Yering Station Reserve Shiraz Viognier
96	2001 Yering Station Reserve Shiraz Viognier
95	2000 Annie's Lane Copper Trail Shiraz Grenache Mourvedre
95	2002 Chalice Bridge Estate Shiraz Cabernet Sauvignon
95	2002 Clonakilla Shiraz Viognier
95	2002 Henschke Johann's Garden Grenache Shiraz Mourvedre

94	**2001 Charles Melton Nine Popes**
94	**2002 d'Arenberg The Laughing Magpie Shiraz Viognier**
94	**2001 Hewitson Old Garden Mourvedre**
94	**2002 Kalleske Old Vine Grenache**
94	**2000 Lindemans Limestone Ridge**
94	**2002 Neagles Rock Grenache Shiraz**
94	**2002 Pondalowie Vineyards Shiraz Viognier**
94	**2000 Rosemount Estate Mountain Blue Shiraz Cabernet**
94	**2002 Temple Bruer Bin 621 Shiraz Blend**
94	**2002 Warrabilla Parola's Limited Release Durif**
94	**2002 Wolf Blass Gold Label Adelaide Hills Shiraz Viognier**
94	**2001 Yering Station Shiraz Viognier**

Cabernet Sauvignon

Last year 28 wines, this year 35. Here the most important factors are the great 2001 red vintage in Margaret River and Great Southern (as expected) and the outcome of the 2001 vintage in Coonawarra (not so expected). These regions provided a little over half of the wines. Here, too, 2002 waits in the wings. (Those on 94 points are listed in abbreviated form in alphabetical running text format.)

96	**2001 Balnaves of Coonawarra The Tally Reserve Cabernet Sauvignon**
96	**1999 Houghton Gladstones Cabernet Sauvignon**
96	**2000 Jamiesons Run Winemakers Reserve Cabernet Sauvignon**
96	**2001 Ladbroke Grove Killian Vineyard Cabernet Sauvignon**
96	**2001 Vasse Felix Cabernet Sauvignon**
95	**2001 Charles Melton Cabernet Sauvignon**
95	**2001 Majella Cabernet Sauvignon**
95	**2001 Punters Corner Cabernet Sauvignon**
95	**2002 Sandalford Margaret River Cabernet Sauvignon**
95	**2001 Suckfizzle Cabernet Sauvignon**
94	**2002 Abercorn A Reserve, 2002 Balgownie Estate, 2001 Balnaves of Coonawarra, 2001 Best's Great Western, 2000 Chain Of Ponds Amadeus, 2000 Dyson Clarice, 2001 Flying Fish Cove Prize Catch, 2001 Flying Fish Cove Upstream Reserve, 2001 Grove Estate The Partner's Reserve, 2002 Heritage Steve Hoff, 2001 House of Certain Views Coonabarabran, 2002 Hugh Hamilton The Villain, 2001 Jamiesons Run Alexander Block Coonawarra, 2001 Mamre Brook, 2001 Maxwell Reserve Lime Cave, 2002 Maygars Hill, 2001 Plantagenet Mount Barker, 2001 Rockfield Estate Reserve, 2002 Sandhurst Ridge,**

1999 Sandstone, 2002 Tyrrell's Lost Block, 2001 We're Wines, 2001 Wirra Wirra The Angelus, 2001 Xanadu, 2001 Zema Estate.

Cabernet blends, and other Bordeaux varieties

The only group with fewer wines than last year, though not by much. Cooler regions dominate, and are the reason for the strong showing of Merlot as a single variety and as a blend with Cabernet Sauvignon.

96	2000 Majella The Malleea
95	2000 Alkoomi Blackbutt
95	2001 Ferngrove Vineyards The Stirlings
95	2000 Wolf Blass Black Label Cabernet Sauvignon Shiraz
95	1999 Yalumba Signature Cabernet Shiraz
94	2001 Balnaves of Coonawarra The Blend
94	2000 Brand's of Coonawarra Patron's Reserve
94	2002 Cullen Diana Madeline Cabernet Sauvignon Merlot
94	2001 d'Arenberg The Galvo Garage Cabernet Sauvignon Merlot Cabernet Franc
94	2001 Devil's Lair Margaret River
94	2001 Grosset Gaia
94	2001 Haan Wilhelmus
94	2002 Leabrook Estate Cabernet Franc
94	2001 Paracombe Wines The Reuben
94	2001 Parker Coonawarra Estate First Growth
94	2002 Pettavel Platina Merlot Petit Verdot
94	2001 Vasse Felix Heytesbury
95	2001 Plantagenet Rocky Horror Vineyard Merlot
94	2001 Barwang Vineyard Special Release Merlot
94	2002 Capel Vale Howecroft Merlot
94	2002 Farr Rising Geelong Merlot
94	2002 Hackersley Merlot
94	2001 Rosemount Estate Rose Label Orange Vineyard Merlot
94	2002 Shaw & Smith Adelaide Hills Merlot

Fortified wines

An Australian treasure-trove, recently discovered by Robert Parker and the *Wine Spectator*, and long before that by Californian retailer and noted wine judge, Darrell Corti. If there were a single scale simultaneously applied to all Australian wines, you would need to add five points to these scores, or deduct five points from table wine scores.

97	NV All Saints Estate Rare Rutherglen Muscat Museum Release
97	NV All Saints Estate Rare Rutherglen Tokay Museum Release
97	NV Campbells Isabella Rare Rutherglen Tokay
97	NV Chambers Rosewood Rare Rutherglen Muscat
97	NV Morris Old Premium Rare Rutherglen Muscat
97	NV Morris Old Premium Rare Rutherglen Tokay
97	1904 Seppelt 100 Year Old Para Liqueur
97	NV Seppelt Rare Rutherglen Tokay DP59
97	NV Seppelt Show Tawny Port DP90
96	NV All Saints Estate Rare Rutherglen Muscat
96	NV All Saints Estate Rare Rutherglen Tokay
96	NV Seppelt Rare Rutherglen Muscat GR113
96	NV Stanton & Killeen Rare Rutherglen Muscat
95	NV Campbells Grand Rutherglen Tokay
95	NV Campbells Merchant Prince Rare Rutherglen Muscat
95	NV Westfield Liqueur Muscat
95	NV Morris Cellar Reserve Grand Rutherglen Tokay
95	NV Seppelt Show Oloroso Sherry DP38
94	NV All Saints Estate Grand Rutherglen Muscat, NV All Saints Estate Grand Rutherglen Tokay, NV Bullers Calliope Rare Rutherglen Liqueur Tokay, NV Chambers Rosewood Grand Rutherglen Muscat, NV De Bortoli Black Noble, NV Morris Cellar Reserve Grand Rutherglen Muscat, NV Seppelt Amontillado Sherry DP116, NV Seppelt Grand Rutherglen Muscat DP63, NV Seppelt Grand Rutherglen Tokay DP57, NV Seppelt Para Liqueur Port, NV Stanton & Killeen Grand Rutherglen Muscat, 1999 Stanton & Killeen Vintage Port.

Special value wines

As always, these are lists of ten of the best value wines, not the ten best wines in each price category. There are literally dozens of wines with similar points and prices, and the choice is necessarily an arbitrary one. This year, too, space has limited the number of categories to four.

Ten of the best value whites under $10

87	2003 De Bortoli Sacred Hill Semillon Chardonnay $5.50
86	2003 De Bortoli Sacred Hill Traminer Riesling $6.00
86	2003 Yalumba Oxford Landing Sauvignon Blanc $7.95
89	2003 Orlando Jacob's Creek Riesling $8.95
87	2003 Orlando Jacob's Creek Chardonnay $8.95
86	2003 Dominion Vinus Chardonnay $9.95
86	2003 Logan Apple Tree Flat Semillon Sauvignon Blanc $9.95
90	2003 Angove's Long Row Sauvignon Blanc $9.99
86	2003 Evans & Tate Salisbury Chardonnay $9.99
87	2003 Zilzie Buloke Reserve Chardonnay $9.99

Ten of the best value reds under $10

87	2002 Yalumba Oxford Landing Shiraz $6.50
87	2002 Lindemans Cawarra Merlot $7.80
86	2003 McPherson Murray Darling Shiraz Cabernet $8.50
87	2002 Orlando Jacob's Creek Shiraz $8.95
86	2002 Angove's Long Row Cabernet Sauvignon $9.99
87	2001 Carramar Estate Shiraz $9.99
87	2003 Evans & Tate Salisbury Shiraz Cabernet $9.99
86	2002 Poet's Corner PC Merlot $9.99
88	2003 Zilzie Buloke Reserve Alternative Tempranillo $9.99
87	2003 Zilzie Buloke Reserve Alternative Petit Verdot $9.99

Ten of the best value whites $10–$15

91	**2002 Sirromet Vineyard Selection Queensland Semillon** $12.00
94	**2003 Ferngrove Vineyards Semillon Sauvignon Blanc** $13.00
92	**2002 Henry Lawson Semillon** $13.00
93	**2003 Pfeiffer Carlyle Riesling** $14.99
92	**2003 Chapel Hill Unwooded Chardonnay** $14.00
93	**2003 Elliot Rocke Estate Semillon** $14.95
94	**2002 Montrose Stony Creek Chardonnay** $14.99
92	**2003 Angus Sturt Ridge Semillon** $15.00
91	**2003 Bochara Sauvignon Blanc** $15.00
93	**2003 S Kidman Coonawarra Riesling** $15.00

Ten of the best value reds $10–$15

90	**2002 The Long Flat Wine Co Yarra Valley Pinot Noir** $12.00
91	**2003 De Bortoli Windy Peak Pinot Noir** $12.00
90	**2002 Bidgeebong Triangle Shiraz** $12.95
90	**NV Drinkmoor Shiraz** $13.80
91	**2002 St Hallett Gamekeeper's Reserve** $13.95
93	**2001 Andrew Harris Vineyards Shiraz** $14.95
90	**2002 Ceravolo Sangiovese** $15.00
91	**2002 Tuart Ridge Shiraz** $15.00
92	**2002 Wangolina Station Cabernet Sauvignon Shiraz** $15.00
91	**2002 Warby Range Estate Durif** $15.00

Ten of the best new wineries

All these wineries have earned a five-star rating on their first entry into the *Australian Wine Companion*. With the exception of Eagle Vale, Journeys End and Watershed Wines, production is very small, so getting your name on the mailing list is the best way of getting access to the wines.

Eagle Vale MARGARET RIVER page 157

A League of Nations joint venture between property owners Steve (born in Colorado, US) and Wendy Jacobs and the winemaking/operational team of Guy, Chantal and Karl Gallienne (Loire Valley, France); Guy adding an Adelaide University winemaking degree. Both white and red wines excellent.

Journeys End Vineyards WAREHOUSE page 260

A virtual winery using the winemaking skills of Ben Riggs and carefully chosen contract grape growers in various parts of McLaren Vale, the major focus being Shiraz. Slick names and packaging have been developed with exports (to the US in particular) the business driver.

Kalleske Wines BAROSSA VALLEY page 263

After more than a century as grape growers, the Kalleske family made a trial vintage in 1999, and, sufficiently encouraged, established a small on-site winery in time for the 2002 vintage. That vintage no doubt helped, but the Greenock Shiraz and Old Vine Grenache are superb examples of the richest Barossa style.

Peter Howland Wines WAREHOUSE page 399

Peter Howland's background is impeccable: in 1997 graduating with first class Honours in oenology from Adelaide University, and practical experience in regions of ultimate diversity – Hunter Valley, Margaret River, Hastings Valley, Macedon Ranges and Puglia, Italy. His selection of grapes for his first five wines (from 2002) reflects the same diversity, and are of great quality.

Redesdale Estate Wines HEATHCOTE page 428

When Peter Williams and wife Suzanne Arnall-Williams purchased their 25-hectare property in 1988 the vineyard, originally planted in 1982, was in a state of neglect. They rehabilitated the vineyard, started a garden (which is now part of the Victorian Open

xxxii | James Halliday

Garden Scheme), erected a two-storey luxury guest cottage and finally (in 1999) decided to keep part of the crop for their own label. The Shiraz and Cabernets are made by Tobias Ansted at Balgownie, and are of the highest quality.

Schubert Estate BAROSSA VALLEY page 463

The late Max Schubert was not a close relation of Steve and Cecilia Schubert, but I am sure he would be impressed with the estate's Shiraz. Output is tiny, but the quality is truly outstanding, and will repay prolonged cellaring – a feature which Max Schubert sought to achieve when he embarked on the creation of Grange in the early 1950s.

Tintagel MARGARET RIVER page 527

The Westphal family began the establishment of their 8-hectare vineyard in 1993, planted not far from Devil's Lair and Leeuwin Estate. Much of the crop is sold to other makers, but when the decision was taken to have part vinified, it met with immediate success for both wines, Semillon and Shiraz.

Ulithorne MCLAREN VALE page 542

The Ulithorne vineyard was planted in 1971 with the idea that it would absorb the effluent from a piggery which owner Frank Harrison wanted to establish. The local council wasn't convinced, and when son Sam Harrison and partner Rose Kentish purchased the property in 1997 the vineyard was near-derelict. Their hard work in restoring it has paid big dividends.

Watershed Wines MARGARET RIVER page 557

Ownership syndicates of investors seeking income tax relief don't have a great track record. This one does: no expense has been spared in establishing the 40-hectare vineyard and building a striking cellar door sales area complete with a 200-seat café/restaurant. Highly skilled winemaking by Cathy Spratt and consultant John Wade has produced a string of excellent wines since the inaugural 2001 vintage.

Wehl's Mount Benson Vineyards MOUNT BENSON page 560

Peter and Leah Wehl were the first movers in Mount Benson when they planted shiraz and cabernet sauvignon in 1989. For a long time thereafter they sold all the grapes, but eventually moved cautiously into winemaking. Their success was so convincing they have grafted some of the old vines to Sauvignon Blanc and Merlot (to widen the product range) and have upgraded the cellar door, which is open 7 days a week.

Best wineries of the regions

After some soul-searching, I have decided to restrict this listing to five-star wineries; the most immediate consequence being the omission of many regions which are not (this year, or perhaps ever) able to sustain higher winery ratings. This may be particularly hard on four and a half-star (or even four-star) wineries, which may well have had a five-star rating in the past and/or achieve it again in the future. For a start, these ratings are vintage-sensitive, but there are many other variables which affect the outcome. The list is, if you will, a generalisation, as like as not to be proved by the exception. This apart, it represents a little under 10 per cent of the total number of wineries.

ADELAIDE HILLS
Ashton Hills
Barratt
Geoff Weaver
Leabrook Estate
Nepenthe Vineyards
Petaluma
Setanta Wines
Shaw & Smith
The Lane

ALBANY
Phillips Brook Estate

BAROSSA VALLEY
Charles Melton
Dutschke Wines
Heritage Wines
Kaesler Wines
Kalleske Wines
Leo Buring
Penfolds
Schubert Estate
Seppelt
Torbreck Vintners
Wolf Blass

BEECHWORTH
Giaconda

BENDIGO
Sandhurst Ridge

CANBERRA DISTRICT
Brindabella Hills
Clonakilla

CLARE VALLEY
Annie's Lane
Cardinham Estate
Grosset
Jeanneret Wines
Kilikanoon
Leasingham
Neagles Rock Vineyards
O'Leary Walker Wines
Wendouree

COONAWARRA
Balnaves of Coonawarra
Brand's of Coonawarra
Jamiesons Run
Majella
Parker Coonawarra Estate
Punters Corner
Zema Estate

DENMARK
West Cape Howe Wines

EDEN VALLEY
Henschke
Pewsey Vale

FRANKLAND
Alkoomi
Ferngrove Vineyards

GEELONG
Bannockburn Vineyards
by Farr
Clyde Park Vineyard
Curlewis Winery
Farr Rising
Provenance Wines
Scotchmans Hill
Shadowfax Vineyard and
    Winery

GEOGRAPHE
Capel Vale

GIPPSLAND
Bass Phillip
Caledonia Australis

GRAMPIANS
Armstrong Vineyards
Best's Wines
Seppelt Great Western

GRANITE BELT
Robert Channon Wines

HEATHCOTE
Domaines Tatiarra
Jasper Hill
Redesdale Estate Wines

HENTY
Crawford River Wines
Tarrington Vineyards

HILLTOPS
Barwang Vineyard
Chalkers Crossing

LANGHORNE CREEK
Bremerton Wines

LOWER HUNTER VALLEY
Brokenwood
Chateau Pâto
Chatto Wines
Keith Tulloch Wine
Lake's Folly
McWilliam's
    Mount Pleasant
Tyrrell's

MACEDON RANGES
Bindi Wine Growers
Curly Flat
Farawell Wines
Granite Hills
Patrick's Vineyard
Virgin Hills

MARGARET RIVER
Cullen Wines
Devil's Lair
Eagle Vale
Flying Fish Cove
Howard Park
Juniper Estate
Leeuwin Estate
Pierro
Suckfizzle & Stella Bella
Tintagel Wines
Vasse Felix
Voyager Estate
Watershed Wines
We're Wines
Xanadu Normans Wines

McLAREN VALE
d'Arenberg
Gemtree Vineyards
Hardys Reynella
Maxwell Wines
Mitolo Wines
Mr Riggs Wine Company
Reynell
Rosemount Estate
Ulithorne
Wirra Wirra

MORNINGTON PENINSULA
Eldridge Estate
Main Ridge Estate
Merricks Creek Wines
Montalto Vineyards
Moorooduc Estate
Paringa Estate
Port Phillip Estate
Red Hill Estate
Scorpo Wines

MOUNT BARKER
Gilberts
Plantagenet

MOUNT BENSON
Wehl's Mount Benson
    Vineyards

MUDGEE
Huntington Estate

PEMBERTON
Merum
Picardy
Wine & Truffle Company

PYRENEES
Dalwhinnie
Summerfield

RUTHERGLEN
All Saints Estate
Bullers Calliope
Campbells
Chambers Rosewood
Morris
Stanton & Killeen Wines
Warrabilla

SOUTH WEST
AUSTRALIA ZONE
WJ Walker Wines

SUNBURY
Arundel
Craiglee

SWAN VALLEY
Houghton
Sandalford

TASMANIA
Clover Hill
Craigow
Domaine A
Elsewhere Vineyard
Freycinet
Frogmore Creek
Jansz
Milford Vineyard
Moorilla Estate
Pipers Brook Vineyard
Providence Vineyards
Tamar Ridge
Wellington

WAREHOUSE
Hewitson
Journeys End Vineyards
Lengs & Cooter
Peter Howland Wines
Two Hands Wines

YARRA VALLEY
Carlei Estate & Green
    Vineyards
De Bortoli
Diamond Valley Vineyards
Domaine Chandon
Dominique Portet
Lillydale Estate
Metier Wines
Mount Mary
Seville Estate
Yarrabank
Yarra Yarra
Yarra Yering
Yering Station

Australia's Geographical Indications

The process of formally mapping Australia's wine regions continues to ever-so-slowly inch forward. The division into states, zones, regions and subregions follows; those regions or subregions marked with an asterisk are variously in an early or late stage of determination. In two instances I have gone beyond the likely finalisation: it makes no sense to me that the Hunter Valley should be a zone, the region Hunter, and then subregions which are all in the Lower Hunter Valley. I have elected to stick with the traditional division between the Upper Hunter Valley on the one hand, and the Lower on the other.

I am also in front of the game with Tasmania, dividing it into Northern and Southern, and, to a lesser degree, have anticipated that the Coastal Hinterland Region of Queensland will seek recognition under this or some similar name. Those regions and subregions marked with an asterisk have taken, or are likely to take, steps to secure registration; they may or may not persevere.

State/Zone	Region	Subregion
NEW SOUTH WALES		
Big Rivers	Murray Darling Perricoota Riverina Swan Hill	
Central Ranges	Cowra Mudgee Orange	
Hunter Valley	Hunter	Allandale* Belford* Broke Fordwich Dalwood* Pokolbin* Rothbury*
Northern Rivers	Hastings River	
Northern Slopes		
South Coast	Shoalhaven Coast Southern Highlands	

Southern NSW	Canberra District Gundagai Hilltops Tumbarumba	
Western Plains		
SOUTH AUSTRALIA		
Adelaide (Super Zone, above Mount Lofty Ranges, Fleurieu and Barossa)		
Barossa	Barossa Valley Eden Valley	High Eden Springton*
Far North	Southern Flinders Ranges	
Fleurieu	Currency Creek Kangaroo Island Langhorne Creek McLaren Vale Southern Fleurieu	Clarendon*
Limestone Coast	Coonawarra Mount Benson Penola* Padthaway Wrattonbully*	
Lower Murray	Riverland	
Mount Lofty Ranges	Adelaide Hills Adelaide Plains Clare Valley	Gumeracha* Lenswood Piccadilly Valley Auburn* Clare* Hill River* Polish Hill River* Sevenhill* Watervale*
The Peninsulas	Southern Eyre Peninsula*	
VICTORIA		
Central Victoria	Bendigo Goulburn Valley Heathcote Strathbogie Ranges Upper Goulburn	Nagambie Lakes
Gippsland		

North East Victoria	Alpine Valleys	Kiewa Valley*
		Ovens Valley*
	Beechworth	
	Glenrowan	
	King Valley*	Myrrhee*
		Whitlands*
	Rutherglen	Wahgunyah*
North West Victoria	Murray Darling	
	Swan Hill	
Port Phillip	Geelong	
	Macedon Ranges	
	Mornington Peninsula	
	Sunbury	
	Yarra Valley	
Western Victoria	Grampians	
	Henty	
	Pyrenees	

WESTERN AUSTRALIA

Central Western Australia		
Eastern Plains, Inland and North of WA		
Greater Perth	Peel	
	Perth Hills	
	Swan District	Swan Valley
South West Australia	Blackwood Valley	
	Geographe	
	Great Southern	Albany
		Denmark
		Frankland River
		Mount Barker
		Porongurup
	Manjimup*	
	Margaret River	
	Pemberton*	
WA South East Coastal	Esperance*	

QUEENSLAND

Queensland	Granite Belt	
	Coastal Hinterland*	
	South Burnett	

TASMANIA

AUSTRALIAN CAPITAL TERRITORY

NORTHERN TERRITORY

Australian vintage 2004: a snapshot

The best winter rains for several years and mild weather during flowering set the scene for above average yields in many parts of Australia. In turn, it was berry and bunch size that were the principal causes of increased yield, and which prompted severe bunch thinning, both during and after veraison. As the season moved through autumn, dehydration also had an impact in some regions, creating a complex pattern of above average (white) to average (both white and red) and below average (red) yields, the last an exception to prove the rule.

New South Wales

Both the **LOWER** and **UPPER HUNTER VALLEY** experienced the wild swings of weather which so often bedevil these regions. A dry, mild to hot spring got things off to a promising start, followed by Christmas/New Year temperatures of 40–45 degrees C, then mid-January rain (25 mm), then 40 degrees C, then 25–55 mm rain, then more extreme heat, and another 20 mm of rain – all before the end of January. Three weeks of fine, mild weather ended abruptly with 45 degrees C on February 21, then 125 mm of rain falling between February 25 and 27. Early harvested Semillon and Chardonnay fared best, the Shiraz succeeding only with old vines and inspired guesses about picking dates.

MUDGEE fared much better, with good spring weather (apart from severe but isolated frosts) and a warm to hot summer. February brought the two weeks of extreme heat and rainfall (178 mm) experienced in the Hunter, but from there on conditions were perfect, with warm days, cool nights and little rain. The yields were average, white wines fair, the red wines outstanding. **ORANGE** went one better, with both whites and reds excelling thanks to perfect late summer and autumn weather, spring frosts and the burst of February heat the only blemishes. Mudgee picks later than the Hunter, Orange much later, hence the February weather had less impact.

HILLTOPS had its hot weather in the last two weeks of December and in January, whereafter conditions cooled down and remained dry. The white wines will be good especially Riesling; Shiraz and Cabernet Sauvignon better still. **COWRA** had little cause for celebration, the overall quality being described as fair. The **HASTINGS VALLEY** experienced the February heatwave, but all the white wines had been picked by then: Semillon and Verdelho the most successful. The **NORTHERN SLOPES** ran along a similar timetable, the February heat coming just prior to the commencement of harvesting of the white varieties; the prolonged, mild and dry autumn provided ideal conditions for the later-ripening varieties of Shiraz, Merlot, Barbera and Cabernet Sauvignon.

The **CANBERRA DISTRICT** season opened with good rains, no frost, good flowering and fruit set – ideal. There was some rain in January, then a prolonged period of 15 days up to 35 degrees C late January to early February. From this point on there was no rainfall, the growing season being the driest on record. Shiraz fared best, and Cabernet did quite well; the white varieties struggled under the extreme conditions.

Victoria

Good winter rains were widespread, although not enough to fully break the drought. A warm December, and one or two hot days in January were followed by a prolonged, dry and mild to warm Indian summer, with nigh on perfect harvest weather. For **BEECHWORTH** Chardonnay was the star, but the reds also have above average quality. **GEELONG**, **GIPPSLAND**, **MACEDON RANGES**, **SUNBURY**, **MORNINGTON PENINSULA** and **YARRA VALLEY** all experienced roughly similar conditions: adequate winter rainfall, a dry and cool spring (frosts in some patches), a warm to very warm December, then an outstanding late summer and autumn, with temperatures in the mid 20s, cloudless blue skies and little or no wind for week after week. Berry and bunch size of Pinot Noir may limit its quality, but the white wines, headed by Chardonnay, will be quite outstanding.

The Central Victorian regions of **BENDIGO**, **GRAMPIANS**, **GOULBURN VALLEY/ NAGAMBIE LAKES**, **PYRENEES** and **STRATHBOGIE RANGES** all tell a similar tale, with some winter rainfall, significant spring frosts in some areas (though far from all), and then a prolonged warm and totally dry growing season through to the end of the third week of April. For some, the white wines are marginally better than the red, for others there was little to chose between the two; while for others still the outstanding quality of the Shiraz and Cabernet Sauvignon is the highlight of the year.

In the far west, **HENTY** had a similar weather pattern, with Riesling and Cabernet Sauvignon the pick, Pinot Noir held back by the widespread issue of berry and bunch size. In the north of Victoria, the **KING VALLEY** and **RUTHERGLEN** have had near identical outcomes, with a prolonged, bone-dry summer and autumn producing good whites, excellent reds and (in the case of Rutherglen) outstanding fortified wines.

South Australia

The pattern was much the same for all of its numerous regions: winter rains partially replenishing ground water and filling dams; excellent weather during flowering pointing to above-average yields; a very warm December followed by one of the coldest Januarys on record; a burst of heat in February; then fine and very mild weather in March and April favouring vineyards which had been severely crop-thinned. Nowhere was this more evident than in **COONAWARRA**, the outcome hanging on a knife's edge as at late April, with 2–3 weeks of solid harvesting facing most of the growers. The best outcome would be a vintage like 2001, and then only for those who had aggressively crop-thinned.

In the **ADELAIDE HILLS** Sauvignon Blanc, Chardonnay and Pinot Noir look to be the most promising; in the **BAROSSA VALLEY** it is not a vintage for white wines, and if Cabernet Sauvignon and Shiraz (the best of the reds) are to impress, it will be thanks to the weather right at the end of the growing season. The outcome in the **CLARE VALLEY** looks to be better than most, with Riesling, Shiraz and old vine Cabernet Sauvignon all being picked at optimum maturity. The **EDEN VALLEY**, too, may surprise, with a similar set of weather conditions prevailing.

McLAREN VALE and **LANGHORNE CREEK** both enjoyed a perfect mild, dry and still autumn, leading to outstanding Shiraz, Grenache, Cabernet Sauvignon and Malbec from old vines, but younger vines carrying problematic crops thanks to the size of the bunches. For **MOUNT BENSON** Semillon and Sauvignon Blanc were the star performers, the Shiraz the best of the reds, while in **PADTHAWAY** (more successful than Coonawarra) Chardonnay developed excellent flavour at low baumes (as it did in southern Victoria) and Cabernet Sauvignon and Shiraz from old vines look very good indeed.

Tasmania

As at the end of April the outlook was uncertain: a cool spring with appropriate rainfall was followed by a very cool January (complete with significant frosts). Autumn – particularly April – was a mixed bag of cold and wet weather, with some bursts of sunshine. The aromatic wines look the best, and sparkling wines, too, will be good.

Western Australia

MARGARET RIVER had a near ideal spring, with adequate rain and good weather leading to above average crops, especially for the white wines. A mild summer, with only a few spikes of extreme heat led into a fine and mild autumn. Chardonnay, Merlot and Cabernet Sauvignon are excellent, as is Semillon; Sauvignon Blanc may be a touch flat. **MANJIMUP**, too, had a cool and dry growing season which, at all times, favoured the development of flavour in the white grapes at relatively low baumes. Riesling, Sauvignon Blanc and Chardonnay should all be outstanding, Shiraz and Merlot being the pick of the reds. A near identical pattern emerged for **PEMBERTON**, with a unanimous nine out of ten rating for the white wines, and a unanimous eight out of ten rating for the red wines. Despite similar weather conditions **GEOGRAPHE** went against the flow, Shiraz and Cabernet Sauvignon performing better than Sauvignon Blanc, Chardonnay and Riesling.

In the **SWAN VALLEY** and **PERTH HILLS** typically warm and dry weather produced good Chardonnay and Verdelho, excellent Shiraz, and outstanding Muscat for fortified wines.

Queensland

After a prolonged drought, the common feature across all regions was the heavy, drought-breaking rainfall of January and early February. The **GRANITE BELT** was on a knife's edge after the rain, but late summer and autumn was generally dry and warm, with more even ripening conditions. Verdelho, Chardonnay, Merlot and Cabernet Sauvignon were the best.

SOUTH BURNETT had a relatively cool (for the region) and dry spring, then the January/February rain, with all the fruit picked by the end of February. Verdelho, some Chardonnay and Pinot Gris did best; Merlot and some Shiraz did well, but it was not a great vintage. **QUEENSLAND COASTAL** had a warm to hot opening in September, followed by a mix of rain and hot weather through October, November and December and conditions became even more extreme in late January and February. Chambourcin, built to stand up to such conditions, did best in a very difficult vintage.

Wine and food or food and wine?

It all depends on your starting point: there are conventional matches for overseas classics such as caviar (Champagne), fresh foie gras (Sauternes, Riesling or Rose), and new season Italian white truffles (any medium-bodied red). Here the food flavour is all important, the wine merely incidental.

At the other extreme come 50-year-old classic red wines: Grange, Grand Cru Burgundy, First Growth Bordeaux, or a Maurice O'Shea Mount Pleasant Shiraz. Here the food is, or should be, merely a low-key foil, but at the same time must be of high quality.

In the Australian context I believe not enough attention is paid to the time of year, which – particularly in the southern states – is or should be a major determinant in the choice of both food and wine. And so I shall present my suggestions in this way, always bearing in mind how many ways there are to skin a cat.

Spring

SPARKLING
Oysters, cold crustacea, tapas, any cold hors d'oeuvres

YOUNG RIESLING
Cold salads, sashimi

GEWURZTRAMINER
Asian

YOUNG SEMILLON
Antipasto, vegetable terrine

PINOT GRIS, COLOMBARD
Crab cakes, whitebait

VERDELHO, CHENIN BLANC
Cold smoked chicken, gravlax

MATURE CHARDONNAY
Grilled chicken, chicken pasta, turkey, pheasant

ROSE
Caesar salad, trout mousse

YOUNG PINOT NOIR
Seared kangaroo fillet, grilled quail

MERLOT
Pastrami, warm smoked chicken

YOUNG MEDIUM-BODIED CABERNET SAUVIGNON
Rack of baby lamb

LIGHT TO MEDIUM-BODIED COOL CLIMATE SHIRAZ
Rare eye fillet of beef

YOUNG BOTRYTISED WINES
Fresh fruits, cake

Summer

CHILLED FINO
Cold consommé

2–3-YEAR-OLD SEMILLON
Gazpacho

2–3-YEAR-OLD RIESLING
Seared tuna

**YOUNG BARREL-FERMENTED
SEMILLON SAUVIGNON BLANC**
Seafood or vegetable tempura

YOUNG OFF-DRY RIESLING
Prosciutto and melon/pear

COOL CLIMATE CHARDONNAY
Abalone, lobster, Chinese-style prawns

10-YEAR-OLD SEMILLON OR RIESLING
Braised pork neck

MATURE CHARDONNAY
Smoked eel, smoked roe

OFF-DRY ROSE
Chilled fresh fruit

YOUNG LIGHT-BODIED PINOT NOIR
Grilled salmon

AGED PINOT NOIR (5+ YEARS)
Coq au vin, wild duck

YOUNG GRENACHE/SANGIOVESE
Osso bucco

MATURE CHARDONNAY (5+ YEARS)
Braised rabbit

HUNTER VALLEY SHIRAZ (5–10 YEARS)
Beef spare ribs

MERLOT
Saltimbocca, roast pheasant

**MEDIUM-BODIED CABERNET
SAUVIGNON (5 YEARS)**
Barbequed butterfly leg of lamb

ALL WINES
Parmigiana

Autumn

AMONTILLADO
Warm consommé

BARREL-FERMENTED MATURE WHITES
Smoked roe, bouillabaisse

COMPLEX MATURE CHARDONNAY
Sweetbreads, brains

FULLY AGED RIESLING
Char-grilled eggplant, stuffed capsicum

AGED MARSANNE
Seafood risotto, Lebanese

AGED PINOT NOIR
Grilled calf's liver, roast kid, lamb or
pig's kidneys

**MATURE MARGARET RIVER
CABERNET MERLOT**
Lamb fillet, roast leg of lamb with
garlic and herbs

SOUTHERN VICTORIAN PINOT NOIR
Peking duck

COOL CLIMATE MERLOT
Lamb loin chops

MATURE GRENACHE/RHÔNE BLENDS
Moroccan lamb

RICH, FULL-BODIED HEATHCOTE SHIRAZ
Beef casserole

YOUNG MUSCAT
Plum pudding

Winter

DRY OLOROSO SHERRY
Full-flavoured hors d'oeuvres

SPARKLING BURGUNDY
Borscht

VIOGNIER
Pea and ham soup

AGED (10+ YEARS) SEMILLON
Vichyssoise (hot)

SAUVIGNON BLANC
Coquilles St Jacques, pan-fried scallops

MATURE CHARDONNAY
Quiche Lorraine

CHARDONNAY (10+ YEARS)
Cassoulet

MATURE SEMILLON SAUVIGNON BLANC
Seafood pasta

YOUNG TASMANIAN PINOT NOIR
Squab, duck breast

MATURE PINOT NOIR
Mushroom ragout, ravioli

MATURE MERLOT
Pot au feu

10-YEAR-OLD HEATHCOTE SHIRAZ
Char-grilled rump steak

**15–20-YEAR-OLD FULL-BODIED
BAROSSA SHIRAZ**
Venison, kangaroo fillet

COONAWARRA CABERNET SAUVIGNON
Braised lamb shanks/shoulder

MUSCAT (OLD)
Chocolate-based desserts

TOKAY (OLD)
Crème brûlée

VINTAGE PORT
Dried fruits, salty cheese

Grape variety plantings

The planting figures from the Australian Bureau of Statistics (ABS) include both multipurpose grapes and wine grapes. The multipurpose grapes are chiefly the white varieties of muscat gordo blanco and sultana. While the lion's share of muscat gordo blanco went to winemaking in 2003 (44 553 tonnes out of a total of 48 953 tonnes) the reverse is true of sultana, where 36 032 tonnes out of a total of 128 000 tonnes went to winemaking, 72 768 tonnes to drying and 19 200 tonnes to table usage.

This split varies significantly from year to year according to supply and demand, but if you look back to 1996 you will see how the 'other white' tonnage has decreased in absolute terms and plummeted from 63 per cent to 35 per cent of the total white crush.

The share of the total crush (red and white) contributed by 'other white' has fallen even more dramatically from 42.8 per cent to 14.8 per cent, reflecting the radical restructuring of the Australian industry over a mere eight vintages.

The foregoing apart, the raw ABS figures showed a decline in total plantings for 2003 compared to 2002. Unofficial discussions with informed statisticians suggest there was a minor flaw in the supply of statistics (not the fault of the ABS) and that plantings in fact increased by around 1 per cent, and I have adopted that measure.

	1996	1997	1998
CHARDONNAY			
hectares	11,721	13,713	14,662
tonnes	92,258	119,678	148,515
RIESLING			
hectares	3,412	3,423	3,345
tonnes	37,135	32,907	33,811
SAUVIGNON BLANC			
hectares	1,538	1,725	1,904
tonnes	15,009	13,328	18,405
SEMILLON			
hectares	4,079	4,803	5,287
tonnes	45,062	52,829	57,112
OTHER WHITE			
hectares	26,372	27,047	25,566
tonnes	326,894	265,288	271,620
TOTAL WHITE			
hectares	**47,122**	**50,711**	**50,764**
tonnes	**516,358**	**484,030**	**529,463**
CABERNET SAUVIGNON			
hectares	8,752	11,219	14,695
tonnes	68,839	67,015	91,876
GRENACHE			
hectares	1,940	2,014	1,988
tonnes	26,212	24,198	23,842
MOURVEDRE			
hectares	583	614	696
tonnes	8,821	7,629	8,238
MERLOT			
hectares	1,246	2,461	3,802
tonnes	9,227	10,331	13,881
PINOT NOIR			
hectares	1,748	1,896	2,192
tonnes	14,801	13,924	19,123
SHIRAZ			
hectares	10,389	13,410	17,930
tonnes	81,674	94,848	131,427
OTHER RED			
hectares	5,902	6,149	6,372
tonnes	36,469	34,503	38,224
TOTAL RED			
hectares	**30,560**	**37,763**	**47,675**
tonnes	**246,043**	**252,448**	**326,611**
TOTAL GRAPES			
hectares	**77,682**	**88,474**	**98,439**
tonnes	**762,401**	**736,478**	**856,074**
PERCENTAGE (TONNES)			
White	**67.73%**	**65.73%**	**61.85%**
Red	**32.27%**	**34.27%**	**38.15%**

1999	2000	2001	2002	2003
16,855	18,526	18,434	21,724	24,138
210,770	201,248	245,199	256,328	233,747
3,347	3,658	3,558	3,962	3,987
30,144	26,800	26,980	27,838	28,994
2,413	2,706	2,766	2,914	2,953
22,834	21,487	25,326	28,567	21,028
6,044	6,832	6,803	6,610	6,283
80,191	77,506	88,427	100,785	77,096
26,331	27,873	25,781	26,215	24,700
282,459	265,196	232,334	255,253	196,209
54,990	**59,595**	**57,342**	**61,425**	**62,051**
626,398	**592,237**	**618,266**	**666,771**	**557,074**
21,169	26,674	28,609	29,573	28,171
127,494	159,358	249,288	257,223	225,723
2,255	2,756	2,427	2,528	2,322
24,196	23,998	22,563	26,260	19,866
866	1,147	1,128	1,238	1,092
9,217	10,496	11,624	12,452	11,822
6,387	8,575	9,330	10,101	10,352
31,801	51,269	80,142	104,423	92,865
2,996	3,756	4,142	4,414	4,270
19,668	19,578	29,514	21,341	27,949
25,596	32,327	33,676	37,031	37,106
192,330	224,394	311,045	326,564	309,000
8,656	11,347	11,621	12,284	12,268
45,103	57,255	68,640	99,467	85,297
67,925	**86,582**	**90,933**	**97,169**	**95,491**
449,809	**546,348**	**772,816**	**847,730**	**772,522**
122,915	**146,177**	**148,275**	**158,594**	**157,492**
1,076,207	**1,138,585**	**1,391,082**	**1,514,501**	**1,329,596**
59.21%	52.02%	44.45%	44.02%	41.90%
41.79%	47.98%	55.55%	55.98%	58.10%

Australian Wineries and Wines 2005

Abbey Creek Vineyard ★★★★

1091 Porongurup Road, Porongurup, WA 6324 **REGION** Great Southern
T (08) 9853 1044 **F** (08) 9853 1040 **OPEN** By appointment
WINEMAKER Robert Diletti (Contract) **EST.** 1990 **CASES** 800
PRODUCT RANGE ($17–22 CD) Riesling, Pinot Noir, Cabernet Sauvignon Merlot.
SUMMARY This is the family business of Mike and Mary Dilworth; the name comes from a winter creek running alongside the vineyard, and a view of The Abbey in the Stirling Range. The vineyard is only 1.5 hectares, roughly split between riesling, pinot noir, cabernet sauvignon and a little merlot, the pinot noir and riesling planted in 1990, the remainder in 1993. Another 0.5 hectare of riesling may follow in the near future. The Rieslings, in particular, have had significant show success.

ΥΥΥΥΥ **Riesling 2002** Flowery, spice and apple blossom aromas; a refined and classic structure; pity no screwcap. 2003 Winewise Best Riesling. **RATING** 94 **DRINK** 2008 $17

ΥΥΥΥ **Pinot Noir 2002** Stylish, but very light. Restraint in the winery has produced as much as possible from the fruit. **RATING** 88 **DRINK** Now $21

ΥΥΥΥ **Cabernet Merlot 2002** Aromatic, light to medium-bodied; spice, herb and red berries; distinctive cool-grown style and acidity. **RATING** 86 **DRINK** 2009 $22

Abbey Rock NR

67 Payneham Road, College Park, SA 5069 (postal) **REGION** Murray Darling
T (08) 8362 0677 **F** (08) 8362 9218 **OPEN** Not
WINEMAKER Les Sampson **EST.** 2001
PRODUCT RANGE ($15 R) The basic wines, made from contract-grown grapes in the Murray Darling and Wrattonbully regions, are a Chardonnay, Shiraz and Cabernet Merlot. More extensive wines at various higher price points are being made from a mix of estate-owned vineyards and contract vineyards in the Adelaide Hills, Clare Valley and elsewhere. These wines, including Pinot Noir, Chardonnay and Cabernet Sauvignon, will be progressively brought onto the market over the next 12 months.
SUMMARY A new but rapidly expanding business with wines sourced from a number of regions across South Australia. The premium wines will be made from pinot noir (2.2 hectares) and chardonnay (3.5 hectares) near Hahndorf in the Adelaide Hills, and from chardonnay (2 hectares), semillon (6.5 hectares), shiraz (8 hectares) and grenache (2 hectares) in the Clare Valley. Plans are afoot to increase both the Adelaide Hills and the Clare Valley plantings.

AbbeyVale NR

392 Wildwood Road, Yallingup, WA 6282 **REGION** Margaret River
T (08) 9755 2121 **F** (08) 9755 2121 **OPEN** 7 days 10–5
WINEMAKER Philip May **EST.** 1986 **CASES** 10 000
PRODUCT RANGE Three ranges: at the top, Reserve, limited to the best white and red wine made each year; Reward, featuring a duo of high quality; and the entry price point Vat range of varietal and regional blends.
SUMMARY The new AbbeyVale is a completely different business from that which operated prior to May 2003, when a 19-member grower group contributed $1.25 million for start-up capital, coupled with grape supply agreements. Well-known and highly skilled vigneron Philip May heads the operation (indeed he is the only director) and the services of two equally skilled and experienced winemaking consultants, Richard Rowe and Bruce Dukes have been secured.

ΥΥΥΥ **Vat 351 Chardonnay 2003** **RATING** 84 **DRINK** Now $13

Abercorn ★★★★☆

Cassilis Road, Mudgee, NSW 2850 **REGION** Mudgee
T 1800 000 959 **F** (02) 6373 3108 **OPEN** Thurs–Mon 10.30–4.30
WINEMAKER Tim Stevens **EST.** 1996 **CASES** 8000
PRODUCT RANGE ($15.95–49.95 R) Chardonnay, Unwooded Chardonnay, A Reserve Chardonnay, Pinot Noir, Shiraz, A Reserve Shiraz, A Reserve Shiraz Cabernet, A Reserve Cabernet; Barons Court is second label, comprising Chardonnay and Shiraz.

SUMMARY Tim and Connie Stevens acquired the 25-year-old Abercorn Vineyard, admirably located next door to Huntington Estate, in 1996. It has consistently produced good-quality wines under the Stevens' ownership. National distribution through National Wine & Beer Distributors; exports to the UK.

ŸŸŸŸŸ **A Reserve Shiraz 2002** Very complex and powerful; plum, blackberry and anise fruit; well-handled new oak. **RATING** 94 **DRINK** 2017 $49.95
A Reserve Cabernet Sauvignon 2002 Classic blackcurrant varietal character; a perfectly poised and weighted palate, supple and smooth. **RATING** 94 **DRINK** 2012 $49.95

ŸŸŸŸŸ **Reserve Shiraz Cabernet 2002** A powerful wine with savoury aspects to its spice, earth and black fruit flavours; fine tannins; an altogether elegant wine. Gold medal 2003 Mudgee Wine Show. **RATING** 93 **DRINK** 2017 $49.95
Cabernet Shiraz 2002 Medium-bodied; a rich mix of blackcurrant, blackberry and dark chocolate; good extract and length. **RATING** 90 **DRINK** 2012 $17.95

ŸŸŸŸ **Reserve Chardonnay 2001** Complex yellow peach, stone fruit and honey; some bottle-developed toasty notes; lots of character. **RATING** 89 **DRINK** 2007 $29.95
Red Heifer 2002 A smooth and supple mix of blackberry, blackcurrant, chocolate and vanilla; supple tannins and a subliminal hint of sweetness. **RATING** 89 **DRINK** 2012 $12

ŸŸŸŸ **Shiraz Cabernet Merlot 2003** **RATING** 86 **DRINK** 2008 $17.95
Cabernet Sauvignon 2002 **RATING** 86 **DRINK** 2009 $19.95
Unwooded Chardonnay 2003 **RATING** 85 **DRINK** Now $15
Shiraz 2002 **RATING** 84 **DRINK** 2007 $19.95

ŸŸŸ **Shiraz 2001** **RATING** 83 $19.95

Ada River ★★★★☆

2330 Main Road, Neerim South, Vic 3831 **REGION** Gippsland
T (03) 5628 1661 **F** (03) 5628 1661 **OPEN** 10–6 weekends and public holidays
WINEMAKER Peter Kelliher, Chris Kelliher **EST.** 1983 **CASES** 2000
PRODUCT RANGE ($14–27 CD) From Gippsland-grown grapes, Chardonnay, Pinot Noir, Merlot, Cabernet Sauvignon, Cabernets; Heathcote Shiraz, Baw Baw Port.
SUMMARY The Kelliher family first planted vines on their dairy farm at Neerim South in 1983, extending the original Millstream Vineyard in 1989 and increasing plantings even further by establishing the nearby Manilla Vineyard in 1994. Until 2000, Ada River leased a Yarra Valley vineyard; it has since relinquished that lease and in its place established a vineyard at Heathcote, in conjunction with a local grower.

ŸŸŸŸŸ **Heathcote Shiraz 2002** Inky dense colour; redolent with lush blackberry and satsuma plum fruit; not over-extracted. Cork condition a worry. **RATING** 93 **DRINK** 2012 $27
Heathcote Cabernet Sauvignon 2002 Opens quietly on the bouquet, rapidly gathering pace on the palate; blackcurrant, chocolate and mocha; persistent but balanced tannins. **RATING** 91 **DRINK** 2012 $22
Gippsland Chardonnay 2001 Bright, light green straw; barrel-ferment oak is obvious, but well integrated with attractive ripe stone fruit; good balance. Value. **RATING** 90 **DRINK** Now $16

ð Adinfern NR

Bussell Highway, Cowaramup, WA 6284 **REGION** Margaret River
T (08) 9755 5272 **F** (08) 9755 5206 **OPEN** 7 days 11–5.30
WINEMAKER Kevin McKay (Contract) **EST.** 1996 **CASES** 1800
PRODUCT RANGE ($16–24 CD) Sauvignon Blanc, Shepherd's Rhapsody (Semillon Sauvignon Blanc), Shepherd's Serenade (Autumn Harvest Semillon), Shiraz, Merlot, Cabernet Sauvignon, Shepherd's Harmony (Autumn Harvest Cabernet), Vintage Ruby Port.
SUMMARY Merv and Jan Smith have farmed their Cowaramup property as a fine wool and lamb producer for over 30 years, but in 1996 diversified by commencing the development of 16 hectares of vineyard planted to sauvignon blanc, semillon, chardonnay, pinot noir, merlot, shiraz, cabernet

sauvignon and malbec. They also built two self-contained rammed earth cottages. The wines (which have had show success) are sold through the cellar door, by mail order and via Adinfern's website <www.adinfern.com>.

TTTTY Shiraz 2002 Medium-bodied; supple, sweet and smooth blackberry fruit; subtle oak and good mouthfeel; clever winemaking. **RATING** 90 **DRINK** 2010 **$** 24

Affleck   NR

154 Millynn Road off Bungendore Road, Bungendore, NSW 2621 **REGION** Canberra District
T (02) 6236 9276 **F** (02) 6236 9090 **OPEN** 7 days 9–5
WINEMAKER Ian Hendry **EST.** 1976 **CASES** 500
PRODUCT RANGE ($12–25 CD) Chardonnay, Chardonnay Reserve, Late Picked Sauvignon Blanc, Sweet White, Pinot Noir, Cabernet Shiraz, Muscat, Vintage Port.
SUMMARY The cellar-door and mail-order price list says that the wines are 'grown, produced and bottled on the estate by Ian and Susie Hendry with much dedicated help from family and friends'. The original 2.5-hectare vineyard has been expanded to 7 hectares, and a tasting room (offering light lunches) opened in 1999.

Ainsworth Estate   ★★★★

110 Ducks Lane, Seville, Vic 3139 **REGION** Yarra Valley
T (03) 5964 4711 **F** (03) 5964 4311 **OPEN** Thurs–Mon 10.30–5
WINEMAKER Denis Craig **EST.** 1994 **CASES** 3000
PRODUCT RANGE ($18–35 CD) Unoaked Chardonnay, Chardonnay, Pinot Noir, Shiraz, Reserve Shiraz, Cabernet Sauvignon Cabernet Franc, Cabernet Merlot, Cabernet Sauvignon.
SUMMARY Denis Craig and wife Kerri planted their first 2 hectares of chardonnay and shiraz near Healesville in 1994, thereafter establishing a second vineyard at Ducks Lane, Seville, with another 2 hectares of vines, here planted to shiraz and pinot noir. They have also turned from selling to purchasing grapes, with a total of just under 3 hectares of chardonnay, shiraz and cabernet sauvignon grown for them under contract. For the time being, at least, Denis Craig and Al Fencaros make the wines at Fencaros' Allinda Winery in Dixons Creek. Three executive apartments overlooking the vineyard are also available for rent.

TTTTY Chardonnay 2002 Complex; attractive funky/smoky aromas; intense palate reflecting tiny yield. **RATING** 92 **DRINK** 2012 **$** 23

TTTT Pinot Noir 2002 Savoury, spicy aromas and flavours; not as rich as most Pinots of the vintage, but has elegance. **RATING** 88 **DRINK** 2009 **$** 25
Cabernet Sauvignon Cabernet Franc 2002 Light to medium-bodied; sweet, small red berry and cassis flavours; minimal tannins and oak. **RATING** 88 **DRINK** 2010 **$** 25
Cabernet Sauvignon Merlot 2002 Light to medium-bodied; sweet blackcurrant fruit; minimal tannins. **RATING** 87 **DRINK** 2008 **$** 25

Akrasi Wines/New Mediterranean Winery   NR

35 Holloway Street, Boort, Vic 3537 **REGION** Central Victorian Zone
T (03) 5455 2244 **F** (03) 5455 2615 **OPEN** By appointment
WINEMAKER George Tallis **EST.** 1997
PRODUCT RANGE Marsanne, Shiraz, Cabernet Sauvignon.
SUMMARY It is a reasonably safe bet that you will not come across Boort by accident. It falls roughly between the Calder and Loddon Highways as they wend their way north towards the Murray River and the NSW border; Kerang, 51 kilometres to the north, is the nearest landmark of any significance. Hence the Central Victorian Zone, but the absence of any region. George Tallis commenced home winemaking in the early 1990s, initially simply for his own benefit and that of his immediate family. Success at this level led to relatively small commercial winemaking, strongly influenced by Tallis' Greek ancestry. Indeed, the word 'Akrasi' comes from the Greek name of George Tallis' home town. Taking away the letter 'A' you are left with krasi, which in Greek means wine.

TTT New Mediterranean Shiraz 2002 RATING 82

Albert River Wines ★★★

1–117 Mundoolun Connection Road, Tamborine, Qld 4270 **REGION** Queensland Coastal
T (07) 5543 6622 **F** (07) 5543 6627 **OPEN** 7 days 10–4
WINEMAKER Peter Scudamore-Smith MW (Consultant) **EST.** 1998 **CASES** 5000
PRODUCT RANGE ($17–29 CD) Jacaranda Semillon, Unwooded Chardonnay, Chardonnay, Sparkling White, Sparkling Red, Grand Masters Sparkling Shiraz, Roundelay (Shiraz Merlot Cabernet blend), Grand Masters Shiraz, Merlot, Shiraz Cabernet Merlot, Red Belly Black Port.
SUMMARY Albert River is yet another high-profile winery to open on the Gold Coast hinterland, with all of its distribution through the cellar door, by mail order and in local restaurants. The proprietors are David and Janette Bladin, with a combined 30 years' experience in tourism and hospitality, who have acquired and relocated two of Queensland's most historic buildings, Tamborine House and Auchenflower House. The winery itself is housed in an annex to Auchenflower House; the Bladins have established 10 hectares of vineyards on the property, and have another 50 hectares under contract. Exports to Japan.

ΨΨΨΨ **Cabernet Shiraz Merlot 2001 RATING** 85 **DRINK** Now **$** 25
Red Belly Black Tawny Port NV RATING 85 **DRINK** Now **$** 20

ΨΨΨ **Jacaranda Verdelho 2003 RATING** 81 **$** 18
Grand Masters Sparkling Shiraz 2000 RATING 80 **$** 29

ΨΨΨ **Grand Masters Sparkling White 2001 RATING** 79 **$** 29

Aldgate Ridge NR

23 Nation Ridge Road, Aldgate, SA 5154 **REGION** Adelaide Hills
T (08) 8388 5225 **F** (08) 8388 5856 **OPEN** By appointment
WINEMAKER David Powell (Contract) **EST.** 1992 **CASES** 400
PRODUCT RANGE ($23–31 CD) Sauvignon Blanc, Pinot Noir.
SUMMARY Jill and Chris Whisson acquired their vineyard property in 1988, when the land was still being used as a market garden. The 2.5 hectares of pinot noir now established were planted in two stages, in 1992 and 1997, the first block with some of the first of the new Burgundian clones to be propagated in Australia. Further plantings of pinot noir and a small block of sauvignon blanc have been added. The vineyard is typical of the Adelaide Hills region, on a rolling to steep southeast-facing hillside at the 440-metre altitude line. The wine is contract-made by the celebrated David Powell of Torbreck Wines in the Barossa Valley, and apart from mail order, has limited fine wine retail distribution.

ΨΨΨ **Sauvignon Blanc 2003 RATING** 79 **$** 23

Aldinga Bay Winery ★★★

Main South Road, Aldinga, SA 5173 **REGION** McLaren Vale
T (08) 8556 3179 **F** (08) 8556 3350 **OPEN** 7 days 10–5
WINEMAKER Nick Girolamo **EST.** 1979 **CASES** 8000
PRODUCT RANGE ($13–21 CD) Verdelho, Chardonnay, Shiraz, Sangiovese, Petit Verdot, Reserve Tawny Port.
SUMMARY The former Donolga Winery has had a name and image change since Nick Girolamo, the son of founders Don and Olga Girolamo, returned from Roseworthy College with a degree in oenology. Nick Girolamo has taken over both the winemaking and the marketing; prices remain modest, though not as low as they once were, reflecting an increase in the quality and an upgrade in packaging. Aldinga Bay also has some very interesting varietal plantings, 16 varieties in all, including petit verdot, nebbiolo, barbera and sangiovese.

Alexandra Bridge Wines ★★★★

101 Brockman Highway, Karridale, WA 6288 **REGION** Margaret River
T (08) 9758 5999 **F** (08) 9758 5988 **OPEN** 7 days 10–4.30
WINEMAKER Philip Tubb, Julian Scott **EST.** 1999 **CASES** 12 000
PRODUCT RANGE ($19.50–48 R) Sauvignon Blanc, Semillon Sauvignon Blanc, Unwooded Chardonnay, Shiraz, Cabernet Merlot; Reserve range of Semillon, Chardonnay, Shiraz and Cabernet Sauvignon. Top of the range 101 series introduced in 2003, representing the best of vintage. The name comes from Alexandra Bridge's address.

SUMMARY To say that in the first few years of this decade Alexandra Bridge had a complicated and convoluted history is to put it mildly. However, it is the outcome which matters. Since July 2002 it has become the operating arm of Australian Wine Holdings; its 800-tonne winery, commissioned in February 2000, was the first built in the Karridale area at the southern end of the Margaret River. The Brockman Vineyard, planted in three stages commencing in 1995, is estate-owned and has a total of 30 hectares of semillon, sauvignon blanc, chardonnay, shiraz and cabernet sauvignon. The grapes coming from the Brockman Vineyard are supplemented by long-term supply agreements with other Margaret River growers. The quality of the wines has not suffered during the period of corporate turmoil. The wines are exported to Europe and South-East Asia.

ΥΥΥΥΥ **101 Cabernet Sauvignon 2001** Fully ripe, luscious blackcurrant and bitter chocolate; good oak and tannin management; fine texture. **RATING** 92 **DRINK** 2016 $ 48

ΥΥΥΥ **101 Semillon 2001** Bright green-gold; rich, full-bodied, no-holds-barred 13.5 degrees alcohol. **RATING** 88 **DRINK** Now $ 38

ΥΥΥ **101 Shiraz 2001 RATING** 82 $ 48

Alkoomi ★★★★★

Wingebellup Road, Frankland, WA 6396 **REGION** Frankland
T (08) 9855 2229 **F** (08) 9855 2284 **OPEN** 7 days 10.30–5
WINEMAKER Michael Staniford, Merv Lange **EST.** 1971 **CASES** 80 000
PRODUCT RANGE ($14–59 R) Frankland River Riesling, Wandoo (Semillon), Sauvignon Blanc, Chardonnay, Shiraz Viognier, Jarrah Shiraz, Cabernet Sauvignon, Blackbutt; cheaper Southlands range.
SUMMARY For those who see the wineries of Western Australia as suffering from the tyranny of distance, this most remote of all wineries shows there is no tyranny after all. It is a story of unqualified success due to sheer hard work, and no doubt to Merv and Judy Lange's aversion to borrowing a single dollar from the bank. The substantial production is entirely drawn from the ever-expanding estate vineyards, which by 2003 amounted to over 80 hectares. Wine quality across the range is impeccable, always with precisely defined varietal character. National retail distribution; exports to Hong Kong, Singapore, Japan, Thailand, Malyasia, the UK, the US, Canada, The Netherlands, Switzerland and France.

ΥΥΥΥΥ **Blackbutt 2000** Fine, fragrant blackcurrant and a hint of raspberry; beautifully balanced and poised; finesse and length. **RATING** 95 **DRINK** 2015 $ 59
Wandoo 2001 Aromatic herbs, spice and grass on the bouquet; exceptional intensity and length; acidity to sustain prolonged cellaring. Pity about the cork finish. **RATING** 94 **DRINK** 2016 $ 33

ΥΥΥΥΥ **Frankland River Chardonnay 2002** Complex barrel-ferment aromas come through strongly before elegant, fine grapefruit and stone fruit drive the palate. Screwcap. **RATING** 93 **DRINK** 2012 $ 21
Frankland River Riesling 2003 Clean and crisp; lime, passionfruit and mineral; tight but balanced. **RATING** 91 **DRINK** 2010 $ 19
Frankland River Sauvignon Blanc 2003 Spotlessly clean, crisp minerally aromas; excellent flavour and balance; ripe gooseberry and tropical fruit. **RATING** 91 **DRINK** 2007 $ 19
Frankland River Shiraz Viognier 2002 Scented, spicy blackberry and plum aromas; a particular juicy flavour and texture ex viognier and 18 months in French oak. **RATING** 90 **DRINK** 2012 $ 21
Frankland River Cabernet Sauvignon 2001 A medium-bodied mix of blackcurrant, cedar and earth; subtle oak, finely grained tannins. **RATING** 90 **DRINK** 2011 $ 24

ΥΥΥΥ **Jarrah Shiraz 2001** Elegant, medium-bodied; more savoury, spicy than usual; gentle tannins. **RATING** 89 **DRINK** 2010 $ 40

Allandale ★★★★

Allandale Road, Allandale via Pokolbin, NSW 2321 **REGION** Lower Hunter Valley
T (02) 4990 4526 **F** (02) 4990 1714 **OPEN** Mon–Sat 9–5, Sun 10–5
WINEMAKER Bill Sneddon **EST.** 1978 **CASES** 25 000

PRODUCT RANGE ($12–50 CD) Semillon, Sauvignon Blanc, Verdelho, Chardonnay, William Methode Champenoise, Late Harvest Semillon Sauvignon Blanc, Fleur (dessert), Lombardo (light red), Hilltops Shiraz, Hilltops Cabernet Sauvignon, Orange Cabernet Sauvignon, Mudgee Cabernet Sauvignon, Reserve Red.

SUMMARY Without ostentation, this medium-sized winery has been under the control of winemaker Bill Sneddon for well over a decade. Allandale has developed something of a reputation as a Chardonnay specialist, but does offer a broad range of wines of consistently good quality, with several red wines sourced from outside the Hunter Valley. The wines are exported to the UK, the US, Singapore, Malaysia and Fiji.

ＹＹＹＹＹ **Hunter Valley Semillon 2002** Excellent bright green tints; tight, herb/grass/citrus flavours; bright finish. **RATING** 92 **DRINK** 2010 $ 17

ＹＹＹＹ **Verdelho 2003 RATING** 85 **DRINK** Now $ 17

Allinda
NR

119 Lorimers Lane, Dixons Creek, Vic 3775 **REGION** Yarra Valley
T (03) 5965 2450 **F** (03) 5965 2467 **OPEN** Weekends and public holidays 11–5
WINEMAKER Al Fencaros **EST.** 1991 **CASES** 2500
PRODUCT RANGE ($16.50–24.50 CD) Riesling, Sauvignon Blanc, Chardonnay, Late Harvest Riesling, Shiraz, Cabernets.
SUMMARY Winemaker Al Fencaros has a Bachelor of Wine Science (Charles Sturt University) and was formerly employed by De Bortoli in the Yarra Valley. All of the Allinda wines are produced on-site; all except the Shiraz (from Heathcote) are estate-grown from a little over 3 hectares of vineyards. Limited retail distribution in Melbourne and Sydney.

All Saints Estate
★★★★★

All Saints Road, Wahgunyah, Vic 3687 **REGION** Rutherglen
T (02) 6035 2222 **F** (02) 6035 2200 **OPEN** Mon–Sat 9–5.30, Sun 10–5.30
WINEMAKER Dan Crane **EST.** 1864 **CASES** 35 000
PRODUCT RANGE ($14–395 CD) The Carlyle range tops the table wines; then come a range of varietals under the All Saints label and the Images range; Tokays and Muscats in the official Rutherglen 3-tiered classification starting with Classic, then Grand and, finally, Rare.
SUMMARY The winery rating reflects the fortified wines, but the table wines are more than adequate. The Terrace restaurant (open 7 days for lunch and Saturday night for dinner) makes this a compulsory and most enjoyable stop for any visitor to the northeast. All Saints and St Leonards are now wholly owned by Peter Brown; the vast majority of the wines are sold through the cellar door and by mailing list. Exports to the US. The faux castle, modelled on a Scottish castle beloved of the founder, is now classified by the Historic Buildings Council.

ＹＹＹＹＹ **Rare Rutherglen Tokay Museum Release NV** Dark olive-brown; the extreme age shows most clearly in the incredible length, finish and aftertaste of the wine; not a trace of staleness. **RATING** 97 **DRINK** Now $ 434.50
Rare Rutherglen Muscat Museum Release NV An exceedingly complex wine that retains elegance, and, like the Museum Tokay, has no hint of staleness. The description of flavours is endless, as is the lingering finish. **RATING** 97 **DRINK** Now $ 434.50
Rare Rutherglen Tokay NV Far, far deeper colour than the Grand; layer upon layer of lusciously rich varietal fruit, moving beyond tea leaf into the Christmas cake/Christmas pudding spectrum. **RATING** 96 **DRINK** Now $ 107.50
Rare Rutherglen Muscat NV Deep, dark brown, dark olive rim; very complex, with a balance of aged raisiny material and a touch of youthful freshness; the equally complex, powerful palate has a strong nutty, rancio framework yet has great balance and suppleness, then a cleansing, dry finish. **RATING** 96 **DRINK** Now $ 107.50
Grand Rutherglen Tokay (375 ml) NV Lusciously rich and complex, with Christmas cake and dried fruit flavours, along with the hallmark echoes of tea leaf and butterscotch, and a lovely skein of sweet fruit running through the mid-palate; the structure is fine and intense. **RATING** 94 **DRINK** Now $ 55

Grand Rutherglen Muscat (375 ml) NV Deep, olive-rimmed brown; a very complex, extremely rich bouquet with intense rancio and some volatile lift. An ultra-rich and dense palate with abundant raisin and plum pudding flavours, the twist of volatility on the finish well within bounds. **RATING** 94 **DRINK** Now $ 55

ΥΥΥΥΫ **Classic Rutherglen Tokay (500 ml) NV** Tea leaf, smoke, toffee and butterscotch aromas lead into an intense, long and lingering palate with abundant weight. Future releases might well see a little more fresh, younger material in the blend. **RATING** 91 **DRINK** Now $ 30.50
Cabernet Sauvignon 2002 Attractive wine; cedar and blackberry; fine, ripe tannins, good extract/oak handling. **RATING** 90 **DRINK** 2012 $ 22
Classic Rutherglen Muscat (500 ml) NV Distinct olive hints to the full tawny colour; the bouquet and palate show considerable rancio, complexity and depth. Just a suggestion of the pendulum swinging a little too far towards aged material. **RATING** 90 **DRINK** Now $ 30.50

ΥΥΥΥ **Shiraz 2002** Powerful black fruits on entry, with some savoury notes; medium-bodied, fine tannins. **RATING** 88 **DRINK** 2010 $ 22
Sparkling Cabernet Sauvignon NV Lots of cassis, blackberry and chocolate in the base wine works better than most. **RATING** 87 **DRINK** 2008 $ 27.50

ΥΥΥΫ **Riesling 2003** **RATING** 86 **DRINK** 2010 $ 17.50
Merlot 2002 **RATING** 86 **DRINK** 2009 $ 22
Chardonnay 2003 **RATING** 85 **DRINK** Now $ 16

🐢 Allison Valley Wines   NR

RSM 457 North Jindong Road, Busselton, WA 6280 (postal) **REGION** Margaret River
T (08) 9755 4873 **F** (08) 9474 1804 **OPEN** Not
WINEMAKER Paul Green (Contract) **EST.** 1997
PRODUCT RANGE ($11.99–13.99 ML) Semillon Sauvignon Blanc, Sauvignon Blanc, Shiraz, Cabernet Sauvignon.
SUMMARY The Porter family planted 10 hectares of semillon, sauvignon blanc, shiraz and cabernet sauvignon with the sole intention of selling the grapes to other winemakers in the region. However, as has been the case with hundreds of other such ventures, the family has decided to have some of the production vinified under the Allison Valley Wines label. There is no cellar door, the small amount of wine being sold by mail order.

Allusion Wines   NR

Smith Hill Road, Yankalilla, SA 5203 **REGION** Southern Fleurieu
T (08) 8558 3333 **F** (08) 8558 3333 **OPEN** Thurs–Sun 11–5
WINEMAKER Contract (previously Normans) **EST.** 1996 **CASES** 750
PRODUCT RANGE ($17–35 CD) Semillon Sauvignon Blanc, Viognier, Shiraz Viognier, Cabernet Sauvignon.
SUMMARY Steve and Wendy Taylor purchased the property on which Allusion Wines is established in 1980, and have since planted 4 hectares of vines and 35 000 trees. Steve Taylor's 20 years as a chef have strongly influenced both the varietal plantings and the wine styles made: not altogether surprisingly, they are designed to be consumed with good food. The wine is fermented off-site, then matured on-site before being contract-bottled.

Allyn River Wines   NR

Torryburn Road, East Gresford, NSW 2311 **REGION** Upper Hunter Valley
T (02) 4938 9279 **F** (02) 4938 9279 **OPEN** Fri–Mon and public holidays 9–5, or by appointment
WINEMAKER David Hook (Contract) **EST.** 1996 **CASES** 650
PRODUCT RANGE ($14.50–16.50 CD) Semillon, Chardonnay Semillon, Dessert Semillon, Chambourcin.
SUMMARY Allyn River is situated on the alluvial soils on the banks of the stream which has given the vineyard its name. The plantings of 1.5 hectares each of semillon and chambourcin were in part inspired by the knowledge that Dr Henry Lindeman had established his famous Cawarra Vineyard in the locality, and since Allyn River's foundation in 1996, others have moved to the area, establishing

vineyards totalling more than 20 hectares within a 10-kilometre radius of Allyn River. As well as a wine tasting room and picnic facilities, self-contained cottage accommodation, known as the Maples Cottage, is available on the property.

Amarillo Vines

NR

27 Marlock Place, Karnup, WA 6176 **REGION** Peel
T (08) 9537 1800 **OPEN** 7 days by appointment
WINEMAKER Phil Franzone (Contract) **EST.** 1995 **CASES** 665
PRODUCT RANGE ($12–16 CD) Verdelho, Chardonnay, Shiraz, Grenache, Merlot, Cabernet Sauvignon.
SUMMARY The Ashby family have market garden and landscaping backgrounds, and the establishment of a small vineyard on the block of land in which their house sits seemed a natural thing to do. What is unusual is the density of the planting, the utilisation of a lyre trellis, and the permanent netting erected around the vineyard. So it is that they do not speak of acres or hectares, but of the 2500 vines planted, and of the production as 8000 bottles.

Amarok Estate

Lot 547 Caves Road, Wilyabrup, WA 6284 (postal) **REGION** Margaret River
T (08) 9756 6888 **F** (08) 9756 6555 **OPEN** Not
WINEMAKER Kevin McKay (Contract) **EST.** 1999 **CASES** 1500
PRODUCT RANGE ($16–24 ML) Semillon Sauvignon Blanc, Sauvignon Blanc, Shiraz, Merlot, Cabernet Sauvignon.
SUMMARY John and Libby Staley, with their youngest daughter Megan, her husband Shane (and youngest grandson Lewis) have all had hands-on involvement in the establishment of 20 hectares of vineyards, clearing bushland, ripping, rock picking, stick picking and planting, etc. The soils are gravelly loam over a clay granite base, the vineyard having a western aspect and being 5 kilometres from the Indian Ocean. The Staleys senior have built a home on the property, and Shane and Megan carry out all of the viticultural tasks. Production will increase significantly in the years ahead as the vines come into full bearing.

Amberley Estate

Thornton Road, Yallingup, WA 6282 **REGION** Margaret River
T (08) 9755 2288 **F** (08) 9755 2171 **OPEN** 7 days 10–4.30
WINEMAKER Eddie Price, David Watson **EST.** 1986 **CASES** 90 000
PRODUCT RANGE ($15–70 R) Chenin Blanc, Sauvignon Blanc, Semillon Sauvignon Blanc, Chardonnay, Shiraz, Cabernet Merlot, Cabernet Sauvignon; First Selection Semillon, Shiraz, Chardonnay; Charlotte Street Chardonnay, Merlot.
SUMMARY Based its initial growth on the basis of its ultra-commercial, fairly sweet Chenin Blanc, which continues to provide the volume for the brand, selling out well prior to the following release. However, the quality of all of the other wines has risen markedly over recent years as the 31 hectares of estate plantings have become fully mature. Exports to the UK, France, Germany, Singapore, Japan, Hong Kong and the US. Purchased by Canadian company Vincorp in early 2004.

ŦŦŦŦŦ **First Selection Semillon 2001** Good length and oak balance; herb and oak flavours; nice dry finish. **RATING** 90 **DRINK** 2009 $ 36.85

Ambrook Wines

NR

114 George Street, West Swan, WA 6055 **REGION** Swan Valley
T (08) 9274 1003 **F** (08) 9379 0334 **OPEN** Wed–Fri 12–5, weekends and public holidays 10–5
WINEMAKER Rob Marshal **EST.** 1990 **CASES** 1200
PRODUCT RANGE ($13–16 CD) Semillon, Chenin, Classic White, Late Harvest Semillon, Sweet, Shiraz, Cabernet Sauvignon.
SUMMARY Michele Amonini has established 4 hectares of chenin blanc, semillon, verdelho, shiraz, cabernet sauvignon and merlot, and then went about quietly producing a solid range of varietal estate-based wines which have had their fair share of success at the various West Australian regional wine shows. Modest pricing increases the appeal.

🐛 Amherst Winery NR

Talbot–Avoca Road, Amherst, Vic 3371 **REGION** Pyrenees
T (03) 5463 2105 **F** (03) 5463 2091 **OPEN** Weekends and public holidays 10–5
WINEMAKER Contract **EST.** 1991
PRODUCT RANGE ($12–25 CD) Chardonnay, Daisy Creek Chardonnay, Dunn's Paddock Shiraz, Daisy Creek Cabernet Shiraz.
SUMMARY Norman and Elizabeth Jones have planted 4 hectares of vines on a property with an extraordinarily rich and interesting history, a shorthand reflection of which is the naming of Dunn's Paddock Shiraz. This variety dominates the planting, with 3.4 hectares, 0.6 hectare cabernet sauvignon and 0.2 hectare of chardonnay. Samuel Dunn was a convict who arrived in Van Diemen's Land in 1838 and endured continuous punishment thereafter until fleeing to South Australia in 1846 and changing his name from Samuel Knowles to Samuel Dunn. When he married 18-year-old Mary Therese Taaffe in Adelaide at the end of 1851, they walked from Adelaide to Amherst pushing a wheelbarrow carrying their belongings. They had 14 children, and Samuel Dunn died in 1898, a highly respected citizen; his widow lived until 1923.

Amietta Vineyard and Winery ★★★☆

30 Steddy Road, Lethbridge, Vic 3332 **REGION** Geelong
T (03) 5281 7407 **F** (03) 5281 7427 **OPEN** By appointment
WINEMAKER Nicholas Clark, Janet Cockbill **EST.** 1995 **CASES** 150
PRODUCT RANGE ($18–30 ML) Riesling, Chardonnay, Rose, Shiraz, Cabernet Franc Merlot.
SUMMARY Janet Cockbill and Nicholas Clark are multi-talented. Both are archaeologists, but Janet manages to combine part-time archaeology, part-time radiography at Geelong Hospital and part-time organic viticulture. Nicholas Clark has nearly completed a viticulture degree at Charles Sturt University, and both he and Janet worked a vintage in France at Michel Chapoutier's biodynamic Domaine de Beates in Provence in 2001. Production is tiny, because of their unwillingness to release wines which they consider not up to standard, and also because of poor weather at flowering. Indeed, part of the minuscule production comes from locally grown purchased grapes. All of that said, Amietta is producing cameo wines of some beauty.

Amulet Vineyard ★★★☆

Wangaratta Road, Beechworth, Vic 3747 **REGION** Beechworth
T (03) 5727 0420 **F** (03) 5727 0421 **OPEN** Fri–Mon, public and school holidays 10–5, or by appointment
WINEMAKER Sue Thornton (Contract) **EST.** 1998 **CASES** 1300
PRODUCT RANGE ($15–25 CD) Chardonnay Orange Muscat, Reserve Scintilla Rosso (sparkling Sangiovese) Rosato, Shiraz, Sangiovese Shiraz, Barbera, Orange Muscat.
SUMMARY Sue and Eric Thornton have planted a patchwork quilt 4-hectare vineyard, with sangiovese taking 1 hectare, the other varieties 0.5 hectare or less each (in descending order of magnitude, barbera, shiraz, cabernet sauvignon, merlot, nebbiolo, orange muscat, pinot gris and pinot blanc). The vineyard (and cellar door) is 11 kilometres west of Beechworth on the road to Wangaratta; the vines are planted on gentle slopes at an elevation of 300 metres. The cellar door enjoys panoramic views, and wine sales are both by the glass and by the bottle.

Anderson NR

Lot 12 Chiltern Road, Rutherglen, Vic 3685 **REGION** Rutherglen
T (02) 6032 8111 **F** (02) 6032 9028 **OPEN** 7 days 10–5
WINEMAKER Howard Anderson **EST.** 1992 **CASES** 1600
PRODUCT RANGE ($12.50–28 CD) Chenin Blanc, Doux Blanc, Unoaked Chardonnay, Chardonnay, Dulcette, Shiraz, Merlot, Durif, Cabernet Merlot, Cabernet Sauvignon, Late Harvest Tokay, Methode Champenoise range of Pinot Noir Chardonnay, Chenin Blanc, Doux Blanc, Shiraz.
SUMMARY Having notched up a winemaking career spanning over 30 years, including a stint at Seppelt Great Western, Howard Anderson and family started their own winery, initially with a particular focus on sparkling wine but now extending across all table wine styles. There are 4 hectares of estate shiraz, and 1 hectare each of durif and petit verdot, with yields controlled at a very low 2.5 tonnes per hectare (or, in the old money, 1 tonne per acre).

Andraos Bros

NR

Winilba Vineyard, 150 Vineyard Road, Sunbury, Vic 3429 **REGION** Sunbury
T (03) 9740 9703 **F** (03) 9740 9795 **OPEN** Fri–Sun and public holidays 11–5, or by appointment
WINEMAKER Fred Andraos, Mario Marson (Consultant) **EST.** 1989 **CASES** 2500
PRODUCT RANGE ($18–70 CD) Released under the Olde Winilba label are Riesling, Semillon, Semillon Sauvignon Blanc, Chardonnay, Pinot Shiraz, Pinot Noir, Shiraz, Cabernet Shiraz and Cabernet Sauvignon.
SUMMARY The original Winilba Vineyard was first planted in 1863, and remained in production until 1889. Exactly 100 years later the Andraos brothers commenced replanting the vineyard on the property they had purchased 5 years earlier. Over the following years they built a winery from the ruins of the original bluestone cellar, making the inaugural vintage in 1996. They have also established Estelle's Cellar Restaurant on the second floor of the building; it is open for dinner from Tuesday to Sunday and for lunch on Friday, Saturday, Sunday and public holidays.

Andrew Garrett

Ingoldby Road, McLaren Flat, SA 5171 **REGION** McLaren Vale
T (08) 8383 0005 **F** (08) 8383 0790 **OPEN** 7 days 10–4
WINEMAKER Charles Hargrave **EST.** 1983 **CASES** 170 000
PRODUCT RANGE Chardonnay, Pinot Noir Chardonnay, Sparkling Burgundy, Shiraz; Garrett Sparkling Chardonnay.
SUMMARY Andrew Garrett has long been owned by the Beringer Blass wine group, with many of the wines now not having a sole McLaren Vale source but instead being drawn from regions across southeastern Australia. Over the past few years, winemaker Charles Hargrave has produced some excellent wines which provide great value for money.

ŶŶŶŶŶ **Ingoldby Reserve Shiraz 2001** Rich, ripe, supple mouthfilling dark chocolate, blackberry and plum; good structure and length; deft oak. Multiple gold medal winner. **RATING** 91 **DRINK** 2021 $43

Andrew Harris Vineyards

Sydney Road, Mudgee, NSW 2850 **REGION** Mudgee
T (02) 6373 1213 **F** (02) 6373 1296 **OPEN** 7 days 9–5
WINEMAKER Frank Newman, Damian Grindley **EST.** 1991 **CASES** 65 000
PRODUCT RANGE ($14.95–39.95 R) Flagships are The Vision (Shiraz Cabernet Sauvignon) and Double Vision (sparkling Shiraz); next down the scale are Personal Selection (previously Reserve) Chardonnay, Merlot Cabernet, Shiraz, Cabernet Sauvignon; at the bottom is the varietal range of Verdelho, Chardonnay, Merlot, Shiraz and Cabernet Sauvignon.
SUMMARY Andrew and Deb Harris lost no time after purchasing a 300-hectare sheep station southeast of Mudgee in 1991. The first 6 hectares of vineyard were planted in that year; they have since been expanded to 106 hectares. A substantial portion of the production is sold to others, but production under the Andrew Harris label has risen significantly in recent years. There is now a spread of price and quality, with a string of difficult vintages also impacting, so some care is needed in choosing the wines. Exports to the US, Canada, Singapore, Malaysia, Japan and New Zealand.

ŶŶŶŶŶ **Shiraz 2001** Seductively rounded, supple and smooth; black fruits, chocolate, cherry; polished, ripe tannins. **RATING** 93 **DRINK** 2012 $14.95

ŶŶŶŶ **Merlot 2002** A nice varietal savoury/woodsy substrate to small red fruits; light to medium-bodied and not swamped by oak. **RATING** 87 **DRINK** 2008 $15.95

ŶŶŶŶ **Shiraz 2002 RATING** 86 **DRINK** 2009 $14.95
Premium Chardonnay 2003 RATING 84 **DRINK** Now $15.95

ŶŶŶ **Shiraz 2000 RATING** 83 $14.95
Verdelho 2003 RATING 82 $14.95

ŶŶŶ **Premium Cabernet Sauvignon 2002 RATING** 79 $24.95

Andrew Peace Wines ★★★

Murray Valley Highway, Piangil, Vic 3597 **REGION** Swan Hill
T (03) 5030 5291 **F** (03) 5030 5605 **OPEN** Mon–Fri 8–5, Sat 10–4, Sun by appointment
WINEMAKER Andrew Peace, Bill Small **EST.** 1995 **CASES** 300 000
PRODUCT RANGE ($9–15 CD) Mighty Murray White, Chardonnay, Chardonnay Reserve, Mighty Murray Rose, Mighty Murray Red, Shiraz, Shiraz Reserve, Shiraz Malbec, Cabernet Merlot.
SUMMARY The Peace family has been a major Swan Hill grape grower since 1980, with almost 90 hectares of vineyards, and moved into winemaking with the opening of a $3 million winery in 1997. The modestly priced wines are aimed at supermarket-type outlets in Australia and, in particular, at the export market in the major destinations for Australian wine.

ŢŢŢ **Mighty Shiraz 2002 RATING** 83 **DRINK** Now $12

Andrew Pirie NR

17 High Street, Launceston, Tas 7250 (postal) **REGION** Northern Tasmania
T (03) 6334 7772 **F** (03) 6334 0751 **OPEN** Not
WINEMAKER Andrew Pirie **EST.** 2004 **CASES** 5000
PRODUCT RANGE ($25–60 R) Under the Andrew Pirie label, very limited volumes of Riesling, Chardonnay and Pinot Noir in the $35 to $60 price range. Supplementary Tasmanian Regional range will be focused on Pinot Noir at a price of around $25.
SUMMARY After a relatively short break, Andrew Pirie has re-established his winemaking activities in Tasmania, while retaining his chief executive management role for Parker Estate in Coonawarra. He has leased the Rosevears Winery, where he will produce the wines for the Rosevears Group, for his own brands, and for others on a contract basis. For the foreseeable future he will rely on contract-grown fruit of the highest possible quality.

Angas Plains Estate ★★★☆

PO Box 283, Strathalbyn, SA 5255 **REGION** Langhorne Creek
T (08) 8537 3159 **F** (08) 8537 3353 **OPEN** At Bremer Restaurant, Langhorne Creek, 7 days 11–5
WINEMAKER Judy Cross (Contract) **EST.** 2000 **CASES** 500
PRODUCT RANGE ($15–18 CD) PJ's Chardonnay, PJ's Shiraz, PJ's Cabernet Sauviginon.
SUMMARY A family-operated business, with 14 hectares of shiraz, 10 hectares of cabernet sauvignon and 1 hectare of chardonnay; it is situated 10 minutes' drive south from the historic town of Strathalbyn, and on the banks of the Angas River. The wines are available through the Bremer Restaurant, which offers tastings of a number of wines from local wineries.

ŢŢŢŢ **PJ's Cabernet Sauvignon 2002** Medium-bodied; sweet blackcurrant and cassis fruit; soft tannins, subtle oak. **RATING** 88 **DRINK** 2010 $18

ŢŢŢ꒱ **PJ's Unwooded Chardonnay 2003 RATING** 85 **DRINK** Now $15

Angas Vineyards NR

PO Box 53, Langhorne Creek, SA 5255 **REGION** Langhorne Creek
T (08) 8537 3337 **F** (08) 8537 3231 **OPEN** Not
WINEMAKER Ben Glaetzer (Contract) **EST.** 1997
PRODUCT RANGE A range of varietally denominated table wines reflecting the plantings.
SUMMARY Angas Vineyards is the umbrella organisation for a number of separately marketed brands. Its principal viticultural resource is 222 hectares of vineyards, with multiple examples of ultra-trendy varietals: verdelho, viognier, pinot gris, grenache, cabernet sauvignon, merlot, malbec, shiraz, mataro, petit verdot, sangiovese, barbera, dolcetto, lagrein and tempranillo. Most of the wine is exported to England, Germany, Ireland, Norway and the US under either the Angas Vineyards, Heartland or Bushy Road Vineyard brand.

Angove's ★★★☆

Bookmark Avenue, Renmark, SA 5341 **REGION** Riverland
T (08) 8580 3100 **F** (08) 8580 3155 **OPEN** Mon–Fri 9–5
WINEMAKER Warrick Billings, Shane Clohesy, Tony Ingle **EST.** 1886 **CASES** 1.3 million
PRODUCT RANGE ($3–220 CD) At the top, Sarnia Farm Chardonnay, Shiraz, Cabernet Sauvignon;
Classic Reserve, covering virtually all varieties; then the Bear Crossing range; underneath that,
Butterfly Ridge; and bringing up the rear, Misty Vineyards; also leading producer of brandy at
various price points (including St Agnes).
SUMMARY Exemplifies the economies of scale achievable in the Australian Riverland without
compromising potential quality. Very good technology provides wines which are never poor and
which can sometimes exceed their theoretical station in life; the white varietals are best. Angove's
expansion into Padthaway has resulted in estate-grown premium wines at the top of the range. As
well as national distribution, Angove's is exported to virtually all the major markets in Europe, North
America and Asia. For good measure, it also acts as a distributor of Perrier Jouet Champagne and
several small Australian wineries.

TTTTT **Long Row Sauvignon Blanc 2003** Clearly expressed ripe varietal character; gooseberry
and passionfruit; well-balanced acidity. Exceptional achievement. Screwcap. **RATING** 90
DRINK Now $ 9.99
Red Belly Black Shiraz 2002 Rich, full of ripe blackberry and plum; supple mouthfeel;
delivers on price. **RATING** 90 **DRINK** Now $ 14.99

TTTT **Vineyard Select Riesling 2003** Rich, potent herb and lime aromas and flavours; on the
big side of the divide. **RATING** 89 **DRINK** 2007 $ 16
Long Row Chardonnay 2002 Well-made tangy melon and stone fruit; whisper of oak;
good balance. Screwcap. **RATING** 87 **DRINK** Now $ 9.99
Anchorage Old Tawny Port NV In fact as much young and old (up to 30 years), but has
buckets of spicy, biscuity flavours. **RATING** 87 **DRINK** Now $ 16

TTTT **Long Row Cabernet Sauvignon 2002 RATING** 86 **DRINK** 2008 $ 9.99
Stonegate Limited Release Verdelho 2003 RATING 85 **DRINK** Now $ 8.99
Sarnia Farm Shiraz 2001 RATING 85 **DRINK** 2007 $ 13.99
Sarnia Farm Cabernet Sauvignon 2000 RATING 85 **DRINK** 2008 $ 13.99
Vineyard Select Riesling 2002 RATING 84 **DRINK** Now $ 16
Long Row Merlot 2002 RATING 84 **DRINK** Now $ 9.99
Vineyard Select Coonawarra Cabernet Sauvignon 2001 RATING 84 **DRINK** Now $ 24

TTT **Long Row Pinot Noir 2003 RATING** 82 $ 9.99
Premium Port Ref 18F60 1996 RATING 82 $ 12.99
Bear Crossing Cabernet Merlot 2002 RATING 81 $ 8.99

Angus Wines ★★★★☆

Captain Sturt Road, Hindmarsh Island, SA 5214 **REGION** Southern Fleurieu
T (08) 8555 2320 **F** (08) 8555 2323 **OPEN** Weekends and public holidays 10–5
WINEMAKER Mike Farmilo **EST.** 1995 **CASES** 2000
PRODUCT RANGE ($15–48 CD) Semillon, Shiraz, Cabernet Sauvignon.
SUMMARY Susan and Alistair Angus are the pioneer viticulturists on Hindmarsh Island, an island
which has never been far from the headlines, but for reasons entirely divorced from viticulture. If
the Bridge has had problems to contend with, so have the Anguses as they have progressed from a
test plot of vines planted in 1992 through to the first tiny commercial crop in 1998 and a far larger
crop in 1999. They have established 4.5 hectares of shiraz, and 1.5 hectares of semillon, the wine
being contract-made for them by Mike Farmilo at The Fleurieu Winery in McLaren Vale. Part is
bottled under the Angus Wines label, but a larger amount is sold in bulk to other wineries. Every
aspect of packaging and marketing the wine has a sophisticated touch. Exports to the UK and
Belgium.

TTTTT **Sturt Ridge Semillon 2003** Aromatic herb, grass and hay aromas and flavours, with
lemony acidity giving length. **RATING** 92 **DRINK** 2010 $ 15

Sturt Ridge Shiraz 2001 Blackberry, plum, prune and dark chocolate; excellent richness, ripeness and mouthfeel. No green tannins. **RATING** 92 **DRINK** 2011 $ 22

Sturt Ridge Semillon 2002 Clean and pure; classic taut, grassy flavours; firm, long finish. Needs time. **RATING** 90 **DRINK** 2008 $ 15

Annapurna Wines   NR

Simmonds Creek Road, Mount Beauty, Vic 3698 **REGION** Alpine Valleys
T (03) 9739 1184 **F** (03) 9739 1184 **OPEN** Wed–Sun 10–5
WINEMAKER Frank Minutello **EST.** 1989
PRODUCT RANGE ($11.30–28.5 CD) Pinot Gris, Chardonnay, Methode Traditionelle, Pinot Noir, Pinot Noir Reserve, Reserve Alfresco (light red), Merlot.
SUMMARY Ezio and Wendy Minutello began the establishment of the 18-hectare vineyard at 550 metres on Mount Beauty in 1989, planting to pinot noir, chardonnay and pinot gris. The decision to produce some wine under the Annapurna label was taken in 1995, and the following year Annapurna was named the Victorian Wines Show Vineyard of the Year (assessed purely on the viticulture, not the wines). Finally, in 1999, the first wines were released. Annapurna, the second-highest mountain after Mount Everest, is Nepalese for 'goddess of bountiful harvest and fertility'. Frank Minutello makes a small amount of wine each year in a small on-site winery, but the lion's share of the grapes is sold to other makers.

Annie's Lane   ★★★★★

Quelltaler Road, Watervale, SA 5452 **REGION** Clare Valley
T (08) 8843 0003 **F** (08) 8843 0096 **OPEN** Mon–Fri 8.30–5, weekends 11–4
WINEMAKER Caroline Dunn **EST.** 1851 **CASES** 120 000
PRODUCT RANGE ($12–45 CD) Riesling, Semillon, Reserve Semillon, Shiraz, Copper Trail Shiraz, Old Vine Shiraz, Grenache Mourvedre, Clare/Barossa Cabernet Merlot.
SUMMARY The Clare Valley portfolio of Beringer Blass formerly made at the historic Quelltaler winery is sold under the Annie's Lane label, the name coming from Annie Weyman, a turn-of-the-century local identity. Since 1996, a series of outstanding wines have appeared under the Annie's Lane label.

♥♥♥♥♥ **Copper Trail Shiraz 2000** Filled to the brim with blackberry and dark chocolate; excellent fruit/oak balance and integration; ripe, soft tannins. **RATING** 95 **DRINK** 2020 $ 55
Copper Trail Shiraz Grenache Mourvedre 2000 Very fragrant spice, chocolate, earth and black fruits; succulent, smooth and long; elegant finish. **RATING** 95 **DRINK** 2010 $ 37

♥♥♥♥♡ **Cabernet Merlot 2002** Powerful super-rich, concentrated and luscious blackcurrant, plum and prune fruit, with ample soft tannins and oak somewhere in the depths. Great value. **RATING** 92 **DRINK** 2015 $ 19

♥♥♥♥ **Riesling 2003** A ripe and powerful wine; tropical/pineapple fruit; somewhat broad.
RATING 89 **DRINK** 2009 $ 18

♥♥♥♡ **Chardonnay 2003 RATING** 85 **DRINK** Now $ 18

Annvers Wines

Lot 10, Razorback Road, Kangarilla, SA 5157 **REGION** Adelaide Hills
T (08) 8374 1787 **F** (08) 8374 2102 **OPEN** Not
WINEMAKER Duane Coates **EST.** 1998 **CASES** 5000
PRODUCT RANGE ($22–42 R) Shiraz, Shiraz Cabernet Sauvignon, Cabernet Sauvignon, Tawny Reserve.
SUMMARY Myriam and Wayne Keoghan established Annvers Wines with the emphasis on quality rather than quantity. The first Cabernet Sauvignon was made in 1998, and volume has increased year by year since then. The grapes come from vineyards in Langhorne Creek, McLaren Vale and the Annvers Estate Vineyard in the Adelaide Hills. Since the wine was first released, it has been sold in the US and Singapore, and has limited retail distribution in South Australia, New South Wales and Queensland. Exports to the US, Canada, the UK, Belgium, Switzerland and Singapore.

ŦŦŦŦ♀ **Shiraz Cabernet 2002** Offers a complex web of black fruits, spice, chocolate and vanilla; excellent texture and structure. **RATING** 93 **DRINK** 2012 $ 22

Reserve Shiraz 2001 Stylish, complex, medium-bodied; full of black fruits; excellent texture, not extractive nor oaky. **RATING** 92 **DRINK** 2011 $ 38

Antcliff's Chase ★★★☆

RMB 4510, Caveat via Seymour, Vic 3660 **REGION** Strathbogie Ranges
T (03) 5790 4333 **F** (03) 5790 4333 **OPEN** Weekends 10–5
WINEMAKER Chris Bennett, Ian Leamon **EST.** 1982 **CASES** 800
PRODUCT RANGE ($14–30 CD) Riesling, Chardonnay, Pinot Noir, Ultra Pinot Noir, Cabernet Merlot.
SUMMARY A small family enterprise which commenced planting the vineyards at an elevation of 600 metres in the Strathbogie Ranges in 1982, and commenced wine production from the 4-hectare vineyard in the early 1990s. After an uncertain start, wine quality has picked up considerably.

ŦŦŦŦ **Ultra Pinot Noir 2001** Ripe, rich plum and black cherry fruit fill a wine with good depth, length and varietal character. A surprise for the Strathbogies. **RATING** 88 **DRINK** 2011 $ 22

ŦŦŦ **Chardonnay 2001** **RATING** 82 $ 20

ŦŦ♀ **Riesling 2001** **RATING** 79 $ 20

Anthony Dale ★★★☆

Lot 202 Robe Road, Bray, SA 5276 (postal) **REGION** Mount Benson
T (08) 8735 7255 **F** (08) 8735 7255 **OPEN** Not
WINEMAKER John Bird (Contract) **EST.** 1994 **CASES** 1750
PRODUCT RANGE ($38 R) Shiraz Cabernet Sauvignon.
SUMMARY Anthony Dale has meticulously planned every aspect and detail of the vineyard and winery which bears his name. The vineyard was planted from 1995 to 1998 inclusive; situated on the leeward side of the Woakwine Range, the light sandy soil is heavily impregnated with limestone. The decision has been taken to limit the crop to 1 tonne per acre (2.5 tonnes per hectare). Only one wine is made: a blend of shiraz and cabernet sauvignon; the winemaker is John Bird, a former senior Penfolds red winemaker with experience in helping make all of the Penfolds top red wines (including Grange). As well as limited local and Queensland distribution, the wines are exported to the US and Switzerland.

Apsley Gorge Vineyard ★★★★☆

The Gulch, Bicheno, Tas 7215 **REGION** Southern Tasmania
T (03) 6375 1221 **F** (03) 6375 1589 **OPEN** By appointment
WINEMAKER Brian Franklin **EST.** 1988 **CASES** 3000
PRODUCT RANGE ($230–40 CD) Chardonnay, Pinot Noir.
SUMMARY While nominally situated at Bicheno on the east coast, Apsley Gorge is in fact some distance inland, and takes its name from a mountain pass. Clearly, it shares with the other east coast wineries the capacity to produce Chardonnay and Pinot Noir of excellent quality.

Apthorpe Estate NR

Lot 1073 Lovedale Road, Lovedale, NSW 2321 **REGION** Lower Hunter Valley
T (02) 4930 9177 **F** (02) 4930 9188 **OPEN** Fri and Mon 10–4, weekends 10–5
WINEMAKER Mark Apthorpe, Jim Chatto (Contract) **EST.** 1996 **CASES** 1200
PRODUCT RANGE ($16–22 CD) Semillon, Chardonnay, Rose, Sparkling Chambourcin, Chambourcin, Cabernet Franc, The Convict Vintage Port.
SUMMARY Samuel Apthorpe was given 14 years' imprisonment as a convict in Australia for stealing a few teaspoons. In the mid-1850s, after he had completed his sentence, he established a vineyard in the Hunter Valley at Bishops Bridge. In 1996 his great-great-great-grandson, Mark Apthorpe, continued the tradition when he planted 2.5 hectares of cabernet franc and 2.5 hectares of chambourcin at nearby Lovedale. The wines are made at Monarch under the direction of Jim Chatto, with input from Mark Apthorpe, and it can be safely assumed that the quality is good.

Aquila Estate ★★★☆

85 Carabooda Road, Carabooda, WA 6033 **REGION** Swan District
T (08) 9561 8166 **F** (08) 9561 8177 **OPEN** Weekends and public holidays 11–5, Mon–Fri by appointment
WINEMAKER Andrew Spencer-Wright **EST.** 1993 **CASES** 20 000
PRODUCT RANGE ($15–40 CD) Riesling, Chenin Blanc, Sauvignon Blanc, Reflections (white blend), Chardonnay, Shiraz, Merlot, Flame (red blend), Cabernet Sauvignon.
SUMMARY As Aquila Estate has matured, so have its grape sources, which are centred on the Margaret River (principally) and Blackwood Valley. The competitively priced wines are in many instances a blend of Blackwood Valley and Margaret River grapes. Exports to the US, Canada, Singapore, Mauritius and Japan.

Arakoon ★★★★☆

229 Main Road, McLaren Vale, SA 5171 **REGION** McLaren Vale
T (08) 8323 7339 **F** (02) 6566 6288 **OPEN** Fri–Sun 10–5, or by appointment
WINEMAKER Patrik Jones, Raymond Jones **EST.** 1999 **CASES** 2000
PRODUCT RANGE ($20–50 R) Chardonnay, Pinot Black (Pinot Noir), Blewitt Springs Shiraz, Doyen Shiraz, Reserve Shiraz, Sellicks Beach Shiraz Grenache, The Lighthouse Cabernet Sauvignon Shiraz.
SUMMARY Ray and Patrik Jones' first venture into wine came to nothing: a 1990 proposal for a film about the Australian wine industry with myself as anchorman. Five years too early, say the Joneses. In 1991 they opened an agency for Australian wine in Stockholm, and they started exporting wine to that country, the UK, Germany and Switzerland in 1994. (They now also export to the US, Belgium, Malaysia, Denmark and Sweden.) In 1999 they took the plunge into making their own wine, and exporting it as well as the wines of others. Patrik is the winemaker, having completed a degree at the Waite Campus of the University of Adelaide. New label and packaging designs are totally appropriate for wines of this quality.

▼▼▼▼▽ **Doyen Shiraz 2002** Dense, deep colour; extremely powerful and concentrated black fruits; ripe tannins in balance. Screwcap; cellaring special. **RATING** 93 **DRINK** 2022 $ 50
Blewitt Springs Shiraz 2002 A rich blend of blackberry, chocolate and a splash of oak; good structure and tannins. Screwcap. **RATING** 91 **DRINK** 2012 $ 40
Sellicks Beach Shiraz Grenache 2002 A generous serving of juicy black fruits in a light to medium-bodied structure; clean finish; really nice wine. Screwcap. **RATING** 90 **DRINK** 2008 $ 20
The Lighthouse Fleurieu Peninsula Cabernet Sauvignon 2002 Tightly knit blackcurrant, mocha, chocolate, vanilla and ripe tannins; excellent overall mouthfeel. Screwcap. **RATING** 90 **DRINK** 2012 $ 20

Archer Falls Vineyard & Winery NR

1253 Newrum Road, Kilcoy via Woodford, Qld 4514 **REGION** Queensland Coastal
T (07) 5496 3507 **F** (07) 5496 3507 **OPEN** Weekends and public holidays 10–5
WINEMAKER Ronald Field **EST.** 1995
PRODUCT RANGE A range of varietally denominated table wines reflecting the plantings.
SUMMARY Ronald Field has a small vineyard of chardonnay and shiraz, using the very experienced Brian Wilson as contract winemaker. The wine is sold through the cellar door and by mail order, with the usual cellar door facilities, including barbecue and picnics.

Arlewood Estate ★★★★☆

Harmans Road South, Wilyabrup, WA 6284 **REGION** Margaret River
T (08) 9755 6267 **F** (08) 9755 6267 **OPEN** Weekends 11–5
WINEMAKER Voyager Estate (Contract) **EST.** 1988 **CASES** 6000
PRODUCT RANGE ($19–35 CD) Semillon, Sauvignon Blanc, Reserve Chardonnay, Pinot Noir, Shiraz, Cabernet Merlot, Cabernet Reserve (Cabernet Sauvignon Merlot Cabernet Franc).
SUMMARY The Heydon and Gosatti families acquired Arlewood Estate in October 1999, having previously established a small vineyard in Cowaramup in 1995. George Heydon is a Perth dentist whose passion for wine has led him to study viticulture at the University of Western Australia, while Garry Gosatti has been involved in the boutique brewing and hospitality industries for many years.

The area under vine has now been expanded to 15 hectares, and Arlewood has entered into a long-term winemaking contract with Voyager Estate, with consultancy advice from Janice McDonald. The quality and consistency of the wines is now impeccable. Retail distribution in most States, and exports to the US and the UK.

ŢŢŢŢŢ Semillon 2003 Finely delineated; crisp, lemony, long; deft use of oak. **RATING** 93 **DRINK** 2012 $19

Armstrong Vineyards

Lot 1 Military Road, Armstrong, Vic 3381 **REGION** Grampians
T (08) 8277 6073 **F** (08) 8277 6035 **OPEN** Not
WINEMAKER Tony Royal **EST.** 1989 **CASES** 800
PRODUCT RANGE ($48 R) Shiraz.
SUMMARY Armstrong Vineyards is the brain- or love-child of Tony Royal, the former Seppelt Great Western winemaker who now runs the Australian business of Seguin Moreau, the largest of the French coopers. Armstrong Vineyards has 5 hectares of shiraz, the first 2 hectares planted in 1989, the remainder in 1995–96. Low yields (4.5 to 5.5 tonnes per hectare) mean the wine will always be produced in limited quantities.

ŢŢŢŢ Shiraz 2002 Harmonious and seamless fusion of blackberry fruit, oak and fine, ripe tannins; long finish. **RATING** 93 **DRINK** 2015 $48

Arranmore Vineyard ★★★

Rangeview Road, Carey Gully, SA 5144 **REGION** Adelaide Hills
T (08) 8390 3034 **F** (08) 8390 0005 **OPEN** By appointment
WINEMAKER John Venus **EST.** 1998 **CASES** 400
PRODUCT RANGE ($15–35 CD) Sauvignon Blanc, Chardonnay, Adelaide Hills Pinot Noir, Black Pinot Noir, Curate's Closet Merlot.
SUMMARY One of the tiny operations which are appearing all over the beautiful Adelaide Hills. At an altitude of around 550 metres, the 2-hectare vineyard is planted to clonally selected pinot noir, chardonnay and sauvignon blanc; the wines are distributed by Australian Premium Boutique Wines, and sold by mail order. Exports to the UK.

ŢŢŢŢ Adelaide Hills Sauvignon Blanc 2003 **RATING** 85 **DRINK** Now $15
Black Pinot Noir 2002 **RATING** 84 **DRINK** Now $35

Arrowfield ★★☆

Denman Road, Jerry's Plains, NSW 2330 **REGION** Upper Hunter Valley
T (02) 6576 4041 **F** (02) 6576 4144 **OPEN** 7 days 10–5
WINEMAKER Tim Pearce **EST.** 1968 **CASES** 70 000
PRODUCT RANGE ($9–20 R) Top-of-the-range Show Reserve range of Chardonnay, Semillon, Shiraz, Merlot, Cabernet Sauvignon, Late Harvest Botrytis Semillon; Hunter Valley Chardonnay, Semillon, Shiraz; Cowra Chardonnay, Merlot; Arrowfield varietals Chardonnay, Semillon Chardonnay, Sauvignon Blanc, Verdelho, Sauvignon Blanc, Shiraz, Cabernet Merlot.
SUMMARY After largely dropping the Arrowfield name in favour of Mountarrow and a plethora of other brands, this Japanese-owned company has come full circle, once again marketing the wines solely under the Arrowfield label. Its principal grape sources are Cowra and the Upper Hunter, but it does venture further afield from time to time. Exports to all major markets.

ŢŢŢ Hunter Valley Shiraz 2001 **RATING** 83 $15
Show Reserve McLaren Vale Shiraz 1999 **RATING** 83 $21

Artamus

PO Box 489, Margaret River, WA 6285 **REGION** Margaret River
T (08) 9757 8131 **F** (08) 9757 8131 **OPEN** Not
WINEMAKER Michael Gadd **EST.** 1994 **CASES** 280
PRODUCT RANGE ($16.25 R) Chardonnay.

SUMMARY Ann Dewar and Ian Parmenter (the celebrated television food presenter) planted a hectare of chardonnay cuttings (from Cape Mentelle) at their property on the north bank of the Margaret River. Their first wine was produced in 1998, made for them by Michael Gadd, and the style of each succeeding vintage has been remarkably consistent.

Arthurs Creek Estate ★★★★

Strathewen Road, Arthurs Creek, Vic 3099 **REGION** Yarra Valley
T (03) 9714 8202 **F** (03) 9824 0252 **OPEN** Not
WINEMAKER Tom Carson (Contract), Gary Baldwin (Consultant) **EST.** 1975 **CASES** 1500
PRODUCT RANGE ($28–46 R) Chardonnay, Cabernet Sauvignon.
SUMMARY A latter-day folly of leading Melbourne QC S E K Hulme, who began the planting of 3 hectares of chardonnay, 4.3 hectares of cabernet sauvignon and 0.7 hectare of merlot at Arthurs Creek in the mid-1970s, and had wine made by various people for 15 years before deciding to sell any of it. A ruthless weeding-out process followed, with only the best of the older vintages offered. Exports to the UK, the US, Denmark and Japan.

Arundel ★★★★★

Arundel Farm Estate, PO Box 136, Keilor, Vic 3036 **REGION** Sunbury
T (03) 9335 3422 **F** (03) 9335 4912 **OPEN** Not
WINEMAKER Bianca Hayes **EST.** 1995 **CASES** 200
PRODUCT RANGE ($25 ML) Shiraz.
SUMMARY Arundel has been built around a single acre of cabernet and shiraz planted by a previous owner in the 1970s, but abandoned for many years. When the Conwell family purchased the property in the early 1990s, the vineyard was resurrected, the first vintage being made by Rick Kinzbrunner in 1995. Thereafter the cabernet was grafted over to shiraz, the block being slowly increased to 1.6 hectares. After the 1999 vintage, Bianca Hayes took over the responsibility for winemaking on-site. An additional 4 hectares of shiraz and 1.6 hectares of viognier and marsanne have been planted, which will lead to significantly increased production in the future.

ŸŸŸŸŸ **Shiraz 2002** Rich, layered and powerful licorice, plum, blackberry and boot leather; complex, rich tannins; thoroughly impressive. **RATING** 94 **DRINK** 2017 $ 25

Ashbrook Estate ★★★★

Harmans Road South, Wilyabrup via Cowaramup, WA 6284 **REGION** Margaret River
T (08) 9755 6262 **F** (08) 9755 6290 **OPEN** 7 days 11–5
WINEMAKER Tony Devitt, Brian Devitt **EST.** 1975 **CASES** 8000
PRODUCT RANGE ($15–25 CD) Gold Label Riesling, Black Label Riesling, Semillon, Semillon Reserve, Sauvignon Blanc, Verdelho, Chardonnay, Shiraz, Cabernet Merlot.
SUMMARY A fastidious maker of consistently excellent estate-grown table wines, this winery shuns publicity and the wine show system alike and is less well-known than it deserves to be, selling much of its wine through the cellar door and to an understandably very loyal mailing list clientele. All of the white wines are of the highest quality, year in, year out. Small quantities of the wines now find their way to Canada, Japan, Singapore, Hong Kong and the UK.

ŸŸŸŸŸ **Sauvignon Blanc 2003** Full-on complexity, funky/smoky; very rich, very ripe; almost sweet. **RATING** 91 **DRINK** Now $ 17

ŸŸŸŸ **Cabernet Merlot 1999** **RATING** 86 **DRINK** 2009 $ 25

Ashley Estate NR

284 Aldersyde Road, Bickley, WA 6076 **REGION** Perth Hills
T (08) 9257 2313 **F** (08) 9257 3403 **OPEN** Sunday and public holidays by appointment
WINEMAKER John Griffiths (Contract) **EST.** 1988
PRODUCT RANGE Pinot Noir.
SUMMARY Ashley Estate (formerly Ashley Park) has 8 hectares of vines planted exclusively to pinot noir by proprietor John Ashley. Highly experienced winemaker John Griffiths is responsible for winemaking, and the wine is sold through the cellar door in its garden setting.

Ashton Hills

Tregarthen Road, Ashton, SA 5137 **REGION** Adelaide Hills
T (08) 8390 1243 **F** (08) 8390 1243 **OPEN** Weekends 11–5.30
WINEMAKER Stephen George **EST.** 1982 **CASES** 1500
PRODUCT RANGE ($20–42 CD) Riesling, Chardonnay, Three (Gewurztraminer Pinot Gris Riesling),
Salmon Brut, Pinot Noir, Piccadilly Valley Pinot Noir, Burra Burra Lone Star Shiraz, Five (Merlot
Cabernet Sauvignon Malbec Cabernet Franc Petit Verdot).
SUMMARY Stephen George wears three winemaker hats: one for Ashton Hills, drawing upon a
3.5-hectare estate vineyard high in the Adelaide Hills; one for Galah Wines; and one for Wendouree.
It would be hard to imagine three wineries producing more diverse styles, with the elegance and
finesse of Ashton Hills at one end of the spectrum, the awesome power of Wendouree at the other.
The Riesling, Chardonnay and Pinot Noir have moved into the highest echelon. The grapes for this
wine come from a vineyard established and owned by Stephen George's father. Exports to the UK and
the US.

ŸŸŸŸŸ **Chardonnay 2002** Fine, elegant and sophisticated; stone fruit, citrus and cashew; subtle
oak; perfect balance. **RATING** 94 **DRINK** 2010 $ 30
Pinot Noir 2002 Strong colour; complex spice, plum and forest aromas; great length and
depth to the multiple flavours of the palate; shows tiny crop concentration. **RATING** 94
DRINK 2012 $ 42

ŸŸŸŸŸ **Riesling 2003** Lime and apple blossom aromas; elegant, crisp, gentle citrus palate; very
stylish. **RATING** 93 **DRINK** 2013 $ 20
Burra Burra Lone Star Shiraz 2001 Intense and deep colour; black fruits, dark chocolate,
lingering acid and tannins to close. **RATING** 90 **DRINK** 2016 $ 25

ŸŸŸŸ **Three 2003** The full dish of fruit salad plus some acidity to tidy up the finish. Pinot Gris,
Gewurztraminer and Riesling. **RATING** 88 **DRINK** Now $ 20
Five 2001 More red fruits and extract than the '00 vintage; nice flicks of spice. A blend of
Merlot, Cabernet Sauvignon, Malbec, Cabernet Franc and Petit Verdot. **RATING** 87
DRINK 2009 $ 25

ŸŸŸŸ **Five 2000** **RATING** 86 **DRINK** 2007 $ 25

Ashworths Hill

NR

104 Ashworths Road, Lancefield, Vic 3435 **REGION** Macedon Ranges
T (03) 5429 1689 **F** (03) 5429 1689 **OPEN** Thurs–Mon 10–6
WINEMAKER Anne Manning, John Ellis **EST.** 1982 **CASES** 100
PRODUCT RANGE ($15–25 CD) Victorian Riesling, Victorian Chardonnay, Macedon Ranges Pinot Noir,
Macedon Ranges Cabernet Sauvignon, fortifieds.
SUMMARY Peg and Ken Reaburn offer light refreshments throughout the day, and the 4-hectare
property has scenic views of the Macedon Ranges.

Audrey Wilkinson

Oakdale, De Beyers Road, Pokolbin, NSW 2320 **REGION** Lower Hunter Valley
T (02) 4998 7411 **F** (02) 4998 7303 **OPEN** Mon–Fri 9–5, weekends 9.30–5
WINEMAKER Mark Woods **EST.** 1999 **CASES** 15 000
PRODUCT RANGE ($16–25.5 CD) Traminer, Semillon, Reserve Semillon, Semillon Verdelho, Verdelho,
Unwooded Chardonnay, Chardonnay, Zinfandel Shiraz Merlot, Merlot, Shiraz, Reserve Shiraz,
Reserve Coonawarra Cabernet Sauvignon.
SUMMARY One of the most historic properties in the Hunter Valley, set in a particularly beautiful
location. The four wines come from the old plantings on the property, which has a very attractive
cellar door. It is part of the James Fairfax wine group (headed by Pepper Tree).

ŸŸŸŸŸ **Reserve Shiraz 2000** Elegant, supple red fruits; fine-grained tannins; subtle oak and
good length. **RATING** 92 **DRINK** 2010 $ 30
Malbec 2003 As usual, very clear varietal raspberry jam flavours; good weight and
structure. **RATING** 90 **DRINK** 2010 $ 20

ŸŸŸŸ **Merlot Cabernet 2003** Clean, fresh, juicy red fruits; attractive, early drinking. **RATING** 87 **DRINK** Now $20

ŸŸŸⱷ **Hillside Shiraz 2003 RATING** 86 **DRINK** 2008 $12

ŸŸŸ **Traminer 2003 RATING** 83 $19
Verdelho 2003 RATING 83 $19

Auldstone ★★★

Booths Road, Taminick via Glenrowan, Vic 3675 **REGION** Glenrowan
T (03) 5766 2237 **F** (03) 5766 2131 **OPEN** Thurs–Sat and school holidays 9–5, Sun 10–5
WINEMAKER Michael Reid **EST.** 1987 **CASES** 2000
PRODUCT RANGE ($14–30 CD) Riesling, Traminer Riesling, Chardonnay, Late Picked Riesling, Sparkling Shiraz, Shiraz, Merlot, Cabernet Merlot, Cabernet Sauvignon, Herceynia Tawny Port, Liqueur Muscat.
SUMMARY Michael and Nancy Reid have restored a century-old stone winery and have replanted the largely abandoned 26-hectare vineyard around it. All of the Auldstone varietal and fortified wines have won a string of medals (usually bronze) in Australian wine shows. Gourmet lunches are available on weekends.

ŸŸŸ **Traminer Riesling 2002 RATING** 82 $14

Austin's Barrabool ★★★★

870 Steiglitz Road, Sutherlands Creek, Vic 3331 **REGION** Geelong
T (03) 5281 1799 **F** (03) 5281 1673 **OPEN** By appointment
WINEMAKER Scott Ireland (Contract), Pamela Austin **EST.** 1982 **CASES** 8000
PRODUCT RANGE ($20–45 CD) Riesling, Sauvignon Blanc, Chardonnay, Ellyse-Chardonnay, Pinot Noir, Reserve Pinot Noir, Shiraz, Cabernet Sauvignon.
SUMMARY Pamela and Richard Austin have quietly built their business from a tiny base, but it has flourished. The vineyard has been progressively extended to 56 hectares, and production has risen from 700 cases in 1998 to 8000 cases in 2004, underwritten by the construction of a new on-site winery. Exports to Asia.

ŸŸŸŸⱷ **Reserve Pinot Noir 2002** More evolved colour than the varietal; highly aromatic, complex spice/briar/bramble/plum; powerful and long; better controlled. **RATING** 91 **DRINK** 2010 $45
Ellyse Chardonnay 2001 Smoky barrel-ferment aromas; complex, restrained, slow-developing palate; creamy cashew notes, but fruit to the fore. **RATING** 90 **DRINK** 2007 $28
Reserve Pinot Noir 2001 Ripe but not jammy plum aromas; full-on palate; spice, cedar, plum and forest. **RATING** 90 **DRINK** 2008 $45

ŸŸŸŸ **Chardonnay 2002** Powerful wine; oak and ripe, concentrated fruit battle for supremacy; punches above its 13 degrees alcohol. **RATING** 89 **DRINK** Now $25
Shiraz 2000 Elegant, well-balanced plum and berry fruit; subtle oak, soft tannins. **RATING** 89 **DRINK** 2010 $40
Riesling 2003 Ripe, rich and full style; abundant lime/tropical flavours; drink now. **RATING** 88 **DRINK** 2007 $20
Pinot Noir 2002 Ripe tobacco leaf, spice and plum aromas and flavours; huge palate; alcohol, extract and ripe fruit. **RATING** 88 **DRINK** 2009 $22
Cabernet Sauvignon 2001 Light to medium-bodied; sweet cassis, with touches of mint and leaf; fine tannins; long finish. **RATING** 87 **DRINK** 2008 $25

ŸŸŸⱷ **Shiraz 2001 RATING** 86 **DRINK** 2007 $40
Merlot 2001 RATING 85 **DRINK** Now $22

Australian Domaine Wines NR

95a Walkerville Terrace, Walkerville, SA 5081 **REGION** Clare Valley
T (08) 8342 3395 **F** (08) 8269 4008 **OPEN** By appointment
WINEMAKER Neil Pike (Polish Hill River Winery) **EST.** 1993 **CASES** 3000
PRODUCT RANGE ($9–11 CD) Shiraz, Old Vine Grenache Shiraz.

SUMMARY Australian Domaine Wines is the reincarnation of Barletta Bros, who started their own brand business for leading Adelaide retailer Walkerville Cellars, which they then owned. The wines are made at Pike's Polish Hill River Winery using tanks and barrels owned by the Barlettas. Retail distribution in South Australia and Melbourne; exports to the US, Canada, Singapore, the UK and Germany.

Avalon Vineyard ★★★☆

RMB 9556 Whitfield Road, Wangaratta, Vic 3678 **REGION** King Valley
T (03) 5729 3629 **F** (03) 5729 3635 **OPEN** 7 days 10–5
WINEMAKER Doug Groom **EST.** 1981 **CASES** 1000
PRODUCT RANGE ($12–20 CD) Riesling, Semillon, Sauvignon Blanc, Chardonnay, Late Harvest Semillon, Pinot Noir, Shiraz, Cabernet Sauvignon, Pinot Noir Methode Champenoise.
SUMMARY Avalon Vineyard is situated in the King Valley, 4 kilometres north of Whitfield. Much of the production from the 10-hectare vineyard is sold to other makers, with limited quantities made by Doug Groom, a graduate of Roseworthy, and one of the owners of the property. Exports to the US.

ΨΨΨΨ **Cabernet Sauvignon Merlot 2002** Abundant rich and ripe sweet blackberry; round and mouthfilling. **RATING** 88 **DRINK** 2012

Avalon Wines NR

1605 Bailey Road, Glen Forrest, WA 6071 **REGION** Perth Hills
T (08) 9298 8049 **F** (08) 9298 8049 **OPEN** By appointment
WINEMAKER Rob Marshall (Contract) **EST.** 1986 **CASES** 700
PRODUCT RANGE ($13–17 CD) Semillon, Chardonnay, Cane-Cut Semillon, Cabernet Merlot.
SUMMARY One of the smaller wineries in the Perth Hills, drawing upon 0.75 hectare each of chardonnay, semillon and cabernet sauvignon.

Avenel Park/Hart Wines ★★★

24/25 Ewings Road, Avenel, Vic 3664 **REGION** Goulburn Valley
T (03) 9347 5444 **F** (03) 9349 3278 **OPEN** Sunday 11–4, or by appointment
WINEMAKER David Traeger, Sam Plunkett (Contract) **EST.** 1994 **CASES** 1000
PRODUCT RANGE ($12–24 CD) Lovers Hill Unwooded Chardonnay, Lovers Hill Rose, Shiraz, Shiraz Cabernet Sauvignon, Cabernet Sauvignon; under the Hart label, Shiraz, Cabernet Sauvignon.
SUMMARY Jed and Sue Hart have, in their words, 'turned the rocky, ironstone soils of Lovers Hill into a 22-acre vineyard over some back-breaking years'. Seven of the 10 hectares are planted to shiraz and cabernet sauvignon, with a small amount each of merlot, semillon and chardonnay. Most of the grapes have been and will continue to be sold to Southcorp, but since 2000 the equivalent of 1000 cases of wine have been retained and contract-made by David Traeger. Nonetheless, the Harts' main viticultural business (Jed Hart is in aviation) will be grape growing.

Aventine Wines NR

86 Watters Road, Ballandean, Qld 4382 **REGION** Granite Belt
T (07) 4684 1301 **F** (07) 3844 2652 **OPEN** Weekends and public holidays 8–6
WINEMAKER Bruce Humphery-Smith **EST.** 1995 **CASES** 1000
PRODUCT RANGE ($12–22 CD) White Flame range of White, Classic Dry White, Red; Black Label range of Chardonnay, Shiraz, Cabernet Sauvignon, Liqueur Muscat, Port; Sparkling Shiraz.
SUMMARY The 8-hectare Aventine vineyard is situated at an elevation of approximately 1000 metres, on a north-facing hill high above the Ballandean Valley. The highest portions of the site are planted to nebbiolo and sangiovese, the soils being a shallow, weathered granite. The wines released under the Aventine label all come from estate-grown grapes, which also include shiraz, cabernet sauvignon and muscat.

🐦 Avonbrook Wines   NR

7 Benrua Road, Clackline, WA 6564 **REGION** Central Western Australia Zone
T (08) 9574 1276 **F** (08) 9574 1070 **OPEN** Weekends and public holidays 10–5
WINEMAKER Peter Murfit **EST.** 1993
PRODUCT RANGE Chenin Blanc, Verdelho, Chardonnay, Shiraz, Merlot.
SUMMARY Avonbrook Wines is loosely based on 2.3 hectares of vineyards planted to chenin blanc,
chardonnay, verdelho, merlot and shiraz by winemaker/viticulturist Peter Murfit. The wines are
exported to England and the US under various brands.

Avonmore Estate   ★★★

Mayreef–Avonmore Road, Avonmore, Vic 3558 **REGION** Bendigo
T (03) 5432 6291 **F** (03) 5432 6291 **OPEN** Thurs–Sun and public holidays 11–5, or by appointment
WINEMAKER Shaun Bryans, Don Buchanan (Contract) **EST.** 1996 **CASES** 1500
PRODUCT RANGE ($20 CD) Shaun's Shiraz, Saxon's Shiraz, Blake's Blend (Cabernet Shiraz),
Sangiovese, Rachel's Red (Cabernet Sauvignon).
SUMMARY Rob and Pauline Bryans own and operate a certified Grade A Bio-Dynamic farm,
producing and selling beef, lamb and cereals as well as establishing 9 hectares of viognier, sangiovese,
cabernet sauvignon, cabernet franc and shiraz, which produced its first crop in 2000. Most of the
wine is contract-made by Don Buchanan at the Tisdall Winery at Echuca, but a small amount is
made on the property. The wine will be marketed under the Avonmore Estate label, but with the
worldwide Demeter logo. Several of the unbottled wines have been awarded medals at Victorian
wine shows, and the Bryans' cellar door is now open.

♼♼♼♼   **Sangiovese 2003** Typical light colour and fruit depth; savoury, persistent fine tannins, all
          part of authentic varietal character. **RATING** 87 **DRINK** Now $ 20

♼♼♼♼   **Cabernet Sauvignon 2002** **RATING** 84 **DRINK** 2009 $ 20

🐦 Baarrooka Vineyard   NR

Coach Road, Strathbogie, Vic 3666 **REGION** Strathbogie Ranges
T (03) 5790 5288 **F** (03) 5790 5205 **OPEN** Weekends and public holidays 11–5 Sept–May, or by
appointment
WINEMAKER Paul Evans, Travis Bush, Russell Synnot **EST.** 1996 **CASES** 1200
PRODUCT RANGE ($18–25 R) Riesling, Sauvignon Blanc, Chardonnay, Pinot Noir, Shiraz, Merlot, CSM
(Cabernet Sauvignon, Shiraz, Merlot), Cabernet Sauvignon.
SUMMARY The establishment of the 32-hectare Baarrooka Vineyard began in 1995, on a north-facing
slope at an elevation of 550 metres. Plantings consist of riesling, sauvignon blanc, chardonnay, pinot
noir, cabernet sauvignon, shiraz, merlot, zinfandel and small blocks of petit verdot, cabernet franc and
malbec. The majority of the grapes are sold under contract into the Yarra Valley, but a small quantity will
be released under the Baarrooka label, the quantities and varieties varying according to the vintage.

♼♼♼   **Chardonnay 2002** **RATING** 81 $ 20

Bacchanalia Estate   NR

Taverner Street, Bacchus Marsh, Vic 3340 **REGION** Sunbury
T (03) 5367 6416 **F** (03) 5367 6416 **OPEN** Sundays by appointment
WINEMAKER Pat Carmody (Contract), John Reid **EST.** 1994 **CASES** 500
PRODUCT RANGE ($15–25 R) Semillon, Shiraz.
SUMMARY Noted ABC broadcaster and journalist John Reid, and wife Val, established Bacchanalia
Estate in 1994 on the fertile black soils of Bacchus Marsh, adjacent to the Werribee River. Consultancy
viticultural advice from Dr Richard Smart pointed to the inevitably vigorous growth to be expected
from the rich black soil, so a Geneva Double Curtain (GDC) trellis and canopy was utilised from the
outset. Two hectares of shiraz, 0.6 hectare semillon, 0.4 hectare cabernet sauvignon and 0.2 hectare
viognier have been established. For several years now Pat Carmody (of Craiglee) has been making the
wine; this is the only wine he makes other than for his own label. Apart from local distribution through
Geelong and Ballarat, the wine is available at Nick's Wine Merchants throughout Melbourne.

Bacchus Hill

NR

115 Lerderderg Park Road, Bacchus Marsh, Vic 3340 **REGION** Sunbury
T 0412 124 166 **OPEN** Not
WINEMAKER Bruno Tassone **EST.** 2000
SUMMARY Lawyer Bruno Tassone migrated from Italy when he was 8 years old, and watched his father carry on the Italian tradition of making wine for home consumption. Tassone followed the same path before purchasing a 35-hectare property at Bacchus Marsh together with his wife Jennifer. Here they have planted 2 hectares each of riesling, semillon, sauvignon blanc, chardonnay, pinot noir, merlot, shiraz and cabernet sauvignon, plus 1 hectare each of chenin blanc and nebbiolo. It was known locally as the Hill Property, and Bacchus Hill Winery became the obvious name. The Tassones are awaiting building approval for the construction of a winery and cellar door, and, all being well, are looking forward to their first vintage in 2005. The plan is to sell most of the wine through local outlets and the cellar door. The property is prominently situated just off the Western Highway, less than 50 kilometres from Melbourne.

Badger's Brook

874 Maroondah Highway, Coldstream, Vic 3770 **REGION** Yarra Valley
T (03) 5962 4130 **F** (03) 5962 4238 **OPEN** Thurs–Mon 11–5
WINEMAKER Contract **EST.** 1993 **CASES** 5000
PRODUCT RANGE ($17–25 CD) The Badger's Brook range, all of which are from the Yarra Valley, mostly said to be estate-grown, and the Storm Ridge range, coming from various regions including the Mornington Peninsula and as far away as Margaret River, but also with some Yarra component.
SUMMARY Situated prominently on the Maroondah Highway, next door to the well-known Rochford's Eyton. Location is all, although not for all the wines. As is proper, the Badger's Brook-branded wines are significantly better than the Storm Ridge range. Domestic distribution on the east coast by The Wine Company. Exports to Germany, the Philippines, Singapore and Malaysia.

ΨΨΨΨ **Yarra Valley Shiraz 2001** Good blackberry and black cherry; hints of spice and dark chocolate; medium-bodied, not over-extracted **RATING** 89 **DRINK** 2011 **$** 25
Yarra Valley Pinot Noir 2002 Fully ripe, complex, intense, dark plum; even a touch of licorice; slight hardness, but may soften with age. **RATING** 88 **DRINK** 2009 **$** 25
Storm Ridge Cabernet Merlot 2001 Very well put together; light to medium-bodied; gently sweet red berry fruits, then a pleasing savoury finish. **RATING** 87 **DRINK** 2008 **$** 20

ΨΨΨΨ **Yarra Valley Chardonnay 2003 RATING** 86 **DRINK** 2007 **$** 20
Storm Ridge Unoaked Chardonnay 2003 RATING 85 **DRINK** Now **$** 17

ΨΨΨ **Storm Ridge Chardonnay Pinot Noir NV RATING** 82 **$** 22

Bago Vineyards

★★★

Milligans Road, off Bago Road, Wauchope, NSW 2446 **REGION** Hastings River
T (02) 6585 7099 **F** (02) 6585 7099 **OPEN** 7 days 11–5
WINEMAKER Jim Mobbs, John Cassegrain (Consultant) **EST.** 1985 **CASES** 6000
PRODUCT RANGE ($10–25 CD) Chardonnay, Jazz White Classic, Verdelho, Chambourcin, Merlot Chambourcin, Jazz Red Classic, Sparkling Pinot Noir Chardonnay, Sparkling Chambourcin, Tawny Port.
SUMMARY Jim and Kay Mobs commenced planting the Broken Bago Vineyards in 1985 with 1 hectare of chardonnay and have now increased the total plantings to 12.5 hectares. Regional specialist John Cassegrain is consultant winemaker.

Baileys of Glenrowan

Cnr Taminick Gap and Upper Taminick Roads, Glenrowan, Vic 3675 **REGION** Glenrowan
T (03) 5766 2392 **F** (03) 5766 2596 **OPEN** Mon–Fri 9–5, weekends 10–5
WINEMAKER Matt Steel **EST.** 1870 **CASES** 15 000
PRODUCT RANGE ($16–40 R) Shiraz, 1904 Block Shiraz, 1920's Block Shiraz, Cabernet Sauvignon are the principal wines; Founder Tokay, Muscat and Port.

SUMMARY Now part of the sprawling Beringer Blass empire, inherited via the Rothbury takeover. Has made some excellent Shiraz in recent years, but its greatest strength lies in its fortified wines. Strangely, no tastings since mid-2003.

Bainton Family Wines

390 Milbrodale Road, Bulga, NSW 2330 **REGION** Lower Hunter Valley
T (02) 9968 1764 **F** (02) 9960 3454 **OPEN** Not
WINEMAKER Tony Bainton **EST.** 1998 **CASES** 3500
PRODUCT RANGE ($15–25 ML) Wollemi Semillon, Unwooded Chardonnay, Shiraz; Q Shiraz Chambourcin; Wollemi Gold Botrytis Semillon, Wollemi Gold Shiraz.
SUMMARY The Bainton family, headed by eminent Sydney QC Russell Bainton, has 48 hectares of vineyard, with the oldest semillon planted over 80 years ago (1923), most in 1940. The major part of the shiraz dates back to plantings in 1950 and 1955.

TTTT   **Wollemi Gold Shiraz 2000** Rich, very ripe licorice, raisin, black plum and earth; fruit-driven; has swallowed up the French/American oak. **RATING** 89 **DRINK** 2013 $ 25

Bald Mountain

Hickling Lane, Wallangarra, Qld 4383 **REGION** Granite Belt
T (07) 4684 3186 **F** (07) 4684 3433 **OPEN** 7 days 10–5
WINEMAKER Simon Gilbert (Contract) **EST.** 1985 **CASES** 5000
PRODUCT RANGE ($11–22 CD) Classic Queenslander Dry White (in fact 100 per cent Sauvignon Blanc), Chardonnay, Reserve Chardonnay, Dancing Brolga (Sauvignon Blanc Verdelho), Late Harvest Sauvignon Blanc, Shiraz, Reserve Shiraz, Shiraz Cabernet, Reserve Shiraz Cabernet.
SUMMARY Denis Parsons is a self-taught but exceptionally competent vigneron who turned Bald Mountain into one of the viticultural showpieces of the Granite Belt. The two Sauvignon Blanc-based wines, Classic Queenslander and the occasional non-vintage Late Harvest Sauvignon Blanc, are interesting alternatives to the mainstream wines. Future production will also see grapes coming from new vineyards near Tenterfield, just across the border in New South Wales. Significant exports to The Netherlands.

Balgownie Estate ★★★★☆

Hermitage Road, Maiden Gully, Vic 3551 **REGION** Bendigo
T (03) 5449 6222 **F** (03) 5449 6506 **OPEN** 7 days 11–5
WINEMAKER Tobias Ansted **EST.** 1969 **CASES** 5000
PRODUCT RANGE ($15–29 CD) Chardonnay, Pinot Noir, Shiraz, Cabernet Sauvignon; Maiden Gully Chardonnay, Cabernet Shiraz.
SUMMARY Balgownie Estate continues to grow in the wake of its acquisition by the Forrester family. A $3 million upgrade of the winery coincided with a doubling of the size of the vineyard to 35 hectares, and in 2003 Balgownie Estate opened a separate cellar door in the Yarra Valley (Cnr Melba Highway and Gulf Road, Yarra Glen, **T** (03) 9730 2669). As well as national distribution through Negociants, exports to the UK, the US, Indonesia, Singapore, Malaysia and Hong Kong.

TTTTT   **Cabernet Sauvignon 2002** Powerful, intense, focused cassis and blackberry; long palate; subtle oak, good tannins. **RATING** 94 **DRINK** 2017 $ 32

TTTTY   **Shiraz 2002** Flooded with blackberry and plum fruit, though not the least heavy nor (obviously) alcoholic. **RATING** 93 **DRINK** 2017 $ 32

TTTT   **Pinot Noir 2002** Dark plum and forest; from the biggest end of town, in fully powerful mode; has potential. **RATING** 89 **DRINK** 2010 $ 22

TTTY   **Chardonnay 2002** **RATING** 86 **DRINK** Now $ 29

Ballabourneen Wines

Talga Road, Rothbury, NSW 2320 **REGION** Lower Hunter Valley
T (02) 4930 7027 **F** (02) 4930 9180 **OPEN** Thurs–Sun 10–5, or by appointment
WINEMAKER Alasdair Sutherland, Andrew Thomas **EST.** 1994 **CASES** 900

PRODUCT RANGE ($9–20 CD) Verdelho, Chardonnay Verdelho, The Stuart Chardonnay, Shiraz.
SUMMARY Alex and Di Stuart planted their first vines, 1.6 hectares of chardonnay and 1.2 hectares of verdelho, in 1994. They followed up these plantings in 1998 with 1.6 hectares of shiraz; the viticulture uses natural sprays, fertilisers, mulches and compost, with a permanent sward maintained between the rows. Competent contract winemaking by Alasdair Sutherland has brought show success for the Verdelho, the high point being a trophy at the 1999 Hunter Valley Wine Show.

ΨΨΨ   **The Stuart Chardonnay 2003 RATING** 83 **$** 20
        Verdelho 2003 RATING 83 **$** 20

Ballandean Estate

Sundown Road, Ballandean, Qld 4382 **REGION** Granite Belt
T (07) 4684 1226 **F** (07) 4684 1288 **OPEN** 7 days 9–5
WINEMAKER Dylan Rhymer, Angelo Puglisi **EST.** 1970 **CASES** 18 000
PRODUCT RANGE ($12–40 CD) Semillon, Semillon Sauvignon Blanc, Black Label Sauvignon Blanc, Black Label Viognier, Black Label Chardonnay, Classic White, Sylvaner Late Harvest, White Pearl (semi-sweet white), lambrusco, Estate Shiraz, Black Label Shiraz, Black Label Cabernet Merlot, Cabernet Sauvignon, fortifieds.
SUMMARY The senior winery of the Granite Belt and by far the largest. The white wines are of diverse but interesting styles, the red wines smooth and usually well made. The estate specialty, Sylvaner Late Harvest, is a particularly interesting wine of great character and flavour if given 10 years' bottle age, but isn't made every year. Exports to the UK and the US.

Ballast Stone Estate Wines

Myrtle Grove Road, Currency Creek, SA 5214 **REGION** Currency Creek
T (08) 8555 4215 **F** (08) 8555 4216 **OPEN** 7 days 10.30–4.30
WINEMAKER F John Loxton **EST.** 2001 **CASES** 15 000
PRODUCT RANGE ($10–19 CD) Riesling, Sauvignon Blanc, Chardonnay, Pinot Chardonnay, Late Harvest, Shiraz, Grenache, Merlot, Petit Verdot, Cabernet Sauvignon.
SUMMARY The Shaw family had been grape growers in McLaren Vale for 25 years before deciding to establish a large vineyard in Currency Creek in 1994. Two hundred and fifty hectares have been planted, mainly cabernet sauvignon and shiraz, with much smaller quantities of eight other trendy varieties. A large on-site winery has been built, managed by Philip Shaw (no relation to Rosemount's Philip Shaw) and John Loxton (formerly senior winemaker at Maglieri). It handled the 1500 tonnes of grapes crushed in 2001; the crush rose to over 5000 tonnes by 2004. Only a small part of the production will be sold under the Ballast Stone Estate label; most will be sold in bulk. A cellar door is to be established on the main Strathalbyn to Victor Harbour Road, tapping into the tourism trade of the Southern Fleurieu Peninsula. Exports to the UK and Germany.

ΨΨΨΨΨ   **Shiraz 2002** Powerful blackberry and plum, with a spicy, savoury extension to the finish.
          RATING 90 **DRINK** 2012 **$** 19

ΨΨΨΨ   **Currency Creek Chardonnay 2002** Gentle, melon and cashew; well balanced, light to
         medium-bodied; ageing quietly. **RATING** 88 **DRINK** 2007 **$** 14
         Merlot 2001 Attractive medium-bodied wine with abundant red berry fruits and soft
         tannins, though not particularly varietal. **RATING** 87 **DRINK** 2009 **$** 18

ΨΨΨΨ   **Shiraz 2001 RATING** 85 **DRINK** Now **$** 19

Balnaves of Coonawarra

★★★★★

Main Road, Coonawarra, SA 5263 **REGION** Coonawarra
T (08) 8737 2946 **F** (08) 8737 2945 **OPEN** Mon–Fri 9–5, weekends 10–5
WINEMAKER Peter Bissell **EST.** 1975 **CASES** 10 000
PRODUCT RANGE ($16–80 R) Chardonnay, Sparkling Cabernet, Cheeky Red, Shiraz, The Blend (Merlot Cabernet Franc), Cabernet Merlot, Cabernet Sauvignon, The Tally Reserve Cabernet Sauvignon.
SUMMARY Former Hungerford Hill vineyard manager and now viticultural consultant-cum-grape grower Doug Balnaves established his vineyard in 1975 but did not launch into winemaking until 1990, with colleague Ralph Fowler as contract-maker in the early years. A striking 300-tonne winery

was built in 1996, with former Wynns Coonawarra Estate assistant winemaker Peter Bissell in charge. The expected leap in quality has indeed materialised and been maintained. The wines are exported to the UK, the US, Canada, Switzerland, The Netherlands, Singapore and Japan.

ΨΨΨΨΨ The Tally Reserve Cabernet Sauvignon 2001 Dense colour; saturated black fruits, opulent mouthfeel, but tightened and lengthened by cedary oak and lingering tannins. **RATING** 96 **DRINK** 2021 $ 80

Shiraz 2001 Dense hue; exceptional texture; fine tannins woven through luscious blackberry and spice fruit. **RATING** 95 **DRINK** 2020 $ 24

Chardonnay 2002 Thoroughly elegant wine with a mix of mineral, faintly smoky oak and citrus fruit on the bouquet; excellent fruit and oak balance and length. Screwcap. **RATING** 94 **DRINK** 2007 $ 28

Cabernet Sauvignon 2001 Abundant ripe blackcurrant fruit; judicious cedary oak; hallmark tannin structure and finesse. **RATING** 94 **DRINK** 2016 $ 31

The Blend 2001 Great texture and mouthfeel; cedar, cigar box, spice and blackcurrant; ultra-fine tannins; great wine at the price. **RATING** 94 **DRINK** 2011 $ 19

ΨΨΨΨΫ Cabernet Merlot 2001 Ripe, concentrated blackcurrant/blackberry fruit; ample structure and tannins; needs patience. **RATING** 90 **DRINK** 2016 $ 24

Balthazar of the Barossa ★★★★

Lot 10 Stonewell Road, Marananga, SA 5355 **REGION** Barossa Valley
T (08) 8562 2949 **F** (08) 8562 2949 **OPEN** Not
WINEMAKER Anita Bowen **EST.** 1999 **CASES** 1000
PRODUCT RANGE ($60 R) Shiraz.
SUMMARY In announcing her occupation as 'a 40-something sex therapist with a 17-year involvement in the wine industry' Anita Bowen hides part of her light under a bushel, for she is the wife of the experienced winemaker Randall Bowen. Be that as it may, she has increased the make of Shiraz coming from her 26-hectare vineyard on Stonewell Road, Marananga, with Torbreck and Greenock Creek as neighbours. She undertook her first vintage at Mudgee, then moved to McLaren Vale, and ultimately the Barossa, where she worked at St Hallet while studying at Roseworthy College. A versatile lady, indeed. As to her wine, she says, 'Anyway, prepare a feast, pour yourself a glass (no chalices, please) of Balthazar and share it with your concubines. Who knows? It may help to lubricate thoughts, firm up ideas and get the creative juices flowing!' Exports to the UK and the US.

ΨΨΨΨΫ Shiraz 2002 Big, powerful, plum, blackberry and a dash of prune; still locked up, but the balance is there. **RATING** 90 **DRINK** 2012 $ 60

ΨΨΨΨ Shiraz 2001 Complex, rich and ripe leather and plum fruit; shows 22 months' maturation in French and American oak; power, not finesse, but is sure to improve. **RATING** 88 **DRINK** 2016 $ 60

Bamajura NR

775 Woodbridge Hill Road, Gardners Bay, Tas 7112 **REGION** Southern Tasmania
T (03) 6295 0294 **F** (03) 6295 0294 **OPEN** By appointment
WINEMAKER Scott Polley **EST.** 1987
PRODUCT RANGE Pinot Noir.
SUMMARY Bamajura's name is derived from the first two letters of the names of the late Ray Polley and his sisters Barbara, Margaret and Judy. The vineyard was planted by Ray Polley, and son Scott took over in the early 1990s; having undertaken the TAFE Tasmania viticulture course, he converted the vineyard to the Scott Henry trellis. In 2002 he took over the winemaking mantle from Michael Vishacki.

Banks Thargo Wines

Racecourse Road, Penola, SA 5277 **REGION** Coonawarra
T (08) 8737 2338 **F** (08) 8737 3369 **OPEN** Not
WINEMAKER Banks Kidman, Jonathon Kidman **EST.** 1980 **CASES** 1200
PRODUCT RANGE ($20 R) Merlot, Cabernet Sauvignon.

SUMMARY The unusual name comes directly from family history. One branch of the Kidman family moved to the Mount Gambier district in 1858, but Thomas Kidman (who had been in the foster care of the Banks family from the age of 2 until he was 13) moved to the Broken Hill/southwest Queensland region to work for the famous Kidman Bros pastoral interests. When he 'retired' from the outback, in 1919, he bought the property presently owned by the family in Coonawarra. His second son was named Banks Thargomindah Kidman, and it is he and wife Jenny who decided to diversify their grazing activities by planting vines in the 1980s. Sixteen and a half hectares are under contract, leaving 1.3 hectares each of merlot and cabernet sauvignon for the subsequently established Banks Thargo brand. It is available by mail order and in Melbourne it is distributed by Richwood Agencies.

Bannockburn Vineyards ★★★★★

Midland Highway, Bannockburn, Vic 3331 **REGION** Geelong
T(03) 5281 1363 **F**(03) 5281 1349 **OPEN** Not
WINEMAKER Gary Farr **EST.** 1974 **CASES** 10 000
PRODUCT RANGE ($21–50 R) Riesling, Sauvignon Blanc, Chardonnay, SRH Chardonnay (named in honour of the late Stuart Reginald Hooper, founder of Bannockburn), Pinot Noir, Saignee (Rose), Serre Pinot Noir, Shiraz, Cabernet Sauvignon Merlot.
SUMMARY With the qualified exception of the Cabernet Merlot, which can be a little leafy and gamey, produces outstanding wines across the range, all with individuality, style, great complexity and depth of flavour. The low-yielding estate vineyards play their role, but so does the French-influenced winemaking of Gary Farr. The Serre Pinot Noir, from a close-planted block, is absolutely outstanding. Export markets have been established in the UK, Belgium, the US, Canada, Hong Kong, Japan, Singapore, New Zealand and Malaysia.

▼▼▼▼▼ **Shiraz 2002** High-toned, penetrating northern Rhône lookalike; exotic, piercing blackberry and licorice; long finish. **RATING** 96 **DRINK** 2012 $50
Pinot Noir 2002 Complex, savoury/spicy/woodsy aromas; intensely powerful and focused palate; plum, spice and Christmas cake; long finish. **RATING** 95 **DRINK** 2010 $50
Serre Pinot Noir 2000 Very Burgundian in style, though with extra power. Plum, spice, forest floor and oak all intermingle seamlessly. **RATING** 95 **DRINK** 2012 $110
Shiraz 2001 The complex bouquet ranges through spice, licorice, earth, pepper and black fruits, much like Côte Rôtie. The palate is at once elegant and sensual, the flavours rippling to a long finish. **RATING** 95 **DRINK** 2016 $50
Chardonnay 2002 Ultra-complex bouquet; strong White Burgundy characteristics; a rich, layered nectarine and peach-driven palate. **RATING** 94 **DRINK** 2008 $50

▼▼▼▼ **Sauvignon Blanc 2003** Complex, but relatively subdued aromas and flavours; powerful, tightly knit; towards White Bordeaux. **RATING** 89 **DRINK** 2007 $21

Banrock Station ★★★☆

Holmes Road, off Sturt Highway, Kingston-on-Murray, SA 5331 **REGION** Riverland
T(08) 8583 0299 **F**(08) 8583 0288 **OPEN** 7 days 10–4, closed public holidays
WINEMAKER Mark Zeppel **EST.** 1994 **CASES** 1.9 million
PRODUCT RANGE ($7.99–12.99 R) Semillon Chardonnay, Chardonnay, Shiraz Cabernet, Cabernet Merlot; Premium Range includes Wigley Reach Unwooded Chardonnay, Napper's Verdelho, Ball Island Shiraz, Cave Cliff Merlot and Sparkling Chardonnay and Shiraz; The Reserve range includes Chardonnay, Shiraz and Petit Verdot.
SUMMARY The $1 million visitors centre at Banrock Station was opened in February 1999. Owned by BRL Hardy, the Banrock Station property covers over 1700 hectares, with 240 hectares being vineyard and the remainder being a major wildlife and wetland preservation area. The wines have consistently offered excellent value for money.

▼▼▼▼ **The Reserve Merlot 2002** Clever winemaking, with lots of sweet, spicy oak, soothing mouthfeel, and surprising length. **RATING** 87 **DRINK** Now $12.99

▼▼▼ **White Shiraz 2003** **RATING** 83 $7

Baptista

139 High Street, Nagambie, Vic 3608 **REGION** Nagambie Lakes
T (03) 5794 2514 **F** (03) 5794 1776 **OPEN** 7 days 10–5
WINEMAKER David Traeger **EST.** 1993 **CASES** 400
PRODUCT RANGE ($115 R) The Graytown Shiraz.
SUMMARY In 1993 David Traeger acquired a vineyard he had coveted for many years, and which had been planted by Baptista Governa in 1891. He has been buying grapes from the vineyard since 1988, but it was in a run-down condition, and required a number of years of rehabilitation before he felt the quality of the grapes was sufficient for a single-vineyard release. Ownership of the business did not pass to Dromana Estate when that company acquired the David Traeger brand; it is jointly owned by David Traeger and the Wine Investment Fund, the latter a majority shareholder in Dromana Estate. Apart from through the cellar door, the wine is distributed by The Wine Company.

Barak Estate NR

Barak Road, Moorooduc, Vic 3933 **REGION** Mornington Peninsula
T (03) 5978 8439 **F** (03) 5978 8439 **OPEN** Weekends and public holidays 11–5
WINEMAKER James Williamson **EST.** 1996 **CASES** 500
PRODUCT RANGE ($17–20 CD) Chardonnay, Shiraz, Cabernet Sauvignon.
SUMMARY When James Williamson decided to plant vines on his 4-hectare Moorooduc property and establish a micro-winery, he already knew it was far cheaper to buy wine by the bottle than to make it. Undeterred, he ventured into grape growing and winemaking, picking the first grapes in 1993 and opening Barak Estate in 1996. Old telegraph poles, railway sleepers, old palings and timber shingles have all been used in the construction of the picturesque winery.

Barambah Ridge

79 Goschnicks Road, Redgate via Murgon, Qld 4605 **REGION** South Burnett
T (07) 4168 4766 **F** (07) 4168 4770 **OPEN** 7 days 10–5
WINEMAKER Stuart Pierce **EST.** 1995 **CASES** 10 000
PRODUCT RANGE ($15–24.95 CD) Semillon, Chardonnay Semillon, Ridge White, Verdelho, Unwooded Chardonnay, Reserve Chardonnay, Barambah Bubbles, Sparkling Shiraz, Laura Rose, Ridge Red, Classic Dry Red, Reserve Shiraz, Cabernet Sauvignon, Old Feedlot Port, Mayoral Muscat, Honey Mead.
SUMMARY Barambah Ridge is owned by Tambarambah Limited, an unlisted public company, and since its inception in 1995 it has quickly established itself as one of the major players in the Queensland wine scene. Its estate plantings at Redgate include chardonnay, semillon, shiraz, verdelho and cabernet sauvignon, and produced their first vintage in 1997. A modern winery was built in 1998, and in 2003 crushed 500 tonnes of grapes, much of it as contract winemaker for many other Queensland wineries. The quality of the wines under the Barambah Ridge label is impressive. Full details of its three retail outlets are at www.barambahridge.com.au.

ΥΥΥΥ **Reserve Shiraz 2001** Fully reflective of complex winemaking techniques used; a savoury cascade of flavours; finely textured. **RATING** 90 **DRINK** 2011 $30

ΥΥΥΥ **Semillon 2002** Moderately intense but clear-cut varietal fruit; herb and citrus; crisp finish. **RATING** 87 **DRINK** Now $15.90
Reserve Merlot 2002 Distinctive savoury/earthy/spicy varietal fruit; fine and quite ripe tannins; good oak handling. **RATING** 87 **DRINK** 2008 $24.95

ΥΥΥ **Reserve Chardonnay 2001** **RATING** 86 **DRINK** Now $24.95

ΥΥΥ **Unwooded Chardonnay 2003** **RATING** 83 **DRINK** Now $15.90
Verdelho 2003 **RATING** 83 $17.90
Classic Dry Red NV **RATING** 83 $15

Baratto's

NR

Farm 678, Hanwood, NSW 2680 **REGION** Riverina
T (02) 6963 0171 **F** (02) 6963 0171 **OPEN** 7 days 10–5
WINEMAKER Peter Baratto **EST.** 1975 **CASES** 6250
PRODUCT RANGE ($6–18 CD) Chardonnay, Trebbiano Semillon (Late Harvest), Botrytis Semillon, Shiraz Cabernet Sauvignon, Cabernet Sauvignon; also, a variety of casks and cleanskins.
SUMMARY Baratto's is in many ways a throwback to the old days. Peter Baratto has 15 hectares of vineyards and sells the wine in bulk or in 10- and 20-litre casks from the cellar door at old-time prices, from as little as a few dollars per litre.

🐌 Barfold Estate

★★★★

57 School Road, Barfold, Vic 3444 **REGION** Heathcote
T (03) 5423 4244 **F** (03) 5423 4225 **OPEN** 7 days 10–5
WINEMAKER Craig Aitken **EST.** 1998 **CASES** 450
PRODUCT RANGE ($25–35 ML) Shiraz.
SUMMARY Craig and Sandra Aitken acquired their farm property in the southwestern corner of the Heathcote wine region with the specific intention of growing premium grapes. They inspected more than 70 properties over the 18 months prior to purchasing Barfold, and are in fact only the second family to own the property since the 1850s. So far they have planted 3.4 hectares of shiraz, and 0.6 hectare of cabernet sauvignon; a small planting of viognier is planned for the future.

🍷🍷🍷🍷 **Heathcote Shiraz 2002** Good colour; fresh black cherry, plum and spice; medium-bodied; fine tannins, subtle oak. Gold medal Ballarat Wine Show 2003. **RATING** 90
DRINK 2009 $30

Barnadown Run

★★★★

390 Cornella Road, Toolleen, Vic 3551 **REGION** Heathcote
T (03) 5433 6376 **F** (03) 5433 6386 **OPEN** 7 days 10–5
WINEMAKER Andrew Millis **EST.** 1995 **CASES** 1500
PRODUCT RANGE ($35–45 CD) Shiraz, Merlot, Cabernet Sauvignon, Henry Bennett's Voluptuary.
SUMMARY Named after the original pastoral lease of which the vineyard forms part, and established on rich terra rossa soil for which the best Heathcote vineyards are famous. Owner Andrew Millis carries out both the viticulture and winemaking at the 5-hectare vineyard. Exports to the US and the UK.

🐌 Barossa Cottage Wines

NR

Nuriootpa–Angaston Road, Angaston, SA 5353 **REGION** Eden Valley
T (08) 8562 3212 **F** (08) 8562 3243 **OPEN** Mon–Sat and public holidays 10–4.30
WINEMAKER Rod Chapman **EST.** 1990
PRODUCT RANGE ($10–28 CD) Riesling, Unwooded Chardonnay, Chardonnay, Late Harvest Riesling, Shiraz, Family Reserve Blend.
SUMMARY Heather and Ray Bartsch have been grape growers for over 20 years, and they are direct descendants of Gottfried Harwig, who settled in the Eden Valley in 1860. They have a substantial holding, with 26 hectares of vines in the Eden Valley and 12 hectares at Angaston. Almost all (95 per cent) of the 300 tonnes of annual grape production is sold to others; only 5 per cent goes to contract winemaker Rod Chapman, to be made into a modestly priced but wide range of wines.

Barossa Ridge Wine Estate

★★★★

Light Pass Road, Tanunda, SA 5352 **REGION** Barossa Valley
T (08) 8563 2811 **F** (08) 8563 2811 **OPEN** By appointment
WINEMAKER Marco Litterini **EST.** 1987 **CASES** 2000
PRODUCT RANGE ($26–28 CD) Valley of Vines (Classic red blend), Old Creek Shiraz, Mardia's Vineyard Cabernet Franc, Bamboo Creek Merlot, The Omega Petit Verdot, Rocky Valley Cabernet Sauvignon.

SUMMARY A grape grower turned winemaker with a small list of interesting red varietals, including the Valley of Vines blend of Merlot, Cabernet Franc, Cabernet Sauvignon and Petit Verdot. All of its wines are built in an impressively heroic style. Increasing retail distribution in Australia, and exports to Switzerland, Germany, Malaysia and Thailand.

ϤϤϤϤϤ **The Omega Petit Verdot 2002** Densely coloured; crammed with black fruits, some earth and chocolate; solid, not aggressive, tannins. For the long haul. RATING 90 DRINK 2015 $ 28

ϤϤϤϤ **Old Creek Shiraz 2001** Blackberry, chocolate and vanilla; medium to full-bodied, but supple and rounded; good balance. RATING 89 DRINK 2016 $ 28
Rocky Valley Cabernet Sauvignon 2001 A coruscating mix of blackcurrant, cassis, herb and mint, then a smooth finish. RATING 89 DRINK 2011 $ 28
Valley of Vines 2001 Spicy/minty overtones to a light to medium-bodied wine; supple Merlot mid-palate and some grip on the finish ex Cabernet Sauvignon and Petit Verdot. RATING 88 DRINK 2010 $ 26
Mardia's Vineyard Cabernet Franc 2002 Cedar, leaf, earth and olive; light to medium-bodied; shades of the Loire Valley; nice length. RATING 87 DRINK 2008 $ 28

ϤϤϤϤ **Bamboo Creek Merlot 2001** RATING 85 DRINK 2008 $ 26

Barossa Settlers ★★★☆

Trial Hill Road, Lyndoch, SA 5351 REGION Barossa Valley
T (08) 8524 4017 F (08) 8524 4519 OPEN 7 days 11–3
WINEMAKER Jane Haese EST. 1983 CASES 500
PRODUCT RANGE ($19–25 CD) Semillon, Chardonnay, Pinot Chardonnay, Shiraz, Finale Hoffnungsthal Settlement Shiraz, Joan's Block Grenache, Cabernet Sauvignon, Finale Cabernet Sauvignon, Port, Sherry.
SUMMARY A superbly located cellar door (dating back to 1860) is the only outlet (other than mail order) for the wines from this excellent vineyard owned by the Haese family; the shiraz was planted in 1887. Production has slowed in recent years, with the grapes from the 31-hectare vineyard being sold to others.

ϤϤϤϤϤ **Shiraz 2002** Masses of deliciously concentrated blackberry fruit; particularly good finish and aftertaste; unexpected finesse. RATING 92 DRINK 2017 $ 25

ϤϤϤ **Semillon 2003** RATING 83 $ 21

Barossa Valley Estate ★★★☆

Seppeltsfield Road, Marananga, SA 5355 REGION Barossa Valley
T (08) 8562 3599 F (08) 8562 4255 OPEN 7 days 10–4.30
WINEMAKER Stuart Bourne EST. 1984 CASES 100 000
PRODUCT RANGE ($9.99–59.99 R) Spires Chardonnay Semillon, Shiraz Cabernet Sauvignon; Moculta Chardonnay, Shiraz, Grenache, Cabernet Merlot; Ebenezer Chardonnay, Shiraz, Cabernet Sauvignon Merlot; and the premium E&E Sparkling Shiraz and Black Pepper Shiraz.
SUMMARY Barossa Valley Estate is part-owned by BRL Hardy, marking the end of a period during which it was one of the last significant co-operative-owned wineries in Australia. Across the board, the wines are full flavoured and honest. E&E Black Pepper Shiraz is an upmarket label with a strong reputation and following, the Ebenezer range likewise. Over-enthusiastic use of American oak (particularly with the red wines) has been the Achilles heel in the past. The wines are distributed in Australia and the UK by BRL Hardy, and by independent distributors in North America.

ϤϤϤϤ **E&E Black Pepper Shiraz 2000** Complex, intense blackberry and powerful oak aromas; however, the mid-palate doesn't deliver up to expectations. RATING 87 DRINK 2011 $ 68
Estate Ebenezer Shiraz 2000 Earth, vanilla, red and blackberry aromas; luscious fruit, good mouthfeel and length. RATING 87 DRINK 2010 $ 28

ϤϤϤϤ **Ebenezer Cabernet Merlot 2001** RATING 84 DRINK 2011 $ 28

ϤϤϤ **Epiphany Shiraz 2001** RATING 83 $ 13

Barramundi Wines ★★☆

Walla Avenue, Griffith, NSW 2680 **REGION** Riverina
T (02) 6966 9600 **F** (02) 6962 2888 **OPEN** Not
WINEMAKER Krister Jonsson, Eddie Bonato, Sam Mittiga **EST.** 1976
PRODUCT RANGE ($6–25.50 CD) Barramundi, Aldridge Estate and Cedar Creek brands for export.
SUMMARY Formerly a listed public company, Cranswick Estate was acquired by Evans & Tate in March 2003. Over the ensuing 15 months there has been a major restructure and brand shuffling exercise. Cranswick has now become Barramundi Wines, and Milburn Park has become a brand under the Salisbury Winery umbrella.

Barratt ★★★★★

Uley Vineyard, Cornish Road, Summertown, SA 5141 **REGION** Adelaide Hills
T (08) 8390 1788 **F** (08) 8390 1788 **OPEN** Weekends and public holidays 11.30–5, or by appointment
WINEMAKER Lindsay Barratt, Jeffrey Grosset (Contract) **EST.** 1993 **CASES** 1200
PRODUCT RANGE ($20.50–39 CD) Sauvignon Blanc, Chardonnay, The Bonython Pinot Noir, The Reserve Pinot Noir, Merlot.
SUMMARY Former medical practitioner Lindsay and Carolyn Barratt own two vineyards at Summertown: the Uley Vineyard, purchased from the late Ian Wilson in August 1990, and the Bonython Vineyard. They have 8.4 hectares of vines, some coming into production, and added Sauvignon Blanc and Merlot to the wine range from 2002. Part of the production from the vineyards is sold to other makers; Jeffrey Grosset is the maker of the Chardonnay and Pinot Noir. Arrangements were finalised for a winery facility at the Adelaide Hills Business and Tourism Centre at Lobethal in time for the 2003 vintage. Limited quantities are sold in the UK, the US and Canada.

♥♥♥♥♥ **The Reserve Pinot Noir 2002** A finer and more elegant, but still remarkably complex, intense and long wine, with a great finish and aftertaste. **RATING** 96 **DRINK** 2010 $ 39
The Bonython Pinot Noir 2002 Potent, intense, complex aromas; dark plum, spice, sous bois and oak are all happening. The palate follows on precisely: rich, ripe and full but not jammy. **RATING** 95 **DRINK** 2010 $ 20.50
Chardonnay 2002 Fine, elegantly chiselled nectarine and citrus fruit; perfectly integrated, subtle French oak; long finish. **RATING** 94 **DRINK** 2007 $ 26

♥♥♥♥ **Merlot 2002** Savoury aromas, then a surprisingly sweet berry and mint mid-palate, before heading back to a savoury finish. **RATING** 88 **DRINK** Now $ 20.50

🐟 Barrecas NR

South West Highway, Donnybrook, WA 6239 **REGION** Geographe
T (08) 9731 1716 **F** (08) 9731 1716 **OPEN** 7 days 10–6
WINEMAKER Iolanda Ratcliffe **EST.** 1994
PRODUCT RANGE ($8.50–13.50 CD) Shiraz, Shiraz Merlot, Cabernet Malbec.
SUMMARY Three generations of the Barreca family have been involved in winemaking, first in Italy and ultimately in Donnybrook. Third-generation Tony Barreca sold his orchard in 1994, using the proceeds to buy the site upon which he has since established 26 hectares, planted to a Joseph's Coat of 26 different varieties. Most of the grapes are sold under contract, but a small, modern winery was erected on-site in 2002 for the production of a limited amount of wine.

Barretts Wines ★★★★

Portland–Nelson Highway, Portland, Vic 3305 **REGION** Henty
T (03) 5526 5251 **OPEN** 7 days 11–5
WINEMAKER Rod Barrett **EST.** 1983 **CASES** 1000
PRODUCT RANGE ($16–20 CD) Riesling, Traminer, Late Harvest Riesling, Pinot Noir, Cabernet Sauvignon.
SUMMARY Has a low profile, selling its wines locally. The initial releases were made at Best's, but since 1992 all wines have been made on the property by Rod Barrett. The 5.5-hectare vineyard is planted to riesling, pinot noir and cabernet sauvignon.

ᵀᵀᵀᵀᵧ **Riesling 2001** A powerful and complex wine in Germanic Rheingau style; now moving into its bottle development phase. **RATING** 91 **DRINK** 2007 $16

ᵀᵀᵀᵧ **Pinot Noir 2001** At the extreme spicy/savoury/foresty end of the varietal spectrum. **RATING** 86 **DRINK** Now $20

Barringwood Park ★★★★

60 Gillams Road, Lower Barrington, Tas 7306 **REGION** Northern Tasmania
T (03) 6492 3140 **F** (03) 6492 3360 **OPEN** Wed–Sun and public holidays 10–5
WINEMAKER Tamar Ridge (Contract) **EST.** 1993 **CASES** 1200
PRODUCT RANGE ($18–24 CD) Pinot Gris, Schonburger, Chardonnay, Reserve Chardonnay, Pinot Chardonnay, Pinot Noir, Mill Block Pinot Noir, Forest Raven Pinot Noir.
SUMMARY Judy and Ian Robinson operate a sawmill at Lower Barrington, 15 minutes south of Devonport on the main tourist trail to Cradle Mountain, and when they planted 500 vines in 1993 the aim was to do a bit of home winemaking for themselves and a few friends. In a thoroughly familiar story, the urge to expand the vineyard and make wine on a commercial scale came almost immediately, and they embarked on a 6-year plan, planting 1 hectare a year for the first 4 years (doing all the work themselves while also running their sawmill), and then built the cellar and tasting rooms during the following 2 years. They have planted pinot noir, chardonnay, pinot gris, schonburger and pinot meunier, and many of the wines have won show medals.

ᵀᵀᵀᵀᵀ **Chardonnay 2002** Clean, ripe nectarine, melon and citrus; subtle oak; good line and length. **RATING** 94 **DRINK** 2010 $20

ᵀᵀᵀᵀ **Chardonnay 2001** Sweet nectarine fruit caresses the mouth; the oak is merely a prop. **RATING** 89 **DRINK** 2008 $20
I/J Pinot Noir Chardonnay 2000 Fine, elegant sweet fruit on entry, then lingering acidity on the finish; crisp, stylish. **RATING** 89 **DRINK** Now $28
Pinot Noir 2001 At the extreme light-bodied end of the spectrum, but varietal character and length undoubted. **RATING** 88 **DRINK** Now $20
Schonburger 2003 Sweet, aromatic, grapey muscaty fruit balanced by citrussy acidity. **RATING** 87 **DRINK** Now $22

ᵀᵀᵀᵧ **Pinot Gris 2003** **RATING** 85 **DRINK** 2007 $22

Barrymore Estate ★★★☆

76 Tuerong Rod, Tuerong, Vic 3933 **REGION** Mornington Peninsula
T (03) 5974 8999 **F** (03) 9789 0821 **OPEN** Weekends 11–5, or by appointment
WINEMAKER Peter J Cotter **EST.** 1998 **CASES** 1500
PRODUCT RANGE ($16–35 CD) Sauvignon Blanc, Pinot Gris, Pinot Grigio, Chardonnay, Retro Rose, Pinot Noir, Pinot Noir Reserve; associated brands are Tuerong Station, Peninsula Pinot Noir and Tuerong Valley.
SUMMARY Barrymore Estate is part of a much larger property that was first settled in the 1840s; the abundance of water and wetlands, with the confluence of the Devil Bend and Balcombe Creeks nearby, has sustained grazing and farming since the first settlement. Peter Cotter has planted 8.5 hectares of pinot noir, 1 hectare each of chardonnay and sauvignon blanc, and 0.5 hectare of pinot gris, selling part of the grapes and making part under the Barrymore label.

ᵀᵀᵀᵀ **Reserve Pinot Noir 2002** Light, spicy, savoury style; has good length; no forced extraction. **RATING** 89 **DRINK** 2007 $45

ᵀᵀᵀᵧ **Pinot Gris 2003** Light straw-green; an interesting contrast to the Pinot Grigio: picked later and with more flavour, the residual sweetness useful at the cellar door. **RATING** 86 **DRINK** Now $24
Pinot Noir 2002 **RATING** 86 **DRINK** 2007 $20
Retro Rose 2003 **RATING** 85 **DRINK** Now $18
Pinot Grigio 2003 **RATING** 84 **DRINK** Now $20

Barwang Vineyard

Barwang Road, Young, NSW 2594 **REGION** Hilltops
T (02) 6382 3594 **F** (02) 6382 2594 **OPEN** Not
WINEMAKER Jim Brayne, Russell Cody, Scott Zrna **EST.** 1969
PRODUCT RANGE ($15.95–31.50 R) Chardonnay, Semillon, Shiraz, Merlot, Cabernet Sauvignon.
SUMMARY Peter Robertson pioneered viticulture in the Young region when he planted his first vines in 1969 as part of a diversification program for his 400-hectare grazing property. When McWilliam's acquired Barwang in 1989, the vineyard amounted to 13 hectares; today the plantings exceed 100 hectares. Wine quality has been exemplary from the word go: always elegant, restrained and deliberately understated, repaying extended cellaring.

TTTTT Special Release Merlot 2001 Savoury, olivaceous, earthy notes meld with fully ripe berry fruit and the finest possible tannins. **RATING** 94 **DRINK** 2010 $ 31.50

TTTTT Shiraz 2001 Black plum and blackberry with a twist of spice; smooth, medium-bodied, fruit-driven; long, fine tannins. **RATING** 92 **DRINK** 2011 $ 24
Chardonnay 2001 Convincing rich peach and melon bottle-developed style; not broad or heavy; soft, mouthfilling. **RATING** 91 **DRINK** Now $ 20
Chardonnay 2002 Complex; both barrel ferment and bottle development add impact to the stone fruit and fig; good acidity. **RATING** 90 **DRINK** 2007 $ 20

Barwick Wines

Level 1, 256 St Georges Terrace, Perth, WA 6000 **REGION** South West Australia Zone
T (08) 9765 1216 **F** (08) 9765 1836 **OPEN** Not
WINEMAKER John Griffiths, Flying Fish Cove (Contract) **EST.** 1997 **CASES** 80 000
PRODUCT RANGE ($10–12 ML) Chardonnay, St John's Brook Shiraz, Dwalganup Shiraz Cabernet, Dwalganup Cabernet Sauvignon.
SUMMARY The production of 80 000 cases, planned to rise in stages to over 100 000 cases, gives some guide to the size of the operation. Since 1997, Barwick Wines has been supplying grapes and bulk wine to some of the best known names in Western Australia and the eastern States from three very large vineyards. The first is the 83-hectare Dwalganup Vineyard in the Blackwood Valley region, the second the 38-hectare St John's Brook Vineyard in the Margaret River, and the third the 73-hectare Treenbrook Vineyard in Pemberton. The wines are contract-made at two locations, and sell for thoroughly old-fashioned prices. The owners of the business are four syndicates which have established the vineyards, and the business plan envisages that 80 per cent of production will be exported to over ten countries, with local sales coming from what the owners describe as 'friends of Barwick'.

TTTT St John's Brook Margaret River Shiraz 2002 Light to medium-bodied; spice, clove, cedar, raspberry and blackberry; fine tannins through the palate, sweet fruit on the finish. Exceptional value. The Flying Fish Cove stamp is on the wine. **RATING** 89 **DRINK** 2008 $ 12

TTTT Dwalganup Blackwood Valley Cabernet Sauvignon 2002 RATING 86 **DRINK** 2008 $ 12

Basedow

c/- James Estate, 951 Bylong Valley Way, Baerami via Denman, NSW 2333 **REGION** Barossa Valley
T 1300 887 966 **F** (02) 6574 5164 **OPEN** Not
WINEMAKER Peter Orr **EST.** 1896 **CASES** 75 000
PRODUCT RANGE ($12.50–65 CD) A unchanged core range of Barossa Valley varietal table and fortified wines; Johannes Barossa Shiraz is the flagship wine.
SUMMARY An old and proud label, once particularly well known for its oak-matured Semillon, which has changed hands on a number of occasions before passing into the ownership of James Estate in 2003. At the time of going to print, the new cellar door has not been established, but it will be opened sometime in 2004.

Basket Range Wines

NR

PO Box 65, Basket Range, SA 5138 **REGION** Adelaide Hills
T (08) 8390 1515 **F** (08) 8390 1515 **OPEN** Not
WINEMAKER Phillip Broderick **EST.** 1980 **CASES** 500
PRODUCT RANGE ($20 ML) A single Bordeaux-blend of Cabernet Sauvignon, Cabernet Franc, Merlot, Malbec drawn from 3 hectares of estate plantings.
SUMMARY A tiny operation known to very few, run by civil and Aboriginal rights lawyer Phillip Broderick, a most engaging man with a disarmingly laid-back manner.

Bass Fine Wines

1337 Pipers River Road/4238 Bridport Road, Pipers Brook, Tas 7254 **REGION** Northern Tasmania
T (03) 6331 0136 **F** (03) 6331 0136 **OPEN** Not
WINEMAKER Guy Wagner **EST.** 1999 **CASES** 1700
PRODUCT RANGE ($17–28 R) Pinot Gris, Strait Chardonnay, Block 1 Pinot Noir, Strait Pinot Noir.
SUMMARY Bass Fine Wines runs entirely counter to the usual Tasmanian pattern of tiny, estate-based businesses. Guy Wagner has set up Bass as a classic negociant operation, working backwards from the marketplace. He has completed a wine marketing degree at the University of Adelaide and intends to continue studies in oenology. The wines have been purchased from various vineyards in bottle and in barrel, but from the 2000 vintage he has also purchased grapes. The winery has been set up to focus on Pinot Noir, with three levels of Pinot in the business plan: Strait Pinot in the fighting varietal sector of the market, then Bass as a premium brand, and ultimately a super-premium Pinot, possibly to come from 30-year-old plantings which have been contracted.

Strait Chardonnay 2003 RATING 85 DRINK Now $18

Bass Phillip

Tosch's Road, Leongatha South, Vic 3953 **REGION** Gippsland
T (03) 5664 3341 **F** (03) 5664 3209 **OPEN** By appointment
WINEMAKER Phillip Jones **EST.** 1979 **CASES** 1500
PRODUCT RANGE ($27–145) Tiny quantities of Pinot Noir in three categories: standard, Premium and an occasional barrel of Reserve. A hatful of Chardonnay also made, plus Pinot Rose and Gamay.
SUMMARY Phillip Jones has retired from the Melbourne rat-race to handcraft tiny quantities of superlative Pinot Noir which, at its best, has no equal in Australia. Painstaking site selection, ultra-close vine spacing and the very, very cool climate of South Gippsland are the keys to the magic of Bass Phillip and its eerily Burgundian Pinots.

Bass Valley Estate Wines

NR

175 Nyora–St Helier Road, Loch, Vic 3945 **REGION** Gippsland
T (03) 5659 6321 **F** (03) 5659 0256 **OPEN** 7 days 10–6
WINEMAKER Robert Cutler, Roger Cutler **EST.** 1991
PRODUCT RANGE Riesling, Shiraz, Cabernet Sauvignon.
SUMMARY The Cutler family have established 3 hectares of riesling, pinot noir, cabernet sauvignon and shiraz on the eastern slopes of the Bass River Valley. The cellar door has barbecue and picnic facilities which take full advantage of the expansive views over the valley.

Batchelor's Terrace Vale

Deasey's Lane, Pokolbin, NSW 2321 **REGION** Lower Hunter Valley
T (02) 4998 7517 **F** (02) 4998 7814 **OPEN** 7 days 10–4
WINEMAKER Alain Leprince **EST.** 1971 **CASES** 9000
PRODUCT RANGE ($14.50–40 CD) Collectors Series Cabernet Sauvignon is top of the range; Old Vine Series varietals are followed by the Cellar Reserve Series, dessert wines, and Strawman Jack Semillon, Rose and Shiraz Cabernet.
SUMMARY In April 2001, the Batchelor family acquired Terrace Vale, but little else has changed. Alain Leprince remains as winemaker, and the wines still come from the 30-year-old estate plantings.

ΨΨΨΨ **Campbells Old Vine Semillon 2003** Powerful wine in all respects; long, intense and lingering; atypical Hunter but lots of character. **RATING** 89 **DRINK** 2009 $ 25

Family Reserve Elizabeth Sauvignon Blanc 2002 Limey, lemony, zesty style; botrytis lusciousness offset by lingering acidity. Serve with a chilled fresh peach. **RATING** 89 **DRINK** 2008 $ 19.50

Lachlans Old Vine Chardonnay 2002 Rounded yellow peach and nicely integrated oak; medium to full-bodied, but not heavy. **RATING** 88 **DRINK** Now $ 27.50

Collectors Series Chardonnay 2003 Very complex, strong barrel-ferment oak aromas; the palate likewise dominated by oak (a pity). **RATING** 87 **DRINK** 2008 $ 32.50

Le Prince Cabernet Sauvignon 2002 Light to medium-bodied; clean, blackcurrant fruit-driven; subtle tannins and oak. **RATING** 87 **DRINK** 2010 $ 27.50

ΨΨΨΨ **Old Vine Pinot Noir Shiraz 2002** **RATING** 86 **DRINK** 2007 $ 25

Cellar Reserve Merlot Cabernet Sauvignon 2002 **RATING** 86 **DRINK** Now $ 23

Batista
NR

Franklin Road, Middlesex, WA 6258 **REGION** Manjimup
T (08) 9772 3530 **F** (08) 9772 3530 **OPEN** By appointment
WINEMAKER Bob Peruch **EST.** 1993 **CASES** 1200
PRODUCT RANGE ($19–28 CD) Pinot Noir, Shiraz, Shiraz Cabernet, Pinot Chardonnay Reserve Brut.
SUMMARY Batista is in fact the baptismal name of owner Bob Peruch, a Pinot Noir devotee whose father planted 1 hectare of vines back in the 1950s, although these have since gone. Between 1993 and 1996 Bob Peruch has planted 1.5 hectares of pinot noir, 1.85 hectares of shiraz and the cabernet family, and 0.5 hectare of chardonnay destined for sparkling wine. The estate has two vineyards, one selected for pinot noir and chardonnay, and the other, 2 kilometres away, for shiraz, cabernet sauvignon, cabernet franc and merlot. The well-drained soils are of quartz and ironstone gravel; yields are restricted to around 7 tonnes per hectare.

Battely Wines
★★★★

Everton Ridge, PO Box 548, Beechworth, Vic 3747 **REGION** Beechworth
T (03) 5727 0505 **F** (03) 5727 0506 **OPEN** By appointment
WINEMAKER Russell Bourne **EST.** 1998 **CASES** 450
PRODUCT RANGE ($16–44 ML) Rose, Syrah, Merlot, Durif.
SUMMARY Dr Russell Bourne is an anaesthetist and former GP (at Mount Beauty), who has always loved the food, wine and skiing of northeast Victoria. He completed his oenolgody degree at Charles Sturt University in 2002 following his acquisition of the former Brown Brothers Everton Hills vineyard. Last year I shared in a bottle of 1964 Everton Hills Cabernet Shiraz which had been entombed at Brown Brothers for over 35 years. The vineyard was sold by Brown Brothers many years ago (low yields made it uneconomic) and was overgrown and abandoned when Dr Bourne purchased it in 1998. In that year he planted 1.6 hectares of shiraz; viognier was planted in the spring of 2001; further Rhône Valley varietal plantings are planned, including counoise. Until the vineyard comes into production the wines are being made from purchased grapes grown in Beechworth. Exports to the US.

ΨΨΨΨΨ **Beechworth Shiraz 2002** Powerful black cherry, licorice and spice aromas, more to blackberry and spice on the rich, lush, mouthfilling palate. **RATING** 92 **DRINK** 2015 $ 44

ΨΨΨΨ **Beechworth Durif 2002** Perversely, less powerful and concentrated than the Shiraz; simple red fruits, but with some spicy nuances. **RATING** 87 **DRINK** 2008 $ 28

Battunga Vineyards
NR

RSD 25A Tynan Road, Meadows, SA 5201 (postal) **REGION** Adelaide Hills
T (08) 8388 3866 **F** (08) 8388 3877 **OPEN** Not
WINEMAKER Robert Mann, Simon White **EST.** 1997 **CASES** A few
PRODUCT RANGE Chardonnay.
SUMMARY The development of this substantial vineyard venture began in 1997 under the direction of David Eckert. The plantings extend to pinot noir (7 hectares), merlot (3.6 hectares), sauvignon blanc (3.4 hectares), chardonnay (2.3 hectares), shiraz (2 hectares), pinot gris (1.8 hectares) and viognier (1.8 hectares), but only a limited amount of wine is made and released under the Battunga Vineyards brand.

Baudin Rock Wines   NR

RSD 109, Kingston SE, SA 5275 (postal) **REGION** Mount Benson
T (08) 8768 6217 **F** (08) 8768 6217 **OPEN** Not
WINEMAKER Contract **EST.** 1997
PRODUCT RANGE Shiraz, Cabernet Sauvignon.
SUMMARY The Ling family, headed by Robin Ling, began the development of Baudin Rock Wines in 1997, and now has 40 hectares planted to sauvignon blanc, cabernet sauvignon, merlot and shiraz. The wines are made under contract, but with assistance from James Ling; the viticulturist is Paul Ling, and the production manager Robin Ling. Only a small amount of the wine is made under the Baudin Rock label; most of the production is sold.

Baxter Stokes Wines   NR

65 Memorial Avenue, Baskerville, WA 6065 **REGION** Swan Valley
T (08) 9296 4831 **F** (08) 9296 4831 **OPEN** weekends and public holidays 9.30–5
WINEMAKER Greg Stokes **EST.** 1988 **CASES** 750
PRODUCT RANGE ($10–14 CD) Chardonnay, Verdelho, Shiraz Pinot Noir, Shiraz Cabernet Sauvignon.
SUMMARY A weekend and holiday operation for Greg and Lucy Stokes, with the production sold by mail order and through the cellar door.

Bay of Fires   ★★★★

40 Baxters Road, Pipers River, Tas 7252 **REGION** Northern Tasmania
T (03) 6382 7622 **F** (03) 6382 7225 **OPEN** 7 days 10–5
WINEMAKER Fran Austin **EST.** 2001 **CASES** 3000
PRODUCT RANGE ($21.85–32.60 R) Riesling, Sauvignon Blanc, Pinot Gris, Chardonnay, Pinot Noir, Pinot Chardonnay.
SUMMARY In 1994 BRL Hardy purchased its first grapes from Tasmania, with the aim of further developing and refining its sparkling wines, a process which quickly gave birth to Arras. The next stage was the inclusion of various parcels of chardonnay from Tasmania in the 1998 Eileen Hardy, and then the development in 2001 of the Bay of Fires brand, offering wines sourced from various parts of Tasmania. As one would expect, there is great potential for the brand. The winery was originally that of Rochecombe, then Ninth Island, and now, of course, Bay of Fires.

ŸŸŸŸŸ **Pinot Noir 2002** Saturated colour and flavour; rich, ripe plum and cherry; tending tadpole in style. **RATING** 91 **DRINK** 2010 $ 32.60

Tigress Riesling 2003 Spice, herb and mineral aromas; delicate but good mouthfeel, flow and balance. Screwcap. **RATING** 90 **DRINK** 2012 $ 22

Tigress Pinot Noir 2002 A complex, rich and ripe mix of black fruits; touch of sous bois. Powerful style, on the edge. Patience. **RATING** 90 **DRINK** 2008 $ 24

ŸŸŸŸ **Tigress Pinot Chardonnay NV** Light straw-green, with excellent mousse. Lively citrus fruit offset by lingering acidity in typical Tasmanian mould. **RATING** 89 **DRINK** 2005 $ 22

ŸŸŸŸ **Tigress Sauvignon Blanc 2003 RATING** 86 **DRINK** Now $ 22

Chardonnay 2002 Tangy, citrussy, entirely fruit-driven; less intense than expected from this vintage. **RATING** 86 **DRINK** 2007 $ 22

Tigress Rose 2002 RATING 86 **DRINK** Now $ 21

Tigress Chardonnay 2002 RATING 85 **DRINK** 2007 $ 21.85

Tigress Pinot Gris 2003 RATING 85 **DRINK** 2007 $ 22

Tigress Pinot Noir 2001 RATING 85 **DRINK** Now $ 24

Bay of Shoals   NR

19 Flinders Avenue, Kingscote, Kangaroo Island, SA 5223 (postal) **REGION** Kangaroo Island
T (08) 8553 2229 **F** (08) 8553 2229 **OPEN** Not
WINEMAKER Bethany Wines (Contract) **EST.** 1994 **CASES** 500
PRODUCT RANGE ($17.50–23 R) Riesling, Sauvignon Blanc, Chardonnay, Shiraz, Cabernet Sauvignon.

SUMMARY John Willoughby's vineyard overlooks the Bay of Shoals, which is the northern boundary of Kingscote, Kangaroo Island's main town. Planting of the vineyard began in 1994, and has now reached 10 hectares of riesling, chardonnay, sauvignon blanc, cabernet sauvignon and shiraz. In addition, 460 olive trees have been planted to produce table olives.

Bayview Estate   NR

365 Purves Road, Main Ridge, Vic 3928 **REGION** Mornington Peninsula
T (03) 5989 6130 **F** (03) 5989 6373 **OPEN** 7 days 11–7
WINEMAKER Dean Burford **EST.** 1984 **CASES** 10 000
PRODUCT RANGE ($12–30 CD) Three ranges: at the top, varietals under the Bayview Estate label; next, the Big Pig range of varietals; and finally a red and white under the equally tasty Ken and Dean's Piss label.
SUMMARY Few enterprises have cast such a broad net over the tourist traffic in the Mornington Peninsula. The estate has the Pig & Whistle Tavern and cellar door, the five-star Views Restaurant (which also serves the 70 local and imported beers), an 80-seat beer garden, a produce store, fly fishing, antiques and rose and lavender gardens. Almost incidental are the 7 hectares of pinot gris, pinot noir and pinot grigio which produce 10 000 cases of wine a year sold through the cellar door, the Hilton Hotel and Crown Casino and several Mornington Peninsula restaurants.

B'darra Estate

1415 Stumpy Gully Road, Moorooduc, Vic 3933 **REGION** Mornington Peninsula
T 0418 310 638 **OPEN** By appointment
WINEMAKER Gavin Perry **EST.** 1998 **CASES** 2000
PRODUCT RANGE ($24–28 ML) Chardonnay, Shiraz, Cabernet Sauvignon; fruit wine.
SUMMARY Gavin and Linda Perry fell in love with Bedarra Island (off the north Queensland coast) when they stayed there, hence the name of their property, which they acquired in 1998, planting just under 5 hectares of vines in 1999. They are progressively developing the 21-hectare holding, with a revegetation and wetland creation planned, of which a lake and two big dams form part. Gavin Perry made his first wine in 1993 (from grapes grown on the Peninsula) while completing a Winery Supplies course. Since that time he has won numerous trophies and gold medals, including Most Successful Exhibitor in 1997, 1999 and 2000 in the Amateur section of the Victorian Wines Show. Given the quality of the 2001 and 2002 B'darra Estate wines, I can only assume he will no longer be entering the Amateur wine section; this would be decidedly unfair, for these were very well made wines.

Beattie Wines   NR

53 Andrew Street, Windsor, Vic 3181 (postal) **REGION** Upper Goulburn
T 0411 187 871 **F** (03) 9682 3630 **OPEN** Not
WINEMAKER Brendon Beattie **EST.** 1998
PRODUCT RANGE Chardonnay, Cabernet Merlot.
SUMMARY Brendon Beattie has planted chardonnay, cabernet sauvignon and merlot at his Kanumbra vineyard. The small production is sold by mail order.

Beaumont Estate

Lot 20, 155 Milbrodale Road, Broke, NSW 2330 (postal) **REGION** Lower Hunter Valley
T 0419 616 461 **F** (07) 5474 3722 **OPEN** Not
WINEMAKER Contract **EST.** 1998
PRODUCT RANGE ($21–25 ML) Hand Picked Semillon, Merlot.
SUMMARY The estate vineyards were planted in September 1999 on the river flats of Parson Creek, nestled between the Yengo and Wollemi National Parks. The soils were enhanced with organic preparations, and after 17 months the 2.2 hectares of semillon and 1.3 hectares of merlot produced a substantial crop; the vine growth, it is said, was equivalent to 3 years under normal conditions. The intention is to continue the organic farming approach, and to eventually become certified Biodynamic. Currently the wines are sold by phone, mail order and email, and future plans include a cellar door. Profits from wine sales will support a respite facility for limited life children, which is currently being constructed on the property.

ＹＹＹＹ **Hand Picked Semillon 2003** Aromas of lemon, grass, mineral and lanolin lead into a palate with good acidity and length; the cork closure suggests caution with cellaring. **RATING** 88 **DRINK** 2010 $ 21

Beckett's Flat ★★★★

Beckett Road, Metricup, WA 6280 **REGION** Margaret River
T (08) 9755 7402 **F** (08) 9755 7344 **OPEN** 7 days 10–6
WINEMAKER Belizar Ilic **EST.** 1992 **CASES** 6000
PRODUCT RANGE ($15–35 CD) Sauvignon Blanc, Verdelho, Chardonnay, Autumn Harvest, Liqueur Chardonnay, Crackling Rose; Belizar's Shiraz, Reserve Justinian (Merlot blend), Cabernet Merlot.
SUMMARY Bill and Noni Ilic opened Beckett's Flat in September 1997. Situated just off the Bussell Highway at Metricup, midway between Busselton and the Margaret River, it draws upon 14 hectares of estate vineyards which were first planted in 1992. From 1998 onwards the wines have been made at the on-site winery. Accommodation is available.

ＹＹＹＹＹ **Belizar's Reserve Justinian 2002** Fresh, clean, juicy fruit; good balance in typical light to medium-bodied mode; has elegance. Bordeaux blend. **RATING** 90 **DRINK** 2011 $ 35

ＹＹＹＹ **Belizar's Shiraz 2002** Light to medium-bodied, elegant style; oak is a major contributor, but has integrated well. **RATING** 89 **DRINK** 2012 $ 25
Chardonnay 2002 Generous, full-bodied, ripe and sweet stone fruit; subtle French oak; slightly hot finish. **RATING** 88 **DRINK** 2007 $ 25
Belizar's Cabernet Merlot 2002 Clean, fresh, light to medium-bodied; bright red fruits; good extract management. **RATING** 88 **DRINK** 2010 $ 25
Sauvignon Blanc 2003 Crisp, clean mineral, slate and leaf aromas; ultra-delicate palate needing more punch. **RATING** 87 **DRINK** Now $ 17.50
Verdelho 2003 Clear fruit salad varietal character; good balance and length. **RATING** 87 **DRINK** Now $ 19

Beckingham Wines ★★★

6-7/477 Warrigal Road, Moorabbin, Vic 3189 **REGION** Mornington Peninsula/Goulburn Valley
T (03) 9258 7352 **F** (03) 9360 0713 **OPEN** Weekends 10–5
WINEMAKER Peter Beckingham **EST.** 1998 **CASES** 1700
PRODUCT RANGE ($9–25 CD) A kaleidoscopic array of regional and varietal table and fortified wines.
SUMMARY Peter Beckingham is a chemical engineer who has turned a hobby into a part-time business, moving operations from the driveway of his house to a warehouse in Moorabbin. The situation of the winery may not be romantic, but it is eminently practical, and more than a few winemakers have adopted the same solution in California. His friends grow the grapes and he makes the wine, with the Mornington Peninsula, Echuca and the Strathbogie Ranges the prime source of grapes; other regions (such as the Yarra Valley) contribute from time to time. Peter Beckingham professes to be passionate about his wines, and is doubtless learning more as each vintage goes by.

ＹＹＹＹ **Edgehill Chardonnay 2003** Clean, well made; nectarine, melon and citrus fruit; unoaked, but has good length. **RATING** 87 **DRINK** Now $ 15
Chardonnay Liqueur NV Strongly spirity; shows the making techniques: barely fermented before alcohol added; Mistella style. **RATING** 87 **DRINK** Now $ 11

ＹＹＹＹ **Cornelia Creek Cabernet 2000** **RATING** 86 **DRINK** Now $ 18
Cornelia Creek Cabernet 2002 **RATING** 85 **DRINK** 2007 $ 18
Pas de Deux Pinot Chardonnay 2000 **RATING** 85 **DRINK** Now $ 18
Pinot Liqueur NV **RATING** 85 **DRINK** Now $ 13
Pas de Deux Pinot Chardonnay 1998 **RATING** 84 **DRINK** Now $ 18

Beechwood Wines NR

PO Box 869, Echuca, Vic 3564 **REGION** Goulburn Valley
T (03) 5482 4276 **F** (03) 5482 1185 **OPEN** Not
WINEMAKER Gavin Beech **EST.** 1995

PRODUCT RANGE Verdelho, Shiraz, Cabernet Sauvignon.

SUMMARY The Beech family (headed by Gavin and Keith) have planted 4.5 hectares of verdelho, shiraz and cabernet sauvignon. There are no cellar door facilities, and the wine is distributed by Brian Downie.

Beelgara Estate ★★★

Farm 576, Beelbangera, NSW 2686 REGION Riverina
T (02) 6966 0200 F (02) 6966 0298 OPEN Mon–Sat 10–5, Sun 11–3
WINEMAKER James Ceccato, Belinda Morandin, Andrew Shulz, Danny Toaldo EST. 1930 CASES 600 000
PRODUCT RANGE ($5–16 CD) Wattleglen Semillon Sauvignon Blanc Chardonnay, Shiraz Cabernet Sauvignon; the Silky Oak range (around $8) of Sauvignon Blanc, Verdelho, Chardonnay, Shiraz, Merlot, Cabernet Merlot, St Macaire; the Woorawa range (around $10) of Riesling, Chardonnay, Old Vine Shiraz, Cabernet Merlot; the Promenade range (around $15) of Semillon, Chardonnay, Botrytis Semillon, Old Vine Shiraz, Chambourcin, Cabernet Sauvignon; sparkling, dessert, Lambrusco, fortifieds.
SUMMARY Beelgara Estate was formed in 2001 after the purchase of the 60-year-old Rossetto family winery in the Riverina district of NSW by a group consisting of growers, distributors and investors. The name Beelgara is a contraction of the Beelbangera region, where the group is headquartered. The new management is placing far greater emphasis on bottled table wine (albeit at low prices), but continues to supply bulk, cleanskin and fully packaged product for both domestic and export markets.

ΥΥΥΥ **Winemakers Selection Cabernet Sauvignon 2002** Generous blackcurrant with a dusting of chocolate and vanilla; good structure and length; a vintage tribute. RATING 88 DRINK 2009 $16
Winemakers Selection Old Vine Shiraz 2002 Densely coloured; blackberry, mocha and chocolate; soft tannins. RATING 87 DRINK 2007 $16

ΥΥΥΫ **Winemakers Selection Semillon 2002** Bright yellow-green; soft, already showing bottle development; flavoursome, early-drinking style. RATING 86 DRINK Now $16
Promenade Cabernet Sauvignon 2002 RATING 86 DRINK 2010 $16
Winemakers Selection Chambourcin 2002 Light to medium-bodied; fair balance; nice flavour, raspberry and plum; lacks structure. RATING 86 DRINK Now $16
Woorawa Cabernet Merlot 2002 RATING 85 DRINK Now $12
Two Thumbs Chardonnay 2002 RATING 84 DRINK Now $14.95

ΥΥΥ **Woorawa Verdelho 2003** RATING 83 $12
Woorawa Chardonnay 2003 RATING 82 $12

Beer Brothers NR

Pheasant Farm Road, Nuriootpa, SA 5355 REGION Barossa Valley
T (08) 8562 4477 F (08) 8562 4757 OPEN 7 days 10–5
WINEMAKER Contract EST. 1997 CASES 500
PRODUCT RANGE ($12–42 CD) Riesling, Chardonnay, Shiraz, Old Vine Shiraz, White Port.
SUMMARY Yes, they really are Beer brothers, and, yes, they grow grapes and make wine, not beer. The brothers in question are Colin Beer (brother of famed chef and author Maggie Beer) and Bruce, who became a partner in the grape-growing venture in 1987. Ten years later they decided to venture into a relatively small amount of winemaking, using the winemaking team at Yalumba (to whom they sell the lion's share of the grape production) and, after selling some of the 40-year-old Barossa Shiraz to Rockford for inclusion in the Basket Press Red, persuaded Dave Powell (of Torbreck) to make 1000 bottles of a 2001 Old Vine Barossa Shiraz, which received high praise from Huon Hooke. The brothers' second vineyard is at Cobdogla, on the River Murray. Visitors to the cellar door won't have the food which Maggie Beer made famous at the Pheasant Farm, but light meals are provided plus local produce; no guesses required to work out what that might be.

Belgenny Vineyard ★★★☆

92 De Beyers Road, Pokolbin, NSW 2320 REGION Lower Hunter Valley
T (02) 9247 5300 F (02) 9247 7273 OPEN Not
WINEMAKER Monarch Winemaking Services (Contract) EST. 1990 CASES 7000

PRODUCT RANGE ($15–30 R) Semillon, Verdelho, Unwooded Chardonnay, Partner's Reserve Chardonnay, Chardonnay, Proprietor's Reserve Chardonnay, Petit Rose, Merlot, Shiraz, Cabernet Sauvignon.
SUMMARY In 1999, partners Norman Seckold and Dudley Leitch realised a long-held ambition to establish a vineyard in the Hunter Valley with the acquisition of their 17-hectare site. Plantings have steadily increased and are presently chardonnay (5.7 hectares), shiraz (4.9 hectares), merlot (2 hectares), semillon (1.2 hectares), and a carefully thought out marketing strategy has been put in place. A cellar door and restaurant are planned. Exports to Hong Kong and Singapore.

🍇 Belgravia Vineyards ★★★★

Belgravia Road, Orange, NSW 2800 **REGION** Orange
T (02) 6365 0633 **F** (02) 6365 0646 **OPEN** By appointment
WINEMAKER David Lowe, Jane Wilson (Contract) **EST.** 2003 **CASES** 6000
PRODUCT RANGE ($12–23 ML) Chardonnay, Reserve Viognier, Late Harvest Semillon, Rose, Reserve Shiraz, Reserve Shiraz Viognier, Cabernet Shiraz Merlot.
SUMMARY Belgravia is an 1800-hectare mixed farming property (sheep, cattle and vineyards) 20 kilometres north of Orange. The first plantings took place in 1996, and there are now 180 hectares contracted to Southcorp, and 10 hectares set aside for the Belgravia wine brand. Owner Richard Hattersley has assembled an impressive team under the direction of general manager Alan Hardy, and the seriousness of the venture is also evidenced by the fact that the first vintages were exported to the UK and Denmark; it is only recently that they have been released onto the domestic market. The property also has a bed and breakfast cottage, and is presently restoring 300 hectares of grassy whitebox woodland.

ΨΨΨΨΨ **Reserve Shiraz Viognier 2002** Fragrant and aromatic; the Viognier influence is obvious throughout; a mix of black cherry and blackberry with a twist of citrus. **RATING** 92 **DRINK** 2012 $ 23
Reserve Orange Shiraz 2001 Appealing array of fruits from raspberry and plum to blackberry and spice; fine extract and tannins; good finish. **RATING** 90 **DRINK** 2011 $ 23

ΨΨΨΨ **Reserve Viognier 2003** Clean, fruit-driven, honeysuckle and peach; subliminal oak; good length. **RATING** 89 **DRINK** Now $ 23
Late Harvest Semillon 2002 A rich, complex and intensely luscious cornucopia of tropical fruits; good balancing acidity. **RATING** 89 **DRINK** 2007 $ 15
Chardonnay 2003 Stone fruit, peach and ripe melon; medium-bodied; slightly short, but flavoursome; from Orange and Mudgee. **RATING** 87 **DRINK** Now $ 19

ΨΨΨΨ **Cabernet Shiraz Merlot 2001** **RATING** 85 **DRINK** 2007 $ 19

🍇 Bell River Estate NR

Mitchell Highway, Neurea, NSW 2820 **REGION** Central Ranges Zone
T (02) 6846 7277 **F** (02) 6846 7277 **OPEN** 7 days 9–6
WINEMAKER Sandra Banks **EST.** 1974 **CASES** 500
PRODUCT RANGE ($10–16 ML) Riesling, Chardonnay, Sweet White, Shiraz, Soft Red (Muscat Grenache Cabernet Sauvignon), Hope Royal Cabernet Sauvignon, and a wide range of fortified wines.
SUMMARY Situated 15 kilometres south of Wellington, Bell River Estate was formerly known as Markeita Cellars, the name change due to its purchase by Michael and Sandra Banks. They have 2.5 hectares of grenache, cabernet sauvignon, shiraz and muscat, and as well as producing Bell River Estate wines, offer bottling, contract winemaking and viticultural services. The wines can be ordered through the website <www.bellriverestate.com.au>.

🍇 Bell's Lane Wines NR

Mangoola Road, Denman, NSW 2328 **REGION** Upper Hunter Valley
T (02) 6547 1191 **F** (02) 6547 1191 **OPEN** Weekends 10–5, or by appointment
WINEMAKER John Hordern **EST.** 1998
PRODUCT RANGE ($18.50–20 CD) Semillon, Verdelho, Chardonnay, Shiraz.

SUMMARY In the words of Paul and Megan Melville, 'We were a typical hard-working Sydney couple, but we were tired of the daily slog of city life and conversations about real estate prices, so we uprooted the kids, sold the house, cleared the land and started planting the vines — 30 000 in all.' Thus was born Bell's Lane Vineyard, 3 kilometres from Denman, in 1998. A dilapidated dairy on the property has been converted to a cellar door, which serves light lunches on weekends. The wines are also sold through selected bottle shops and by mail order.

Bellarine Estate   ★★★★

2270 Portarlington Road, Bellarine, Vic 3222 **REGION** Geelong
T (03) 5259 3310 **F** (03) 5259 3393 **OPEN** 7 days 10–4
WINEMAKER Robin Brockett **EST.** 1995 **CASES** 7000
PRODUCT RANGE ($21–25 CD) The premium varietal range under the Bellarine Estate label; the second range of Portarlington Ridge comes from various Victorian sources.
SUMMARY A relatively recent arrival on the Bellarine Peninsula, but a substantial one, with 4 hectares each of chardonnay and pinot noir, 3 hectares of shiraz (producing an excellent wine with a dash of viognier), 1 hectare of merlot and 0.5 hectare each of pinot gris and viognier. The wines are made by Robin Brockett at Scotchmans Hill. Bella's restaurant is open for lunch 7 days and dinner on Friday and Saturday.

ꔪꔪꔪꔪ **James' Paddock Chardonnay 2002** Complex and intense; barrel ferment and malolactic ferments plus bottle development plus cool vintage all add to the texture and intensity. **RATING** 92 **DRINK** 2009 $ 24.50
Phil's Fetish Pinot Noir 2002 Concentrated, ultra-ripe plum, spice and prune; voluptuously rich and concentrated, but not tannic. **RATING** 92 **DRINK** 2012 $ 23

ꔪꔪꔪ **James' Paddock Chardonnay 2001** Obvious barrel-ferment inputs provide complexity; stone fruit comes through on the palate and long finish; developing slowly. **RATING** 89 **DRINK** Now $ 24.50
Julian's Merlot 2001 Aromatic and tangy; light to medium-bodied but intense; lingering red berry and olive finish; clear varietal character. **RATING** 89 **DRINK** 2011 $ 32.90

ꔪꔪꔪ **Portarlington Ridge The Pump Chardonnay 2001** **RATING** 86 **DRINK** 2007 $ 19.50

Bellendena   NR

240 Tinderbox Road, Tinderbox, Tas 7054 **REGION** Southern Tasmania
T (03) 6229 8264 **F** (03) 6229 8307 **OPEN** By appointment
WINEMAKER Andrew Hood **EST.** 1995 **CASES** 12
PRODUCT RANGE ($20–25 ML) Chardonnay, Pinot Noir.
SUMMARY A typical micro-operation only made possible by Andrew Hood's willingness to make 1 or 2 barrels for growers wanting to have their own wine. Andrew and Jane Elek, the former a consultant in international economic policy, the latter a biologist and entomologist, have established 0.5 hectare of vineyard, planted equally to chardonnay and pinot noir. The name Bellendena comes from the botanical name of a native Tasmanian plant, *Bellendena montana*, commonly known as Mountain Rocket. The label depicts the red seed capsules of the plant viewed from above. The wine is sold by mail order only. At 12 cases, this was surely the smallest commercial winery in the 2003 vintage.

Belubula Valley Vineyards   NR

Golden Gully, Mandurama, NSW 2798 **REGION** Orange
T (02) 6367 5236 **F** (02) 6362 4726 **OPEN** Not
WINEMAKER David Somervaille **EST.** 1986 **CASES** 650
PRODUCT RANGE ($18.50–21 R) Cabernet Sauvignon.
SUMMARY Belubula Valley is a foundation member of the Central Highlands Grapegrowers Association (now ORVA), centred on Orange; the vineyard is located on the Belubula River, near Carcoar, and the small amounts of wine made to date have not yet been commercially released. David Somervaille, incidentally, was the chairman of partners of the national law firm Blake Dawson Waldron. Like me, he is a self-taught winemaker, his early experience with wine coming through his participation in a partnership which operated the Oakdale Vineyard (now Audrey Wilkinson) in the Hunter Valley; this was, however, sold in 1980.

Ben's Run ★★★★

71 Adams Peak Road, Broke, NSW 2330 (postal) **REGION** Lower Hunter Valley
T (02) 6579 1310 **F** (02) 6579 1370 **OPEN** Not
WINEMAKER Contract **EST.** 1997 **CASES** 550
PRODUCT RANGE ($27 R) Shiraz.
SUMMARY Ben's Run has an interesting, almost schizophrenic, background. On the one hand, say the owners, 'it is named for our kelpie dog for graciously allowing part of his retirement run to be converted into a showpiece shiraz-only vineyard'. On the other hand, patriarch Norman Marran was one of the pioneers of the Australian cotton industry, and has had a long and distinguished career as a director of both the Australian Wheat Board and the Grains Research Corporation, and is currently chairman of a leading food research company. The decision has been taken to produce only 500 cases of wine a year from the 3-hectare, low-yielding shiraz-only vineyard, the remainder being sold to Andrew Margan.

Benarra Vineyards ★★★☆

PO Box 1081, Mount Gambier, SA 5290 **REGION** Mount Gambier
T (08) 8738 9355 **F** (08) 8738 9355 **OPEN** Not
WINEMAKER Martin Slocombe **EST.** 1998 **CASES** 150
PRODUCT RANGE Flint Bed Pinot Noir.
SUMMARY Lisle Pudney has planted a substantial vineyard, with the help of investors. In all there are over 26 hectares of pinot noir and 4 hectares each of sauvignon blanc and chardonnay, with another 40 hectares to be planted over the next 3 years. The vineyard is situated 20 kilometres from the Southern Ocean on ancient flint beds; a million-year-old mollusc found on the property by Lisle Pudney is depicted on the label of the Pinot Noir. Most of the grapes are sold; a small portion is contract-made for the Benarra label, and is of good quality and varietal character.

Bendigo Wine Estate NR

682 Axedale–Goornong Road, Axedale, Vic 3551 **REGION** Bendigo
T (03) 5439 7444 **F** (03) 5439 7433 **OPEN** 7 days
WINEMAKER Contract **EST.** 2000
PRODUCT RANGE Riesling, Chardonnay, Verdelho, Pinot Noir, Shiraz, Cabernet Merlot.
SUMMARY A quite substantial operation, with plantings of riesling, chardonnay, verdelho, pinot noir, cabernet sauvignon, merlot, malbec, shiraz and mourvedre, producing both table and sparkling wines. The wines are chiefly sold by mail order and through the cellar door, which has barbecue and picnic facilities, and periodically stages events.

Bent Creek Vineyards ★★★★

Lot 10 Blewitt Springs Road, McLaren Flat, SA 5171 **REGION** McLaren Vale
T (08) 8383 0414 **F** (08) 8239 1538 **OPEN** Sundays and public holidays 11–5
WINEMAKER Michael Scarpantoni **EST.** 2001 **CASES** 5000
PRODUCT RANGE ($13–49 CD) Riesling, Unwooded Chardonnay, Nero Sparkling Shiraz, The Nude Shiraz, Black Dog Shiraz, Reserve Shiraz, Cabernet, Tawny Port.
SUMMARY Loretta and Peter Polson became wine drinkers and collectors a decade before they acquired a small patch of 40-year-old dry-grown chardonnay and shiraz at McLaren Flat; this was followed by the purchase of another small property at McLaren Vale, planted to grenache, cabernet franc and chardonnay. Say the Polsons, 'Land barons? Hardly: 10 acres in all, but you will appreciate that it is enough for one man to look after and hand prune.' Until recently, all of the grapes were sold to d'Arenberg, but now a small proportion is kept back for the Bent Creek Vineyards. Exports to Canada and Belgium.

 The Nude Shiraz 2002 Massively powerful and dense; black fruits, licorice and loads of vanilla oak and tannins. **RATING** 91 **DRINK** 2017 $39

The Black Dog Shiraz 2002 Traditional style; blackberry and chocolate swathed in vanilla. **RATING** 89 **DRINK** 2012 $21
Nero Sparkling Shiraz 2002 Lots of black cherry and dark chocolate fruit; not too sweet; a pleasant surprise. **RATING** 88 **DRINK** Now $19

Cabernet Sauvignon 2002 Clean, fresh; light to medium-bodied; black and redcurrant; no frills. **RATING** 87 **DRINK** 2009 $17

ŸŸŸŸ **Unwooded Chardonnay 2003 RATING** 86 **DRINK** 2007 $17
Riesling 2003 RATING 84 **DRINK** 2007 $15

Beresford Wines ★★★

26 Kangarilla Road, McLaren Vale, SA 5171 **REGION** McLaren Vale
T (08) 8323 8899 **F** (08) 8323 7911 **OPEN** Mon–Fri 9–5, weekends 10–5
WINEMAKER Scott McIntosh **EST.** 1985 **CASES** 100 000
PRODUCT RANGE ($7.50–40 CD) At the bottom of the three-tier structure come the Beacon Hill varietals; the second level is the Highwood range; then under the premium Beresford label are Clare Valley Riesling, Adelaide Hills Chardonnay, McLaren Vale Chardonnay, Clare Valley Shiraz, McLaren Vale Shiraz and McLaren Vale Cabernet Sauvignon.
SUMMARY The Beresford brand sits at the top of a range of labels primarily and successfully aimed at export markets in the UK, the US, Hong Kong and China. The intention is that ultimately most, if not all, of the wines will be sourced from grapes grown in McLaren Vale; a new cellar door and boutique winery recently opened as planned. Incidentally, it is run as an entirely separate operation from its sister winery, Step Road in Langhorne Creek.

ŸŸŸŸ **McLaren Vale Chardonnay 2001** Attractive nectarine and melon fruit are dominant; slightly high adjusted acidity; oak barely perceptible **RATING** 86 **DRINK** Now $18

Berri Estates ★★☆

Sturt Highway, Glossop, SA 5344 **REGION** Riverland
T (08) 8582 0300 **F** (08) 8583 2224 **OPEN** Mon–Sat 9–5, Sundays on long weekends 10–4
WINEMAKER Paul Kasselbaum, Peter Hensel, Graham Buller **EST.** 1916
PRODUCT RANGE ($4.99 R) Light Fruity Lexia, Fruity Gordo Moselle, Chablis, Claret, Rose, White Lambrusco, all in cask form.
SUMMARY Part of the BRL Hardy Group, with no pretensions to grandeur, its visible business almost entirely restricted to 5-litre casks, many with generic names to be phased out under Australia's wine agreement with the EU.

Berrys Bridge ★★★★

Forsters Road, Carapooee, St Arnaud, Vic 3478 **REGION** Pyrenees
T (03) 5496 3220 **F** (03) 5496 3322 **OPEN** Weekends by appointment
WINEMAKER Jane Holt **EST.** 1990 **CASES** 1500
PRODUCT RANGE ($42–45 CD) Shiraz, Merlot, Cabernet Sauvignon.
SUMMARY While the date of establishment is 1990, Roger Milner purchased the property in 1975, intending to plant a vineyard; he had already worked for 3 years at Reynell winery in South Australia. In the mid-1980s he returned with Jane Holt, and together they began the construction of the stone house-cum-winery. Planting of existing 7 hectares of vineyard commenced in 1990, around the time that Jane commenced her viticultural studies at Charles Sturt University (completed in 1993, and followed by a wine science degree in 2000). Until 1997 the grapes were sold to others, the first vintage (from 1997) being released in November 1998 when Ian McDonald joined the business and became responsible for marketing and export. The wines are distributed in Victoria through Winestock to a number of well-known retailers. Not surprisingly, the limited quantity sells out with great speed. Exports to the US, Germany and Switzerland.

Best's Wines ★★★★★

111 Best's Road, Great Western, Vic 3377 **REGION** Grampians
T (03) 5356 2250 **F** (03) 5356 2430 **OPEN** Mon–Sat 10–5, Sun 11–4
WINEMAKER Viv Thomson, Hamish Seabrook **EST.** 1866 **CASES** 30 000
PRODUCT RANGE ($14–82 R) Three ranges: at the top are wines in the Great Western range (headed by Thomson Family), then the Kindred Spirits and Victoria ranges.

SUMMARY Best's Great Western winery and vineyards are among the best-kept secrets of Australia. Indeed the vineyards, with vines dating back to 1867, have secrets which may never be revealed: for example, certain vines planted in the Nursery Block have defied identification and are thought to exist nowhere else in the world. The cellars, too, go back to the same era: they were constructed by butcher-turned-winemaker, Joseph Best, and his family. Since 1920, the Thomson family has owned the property, with father Viv and sons Ben, Bart and Marcus representing the fourth and fifth generations. They consistently produce elegant, supple wines which deserve far greater recognition than they receive. The Shiraz is a classic; the Thomson Family Shiraz magnificent. Exports to the UK, the US, Canada, The Netherlands, Belgium, Switzerland, Japan, Singapore, Germany and Malaysia.

ŶŶŶŶŶ **Thomson Family Shiraz 2001** Succulently rich and supple black fruits and perfectly integrated French oak; graceful and elegant despite the richness. **RATING** 96 **DRINK** 2016 $65
Bin O Shiraz 2001 Savoury, gently earthy edges to blackberry/cherry aromas blend into a supple palate; the fruit has a very long carry, with the tannins fine and soft. **RATING** 94 **DRINK** 2011 $35
Great Western Cabernet Sauvignon 2001 A highly sophisticated wine; great fusion of fruit, oak and tannins; outstanding texture, structure and overall mouthfeel. **RATING** 94 **DRINK** 2015 $30

ŶŶŶŶŶ **Great Western Riesling 2003** Bright straw-green; fragrant citrussy mineral aromas; firm palate, long finish. **RATING** 92 **DRINK** 2009 $18
Great Western Chardonnay 2001 Ageing slowly; subtle oak and malolactic inputs; cashew and melon; good length and balance. **RATING** 90 **DRINK** 2008 $28

ŶŶŶŶ **Victoria Shiraz 2002** Highly aromatic cherry/cherry jam aromas; medium-bodied; red fruits backed by fine tannins. **RATING** 89 **DRINK** 2007 $16
Kindred Spirits Merlot 2001 Elegant, long, fine and supple; excellent varietal character in bright, fresh small fruits; minimal tannins. **RATING** 87 **DRINK** 2008 $19.50

ŶŶŶŶ **Victoria Riesling 2003** **RATING** 86 **DRINK** 2007 $14
Victoria Chardonnay 2003 **RATING** 86 **DRINK** Now $14
Great Western Pinot Noir 2001 **RATING** 86 **DRINK** 2007 $24.95
Victoria Shiraz 2001 **RATING** 86 **DRINK** 2007 $16
Kindred Spirits Chardonnay 2003 **RATING** 85 **DRINK** Now $19.50
Victoria Cabernet Sauvignon 2001 **RATING** 85 **DRINK** 2008 $16

Bethany Wines ★★★☆

Bethany Road, Bethany via Tanunda, SA 5352 **REGION** Barossa Valley
T (08) 8563 2086 **F** (08) 8563 0046 **OPEN** Mon–Sat 10–5, Sun 1–5
WINEMAKER Geoff Schrapel, Robert Schrapel **EST.** 1977 **CASES** 25 000
PRODUCT RANGE ($14.50–65 CD) An interesting range of Eden Valley, Barossa Valley and Kangaroo Island-sourced varietal table wines, headed by GR6 Reserve Shiraz and GR5 Reserve Cabernet Sauvignon. Also fortifieds and sparklings.
SUMMARY The Schrapel family has been growing grapes in the Barossa Valley for over 140 years, but the winery has only been in operation since 1977. Nestling high on a hillside in the site of an old quarry, it is run by Geoff and Rob Schrapel, who produce a range of consistently well-made and attractively packaged wines. They have 36 hectares of vineyards in the Barossa Valley, 8 in the Eden Valley and (recently and interestingly) 2 hectares each of chardonnay and cabernet sauvignon on Kangaroo Island. The wines enjoy national distribution in Australia, and are exported to the UK, Germany, Sweden, The Netherlands, New Zealand, Japan and Singapore.

ŶŶŶŶ **Shiraz 2001** Ripe, luscious red and black fruits; soft tannins, good overall flavour. **RATING** 89 **DRINK** 2011 $25
Riesling 2003 Rich, full-bodied, ripe tropical/citrus fruit in traditional style. **RATING** 87 **DRINK** Now $14.50
Select Late Harvest Cordon Cut Riesling 2003 Rich, direct tropical fruit; fully sweet, but good acid balance. **RATING** 87 **DRINK** 2008 $18

ŶŶŶŶ **Barrel Fermented Semillon 2002** **RATING** 85 **DRINK** Now $14
Grenache Pressings 2002 **RATING** 84 **DRINK** Now $15.90

⚘ Bettenay's

Lot 1685, Cnr Harmans South and Miamup Roads, Wilyabrup, WA 6284 **REGION** Margaret River
T (08) 9755 5539 **F** (08) 9755 5539 **OPEN** 7 days 10–5
WINEMAKER Peter Stanlake (Contract) **EST.** 1989 **CASES** 1500
PRODUCT RANGE ($14–45 CD) Semillon, Sauvignon Blanc, Semillon Sauvignon Blanc, Chardonnay, Lost Plot Red Blend, Shiraz, Merlot, Cabernet Merlot, Lost Plot White Port.
SUMMARY Greg Bettenay began the development of 10 hectares of vineyards in 1989, planted to sauvignon blanc, semillon, chardonnay, cabernet sauvignon, merlot and shiraz. The development now extends to two farm vineyard cottages and a luxury tree-top spa apartment known as The Leafy Loft.

ⓎⓎⓎⓎ **Merlot 2001** Elegant, supple and fine red berry fruits with an appropriate touch of olive; balanced tannins and oak. **RATING** 93 **DRINK** 2011 $45

ⓎⓎⓎⓎ **Shiraz 2002** Medium-bodied black cherry and spice, vibrant palate; nice oak handling. **RATING** 88 **DRINK** 2010 $27

ⓎⓎⓎⓎ **Chardonnay 2002** Complex, funky barrel-ferment inputs; plenty of flavour; slightly sweet. **RATING** 86 **DRINK** Now $36

⚘ Bettio Wines

RMB 9329 Whitfield Road, King Valley, Vic 3678 **REGION** King Valley
T (03) 5727 9308 **F** (03) 5727 9344 **OPEN** By appointment
WINEMAKER Daniel Bettio **EST.** 1995 **CASES** 2000
PRODUCT RANGE ($16–25 CD) Sauvignon Blanc, Chardonnay, Merlot, Cabernet Sauvignon.
SUMMARY The Bettio family, with Paul and Daniel at the helm, have established 20 hectares of vines in the King Valley and 5 hectares at Cheshunt. The plantings are of sauvignon blanc, chardonnay, merlot and cabernet sauvignon, and the wines are chiefly sold through the cellar door and by mail order. A range of back vintages going back to 1997 are available at the cellar door or by mail order.

ⓎⓎⓎ **Chardonnay 2002** **RATING** 83 $16
Sauvignon Blanc 2002 **RATING** 82 $16

Beyond Broke Vineyard NR

Cobcroft Road, Broke, NSW 2330 **REGION** Lower Hunter Valley
T (02) 6026 2043 **F** (02) 6026 2043 **OPEN** Tastings available at Broke Village Store 10–4
WINEMAKER Pete Howland (Contract) **EST.** 1996 **CASES** 4000
PRODUCT RANGE ($14–22 R) Semillon, Verdelho, Chardonnay, Unwooded Chardonnay, Sparkling Semillon, Shiraz.
SUMMARY Beyond Broke Vineyard is the reincarnation of a former Lindemans vineyard purchased by Bob and Terry Kennedy in 1996. In a more than slightly ironical twist, the 1997 Beyond Broke Semillon won 2 trophies at the Hunter Valley Wine Show of that year, the first for the Best Current Vintage Semillon and the second, the Henry John Lindeman Memorial Trophy for the Best Current Vintage Dry White Wine. Subsequent shows have been less spectacularly kind, but there is nothing surprising in that, and its turn will come again when vintage conditions permit.

Bianchet ★★★☆

187 Victoria Road, Lilydale, Vic 3140 **REGION** Yarra Valley
T (03) 9739 1779 **F** (03) 9739 1277 **OPEN** Thurs–Fri 10–4, weekends 10–5
WINEMAKER Gary Mills **EST.** 1976 **CASES** 2500
PRODUCT RANGE ($15–27 CD) Copestone Semillon Sauvignon Blanc, Marsanne, Chardonnay, Chardonnay Cuvee, Duet (Gewurztraminer Semillon), Verduzzo, Pinot Noir, Shiraz, Merlot, Cabernet.
SUMMARY Owned by a small Melbourne-based syndicate, which acquired the business from the founding Bianchet family. One of the most unusual wines from the winery is Verduzzo Gold, a late-harvest sweet white wine made from the Italian grape variety. The wines are still basically sold through the cellar door.

Bidgeebong Wines

352 Byrnes Road, Bomen, NSW 2650 **REGION** Southern New South Wales Zone
T (03) 9853 6207 **F** (03) 9853 5499 **OPEN** Mon–Fri 9–4
WINEMAKER Andrew Birks **EST.** 2000 **CASES** 15 000
PRODUCT RANGE ($16–20.50 R) Tumbarumba Chardonnay, Gundagai Shiraz, Tumbarumba Merlot.
SUMMARY Encompasses what the founders refer to as the Bidgeebong triangle lying between Young, Wagga Wagga, Tumbarumba and Gundagai, which provide grapes for the Bidgeebong brand. Two of the partners are Andrew Birks, with a 30-year career as a lecturer and educator at Charles Sturt University, and Simon Robertson, who studied viticulture and wine science at Charles Sturt University, and after working in Europe and the Barwang Vineyard established by his father Peter in 1969, built a substantial viticultural management business in the area. A winery was completed for the 2002 vintage, and will eventually be capable of handling 2000 tonnes of grapes, for Bidgeebong's own needs and those of other local growers and larger producers who purchase grapes from the region. Exports to the UK.

TTTTT Gundagai Shiraz 2002 Ultra-concentrated, complex and rich; blackberry, black cherry, licorice, spice and dark chocolate flood the mouth, balanced by good tannins. Festooned with medals. **RATING** 95 **DRINK** 2017 $ 24.95

TTTTT Triangle Shiraz 2002 Abundant blackberry, dark fruits and chocolate; a mouthfilling and rich junior brother to the Gundagai Shiraz. Screwcap. **RATING** 90 **DRINK** 2015 $ 12.95

TTTT Triangle Chardonnay 2003 Subtle but complex winemaking techniques result in a wine with soft melon and fig flavours; creamy mouthfeel. **RATING** 88 **DRINK** Now $ 12.95
Tumbarumba Merlot 2002 Wholly appropriate weight and structure for the variety; redcurrant/raspberry fruit; subtle oak. **RATING** 88 **DRINK** 2009 $ 19.95

Big Barrel Vineyard and Winery NR

787 Landsborough Road, Maleny, Qld 4551 **REGION** Queensland Coastal
T (07) 5429 6300 **F** (07) 5429 6331 **OPEN** 7 days 10–5
WINEMAKER Stuart Pierce **EST.** 2000 **CASES** 1280
PRODUCT RANGE ($12.90–20 CD) Ridge White, Chardonnay Semillon, Verdelho, Unwooded Chardonnay, Chardonnay, Barambah Bubbles, Sparkling Shiraz, Ridge Red, Classic Dry Red, Reserve Shiraz, Durif, Merlot, Glasshouse Tawny Port.
SUMMARY The Pagano family's forebears made wine on the foothills of Mount Etna for many generations, and the family has been involved in the Australian wine industry for over 40 years. But it was not until 12 years ago that father Sebastian and wife Maria Pagano saw the Maleny area with its Glasshouse Mountain and surrounding Blackall Range, reminiscent of a scaled-down Mount Etna. They have now planted 4 hectares of chambourcin on-site, and opened a tasting room in the shape of a giant barrel; there is a wide range of wines sourced from elsewhere in Australia. In best Queensland tradition, there are plenty of attractions for tourists, including vineyard tours, light foccacia lunches through Monday to Saturday, and a continental buffet lunch on Sunday.

Big Hill Vineyard

Cnr Calder Highway and Belvoir Park Road, Big Hill, Bendigo, Vic 3550 **REGION** Bendigo
T (03) 5435 3366 **F** (03) 5435 3311 **OPEN** 7 days 10–5
WINEMAKER John Ellis, Robert Fiumara (Contract) **EST.** 1998 **CASES** 1200
PRODUCT RANGE ($11–30 CD) Granite White, Sauvignon Blanc, Verdelho, Chardonnay, Bendigo Chardonnay, Granite Botrytis, Granite Red, Bendigo Shiraz, Reserve Shiraz, Cabernet Sauvignon, Granite Port, Curly Port, Curly Muscat.
SUMMARY A partnership headed by Nick Cugura began the re-establishment of what is now called Big Hill Vineyard on a site which was first planted to grapes almost 150 years ago. That was in the height of the gold rush, and there was even a long-disappeared pub, the Granite Rock Hotel. The wheel has come full circle, for Big Hill Vineyard now has a café-restaurant overlooking the vineyard, with plans for bed and breakfast cottages. The restaurant specialises in wedding receptions, and provides limited conference facilities. The modern-day plantings began with 2 hectares of shiraz in 1998 (which provided the first wine in May 2000), followed by 1 hectare each of merlot and cabernet sauvignon.

Big Shed Wines ★★★★

1289 Malmsbury Road, Glenlyon, Vic 3461 **REGION** Macedon Ranges
T (03) 5348 7825 **F** (03) 5348 7825 **OPEN** 7 days, winter 10–6, summer 10–7
WINEMAKER Ken Jones **EST.** 1999 **CASES** 1200
PRODUCT RANGE ($15–25 CD) Intrigue (Spatlese Lexia), Chardonnay, Pinot Noir, Shiraz, Reserve
Shiraz, Merlot, Cabernet Sauvignon, Sticky Stuff (10-year-old Muscat).
SUMMARY Founder and winemaker Ken Jones was formerly a geneticist and molecular biologist at
Edinburgh University, and the chemistry of winemaking comes easily. The estate-based wine comes
from the 2 hectares of pinot noir; the other wines are made from purchased grapes grown in various
parts of Central Victoria.

ŶŶŶŶŶ **Reserve Shiraz 2002** An attractive mix of black cherry, plum, spice and licorice; good
structure, soft tannins. **RATING** 91 **DRINK** 2012 $ 22
Pinot Noir 2002 Very complex tomato vine/rhubarb/spice aromas; abundant fruit flavour
in the mouth, more to ripe, spicy plum. **RATING** 90 **DRINK** 2007 $ 25

ŶŶŶŶ **Chardonnay 2001** Solid wine; nectarine/peach fruit; good balance. **RATING** 87
DRINK 2009 $ 24
Merlot 2002 Very ripe voluptuous fruit; soft tannins and minimal oak. **RATING** 87
DRINK 2009 $ 22
Cabernet Sauvignon 2002 Blackberry and raspberry aromas and flavours; relatively soft.
RATING 87 **DRINK** 2008 $ 23

ŶŶŶŶ **Chardonnay 2003 RATING** 86 **DRINK** 2007 $ 24

Bimbadgen Estate ★★★★

Lot 21 McDonalds Road, Pokolbin, NSW 2321 **REGION** Lower Hunter Valley
T (02) 4998 7585 **F** (02) 4998 7732 **OPEN** 7 days 9.30–5
WINEMAKER Simon Thistlewood **EST.** 1968 **CASES** 70 000
PRODUCT RANGE ($12.50–48 R) Three tiers: Grand Ridge varietals at the bottom; then varietals under
the Bimbadgen label; the Signature Range is the super-premium.
SUMMARY Established as McPherson Wines, then successively Tamalee, then Sobels, then Parker
Wines and now Bimbadgen, this substantial winery has had what might politely be termed a
turbulent history. It has the great advantage of having 109 hectares of estate plantings, mostly with
now relatively old vines, supplemented by a separate estate vineyard at Yenda for the lower-priced
Grand Ridge series. The restaurant is open 7 days for lunch and from Wednesday to Saturday
inclusive for dinner. Exports to Hong Kong, Japan, the UK and the US.

ŶŶŶŶŶ **Signature Individual Vineyard Shiraz 2002** Very deep red-purple; rich, complex, but
highly focused blackberry/cherry fruit; ripe tannins and good oak. Top-flight wine.
RATING 94 **DRINK** 2017 $ 48

ŶŶŶŶŶ **Signature Semillon 2001** Mineral, herb and lemon aromas; generous flavour, easing
towards maturity without any fuss. **RATING** 91 **DRINK** 2009 $ 25
Semillon 2003 Fuller style, but not the least bit coarse; ripe fruit, good acidity and length.
Screwcap. **RATING** 90 **DRINK** 2008 $ 17.50

ŶŶŶŶ **Museum of Contemporary Art Semillon Sauvignon Blanc 2003** Delicate but synergistic
blend of varieties and regions (sauvignon blanc from Orange); faintly tropical flavour;
crisp, clean finish. **RATING** 89 **DRINK** 2007 $ 20
Myall Road Botrytis Semillon (375 ml) 2002 Surprisingly direct; very sweet lemony
fruit, the acidity still to integrate back into the palate. **RATING** 87 **DRINK** 2009 $ 18.50

ŶŶŶŶ **Museum of Contemporary Art Sangiovese 2003** Fresh, vibrant cross between dry red
and rose; cherry flavours; well-balanced summer red. **RATING** 86 **DRINK** Now $ 20
Signature Pinot Chardonnay NV RATING 85 **DRINK** Now $ 25
Hunter Valley Verdelho 2003 RATING 84 **DRINK** Now $ 17.50

ŶŶŶ **Grand Ridge Sparkling Semillon NV RATING** 83 $ 12.50

Bindaree Estate

NR

Fish Fossil Drive, Canowindra, NSW 2804 **REGION** Cowra
T (02) 6344 1214 **F** (02) 6344 3217 **OPEN** Wed–Fri 11–5, weekends 10–5
WINEMAKER Contract **EST.** 1998 **CASES** 2000
PRODUCT RANGE ($12–20 CD) Unwooded Chardonnay, Reserve Chardonnay, Shiraz, Reserve Shiraz, Dry Red, Cabernet Sauvignon, Reserve Cabernet Sauvignon.
SUMMARY The Workman family have established their property in the foothills of the Belubula River Valley, near Canowindra. They have planted 1 hectare of chardonnay, and 3 hectares each of cabernet sauvignon and shiraz. The first vintage (2001) was successful in the 2002 Cowra Wine Show, the Reserve Chardonnay winning silver and the Unwooded Chardonnay bronze.

Bindi Wine Growers

343 Melton Road, Gisborne, Vic 3437 (postal) **REGION** Macedon Ranges
T (03) 5428 2564 **F** (03) 5428 2564 **OPEN** Not
WINEMAKER Michael Dhillon, Stuart Anderson (Consultant) **EST.** 1988 **CASES** 1200
PRODUCT RANGE ($30–65 ML) Chardonnay, Quartz Chardonnay, Macedon Methode Champenoise Cuvee II, Original Vineyard Pinot Noir, Block 5 Pinot Noir, Bundaleer Shiraz.
SUMMARY One of the icons of Macedon, indeed Victoria. The Chardonnay is top-shelf, the Pinot Noir as remarkable (albeit in a very different idiom) as Bass Phillip, Giaconda or any of the other tiny-production icon wines. The addition of the Heathcote-sourced Shiraz under the Bundaleer label simply confirms Bindi as one of the greatest small producers in Australia. Notwithstanding the tiny production, the wines are exported (in small quantities, of course) to the UK, The Netherlands, Italy, Hong Kong and the US.

🍷🍷🍷🍷🍷 **Chardonnay 2002** Very complex barrel-ferment aromas, but the oak is balanced and integrated; a super-powerful and concentrated palate almost takes one's breath away, and lingers for an impossibly long time. It's not the alcohol (13.5 degrees); it's the yield of less than 1 tonne to the acre. **RATING** 96 **DRINK** 2015 $ 30
Quartz Chardonnay 2002 A slightly more restrained bouquet, but again, extraordinary concentration, length and aftertaste. The same dynamics at work. **RATING** 96 **DRINK** 2015 $ 50
Original Vineyard Pinot Noir 2002 Deep colour; lusciously ripe plum aromas leap from the glass; a predictably rich, complex, very intense and powerful palate. Only 13 degrees alcohol and a minute cropping level. **RATING** 95 **DRINK** 2010 $ 50

🍷🍷🍷🍷🍷 **Bundaleer Shiraz 2002** Vivid, deep purple-red; a luscious array of plum, blackberry and licorice; rich, full, fruit-driven; soft tannins. **RATING** 92 **DRINK** 2012 $ 19
Bundaleer Shiraz 2001 Spicy/savoury/earthy aromas and edges to the small black fruits of the wine; medium-bodied; good texture and structure in an elegant mode. **RATING** 90 **DRINK** 2009 $ 19

Bird in Hand

Bird in Hand Road, Woodside, SA 5244 **REGION** Adelaide Hills
T (08) 8232 9033 **F** (08) 8232 9066 **OPEN** Not
WINEMAKER Andrew Nugent **EST.** 1997 **CASES** 8000
PRODUCT RANGE ($20–70 R) Bird in Hand estate-grown, single-variety wines; Two In The Bush estate-grown blended wines; Nest Egg varietals produced in outstanding vintages.
SUMMARY This substantial wine and olive oil-making property is situated on the Bird in Hand Road at Woodside, which in turn took its name from a 19th century gold mine called Bird in Hand. It is the venture of the Nugent family, headed by Dr Michael Nugent, who was formerly an owner and director of Tatachilla, and who acquired the property in 1997. Son Andrew Nugent is a Roseworthy graduate, and has had a successful career managing vineyards in various parts of South Australia. (Andrew's wife Susie manages the olive oil side of the business.) Retail distribution is being set up throughout Australia, with exports to the UK underway, and planned for the US, Singapore and the Philippines. The family also has properties on the Fleurieu Peninsula and in the Clare Valley; the latter provide both riesling and shiraz (and olives from 100-year-old wild olive trees).

♢♢♢♢♢ **Two in the Bush Sauvignon Blanc Semillon 2003** Lingering, clean, fresh and crisp aromas; sweet lemony acidity; very good mouthfeel. Screwcap. **RATING** 92 **DRINK** 2007 $ 20

Merlot 2002 Medium-bodied; strongly varietal savoury, spicy edges around a core of dark fruits; very well made. **RATING** 92 **DRINK** 2007 $ 35

Sauvignon Blanc 2003 Delicate gooseberry flavours and structure; extremely subtle use of oak; clever making. Slight cork taint ignored. **RATING** 90 **DRINK** Now $ 25

♢♢♢♢ **Joy Sparkling NV** Pronounced strawberry and nutmeg spice; lots of flavour; sweet fruit rather than dosage. **RATING** 89 **DRINK** 2007

Two in the Bush Merlot Cabernet 2002 Tangy, savoury; more pronounced tannins and less charming than the Merlot, though in the same family. **RATING** 88 **DRINK** 2009 $ 25

Nest Egg Cabernet Sauvignon 2001 Fragrant, fresh berry and mint aromas; light to medium-bodied, light tannins. **RATING** 87 **DRINK** 2009 $ 50

Birdwood Estate ★★★★

Mannum Road, Birdwood, SA 5234 **REGION** Adelaide Hills
T (08) 8263 0986 **F** (08) 8263 0986 **OPEN** Not
WINEMAKER Oli Cucchiarelli **EST.** 1990 **CASES** 700
PRODUCT RANGE ($16–21 ML) Chardonnay, Riesling, Pinot Noir, Merlot, Cabernet Merlot, Cabernet Sauvignon.
SUMMARY Birdwood Estate draws upon 7 hectares of estate vineyards progressively established since 1990. The quality of the white wines, and in particular the Chardonnay, has generally been good. The tiny production is principally sold through retail outlets in Adelaide, with limited distribution in Sydney and Melbourne.

♢♢♢♢ **Pinot Noir 2003** Spicy, savoury, plummy fruit; light to medium-bodied; fine structure, good balance and finish. Screwcap. **RATING** 89 **DRINK** 2007 $ 19

Cabernet Merlot 2001 A tangy, savoury mix of blackcurrant plus touches of plum and raspberry; sweet oak. **RATING** 89 **DRINK** 2012 $ 21

Birnam Wood Wines NR

Turanville Road, Scone, NSW 2337 **REGION** Upper Hunter Valley
T (02) 6545 3286 **F** (02) 6545 3431 **OPEN** Weekends and public holidays 11–4
WINEMAKER Monarch Winemaking Services (Contract) **EST.** 1994 **CASES** 8000
PRODUCT RANGE ($7–20 R) The Shakespeare Range at the bottom; then the Family range of varietals; at the top, Premium Reserve Chardonnay and Premium Reserve Shiraz.
SUMMARY Former Sydney car dealer Mike Eagan and wife Min moved to Scone to establish a horse stud; the vineyard came later (in 1994) but is now a major part of the business, with 32 hectares of vines. Most of the grapes are sold; only some are vinified for Birnam Wood. Exports to Switzerland, Canada and China. Son Matthew has now joined the business after working for 5 years for Tyrrell's in its export department.

🐚 Bishop Grove Wines NR

Lot 136 Old Maitland Road, Bishops Bridge, NSW 2326 **REGION** Lower Hunter Valley
T (02) 4930 4698 **F** (02) 4930 4698 **OPEN** By appointment
WINEMAKER Greg Silkman (Contract) **EST.** 1990
PRODUCT RANGE ($17–23.50 ML) Harmonee Chardonnay Verdelho, Verdelho, Unwooded Chardonnay, Chardonnay, Harry Shiraz.
SUMMARY Planting of the vineyard was begun in 1990 by retired engineer Harry Wells, who chose chardonnay, verdelho and shiraz. Initially the grapes were sold to others, but then Harry's daughter Beth and son-in-law Peter Parkinson began producing wines under the Bishop Grove Label. Thanks to skilled contract winemaking, and also to the mature vines, Bishop Grove has had significant show success, including the top gold and trophy for Best 2002 Chardonnay at the NSW Boutique Winemakers Show of that year. A large house is available for rent; the wines are sold by mail order.

Black George

NR

Black Georges Road, Manjimup, WA 6258 **REGION** Manjimup
T (08) 9772 3569 **F** (08) 9772 3102 **OPEN** 7 days 10.30–4.45
WINEMAKER Gregory Chinery **EST.** 1991 **CASES** 3750
PRODUCT RANGE ($15–40 CD) Sauvignon Blanc, Sauvignon Blanc Chardonnay, Verdelho, Pinot Noir, Merlot Cabernet Franc, Cabernet Merlot, Cabernet Sauvignon, White Port.
SUMMARY Black George arrived with particular aspirations to make high-quality Pinot Noir. As with so much of the Manjimup region, it remains to be seen whether the combination of soil and climate will permit this; the quality of the Black George Merlot Cabernet Franc once again points in a different direction. Retail distribution in New South Wales, Victoria, Western Australia and Queensland; exports to the UK and The Netherlands.

Blackgum Estate

NR

166 Malmsbury Road, Metcalfe, Vic 3448 **REGION** Macedon Ranges
T (03) 5423 2933 **F** (03) 5423 2944 **OPEN** Not
WINEMAKER Simonette Sherman **EST.** 1990 **CASES** 400
PRODUCT RANGE ($15–25 CD) Riesling, Chardonnay, Cabernet Sauvignon.
SUMMARY Simonette Sherman is the sole proprietor, executive winemaker and marketing manager of Blackgum Estate. It is situated 9 kilometres northeast of the historic village of Malmsbury, and 1.6 kilometres from the town of Metcalfe. The 4.5-hectare 10-year-old vineyard is planted to riesling, chardonnay, shiraz and cabernet sauvignon, with a planting of sagrantino (which sent me scuttling to Jancis Robinson's *Oxford Companion to Wine*) planned for the near future. It is a red variety grown strictly around the Italian university town of Perugia, and is said to produce wines of great concentration and, usually, liveliness, with deep ruby colour and some bitterness. So there; the varietal atlas of Australia continues to expand. Ms Sherman retains Llew Knight of Granite Hills to make the Riesling, while the Cabernet Sauvignon and Chardonnay were made on-site in consultation with Tom Gyorffy.

BlackJack Vineyards

 ★★★☆

Cnr Blackjack Road and Calder Highway, Harcourt, Vic 3453 **REGION** Bendigo
T (03) 5474 2355 **F** (03) 5474 2355 **OPEN** Weekends and public holidays 11–5, when stock available
WINEMAKER Ian McKenzie, Ken Pollock **EST.** 1987 **CASES** 2500
PRODUCT RANGE ($25–30 CD) Shiraz, Cabernet Merlot; second label is Chortle's Edge.
SUMMARY Established by the McKenzie and Pollock families on the site of an old apple and pear orchard in the Harcourt Valley. Best known for some very good Shirazs. Ian McKenzie, incidentally, is not to be confused with Ian McKenzie of Seppelt Great Western. Exports to New Zealand.

 ♥♥♥♥ **Cabernet Merlot 2001** Offers a fragrant mix of mint, red berry, spice and leaf aromas and flavours in a medium-bodied, well-balanced frame. **RATING** 87 **DRINK** 2011 $25

 ♥♥♥♡ **Shiraz 2001 RATING** 86 **DRINK** 2011 $25

 ♥♥♥ **Chortle's Edge Shiraz 2001 RATING** 83 $18

Blackwood Crest Wines

NR

RMB 404A, Boyup Brook, WA 6244 **REGION** Blackwood Valley
T (08) 9767 3029 **F** (08) 9767 3029 **OPEN** 7 days 10–6
WINEMAKER Max Fairbrass **EST.** 1976 **CASES** 1500
PRODUCT RANGE ($15–25 CD) Riesling, Sauvignon Blanc, Semillon Sauvignon Blanc, Chardonnay, Shiraz, Cabernet Sauvignon, Ruby Port, Liqueur Muscat.
SUMMARY A remote and small winery which has produced one or two notable red wines full of flavour and character; however, quality does fluctuate somewhat.

Blackwood Wines ★★☆

Kearney Street, Nannup, WA 6275 **REGION** Blackwood Valley
T (08) 9756 0088 **F** (08) 9756 0089 **OPEN** Thurs–Tues 10–4
WINEMAKER Andrew Mountford (Contract) **EST.** 1998 **CASES** 5000
PRODUCT RANGE ($17–29 CD) Blackwood White, Chenin Blanc, Unwooded Chardonnay, Late Harvest Verdelho, Pinot Noir, Merlot Cabernet Sauvignon, Merlot Cabernet Franc Malbec. A new range under the Fishbone label has been added.
SUMMARY Blackwood Wines draws upon 1 hectare each of chardonnay, merlot and chenin blanc and 0.5 hectare of pinot noir, supplemented by contract-grown fruit, which significantly broadens the product range. It also operates a Cellar Club with discounted prices for members, and a restaurant is open each day except Wednesday. Exports to the UK and Denmark.

TTTΥ **Fishbone Cabernet Shiraz 2002** **RATING** 86 **DRINK** 2007 $ 14
Cabernet Merlot 2001 **RATING** 85 **DRINK** Now $ 20
Fishbone Semillon Chenin Blanc 2002 **RATING** 84 **DRINK** Now $ 13
Fishbone Shiraz 2002 **RATING** 84 **DRINK** Now $ 14

TTT **Fishbone Late Harvest Verdelho 2003** **RATING** 83 $ 18
Fishbone Chenin Verdelho 2003 **RATING** 82 $ 13

Blanche Barkly Wines ★★★☆

Rheola Road, Kingower, Vic 3517 **REGION** Bendigo
T (03) 5438 8223 **OPEN** Weekends and public holidays 10–5, or by appointment
WINEMAKER David Reimers, Arleen Reimers **EST.** 1972 **CASES** 1000
PRODUCT RANGE ($25 CD) Mary Eileen Kingower Shiraz, Johann Kingower Cabernet Sauvignon.
SUMMARY After a long hiatus, tastings of the 2000 and 2001 vintage wines happily renewed my acquaintance with the winery. Unfortunately, the 2002 vintages were being bottled at the time of writing and samples unavailable for tasting.

Bleasdale Vineyards ★★★★

Wellington Road, Langhorne Creek, SA 5255 **REGION** Langhorne Creek
T (08) 8537 3001 **F** (08) 8537 3224 **OPEN** Mon–Sat 9–5, Sun 10–5
WINEMAKER Michael Potts, Renae Hirsch **EST.** 1850 **CASES** 100 000
PRODUCT RANGE ($9–28 CD) Langhorne Crossing White and Red; Verdelho, Chardonnay, Late Picked Verdelho, Sparkling Shiraz, Shiraz Rose, Generations Shiraz, Bremerview Vineyard Shiraz, Petrel Reserve Shiraz, Cabernet Shiraz, Malbec, Frank Potts (Cabernet Malbec Merlot Petit Verdot), Mulberry Tree Cabernet Sauvignon, fortified.
SUMMARY One of the most historic wineries in Australia, drawing upon vineyards that are flooded every winter by diversion of the Bremer River, which provides moisture throughout the dry, cool, growing season. The wines offer excellent value for money, all showing that particular softness which is the hallmark of the Langhorne Creek region. Production has soared; export markets established in the UK, the US, New Zealand, Switzerland and Germany.

TTTTΥ **Petrel Reserve Shiraz 1999** Obvious oak inputs; tangy, savoury edges to the fruit; scores a bull's eye with its length and persistence. **RATING** 93 **DRINK** 2014 $ 28
Frank Potts 2002 A smooth, supple and luscious array of black fruits rounded off with soft, lingering tannins. **RATING** 92 **DRINK** 2017 $ 28

TTTT **Bremerview Vineyard Shiraz 2001** Medium to full-bodied; good depth of blackberry, chocolate and mocha-accented fruit; fine, ripe tannins. **RATING** 89 **DRINK** 2009 $ 16.50
Sparkling Shiraz NV Generous, luscious red fruits; good finish, not phenolic; will age well on cork. **RATING** 89 **DRINK** 2010 $ 17.50

TTTΥ **Shiraz Cabernet 2001** **RATING** 84 **DRINK** Now $ 13

Bloodwood ★★★★☆

4 Griffin Road, Orange, NSW 2800 **REGION** Orange
T (02) 6362 5631 **F** (02) 6361 1173 **OPEN** By appointment
WINEMAKER Stephen Doyle **EST.** 1983 **CASES** 4000
PRODUCT RANGE ($15–35 ML) Riesling, Chardonnay, Schubert Chardonnay, Chirac (Pinot Chardonnay), Noble Riesling, Big Men in Tights (Rose), Rose of Malbec, Maurice (Bordeaux blend), Merlot Noir, Cabernet Sauvignon.
SUMMARY Rhonda and Stephen Doyle are two of the pioneers of the burgeoning Orange district. The wines are sold mainly through the cellar door and an energetically and informatively run mailing list; the principal retail outlet is Ian Cook's Fiveways Cellar in Paddington, Sydney. Bloodwood has done best with elegant but intense Chardonnay and the intermittent releases of super-late-harvest Ice Riesling. Exports to the UK.

ҮҮҮҮ **Chardonnay 2002** Very good balance, flavour and mouthfeel; ripe melon and stone fruit; subtle oak infusion. **RATING** 91 **DRINK** 2008 **$** 22
Noble Riesling 2003 Zippy, lively, zesty lemony fruit and acidity; will develop. **RATING** 90 **DRINK** 2010 **$** 22

ҮҮҮҮ **Riesling 2003** Spotless lemon, herb and mineral aromas; an accessible and relatively soft palate. Drink-now style. **RATING** 87 **DRINK** 2008 **$** 18
Big Men in Tights 2003 In usual style; aromatic berry fruits; dry finish; food style. **RATING** 87 **DRINK** Now **$** 15

ҮҮҮ **Chirac 2000** **RATING** 84 **DRINK** Now **$** 30

🍷 Blown Away ★★★★

PO Box 108, Willunga, SA 5172 **REGION** McLaren Vale
T (08) 8557 4554 **F** (08) 8557 4554 **OPEN** Not
WINEMAKER Trevor Tucker (Contract) **EST.** 2001 **CASES** 150
PRODUCT RANGE ($18–28 ML) Grenache, Bare Bottom Hills Shiraz, Summer Cabernet Sauvignon.
SUMMARY Dave and Sue Watson purchased their property, situated on the corner of Plains and Rogers Roads at the base of Sellicks Hill, in 1993. It had 0.8 hectare of old shiraz and cabernet sauvignon, and a little over 3 hectares of almond trees. In 1995 they removed the trees and planted the area to shiraz and grenache. Somewhat reluctantly, they sold the grapes to a local winery, but in 2001 had a small amount of Grenache and Cabernet made as a blend under the Summer of 2001 label. The grenache was sold the following year, but they retained the grapes from the old plantings of cabernet sauvignon and shiraz, and had the wines made by Trevor Tucker. The label, incidentally, features a painting by Sue Watson.

ҮҮҮҮҮ **Bare Bottom Hills Shiraz 2002** Impenetrable, saturated purple; luscious, voluptuous blackberry fruit; excellent oak and tannin balance. Basket-pressed French oak. **RATING** 94 **DRINK** 2017 **$** 28

ҮҮҮҮ **Summer of 2002 Cabernet Sauvignon** Medium red-purple. Surprisingly light in body compared with the Shiraz; elegant red and blackcurrant fruit; unforced style. **RATING** 87 **DRINK** 2007 **$** 28

🍷 Blueberry Hill Vineyard NR

Cnr McDonalds and Coulson Roads, Pokolbin, NSW 2320 **REGION** Lower Hunter Valley
T (02) 4998 7295 **F** (02) 4998 7296 **OPEN** 7 days 10–5, until 6.30 Fri–Sat in summer
WINEMAKER Greg Silkman (Contract) **EST.** 1973 **CASES** 2000
PRODUCT RANGE ($21–40 CD) Chardonnay Sauvignon Blanc, Chardonnay, Reserve Chardonnay, Blanc de Noir, Rouge de Noir, Pinot Noir, Shiraz, Merlot.
SUMMARY Blueberry Hill Vineyard is part of the old McPherson Estate, with fully mature plantings of chardonnay, sauvignon blanc, shiraz, pinot noir, merlot and cabernet sauvignon. Until 2000 the grapes were sold to other winemakers, but since that year part of the crush goes towards the extensive Blueberry Hill range.

Bluebush Estate
NR

Wilderness Road, Cessnock, NSW 2325 **REGION** Lower Hunter Valley
T (02) 4930 7177 **F** (02) 4930 7666 **OPEN** Not
WINEMAKER Contract **EST.** 1991 **CASES** 200
PRODUCT RANGE ($15 R) Chardonnay, Shiraz.
SUMMARY Two hectares of vineyards (half chardonnay, half shiraz) have been established by Robyn and David McGain; the wines are contract-made and sold by mail order, and there is bed and breakfast and self-contained accommodation (Bluebush Cottage and Bridstowe Barn) overlooking the vineyard.

Blue Pyrenees Estate
★★★☆

Vinoca Road, Avoca, Vic 3467 **REGION** Pyrenees
T (03) 5465 3202 **F** (03) 5465 3529 **OPEN** Mon–Fri 10–4.30, weekends and public holidays 10–5
WINEMAKER Andrew Koerner **EST.** 1963 **CASES** 100 000
PRODUCT RANGE ($13.50–72 CD) At the top come the Estate Reserve wines of The Richardson, Reserve Red and Reserve Chardonnay; next are the varietal wines; and at the bottom are the budget-priced Fiddlers Creek wines. Also Blue Pyrenees sparkling wines.
SUMMARY Forty years after Remy Cointreau established Blue Pyrenees Estate (then known as Chateau Remy), it sold the business to a small group of Sydney businessmen led by John Ellis (no relation to the John Ellis of Hanging Rock). The winemaking and marketing teams continue in place, although John Ellis has become involved in all areas of the business. The core of the business is the 180-hectare estate vineyard, much of it fully mature. Exports to all major markets.

▼▼▼▼ **Midnight Cuvee 1998** Crisp and citrussy, very fresh; good length and attractive finish.
RATING 89 **DRINK** 2007 $34

Blue Wren
★★★★

1 Cassilis Road, Mudgee, NSW 2850 **REGION** Mudgee
T (02) 6372 6205 **F** (02) 6372 6206 **OPEN** 7 days 10.30–4.30
WINEMAKER Various contract **EST.** 1985 **CASES** 2000
PRODUCT RANGE ($14–28 CD) Semillon, Verdelho, Chardonnay, Late Picked Semillon, Merlot, Shiraz, Cabernet Sauvignon, Port.
SUMMARY James and Diana Anderson have two vineyards, the first called Stoney Creek, planted in 1985 and acquired from the Britten family in early 1999. It has 2 hectares each of chardonnay and semillon, 1.5 hectares of cabernet and 0.5 hectare of merlot, situated 20 kilometres north of Mudgee, and the vines are dry-grown. The second vineyard has been planted to 2.4 hectares of shiraz and 1.4 hectares of verdelho, leaving more than 20 hectares as yet unplanted. The Bombira Vineyard, as it is known, is adjacent to the old Augustine vineyards owned by Beringer Blass. The capacious on-site restaurant is recommended — as are the wines.

▼▼▼▼▽ **Shiraz 2002** Strong colour; rich, ripe, multi-flavoured blackberry, spice and mocha; fine, savoury tannins. **RATING** 90 **DRINK** 2010 $28
Merlot 2002 Plenty of varietal character throughout bouquet and palate; savoury spice, olive and small berry fruits; particularly convincing finish. Screwcap. **RATING** 90 **DRINK** 2012 $28

▼▼▼▼ **Semillon 2001** Bright, light straw-green; has excellent structure, length and acidity, although the flavours are slightly suppressed as the wine enters its transition phase. **RATING** 88 **DRINK** 2008 $16
Cabernet Sauvignon 2002 Bright, snappy blackcurrant/redcurrant fruit; light tannin and oak. Screwcap. **RATING** 87 **DRINK** 2010 $28
Cabernet Sauvignon 2001 A softer style of similar quality. Cork finished. **RATING** 87 **DRINK** 2009 $28

▼▼▼▽ **Chardonnay 2001** Plenty of impact and length; seems riper than 12.5 degrees alcohol; nectarine fruit, acidity balanced by a touch of sweetness. **RATING** 86 **DRINK** Now $16
Semillon 2002 RATING 84 **DRINK** 2007 $16
Semillon Chardonnay 2001 RATING 84 **DRINK** Now $16

ŢŢŢ **Shiraz 2001** RATING 81 $28
Verdelho 2003 RATING 80 $16

ŢŢŢ **Chardonnay 2002** RATING 79 $16

Boatshed Vineyard ★★★

703 Milbrodale Road, Broke, NSW 2330 (postal) **REGION** Lower Hunter Valley
T (02) 9876 5761 **F** (02) 9876 5761 **OPEN** Not
WINEMAKER Tamburlaine (Contract) **EST.** 1989 **CASES** 3500
PRODUCT RANGE ($15–18 ML) Verdelho, Estate Chardonnay, Botrytis Chardonnay, Chardonnay Pinot Noir, Chambourcin, Shiraz, Merlot, Cabernet Merlot, Cabernet Sauvignon.
SUMMARY Mark and wife Helen Hill acquired the property in June 1998. At that time it had 5 hectares of chardonnay, and in the spring of 1999 the plantings were extended with 2 hectares each of verdelho, merlot, chambourcin, shiraz and cabernet sauvignon. As Mark Hill says, the new name of the vineyard has much more to do with his lifetime involvement with rowing, first as a schoolboy competitor and thereafter as a coach of his school's senior IVs. Sustainable viticultural practices are used, and no insecticides have been applied for the past 15 years. The wines are made under contract at Tamburlaine, with approximately 25 per cent of the wine made and bottled for Boatshed, the remainder being taken by Tamburlaine. There is no cellar door, and all sales are mail order or ex the vineyard on a wholesale basis to Sydney restaurants. Viticulture has been in the hands of Christopher Hill since the 2000 vintage.

ŢŢŢ **Verdelho 2003** RATING 84 **DRINK** Now $15

Bochara Wines ★★★★☆

Glenelg Highway, Bochara, Vic 3300 **REGION** Henty
T (03) 5571 9309 **F** (03) 5570 8334 **OPEN** Thurs–Mon 11–5, or by appointment
WINEMAKER Martin Slocombe **EST.** 1998 **CASES** 1000
PRODUCT RANGE ($12–22 CD) Sauvignon Blanc, Chardonnay, Arcadia Brut Cuvee, Picnic Train Rose, Pinot Noir, Merlot Cabernet Franc, Shiraz Cabernet Sauvignon.
SUMMARY This is the small husband and wife business of experienced winemaker Martin Slocombe and former Yalumba viticulturist Kylie McIntyre. They have established 1 hectare each of pinot noir and sauvignon blanc, together with 0.5 hectare of pinot meunier, supplemented by grapes purchased from local grape growers. The modestly priced but well made wines are principally sold through the cellar door sales cottage on the property, transformed from a decrepit weatherboard shanty with one cold tap to a fully functional two-room tasting area. The wines are also available through a number of local restaurants and bottle shops. The label design, incidentally, comes from a 1901 poster advertising the subdivision of the original Bochara property into smaller farms.

ŢŢŢŢ **Chardonnay 2001** Finely tempered and elegant; intense and long grapefruit and nectarine; subtle oak. **RATING** 93 **DRINK** 2011 $25
Sauvignon Blanc 2003 Herb, grass and flint aromas, then an unexpectedly rich and concentrated passionfruit and gooseberry palate. **RATING** 91 **DRINK** Now $15
Shiraz Cabernet 2002 Aromatic spiced plum aromas; intensely focused on red fruits; gentle fine tannins. **RATING** 90 **DRINK** 2012 $18

Boggy Creek Vineyards ★★★☆

1657 Boggy Creek Road, Myrrhee, Vic 3732 **REGION** King Valley
T (03) 5729 7587 **F** (03) 5729 7600 **OPEN** By appointment
WINEMAKER Contract **EST.** 1978
PRODUCT RANGE ($14–18 ML) Riesling, Sauvignon Blanc, Pinot Gris, Chardonnay, Unwooded Chardonnay, Rose, Shiraz, Barbera, Cabernet Sauvignon.
SUMMARY Graeme and Maggie Ray started their vineyard as a hobby in 1978, planting small quantities of riesling and chardonnay. Since then the vineyard has grown to over 30 hectares, with the addition of cabernet sauvignon, shiraz, barbera, pinot gris and other experimental lots. It is situated on northeast-facing slopes at an altitude of 350 metres, with warm summer days and cool nights.

ŶŶŶŶ **Barbera Sangiovese 2003** Attractive rose style; fresh, direct; good balance; not sweet. **RATING** 87 **DRINK** Now $ 16

ŶŶŶ **Chardonnay 2002 RATING** 83 $ 18
Pinot Gris 2002 RATING 81 $ 16

Bogong Estate

NR

Cnr Mountain Creek and Damms Roads, Mount Beauty, Vic 3699 **REGION** Alpine Valleys
T 0419 567 588 **F** (03) 5754 4946 **OPEN** 7 days 10–5
WINEMAKER Bill Tynan **EST.** 1997 **CASES** 2500
PRODUCT RANGE ($15–20 CD) Pinotnoir.com.au Pinot Noir, Pinot Forte (Port).
SUMMARY In the flesh, Bill Tynan looks exactly as a tax partner for a large accounting firm should look: slim, quietly spoken and self-deprecating. His business card, featuring the imprint in vivid pink of an impression of Marilyn Monroe's lips, tells you all is not what it seems. He has in fact given up accounting, and wagered everything by planting 10 hectares of pinot noir in the upper reaches of Kiewa River Valley, with no near neighbours to keep him company. Winemaking is all about fermenting pinot noir in large plastic bags with gas valves, a system developed by the Hickinbotham family. Marketing the wine is no less lateral: Pinotnoir.com.au 2002 Pinot Noir is aimed at the younger, faster movers of Melbourne and Sydney. The estate wine is directed to the serious, probably older, market.

Boireann

★★★★

Donnellys Castle Road, The Summit, Qld 4377 **REGION** Granite Belt
T (07) 4683 2194 **OPEN** 7 days 10–4.30
WINEMAKER Peter Stark **EST.** 1998 **CASES** 500
PRODUCT RANGE ($15–35 CD) Grenache Mourvedre Shiraz, Reserve Shiraz Viognier, Petit Verdot, Merlot, Cabernet Merlot, Reserve Cabernet Sauvignon.
SUMMARY Peter and Therese Stark have a 10-hectare property set amongst the great granite boulders and trees which are so much part of the Granite Belt. They have established 0.7 hectare of vines planted to no less than 11 varieties, including the four Bordeaux varieties which go to make a Bordeaux blend; grenache and mourvedre for a Rhône blend; and there will also be a straight Merlot. Tannat (French) and barbera and nebbiolo (Italian) make up the viticultural League of Nations.

ŶŶŶŶŶ **Shiraz Viognier 2002** Deeply coloured; very opulent rich and striking dark plum and blackberry; excellent texture and balance aided by 7 per cent Viognier component. Highest-pointed red wine from Queensland to date. **RATING** 94 **DRINK** 2012 $ 35

ŶŶŶŶ **Reserve Cabernet Sauvignon 2002** Densely coloured; powerful blackcurrant fruit; fraction jammy; good French oak. **RATING** 89 **DRINK** 2012 $ 35
Special Release Cabernet Merlot 2002 Rich blackcurrant fruit; some oak evident but not overdone; powerful, sustained finish. **RATING** 88 **DRINK** 2012 $ 24

ŶŶŶŶ **Grenache Shiraz Mourvedre 2002 RATING** 86 **DRINK** 2009 $ 29
Cabernet Merlot 2002 RATING 85 **DRINK** 2007 $ 15

ŶŶŶ **Petit Verdot 2002 RATING** 78 $ 20

Boneo Plains

NR

RMB 1400 Browns Road, South Rosebud, Vic 3939 **REGION** Mornington Peninsula
T (03) 5988 6208 **F** (03) 5988 6208 **OPEN** By appointment
WINEMAKER R D Tallarida **EST.** 1988 **CASES** 2500
PRODUCT RANGE ($10–22 CD) Chardonnay, Cabernet Sauvignon; Roch Unwooded Chardonnay, Roch Rose.
SUMMARY A 9-hectare vineyard and winery established by the Tallarida family, well known as manufacturers and suppliers of winemaking equipment to the industry. The Chardonnay is the best of the wines so far released.

Bonneyview

NR

Sturt Highway, Barmera, SA 5345 **REGION** Riverland
T (08) 8588 2279 **OPEN** 7 days 9–5.30
WINEMAKER Robert Minns **EST.** 1975 **CASES** 2500
PRODUCT RANGE ($10–13 CD) Unoaked Chardonnay, Late Picked Frontignan, Shiraz Petit Verdot, Petit Verdot Merlot, Cabernet Blend.
SUMMARY The smallest Riverland winery selling exclusively through the cellar door, with an ex-Kent cricketer and Oxford University graduate as its owner/winemaker. The Shiraz Petit Verdot (unique to Bonneyview) and Cabernet Petit Verdot add a particular dimension of interest to the wine portfolio.

Boora Estate

NR

'Boora', Warrie Road, Dubbo, NSW 2830 **REGION** Western Plains Zone
T (02) 6884 2600 **F** (02) 6884 2600 **OPEN** Sat–Tues 10–5, or by appointment
WINEMAKER Frank Ramsay **EST.** 1984
PRODUCT RANGE ($15–22.50 CD) Semillon, Chardonnay, Shiraz, Merlot, Cabernet Sauvignon Cabernet Franc.
SUMMARY The wheel comes full circle with Boora Estate, where Frank Ramsay has established approximately 0.5 hectare each of chardonnay, semillon, cabernet franc, cabernet sauvignon, merlot, tempranillo and shiraz. In the 1870s and 1880s Dubbo supported a significant winemaking industry, with Eumalga Estate (owned and run by French-born J E Serisier) said (by the local newspaper of the time) to have the second-largest winery in Australia (which I doubt). Mount Olive won a number of awards in international exhibitions in the 1880s. That achievement was matched 120 years later by Boora Estate winning a silver medal at the 2001 Brisbane Wine Show with its 2000 Shiraz, competing against wines from all parts of Australia.

Borambola Wines

Sturt Highway, Wagga Wagga, NSW 2650 **REGION** Gundagai
T (02) 6928 4210 **F** (02) 6928 4210 **OPEN** 7 days 11–4
WINEMAKER Andrew Birks, Michael Hatcher **EST.** 1995 **CASES** 3000
PRODUCT RANGE ($10–16 CD) Chardonnay, Shiraz, Cabernet Merlot.
SUMMARY Borambola Homestead was built in the 1880s, and in the latter part of that century was the centre of a pastoral empire of 1.4 million hectares; ownership passed to the McMullen family in 1992. It is situated in rolling foothills 25 kilometres east of Wagga Wagga in the newly declared Gundagai region. Just under 10 hectares of vines surround the homestead (4 hectares shiraz, 3.5 hectares cabernet sauvignon, 2.2 hectares chardonnay) and the wines are made for Borambola by the Charles Sturt winemakers Andrew Birks and Michael Hatcher.

▼▼▼▼ **Premium Gundagai Shiraz NV** A massively powerful prune, plum, blackberry and dark chocolate mix; 15.9 degrees alcohol not its greatest asset, but ... **RATING** 87 **DRINK** 2015
$10

Boston Bay Wines

Lincoln Highway, Port Lincoln, SA 5606 **REGION** Southern Eyre Peninsula
T (08) 8684 3600 **F** (08) 8684 3637 **OPEN** Weekends, school/public holidays 11.30–4.30
WINEMAKER David O'Leary, Nick Walker **EST.** 1984 **CASES** 3000
PRODUCT RANGE ($13–24 CD) The Clare Riesling, Spatlese Riesling, The Oakbank Chardonnay, Riesling Mistelle, Shiraz, Baudin's Blend (Shiraz Cabernet Sauvignon Merlot), Merlot, Cabernet Sauvignon.
SUMMARY A strongly tourist-oriented operation which has extended the viticultural map in South Australia. It is situated at the same latitude as Adelaide, overlooking the Spencer Gulf at the southern tip of the Eyre Peninsula. Say proprietors Graham and Mary Ford, 'It is the only vineyard in the world to offer frequent sightings of whales at play in the waters at its foot.'

Bosworth ★★★★

Edgehill Vineyards, Gaffney Road, Willunga, SA 5172 **REGION** McLaren Vale
T (08) 8556 2441 **F** (08) 8556 4881 **OPEN** By appointment
WINEMAKER Ben Riggs (Contract) **EST.** 1996 **CASES** 1000
PRODUCT RANGE ($26 CD) Battle of Bosworth Shiraz, Battle of Bosworth Cabernet Sauvignon.
SUMMARY The Edgehill Vineyard, established many years ago, was taken over by son Joch Bosworth in 1996. He set about converting 6.5 hectares of shiraz and cabernet sauvignon to fully certified A-grade organic viticulture, and is now in the process of converting the chardonnay (which takes 4 years). The regime prohibits the use of herbicides and pesticides; the weeds are controlled by soursob, the pretty yellow flower considered a weed by many, which carpets the vineyards in winter, but dies off in early spring as surface moisture dries, forming a natural weed mat. But organic viticulture is never easy, and when Joch Bosworth moved to make the first wines from the vines, the Battle of Bosworth name was a neat take. Joch's partner, Louise Hemsley-Smith, runs the marketing and promotion side of the business in her spare time: her day job is with Penny's Hill.

♟♟♟♟ **Battle of Bosworth Shiraz 2001** Savoury, spicy, earthy aromas; light to medium-bodied, in a fine and elegant style, with a touch of regional chocolate. Totally counter-cultural for the region. **RATING** 88 **DRINK** 2008 $ 26
Battle of Bosworth Cabernet Sauvignon 2001 Fragrantly savoury and earthy, not dissimilar to the Shiraz; light to medium-bodied, but has length to the blackcurrant, redcurrant and mint-accented palate. **RATING** 88 **DRINK** 2009 $ 26

Botobolar ★★★☆

89 Botobolar Road, Mudgee, NSW 2850 **REGION** Mudgee
T (02) 6373 3840 **F** (02) 6373 3789 **OPEN** Mon–Sat 10–5, Sun 10–3
WINEMAKER Kevin Karstrom **EST.** 1971 **CASES** 4000
PRODUCT RANGE ($9–24 CD) Sauvignon Blanc, Rain Goddess Dry White, Rain Goddess Sweet White, Marsanne, Chardonnay, Rain Goddess Red, Pinot Noir, Merlot, Shiraz, R&B Shiraz, Cabernet Sauvignon; The King, The Saviour (both Cabernet Shiraz blends); Low Preservative Chardonnay and Preservative Free Shiraz.
SUMMARY One of the first organic vineyards in Australia, with present owner Kevin Karstrom continuing the practices established by founder Gil Wahlquist. Preservative Free Dry White and Dry Red extend the organic practice of the vineyard to the winery. Shiraz is consistently the best wine to appear under the Botobolar label. Exports to the UK, Denmark and Germany.

♟♟♟♟♟ **Special Release Cabernet Sauvignon 2001** Solid, rich blackberry and blackcurrant mix; touches of chocolate and vanilla; good tannins on long finish. **RATING** 90 **DRINK** 2012 $ 19

♟♟♟♟ **Merlot 2003** Abundant ripe, red fruits, powerful tannins; in your face, and needs to back away. Screwcap. **RATING** 86 **DRINK** 2013 $ 17

♟♟♟ **Marsanne 2002** **RATING** 82 $ 12

♟♟♟ **Shiraz 2002** **RATING** 79 $ 14

Bowen Estate ★★★★

Riddoch Highway, Coonawarra, SA 5263 **REGION** Coonawarra
T (08) 8737 2229 **F** (08) 8737 2173 **OPEN** 7 days 10–5
WINEMAKER Doug Bowen, Emma Bowen **EST.** 1972 **CASES** 12 000
PRODUCT RANGE ($20.25–55 R) Chardonnay, Shiraz, Ampelon (Shiraz), The Blend, Cabernet Sauvignon.
SUMMARY One of the best-known names among the smaller Coonawarra wineries, with a great track record of red winemaking. Full-bodied reds at the top end of the ripeness spectrum were the winery trademarks, but there seems to be a change in style to less overtly ripe fruit. Exports to all major markets.

♟♟♟♟♟ **Cabernet Sauvignon 2001** Light to medium-bodied; savoury/earthy regional overtones to the blackcurrant fruit; only 13.5 degrees alcohol; nice freshness. **RATING** 90 **DRINK** 2010 $ 27.50

ΨΨΨΨ **Shiraz 2001** Medium-bodied; restrained plum, mint and blackberry; gentle oak and tannins; a new style direction. **RATING** 89 **DRINK** 2011 $ 26.50
The Blend 2001 Clean, fragrant red and blackcurrant fruit in a fresh, light to medium-bodied, confirming the Bowen change of style. **RATING** 88 **DRINK** 2011 $ 25

ΨΨΨΨ **Chardonnay 2002 RATING** 85 **DRINK** Now $ 20.25

Bowmans Wines ★★★

RMB 543 Springs Road, Mount Barker, WA 6324 (postal) **REGION** Mount Barker
T (08) 9857 6083 **F** (08) 9857 6083 **OPEN** Not
WINEMAKER Porongorup Winery (Contract) **EST.** 1998 **CASES** 1000
PRODUCT RANGE ($14–16 R) Sauvignon Blanc, Shiraz.
SUMMARY Bowmans Wines is situated on a beef cattle farm owned by Gerald and Marion Jenkins. Six hectares of vines, planted on picturesque slopes, have been progressively established between 1998 and 2001. The first vintage of sauvignon blanc and shiraz came in 2001, and the wines have retail distribution in all of the local towns, as well as outlets in Perth.

Box Stallion ★★★★

64 Turrarubba Road, Merricks North, Vic 3926 **REGION** Mornington Peninsula
T (03) 5989 7444 **F** (03) 5989 7688 **OPEN** 7 days 11–5
WINEMAKER Alex White **EST.** 2001 **CASES** 9000
PRODUCT RANGE ($16–38 CD) Sauvignon Blanc, Moscato, Arneis, Red Barn Chardonnay, The Enclosure Chardonnay, Sweet Harmony, Blaze Rose, Dolcetto, Tempranillo, Pinot Meunier, Shiraz.
SUMMARY Box Stallion is the joint venture of Stephen Wharton, John Gillies and Garry Zerbe, who have linked two vineyards, one at Bittern and one at Merricks North, and planted 20 hectares of vines between 1997 and 2003. What once was a thoroughbred stud has now become a vineyard, with the Red Barn (in their words) 'now home to a stable of fine wines'. Those wines are made at the jointly owned winery with Alex White as winemaker, and won 2 trophies (Shiraz and Pinot Noir) at the 2003 Concours des Vins du Victoria. The café is open daily from 11 am to 5 pm.

ΨΨΨΨ **Pinot Noir 2002** Very complex spice, black cherry, plum; powerful, concentrated mid-palate; tails away fractionally on the finish. **RATING** 92 **DRINK** 2007 $ 35

Boynton's ★★★☆

Great Alpine Road, Porepunkah, Vic 3741 **REGION** Alpine Valleys
T (03) 5756 2356 **F** (03) 5756 2610 **OPEN** 7 days 10–5
WINEMAKER Kel Boynton, Eleana Anderson **EST.** 1987 **CASES** 11 000
PRODUCT RANGE ($14–60 CD) Riesling, Sauvignon Blanc, Chardonnay, Boynton's Gold (Noble Riesling Chardonnay blend), Pinots (Pinot Meunier Pinot Noir), Shiraz, Merlot, Cabernet Sauvignon, Alluvium (Cabernet Sauvignon Merlot Petit Verdot), Vintage Brut; Paiko range of Chardonnay, Regent Reserve, Sangiovese, Merlot.
SUMMARY The original 12.5-hectare vineyard, expanded to almost 16 hectares by 1996 plantings of pinot gris, durif and sauvignon blanc, is situated in the Ovens Valley north of the township of Bright, under the lee of Mount Buffalo. In the early years a substantial part of the crop was sold, but virtually all is now vinified at the winery. Overall, the red wines have always outshone the whites, initially with very strong American oak input, but in more recent years with better fruit/oak balance. Striking, indeed strident, new labelling has led to a minor name change — the dropping of the words 'of Bright'. This also reflects the arrival of vine nurseryman Bruce Chalmers as a partner in the business. The wines have distribution through the east coast of Australia; exports to Germany, Austria and the US.

ΨΨΨΨ **Alluvium Reserve 2001** An extra dimension of structure, texture and sweet fruit; blackberry to blackcurrant; soft, but definite, tannins. Bordeaux blend. **RATING** 91 **DRINK** 2014 $ 42

ΨΨΨΨ **Paiko Pinot Gris 2003** Quite flowery and aromatic; a core of apple and pear, fleshed out by a flick of residual sugar. Surprising result from the warm Murray Darling climate. **RATING** 87 **DRINK** Now $ 14.30

Shiraz 2000 Holding hue well; a pleasing marriage of red and black fruits, vanilla oak and tannins; medium-bodied, eminently approachable. **RATING** 87 **DRINK** 2008 $20.30
Cabernet Sauvignon 2000 Quite sweet and soft red and black fruits holding their freshness; very similar in overall effect to the Shiraz. **RATING** 87 **DRINK** 2009 $20.30

ŸŸŸŸ **Paiko Shiraz 2001 RATING** 86 **DRINK** Now $16.55
Paiko Merlot 2001 RATING 85 **DRINK** Now $17
Merlot 2000 RATING 85 **DRINK** Now $20.30
Paiko Regent Reserve 2001 RATING 84 **DRINK** Now $18
Paiko Sangiovese 2002 RATING 84 **DRINK** Now $18

ŸŸŸ **Paiko Chardonnay 2001 RATING** 83 $15

Bracken Hill   NR

81 Tinderbox Road, Tinderbox, Tas 7052 **REGION** Southern Tasmania
T (03) 6229 6475 **OPEN** Annual open weekends in March and October
WINEMAKER Contract **EST.** 1993 **CASES** 120
PRODUCT RANGE ($20 ML) Gewurztraminer.
SUMMARY Max Thalmann came here from Switzerland in 1961, retired 30 years later, and took the decision to plant his 0.4-hectare vineyard entirely to gewurztraminer. As Tasmanian writer Phil Laing has pointed out, it is probably the only specialist Gewurztraminer producer in the southern hemisphere, making Thalmann's decision all the more curious, because he prefers red wine to white wine. His logic, however, was impeccable: he could sell the grapes and/or the wine from his vineyard and use the money to buy red wines of his choice. Bracken Hill has its open weekend in October, and participates in the annual Tasmanian cellar door open weekend in March. The label, incidentally, comes from a painting by Max Thalmann, which proves he is a man of many talents.

Braewattie   ★★★★

351 Rochford Road, Rochford, Vic 3442 **REGION** Macedon Ranges
T (03) 9818 5742 **F** (03) 9818 8361 **OPEN** By appointment
WINEMAKER John Flynn, John Ellis **EST.** 1993 **CASES** 250
PRODUCT RANGE ($25–29 ML) Chardonnay, Pinot Noir, Macedon Brut (Pinot Noir Chardonnay).
SUMMARY Des and Maggi Ryan bought Braewattie in 1990; Maggi's great-grandfather, James McCarthy, had acquired the property in the 1880s, and it remained in the family until 1971. When the property came back on the market the Ryans seized the opportunity to reclaim it, complete with a small existing planting of 300 pinot noir and chardonnay vines. Those plantings now extend to 9.7 hectares, part of the production being sold as grapes, and a small amount contract-made. The Macedon Brut is a particularly good wine.

ŸŸŸŸ **Macedon Brut Pinot Noir Chardonnay NV RATING** 86 **DRINK** Now $29

ŸŸŸ **Pinot Noir 2002 RATING** 83 $25

Brahams Creek Winery   NR

Woods Point Road, East Warburton, Vic 3799 **REGION** Yarra Valley
T (03) 9566 2802 **F** (03) 9566 2802 **OPEN** Weekends and public holidays 11–5
WINEMAKER Geoff Richardson, Chris Young **EST.** 1990 **CASES** 1200
PRODUCT RANGE ($11–13.50 CD) Chardonnay, Pinot Noir, Merlot, Cabernet Sauvignon, Tawny Port.
SUMMARY Owner Geoffrey Richardson did not start marketing his wines until 1994, and a string of older vintages are available for sale at the cellar door at an enticing price. Part of the grape production is sold to other Yarra Valley winemakers.

Bramley Wood   NR

RMB 205 Rosa Brook Road, Margaret River, WA 6285 (postal) **REGION** Margaret River
T (08) 9757 9291 **F** (08) 9757 9291 **OPEN** Not
WINEMAKER Cliff Royle, Mike Edwards (Voyager Estate) **EST.** 1994 **CASES** 200
PRODUCT RANGE ($25 ML) Bob's Vineyard Cabernet Sauvignon.

SUMMARY David and Rebecca McInerney planted 2 hectares of cabernet sauvignon in 1994, with an inaugural vintage in 1998, released in December 2000. Encouraged by the quality of that wine and, in particular, the 1999 which followed it, the McInerneys plan to one day expand their plantings. For the time being, the tiny production is sold by mail order and through the two self-contained chalets on the property, each capable of hosting 4–6 adults.

Brand's of Coonawarra ★★★★★

Riddoch Highway, Coonawarra, SA 5263 **REGION** Coonawarra
T (08) 8736 3260 **F** (08) 8736 3208 **OPEN** Mon–Fri 8–5, weekends 10–4
WINEMAKER Jim Brand, Jim Brayne **EST.** 1966
PRODUCT RANGE ($19–73 R) Riesling, Chardonnay, Sparkling Cabernet Sauvignon, Cabernet Merlot, Shiraz, Stentiford's Reserve Shiraz, Merlot, Cabernet Sauvignon, Patron's Reserve.
SUMMARY Part of a very substantial investment in Coonawarra by McWilliam's, which first acquired a 50 per cent interest from the founding Brand family then moved to 100 per cent, and followed this with the purchase of 100 hectares of additional vineyard land. Significantly increased production of the smooth wines for which Brand's is known has followed.

ΥΥΥΥΥ Patron's Reserve 2000 Dense, dark fruit, chocolate and integrated French oak; good tannin; complex and complete. **RATING** 94 **DRINK** 2016 $ 73

ΥΥΥΥΥ Stentiford's Reserve Shiraz 2000 Opens up convincingly on a long and complex, fruit-driven palate, with a mix of raspberry and blackberry fruit; integrated oak and fine tannins. Great outcome for a difficult vintage. **RATING** 93 **DRINK** 2015 $ 73
Special Release Merlot 2001 Clear cut redcurrant and blackcurrant varietal fruit; supple, fine tannins; cedary notes and excellent texture. **RATING** 92 **DRINK** 2011 $ 31.50
Shiraz 2002 Intense and long; concentrated, low yield; blackberry with a twang. **RATING** 90 **DRINK** 2012 $ 25
Cabernet Sauvignon 2001 Firm, focused earthy black fruits in a tightly built frame; will age slowly and gracefully. **RATING** 90 **DRINK** 2016 $ 24

ΥΥΥΥ Riesling 2002 Clean, slightly subdued bouquet; nicely balanced, gently spiced lime juice palate; in transition. **RATING** 89 **DRINK** 2010 $ 19
Chardonnay 2003 Fine, fragrant, citrussy stone fruit and melon; subtle oak; long finish. **RATING** 89 **DRINK** 2008 $ 20
Riesling 2003 Abundant apple, lime and mineral aromas, the palate of moderate length and intensity. **RATING** 87 **DRINK** 2011 $ 19
Chardonnay 2002 Well balanced and integrated components of stone fruit, cashew malolactic and subtle oak; suave complexity. **RATING** 87 **DRINK** 2007 $ 20
Shiraz 2001 Elegant rather than fulsome, with savoury, earthy edges to the fruit. **RATING** 87 **DRINK** 2009 $ 25

Brangayne of Orange ★★★★☆

49 Pinnacle Road, Orange, NSW 2880 **REGION** Orange
T (02) 6365 3229 **F** (02) 6365 3170 **OPEN** By appointment
WINEMAKER Simon Gilbert (Contract), Richard Bateman **EST.** 1994 **CASES** 3500
PRODUCT RANGE ($22–29 CD) Sauvignon Blanc, Chardonnay, Premium Chardonnay, Isolde Reserve Chardonnay, Pinot Noir, The Tristan (Cabernet blend).
SUMMARY Orchardists Don and Pamela Hoskins decided to diversify into grape growing in 1994 and have progressively established 25 hectares of high-quality vineyards. With viticultural consultancy advice from Dr Richard Smart and skilled contract winemaking by Simon Gilbert, Brangayne made an extraordinarily auspicious debut, underlining the potential of the Orange region. Daughter Nicola, having had experience at the marketing coal-face in Melbourne and Sydney, has returned to Orange and taken over responsibility for the day-to-day management of the business. Exports to the UK and Singapore.

ΥΥΥΥΥ The Tristan 2001 A vibrantly flavoured and spicy mix of red and black fruits; silky tannins; good use of oak. **RATING** 91 **DRINK** 2011 $ 29

Bream Creek ★★★

Marion Bay Road, Bream Creek, Tas 7175 **REGION** Southern Tasmania
T (03) 6231 4646 **F** (03) 6231 4646 **OPEN** At Potters Croft, Dunally **T** (03) 6253 5469
WINEMAKER Steve Lubiana, Julian Alcorso (Contract) **EST.** 1975 **CASES** 3500
PRODUCT RANGE ($18–24 CD) Riesling, Traminer, Sauvignon Blanc, Schonburger, Chardonnay, Pinot Noir Rose, Pinot Noir, Cabernet Sauvignon.
SUMMARY Until 1990 the Bream Creek fruit was sold to Moorilla Estate, but since that time the winery has been independently owned and managed under the control of Fred Peacock, legendary for the care he bestows on the vines under his direction. Peacock's skills have seen both an increase in production and also a vast lift in wine quality across the range, headed by the Pinot Noir. The 1996 acquisition of a second vineyard in the Tamar Valley has significantly strengthened the business base of the venture.

🍷🍷🍷🍸 **Sauvignon Blanc 2003** **RATING** 86 **DRINK** Now **$** 19
Schonburger 2003 **RATING** 84 **DRINK** Now **$** 18

🍷🍷🍷 **Chardonnay 2003** **RATING** 83 **$** 19
Riesling 2003 **RATING** 82 **$** 18

Bremerton Wines ★★★★

Strathalbyn Road, Langhorne Creek, SA 5255 **REGION** Langhorne Creek
T (08) 8537 3093 **F** (08) 8537 3109 **OPEN** 7 days 10–5
WINEMAKER Rebecca Willson **EST.** 1988 **CASES** 23 000
PRODUCT RANGE ($16–35 CD) Sauvignon Blanc, Verdelho, Old Adam Shiraz, Selkirk Shiraz, Walter's Cabernet Sauvignon, Tamblyn (Cabernet Shiraz Malbec Merlot), Ciel Botrytised and Fortified Chenin Blanc.
SUMMARY The Willsons have been grape growers in the Langhorne Creek region for some considerable time but their dual business as grape growers and winemakers has expanded significantly over the past few years. Their vineyards have more than doubled to over 100 hectares (predominantly cabernet sauvignon, shiraz and merlot), as has their production of wine under the Bremerton label, no doubt in recognition of the quality of the wines. In February 2004 sisters Rebecca and Lucy (marketing) took control of the business, marking the event with (guess what) revamped label designs. Wholesale distribution in all States of Australia; exports to the UK, the US, Canada, Singapore, The Netherlands, Germany, Switzerland and New Zealand.

🍷🍷🍷🍷🍷 **Old Adam Shiraz 2001** Ripe black fruits/blackberry/prune aromas joined by loads of bitter chocolate à la McLaren Vale on the palate; great finish and aftertaste; superb tannins. **RATING** 95 **DRINK** 2016 **$** 35

🍷🍷🍷🍷🍸 **Selkirk Shiraz 2001** Powerful, gutsy licorice and blackberry; a hint of game. **RATING** 90 **DRINK** 2016 **$** 22

🍷🍷🍷🍷 **Walter's Cabernet Sauvignon 2000** Some bottle-developed earthy/savoury overtones to the fruit; also elements of chocolate and oak. Reflects the vintage. **RATING** 87 **DRINK** 2008 **$** 27
Tamblyn 2001 Very savoury, cedary, earthy, spicy, lemony, with a silky texture and fine tannins. **RATING** 87 **DRINK** 2008 **$** 17.50

Bress ★★★

Modesty Cottage, Church Street, Fryerstown, Vic 3451 (postal) **REGION** Warehouse
T 0409 566 773 **OPEN** Not
WINEMAKER Adam Marks **EST.** 2001 **CASES** 1200
PRODUCT RANGE ($19.99–29.99 ML) There are two tiers, the Silver Label Margaret River Semillon Sauvignon Blanc and Yarra Valley Pinot Noir, and the Gold Label Heathcote Shiraz.
SUMMARY Adam Marks won the Ron Potter Scholarship in 1991 to work as assistant winemaker to Rodney Hooper at the Charles Sturt University. Since that time he has made wine in all parts of the world, then was winemaker at Dominion Wines for 2 years before taking the brave decision (during his honeymoon in 2000) to start his own business. He has selected Margaret River semillon and sauvignon blanc as the best source of White Bordeaux-style wine in Australia; Yarra Valley pinot noir

as the best pinot noir region; and shiraz from Heathcote for precisely the same reason. The majority of the wine is sold to mailing list clients through the website <www.bress.com.au>, with some direct distribution to select restaurants and independent retailers. As at 2004 he is being challenged by French authorities who believe his wines may be confused with chickens coming from the French region of Bress.

ŸŸŸŸŸ **Unfiltered Heathcote Shiraz 2002** Dense colour; opulent blackberry, dark chocolate and plum, yet paradoxically restrained. **RATING** 92 **DRINK** 2017 $ 37.99

ŸŸŸŸ **Yarra Valley Pinot Noir 2003** Spotless cherry/plum fruit in a direct, light to medium-bodied style. Needs time. Screwcap. **RATING** 88 **DRINK** 2008 $ 19.99

ŸŸŸŸ **Margaret River Semillon Sauvignon Blanc 2003 RATING** 85 **DRINK** Now $ 20

Brewery Hill Estates   NR

PO Box 640, Unley, SA 5061 **REGION** McLaren Vale
T (08) 8272 1911 **F** (08) 8272 1944 **OPEN** Not
WINEMAKER Contract **EST.** 1869
PRODUCT RANGE ($8–16.50 ML) Dry White, Artisan Chardonnay, Ardent Estates Margaret River Chardonnay, Sparkling Cabernet Sauvignon, Sparkling Burgundy, Ardent Estates McLaren Vale Shiraz, Classic Dry Red, Coonawarra Merlot, Ardent Estates McLaren Vale Cabernet Franc, Ardent Estates Limestone Coast Cabernet Sauvignon, Smooth Old Tawny Port.
SUMMARY A change of name and of address for the former St Francis Winery, which has moved into the former Manning Park Winery and is now known as Brewery Hill Winery. It is now part of ewinexchange Limited, with the wines being sold primarily by mail order and through the internet.

Briagolong Estate   ★★★★

Valencia–Briagolong Road, Briagolong, Vic 3860 **REGION** Gippsland
T (03) 5147 2322 **F** (03) 5147 2400 **OPEN** By appointment
WINEMAKER Gordon McIntosh **EST.** 1979 **CASES** 400
PRODUCT RANGE ($35 ML) Chardonnay, Pinot Noir.
SUMMARY This is very much a weekend hobby for medical practitioner Gordon McIntosh, who tries hard to invest his wines with Burgundian complexity. Six years of continuous drought, with one break in 2002 when hail destroyed the crop, has meant no Chardonnay in 2000, 2001 or 2002, nor Pinot for 2002 (the 2001 is in doubt). Given the quality of the 2000 Pinot, the loss is all the keener. The one ray of sunshine comes in the form of micro-releases of prior vintages (back to 1996) for mailing list customers, and a last offering of 2000 Pinot Noir.

Brian Barry Wines   ★★★

PO Box 128, Stepney, SA 5069 **REGION** Clare Valley
T (08) 8363 6211 **F** (08) 8362 0498 **OPEN** Not
WINEMAKER Brian Barry, Judson Barry **EST.** 1977 **CASES** 6000
PRODUCT RANGE ($20–35 R) Jud's Hill Handpicked Riesling, Handpicked Merlot, Handpicked Cabernet Sauvignon; Special Reserve Shiraz.
SUMMARY Brian Barry is an industry veteran with a wealth of winemaking and show-judging experience. His is nonetheless in reality a vineyard-only operation, with a substantial part of the output sold as grapes to other wineries and the wines made under contract at various wineries, albeit under Brian Barry's supervision. As one would expect, the quality is reliably good. Retail distribution through all States, and exports to the UK and the US.

ŸŸŸŸ **Jud's Hill Handpicked Riesling 2003** Herb and pine needle aromas; solid, but rather diffuse. **RATING** 86 **DRINK** 2007 $ 18

Briar Ridge   ★★★★

Mount View Road, Mount View, NSW 2325 **REGION** Lower Hunter Valley
T (02) 4990 3670 **F** (02) 4990 7802 **OPEN** 7 days 10–5
WINEMAKER Karl Stockhausen, Steven Dodd **EST.** 1972 **CASES** 27 000

PRODUCT RANGE ($19.50–28.50 CD) Premium range of Early Harvest Semillon, Crop Thinned Verdelho, Hand Picked Chardonnay, Methode Champenoise, Old Vines Shiraz; Signature Release range of Stockhausen Semillon, Chardonnay, Stockhausen Shiraz.
SUMMARY Semillon and Hermitage, each in various guises, have been the most consistent performers, underlying the suitability of these varieties to the Hunter Valley. The Semillon, in particular, invariably shows intense fruit and cellars well. Briar Ridge has been a model of stability with the winemaking duo of Karl Stockhausen and Steven Dodd, and also has the comfort of over 48 hectares of estate vineyards from which it is able to select the best grapes. Exports to the US and Canada.

ＹＹＹＹＹ **Signature Release Steve Dodd Chardonnay 2003** Subtle style; seamless interweaving of components; melon fruit; creamy feel, not sweet. **RATING** 91 **DRINK** 2007 $ 25

ＹＹＹＹ **Hand Picked Chardonnay 2003** A subtle but complex interplay of melon, oak and cashew influences; good balance. **RATING** 89 **DRINK** Now $ 19.50
Early Harvest Semillon 2003 Excellent colour; smooth, with good balance and length; early maturing style. **RATING** 88 **DRINK** 2009 $ 19.50
Old Vines Shiraz 2002 Light to medium-bodied; lively cherry and spice. Drink soon. **RATING** 88 **DRINK** 2007 $ 20
Signature Release Karl Stockhausen Shiraz 2002 Deeper colour than the Old Vines; pungent bacony oak is over the top; time may or may not heal. **RATING** 87 **DRINK** 2011 $ 28.50

ＹＹＹＹ **Crop Thinned Verdelho 2003** Thinning has certainly worked to increase flavour; varietal limitations are still apparent. Some fruit salad, not too sweet. **RATING** 86 **DRINK** Now $ 19.50
Stockhausen Semillon 2003 **RATING** 85 **DRINK** 2009 $ 25
Verdelho 2003 **RATING** 85 **DRINK** Now $ 19.50

Briarose Estate ★★★★

Bussell Highway, Augusta, WA 6290 **REGION** Margaret River
T (08) 9758 4160 **F** (08) 9758 4161 **OPEN** 7 days 10–4.30
WINEMAKER Cath Oates **EST.** 1998 **CASES** 12 000
PRODUCT RANGE ($15–26 CD) Semillon, Sauvignon Blanc, Semillon Sauvignon Blanc, Merlot, Cabernet Franc, Cabernet Merlot, Blackwood Cove (Cabernet Sauvignon Merlot Cabernet Franc); Reserve range includes Merlot, Cabernet Sauvignon.
SUMMARY Brian and Rosemary Webster began the development of the estate plantings in 1998, which now comprise sauvignon blanc (2.33 hectares), semillon (1.33 hectares), cabernet sauvignon (6.6 hectares), merlot (2.2 hectares) and cabernet franc (1.1 hectares). It is situated at the southern end of the Margaret River region, 6 kilometres north of Augusta, and as Briarose and other new winery developments in the area have shown, the climate is distinctly cooler than that of the Margaret River proper.

ＹＹＹＹＹ **Sauvignon Blanc Semillon 2003** Spotlessly clean herb and mineral aromas, with riper, more tropical fruit on the palate; clean, long and crisp; good finish. **RATING** 90 **DRINK** Now $ 17
Reserve Cabernet Sauvignon 2001 Good structure, texture and length; blackcurrant with touches of earth, briar and spice; good lingering tannins. **RATING** 90 **DRINK** 2010 $ 23

ＹＹＹＹ **Sauvignon Blanc 2003** Powerful, ripe and complex fruit in the tropical spectrum gives an overall impression of sweetness. Screwcap. **RATING** 89 **DRINK** Now $ 19
Reserve Merlot 2002 Distinctly savoury in an unambiguous varietal mode; good mouthfeel and finish. **RATING** 88 **DRINK** 2009 $ 19
Blackwood Cove 2001 Medium-bodied; savoury blackcurrant and earth; the cool site/subregion influence obvious; good length. **RATING** 87 **DRINK** 2010 $ 26

ＹＹＹＹ **Blackwood Cove 2002** Light to medium-bodied; savoury/briary characters throughout; needs more sweet fruit, but has length. **RATING** 86 **DRINK** 2012 $ 26
Cabernet Merlot 2001 **RATING** 86 **DRINK** 2009 $ 19
Reserve Cabernet Sauvignon 2002 **RATING** 86 **DRINK** 2009 $ 23
Cabernet Franc 2001 **RATING** 86 **DRINK** 2008 $ 19
Cabernet Merlot 2002 **RATING** 85 **DRINK** 2009 $ 19

Bridgeman Downs

NR

Barambah Road, Moffatdale via Murgon, Qld 4605 **REGION** South Burnett
T (07) 4168 4784 **F** (07) 4168 4767 **OPEN** Thurs–Mon 10–4
WINEMAKER Bruce Humphery-Smith
PRODUCT RANGE ($12–18.50 CD) Cellar White and Red; Chardonnay, Verdelho, Shiraz, Merlot Cabernet.
SUMMARY A substantial, albeit new, vineyard with 4 hectares of vines, the major plantings being of verdelho, chardonnay and shiraz, with lesser amounts of merlot and cabernet sauvignon. The perpetual-motion Bruce Humphery-Smith has been retained as consultant winemaker, which should ensure wine quality. However, no tastings.

Bridgewater Mill

★★★★

Mount Barker Road, Bridgewater, SA 5155 **REGION** Adelaide Hills
T (08) 8339 3422 **F** (08) 8339 5311 **OPEN** Mon–Fri 9.30–5, weekends 10–5
WINEMAKER Brian Croser **EST.** 1986 **CASES** 50 000
PRODUCT RANGE ($19–21 CD) 3 Districts Sauvignon Blanc, Chardonnay, Millstone Shiraz.
SUMMARY The second label of Petaluma, which consistently provides wines most makers would love to have as their top label. The fruit sources are diverse, with the majority of the sauvignon blanc and chardonnay coming from Petaluma-owned or managed vineyards, while the Shiraz is made from purchased grapes. Exports to the UK, the US and New Zealand.

ŸŸŸŸŸ **Three Districts Sauvignon Blanc 2003** Spotlessly clean; fine, delicate but long and well balanced; passionfruit. **RATING** 90 **DRINK** Now $19

ŸŸŸŸ **Millstone Shiraz 2001** Scented red fruits; light to medium-bodied, finely textured mix of red and dark fruits; cool-climate component obvious. **RATING** 88 **DRINK** 2009 $21

Briery Estate

NR

Lot 16 Briar Lane, Bindoon, WA 6502 **REGION** Perth Hills
T (08) 9576 1417 **F** (08) 9576 1417 **OPEN** Wed–Mon 10–6, Tuesday by appointment
WINEMAKER Ron Waterhouse **EST.** 1994 **CASES** 500
PRODUCT RANGE ($10–20 CD) Classic Dry White, Mellorose, Rosalinda, Carina, Cabernet Shiraz, Briar Muscat, Ruby Port.
SUMMARY Ron Waterhouse and Christine Smart run Briery Estate (formerly Jacaranda Homestead) in the hills of Bindoon. There they have 9 hectares of verdelho, pinot noir, grenache, shiraz, cabernet sauvignon, muscat, furmint and harslevelu, although they steer around varietal naming of their wines. The wines are chiefly sold by mail order and through the cellar door, which has barbecue, picnic facilities and crafts.

Brindabella Hills

★★★★★

Woodgrove Close, via Hall, ACT 2618 **REGION** Canberra District
T (02) 6230 2583 **F** (02) 6230 2023 **OPEN** Weekends, public holidays 10–5
WINEMAKER Dr Roger Harris **EST.** 1986 **CASES** 2000
PRODUCT RANGE ($18–25 CD) Riesling, Sauvignon Blanc Semillon, Chardonnay, Reserve Chardonnay, Shiraz, Shiraz Cabernet Franc, Tumbarumba Merlot, Cabernets, Cabernet Shiraz, Cabernet, Reserve Cabernet.
SUMMARY Distinguished research scientist Dr Roger Harris presides over Brindabella Hills, which increasingly relies on estate-produced grapes, with small plantings of cabernet sauvignon, cabernet franc, merlot, shiraz, chardonnay, sauvignon blanc, semillon and riesling. Wine quality has been consistently impressive. Limited retail distribution in New South Wales and the ACT.

ŸŸŸŸŸ **Shiraz 2002** Fragrant spicy aromas; elegant but intense and extremely long palate of black fruits, spice and fine tannins. **RATING** 94 **DRINK** 2015 $25

ŸŸŸŸŸ **Riesling 2003** Spice, lime and herb aromas, then a crisp, delicate palate with minerally acidity and good length. Screwcap. **RATING** 92 **DRINK** 2013 $20
Sauvignon Blanc Semillon 2003 Spotlessly clean, crisp, tightly focused but delicate; faint tropical fruit, good finish. Screwcap. **RATING** 90 **DRINK** 2007 $18

Tumbarumba Merlot 2002 RATING 86 DRINK 2007 $ 18
Cabernet Shiraz 2002 RATING 85 DRINK 2007 $ 20

🐌 Brischetto Wines
NR

106 Hughes Road, Bargara, Qld 4670 **REGION** Queensland Coastal
T (07) 4159 0862 **F** (07) 4159 0860 **OPEN** 7 days 8–5
WINEMAKER Angelo Puglisi (Contract), Joe Brischetto **EST.** 1996
PRODUCT RANGE Chardonnay, Shiraz Cabernet, Cabernet Sauvignon; Mellow Shiraz, Coral Coast Sweet Red.
SUMMARY Joe and Elizabeth Brischetto planted the first vines in 1996, expanding the vineyard to its present size of 12 000 vines (around 20 acres) the following year. The winery is located at the coastal town of Bargara, 12 kilometres from Bundaberg, offering views of the sea and vineyards from the outdoor tasting area.

🐌 Bristol Farm
★★★★

59 Bellingham Road, Main Ridge, Vic 3928 **REGION** Mornington Peninsula
T (03) 9830 1453 **F** (03) 9888 6794 **OPEN** By appointment
WINEMAKER Contract **EST.** 1997 **CASES** 250
PRODUCT RANGE ($50 ML) Lionheart Pinot Noir, Monty's Paddock Pinot Noir.
SUMMARY Bristol Farm is a pinot noir specialist; Wayne Condon has established slightly over 1 hectare of multiple clones of the variety and, for good measure, has not used irrigation in their establishment or ongoing growing. Monty's Paddock is the premium release, made only in the best vintages; Lionheart is the normal label. The tiny production is sold by mail order.

 Monty's Paddock Pinot Noir 2000 Intense and stylish, with sappy pinot aromas; powerful, long and lingering, full of character and style. **RATING** 93 **DRINK** 2010 $ 50

 Pinot Noir 2001 RATING 86 DRINK Now

Britannia Creek Wines
NR

75 Britannia Creek Road, Wesburn, Vic 3799 **REGION** Yarra Valley
T (03) 5967 1006 **F** (03) 5780 1426 **OPEN** Weekends 10–6
WINEMAKER Charlie Brydon **EST.** 1982 **CASES** 1600
PRODUCT RANGE ($12–24 CD) Semillon, Sauvignon Blanc, Cabernets, Cabernets Reserve.
SUMMARY The wines (from Britannia Creek Wines) are made under the Britannia Falls label from 4 hectares of estate-grown grapes. A range of vintages are available from the cellar door, with some interesting, full-flavoured Semillon.

Broadview Estate
★★★☆

Rowbottoms Road, Granton, Tas 7030 **REGION** Southern Tasmania
T (03) 6263 6882 **F** (03) 6263 6840 **OPEN** Tues–Sun 10–5
WINEMAKER Andrew Hood (Contract) **EST.** 1996 **CASES** 250
PRODUCT RANGE ($16–18 CD) Stoney Ridge Riesling, Erin Vale Chardonnay.
SUMMARY David and Kaye O'Neil planted 0.5 hectare of chardonnay and 0.25 hectare each of riesling and pinot noir in the spring of 1996, producing limited quantities of normally very good Riesling and Chardonnay.

Stoney Ridge Riesling 2003 RATING 86 DRINK 2010 $ 16

Brockville Wines
★★★

15th Street Ext, Irymple South, Vic 3498 **REGION** Murray Darling
T (03) 5024 5143 **OPEN** 7 days 10–4
WINEMAKER Contract **EST.** 1999 **CASES** 800
PRODUCT RANGE ($14 CD) Cabernet Sauvignon.

SUMMARY Mark Bowring, a great-grandson of W B Chaffey (responsible for the design and implementation of the irrigation scheme in the Sunraysia district in the 1880s), and wife Leigh have been growing grapes since 1975. They have 10 hectares of chardonnay, 4.4 hectares of cabernet sauvignon and 1 hectare of shiraz. Most of the grapes are sold to local wineries, but in 1999 the Bowrings decided to have a small portion of cabernet sauvignon vinified for their own label. They chose Brockville as the name, as it is (or was) the Canadian hometown of W B Chaffey. More recently (in 2003) they acquired an additional 23 hectares of vineyard directly across the road from their original plantings, and have opened a cellar door.

ΨΨΨΨ **Cabernet Sauvignon 2002** **RATING** 86 **DRINK** 2007 $ 14

Broke Estate/Ryan Family Wines ★★★☆

Wollombi Road, Broke, NSW 2330 **REGION** Lower Hunter Valley
T (02) 9664 3000 **F** (02) 9665 3303 **OPEN** Weekends and public holidays 10–5, or by appointment
WINEMAKER Matthew Ryan **EST.** 1988 **CASES** 18 000
PRODUCT RANGE ($12–35 CD) Broke Estate is the premium label, with Semillon, Chardonnay, Moussant Cabernets (sparkling), Lacrima Angelorum (sweet white) and Cabernet Sauvignon; the second label is Ryan Free Run Chardonnay and Single Vineyard Cabernets.
SUMMARY With a high-profile consultant viticulturist (Dr Richard Smart) achieving some spectacular early results, Broke Estate is seldom far from the headlines. Some good wines were made in 2000 and 2001.

🐝 Broken Earth NR

PO Box 454, Berri, SA 5343 **REGION** Riverland
T (08) 8583 6500 **F** (08) 8583 6599 **OPEN** 7 days 10–4
WINEMAKER Stuart Auld, Gary Magilton, John Lempens **EST.** 1998 **CASES** 75 000
PRODUCT RANGE ($12.50–12.95 ML) Chardonnay, Viognier, Verdelho, Petit Verdot, Sangiovese, Shiraz, Merlot, Cabernet Sauvignon; and a range of Kosher wines.
SUMMARY Broken Earth Wines is a subsidiary of a diversified public company which has 17 000 hectares of land 142 kilometres southeast of Broken Hill and 50 kilometres from Mildura. At its Millewa vineyard, 450 hectares of vines have been established, planted to chardonnay, verdelho, cabernet sauvignon, merlot, shiraz and sangiovese. A winery with a 21 000-tonne capacity has been built, and produces a range of wine sold in bulk, as cleanskin bottles and under the proprietary Broken Earth brand.

🐝 Broken Gate Wines ★★★★

101 Munster Terrace, North Melbourne, Vic 3051 **REGION** Warehouse
T (03) 9843 3211 **F** (03) 9416 3676 **OPEN** Not
WINEMAKER Contract **EST.** 2001
PRODUCT RANGE Chardonnay, Pinot Noir, Shiraz, Cabernet Sauvignon.
SUMMARY Broken Gate is a partnership between Brendan Chapman and Joseph Orbach. Chapman has an extensive liquor retailing background, and is presently bulk wine buyer for swords wines, responsible for the purchase of 160 000 litres of wine across Australia. It is he who doubtless provides the entree cards for the wines released under the Broken Gate label. Joseph Orbach lived and worked in the Clare Valley from 1994 to 1998 at Leasingham Wines, while also leading the restoration of the Clarevale Winery Co-op building. If this were not enough, he was the head chef and team leader in Tasting Australia, representing the Clare Valley, and the designer and creator of a prism-shaped wine cask, now selling at Sainsbury wine stores in the UK, full of Chilean Chardonnay and Merlot.

ΨΨΨΨΨ **Heathcote Shiraz 2002** Abundant blackcurrant fruit; appealing, gently savoury tannins; hint of olive. **RATING** 90 **DRINK** 2012
Sunbury Shiraz 2001 Clean raspberry, cherry and blackberry fruits; some spice; subtle oak, fine tannins; true finesse. **RATING** 90 **DRINK** 2011

ΨΨΨΨ **Geelong Pinot Noir 2003** Good colour; plum and a touch of mint; light to medium-bodied; low pH style. **RATING** 86 **DRINK** 2008

Brokenwood

McDonalds Road, Pokolbin, NSW 2321 **REGION** Lower Hunter Valley
T (02) 4998 7559 **F** (02) 4998 7893 **OPEN** 7 days 10–5
WINEMAKER Iain Riggs **EST.** 1970 **CASES** 70 000
PRODUCT RANGE ($10–90 CD) An increasingly diverse range of varietal wines from different regions.
Semillon is the volume cornerstone; ILR Reserve Semillon, Graveyard Chardonnay and Graveyard
Shiraz the icons.
SUMMARY Deservedly fashionable winery producing consistently excellent wines. Cricket Pitch
Sauvignon Blanc Semillon has an especially strong following, as has Cabernet Sauvignon; the Graveyard
Shiraz is one of the best Hunter reds available today, and the unwooded Semillon is a modern classic. The
investment in Seville Estate (Yarra Valley) by Brokenwood has been restructured; for details see the
Seville Estate entry. National distribution in Australia; exports to the US, the UK, Canada and Sweden.

ΥΥΥΥΥ **Graveyard Shiraz 2001** The black fruits of the bouquet have touches of regional earth
backed by subtle oak; the palate offers much sweeter flavours, mixing blackberry and
cherry through to a long finish. **RATING** 95 **DRINK** 2021 $ 90
ILR Reserve Semillon 1998 Highly scented, aromatic, touches of spice and toast; intense
and long; excellent balance and finish. Top in the Tri Nations Semillon class. **RATING** 94
DRINK 2013 $ 35

ΥΥΥΥΫ **Indigo Vineyard Viognier 2002** Clear varietal fruit; pastille, peach, fig and apricot;
acidity prevents cloying. **RATING** 92 **DRINK** 2007 $ 30
Forest Edge Chardonnay 2002 Very powerful and complex, with strongly Burgundian
overtones, but less idiosyncratic than its predecessor, which was nicknamed 'Mr Stinky'.
RATING 90 **DRINK** 2007 $ 35
Indigo Pinot Noir 2002 Deeply coloured; complex dark fruit and forest floor aromas; equally
complex structure and length; confronting, ageworthy style. **RATING** 90 **DRINK** 2007 $ 30
Forest Edge Pinot Noir 2002 Appealing and fragrant cherry, plum and spice varietal
fruit; not overly complex, but should build. **RATING** 90 **DRINK** 2008 $ 30

ΥΥΥΥ **Semillon 2003** Spotlessly clean; very pale colour; still to develop its personality; fraction
short. **RATING** 88 **DRINK** 2008 $ 17

Broke's Promise Wines

725 Milbrodale Road, Broke, NSW 2330 **REGION** Lower Hunter Valley
T (02) 6579 1165 **F** (02) 9438 4985 **OPEN** By appointment
WINEMAKER Andrew Margan (Contract) **EST.** 1996 **CASES** 2000
PRODUCT RANGE ($17.50–20 R) Hunter Valley Semillon, Beholden Chardonnay, Hunter Valley Shiraz,
Hunter Valley Barbera.
SUMMARY Jane Marquard and Dennis Karp (and their young children) have established Broke's
Promise on the banks of the Wollombi Brook adjacent to the Yengo National Park. They have
followed tradition in planting shiraz, chardonnay and semillon, and broken with it by planting
barbera and olive trees — the latter two inspired by a long stay in Italy. Exports to the UK and Asia.

Brook Eden Vineyard

Adams Road, Lebrina, Tas 7254 **REGION** Northern Tasmania
T (03) 6395 6244 **F** (03) 6395 6211 **OPEN** 7 days 10–5
WINEMAKER Mike Fogarty (Contract) **EST.** 1988 **CASES** 500
PRODUCT RANGE ($17–28 CD) Riesling, Unwooded Chardonnay, Tribute Chardonnay, Pinot Noir,
Pinot Noir Reserve.
SUMMARY Sheila and the late Jan Bezemer established a 2.2-hectare vineyard on the 60-hectare
Angus beef property which they purchased in 1987. The vineyard site is beautiful, with viticultural
advice from the noted Fred Peacock.

ΥΥΥΥ **Chardonnay 2002** Clean, supple and elegant; good balance and line. **RATING** 89
DRINK 2010 $ 22

ΥΥΥΫ **Riesling 2003** **RATING** 85 **DRINK** 2011 $ 21
Pinot Noir 2002 **RATING** 85 **DRINK** 2003 $ 25

Brookhampton Estate ★★★☆

South West Highway, Donnybrook, WA 6239 **REGION** Geographe
T (08) 9731 0400 **F** (08) 9731 0500 **OPEN** Wed–Sun 10–4
WINEMAKER Contract **EST.** 1998 **CASES** 4000
PRODUCT RANGE ($16–18 CD) Sauvignon Blanc, Chardonnay, Shiraz, Cabernet Merlot, Cabernet
Sauvignon.
SUMMARY Brookhampton Estate, situated 3 kilometres south of Donnybrook, has wasted no time
since its establishment in 1998. One hundred and twenty 7 hectares of vines have been established
with three fashionable red varietals to the fore: cabernet sauvignon (34 hectares), shiraz (29
hectares) and merlot (22 hectares). One hectare of tempranillo and 3 hectares of grenache can safely
be classed as experimental. The three white varieties planted are chardonnay, sauvignon blanc and
semillon. The first contract-made vintage was in 2001, understandably in small quantities given the
youth of the vineyard.

Brookland Valley ★★★★

Caves Road, Wilyabrup, WA 6284 **REGION** Margaret River
T (08) 9755 6250 **F** (08) 9755 6214 **OPEN** 7 days 10–5
WINEMAKER Robert Bowen **EST.** 1984 **CASES** 2800
PRODUCT RANGE ($16.99–59.99 R) Sauvignon Blanc, Chardonnay, Merlot, Cabernet Merlot; Verse 1
Semillon Sauvignon Blanc, Chardonnay, Shiraz, Cabernet Sauvignon Merlot.
SUMMARY Brookland Valley has an idyllic setting, with its much enlarged Flutes Café one of the best
winery restaurants in the Margaret River region, and its Gallery of Wine Arts, which houses an
eclectic collection of wine and food-related art and wine accessories. In 1997 BRL Hardy acquired a
50 per cent interest in the venture and took responsibility for viticulture and winemaking. The move
towards richer and more complex red wines evident before the takeover has continued; the white
wines have an extra degree of finesse and elegance. Exports to the UK, Germany, Switzerland, Japan
and Hong Kong.

ᵀᵀᵀᵀ **Chardonnay 2001** Developing slowly; subtle stone fruit and grapefruit mix; neatly
balanced and integrated barrel-ferment characters. **RATING** 92 **DRINK** 2009 $ 33
Merlot 2000 Medium-bodied; very savoury, with olive and earth varietal character; fine,
supple tannins; long finish. **RATING** 90 **DRINK** 2010 $ 38

ᵀᵀᵀᵀ **Verse 1 Semillon Sauvignon Blanc 2003** Highly aromatic tropical and herb aromas and
flavours; intense and long. **RATING** 89 **DRINK** 2008 $ 17
Reserve Chardonnay 2002 Complex wine from start to finish; some minerally offsets to
the fruit, and plenty of oak. **RATING** 88 **DRINK** 2007 $ 31.99
Verse 1 Chardonnay 2003 Crisp and light, with very subtle use of oak; needs to build
more body. **RATING** 87 **DRINK** 2007 $ 17.99

ᵀᵀᵀᵀ **Sauvignon Blanc 2003 RATING** 84 **DRINK** Now $ 24.99

Brookside Vineyard NR

5 Loaring Road, Bickley Valley, WA 6076 **REGION** Perth Hills
T (08) 9291 8705 **F** (08) 9291 5316 **OPEN** Weekends and public holidays 11–5
WINEMAKER Darlington Estate (Contract) **EST.** 1984 **CASES** 375
PRODUCT RANGE ($17–20 CD) Chardonnay, Cabernet Sauvignon, Cobbler's Leap Cabernet Sauvignon,
Methode Champenoise.
SUMMARY Brookside is one of the many doll's house-scale vineyard operations which dot the Perth
Hills. It has 0.25 hectare each of chardonnay and cabernet sauvignon, basically selling the wine
through a mailing list. It does, however, offer bed and breakfast accommodation at the house, which
has attractive views of the Bickley Valley.

Brookwood Estate ★★★

Treeton Road, Cowaramup, WA 6284 **REGION** Margaret River
T (08) 9755 5604 **F** (08) 9755 5870 **OPEN** 7 days 10–6
WINEMAKER Trevor Mann, Lyn Mann **EST.** 1999 **CASES** 2500
PRODUCT RANGE ($18–24 R) Sauvignon Blanc, Semillon Sauvignon Blanc, Chenin Blanc, Mellow
Rouge, Shiraz, Cabernet Sauvignon.
SUMMARY Trevor and Lyn Mann began the development of their 50-hectare property in 1996, and now
have 1.3 hectares each of shiraz, cabernet sauvignon, semillon, sauvignon blanc and chenin blanc planted.
An on-site winery was constructed in 1999 to accommodate the first vintage. Viticultural consultants
provide advice on management in the vineyard, and the Manns are looking to establish export markets.

ȲȲȲȲ **Sauvignon Blanc 2003** Clean, crisp, light aromas are joined by a touch of gooseberry on
the palate; nice feel, balance and length. **RATING** 88 **DRINK** Now $ 22

ȲȲȲȲ **Chenin Blanc 2003** **RATING** 84 **DRINK** Now $ 18

ȲȲȲ **Semillon Autumn Harvest 2003** **RATING** 82 $ 20

🐎 Broomstick Estate ★★★☆

4 Frances Street, Mount Lawley, WA 6050 (postal) **REGION** Margaret River
T (08) 9271 9594 **F** (08) 9271 9741 **OPEN** Not
WINEMAKER Andrew Gaman (Contract) **EST.** 1997 **CASES** 300
PRODUCT RANGE ($15 R) Shiraz.
SUMMARY Robert Holloway and family purchased the property on which the vineyard is now
established in 1993 as an operating dairy farm. In 1997 the first block of 6 hectares of shiraz was
planted. Over the following years 5.5 hectares of merlot, and then (in 2004) 5.2 hectares of
chardonnay and 2 hectares of sauvignon blanc, for a total area of 18.7 hectares. The picturesque
winery, situated alongside a large freshwater dam, is the first wine grape vineyard in Western
Australia to be awarded the SQF 2000 Quality Assurance Certification. The Holloways see
themselves as grape growers first and foremost, but have kept back enough shiraz to make 300 cases
a year, offered by the case freight-free anywhere in Australia.

ȲȲȲȲ **Shiraz 2002** Clean, light to medium-bodied and elegant; plum and spice flavours; subtle
oak. **RATING** 88 **DRINK** 2009 $ 15

Brothers in Arms ★★★☆

PO Box 840, Langhorne Creek, SA 5255 **REGION** Langhorne Creek
T (08) 8537 3070 **F** (08) 8537 3415 **OPEN** Not
WINEMAKER David Freschi **EST.** 1998 **CASES** 18 000
PRODUCT RANGE ($20–40 R) Shiraz, No. 6 Shiraz Cabernet Sauvignon.
SUMMARY The Adams family has been growing grapes at Langhorne Creek since 1891, when the first
vines at the famed Metala vineyards were planted. Tom and Guy Adams are the fifth generation to own
and work the vineyard, and over the past 20 years have both improved the viticulture and expanded the
plantings to the present 40 hectares (shiraz and cabernet sauvignon). It was not until 1998 that they
took the next step, deciding to hold back a small proportion of the production for vinification under the
Brothers in Arms brand. Exports to the US (The Grateful Palate), Canada, the UK and Singapore.

ȲȲȲȲ **Shiraz 2001** **RATING** 86 **DRINK** 2012 $ 40

Brown Brothers ★★★★

Snow Road, Milawa, Vic 3678 **REGION** King Valley
T (03) 5720 5500 **F** (03) 5720 5511 **OPEN** 7 days 9–5
WINEMAKER Terry Barnett, Wendy Cameron **EST.** 1885 **CASES** 790 000
PRODUCT RANGE ($9.90–46.80 R) A kaleidoscopic array of varietal wines, with a cross-hatch of
appellations, the broadest being Victorian, more specific being King Valley and Milawa, then the
Limited Release, Family Selection and the Family Reserve ranges. A new super-premium range of
wines was released in March 2003 under the Patricia label (the matriarch of the family). There is also
a tempting array of cellar door-only varietal wines.

SUMMARY Brown Brothers draws upon a considerable number of vineyards spread throughout a range of site climates, ranging from very warm to very cool, with the climate varying according to altitude. It is also known for the diversity of varieties with which it works, and the wines represent good value for money. Deservedly one of the most successful family wineries in Australia. The wines are exported to over 27 countries in Europe, the UK, Asia and the Far East, and (after a long, self-imposed absence) the US.

ŶŶŶŶŶ **Patricia Pinot Noir Chardonnay Brut 1997** Exceedingly fine but complex; long and lingering; excellent balance and classic restraint. Five years on yeast lees. RATING 95 DRINK 2008 $39
Patricia Noble Riesling 1999 Immensely complex cumquat, mandarin and box honey; perfect balancing acidity; great length. RATING 95 DRINK 2008 $26

ŶŶŶŶŶ **Liqueur Muscat NV** Complex, intense raisiny fruit; very rich; an excellent blend of younger and older material. RATING 92 DRINK Now $29.80
Pinot Chardonnay Brut NV A fragrant, flowery, citrussy bouquet is followed by a lively, fresh, crisp and lingering palate. RATING 90 DRINK Now $18.30

ŶŶŶŶ **Cellar Door Release Sparkling Shiraz 2001** Impressively rich and powerful fruit immediately proclaims the Heathcote source; will richly repay cellaring. RATING 89 DRINK 2011 $24.40
Very Old Port NV Rich Christmas cake flavours; again a pleasing dry finish. RATING 89 DRINK Now $27.50
Very Old Tokay NV Sweet tea leaf and cake; quite luscious; 'very old' a highly subjective term. A balanced but not overly complex wine. RATING 89 DRINK Now $27.90
Everton Chardonnay Sauvignon Blanc Pinot Grigio 2003 Aromatic; quite intense citrus, passionfruit and stone fruit; the contribution of the pinot grigio is not obvious. RATING 88 DRINK Now $13
Reserve Muscat NV Positive raisin/grapey fruit flavours are strongly varietal; acidity to balance. RATING 88 DRINK Now $18
Cellar Door Release King Valley Riesling 2003 Floral, minerally, lighter style; pleasing fruity finish. RATING 87 DRINK 2007 $14.10
Cellar Door Release King Valley Riesling 2001 Soft, round, nicely matured; good balance and flavour. RATING 87 DRINK Now $14.10
Cellar Door Release Roussanne 2003 Excellent colour; nice touch of citrus along with apricot. RATING 87 DRINK 2007 $15.40
Moscato 2003 Grapey, juicy, fresh and sweet semi-sparkling; balancing acidity. RATING 87 DRINK Now $13.70
Orange Muscat & Flora 2003 Laden with tropical fruit; spatlese level of sweetness. RATING 87 DRINK Now $16.40
Cellar Door Release Milawa Graciano 2001 Great colour, still purple; pleasant, soft mid-palate red fruit; savoury tannins on the finish aid length. RATING 87 DRINK 2008 $18.90
Spatlese Lexia 2003 Tangy lemon blossom; gently sweet fruit and finish; a classic style. RATING 87 DRINK Now $11.90
Reserve Port NV Clean, nicely balanced and aged; spicy, biscuity flavours; nice dry finish. RATING 87 DRINK Now $14.10

ŶŶŶŶ **Victorian Shiraz 2002** RATING 86 DRINK 2009 $18.60
Everton Cabernet Sauvignon Shiraz Malbec 2001 RATING 86 DRINK 2007 $13
Cellar Door Sangiovese 2002 Bright, breezy, fresh cherry and spice aromas and flavours; minimal tannins. From Heathcote. RATING 86 DRINK Now $18.90
Special Late Harvested Orange Muscat & Flora 2003 RATING 86 DRINK Now $9.90
Victorian Chardonnay 2002 RATING 85 DRINK Now $18.60
Pinot Grigio 2003 RATING 85 DRINK Now $15.60
King Valley Merlot 2001 RATING 85 DRINK Now $17.20
Victorian Merlot 2001 RATING 85 DRINK 2007 $17.20
Cabernet Sauvignon 2001 RATING 84 DRINK Now $18.60

ŶŶŶ **Sauvignon Blanc 2003** RATING 83 $17.20
Chenin Blanc 2003 RATING 83 $12.30
Tarrango 2003 RATING 83 $11.90
Crouchen Riesling 2003 RATING 81 $11.90

Brown Hill Estate

Cnr Rosa Brook Road and Barrett Road, Rosa Brook, WA 6285 **REGION** Margaret River
T (08) 9757 4003 **F** (08) 9757 4004 **OPEN** 7 days 10–5
WINEMAKER Nathan Bailey **EST.** 1995 **CASES** 3000
PRODUCT RANGE ($12–35 CD) Charlotte Sauvignon Blanc, Lakeview Semillon Sauvignon Blanc, Autumn Mist, Desert Rose, Chaffers Shiraz, Hannans Cabernet Sauvignon, Ivanhoe Reserve Cabernet Sauvignon.
SUMMARY The Bailey family's stated aim is to produce top-quality wines at affordable prices. This is to be achieved by uncompromising viticultural practices emphasising low yields per hectare, in conjunction with the family being involved in all stages of production with minimum outside help. They have established 7 hectares each of shiraz and cabernet sauvignon, 4 hectares of semillon, and 2 hectares each of sauvignon blanc and merlot, and by the standards of the Margaret River, the prices are indeed affordable.

ŶŶŶŶŶ **Hannans Cabernet Sauvignon 2002** Spotlessly clean, succulent blackcurrant fruit; good control of extract and oak; soft tannins. Lovely wine. **RATING** 92 **DRINK** 2012 $18
Chaffers Shiraz 2002 Quite fragrant; excellent black cherry and spice fruit; good texture, length and balance. **RATING** 91 **DRINK** 2012 $16
Ivanhoe Reserve Cabernet Sauvignon 2001 A complex array of sweet and more savoury fruits plus cedary oak; soft, lingering tannins. **RATING** 90 **DRINK** 2011 $35

ŶŶŶŶ **Lakeview Semillon Sauvignon Blanc 2003** Similarly clean; slightly more lemony bite and complexity from an airbrush of oak. **RATING** 88 **DRINK** 2007 $12
Charlotte Sauvignon Blanc 2003 Fresh, clean; nicely balanced tropical fruit; moderate length. **RATING** 87 **DRINK** Now $14

ŶŶŶ **Desert Rose 2003** **RATING** 83 $13

Browns of Padthaway

Keith Road, Padthaway, SA 5271 **REGION** Padthaway
T (08) 8765 6063 **F** (08) 8765 6083 **OPEN** At Padthaway Estate
WINEMAKER Contract **EST.** 1993 **CASES** 35 000
PRODUCT RANGE ($10–21 R) Classic Diamond, Riesling, Sauvignon Blanc, Non Wooded Chardonnay, Verdelho, T-Trellis Shiraz, Ernest Shiraz, Redwood Cabernet Malbec, Myra Family Reserve Cabernet Sauvignon, Sparkling Shiraz.
SUMMARY The Brown family has for many years been the largest independent grape grower in Padthaway, a district in which most of the vineyards were established and owned by Wynns, Seppelt, Lindemans and Hardys, respectively. After a slow start, has produced some excellent wines since 1998, and wine production has increased accordingly.

ŶŶŶŶ **Ernest Family Reserve Shiraz 2001** Powerful, concentrated prune and blackberry aromas and flavours; some vanilla. Alcohol (14.5 degrees) pokes through on the finish. **RATING** 87 **DRINK** 2011 $25

ŶŶŶŶ **Unwooded Chardonnay 2001** **RATING** 86 **DRINK** Now $17
T-Trellis Shiraz 2001 **RATING** 86 **DRINK** 2010 $18
Myra Family Reserve Cabernet Sauvignon 2001 **RATING** 85 **DRINK** 2009 $21

🐎 Brumby Wines
★★★☆

Sandyanna, 24 Cannon Lane, Wood Wood, Vic 3596 **REGION** Swan Hill
T 0438 305 364 **F** (03) 5030 5366 **OPEN** Mon–Fri 9–5
WINEMAKER Neil Robb, John Ellis, Glen Olsen (Contract) **EST.** 2001 **CASES** 3500
PRODUCT RANGE ($13–21 CD) Chardonnay, Shiraz, Durif, Cabernet Sauvignon.
SUMMARY The derivation of the name is even more direct and simple than you might imagine: the owners are Stuart and Liz Brumby, who decided to plant grapes for supply to others before moving to having an increasing portion of their production from the 15 hectares of chardonnay, cabernet sauvignon, shiraz and durif vinified under their own label. For the time being, sales are through the cellar door, by mailing list and via the website <www.brumbywines.com.au>, but the plan is to establish retail sales and exports.

ΨΨΨΫ **Durif 2002** Dense red-purple; true varietal power; dense, deep black fruits; evenly weighted through palate. **RATING** 90 **DRINK** 2012 $ 21

ΨΨΨΫ **Shiraz 2002 RATING** 86 **DRINK** 2007 $ 14

Brunswick Hill Wines   NR

34 Breese Street, Brunswick, Vic 3056 **REGION** Port Phillip Zone
T (03) 9383 4681 **F** (03) 9386 5699 **OPEN** By appointment
WINEMAKER Peter Atkins, Graeme Rojo **EST.** 1999
PRODUCT RANGE ($16–34 ML) Sauvignon Blanc, Yarra Valley Chardonnay, Anstey Shiraz, Shiraz, Shiraz Cabernet, Merlot, Yarra Valley Cabernet Sauvignon.
SUMMARY Peter Atkins and Graeme Rojo are partners in the Brunswick Hill Wines venture, which is claimed to be Melbourne's only urban winery, situated in the heart of urban Brunswick, 15 minutes from the CBD. Studley Park Vineyard is even closer, but its grapes are sent to Granite Hills for winemaking. The ability to open the winery where it is doubtless reflects Peter Atkins' background as an environmental and urban planner, and his present position as a senior manager in the Department of Natural Resources and the Environment. A member of the Eltham and District Winemakers Guild, Atkins moved to commercial winemaking after 10 years as an amateur. Brunswick Hill Wines takes grapes from a number of Victorian regions, ranging from cool to warm. 1999 was the first fully fledged commercial vintage, and a number of vintages are available by mail order and through the cellar door on Saturdays.

Brush Box Vineyard   NR

c/- 6 Grandview Parade, Mona Vale, NSW 2103 **REGION** Lower Hunter Valley
T (02) 9979 4468 **F** (02) 9999 5303 **OPEN** Not
WINEMAKER Contract **EST.** 1997 **CASES** 1000
PRODUCT RANGE ($13–17 ML) Verdelho, Chardonnay, Cabernet Merlot.
SUMMARY Paul and Suzanne Mackay have established their 6.5-hectare Brushbox Vineyard at Broke. It is situated in a secluded part of the Fordwich Hills, with views across the Wollombi Valley to the northern perimeter of Yengo National Park. It is planted to chardonnay, verdelho, cabernet sauvignon and merlot; the wine is sold by mail order only.

Bulga Wine Estates

Bulga Road, Swan Hill, Vic 3585 **REGION** Swan Hill
T (03) 5037 6685 **F** (03) 5037 6992 **OPEN** By appointment
WINEMAKER Rod Bouchier **EST.** 1999
PRODUCT RANGE ($15 R) Chardonnay, Shiraz.
SUMMARY Bulga Wine Estates draws on a little over 50 hectares of vines: chardonnay (10 hectares), cabernet sauvignon (10 hectares), the remainder shiraz and a little colombard. Only part of the wine is vinified under the Bulga Wine Estates label, and handsomely so.

Bullers Beverford

Murray Valley Highway, Beverford, Vic 3590 **REGION** Swan Hill
T (03) 5037 6305 **F** (03) 5037 6803 **OPEN** Mon–Sat 9–5
WINEMAKER Richard Buller (Jnr) **EST.** 1951 **CASES** 50 000
PRODUCT RANGE ($5.50–14 CD) A comprehensive range of basic varietal wines under the Sails, Victoria and Magee flags; likewise budget-priced Port, Tokay and Muscat.
SUMMARY This is a parallel operation to the Calliope winery at Rutherglen, similarly owned and operated by third-generation Richard and Andrew Buller, offering traditional wines which in the final analysis reflect both their Riverland origin and a fairly low-key approach to style in the winery. It is, however, one of the few remaining sources of reasonable-quality bulk fortified wine available to the public, provided in 22-litre Valorex barrels at $5.50 per litre.

ΨΨΨΫ **Sails Durif 2002** Good colour; light to medium-bodied; fresh red berry fruits show the durability of the variety in the Riverland. **RATING** 86 **DRINK** Now $ 14
Cabernet Sauvignon 2001 RATING 85 **DRINK** 2007 $ 13
Sails Cabernet Rose 2003 RATING 84 **DRINK** Now $ 14

ΥΥΥ **Victoria Shiraz Grenache Mourvedre 2002** RATING 83 $13
Magee Cabernet Shiraz 2001 RATING 83 $11
Chardonnay 2003 RATING 81 $9
Victoria Rose 2003 RATING 80 $9
Merlot 2001 RATING 80 $13

Bullers Calliopes ★★★★★

Three Chain Road, Rutherglen, Vic 3685 REGION Rutherglen
T (02) 6032 9660 F (02) 6032 8005 OPEN Mon–Sat 9–5, Sun 10–5
WINEMAKER Andrew Buller EST. 1921 CASES 4000
PRODUCT RANGE ($14–60 CD) Limited Release range of Marsanne, Chardonnay, Shiraz, Merlot Cabernet Franc; Mondeuse Shiraz, Shiraz, Durif, fortifieds.
SUMMARY The Buller family is very well known and highly regarded in northeast Victoria, and the business benefits from vines that are now 80 years old. The rating is for the superb releases of Museum fortified wines. Limited releases of Calliope Shiraz and Shiraz Mondeuse can also be very good.

ΥΥΥΥΥ **Rare Rutherglen Liqueur Tokay NV** Medium deep golden-brown; a mix of sweet tea leaf and Christmas cake is a highly aromatic entry point for the bouquet; the palate has a sweet core of muscadelle fruit, and rancio, tea leaf, nutty and cake elements surrounding the core. RATING 94 DRINK Now $60

ΥΥΥΥΥ **Fine Old Classic Rutherglen Muscat NV** The deepest coloured of the Classic muscats, full tawny, olive on the rim; rich and generous, with grapey/raisiny fruit offset by an airbrush of wood-aged rancio; the palate is still fruit-forward but with a compelling skein of complexity. RATING 92 DRINK Now $18

ΥΥΥΥ **Fine Old Classic Rutherglen Tokay NV** A mix of tea leaf and dried muscadelle aromas, the palate following down the same track, with distilled muscadelle fruit stemming directly (in flavour terms) from the fruit base. Good balance and richness. RATING 89 DRINK Now $18

Bulong Estate ★★★☆

70 Summerhill Road, Yarra Junction, Vic 3797 (postal) REGION Yarra Valley
T (03) 5967 2487 F (03) 5967 2487 OPEN Not
WINEMAKER Contract EST. 1994 CASES 3000
PRODUCT RANGE ($16–21 ML) Sauvignon Blanc, Pinot Gris, Chardonnay, Pinot Noir, Merlot, Cabernet Sauvignon.
SUMMARY Judy and Howard Carter purchased their beautifully situated 45-hectare property in 1994: it looks down into the valley below and across to the nearby ranges with Mount Donna Buang at their peak. Most of the grapes from the immaculately tended vineyard are sold, with limited quantities made for the Bulong Estate label. Exports to the UK.

ΥΥΥΥ **Chardonnay 2003** Attractive, light to medium-bodied; citrus, melon and grapefruit; touch of French oak. RATING 89 DRINK 2007 $21
Sauvignon Blanc 2003 Delicate, clean and crisp; light passionfruit and gooseberry flavours; good length and balance. RATING 87 DRINK Now $16

ΥΥΥΥ **Pinot Gris 2003** RATING 86 DRINK Now $18
Merlot 2001 RATING 86 DRINK Now $21
Cabernet Sauvignon 2002 RATING 85 DRINK 2007 $21

Bundaleer Wines ★★★★

41 King Street, Brighton, SA 5048 (postal) REGION Southern Flinders Ranges
T (08) 8296 1231 F (08) 8296 2484 OPEN Not
WINEMAKER Angela Meaney EST. 1998 CASES 600
PRODUCT RANGE ($18–20 R) Shiraz, Shiraz Cabernet Sauvignon.
SUMMARY Bundaleer is a joint venture between third-generation farmer Des Meaney and manufacturing industry executive Graham Spurling (whose family originally came from the

Southern Flinders). Planting of the 8-hectare vineyard began in 1998, the first vintage coming in 2001. It is situated in a region known as the Bundaleer Gardens, on the edge of the Bundaleer Forest, 200 kilometres north of Adelaide, at an altitude of 500 metres. Bundaleer Wines is one of five growers with their own labels in the newly declared Southern Flinders region. The wines are made under the care of industry veteran Angela Meaney at Paulett Winery in the Clare Valley. This should not be confused with the Bundaleer Shiraz brand made by Bindi.

Bundaleera Vineyard ★★★★

449 Glenwood Road, Relbia, Tas 7258 **REGION** Northern Tasmania
T (03) 6343 1231 **F** (03) 6343 1250 **OPEN** Not
WINEMAKER Rosevears Estate (Contract) **EST.** 1996 **CASES** 1000
PRODUCT RANGE ($16.50–27.50 CD) Riesling, Unwooded Chardonnay, Chardonnay, Pinot Noir.
SUMMARY David (a consultant metallurgist in the mining industry) and Jan Jenkinson have established 2.5 hectares of vines in a sunny, sheltered north to northeast position in the North Esk Valley. The 12-hectare property on which their house and vineyard are established give them some protection from the urban sprawl of Launceston. Jan is the full-time viticulturist and gardener for the immaculately tended property.

ŢŢŢ **Unwooded Chardonnay 2003** **RATING** 83 $16.50

Bungawarra NR

Bents Road, Ballandean, Qld 4382 **REGION** Granite Belt
T (07) 4684 1128 **F** (07) 4684 1128 **OPEN** 7 days 10–4.30
WINEMAKER Jeff Harden **EST.** 1975 **CASES** 1300
PRODUCT RANGE ($10–18 CD) Traminer, Thomas Semillon, Foundation Chardonnay, Reserve Chardonnay, Bliss, Festival Red, Paragon, Shiraz, Cabernet Sauvignon, Liquid Amber, Paragon Liqueur Muscat.
SUMMARY Now owned by Jeff Harden. It draws upon 5 hectares of mature vineyards which over the years have shown themselves capable of producing red wines of considerable character.

Bunnamagoo Estate ★★★☆

Bunnamagoo, Rockley, NSW 2795 **REGION** Central Ranges Zone
T 1300 304 707 **F** (02) 6377 5231 **OPEN** Not
WINEMAKER Jon Reynolds (Contract) **EST.** 1995 **CASES** 1000
PRODUCT RANGE ($21.40–27.40 ML) Chardonnay, Cabernet Sauvignon.
SUMMARY Bunnamagoo Estate (on one of the first land grants in the region) is situated near the historic town of Rockley, itself equidistant to Bathurst and Oberon. Here a 7-hectare vineyard planted to chardonnay, merlot and cabernet sauvignon has been established by Paspaley Pearls, a famous name in the pearl industry. The wines are contract-made under the direction of Jon Reynolds at the Cabonne Winery in Orange, and are sold by mail order.

ŢŢŢŢ **Chardonnay 2001** Complex barrel-ferment inputs; rich, sweet peachy fruit; abundant mid-palate flesh; well made. **RATING** 89 **DRINK** Now $23.60

ŢŢŢŢ **Cabernet Sauvignon 2001** **RATING** 86 **DRINK** 2009 $27.40

Burge Family Winemakers ★★★★

Barossa Way, Lyndoch, SA 5351 **REGION** Barossa Valley
T (08) 8524 4644 **F** (08) 8524 4444 **OPEN** Thurs–Mon 10–5
WINEMAKER Rick Burge **EST.** 1928 **CASES** 3000
PRODUCT RANGE ($16–38 CD) Olive Hill Riesling, Olive Hill Semillon, Olive Hill Shiraz Grenache Mourvedre, The Renoux (Shiraz Merlot Cabernet), Clochmerle (Grenache Cabernet), Garnacha Old Vine Grenache, A Nice Red (Merlot Cabernet), Draycott Shiraz.
SUMMARY Rick Burge (not to be confused with Grant Burge, although the families are related) has established himself as an icon producer of exceptionally rich, lush and concentrated Barossa red wines. Rick's sense of humour is evident with the Clochmerle Grenache Cabernet, and even more with the Merlot Cabernet blend made for those who come to cellar door and ask 'Do you have a nice red?' He is happy to provide precisely what they ask for.

ΥΥΥΥ **The Renoux Shiraz Merlot Cabernet 2002** Fragrant aromas of sweet red fruits and spices; clean, light to medium-bodied; fruit-driven, fine tannins. **RATING** 90 **DRINK** 2010 $ 24

ΥΥΥΥ **Olive Hill Shiraz Grenache Mourvedre 2002** A quite intense and complex bouquet; multi-faceted black fruit flavours; no jam. Good structure. **RATING** 89 **DRINK** 2010 $ 29

ΥΥΥ **Muscat Blanc Late Harvest 2003** **RATING** 83 $ 16

🐌 Burgi Hill Vineyard   NR

290 Victoria Road, Wandin North, Vic 3139 **REGION** Yarra Valley
T (03) 5964 3568 **F** (03) 5964 3568 **OPEN** By appointment
WINEMAKER Christopher Sargeant **EST.** 1974 **CASES** 300
PRODUCT RANGE ($18–23 ML) Sauvignon Blanc, Chardonnay, Pinot Noir, Cabernet Merlot.
SUMMARY The small 4.5-hectare vineyard now operated by Christopher Sargeant and family was established 30 years ago. For many years the grapes were sold, but they are now being partly vinified for the Burgi Hill label. The varieties planted are chardonnay, sauvignon blanc, pinot noir, merlot and cabernet sauvignon.

Burke & Hills

Cargo Road, Lidster, NSW 2800 **REGION** Orange
T (02) 6365 3456 **F** (02) 6365 3456 **OPEN** Fri–Mon 11–5 at Lakeside Café, Lake Canobolas
WINEMAKER Christophe Derrez, Lucy Maddox **EST.** 1999 **CASES** 3500
PRODUCT RANGE ($18–32 CD) Sauvignon Blanc, Chardonnay, Pinot Noir; others in the pipeline include a Bordeaux-style red blend and sparkling.
SUMMARY Now this is an interesting venture: in an unofficial background response to my standard request for insight into motives and goals, founder Doug Burke wrote, 'I guess you would scream if you heard another new small vineyard/winery prattling on about small volumes, low yields, best practice ... in a quest for great quality, subtlety and complexity.' Very likely, but here the facts speak for themselves: a non-fatal search led to the selection of a steeply sloping, frost-free north-facing slope rising to an altitude of 940 metres on Mount Lidster; the planting of 10 hectares of classic varieties, but including an excellent mix of MV6, 114, 115 and 777 clones of pinot noir; the appointment of Brett Wilkins as viticulturist (with leading consultant Di Davidson in the background) and former Gevrey Chambertin-cum-Flying Winemaker Christophe Derrez; the erection of a 200-tonne capacity winery to supplement cash flow by undertaking contract winemaking; and the running of the Lakeside Café at Lake Canobolas, 2 kilometres from the winery ... All of these things point to a carefully structured business plan with one objective: in Burke's words, 'Don't go broke.'

ΥΥΥΥ **Sauvignon Blanc 2002** Clean grassy and orange peel aromas; the palate lifted by a touch of French oak. **RATING** 88 **DRINK** Now $ 22
Chardonnay 2003 In winery style, full and generous; ripe stone fruit and well-integrated oak. **RATING** 88 **DRINK** 2007 $ 23
Pinot Noir 2002 Again shows winemaker preference for very ripe fruit; a sweet plum and cherry mix; powerful finish. **RATING** 88 **DRINK** 2007 $ 32
Sauvignon Blanc 2003 Big, rich, powerful, mouthfilling wine; partial barrel ferment adds significantly to texture and structure, though not to varietal character. **RATING** 87 **DRINK** Now $ 22
Chardonnay 2002 Spicy barrel-ferment inputs to melon and peach fruit; two pickings, one month apart. **RATING** 87 **DRINK** Now $ 23

🐌 Burke and Wills Winery

3155 Burke and Wills Track, Mia Mia, Vic 3444 **REGION** Heathcote
T (03) 5425 5400 **F** (03) 5425 5401 **OPEN** By appointment
WINEMAKER Andrew Pattison **EST.** 2003 **CASES** 1000
PRODUCT RANGE ($18–40 ML) The premium releases are the Pattison Reserve Shiraz, Cabernet Merlot; cheaper varietals under The Dig Tree label include Chardonnay, Pinot Noir, Merlot and Cabernet Sauvignon.

SUMMARY Andrew Pattison established Burke and Wills Winery in 2003, after selling Lancefield Winery. He is in the course of establishing 1 hectare of shiraz, 0.5 hectare each of gewurztraminer, and has 1 hectare each of chardonnay and cabernets at Malmsbury, plus 0.5 hectare of pinor noir, supplemented by contract-grown grapes from a Macedon Ranges vineyard supplying chardonnay, pinot noir and cabernets. Not to be confused with Burke & Hills.

♈♈♈♈♈ **Pattison Reserve French Oak Shiraz 2001** Rich, loaded with spicy/plummy fruit, and lots and lots of oak; Guigal super-cuvee style. **RATING** 94 **DRINK** 2017 $30

♈♈♈♈♈ **White Heather Unoaked Chardonnay 2002** Crisp, tangy and lively; excellent length; bright finish and balanced acidity. **RATING** 90 **DRINK** Now $17

♈♈♈♈ **Pattison Cabernet Sauvignon Cabernet Franc Merlot 2001** Rich, sweet black berries and plum fruit; soft tannins. **RATING** 87 **DRINK** 2009 $22
Chardonnay Brut NV Strangely, a deep bronze colour, belying its varietal make-up; very rich, full-bodied; balanced dosage. **RATING** 87 **DRINK** Now $20

♈♈♈♈ **Malmsbury Pinot Noir 2002 RATING** 86 **DRINK** Now $18
Gewurztraminer 2003 RATING 85 **DRINK** 2007 $25
Malmsbury Chardonnay 2001 RATING 85 **DRINK** 2007 $18
White Heather Unoaked Chardonnay 2003 RATING 84 **DRINK** 2007 $17

Burnbrae   ★★★☆

Hill End Road, Erudgere via Mudgee, NSW 2850 **REGION** Mudgee
T (02) 6373 3504 **F** (02) 6373 3601 **OPEN** Wed–Mon 9–5
WINEMAKER Alan Cox **EST.** 1976
PRODUCT RANGE ($10–25 CD) Sauvignon Blanc, Chardonnay, Pinot Noir, Shiraz, Malbec, Cabernet Shiraz, Cabernet Sauvignon, Vintage Port, Liqueur Muscat.
SUMMARY The founding Mace family sold Burnbrae to Alan Cox in 1996. It continues as an estate-based operation with 23 hectares of vineyards. Since that time the Burnbrae wines have gone from strength to strength, improving beyond all recognition, attesting to the value of the old, dry-grown vines and the accumulation of winemaking experience by Alan Cox.

♈♈♈♈ **Cabernet Sauvignon 2002** Abundant dark chocolate, sweet blackcurrant and blackberry fruit, the tannins still needing to soften and come back into balance. **RATING** 88
DRINK 2015 $25
Chardonnay 2002 Clean, fresh and tangy; an early-picked style showing little, if any, oak influence, but good length. **RATING** 87 **DRINK** 2007 $15

♈♈♈♈ **Shiraz 2002 RATING** 86 **DRINK** 2010 $25
Merlot 2002 RATING 84 **DRINK** 2007 $17

♈♈♈ **Chardonnay 2003 RATING** 83 $15
Pinot Noir 2003 RATING 83 $17
Pinot Noir 2002 RATING 83 $17

Burramurra   ★★★☆

Barwood Park, High Street, Nagambie, Vic 3608 **REGION** Nagambie Lakes
T (03) 5794 2181 **F** (03) 5794 2755 **OPEN** Fri–Sun and public holidays 10–5, or by appointment
WINEMAKER Mitchelton (Contract) **EST.** 1988 **CASES** 1000
PRODUCT RANGE ($15–18 R) Sauvignon Blanc, Cabernet Sauvignon Merlot.
SUMMARY Burramurra is the relatively low-profile vineyard operation of the Honourable Pat McNamara. Most of the grapes are sold to Mitchelton; a small amount is contract-made for the Burramurra label. Glowing reviews in the US have led to brisk export business with that country and to the selection of Burramurra by various international airlines.

Burrundulla

NR

Sydney Road, Mudgee, NSW 2850 **REGION** Mudgee
T (02) 6372 1620 **F** (02) 6372 4058 **OPEN** Not
WINEMAKER Contract **EST.** 1996
PRODUCT RANGE Semillon.
SUMMARY A very substantial venture but one which is still in its infancy; the Cox family (Chris, Michael and Ted) are in the course of establishing 54 hectares of vineyards planted to chardonnay, shiraz and cabernet sauvignon.

ΥΥΥ **Semillon 2003 RATING** 82

Burton Premium Wines

★★★☆

PO Box 242, Killara, NSW 2071 **REGION** Warehouse
T (02) 9416 6631 **F** (02) 9416 6681 **OPEN** Not
WINEMAKER Mike Farmilo, Pat Tocacui (Contract) **EST.** 1998 **CASES** 4000
PRODUCT RANGE ($18–35 ML) McLaren Vale Chardonnay, McLaren Vale Shiraz, Limestone Coast Merlot, Southeast Australia Cabernet Merlot, Coonawarra Cabernet Sauvignon, Reserve Coonawarra Cabernet Sauvignon, Limestone Coast Cabernet Sauvignon.
SUMMARY Burton Premium Wines has neither vineyards nor winery, purchasing its grapes and having the wines made in various locations by contract winemakers. It brings together the marketing and financial skills of managing director Nigel Burton, and the extensive wine industry experience (as a senior judge) of Dr Ray Healy, who is director in charge of all aspects of winemaking. Exports to the UK, the US, Canada and Japan.

ΥΥΥΥ **Limestone Coast Merlot 2001** Savoury varietal character and structure; sweet leather, spice, bitter chocolate and redcurrant; fine tannins **RATING** 87 **DRINK** 2010 $ 27.50
The Limestone Coast Cabernet Sauvignon 2001 Clean, ripe, blackcurrant, cassis and mint supported by well-balanced and integrated oak. **RATING** 87 **DRINK** 2011 $ 24.50

ΥΥΥΫ **McLaren Vale Shiraz 2001 RATING** 85 **DRINK** Now $ 30
Coonawarra Cabernet Sauvignon 2001 RATING 85 **DRINK** Now $ 35

ΥΥΥ **McLaren Vale Chardonnay 2002 RATING** 83 $ 19.50

Bush Piper Vineyard

NR

Badenoch, Horspool Way via Molong Road, Orange, NSW 2800 **REGION** Orange
T (02) 6361 8280 **F** (02) 6361 8432 **OPEN** By appointment
WINEMAKER Mark Davidson (Tamburlaine) **EST.** 1996 **CASES** 3000
PRODUCT RANGE ($15–20 CD) Sauvignon Blanc, Shiraz, Cabernet Sauvignon.
SUMMARY Shortly after Jo and Richard Cummins moved to Orange, they realised their property was ideal viticultural land. Planting began in 1996 with cabernet sauvignon, followed the next year by further blocks of cabernet and shiraz. The wines are sold by mail order and through select restaurants.

by Farr

★★★★★

PO Box 72, Bannockburn, Vic 3331 **REGION** Geelong
T (03) 5281 1979 **F** (03) 5281 1979 **OPEN** Not
WINEMAKER Gary Farr **EST.** 1999 **CASES** 2000
PRODUCT RANGE ($49.99–51.99 R) Viognier, Chardonnay, Pinot Noir, Shiraz.
SUMMARY In 1994 Gary Farr and family planted 11 hectares of clonally selected viognier, chardonnay, pinot noir and shiraz, at a density of 7000 per hectare, on a north-facing hill which is directly opposite the Bannockburn Winery; they had acquired the land from the late Stuart Hooper (Bannockburn's then owner). For a multiplicity of reasons, in 1999 Farr decided to establish his own label for part of the grapes coming from the vineyard; the remainder goes to Bannockburn. The quality of the wines is exemplary, and their character subtly different from those of Bannockburn itself; this is due, in Farr's view, to the interaction of the terroir of the hill and the clonal selection. As from 2000, the reference to Bannockburn was removed from the front label. Exports to the US, the UK, Japan, Denmark, Hong Kong, Singapore and Malaysia.

ΨΨΨΨΨ **Shiraz by Farr 2002** Pure blackberry, cherry, anise, spice and licorice; powerful but elegant; great structure. Seven per cent Viognier really does the trick. **RATING** 95 **DRINK** 2017 $ 51.99

Chardonnay by Farr 2002 Very complex style with barrel ferment, malolactic ferment, lees inputs to the rich, ripe stone fruit; suitably long finish. **RATING** 94 **DRINK** 2009 $ 49.99

ΨΨΨΨΨ **Pinot Noir by Farr 2002** Deep purple; ghetto blaster black plum, sous bois, leather and heaven knows what else. **RATING** 91 **DRINK** 2008 $ 51.99

ΨΨΨΨ **Viognier by Farr 2002** Ultra-complex and ultra-powerful, with layers of orange peel, honey and apricot; shows its 14.5 degrees alcohol. **RATING** 89 **DRINK** 2007 $ 51.99

🦥 Byramgou Park   NR

Wade Road, Brookhampton, WA 6239 **REGION** Geographe
T (08) 9731 8248 **F** (08) 9731 8248 **OPEN** 7 days 10–6
WINEMAKER Siobhan Lynch **EST.** 1997 **CASES** 700
PRODUCT RANGE ($12–15 CD) Shiraz Grenache, Grenache.
SUMMARY The unusual name comes courtesy of the great-great-grandfather of Richard Knox, the proprietor of the business (with Geraldine Knox). It was the name of the ship which his forebear sailed to Arabia in 1821; he received a gold cup, depicted on the label, for his deeds. These details to one side, there are 5 hectares of chardonnay, grenache, shiraz and cabernet sauvignon, and the wine is made by Siobhan Lynch, a district veteran whose father, Ken Lynch, established Chatsfield many years ago. It hardly need be said that the wines meet their aim of representing value for money.

🦥 Cahillton   ★★★☆

93A Killara Road, Gruyere, Vic 3770 **REGION** Yarra Valley
T (03) 5964 9000 **F** (03) 5964 9313 **OPEN** Not
WINEMAKER Peter Wilson **EST.** 1999 **CASES** 2000
PRODUCT RANGE ($20–36 ML) Sauvignon Blanc, Chardonnay, Pinot Noir, Shiraz, Cabernet Sauvignon.
SUMMARY The Indonesian Widjaja family have major palm oil plantations in Java, with downstream refining. Under the direction of Hendra Widjaja, it has decided to diversify into the Australian wine business, establishing two very significant vineyards, one in the Yarra Valley planted to no less than 12 varieties, and an even larger one in Heathcote with seven varieties, headed by shiraz, supplemented by nebbiolo, tempranillo, merlot, cabernet sauvignon, viognier and chardonnay. Between them the two vineyards cover 128 hectares. From 2004, all of the wines are being made at a new $7 million winery built at Heathcote. While the major part of the production will be exported to Asia and the US, direct sales are being made in Australia.

ΨΨΨΨΨ **Pinot Noir 2002** Excellent black cherry, plum and all-spice fruit; good length; needs time. **RATING** 90 **DRINK** 2008 $ 29

ΨΨΨΨ **Shiraz 2002** **RATING** 86 **DRINK** 2012 $ 35
Cabernet Sauvignon 2002 **RATING** 85 **DRINK** 2007 $ 29
Chardonnay 2002 **RATING** 84 **DRINK** Now $ 23

ΨΨΨ **Sauvignon Blanc 2003** **RATING** 83 $ 23

Calais Estate   NR

Palmers Lane, Pokolbin, NSW 2321 **REGION** Lower Hunter Valley
T (02) 4998 7654 **F** (02) 4998 7813 **OPEN** 7 days 9–5
WINEMAKER Adrian Sheridan **EST.** 1987 **CASES** 11 000
PRODUCT RANGE ($14.50–40 CD) Semillon, Viognier, Shiraz, Chambourcin.
SUMMARY Richard and Susan Bradley purchased the substantial Calais Estate winery in April 2000. Long-serving winemaker Adrian Sheridan continues his role, and the estate offers a wide range of facilities for visitors, ranging from private function rooms to picnic spots to an undercover outdoor entertaining area.

Caledonia Australis

PO Box 54, Abbotsford, Vic 3067 **REGION** Gippsland
T (03) 9416 4156 **F** (03) 9416 4157 **OPEN** Not
WINEMAKER MasterWineMakers (Contract)
PRODUCT RANGE ($18.65–40.50 ML) Chardonnay, Mount Macleod Pinot Noir, Pinot Noir, Pinot Noir Reserve.
SUMMARY The reclusive Caledonia Australis is a Pinot Noir and Chardonnay specialist, with a total of 18 hectares planted to chardonnay and pinot noir in three separate vineyard locations. All of the vineyards are in the Leongatha area, on red, free-draining, high-ironstone soils, on a limestone or marl base, and the slopes are east to northeast facing. Small-batch winemaking has resulted in consistently high-quality wines.

TTTTT **Chardonnay 2001** Powerful, yet has great texture and balance; the full panoply of barrel ferment, malolactic ferment and (possibly) wild yeast; fig, peach and grilled nuts; subtly creamy texture. **RATING** 95 **DRINK** 2008 $ 31

Calem Blue/Shelton Wines NR

PO Box 4132, Wembley, WA 6913 **REGION** Margaret River
T (08) 6380 1511 **F** (08) 6380 1522 **OPEN** Not
WINEMAKER Flying Fish Cove, Bill Crappsley (Contract) **EST.** 1996
PRODUCT RANGE ($12.50–19.60 ML) Calem Blue range of Sauvignon Blanc Semillon, Chardonnay, Shiraz; Bin 168 Cabernet Sauvignon.
SUMMARY David and Nicky Shelton are vineyard holders within the 80-hectare Margaret River Vineyards Estate in Clews Road, Cowaramup. The estate is a relatively rare example of so-called *clos* farming being an unqualified success, with a generally high level of viticulture throughout, and substantial on-site amenities for the vineyard holders. The name Calem is a combination of the Sheltons' children's names: Cal and Emma. The vineyard was planted in 1996, and the first vintage was produced in 2000. The viticulture is under the control of Ian Davies, and winemaking is by the powerful duo of Flying Fish Cove and Bill Crappsley. The show success of the wines comes as no surprise, and the wines have secured wholesale distribution throughout Queensland, South Australia and the Northern Territory. One wine, Bin 168 Cabernet Sauvignon, has been specifically developed for the Asian market, and is available only by mail order.

Callipari Wine NR

Cureton Avenue, Nichols Point, Vic 3501 **REGION** Murray Darling
T (03) 5023 4477 **F** (03) 5021 0988 **OPEN** Weekends and public holidays 10–4
WINEMAKER Michael Callipari **EST.** 1999 **CASES** 3000
PRODUCT RANGE ($12.85–16.50 CD) Shiraz, Shiraz Cabernet, Grenache Cabernet Franc Shiraz, Cabernet Merlot, Cabernet Sauvignon, Ned's Red.
SUMMARY Michael Callipari is among the third generation of the Callipari family, the first members of which left Calabria, Sicily in May 1951. Various members of the family have developed vineyards over the years, and Callipari Wine & Food now has over 23 hectares of vines on two properties available for its wines. Mother Giuseppa Callipari makes the food products grown on the family farm, sold through the cellar door and at tourism outlets and shops in the district. Ned's Red, incidentally, is described as a 'premium red wine with a dash of orange and lemon'.

Calyla Vines Estate NR

PO Box 523, Brighton, SA 5048 **REGION** Warehouse
T (08) 8298 8877 **F** (08) 8298 8878 **OPEN** Not
WINEMAKER Contract **EST.** 1999
PRODUCT RANGE Chardonnay, Cabernet Sauvignon.
SUMMARY This is a virtual winery run by Gerald Lopez, with chardonnay and cabernet sauvignon contract-grown and contract-made; there are no local sales, only exports to the US, France and Japan.

Cambewarra Estate ★★★☆

520 Illaroo Road, Cambewarra, NSW 2540 **REGION** Shoalhaven Coast
T (02) 4446 0170 **F** (02) 4446 0170 **OPEN** Thurs–Sun and public and school holidays 10–5
WINEMAKER Tamburlaine (Contract) **EST.** 1991 **CASES** 3500
PRODUCT RANGE ($15.50–36 CD) Amanda Verdelho, Unwooded Chardonnay, John Chardonnay, Botrytis Chardonnay, Sparkling Chambourcin, Petit Rouge, Michael Chambourcin, Cabernet Sauvignon, Vintage Port.
SUMMARY Geoffrey and Louise Cole founded Cambewarra Estate near the Shoalhaven River on the central southern coast of New South Wales, with contract winemaking competently carried out (a considerable distance away) at Tamburlaine Winery in the Hunter Valley. Cambewarra continues to produce attractive wines which have had significant success in wine shows.

ᵀᵀᵀᵀ **John Chardonnay 2003** Clean, fresh stone fruit, melon and citrus; airbrush of oak; good length. **RATING** 89 **DRINK** Now $20
Michael Chambourcin 2002 Holding hue well; a nice basket of red and dark berry fruits of every description; clean, soft finish. **RATING** 89 **DRINK** 2008 $21
Cabernet Sauvignon 2001 Tangy blackcurrant, leaf, mint and herb; fine tannins; belies 13.5 degrees alcohol. **RATING** 87 **DRINK** 2009 $29.50

ᵀᵀᵀ **Amanda Verdelho 2003 RATING** 83 $19

Camden Estate Vineyards NR

172 Macarthur Road, Spring Farm, NSW 2570 **REGION** Sydney Basin
T 0414 913 089 **F** (02) 4568 0110 **OPEN** Not
WINEMAKER Evans Wine Company **EST.** 1975 **CASES** 800
PRODUCT RANGE ($12–16 R) Chardonnay.
SUMMARY Camden Estate Vineyards was originally known as Bridge Farm Wines when it was established by Norman Hanckel. The 17 hectares of chardonnay he planted in the 1970s was one of the largest single plantings in Australia at the time, if not the largest. Over the years, most of the grapes were sold to other producers, various estate labels appearing and then disappearing in relatively short order. The grapes are now sold to the Evans Wine Company, which makes and distributes the wine from the vineyard under the Camden Park label.

Campbells ★★★★★

Murray Valley Highway, Rutherglen, Vic 3685 **REGION** Rutherglen
T (02) 6032 9458 **F** (02) 6032 9870 **OPEN** Mon–Sat 9–5, Sun 10–5
WINEMAKER Colin Campbell **EST.** 1870 **CASES** 60 000
PRODUCT RANGE ($9–94 CD) A range of table wines, with Bobbie Burns and The Barley Durif at the top; Muscats and Tokays in Classic, Grand and Rare Rutherglen Classification hierarchy.
SUMMARY A wide range of table and fortified wines of ascending quality and price, which are always honest; as so often happens in this part of the world, the fortified wines are the best, with the extremely elegant Isabella Rare Tokay and Merchant Prince Rare Muscat at the top of the tree; the winery rating is for the fortified wines. A feature of the cellar door is an extensive range of back vintage releases of small parcels of wine not available through any other outlet. National distribution through Red+White; exports to the UK, the US, Canada and New Zealand.

ᵀᵀᵀᵀᵀ **Isabella Rare Rutherglen Tokay NV** Very deep olive-brown; broodingly complex, deep and concentrated aromas, then layer upon layer of flavour in the mouth. Incredibly intense and complex, with varietal tea leaf/muscadelle fruit continuity. **RATING** 97 **DRINK** Now $94
Grand Rutherglen Tokay NV Deep mahogany, olive rim. An intensely complex bouquet, with hints of smoke, abundant rancio. Glorious malty, tea leaf flavours linger long in the mouth; great style and balance. **RATING** 95 **DRINK** Now
Merchant Prince Rare Rutherglen Muscat NV Dark brown, with olive-green on the rim; particularly fragrant, with essencey, raisiny fruit; supple, smooth and intense wine floods every corner of the mouth, but retains elegance, and continues the house style to perfection. **RATING** 95 **DRINK** Now $94

ᵧᵧᵧᵧ **Classic Rutherglen Tokay NV** Medium brown; a complex bouquet with dried muscadelle fruit; deliciously idiosyncratic. The faintly smoky palate has power and depth, again with dried muscadelle grapes reflecting the bouquet. **RATING** 93 **DRINK** Now $ 34.60
Grand Rutherglen Muscat NV Full olive-brown; highly aromatic; a rich and complex palate is silky smooth, supple and long, the raisiny fruit perfectly balanced by the clean, lingering acid (and spirit) cut on the finish. **RATING** 93 **DRINK** Now
Classic Rutherglen Muscat NV Spicy/raisiny complexity starting to build; in typical Campbells style, lively, clearly articulated, with good balance and length. **RATING** 92 **DRINK** Now $ 34.60
Rutherglen Tokay NV Bright, light golden-brown; classic mix of tea leaf and butterscotch aromas lead into an elegant wine which dances in the mouth; has balance and length. **RATING** 92 **DRINK** Now $ 16.70
Rutherglen Muscat NV Bright, clear tawny-gold; a highly aromatic bouquet, spicy and grapey, is mirrored precisely on the palate, which has nigh on perfect balance. **RATING** 90 **DRINK** Now $ 16.70

ᵧᵧᵧᵧ **Bobbie Burns Shiraz 2002** Very ripe plum, prune and blackberry flavours; fruit-driven, with a relatively soft finish; departing twitch of alcohol. **RATING** 89 **DRINK** 2010 $ 18.80

ᵧᵧᵧ **Chardonnay 2003** **RATING** 83 $ 13.30
Bobbie Burns Shiraz 2001 **RATING** 83 $ 18.80
The Barkly Durif 2001 **RATING** 83 **DRINK** 2010 $ 39
Shiraz Durif Cabernet Sauvignon 2001 **RATING** 81 $ 15

Camyr Allyn Wines ★★★☆

Camyr Allyn North, Allyn River Road, East Gresford, NSW 2311 **REGION** Upper Hunter Valley
T (02) 4938 9576 **F** (02) 4938 9576 **OPEN** 7 days 10–5
WINEMAKER Geoff Broadfield, James Evers **EST.** 1999 **CASES** 3000
PRODUCT RANGE ($16–20 CD) Verdelho, Rose, Sparkling Shiraz, Shiraz, Merlot.
SUMMARY John and Judy Evers purchased the property known as Camyr Allyn North in 1997, and immediately set about planting 1.7 hectares of verdelho, 1.4 hectares of merlot and 1.3 hectares of shiraz. The wines are made at the new Northern Hunter winery at East Gresford by resident winemaker Geoff Broadfield and the owner's son, James Evers, who worked for Mildara Blass in Coonawarra for some time. The promotion and packaging of the wines is innovative and stylish.

ᵧᵧᵧᵧ **Merlot 2002** Pleasantly savoury, with obvious varietal character; earth, olive and red berry; a surprise. **RATING** 88 **DRINK** 2009 $ 18.50
Shiraz 2002 Light to medium-bodied; regional earthy/spicy style; good savoury tannins. **RATING** 87 **DRINK** 2008 $ 18.50
Sparkling Shiraz 2002 Made in the 'modern' dry style using a light base which avoids the necessity for residual sugar to balance the phenolics. **RATING** 87 **DRINK** 2008 $ 20

ᵧᵧᵧᵧ **Rose 2003** **RATING** 85 **DRINK** Now $ 16

ᵧᵧᵧ **Verdelho 2003** **RATING** 83 $ 18

Candlebark Hill ★★★★

Fordes Lane, Kyneton, Vic 3444 **REGION** Macedon Ranges
T (03) 9836 2712 **F** (03) 9836 2712 **OPEN** By appointment
WINEMAKER David Forster, Vincent Lakey, Llew Knight (Consultant) **EST.** 1987 **CASES** 600
PRODUCT RANGE ($25–49 CD) Chardonnay, Pinot Noir, Cabernet Merlot, Cabernet Shiraz; Reserve Pinot Noir, Cabernet Merlot.
SUMMARY Candlebark Hill has been established by David Forster on the northern end of the Macedon Ranges, and enjoys magnificent views over the central Victorian countryside north of the Great Dividing Range. The vineyard is planted to pinot noir (1.5 hectares) together with 1 hectare each of chardonnay and the three main Bordeaux varieties, complete with 0.5 hectare of shiraz and malbec. The Reserve Pinot Noir is especially meritorious.

ΨΨΨΨΨ **Reserve Pinot Noir 2000** Excellent colour; powerful, intense; cherry and plum fruit; good balance and length. RATING 94 DRINK 2010 $ 35

ΨΨΨΨΫ **Pinot Noir 2000** Intense and complex; savoury/cherry/spicy aromas and flavours. Developing very well. RATING 90 DRINK 2007 $ 29

ΨΨΨΫ **Cabernet Merlot 2001** RATING 85 DRINK 2008 $ 25

ΨΨΨ **Pinot Noir 2002** RATING 83 $ 29

Cannibal Creek Vineyard ★★★★

260 Tynong North Road, Tynong North, Vic 3813 REGION Gippsland
T (03) 5942 8380 F (03) 5942 8202 OPEN 7 days 11–5
WINEMAKER Patrick Hardiker EST. 1997 CASES 1600
PRODUCT RANGE ($16–28 CD) Sauvignon Blanc, Chardonnay, Chardonnay, Pinot Noir, Merlot, Cabernet Sauvignon.
SUMMARY The Hardiker family moved to Tynong North in 1988, initially only grazing beef cattle, but aware of the viticultural potential of the sandy clay loam and bleached sub-surface soils weathered from the granite foothills of Tynong North. Plantings began in 1997, using organic cultivation methods, and by 1999 the vines were already producing grapes. The family decided to make their own wine, and a heritage-style shed built from locally milled timber has been converted into a winery and small cellar-door facility.

ΨΨΨΨΫ **Chardonnay 2002** Attractive nectarine, melon and citrus mix; excellent balance and length; minimal oak. RATING 92 DRINK 2007 $ 20
Sauvignon Blanc 2003 Spotlessly clean; appealing range of gooseberry, kiwi fruit and passionfruit; even flow. RATING 90 DRINK Now $ 16

ΨΨΨΨ **Merlot 2002** Spice, redcurrant and plum aromas; more savoury/briary edges on the palate; sweet tannins. RATING 87 DRINK 2010 $ 28
Cabernet Sauvignon 2002 Light to medium-bodied; some savoury characters; blackcurrant and a touch of raspberry on the finish. RATING 87 DRINK 2011 $ 28

Canobolas-Smith ★★★

Boree Lane, off Cargo Road, Lidster via Orange, NSW 2800 REGION Orange
T (02) 6365 6113 F (02) 6365 6113 OPEN Weekends, public holidays 11–5
WINEMAKER Murray Smith EST. 1986 CASES 2000
PRODUCT RANGE ($10–35 CD) Highland Chardonnay, Chardonnay, Shine Methode Champenoise, Shine Botrytis Chardonnay, Highland Red, Pinot Noir, Chambourcin Cabernet, Catombal Range, Alchemy (Cabernet blend), Cabernets.
SUMMARY Canobolas-Smith has established itself as one of the leading Orange district wineries with its distinctive blue wrap-around labels. Much of the wine is sold through the cellar door, which is well worth a visit. Exports to the US and Asia.

Canonbah Bridge ★★★☆

Merryanbone Station, Warren, NSW 2824 REGION Western Plains Zone
T (02) 6833 9966 F (02) 6833 9980 OPEN Not
WINEMAKER John Hordern (Contract) EST. 1999 CASES 10 000
PRODUCT RANGE ($15–30 ML) Varietal wines in three price tiers: Canonbah Bridge Reserve at the top, then Canonbah Bridge, followed by Ram's Leap.
SUMMARY If you ever wondered why the Central Western New South Wales Zone was the largest in New South Wales, Canonbah Bridge provides an answer. The 29-hectare vineyard has been established by Shane McLaughlin on the very large Merryanbone Station, a Merino sheep stud which has been in the family for four generations. If you head out of Dubbo towards Bourke, you will pass by Warren, northwest of Dubbo. The wines are contract-made by John Hordern, and in some instances incorporate grapes grown in McLaren Vale and elsewhere; these are typically released under the Ram's Leap second label. The wines are available in Australia by mail order and in select Sydney restaurants and wine shops; the majority is exported to the US, the UK, Canada, Malaysia and Hong Kong.

ŸŸŸŸ **Drought Reserve Shiraz 2001** Complex wild herbs (Provence) and spice; overall, savoury, medium-bodied; good length. **RATING** 89 **DRINK** 2011 $ 30
Semillon Sauvignon Blanc 2002 Well constructed and balanced; clean, complex mix of gooseberry and lime/lemon; more weight, less elegance. **RATING** 88 **DRINK** Now $ 20
Ram's Leap Semillon Sauvignon Blanc 2002 Aromatic, clean, zesty aromas; clearly articulated fruit; a blend of Western Plains and Orange material. **RATING** 88 **DRINK** 2007 $ 15

ŸŸŸŸ **Ram's Leap Merlot 2002 RATING** 86 **DRINK** 2010 $ 15
Ram's Leap Shiraz 2002 RATING 85 **DRINK** 2008 $ 15

ŸŸŸ **Ram's Leap Chardonnay 2002 RATING** 83 $ 15

Canungra Valley Vineyards   NR

Lamington National Park Road, Canungra Valley, Qld 4275 **REGION** Queensland Coastal
T (07) 5543 4011 **F** (07) 5543 4162 **OPEN** 7 days 10–5
WINEMAKER Stuart Pierce, Mark Davidson (Contract) **EST.** 1997 **CASES** 5000
PRODUCT RANGE ($13.50–30 CD) Picnic range at the bottom; then Platypus Play; then the Reserve range of O'Reilly varietals and sundry fortifieds.
SUMMARY Canungra Valley Vineyards has been established in the hinterland of the Gold Coast with a clear focus on broad-based tourism. Eight hectares of vines have been established around the 19th-century homestead (relocated to the site from its original position in Warwick), but these provide only a small part of the wine offered for sale. In deference to the climate, 70 per cent of the estate plantings is chambourcin, the rain and mildew-resistant hybrid, the remainder being semillon. All the wine being offered at this early stage has been purchased from other winemakers. Canungra Valley offers a great deal of natural beauty for the general tourist.

🐌 Cape Barren Wines   ★★★★☆

Lot 20 Little Road, Willunga, SA 5172 **REGION** McLaren Vale
T (08) 8556 4374 **F** (08) 8556 4364 **OPEN** By appointment
WINEMAKER Brian Light (Contract) **EST.** 1999 **CASES** 1600
PRODUCT RANGE ($32.95 R) Old Vine Shiraz.
SUMMARY Lifelong friends and vignerons Peter Matthews and Brian Ledgard joined forces in 1999 to create Cape Barren Wines. It is a single-vineyard, one-wine business, sourced from 4 hectares of 70-year-old shiraz vines at Blewitt Springs. It comes as no surprise that the 2002 Old Vine Shiraz won a gold medal at its first wine show entry, at the all-important local derby of the McLaren Vale Wine Show.

ŸŸŸŸŸ **Old Vine Shiraz 2002** Archetypal McLaren Vale style; lashings of dark chocolate wrapped around a core of blackberry fruit; 15 months in French and American oak barely shows.
RATING 92 **DRINK** 2022 $ 32.95

Cape Bouvard   NR

Mount John Road, Mandurah, WA 6210 **REGION** Peel
T (08) 9739 1360 **F** (08) 9739 1360 **OPEN** 7 days 10–5 **EST.** 1990 **CASES** 2000
PRODUCT RANGE ($13–20 CD) Chenin Blanc, Dry White, Tuart Shiraz, Cabernet Sauvignon, Port.
SUMMARY While it continues in operation after its sale in 2003, there have been recent changes, the details of which are still unavailable.

Cape d'Estaing   NR

PO Box 214, Kingscote, Kangaroo Island, SA 5223 **REGION** Kangaroo Island
T (08) 8383 6299 **F** (08) 8383 6299 **OPEN** Not
WINEMAKER Mike Farmilo (Contract), Robin Moody **EST.** 1994 **CASES** 4000
PRODUCT RANGE Shiraz, Sparkling Shiraz, Shiraz Cabernet, Cabernet.
SUMMARY Graham and Jude Allison, Alan and Ann Byers, Marg and Wayne Conaghty and Robin and Heather Moody have established 9 hectares of cabernet sauvignon and shiraz near Wisanger on

Kangaroo Island. Robin Moody was a long-serving senior employee of Southcorp, with a broad knowledge of all aspects of grape growing and winemaking. It's he who joins with contract winemaker Mark Farmilo each year. There is limited retail distribution in Adelaide, and exports to US. The wines are also available by mail order.

Cape Grace ★★★★☆

Fifty One Road, Cowaramup, WA 6284 **REGION** Margaret River
T (08) 9755 5669 **F** (08) 9755 5668 **OPEN** 7 days 10–5
WINEMAKER Robert Karri-Davies, Mark Messenger (Consultant) **EST.** 1996 **CASES** 1500
PRODUCT RANGE ($16–38 CD) Chenin Blanc, Chardonnay, Shiraz, Cabernet Sauvignon.
SUMMARY Cape Grace Wines can trace its history back to 1875, when timber baron MC Davies settled at Karridale, building the Leeuwin lighthouse and founding the township of Margaret River. One hundred and twenty years later, Robert and Karen Karri-Davies planted just under 6 hectares of vineyard to chardonnay, shiraz and cabernet sauvignon, with smaller amounts of merlot, semillon and chenin blanc. They make a good team: Robert is a self-taught viticulturist, keeping up to date through reading and field seminars. Karen Karri-Davies has over 15 years of international sales and marketing experience in the hospitality industry in Canada, Australia and Indonesia. Winemaking is carried out on the property under the direction of consultant Mark Messenger, a veteran of the Margaret River region, with over 9 years' experience at Cape Mentelle and 3 years at Juniper Estate.

ŶŶŶŶ♀ **Cabernet Sauvignon 2002** Deeply coloured; luscious, ripe blackcurrant and redcurrant fruit; powerful tannins; needs time, which it will repay. **RATING** 93 **DRINK** 2017 $ 38
Shiraz 2002 Fresh, fragrant red fruits, quite different from the 2001; medium-bodied; excellent fruit/oak balance; fine, soft tannins. **RATING** 91 **DRINK** 2012 $ 29

ŶŶŶŶ **Chardonnay 2002** Light to medium-bodied; well-balanced melon/nectarine fruit and oak; will develop well. **RATING** 89 **DRINK** 2007 $ 29

Cape Horn Vineyard ★★★

Echuca–Picola Road, Kanyapella, Vic 3564 **REGION** Goulburn Valley
T (03) 5480 6013 **F** (03) 5480 6013 **OPEN** 7 days 10.30–5
WINEMAKER John Ellis (Contract) **EST.** 1993 **CASES** 1500
PRODUCT RANGE ($15–29 CD) Marsanne, Chardonnay, Sparkling Durif Shiraz, Rose, Shiraz, Durif, Cabernet Sauvignon.
SUMMARY The unusual name comes from a bend in the Murray River which was considered by the riverboat owners of the 19th century to resemble Cape Horn, a resemblance now depicted on the wine label. The property was acquired by Echuca GP Dr Sue Harrison and her schoolteacher husband Ian in 1993. Ian Harrison has progressively established their 9-hectare vineyard, planted to chardonnay, shiraz, zinfandel, cabernet sauvignon, marsanne and durif.

ŶŶŶŶ **Echuca Durif 2001** Still with vivid, bright, deep purple colour; fresh, concentrated fruit; needs a decade or more. **RATING** 89 **DRINK** 2016 $ 21
Echuca Marsanne 2003 Honeysuckle, spiced pear and baked apple flavours; fluffy finish. **RATING** 87 **DRINK** Now $ 18

ŶŶŶ♀ **Echuca Cabernet Sauvignon 2001** **RATING** 86 **DRINK** 2008 $ 19
Echuca Chardonnay 2002 **RATING** 84 **DRINK** Now $ 18

ŶŶŶ **Echuca Rose 2003** **RATING** 83 $ 15
Echuca Shiraz 2001 **RATING** 83 $ 19

Cape Jaffa Wines ★★★★

Limestone Coast Road, Cape Jaffa, SA 5276 **REGION** Mount Benson
T (08) 8768 5053 **F** (08) 8768 5040 **OPEN** 7 days 10–5
WINEMAKER Derek Hooper **EST.** 1993 **CASES** 18 000
PRODUCT RANGE ($19–35 CD) Unwooded Chardonnay (McLaren Vale), Semillon Sauvignon Blanc, Sauvignon Blanc, Unwooded Chardonnay, Barrel Fermented Chardonnay (Mount Benson and Padthaway), Shiraz (McLaren Vale), Siberia Shiraz, Cabernet Sauvignon (Mount Benson), Brocks Reef Cabernet Merlot.

SUMMARY Cape Jaffa is the first of the Mount Benson wineries to come into production, albeit with most of the initial releases coming from other regions. Ultimately all of the wines will come from the substantial estate plantings of 25 hectares, which include the four major Bordeaux red varieties, as well as shiraz, chardonnay, sauvignon blanc and semillon. It is a joint venture between the Hooper and Fowler families, and the winery (built of local paddock rock) has been designed to allow eventual expansion to 1000 tonnes, or 70 000 cases. Exports to the UK, the US, China, Hong Kong, Singapore, the Philippines and New Zealand.

ŢŢŢŢŢ **Sauvignon Blanc 2003** Clean, fresh, tight mineral and green pea aromas and flavours; lingering, bone-dry finish. **RATING** 90 **DRINK** 2007 $ 19

ŢŢŢŢ **Semillon Sauvignon Blanc 2003** Crisp, tight, grassy mineral flavours; light-bodied, but good length and finish. **RATING** 89 **DRINK** 2007 $ 19
Mount Benson Shiraz 2000 Complex gamey/blackberry/licorice/leather aromas flow through to a smooth, blackberry, raspberry and spice palate. Excellent value. **RATING** 89 **DRINK** 2012 $ 34.95
Mount Benson Shiraz 2001 Spicy black pepper and black cherry; lively and fresh; fruit-driven. **RATING** 87 **DRINK** 2010 $ 34.95

ŢŢŢŢ **Unwooded Chardonnay 2003** **RATING** 84 **DRINK** Now $ 19
Mount Benson Cabernet Sauvignon 2001 **RATING** 84 **DRINK** 2007 $ 23

Capel Vale ★★★★★

Lot 5 Stirling Estate, Mallokup Road, Capel, WA 6271 **REGION** Geographe
T (08) 9727 1986 **F** (08) 9727 1904 **OPEN** Cellar door and restaurant 7 days 10–4
WINEMAKER Rebecca Catlin **EST.** 1979 **CASES** 100 000
PRODUCT RANGE ($12.50–50 CD) A carefully structured hierarchy of varietals with the CV range at the bottom; then the Capel Vale Fine Dining range of all major varietals; at the top, Connoisseur range of Whispering Hill Riesling, Seven Day Road Sauvignon Blanc, Frederick Chardonnay, Kinnaird Shiraz, Howecroft Merlot, Collector's Release Pwakenback Shiraz, Middleton Shiraz and Whispering Hill Shiraz.
SUMMARY Capel Vale continues to expand its viticultural empire, its contract-grape sources and its marketing, the last through the introduction of a series of vineyard, or similarly named, super-premium wines. Against the run of play, the most successful of these super-premiums are the red wines, for it was the Riesling which first captured attention. The strong marketing focus the company has always had is driven by its indefatigable owner, Dr Peter Pratten, who has developed export markets throughout Europe, Asia and the US.

ŢŢŢŢŢ **Kinnaird Shiraz 2002** Super-ripe plum, prune and dark chocolate; sumptuous and rich; silky tannins. **RATING** 94 **DRINK** 2017 $ 50
Howecroft Merlot 2002 A classy wine from start to finish; savoury dark fruits; fine-grained, lingering tannins; velvet glove stuff. **RATING** 94 **DRINK** 2015 $ 50

ŢŢŢŢ **Special Collector's Release Pwakenbak Shiraz 2002** Excellent red-purple; the richest and deepest of the three Special Collector's Shirazs, all sourced from the Whispering Vineyard; plummy/blackberry fruit; fine, ripe tannins. **RATING** 91 **DRINK** 2012 $ 33.50
Whispering Hill Riesling 2003 Spotlessly clean aromatic, mineral and citrus; well balanced; appealing finish. **RATING** 90 **DRINK** 2008 $ 24

ŢŢŢŢ **Chardonnay 2001** Complex array of fig, cashew and melon; rich, mouthfilling, layered yet smooth, creamy. **RATING** 89 **DRINK** Now $ 23
Howecroft Merlot 2001 Cedary, sexy oak handling; good texture and balance; twists of earth and berry. **RATING** 89 **DRINK** 2011 $ 50

ŢŢŢŢ **Special Cellar Release Pinot Noir 2001** **RATING** 86 **DRINK** Now $ 30
CV Shiraz 2001 **RATING** 85 **DRINK** 2008 $ 15
Verdelho 2003 **RATING** 84 **DRINK** Now $ 17

Cape Mentelle ★★★★

Off Wallcliffe Road, Margaret River, WA 6285 **REGION** Margaret River
T (08) 9757 0888 **F** (08) 9757 3233 **OPEN** 7 days 10–4.30
WINEMAKER John Durham, Eloise Jervis, Simon Burnell **EST.** 1970 **CASES** 55 000
PRODUCT RANGE ($15.35–60 R) Semillon Sauvignon Blanc, Sauvignon Blanc Semillon Wallcliffe Reserve, Georgiana, Marmaduke, Chardonnay, Shiraz, Zinfandel, Cabernet Merlot Trinders Vineyard, Cabernet Sauvignon.
SUMMARY After more than 20 years at the helm, David Hohnen has retired to follow other wine interests. The Chardonnay and Semillon Sauvignon Blanc are among Australia's best, the potent Shiraz usually superb, and the berry/spicy Zinfandel makes one wonder why this grape is not as widespread in Australia as it is in California. Part of the LVMH (Louis Vuitton Möet Hennessy) group, and since the advent of Dr Tony Jordan as Australasian CEO there has been a concerted and successful campaign to rid the winery of the brettanomyces infection, which particularly affected the Cabernet Sauvignon. Exports to all the major markets.

ȲȲȲȲȲ **Chardonnay 2002** Complex array of fig, cashew and melon; rich, mouthfilling, layered yet smooth, creamy. **RATING** 94 **DRINK** 2009 $ 36.50

ȲȲȲȲȲ **Shiraz 2002** Deep colour; powerful, concentrated, clean blackberry fruit; good structure and tannin texture. **RATING** 92 **DRINK** 2017 $ 32.40

ȲȲȲȲ **Zinfandel 2002** Very ripe prune, spice and black plums; massive mouthfeel; Robert Parker, here we come. **RATING** 89 **DRINK** 2008 $ 38.20
Semillon Sauvignon Blanc 2003 Tight and youthful, with semillon doing much of the talking; good length and persistent finish; subliminal oak. **RATING** 88 **DRINK** 2009 $ 22.40
Trinders Vineyard Cabernet Merlot 2002 Medium-bodied; sweet red and black fruits with savoury edges; positive oak use. **RATING** 87 **DRINK** 2010 $ 28.25

ȲȲȲȲ **Marmaduke Shiraz Grenache Mataro 2002** **RATING** 86 **DRINK** 2007 $ 15.35

Capercaillie ★★★★

Londons Road, Lovedale, NSW 2325 **REGION** Lower Hunter Valley
T (02) 4990 2904 **F** (02) 4991 1886 **OPEN** Mon–Sat 9–5, Sun 10–5
WINEMAKER Alasdair Sutherland **EST.** 1995 **CASES** 6000
PRODUCT RANGE ($17–40 CD) Watervale Riesling, Hunter Valley Gewurztraminer, Hunter Valley Semillon, Orange Highlands Sauvignon Blanc, Hunter Valley Chardonnay, Dessert Chardonnay, C Sparkling Red, Hunter Valley Rose, Hunter Valley Chambourcin, The Ghillie Shiraz, Ceilidh Shiraz, Hunter Valley Shiraz, Orange Highlands Merlot, The Clan (Cabernet Sauvignon Merlot Cabernet Franc).
SUMMARY The former Dawson Estate, now run by Hunter Valley veteran Alasdair Sutherland (no relation to Neil Sutherland of Sutherland Estate). The Capercaillie wines are very well made, with generous flavour. Following the example of Brokenwood, its fruit sources are spread across southeastern Australia. The wines are exported to the UK and New Zealand.

ȲȲȲȲȲ **The Ghillie Shiraz 2002** Sweet dark plum, spice and a touch of regional leather; soft, quite velvety mouthfeel; very good finish. **RATING** 93 **DRINK** 2012 $ 40
Hunter Valley Semillon 2003 Strong green-yellow; long and intense herb, grass and mineral; lots of character and length. Volatility not a problem for me. **RATING** 90 **DRINK** 2013 $ 19

ȲȲȲȲ **Orange Highlands Merlot 2002** Fragrant red berry, raspberry and mint aromas; light to medium-bodied, the oak not overplayed. **RATING** 87 **DRINK** 2009 $ 27

ȲȲȲȲ **Dessert Style Gewurztraminer 2003** **RATING** 86 **DRINK** Now $ 18
Hunter Valley Gewurztraminer 2003 **RATING** 85 **DRINK** Now $ 19
Hunter Valley Rose 2003 **RATING** 85 **DRINK** Now $ 18
Hunter Valley Chambourcin 2002 **RATING** 85 **DRINK** Now $ 21
Hunter Valley Chardonnay 2003 **RATING** 84 **DRINK** Now $ 19
Hunter Valley Shiraz 1998 **RATING** 84 **DRINK** 2008 $ 50

ȲȲȲ **Sparkling Sauvignon Blanc 2003** **RATING** 83 $ 25

Capogreco Winery Estate

NR

Riverside Avenue, South Mildura, Vic 3500 **REGION** Murray Darling
T (03) 5022 1431 **F** (03) 5022 1431 **OPEN** Mon–Sat 10–5
WINEMAKER Bruno Capogreco **EST.** 1976
PRODUCT RANGE ($8–12 CD) Riesling, Moselle, Shiraz Mataro, Cabernet Sauvignon, Claret, Rose, fortifieds.
SUMMARY Italian-owned and run, the wines are a blend of Italian and Australian Riverland influences. The estate has 13 hectares of chardonnay, 14 hectares of shiraz and 6 hectares of cabernet sauvignon, but also purchases other varieties.

Captains Creek Organic Wines

NR

160 Mays Road, Blampied, Vic 3364 **REGION** Ballarat
T (03) 5345 7408 **F** (03) 5345 7408 **OPEN** By appointment
WINEMAKER Alan Cooper, Norman Latta, David Cowburn **EST.** 1994 **CASES** 400
PRODUCT RANGE ($23–25 ML) Unwooded Chardonnay, Chardonnay, Pinot Noir.
SUMMARY Doug and Carolyn May are third-generation farmers at the Captains Creek property, and have been conducting the business for over 20 years without using any chemicals. When they began their establishment of the vineyard in 1994, with 1 hectare each of chardonnay and pinot noir, they resolved to go down the same path, eschewing the use of insecticides or systematic fungicides, instead using preventive spray programs of copper and sulphur. Thermal flame weeding and beneficial predatory insects control weeds and mites. There is also a neat historical connection, as Blampied takes its name from 20-year-old Anne-Marie Blampied and her 15-year-old brother Emille, who emigrated from Lorraine in France in 1853, lured by gold. Anne-Marie married Jean-Pierre Trouette, another Frenchman, and Trouette and Blampied were the first to plant vines in the Great Western region, in 1858.

Captain's Paddock

NR

18 Millers Road, Kingaroy, Qld 4610 **REGION** South Burnett
T (07) 4162 4534 **F** (07) 4162 4502 **OPEN** 7 days 10–5
WINEMAKER Ross Whitford **EST.** 1995 **CASES** 2000
PRODUCT RANGE ($10–16 CD) Chardonnay, Captain's White, Shiraz, Shiraz Cabernet Sauvignon Merlot, Captain's Red (semi-sweet).
SUMMARY Don and Judy McCallum planted the first hectare of vineyard in 1995, followed by a further 3 hectares in 1996, focusing on shiraz and chardonnay. It is a family affair; the mudbrick cellar door building was made with bricks crafted by Don McCallum, and Judy's screen printing adorns the tables and chairs and printed linen for sale to the public. Their two children are both sculptors, with works on display at the winery. Captain's Paddock is fully licensed, offering either light platters or full dishes incorporating local produce. Meals are served either inside or alfresco in the courtyard, with its views over the Booie Ranges.

Carabooda Estate

NR

297 Carabooda Road, Carabooda, WA 6033 **REGION** Swan District
T (08) 9407 5283 **F** (08) 9407 5283 **OPEN** 7 days 10–6
WINEMAKER Terry Ord **EST.** 1989 **CASES** 1500
PRODUCT RANGE ($16–25 CD) Sauvignon Blanc, Semillon Sauvignon Blanc, Sweet Chenin, Shiraz, Cabernet Shiraz, Cabernet Sauvignon, Vintage Port.
SUMMARY 1989 is the year of establishment given by Terry Ord, but it might as well have been 1979 (when he made his first wine) or 1981 (when he and wife Simonne planted their first vines). It has been a slowly, slowly exercise, with production from the 3 hectares of estate plantings now supplemented by purchased grapes, the first public release not being made until mid-1994. Since that time production has risen significantly.

Carbunup Crest Vineyard

★★★★

PO Box 235, Busselton, WA 6280 **REGION** Margaret River
T (08) 9754 2618 **F** (08) 9754 2618 **OPEN** Not
WINEMAKER Flying Fish Cove **EST.** 1998 **CASES** 2000

PRODUCT RANGE ($7.50–20 ML) Cella Rage range of Classic White, Chardonnay Verdelho, Chardonnay, Shiraz, Merlot, Cabernet Merlot, Cabernet Sauvignon.

SUMMARY Carbunup Crest is operated by three local families, with Kris Meares managing the business. Initially it operated as a grapevine rootling nursery, but it has gradually converted to grape growing and winemaking. There are 6 hectares of vineyard, all of which are all now in production, but with plans to extend the plantings to 20 hectares in the years ahead (the property is 53 hectares in total). The contract-made wines are of great value, even if the names are kitschy. This is certainly a producer to watch.

🍷🍷🍷🍷 **Cella Rage Shiraz 2002** Brimming with plum, blackberry, prune, spice and chocolate, the tannins are soft, oak minimal. **RATING** 93 **DRINK** 2011 $ 12
Cella Rage Cabernet Sauvignon Merlot 2002 Clean, medium-bodied; appealing red fruits; soft texture and structure; clever winemaking. **RATING** 90 **DRINK** 2007 $ 14.50

🍷🍷🍷 **Cella Rage Merlot Cabernet 2002 RATING** 86 **DRINK** 2007 $ 14.50
Cella Rage Cabernet Sauvignon 2002 RATING 86 **DRINK** 2008 $ 12.25
Cella Rage Chardonnay 2003 RATING 85 **DRINK** Now $ 13.75
Cella Rage Classic White 2003 RATING 84 **DRINK** Now $ 9.90

Cardinham Estate

Main North Road, Stanley Flat, SA 5453 **REGION** Clare Valley
T (08) 8842 1944 **F** (08) 8842 1955 **OPEN** 7 days 10–5
WINEMAKER Smith John Wine Co. **EST.** 1980 **CASES** 3000
PRODUCT RANGE ($18–30 CD) Clare Valley Riesling, Chardonnay, Sangiovese, Stradbrooke Shiraz, Cabernet Merlot, Cabernet Sauvignon.
SUMMARY The Smith family has progressively increased the vineyard size to its present level of 60 hectares, the largest plantings being of cabernet sauvignon (23 hectares), shiraz (15 hectares) and riesling (10.5 hectares). It entered into a grape supply contract with Wolf Blass, which led to an association with then Quelltaler winemaker Stephen John. After 15 years supplying Wolf Blass and others, Stephen John and the Smiths formed the Smith John Wine Company in 1999. Its purpose is to provide contract winemaking services to small producers in the valley, and to supply bulk wine to others. The development of the Cardinham brand is a small but important part of the business. This has seen production rise to 3000 cases, with the three staples of Riesling, Cabernet Merlot and Stradbroke Shiraz available from the winery and through retail distribution, and additional wines made in small volume available only at the cellar door and by mail order. Exports to Singapore.

🍷🍷🍷🍷🍷 **Stradbrooke Shiraz 2002** Great colour; luscious, velvety, smooth dark plum and blackberry fruit has soaked up the oak; very good balance; great value. **RATING** 94 **DRINK** 2015 $ 20

🍷🍷🍷🍷 **Clare Valley Riesling 2003** Aromatic and flowery lime blossom, spice and a hint of apple; a fresh and lively palate, and a long, lingering finish. Screwcap. **RATING** 93 **DRINK** 2013 $ 18
Cabernet Merlot 2002 High-toned, vibrant cassis/berry fruit; fresh finish, tannins and acidity; still to settle down; pointed as it is now. **RATING** 90 **DRINK** 2012 $ 20

🍷🍷🍷 **Chardonnay 2002 RATING** 86 **DRINK** Now $ 18

Cargo Road Wines NR

Cargo Road, Orange, NSW 2800 **REGION** Orange
T (02) 6365 6100 **F** (02) 6365 6001 **OPEN** Weekends and public holidays 11–5, or by appointment
WINEMAKER James Sweetapple **EST.** 1983 **CASES** 1800
PRODUCT RANGE ($14–25 CD) Riesling, Gewurztraminer, Sauvignon Blanc, Merlot, Zinfandel, Cabernet Merlot.
SUMMARY Originally called The Midas Tree, the vineyard was planted in 1984 by Roseworthy graduate John Swanson. He established a 2.5-hectare vineyard that included zinfandel 15 years ahead of his time. The property was acquired in 1997 by a syndicate, which is expanding the vineyard, particularly zinfandel. Unfortunately, wine samples sent in 2004 were lost in action.

Carilley Estate ★★★☆

Lot 23 Hyem Road, Herne Hill, WA 6056 **REGION** Swan Valley
T (08) 9296 6190 **F** (08) 9296 6190 **OPEN** 7 days 10.30–5
WINEMAKER Rob Marshall **EST.** 1985 **CASES** 2000
PRODUCT RANGE ($8.50–20 R) Chenin Blanc, Chardonnay, Shiraz, Reserve Shiraz, Titian Port.
SUMMARY Doctors Laura and Isavel Carija have 8 hectares of vineyard planted to shiraz, chardonnay, viognier and merlot. Most of the grapes are sold, with only a small proportion made under the Carilley Estate label, with very limited distribution (retail or by mail order). The winery café supplies light Mediterranean food.

Carindale Wines ★★★☆

Palmers Lane, Pokolbin, NSW 2321 **REGION** Lower Hunter Valley
T (02) 4998 7665 **F** (02) 4998 7065 **OPEN** Wed–Mon 10–5
WINEMAKER Brian Walsh (Contract) **EST.** 1996 **CASES** 4000
PRODUCT RANGE ($26.50–31 CD) Chardonnay, Sparkling Chardonnay, Sparkling Merlot, Blackthorn (Cabernet blend), Liqueur Muscat.
SUMMARY Carindale draws upon 2 hectares of chardonnay, 1.2 hectares of cabernet franc and 0.2 hectare of merlot (together with few muscat vines). Exports to Singapore.

▼▼▼▼ **Chardonnay 2000** Attractive bottle-developed characters; smooth, light to medium-bodied and supple; emphatic drink-now style. **RATING** 88 **DRINK** Now $ 21

▼▼▼▽ **Sparkling Merlot NV** **RATING** 86 **DRINK** Now $ 32

Carlei Estate & Green Vineyards ★★★★★

1 Albert Road, Upper Beaconsfield, Vic 3808 **REGION** Yarra Valley
T (03) 5944 4599 **F** (03) 5944 4599 **OPEN** Weekends by appointment
WINEMAKER Sergio Carlei **EST.** 1994 **CASES** 10 000
PRODUCT RANGE ($16–59 ML) The wines are released in two ranges: Carlei Green Vineyards for varietals made from specified regions; and the Carlei Estate wines, which are vineyard-specific and, with one exception, sell for significantly more than the Green Vineyards range.
SUMMARY Carlei Estate & Green Vineyards has come a long way in a little time, with Sergio Carlei graduating from home winemaking in a suburban garage to his own (real) winery in Upper Beaconsfield, which happens to fall just within the boundaries of the Yarra Valley. Along the way Carlei acquired a Bachelor of Wine Science degree from Charles Sturt University, Wagga Wagga. He also established a 2.25-hectare vineyard with organic and biodynamic accreditation adjacent to the Upper Beaconsfield winery. As each vintage has passed, more and more irresistible parcels of quality wine from here, there and everywhere have led to a bewildering but usually excellent array of wines made in quantities as little as 50 cases.

▼▼▼▼▼ **Carlei Estate Yarra Valley Chardonnay 2002** Very complex flavour and structure; intense, tangy citrus and nectarine, hallmark Yarra length. **RATING** 95 **DRINK** 2012 $ 39

▼▼▼▼▽ **Green Vineyards Yarra Valley Chardonnay 2002** Complex aromas suggesting wild yeast and lots of lees contact; long melon and citrus fruit; lingering finish. **RATING** 93 **DRINK** 2010 $ 26
Green Vineyards Central Victoria Shiraz 2002 Dense colour; concentrated, saturated black plum and blackberry; a soft but persistent oak and tannin backdrop. **RATING** 90 **DRINK** 2011 $ 29
Green Vineyards Bendigo Cabernet Sauvignon 2002 Solid, dark, blackberry fruit; hints of prune and chocolate; fruit-driven, then sweet tannin finish. **RATING** 90 **DRINK** 2012 $ 30

▼▼▼▼ **Carlei Estate Yarra Valley Cabernets 2001** Earthy, cedary black fruits; light to medium-bodied; overall savoury, with firm, fine tannins. **RATING** 89 **DRINK** 2011 $ 39
Carlei Estate Tre Rossi 2001 Light to medium-bodied cherry, raspberry, plum and blackberry fruits; subtle oak; 14 degrees alcohol but seems lighter; Heathcote, with an unusual but pleasing spin. **RATING** 89 **DRINK** 2011 $ 49

▼▼▼▽ **Carlei Estate Tre Bianchi 2003** **RATING** 86 **DRINK** Now $ 24

Carn Estate

NR

Eleventh Street, Nichols Point, Vic 3501 **REGION** Murray Darling
T (03) 5024 7393 **F** (03) 5021 2929 **OPEN** 7 days
WINEMAKER Contract **EST.** 1997
PRODUCT RANGE Colombard, Shiraz, Merlot, Cabernet Sauvignon.
SUMMARY Richard Carn has established 9 hectares of colombard, cabernet sauvignon, merlot and shiraz on two vineyard sites, and has the wine contract-made. In a relatively short time, exports to England have been established; the cellar door offers light meals, barbecue and picnic facilities.

Carosa

★★★★

310 Houston Street, Mount Helena, WA 6082 **REGION** Perth Hills
T (08) 9572 1603 **F** (08) 9572 1604 **OPEN** Weekends, holidays 11–5, or by appointment
WINEMAKER James Elson **EST.** 1984 **CASES** 800
PRODUCT RANGE ($15–19 CD) Jessica Semillon, Summer White, Classic Dry White, Chardonnay, Isabella Pinot Noir, Hannah Shiraz, Grenache Shiraz, Lucian Merlot, Cabernet Merlot, Cabernet Sauvignon.
SUMMARY Very limited production and small-scale winemaking result in wines which can only be described as rustic, but which sell readily enough into the local market. Winemaker Jim Elson had extensive eastern Australia winemaking experience (with Seppelt). The wines are sold through the cellar door and by mailing list.

Carpinteri Vineyards

NR

PO Box 61, Nyah, Vic 3594 **REGION** Swan Hill
T (03) 5030 2569 **F** (03) 5030 2680 **OPEN** Not
WINEMAKER Michael Kyberd (Contract) **EST.** 1945 **CASES** 900
PRODUCT RANGE ($50–111 per case) Unwooded Chardonnay, Medium Sweet White, Shiraz, Grenache Mataro, Shiraz Grenache Mataro.
SUMMARY Vince and Con Carpinteri are primarily grape growers, with 30 hectares planted to chardonnay, grenache, malbec, shiraz, mourvedre, black muscat and sultana. A small amount of wine is made under contract by Michael Kyberd at Red Hill Estate in the Mornington Peninsula, and the wines are sold by mail order. The wines are also sold through East Melbourne Cellars.

Casa Fontana

NR

4 Cook Street, Lutana, Tas 7009 **REGION** Southern Tasmania
T (03) 6272 3180 **OPEN** Not
WINEMAKER Mark Fontana, Steve Lubiana (Contract) **EST.** 1994 **CASES** 250
PRODUCT RANGE ($22 ML) Chardonnay, Pinot Noir.
SUMMARY Mark Fontana and his Japanese wife Shige planted their first pinot noir in 1994 and over the following 2 years expanded the vineyard to its present level of 2.6 hectares, 1 hectare each of pinot noir and chardonnay, and 0.6 hectare of riesling. Mark Fontana is a metallurgist with Pasminco and came into grape growing through his love of fine wine.

Casa Freschi

★★★☆

30 Jackson Avenue, Strathalbyn, SA 5255 **REGION** Langhorne Creek
T (08) 8536 4569 **F** (08) 8536 4569 **OPEN** Not
WINEMAKER David Freschi **EST.** 1998 **CASES** 1000
PRODUCT RANGE ($38–58 R) Profondo, La Signora.
SUMMARY David Freschi graduated with a degree in Oenology from Roseworthy in 1991, and spent most of the next decade working overseas in California, Italy and New Zealand, culminating in a senior winemaking position with Corbans in New Zealand in 1997. In 1998 he and his wife decided to trade in the corporate world for a small family-owned winemaking business, with a core of 2.5 hectares of vines established by David Freschi's parents in 1972, and an additional 2 hectares of nebbiolo planted adjacent to the original vineyard. Says David Freschi, 'the names of the wines were chosen to best express the personality of the wines grown in our vineyard, as well as to express our heritage.' Exports to the US, Germany, Switzerland, Singapore and New Zealand.

ŸŸŸŸ **La Signora 2001** In the lifted style seemingly favoured by Casa Freschi; a lively array of red and black fruits, complemented by fine, savoury tannins. **RATING** 89 **DRINK** 2011 $ 38

ŸŸŸŸ **Profondo 2001** **RATING** 86 **DRINK** 2011 $ 58

Casas Wines ★★★★

RMB 236D Rosa Brook Road, Margaret River, WA 6285 **REGION** Margaret River
T (08) 9757 4542 **F** (08) 9757 4006 **OPEN** By appointment
WINEMAKER Janice MacDonald **EST.** 1992 **CASES** 2000
PRODUCT RANGE ($16.50–34 CD) Sauvignon Blanc, Chardonnay, Shiraz, Cabernet Sauvignon.
SUMMARY John Casas has established 5 hectares of shiraz, 4 hectares of cabernet sauvignon and 1 hectare each of chardonnay and sauvignon blanc. The vineyard is managed to produce low yields of between 1 and 2 tonnes per acre, with the aim of making a wine of sufficient power and density to merit barrel maturation of between one-and-a-half and two-and-a-half years. Domestic distribution by the quirkily named Medicinal Purposes Wine Co. (0438 250 372) supplements website sales to private customers and selected restaurants. The wines are also exported to the UK and the US, in the latter instance through Epicurean Wines of Seattle.

ŸŸŸŸŸ **Cabernets 2001** Excellent texture, structure and balance; black fruits and chocolate supported by sweet oak and ripe tannins. **RATING** 91 **DRINK** 2011 $ 25

ŸŸŸŸ **Shiraz 2001** Spicy, cedary overtones to gentle red berry fruit; good balance. **RATING** 88 **DRINK** 2010 $ 25

Cascabel ★★★★

Rogers Road, Willunga, SA 5172 **REGION** McLaren Vale
T (08) 8557 4434 **F** (08) 8557 4435 **OPEN** Not
WINEMAKER Susana Fernandez, Duncan Ferguson **EST.** 1997 **CASES** 2500
PRODUCT RANGE ($22–38 R) Eden Valley Riesling, Fleurieu Shiraz, McLaren Vale Grenache et al, Tempranillo Graciano, Monastrell.
SUMMARY Cascabel's proprietors, Duncan Ferguson and Susana Fernandez, established Cascabel when they purchased a property at Willunga on the Fleurieu Peninsula and planted it to a mosaic of nine southern Rhône and Spanish varieties: 5 hectares in all. The choice of grapes reflects the winemaking experience of the proprietors in Australia, the Rhône Valley, Bordeaux, Italy, Germany and New Zealand — and also Susana Fernandez's birthplace, Spain. Both are fully qualified and have moved the production base steadily towards the style of the Rhône Valley, Rioja and other parts of Spain. The wines have consistently impressed. Exports to the US, the UK, Switzerland, Hong Kong and Japan.

ŸŸŸŸŸ **Eden Valley Riesling 2003** Spotless flowery, lemon blossom aromas; finely boned and structured; classic tightness. **RATING** 92 **DRINK** 2023 $ 22

ŸŸŸŸ **Monastrell 2002** Spicy, cedary, earthy, house-style aromas, the palate with more weight to the dark fruits/dark chocolate flavours and tannins. **RATING** 89 **DRINK** 2012 $ 38
Tempranillo Graciano 2002 An aromatic mix of cedar, cigar and prune, then an intensely tangy, striking palate, almost citrussy, off in another direction. **RATING** 88 **DRINK** 2009 $ 38

ŸŸŸŸ **Grenache et al 2002** **RATING** 86 **DRINK** Now $ 23
Fleurieu Peninsula Shiraz 2002 **RATING** 85 **DRINK** Now $ 30

Casella Estate ★★★

Wakely Road, Yenda, NSW 2681 **REGION** Riverina
T (02) 6968 1346 **F** (02) 6968 1196 **OPEN** Not
WINEMAKER Alan Kennett, Con Simos, John Quarisa **EST.** 1969 **CASES** 5 million
PRODUCT RANGE ($4.95–19.50 R) A wide number of varietal wines starting at the lowest end with Crate 31, then moving through Cottlers Bridge, Carramar Estate, Yenda Vale and, at the top, Casella Estate. All pale into insignificance when viewed against the yellow tail range, priced domestically at $9.95.

SUMMARY One of the modern-day fairytale success stories, transformed overnight from a substantial, successful but non-charismatic business shown as making 650 000 cases in the 2000 edition of *Wine Companion*. Its opportunity came when the American distribution of Lindemans Bin 65 Chardonnay was taken away from WJ Deutsch & Sons, leaving a massive gap in its portfolio, which was filled by yellow tail. It has built its US presence at a faster rate than any other wine or brand in history. The storm clouds on the horizon are the ever-strengthening Australian dollar: all of the financial and marketing skills of Casella and WJ Deutsch will be needed if the brand is to avoid a hard landing.

ﾟﾟﾟﾟﾟ **Yenda Vale Limited Release Sangiovese 2002** An interesting mix of spice, tobacco, cedar and cherry; typical fine, lingering, almost lemony, tannins. A particularly good example of the variety. **RATING** 90 **DRINK** 2007 $ 17.60

ﾟﾟﾟﾟ **Yenda Vale Limited Release Viognier 2003** Pleasant, unoaked wine with nice soft peach and pastille fruit; well balanced; simple. Amazingly, won the trophy for Best Current Vintage Dry White, Melbourne Wine Show 2003. **RATING** 89 **DRINK** Now $ 17.60
Carramar Estate Shiraz 2001 Pleasant, medium-bodied; gently sweet fruit; well balanced. **RATING** 87 **DRINK** 2008 $ 9.99

ﾟﾟﾟﾟ **yellow tail Reserve Shiraz 2002** **RATING** 86 **DRINK** 2008 $ 18
Yenda Vale Limited Release Pinot Grigio 2003 **RATING** 85 **DRINK** Now $ 17.60
Yenda Vale Limited Release Viognier 2002 **RATING** 84 **DRINK** Now $ 17.60
Phillips Landing Shiraz 2002 **RATING** 84 **DRINK** 2007 $ 18

ﾟﾟﾟ **yellow tail Merlot 2003** **RATING** 81 $ 9.95
yellow tail Chardonnay 2003 **RATING** 80 $ 9.95
yellow tail Shiraz 2003 **RATING** 80 $ 9.95

🐚 Casley Mount Hutton Winery　　　　　　　　　NR

'Mount Hutton', Texas Road, via Stanthorpe, Qld 4380 **REGION** Granite Belt
T (07) 4683 6316 **F** (07) 4683 6345 **OPEN** Fri–Sun 10–5
WINEMAKER Grant Casley **EST.** 1999
PRODUCT RANGE A range of varietally denominated table wines reflecting the plantings.
SUMMARY Grant and Sonya Casley have established 9 hectares of sauvignon blanc, chenin blanc, semillon, chardonnay, cabernet sauvignon, merlot and shiraz, making the wine on-site. The chief wine sales are by mail order and through the cellar door, which offers all of the usual facilities, and meals by prior arrangement.

Cassegrain　　　　　　　　　　　★★★★

Hastings River Winery, Fernbank Creek Road, Port Macquarie, NSW 2444 **REGION** Hastings River
T (02) 6583 7777 **F** (02) 6584 0354 **OPEN** 7 days 9–5
WINEMAKER John Cassegrain **EST.** 1980 **CASES** 45 000
PRODUCT RANGE ($12–28.10 CD) A wide range of interesting varietal table wines (regional/varietal) headed by the Collection series of Reserve Semillon, Reserve Fromenteau, Brut, Reserve Chambourcin, Reserve Shiraz, Reserve Cabernet Merlot.
SUMMARY A very substantial operation based in the Hastings Valley on the north coast of New South Wales. In earlier years it drew fruit from many parts of Australia, but it is now entirely supplied by the 154 hectares of estate plantings which offer 14 varieties, including chambourcin, a French-bred cross. In February 2002 Cassegrain purchased Hungerford Hill from Southcorp, and secured the services of Phillip John as senior Hungerford Hill winemaker. The identity of Hungerford Hill as a separate venture has been preserved, and it is thus separately listed in this book. Exports to the UK, The Netherlands, Malaysia, Thailand, the Philippines, Singapore and Japan.

ﾟﾟﾟﾟﾟ **Fromenteau Reserve Chardonnay 2002** Very harmonious and supple; a seamless fusion of melon fruit, spicy oak and cashew; elegant and perfectly balanced. **RATING** 94
DRINK 2007 $ 26.95

ﾟﾟﾟﾟ **Hastings River Reserve Semillon 1997** Glowing yellow-green; complex toast and honey, then lemony acidity. Has developed superbly over the past 5 years. **RATING** 92 **DRINK** Now
$ 26.95

Reserve Cabernet Sauvignon Merlot 2002 Very attractive blend of redcurrant, blackberry, spice and mocha; elegant, light to medium-bodied; fine tannins, good length. Northern Slopes Zone. **RATING** 91 **DRINK** 2012 $26.95

Chardonnay 2003 Fresh, complex, smoky barrel-ferment nuances; relatively light-bodied but lively grapefruit and melon flavours; clean, lingering finish. Tumbarumba, Sydney Basin and Hastings River. **RATING** 90 **DRINK** 2008 $18.95

Reserve Shiraz 2002 Medium-bodied; blackberry, plum and prune, but not jammy; fine, savoury tannins, and good length. Northern Slopes Zone. **RATING** 90 **DRINK** 2012 $26.95

ȲȲȲȲ **Stone Circle Semillon Sauvignon Blanc 2003** Clean, attractive, lemony/grassy fruit aromas; some passionfruit and lemon fruit before tailing off. Good value, as are most of the wines in the Stone Circle range. **RATING** 87 **DRINK** Now $12.95

Reserve Shiraz 2001 Clean, moderately ripe plum, spice and raspberry aromas, adding blackberry to the mix on the palate; soft tannins and vanilla oak. Hastings River and the Northern Slopes Zone. **RATING** 87 **DRINK** 2011 $26.95

ȲȲȲȲ **Discovery Rose 2003** **RATING** 86 **DRINK** Now $16.95

Unwooded Chardonnay 2003 **RATING** 85 **DRINK** Now $16.95

Stone Circle Chardonnay 2003 **RATING** 85 **DRINK** Now $12.95

Shiraz 2002 **RATING** 85 **DRINK** 2009 $18.95

Verdelho 2003 **RATING** 84 **DRINK** Now $16.95

Stone Circle Shiraz 2002 **RATING** 84 **DRINK** 2007 $12.95

Stone Circle Merlot 2002 **RATING** 84 **DRINK** 2007 $12.95

Northern Slopes Merlot Cabernet Sauvignon 2002 **RATING** 84 **DRINK** 2007 $18.95

Castagna Vineyard ★★★★☆

Ressom Lane, Beechworth, Vic 3747 **REGION** Beechworth
T (03) 5728 2888 **F** (03) 5728 2898 **OPEN** By appointment
WINEMAKER Julian Castagna **EST.** 1997 **CASES** 2000
PRODUCT RANGE ($23–75 ML) Allegro, Ingenue (Viognier), Genesis Syrah, La Chiave.
SUMMARY The elegantly labelled wines of Castagna will ultimately come from 4 hectares of estate shiraz and viognier in the course of establishment (the latter making up 15 per cent of the total). Winemaker Julian Castagna is intent on making wines which reflect the terroir as closely as possible, declining to use cultured yeast or filtration. Genesis Syrah deserves its icon status.

Castle Glen Vineyard NR

Amiens Road, The Summit, Qld 4377 **REGION** Granite Belt
T (07) 4683 2363 **F** (07) 4683 2169 **OPEN** 7 days 10–5
WINEMAKER Cedric Millar **EST.** 1990
PRODUCT RANGE Table, fortified and sparkling wines.
SUMMARY Unashamedly caters for the general tourist, with a large castle boasting an open fire set in 40 hectares, and specialising in 27 liqueur-style fruit wines, but with Chardonnay, Shiraz, Merlot, Cabernet Sauvignon, Semillon and White Muscat also available.

Castle Rock Estate ★★★★

Porongurup Road, Porongurup, WA 6324 **REGION** Porongurup
T (08) 9853 1035 **F** (08) 9853 1010 **OPEN** Mon–Fri 10–4, weekends and public holidays 10–5
WINEMAKER Robert Diletti **EST.** 1983 **CASES** 5000
PRODUCT RANGE ($15–23 CD) Riesling, Chardonnay, Late Harvest Riesling, Pinot Noir, Cabernet Sauvignon Merlot, Liqueur Muscat, Robert Reserve White & Red.
SUMMARY An exceptionally beautifully sited vineyard, winery and cellar-door sales area on a 55-hectare property with sweeping vistas from the Porongurups, operated by the Diletti family. The standard of viticulture is very high, and the site itself ideally situated (quite apart from its beauty). The two-level winery, set on the natural slope, was completed in time for the 2001 vintage, and maximises gravity flow, in particular for crushed must feeding into the press. The Rieslings have always been elegant, and handsomely repaid time in bottle.

ᵀᵀᵀᵀ Riesling 2003 Mineral, apple, herb and lime aromas, moving more to lime/citrus on the smooth, balanced palate; good length, cellaring special. Screwcap. RATING 92 DRINK 2013 $18

ᵀᵀᵀᵀ Pinot Noir 2002 Big, solid, dark plum fruit, generous and fleshy. RATING 89 DRINK 2007 $23
Robert Reserve Red 2001 Sweet fruit amplified by sweet oak; light to medium-bodied; well balanced, gently ripe tannins. RATING 87 DRINK 2008 $17

ᵀᵀᵀᵀ Robert Reserve White 2003 Clean, fresh, dry, crisp citrus; no concession to cellar-door sweetness. Screwcap. RATING 86 DRINK 2007 $15
Cabernet Merlot 2000 RATING 85 DRINK 2007 $19

Cathcart Ridge Estate

NR

Moyston Road, Cathcart via Ararat, Vic 3377 REGION Grampians
T (03) 5352 1997 F (03) 5352 1558 OPEN 7 days 10–5
WINEMAKER David Farnhill EST. 1977 CASES 5000
PRODUCT RANGE ($12.95–80 CD) Estate range of Shiraz, Chasselas, Grampians Shiraz, Grampians Merlot, Grampians Cabernet and flagship The Grampian Shiraz; Rhymney Reef Chardonnay, Shiraz, Cabernet Merlot and Old Tawny Port; and, at the bottom of the price range, Mount Ararat Classic Dry White, Shiraz, Merlot, Cabernet Merlot and Cabernet Sauvignon.
SUMMARY In recent years has raised capital to fund a significant expansion program of both vineyards and the winery, but is still little known in the wider retail trade. Sporadic tastings haven't been particularly exciting. Mount Ararat Estate is a parallel operation to Cathcart Ridge, David Farnhill being the Chief Executive of both. There are 2.5 hectares of vineyard within the Grampians region, and another 7.5 hectares at Mildura, providing riesling, chardonnay, colombard, grenache and shiraz. Exports to the UK.

Cathedral Lane Wines

 ★★★★

228 Cathedral Lane, Taggerty, Vic 3714 REGION Upper Goulburn
T (03) 5774 7305 F (03) 5774 7696 OPEN By appointment
WINEMAKER MasterWineMakers (Contract) EST. 1997 CASES 450
PRODUCT RANGE ($25 ML) Pinot Noir.
SUMMARY Rod Needham and Heather Campbell formed the Acheron Valley Wine Company, which makes the Cathedral Lane wines, in 1997. The 3.2-hectare vineyard is situated on the lower slopes of Mount Cathedral at a height of 280 metres. A variant of the Scott Henry trellis system, with high-density 1-metre spacing between the vines, alternately trained up or down, has been employed. The vineyard planning was supervised by former Coldstream Hills viticulturist Bill Christophersen.

ᵀᵀᵀᵀ Pinot Noir 2002 Light to medium-bodied but clear varietal character in a savoury/foresty mode; fine, supple and unforced; very different from the '02 vintage, and the best yet. RATING 89 DRINK Now $25

🐌 Catherine's Ridge

NR

Fish Fossil Drive, Canowindra, NSW 2804 REGION Cowra
T (02) 6344 3212 F (02) 6344 3242 OPEN By appointment
WINEMAKER Contract EST. 1999
PRODUCT RANGE ($12–18 CD) Chardonnay, Verdelho, Shiraz.
SUMMARY Kay and David Warren have 18 hectares of chardonnay, verdelho, shiraz and cabernet sauvignon. The wine is made under contract from part of the annual grape production.

Catherine Vale Vineyard

 ★★★

656 Milbrodale Road, Bulga, NSW 2330 REGION Lower Hunter Valley
T (02) 6579 1334 F (02) 6579 1334 OPEN Weekends and public holidays 10–5, or by appointment
WINEMAKER John Hordern (Contract) EST. 1994 CASES 1500
PRODUCT RANGE ($12–19 CD) Semillon, Semillon Chardonnay, Chardonnay, Late Harvest Semillon, Dolcetto.

SUMMARY Former schoolteachers Bill and Wendy Lawson have established Catherine Vale as a not-so-idle retirement venture. Both were involved in school athletics and sports programs, handy training for do-it-yourself viticulturists. Most of the grapes from the 5.8-hectare vineyard are sold to contract winemaker John Hordern; a small proportion is vinified for the Catherine Vale label.

ŸŸŸŸ **Chardonnay 2002** Nectarine and white peach, with a substrate of subtle barrel-ferment/malolactic and lees contact; impressive value. **RATING** 89 **DRINK** Now $ 16
Semillon 2002 Clean, with a touch of sweetness adding to the palate depth; drink sooner rather than later. **RATING** 87 **DRINK** Now $ 14

ŸŸŸŸ **Gabrielle Dolcetto 2003** **RATING** 84 **DRINK** Now $ 15

ŸŸŸ **Semillon Chardonnay 2002** **RATING** 83 $ 12

Catspaw Farm NR

Texas Road, Stanthorpe, Qld 4380 **REGION** Granite Belt
T (07) 4683 6229 **F** (07) 4683 6386 **OPEN** Thurs–Sun and public holidays 10–5, 7 days at Easter and June and September Queensland school holidays
WINEMAKER Christopher Whitfort **EST.** 1989 **CASES** 300
PRODUCT RANGE ($12–22 CD) Sauvignon Blanc Semillon, Chardonnay, Golden Queen, Shiraz Merlot, Chambourcin, Cabernet Shiraz, Cats Whiskers Liqueur Muscat and Gold Label Muscat.
SUMMARY The foundations for Catspaw Farm were laid back in 1989, when planting of the vineyard began with chardonnay, riesling, cabernet franc, cabernet sauvignon, merlot, chambourcin and shiraz, totalling 4.6 hectares. More recently, Catspaw has moved with the times in planting roussanne, semillon, barbera and sangiovese, lifting total plantings to just under 8 hectares. The newer plantings are yet to come into bearing and the wines are some time away from release. In the meantime, a mixed bag of wines are available, some dating back to 1998. Catspaw, incidentally, also offers on-farm accommodation in a self-contained farmhouse (with disabled access) and picnic facilities.

Cawdor Wines

Old Mount Barker Road, Echunga, SA 5153 **REGION** Adelaide Hills
T (08) 8388 8456 **F** (08) 8388 8807 **OPEN** By appointment
WINEMAKER Contract **EST.** 1999 **CASES** 350
PRODUCT RANGE ($18 R) Sauvignon Blanc.
SUMMARY Jock Calder and his family began the establishment of Cawdor Wines with the purchase of 22 hectares near the township of Echunga. Five hectares of sauvignon blanc were planted in their first year, with a further 2.6 hectares of sauvignon blanc, 7.9 hectares of shiraz and 2.7 hectares of riesling in the following year. The major part of the production is sold to Nepenthe Wines, but Cawdor nominates how much it wishes to have vinified under its own label each year. It has followed a softly, softly approach, with only small amounts being made; there is no cellar door, nor is one planned. The wine is sold via fax, email, phone, etc, with limited wholesale distribution through David Turner Agencies.

Ceccanti Kiewa Valley Wines NR

Bay Creek Lane, Mongans Bridge, Vic 3691 **REGION** Alpine Valleys
T (03) 5754 5236 **F** (03) 5754 5353 **OPEN** 7 days 11–5
WINEMAKER Angelo Ceccanti, Moya Ceccanti, Danny Ceccanti **EST.** 1988
PRODUCT RANGE ($13.90–18 CD) Riesling, Shiraz, Merlot, Cabernet Sauvignon.
SUMMARY Parents Angelo and Moya Ceccanti, with son Danny, have established 16 hectares of vines, and now use all of the production for their wines, which are made on-site by the family. Angelo, raised in Tuscany, had extensive exposure to viticulture and winemaking, but it is Moya and Danny who have the technical knowledge.

Cedar Creek Estate

104–144 Hartley Road, Mount Tamborine, Qld 4272 **REGION** Queensland Coastal
T (07) 5545 1666 **F** (07) 5545 4762 **OPEN** 7 days 10–5
WINEMAKER Contract **EST.** 2000 **CASES** 1500

PRODUCT RANGE ($14.50–23.90 CD) A range of varietally identified table wines plus generic and fortified wines.

SUMMARY Opened in November 2000, Cedar Creek Estate takes its name from the creek which flows through the property at an altitude of 550 metres on Tamborine Mountain. A 3.7-hectare vineyard has been planted to chambourcin and verdelho, supplemented by grapes grown elsewhere. The focus will always be on general tourism, with a host of facilities, including a restaurant, for visitors, and it also offers wines from Ballandean Estate.

▼▼▼ **Late Harvest Semillon 2003** RATING 83 $17.90
Shiraz 2002 RATING 82 $16.50
Verdelho 2002 RATING 81 $15
Unwooded Chardonnay 2002 RATING 80 $17.50
Verdelho 2003 RATING 80 $15

Cellarmasters ★★★☆

Cnr Barossa Valley Way and Siegersdorf Road, Tanunda, SA 5352 **REGION** Barossa Valley
T (08) 8561 2200 **F** (08) 8561 2299 **OPEN** Not
WINEMAKER Simon Adams, Steve Chapman, Nick Badrice, John Schwartzkopff, Sally Blackwell, Mark Starick **EST.** 1982
PRODUCT RANGE ($16–40 ML) Produces a substantial number of wines under proprietary labels (Dorrien Estate, Rare Print, New Eden, Avon Brae) for the Cellarmaster Group; notable are Storton Hill, Di Fabio, Black Wattle Mount Benson, Wright's Bay, Amberton, Addison Selection 49, Bosworth Edge and Vasarelli.
SUMMARY The Cellarmaster Group was acquired by Beringer Blass in 1997. Dorrien Estate is the physical base of the vast Cellarmaster network which, wearing its retailer's hat, is by far the largest direct-sale outlet in Australia. It buys substantial quantities of wine from other makers either in bulk or as cleanskin, or with recognisable but subtly different labels of the producers concerned. It is also making increasing quantities of wine on its own account at Dorrien Estate, many of which are quite excellent, and of trophy quality. The labelling of these wines is becoming increasingly sophisticated, giving little or no clue to the Cellarmaster link. Chateau Dorrien is an entirely unrelated business.

▼▼▼▼ **The Ridge Coonawarra Chardonnay 2002** Quite complex barrel-ferment aromas; tightens up on the palate; good length. **RATING** 89 **DRINK** 2007 $14.99
Avon Brae Eden Valley Shiraz 2001 Very sweet minty/berry, medium-bodied palate; touches of chocolate and earth underneath. **RATING** 87 **DRINK** 2010 $19.99

▼▼▼▽ **Mum's Block Shiraz 2000** RATING 86 DRINK 2010 $33
The Ridge Coonawarra Cabernet 2001 RATING 86 DRINK 2007 $20.50
Storten Vineyards Riesling 2003 RATING 85 DRINK 2008 $17.50

▼▼▼ **Dorrien Estate Lysander Mount Benson Sauvignon Blanc 2003** RATING 83 $13.99
Fowler Blair House Limestone Coast Shiraz 2001 RATING 81 $18.50

Celtic Farm ★★★★

39 Sweyn Street, North Balwyn, Vic 3104 (postal) **REGION** Warehouse
T (03) 9857 3600 **F** (03) 9857 3601 **OPEN** Not
WINEMAKER Gerry Taggert **EST.** 1997 **CASES** 4000
PRODUCT RANGE ($18–28.50 R) South Block Riesling (Clare Valley), The Gridge Pinot Grigio (King Valley), Revenge Botrytis Semillon, Firkin Hall Yarra Valley Shiraz, Raisin Hell Rutherglen Muscat.
SUMMARY Yet another warehouse winery, these days owned and run by co-founder Gerry Taggert, joined by long-time friends Mark McNeill and Mike Shields — all fine Celts, according to Taggert. Taggert says, 'Celtic Farm is produced from classic varieties selected from Australia's premium wine regions and made with a total commitment to quality. While we have a desire to pay homage to our Celtic (drinking) heritage we are also acutely aware that wine should be about enjoyment, fun and not taking yourself too seriously.' Unsurprisingly, the team is negotiating with importers in Ireland, and in conjunction with the Celtic Farm brand, may develop an exclusive export label.

🐚 Centennial Vineyards ★★★★☆

'Woodside', Centennial Road, Bowral, NSW 2576 **REGION** Southern Highlands
T (02) 4861 8700 **F** (02) 4681 8777 **OPEN** 7 days 10–5
WINEMAKER Tony Cosgriff **EST.** 2002 **CASES** 9000
PRODUCT RANGE ($17–25 CD) Sauvignon Blanc, Verdelho, Chardonnay, Late Harvest Semillon, Rose,
Pinot Noir, Shiraz Cabernet, Cabernet Merlot, Cabernet Sauvignon; Bong Bong White, Chardonnay
and Red.
SUMMARY Centennial Vineyards is a substantial development jointly owned by wine professional
John Large and investor Mark Dowling, covering 133 hectares of beautiful grazing land, with over 30
hectares planted to sauvignon blanc, riesling, verdelho, chardonnay, merlot, pinot noir, cabernet
sauvignon and tempranillo. Production from the estate vineyards (the vines of which age from 4 to
7 years) is supplemented by purchases of grapes from other regions, including Orange. Also, releases
of ultra-obscure varieties, including rondinella and corvina, come on-stream in 2004. The new
on-site winery has a 120-tonne capacity, and worked close to this capacity in 2003. A substantial and
very popular restaurant is open 7 days. Sales are mainly through local distribution, the cellar door, a
mailing list and some exports.

ΨΨΨΨΨ **Reserve Cabernet Sauvignon 2002** Blackcurrant, mint and cassis; spotlessly clean, fruit-
driven; fine tannins and subtle oak. **RATING** 91 **DRINK** 2010 $ 27.99
Sauvignon Blanc 2002 Pronounced pungent and aromatic varietal character which,
praise be, is not sweaty. Gooseberry, asparagus palate; good length and crisp finish. **RATING**
90 **DRINK** Now $ 19

ΨΨΨΨ **Reserve Cabernet Merlot 2002** Fragrant, ripe raspberry, redcurrant and blackcurrant
aromas and flavours; very pure fruit, though does thin out slightly on the finish. **RATING** 88
DRINK 2009 $ 27.99
Woodside Chardonnay 2002 Fragrant citrus and apple; focused palate; subtle oak. From
Bowral region vineyards. **RATING** 87 **DRINK** Now $ 17
Rose 2003 Fresh, lively strawberry and citrus flavours; 11 degrees alcohol is a plus; acidity
lengthens the finish. Screwcap; good packaging. **RATING** 87 **DRINK** Now $ 16.99

ΨΨΨΨ **Bong Bong Red 2002** **RATING** 86 **DRINK** Now $ 17
Verdelho 2003 **RATING** 85 **DRINK** Now $ 18.99
Late Harvest Semillon 2002 **RATING** 84 **DRINK** Now $ 21.99

ΨΨΨ **Bong Bong White 2002** **RATING** 80 $ 17

Ceravolo Wines ★★★☆

Suite 16, Tranmere Village, 172 Glynburn Road, Tranmere, SA 5073 (postal) **REGION** Adelaide Plains
T (08) 8336 4522 **F** (08) 8365 0538 **OPEN** Not
WINEMAKER Colin Glaetzer, Ben Glaetzer (Contract) **EST.** 1995 **CASES** 10 000
PRODUCT RANGE ($15–25 R) Chardonnay, Shiraz, Merlot, Petit Verdot, Sangiovese; under the larger
volume and cheaper Red Earth label are Chardonnay, Shiraz and Cabernet Sauvignon.
SUMMARY The Ceravolo family has established a substantial business in the Adelaide Plains region,
moving from contract grape growing to grape growing and winemaking. A name change to Ceravolo
Premium Wines and smart new packaging should lift the profile of the business. The principals are
parents Joe and Heather Ceravolo, and son Dr Joe Ceravolo, who still continues his dental practice,
doubling up as vigneron and director of St Andrews Estate. In 1999 the label was launched, centred
around Shiraz, but with Chardonnay and Merlot in support. Conspicuous success at the London
International Wine Challenge led both to exports and the registration of the Adelaide Plains region
under the GI legislation.

ΨΨΨΨΨ **Sangiovese 2002** Nicely modulated and balanced; small red fruits; silky tannins;
excellent varietal character. **RATING** 90 **DRINK** 2008 $ 15

ΨΨΨΨ **Petit Verdot 2002** Deep colour; powerful, brooding dark fruits; structure still locked up;
needs time. **RATING** 88 **DRINK** 2012 $ 25
Adelaide Plains Merlot 2002 Fragrant raspberry and mint aromas and flavours; light-
bodied, early-drinking style. **RATING** 87 **DRINK** Now $ 18

ΨΨΨΨ **Unwooded Chardonnay 2003** **RATING** 86 **DRINK** Now $ 15

Chain of Ponds ★★★★

Adelaide Road, Gumeracha, SA 5233 **REGION** Adelaide Hills
T (08) 8389 1415 **F** (08) 8389 1877 **OPEN** Mon–Fri 11–4, weekends and public holidays 10.30–4.30
WINEMAKER Neville Falkenberg **EST.** 1993 **CASES** 17 500
PRODUCT RANGE ($14.95–35 CD) Purple Patch Riesling, Square Cut Semillon, Black Thursday Sauvignon Blanc, Nether Hill Unwooded Chardonnay, Corkscrew Road Chardonnay, Salem Selection Pinot Noir, Ledge Shiraz, Jupiter's Blood Sangiovese, Amadeus Cabernet Sauvignon, Diva Sparling; Cabochon White and Red; Novello Bianco, Rosso and Nero.
SUMMARY Chain of Ponds is the largest grower in the Adelaide Hills, with 100 hectares of vines at Gumeracha and 300 acres at Kersbrook. It produces 1000 tonnes of grapes a year; almost all are sold to other wineries, but a small amount of wine is made under the Chain of Ponds label, and it enjoys consistent show success. The Vineyard Balcony Restaurant is open for lunch on weekends and public holidays.

▼▼▼▼▼ **Amadeus Cabernet Sauvignon 2000** Medium to full-bodied; supple, rich, blackcurrant/cassis fruit; fine, ripe tannins; good length and line. **RATING** 94 **DRINK** 2020 $35

▼▼▼▼▽ **Purple Patch Riesling 2003** Intense herb, spice and lanolin aromas; an abundance of generous flavour, nicely balanced. **RATING** 90 **DRINK** 2009 $17.50
Novello Rosso 2003 Aromatic cherry blossom aromas; like any Rose, light-bodied, but with a long, cleansing palate; crisp acidity to close. **RATING** 90 **DRINK** Now $14.99

▼▼▼▼ **Black Thursday Sauvignon Blanc 2003** Clean and crisp; touches of asparagus and grass aromas; builds flavour, though not varietal character, on the palate. **RATING** 88 **DRINK** Now $17.50
Novello Nero 2003 Fragrant, spicy black cherry/berry aromas and flavours, the sweet spicy characters on the palate offset by savoury tannins. **RATING** 88 **DRINK** Now $14.95
Cabochon Red 2001 Controlled barrel-ferment inputs; moderately intense nutty overtones to slightly sweet, figgy fruit. **RATING** 88 **DRINK** 2007 $18.95

▼▼▼▽ **Corkscrew Road Chardonnay 2001** **RATING** 86 **DRINK** 2007 $35
Viognier 2003 **RATING** 86 **DRINK** 2008 $20
Ledge Shiraz 2000 **RATING** 86 **DRINK** 2007 $35
Cabochon White 2002 **RATING** 84 **DRINK** Now $20

Chalice Bridge Estate ★★★★

Rosa Glen Road, Margaret River, WA 6285 **REGION** Margaret River
T (08) 9388 6088 **F** (08) 9382 1887 **OPEN** By appointment
WINEMAKER Tim Mortimer **EST.** 1998 **CASES** 12 000
PRODUCT RANGE ($16–28 ML) Semillon Sauvignon Blanc, Chardonnay, Unwooded Chardonnay, Shiraz, Cabernet Shiraz, Cabernet Sauvignon.
SUMMARY Chalice Bridge Estate is a recent arrival in wine terms, but has a long history, dating back to 1924, when it was densely forested with jarrah and marri trees. A group of English settlers arrived with the aim of converting the forest to grazing land. Most gave up, but the Titterton family persevered, eventually selling the property in 1977. Planting of the vineyard began in 1987; there are now 47 hectares of cabernet sauvignon, 29 hectares of shiraz and 27 hectares of chardonnay, with lesser plantings of semillon, sauvignon blanc and merlot making up the total plantings of 121 hectares, the second-largest single vineyard in the Margaret River region.

▼▼▼▼▼ **Shiraz Cabernet Sauvignon 2002** Delicious raspberry and redcurrant fruit; a wine of elegance, with excellent balance and oak use. **RATING** 95 **DRINK** 2017 $28

▼▼▼▼▽ **Shiraz 2002** Finely structured but intense black cherry and plum fruit; subtle oak and silky tannins. **RATING** 92 **DRINK** 2012 $22

▼▼▼▼ **Sauvignon Blanc 2003** Clean, positive varietal aromatics; gooseberry/tropical fruit, the faintest hint of sweetness balanced by acidity. **RATING** 89 **DRINK** Now $20
Semillon Sauvignon Blanc 2003 Spotlessly clean; tight, crisp mineral and herb flavours, dry finish; will grow with age. **RATING** 87 **DRINK** 2007 $16

▼▼▼▽ **Unwooded Chardonnay 2003** **RATING** 84 **DRINK** Now $16

Chalkers Crossing   ★★★★★

387 Grenfell Road, Young, NSW 2594 **REGION** Hilltops
T (02) 6382 6900 **F** (02) 6382 5068 **OPEN** 7 days 10–4
WINEMAKER Celine Rousseau **EST.** 2000 **CASES** 10 000
PRODUCT RANGE ($15–25 CD) Hilltops range of Riesling, Semillon, Shiraz, Shiraz Second Label,
Cabernet Sauvignon Merlot, Cabernet Sauvignon; Tumbarumba range of Sauvignon Blanc,
Frontignan, Chardonnay, Rose, Pinot Noir.
SUMMARY Owned and operated by Ted and Wendy Ambler, Chalkers Crossing is based near Young,
where the first vines were planted at the Rockleigh vineyard in late 1997, with follow-up plantings in
1998 lifting the total to 10 hectares. It also purchases grapes from Tumbarumba and Gundagai to
supplement the intake. A winery was opened for the 2000 vintage, with Celine Rousseau as
winemaker. Born in France's Loire Valley and trained in Bordeaux, Rousseau has worked in
Bordeaux, Champagne, Languedoc, Margaret River and in the Perth Hills, an eclectic mix of climates
if ever there was one. This French Flying Winemaker (now an Australian citizen) has exceptional
skills and dedication. Exports to France, Hong Kong and the UK.

ΥΥΥΥΥ **Tumbarumba Chardonnay 2002** Very elegant yet intense and long cool-climate style;
citrus and nectarine fruit do all of the work. **RATING** 94 **DRINK** 2010 $ 18

ΥΥΥΥΥ **Hilltops Riesling 2003** Mineral, earth, slate and citrus aromas; quite lean citrus fruit on
entry, building on the finish. **RATING** 90 **DRINK** 2010 $ 16.50

Chalk Hill   ★★★★☆

PO Box 205, McLaren Vale, SA 5171 (postal) **REGION** McLaren Vale
T (08) 8556 2121 **F** (08) 8556 2221 **OPEN** Not
WINEMAKER Emma Bekkers **EST.** 1973 **CASES** 2500
PRODUCT RANGE ($15–25 CD) Unwooded Chardonnay, Shiraz, Barbera, Sangiovese, Cabernet
Sauvignon.
SUMMARY Chalk Hill is in full flight again, drawing upon three vineyards (Slate Creek, Wit's End and
Chalk Hill) of grape-growing owners John and Di Harvey, who acquired Chalk Hill in 1995. There
has been considerable work on the Chalk Hill home vineyard since its acquisition, part being re-
trellised, and riesling replaced by new plantings of shiraz and cabernet sauvignon, plus small
amounts of barbera and sangiovese. Domestic distribution is solely by mail order; a small portion is
exported to The Netherlands, Canada and the US (under Wits End label).

ΥΥΥΥΥ **Barbera 2002** Complex spice and cigar box aromas; abundant, sweet, dark berry fruits;
nice, dry lingering finish and fine tannins. **RATING** 93 **DRINK** 2009 $ 18
Sangiovese 2002 Good colour; medium-bodied and well balanced; spicy cherry fruit and
fine oak; no stringy or thin characters. Impressive. **RATING** 92 **DRINK** 2010 $ 18
Cabernet Sauvignon 2001 Stacks of dark chocolate; ripe blackcurrant also in abundance;
all comes together very well. **RATING** 90 **DRINK** 2013 $ 25

ΥΥΥΥ **Shiraz 2000** A deep and complex array of black fruits; touches of earth and game; big
mid-palate, less on the finish. **RATING** 88 **DRINK** 2010 $ 25

Chambers Rosewood   ★★★★★

Barkly Street, Rutherglen, Vic 3685 **REGION** Rutherglen
T (02) 6032 8641 **F** (02) 6032 8101 **OPEN** Mon–Sat 9–5, Sun 11–5
WINEMAKER Bill Chambers, Stephen Chambers **EST.** 1858 **CASES** 10 000
PRODUCT RANGE ($6–180 CD) A wide range of table wines, including such rarities as Gouias, Blue
Imperial (which is in fact Cinsaut) and a wide range of fortified wines. The supremely great wines are
the Rare Tokay and Rare Muscat, and the very good Special Muscat and Special Tokay. These are now
offered in 375 ml bottles at prices which are starting to reflect their intrinsic value, and are rather
higher than the prices for the same wines when they were last offered in 750 ml bottles.
SUMMARY The winery rating is given for the Special Muscat and Tokay (rated 'Grand' under the
Rutherglen Classification system) and the Rare wines, which are on a level all of their own,
somewhere higher than five stars. The chief virtue of the table wines is that they are cheap. Exports to
the US, the UK, Singapore and New Zealand.

ᵀᵀᵀᵀᵀ **Rare Rutherglen Muscat (375ml) NV** Very deep mahogany-brown, olive rim; the bouquet comes on like a blitzkrieg, so powerful and complex it very nearly imprisons the senses. The palate is a magical combination of extreme rancio, driving the length and finish, but seamlessly filled out by essence-like raisin fruit. **RATING** 97 **DRINK** Now $180
Grand Rutherglen Muscat (375ml) NV Full olive-brown; ultra-complex aromas, with a piercing strand of rancio; layer upon layer of flavour, balanced and integrated — no one flavour is dominant. **RATING** 94 **DRINK** Now $40

ᵀᵀᵀᵀᵀ **Rutherglen Muscat NV** Lovely, fresh rose petal muscat fruit aromas leap from the glass, the flavour impact similarly fresh and immediate; wonderfully sweet, but doesn't cloy. **RATING** 90 **DRINK** Now $13

ᵀᵀᵀ **Gouais 2001 RATING** 81 $12

Channybearup Vineyard ★★★★

Lot 4 Channybearup Road, Pemberton, WA 6260 (postal) **REGION** Pemberton
T (08) 9776 0042 **F** (08) 9776 0043 **OPEN** Not
WINEMAKER Larry Cherubino **EST.** 1999 **CASES** 11 000
PRODUCT RANGE ($16–25 R) Fly Brook range of Unwooded Chardonnay, Verdelho, Pinot Noir, Merlot, Shiraz, Cabernet Sauvignon; second label is Wild Fly.
SUMMARY Channybearup has been established by a small group of Perth businessmen, who have been responsible for the establishment of 62 hectares of vineyards (the majority planted in 1999 and 2000). The principal varieties are chardonnay (22 hectares), pinot noir (10 hectares), merlot (10 hectares), shiraz (9 hectares), cabernet sauvignon (7.5 hectares), pinot noir (7 hectares), with lesser amounts of verdelho and sauvignon blanc. While principally established as a grape supplier to other makers, a tiny range of wines is being marketed. Exports to the US.

ᵀᵀᵀᵀᵀ **Fly Brook Merlot 2002** Good colour; considerable but well-integrated oak ex barrel fermentation; excellent mouthfeel. **RATING** 92 **DRINK** 2012 $19
Fly Brook Cabernet Sauvignon 2002 Light to medium-bodied; blackcurrant, touches of olive and spice; good texture/structure from fine-grained tannins. **RATING** 91 **DRINK** 2012 $19
Fly Brook Shiraz 2002 Blackberry, licorice and spice; still very firm, but well-integrated French oak; full of promise. **RATING** 90 **DRINK** 2015 $19

ᵀᵀᵀᵀ **Fly Brook Unwooded Chardonnay 2003** Excellent bouquet, ripe, sweet stone fruit; however, needs a touch more acidity on the palate. **RATING** 87 **DRINK** Now $18

ᵀᵀᵀ **Fly Brook Verdelho 2003 RATING** 83 $16
Wild Fly Cabernet Merlot 2002 RATING 82 $13

Chanters Ridge ★★★☆

440 Chanters Lane, Tylden, Vic 3444 **REGION** Macedon Ranges
T 0427 511 341 **F** (03) 9509 8046 **OPEN** Weekends 10–4 by appointment
WINEMAKER John Ellis **EST.** 1995 **CASES** 500
PRODUCT RANGE ($25 CD) Pinot Noir.
SUMMARY Orthopaedic surgeon Barry Elliott, as well as running the surgery unit at Melbourne's Alfred Hospital, became involved with the Kyneton Hospital 5 years ago. Through a convoluted series of events, he and his wife acquired the 24-hectare property without any clear idea of what they might do with it; later his lifelong interest in wine steered him towards the idea of establishing a vineyard. He retained local overlord John Ellis as his consultant, and this led to the planting of 2 hectares of pinot noir, and the first tiny make in 2000. Barry Elliott intends to retire from surgery and devote himself full-time to the challenge of making Pinot Noir in one of the more difficult parts of Australia, but one which will richly reward success.

Chapel Hill

Chapel Hill Road, McLaren Vale, SA 5171 **REGION** McLaren Vale
T (08) 8323 8429 **F** (08) 8323 9245 **OPEN** 7 days 12–5
WINEMAKER Pam Dunsford (Consultant), Angela Meaney **EST.** 1979 **CASES** 55 000
PRODUCT RANGE ($14–50 CD) Verdelho, Unwooded Chardonnay, Reserve Chardonnay, McLaren Vale
Shiraz, McLaren Vale/Coonawarra Cabernet Sauvignon, The Vicar, The Devil Tawny Port.
SUMMARY A leading medium-sized winery in the region; in the second half of 2000 Chapel Hill was
sold to the diversified Swiss Thomas Schmidheiny group, which owns the respected Cuvaison winery
in California, as well as vineyards in Switzerland and Argentina. From my knowledge of Cuvaison,
stretching back 15 years or so, I am confident Chapel Hill is in safe hands. Exports to the UK, the US,
Canada, Switzerland, Germany and Hong Kong.

ŸŸŸŸŸ **Unwooded Chardonnay 2003** Has exceptional length; a fruit-driven mix of melon and
citrus; pleasingly dry finish. **RATING** 92 **DRINK** 2007 $ 14
Reserve Chardonnay 2002 Fragrant, subtle barrel-ferment inputs; supple, creamy fig
and cashew mouthfeel. **RATING** 91 **DRINK** 2008 $ 24
McLaren Vale/Coonawarra Cabernet Sauvignon 2001 Elegant cassis/blackcurrant fruit
with good carry; subtle oak and minimal tannins **RATING** 90 **DRINK** 2011 $ 25

ŸŸŸŸ **The Vicar Cabernet Shiraz 2001** Light to medium-bodied; minty/savoury black fruits;
minimal oak. **RATING** 88 **DRINK** 2011 $ 43

Chapman's Creek Vineyard

NR

RMS 447 Yelverton Road, Wilyabrup, WA 6280 **REGION** Margaret River
T (08) 9755 7545 **F** (08) 9755 7571 **OPEN** 7 days 10.30–4.30
WINEMAKER Various Contract **EST.** 1989 **CASES** 5000
PRODUCT RANGE ($15–26 R) Chenin Blanc, Unoaked Chardonnay, Chardonnay, Merlot, Cabernet
Merlot, Tawny Port.
SUMMARY Chapman's Creek was founded by the late Tony Lord, an extremely experienced wine
journalist who for many years was editor and part-owner of *Decanter* magazine of the UK, one of the
leaders in the field. Notwithstanding this, he was always reticent about seeking any publicity for
Chapman's Creek; why, I do not know. Regrettably, it is now too late to find out, as he died in
February 2002. Chapman's Creek will continue to be managed by his long-term pal, Chris Leach,
who was one of those who kept an eye on him throughout his prolonged illness.

🐌 Chapman Valley Wines

Lot 14 Howatharra Road, Nanson, Chapman Valley via Geraldton, WA 6530
REGION Central Western Australia Zone
T (08) 9920 5148 **F** (08) 9920 5206 **OPEN** 7 days 10–5
WINEMAKER Stephen Murfit (Contract) **EST.** 1995 **CASES** 5500
PRODUCT RANGE ($14.50–18 CD) Semillon Sauvignon Blanc, Verdelho, Classic White, Cayley Springs
White, Chenin Blanc, Chardonnay, Shiraz, Merlot, Zinfandel, Cabernet Sauvignon Merlot, Vintage
Port.
SUMMARY Chapman Valley Wines is Western Australia's most northern winery, situated 30
kilometres northeast of Geraldton in the picturesque valley which gives the business its name. A
hobby vineyard on a nearby property led to the establishment of 5 hectares of vines in 1995, followed
by a further 3 hectares in 1999. The varieties are varied but strictly mainstream: semillon, chenin
blanc, chardonnay, verdelho, sauvignon blanc, shiraz, merlot, cabernet sauvignon and (somewhat
rarer) zinfandel. The wines are made by Steve Murfit at Lilac Hill Estate in the Swan Valley. The
wines are chiefly sold by mail order and through the cellar door, which is complemented by a
restaurant with a full food selection, offering inside or outdoor seating under gazebos. It also caters
for evening functions by arrangement.

ŸŸŸŸ **Merlot 2002** Light to medium-bodied and clean; fresh red fruits; clever use of spicy oak.
RATING 88 **DRINK** 2009 $ 18

Charles Cimicky

NR

Gomersal Road, Lyndoch, SA 5351 **REGION** Barossa Valley
T (08) 8524 4025 **F** (08) 8524 4772 **OPEN** Tues–Sat 10.30–4.30
WINEMAKER Charles Cimicky **EST.** 1972 **CASES** 15 000
PRODUCT RANGE ($15–25 CD) Sauvignon Blanc, Chardonnay, Cabernet Franc, Classic Merlot, Cabernet Sauvignon, Signature Shiraz, Old Fireside Tawny Port.
SUMMARY These wines are of very good quality, thanks to the lavish (but sophisticated) use of new French oak in tandem with high-quality grapes. The intense, long-flavoured Sauvignon Blanc has been a particularly consistent performer, as has the rich, voluptuous American-oaked Signature Shiraz. No tastings, regrettably; I am sure the wines would score well. Limited retail distribution in South Australia, Victoria, New South Wales and Western Australia, with exports to the UK, the US, Switzerland, Canada, Malaysia and Hong Kong.

Charles Melton

Krondorf Road, Tanunda, SA 5352 **REGION** Barossa Valley
T (08) 8563 3606 **F** (08) 8563 3422 **OPEN** 7 days 11–5
WINEMAKER Charlie Melton **EST.** 1984 **CASES** 15 000
PRODUCT RANGE ($17.90–36.90 CD) Rose of Virginia, Pinot Meunier, Shiraz, Laura Shiraz, Nine Popes (Shiraz Grenache Mourvedre), Grenache, Cabernet Sauvignon, Sotto di Ferro (sweet white).
SUMMARY Charlie Melton, one of the Barossa Valley's great characters, with wife Virginia by his side, makes some of the most eagerly sought à la mode wines in Australia. Inevitably, the Melton empire grew in response to the insatiable demand, with a doubling of estate vineyards to 13 hectares (and the exclusive management and offtake of a further 10 hectares) and the erection of a new barrel store in 1996. The expanded volume has had no adverse effect on the wonderfully rich, sweet, well made wines. Exports to the UK, Ireland, Switzerland, France, the US and South-East Asia.

ŸŸŸŸŸ **Cabernet Sauvignon 2001** Supple, round, velvety and smooth mix of cassis, blackcurrant and spice. **RATING** 95 **DRINK** 2016 $ 41.90
Nine Popes 2001 Fragrant blackberry, plum and anise; excellent balance and structure; fine tannins and subtle oak. **RATING** 94 **DRINK** 2011 $ 44.90

ŸŸŸŸŸ **Shiraz 2001** Sweet black cherry and blackberry aromas; a smooth and supple palate, with excellent texture, length and balance. **RATING** 93 **DRINK** 2014 $ 44.90
Rose of Virginia 2003 Cherry, cherry blossom and a citrus twist; clean, long and fresh. **RATING** 90 **DRINK** Now $ 18.50

Charles Reuben Estate

NR

777 Middle Tea Tree Road, Tea Tree, Tas 7017 **REGION** Southern Tasmania
T (03) 6268 1702 **F** (03) 6231 3571 **OPEN** Wed–Sun 10–5
WINEMAKER Tim Krushka **EST.** 1990 **CASES** 350
PRODUCT RANGE ($15–22 CD) Riesling, Chardonnay, Unwooded Chardonnay, Pinot Noir.
SUMMARY Charles Reuben Estate has 1.5 hectares of pinot noir, 0.5 hectare of chardonnay and a few rows of riesling in production. It has also planted 1.2 hectares of the four Bordeaux varieties, headed by cabernet sauvignon, with a little cabernet franc, merlot and petit verdot, and 0.6 hectare of sauvignon blanc accompanied by a few rows of semillon.

Charles Sturt University Winery

McKeown Drive (off Coolamon Road) Wagga Wagga, NSW 2650 **REGION** Southern New South Wales Zone
T (02) 6933 2435 **F** (02) 6933 4072 **OPEN** Mon–Fri 11–5, weekends 11–4
WINEMAKER Andrew Drumm **EST.** 1977 **CASES** 15 000
PRODUCT RANGE ($13.20–20 CD) The precise composition varies from one release to the next, but is divided into two sections: the top-of-the-range Limited Release Series (Pinot Gris, Chardonnay, Methode Champenoise, Cabernet Sauvignon, Botrytis Semillon, Liqueur Port and Liqueur Muscat, for example) and a basic range of lower-priced varietals including Traminer Riesling, Sauvignon Blanc Semillon, Chardonnay, Shiraz and Cabernet Sauvignon Merlot.

SUMMARY A totally new $2.5 million commercial winery (replacing the 1977 winery) was opened on 9 April 2002, complementing the $1 million experimental winery opened in June 2001. The commercial winery has been funded through the sale of wines produced under the Charles Sturt University brand, wines which always offer the consumer good value. It seems reasonable to expect that the quality will rise in the wake of the opening of the two new facilities. Interestingly, this teaching facility is using screwcaps on all of its wines, both white and red.

ŸŸŸŸŸ **Limited Release Chardonnay 2002** Surprisingly sweet peachy/apricot fruit; climate shows in the bright acidity and length. From Orange. **RATING** 90 **DRINK** 2008 $ 18.15

ŸŸŸŸ **Limited Release Cabernet Sauvignon Merlot Cabernet Franc 2002** Predominantly sweet redcurrant/raspberry aromas and flavours; lingering, fine tannins. Screwcap. Hilltops and Orange. **RATING** 88 **DRINK** 2009 $ 19.80
Shiraz 2002 A mix of spice, briar, leather and black fruits; balanced tannins and oak. Big Rivers and Gundagai. **RATING** 87 **DRINK** 2008 $ 13.20

ŸŸŸŸ **Sauvignon Blanc 2003** **RATING** 86 **DRINK** Now $ 13.20
Chardonnay 2003 Quite fragrant citrus and nectarine; light to medium-bodied, with a subtle whiff of oak. Screwcap. From Big Rivers and Orange. **RATING** 86 **DRINK** 2007 $ 13.20
Cabernet Sauvignon Merlot 2002 **RATING** 84 **DRINK** Now $ 13.20

Charlotte Plains

NR

RMB 3180 Dooleys Road, Maryborough, Vic 3465 **REGION** Bendigo
T (03) 5361 3137 **OPEN** By appointment
WINEMAKER Roland Kaval **EST.** 1990 **CASES** 80
PRODUCT RANGE ($16 ML) Shiraz.
SUMMARY Charlotte Plains is a classic example of miniaturism. Production comes from a close-planted vineyard which is only 1.6 hectares, part being shiraz, the remainder sauvignon blanc. The minuscule production is sold solely through the mailing list and by phone.

Charlotte's Vineyard

★★★★

Kentucky Road, Merricks North, Vic 3926 **REGION** Mornington Peninsula
T (03) 5989 7266 **F** (03) 5989 7500 **OPEN** 7 days 11–5
WINEMAKER Michael Wyles **EST.** 1987
PRODUCT RANGE ($18–26 CD) Chardonnay, Pinot Noir, Shiraz, Cabernet Sauvignon.
SUMMARY Susan Wyles has purchased the former 3-hectare Hanns Creek Vineyard and renamed it Charlotte's Vineyard. She says she and Michael Wyles are going through a very sharp learning curve, but you certainly wouldn't guess that by looking at the first-up releases from Charlotte's Vineyard.

ŸŸŸŸŸ **Pinot Noir 2002** Complex and rich; very intense, obvious low yield; strong varietal plummy character; lingering spicy notes. **RATING** 94 **DRINK** 2009

ŸŸŸŸ **Chardonnay 2002** Well made; obvious barrel-ferment oak inputs; some malolactic, too, around a core of melon and white peach. Ageing nicely. **RATING** 89 **DRINK** 2007

Chartley Estate

★★★★

38 Blackwood Hills Road, Rowella, Tas 7270 **REGION** Northern Tasmania
T (03) 6394 7198 **F** (03) 6394 7598 **OPEN** 7 days 10–5
WINEMAKER Julian Alcorso, Leigh Clarnette (Contract) **EST.** 2000 **CASES** 180
PRODUCT RANGE ($12.95–28 R) Riesling, Pinot Gris, Pinot Noir.
SUMMARY The Kossman family began the establishment of 2 hectares each of riesling, sauvignon blanc and pinot noir, and 1 hectare of pinot gris, in 2000. As the vines come into full bearing, the production will increase substantially; if the 2003 Pinot Gris is any guide, wine quality will be excellent, which is not surprising given the skills of the contract winemaking team of Julian Alcorso and Leigh Clarnette.

ŸŸŸŸŸ **Pinot Gris 2003** Highly aromatic apple blossom, pear and spice; abundant flavour and mouthfeel; very good varietal example; has developed in bottle. **RATING** 90 **DRINK** 2007 $ 23.95

Chateau Champsaur
NR

Wandang Lane, Forbes, NSW 2871 **REGION** Central Ranges Zone
T (02) 6852 3908 **F** (02) 6852 3902 **OPEN** Saturday 10–5, or by appointment
WINEMAKER Pierre Dalle, Andrew McEwin **EST.** 1866 **CASES** 200
PRODUCT RANGE ($10–13 CD) Colombard Semillon, Chateau Dry White, Shiraz, Shiraz Cabernet, fortified.
SUMMARY The establishment date of 1866 is correct. In that year Frenchmen Joseph Bernard Raymond and Auguste Nicolas took up a 130-hectare selection and erected a large wooden winery and cellar, with production ranging up to 360 000 litres in a year in its heyday. They named it Champsaur after Raymond's native valley in France, and it is said to be the oldest French winery in the southern hemisphere. In recent years it traded as Lachlan Valley Wines, but under the ownership of Pierre Dalle has reverted to its traditional name and French ownership.

Chateau Dore
NR

303 Mandurang Road, Mandurang near Bendigo, Vic 3551 **REGION** Bendigo
T (03) 5439 5278 **OPEN** 7 days 10–5
WINEMAKER Ivan Grose **EST.** 1860 **CASES** 1000
PRODUCT RANGE ($19–25 CD) Riesling, Shiraz, Cabernet Sauvignon, Tawny Port.
SUMMARY Has been in the ownership of the Grose family since 1860, with the winery buildings dating back respectively to 1860 and 1893. All wine is sold through the cellar door and function centre.

Chateau Dorrien

Cnr Seppeltsfield Road and Barossa Valley Way, Dorrien, SA 5352 **REGION** Barossa Valley
T (08) 8562 2850 **F** (08) 8562 1416 **OPEN** 7 days 10–5
WINEMAKER Fernando Martin, Ramon Martin **EST.** 1985 **CASES** 2000
PRODUCT RANGE ($10–18 CD) A full range of varietal white and red wines focused around Riesling, Chardonnay, Shiraz, Mourvedre, Cabernet Merlot, Cabernet Sauvignon plus fortified wines, and range of meads in various forms; also Twin Valley wines.
SUMMARY The Martin family, headed by Fernando and Jeanette, purchased the old Dorrien winery from the Seppelt family in 1984, officially opening it as Chateau Dorrien on 13 January 1985. In 1990 the family purchased Twin Valley Estate, and moved the winemaking operations of Chateau Dorrien to the Twin Valley site. All of the Chateau Dorrien group wines are sold at Chateau Dorrien, Twin Valley being simply a production facility. Exports to Singapore and the US.

TTTT **Shiraz 1999** Nice bottle-developed style; light to medium-bodied; blackberry, mocha and chocolate; fine tannins, good finish. **RATING** 88 **DRINK** 2009 $ 20

TTTT **Cabernet Sauvignon 2000** **RATING** 86 **DRINK** 2008 $ 20
Cabernet Sauvignon 1999 **RATING** 86 **DRINK** 2007 $ 20
Cabernet Merlot 2000 **RATING** 85 **DRINK** Now $ 20
Land's End Chardonnay 2003 **RATING** 84 **DRINK** 2007 $ 14

TTT **Eden Valley Riesling 2003** **RATING** 81 $ 15
Golden Harvest Riesling 2003 **RATING** 80 $ 14
Primavera Rose NV **RATING** 80 $ 10

Chateau Francois
NR

Broke Road, Pokolbin, NSW 2321 **REGION** Lower Hunter Valley
T (02) 4998 7548 **F** (02) 4998 7805 **OPEN** Weekends 9–5, or by appointment
WINEMAKER Don Francois **EST.** 1969 **CASES** 700
PRODUCT RANGE Pokolbin Mallee Semillon, Chardonnay, Shiraz Pinot Noir.
SUMMARY The retirement hobby of former NSW Director of Fisheries, Don Francois. Soft-flavoured and structured wines which frequently show regional characters but which are modestly priced and are all sold through the cellar door and by mailing list to a loyal following. The tasting room is available for private dinners for 12–16 people. Don Francois sailed through a quadruple-bypass followed by a mild stroke with his sense of humour intact, if not enhanced. A subsequent newsletter

said (inter alia) '... my brush with destiny has changed my grizzly personality and I am now sweetness and light ... Can you believe? Well, almost!' He even promises comfortable tasting facilities.

ΨΨΨΨ **Semillon 2002** Mineral, slate and herb aromas repeated in the crisp, tight and youthful palate. **RATING** 87 **DRINK** 2009

ΨΨΨ **Semillon 1999 RATING** 82

Chateau Leamon ★★★★

5528 Calder Highway, Bendigo, Vic 3550 **REGION** Bendigo
T (03) 5447 7995 **F** (03) 5447 0855 **OPEN** Wed–Mon 10–5
WINEMAKER Ian Leamon **EST.** 1973 **CASES** 2500
PRODUCT RANGE ($17–38 CD) Riesling, Semillon, Chardonnay, Shiraz, Reserve Shiraz, Cabernet Sauvignon Cabernet Franc Merlot, Reserve Cabernet Sauvignon.
SUMMARY One of the longest-established wineries in the region, with estate and locally grown shiraz and cabernet family grapes providing the excellent red wines. Limited retail distribution in Victoria, New South Wales and Queensland; exports to Asia, the US, Canada, the UK and Germany.

ΨΨΨΨΨ **Reserve Shiraz 2002** A complex array of licorice, spice, anise, blackberry and black cherry aromas and flavours; satiny texture. **RATING** 93 **DRINK** 2017 $ 38

ΨΨΨΨ **Cabernet Sauvignon Cabernet Franc Merlot 2002** A light to medium-bodied mix of red berry, leaf and mint; savoury, light tannins. **RATING** 87 **DRINK** 2008 $ 22

ΨΨΨΨ **Reserve Cabernet Sauvignon 2002 RATING** 86 **DRINK** 2010 $ 38

Chateau Pâto ★★★★★

Thompson's Road, Pokolbin, NSW 2321 **REGION** Lower Hunter Valley
T (02) 4998 7634 **F** (02) 4998 7860 **OPEN** By appointment
WINEMAKER Nicholas Paterson **EST.** 1980 **CASES** 300
PRODUCT RANGE ($38 CD) Shiraz.
SUMMARY Nicholas Paterson took over responsibility for this tiny winery following the death of father David Paterson during the 1993 vintage. Two and a half hectares of shiraz, 1 hectare of chardonnay and 0.5 hectare of pinot noir; most of the grapes are sold, with a tiny quantity of shiraz being made into a marvellous wine. David Paterson's inheritance is being handsomely guarded.

ΨΨΨΨΨ **Shiraz 2002** Twenty-five-year-old vines give that extra concentration; lovely red and black fruits; fine, silky tannins. **RATING** 94 **DRINK** 2015 $ 38

Chateau Tanunda ★★★

9 Basedow Road, Tanunda, SA 5352 **REGION** Barossa Valley
T (08) 8563 3888 **F** (08) 8563 1422 **OPEN** 7 days 10–5
WINEMAKER Simon Gilbert, Ralph Fowler (Contract) **EST.** 1890 **CASES** 8000
PRODUCT RANGE ($17–45 CD) The Chateau Riesling, Botrytis Semillon, Shiraz, Merlot Cabernet; Chateau Tanunda Pinot Noir Chardonnay, Shiraz, Cabernet Sauvignon; Grand Barossa Shiraz.
SUMMARY This is one of the most imposing winery buildings in the Barossa Valley, built from stone quarried at nearby Bethany in the late 1880s. It started life as a winery, then became a specialist brandy distillery until the death of the Australian brandy industry, whereafter it was simply used as storage cellars. It has now been completely restored, and converted to a major convention facility catering for groups up to 400. The large complex also houses a cellar door where the Chateau Tanunda wines are sold; Chateau Bistro, gardens and a croquet lawn; the Barossa Small Winemakers Centre, offering wines made by small independent winemakers in the region; and, finally, specialist support services for tour operators. It is a sister winery to Cowra Estate; both are owned by the Geber family.

ΨΨΨΨ **Grand Barossa Shiraz 2001** Pleasant medium-bodied Shiraz in traditional Barossa Valley style. **RATING** 87 **DRINK** 2010 $ 45

ΨΨΨΨ **Pinot Chardonnay 2001 RATING** 86 **DRINK** Now $ 17
The Chateau Shiraz 2001 RATING 85 **DRINK** 2007 $ 28

Chatsfield

O'Neil Road, Mount Barker, WA 6324 **REGION** Mount Barker
T (08) 9851 1704 **F** (08) 9851 1704 **OPEN** Tues–Sun, public holidays 10.30–4.30
WINEMAKER Dionne Miller **EST.** 1976 **CASES** 7000
PRODUCT RANGE ($10–20 CD) Riesling, Sauvignon Blanc, Gewurztraminer, Chardonnay, Indulge (sweet white), Shiraz, Cabernet Franc.
SUMMARY Irish-born medical practitioner Ken Lynch can be proud of his achievements at Chatsfield, as can most of the various contract winemakers who have taken the high-quality estate-grown material and made some impressive wines, notably the Riesling, vibrant Cabernet Franc (as an unwooded nouveau style) and spicy licorice Shiraz. Exports to the UK, the US, Japan and Hong Kong.

ᵀᵀᵀᵀᵀ Mount Barker Shiraz 2002 Elegant, spicy blackberry/cherry fruit. A long palate and fine tannins to close; has finesse. **RATING** 92 **DRINK** 2010 **$** 20
Mount Barker Chardonnay 2002 Complex, cool-grown fruit aromas; elegant, light to medium-bodied stone fruit and subtle oak ex 9 months in wood; great value. **RATING** 90 **DRINK** 2007 **$** 15

Chatto Wines

McDonalds Road, Pokolbin, NSW 2321 **REGION** Lower Hunter Valley
T 0417 109 794 **F** (02) 4998 7294 **OPEN** 7 days 9–5
WINEMAKER Jim Chatto **EST.** 2000 **CASES** 750
PRODUCT RANGE ($19.50–35 R) Hunter Valley Semillon; Tamar Valley Riesling and Pinot Noir.
SUMMARY Jim Chatto spent several years in Tasmania as the first winemaker at Rosevears Estate, and indeed helped design the Rosevears winery. He has since moved to the Hunter Valley to work for Monarch Winemaking Services, but has used his Tasmanian contacts to buy small parcels of riesling and pinot noir. Possessed of a particularly good palate, he has made wines of excellent quality under the Chatto label. Exports to Canada.

ᵀᵀᵀᵀᵀ Tamar Valley Pinot Noir 2002 Amazing colour; exceptional breadth and depth of flavour, oozing black plums and dark cherries; the tiny crop is obvious, making it difficult to avoid some tadpole effect. **RATING** 94 **DRINK** 2012 **$** 35

ᵀᵀᵀᵀᵀ Hunter Valley Semillon 2001 Herbs, snow peas, grass and lanolin aromas; very good line and length; simply requires time. **RATING** 91 **DRINK** 2011 **$** 19.50
Tamar Valley Riesling 2000 Already showing classic bottle-developed aromas and flavours; lime blossom fruit; shortens fractionally, but has great flavour. **RATING** 90 **DRINK** Now **$** 19.50

Chepstowe Vineyard

Fitzpatricks Lane, Carngham, Vic 3351 **REGION** Ballarat
T (03) 5344 9412 **F** (03) 5344 9403 **OPEN** 7 days 10–5
WINEMAKER John Ellis (Contract) **EST.** 1994 **CASES** 700
PRODUCT RANGE ($25–30 CD) Chardonnay, Pinot Noir.
SUMMARY Way back in 1983 Bill Wallace asked the then Yellowglen winemaker Dominique Landragin what he thought about the suitability of a block of steeply sloping grazing land on the side of the Chepstowe Hill, looking northeast across to the Grampians and its various mountains, including Mount Misery. Landragin replied, 'It might be possible to grow grapes there', and Wallace subsequently acquired the property. It was not until November 1994 that 1 hectare each of pinot noir and chardonnay was planted, followed by an additional hectare of pinot noir in 1996. In the warmest of vintages it is possible to obtain full ripeness for table wines, but in normal years I suspect sparkling wine (of potentially high quality) might be the best option.

Chestnut Grove

★★★☆

Chestnut Grove Road, Manjimup, WA 6258 **REGION** Manjimup
T (08) 9772 4345 **F** (08) 9772 4543 **OPEN** 7 days 10–4
WINEMAKER Mark Aitken **EST.** 1988 **CASES** 13 000

PRODUCT RANGE ($10–50 R) Platinum (Verdelho Sauvignon Blanc), Verdelho, Chardonnay, Autumn Harvest, Scintillement (sparkling), Pinot Noir, Cabernet Merlot, Merlot, Vermilion (Shiraz Cabernet Sauvignon).

SUMMARY A substantial vineyard which is now reaching maturity and the erection of an on-site winery are the most obvious signs of change, but ownership, too, has been passed on by the late founder Vic Kordic to his sons Paul (a Perth lawyer) and Mark (who is the general manager of the wine business) and thence (in 2002) to Mike Calneggia's Australian Wine Holdings Limited group. Exports to Canada, Denmark, Germany, Hong Kong, Singapore and the UK.

ŸŸŸŸ **Verdelho 2003** RATING 84 DRINK Now $ 20

Chestnut Hill Vineyard ★★★★

1280 Pakenham Road, Mount Burnett, Vic 3781 **REGION** Gippsland
T (03) 5942 7314 **F** (03) 5942 7314 **OPEN** Weekends and public holidays 10.30–5.30, or by appointment
WINEMAKER Charlie Javor **EST.** 1995 **CASES** 1200
PRODUCT RANGE ($24–27.50 CD) Sauvignon Blanc, Liberty Chardonnay, Pinot Noir.
SUMMARY Charlie and Ivka Javor started Chestnut Hill with small plantings of chardonnay and shiraz in 1985 and have slowly increased the vineyards to their present total of a little over 3 hectares. The first wines were made in 1995, and all distribution is through the cellar door and direct to a few restaurants. Situated less than 1 hour's drive from Melbourne, the picturesque vineyard is situated among the rolling hills in the southeast of the Dandenongs, near Mount Burnett. The label explains, 'Liberty is a gift we had never experienced in our homeland', which was Croatia, from which they emigrated in the late 1960s.

ŸŸŸŸŸ **Sauvignon Blanc 2003** Crisp, clean gooseberry and asparagus flavours; lingering acidity; very good finish. **RATING** 90 **DRINK** Now $ 24

ŸŸŸŸ **Liberty Chardonnay 2001** Elegant melon and stone fruit; fine line and length; developing slowly and most impressively. **RATING** 89 **DRINK** Now $ 27.50
Pinot Noir 2001 Elegant light-bodied style; savoury and spicy, but not a lot of flesh. **RATING** 88 **DRINK** Now $ 27.50

Cheviot Bridge/Long Flat ★★★★

10/499 St Kilda Road, Melbourne, Vic 3004 (postal) **REGION** Upper Goulburn
T (03) 9820 9080 **F** (03) 9820 9070 **OPEN** Not
WINEMAKER Hugh Cuthbertson **EST.** 1998
PRODUCT RANGE ($12.95–25 R) In descending order of price, but ascending order of volume: Cheviot Bridge Yea Valley Range ($24), CB Range ($14), The Long Flat Wine Co. ($12) and Long Flat (ex Tyrrell's) ($7.99). Kissing Bridge and Thirsty Lizard are export-only labels.
SUMMARY Cheviot Bridge/Long Flat brings together a highly experienced team of wine industry professionals and investors who provided the 10 million plus required to purchase the Long Flat range of wines from Tyrrell's, the purchase taking place in the second half of 2003. The wines are being contract-made by Tyrrell's and others, but with substantial input from the Cheviot Bridge partners, in terms of both sourcing and wine style. The major market is the US, and the key is a structure set up by Cheviot Bridge to eliminate one of the profit levels typically encountered by the three-tiered US distribution system. Also exports to many other parts of the world; and, of course, very substantial local distribution.

ŸŸŸŸŸ **The Long Flat Wine Co. Yarra Valley Pinot Noir 2002** Altogether impressive; abundant black cherry/plum/spice aromas and flavours; good focus, balance and length. Great value. **RATING** 90 **DRINK** 2009 $ 12
Cheviot Bridge Yea Valley Cabernet Merlot 2001 Complex, briary/brambly aromas; concentrated and quite sweet fruit on the palate; smooth finish. **RATING** 90 **DRINK** 2011 $ 24

ŸŸŸŸ **The Long Flat Wine Co. Coonawarra Cabernet Sauvignon 2001** Good wine; medium-bodied, and not over-worked or extracted; blackcurrant and mulberry fruit; gentle oak, fine tannins. **RATING** 88 **DRINK** 2011 $ 12

The Long Flat Wine Co. Eden Valley Riesling 2003 Rich, full, almost fleshy; sweet, tropical lime juice; ready now. Screwcap. **RATING** 87 **DRINK** Now $ 12

The Long Flat Wine Co. Barossa Valley Shiraz 2002 Clean, fresh, light to medium-bodied; bright red and black fruits, minimal oak influence; drink-now style. **RATING** 87 **DRINK** Now $ 12

ȲȲȲȲ **The Long Flat Wine Co. Yarra Valley Chardonnay 2003** Clean, gentle melon and nectarine; no obvious oak, easy style. Screwcap. **RATING** 86 **DRINK** Now $ 12

Long Flat White 2002 RATING 84 **DRINK** Now $ 8.50

ȲȲȲ **Long Flat Chardonnay 2002 RATING** 83 $ 8.50

Long Flat Shiraz 2002 RATING 83 $ 8.50

Long Flat Red 2002 RATING 83 $ 8.50

Long Flat Brut NV RATING 83 $ 8.50

Long Flat Merlot 2002 RATING 82 $ 8.50

🍃 Chidlow's Well Estate   NR

PO Box 84, Chidlow, WA 6556 **REGION** Perth Hills
T (08) 9572 3770 **F** (08) 9572 3750 **OPEN** By appointment
WINEMAKER Rob Marshall (Contract) **EST.** 2002 **CASES** 500
PRODUCT RANGE ($15–18 CD) Chenin Blanc, Reserve Chardonnay, Shiraz.
SUMMARY Chidlow is around 60 kilometres east of Perth, and was originally known as Chidlows Well, its railway station a hub for train services to the interior of the State. While within the Perth Hills region, it is some way distant from the majority of the wineries in the Hills. Rod and Marilyn Lange have 3 hectares of chardonnay, chenin blanc and shiraz, using the experience and skill of Rob Marshall as contract winemaker. The sales are by word of mouth, mail order and through the cellar door.

🍃 Chittering Valley Winery/Nesci Estate Wines   NR

Lot 12 Great Northern Highway, Chittering, WA 6084 **REGION** Perth Hills
T (08) 9571 4102 **F** (08) 9571 4288 **OPEN** Not
WINEMAKER Kevin Nesci **EST.** 1948
PRODUCT RANGE Chenin Blanc, Sauvignon Blanc, Chardonnay, Shiraz, Cabernet Sauvignon.
SUMMARY The roots of this business go back well over 50 years. Kevin Nesci has 25 hectares of sauvignon blanc, chenin blanc, semillon, chardonnay, pinot noir, grenache, merlot, shiraz, cabernet sauvignon, zinfandel and pedro ximenes. Most of the grape production is sold, a lesser amount made on-site; the latter is sold by mail order.

🍃 Chiverton   NR

605 Mid Western Highway, Cowra, NSW 2794 **REGION** Cowra
T (02) 6342 9308 **F** (02) 6342 9314 **OPEN** Weekends and public holidays 10–4
WINEMAKER Simon Gilbert (Contract) **EST.** 1994
PRODUCT RANGE Verdelho, Chardonnay, Shiraz, Cabernet Sauvignon.
SUMMARY Greg Thompson began the development of Chiverton in 1994; in 1998 a cellar door and small tasting room attached to the Chiverton Homestead were opened. The wines are sold under the Chiverton, Billygoat Hill and Nude Estate labels, with exports to England. Much of the production from the 107 hectares of semillon, chardonnay, verdelho, cabernet sauvignon, merlot and shiraz is sold to other wineries.

Chrismont Wines

Upper King Valley Road, Cheshunt, Vic 3678 **REGION** King Valley
T (03) 5729 8220 **F** (03) 5729 8253 **OPEN** 7 days 11–5
WINEMAKER Warren Proft **EST.** 1980
PRODUCT RANGE ($14–25 CD) Riesling, Chardonnay, Shiraz, Cabernet Merlot; La Zona range of Marzemino, Pinot Grigio, Barbera.

SUMMARY Arnold (Arnie) and Jo Pizzini have established 80 hectares of vineyards in the Whitfield area of the Upper King Valley. They have planted riesling, sauvignon blanc, chardonnay, pinot gris, cabernet sauvignon, merlot, shiraz, barbera, marzemino and arneis. The La Zona range ties in the Italian parentage of the Pizzinis, and is part of their intense interest in all things Italian.

ΥΥΥΥ   **Riesling 2003** Perfumed, aromatic; considerable intensity and length, with a touch of spritz. **RATING** 89 **DRINK** 2007 $14

Christmas Hill   NR

RSD 25C, Meadows, SA 5201 (postal) **REGION** Adelaide Hills
T (08) 8235 3000 **F** (08) 332 2398 **OPEN** Not
WINEMAKER Peter Leske (Contract) **EST.** 2000 **CASES** 750
PRODUCT RANGE ($14 ML) Sauvignon Blanc.
SUMMARY Christmas Hill is primarily a grape grower, selling all but a small part of its production of chardonnay (3.8 hectares), sauvignon blanc (3.5 hectares), shiraz (1.2 hectares), cabernet sauvignon (2.6 hectares) and pinot noir (1.4 hectares), but keeping back the equivalent of 750 cases of Sauvignon Blanc which is made for Christmas Hill by Peter Leske at Nepenthe Wines. It is primarily sold to two leading Adelaide clubs, a restaurant, and through Christmas Hills' mailing list, with a dribble finding its way onto the Adelaide retail market. It is offered only by the case to mailing list customers.

Churchview Estate   ★★★☆

Cnr Bussell Highway and Gale Road, Metricup, WA 6280 **REGION** Margaret River
T (08) 9755 7200 **F** (08) 9755 7300 **OPEN** Mon–Sat 9.30–5.30
WINEMAKER Bill Crappsley (Contract) **EST.** 1998 **CASES** 18 000
PRODUCT RANGE ($14.50–24.50 CD) Riesling, Semillon Sauvignon Blanc, Marsanne, Unwooded Chardonnay, Chardonnay, Rose, Shiraz, Cabernet Merlot, Cabernet Sauvignon, Private Bin Vintage Port.
SUMMARY The Fokkema family, headed by Spike Fokkema, immigrated from The Netherlands in the 1950s. Their business success in the following decades led to the acquisition of the 100-hectare Churchview Estate property in 1997, and to the progressive establishment of 56 hectares of vineyards; another 14 hectares are scheduled for planting by 2007. This will result in production rising from the present 18 000 cases to 60 000 cases, sustained by exports to Asia and The Netherlands. The family lives on-site, and carries out much of the viticultural work, with the vineyard canopy managed on the Smart Dyson model. Yields are controlled to 10 tonnes per hectare, and veteran West Australian winemaker Bill Crappsley is in charge, producing consistently good wines.

ΥΥΥΥ   **Premium Range Chardonnay 2003** Spotlessly clean, light to medium-bodied; the peach and melon fruit has soaked up the oak; fractionally sweet overall, possibly ex alcohol. **RATING** 89 **DRINK** 2008 $22.50
     Premium Range Marsanne 2003 Powdery/chalky/stoney varietal aromas; some crushed citrus leaves on the palate; impressive intensity and length. Screwcap. **RATING** 89 **DRINK** 2007 $14.50
     Unwooded Chardonnay 2003 Clean and fresh; melon, apple and citrus; good line and length. **RATING** 88 **DRINK** 2007 $19.50
     Cabernet Sauvignon 2002 Fresh, bright and youthful; light to medium-bodied; cassis/red fruits, minimal tannins. **RATING** 87 **DRINK** 2008 $18.50
     Private Bin Vintage Port 2002 Nice dry style, firm and clean; blackberries and spices; too good for cellar door. **RATING** 87 **DRINK** 2012 $18.50

ΥΥΥΫ   **Rose 2003** **RATING** 86 **DRINK** Now $14.50
     Premium Range Riesling 2003 **RATING** 85 **DRINK** Now $19.50
     Shiraz 2002 **RATING** 85 **DRINK** 2009 $24.50
     Cabernet Sauvignon Merlot 2002 **RATING** 85 **DRINK** 2009 $22.50

Ciavarella ★★★

Evans Lane, Oxley, Vic 3678 **REGION** King Valley
T (03) 5727 3384 **F** (03) 5727 3384 **OPEN** Mon–Sat 9–6, Sun 10–6
WINEMAKER Cyril Ciavarella **EST.** 1978 **CASES** 3000
PRODUCT RANGE ($10–28 CD) Aucerot, Semillon Aucerot, Semillon, Verdelho, Viognier, Unwooded Chardonnay, Chardonnay, Bianca (sweet white), Rosina, Durif, Dolcino (medium-bodied sweet red), Cabernet Sauvignon.
SUMMARY Cyril and Jan Ciavarella both entered the wine industry from other professions and have been producing wine since 1992. The vineyard was planted in 1978, with plantings and varieties being extended over the years. One variety, aucerot (first released in 375 ml bottles in late 2001) was produced by Maurice O'Shea of McWilliam's Mount Pleasant in the Hunter Valley 50 or more years ago; the Ciavarella vines have been grown from cuttings collected from an old Glenrowan vineyard before the parent plants were removed in the mid-1980s.

ΨΨΨΨ **Semillon Aucerot 2002** Quite lusciously fruit-sweet, predominantly peach/stone fruit; good balance and acidity. Interesting use of very rare grape variety. **RATING** 87 **DRINK** Now $ 25

Clairault ★★★★

Caves Road, Wilyabrup, WA 6280 **REGION** Margaret River
T (08) 9755 6225 **F** (08) 9755 6229 **OPEN** 7 days 10–5
WINEMAKER Will Shields **EST.** 1976 **CASES** 40 000
PRODUCT RANGE ($14.50–50 CD) Riesling, Semillon, Sauvignon Blanc, Semillon Sauvignon Blanc, Chardonnay, Claireau (sweet white), Cape Pink, Cabernet Merlot, Cabernet Sauvignon, The Clairault Claddah Reserve; also Swagman's Kiss Chardonnay, White and Red.
SUMMARY Bill and Ena Martin, with sons Conor, Brian and Shane, acquired Clairault several years ago; this has led to a major expansion of the vineyards on the 120-hectare property. The 12 hectares of vines established by the Lewises, which are up to 25 years old, are being supplemented by the development of another 70 hectares of vines on the property, with an end-point ratio of 70 per cent red varieties to 30 per cent white varieties. A restaurant is open for lunch 7 days. Domestic distribution throughout all States; exports to the US, Canada, the UK and Germany.

Clancy's of Conargo NR

Killone Park, Conargo Road, Deniliquin, NSW 2710 **REGION** Riverina
T (03) 5884 6684 **F** (03) 5884 6779 **OPEN** 7 days 10–6
WINEMAKER Bernard Clancy, Jason Clancy **EST.** 1999 **CASES** 1000
PRODUCT RANGE ($10–15 CD) Semillon Chardonnay, Verdelho, Taminga, Mataro, Grenache, Shiraz, Cabernet Sauvignon
SUMMARY The Clancy family has been carrying on a mixed farming enterprise on their property north of Deniliquin for over 25 years, including lucerne growing, cropping and sheep production. A tiny planting of taminga was made in 1988, but it was not until 6 hectares were planted in 1997 that the Clancys ventured into commercial grape growing and winemaking. The predominant varieties are shiraz and semillon. All of the production is sold locally and through the cellar door.

Clarence Hill ★★★

PO Box 530, McLaren Vale, SA 5171 **REGION** McLaren Vale
T (08) 8323 8946 **F** (08) 8323 9644 **OPEN** Not
WINEMAKER Claudio Curtis, Brian Light (Contract) **EST.** 1990
PRODUCT RANGE ($10–35 ML) Clarence Hill range of Riesling, Semillon, Sauvignon Blanc, Chardonnay, Shiraz, Grenache Shiraz, Cabernet Sauvignon Merlot, Cabernet Sauvignon, La Cavata Old Port; Landcross range of Sauvignon Blanc Semillon, Shiraz Cabernet Sauvignon.
SUMMARY This is indeed a complicated story, with the Curtis family as its core, encompassing a wine history dating back to the 15th century in Italy. In 1956 the family emigrated to Australia, purchasing its first vineyard land from one Clarence William Torrens Rivers; they renamed it Clarence Hill. Further land was acquired in the 1980s and 1990s, establishing the Landcross Farm and California Rise vineyards, which, together with Clarence Hill, now have over 100 hectares in production. In

1990 Claudio Curtis, having previously acquired a science degree from the University of Adelaide, formed the Tiers Wine Co. (Australia) Pty Ltd to undertake wine production and sales. That company, obviously enough, has nothing to do with Petaluma, and just to complicate matters further, a new winery adjacent to the company's vineyards, operational for the 2002 vintage, is called Landcross Estate Winery. Exports to the UK, Canada, Switzerland and Thailand.

Clarendon Hills

Brookmans Road, Blewitt Springs, SA 5171 **REGION** McLaren Vale
T (08) 8364 1484 **F** (08) 8364 1484 **OPEN** By appointment
WINEMAKER Roman Bratasiuk **EST.** 1989 **CASES** 12 000
PRODUCT RANGE ($65–250 R) Individual vineyard releases of Pinot Noir, Syrah, Shiraz, Grenache and Cabernet Sauvignon.
SUMMARY Age and experience, it would seem, have mellowed Roman Bratasiuk — and the style of his wines. Once formidable and often rustic, they are now far more sculpted and smooth, at times bordering on downright elegance. Exports to New Zealand, the US, Canada, Germany, Switzerland, Belgium, The Netherlands, Sweden, the UK and Japan.

ŸŸŸŸŸ **Hickinbotham Vineyard Shiraz 2001** A mix of bright red berry fruit and bitter chocolate; quality oak and lingering, fine tannins. **RATING** 92 **DRINK** 2011 **$** 100
Brookman Vineyard Shiraz 2001 Cool-grown herb, leaf, mint and chocolate flavours run through a medium-bodied but long palate. **RATING** 90 **DRINK** 2010 **$** 100

Classic McLaren Wines

Lot B Coppermine Road, McLaren Vale, SA 5171 **REGION** McLaren Vale
T (08) 8323 9551 **F** (08) 8323 9551 **OPEN** By appointment
WINEMAKER Tony De Lisio **EST.** 1996 **CASES** 7100
PRODUCT RANGE ($16.55–100 R) CMC range of Shiraz, Grenache, Cabernet Merlot; and La Testa range of Chardonnay, Shiraz, Blend (Shiraz Grenache Cabernet Sauvignon), Merlot, Grenache, Cabernet Sauvignon.
SUMMARY Tony and Krystina De Lisio have established a substantial business in a relatively short period of time. They have established vineyard plantings of shiraz (20.47 hectares), merlot (11.34 hectares), cabernet sauvignon (9.29 hectares), semillon (3.9 hectares) and chardonnay (0.41 hectares), and are currently building a new winery and underground cellar storage for wine in barrel and packaged wine. When the new buildings are completed, there will be facilities for tastings, promotions and the possibility of limited cellar-door sales. The wines are distributed in Sydney and Melbourne by Ultimo Wine Centre; Adelaide is serviced direct from the winery. Exports to the UK, the US, Thailand, Germany, Belgium, Switzerland and New Zealand have been established at impressively high prices.

Clayfield Wines

Wilde Lane, Moyston, Vic 3377 **REGION** Grampians
T (03) 5354 2689 **OPEN** Mon–Sat 10–5, Sun 11–4
WINEMAKER Simon Clayfield **EST.** 1997 **CASES** 500
PRODUCT RANGE ($45 CD) Shiraz.
SUMMARY Former long-serving Best's winemaker Simon Clayfield and wife Kaye are now doing their own thing. They planted 2 hectares of shiraz between 1997 and 1999, and after early vintages from 1999 to 2001, would have produced a substantial crop in 2002 were it not for a grass fire a month before vintage. The volumes so far made are tiny, and the Clayfields expect to be producing more than 750 cases of Shiraz by 2005. The splendid Black Label Shiraz is sold for $45 at the cellar door and distributed through Woods Wines Pty Ltd (03) 9381 2263; retail it is available at Armadale Cellars, High Street, Prahran. Currently one-third of the production is exported to the US.

Claymore Wines

Leasingham Road, Leasingham, SA 5452 **REGION** Clare Valley
T 0412 822 250 **F** (08) 8284 2899 **OPEN** Weekends and public holidays 10–5
WINEMAKER Justin Ardill **EST.** 1998 **CASES** 3000

PRODUCT RANGE ($16–30 CD) Joshua Tree Clare Valley Riesling, Joshua Tree Watervale Riesling, Duet Semillon Chardonnay, Duet Grenache Shiraz, Nocturne Shiraz, Dark Side of the Moon Shiraz, Merlot, Nocturne Cabernet.

SUMMARY Claymore Wines draws on various vineyards, some situated in the Clare Valley, others in McLaren Vale. The Kupu-Kupu Vineyard at Penwortham has 9 hectares of shiraz and 2 hectares of merlot planted in 1997; the Nocturne series of wines come from the Wilpena and Moray Park Vineyards owned by the Trott family; and the Joshua Tree Watervale Riesling comes from old vines on the Leasingham to Mintaro road; these are not, however, estate-owned (although the story is, I must admit, somewhat complex). It is the Joshua Tree Rieslings which have attracted high ratings from magazines and at the Clare Valley Wine Show.

Clearview Estate Mudgee ★★☆

Cnr Sydney and Rocky Water Hole Roads, Mudgee, NSW 2850 **REGION** Mudgee
T (02) 6372 4546 **F** (02) 6372 7577 **OPEN** Fri–Mon 10–4, or by appointment
WINEMAKER Letitia (Tish) Cecchini **EST.** 1995 **CASES** 2200
PRODUCT RANGE ($14–19 CD) Church Creek Chardonnay (oaked and unoaked); Rocky Waterhole Red Shiraz, Cabernet Sauvignon, Merlot.
SUMMARY No relationship with the famous Hawke's Bay winery, but doubtless John E Hickey and family would be delighted to achieve the same quality. They have progressively planted 4.23 hectares of shiraz, 2.27 hectares each of chardonnay and cabernet sauvignon, 1.2 hectare of merlot, and small amounts of cabernet franc, semillon, pinot grigio, barbera and sangiovese (yet to come into bearing) since 1995, and send the grapes to the Hunter Valley to be contract-made. An 'Aussie Farm'-style cellar door with a timber deck looking out over the vineyard and surrounding vista was opened in September 2000. Exports to the US.

ŦŦŦŸ **Cabernet Shiraz 2002 RATING** 84 **DRINK** 2007 **$** 19

ŦŦŦ **Rocky Waterhole Red Shiraz 2001 RATING** 83 **$** 18
Merlot 2002 RATING 82 **$** 19
Rocky Waterhole Red Merlot 2002 RATING 82 **$** 19
Church Creek Chardonnay 2002 RATING 80 **$** 17

🐦 Cleggett Wines NR

'Shalistin', Langhorne Creek, SA 5255 (postal) **REGION** Langhorne Creek
T (08) 8537 3133 **F** (08) 8537 3102 **OPEN** At Bremer Centre, Langhorne Creek, 7 days 11–5
WINEMAKER Contract **EST.** 2000 **CASES** 2000
PRODUCT RANGE ($12–20 ML) Shalistin, Malian, Cabernet Sauvignon.
SUMMARY The Cleggett family first planted grape vines at Langhorne Creek in 1911. In 1977 a sport (a natural mutation) of cabernet sauvignon produced bronze-coloured grapes; cuttings were taken and increasing quantities of the vine were gradually established, and called malian. Ten years later one of the malian vines itself mutated to yield golden-white bunches, and this in turn was propagated with the name shalistin. There are now 4 hectares of shalistin and 2 hectares of malian in bearing. Shalistin is made as a full-bodied but unoaked white wine; malian produces both an early and a late harvest wine, the former in a rose style, the latter with significant residual sugar, but again in a rose style. These wines are available, along with Cabernet Sauvignon, direct from the winery, in selected liquor outlets and restaurants, or direct from the winery.

Clemens Hill ★★★☆

686 Richmond Road, Cambridge, Tas 7170 **REGION** Southern Tasmania
T (03) 6248 5985 **F** (03) 6248 5985 **OPEN** By appointment
WINEMAKER Julian Alcorso (Contract) **EST.** 1994 **CASES** 650
PRODUCT RANGE ($16.50–25 CD) Sauvignon Blanc, Chardonnay, Pinot Noir.
SUMMARY The Shepherd family acquired Clemens Hill in June 2001 after selling their Rosabrook winery in the Margaret River to Palandri Wines. They also have a shareholding in Winemaking Tasmania, the newly established contract winemaking facility run by Julian Alcorso, who will henceforth make the Clemens Hill wines. The estate vineyards have now been increased to 2.1 hectares.

ŸŸŸŸ **Sauvignon Blanc 2003** Clean; gooseberry and a touch of herb, moderately varietal; light to medium-bodied; good length and mouthfeel. **RATING** 87 **DRINK** Now $ 16.50
Pinot Noir 2002 Light to medium-bodied; silky mouthfeel; plum and cherry fruit; good length. **RATING** 87 **DRINK** 2008 $ 25

ŸŸŸŸ **Chardonnay 2002** **RATING** 84 **DRINK** 2007 $ 16.50

Cleveland ★★★

Shannons Road, Lancefield, Vic 3435 **REGION** Macedon Ranges
T (03) 5429 9000 **F** (03) 5429 2143 **OPEN** 7 days 9–5
WINEMAKER David Cowbrun, Kilchurn Wines (Contract) **EST.** 1985 **CASES** 2500
PRODUCT RANGE ($10–45 CD) Chardonnay, Dunsford Run Chardonnay, Pinot Gris, Macedon Brut, Brut Rose, Dunsford Run Rose, Pinot Noir, Dunsford Run Shiraz, Shiraz, Minus Five Cabernet Merlot; Brien Family Chardonnay Gordo, Muscat Gordo Blanco, Shiraz.
SUMMARY The Cleveland homestead was built in 1889 in the style of a Gothic Revival manor house, but had been abandoned for 40 years when purchased by the Briens in 1983. It has since been painstakingly restored, and 3.8 hectares of surrounding vineyard established. In January 2002 the new owner — Grange Group of Conference Centres —initiated fast-track development of The Grange at Cleveland Winery, with 22 suites, plus a large conference room and facilities alongside a new winery and warehouse.

ŸŸŸŸ **Macedon Brut 2000** Lively, fresh and zippy, acidity providing length. **RATING** 88
DRINK Now $ 20
Pinot Noir 2000 Attractive cherry and plum fruit; good mouthfeel and balance. **RATING** 87
DRINK 2008 $ 26

ŸŸŸ **Pinot Gris 2002** **RATING** 81 $ 19

Cliff House NR

57 Camms Road, Kayena, Tas 7270 **REGION** Northern Tasmania
T (03) 6394 7454 **F** (03) 6394 7454 **OPEN** By appointment
WINEMAKER Julian Alcorso (Contract) **EST.** 1983 **CASES** 2500
PRODUCT RANGE ($18–20 R) Riesling, Chardonnay, Pinot Noir, Devil's Elbow (Pinot Cabernet blend), Cabernet Sauvignon.
SUMMARY Cliff House has undergone a metamorphosis. In 1999 Geoff and Cheryl Hewitt sold the 4-hectare vineyard they established in the Tamar Valley area in 1983. They have now turned a two-hole golf course around their house into a vineyard, planted to riesling and pinot noir.

Clonakilla ★★★★★

Crisps Lane, Murrumbateman, NSW 2582 **REGION** Canberra District
T (02) 6227 5877 **F** (02) 6227 5871 **OPEN** 7 days 11–5
WINEMAKER Tim Kirk **EST.** 1971 **CASES** 5000
PRODUCT RANGE ($18–56 CD) Riesling, Semillon Sauvignon Blanc, Viognier, Chardonnay, Shiraz Viognier, Hilltops Shiraz, Cabernet Merlot.
SUMMARY The indefatigable Tim Kirk, who has many of the same personality characteristics as Frank Tate (of Evans & Tate), has taken over the management of Clonakilla from father and scientist Dr John Kirk. The quality of the wines is excellent, none more so than the highly regarded Shiraz Viognier, which sells out quickly every year. Exports to the UK, the US, Canada, Singapore and Hong Kong.

ŸŸŸŸŸ **Shiraz Viognier 2002** Excellent colour; fragrant, stylish and complex, rippling with licorice/anise, spice and black cherry; fine texture and mouthfeel; ripe tannins. Another outstanding wine. Six per cent viognier. **RATING** 95 **DRINK** 2012 $ 56
Hilltops Shiraz 2002 Complex; great structure with good acidity and length to the blackberry and spice palate. **RATING** 94 **DRINK** 2015 $ 24

ŸŸŸŸŸ **Riesling 2003** Fresh, crisp, mineral aromas; tingling citrus and apple flavours; excellent length. **RATING** 93 **DRINK** 2012 $ 20

Hilltops Shiraz 2003 Dense, deep purple hue; a powerful mix of blackberry, plum, prune and blackcurrant has totally absorbed the oak; balanced tannins. **RATING** 93 **DRINK** 2015 $ 24

Viognier 2002 Deep, rich, clear varietal character and mouthfeel; neither phenolic nor oily; top-class example. **RATING** 92 **DRINK** Now $ 36

Viognier 2003 Brilliant green-straw; mouthfilling and powerful; out-punches its 13.5 degrees alcohol; pastille, baked fruits and some spice; not phenolic. **RATING** 90 **DRINK** 2008 $ 36

Hilltops Shiraz 2001 Excellent colour; complex black fruits and Côte Rôtie-like game and spice; intense finish. **RATING** 90 **DRINK** 2014 $ 24

ΥΥΥΥ **Cabernet Merlot 2001 RATING** 86 **DRINK** 2007 $ 28

Clos Clare

Old Road, Watervale, SA 5452 **REGION** Clare Valley
T (08) 8843 0161 **F** (08) 8843 0161 **OPEN** Weekends and public holidays 10–5
WINEMAKER Various Contract **EST.** 1993 **CASES** 1200
PRODUCT RANGE ($19–24 CD) Riesling, Shiraz.
SUMMARY Clos Clare is based on a small (2 hectares), unirrigated section of the original Florita Vineyard once owned by Leo Buring, which produces Riesling of extraordinary concentration and power. Exports to the US and Singapore.

ΥΥΥΥΥ **Shiraz 2002** Blackberry, pepper, spice and earth provide lots of light and shade to the complex flavours; balanced and integrated oak, lingering tannins. **RATING** 90 **DRINK** 2015 $ 24

Clovely Estate ★★★

Steinhardts Road, Moffatdale via Murgon, Qld 4605 **REGION** South Burnett
T (07) 3216 1088 **F** (07) 3216 1050 **OPEN** Fri–Sun 10–5
WINEMAKER David Lowe, Luke Fitzpatrick (Contract) **EST.** 1998 **CASES** 63 000
PRODUCT RANGE ($12.95–14.95 CD) Reserve Chardonnay, Shiraz Cabernet; Left Field Semillon, Semillon Chardonnay, Verdelho, Chardonnay, Merlot, Shiraz, Cabernet Merlot, Cabernet Sauvignon; Queensland varietal range; Fifth Row Chardonnay, Shiraz Cabernet.
SUMMARY Although new-born, Clovely Estate has the largest vineyards in Queensland, having established 173 hectares of vines at two locations just to the east of Murgon in the Burnett Valley. There are 127 hectares of red grapes (including 74 hectares of shiraz) and 47 hectares of white grapes. The attractively packaged wines are sold in four tiers: Clovely Estate at the top end, and which will not be produced every year; Left Field, strongly fruity and designed to age; Fifth Row, for early drinking; and Queensland, primarily designed for the export market.

ΥΥΥΥ **Reserve Chardonnay 2002** A rich wine with lots of ripe nectarine and peach fruit; round and full; has demolished the French oak in which it was matured. **RATING** 88 **DRINK** Now $ 24

ΥΥΥΥ **Reserve Shiraz Cabernet 2001 RATING** 85 **DRINK** 2007 $ 24

Clover Hill

Clover Hill Road, Lebrina, Tas 7254 **REGION** Northern Tasmania
T (03) 6395 6114 **F** (03) 6395 6257 **OPEN** 7 days 10–5, by appointment in winter
WINEMAKER Leigh Clarnette, Loic Le Calvez, Mark Laurence **EST.** 1986 **CASES** 4000
PRODUCT RANGE ($35 R) Clover Hill (sparkling).
SUMMARY Clover Hill was established by Taltarni in 1986 with the sole purpose of making a premium sparkling wine. Its 20 hectares of vineyards, made up of 12 hectares of chardonnay, 6.5 of pinot noir and 1.5 of pinot meunier, are now all in bearing, although extensive re-trellising took place in 2002. The sparkling wine quality is excellent, combining finesse with power and length.

ΥΥΥΥΥ **Clover Hill 1999** A classic mineral, nectarine and brioche bouquet is followed by a delicate but intense stone fruit palate, lengthened by lingering acidity. **RATING** 95 **DRINK** Now $ 35

Clyde Park Vineyard

★★★★★

2490 Midland Highway, Bannockburn, Vic 3331 **REGION** Geelong
T (03) 5281 7274 **F** (03) 5281 7274 **OPEN** Weekends and public holidays 11–4
WINEMAKER Terry Jongebloed, Ben Tyler **EST.** 1979 **CASES** 2800
PRODUCT RANGE ($18–30 CD) Sauvignon Blanc, Pinot Gris, Chardonnay, Pinot Noir, Shiraz; Reserve Chardonnay, Pinot Noir.
SUMMARY Clyde Park Vineyard was established by Gary Farr, but then sold many years ago. It has passed through several changes of ownership, but is now owned by Terry Jongebloed and Sue Jongebloed-Dixon. It has significant, mature plantings of pinot noir (3.4 hectares), chardonnay (3.1 hectares), sauvignon blanc (1.5 hectares), shiraz (1.2 hectares) and pinot gris (0.9 hectare). Wine quality is excellent, no doubt aided by the mature vineyard.

ＹＹＹＹＹ **Shiraz 2002** Fragrant, spicy, licorice and black cherry; very regional; wonderful mouthfeel and texture; fine, filigreed tannins and lingering finish. **RATING** 96 **DRINK** 2017 $23.50
Reserve Chardonnay 2002 Tight and fine, much more elegant than the varietal release; great length and acidity; has eaten up the new oak. **RATING** 94 **DRINK** 2010 $29

ＹＹＹＹＹ **Chardonnay 2001** Funky, complex barrel-ferment and bottle-developed characters; rich, full-on style. **RATING** 91 **DRINK** 2007 $20.80
Pinot Noir 2001 Complex, with some forest floor emerging; plum and spice; long finish, fine tannins. **RATING** 91 **DRINK** Now $23.50
Chardonnay 2002 Concentrated but smooth nectarine and peach fruit; well-integrated oak. **RATING** 90 **DRINK** 2008 $20.80
Pinot Gris 2002 Apple, ripe pear and some musk; lots of round and supple mouthfeel. **RATING** 90 **DRINK** 2007 $20.80

ＹＹＹＹ **Pinot Noir 2002** Aromatic, fragrant spice, stem and brush aromas and flavours; a slightly green/minty element. **RATING** 88 **DRINK** Now $23.50

ＹＹＹＹ **Sauvignon Blanc 2002** **RATING** 86 **DRINK** Now $20.80
Reserve Chardonnay 1999 **RATING** 84 **DRINK** Now $29

Coal Valley Vineyard

★★★☆

257 Richmond Road, Cambridge, Tas 7170 **REGION** Southern Tasmania
T (03) 6248 5367 **F** (03) 6248 4175 **OPEN** 7 days 10–4, Friday evening tapas 4–8
WINEMAKER Andrew Hood (Contract) **EST.** 1991 **CASES** 500
PRODUCT RANGE ($18–35 CD) Riesling, Chardonnay, Pinot Noir, Cabernet Merlot.
SUMMARY Coal Valley Vineyard is the new name for Treehouse Vineyard and Wine Centre; the change was brought about by the fact that Treehouse had been trademarked by the Pemberton winery, Salitage. The vineyard was purchased by Todd Goebel and wife Gillian Christian in 1999. They have set about doubling the size of the existing riesling vineyard, and establishing 1.5 hectares of another vineyard planted to pinot noir, with a few vines of cabernet. The Wine Centre now incorporates a full commercial kitchen and overlooks the existing vineyard and the Coal River Valley.

ＹＹＹＹ **Chardonnay 2003** **RATING** 85 **DRINK** 2007 $25
Riesling 2003 **RATING** 84 **DRINK** 2008 $21

Coalville Vineyard

NR

RMB 4750 Moe South Road, Moe South, Vic 3825 **REGION** Gippsland
T (03) 5127 4229 **F** (03) 5127 2148 **OPEN** 7 days 10–5
WINEMAKER Peter Beasley **EST.** 1985 **CASES** 3000
PRODUCT RANGE ($15–18 CD) Chardonnay, Malbec, Merlot, Cabernet Merlot, Cabernet Sauvignon.
SUMMARY This is the new name for Mair's Coalville, following the sale of the property by Dr Stewart Mair to Peter Beasley, who has significantly increased not only the volume but also the range of wines available.

Cobaw Ridge ★★★★☆

31 Perc Boyer's Lane, East Pastoria via Kyneton, Vic 3444 **REGION** Macedon Ranges
T (03) 5423 5227 **F** (03) 5423 5227 **OPEN** 7 days 10–5
WINEMAKER Alan Cooper **EST.** 1985 **CASES** 1200
PRODUCT RANGE ($30–45 CD) Chardonnay, Lagrein, Pinot Noir, Shiraz Viognier.
SUMMARY Nelly and Alan Cooper established Cobaw Ridge's 6-hectare vineyard at an altitude of 610 metres in the hills above Kyneton, complete with self-constructed pole-framed mudbrick house and winery. The plantings of cabernet sauvignon have been removed and partially replaced by lagrein, a variety which sent me scuttling to Jancis Robinson's seminal book on grape varieties, from which I learned that it is a northeast Italian variety typically used to make delicate Rose; at Cobaw Ridge it is made into an impressive full-bodied dry red. The planned sale of Cobaw Ridge did not proceed, and the Coopers now intend to stay, a sensible decision given the very high quality of the releases current in 2004. Exports to the UK and the US.

ΥΥΥΥΥ **Shiraz Viognier 2002** Highly aromatic and spicy; black cherry threaded through with fine, ripe and soft tannins; spotlessly clean and great mouthfeel. **RATING** 93 **DRINK** 2012 $ 38
Lagrein 2002 A fragrant mix of red and black cherry and spice; light to medium-bodied and silky until the appealing crisp acidity on the finish. **RATING** 91 **DRINK** 2010 $ 45

ΥΥΥΥ **Chardonnay 2002** Rich and full, with glycerol sweetness; ripe pineapple fruit, very similar to the equally rich and lush '00. **RATING** 89 **DRINK** 2007 $ 30

Cobbitty Wines NR

Cobbitty Road, Cobbitty, NSW 2570 **REGION** South Coast Zone
T (02) 4651 2281 **F** (02) 4651 2671 **OPEN** Mon–Sat 9.30–5.30, Sun 11–5.30
WINEMAKER Giovanni Cogno **EST.** 1964 **CASES** 5000
PRODUCT RANGE ($5–14 CD) A full range of generic table, fortified and sparkling wines under the Cobbitty Wines label; also cocktail wines.
SUMMARY Draws upon 10 hectares of estate plantings of muscat, barbera, grenache and trebbiano, relying very much on local and ethnic custom.

Cobb's Hill ★★★☆

Oakwood Road, Oakbank, SA 5243 **REGION** Adelaide Hills
T (08) 8388 4054 **F** (08) 8388 4820 **OPEN** Not
WINEMAKER Shaw & Smith (Contract) **EST.** 1997 **CASES** 700
PRODUCT RANGE ($15 ML) Riesling, Sauvignon Blanc, Chardonnay, Merlot.
SUMMARY Sally and Roger Cook have a 140-hectare property in the Adelaide Hills that takes its name from Cobb and Co., which used it as a staging post and resting place for 1000 horses. The Cooks now use the property to raise Angus cattle, grow cherries and, more recently, grow grapes. Three different sites on the property, amounting to just over 10 hectares, were planted to selected clones of sauvignon blanc, chardonnay, semillon, riesling and merlot. Part of the production is sold to Shaw and Smith, who vinify the remainder for Cobb's Hill. The Sauvignon Blanc won the Advertiser/Hyatt Wine of the Year award in its category in 2003.

ΥΥΥΥ **Sauvignon Blanc 2003** Comes through powerfully on the palate, with a mix of tropical and gooseberry fruit; good length. **RATING** 88 **DRINK** Now $ 15

🦜 Cockatoo Ridge NR

PO Box 855, Nuriootpa, SA 5355 **REGION** Riverland
T (08) 8563 6400 **F** (08) 8563 1117 **OPEN** Not
WINEMAKER Stephen Obst **EST.** 1990
PRODUCT RANGE ($9.95 R) Chardonnay, Premium Reserve Chardonnay, Brut Reserve NV, Premium Reserve Eyrie Vintage Cuvee, Cockatoo Black Sparkling Red, Shiraz, Premium Reserve Shiraz, Cabernet Merlot.
SUMMARY Cockatoo Ridge was established by Geoff Merrill, and rapidly built volume by sales through the large retail chains, the extremely colouful label standing out on the shelf. The business

was already a large one when it was acquired by a company headed by ex-Orlando winemaker Ivan Limb. The wine is now distributed by Tucker Seabrook through a wide range of outlets, as well as to all of Australia's major export destinations. The large production is based in part on estate plantings of 98 hectares at Waikerie on the River Murray, and supplemented by grapes grown under contract in the Barossa Valley.

Cockfighter's Ghost

Lot 251 Milbrodale Road, Broke, NSW 2330 **REGION** Lower Hunter Valley
T (02) 9563 2500 **F** (02) 9563 2555 **OPEN** At Poole's Rock
WINEMAKER Patrick Auld **EST.** 1994 **CASES** 30 000
PRODUCT RANGE ($16.50–28.50 R) Clare Valley Riesling, Semillon, Verdelho, Unwooded Chardonnay, Chardonnay, Pinot Noir, Shiraz, Merlot, Coonawarra Premium Reserve Cabernet Sauvignon.
SUMMARY Like Poole's Rock Vineyard, part of a rapidly expanding wine empire owned by eminent Sydney merchant banker David Clarke; housed at the former Tulloch winery since 2003. Accommodation is available at the Milbrodale property. The wine has retail distribution throughout Australia and is exported to the UK, the US, Canada, New Zealand and Asia.

▼▼▼ **Verdelho 2003 RATING** 83 $16.95

Cody's NR

New England Highway, Ballandean, Qld 4382 **REGION** Granite Belt
T (07) 4684 1309 **F** (07) 5572 6500 **OPEN** 7 days 10–5
WINEMAKER Adam Chapman (Contract) **EST.** 1995 **CASES** 500
PRODUCT RANGE ($18–20 CD) Shiraz, Cabernet Merlot.
SUMMARY John Cody has established 2.5 hectares of cabernet sauvignon, merlot and shiraz at his Ballandean vineyard. The wines are contract-made by Adam Chapman at Sirromet, and are sold by mail order and through the cellar door, which offers the usual facilities.

Cofield Wines

Distillery Road, Wahgunyah, Vic 3687 **REGION** Rutherglen
T (02) 6033 3798 **F** (02) 6033 0798 **OPEN** Mon–Sat 9–5, Sun 10–5
WINEMAKER Max Cofield, Damien Cofield **EST.** 1990 **CASES** 11 000
PRODUCT RANGE ($15–28 CD) Semillon, Semillon Sauvignon Blanc, Semillon Chardonnay, Chenin Blanc, Max's Blend White, Chardonnay, Late Harvest Muscadelle, Shiraz, Gamay, Merlot, Max's Blend Red, Cabernet Franc, Cabernet Sauvignon, sparkling, fortified; Quartz Vein Vineyard varietals are top of the range.
SUMMARY District veteran Max Cofield, together with wife Karen and sons Damien, Ben and Andrew, is developing a strong cellar-door sales base by staging in-winery functions with guest chefs, and also providing a large barbecue and picnic area. (The Pickled Sisters Café is open for lunch Wed–Mon; telephone (02) 6033 2377.) Limited retail distribution through Prime Wines in Melbourne, exports to the US.

Coldstream Hills NR

31 Maddens Lane, Coldstream, Vic 3770 **REGION** Yarra Valley
T (03) 5964 9410 **F** (03) 5964 9389 **OPEN** 7 days 10–5
WINEMAKER Andrew Fleming, Greg Jarratt, James Halliday (Consultant) **EST.** 1985 **CASES** 55 000
PRODUCT RANGE ($24.50–75.90 CD) Pinot Gris, Sauvignon Blanc, Chardonnay, Reserve Chardonnay, Pinot Noir, Reserve Pinot Noir, Merlot, Reserve Merlot, Briarston (Cabernet Merlot), Reserve Cabernet Sauvignon, Pinot Noir Chardonnay Brut; occasional limited release wines sold chiefly through the cellar door.
SUMMARY Founded by the author, who continues to be involved with the winemaking, but acquired by Southcorp in mid-1996. Expansion plans already then underway have been maintained, with well in excess of 100 hectares of owned or managed estate vineyards as the base. Chardonnay and Pinot Noir continue to be the principal focus; Merlot came on-stream from the 1997 vintage. Vintage conditions permitting, these three wines are made in both varietal and Reserve form, the latter in restricted quantities.

Sauvignon Blanc 2003 Spotlessly clean, with intense varietal aromas and a touch of snow pea; a delicate, but well-balanced palate building intensity on a long, lingering finish. **NR DRINK** Now $ 24.50

Chardonnay 2003 Attractive white peach, melon and quince fruit; subtle cashew barrel-ferment overtones and toasty integrated oak. **NR DRINK** 2008 $ 26.50

Pinot Noir 2002 Intense and tight spicy/savoury plum flavours; long, lingering finish and excellent acidity. **NR DRINK** 2011 $ 26.50

Merlot 2001 Strongly varietal, with a mix of dark berry/blackcurrant fruit and hints of spice and olive; cedary French oak, good tannin structure. **NR DRINK** 2011 $ 27.50

Chardonnay Pinot 1999 Rich, complex, bready and berry fruit aromas. Well balanced; fruit flavours ranging from ripe pear to citrus. **NR DRINK** Now $ 26.50

🐦 Coliban Valley Wines ★★★★

Metcalfe–Redesdale Road, Metcalfe, Vic 3448 **REGION** Heathcote
T (03) 9813 3895 **F** (03) 9813 3895 **OPEN** Weekends 10–5
WINEMAKER Helen Miles **EST.** 1997 **CASES** 100
PRODUCT RANGE ($20–25 CD) Cabernet Merlot.
SUMMARY Helen Miles (with a degree in science) and partner Greg Miles have planted 3.5 hectares of shiraz, 0.75 hectare of cabernet and 0.25 hectare of merlot near Metcalfe, at the southern end of the Heathcote wine region. The granitic soils, with a band of clay, minimise the need for irrigation; the vines are mulched with material from the surrounding paddocks. The climate also means minimal spraying, predominantly copper and sulphur, with some biological spraying. At the present time, most of the production is sold as grapes to others, but it is intended to increase the amount made under the Coliban Valley label, and also to evaluate a small trial planting of sangiovese as a possible blend mate with cabernet sauvignon.

ΥΥΥΥ **Cabernet Merlot 2001** Similar to the '02, but with slightly more structure. **RATING** 89 **DRINK** 2009 $ 20
Cabernet Merlot 2002 Clean, lifted blackcurrant aromas; elegant light to medium-bodied palate; red and black fruits and fine tannins. **RATING** 88 **DRINK** 2009 $ 25

Colmaur ★★★★

447 Native Corners Road, Campania, Tas 7026 **REGION** Southern Tasmania
T (03) 6260 4312 **F** (03) 6260 4580 **OPEN** By appointment
WINEMAKER Michael Vishacki (Contract) **EST.** 1994 **CASES** 120
PRODUCT RANGE ($20–22 CD) Chardonnay, Pinot Noir.
SUMMARY Colmaur is sufficiently small for the vines to be counted: presently 1100 chardonnay and 1700 pinot noir are in production. In 2000/2001 a further 600 chardonnay, 1350 pinot noir and 250 cabernet sauvignon were planted, and that will be the total extent of the vineyard. Likewise, production will be limited to the five new French oak barrels purchased in 2000, producing 100 to 120 cases of wine per year; any surplus grapes will be sold. There are also 700 olive trees in production, and Colmaur has its own oil press.

🐦 Colvin Wines

19 Boyle Street, Mosman, NSW 2088 (postal) **REGION** Lower Hunter Valley
T (02) 9908 7886 **F** (02) 9908 7885 **OPEN** Not
WINEMAKER Andrew Spinaze, Trever Drayton (Contract) **EST.** 1999 **CASES** 6500
PRODUCT RANGE ($24 ML) Semillon, Sangiovese.
SUMMARY Sydney lawyer John and wife Robyn Colvin purchased the De Beyer Vineyard in 1990, with its history going back to the second half of the 19th century. By 1967, when a syndicate headed by Douglas McGregor purchased 35 hectares of the original vineyard site, no vines remained. The syndicate planted semillon on the alluvial soil of the creek flats, and shiraz on the red clay hillsides. When the Colvins acquired the property in 1990 the vineyard was in need of attention. Up to 1998, all of the grapes were sold to Tyrrell's, but since 1999 quantities have been made for distribution under the Colvin Wines label. These include Sangiovese, coming from a little over 1 hectare of the variety planted by John Colvin in 1996, inspired by his love of the wines of Tuscany.

ΨΨΨΨΨ **Semillon 2002** Very powerful, potent and intense wine, with great length; some CO_2. 100 cases made. **RATING** 94 **DRINK** 2010 $ 24

ΨΨΨΨ **Semillon 2003** Herb, grass and mineral aromas; the wine sweetens briefly on entry to the mouth, then tightens up. **RATING** 87 **DRINK** 2010 $ 24
Sangiovese 2000 Light-bodied and not forced; sweet cherry fruit at core with savoury, almost lemony, surrounds. Quite varietal. **RATING** 87 **DRINK** 2007 $ 24

ΨΨΨΨ **Sangiovese 1999** **RATING** 84 **DRINK** Now $ 24

Connor Park Winery

NR

59 Connors Road, Leichardt, Vic 3516 **REGION** Bendigo
T (03) 5437 5234 **F** (03) 5437 5204 **OPEN** 7 days 10–6
WINEMAKER Ross Lougoon **EST.** 1994 **CASES** 10 000
PRODUCT RANGE ($12–28 CD) Riesling, Semillon, Marsanne, Seanne, Sparkling Shiraz, Merlot, Shiraz, Cabernet, Port, Muscat.
SUMMARY The original planting of 2 hectares of vineyard dates back to the mid-1960s and to the uncle of the present owners, who had plans for designing an automatic grape harvester. The plans came to nothing, and when the present owners purchased the property in 1985 the vineyard had run wild. They resuscitated it (it formed part of a much larger mixed farming operation), and until 1994 were content to sell the grapes to other winemakers. Since then the vineyard has been expanded to 10 hectares. Production has risen from 2000 to 10 000 cases, with exports to the US and retail distribution in Melbourne supplementing cellar door and mailing list sales.

Constable & Hershon

★★★

1 Gillards Road, Pokolbin, NSW 2320 **REGION** Lower Hunter Valley
T (02) 4998 7887 **F** (02) 4998 6555 **OPEN** 7 days 10–5
WINEMAKER Neil McGuigan (Contract) **EST.** 1981 **CASES** 3000
PRODUCT RANGE ($20–26 CD) Semillon, Chardonnay, Unwooded Chardonnay, Vintage Collection Chardonnay, Sparkling Shiraz, Botrytis Semillon, Shiraz, Merlot.
SUMMARY Features four spectacular formal gardens, the Rose, Knot and Herb, Secret and Sculpture; a free garden tour (lasting 30 minutes) is conducted Monday to Friday at 10.30 am. The 12-hectare vineyard is itself spectacularly situated under the backdrop of the Brokenback Range. Typically offers a range of several vintages of each variety ex cellar door or by mailing list.

ΨΨΨΨ **Semillon 2001** Complex, slightly funky aromas; good intensity on palate; a crisp mineral and herb mix. **RATING** 88 **DRINK** 2011 $ 21.50
Sparkling Shiraz 2002 Lively, fresh black cherry fruit; low phenolics help achieve balance without excessive sweetness. **RATING** 88 **DRINK** 2007 $ 24.50

ΨΨΨΨ **Merlot 2002** **RATING** 86 **DRINK** 2007 $ 26
Cabernet Merlot 2002 **RATING** 86 **DRINK** 2008 $ 26
Unwooded Chardonnay 2002 **RATING** 85 **DRINK** Now $ 19.95
Shiraz 2002 **RATING** 85 **DRINK** 2007 $ 24

ΨΨΨ **Semillon 2002** **RATING** 82 $ 21.50
Chardonnay 2002 **RATING** 81 $ 23.50

Coolangatta Estate

★★★☆

1335 Bolong Road, Shoalhaven Heads, NSW 2535 **REGION** Shoalhaven Coast
T (02) 4448 7131 **F** (02) 4448 7997 **OPEN** 7 days 10–5
WINEMAKER Tyrrell's (Contract) **EST.** 1988 **CASES** 5000
PRODUCT RANGE ($16–22 CD) Semillon, Sauvignon Blanc Chardonnay, Sauvignon Blanc Verdelho, Classic Dry White, Alexander Berry Chardonnay, Verdelho, Chambourcin, Merlot Shiraz, Cabernet Sauvignon, Vintage Port.
SUMMARY Coolangatta Estate is part of a 150-hectare resort with accommodation, restaurants, golf course, etc, with some of the oldest buildings convict-built in 1822. It might be thought that the wines are tailored purely for the tourist market, but in fact the standard of viticulture is exceptionally high (immaculate Scott-Henry trellising), and the winemaking is wholly professional (by Tyrrell's).

ΫΫΫΫΫ **Semillon 1998** Slowly developing exactly as expected, and still with life in it; plenty of juicy fruit, and years to go. A re-release; well worth the price. **RATING** 92 **DRINK** 2010 $22

ΫΫΫΫ **Alexander Berry Chardonnay 2003** Attractive, soft, peachy wine; subtle French oak; gentle acidity. **RATING** 88 **DRINK** Now $22
Eileen Chambourcin 2003 Typical vivid colour; light to medium-bodied, with bright, juicy red fruits and zero tannins. **RATING** 88 **DRINK** Now $19
Elizabeth Berry Cabernet Sauvignon 2003 Light-bodied; clean, supple blackcurrant fruit; well balanced, not forced. **RATING** 87 **DRINK** 2008 $22

ΫΫΫΫ **Verdelho 2003** **RATING** 86 **DRINK** Now $18
Merlot Shiraz 2003 **RATING** 84 **DRINK** Now $19

Coombe Farm Vineyard NR

11 St Huberts Road, Coldstream, Vic 3770 **REGION** Yarra Valley
T (03) 9739 1136 **F** (03) 9739 1136 **OPEN** Not
WINEMAKER Yering Station (Contract) **EST.** 1999
PRODUCT RANGE ($24–30 R) Chardonnay, Pinot Noir.
SUMMARY Coombe Farm Vineyard is owned by Pamela, Lady Vestey, Lord Samuel Vestey and The Right Honourable Mark Vestey, Lady Vestey being Dame Nellie Melba's grand-daughter. After a small initial planting, the decision was taken in 1999 to very significantly extend the vineyard; there are now 25 hectares of pinot noir, 18 hectares of chardonnay, 7.4 hectares of merlot, 5.4 hectares of cabernet sauvignon, 1.9 hectares of marsanne and 0.7 hectare of arneis. The vast majority of the fruit is sold, a small amount being made for the Coombe Farm Vineyard label at Yering Station.

Coombend Estate ★★★☆

Coombend via Swansea, Tas 7190 **REGION** Southern Tasmania
T (03) 6257 8881 **F** (03) 6257 8484 **OPEN** 7 days 9–6
WINEMAKER Andrew Hood (Contract) **EST.** 1985 **CASES** 2000
PRODUCT RANGE ($15–28 CD) Riesling, Sauvignon Blanc, Late Harvest, Fleurieu Bay Rose, Cabernet Sauvignon.
SUMMARY John Fenn Smith originally established 1.75 hectares of cabernet sauvignon, 2.25 hectares of sauvignon blanc and 0.3 hectare of riesling (together with a little cabernet franc) on his 2000-hectare sheep station, choosing that part of his property which is immediately adjacent to Freycinet. This slightly quixotic choice of variety has been justified by the success of the wine in limited show entries. In December 1998 Coombend opened a purpose-built cellar-door sales area; it has also significantly expanded its plantings to include riesling and sauvignon blanc. Exports to Hong Kong and the UK.

ΫΫΫΫ **Sauvignon Blanc 2003** Very delicate oak infusion, more structural than flavour; gentle tropical and passionfruit backdrop. **RATING** 87 **DRINK** Now $24

ΫΫΫΫ **Riesling 2003** **RATING** 85 **DRINK** 2009 $22

Cooperage Estate NR

15 Markovitch Lane, Junortoun, Vic 3551 **REGION** Bendigo
T 0418 544 743 **OPEN** Not
WINEMAKER Graham Gregurek **EST.** 1995
SUMMARY The Gregurek family has established 2.2. hectares of shiraz and cabernet sauvignon at their vineyard on the southern outskirts of the town of Bendigo. As the name suggests, there is also a cooperage on-site.

Cooper Wines ★★☆

Lovedale Road, Lovedale, NSW 2321 **REGION** Lower Hunter Valley
T (02) 4930 7387 **F** (02) 4930 7900 **OPEN** Mon–Fri 10–5, weekends 9.30–5
WINEMAKER Greg Silkman (Contract) **EST.** 2001 **CASES** 2000

PRODUCT RANGE ($17–25 CD) Semillon, Semillon Sauvignon Blanc, Verdelho, Chardonnay Semillon, Unoaked Chardonnay, Chardonnay, Chambourcin, Shiraz.

SUMMARY Max Cooper is a Qantas pilot who purchased the former Allanmere Winery and Vineyard, leasing the winery back to Allanmere but retaining the vineyards. The chardonnay is estate-grown; the other wines made from grapes purchased from growers in the region.

ϒϒϒ **Semillon 2003 RATING** 83 $ 17

Coorinja ★★☆

Toodyay Road, Toodyay, WA 6566 **REGION** Greater Perth Zone
T (08) 9574 2280 **OPEN** Mon–Sat 10–5
WINEMAKER Michael Wood **EST.** 1870 **CASES** 3200
PRODUCT RANGE ($8–10.50 CD) Dry White, Claret, Hermitage, Burgundy, fortifieds; the latter account for 50 per cent of Coorinja's production.
SUMMARY An evocative and historic winery nestling in a small gully which seems to be in a time warp, begging to be used as a set for a film. A recent revamp of the packaging accompanied a more than respectable Hermitage, with lots of dark chocolate and sweet berry flavour, finishing with soft tannins.

Cooyal Grove ★★☆

Lot 9 Stoney Creek Road, Mudgee, NSW 2850 **REGION** Mudgee
T (02) 6373 3344 **F** (02) 6373 3344 **OPEN** 7 days by appointment
WINEMAKER Michael Slater (Contract) **EST.** 1990 **CASES** 500
PRODUCT RANGE ($15–18 ML) Chardonnay, Merlot.
SUMMARY In late 2002 Cooyal Grove was purchased from its Italian founder by Sydney publican John Lenard and Paul and Lydele Walker, a local Mudgee vigneron and his wife. At the time the 10-hectare property had a mix of vines, pistachio nut trees and olives. In their own words, the partners say, 'Since purchasing the property we have worked almost every weekend in the vineyard and grove undertaking every task from planting new blocks to pruning, training, harvesting, bottling and labelling. Given that all of the partners are only 30 years old and not yet financially able to employ outside labour, we seem to call on every friend, relative and friend's relatives to assist in the production of the crops. This has made for a feeling of building something from scratch which we are proud of.' In addition to the olive oil and pistachio nut production, the vineyards have now been expanded to 4.5 hectares in total, with chardonnay, semillon, sauvignon blanc, merlot, shiraz and cabernet sauvignon. The wines are principally sold by mail order, with distribution through Cape Karoo Wine Agencies in northern New South Wales and Queensland; hotels and bottle shops in Mudgee; and at three Sydney outlets: Hornsby Railway Hotel, Patricks Pennant Hills and Shergolds Liquor, Lane Cove.

ϒϒϒϒ **Merlot 2002** Big-framed wine with lots of muscle; plenty of red fruits but the tannins are unbalanced. May soften with time. **RATING** 86 **DRINK** 2010 $ 18
Chardonnay 2003 RATING 84 **DRINK** Now $ 15

Cope-Williams ★★★★

Glenfern Road, Romsey, Vic 3434 **REGION** Macedon Ranges
T (03) 5429 5428 **F** (03) 5429 5655 **OPEN** 7 days 11–5
WINEMAKER David Cowburn **EST.** 1977 **CASES** 7000
PRODUCT RANGE ($14–25 R) Chardonnay, Cabernet Merlot; d'Vine is second label with Riesling, Chardonnay and Cabernet Sauvignon; also Kithbrook Estate Sparkling; winery specialty is sparkling wine, Macedon R.O.M.S.E.Y.
SUMMARY One of the high-country Macedon pioneers, specialising in sparkling wines which are full flavoured, but also producing excellent Chardonnay and Pinot Noir table wines in the warmer vintages. A traditional 'English Green'-type cricket ground is available for hire and booked out most days of the week from spring through till autumn.

ϒϒϒϒϒ **Chardonnay 2000** Superb colour; elegant but full of fruit flavour; perfect oak balance and integration. **RATING** 95 **DRINK** 2010 $ 24

ϒϒϒϒϒ **R.O.M.S.E.Y. Vintage Brut 1996** Complex, medium-bodied sparkling, with a fleeting hint of vanilla; freshness and grip to the finish. **RATING** 90 **DRINK** 2007 $ 26

ŸŸŸŸ **Kithbrook Estate Sparkling 1998** Intensely aromatic and flowery; clean, lingering, tangy and zesty; lingering acidity. Pinot Noir and Chardonnay sourced from the Strathbogie Ranges. **RATING** 89 **DRINK** Now

ŸŸŸ **Pinot Noir 1998 RATING** 83 $ 24

Copper Bull Wines   NR

19 Uplands Road, Chirnside Park, Vic 3116 **REGION** Yarra Valley
T (03) 9726 7111 **OPEN** Wed–Sun 11–6
WINEMAKER David Schliefert **EST.** 1982 **CASES** 800
PRODUCT RANGE Semillon, Sangiovese, Cabernet Sauvignon.
SUMMARY Copper Bull is the reincarnation of Halcyon Daze. The Rackleys, having gone into semi-retirement, have leased the vineyard, winery and cellar door to David and Janie Schliefert, who produced the first wines under the Copper Bull label in 2003. David Schliefert spent 19 years at Lindemans Karadoc winery, becoming a cellar supervisor in the process, while wife Janie worked in quality management at Lindemans. The small production will be sold from the cellar door as and when it comes on-stream.

Copper Country   NR

Lot 6 Kingaroy Road, Nanango, Qld 4615 **REGION** South Burnett
T (07) 4163 1011 **F** (07) 4163 1122 **OPEN** 7 days 9–5
WINEMAKER Contract **EST.** 1995 **CASES** 1000
PRODUCT RANGE ($10–16 CD) Shiraz.
SUMMARY The Winter family (Derek, Helena, Stephen and Justyne) were restaurateurs before venturing into grape growing and winemaking. The name of the vineyard and the restaurant is recognition of the fact that copper was the first mineral mined in the region. As well as grape growing, the Winters make cheese, the principal outlet for their products being their restaurant and cellar door.

Coriole   ★★★★☆

Chaffeys Road, McLaren Vale, SA 5171 **REGION** McLaren Vale
T (08) 8323 8305 **F** (08) 8323 9136 **OPEN** Mon–Fri 10–5, weekends and public holidays 11–5
WINEMAKER Grant Harrison **EST.** 1967 **CASES** 34 000
PRODUCT RANGE ($15.25–75 R) Semillon, Lalla Rookh Semillon, Semillon Sauvignon Blanc, Chenin Blanc, Shiraz, Lloyd Reserve Shiraz, Redstone Shiraz Cabernet, Sangiovese, Nebbiolo, Mary Kathleen Cabernet Merlot, Cabernet Sauvignon.
SUMMARY Justifiably best known for its Shiraz, which — both in the rare Lloyd Reserve and standard forms — is extremely impressive. It has spread its wings in recent years, being one of the first wineries to catch onto the Italian fashion with its Sangiovese, but its white varietal wines lose nothing by comparison. It is also a producer of high-quality olive oil distributed commercially through all Australian states. The wines are exported to the UK, the US, Canada, Switzerland, Germany, The Netherlands, Sweden, Taiwan, Malaysia, Japan, Singapore and New Zealand.

ŸŸŸŸŸ **Lloyd Reserve Shiraz 2001** A powerful, potent and complex bouquet of blackberry and spice; regional chocolate and lots of oak add to the palate flavour; long finish. **RATING** 93 **DRINK** 2015 $ 70

Shiraz 2002 Black fruits, spice and mocha; medium-bodied; has finesse and length; fine tannins, clean finish. **RATING** 92 **DRINK** 2015 $ 25

Mary Kathleen Reserve Cabernet Merlot 2001 A rich and supple blend of blackcurrant, redcurrant and chocolate; fine tannins; good oak. **RATING** 92 **DRINK** 2011 $ 39

Shiraz 2001 Lovely medium-bodied black cherry fruit; ripe tannins; good length and balance. **RATING** 91 **DRINK** 2011 $ 25

Mary Kathleen Reserve Cabernet Merlot 2001 Clean and aromatic, with a range of blackcurrant, earth, chocolate, spice and mint flavours; good tannins. **RATING** 91 **DRINK** 2010 $ 39

Contour 4 Sangiovese Shiraz 2001 A spicy, tangy, savoury cascade of flavours from blackberry through to raspberry to cherry, all with a twist of lemon. Screwcap. **RATING** 90 **DRINK** 2010 $ 13

ΨΨΨΨ **Lalla Rookh Grenache Shiraz 2001** An elegant, medium-bodied wine in the savoury spectrum; lingering, fine tannins. **RATING** 89 **DRINK** 2008 $28.99
Sangiovese 2002 Spice, earth, dried herb and cherry fruit; long, savoury, fine tannins, but not too dry. **RATING** 88 **DRINK** 2008 $17.99
Semillon Sauvignon Blanc 2003 Full flavoured and generous; ripe tropical fruit with a touch of citrus. Screwcap. **RATING** 87 **DRINK** Now $15
Nebbiolo 2002 Typical light colour; red cherry, lemon and mint; fine-grained tannins; distinctly varietal, but ... **RATING** 87 **DRINK** 2007 $29.99

ΨΨΨΨ **Redstone 2001 RATING** 86 **DRINK** 2009 $19.99
Chenin Blanc 2003 RATING 84 **DRINK** Now $13

Cosham ★★★

101 Union Road, Carmel via Kalamunda, WA 6076 **REGION** Perth Hills
T (08) 9293 5424 **F** (08) 9293 5062 **OPEN** Weekends and public holidays 10–5
WINEMAKER Jane Brook Estate (Contract) **EST.** 1989 **CASES** 1000
PRODUCT RANGE ($14–22 CD) Chardonnay, Pinot Noir, Cabernet Merlot, Methode Champenoise Brut.
SUMMARY Has grown significantly over recent years, though admittedly from a small base. A complex Methode Champenoise and savoury/earth Cabernet Merlot are both creditable wines, and the Chardonnay very good. The vineyard is planted on an old orchard, and consists of 2 hectares of cabernet sauvignon, merlot, shiraz, pinot noir, cabernet franc, chardonnay and petit verdot, established between 1990 and 1995. They grow in gravelly loam with some clay, but overall in a well-drained soil with good rainfall. Depending on the grape variety, vintage ranges from late February to early April.

ΨΨΨΨ **Chardonnay 2001** Nicely balanced; ripe stone fruit and subtle oak; ageing well, and good value. **RATING** 87 **DRINK** 2008 $15

ΨΨΨΨ **Cabernet Merlot 2000 RATING** 86 **DRINK** 2009 $18

🐦 Cow Hill NR

PO Box 533, Beechworth, Vic 3747 **REGION** Beechworth
T 0411 249 704 **OPEN** Not
WINEMAKER Andrew Doyle **EST.** 2001
PRODUCT RANGE ($22–25 R) Chardonnay, Shiraz.
SUMMARY Andrew Doyle began the development of Cow Hill with the planting of 1.5 hectares each of viognier and nebbiolo on very steep mudstone, slate and shale soils. Tempranillo and muscat, and possibly shiraz, are to follow, and take the plantings to a total of 10 hectares. In the meantime, Doyle is buying grapes from other vineyards in the Beechworth region to produce his wines.

Cowra Estate ★★★☆

Boorowa Road, Cowra, NSW 2794 **REGION** Cowra
T (02) 9907 7735 **F** (02) 9907 7734 **OPEN** Tues–Sun 10–4 at The Quarry Restaurant
WINEMAKER Simon Gilbert (Contract) **EST.** 1973 **CASES** 6000
PRODUCT RANGE ($15–25 CD) Cowra Estate Chardonnay, Cabernet Rose, Cabernets; Eagle Rock Chardonnay, Cabernet Merlot and Classic Bat Cabernet Merlot are sold through the cellar door and selected restaurants.
SUMMARY Cowra Estate was purchased from the family of founder Tony Gray by South African-born food and beverage entrepreneur John Geber in 1995. A vigorous promotional campaign has gained a higher domestic profile for the once export-oriented brand. John Geber is actively involved in the promotional effort and rightly proud of the excellent value for money which the wines represent. The Quarry Wine Cellars and Restaurant offer visitors a full range of all of the Cowra Estate's wines, but also wines from the other producers in the region. The relabelled Eagles Rock series significantly lifts the quality bar. The Geber family, incidentally, also owns Chateau Tanunda in the Barossa Valley.

ΨΨΨΨΨ **Eagle Rock Chardonnay 2001** Quite complex, rich and intense; good French oak; very much a cut above any prior wine from Cowra Estate; drink asap. **RATING** 92 **DRINK** Now $19

TTTT **Eagle Rock Cabernet Merlot 2000** Pronounced savoury varietal character; good structure and concentration. **RATING** 87 **DRINK** Now $ 19

TTTY **Cabernet Rose 2003** **RATING** 84 **DRINK** Now $ 15

TTT **Classic Bat Cabernet Merlot 2001** **RATING** 83 $ 19

Crabtree of Watervale ★★★★

North Terrace, Watervale SA 5452 **REGION** Clare Valley
T (08) 8843 0069 **F** (08) 8843 0144 **OPEN** Mon–Sat 11–5
WINEMAKER Robert Crabtree **EST.** 1979 **CASES** 5000
PRODUCT RANGE ($20 CD) Riesling, Semillon, Bay of Biscay Rose, Picnic Hill Shiraz, Windmill Vineyard Cabernet Sauvignon, Zibibbo, Muscat of Alexandria, Windmill Tawny.
SUMMARY The gently mannered Robert Crabtree and wife Elizabeth are the drivers of the business, making full-flavoured, classic Clare Valley styles with outstanding success in some recent vintages. Exports to New Zealand, Canada and Malaysia.

TTTTY **Riesling 2003** Floral, lime blossom aromas to open with, then rich, luscious, mouthfilling lime and tropical fruit; at the rich end of the vintage style, and totally seductive. **RATING** 93 **DRINK** 2009 $ 20
Picnic Hill Vineyard Shiraz 2002 Vivid colour; rich, round black cherry and blackberry; soft, ripe tannins. Screwcap. **RATING** 90 **DRINK** 2015 $ 20

TTTT **Centinas Gaze Tempranillo 2003** Very fragrant and fresh; a rose with attitude; raspberry and cherry fruit for summer drinking; has totally absorbed the French oak. Screwcap. **RATING** 87 **DRINK** Now $ 20

TTTY **Semillon 2000** **RATING** 86 **DRINK** Now $ 20
Clare Valley Muscat NV **RATING** 86 **DRINK** Now $ 20
Bay of Biscay Rose 2003 **RATING** 85 **DRINK** Now $ 20

Craig Avon Vineyard ★★★

Craig Avon Lane, Merricks North, Vic 3926 **REGION** Mornington Peninsula
T (03) 5989 7465 **F** (03) 5989 7615 **OPEN** By appointment
WINEMAKER Ken Lang **EST.** 1986 **CASES** 1000
PRODUCT RANGE ($30–34 CD) Chardonnay, Pinot Noir, Cabernet.
SUMMARY The wines are competently made, clean, and with pleasant fruit flavour. All of the wines are sold through the cellar door and by mailing list.

Craigie Knowe NR

80 Glen Gala Road, Cranbrook, Tas 7190 **REGION** Southern Tasmania
T (03) 6259 8252 **F** (03) 6259 8252 **OPEN** 7 days by appointment
WINEMAKER Dr John Austwick **EST.** 1979 **CASES** 500
PRODUCT RANGE ($25 CD) Pinot Noir, Cabernet Sauvignon.
SUMMARY John Austwick makes a small quantity of full-flavoured, robust Cabernet Sauvignon in a tiny winery as a weekend relief from a busy metropolitan dental practice. The Pinot Noir is made in a style which will appeal to confirmed Cabernet Sauvignon drinkers.

Craiglee ★★★★★

Sunbury Road, Sunbury, Vic 3429 **REGION** Sunbury
T (03) 9744 4489 **F** (03) 9744 4489 **OPEN** Sun, public holidays 10–5, or by appointment
WINEMAKER Patrick Carmody **EST.** 1976 **CASES** 3000
PRODUCT RANGE ($16–38 CD) Sauvignon Blanc, Chardonnay, Pinot Noir, Shiraz, Cabernet Sauvignon.
SUMMARY A historic winery with a proud 19th-century record, which recommenced winemaking in 1976 after a prolonged hiatus. Produces one of the finest cool-climate Shirazs in Australia, redolent of cherry, licorice and spice in the better (i.e. warmer) vintages, lighter-bodied in the cooler ones. Maturing vines and improved viticulture have made the wines more consistent (and even better) over the past 10 years or so. Exports to the UK, the US and New Zealand.

Craigow ★★★★★

528 Richmond Road, Cambridge, Tas 7170 **REGION** Southern Tasmania
T (03) 6248 5379 **F** (03) 6248 5482 **OPEN** 7 days Christmas to Easter (except public holidays), or by appointment
WINEMAKER Julian Alcorso (Contract) **EST.** 1989 **CASES** 2000
PRODUCT RANGE ($25–35 CD) Riesling, Gewurztraminer, Chardonnay, Botrytis Riesling, Pinot Noir.
SUMMARY Craigow has substantial vineyards, with 5 hectares of pinot noir and another 5 hectares divided among riesling, chardonnay and gewurztraminer. Barry and Cathy Edwards have moved from being grape growers with only one wine made for sale to a portfolio of five wines, while continuing to sell most of their grapes. Exports to the UK.

🍷🍷🍷🍷🍷 **Botrytis Riesling 2001** Highly fragrant; intense citrus blossom and honey; focused, with fine lingering acidity. **RATING** 95 **DRINK** 2008 $35
Gewurztraminer 2003 Floral rose petal aromas; delicate, silky texture; some lychee; quite delicious. **RATING** 94 **DRINK** 2009 $24

🍷🍷🍷🍷🍷 **Riesling 2003** Fragrant apple blossom and passionfruit; long, clean, lingering finish. **RATING** 90 **DRINK** 2014 $21

🍷🍷🍷🍷 **Chardonnay 2002** Nectarine and peach; even flow; good balance. **RATING** 86 **DRINK** 2008 $22.50

🍷🍷🍷 **Pinot Noir 2002** **RATING** 83 $28

Craneford ★★★★

Moorundie Street, Truro, SA 5356 **REGION** Barossa Valley
T (08) 8564 0003 **F** (08) 8564 0008 **OPEN** 7 days 10–5
WINEMAKER John Zilm, Colin Forbes (Consultant) **EST.** 1978 **CASES** 25 000
PRODUCT RANGE ($14–33 CD) Eden Valley Riesling, Barossa Semillon, Barossa Valley Chardonnay, Barossa Valley Unwooded Chardonnay, Shiraz, Quartet (Petit Verdot Cabernet Sauvignon Cabernet Franc Shiraz), Grenache, Coonawarra Cabernet Sauvignon, Mistelle (fortified), Sparkling Shiraz Petit Verdot.
SUMMARY The purchase of Craneford by owner/winemaker John Zilm has wrought many changes. It has moved to a new winery (and café) and is supported by contract-grown grapes, with the purchase price paid per hectare, not per tonne, giving Craneford total control over yield and (hopefully) quality. Colin Forbes continues to provide consultancy advice. Retail distribution in Sydney and Melbourne, and exports to Japan through Australian Prestige Wines.

Crane Winery NR

Haydens Road, Kingaroy, Qld 4610 **REGION** South Burnett
T (07) 4162 7647 **F** (07) 4162 8381 **OPEN** 7 days 10–4
WINEMAKER John Crane **EST.** 1996 **CASES** 4000
PRODUCT RANGE ($12–25 CD) Semillon, Semillon Chardonnay, Verdelho, Marsanne, Hillside White, Chardonnay, Late Harvest Frontignac, Noble Chardonnay Botrytis, Sparkling Burgundy, Pinot Semillon Chardonnay Sparkling, Estate Sparkling Cuvee, Hillside Red, Pinot Noir, Shiraz, Merlot, Liqueur Shiraz, Cream Sherry.
SUMMARY Established by John and Sue Crane, Crane Winery is one of several in the burgeoning South Burnett in Queensland, drawing upon 4 hectares of estate plantings but also purchasing grapes from 20 other growers in the region. Interestingly, Sue Crane's great-grandfather established a vineyard planted to shiraz 100 years ago (in 1898), and it remained in production until 1970.

Crawford River Wines ★★★★★

Hotspur Upper Road, Condah, Vic 3303 **REGION** Henty
T (03) 5578 2267 **F** (03) 5578 2240 **OPEN** By appointment
WINEMAKER John Thomson **EST.** 1975 **CASES** 4000
PRODUCT RANGE ($22–36 CD) Riesling, Reserve Riesling, Semillon, Semillon Sauvignon Blanc, Cabernet Merlot, Cabernet Sauvignon, Nektar.

SUMMARY Time flies, and it seems incredible that Crawford River should be approaching its 30th birthday. Once a tiny outpost in a little-known wine region, Crawford River has now established itself as one of the foremost producers of Riesling (and other excellent wines), thanks to the unremitting attention to detail and skill of its founder and winemaker, John Thomson. Exports to the UK and Denmark.

ŸŸŸŸ **Riesling 2003** Flowery, piercing passionfruit, lime and spice; delicate yet flavour-packed. **RATING** 94 **DRINK** 2013 $30

ŸŸŸŸŸ **Semillon Sauvignon Blanc 2003** Fragrant lime blossom aromas, moving to more herbal and mineral notes on the palate; typical Crawford River length. **RATING** 92 **DRINK** 2008 $22
Nektar 2003 Fine, elegant understated Germanic auslese style; perfect balancing acidity; will richly repay patience. **RATING** 92 **DRINK** 2013 $27
Cabernet Merlot 2002 Elegantly proportioned and finely chiselled, as are all of the wines from this winery; cedar, spice and blackcurrant; fine silky tannins; uncompromisingly cool climate. **RATING** 90 **DRINK** 2012 $28

ŸŸŸŸ **Cabernet Sauvignon 2001** Light to medium-bodied Bordeaux style; berries and forest; minimal tannins. **RATING** 87 **DRINK** 2008 $36

Crisford Winery   NR

556 Hermitage Road, Pokolbin, NSW 2320 **REGION** Lower Hunter Valley
T (02) 9387 1100 **F** (02) 9387 6688 **OPEN** Not
WINEMAKER Steve Dodd **EST.** 1990 **CASES** 340
PRODUCT RANGE A single wine — Synergy (Merlot Cabernet Franc blend).
SUMMARY Carol and Neal Crisford have established 2.6 hectares of merlot and cabernet franc which go to produce Synergy (a name which I fancy has been trademarked by Richard Hamilton). Neal Crisford produces educational videos on wine used in TAFE colleges and by the Australian Society of Wine Education. The wine is sold through the Hunter Valley Wine Society.

✿ Crittenden at Dromana

25 Harrisons Road, Dromana, Vic 3936 **REGION** Mornington Peninsula
T (03) 5981 8322 **F** (03) 5981 8366 **OPEN** 7 days 11–5
WINEMAKER Garry Crittenden **EST.** 2003 **CASES**
PRODUCT RANGE ($15–25 CD) Chardonnay, Pinot Noir; Pinocchio Arneis, Sangiovese; Schinus range of Sauvignon Blanc, Pinot Gris, Chardonnay, Merlot, Shiraz.
SUMMARY Like a phoenix from the ashes, Garry Crittenden has risen again, soon after his formal ties with Dromana Estate Limited were severed (son Rollo remains chief winemaker at Dromana Estate). He took with him the Schinus range; has Sangiovese and Arneis due for progressive release under the Pinocchio label; and, under the premium Crittenden at Dromana label, is making wines from the 22-year-old 5-hectare vineyard surrounding the family house and cellar door. The wines are distributed by Red+White.

ŸŸŸŸŸ **Chardonnay 2002** Super-fine elegant style reflecting whole-bunch pressing; melon and cashew; oak in the back seat. **RATING** 92 **DRINK** 2010 $25

ŸŸŸŸ **Pinot Noir 2002** Shows some fruit-shrivel characters, but has good length and positive varietal character. **RATING** 87 **DRINK** 2008 $25
Schinus Merlot 2002 Light to medium-bodied; supple red fruits are supported by gentle tannins. **RATING** 87 **DRINK** 2007 $15

ŸŸŸŸ **Schinus Sauvignon Blanc 2003 RATING** 85 **DRINK** Now $15
Schinus Chardonnay 2003 RATING 85 **DRINK** Now $15
Schinus Pinot Gris 2003 RATING 84 **DRINK** Now $18
Schinus Shiraz 2001 RATING 84 **DRINK** Now $15

Crooked River Wines

11 Willow Vale Road, Gerringong, NSW 2534 **REGION** Shoalhaven Coast
T (02) 4234 0975 **F** (02) 4234 4477 **OPEN** 7 days 10.30–4.30
WINEMAKER Bevan Wilson **EST.** 1998 **CASES** 6500

PRODUCT RANGE ($19.50–24 CD) Arneis, Verdelho, Chardonnay, Illawarra Flame, Rose, Shiraz, Chambourcin, Sweet Chambourcin, Sangiovese, Premium Shiraz, Merlot, Cabernet Merlot, Cabernet Sauvignon.

SUMMARY With 14 hectares of vineyard planted to chardonnay, verdelho, arneis, shiraz, cabernet sauvignon, merlot, ruby cabernet, sangiovese and chambourcin, Crooked River Wines has the largest vineyard on the south coast. Production is expected to increase to 10 000 cases through an on-site winery. Cellar-door sales, craft shop and café opened in December 2001.

🍷🍷🍷🍷 **Premium Shiraz 2003** Vivid, youthful red-purple; light to medium-bodied; fresh plum and blackberry fruit, light touch of American oak. **RATING** 87 **DRINK** Now $24

🍷🍷🍷🍷 **Arneis 2003** **RATING** 84 **DRINK** Now $22

🍷🍷🍷 **Unwooded Chardonnay 2003** **RATING** 83 $22
Chardonnay Softly Wooded 2003 **RATING** 83 $19.50
Verdelho 2003 **RATING** 83 $19.50
Premium Cabernet Merlot 2003 **RATING** 83 $24
Premium Cabernet Sauvignon 2003 **RATING** 82 $24
Sangiovese Cabernet Sauvignon 2003 **RATING** 82 $22
Sangiovese 2003 **RATING** 82 $22
Merlot 2003 **RATING** 81 $19.50
Chambourcin 2003 **RATING** 81 $19.50

Cross Rivulet   NR

334 Richmond Road, Cambridge, Tas 7170 **REGION** Southern Tasmania
T (03) 6228 5406 **OPEN** First weekend March, or by appointment
WINEMAKER Lloyd Mathews **EST.** 1980 **CASES** 350
PRODUCT RANGE Riesling, Gewurztraminer, Muller Thurgau, Unwooded Chardonnay, Pinot Noir.
SUMMARY Geologist Lloyd Mathews is a self-taught viticulturist and winemaker, readily confessing that his main experience is learning from mistakes, a short adult education course on winemaking notwithstanding.

Crosswinds Vineyard   ★★★☆

10 Vineyard Drive, Tea Tree, Tas 7017 **REGION** Southern Tasmania
T (03) 6268 1091 **F** (03) 6268 1091 **OPEN** Mon–Fri 10–5
WINEMAKER Andrew Vasiljuk **EST.** 1990 **CASES** 650
PRODUCT RANGE ($18–60 CD) Non Wooded Chardonnay, Barrel Fermented Chardonnay, sparkling, Non Wooded Pinot Noir, Barrel Matured Pinot Noir, Reserve Pinot Noir.
SUMMARY Crosswinds has two vineyards: the 1-hectare Tea Tree Vineyard and the 2-hectare Margate Vineyard. As well as cellar-door sales, has retail distribution in Melbourne and small exports to the UK and South-East Asia. Both Chardonnay and Pinot Noir have excelled in recent years.

🍷🍷🍷🍷 **Vintage Sparkling 1999** Strong green-yellow; aromatic and intense fruit; long, lingering, high acid finish. **RATING** 87 **DRINK** 2007
Sparkling NV Deep colour; highly aromatic; intense fruit; lingering acidity demands understanding. **RATING** 87 **DRINK** 2010

Cruickshank Callatoota Estate

2656 Wybong Road, Wybong, NSW 2333 **REGION** Upper Hunter Valley
T (02) 6547 8149 **F** (02) 6547 8144 **OPEN** 7 days 9–5
WINEMAKER John Cruickshank, Laurie Nicholls, Andrew Thomas (Consultant) **EST.** 1973 **CASES** 5000
PRODUCT RANGE ($10–25 CD) Cabernet Rose, Shiraz, Cabernet Franc, Two Cabernets, Summer Cabernet, Cabernet Sauvignon, Cabernet Sauvignon Carbonic Maceration, Cabernet Sauvignon Pressings, Show Reserve Cabernet Sauvignon, Old Tawny Port.
SUMMARY Owned by Sydney management consultant John Cruickshank and family. There is continued improvement in wine quality and style, presumably reflecting the input of Andrew Thomas. The Rose continues its good form, but it is with the younger table wines that the improvement is obvious.

ΨΨΨΨ **Shiraz 2002** Solid and quite rich; a mix of dark fruits, chocolate and good tannins. **RATING** 89 **DRINK** 2012 $11.60

Cabernet Rose 2003 Well balanced; clear varietal fruit expression; length and freshness; impressive example. **RATING** 88 **DRINK** Now $12.50

Cabernet Sauvignon Pressings 2002 Clean, solid blackberry/blackcurrant fruit; the tannins are neither abrasive nor excessive. **RATING** 88 **DRINK** 2013 $15

ΨΨΨΨ **Cabernet Sauvignon Pressings 1999** **RATING** 84 **DRINK** 2007 $15

ΨΨΨ **Summer Cabernet Sauvignon 2002** **RATING** 83 $10

Cullen Wines ★★★★★

Caves Road, Cowaramup, WA 6284 **REGION** Margaret River
T (08) 9755 5277 **F** (08) 9755 5550 **OPEN** 7 days 10–4
WINEMAKER Vanya Cullen, Trevor Kent **EST.** 1971 **CASES** 20 000
PRODUCT RANGE ($18–82 CD) Flagship wines: Semillon Sauvignon Blanc, Chardonnay, Pinot Noir, Mangan Malbec Petit Verdot Merlot, Diana Madeline Cabernet Sauvignon Merlot; premium wines: Robinson's Riesling, Classic Dry White, Velvet Red, Autumn Harvest; Ellen Bussell White and Red.
SUMMARY One of the pioneers of Margaret River and has always produced long-lived wines of highly individual style from the substantial and mature estate vineyards. Since the 2003 vintage the vineyard has received A grade certification from the Biological Farmers Association, and received the award as best runner-up for best organic producer (all crops) with less than 5 years' certification. Winemaking is now in the hands of Vanya Cullen, daughter of the founders; she is possessed of an extraordinarily good palate. The Chardonnay is superb, while the Cabernet Merlot goes from strength to strength; indeed, I would rate it among Australia's best. The wines are distributed throughout Australia and also make their way to significant export markets in the UK, the US, Europe and Asia.

ΨΨΨΨΨ **Semillon Sauvignon Blanc 2003** Multi-dimensional and complex, the barrel ferment is evident but not over the top; sweet citrus and passionfruit run through a very long palate; lingering finish. **RATING** 96 **DRINK** 2012 $29

Chardonnay 2002 Beautifully made, proportioned and balanced; elegance and finesse; citrus, melon and stone fruit combined with a touch of creamy cashew. **RATING** 96 **DRINK** 2009 $50

Diana Madeline Cabernet Sauvignon Merlot 2002 Spotlessly clean but complex blackcurrant/blackberry and briar fruit; long palate strengthened and lengthened by tannins on the finish. Fruit, not oak, driven. **RATING** 94 **DRINK** 2022 $82

ΨΨΨΨ **Mangan Malbec Petit Verdot Merlot 2002** An avant-garde blend, vivid purple, with cascades of cassis, blackcurrant and blackberry fruits plus fine-grained tannins. **RATING** 92 **DRINK** 2012 $45

Mangan Malbec Petit Verdot Merlot 2003 Swimming with sweet fruit from blackcurrant to raspberry; minimal tannins; diametrically opposite to usual Cullen style. **RATING** 90 **DRINK** 2008 $45

ΨΨΨΨ **Ellen Bussell White 2003** A fragrant and flowery mix of fresh herbs and blossom aromas; crisp and crunchy, with excellent acidity and length. **RATING** 89 **DRINK** 2009 $18

Ellen Bussell Red 2002 Fresh and lively redcurrant aromas move to a raspberry and blackcurrant fruit mix in the mouth. Delicious fruit. Screwcap. **RATING** 88 **DRINK** 2007 $23

Curlewis Winery ★★★★★

55 Navarre Road, Curlewis, Vic 3222 **REGION** Geelong
T (03) 5250 4567 **F** (03) 5250 4567 **OPEN** By appointment
WINEMAKER Rainer Breit **EST.** 1998 **CASES** 1000
PRODUCT RANGE ($18–57 R) Pinot Gris, Chardonnay, Bellarine Selection Pinot Noir, Pinot Noir, Reserve Pinot Noir, Shiraz.
SUMMARY Rainer Breit and partner Wendy Oliver have achieved a great deal in a remarkably short period of time. In 1996 they purchased their property at Curlewis with 1.6 hectares of what were

then 11-year-old pinot noir vines; previously (and until 1998) the grapes had been sold to Scotchmans Hill. They set to and established an on-site winery, making 800 cases of very good Pinot Noir in their first vintage, 1998. Rainer Breit is a self-taught winemaker, but the full bag of pinot noir winemaking tricks is used: cold-soaking, hot-fermentation, post-ferment maceration, part inoculated and partly wild yeast use, prolonged lees contact, and bottling the wine neither fined nor filtered. While Breit and Oliver are self-confessed 'pinotphiles', they have planted a little chardonnay and buy a little locally grown shiraz and chardonnay. The wines are sold into Australia's best restaurants or by mail order, and rarely hit retail shelves. Exports to Singapore, Japan and Malaysia.

ŸŸŸŸŸ **Reserve Pinot Noir 2002** Very complex aromas and flavours; an intense mix of plum, black cherry and forest; long, lingering finish; excellent acidity. **RATING** 96 **DRINK** 2010 $ 57

Chardonnay 2002 Very complex and rich array of barrel-ferment, malolactic-ferment and bottled-developed aromas; ripe stone fruit and French oak coalesce on the intense and textured palate; good acidity. **RATING** 94 **DRINK** 2009 $ 30

Curly Flat   ★★★★★

Collivers Road, Lancefield, Vic 3435 **REGION** Macedon Ranges
T (03) 5429 1956 **F** (03) 5429 2256 **OPEN** First Sunday of each month, or by appointment
WINEMAKER Phillip Moraghan, Jillian Ryan **EST.** 1991 **CASES** 2500
PRODUCT RANGE ($24–44 ML) Chardonnay, Lacuna Chardonnay (unwooded), Pinot Noir.
SUMMARY Phillip and Jeni Moraghan began the development of Curly Flat in 1992, drawing in part upon the inspiration Phillip Moraghan experienced when working in Switzerland in the late 1980s, and with a passing nod to Michael Leunig. With ceaseless help and guidance from the late Laurie Williams (who died unexpectedly in mid-2001), the Moraghans have painstakingly established 14 hectares of vineyard, principally pinot noir, with lesser amounts of chardonnay and pinot gris. A multi-level, gravity-flow winery was commissioned for the 2002 vintage. Phillip Moraghan is very happy with the quality of the 2002 wines, made with advice from Gary Farr. Exports to the US and the UK.

ŸŸŸŸŸ **Pinot Noir 2001** Very complex wine; lots of flavour and texture; shows some whole-bunch/stalky characters which add to the appeal. Trophy 2003 Macedon Ranges Wine Show. **RATING** 94 **DRINK** 2007 $ 48

ŸŸŸŸŸ **Chardonnay 2002** Elegant and subtle; sophisticated winemaking; barrel-ferment and malolactic-ferment inputs to cashew, melon and fig flavours; harmonious. **RATING** 92 **DRINK** 2009 $ 38

Pinot Noir 2002 Abundant, rich, ripe plum on entry; more savoury mid-palate and finish; will develop more complexity by release date in March '05. **RATING** 92 **DRINK** 2010 $ 48

Chardonnay 2001 Bright colour; sophisticated melon, creamy cashew aromas and flavours; controlled barrel-ferment inputs; very good line and length. **RATING** 91 **DRINK** 2008 $ 38

Currency Creek Estate   ★★★

Winery Road, Currency Creek, SA 5214 **REGION** Currency Creek
T (08) 8555 4069 **F** (08) 8555 4100 **OPEN** 7 days 10–5
WINEMAKER John Loxton **EST.** 1969 **CASES** 7000
PRODUCT RANGE ($3.95–25.95 CD) Sedgeland Sauvignon Blanc, The Creek Station Semillon Sauvignon Blanc, The Creek Station Semillon, Reserve Brut, Princess Alexandrina Noble Semillon, Ostrich Hill Shiraz, The Creek Station Grenache Shiraz, The Creek Station Cabernet Grenache, Cabernet Sauvignon; fortifieds.
SUMMARY Constant name changes early in the piece (Santa Rosa and Tonkins were also tried) did not help the quest for identity or recognition in the marketplace, but the winery has nonetheless produced some outstanding wood-matured whites and pleasant, soft reds selling at attractive prices.

ŸŸŸŸ **Ostrich Hill Shiraz 2001** **RATING** 86 **DRINK** 2010 $ 19.95

🐦 Cuttaway Hill Estate ★★★☆

PO Box 2034, Bowral, NSW 2576 **REGION** Southern Highlands
T (02) 4862 4551 **F** (02) 4862 2326 **OPEN** Not
WINEMAKER Jim Chatto, Mark Bourne **EST.** 1998 **CASES** 5000
PRODUCT RANGE ($16.50–28 R) Semillon Sauvignon Blanc, Pinot Gris, Chardonnay, Reserve Chardonnay, Merlot, Cabernet Sauvignon.
SUMMARY Owned by the O'Neil family, Cuttaway Hill Estate is the largest vineyard property in the Southern Highlands, with a total of 38 hectares on three vineyard sites. The original Cuttaway Hill vineyard at Mittagong has 17 hectares of chardonnay, merlot, cabernet sauvignon and shiraz. The Allambie vineyard of 6.9 hectares is established on the light sandy loam soils of Ninety Acre Hill, and is planted to sauvignon blanc, pinot gris and pinot noir. The third and newest vineyard of 14.2 hectares is Maytree, situated west of Moss Vale in a relatively dryer and warmer meso-climate. Here cabernet sauvignon, merlot and pinot noir (and a small amount of chardonnay) have been planted, to provide fully mature grapes and more intensely flavoured wines. The standard of both viticulture and contract winemaking under the direction of Jim Chatto at Monarch Winemaking Services is evident in the quality of the wines.

ΨΨΨΨΨ **Semillon Sauvignon Blanc 2003** Clean, fragrant and crisp aromas; attractive passionfruit and citrus; clean, well made, and with good length. Screwcap. **RATING** 90 **DRINK** Now $ 20

ΨΨΨΨ **Chardonnay 2001** Still holding bright colour; well made; fig, cashew and nectarine; subtle malolactic and oak inputs. **RATING** 87 **DRINK** Now $ 20

ΨΨΨΨ **Pinot Gris 2003** Plenty of apple and musk flavour; builds on the finish, and has a clean aftertaste. **RATING** 86 **DRINK** Now $ 22
Merlot 2002 **RATING** 85 **DRINK** 2007 $ 20
Cabernet Sauvignon 2001 **RATING** 84 **DRINK** 2007 $ 20

Dalfarras ★★★☆

PO Box 123, Nagambie, Vic 3608 **REGION** Nagambie Lakes
T (03) 5794 2637 **F** (03) 5794 2360 **OPEN** Not
WINEMAKER Alister Purbrick, Alan George **EST.** 1991 **CASES** 18 000
PRODUCT RANGE ($13.50–15.95 R) Sauvignon Blanc, Verdelho, Shiraz, Merlot.
SUMMARY The personal project of Alister Purbrick and artist-wife Rosa (nee) Dalfarra, whose paintings adorn the labels of the wines. Alister, of course, is best known as winemaker at Tahbilk, the family winery and home, but this range of wines is intended to (in Alister's words) 'allow me to expand my winemaking horizons and mould wines in styles different from Tahbilk'. It now draws upon 23 hectares of its own plantings in the Goulburn Valley, and the business continues to grow year by year.

ΨΨΨΨ **Shiraz 2000** **RATING** 85 **DRINK** Now $ 14.95

Dalrymple ★★★☆

1337 Pipers Brook Road, Pipers Brook, Tas 7254 **REGION** Northern Tasmania
T (03) 6382 7222 **F** (03) 6382 7222 **OPEN** 7 days 10–5
WINEMAKER Bertel Sundstrup **EST.** 1987 **CASES** 4500
PRODUCT RANGE ($15–35 CD) Chardonnay, Unwooded Chardonnay, Sauvignon Blanc, Blanc de Blancs, Pinot Noir, Pinot Noir Special Bin.
SUMMARY A partnership between Jill Mitchell and her sister and brother-in-law, Anne and Bertel Sundstrup, inspired by father Bill Mitchell's establishment of the Tamarway Vineyard in the late 1960s. In 1991 Tamarway reverted to the Sundstrup and Mitchell families and it, too, will be producing wine in the future, probably under its own label but sold ex the Dalrymple cellar door. As production has grown (significantly), so has that of wine quality across the board, often led by its Sauvignon Blanc.

ΨΨΨΨ **Chardonnay 2002** Obvious, slightly funky barrel-ferment aromas; tighter palate; fresher, more lively. **RATING** 88 **DRINK** 2009 $ 25

ΥΥΥΥ **Sauvignon Blanc 2003** RATING 86 DRINK Now $ 30
Chardonnay 2003 RATING 86 DRINK 2007 $ 25
Unwooded Chardonnay 2003 RATING 85 DRINK Now $ 20

ΥΥΥ **Pinot Noir 2002** RATING 83 $ 30

Dalwhinnie ★★★★★

448 Taltarni Road, Moonambel, Vic 3478 **REGION** Pyrenees
T (03) 5467 2388 **F** (03) 5467 2237 **OPEN** 7 days 10–5
WINEMAKER David Jones, Gary Baldwin (Consultant) **EST.** 1976 **CASES** 5500
PRODUCT RANGE ($35–55 CD) Dalwhinnie Pinot Noir; Moonambel Chardonnay, Shiraz and
Cabernet; Eagle Series Shiraz.
SUMMARY David and Jenny Jones are making outstanding wines right across the board. The wines
all show tremendous depth of fruit flavour, reflecting the relatively low-yielding but very well-
maintained vineyards. It is hard to say whether the Chardonnay, the Cabernet Sauvignon or the
Shiraz is the more distinguished, the Pinot Noir a startling arrival from out of nowhere. A further 8
hectares of shiraz (with a little viognier) were planted in the spring of 1999 on a newly acquired
block on Taltarni Road, permitting the further development of exports to the UK, Spain,
Switzerland, the US, Canada, New Zealand and Hong Kong. A 50-tonne contemporary high-tech
winery was built prior to the 2002 vintage allowing the Eagle Series Shiraz and Pinot Noir to be
made on-site.

ΥΥΥΥΥ **Moonambel Shiraz 2002** A complex web of blackberry, leather, mocha and game;
excellent tannin structure on the finish. **RATING** 93 **DRINK** 2015 $ 48
Moonambel Cabernet Sauvignon 2002 Focused, concentrated blackcurrant and earth
varietal fruit; long, persuasive tannins; overall distinctly savoury. **RATING** 92 **DRINK** 2014
$ 42
Pinot Noir 2002 A potent mix of wild berry fruits, plums and forest floor; long and
brooding. **RATING** 91 **DRINK** 2007 $ 38

ΥΥΥΥ **Moonambel Chardonnay 2002** Very complex, strong spicy oak; a big wine in every
respect, already showing considerable development. **RATING** 89 **DRINK** Now $ 35

Dalyup River Estate NR

Murrays Road, Esperance, WA 6450 **REGION** Southwest Australia Zone
T (08) 9076 5027 **F** (08) 9076 5027 **OPEN** Weekends 10–4 Oct–May
WINEMAKER Tom Murray **EST.** 1987 **CASES** 1000
PRODUCT RANGE ($13–17 CD) Hellfire White, Esperance Chardonnay (unwooded), Chardonnay,
Esperance Shiraz, Esperance Cabernet Sauvignon.
SUMMARY Arguably the most remote winery in Australia other than Chateau Hornsby in Alice
Springs, drawing upon 2.5 hectares of estate vineyards. The quantities are as small as the cellar-door
prices are modest; this apart, the light but fragrant wines show the cool climate of this ocean-side
vineyard. Came from out of the clouds to win the trophy for Best Wine of Show at the West
Australian Show in 1999 with its Shiraz, but hasn't repeated that success.

Dal Zotto Estate ★★★★

1944 Edi Road, Cheshunt, Vic 3678 **REGION** King Valley
T (03) 5729 8321 **F** (03) 5729 8490 **OPEN** 7 days 11–5
WINEMAKER Otto Dal Zotto, Michael Dal Zotto **EST.** 1987 **CASES** 10 000
PRODUCT RANGE ($20–35 CD) Riesling, Chardonnay, Family Reserve Shiraz, Barbera, Sangiovese,
Merlot, Cabernet Merlot, Cabernet Sauvignon.
SUMMARY Dal Zotto Wines remains primarily a contract grape grower, with 48 hectares of vineyards
(predominantly chardonnay, cabernet sauvignon and merlot, with smaller plantings of riesling, pinot
gris, shiraz, sangiovese, barbera and marzemino). Increasing amounts are made under the Dal Zotto
label, with retail distribution in New South Wales and exports to the US and Japan.

Danbury Estate NR

Billimari, NSW 2794 (PO Box 605, Cowra, NSW 2794) **REGION** Cowra
T (02) 6341 2204 **F** (02) 6341 4690 **OPEN** Tues–Sun 10–4 at Chill Restaurant, Japanese Garden, Cowra
WINEMAKER Hope Estate (Contract) **EST.** 1996 **CASES** 6000
PRODUCT RANGE ($12.95–15.30 CD) Middleton Chardonnay, Middleton Sparkling, Reserve.
SUMMARY A specialist Chardonnay producer established by Jonathon Middleton, with 22 hectares in
production and the wines made under contract. The Quarry Restaurant is open Tuesday to Sunday 10–4.

d'Arenberg

Osborn Road, McLaren Vale, SA 5171 **REGION** McLaren Vale
T (08) 8323 8206 **F** (08) 8323 8423 **OPEN** 7 days 10–5
WINEMAKER Chester Osborn, Phillip Dean **EST.** 1912 **CASES** 180 000
PRODUCT RANGE ($11.95–60 R) A daunting array of whimsically labelled varietals such as Dry Dam
Riesling, Broken Fishplate Sauvignon Blanc, Last Ditch Viognier, Money Spider Roussanne, Stump
Jump Sauvignon Blanc Chardonnay, Hermit Crab Marsanne Viognier, Olive Grove Chardonnay,
Other Side Chardonnay, Lucky Lizard Chardonnay, Noble Riesling, Noble Semillon, Noble Traminer
Riesling, Peppermint Paddock Sparkling Chambourcin, Feral Fox Pinot Noir, Dead Arm Shiraz,
Footbolt Old Vine Shiraz, Laughing Magpie Shiraz Viognier, Twenty Eight Road Mourvedre, d'Arry's
Original Shiraz Grenache, Stump Jump Grenache Shiraz, Ironstone Pressings Grenache Shiraz
Mourvedre, Custodian Grenache, Galvo Garage Cabernet Sauvignon Merlot Cabernet Franc, High
Trellis Cabernet Sauvignon, Coppermine Road Cabernet Sauvignon; Vintage Fortified Shiraz,
Nostalgia Rare Tawny.
SUMMARY Originally a conservative, traditional business (albeit successful), d'Arenberg adopted a
much higher profile in the second half of the 1990s, with a cascade of volubly worded labels and the
opening of a spectacularly situated and high-quality restaurant, d'Arry's Verandah. Happily, wine
quality has more than kept pace with the label uplifts. An incredible number of export markets
spread across Europe, North America and Asia, with all of the major countries represented.

TTTTT **The Laughing Magpie Shiraz Viognier 2002** Oozing licorice, spice, blackberry and
    chocolate; very ripe and rich; tannins not overdone. **RATING** 94 **DRINK** 2012 $ 31.50
    The Galvo Garage Cabernet Sauvignon Merlot Cabernet Franc 2001 Absurdly named
    but a delicious wine from the first second to the last, with an array of lush black and red
    fruits, spicy, fluffy tannins and good oak handling. Fully deserves its gold medals.
    RATING 94 **DRINK** 2011 $ 31.50

TTTTY **The Lucky Lizard Chardonnay 2002** Very funky, solids/wild yeast aromas, then a striking,
    long, intense citrus and melon palate. **RATING** 93 **DRINK** 2008 $ 25
    The Dead Arm Shiraz 2001 Complex, rich licorice and blackberry aromas; palate
    crammed with opulent, ripe fruit flavour. **RATING** 93 **DRINK** 2016 $ 65
    The Ironstone Pressings 2002 Deep colour; massive wine with great depth of multi-
    flavoured black fruits and tannins. **RATING** 93 **DRINK** 2017 $ 65
    The Footbolt Old Vine Shiraz 2001 Full-on style; licorice, spice, game and blackberry;
    abundant texture and structure, but not over the top. **RATING** 92 **DRINK** 2011 $ 19.95
    The Coppermine Road Cabernet Sauvignon 2001 Quite fragrant, fully ripe
    cassis/blackcurrant aromas; full-bodied, gutsy tannins. **RATING** 92 **DRINK** 2016 $ 65
    Sticks & Stones Tempranillo Grenache Souzao 2002 Concentrated dark berry fruit plus
    splashes of spice; ripe, lingering tannins. **RATING** 92 **DRINK** 2012 $ 35
    The Ironstone Pressings 2000 Savoury, spicy, chocolaty; round mouthfeel; fine filigree of
    tannins. **RATING** 91 **DRINK** 2007 $ 65
    d'Arry's Original Shiraz Grenache 2001 Complex dark fruit/plum/spice aromas, then a
    similarly rich and complex palate with ample structure; good tannins to close. **RATING** 91
    DRINK 2011 $ 19.95
    The High Trellis Cabernet Sauvignon 2001 Earthy/savoury/blackberry aromas; swells
    on the palate; lots of rich black fruits. **RATING** 91 **DRINK** 2016 $ 19.95
    The Custodian Sand on Clay Grenache 2002 At the savoury end of the spectrum, but
    with good structure. **RATING** 90 **DRINK** 2009 $ 20
    The Custodian Grenache 2000 Developed red; interesting bottle developed characters ex
    Southern Rhône, tangy and savoury; fine tannins linger. **RATING** 90 **DRINK** 2007 $ 19.95

ΥΥΥΥ **The Last Ditch Viognier 2002** Honeysuckle, blossom, pastille aromas, the full-flavoured palate with nice viscosity and length; carries French oak and 14.5 degrees alcohol with ease. **RATING** 88 **DRINK** 2007 $ 20

Twenty Eight Road Mourvedre 2002 Powerful wine; very typical of the variety; deeply coloured; slightly hard edges, but flavoursome. **RATING** 88 **DRINK** 2012 $ 35

ΥΥΥΥ **The Derelict Vineyard Grenache 2002** **RATING** 86 **DRINK** 2007 $ 30

The Custodian Loam Grenache 2002 **RATING** 86 **DRINK** 2008 $ 20

The Stump Jump Grenache Shiraz Mourvedre 2002 **RATING** 86 **DRINK** Now $ 11.95

The Stump Jump Riesling Sauvignon Blanc Marsanne 2002 **RATING** 85 **DRINK** Now $ 11.95

The Custodian Deep Sand Grenache 2002 **RATING** 85 **DRINK** 2007 $ 20

The Money Spider Roussanne 2002 **RATING** 84 **DRINK** Now $ 20

ΥΥΥ **The Hermit Crab Marsanne Viognier 2002** **RATING** 83 $ 15

Dargo Valley Winery   NR

Lower Dargo Road, Dargo, Vic 3682 **REGION** Gippsland
T (03) 5140 1228 **F** (03) 5140 1388 **OPEN** Mon–Thurs 12–8, weekends, holidays 10–8 (closed Fridays)
WINEMAKER Hermann Bila **EST.** 1985 **CASES** 500
PRODUCT RANGE ($12.50–14.50 CD) Rhine Riesling, Sauvignon Blanc, Chardonnay, Pinot Noir, Cabernet Sauvignon, Port, Muscat.
SUMMARY Two and a half hectares are situated in mountain country north of Maffra and looking towards the Bogong National Park. Hermann Bila comes from a family of European winemakers; there is an on-site restaurant, and Devonshire teas and ploughman's lunches are served — very useful given the remote locality. The white wines tend to be rustic, the sappy/earthy/cherry Pinot Noir the pick of the red wines. Bed and breakfast accommodation is available.

Darling Estate   ★★☆

Whitfield Road, Cheshunt, Vic 3678 **REGION** King Valley
T (03) 5729 8396 **F** (03) 5729 8396 **OPEN** By appointment
WINEMAKER Guy Darling **EST.** 1990 **CASES** 500
PRODUCT RANGE ($10–30 CD) Under the Koombahla label are Riesling, Chardonnay, Pinot Noir, Shiraz, Cabernet Franc, Cabernet Sauvignon; Nambucca Chenin Blanc and Gamay.
SUMMARY Guy Darling was one of the pioneers of the King Valley when he planted his first vines in 1970. For many years the entire production was purchased by Brown Brothers, providing their well-known Koombahla Estate label. Much of the production from the 23 hectares is still sold to Brown Brothers (and others), but in 1991 Guy Darling established a fully functional winery, making a small portion of the production into wine — which was, in fact, his original motivation for planting the first vines.

ΥΥΥ **Nambucca Gamay 2002** **RATING** 83 $ 13

Nambucca Gamay Pressings 2002 **RATING** 83 $ 12

Darling Park   ★★★★

232 Red Hill Road, Red Hill, Vic 3937 **REGION** Mornington Peninsula
T (03) 5989 2324 **F** (03) 5989 2324 **OPEN** Weekends and public holidays 11–5, 7 days in January
WINEMAKER Josh Liberman **EST.** 1986 **CASES** 3000
PRODUCT RANGE ($17–38 CD) Sauvignon Blanc, Madhatters Sparkling, Querida (Rose), Te Quiero, Decadence, Pinot Noir, Estate Merlot, Cabernet Merlot, Estate Cabernet Sauvignon.
SUMMARY Josh Liberman (and wife Karen) and David Coe purchased Darling Park prior to the 2002 vintage. The Winenet consultancy group is providing advice on both the viticultural and winemaking side, and the product range has been revamped.

ΥΥΥΥΥ **Arthur Boyd Collection Te Quiero 2001** Strong purple-red; abundant cassis fruit and soft, persistent tannins; nice touches of oak and chocolate. **RATING** 90 **DRINK** 2011 $ 28

YYYY **Pinot Noir 2002** Inky colour; powerful, dark plummy, foresty; super-concentrated, powerful and tannic. Needed a gentler hand. **RATING** 89 **DRINK** 2012 $38
Querida Rose 2003 Brilliant colour; fresh cherry and strawberry aromas and flavours; balanced, dry finish; good acidity. unconventional blend of Pinot Noir, Pinot Gris and Chardonnay. **RATING** 87 **DRINK** Now $17

YYYY **Chardonnay 2002 RATING** 85 **DRINK** Now $22
Arthur Boyd Collection Adelaide Hills Merlot 2002 RATING 85 **DRINK** 2007 $28

Darlington Estate   NR

Lot 39 Nelson Road, Darlington, WA 6070 **REGION** Perth Hills
T (08) 9299 6268 **F** (08) 9299 7107 **OPEN** Thurs–Sun and holidays 12–5
WINEMAKER Caspar van der Meer **EST.** 1983 **CASES** 3000
PRODUCT RANGE ($13–30 CD) Sonata (Sauvignon Blanc), Semillon, Chardonnay, Symphony (Verdelho), Serenade (Chardonnay), Shiraz, Cabernet Sauvignon, Brut, Ruby Port; Darling Red (Grenache), Darling White (Unwooded Chardonnay), Darling Rose (Grenache).
SUMMARY Established by the van der Meer family, it is one of the oldest — and was once the largest — wineries in the Perth Hills, for a while setting the standard. After an intermission, Caspar van der Meer has returned to the winemaking role.

Darlington Vineyard   ★★★☆

Holkam Court, Orford, Tas 7190 **REGION** Southern Tasmania
T (03) 6257 1630 **F** (03) 6257 1630 **OPEN** Thurs–Mon 10–5
WINEMAKER Andrew Hood **EST.** 1993 **CASES** 450
PRODUCT RANGE ($15–20 CD) Riesling, Sauvignon Blanc, Chardonnay, Pinot Noir.
SUMMARY Peter and Margaret Hyland planted a little under 2 hectares of vineyard in 1993. The first wines were made from the 1999 vintage, forcing retired builder Peter Hyland to complete their home so the small building in which they had been living could be converted to a cellar door. The vineyard looks out over the settlement of Darlington on Maria Island, the site of Diego Bernacci's attempt to establish a vineyard and lure investors by attaching artificial bunches of grapes to his vines. The outline of Maria Island is depicted on the label.

David Traeger   ★★★☆

139 High Street, Nagambie, Vic 3608 **REGION** Nagambie Lakes
T (03) 5794 2514 **F** (03) 5794 1776 **OPEN** 7 days 10–5
WINEMAKER David Traeger **EST.** 1986 **CASES** 10 000
PRODUCT RANGE ($11–29.50 R) Verdelho, Shiraz, Cabernet; Helvetia (cellar door only), Classic Dry (Riesling Semillon), Late Harvest (Riesling Verdelho), Cabernet Dolce, Cabernet Shiraz Merlot, Tawny Port.
SUMMARY David Traeger learned much during his years as assistant winemaker at Mitchelton, and knows central Victoria well. The red wines are solidly crafted, the Verdelho interesting but more variable in quality. In late 2002 the business was acquired by the Dromana Estate group, but David Traeger has stayed on as winemaker. See also separate Baptista entry.

Dawson Estate   NR

Cnr Old Naracoorte and Kangaroo Hill Roads, Robe, SA 5276 **REGION** Mount Benson
T (08) 8768 2427 **F** (08) 8768 2987 **OPEN** Not
WINEMAKER Derek Hooper (Contract) **EST.** 1998 **CASES** 500
PRODUCT RANGE ($18–25 R) Shiraz, Cabernet Sauvignon.
SUMMARY Anthony Paul and Marian Dawson are busy people. In addition to establishing over 20 hectares of chardonnay, pinot noir, shiraz and cabernet sauvignon, they are in the process of opening a wine bar/restaurant in Robe, and intend to continue extending the vineyard on a further 16 hectares of plantable land. All of this is largely financed by the crayfishing boat which Anthony runs in the crayfish season.

Dawson's Patch Valley

NR

71 Kallista-Emerald Road, The Patch, Vic 3792 (postal) **REGION** Yarra Valley
T 0419 521 080 **OPEN** Not
WINEMAKER Paul Evans (Contract) **EST.** 2000 **CASES** 400
PRODUCT RANGE ($15 R) Chardonnay.
SUMMARY In 1996 James and Jody Dawson planted 1.2 hectares of chardonnay on their vineyard at the southern end of the Yarra Valley. The climate here is particularly cool, and the grapes do not normally ripen until late April. Jody Dawson manages the vineyards, and is completing a degree in viticulture through Charles Sturt University. The tiny production is basically sold through local restaurants and cellars in the Olinda/Emerald/Belgrave area. So far only a barrel-fermented (French oak) wine has been produced, but it may be that an unoaked version will join the roster some time in the future.

Deakin Estate

Kulkyne Way, via Red Cliffs, Vic 3496 **REGION** Murray Darling
T (03) 5029 1666 **F** (03) 5024 3316 **OPEN** Not
WINEMAKER Phil Spillman **EST.** 1980 **CASES** 500 000
PRODUCT RANGE ($10.50–15 R) Sauvignon Blanc, Colombard, Chardonnay, Brut, Shiraz, Merlot, Cabernet Sauvignon; Select range of Chardonnay, Sparkling Shiraz, Shiraz, Merlot.
SUMMARY Effectively replaces the Sunnycliff label in the Katnook Estate, Riddoch and (now) Deakin Estate triumvirate, which constitutes the Wingara Wine Group, now 60 per cent owned by Freixenet of Spain. Sunnycliff is still used for export purposes but appears on the domestic market. Deakin Estate draws on over 300 hectares of its own vineyards, making it largely self-sufficient, and produces competitively priced wines of consistent quality and impressive value. Exports to the UK, the US, Canada, New Zealand and Asia.

ŢŢŢŢ **Select Shiraz 2001** Still retaining fresh, bright red and dark berry fruits; good oak handling, well made. Shiraz gold medal winner 2003 International Wine & Spirit Competition. **RATING** 89 **DRINK** Now $ 15
Shiraz 2002 Quite rich and complex; lots of dark berry fruit and a twist of oak; shows the outstanding 2002 vintage. Great value. **RATING** 87 **DRINK** Now $ 10

ŢŢŢŢ **Cabernet Sauvignon 2002 RATING** 86 **DRINK** Now $ 10
Merlot 2002 RATING 85 **DRINK** Now $ 10
Chardonnay 2003 RATING 84 **DRINK** Now $ 10
Brut NV RATING 84 **DRINK** Now $ 10

ŢŢŢ **Sauvignon Blanc 2003 RATING** 83 $ 10
Select Shiraz 2000 RATING 82 $ 15

De Bortoli

De Bortoli Road, Bilbul, NSW 2680 **REGION** Riverina
T (02) 6966 0100 **F** (02) 6966 0199 **OPEN** Mon–Sat 9–5, Sun 9–4
WINEMAKER Darren De Bortoli, Ralph Graham, Julie Mortlock, Helen Foggo-Paschkow **EST.** 1928
CASES 3 million
PRODUCT RANGE ($4.90–42.50 CD) Noble One Botrytis Semillon is the flagship wine; premium varietals under Deen De Bortoli label; mid-priced range of varietal and blended wines under the Montage and Wild Vine labels; low-priced range of varietal and generic wines under the Sacred Hill label; sparkling, Fortified. Substantial exports in bulk.
SUMMARY Famous among the cognoscenti for its superb Botrytis Semillon, which in fact accounts for only a minute part of its total production, this winery turns around low-priced varietal and generic wines which are invariably competently made and equally invariably provide value for money. These come in part from 250 hectares of estate vineyards, but mostly from contract-grown grapes. The death of founder Deen De Bortoli in 2003 was widely mourned by the whole industry. Exports include Canada, Singapore, Japan, Hong Kong, Sweden and Thailand.

ŢŢŢŢŢ **Noble One 2002** In style heartland; luscious apricot, cumquat and honey offset by lingering, balancing acidity. **RATING** 94 **DRINK** 2011 $ 24

Noble One 2001 Glowing gold; archetypal, complex cumquat, honey, citrus and honeycomb; balancing acidity and subtle oak. **RATING** 94 **DRINK** 2010 $ 24

Black Noble NV Utterly unique style; very intense, long, lingering palate and aftertaste; excellent acidity provides a clean finish; the botrytis semillon origins long gone. **RATING** 94 **DRINK** Now $ 28

ᵀᵀᵀᵀᵀ **Old Boys Tawny Port NV** A fine example of aged tawny (average 21 years) at the sweeter end of the spectrum; good nutty rancio characters, length and balance. **RATING** 90 **DRINK** Now $ 28

Show Liqueur Muscat NV Luscious, full-on grapey/raisiny muscat; good rancio; top value. **RATING** 90 **DRINK** Now $ 16.50

ᵀᵀᵀᵀ **Deen De Bortoli Vat 5 Botrytis Semillon (375 ml) 2000** Glowing gold; moderately sweet tropical fruits and crisp acidity; has benefitted from time in bottle. **RATING** 89 **DRINK** 2007 $ 10

Rare Dry Botrytis Semillon 1996 A quirky style unique to De Bortoli in this country, but with parallels in Sauternes. Golden bronze, with complex, biscuity, dried fruit aromas and flavours. The power of the wine all but obscures the modest amount of residual sugar. Strongly recommended as something out of the ordinary. **RATING** 89 **DRINK** Now $ 17.85

Rare Dry Botrytis Semillon 1997 Complex toasty/nutty aromas and flavours in the tradition of this style, but a drier finish than usual. **RATING** 88 **DRINK** 2007 $ 17.85

Sacred Hill Semillon Chardonnay 2003 Tangy and lively; sweet citrussy fruit; surprising length. **RATING** 87 **DRINK** Now $ 5.50

Deen Vat 9 Cabernet Sauvignon 2002 Lots of cassis blackberry fruit; good structure; seriously good wine for $11 or less. **RATING** 87 **DRINK** Now $ 11

ᵀᵀᵀᵀ **Deen Vat 2 Sauvignon Blanc 2003** **RATING** 86 **DRINK** Now $ 10

Sacred Hill Traminer Riesling 2003 Spicy floral varietal character from the traminer, more evident than in most higher priced versions. As always, a slightly sweet finish; ideal for Asian food. Outstanding value. **RATING** 86 **DRINK** Now $ 6

Deen Vat 8 Shiraz 2002 **RATING** 86 **DRINK** 2008 $ 10

Emeri Brut Chardonnay Pinot NV Highly fragrant and fruit; against expectations, isn't particularly sweet; cheerful fizz. **RATING** 86 **DRINK** Now $ 10.50

8 Year Old Tawny Port NV **RATING** 86 **DRINK** Now $ 28

Deen Vat 9 Verdelho 2003 **RATING** 85 **DRINK** Now $ 11

Deen Vat 4 Petit Verdot 2001 **RATING** 85 **DRINK** 2007 $ 10

Wild Vine Shiraz 2003 **RATING** 84 **DRINK** 2007 $ 7.50

ᵀᵀᵀ **Sacred Hill Rhine Riesling 2003** **RATING** 83 $ 6.50

Wild Vine Chardonnay 2003 **RATING** 83 $ 8.50

Sacred Hill Shiraz Cabernet 2003 **RATING** 83 $ 6.50

Sacred Hill Cabernet Merlot 2003 **RATING** 83 $ 7

Sacred Hill Colombard Chardonnay 2003 **RATING** 82 $ 6.50

Montage Chardonnay Semillon 2002 **RATING** 80 $ 7.90

De Bortoli (Hunter Valley)   ★★★☆

Lot 1, Branxton Road, Pokolbin, NSW 2320 **REGION** Lower Hunter Valley
T (02) 4993 8800 **F** (02) 4993 8899 **OPEN** 7 days 10–5
WINEMAKER Scott Stephens **EST.** 2002 **CASES** 40 000

PRODUCT RANGE ($15–200 CD) Hunter Valley range of Semillon, Verdelho, Chardonnay, Winemakers Selection Merlot; Black Creek range of Semillon Sauvignon Blanc, Verdelho, Chardonnay, Late Harvest Semillon, Rose, Sparkling Shiraz, Shiraz, Cabernet Merlot; Murphy Semillon.

SUMMARY De Bortoli extended its wine empire in 2002 with the purchase of the former Wilderness Estate, giving it an immediate and substantial presence in the Hunter Valley courtesy of the 26 hectares of established vineyards, to be expanded significantly by the subsequent purchase of an adjoining 40-hectare property. The wines will be released in three price ranges: at the top the Hunter Valley Semillon and Chardonnay, made from Hunter Valley grapes; then the Black Creek range, utilising three region blends encompassing the Hunter, Yarra and King Valleys (Semillon Sauvignon Blanc and Cabernet Merlot) and Hunter Valley, Heathcote and Yarra Valley (Shiraz).

▼▼▼▼♀ **Murphy's Semillon 2003** Spotlessly clean and delicate; appealing, sweet lemon juice flavours; good length. RATING 92 DRINK 2012 $30
Winemakers Selection Hunter Valley Semillon 2003 Lively, intense and long; sweet, lemony fruit; dry finish. RATING 91 DRINK 2012 $20
Black Creek Muscat 2003 Remarkably rich and complex, obviously Riverina, not Hunter, in origin. A high quality wine which will cause a cellar door stampede. RATING 90
DRINK Now $15

▼▼▼▼ **Black Creek Chardonnay 2003** Fresh, light-bodied, fruit-driven; grapefruit and stone fruit; a blend of Hunter Valley and Tumbarumba grapes. RATING 88 DRINK Now $16
Hunter Valley Semillon 2003 More dusty/herbal aromas; crisp palate; good length. RATING 87 DRINK 2008 $20
Hunter Valley Shiraz 2003 Deep colour; concentrated black cherry fruit; saturated and plush; minimal oak influence. Could blossom in bottle. RATING 87 DRINK 2009 $20

▼▼▼▼♀ **Black Creek Semillon Sauvignon Blanc 2003** RATING 86 DRINK 2007 $15
Black Creek Shiraz 2003 RATING 85 DRINK Now $15
Black Creek Cabernet Merlot 2003 RATING 85 DRINK 2008 $15
Hunter Valley Semillon 2000 RATING 84 DRINK Now $20
Hunter Valley Chardonnay 2001 RATING 84 DRINK Now $20
Black Creek Verdelho 2003 RATING 84 DRINK Now $16

▼▼▼ **Hunter Valley Chardonnay 2003** RATING 83 $20
Hunter Valley Verdelho 2003 RATING 83 $20
Black Creek Rose 2003 RATING 83 $15
Black Creek Sparkling Shiraz NV RATING 83 $16
Black Creek Late Harvest Semillon 2003 RATING 83 $15
Black Creek Liqueur Muscat NV RATING 81 $15

De Bortoli (Victoria) ★★★★★

Pinnacle Lane, Dixons Creek, Vic 3775 REGION Yarra Valley
T (03) 5965 2271 F (03) 5965 2442 OPEN 7 days 10–5
WINEMAKER Stephen Webber, David Slingsby-Smith, Ben Cane, Paul Bridgeman
EST. 1987 CASES 400 000
PRODUCT RANGE ($12–57.50 R) At the top comes the premium Melba (Cabernet blend), followed by Yarra Valley varietals; then comes the intermediate Gulf Station range, also solely from the Yarra Valley; the Windy Peak label is from various Victorian regions.
SUMMARY The quality arm of the bustling De Bortoli group, run by Leanne De Bortoli and husband Stephen Webber, ex-Lindeman winemaker. The top label (Yarra Valley), the second (Gulf Station) and the third label (Windy Peak) offer wines of consistently good quality and excellent value — the complex Chardonnay is of outstanding quality. Exports to the UK, Europe, Asia and the US.

▼▼▼▼▼ **Yarra Valley Pinot Noir 2002** Fine, fragrant, supple and silky smooth plum, cherry and strawberry; good length. RATING 94 DRINK 2009 $29
Yarra Valley Pinot Noir 2001 Very complex and fragrant cherry and strawberry aromas, the palate has a sweet fruit core surrounded by savoury, silky tannins. RATING 94 DRINK Now $29

▼▼▼▼♀ **Windy Peak Pinot Noir 2003** Bright colour; fresh cherry and plum fruit; remarkable structure, length and complexity for a wine at this price. Exceptional value. Is in fact Yarra Valley-sourced. RATING 91 DRINK Now $12
Gulf Station Shiraz 2002 Powerful dark fruits/blackberries; savoury tannin structure. Will flower given time. RATING 90 DRINK 2010 $16

▼▼▼▼ **Gulf Station Chardonnay 2003** Finely structured and very long, so typical of the Yarra; nectarine, melon and citrus fruit; subtle barrel ferment component. RATING 89
DRINK 2008 $16
Gulf Station Pinot Noir 2003 Plenty of depth and power; rich dark plum and spice; will develop. RATING 89 DRINK 2008 $16
Gulf Station Merlot 2003 Clear-cut small berry varietal fruit, albeit at the riper end of the spectrum; fruit-driven, early-drinking style. RATING 88 DRINK 2007 $16

Gulf Station Semillon Sauvignon Blanc 2003 Strong varietal herbal fruit aromas, offset by a hint of sweetness; easy style. **RATING** 87 **DRINK** Now $16

Gulf Station Pinot Noir 2002 A complex array of strawberry, rhubarb and tangy/foresty aromas, then a light to medium-bodied savoury palate. Value. **RATING** 87 **DRINK** 2007 $16

Gulf Station Cabernet Sauvignon 2001 Elegant, light to medium-bodied and unforced; nicely ripened cassis and cedar; fine tannins. **RATING** 87 **DRINK** 2011 $16

Windy Peak Spaetlese Riesling 2002 Lovely wine for those looking for some sweetness; floral lime aromas and flavours; perfect acid balance. **RATING** 87 **DRINK** Now $11.50

▼▼▼♀ **Gulf Station Riesling 2003** **RATING** 86 **DRINK** Now $16

Windy Peak Sauvignon Blanc Semillon 2003 **RATING** 86 **DRINK** Now $15.99

Windy Peak Pinot Noir 2002 **RATING** 86 **DRINK** Now $12

Windy Peak Riesling 2003 **RATING** 85 **DRINK** Now $13

Windy Peak Chardonnay 2003 **RATING** 85 **DRINK** Now $13

Windy Peak Sangiovese 2002 **RATING** 85 **DRINK** Now $12

Windy Peak Shiraz 2001 **RATING** 84 **DRINK** Now $12

Deep Dene Vineyard   NR

36 Glenisla Road, Bickley, WA 6076 **REGION** Perth Hills
T (08) 9293 0077 **F** (08) 9293 0077 **OPEN** By appointment
WINEMAKER Contract **EST.** 1994 **CASES** 4000
PRODUCT RANGE ($25–28 R) Pinot Noir, Shiraz, Sparkling.
SUMMARY Improbably, was once one of the largest Perth Hills vineyards, but no more. It comprises 4 hectares of pinot noir and 0.5 hectare of shiraz, continuing the near obsession of the Perth Hills vignerons with pinot noir in a climate which, to put it mildly, is difficult for the variety, other than its use in sparkling wine.

🍃 Deep Water Estate   NR

12 Morpeth Street, Mount Barker, WA 6324 **REGION** Mount Barker
T (08) 9851 1435 **F** (08) 9851 1435 **OPEN** Wed–Mon 10–5
WINEMAKER Keith McPake **EST.** 2001 **CASES** 1000
PRODUCT RANGE ($13–20 CD) Riesling, Semillon Sauvignon Blanc, Unwooded Chardonnay, Reserve Chardonnay, Pinot Noir, Cabernet Sauvignon Merlot Shiraz; Aviators White, Red and Port.
SUMMARY Keith and Rebecca McPake are newcomers to the wine industry, but have big plans. Its genesis was Keith McPake's desire to make his own wine, cutting out the winemaker/wholesaler/retailer margins, but realised 'after all we can only drink so much ourselves'. He started by leasing the 6-hectare Kincora Vineyard on the northern slopes of Mount Barker, planted to pinot noir, cabernet sauvignon and semillon between 1991 and 1995. They have now begun the development of an estate vineyard, with 4 hectares of cabernet franc, merlot, riesling and chardonnay planted in 2003. Construction of a cellar-door area looms in the near future. Their future plans are for an estate-grown olive oil, Deep Water Estate blend of coffee which they are importing and roasting, and a selection of hand-made chocolates. In the meantime there is a substantial range of wines available at two price levels, Aviators at the lower end and Deep Water Estate at the higher end, in turn headed by Reserve wines.

Deep Woods Estate   ★★★★

Lot 10 Commonage Road, Yallingup, WA 6282 **REGION** Margaret River
T (08) 9756 6066 **F** (08) 9756 6366 **OPEN** Tues–Sun 11–5, 7 days during holidays
WINEMAKER Ben Gould **EST.** 1987 **CASES** 20 000
PRODUCT RANGE ($14–38 CD) Semillon, Semillon Sauvignon Blanc, Ivory (Semillon Sauvignon Blanc Chardonnay), Verdelho, Eden (Botrytis Semillon), Harmony (Rose), Shiraz, Ebony (Cabernet Sauvignon Shiraz), Cabernet Merlot, Cabernet Sauvignon, Cabernet Reserve; Boneyard white and red.
SUMMARY The Gould family acquired Deep Woods Estate in 1991, 4 years after the commencement of the estate plantings. There are 15 hectares of estate vines planted to nine varieties, with the intake supplemented by extended family-grown grapes for the Ebony and Ivory labels. At the top of the tree are the occasional and tiny releases under the Boneyard label. These wines are only available to mail list customers, and are likely to be pre-sold to those on a waiting list, but overall production

continues to steadily increase. The establishment of a second vineyard at Cowaramup will doubtless help: 8 hectares of sauvignon blanc have been planted and another 32 hectares of various varieties will follow. Exports to Switzerland.

ᵀᵀᵀᵀᵀ **Boneyard Chardonnay 2003** Elegant, subtly complex mix of barrel ferment, malaloctic and lees contact influences; creamy cashew and melon; long finish. **RATING** 94 **DRINK** 2010 $ 38

ᵀᵀᵀᵀᵀ **Semillon Sauvignon Blanc 2003** In the heart of Margaret River style; a delicate mix of tropical and more lemony flavours; outstanding length. Screwcap. **RATING** 91 **DRINK** 2007 $ 18

Shiraz 2003 Very rich, ripe and voluptuous blackberry and plum; continues pushing the envelope for Margaret River Shiraz. **RATING** 90 **DRINK** 2013 $ 25

ᵀᵀᵀᵀ **Ebony 2003** Nice wine, outstanding at its price point; supple black fruits; plenty of mid-palate fruit; soft, fluffy tannins. **RATING** 89 **DRINK** 2007 $ 14

ᵀᵀᵀᵀ **Verdelho 2003 RATING** 86 **DRINK** Now $ 18
Harmony 2003 RATING 84 **DRINK** Now $ 14

ᵀᵀᵀ **Ivory 2003 RATING** 83 $ 14

Delacolline Estate   NR

Whillas Road, Port Lincoln, SA 5606 **REGION** Southern Eyre Peninsula
T (08) 8682 5277 **F** (08) 8682 4455 **OPEN** Weekends 9–5
WINEMAKER Andrew Mitchell (Contract) **EST.** 1984 **CASES** 650
PRODUCT RANGE ($10–15 R) Riesling, Fume Blanc, Cabernet Sauvignon.
SUMMARY Joins Boston Bay as the second Port Lincoln producer; the white wines are made under contract in the Clare Valley. The 3-hectare vineyard, run under the direction of Tony Bassett, reflects the cool maritime influence, with ocean currents that sweep up from the Antarctic.

Delamere   ★★★☆

Bridport Road, Pipers Brook, Tas 7254 **REGION** Northern Tasmania
T (03) 6382 7190 **F** (03) 6382 7250 **OPEN** 7 days 10–5
WINEMAKER Richard Richardson **EST.** 1983 **CASES** 2500
PRODUCT RANGE ($18–32 CD) Chardonnay, Chardonnay Reserve, Pinot Noir, Pinot Noir Reserve, Sparkling Rose, Sparkling Cuvee.
SUMMARY Richie Richardson produces elegant, rather light-bodied wines that have a strong following. The Chardonnay has been most successful, with a textured, complex, malolactic-influenced wine with great, creamy feel in the mouth. The Pinots typically show pleasant varietal fruit, but seem to suffer from handling problems. Retail distribution in Victoria through Prime Wines, in Tasmania via Red+White.

ᵀᵀᵀᵀᵀ **Cuvee 1998** Bright colour; delicious palate; creamy fruit and a touch of hazelnut; rich but not heavy. **RATING** 94 **DRINK** 2009 $ 26

ᵀᵀᵀ **Pinot Noir 2002 RATING** 83 $ 18

Delaney's Creek Winery   NR

70 Hennessey Road, Delaneys Creek, Qld 4514 **REGION** Queensland Coastal
T (07) 5496 4925 **F** (07) 5496 4926 **OPEN** Mon–Fri 10–4, weekends and public holidays 10–5
WINEMAKER Barry Leverett **EST.** 1997 **CASES** 3000
PRODUCT RANGE ($10.50–16.50 CD) Verdelho, Chardonnay, Muscat Rose, Pinot Noir, Late Shiraz, fortifieds.
SUMMARY Barry and Judy Leverett established Delaney's Creek Winery in 1997 and by doing so has expanded the vineyard map of Queensland yet further. Delaney's Creek is situated near the town of Woodford, itself not far northwest of Caboolture. In 1998 they planted an exotic mix of 1 hectare each of shiraz, chardonnay, sangiovese, touriga nacional and verdelho. In the meantime they are obtaining their grapes from 4 hectares of contract-grown fruit, including cabernet sauvignon, cabernet franc, merlot, shiraz, chardonnay, marsanne and verdelho.

Delatite ★★★★

Stoneys Road, Mansfield, Vic 3722 **REGION** Upper Goulburn
T (03) 5775 2922 **F** (03) 5775 2911 **OPEN** 7 days 10–5
WINEMAKER Rosalind Ritchie **EST.** 1982 **CASES** 12 000
PRODUCT RANGE ($18–39 CD) Riesling, Dead Man's Hill Gewurztraminer, Sauvignon Blanc, Pinot Gris, Unoaked Chardonnay, Chardonnay, Delmelza Pinot Chardonnay, Late Picked Riesling, Rose, Pinot Noir, Shiraz, Merlot, Malbec, Dungeon Gully, Devil's River (Cabernet Sauvignon Malbec Shiraz), Cabernet Sauvignon, fortifieds; V.S. Limited Edition Riesling, R.J. Limited Edition (Cabernet blend).
SUMMARY With its sweeping views across to the snow-clad alps, this is uncompromising cool-climate viticulture, and the wines naturally reflect the climate. Light but intense Riesling and spicy Traminer flower with a year or two in bottle, and in the warmer vintages the red wines achieve flavour and mouthfeel, albeit with a distinctive mintiness. In spring 2002 David Ritchie (the viticulturist in the family) embarked on a program to adopt biodynamics, commencing with the sauvignon blanc and gewurztraminer. He says: 'It will take time for us to convert the vineyard and change our mindset and practices but I am fully convinced it will lead to healthier soil and vines.' Exports to the UK, Switzerland, Germany, Malaysia and Japan.

ᵀᵀᵀᵀ♀ **Dead Man's Hill Gewurztraminer 2003** Spotlessly clean; subtle spice and lychee aromas, the light to medium-bodied palate crisp, delicate and balanced. **RATING** 91 **DRINK** 2009 $ 20.60

ᵀᵀᵀ♀ **Pinot Gris 2002 RATING** 84 **DRINK** Now $ 20.60

ᵀᵀᵀ **Devil's River 2000 RATING** 81 $ 23.65

del Rios ★★★★

2320 Ballan Road, Anakie, Vic 3221 **REGION** Geelong
T (03) 5284 1221 **F** (03) 9497 4644 **OPEN** Weekends 10–4, bus tours by appointment
WINEMAKER To be appointed **EST.** 1996 **CASES** 5000
PRODUCT RANGE ($18–32 CD) Sauvignon Blanc, Chardonnay, Marsanne, Pinot Noir, Reserve Pinot Noir, Shiraz, Cabernet Merlot, Cabernet Sauvignon, Reserve Cabernet Sauvignon.
SUMMARY German del Rio was born in northern Spain (in 1920) where his family owned vineyards. After three generations in Australia, his family has established 15 hectares of vines on their 104-hectare property on the slopes of Mount Anakie, the principal focus being chardonnay, pinot noir and cabernet sauvignon (4 hectares each) then marsanne, sauvignon blanc, merlot and shiraz (1 hectare each). Planting commenced in 1996, and vintage 2000 was the first commercial release; winemaking moved on-site in 2004.

ᵀᵀᵀᵀᵀ **Reserve Bendigo Pinot Noir 2002** Complex and chock full of interest from the word go; plum and sweet spices; excellent texture and length; a major surprise. **RATING** 94 **DRINK** 2007 $ 32

ᵀᵀᵀᵀ **Bendigo Sauvignon Blanc 2003** High flavoured tropical passionfruit aromas and flavours; plenty happening. **RATING** 89 **DRINK** 2007 $ 18
Bendigo Chardonnay 2002 Complex, rich, ripe yellow peach/stone fruit; mouthfilling 14 degrees alcohol; good value. **RATING** 89 **DRINK** 2007 $ 18

ᵀᵀᵀ♀ **Bendigo Sauvignon Blanc 2002 RATING** 86 **DRINK** Now $ 18
Bendigo Marsanne 2002 RATING 85 **DRINK** Now $ 19

De Iuliis ★★★☆

21 Broke Road, Pokolbin, NSW 2320 **REGION** Lower Hunter Valley
T (02) 4993 8000 **F** (02) 4998 7168 **OPEN** 7 days 10–5
WINEMAKER Michael De Iuliis **EST.** 1990 **CASES** 9 000
PRODUCT RANGE ($14–32 CD) Semillon, Verdelho, Chardonnay, Show Reserve Chardonnay, Pinot Chardonnay, Cordon Cut Semillon, Ruby Rose, Hunter Valley Shiraz, McLaren Vale Shiraz, Show Reserve Shiraz, Show Reserve Merlot, Hunter Valley/McLaren Vale Merlot.
SUMMARY Three generations of the De Iuliis family have been involved in the establishment of their 45-hectare vineyard at Keinbah in the Lower Hunter Valley. The family acquired the property in

1986 and planted the first vines in 1990, selling the grapes from the first few vintages to Tyrrell's but retaining small amounts of grapes for release under the De Iuliis label. Winemaker Michael De Iuliis, third-generation family member, has completed postgraduate studies in oenology at the Roseworthy Campus of Adelaide University. The overall quality of the wines is good and the wines are available through the cellar door and selected restaurants in the Hunter and Sydney, with small amounts coming to Melbourne.

 TTTTY **Show Reserve Shiraz 2002** Strongly regional earthy, leather, spicy aromas; sweet black fruits on the palate; good oak handling. **RATING** 90 **DRINK** 2012 $ 20
Show Reserve Merlot 2002 Surprisingly lush, ripe fruit on the mid-palate, but also a sustained, sweet finish; varietal character not entirely convincing, but it's a seductive wine. **RATING** 90 **DRINK** 2012 $ 27

TTTY **Show Reserve Chardonnay 2002 RATING** 86 **DRINK** Now $ 18
Methode Champenoise Pinot Chardonnay 2000 RATING 86 **DRINK** Now $ 24
Show Reserve Chardonnay 2000 RATING 85 **DRINK** Now $ 18
Shiraz 2001 RATING 85 **DRINK** 2011 $ 20
Semillon 2003 RATING 84 **DRINK** 2009 $ 14

TTT **Show Reserve Verdelho 2002 RATING** 82 $ 16

Demondrille Vineyards ★★★

RMB 97, Prunevale Road, Prunevale via Harden, NSW 2587 **REGION** Hilltops
T (02) 6384 4272 **F** (02) 6384 4292 **OPEN** Weekends 10.30–5, or by appointment
WINEMAKER George Makkas **EST.** 1979 **CASES** 1500
PRODUCT RANGE ($12–22 CD) Riesling, Semillon, Semillon Sauvignon Blanc, Pinot Rose, Cabernet Sauvignon, Pinot Noir, The Raven (Shiraz).
SUMMARY Planted in 1979 and a totally dry land vineyard, Demondrille is set on a ridge between the towns of Harden and Young in NSW. In the past most of the wines were made under contract, however as from the 2002 vintage all wines were made on-site. Greek-born and Australian-raised winemaker George Makkas completed his degree in wine science at Charles Sturt University in 2003. Rob Provan runs the vineyard and cellar door. The Raven (Shiraz) has received several awards.

Dennis ★★★

Kangarilla Road, McLaren Vale, SA 5171 **REGION** McLaren Vale
T (08) 8323 8665 **F** (08) 8323 9121 **OPEN** Mon–Fri 10–5, weekends, holidays 11–5
WINEMAKER Peter Dennis **EST.** 1970 **CASES** 6000
PRODUCT RANGE ($16–40 CD) Sauvignon Blanc, Matilda (Semillon Sauvignon Blanc Chardonnay), Chardonnay, Shiraz, Matilda (Shiraz Merlot Cabernet), Merlot, Cabernet Sauvignon, Egerton Vintage Port, Old Tawny Port.
SUMMARY A low-profile winery which has, from time to time, made some excellent wines, most notably typically full-blown, buttery/peachy Chardonnay. However, in 1998 the pendulum swung towards the Shiraz and Cabernet Sauvignon. Exports to the UK, New Zealand and Canada.

Derwent Estate ★★★☆

329 Lyell Highway, Granton, Tas 7070 **REGION** Southern Tasmania
T (03) 6248 5073 **F** (03) 6248 5073 **OPEN** Not
WINEMAKER Stefano Lubiana (Contract) **EST.** 1993 **CASES** 300
PRODUCT RANGE ($17.50 ML) Riesling, Chardonnay, Pinot Noir.
SUMMARY The Hanigan family has established Derwent Estate as part of a diversification program for their 400-hectare mixed farming property. Five hectares of vineyard have been progressively planted since 1993, initially to riesling, followed by chardonnay and pinot noir.

TTTT **Riesling 2003** Lemon, mineral and herb aromas and flavours; slightly brisk acidity needs to soften. **RATING** 87 **DRINK** 2012

TTT **Unwooded Chardonnay 2003 RATING** 83

Devil's Lair ★★★★★

Rocky Road, Forest Grove via Margaret River, WA 6285 **REGION** Margaret River
T (08) 9757 7573 **F** (08) 9757 7533 **OPEN** Not
WINEMAKER Stuart Pym **EST.** 1985 **CASES** 40 000
PRODUCT RANGE ($18.95–59 R) Chardonnay, Margaret River (Cabernet blend); Fifth Leg Dry White and Dry Red.
SUMMARY Having rapidly carved out a high reputation for itself through a combination of clever packaging and marketing allied with impressive wine quality, Devil's Lair was acquired by Southcorp Wines (Penfolds, etc) in December 1996, and production is projected to increase.

ŸŸŸŸŸ **Chardonnay 2001** A wonderfully fine and long palate; intense stone fruit; subtle oak. Top gold 2003 Qantas Wines Show of Western Australia. **RATING** 96 **DRINK** 2011 $ 39.95
Margaret River 2001 Fragrant, ripe blackcurrant, cassis and mulberry aromas and flavours; great texture, structure and oak integration. **RATING** 94 **DRINK** 2010 $ 59

ŸŸŸŸŸ **Fifth Leg Dry Red 2002** Clean, ripe and sweet (but not jammy) red and blackcurrant fruit; fine tannins. **RATING** 90 **DRINK** 2010 $ 21.80

Diamond Valley Vineyards ★★★★★

2130 Kinglake Road, St Andrews, Vic 3761 **REGION** Yarra Valley
T (03) 9710 1484 **F** (03) 9710 1369 **OPEN** Not
WINEMAKER David Lance, James Lance **EST.** 1976 **CASES** 7000
PRODUCT RANGE ($17.50–65 R) Estate Chardonnay, Pinot Noir, Cabernet; Yarra Valley (formerly Blue Label) Sauvignon Blanc, Chardonnay, Pinot Noir, Cabernet Merlot; Close Planted Pinot Noir.
SUMMARY One of the Yarra Valley's finest producers of Pinot Noir and an early pacesetter for the variety, making wines of tremendous style and crystal-clear varietal character. They are not Cabernet Sauvignon lookalikes but true Pinot Noir, fragrant and intense. The chardonnays show the same marriage of finesse and intensity, and the Cabernet family wines shine in the warmer vintages. Much of the wine is sold through an informative and well-presented mailing list, supplemented by national distribution through Red+White. Exports to the UK, Holland, Belgium, Germany, Denmark, Indonesia, Singapore and Malaysia.

ŸŸŸŸŸ **Close Planted Pinot Noir 2002** Wonderfully complex, intense and long; spicy, savoury notes around a profound core of black cherry/plum fruit. **RATING** 96 **DRINK** 2015 $ 65
Estate Pinot Noir 2002 Wonderfully intense black cherry and spice, yet not the least bit heavy; laden with promise. **RATING** 95 **DRINK** 2010 $ 59
Yarra Valley Chardonnay 2002 Fragrant but fine, the tangy bouquet has melon and citrus aromas, the palate with irresistible pure fruit; great line and length. **RATING** 94
DRINK 2008 $ 21.50
Close Planted Pinot Noir 2001 Intense, yet delicate and stylish red fruit aromas; supple, silky and smooth; understated but seductive in true pinot fashion. **RATING** 94 **DRINK** 2010 $ 65

ŸŸŸŸŸ **Estate Chardonnay 2002** Intense, complex and compact white peach and melon fruit has soaked up the oak. **RATING** 93 **DRINK** 2012 $ 29.95
Yarra Valley Pinot Noir 2002 Starting to show development, with very complex berry/sappy/oak/spice aromas and a lively, intense, savoury palate of considerable length. **RATING** 93 **DRINK** 2007 $ 24.90

ŸŸŸŸ **Yarra Valley Sauvignon Blanc 2003** Spotlessly clean, delicate mix of tropical and gooseberry; fine finish. **RATING** 88 **DRINK** Now $ 17.50

ŸŸŸŸ **Yarra Valley Cabernet Merlot 2002** **RATING** 86 **DRINK** 2008 $ 21.50
Yarra Valley Cabernet Sauvignon Cabernet Franc 2000 **RATING** 86 **DRINK** 2009 $ 29.95

Diggers Rest NR

205 Old Vineyard Road, Sunbury, Vic 3429 **REGION** Sunbury
T (03) 9740 1660 **F** (03) 9740 1660 **OPEN** By appointment
WINEMAKER Peter Dredge **EST.** 1987 **CASES** 1000

PRODUCT RANGE ($16.50–22 CD) Chardonnay, Pinot Noir, Shiraz, Cabernet Sauvignon.
SUMMARY Diggers Rest was purchased from the founders Frank and Judith Hogan in July 1998; the new owners, Elias and Joseph Obeid, intend to expand the vineyard resources and, by that means, significantly increase production.

DiGiorgio Family Wines ★★★★

Riddoch Highway, Coonawarra, SA 5263 **REGION** Coonawarra
T(08) 8736 3222 **F**(08) 8736 3233 **OPEN** 7 days 10–5
WINEMAKER Pat Tocaciu **EST.** 1998 **CASES** 10 000
PRODUCT RANGE ($15–40 CD) Lucindale Chardonnay, Sterita Chardonnay, Chardonnay Pinot Noir Sparkling, Sterita Shiraz, Lucindale Merlot, Sterita Cabernet Merlot, Lucindale Cabernet Sauvignon, Francesco Reserve Cabernet Sauvignon.
SUMMARY Stefano DiGiorgio emigrated from Abbruzzi, Italy, arriving in Australia in July 1952. Over the years, he and his family gradually expanded their holdings at Lucindale, In 1989 the decision was taken to plant 2 hectares each of pinot noir and cabernet sauvignon, resulting in the present holdings of cabernet sauvignon (99 hectares), chardonnay (10 hectares), merlot (9 hectares), shiraz (6 hectares) and pinot noir (2 hectares). In 2002 the family purchased the historic Rouge Homme winery from Southcorp capable of crushing 10 000 tonnes of grapes a year, and its surrounding 13.5 hectares of vines. The Lucindale plantings are outside any existing region, and are simply part of the Limestone Coast Zone, with the likelihood that there will be two product ranges in the future. The enterprise is offering full winemaking services to vignerons in the Limestone Coast Zone. The newly renovated cellar door is now open to the public. Exports to Germany and The Netherlands.

TTTT **Lucindale Chardonnay 2001** Elegant, light to medium-bodied; smooth, supple sweet apple and stone fruit. **RATING** 93 **DRINK** 2010 $18

TTTT **Lucindale Merlot 2001** Elegant, fresh raspberry/red fruits; fine tannins and subtle oak; light to medium-bodied and elegant. **RATING** 88 **DRINK** 2010 $22.50
Lucindale Pinot Chardonnay NV blush pink; attractive, fresh strawberry and nectarine flavours. **RATING** 87 **DRINK** Now $15

TTTT **Sparkling Merlot 2001** **RATING** 85 **DRINK** 2008 $19

Diloreto Wines ★★★★

45 Wilpena Terrace, Kilkenny, SA 5009 (postal) **REGION** Adelaide Plains
T(08) 8345 0123 **OPEN** Not
WINEMAKER Tony Diloreto **EST.** 2001 **CASES** 250
PRODUCT RANGE Shiraz.
SUMMARY The Diloreto family have been growing grapes since the 1960s, with 8 hectares of shiraz, cabernet sauvignon, mourvedre and grenache. The vineyard was founded by father Gesue Diloreto and, in common with so many Adelaide Plains grape growers, the family sold the grapes to South Australian winemakers. However, son Tony and wife Gabriell (herself with a winemaking background from the Rhine Valley in Germany) decided they would jointly undertake a short winemaking course at the end of the 1990s. The results were encouraging, and in 2001 Tony Diloreto entered two wines in the Australian Amateur Wine Show, competing against 700 vignerons from around Australia. Both were Shiraz from the 2001 vintage, one with new oak, the other not. Both won gold medals, and the judges strongly recommended that the wines be sold commercially. Great oaks from little acorns indeed.

di Lusso Wines ★★★★

Eurunderee Lane, Mudgee, NSW 2850 **REGION** Mudgee
T(02) 6373 3125 **F**(02) 6373 3128 **OPEN** Fri–Mon 10–5
WINEMAKER Drew Tuckwell (Contract) **EST.** 1998 **CASES** 3000
PRODUCT RANGE ($14–25 CD) Picolit (sweet white), Barbera, Sangiovese, Super T (Sangiovese Shiraz), Aleatico, Il Palio (Sangiovese, Merlot, Shiraz); Chalkboard Pinot Grigio, Vino Rosato and Mudgee Rosso.
SUMMARY Rob Fairall and partner Luanne Hill have at last been able bring to fruition the vision they have had for some years to establish an Italian 'enoteca' operation, offering Italian varietal wines and foods. The plantings of 2 hectares each of barbera and sangiovese, 1 hectare of nebbiolo and

0.5 hectare of picolit, supplemented by the purchase of aleatico and sangiovese from the Mudgee region, and pinot grigio from Orange, set the tone for the wine which is made by contract winemaker Drew Tuckwell, a specialist in Italian varieties. The estate also produces olives for olive oil and table olives, and it is expected the range of both wine and food will increase over the years. An on-site winery came on-stream in early 2003, and the full cellar door opened. The decision to focus on Italian varieties has been a major success.

ΨΨΨΨΨ **Barbera 2002** Perfumed fruit aromas; light to medium-bodied but impeccably balanced; plum, spice and cedar flavours. **RATING** 90 **DRINK** 2010 $ 26

ΨΨΨΨ **Sangiovese 2002** Clean, fragrant, spice and cherry; unforced; good varietal character; ultra-fine, sweet tannins. **RATING** 89 **DRINK** 2009 $ 25
Chalkboard Pinot Grigio 2003 Water white; deserves grigio name; all about length and structure rather than fruit flavour. **RATING** 87 **DRINK** Now $ 19
il Palio 2002 Difficult to categorise; light-bodied and savoury; interesting allspice flavours on finish. Super Tuscan model; 75 per cent Sangiovese, 20 per cent Merlot, 5 per cent Shiraz. **RATING** 87 **DRINK** 2007 $ 28

ΨΨΨΨ **Aleatico 2003** **RATING** 85 **DRINK** Now $ 23
Picolit 2003 **RATING** 84 **DRINK** Now $ 14

ΨΨΨ **Chalkboard Mudgee Rosso 2002** **RATING** 81 $ 19

🐦 Dindima Wines   NR

Lot 22 Cargo Road, Orange, NSW 2800 **REGION** Orange
T (02) 6365 3388 **F** (02) 6365 3096 **OPEN** Not
WINEMAKER James Bell, Murray Smith (Contract) **EST.** 2002
PRODUCT RANGE Pinot Noir.
SUMMARY David Bell and family acquired the property known as Osmond Wines in 2002, renaming it Dindima Wines, with the first vintage under the new ownership made in 2003 (Pinot Noir, due for release at the end of 2004) from the 4.5-hectare plantings. It is a retirement occupation for Dave Bell and his wife, but both sons intend to become involved with grape growing and, ultimately, winemaking.

🐦 Dingo Creek Vineyard   NR

265 Tandur-Traveston Road, Traveston, Qld 4570 **REGION** Queensland Coastal
T (07) 5485 1731 **F** (07) 5485 0041 **OPEN** Weekends 10–4, or by appointment
WINEMAKER Bruce Humphery-Smith **EST.** 1997
PRODUCT RANGE Sauvignon Blanc, Chardonnay, Merlot, Cabernet Sauvignon; plus a range of fortified and mead wines.
SUMMARY Marg and David Gillespie both had agricultural or viticultural backgrounds before moving to Queensland. Marg Gillespie's father worked in the wine industry, as did Marg, with Bullers Wines. In 1994 they began a search for agriculturally viable land with permanent water to start their own vineyard, and the property at Traveston provided the answer. Planting began in 1997 with chardonnay and cabernet sauvignon, followed a year later with merlot and sauvignon blanc, with a total of 2 hectares under vine. The cellar door offers a full range of tourist facilities, one feature being a 6-metre by 18-metre bird aviary.

ΨΨΨ **Angus Merlot Cabernet 2001** **RATING** 83 $ 18

🐦 Dionysus Winery   NR

1 Patemans Lane, Murrumbateman, NSW 2582 **REGION** Canberra District
T (02) 6227 0208 **F** (02) 6227 0209 **OPEN** Weekends and public holidays 10–5, or by appointment
WINEMAKER Michael O'Dea **EST.** 1998
PRODUCT RANGE ($12–20 CD) Sauvignon Blanc, Unoaked Chardonnay, Chardonnay, Shiraz, Cabernet Sauvignon.
SUMMARY Michael and Wendy O'Dea are both public servants in Canberra seeking weekend and holiday relief from their everyday life at work. In 1996 they purchased their property at Murrumbateman, and, commencing in 1998, planted 4 hectares of chardonnay, sauvignon blanc riesling, pinot noir, cabernet sauvignon and shiraz over the three following years. A small winery was

constructed in 2002, and handled the 2003 vintage. Michael O'Dea has completed an associate degree in winemaking at Charles Sturt University, and is responsible for viticulture and winemaking; Wendy O'Dea has completed various courses at the Canberra TAFE and is responsible for wine marketing and (in their words) 'nagging Michael and being a general slushie'.

Di Stasio NR

Range Road, Coldstream, Vic 3770 **REGION** Yarra Valley
T (03) 9525 3999 **F** (03) 9525 3815 **OPEN** By appointment, or at Café Di Stasio, 31 Fitzroy Street, St Kilda
WINEMAKER Rob Dolan, Kate Goodman (Contract) **EST.** 1995 **CASES** 900
PRODUCT RANGE Chardonnay, Pinot Noir.
SUMMARY Famous Melbourne restaurateur Rinaldo (Ronnie) Di Stasio bought a virgin bushland 32-hectare hillside block in the Yarra Valley in 1994 adjacent to the Warramate Flora and Fauna Reserve. He has since established 2.8 hectares of vineyards, equally split between pinot noir and chardonnay, put in roads and dams, built a substantial house, and also an Allan Powell Monastery, complete with art gallery and tree-filled courtyard sitting like a church on top of the hill. Production has never been great, but did commence in 1999, the wines of that and subsequent vintages being initially sold through Café Di Stasio in St Kilda, a Melbourne icon. In 2003 he took the plunge and appointed Domaine Wine Shippers as his distributor, and the wines are now spread through the smartest restaurants in Melbourne and Sydney. The less said about the scrawled, handwritten labels, the better. Exports to the UK.

Divers Luck Wines ★★★

Hellenvale, Nelson Bay Road, Bobs Farm, Port Stephens, NSW 2316 **REGION** Northern Rivers Zone
T (02) 4982 2471 **F** (02) 4982 2726 **OPEN** 7 days 10–5
WINEMAKER Anthony Adams **EST.** 2000 **CASES** 2000
PRODUCT RANGE ($16.50–30 CD) Semillon, Verdelho, Birubi (Chardonnay Verdelho), Chardonnay, The Divers Sticky, Red Diver (Shiraz Merlot Chambourcin), Red Velvet, Bin 601 Shiraz, The Diver Shiraz, Chambourcin, Port.
SUMMARY Anthony Adams and wife Hellen purchased the property now known as Hellenvale in June 2000, after Anthony Adams had spent the last 10 years as an abalone diver on the far south coast of New South Wales. He was struck down with a severe case of bends in 1999, and after spending 4 days in the re-compression chamber at the Prince of Wales Hospital in Sydney, he wisely decided on a change of career. Together with son Damien, the Adams' have a 3-hectare vineyard planted to chambourcin, merlot, shiraz, verdelho and chardonnay, and built the on-site boutique winery. Three of the wines won bronze medals at the 2003 Hunter Valley Wine Show, and are sold through mail order and cellar door, but with discounted prices for members of the Divers Luck Wine Club.

🍷🍷🍷🍷 **Chardonnay 2002** Youthful, fresh stone fruit and citrus aromas and flavours; delicate; well balanced. **RATING** 87 **DRINK** Now **$** 17

Dixons Run ★★★

5 Carrick St, Mont Albert, Vic 3127 **REGION** Yarra Valley
T (08) 9898 7476 **F** (03) 9349 2434 **OPEN** Not
WINEMAKER Contract **EST.** 2002
PRODUCT RANGE ($19.90–24.90 R) Sauvignon Blanc, Unwooded Chardonnay, Chardonnay, Pinot Noir, Cabernet Sauvignon.
SUMMARY Named after a Mr Dixon who grazed cattle on a squatter's run in the 1840s, his landing stretching over a large distance. The area became known as Dixons Run, and is now home to a number of vineyards and wineries in the Dixons Creek subregion of the Yarra Valley.

🍷🍷🍷🍷 **Cabernet Sauvignon 2002** Light to medium-bodied; fruit-driven, spotlessly clean redcurrant and blackcurrant fruit; minimal tannins. **RATING** 87 **DRINK** 2010 **$** 24.99

🍷🍷🍷🍷 **Pinot Noir 2002** Light, fresh cherry/strawberry aromas and flavours; crisp finish; minimal oak. **RATING** 86 **DRINK** 2007 **$** 24.99
Chardonnay 2002 **RATING** 84 **DRINK** Now **$** 22.99

🍷🍷🍷 **Sauvignon Blanc 2002** **RATING** 83 **$** 19.99

Djinta Djinta Winery ★★☆

10 Stevens Road, Kardella South, Vic 3950 **REGION** Gippsland
T (03) 5658 1163 **OPEN** Weekends and public holidays 10–6, or by appointment
WINEMAKER Peter Harley **EST.** 1991 **CASES** 500
PRODUCT RANGE ($15–20 CD) Semillon, Sauvignon Blanc, Marsanne, Finale (sweet white), Cabernets Merlot.
SUMMARY One of a group of wineries situated between Leongatha and Korumburra, the most famous being Bass Phillip. Vines were first planted in 1986 but were largely neglected until Peter and Helen Harley acquired the property in 1991, and set about reviving the 2 hectares of sauvignon blanc and cabernet sauvignon, planting an additional 3 hectares (in total) of merlot, cabernet franc, cabernet sauvignon, semillon, marsanne, roussane and viognier. The first vintage was 1995, during the time that Peter Harley was completing a Bachelor of Applied Science (Wine Science) at Charles Sturt University. They are deliberately adopting a low-technology approach to both vineyard and winery practices, using organic methods wherever possible.

ΨΨΨΫ **Cabernets Merlot 2001 RATING** 86 **DRINK** 2008 $ 22.70
Marsanne 2000 RATING 85 **DRINK** Now $ 20

ΨΨΨ **Finale 2002 RATING** 83 $ 25
Sauvignon Blanc 2002 RATING 81 $ 20

DogRidge Vineyard NR

RSD 195 Bagshaws Road, McLaren Flat, SA 5171 **REGION** McLaren Vale
T (08) 8383 0140 **F** (08) 8383 0430 **OPEN** By appointment
WINEMAKER Dave Wright, Jen Wright, Fred Howard, Wayne Dutschke (Consultant) **EST.** 1993 **CASES** 2000
PRODUCT RANGE ($28–38 ML) DV7 Shiraz, Wylpena Shiraz, DV6 Cabernet Sauvignon.
SUMMARY Dave and Jan Wright had a combined background of dentistry, art and a Charles Sturt University viticultural degree when they moved from Adelaide to McLaren Flat to become vignerons. They inherited vines planted in the early 1940s as a source for Chateau Reynella fortified wines, and their viticultural empire now has 2 hectares each of cabernet sauvignon and shiraz on the Duck Chase vineyard, and access to 45 hectares of contract-grown grapes. The wines have been variously released under the Wylpena Vineyard label and DogRidge label.

Domain Day NR

24 Queen Street, Williamstown, SA 5351 **REGION** Barossa Valley
T (08) 8524 6224 **F** (08) 8524 6229 **OPEN** By appointment
WINEMAKER Robin Day **EST.** 2000
PRODUCT RANGE ($13.75–22 ML) Riesling, Viognier, One Serious™ Rose; with others following.
SUMMARY This is a classic case of an old dog learning new tricks, and doing so with panache. Robin Day had a long and distinguished career as winemaker, then chief winemaker, then technical director of Orlando; participated in the management buy-out; and profitted substantially from the on-sale to Pernod Ricard. After the sale he remained on as a director, but became a globe trotting advisor, consultant and observer. He has hastened slowly with the establishment of Domain Day, but there is nothing conservative about his approach in establishing his 15-hectare vineyard at Mount Crawford, high in the hills (at 450 metres) of the southeastern extremity of Australia's Barossa Valley wine region, bordering on two sides of the vineyard on the Eden Valley. While the mainstream varieties are merlot, pinot noir and riesling, he has crawled Italy, France and Georgia for the other varieties: viognier, sangiovese, saperavi, lagrein, garganega and sagrantino. It is a venture which I, for one, will watch with considerable interest.

Domaine A ★★★★★

Campania, Tas 7026 **REGION** Southern Tasmania
T (03) 6260 4174 **F** (03) 6260 4390 **OPEN** Mon–Fri 9–4, weekends by appointment
WINEMAKER Peter Althaus, Veltin Tieman **EST.** 1973 **CASES** 5000

PRODUCT RANGE ($20–60 CD) Domaine A is the top label with Lady A Fume Blanc, Pinot Noir, Cabernet Sauvignon; second label is Stoney Vineyard with Aurora (wood-matured Sylvaner), Sauvignon Blanc, Pinot Noir and Cabernet Sauvignon.

SUMMARY The striking black label of the premium Domaine A wine, dominated by the single, multicoloured 'A', signified the change of ownership from George Park to Swiss businessman Peter Althaus many years ago. The wines are made without compromise, and reflect the low yields from the immaculately tended vineyards. They represent aspects of both Old World and New World philosophies, techniques and styles. Exports to the US, Singapore, Hong Kong, the UK, France and Switzerland.

ŦŦŦŦ♈ **Stoney Vineyard Sauvignon Blanc 2003** Very complex and highly aromatic mix of passionfruit and tropical fruit; long palate and finish. **RATING** 92 **DRINK** 2007 $ 30

Domaine Chandon ★★★★★

Green Point, Maroondah Highway, Coldstream, Vic 3770 **REGION** Yarra Valley
T (03) 9739 1110 **F** (03) 9739 1095 **OPEN** 7 days 10.30–4.30
WINEMAKER Dr Tony Jordan, Neville Rowe, James Gosper, John Harris **EST.** 1986 **CASES** 150 000
PRODUCT RANGE ($22.95–38 CD) The most important sparkling wine is the Vintage Brut; then there is a range of special vintage cuvees, rounded off with non-vintage Brut and a sparkling Pinot Shiraz. Table wines under the Green Point label, the Chardonnay and Pinot Noir in both varietal and reserve; also McLaren Vale Shiraz.
SUMMARY Wholly owned by Moet et Chandon, and one of the two most important wine facilities in the Yarra Valley, the Green Point tasting room having a national and international reputation and a number of major tourism awards in recent years. Not only has the sparkling wine range evolved, but there has been increasing emphasis placed on the table wines. The return of Dr Tony Jordan, the first CEO of Domaine Chandon should further strengthen both the focus and quality of the brand. Exports to the UK, Asia and Japan.

ŦŦŦŦŦ **Green Point Reserve Chardonnay 2002** Finer than any previous release; melon and citrus, with all but subliminal oak and malolactic influences; very long finish. **RATING** 95 **DRINK** 2012 $ 35
Green Point Reserve Pinot Noir 2001 Clean, fragrant red fruit, spice and forest aromas lead into a stylish and tangy palate, with a silky texture, opening like the proverbial peacock's tail on the finish and aftertaste. **RATING** 95 **DRINK** 2009 $ 37
Vintage Brut 2001 A classic fine, but complex bouquet; fine, fresh and vigorous in the mouth, significantly more elegant than recent releases. **RATING** 95 **DRINK** Now $ 33.95
Green Point Yarra Valley Reserve Shiraz 2002 Potent blackberry and black cherry fruit; long, smooth and intense; oak incidental; fine tannins. **RATING** 94 **DRINK** 2012 $ 47
Yarra Valley Brut 1997 Toasty lees aromas; taught, fine, racy, minerally/lemony flavours running through to a long, crisp finish; minimal dosage. **RATING** 94 **DRINK** 2007 $ 32.95
Brut Rose 1999 Complex, convincing, supple mouthfilling style; the auto-suggestion of more strawberry; good length and balance; nice acidity. **RATING** 94 **DRINK** Now $ 33.95

ŦŦŦŦ♈ **Green Point Vineyards Chardonnay 2002** Singularly intense and fragrant citrus and melon fruit; tight and focused, long finish. **RATING** 93 **DRINK** 2012 $ 23.95
Green Point Reserve McLaren Vale Shiraz 2002 Big, rich, regionally-accented mix of black fruits and dark chocolate; oak evident but balanced; fine tannins. **RATING** 91 **DRINK** 2012 $ 47
Green Point Cuvee 1995 Complex array of sweet, dried fruit flavours; curious lack of bready/toasty notes from extended lees contact, and a break before brisk acidity on the finish. **RATING** 90 **DRINK** 2007 $ 55
Sparkling Pinot Shiraz NV Complex, spicy, leathery, savoury; far more interest than most sparkling reds; will repay cellaring. **RATING** 90 **DRINK** 2008 $ 24.95

ŦŦŦŦ **Green Point Shiraz 2002** Quite complex blackberry, spice, leather and mocha; oak does show through, but finishes long. Victoria. **RATING** 89 **DRINK** 2010

ŦŦŦ♈ **Green Point Sauvignon Blanc Semillon 2003** **RATING** 85 **DRINK** Now $ 20.95

🐦 Domaines Tatiarra

2/102 Barkers Road, Hawthorn, Vic 3124 (postal) **REGION** Heathcote
T 0411 240 815 **F** (03) 9890 5322 **OPEN** Not
WINEMAKER Ben Riggs (Contract) **EST.** 1991 **CASES** 1800
PRODUCT RANGE ($25–60 R) Cambrian Shiraz, Caravan of Dreams Shiraz Pressings, Trademark Shiraz.
SUMMARY Domaines Tatiarra Limited is an unlisted public company, its core asset being a 60-hectare property of cambrian earth first identified and developed by Bill Hepburn, who sold the project to the company in 1991. It is intended to produce only one varietal wine: Shiraz. The majority of the wine will come from the Tatiarra (Aboriginal word meaning beautiful country) property, but the Trademark Shiraz is an equal blend of McLaren Vale and Heathcote wine. The wines are made at the modern Pettavel Winery in Geelong, Ben Riggs commuting backwards and forwards between McLaren Vale and the winery as required. It is hard to imagine a more auspicious start to a new venture than that provided by the 2002 wines.

🍷🍷🍷🍷🍷 **Cambrian Shiraz 2002** Deep, almost opaque colour; smooth, ripe, concentrated blackberry and plum fruit, complexed by touches of pepper and spice; excellent management of tannins and oak. **RATING** 94 **DRINK** 2017 $40

🍷🍷🍷🍷🍷 **Caravan of Dreams Shiraz Pressings 2002** Even greater richness and complexity than the other two wines, oozing luscious blackberry and plum jam, with touches of spice. Velvety finish. **RATING** 93 **DRINK** 2022 $50

Trademark Shiraz 2002 Deeply coloured, lusciously rich, ripe and powerful; a mix of dark chocolate, earth and blackberry; abundant tannins. **RATING** 90 **DRINK** 2020 $60

Dominion Wines

Upton Road, Strathbogie Ranges via Avenel, Vic 3664 **REGION** Strathbogie Ranges
T (03) 5796 2718 **F** (03) 5796 2719 **OPEN** By appointment
WINEMAKER Travis Bush, Michael Clayden **EST.** 1999 **CASES** 140 000
PRODUCT RANGE ($8.95–19.95 CD) Wines released in three tiers: the cheaper Vinus range of Muscat Gordo, Riesling, Chardonnay, Shiraz Cabernet, Sparkling Shiraz; followed by the Alexander Park label offering Riesling, Sauvignon Blanc, Unwooded Chardonnay, Chardonnay, Pinot Noir, Shiraz, Cabernet Sauvignon; then the Alexander Park Reserve Chardonnay and Shiraz.
SUMMARY Dominion is a major newcomer in the wine industry. Between December 1996 and September 1999, 91 hectares of vines were planted at Alexander Park with sauvignon blanc, chardonnay, pinot noir, shiraz and cabernet sauvignon the principal varieties, and smaller amounts of riesling, verdelho and merlot. Prior to the 2000 vintage a winery designed by award-winning architect Scott Shelton was erected at Alexander Park; at full capacity it will be able to process up to 7500 tonnes of fruit. It has two functions: firstly, the production of the company's own brands of Dominion Estate, Alexander Park and Vinus; secondly, contract winemaking services for other major Australian wine companies.

🍷🍷🍷🍷 **Vinus Chardonnay 2003** **RATING** 86 **DRINK** Now $9.95
Vinus Shiraz Cabernet 2001 **RATING** 84 **DRINK** Now $9.95

Dominique Portet

870–872 Maroondah Highway, Coldstream, Vic 3770 **REGION** Yarra Valley
T (03) 5962 5760 **F** (03) 5962 4938 **OPEN** 7 days 10–5
WINEMAKER Dominique Portet, Marcus Satchell **EST.** 6000 **CASES** 6000
PRODUCT RANGE ($16–40 CD) Sauvignon Blanc, Fontaine Rose, Fontaine (Cabernet Merlot Shiraz), Heathcote Shiraz, Merlot, Cabernet Sauvignon.
SUMMARY Dominique Portet was bred in the purple. He spent his early years at Chateau Lafite (where his father was regisseur) and was one of the very first Flying Winemakers, commuting to Clos du Val in the Napa Valley where his brother is winemaker and helping with the initial vintages. Since 1976 he has lived in Australia, spending more than 20 years as managing director of Taltarni, and also developed the Clover Hill Vineyard in Tasmania. After retiring from Taltarni, he set himself up in the Yarra Valley, a region he had been closely observing since the mid-1980s. In 2001 he found the perfect site he had long looked for, and in a twinkling of an eye, built his winery and cellar door, and

planted a quixotic mix of viognier (0.9 hectare) and merlot (0.7 hectare) next to the winery, also undertaking substantial contract winemaking for others. Exports to the UK, Switzerland, the US, Hong Kong, Japan, Malaysia, Thailand and New Zealand.

ҮҮҮҮҮ **Heathcote Shiraz 2002** Deep colour; concentrated and rich blackberry, plum and raspberry fruits; supple and stylish; good tannin and oak management. **RATING** 94 **DRINK** 2015 $42

ҮҮҮҮҮ **Heathcote Cabernet Sauvignon 2002** Similar characters to the Shiraz; clean, powerful cassis and blackcurrant aromas; masses of lush and generous fruit on the palate; good tannins and oak. **RATING** 92 **DRINK** 2015 $38
Yarra Valley Cabernet Sauvignon 2002 Good hue; an aromatic, distinctly savoury bouquet; cassis comes through strongly throughout the length of the palate; controlled oak and tannins. **RATING** 90 **DRINK** 2017 $40

ҮҮҮҮ **Fontaine Rose 2003** Fragrant cherry blossom aromatics; crisp, fresh and dry; long finish. Screwcapped. **RATING** 88 **DRINK** Now $18.50

ҮҮҮҮ **Yarra Sauvignon Blanc 2003** **RATING** 86 **DRINK** Now $22

Donnelly River Wines   NR

Lot 159 Vasse Highway, Pemberton, WA 6260 **REGION** Pemberton
T (08) 9776 2052 **F** (08) 9776 2053 **OPEN** 7 days 9.30–4.30
WINEMAKER Blair Meiklejohn **EST.** 1986 **CASES** 15 000
PRODUCT RANGE ($13–26 CD) Sauvignon Blanc, Chardonnay, Mist (white blend), Pinot Noir, Shiraz, Karri, Cabernet Sauvignon, Cascade, Mistella, Port, Liqueur Muscat.
SUMMARY Donnelly River Wines draws upon 16 hectares of estate vineyards, planted in 1986 and which produced the first wines in 1990. It has performed consistently well with its Chardonnay. Exports to the UK, Denmark, Germany, Singapore, Malaysia and Japan.

Donnybrook Estate   NR

Hacket Road, Donnybrook, WA 6239 **REGION** Geographe
T (08) 9731 0707 **F** (08) 9731 0707 **OPEN** 7 days 10–5.30
WINEMAKER Gary Greirson **EST.** 1997 **CASES** 5000
PRODUCT RANGE ($10–30 CD) Semillon, Sauvignon Blanc, Verdelho, Unwooded Chardonnay, Chardonnay, Shiraz, Merlot, Tempranillo, Grenache, Graciano, Cinsault, Barbera, Zinfandel, Cabernet Sauvignon; Red and White Port.
SUMMARY Gary Greirson and wife Sally have completed the long-planned move to Donnybrook Estate from Cape Bouvard. The new winery was completed during the 2003 vintage, and Gary Greirson contract-makes a small amount of wine for others in the Donnybrook area. The wines are estate-grown from 11 acres of vineyards.

Donovan Wines   NR

RMB 2017 Pomonal Road, Stawell, Vic 3380 **REGION** Grampians
T (03) 5358 2727 **F** (03) 5358 2727 **OPEN** Mon–Sat 10–5, Sun 12–5
WINEMAKER Chris Peters **EST.** 1977 **CASES** 250
PRODUCT RANGE ($14–27 CD) Chardonnay, Shiraz, Cabernet Sauvignon, Sparkling.
SUMMARY Donovan quietly makes some concentrated, powerful Shiraz, with several vintages of the latter typically on offer. Limited distribution in Melbourne; otherwise most of the wine is sold via mail order with some bottle age. Has 5 hectares of estate plantings.

Doonkuna Estate

Barton Highway, Murrumbateman, NSW 2582 **REGION** Canberra District
T (02) 6227 5811 **F** (02) 6227 5085 **OPEN** 7 days 11–4
WINEMAKER Malcolm Burdett **EST.** 1973 **CASES** 3000
PRODUCT RANGE ($12–26 CD) Riesling, Sauvignon Blanc Semillon, Chardonnay, Cian (Pinot Noir Chardonnay), Rose, Pinot Noir, Shiraz, Cabernet Merlot, Cabernet Sauvignon; Rising Ground

Sauvignon Blanc Semillon, Chardonnay, Shiraz, Cabernet Merlot and Cabernet Sauvignon.
SUMMARY Following the acquisition of Doonkuna by Barry and Maureen Moran in late 1996, the plantings have been increased from a little under 4 hectares to 20 hectares. The cellar door prices remain modest, and increased production will follow in the wake of the new plantings.

ŸŸŸŸ **Chardonnay 2002** Cashew, soft stone fruit and subtle oak; similar style to Rising Group Chardonnay; more fruit depth and length. **RATING** 89 **DRINK** 2010 $ 20
Cabernet Sauvignon 2001 Medium-bodied, clean, direct blackcurrant fruit; touches of spice, cedar and balanced tannins. **RATING** 88 **DRINK** 2011 $ 25
Sauvignon Blanc Semillon 2003 Clean; complex mix of lemon/citrus/herb and grass; faintest hint of oak. **RATING** 87 **DRINK** 2009 $ 16
Rising Ground Chardonnay 2003 Subtle winemaker inputs; gentle cashew and melon; good balance. **RATING** 87 **DRINK** 2008 $ 14
Pinot Noir 2002 **RATING** 87 **DRINK** 2008 $ 20
Shiraz 2001 Clean, gently ripe savoury/leathery fruit; fine tannins. **RATING** 87 **DRINK** 2008 $ 26

ŸŸŸŸ **Riesling 2003** **RATING** 86 **DRINK** 2008 $ 18
Rose 2003 **RATING** 85 **DRINK** Now $ 14
Cian Pinot Chardonnay 2000 **RATING** 84 **DRINK** Now $ 25

Dowie Doole ★★★☆

Tatachilla Road, McLaren Vale, SA 5171 (postal) **REGION** McLaren Vale
T (08) 8323 7428 **F** (08) 8323 7305 **OPEN** At Ingleburne, Willunga Road: Mon–Fri 10–5, weekends and public holidays 11–5
WINEMAKER Brian Light (Contract) **EST.** 1996 **CASES** 7000
PRODUCT RANGE ($15.50–40 CD) Semillon, Chenin Blanc, Shiraz, Reserve Shiraz, Merlot, Cabernet Sauvignon.
SUMMARY The imaginatively packaged and interestingly named Dowie Doole was a joint venture between two McLaren Vale grape growers: architect Drew Dowie and one-time international banker Norm Doole. Between them they have over 40 hectares of vineyards, and only a small proportion of their grapes are used to produce the Dowie Doole wines. In 1999 the partnership was expanded to include industry marketing veteran Leigh Gilligan, who returned to his native McLaren Vale after 5 years in Coonawarra (Gilligan is also involved with Boar's Rock). Exports to Canada, Germany, Denmark, Fiji, Singapore and Hong Kong.

ŸŸŸŸŸ **Reserve Shiraz 2002** Deep, dense colour; intense black fruits and bitter chocolate aromas; concentrated palate, rippling flavours on the finish. **RATING** 93 **DRINK** 2017 $ 40

ŸŸŸŸ **Shiraz 2001** **RATING** 86 **DRINK** 2009 $ 23
Cabernet Sauvignon 2001 **RATING** 86 **DRINK** 2008 $ 21
Merlot 2002 **RATING** 85 **DRINK** 2007 $ 21
Chenin Blanc 2003 **RATING** 84 **DRINK** Now $ 15.50

🍃 Downing Estate Vineyard NR

19 Drummonds Lane, Heathcote, Vic 3523 **REGION** Heathcote
T (03) 5433 3387 **F** (03) 5433 3389 **OPEN** By appointment
WINEMAKER Bob Downing, Joy Downing **EST.** 1994
PRODUCT RANGE Shiraz, Merlot, Cabernet Sauvignon.
SUMMARY Bob and Joy Downing purchased 24 hectares of undulating land in 1994, and have since established the estate vineyard from which all of the wines are made; 75 per cent of the plantings are shiraz, 20 per cent cabernet sauvignon and 5 per cent merlot.

🍃 Drakesbrook Wines NR

PO Box 284, Waroona, WA 6215 **REGION** Peel
T (08) 9446 1383 **F** (08) 9446 1383 **OPEN** Not
WINEMAKER Bernard Worthington **EST.** 1998
PRODUCT RANGE A range of varietally denominated table wines reflecting the plantings.

SUMMARY Bernard (Bernie) Worthington, a Perth-based property specialist, developed a serious interest in wine 10 years ago, and spent 4 years looking for a site which met all his criteria of ample water, easy access to a major population, and supporting tourist attractions. During that time he also completed a part-time 4-year winegrowing course at Charles Sturt University. All his interests coalesced when he found Drakesbrook, a 216-hectare property taking its name from the Drakesbrook River which flows through it. One hour's drive from Perth and at an altitude of 265 metres, it has views out to the ocean and is adjacent to the Lake Navarino tourist resort. He has subdivided the property, retaining 121 hectares and offering the remainder in three lots between 24 and 40 acres in size. His 11.9-hectare vineyard is planted to semillon, chardonnay, shiraz, merlot, petit verdot, cabernet franc and cabernet sauvignon. The wines are made elsewhere with input from Worthington.

Drayton's Family Wines ★★★

Oakey Creek Road, Cessnock, NSW 2321 **REGION** Lower Hunter Valley
T (02) 4998 7513 **F** (02) 4998 7743 **OPEN** Mon–Fri 8–5, weekends and public holidays 10–5
WINEMAKER Trevor Drayton **EST.** 1853 **CASES** 90 000
PRODUCT RANGE ($7–70 CD) Several label ranges including budget-priced Oakey Creek, New Generation and Hunter Valley; Vineyard Reserve Chardonnay, Semillon, Pinot Noir, Shiraz, Merlot; Sparkling and fortifieds; top-of-the-range Limited Release Chardonnay, Shiraz, Susanne Semillon, William Shiraz, Joseph Shiraz, Bin 5555 Shiraz, Botrytis Semillon, Old Vineyard Sherry and Liqueur Muscat.
SUMMARY A family-owned and run stalwart of the Hunter Valley, producing honest, full-flavoured wines which sometimes excel themselves and are invariably modestly priced. The size of the production will come as a surprise to many but it is a clear indication of the good standing of the brand, notwithstanding the low profile of recent years. It is not to be confused with Reg Drayton Wines; national retail distribution with exports to New Zealand, the US, Japan, Singapore, Taiwan, Samoa and Switzerland.

ŸŸŸŸ **Vineyard Reserve Chardonnay 2002** **RATING** 86 **DRINK** Now $21
William Shiraz 2000 **RATING** 86 **DRINK** 2010 $45
Hunter Valley Cabernet Sauvignon 2002 **RATING** 85 **DRINK** 2013 $16.50
Susanne Semillon 2003 **RATING** 84 **DRINK** 2010 $35
Vineyard Reserve Semillon 2003 **RATING** 84 **DRINK** 2010 $21

ŸŸŸ **Semillon 2003** **RATING** 83 $16.50
Vineyard Reserve Chardonnay 2000 **RATING** 81 $21

ŸŸŸ **Hunter Valley Verdelho 2003** **RATING** 79 $16.50

Drews Creek Wines NR

558 Wollombi Road, Broke, NSW 2330 **REGION** Lower Hunter Valley
T (02) 6579 1062 **F** (02) 6579 1062 **OPEN** By appointment
WINEMAKER David Lowe (Contract) **EST.** 1993 **CASES** 300
PRODUCT RANGE ($10–16 R) Chardonnay, Unoaked Chardonnay, Merlot.
SUMMARY Graeme Gibson and his partners are developing Drews Creek step by step. The initial planting of 2 hectares of chardonnay and 3 hectares of merlot was made in 1991, and the first grapes produced in 1993. A further 2.5 hectares of sangiovese were planted in September 1999. Most of the grapes are sold to contract-winemaker David Lowe, but a small quantity of wine is made for sale to friends and through the mailing list. A cellar door has opened, and holiday cabins overlooking the vineyard and Wollombi Brook are planned.

Driftwood Estate ★★★☆

Lot 13 Caves Road, Yallingup, WA 6282 **REGION** Margaret River
T (08) 9755 6323 **F** (08) 9755 6343 **OPEN** 7 days 11–4.30
WINEMAKER Barney Mitchell, Mark Pizzuto **EST.** 1989 **CASES** 15 000
PRODUCT RANGE ($15–29 CD) Classic White, Semillon, Sauvignon Blanc Semillon, Chardonnay, Sparkling Brut, Cane Cut Semillon, Shiraz, Shiraz Cabernet Sauvignon, Merlot, Cabernet Sauvignon, Tawny Port.

SUMMARY Driftwood Estate is now a well-established landmark on the Margaret River scene. Quite apart from offering a brasserie restaurant capable of seating 200 people (open 7 days for lunch and dinner) and a mock Greek open-air theatre, its wines feature striking and stylish packaging (even if strongly reminiscent of that of Devil's Lair) and opulently flavoured wines. The winery architecture is, it must be said, opulent rather than stylish. The wines are exported to Singapore.

ɤɤɤɤ **Reserve Chardonnay 2001** Complex malolactic and barrel ferment inputs; stone fruit and honey flavours, tailing off fractionally on the finish. **RATING** 89 **DRINK** 2007
Cabernet Sauvignon 2001 Clear-cut varietal character in medium-bodied mode; cedar and ripe, but fine tannins; controlled oak. **RATING** 88 **DRINK** 2016 $ 23
Chardonnay 2002 Showing some development; generous peach and stone fruit; early developing. **RATING** 87 **DRINK** 2007 $ 21.90

ɤɤɤɤ **Sauvignon Blanc Semillon 2003** **RATING** 86 **DRINK** Now $ 15.90
Classic White 2003 **RATING** 86 **DRINK** Now $ 15
Shiraz Cabernet Sauvignon 2002 **RATING** 85 **DRINK** 2009 $ 15.90

Drinkmoor Wines ★★★☆

All Saints Road, Wahgunyah, Vic 3687 **REGION** Rutherglen
T (02) 6033 5544 **F** (02) 6033 5645 **OPEN** 7 days 10–5
WINEMAKER Damien Cofield **EST.** 2002 **CASES** 2500
PRODUCT RANGE ($11.80–13.80 CD) Al Dente White, Chenin Blanc, Unoaked Chardonnay, Sticky (Late Harvest Muscadelle), Al Dente Red (Gamay), Shiraz, Cabernet Merlot, Cabernets, Petit Verdot, Traveller (Fortified White).
SUMMARY This is a separate venture of Max and Karen Cofield (who also own Cofield Wines) and son Damien, with a very clear vision and marketing plan. It is to encourage people to make wine their beverage of choice; in other words, don't drink beer or spirits, drink wine instead, or drink more wines. Thus the wines are made in an everyday, easy drinking style, with the cost kept as low as possible. The labelling, too, is designed to take the pretentiousness out of wine drinking, and to provide a bit of fun. Although the Cofields don't say so, this is the heartland of Generation X.

ɤɤɤɤɤ **Shiraz NV** Uncomplicated but very generous; an abundant array of black fruits, and ripe tannins. **RATING** 90 **DRINK** 2008 $ 13.80
Sticky 375 ml NV Super-seductive and aptly named; tropical fruit salad and citrussy acidity. **RATING** 90 **DRINK** 2007 $ 11.80

ɤɤɤɤ **Cabernet Merlot NV** Authentic cassis/blackcurrant varietal fruit; not extractive; good balance. **RATING** 89 **DRINK** 2008 $ 13.80
Cabernets NV Very good colour; abundant black fruits; soft, ripe tannins; good balance. Right in the slot of the style. **RATING** 89 **DRINK** 2008 $ 13.80
Traveller NV Colour has all the indicators of some age, light olive-brown; balanced, biscuity dry finish; impressive fortified, barrel-aged style. **RATING** 88 **DRINK** Now $ 13.80
Petit Verdot NV Deep colour; smooth, dark cherry/raspberry fruit, then a crisp finish. **RATING** 87 **DRINK** Now $ 13.80

ɤɤɤɤ **Unoaked Chardonnay NV** **RATING** 85 **DRINK** Now $ 11.80

ɤɤɤ **Chenin Blanc NV** **RATING** 83 $ 11.80
Al Dente Red NV **RATING** 83 $ 13.80
Al Dente White NV **RATING** 82 $ 11.80

Dromana Estate ★★★☆

RMB 555 Old Moorooduc Road, Tuerong, Vic 3933 **REGION** Mornington Peninsula
T (03) 5974 4400 **F** (03) 5974 1155 **OPEN** Wed–Sun 11–5
WINEMAKER Rollo Crittenden **EST.** 1982 **CASES** 30 000
PRODUCT RANGE ($15–54 CD) Dromana Estate Sauvignon Blanc Semillon, Chardonnay, Reserve Chardonnay, Pinot Noir, Reserve Pinot Noir, Shiraz, Cabernet Merlot; and a range of Italian varietals Arneis, Barbera, Dolcetto, Sangiovese, Nebbiolo and Rosato under the Garry Crittenden i label.
SUMMARY Since it was first established, Dromana Estate has always been near or at the cutting edge, both in marketing terms and in terms of development of new varietals, most obviously the Italian

range under the 'i' label. Crittenden has taken over winemaking responsibilities, and the business is now majority-owned by outside investors. Exports to the UK, Singapore, Canada and Russia.

ŶŶŶŶ **Garry Crittenden i Rosato 2003** Pale salmon; spicy fragrance and zesty, spicy minerally flavours give real character; subliminal sweetness. Screwcap guarantees freshness. **RATING** 89 **DRINK** Now $15

Garry Crittenden i Arneis 2003 Clean, intense pear skin/lemon rind aromatics; steely acidity, good length in the mouth. **RATING** 88 **DRINK** Now $20

Sauvignon Blanc Semillon 2003 Light to medium-bodied; nicely balanced, gentle tropical fruit; user-friendly. **RATING** 87 **DRINK** Now $20

ŶŶŶŸ **Shiraz 2001 RATING** 85 **DRINK** 2008 $29

🍇 Dromana Valley Wines   NR

Cnr Nepean Highway and Pickings Lane, Dromana, Vic 3936 **REGION** Mornington Peninsula
T (03) 5987 2093 **F** (03) 5987 2093 **OPEN** Weekends and public holidays 11–5
WINEMAKER Greg Ray **EST.** 1974
PRODUCT RANGE ($16–28 CD) Chardonnay, Pinot Noir, Shiraz, Cabernet Shiraz, Cabernet Sauvignon.
SUMMARY The Stavropoulos family established Dromana Valley Wines in 1974 with the planting of a small block of shiraz. When the Hickinbotham family purchased the property across the road in 1988 it led to the first Dromana Valley wines being made by Andrew Hickinbotham, and to the extension of the vineyard in 1989, with further plantings in 1997. There is now a little under 2 hectares of chardonnay, over 1 hectare of pinot noir, the remaining 2 hectares divided between shiraz and cabernet sauvignon. In 1997 a new winery was built, and in Easter 1998 the cellar door was opened and wine sales commenced, with a number of vintages on offer. Since 1999 winemaking has been carried out by Greg Ray at the on-site winery.

🍇 Drummonds Corrina Vineyard   ★★★★

85 Wintles Road, Leongatha South, Vic 3953 **REGION** Gippsland
T (03) 5664 3317 **OPEN** Weekends 10–5
WINEMAKER Phillip Jones (Contract) **EST.** 1983
PRODUCT RANGE ($14–35 CD) Sauvignon Blanc, Dinah's Block Pinot Noir, Pinot Noir, Cabernet Sauvignon Merlot.
SUMMARY The Drummond family has 3 hectares of vines (1 hectare each of pinot noir and sauvignon blanc, and 0.5 hectare each of cabernet sauvignon and merlot) which was slowly established without the aid of irrigation. The viticultural methods are those practised by Phillip Jones, who makes the wines for Drummonds; north-south row orientation, leaf plucking on the eastside of the rows, low yields, and all fruit picked by hand. Similarly restrained winemaking methods (no pumping, no filters and low SO_2) follow in the winery. The wines are sold through the cellar door and by mail order only.

ŶŶŶŶ **Pinot Noir 2001** Light, developed colour; at the lighter, savoury end of the spectrum, but has good balance and texture, and does build towards the finish. **RATING** 89 **DRINK** Now $28

Dudley Partners   NR

Porky Flat Vineyard, Penneshaw, Kangaroo Island, SA 5222 (postal) **REGION** Kangaroo Island
T (08) 8553 1509 **F** (08) 8553 1509 **OPEN** Not
WINEMAKER Wine Network (James Irvine) **EST.** 1994
PRODUCT RANGE Peninsula Chardonnay, Porky Flat Shiraz, Shearing Shed Red (Shiraz Cabernet), Hog Bay River Cabernet.
SUMMARY Colin Hopkins, Jeff Howard, Alan Willson and Paul Mansfield have formed a partnership to bring together three vineyards on Kangaroo Island's Dudley Peninsula: the Porky Flat Vineyard of 5 hectares, Hog Bay River of 2 hectares and Sawyers of 4 hectares. It is the quirky vineyard names which give the products there distinctive identities. The partners not only look after viticulture, but also join in the winemaking process. To date, most of the wines are sold through licensed outlets on Kangaroo Island, supplemented by retail sales in Adelaide.

Duerden's Wines

NR

Lot 295 Waggon Road, Victor Harbor, SA 5211 **REGION** Southern Fleurieu
T (08) 8552 8450 **F** (08) 8552 8450 **OPEN** 7 days 9–5
WINEMAKER Harry Duerden **EST.** 1996
PRODUCT RANGE ($14.75–39 CD) Sweet Frontignac, Cabernet Sauvignon Wildfire, Cabernet Sauvignon Bushfire, Waggon Road Cabernet Sauvignon First Press, Waggon Road Cabernet Sauvignon Show Reserve; liqueurs.
SUMMARY Harry Duerden has established 2 hectares of vineyard (90 per cent cabernet sauvignon, 10 per cent frontignac) grown on the Italian pergola system. He cautiously says it is the only known commercial vineyard using this system in Australia, and you could be confident he is right. Deliberately and charmingly eccentric, he suggests the system is ahead of its time, rather than the ancient history others might describe it as. His one-line description of his First Press Cabernet Sauvignon follows down the same track, 'an alternative to alcoholic furniture polish'. If all this were not enough, he produces a range of liqueur-style products, including a quandong-flavoured wine product, with a fortified wine base.

🐦 Due South

NR

PO Box 72, Denmark, WA 6333 **REGION** Denmark
T (08) 9848 3399 **F** (08) 9752 4133 **OPEN** Not
WINEMAKER Brenden Smith (Contract) **EST.** 1999
PRODUCT RANGE ($14.99 R) Unwooded Chardonnay.
SUMMARY Another substantial new development in the Great Southern, with 100 hectares of sauvignon blanc, semillon, chardonnay, pinot noir, shiraz, merlot, cabernet franc, cabernet sauvignon. Part of the grapes produced each year go to make wine under the Due South brand which is stocked exclusively by Vintage Cellars. The remainder is sold as grapes or processed wine to others. The Due South wines are also exported to the UK and available by mail order.

Duke's Vineyard

★★★☆

Porongurup Road, Porongurup, WA 6324 **REGION** Porongurup
T (08) 9853 1107 **F** (08) 9853 1107 **OPEN** 7 days 10–4.30
WINEMAKER Mike Garland (Contract) **EST.** 1998 **CASES** 2500
PRODUCT RANGE ($16–24 CD) Riesling, Autumn Riesling, Shiraz, Cabernet Sauvignon.
SUMMARY When Hilde and Ian (Duke) Ranson sold their clothing manufacturing business in 1998 they were able to fulfil a long-held dream of establishing a vineyard in the Porongurup subregion of Great Southern. It took two abortive efforts before they became third-time-lucky with the acquisition of a 65-hectare farm at the foot of the Porongurup Range. They planted 3 hectares each of riesling and shiraz, and 3.5 hectares of cabernet sauvignon with a hectare of petit verdot to keep the cabernet company. Hilde Ranson is a successful artist, and it was she who designed the beautiful scalloped, glass-walled cellar-door sale area with its mountain blue cladding. The wines are made by Rob Lee at the Porongurup Winery, and have limited New South Wales distribution through Lewis Fine Wines.

    YYYY   **Riesling 2003** Crisp, slatey/minerally, apple, herb and lime. Will repay cellaring.
        RATING 89 **DRINK** 2008 $18

Dulcinea

NR

Jubilee Road, Sulky, Ballarat, Vic 3352 **REGION** Ballarat
T (03) 5334 6440 **F** (03) 5334 6828 **OPEN** 7 days 10–6
WINEMAKER Rod Stott **EST.** 1983 **CASES** 3000
PRODUCT RANGE ($10–16 CD) Sauvignon Blanc, Chardonnay, La Mancha Sparkling Chardonnay, Frontignan, Pinot Noir, Shiraz, Merlot, Cabernet Sauvignon, Tawny Port.
SUMMARY Rod Stott is passionate grape grower and winemaker (with 6 hectares of vineyard) who chose the name Dulcinea from 'The Man of La Mancha', where only a fool fights windmills. With winemaking help from various sources, he has produced a series of interesting and often complex wines. Exports to Japan, Fiji and China.

Dusty Hill Estate

Barambah Road, Moffatdale via Murgon, Qld 4605 **REGION** South Burnett
T (07) 4168 4700 **F** (07) 4168 4888 **OPEN** 7 days 9.30–5
WINEMAKER Stuart Pierce **EST.** 1996 **CASES** 3000
PRODUCT RANGE ($15–30 R) Semillon, Verdelho, Rose, Dusty Rose, Dusty Chill, Shiraz, Merlot, Liqueur Muscat.
SUMMARY Joe Prendergast and family have established 2 hectares each of shiraz and cabernet sauvignon, 1 hectare of verdelho, and semillon and 0.5 hectare each of merlot and black muscat. The vines are crop-thinned to obtain maximum ripeness in the fruit and to maximise tannin extract, although the winery's specialty is the Dusty Rose, continuing a long tradition of rose/Beaujolais style wines from Queensland. They also have a luxury bed and breakfast cottage with three queen-sized bedrooms which takes advantage of the 20 kilometres of waterfront to Lake Barambah.

Dutschke Wines ★★★★★

Lyndoch Valley Road, Lyndoch, SA 5351 (postal) **REGION** Barossa Valley
T (08) 8524 5485 **F** (08) 8524 5489 **OPEN** Not
WINEMAKER Wayne Dutschke **EST.** 1990 **CASES** 4000
PRODUCT RANGE ($18–50 R) Ivy Blondina Frontignac, Oscar Semmler Shiraz, Single Barrel Shiraz, St Jakobi Shiraz, Willowbend Merlot Shiraz Cabernet, The Tawny 22 Year Old Port, The Tokay, The Muscat.
SUMMARY Wayne Dutschke had 10 years of winemaking experience with major wine companies in all the eastern States of Australia and six separate Flying Winemaker stints in France, Spain and California. He returned to South Australia to join his uncle, Ken Semmler, a leading grape grower in the Barossa Valley and now in the Adelaide Hills. Exports to the US, Canada, Germany, Malaysia, Hong Kong and Singapore.

ȲȲȲȲȲ **Oscar Semmler Shiraz 2002** Powerful, but neither jammy nor hot; dark berries and bitter chocolate; fine tannins; excellent handling of French oak. **RATING** 94 **DRINK** 2017 $ 50

ȲȲȲȲȲ **Willow Bend Shiraz Merlot Cabernet 2002** Shows the strength of the vintage; cassis and blackcurrant fruit, with fine, silky tannins. **RATING** 93 **DRINK** 2017 $ 28
St Jakobi Shiraz 2002 Vibrant mix of black and red fruits; perfectly integrated vanillin oak and fine, ripe tannins. Elegant style. **RATING** 92 **DRINK** 2012 $ 35
Oscar Semmler Shiraz 2001 Very ripe blackberry, plum jam and chocolate fruit; luscious and mouthfilling; subtle French oak. Carries 15 degrees alcohol easily. **RATING** 90 **DRINK** 2021 $ 50

ȲȲȲȲ **St Jakobi Shiraz 2001** Opens with savoury, oaky aromas and flavours, but swells with ripe blackberry jam and plum on the palate; notes of vanilla. **RATING** 88 **DRINK** 2016 $ 35

ȲȲȲȲ **Willow Bend Shiraz Merlot Cabernet 2001** **RATING** 86 **DRINK** 2010 $ 28

ȲȲȲ **Ivy Blondina Frontignac 2003** **RATING** 83 $ 15

Dyson Wines

Sherriff Road, Maslin Beach, SA 5170 **REGION** McLaren Vale
T (08) 8386 1092 **F** (08) 8327 0066 **OPEN** 7 days 10–5
WINEMAKER Allan Dyson **EST.** 1976 **CASES** 2000
PRODUCT RANGE ($10–25.50 CD) Chardonnay, Viognier, Liqueur Chardonnay, Cabernet Sauvignon, Ambra Liqueur (White Port).
SUMMARY Allan Dyson, who describes himself as 'a young man of 50-odd years' has recently expanded his 1.5 hectares of viognier with 2.5 hectares each of chardonnay and cabernet sauvignon, and has absolutely no thoughts of slowing down or retiring. Some retail distribution in South Australia and New South Wales supplements direct sales from the cellar door.

ȲȲȲȲȲ **Clarice Cabernet Sauvignon 2000** Lush regional style, laden with blackcurrant fruit and dark chocolate; smooth and supple; a classic wine for cellaring, however good it is now. **RATING** 94 **DRINK** 2015 $ 22.50

ΨΨΨΨ **Chardonnay 2002** Rich but not heavy; ripe peach and nectarine fruit; good oak. **RATING** 89 **DRINK** 2007 $ 22.50

Viognier 2003 Clear varietal character, with full-on pastille fruit, and some alcohol impact. **RATING** 87 **DRINK** Now $ 20

Eagle Vale ★★★★★

51 Caves Road, Margaret River, WA 6285 **REGION** Margaret River
T (08) 9757 6477 **F** (08) 9757 6199 **OPEN** 7 days 10–5
WINEMAKER Guy Gallienne **EST.** 1997 **CASES** 5000
PRODUCT RANGE ($14.50–45 CD) Wood Aged Semillon, Fume Sauvignon Blanc, Semillon Sauvignon Blanc, Chardonnay, Shiraz, Merlot, Cabernet Sauvignon Merlot Cabernet Franc. Jack in the Barrel (sweet wine) is strictly cellar door only.
SUMMARY Eagle Vale is a joint venture between the property owners, Steve and Wendy Jacobs, and the operator/winemaking team of Guy, Chantal and Karl Gallienne. It is a United Nations team; Steve Jacobs was born in Colorado, USA, and has business interests in Bali, Indonesia, while living in Perth with his wife and family. The Galliennes come from the Loire Valley, France, although Guy secured his winemaking degree at Roseworthy College/Adelaide University. The vineyard is managed on a low impact basis, without pesticides (guinea fowls do the work) and minimal irrigation. Eleven and a half hectares have been established, and all the wines are made from estate-grown grapes.

ΨΨΨΨΨ **Chardonnay 2002** Attractive wine; ripe melon, nectarine fruit fills the mouth; well-handled barrel-ferment and malolactic ferment characters; concentrated and focused. **RATING** 94 **DRINK** 2010 $ 45

ΨΨΨΨΨ **Cabernet Sauvignon Merlot 2001** Voluminous cassis and blackcurrant fruit; supple and soft, fine tannins and sure oak. **RATING** 93 **DRINK** 2016 $ 28

Chardonnay 2001 Similar sophistication to the '02, but not as intense. **RATING** 90 **DRINK** 2009

Merlot 2002 Abundant, sweet red and black fruits yet not jammy; fine, savoury tannins add varietal character; good focus. Screwcap. **RATING** 90 **DRINK** 2012 $ 24.50

ΨΨΨΨ **Fume Sauvignon Blanc 2002** In near-identical style to the '03, but with greater length and intensity. **RATING** 89 **DRINK** 2008 $ 26

Shiraz 2002 Very foresty, very gamey; chocolate, spice, licorice aftertaste; long finish. Interpreted as varietal character, but without total conviction. **RATING** 89 **DRINK** 2012 $ 29

Semillon Sauvignon Blanc 2002 Neatly balanced blend of 73 per cent Semillon, 27 per cent Sauvignon Blanc; long, clean and firm citrus/lemon flavours. **RATING** 88 **DRINK** 2009 $ 18

Fume Sauvignon Blanc 2003 Very developed, though healthy colour; a rich, mouthfilling mix of herbal fruit and spicy/smoky oak. **RATING** 87 **DRINK** 2008 $ 26

ΨΨΨ **Wood Aged Semillon 2002** **RATING** 86 **DRINK** 2007 $ 26

East Arm Vineyard ★★★☆

111 Archers Road, Hillwood, Tas 7250 **REGION** Northern Tasmania
T (03) 6334 0266 **F** (03) 6334 1405 **OPEN** Weekends and public holidays, or by appointment
WINEMAKER Bert Sundstrup, Nicholas Butler (Contract) **EST.** 1993 **CASES** 1200
PRODUCT RANGE ($17–31 CD) Riesling, Unwooded Chardonnay, Chardonnay, Pinot Noir.
SUMMARY East Arm Vineyard was established by Launceston gastroenterologist Dr John Wettenhall and partner Anita James, who also happens to have completed the Charles Sturt University Diploma in Applied Science (wine growing). The 2 hectares of vineyard which came into full production in 1998 are more or less equally divided between riesling, chardonnay and pinot noir. It is established on an historic block, part of a grant made to retired British soldiers of the Georgetown garrison in 1821, and slopes down to the Tamar River. The property is 25 hectares, and there are plans for further planting and, somewhere down the track, a winery. The Riesling is always excellent. Exports to Hong Kong.

ΨΨΨΨ **Riesling 2003** Big, rich style; lots of concentration on bouquet and palate; tropical, early developing. **RATING** 87 **DRINK** 2008 $ 20

▼▼▼⧓ **Pinot Noir 2002** RATING 86 DRINK 2007 $ 31

▼▼▼ **Sweet Riesling 2003** RATING 83 $ 16

Eastern Peake   NR

Clunes Road, Coghills Creek, Vic 3364 **REGION** Ballarat
T (03) 5343 4245 **F** (03) 5343 4365 **OPEN** 7 days 10–5
WINEMAKER Norman Latta **EST.** 1983 **CASES** 3000
PRODUCT RANGE ($17–30 CD) Reserve Chardonnay, Persuasion (Pinot Rose), Pinot Noir, Morillon
Pinot Noir, Reserve Pinot Noir.
SUMMARY Norm Latta and Di Pym commenced the establishment of Eastern Peake, situated 25
kilometres northeast of Ballarat on a high plateau overlooking the Creswick Valley, almost 15 years
ago. In the early years the grapes were sold to Trevor Mast of Mount Chalambar and Mount Langi
Ghiran, but the 5 hectares of vines are now dedicated to the production of Eastern Peake wines. The
Pinot Noir is on the minerally/stemmy side; earlier bottling might preserve more of the sweet fruit.
Exports to the UK and Northern Ireland.

Eden Springs   NR

Boehm Springs Road, Springton, SA 5235 **REGION** Eden Valley
T (08) 8564 1166 **F** (08) 8564 1265 **OPEN** Not
WINEMAKER Andrew Ewart (Contract) **EST.** 2000 **CASES** 1500
PRODUCT RANGE ($15.50–22.50 ML) High Eden range of Riesling, Shiraz, Cabernet Sauvignon
Merlot.
SUMMARY Richard Wiencke and Meredith Hodgson opened the Eden Springs wine doors on 1 July
2000, offering the first wines from the 19 hectares of vines made in 1999 (Shiraz and Cabernet
Sauvignon) and the inaugural release of Riesling from 2000, contract-made by Andrew Ewart. It is a
remote vineyard (6 kilometres by dirt road from Springton) and sells its wine through a high-quality
newsletter to mail list customers, and a website <www.edensprings.com.au> which has brought
export orders from the US, Denmark, Singapore and Malaysia.

Edwards & Chaffey   NR

Chaffey's Road, McLaren Vale, SA 5171 **REGION** McLaren Vale
T (08) 8323 8250 **F** (08) 8323 9308 **OPEN** Not
WINEMAKER Stephen Goodwin **EST.** 1850
PRODUCT RANGE ($8.95–34.95R) Semillon Sauvignon Blanc, Unwooded Chardonnay, E&C McLaren
Vale Chardonnay, Sangiovese; Section 353 range of McLaren Vale-sourced Pinot Noir Chardonnay,
Shiraz and Cabernet Sauvignon; Seaview sparkling wines in three ranges, Semi Premium, Special
Reserve and Vintage Reserve.
SUMMARY After a near-death experience, the Edwards & Chaffey range of table and sparkling wines
has been revived and, indeed, expanded by the arrival of Sangiovese; Seaview is restricted to the
sparkling wines.

Edwards Vineyard

Cnr Caves Road and Ellensbrook Road, Cowaramup, WA 6284 **REGION** Margaret River
T (08) 9755 5999 **F** (08) 9755 5988 **OPEN** 7 days 10.30–5.30
WINEMAKER Michael Edwards **EST.** 1994 **CASES** 2000
PRODUCT RANGE ($19–29 CD) Semillon, Sauvignon Blanc, Chardonnay, Shiraz, Cabernet Sauvignon.
SUMMARY This is very much a family affair, headed by parents Brian and Jenny Edwards. Michael
Edwards is the assistant winemaker at Voyager Estate, while overseeing the winemaking of the
Edwards Vineyard wines; Chris Edwards is vineyard manager, while Fiona and Bianca Edwards are
involved in sales and marketing. They have a substantial vineyard, planted to chardonnay (3
hectares), semillon (2.5 hectares), sauvignon blanc (2.1 hectares), shiraz (4.8 hectares) and cabernet
sauvignon (7.6 hectares). One of the local attractions is the Tigermoth 'Matilda', flown from England
to Australia in 1990 as a fundraiser, and which is now kept at the Edwards Vineyard and can be seen
flying locally. Exports to Denmark, Ireland and Spain.

Elan Vineyard

17 Turners Road, Bittern, Vic 3918 **REGION** Mornington Peninsula
T (03) 5983 1858 **F** (03) 5983 2821 **OPEN** First weekend of month, public holidays 11–5, or by appointment
WINEMAKER Selma Lowther **EST.** 1980 **CASES** 400
PRODUCT RANGE ($16–20 CD) Chardonnay, Shiraz, Gamay, Merlot, Cabernet Merlot.
SUMMARY Selma Lowther, then fresh from Charles Sturt University (as a mature-age student) made an impressive debut with her spicy, fresh, crisp Chardonnay, and has continued to make tiny quantities of appealing and sensibly priced wines. Most of the grapes from the 2.5 hectares of estate vineyards are sold; production remains minuscule.

Elderton

3 Tanunda Road, Nuriootpa, SA 5355 **REGION** Barossa Valley
T (08) 8568 7878 **F** (08) 8568 7879 **OPEN** Mon–Fri 8.30–5, weekends, holidays 11–4
WINEMAKER Richard Langford, James Irvine (Consultant) **EST.** 1984 **CASES** 32 000
PRODUCT RANGE ($12.90–85 CD) Riesling, Sauvignon Blanc Verdelho, Unwooded Chardonnay, Chardonnay, Ashmead Family Reserve Sparkling Shiraz, Botrytis Semillon, Cabernet Rose, Shiraz, Friends Shiraz, Tantalus Shiraz Cabernet Sauvignon, Merlot, CSM, Cabernet Sauvignon, Friends Cabernet Sauvignon; Command Shiraz and Ashmead Single Vineyard Cabernet Sauvignon are flagbearers.
SUMMARY The wines are based on some old, high-quality Barossa floor estate vineyards, and all are driven to a lesser or greater degree by lashings of American oak; the Command Shiraz is at the baroque end of the spectrum and has to be given considerable respect within the parameters of its style. National retail distribution, with exports to the UK, the US, Europe and Asia.

TTTTY **Barossa Shiraz 2002** Rich, supple blackberry, plum and licorice; good concentration and focus; background oak. **RATING** 93 **DRINK** 2017 $24.95
Ashmead Single Vineyard Cabernet Sauvignon 2000 Solid blackcurrant fruit; supple texture; well-integrated and balanced French oak; excellent outcome for the vintage. **RATING** 92 **DRINK** 2015 $85
Barossa Cabernet Sauvignon Shiraz Merlot 2000 Complex flavour and structure; long, slippery palate; spicy nuances. Another outstanding outcome. **RATING** 91 **DRINK** 2010 $40
Eden Valley Riesling 2003 Intense lime blossom aromas; full-flavoured but not heavy; early maturing. **RATING** 90 **DRINK** 2008 $14.95
Friends Cabernet Sauvignon 2002 Attractive blackcurrant/cassis fruit does all the talking. **RATING** 90 **DRINK** 2011 $18.95
Barossa Cabernet Sauvignon 2001 Blackcurrant and blackberry fruit; good texture and structure; ripe tannins, positive oak. **RATING** 90 **DRINK** 2011 $23.95

TTTT **Command Shiraz 2000** Mint, vanilla and red berry fruits, with a sweet core; oak dominant. **RATING** 89 **DRINK** 2015 $85

TTTY **Friends Shiraz 2002** **RATING** 86 **DRINK** 2007 $18.95
Barossa Merlot 2000 **RATING** 86 **DRINK** 2010 $28.95
Tantalus Shiraz Cabernet 2002 **RATING** 85 **DRINK** 2007 $13.95

TTT **Unwooded Chardonnay 2003** **RATING** 83 $13.95
Sauvignon Blanc Verdelho 2003 **RATING** 81 $13.95

Eldredge

Spring Gully Road, Clare, SA 5453 **REGION** Clare Valley
T (08) 8842 3086 **F** (08) 8842 3086 **OPEN** 7 days 11–5
WINEMAKER Leigh Eldredge **EST.** 1993 **CASES** 7000
PRODUCT RANGE ($14–40 CD) Watervale Riesling, Semillon Sauvignon Blanc, Sparkling, Late Harvest Riesling, Blue Chip Shiraz, Gilt Edge Shiraz, MSG, Boundary Sangiovese, Cabernet Sauvignon, Tawny Port.
SUMMARY Leigh and Karen Eldredge have established their winery and cellar-door sales area in the Sevenhill Ranges at an altitude of 500 metres, above the town of Watervale. Hit a purple patch with

its 2001 and 2002 white wines, complementing the very good Cabernet Sauvignon. The wines are distributed in Victoria and Queensland and exported to the UK, the US and Canada.

ΥΥΥΥ **Watervale Riesling 2003** Flowery, aromatic lime blossom; abundant tropical fruit in a generous mode. **RATING** 90 **DRINK** 2009 $ 17

ΥΥΥ **Boundary Sangiovese 2001** Varietal savoury, earthy, cherry aromas and flavours; soft, fine tannins. **RATING** 86 **DRINK** 2008 $ 26
Blue Chip Shiraz 2001 **RATING** 85 **DRINK** 2011 $ 26

ΥΥΥ **Blue Chip Shiraz 2002** **RATING** 80 $ 26

Eldridge Estate ★★★★★

120 Arthyrs Seat Road, Red Hill, Vic 3937 **REGION** Mornington Peninsula
T (03) 5989 2644 **F** (03) 5989 2644 **OPEN** Weekends, public holidays and January 1–26 11–5
WINEMAKER David Lloyd **EST.** 1985 **CASES** 800
PRODUCT RANGE ($15–34 CD) Sauvignon Blanc Semillon, North Patch Chardonnay, Chardonnay, Pink Lloyd Rose, Gamay, West Patch Pinot Noir, Pinot Noir, Euroa Creek Shiraz, Cabernet Merlot.
SUMMARY The Eldridge Estate vineyard, with seven varieties included in its 3.5 hectares, was purchased by Wendy and David Lloyd in 1995. Major retrellising work has been undertaken, changing to Scott-Henry, and all of the wines will now be estate-grown and made. David Lloyd has also planted several Dijon-selected pinot noir clones (114, 115 and 777) which have made their contribution since 2004. The wines are available at the Victorian Wine Centre and Tastings, Armadale, in Melbourne, and a few leading restaurants in Melbourne and Sydney.

ΥΥΥΥΥ **Pinot Noir 2002** Superb colour; great power, depth and potency, but not at the expense of varietal character; pristine plum and a dash of spice; long, lingering finish. Screwcap.
RATING 95 **DRINK** 2010 $ 35
Chardonnay 2002 All the intensity and complexity expected of the vintage; layered, tangy citrus-accented fruit; great length. Slight cork taint was disregarded. **RATING** 94
DRINK 2010 $ 35

ΥΥΥΥ **Gamay 2002** Bold, juicy, sweet, and luscious, but not jammy, red berry fruit with appealing spicy notes. Screwcap. Best Gamay yet from Australia. **RATING** 91 **DRINK** Now $ 25

ΥΥΥΥ **Euroa Creek Shiraz 2002** Medium-bodied; a clean mix of red and black cherries; fine texture. Screwcap. Three hundred cases made from unirrigated vines at Euroa. **RATING** 89
DRINK 2010 $ 42

Elgee Park ★★★★

Wallaces Road RMB 5560, Merricks North, Vic 3926 **REGION** Mornington Peninsula
T (03) 5989 7338 **F** (03) 5989 7338 **OPEN** One day a year — Sunday of Queen's Birthday weekend
WINEMAKER Contract **EST.** 1972 **CASES** 1800
PRODUCT RANGE ($18–34 ML) Baillieu Myer Family Reserve Riesling, Viognier, Chardonnay, Pinot Noir, Merlot, Cabernet Merlot; Cuvee Brut
SUMMARY The pioneer of the Mornington Peninsula in its twentieth-century rebirth, owned by Baillieu Myer and family. The wines are now made at Stonier and T'Gallant, Elgee Park's own winery having been closed, and the overall level of activity decreased. Melbourne retail distribution through Flinders Wholesale.

Elgo Estate ★★☆

RMB 6170 James Road, Longwood, Vic 3665 (postal) **REGION** Strathbogie Ranges
T (03) 9328 3766 **F** (03) 5798 5524 **OPEN** Not
WINEMAKER Cameron Atkins **EST.** 1999 **CASES** 15 000
PRODUCT RANGE ($12–28 R) At the top Elgo Estate Upton Hill Reserve varietals ($26–28); in the middle the Elgo Estate Strathbogie Ranges varietals ($16–20); and at the bottom the Allira range ($12–14).
SUMMARY The Taresch family began the development of their vineyard at an altitude of 500 metres in the Upton area, adjacent to Mount Helen, Alexander Park and Plunkett's Blackwood Ridge

vineyards. Grant Taresch manages the vineyard, while Cameron Atkins, who has overseen the vintages made between 2001 and 2003 at other venues, will run the new 800-tonne winery erected for the 2004 vintage. Striking packaging is a feature.

ȚȚȚȚ **Strathbogie Ranges Pinot Noir 2002** RATING 85 DRINK Now $ 26
Upton Hill Pinot Noir 2002 RATING 84 DRINK Now $ 18

Eling Forest Winery ★★★

Hume Highway, Sutton Forest, NSW 2577 REGION Southern New South Wales Zone
T (02) 4878 9499 F (02) 4878 9133 OPEN 7 days 10–5
WINEMAKER Leslie Fritz, Michelle Crockett EST. 1987 CASES 5000
PRODUCT RANGE ($12–35 CD) Riesling, Chardonnay, Lunel (semi sweet), Rose, Pinot Noir, Merlot, Reserve Merlot, Shiraz, Cabernet Sauvignon, Reserve Cabernet Sauvignon, Cherry Port, Peach Brandy.
SUMMARY Eling Forest's mentally agile and innovative founder Leslie Fritz celebrated his 80th birthday not long after he planted the first vines at his Sutton Forest vineyard in 1987. He proceeded to celebrate his 88th birthday by expanding the vineyards from 3 hectares to 4, primarily with additional plantings of the Hungarian varieties. In 2004 Eling Forest was purchased by the partnership of Lucky Gattellari and the local winegrowing Wainberg family. A new winery and cellar door has been built and the vineyard much expanded. Bed and breakfast accommodation is available, and the on-site restaurant also hosts the region's annual wine and food festival.

Eljamar NR

251 Henry Lawson Drive, Mudgee, NSW 2850 REGION Mudgee
T (02) 6373 3874 F (02) 6373 3854 OPEN Fri–Sun and public holidays 9–5
WINEMAKER Ian MacRae EST. 2000
PRODUCT RANGE Secret Garden Chardonnay, Rose, Shiraz, Cabernet Sauvignon.
SUMMARY Eljamar is owned by Ian and Carol MacRae, and is a sister operation to their main business, Miramar Wines. Eljamar has its own estate plantings of 10 hectares of shiraz and about 2 hectares each of cabernet sauvignon and chardonnay. The wines are made at Miramar, the cellar door is open on-site at Eljimar. The property is only 5 kilometres from the town of Mudgee on Henry Lawson Drive and also fronts Craigmoor Road, giving it a prime position in the so-called 'golden triangle'.

Ellender Estate ★★★☆

260 Green Gully Road Glenlyon, Vic 3461 REGION Macedon Ranges
T (03) 5348 7785 F (03) 5348 4077 OPEN Weekends and public holidays 11–5, or by appointment
WINEMAKER Graham Ellender EST. 1996 CASES 1200
PRODUCT RANGE ($18–33 CD) Chardonnay, Pinot Noir, Cabernet Franc, Shiraz, Merlot, Cabernet Sauvignon.
SUMMARY Former senior lecturer in dental science at the University of Melbourne, Graham Ellender, moved to Daylesford with wife Jenny with the twofold purpose of escaping academia and starting a vineyard and winery, simultaneously establishing dental practices at Daylesford and East Ivanhoe. The Ellenders have established 4 hectares of pinot noir, chardonnay, sauvignon blanc and pinot gris, and also source shiraz and sauvignon blanc from Cowra, cabernet sauvignon from Harcourt, cabernet franc from Macedon and pinot noir from Narre Warren. Formerly called Leura Glen Estate, marketplace confusion with other similar names, and other considerations, has led to the change of name to Ellender Estate.

ȚȚȚȚȚ **Macedon Pinot Noir 2001** Complex wine; rich plum/dark fruits, but also foresty/savoury characters. Impressive. RATING 90 DRINK Now $ 28

ȚȚȚȚ **Chardonnay 2003** Driven by attractive melon and nectarine fruit; good balance and weight; estate-grown. RATING 88 DRINK 2007 $ 28

ȚȚȚȚ **Shiraz 2001** RATING 85 DRINK Now $ 18
Red Nelle Cabernet Sauvignon 2001 RATING 85 DRINK Now $ 18

ȚȚȚ **Moonstruck Vineyard Chardonnay 2003** RATING 77 $ 28
Macedon Ranges Chardonnay 2003 RATING 76 $ 28

Elliot Rocke Estate

Craigmoor Road, Mudgee, NSW 2850 **REGION** Mudgee
T (02) 6372 7722 **F** (02) 6372 0680 **OPEN** 7 days 9–4
WINEMAKER Jim Chatto, Greg Silkman (Monarch Winemaking Services) **EST.** 1999 **CASES** 5000
PRODUCT RANGE ($12.95–19.95 CD) Traminer, Semillon, Unwooded Chardonnay, Premium Chardonnay, Late Harvest, McLaren Vale Shiraz, Cabernet Sauvignon Merlot.
SUMMARY Elliot Rocke Estate is a new label for Mudgee, but planting of its 24.2 hectares of vineyards dates back to 1987, when the property was known as Seldom Seen. Plantings comprise approximately 9 hectares of semillon, 4.3 hectares shiraz and chardonnay, 2.2 hectares merlot and 2 hectares each of cabernet sauvignon and traminer, with 0.5 hectare of doradillo. Contract winemaking by Jim Chatto and Greg Silkman have resulted in medals at the Mudgee and Rutherglen wine shows. The wines are available through the cellar door, by mailing list, and through a number of Sydney retailers.

Semillon 2003 Classic tight, crisp bouquet; long, lingering lemony finish. Gold medal 2003 Mudgee Wine Show. **RATING** 93 **DRINK** 2013 $ 14.95

Unwooded Chardonnay 2003 Fragrant and positive aromas of nectarine and blossom; good balance and length; way above average. Screwcap. **RATING** 89 **DRINK** 2007 $ 14.95
Premium Chardonnay 2002 A subtle lick of oak doesn't threaten the nectarine/melon fruit flavour; light to medium-bodied; good length, well made. **RATING** 89 **DRINK** Now $ 17.95

Traminer 2003 **RATING** 85 **DRINK** Now $ 12.95

Late Harvest Sweet White 2003 **RATING** 81 $ 16.95

Elmslie ★★☆

Upper McEwans Road, Legana, Tas 7277 **REGION** Northern Tasmania
T (03) 6330 1225 **F** (03) 6330 2161 **OPEN** By appointment
WINEMAKER Ralph Power **EST.** 1972 **CASES** 600
PRODUCT RANGE ($18 ML) Pinot Noir, Cabernet Sauvignon.
SUMMARY A small, specialist red winemaker, from time to time blending Pinot Noir with Cabernet. The fruit from the now fully mature vineyard (0.5 hectare of pinot noir and 1.5 hectares of cabernet sauvignon) has depth and character, but operational constraints mean that the style of the wine is often somewhat rustic.

Elmswood Estate ★★★

75 Monbulk-Seville Road, Wandin East, Vic 3139 **REGION** Yarra Valley
T (03) 5964 3015 **F** (03) 5964 3405 **OPEN** 7 days 10–5
WINEMAKER Contract **EST.** 1981 **CASES** 2000
PRODUCT RANGE ($20–30 CD) Unoaked Chardonnay, Chardonnay, Cabernet Rose, Barrel Select Merlot, Cabernet Merlot, Cabernet Sauvignon, Barrel Select Cabernet.
SUMMARY Rod and Dianne Keller purchased their 9.5-hectare vineyard in June 1999; it had been planted in 1981 on the red volcanic soils of the far-southern side of the valley which stretch from Wandin to Warburton. Prior to their acquisition of the vineyard, the grapes had been sold to other Yarra Valley winemakers, but the Kellers immediately set about having their own wine made from the estate. The cellar door offers spectacular views across the Upper Yarra Valley to Mount Donna Buang and Warburton. The wines are sold chiefly through the cellar door and mailing list, with limited restaurant listings.

Cabernet Merlot 2001 Strongly briary/savoury bouquet; medium-bodied palate, with a nice splash of blackcurrant in the savoury mix. Gold medal 2003 Cool Climate Wine Show. **RATING** 89 **DRINK** 2011 $ 26

Barrel Select Cabernet Sauvignon 2001 **RATING** 85 **DRINK** 2008 $ 40
Ralph's Cabernet Rose 2002 **RATING** 84 **DRINK** Now $ 20

Unoaked Chardonnay 2003 **RATING** 83 $ 20

Chardonnay 2002 **RATING** 79 $ 23

Elsewhere Vineyard

42 Dillons Hill Road, Glaziers Bay, Tas 7109 **REGION** Southern Tasmania
T (03) 6295 1228 **F** (03) 6295 1591 **OPEN** Not
WINEMAKER Andrew Hood (Contract), Steve Lubiana (Contract) **EST.** 1984 **CASES** 4000
PRODUCT RANGE ($20–40 ML) Riesling, Chardonnay, Pinot Noir, Methode Champenoise.
SUMMARY Kylie and Andrew Cameron's evocatively named Elsewhere Vineyard used to jostle for
space with a commercial flower farm. It is a mark of the success of the wines that in 1993 some of the
long-established flowers made way for additional chardonnay and riesling, although it is Elsewhere's
long-lived Pinot Noirs that are so stunning and declare the winery rating. The estate-produced range
comes from 6 hectares of pinot noir, 3 hectares of chardonnay and 1 hectare of riesling which
constitute the immaculately tended vineyard.

ŸŸŸŸŸ **Riesling 2003** Bright green-yellow; ultra-expressive, lively and intense; explosive flavour
and length driven by high acidity and substantial residual sugar in perfect balance.
RATING 96 **DRINK** 2016 $ 25

ŸŸŸŸŸ **Pinot Noir 2002** Deep, intense and very powerful; black fruits, anise, shoe leather; over
the top for some, not others. **RATING** 93 **DRINK** 2012 $ 40

Elsmore's Caprera Grove

657 Milbrodale Road, Broke, NSW 2330 **REGION** Lower Hunter Valley
T (02) 6579 1344 **F** (02) 6579 1355 **OPEN** Weekends and public holidays 10–5, or by appointment
WINEMAKER Jim Chatto, Gary Reid (Contract) **EST.** 1995 **CASES** 800
PRODUCT RANGE ($15–25 CD) Verdelho, Chardonnay, Peregrinus Methode Champenoise, Bartolomeo
Botrytis Chardonnay, Shiraz.
SUMMARY Bindy and Chris Elsmore purchased their 16-hectare property at Broke in 1995,
subsequently establishing a little over 4 hectares of chardonnay, verdelho and shiraz, with
chardonnay taking the lion's share of the plantings. Their interest in wine came not from their
professional lives — Chris is a retired commodore of the Royal Australian Navy and Bindy had a
career in advertising, marketing and personnel — but from numerous trips to the wine regions of
France, Italy and Spain.

ŸŸŸŸ **Verdelho 2003** **RATING** 85 **DRINK** Now $ 16
Shiraz 2002 **RATING** 85 **DRINK** 2007 $ 19
Chardonnay 2002 **RATING** 84 **DRINK** Now $ 15

Eltham Vineyards

225 Shaws Road, Arthurs Creek, Vic 3099 **REGION** Yarra Valley
T (03) 9439 4144 **F** (03) 9439 5121 **OPEN** By appointment
WINEMAKER George Apted, John Graves **EST.** 1990 **CASES** 600
PRODUCT RANGE ($18–28 CD) Chardonnay, Pinot Noir, Cabernet Merlot, Cabernet Sauvignon.
SUMMARY Drawing upon vineyards at Arthurs Creek and Eltham, John Graves (brother of David
Graves of the illustrious Californian Pinot producer Saintsbury) produces tiny quantities of quite
stylish Chardonnay and Pinot Noir, the former showing nice barrel-ferment characters. The wines
have been consistent medal winners in regional Victorian wine shows.

ŸŸŸŸ **Chardonnay 2000** Youthful, slow-developing; light stone fruit and subtle oak.
Understated and stylish. **RATING** 89 **DRINK** 2007 $ 25
Pinot Noir 2000 Slightly cloudy, perhaps unfiltered; spicy/stemmy/oaky complexity to
bouquet; has style and grip, some austerity and good length. **RATING** 88 **DRINK** Now $ 25

Elysium Vineyard

393 Milbrodale Road, Broke, NSW 2330 **REGION** Lower Hunter Valley
T (02) 9664 2368 **F** (02) 9664 2368 **OPEN** Weekends 10–5, or by appointment
WINEMAKER Wandin Valley Estate, Tyrrell's (Contract) **EST.** 1990 **CASES** 450
PRODUCT RANGE ($18–50 CD) Verdelho.

SUMMARY Elysium was once part of a much larger vineyard established by John Tulloch. John Tulloch (not part of the Tulloch operation previously owned by Southcorp) continues to look after the viticulture, with the 1 hectare of verdelho being vinified at Tyrrell's. The Elysium Cottage, large enough to accommodate six people, has won a number of tourism awards, and proprietor Victoria Foster conducts wine education weekends on request, with meals prepared by a chef brought in for the occasion. The cost per person for a gourmet weekend is $300–400 per person, depending on numbers.

▼▼▼▼♡ **Limited Release Fordwich Verdelho 1999** Amazingly fresh; an attractive mix of melon and citrus; good length and acidity. Gold medal 2003 Hunter Valley Wine Show in museum class. **RATING** 92 **DRINK** Now $50

▼▼▼ **Verdelho 2003 RATING** 82 $20

🍎 Emma's Cottage Vineyard   NR

Wilderness Road, Lovedale, NSW 2320 **REGION** Lower Hunter Valley
T (02) 4998 7734 **F** (02) 4998 7209 **OPEN** Fri–Mon, public and school holidays 10–5, or by appointment
WINEMAKER David Hook (Contract) **EST.** 1987
PRODUCT RANGE ($14–30 CD) Semillon, Chardonnay Semillon, Chardonnay, Late Harvest Chardonnay, Sparkling Chardonnay, Shiraz, Merlot, Tokay.
SUMMARY Rob and Toni Powys run a combined boutique winery and accommodation business set in a three-bedroom farmhouse, situated on a 12-hectare property at Lovedale. Four hectares of semillon, chardonnay, verdelho, merlot, pinot noir and shiraz have been planted, and a range of varietals and vintages are on offer.

Empress Vineyard   ★★★★☆

Drapers Road, Irrewarra, Vic 3250 (postal Amberley House, 391 Sandy Bay Road, Hobart, Tas 7005) **REGION** Western Victoria Zone
T (03) 6225 1005 **F** (03) 6225 0639 **OPEN** By appointment
WINEMAKER Robin Brockett, Cate Looney, Lisa Togni **EST.** 1998 **CASES** 1000
PRODUCT RANGE ($18–30 CD) Semillon Sauvignon Blanc, Chardonnay, Pinot Noir, Cabernet Sauvignon Merlot.
SUMMARY If the address of Empress and its Geographic Zone seem schizophrenic, don't be alarmed. Allistair Lindsay is in the course of moving to Tasmania, and is selling the restaurant at Irrewarra (although not so far the vineyard) while seeking to re-establish both restaurant and vineyard/winemaking near Hobart. It is uncertain whether both vineyard operations will be kept going in tandem; the quality of the wines from the existing Empress Vineyard must tempt Lindsay to maintain the operation.

▼▼▼▼♡ **Chardonnay 2001** Fine, elegant but complex; barrel ferment and malolactic inputs; melon, nectarine and cashew, with a creamy texture. **RATING** 93 **DRINK** 2008 $22
Semillon Sauvignon Blanc 2002 Intense and highly focused fruit; sweet citrus and gooseberry; excellent back palate and finish. **RATING** 92 **DRINK** 2007 $18

England's Creek   NR

PO Box 6, Murrumbateman, NSW 2582 **REGION** Canberra District
T (02) 6227 5550 **F** (02) 6226 8898 **OPEN** At Barrique Café, Murrumbateman Thurs–Sun
WINEMAKER Ken Helm (Contract) **EST.** 1995 **CASES** 250
PRODUCT RANGE ($17–20 ML) Riesling, Hand Picked Riesling, Shiraz, Hand Picked Shiraz.
SUMMARY The diminutive England's Creek was established in 1995 by Stephen Carney and Virginia Rawling with the planting of 1 hectare each of riesling and shiraz, subsequently doubling the size of each. The wines are available at selected Canberra restaurants and Vintage Cellars, Manuka or by contacting the winery on phone or fax.

Ensay Winery

NR

Great Alpine Road, Ensay, Vic 3895 **REGION** Gippsland
T (03) 5157 3203 **F** (03) 5157 3372 **OPEN** Weekends, public and school holidays 11–5, or by appointment
WINEMAKER David Coy **EST.** 1992 **CASES** 1500
PRODUCT RANGE ($17–20 R) Chardonnay, Pinot Noir, Shiraz, Cabernet Sauvignon.
SUMMARY A weekend and holiday business for the Coy family, headed by David Coy, with 2.5 hectares of chardonnay, pinot noir, merlot, shiraz and cabernet sauvignon.

Epis/Epis & Williams

★★★★

Lot 16 Calder Highway, Woodend, Vic 3442 **REGION** Macedon Ranges
T (03) 5427 1204 **F** (03) 5427 1204 **OPEN** By appointment
WINEMAKER Stuart Anderson **EST.** 1990 **CASES** 850
PRODUCT RANGE ($35–40 R) Epis Chardonnay, Pinot Noir; Epis & Williams Cabernet Sauvignon.
SUMMARY Three legends are involved in the Epis and Epis & Williams wines, two of them in their own lifetime. They are long-term Essendon guru and former player, Alec Epis, who owns the two quite separate vineyards and brands; Stuart Anderson, who makes the wines, with Alec Epis doing all the hard work; and the late Laurie Williams, the father of viticulture in the Macedon region and who established the Flynn & Williams vineyard in 1976. Alec Epis purchased that vineyard from Laurie Williams in 1999, and as a mark of respect (and with Laurie Williams' approval) continued to use his name in conjunction with that of Alec Epis. The cabernet sauvignon comes from this vineyard, the chardonnay and pinot noir from the vineyard at Woodend, where a small winery was completed prior to the 2002 vintage.

Eppalock Ridge

★★★

633 North Redesdale Road, Redesdale, Vic 3444 **REGION** Heathcote
T (03) 5443 7841 **OPEN** By appointment
WINEMAKER Rod Hourigan **EST.** 1979 **CASES** 1500
PRODUCT RANGE ($33 ML) Shiraz, Cabernet Merlot.
SUMMARY While continuing to maintain a low profile as a winemaking operation, the estate plantings have increased to 17 hectares, dominated by shiraz with 10 hectares, and as well as limited domestic retail distribution, exports have been established to the US, New Zealand and Fiji.

ΨΨΨΨ **Shiraz 2001 RATING** 85 **DRINK** 2011 **$** 32

Ermes Estate

NR

2 Godings Road, Moorooduc, Vic 3933 **REGION** Mornington Peninsula
T (03) 5978 8376 **F** (03) 5978 8396 **OPEN** Weekends and public holidays 11–5
WINEMAKER Ermes Zucchet, Denise Zucchet **EST.** 1989 **CASES** 800
PRODUCT RANGE ($10–20 CD) Riesling/Malvasia, Chardonnay, Fresco (rose), Pinot Grigio, Merlot, Cabernet Sauvignon.
SUMMARY Ermes and Denise Zucchet commenced planting of the 2.5-hectare estate in 1989 with chardonnay, riesling, cabernet sauvignon and merlot, adding pinot gris in 1991. In 1994 an existing piggery on the property was converted to a winery and cellar-door area (in the Zucchets' words, 'the pigs having been evicted'), and the modestly priced wines are on sale during the weekends.

ese Vineyards

★★★★

1013 Tea Tree Road, Tea Tree, Tas 7017 **REGION** Southern Tasmania
T 0417 319 875 **F** (03) 6225 1989 **OPEN** 7 days 10–5
WINEMAKER Julian Alcorso (Contract) **EST.** 1994 **CASES** 2600
PRODUCT RANGE ($24.50 CD) Chardonnay, Pinot Noir.
SUMMARY Elvio and Natalie Brianese are an architect and graphic designer couple whose extended family have centuries-old viticultural roots in the Veneto region of northern Italy. Ese has 2.5 hectares of vineyard and got off to a flying start with a gold and silver medal for its 1997 Pinot Noir.

Subsequent vintages have been less exhilarating, but there is no question the potential is there, and a further 4 hectares of pinot noir and chardonnay was planted in 2003-4.

♥♥♥♥♥ Pinot Noir 2002 Very complex, very powerful dark plum, and black cherry plus oak and spice. **RATING** 94 **DRINK** 2012 $ 26

♥♥♥♥ Chardonnay 2002 RATING 85 **DRINK** Now $ 26

Etain   ★★★☆

Boodjidup Road, Margaret River, WA 6285 **REGION** Margaret River
T 0407 445 570 **OPEN** Not
WINEMAKER Conor Lagan, Jurg Muggli **EST.** 2001 **CASES** 5000
PRODUCT RANGE ($16–25 R) Riesling, Semillon Sauvignon Blanc, Merlot, Cabernet Merlot.
SUMMARY Etain is a private label of Conor Lagan, available only to trade through distributor Prime Wines. In Gaelic mythology Etain is the horse goddess, representing birth and rebirth. It is in turn linked to the fascinating story of Conor Lagan's life, which can be found on www.etainwines.com. The wines are sourced from vineyards in the Margaret and Frankland River regions.

Eumundi Winery   NR

2 Bruce Highway, Eumundi, Qld 4562 **REGION** Queensland Coastal
T (07) 5442 7444 **F** (07) 5442 7455 **OPEN** 7 days 10–6
WINEMAKER Andrew Hickinbotham (Contract) **EST.** 1996 **CASES** 2500
PRODUCT RANGE ($12–15 R) Semillon Chardonnay, Taminga, Shiraz, Shiraz Cabernet, Shiraz Durif, Merlot, Chambourcin, Cabernet Sauvignon.
SUMMARY Eumundi Vineyard is set on 21 hectares of riverfront land in the beautiful Eumundi Valley, 12 kilometres inland from Noosa Heads. The climate is hot, wet, humid and maritime, the only saving grace being the regular afternoon northeast sea breeze. It is a challenging environment in which to grow grapes, and over 5 years the owners, Robyn and Gerry Humphrey, have trialled 14 different grape varieties and three different trellis systems. Currently they have tempranillo, shiraz, chambourcin, petit verdot, durif and mourvedre, and verdelho. Plantings in 2001 included tannat and others, which gives some idea of their eclectic approach. The establishment of the vineyard was financed by the sale of a 19-metre charter yacht which used to sail the oceans around northern Australia. Quite a change in lifestyle for the Humphreys.

Evans & Tate   ★★★★

Metricup Road, Wilyabrup, WA 6280 **REGION** Margaret River
T (08) 9755 6244 **F** (08) 9755 6346 **OPEN** 7 days 10.30–5
WINEMAKER Richard Rowe **EST.** 1970
PRODUCT RANGE ($13.50–50 CD) Gnangara range of Sauvignon Blanc, Chenin Blanc, Unwooded Chardonnay, Shiraz, Cabernet Sauvignon; the Margaret River range of Margaret River Classic, Semillon, Sauvignon Blanc Semillon, Verdelho, Chardonnay, Cane Cut Semillon, Shiraz, Classic Shiraz Cabernet Merlot, Merlot, Cabernet Merlot; Redbrook Chardonnay, Cabernet Sauvignon.
SUMMARY From its Swan Valley base 30 years ago, Evans & Tate has grown to the point where it is the largest Margaret River winery and producer, with an uninterrupted pattern of growth. Having multiplied its estate vineyard holdings with the establishment of a large planting in the Jindong subregion, it raised substantial capital by going public, successfully listing on the Stock Exchange. It then turned its attention eastwards, with the acquisition of Oakridge Estate in the Yarra Valley, followed by Cranswick Wines (now called Barramundi) in March 2003. Wine quality is always polished, and, within the Margaret River context, at the lighter end of the spectrum. National distribution and exports to all major wine markets.

♥♥♥♥ Margaret River Merlot 2000 Impressively deep colour; briar, olive and blackcurrant, medium-bodied, with plenty of texture and ripe tannins. **RATING** 93 **DRINK** 2015 $ 29.99

Redbrook Chardonnay 2001 Good regional style; smoky oak, cashew and multi-fruit flavours, peach through to grapefruit. **RATING** 92 **DRINK** 2008 $ 40

Margaret River Shiraz 2002 Distinct spicy varietal fruit; lingering, focused palate; dark plum, blackberry, spice; ripe tannins. **RATING** 91 **DRINK** 2012 $ 20.99

Margaret River Semillon 2002 Complex wine; skilled partial barrel ferment; long, multi-flavoured palate; hints of passionfruit and gooseberry. **RATING** 90 **DRINK** 2009 $19.99

ŢŢŢŢ **Margaret River Sauvignon Blanc Semillon 2003** Clean, crisp, mineral; asparagus/gooseberry/herb aromas and flavours; the barest hint of oak; powerful finish. Screwcap. **RATING** 89 **DRINK** 2007 $18.99
Margaret River Cabernet Sauvignon 2000 In typical winery style, medium-bodied; persistent, blackcurrant fruit and tannin mix; fraction austere. **RATING** 89 **DRINK** 2010 $29.99
Margaret River Classic White 2003 Clean, fresh, crisp lemony/minerally core; herbs and spices add to the appeal. **RATING** 87 **DRINK** Now $18
Salisbury Shiraz Cabernet 2003 Plenty of ripe blackberry, plum and blackcurrant fruit; slightly simple, but lots of flavour. **RATING** 87 **DRINK** 2008 $9.99

ŢŢŢŸ **Gnangara Shiraz 2002** **RATING** 86 **DRINK** Now $13.50
Margaret River Cabernet Merlot 2003 Bright red fruit aromas and on entry to the mouth, then savoury tannins are slightly abrasive. **RATING** 86 **DRINK** 2008 $20.99
Margaret River Cabernet Merlot 2001 **RATING** 86 **DRINK** 2007 $20.99
Gnangara Sauvignon Blanc 2003 **RATING** 85 **DRINK** Now $13.50
Margaret River Verdelho 2003 **RATING** 85 **DRINK** Now $17.99
Gnangara Cabernet Sauvignon 2002 **RATING** 85 **DRINK** Now $13.50

ŢŢŢ **Gnangara Merlot 2002** **RATING** 83 $13.50

Evans & Tate Salisbury ★★★

Campbell Avenue, Irymple, Vic 3498 **REGION** Murray Darling
T (03) 5024 6800 **F** (03) 5024 6605 **OPEN** Mon–Sat 10–4.30, Sun 12–4
WINEMAKER Krister Jonsson, Donna Stephens, Tony Pla Bou **EST.** 1977
PRODUCT RANGE ($4–15 R) Semillon Chardonnay, Semillon Sauvignon Blanc, Chardonnay, Botrytis Semillon, Shiraz Cabernet, Cabernet Merlot; Milburn Park Chardonnay and Shiraz.
SUMMARY This is the former Milburn Park winery; the positions of the Salisbury and Milburn brands have been reversed, with Salisbury now the senior, the re-launched Milburn Park label, sold at cellar door and export only, part of the Salisbury production.

ŢŢŢŢ **Shiraz Cabernet 2002** **RATING** 87 **DRINK** Now $9.99

ŢŢŢŸ **Cabernet Merlot 2002** **RATING** 84 **DRINK** Now $9.99

ŢŢŢ **Chardonnay 2002** **RATING** 83 $9.99

Evans Family Wines ★★★★

151 Palmers Lane, Pokolbin, NSW 2321 **REGION** Lower Hunter Valley
T (02) 4998 7237 **F** (02) 4998 7201 **OPEN** 7 days 10–5
WINEMAKER Toby Evans **EST.** 1979 **CASES** 2600
PRODUCT RANGE ($11.50–24.50 CD) Semillon, Chardonnay, Gamay, Pinot Noir, Shiraz, Muscat; Lounge Lizard Sweet White, Rose, Lazy Red and Shiraz.
SUMMARY In the wake of the acquisition of Rothbury by Mildara Blass, Len Evans' wine interests now focus on Evans Family (estate-grown and produced from vineyards around the family home), the Evans Wine Company (a quite different, part-maker, part-negociant business) and, most recently, Tower Estate. Len Evans continues to persist with the notion that the Hunter Valley can produce Gamay and Pinot Noir of quality and, irritatingly, occasionally produces evidence to suggest he may be half right. There is, of course, no such reservation with the Semillon, the Chardonnay or the Shiraz. Exports to the US.

ŢŢŢŢ **Chardonnay 2003** Bright green-gold; medium to full-bodied; ripe, yellow peach and stone fruit; subtle oak. **RATING** 88 **DRINK** Now $20
Pinot Noir 2002 Spicy, faintly earthy plum and spice aromas and flavours; fine, silky tannins; well constructed, light-bodied red wine. **RATING** 88 **DRINK** Now $22.50

Howard Vineyard Semillon 2001 Clean, fresh, crisp citrus and apple aromas; good line and length. **RATING** 87 **DRINK** 2011 $16.50

Gamay 2001 One hundred per cent regional, and 100 per cent aberrational in terms of varietal character; medium-bodied; spicy brambly earthy flavours; has some length. Reminiscent of Hunter Valley Pinot Noirs. **RATING** 87 **DRINK** Now $13.50

ŸŸŸŸ **Howard Shiraz 2001 RATING** 85 **DRINK** 2009 $28.50

Evelyn County Estate ★★★★☆

55 Eltham-Yarra Glen Road, Kangaroo Ground, Vic 3097 **REGION** Yarra Valley
T (03) 9437 2155 **F** (03) 9437 2188 **OPEN** Mon–Wed 11–5, Thurs–Fri 11 am–10 pm, Sat 9–midnight, Sun 9 am–10 pm
WINEMAKER Robyn Male, James Lance, David Lance (Contract) **EST.** 1994 **CASES** 2000
PRODUCT RANGE ($22–45 CD) Black Paddock range of Sauvignon Blanc, Chardonnay, Sticky, Pinot Noir, Merlot, Cabernet Sauvignon.
SUMMARY The 8-hectare Evelyn County Estate has been established by former Coopers & Lybrand managing partner Roger Male and his wife Robyn, who has completed a degree in Applied Science (Wine Science) at Charles Sturt University. David and James Lance (of Diamond Valley) are currently making the wines, and an architect-designed cellar-door sales, gallery and restaurant opened in April 2001. As one would expect, the quality of the wines is very good. A small planting of tempranillo bore its first crop in 2004 and the wine was be made on-site by Robyn Male.

ŸŸŸŸŸ **Black Paddock Merlot 2002** Strongly varietal olive, earth and spice aromas; small red and black fruits on the palate; fine tannins, lingering finish. **RATING** 91 **DRINK** 2011 $30

Black Paddock Pinot Noir 2002 Strong colour; very complex spicy, gamey, foresty aromas and flavours. Will win some, lose some. **RATING** 90 **DRINK** 2009 $45

Black Paddock Cabernet Sauvignon 2002 Medium-bodied blackcurrant/blackberry/cedar; good texture. **RATING** 90 **DRINK** 2014 $30

Excelsior Peak NR

PO Box 269, Tumbarumba, NSW 2653 **REGION** Tumbarumba
T (02) 6948 5102 **F** (02) 6948 5102 **OPEN** Not
WINEMAKER Contract **EST.** 1980 **CASES** 700
PRODUCT RANGE ($18–22 ML) Chardonnay, Pinot Noir, Methode Champenoise.
SUMMARY Excelsior Peak proprietor Juliet Cullen established the first vineyard in Tumbarumba in 1980. That vineyard was thereafter sold to Southcorp, and Juliet Cullen subsequently established another vineyard, now releasing wines under the Excelsior Peak label. Plantings total over 10 hectares, with most of the grapes sold. Sales only by mail order.

Ey Estate ★★★☆

Main Road, Coonawarra, SA 5263 **REGION** Coonawarra
T (08) 8739 3063 **F** (08) 8739 3069 **OPEN** Not
WINEMAKER Pat Tocaciu (Contract) **EST.** 1989 **CASES** 800
PRODUCT RANGE ($23 R) Chardonnay, Cabernet Sauvignon.
SUMMARY The Ey family arrived in Coonawarra in 1908, establishing a mixed farming business on terra rossa soil just to the north of the Coonawarra township. Between 1988 and 1998 third generation Robin Ey, and fourth generation son Peter Ey, have established 20 hectares of cabernet sauvignon, 4 hectares of chardonnay and 2 hectares of shiraz, planted in five separate blocks. Most of the grapes are sold to Southcorp under contract, with a small amount made by contract winemaker Pat Tocaciu.

ŸŸŸŸ **Cabernet Sauvignon 2000** A fruit-driven, medium-bodied wine with a classic mix of blackcurrant, mulberry and blackberry; minimal oak and tannin inputs. **RATING** 88 **DRINK** 2010 $23

🐚 Eyre Creek

NR

PO Box 162, Auburn, SA 5451 **REGION** Clare Valley
T 0418 818 400 **F** (08) 8849 2266 **OPEN** Not
WINEMAKER Stephen John (Contract) **EST.** 1999
PRODUCT RANGE A range of varietally denominated table wines reflecting the plantings.
SUMMARY John Osborne established Auburn Vintners, the maker of Eyre Creek, in 1999 with 2 hectares of riesling, grenache, cabernet sauvignon and shiraz. The tiny output is sold by mail order and through limited wholesale distribution.

Faber Vineyard

★★★☆

233 Hadrill Road, Baskerville, WA 6056 (postal) **REGION** Swan Valley
T (08) 9296 0619 **F** (08) 9296 0681 **OPEN** Not
WINEMAKER John Griffiths **EST.** 1997 **CASES** 1000
PRODUCT RANGE ($12–40 ML) Verdelho, Chardonnay, Chardonnay Blanc de Blanc, Riche Shiraz, Shiraz, Reserve Shiraz, Shiraz Cabernet.
SUMMARY Former Houghton winemaker and now university lecturer and consultant John Griffiths has teamed with his wife Jane Micallef to found Faber Vineyard. Since 1997 they have established 1 hectare of shiraz, and 0.5 hectare each of chardonnay, verdelho, cabernet sauvignon, petit verdot and brown muscat. Says John Griffiths 'It may be somewhat quixotic, but I'm a great fan of traditional warm area Australia wine styles — those found in areas such as Rutherglen and the Barossa. Wines made in a relatively simple manner that reflect the concentrated ripe flavours one expects in these regions. And when one searches, some of these gems can be found from the Swan Valley.' Possessed of an excellent palate, and with an impeccable winemaking background, the quality of John Griffiths' wines is guaranteed. Unfortunately no Shiraz tasted recently.

♟♟♟♟ **Verdelho 2003 RATING** 86 **DRINK** 2008 $ 12

♟♟♟ **Chardonnay 2003 RATING** 83 $ 12

Fairview Wines

★★★☆

422 Elderslie Road, Branxton, NSW 2335 **REGION** Lower Hunter Valley
T (02) 4938 1116 **F** (02) 4938 1116 **OPEN** Fri–Mon 10–5, or by appointment
WINEMAKER Rhys Eather (Contract) **EST.** 1997 **CASES** 2000
PRODUCT RANGE ($16–25 CD) Semillon, Verdelho, Dolcezza Mia (dessert), Saignee, Shiraz.
SUMMARY Greg and Elaine Searles purchased the property on which they have established Fairview Wines in 1997. For the previous 90 years it had sustained an orchard, but since that time 2 hectares of shiraz, 1 hectare of each of barbera, semillon and 0.5 hectare of chambourcin and verdelho have been established, using organic procedures wherever possible. The Searles operate the cellar door in person; retail distribution in Sydney and exports to the UK have also been established. Accommodation (in a relocated church) is now also available.

♟♟♟♟ **Shiraz 2002** Medium-bodied; savoury/earthy regional overtones to black fruits; scores particularly well on the finish. **RATING** 89 **DRINK** 2010 $ 25

♟♟♟♟ **Dolcezza Mia 2003 RATING** 86 **DRINK** 2007 $ 20

♟♟♟ **Semillon 2003 RATING** 83 $ 18

Faisan Estate

NR

Amaroo Road, Borenore, NSW 2800 **REGION** Orange
T (02) 6365 2380 **OPEN** Not
WINEMAKER Col Walker **EST.** 1992 **CASES** 500
PRODUCT RANGE Semillon, Chardonnay, Canobolas Classic White, Pinot Noir, Britton's Block Cabernet Sauvignon, Cabernet Sauvignon.
SUMMARY Faisan Estate, within sight of Mount Canobolas and 20 kilometres west of the city of Orange, has been established by Trish and Col Walker. They now have almost 10 hectares of vineyards coming into bearing and have purchased grapes from other growers in the region in the interim.

Falls Wines ★★★

Belubula Way, Canowindra, NSW 2804 **REGION** Cowra
T (02) 6344 1293 **F** (02) 6344 1290 **OPEN** 7 days 10–4
WINEMAKER Jon Reynolds (Contract) **EST.** 1997 **CASES** 3200
PRODUCT RANGE ($16–24 CD) Semillon, Fields of Gold Chardonnay, Squatter's Ghost Shiraz, Merlot, Cabernet Merlot, Cabernet Sauvignon.
SUMMARY Peter and Zoe Kennedy have established Falls Vineyard and Retreat (to give it its full name) on the outskirts of Canowindra. They have planted chardonnay, semillon, merlot, cabernet sauvignon and shiraz, with a luxury bed and breakfast accommodation retreat offering large, internal spa baths, exercise facilities, fishing and a tennis court.

TTTT **Fields of Gold Chardonnay 2002** Rich, ripe, mouthfilling yellow peach/tropical fruits; doesn't cloy on the finish; good oak integration. Screwcap. **RATING** 87 **DRINK** 2007 $ 18
Squatter's Ghost Shiraz 2002 Pleasant, medium-bodied wine; well made in a ripe, traditional style, with integrated American oak. **RATING** 87 **DRINK** 2007 $ 24

TTTT **Cabernet Sauvignon 2002** **RATING** 86 **DRINK** 2007 $ 18
Semillon 2002 **RATING** 84 **DRINK** Now $ 16
Merlot 2002 **RATING** 84 **DRINK** Now $ 20

🦐 Faranda Wines NR

768 Wanneroo Road, Wanneroo, WA 6065 **REGION** Swan District
T (08) 9306 1174 **OPEN** Mon–Fri 9–5
WINEMAKER Basil Faranda
PRODUCT RANGE Shiraz, Grenache and a range of fortified wines.
SUMMARY Basil Faranda has 3 hectares of mixed wine and table grapes, planted to grenache, shiraz, muscat, chasselas, cardinal, italia, cannon hall. He makes the wine on-site, selling through local outlets and cellar door.

🦐 Farrawell Wines ★★★★★

60 Whalans Track, Lancefield, Vic 3435 **REGION** Macedon Ranges
T (03) 9817 5668 **F** (03) 9817 7215 **OPEN** Not
WINEMAKER Trefor Morgan, David Cowburn (Contract) **EST.** 2000 **CASES** 200
PRODUCT RANGE ($22–25 ML) Chardonnay, Pinot Noir.
SUMMARY Farrawell had a dream start to its commercial life when its 2001 Chardonnay was awarded the trophy for Best Chardonnay at the 2003 Macedon Ranges Wine Exhibition. Given that slightly less than 1 hectare each of chardonnay and pinot noir are the sole source of wines, production will always be limited, and in the low-yielding 2002 vintage produced only tiny amounts, so small they were not eligible to enter the Macedon Wine Show. Contract winemaker Trefor Morgan is the owner/winemaker of Mount Charlie Winery, perhaps better known as a Professor of Physiology at Melbourne University.

TTTTT **Chardonnay 2001** Fine and elegant; fruit-driven; nectarine, peach and melon; long, stylish finish. Trophy winner Macedon Ranges Wine Exhibition 2003 **RATING** 94
DRINK 2010 $ 22

Farmer's Daughter Wines ★★★☆

791 Cassilis Road, Mudgee, NSW 2850 **REGION** Mudgee
T (02) 6373 3177 **F** (02) 6373 3759 **OPEN** 7 days 9–5
WINEMAKER Joe Lesnik (Contract) **EST.** 1995 **CASES** 6000
PRODUCT RANGE ($17–22 CD) Reserve Semillon, Chardonnay, Late Harvest Semillon, Shiraz, Merlot, Cabernet Sauvignon, Farmer's Port.
SUMMARY The intriguingly named Farmer's Daughter Wines is a family-owned vineyard, run by the daughters of a feed-lot farmer, with contract winemaking by Joe Lesnik. Much of the production from the substantial vineyard of 23 hectares, dominated by shiraz with 13 hectares, the rest taken up with chardonnay, merlot, cabernet sauvignon, and semillon is sold to other winemakers. However, a sufficient amount to produce 6000 cases is retained and contract-made. As well as local retail distribution (and 7-day cellar-door sales) the wines are available through Porters liquor outlets in Sydney.

Farosa Estate

NR

1157 Port Wakefield Road, Waterloo Corner, SA 5110 (postal) **REGION** Adelaide Plains
T 0412 674 655 **F** (08) 8280 6450 **OPEN** Not
WINEMAKER Frank Perre (Contract) **EST.** 2000
PRODUCT RANGE Shiraz.
SUMMARY The family-owned Farosa Estate has 11 hectares of shiraz and 3.6 hectares of mourvedre (mataro) in production. The aim is to produce a full-bodied wine with the least amount of preservatives as possible, with open fermentation and oak maturation varying between 10 and 18 months. To date, contract winemaking has taken place in the Barossa Valley, but the family is contemplating building its own winery.

Farrell's Limestone Creek

NR

Mount View Road, Mount View, NSW 2325 **REGION** Lower Hunter Valley
T (02) 4991 2808 **F** (02) 4991 3414 **OPEN** 7 days 10–5
WINEMAKER Neil McGuigan (Contract) **EST.** 1980 **CASES** 3500
PRODUCT RANGE Semillon, Chardonnay, Shiraz, Merlot, Cabernet Sauvignon Merlot.
SUMMARY The Farrell family purchased 20 hectares on Mount View in 1980 and gradually established 7.3 hectares of vineyards planted to semillon, verdelho, chardonnay, shiraz, cabernet sauvignon and merlot. Most of the grapes are sold to McWilliam's, a lesser amount made for the cellar door and mail list orders.

Farr Rising

27 Maddens Road, Bannockburn, Vic 3331 (postal) **REGION** Geelong
T (03) 5281 1979 **F** (03) 5281 1979 **OPEN** Not
WINEMAKER Nicholas Farr **EST.** 2001 **CASES** 1500
PRODUCT RANGE ($29–35 R) Chardonnay, Saignee, Geelong Pinot Noir, Mornington Pinot Noir, Merlot.
SUMMARY Nicholas Farr is the son of Gary Farr, and with the full encouragement of his father, has launched his own brand. He has learnt his winemaking both in France and Australia, and has access to some excellent base material, hence the quality of the wines.

ΥΥΥΥΥ **Mornington Pinot Noir 2002** Fresh, fragrant, lively and tangy cherry aromas are mirrored in a long, vibrant and intense palate, with plum, cherry and spice; style and finesse. **RATING** 95 **DRINK** 2009 $ 34

Geelong Chardonnay 2002 A stylish, intense, complex yet subtle interplay of citrus/melon fruit and oak; great acidity. **RATING** 94 **DRINK** 2012 $ 34

Geelong Merlot 2002 Ultra-complex and fragrant; strongly reminiscent of right bank Bordeaux; wild herb, spices, multi-small berry fruits. Exhilarating. **RATING** 94 **DRINK** 2012 $ 34

ΥΥΥΥΥ **Geelong Pinot Noir 2002** A complex array of spice, plum, stem and forest aromas, then plum and spice to the fore in the mouth; nice oak. **RATING** 93 **DRINK** 2010 $ 34

ΥΥΥΥ **Saignee 2002** Salmon-tinged colour; quite complex strawberry, plum and spice flavours. **RATING** 87 **DRINK** Now $ 19.50

Felsberg Winery

116 Townsends Road, Glen Aplin, Qld 4381 **REGION** Granite Belt
T (07) 4683 4332 **F** (07) 4683 4377 **OPEN** 7 days 9–5
WINEMAKER Otto Haag **EST.** 1983 **CASES** 2000
PRODUCT RANGE ($13–20 CD) Riesling, Gewurztraminer, Sylvaner, White Classic, Chardonnay, Shiraz, Merlot, Cabernet Shiraz, Cabernet Sauvignon, Mead, Ruby Mead.
SUMMARY Felsberg has a spectacular site, high on a rocky slope, the winery itself built on a single huge boulder. It has been offering wine for sale via the cellar door (and mail list) made by former master brewer Otto Haag for many years; the red wines are the winery strength.

ΥΥΥΥ **Merlot 2002 RATING** 86 **DRINK** 2007 $ 20

ΥΥΥ **Shiraz 2002 RATING** 78

Fenton Views Winery ★★★☆

182 Fenton Hill Road, Clarkefield, Vic 3430 **REGION** Sunbury
T (03) 5428 5429 **F** (03) 5428 5304 **OPEN** Weekends 11–5, or by appointment
WINEMAKER David Spiteri **EST.** 1994 **CASES** 800
PRODUCT RANGE ($15–22 R) Chardonnay, Rose, Pinot Noir, Shiraz.
SUMMARY Situated on the north-facing slopes of Fenton Hill at Clarkefield, just northeast of Sunbury, the Hume and Macedon Ranges providing a spectacular and tranquil setting. It is a small family operation, with plantings of shiraz and chardonnay, followed by pinot noir and cabernet sauvignon. Co-owner David Spiteri studied winemaking at Charles Sturt University, and has had vintage experience both in Australia and California.

ŸŸŸŸŸ Pinot Noir 2002 Packed to the gills with ripe plum and cherry varietal fruit; will build complexity in the years ahead. **RATING** 90 **DRINK** 2008 $ 20

ŸŸŸŸ Shiraz 2001 Similar to the '02, but a fraction sweeter fruit albeit less spice. **RATING** 87 **DRINK** 2008 $ 22

ŸŸŸŸ Shiraz 2002 Ultra-spicy, extreme cool climate style; light to medium-bodied; Chinese food special. **RATING** 86 **DRINK** 2008 $ 22

Chardonnay 2002 RATING 85 **DRINK** Now $ 18

Ferguson Falls Estate NR

Pile Road, Dardanup, WA 6236 **REGION** Geographe
T (08) 9728 1083 **F** (08) 9728 1616 **OPEN** 11–5 weekends and publich holidays or by appointment
WINEMAKER David Crawford (Contract) **EST.** 1983 **CASES** 1000
PRODUCT RANGE Chardonnay, Cabernet Sauvignon.
SUMMARY Peter Giumelli and family are dairy farmers in the lush Ferguson Valley, 180 kilometres south of Perth. In 1983 they planted 3 hectares of cabernet sauvignon, chardonnay and merlot, making their first wines for commercial release from the 1995 and 1996 vintages which confirmed the suitability of the region for the production of premium wine. This in turn led to a doubling of the plantings, including 1 hectare of tempranillo and 0.6 hectare of nebbiolo.

Fergusson ★★★☆

Wills Road, Yarra Glen, Vic 3775 **REGION** Yarra Valley
T (03) 5965 2237 **F** (03) 5965 2405 **OPEN** 7 days 11–5
WINEMAKER Christopher Keyes, Peter Fergusson **EST.** 1968 **CASES** 5000
PRODUCT RANGE ($16–30 CD) There are two basic ranges: the lower-priced Tartan Range sourced from grapes grown outside the Yarra Valley, with Chardonnay, Pinot Noir, Shiraz, Cabernet Sauvignon, Fine Old Tawny Port; and the Estate Range with Victoria Chardonnay, Victoria Reserve Chardonnay, Sparkling Pinot Noir Chardonnay, LJK Pinot Noir, Jeremy Shiraz, Benjamyn Cabernet Sauvignon.
SUMMARY One of the very first Yarra wineries to announce the rebirth of the Valley, now best known as a favoured tourist destination, particularly for tourist coaches, and offering hearty fare in comfortable surroundings accompanied by wines of both Yarra and non-Yarra Valley origin. For this reason the limited quantities of its estate wines are often ignored, but should not be. Exports to the UK and New Zealand.

Fermoy Estate

Metricup Road, Wilyabrup, WA 6280 **REGION** Margaret River
T (08) 9755 6285 **F** (08) 9755 6251 **OPEN** 7 days 11–4.30
WINEMAKER Michael Kelly **EST.** 1985 **CASES** 25 000
PRODUCT RANGE ($17–35 CD) Semillon, Reserve Semillon, Sauvignon Blanc, Chardonnay, Merlot, Shiraz, Cabernet Sauvignon, Reserve Cabernet Sauvignon.
SUMMARY A long-established estate-based winery with 14 hectares of semillon, sauvignon blanc, chardonnay, cabernet sauvignon and merlot. A change of ownership several years ago seemed to

coincide with a distinct shift in style — and improvement in — the wines, notwithstanding the continuation of Michael Kelly as winemaker. Exports to the UK, Holland, Switzerland and the US.

ŸŸŸŸŸ **Chardonnay 2002** Tightly controlled barrel ferment inputs to the complex bouquet; fines up on the palate, with more fruit focus; excellent finish and aftertaste. **RATING** 93 **DRINK** 2010 $ 27

Fernbrook Estate Wines

NR

Bolganup Dam Road, Porongurup, WA 6324 **REGION** Porongurup
T (08) 9853 1030 **F** (08) 9853 1030 **OPEN** By appointment
WINEMAKER David McNamara **EST.** 1978
PRODUCT RANGE Gamay, Cabernet Sauvignon.
SUMMARY Run by Danuta Faulkner and Michelle Faulkner-Pearce, the Estate (formerly Bolganup Heritage Wines) has 4 hectares of cabernet sauvignon and gamay, and makes table, sparkling and organic wines under the Fernbrook Estate label. Exports to the UK, Germany and Sweden are the primary outlet; domestic sales by mail order and through the cellar door by appointment.

Ferngrove Vineyards

 ★★★★★

Ferngrove Road, Frankland, WA 6396 **REGION** Frankland
T (08) 9855 2378 **F** (08) 9855 2368 **OPEN** 7 days 10–4
WINEMAKER Kim Horton **EST.** 1997 **CASES** 20 000
PRODUCT RANGE ($13–40 R) Cossack Riesling, Sauvignon Blanc, Semillon Sauvignon Blanc, Chardonnay, Shiraz, Dragon Shiraz, King Malbec, Merlot, Cabernet Merlot, Majestic Cabernet Sauvignon. Leaping Lizard is Ferngrove's second label.
SUMMARY After 90 years of family beef and dairy farming heritage, Murray Burton decided to venture into premium grape growing and winemaking in 1997. Since that time he has moved with exceptional speed, establishing 414 hectares of grapes on three vineyards in the Frankland River subregion, and a fourth at Mount Barker. The operation centres around the Ferngrove Vineyard, where a large rammed-earth winery and tourist complex was built in 2000. Part of the vineyard production is sold as grapes; part sold as juice or must, part sold as finished wine; and part under the Ferngrove Vineyards own label.

ŸŸŸŸŸ **The Stirlings 2001** Stylish mix of red and black fruits, dark chocolate and fine, ripe tannins. High quality oak in the background. Very impressive Bordeaux style. **RATING** 95 **DRINK** 2016 $ 40
Leaping Lizard Semillon 2003 Lemony, juicy, minerally; clean as a whistle; great length and intensity. **RATING** 95 **DRINK** 2010 $ 15.99
Cossack Riesling 2003 A spotless, highly fragrant lime and mineral bouquet leads into a crisp, bone-dry palate, with great structure, length and finesse for the classicists. **RATING** 94 **DRINK** 2010 $ 23
Semillon Sauvignon Blanc 2003 Abundant flavour and richness throughout; really shines on finish, fresh but flavoursome. **RATING** 94 **DRINK** 2008 $ 13

ŸŸŸŸŸ **Dragon Shiraz 2001** Clean, ripe plum, blackberry and spice fruit; excellent structure, length and cool climate style. **RATING** 92 **DRINK** 2011 $ 24.95
King Malbec 2001 Dense colour; rich, very deep and concentrated black fruits, prune and spice; controlled extract. **RATING** 91 **DRINK** 2016 $ 24.95

ŸŸŸŸ **Riesling 2003** Mineral and citrus; light and fresh, still building character. **RATING** 89 **DRINK** Now $ 17.99
Majestic Cabernet Sauvignon 2001 Medium-bodied; blackberry and blackcurrant fruit with fine but persistent and slightly austere tannins. Needs time. **RATING** 89 **DRINK** 2013 $ 24.95
Cabernet Merlot 2002 Abundant, fresh red and black fruits drive the wine; no frills. **RATING** 87 **DRINK** 2008 $ 14.99

ŸŸŸŸ **Butterfly Chardonnay 2002 RATING** 85 **DRINK** Now $ 22.95
Shiraz 2002 RATING 85 **DRINK** 2007 $ 17.99

Fern Gully Winery

NR

63 Princes Highway, Termeil, NSW 2539 **REGION** Shoalhaven Coast
T (02) 4457 1124 **OPEN** Weekends and holidays 11–5.30 (except Winter)
WINEMAKER Max Staniford **EST.** 1996 **CASES** 350
PRODUCT RANGE ($15–20 CD) Chardonnay, Shiraz, Chambourcin, Cabernet Sauvignon, Vintage Port.
SUMMARY Glenda and Max Staniford planted 0.25 hectare each of chardonnay, shiraz, cabernet sauvignon and chambourcin in the 1996 and 1997 planting seasons, producing the first grapes in 1998. The wines are all estate-grown (hence the limited production) and all of the winemaking takes place on-site. The vineyard is enclosed in permanent netting, and hand picking the grapes ensures the exclusion of diseased fruit. The wines have won a number of silver and bronze medals at (unspecified) shows.

Fern Hill Estate

★★☆

Ingoldby Road, McLaren Flat, SA 5171 **REGION** McLaren Vale
T (08) 8383 0167 **F** (08) 8383 0107 **OPEN** 7 days 10–5 at Marienberg
WINEMAKER Peter Orr **EST.** 1975 **CASES** 5000
PRODUCT RANGE ($14–16 CD) Semillon, Chardonnay, Brut, Shiraz, Cabernet Sauvignon.
SUMMARY Fernhill Estate, along with Marienberg and Basedow, became part of the James Estate empire in 2003. The wines are made under the direction of Peter Orr and sold through the Marienberg cellar door.

Fighting Gully Road

NR

RMB 1315, Whorouly South, Vic 3735 **REGION** Beechworth
T (03) 5727 1434 **F** (03) 5727 1434 **OPEN** By appointment
WINEMAKER Mark Walpole **EST.** 1997
PRODUCT RANGE ($25 CD) Cabernet Merlot.
SUMMARY Mark Walpole (chief viticulturist for Brown Brothers) and partner Carolyn De Poi have begun the development of their Aquila Audax Vineyard, planting the first vines in 1997. It is situated between 530 and 580 metres above sea level, the upper eastern slopes planted to pinot noir and the warmer western slopes to cabernet sauvignon; there are also small quantities of tempranillo, sangiovese and merlot.

Fire Gully

★★★☆

Metricup Road, Wilyabrup, WA 6280 **REGION** Margaret River
T (08) 9755 6220 **F** (08) 9755 6308 **OPEN** By appointment
WINEMAKER Dr Michael Peterkin **EST.** 1988 **CASES** 5000
PRODUCT RANGE ($22–39 R) Semillon, Sauvignon Blanc Semillon, Pinot Noir, Shiraz, Merlot, Cabernet Sauvignon Merlot, Cabernet Sauvignon.
SUMMARY The Fire Gully vineyard (planted in 1988) has been established on what was progressively a dairy and then a beef farm, with a 15-acre lake created in the gully ravaged by bushfires which gave the property its name, and which is stocked with marron. In 1998 Mike Peterkin of Pierro purchased the property, and now manages the vineyard in conjunction with former owners Ellis and Margaret Butcher. He regards the Fire Gully wines as entirely separate to those of Pierro, being estate-grown, with just under 9 hectares planted to cabernet sauvignon, merlot, shiraz, semillon, sauvignon blanc, chardonnay and viognier. Exports to the US, Europe, Asia and Russia.

YYYY **Cabernet Sauvignon 2001** Opens in a savoury mode, offering more blackcurrant and herb fruit on the medium-bodied palate. **RATING** 87 **DRINK** 2009 **$** 39

YYYY **Sauvignon Blanc Semillon 2003** **RATING** 86 **DRINK** Now **$** 22

First Creek Wines

★★★★

Cnr McDonalds Road & Gillards Road, Pokolbin, NSW 2321 **REGION** Lower Hunter Valley
T (02) 4998 7293 **F** (02) 4998 7294 **OPEN** 7 days 9.30–5
WINEMAKER Greg Silkman, Jim Chatto **EST.** 1984 **CASES** 25 000

PRODUCT RANGE ($14.50–20 CD) At the bottom of the range comes the Three Degrees varietals and blends from various NSW regions. Next come the premium varietal range single region wines; a limited range of single vineyard Allanmere wines, and finally the Limited Release range of single vineyard wines with bottle age.

SUMMARY First Creek is the shopfront of Monarch Winemaking Services, which has acquired the former Allanmere wine business and offers a complex range of wines both under the First Creek and Allanmere labels. The quality is very reliable.

ΨΨΨΨΨ **Shiraz 2002** Substantial and complex blackberry, licorice, earth and spice flavours; controlled extract and tannins. **RATING** 90 **DRINK** 2012 $ 20

ΨΨΨΨ **Lightly Oaked Semillon 2003** The oak slightly fills out the structure, but is otherwise barely perceptible on a crisp herb, grass and lemon palate. Screwcap. **RATING** 89 **DRINK** 2007 $ 14.50
Cabernet Sauvignon 2002 Medium-bodied; clear-cut blackcurrant primary varietal fruit; good extract and length. Will develop well. **RATING** 89 **DRINK** 2012 $ 20
Durham Chardonnay 2002 A complex interplay of stone fruit and oak, layered and textured. **RATING** 88 **DRINK** Now $ 16
Shiraz 2001 Better fruit balance and flavour than many from the 2001 vintage, with blackberry fruit supported by good tannin and oak. **RATING** 88 **DRINK** 2011 $ 20
Durham Chardonnay 2003 Very ripe and sweet tropical and stone fruit mix; subtle oak; big wine. **RATING** 87 **DRINK** Now $ 16

ΨΨΨΨ **Pinot Noir 2002** Light to medium-bodied; savoury, with recognisable varietal character, but somehow lacks conviction. **RATING** 86 **DRINK** Now $ 20
Merlot 2002 **RATING** 86 **DRINK** 2008 $ 20
Verdelho 2003 **RATING** 84 **DRINK** Now $ 14.50
Allanmere Verdelho 2003 **RATING** 84 **DRINK** Now

5 Corners Wines ★★★

785 Henry Lawson Drive, Mudgee, NSW 2850 **REGION** Mudgee
T (02) 6373 3745 **F** (02) 6373 3749 **OPEN** 7 days 9.30–5
WINEMAKER Contract **EST.** 2001
PRODUCT RANGE ($14–25 CD) Traminer, Sauvignon Blanc, Chardonnay, Shiraz.
SUMMARY 5 Corners Wines came together in a hurry. Grant and Suzie Leonard came to Mudgee in 2001 for an overnight visit, and promptly fell in love with the region. So much so that they purchased a 40-hectare property with 5 hectares of established vineyard and a small cottage, which formed the basis for the venture. The property (40 hectares in all) now includes the family's house (five children and six dogs come and go), the original cottage (occupied by the vineyard manager), and plantings which have been increased by a further 3 hectares.

ΨΨΨΨ **Mudgee Sauvignon Blanc 2003** **RATING** 84 **DRINK** Now $ 17

🦢 Five Geese/Hillgrove Wines ★★★★☆

RSD 587 Chapel Hill Road, Blewitt Springs, SA 5171 (postal) **REGION** McLaren Vale
T (08) 8383 0576 **F** (08) 8383 0629 **OPEN** Not
WINEMAKER Mike Farmilo (Contract) **EST.** 1999 **CASES** 1000
PRODUCT RANGE ($17.50–24.50 ML) Shiraz, Grenache Shiraz.
SUMMARY Five Geese is produced by Hillgrove Wines, a partnership established between Sue Trott, Joanne Watt and Rob Sumner in July 1999. The wines come from 32 hectares of vines separately owned by Sue Trott, one vineyard planted in 1927, and the other in 1963. The grapes have been sold for many years to companies such as Southcorp and Orlando, but in 1999 Sue Trott took the decision to establish the partnership and make a strictly limited amount of wine from the pick of the vineyards.

ΨΨΨΨΨ **Five Geese McLaren Vale Shiraz 2002** A rich, smooth and velvety array of black fruits, dark chocolate and vanilla/mocha oak. Ripe tannins. Screwcap. **RATING** 93 **DRINK** 2017 $ 23

ΨΨΨΨ **Five Geese McLaren Vale Shiraz 2001** More red fruit flavours; medium-bodied, clean-cut mouthfeel; a certain elegance. **RATING** 89 **DRINK** 2011 $ 23

Five Oaks Vineyard ★★★

60 Aitken Road, Seville, Vic 3139 **REGION** Yarra Valley
T (03) 5964 3704 **F** (03) 5964 3064 **OPEN** Weekends and public holidays 10–5 and by appointment
WINEMAKER Wally Zuk **EST.** 1997 **CASES** 2000
PRODUCT RANGE ($15–45 CD) Riesling, Chardonnay, Merlot, Cabernet Sauvignon Merlot, Cabernet Sauvignon, SGS Cabernet Sauvignon.
SUMMARY Wally Zuk, together with wife Judy run all aspects of Five Oaks, far removed from Wally Zuk's background in nuclear physics. He has, however, completed his wine science degree at Charles Sturt University, and is thus more than qualified to make the Five Oaks wines.

ᵧᵧᵧᵧ **Cabernet Sauvignon 2001** Medium-bodied; clean, direct blackcurrant fruit plus a touch of cassis; good ripe tannin and oak management. **RATING** 88 **DRINK** 2011 $ 27

ᵧᵧᵧᵧ **Cabernet Merlot 2000 RATING** 86 **DRINK** 2007 $ 25
SGS Cabernet Sauvignon 2000 RATING 85 **DRINK** 2009 $ 45

572 Richmond Road ★★★★

572 Richmond Road, Cambridge, Tas 7170 (postal) **REGION** Southern Tasmania
T 0419 878 023 **F** (07) 3391 4565 **OPEN** Not
WINEMAKER Julian Alcorso (Contract) **EST.** 1994 **CASES** 450
PRODUCT RANGE ($20–25 ML) Riesling, Gewurztraminer, Chardonnay, Pinot Noir.
SUMMARY It hardly need be said 572 Richmond Road is both the address and the name of the vineyard. It is owned by John and Sue Carney, medical professionals, and is adjacent to Andrew Hood's winery, hence becoming part of a spectacular vineyard development with various ownerships but all situated close to the winery.

ᵧᵧᵧᵧ **Riesling 2003** Crammed with tropical flavour; softer than the usual style, but has plenty of attitude. **RATING** 89 **DRINK** 2009 $ 19

ᵧᵧᵧᵧ **Gewurztraminer 2003 RATING** 86 **DRINK** Now $ 21

Five Sons Estate ★★★☆

85 Harrison's Road, Dromana, Vic 3936 **REGION** Mornington Peninsula
T (03) 5987 3137 **F** (03) 5981 0572 **OPEN** By appointment
WINEMAKER Contract **EST.** 1998 **CASES** 600
PRODUCT RANGE ($18–28 ML) The wines come in two ranges: the entry point is The Boyz Pinot Noir and Cabernet Shiraz, the premium wines under the Five Sons Estate label.
SUMMARY Bob and Sue Peime purchased the most historically significant viticultural holding in the Mornington Peninsula in 1998. Development of the 68-hectare property began in the early 1930s, with the clearing of woodlands, and the planting of passionfruit. In the 1940s it was sold to a member of the Seppelt family, who took out the passionfruit vines and planted riesling in 1948. Two years later the property was sold to the Broadhurst family, close relatives of Doug Seabrook, who persisted with growing and making riesling until a 1967 bushfire destroyed the vines. Since 1998 10 hectares of pinot noir, 5 hectares of chardonnay, 2.5 hectares of shiraz and 1.2 hectares each of pinot gris and cabernet sauvignon have been planted. The first vintage was made in 2001, and the size and scope of the business will grow rapidly as the vines come into full bearing.

ᵧᵧᵧᵧ **Pinot Noir 2001** Light to medium-bodied, smooth and supple; sweet plummy fruit; easy style. **RATING** 88 **DRINK** Now $ 28

🦡 Flamsteed NR

9 Mellish Street, Beechworth, Vic 3747 **REGION** Beechworth
T 0412 475 328 **F** (03) 5728 1603 **OPEN** By appointment
WINEMAKER Will Flamsteed, Steve Flamsteed **EST.** 2002
PRODUCT RANGE Chardonnay, Shiraz.
SUMMARY Will Flamsteed, wife Sarah and brother Steve Flamsteed have established 3.25 hectares of chardonnay and shiraz, with Sarah Flamsteed filling the role of viticulturist. Sarah's parents, Di and

Pete Smith, established the first vineyard in Beechworth in 1978 with the encouragement of John Brown Jnr of Brown Brothers. Most of the production of the Smith's 2.5 hectares of chardonnay, cabernet sauvignon and merlot is now sold to Shadowfax but the remainder is being vinified by Di and Pete Smith and will (so it seems) be sold under the Flamsteed label, along with a Shiraz from Great Western.

Flinders Bay ★★★★

Davis Road, Witchcliffe, WA 6286 **REGION** Margaret River
T (08) 9757 6281 **F** (08) 9757 6353 **OPEN** Not
WINEMAKER Contract **EST.** 1995 **CASES** 10 000
PRODUCT RANGE ($16–20 R) Pericles Sauvignon Blanc Semillon, Dunsborough Hills Semillon Sauvignon Blanc, Verdelho, Chardonnay, Shiraz, Merlot, Dunsborough Hills Merlot Cabernet Sauvignon, Agincourt Cabernet Malbec Merlot.
SUMMARY Flinders Bay is a joint venture between the Gillespie and Ireland families. The Gillespies have been grape growers and viticultural contractors in the Margaret River region for over 20 years, while Bill and Noel Ireland were very prominent retailers in Sydney from 1979 to 1996. All in all, a potent and synergistic combination. Fifty hectares of vines were planted between 1995 and 1998 at Karridale, an extremely cool subregion (possibly the coolest in Western Australia) with the climate influenced by both the Indian and Southern Oceans. The wines presently being produced are blends of grapes from the northern and central parts of the Margaret River with estate-grown grapes. Ultimately, all of the wines will be estate-produced. The white wines are contract-made at Vasse Felix, which also provides the cellar-door facility for Flinders Bay. Exports to the US.

▼▼▼▼▼ **Shiraz 2001** Medium-bodied, but with great length. Redcurrant, raspberry, cherry, fine tannins and subtle oak. **RATING** 96 **DRINK** 2015 $ 20

▼▼▼▼▽ **Pericles Sauvignon Blanc Semillon 2003** Highly aromatic herb, grass, spice and asparagus aromas and flavours; excellent intensity and length. **RATING** 93 **DRINK** 2007 $ 16
Pericles Sauvignon Blanc Semillon 2003 Clean, crisp, incisive aromas; delicate rather than powerful; perfect balance, good length. **RATING** 90 **DRINK** 2007 $ 16

▼▼▼▼ **Cabernet Sauvignon 2002** Medium-bodied; some fruit sweetness to balance the dusty cabernet varietal character; subtle oak. **RATING** 89 **DRINK** 2010 $ 20
Chardonnay 2003 Elegant citrus and stone fruit; no frills, but good flavour and balance. **RATING** 88 **DRINK** 2007 $ 15.99

▼▼▼▽ **Verdelho 2003 RATING** 85 **DRINK** Now $ 16
Merlot 2002 RATING 85 **DRINK** 2007 $ 15.99

Flint's of Coonawarra ★★★★

PO Box 8, Coonawarra, SA 5263 **REGION** Coonawarra
T (08) 8736 5046 **F** (08) 8736 5146 **OPEN** Not
WINEMAKER Bruce Gregory (Contract) **EST.** 2000 **CASES** 700
PRODUCT RANGE ($23 ML) Gammon's Crossing Cabernet Sauvignon; Rostrevor Shiraz, Cabernet Sauvignon, Merlot.
SUMMARY Six generations of the Flint family have lived and worked in Coonawarra since 1840. Damian Flint and his family began the development of 21 hectares of cabernet sauvignon, shiraz and merlot in 1989, but it was not until 2000 that they decided to keep a small portion of cabernet sauvignon back and have it contract-made by Bruce Gregory at Majella, which is owned by their lifelong friends the Lynn brothers. Ten tonnes (around 700 cases) were vinified, and the wine had immediate show success in Melbourne; another 10 tonnes were diverted from the 2001 vintage, and the first wines were released in 2003.

▼▼▼▼▽ **Gammon's Crossing Cabernet Sauvignon 2001** Medium-bodied; pleasantly ripe cassis fruit with deft oak handling; elegance and line. **RATING** 90 **DRINK** 2010 $ 23

Fluted Cape Vineyard ★★★☆

28 Groombridge Road, Kettering, Tas 7155 **REGION** Southern Tasmania
T (03) 6267 4262 **OPEN** 7 days 10–5
WINEMAKER Andrew Hood (Contract) **EST.** 1993 **CASES** 170
PRODUCT RANGE ($12–25 CD) Unwooded Chardonnay, Chardonnay, Pinot Noir.
SUMMARY For many years Val Dell was the senior wildlife ranger on the central plateau of Tasmania, his wife Jan running the information centre at Liawenee. I met them there on trout fishing expeditions, staying in one of the park huts. They have now retired to the Huon Valley region, having established 0.25 hectare each of pinot noir and chardonnay overlooking Kettering and Bruny Island, said to be a spectacularly beautiful site, which I wouldn't doubt. The high quality wines are made for them by Andrew Hood and are sold from the cellar door, and through Hartzview Cellars in Gardners Bay.

Flying Fish Cove ★★★★★

Lot 125 Caves Road, Wilyabrup, WA 6284 (postal) **REGION** Margaret River
T (08) 9755 6688 **F** (08) 9755 6788 **OPEN** 7 days 11–5
WINEMAKER David Watson **EST.** 2001 **CASES** 10 000
PRODUCT RANGE An array of varietal wines at various prices with Upstream Reserve and Prize Catch at the top.
SUMMARY Flying Fish Cove's major activity is that of a large contract winemaking facility for Margaret River (and other) vignerons. A skilled winemaking team and a high-tech winery is producing a stream of excellent wines (chiefly red) across a range of price points both for its own label and for others.

▼▼▼▼▼ **Margaret River Shiraz 2002** Abounding with black cherry, blackberry fruit, ripe tannins, it is silky smooth and long. **RATING** 94 **DRINK** 2012 $ 16
Upstream Reserve Cabernet Sauvignon 2001 Crammed with cassis/blackcurrant fruit, but not jammy/heavy; clean, medium-bodied; soft, ripe, fine tannins. **RATING** 94 **DRINK** 2016 $ 25
Prize Catch Cabernet Sauvignon 2001 Great colour; superb varietal character; rich, not overripe, blackcurrant fruit; fine tannins. Screwcap. **RATING** 94 **DRINK** 2012 $ 65

▼▼▼▼▽ **Margaret River Cabernet Sauvignon 2002** Powerful and solid; abundant black fruit supported by plenty of tannins; very age-worthy. **RATING** 91 **DRINK** 2017 $ 18
Cabernet Shiraz 2002 Medium to full-bodied; generous, supple mouthfilling dark fruits; dense extract and oak. **RATING** 90 **DRINK** 2012

▼▼▼▼ **Upstream Reserve Chardonnay 2001** Elegant, light to medium-bodied; ripe stone fruit and cashew/creamy notes. **RATING** 89 **DRINK** 2007 $ 22
Upstream Reserve Shiraz 2001 Powerful, chunky, savoury, chocolatey flavours; robust and briary. **RATING** 89 **DRINK** 2016 $ 25

▼▼▼▽ **Pinot Chardonnay 2001 RATING** 86 **DRINK** Now $ 22
Sparkling Shiraz 1999 RATING 86 **DRINK** 2007 $ 25
Semillon Sauvignon Blanc 2003 RATING 84 **DRINK** Now $ 22
The Italian Job 2002 RATING 84 **DRINK** Now $ 22.90

▼▼▼ **Chenin Blanc 2003 RATING** 83 $ 16

Foate's Ridge ★★★

241 Fordwich Road, Broke, NSW 2330 (postal) **REGION** Lower Hunter Valley
T (02) 6579 1284 **F** (02) 9922 4397 **OPEN** Not
WINEMAKER Steve Dodd (Contract) **EST.** 1992 **CASES** 1000
PRODUCT RANGE ($15.95–18.95 ML) Verdelho, Merlot, Cabernet Sauvignon.
SUMMARY The Foate family, headed by Tony Foate, has planted a total of 10 hectares of chardonnay (4 hectares) and verdelho, merlot and cabernet sauvignon (2 hectares each) between 1992 and 2001 on the 36-hectare property purchased in 1991. The soils are the typical light alluvial loam of the region, which promote vigorous vine growth and generous yields, yields which need to be controlled if

quality is to be maximised. Using a Scott Henry trellis, bunch thinning and fewer spur positions have been utilised to reduce the 15 tonne per hectare yields down to 10 tonnes per hectare.

ŸŸŸŸ **Merlot 2003** Light to medium-bodied; clean, fresh red berry fruits; attractive, early drinking. **RATING** 86 **DRINK** Now $16.95

ŸŸŸ **Verdelho 2003 RATING** 83 $15.95

Fonty's Pool Vineyards ★★★★

Seven Day Road, Manjimup, WA 6258 **REGION** Pemberton
T (08) 9777 0777 **F** (08) 9777 0788 **OPEN** 7 days 10–4.30
WINEMAKER Eloise Jarvis **EST.** 1998 **CASES** 20 000
PRODUCT RANGE ($16–20.75 R) Sauvignon Blanc Semillon, Viognier, Chardonnay, Pinot Noir, Shiraz.
SUMMARY This is a joint venture between Cape Mentelle (which makes the wine) and Fonty's Pool Farm. The Fonty's Pool vineyards are part of the original farm owned by pioneer settler Archie Fontanini, who was granted land by the government in 1907. In the early 1920s a large dam was created to provide water for the intensive vegetable farming which was part of the farming activities. The dam became known as Fonty's Pool and to this day remains a famous local landmark and recreational facility. The first grapes were planted in 1989, and at 110 hectares, the vineyard is now one of the region's largest, supplying grapes to a number of leading West Australian wineries. An increasing amount of the production is used for Fonty's Pool, which has now established an on-site cellar door. Exports to the UK and Europe supplement domestic distribution by Moet Hennessy.

ŸŸŸŸŸ **Viognier 2002** Spicy varietal character and controlled oak; thickens momentarily before freshening up on the finish; judicious oak; very stylish. **RATING** 92 **DRINK** 2007 $20.75
Merlot 2001 Strong colour; attractive, ripe blackcurrant/plum/spice flavours; good tannin structure. **RATING** 91 **DRINK** 2011 $20.75

ŸŸŸŸ **Sauvignon Blanc Semillon 2003** Crisp, mineral and passionfruit aromas and flavours; neat finish. **RATING** 87 **DRINK** Now $16

🍇 Fordwich Estate NR

185 Fordwich Road, Broke, NSW 2330 **REGION** Lower Hunter Valley
T (02) 6579 1197 **F** (02) 6579 1197 **OPEN** Not
WINEMAKER Contract **EST.** 1990
PRODUCT RANGE Verdelho, Chardonnay, Merlot.
SUMMARY Warren Moore has 10 hectares of chardonnay, verdelho and merlot in the Broke Fordwich subregion of the Hunter Valley. Part of the production is contract-made, and sold principally by mail order.

🍇 Forester Estate ★★★★☆

Lot 11 Wildwood Road, Yallingup, WA 6282 **REGION** Margaret River
T (08) 9755 2788 **F** (08) 9755 2766 **OPEN** By appointment
WINEMAKER Kevin McKay, Michael Langridge **EST.** 2001 **CASES** 7000
PRODUCT RANGE ($17–28 R) Sauvignon Blanc, Semillon Sauvignon Blanc, Chardonnay, Shiraz, Cabernet Merlot, Cabernet Sauvignon.
SUMMARY The Forester Estate business partners are Kevin McKay, who began the development of Abbey Vale Vineyards in 1986 (remaining with it for 12 months after its sale in 2001) and Redmond Sweeny, a chartered accountant. Winemaker Michael Langridge has a Bachelor of Arts (hons) degree in Psychology and a near-completed Bachelor of Applied Science (Wine Science, Charles Sturt) degree. Bill McKay says 'he is the most over-qualified fork-lift driver in Australia'. Langridge also has six vintages in the Margaret River region under his belt. Together they have built and designed a 500-tonne winery, half devoted to contract winemaking, the other half for the Forester Estate label. Part of the intake comes from the 4.5-hectare estate plantings of sauvignon blanc, cabernet and shiraz, the remainder from nearby growers, one of whom is the operating viticulturist at Forester Estate.

ŸŸŸŸŸ **Shiraz 2002** High-toned, fragrant red and black fruit aromas; an intense palate; black cherry and a nice touch of oak; particularly long finish. 175 cases made. **RATING** 93 **DRINK** 2012 $28

Cabernet Sauvignon 2002 Quite fragrant cassis aromas; powerful, pure cabernet varietal blackcurrant and cassis fruit; good oak, lingering tannins. **RATING** 92 **DRINK** 2012 $ 24.50
Sauvignon Blanc 2003 Clean, floral, crisp herbaceous aromas; intense and powerful, with zesty herb and gooseberry flavours. **RATING** 90 **DRINK** Now $ 20

ᵀᵀᵀᵀ **Cabernet Sauvignon 2001** Blackcurrant/cassis and raspberry fruit; deft use of French oak; good intensity and length; ripe tannins. **RATING** 89 **DRINK** 2011 $ 24.50
Semillon Sauvignon Blanc 2003 Soft, sweet, gently tropical fruit; good depth, sustained through to a long finish. **RATING** 88 **DRINK** Now $ 17
Cabernet Merlot 2002 Pure, clean cassis, redcurrant, raspberry and mint; fruit-driven; fine tannins. **RATING** 88 **DRINK** 2010 $ 17
Shiraz 2001 Spotlessly clean; light to medium-bodied; fine, black cherry spice and cinnamon fruit; fine tannins. **RATING** 87 **DRINK** 2008 $ 28

ᵀᵀᵀᵞ **Chardonnay 2002** **RATING** 86 **DRINK** 2007 $ 22

Forest Hill Vineyard ★★★☆

South Coast Highway, Denmark, WA 6333 **REGION** Mount Barker
T(08) 9381 2911 **F**(08) 9381 2955 **OPEN** 7 days 10–5
WINEMAKER Larry Cherubino, Andrew Marks **EST.** 1966 **CASES** 20 000
PRODUCT RANGE ($14–21 CD) Riesling, Sauvignon Blanc Semillon, Chardonnay, Late Harvest Riesling, Shiraz, Cabernet Sauvignon.
SUMMARY This is one of the oldest 'new' winemaking operations in Western Australia, and was the site for the first grape plantings for the Great Southern region in 1966 on a farming property owned by the Pearce family. The Forest Hill brand became well-known, aided by the fact that a 1975 Riesling made by Sandalford from Forest Hill grapes won 9 trophies in national wine shows. In 1997 the property was acquired by interests associated with Perth stockbroker Tim Lyons, and a program of renovation and expansion of the vineyards commenced. A new winery near Denmark was completed in time for the 2003 vintage, and a new cellar door opened in September 2004.

ᵀᵀᵀᵀ **Riesling 2002** Complex wine, seemingly showing some botrytis influence, which, while adding to the total impact, has also hastened the development somewhat. **RATING** 87
DRINK Now $ 16

Fox Creek Wines ★★★★

Malpas Road, Willunga, SA 5172 **REGION** McLaren Vale
T(08) 8556 2403 **F**(08) 8556 2104 **OPEN** 7 days 10–5
WINEMAKER Chris Dix, Tony Walker **EST.** 1995 **CASES** 35 000
PRODUCT RANGE ($12–70 CD) Semillon Sauvignon Blanc, Sauvignon Blanc, Verdelho, Chardonnay, Vixen (Sparkling Red), Shadow's Run Shiraz Cabernet, Grenache Shiraz, Short Row Shiraz, Reserve Shiraz, Reserve Merlot, Fox and Hounds Shiraz Cabernet Sauvignon, JSM Shiraz Cabernet Franc, Duet Cabernet Merlot, Reserve Cabernet Sauvignon.
SUMMARY Fox Creek has made a major impact since coming on-stream late in 1995. It is the venture of a group of distinguished Adelaide doctors (three are professors), with particular input from the Watts family, which established the vineyard back in 1985. The Reserve red wines, and especially the Reserve Shiraz, are outstanding and have enjoyed considerable show success. As well as comprehensive distribution throughout Australia, the wines are exported to the UK, the US, Canada, Germany, Switzerland, Denmark, Belgium, New Zealand and Thailand.

ᵀᵀᵀᵀᵞ **Short Row Shiraz 2002** Rich and concentrated; abundant blackberry fruit, a touch of vanilla oak, balanced tannins. **RATING** 92 **DRINK** 2015 $ 26
Reserve Shiraz 2002 Densely coloured; rich, plush blackberry, dark chocolate and vanilla; good balance in epic style. **RATING** 92 **DRINK** 2017 $ 70

ᵀᵀᵀᵀ **JSM 2002** Densely coloured; regional black fruits and bitter chocolate; soft tannins to close. **RATING** 89 **DRINK** 2012 $ 22
Shadow's Run Shiraz Cabernet 2002 Bursting with fresh, ripe fruit in very different style to usual; early drinking. **RATING** 89 **DRINK** 2008 $ 12

Duet Cabernet Merlot 2002 Solidly ripe, slightly chunky black fruits with the usual dash of regional dark chocolate. **RATING** 88 **DRINK** 2012 $19

Vixen NV The balance and dosage are better than usual (not too sweet), shiraz and cabernet franc work well together. **RATING** 87 **DRINK** 2007 $22

Foxeys Hangout ★★★☆

795 White Hill Road, Red Hill, Vic 3937 **REGION** Mornington Peninsula
T 0402 117 104 **F** (03) 9809 0495 **OPEN** Not
WINEMAKER Tony Lee **EST.** 1998 **CASES** 3000
PRODUCT RANGE ($13.50–24.50 ML) Pinot Gris, Cordon Cut Pinot Gris, Chardonnay, Rose, Pinot Noir.
SUMMARY Brothers Michael and Tony Lee spent 20 years in the hospitality industry, acquiring a considerable knowledge of wine through the selection of wine lists for two decades, opting for a change of lifestyle and occupation when they planted 2.2 hectares of pinot noir, 2 hectares of chardonnay and 0.5 hectare of pinot gris on the northeast-facing slopes of an old farm. The name (and the catchy label) stems from the true tale of two Mornington Peninsula fox hunters who began a competition with each other in 1936, hanging their kills on the branches of an ancient eucalypt tree to keep count. The corpses have gone, but not the nickname for the area in which the vineyard is planted.

ＹＹＹＹＹ **Pinot Noir 2001** Fragrant, spicy, sappy varietal aromas; light-bodied and elegant; good length is a feature. **RATING** 90 **DRINK** Now $20

ＹＹＹＹ **Pinot Gris 2003** Made from very late-harvested grapes; relatively delicate, sweet, fresh fruit with overtones of spice and honey works quite well. **RATING** 87 **DRINK** Now $17.50

ＹＹＹＹ **Pinot Gris 2001** **RATING** 86 **DRINK** Now $17.50
Chardonnay 2001 **RATING** 84 **DRINK** Now $24

Francois Jacquard

14 Neil Street, Osborne Park, WA 6017 **REGION** Perth Hills
T (08) 9380 9199 **F** (08) 9380 9199 **OPEN** Not
WINEMAKER Francois Jacquard **EST.** 1997 **CASES** 2000
PRODUCT RANGE ($17–42 R) Long Jetty Seafood Reserve Semillon Sauvignon Blanc; Terra Dura Millennium Collection Viognier, Reserve Collection Chardonnay, Millennium Collection Shiraz, De Beaux Vineyards Shiraz Viognier; Duyfken 1606 Replica Cabernet Sauvignon.
SUMMARY Francois (Franky) Jacquard graduated from Dijon University in 1983. He worked that vintage as a cellar hand at Domaine Dujac, then came to Australia for Bannockburn in 1985. Between then and 1992 he worked in both the northern and southern hemispheres, before moving back to become chief winemaker at Chittering Estate in the Perth Hills in 1992, a position he held until 1997 when he established his own brand. He does not have vineyards of his own, leasing one in the Chittering Valley, and having a long-term purchase arrangement with another. He now makes the wines at the new Sitella Winery in the Swan Valley. As Franky Jacquard himself recognises, the style of his wines is most definitely not mainstream Australian. He is much more interested in texture and longevity than primary fruit flavour, and is quite relaxed about a degree of controlled oxidation in his white wine making. The rating reflects previous extensive tastings.

Frankland Estate

Frankland Road, Frankland, WA 6396 **REGION** Frankland
T (08) 9855 1544 **F** (08) 9855 1549 **OPEN** By appointment
WINEMAKER Barrie Smith, Judi Cullam **EST.** 1988 **CASES** 15 000
PRODUCT RANGE ($15–34.50 R) Under the Isolation Ridge label are Riesling, Chardonnay, Shiraz, Cabernet Sauvignon; Rivermist range of Riesling, Shiraz, Cabernets; Olmo's Reward (Bordeaux-blend) is the flagbearer; also Cooladerra Vineyard Riesling and Poison Hill Vineyard Riesling.
SUMMARY A significant Frankland River operation, situated on a large sheep property owned by Barrie Smith and Judi Cullam. The 29-hectare vineyard has been established progressively since 1988, and a winery was built on the site for the 1993 vintage. The recent introduction of an array of single vineyard Rieslings has been a highlight, and all the wines are energetically promoted and

marketed by Judi Cullam. Frankland Estate has held several important International Riesling tastings and seminars over recent years. Murphy has intervened to prevent inclusion of tasting notes for the 2003 Rieslings. Exports to the US, Canada, the UK, Belgium, Switzerland, Denmark, Singapore and Japan.

▼▼▼▼ **Olmo's Reward 2000** A medium-bodied but complex array of secondary/spicy/savoury fruit flavours; pleasantly drying tannins to close. **RATING** 87 **DRINK** 2010 $ 34.50

🐦 Frazer Woods Wines ★★☆

c/- Post Office, Yallingup, WA 6282 **REGION** Margaret River
T (08) 9755 6274 **F** (08) 9755 6295 **OPEN** Not
WINEMAKER Various contract **EST.** 1996 **CASES** 1000
PRODUCT RANGE ($25–27 R) Pinot Chardonnay Sparkling, Sparkling Shiraz, Sparkling White Shiraz, Shiraz.
SUMMARY John Frazer has set up a contract sparkling wine business, called the Champagne Shed, although the winemaking is done off-site. He makes the Frazer Woods own wines from 2 hectares of estate-grown shiraz, the white grapes for the Pinot Chardonnay Sparkling being bought in. The wines are sold through the Margaret River Wine Cellars and Witchcliffe Liquor Store.

▼▼▼▼ **Shiraz 2001** Marked oak aromas; medium-bodied vanilla and blackberry flavours; good length and depth; soft tannins. **RATING** 87 **DRINK** 2011 $ 25

▼▼▼▽ **Shiraz 2002** **RATING** 84 **DRINK** 2007 $ 25

▼▼▼ **Pinot Chardonnay NV** **RATING** 83 $ 27
Sparkling Shiraz 2001 **RATING** 80 $ 25

Freycinet ★★★★★

15919 Tasman Highway via Bicheno, Tas 7215 **REGION** Southern Tasmania
T (03) 6257 8574 **F** (03) 6257 8454 **OPEN** 7 days 9.30–4.30
WINEMAKER Claudio Radenti, Lindy Bull, Paula Kloosterman (Assistant) **EST.** 1980 **CASES** 5000
PRODUCT RANGE ($22–55 CD) Riesling, Schonburger Riesling, Chardonnay, Radenti (Methode Champenoise), Pinot Noir, Cabernet Merlot.
SUMMARY The original 9-hectare Freycinet vineyards are beautifully situated on the sloping hillsides of a small valley. The soils are podsol and decaying granite with a friable clay subsoil, and the combination of aspect, slope, soil and heat summation produce red grapes of unusual depth of colour and ripe flavours. One of Australia's foremost producers of Pinot Noir, with a wholly enviable track record of consistency — rare with such a temperamental variety. Exports to the UK, Hong Kong and The Netherlands.

▼▼▼▼▼ **Pinot Noir 2002** Strong red-purple; complex plum, spice/mace/nutmeg aromas; floods the mouth with varietal fruit; excellent structure. **RATING** 95 **DRINK** 2010 $ 62
Riesling 2003 Intense spicy/minerally aromas lead into a super-intense, long, lemony/minerally palate, with a lingering crisp and dry finish. A cellaring special.
RATING 94 **DRINK** 2013 $ 21

▼▼▼▼▽ **Louis Unwooded Chardonnay 2003** Nectarine and peach; excellent texture, flavour, length and balance. **RATING** 92 **DRINK** 2008 $ 18
Chardonnay 2002 Light to medium-bodied; melon, cashew and creamy malolactic influences; well-balanced oak. **RATING** 90 **DRINK** 2010 $ 30

🐦 Frog Island ★★★★

PO Box 423, Kingston SE, SA 5275 **REGION** Limestone Coast Zone
T (08) 8768 5000 **F** (08) 8768 5008 **OPEN** Not
WINEMAKER Sarah Squire **EST.** 2003 **CASES** 3500
PRODUCT RANGE ($15–18 R) Chardonnay, Sparkling Red, Shiraz, Cabernet Sauvignon.
SUMMARY Sarah Squire (nee Fowler) has decided to do her own thing, with full support from father Ralph. The quixotic name is taken from a small locality inland from the seaside town of Robe, and the wine is deliberately made in a fresh, fruit-forward style.

ᵀᵀᵀᵀ♈ **Shiraz 2001** Powerful, rich, blackberry and dark chocolate; good tannin extract and structure. **RATING** 93 **DRINK** 2012 $18

ᵀᵀᵀᵀ **Chardonnay 2003** Fresh, lively, citrus and melon; plenty of back palate flavour and good length. Screwcap. **RATING** 88 **DRINK** 2007 $20

ᵀᵀᵀ♈ **Cabernet 2001 RATING** 84 **DRINK** 2008 $18

Frogmore Creek ★★★★★

Brinktop Road, Penna, Tas 7171 **REGION** Southern Tasmania
T (03) 6224 6788 **F** (03) 6224 6788 **OPEN** Not
WINEMAKER Andrew Hood (Contract) **EST.** 1997
PRODUCT RANGE Riesling, Traminer, Chardonnay, Iced Riesling, Pinot Noir, Reserve Pinot Noir.
SUMMARY Frogmore Creek is a Pacific Rim joint venture, the two owners being Tony Scherer of Tasmania, and Jack Kidwiler of California. They have commenced the establishment of the only organically certified commercial vineyard in Tasmania, and plan to take the area under vine to 80 hectares over the next 3 to 5 years. An on-site winery will be constructed in three stages over the next 2 years, with Andrew Hood undertaking the winemaking in the interim. When completed, the development will offer visitor centre and cellar-door sales area; an environmental centre with walking trails and lakeside picnic areas; an organic garden; and a restaurant, accommodation and event facilities. The name, incidentally, is taken from the creek which runs through the property. In late 2003 the Frogmore Creek owners acquired the Wellington wine business of Andrew Hood, and for the forseeable future will run the two operations in tandem, handling all organically-grown fruit at the new Frogmore Creek winery, and the remainder at the existing Wellington winery. The brand made a dramatic debut at the 2004 Tasmanian Wines Show with its Reserve Pinot Noir winning the trophy for Best Wine of Show.

ᵀᵀᵀᵀᵀ **Reserve Pinot Noir 2002** Complex and rich, abundant and opulent plummy fruit; good oak and extract. Outstanding wine. **RATING** 96 **DRINK** 2011

Frog Rock ★★★☆

Cassilis Road, Mudgee, NSW 2850 **REGION** Mudgee
T (02) 6372 2408 **F** (02) 6372 6924 **OPEN** 7 days 10–5
WINEMAKER Simon Gilbert, David Lowe (Contract) **EST.** 1973 **CASES** 20 000
PRODUCT RANGE ($14–25 CD) Creek range of Chardonnay, Shiraz, Cabernet Sauvignon; Frog Rock range of Old Vine Semillon, Chardonnay, Rose, Chambourcin, Merlot, Old Vine Shiraz, Old Vine Cabernet Sauvignon; Premium Chardonnay, Shiraz, Cabernet Sauvignon.
SUMMARY Frog Rock is the former Tallara Vineyard, established over 30 years ago by leading Sydney chartered accountant Rick Turner. There are now 60 hectares of vineyard, with 22 hectares each of shiraz and cabernet sauvignon, and much smaller plantings of chardonnay, semillon, merlot, petit verdot and chambourcin. Exports to the UK, the US, Canada, Singapore, Malaysia and Hong Kong.

ᵀᵀᵀᵀ♈ **Old Vine Semillon 2003** Classic young Semillon; herb, stone and lanolin; already building character. **RATING** 91 **DRINK** 2009 $18

ᵀᵀᵀᵀ **Premium Chardonnay 2002** Good depth and focus; stone fruit and a whisper of oak; plenty of presence. **RATING** 89 **DRINK** Now $20
Old Vine Cabernet Sauvignon 2001 Light to medium-bodied; some sweet berry/cassis on the back palate; clean finish. **RATING** 88 **DRINK** 2009 $25
Old Vine Cabernet Sauvignon 2000 Spicy, savoury, multi-flavoured earthy blackberry and blackcurrant; pleasing texture and persistence. **RATING** 88 **DRINK** 2010 $25
Merlot 2003 Bright colour; fresh, clean and vibrant red fruits; simple, early-drinking style. **RATING** 87 **DRINK** Now $22

ᵀᵀᵀᵀ **Rose 2003 RATING** 86 **DRINK** Now $18
Old Vine Shiraz 2001 RATING 86 **DRINK** 2009 $25
Merlot 2002 Again, a wine with attitude; a mix of olive, chocolate and savoury berry fruit; nice tannins. **RATING** 86 **DRINK** 2007 $22

Frogspond

NR

400 Arthurs Seat Road, Red Hill, Vic 3937 **REGION** Mornington Peninsula
T (03) 5989 2941 **F** (03) 9824 7659 **OPEN** By appointment
WINEMAKER David Lloyd **EST.** 1994 **CASES** 190
PRODUCT RANGE ($36–40 R) Chardonnay, Pinot Noir.
SUMMARY The Nelson family has established 2 hectares of chardonnay and pinot noir on an ideal
north-facing slope. The low yields produce grapes with intense fruit flavours, but only a tiny amount
of wine is made, sold primarily by mail order.

Fyffe Field

★★★

1417 Murray Valley Highway, Yarrawonga, Vic 3730 **REGION** Goulburn Valley
T (03) 5748 4282 **F** (03) 5748 4284 **OPEN** 7 days 10–5
WINEMAKER Contract **EST.** 1993 **CASES** 1300
PRODUCT RANGE ($11–15 CD) Verdelho, Late Harvest Semillon, Shiraz, Byramine Classic Red, Merlot,
Cabernet Sauvignon, Tokay, Muscat, Tawny Snort.
SUMMARY Fyffe Field has been established by Graeme and Liz Diamond near the Murray River
between Cobram and Yarrawonga in a mudbrick and leadlight tasting room opposite an historic
homestead. They have 2 hectares of shiraz, 1 hectare each of semillon, verdelho, merlot and cabernet
sauvignon, and 0.5 hectare each of touriga and petit verdot. A highlight is the ornamental pig
collection, a display set up long before Babe was born.

Gabriel's Paddocks Vineyard

NR

Deasys Road, Pokolbin, NSW 2320 **REGION** Lower Hunter Valley
T (02) 4998 7650 **F** (02) 4998 7603 **OPEN** Thurs–Mon 9–5
WINEMAKER Contract **EST.** 1979
PRODUCT RANGE Chenin Blanc, Chardonnay, Pinot Noir, Shiraz, Cabernet Merlot.
SUMMARY Formerly Sutherlands Wines, Gabriel's Paddocks is as much about general tourism and small
conference accommodation as it is about wine production, with two separate buildings able to
accommodate more than 20 people. The 13.6-hectare vineyards are planted to chardonnay, chenin blanc,
pinot noir, merlot, shiraz and cabernet sauvignon; the wines from these varieties are all contract-made.

Galafrey

★★★

Quangellup Road, Mount Barker, WA 6324 **REGION** Mount Barker
T (08) 9851 2022 **F** (08) 9851 2324 **OPEN** 7 days 10–5
WINEMAKER Ian Tyrer **EST.** 1977 **CASES** 10 000
PRODUCT RANGE ($12–50 CD) Riesling, Muller, Semillon Sauvignon Blanc, Chardonnay, Unoaked
Chardonnay, Reserve Botrytis Riesling, Pinot Noir, Shiraz, Merlot, Cabernet Sauvignon, Reserve
Cabernet Sauvignon, Tawny Port; Art Label Semillon Sauvignon Blanc, Shiraz.
SUMMARY Relocated to a new purpose-built but utilitarian winery after previously inhabiting the
exotic surrounds of the old Albany wool store, Galafrey makes wines with plenty of robust, if not
rustic, character, drawing grapes in the main from nearly 13 hectares of estate plantings at Mount
Barker. Exports to Belgium, Holland, Japan and Singapore.

 Semillon Sauvignon Blanc 2002 RATING 86 **DRINK** Now $14

Galah

★★★☆

Tregarthen Road, Ashton, SA 5137 **REGION** Adelaide Hills
T (08) 8390 1243 **F** (08) 8390 1243 **OPEN** Available at Ashton Hills
WINEMAKER Stephen George **EST.** 1986 **CASES** 1500
PRODUCT RANGE ($7.50–35 ML) Unlabelled S.A. range of Semillon Chardonnay, Cabernet Shiraz,
Cabernet Sauvignon; Brut, Clare Valley Sparkling Red, Adelaide Hills Three Sheds Red, Clare Valley
Shiraz, Clare Valley Cabernet Malbec Shiraz, Clare Valley Cabernet Sauvignon.
SUMMARY Over the years, Stephen George has built up a network of contacts across South Australia
from which he gains some very high-quality small parcels of grapes or wine for the Galah label. These
are all sold direct at extremely low prices for the quality. Exports to the UK and the US.

ȲȲȲȲ **Cabernet Sauvignon 2000** Firm, savoury, earth, olive and blackberry; austere but balanced. **RATING** 87 **DRINK** 2010 $ 25

ȲȲȲȲ **Clare Valley Shiraz 2000** **RATING** 85 **DRINK** 2009 $ 25

Gallagher Estate ★★★☆

Dog Trap Road, Murrumbateman, NSW 2582 **REGION** Canberra District
T (02) 6254 9957 **F** (02) 6254 9957 **OPEN** Not
WINEMAKER Greg Gallagher **EST.** 1995 **CASES** 2500
PRODUCT RANGE ($14–20 R) Chardonnay, Shiraz.
SUMMARY Greg Gallagher was senior winemaker at Taltarni for 20 years, where he worked with Dominique Portet. He began planning a change of career at much the same time as did Dominique, and began the establishment of a small vineyard at Murrumbateman in 1995, planting a little over 1 hectare each of chardonnay and shiraz. He has now moved to the region with his family, his major job at the present time being winemaker at the Charles Sturt University Winery, playing a central role in training the winemakers of tomorrow. Retail distribution through Yarra Valley Wine Consultants in Victoria and New South Wales, and Oak Barrel Wines in Canberra.

ȲȲȲȲȲ **Chardonnay 2003** Appealing melon, nectarine and cashew flavours; balance and elegance; best yet. **RATING** 90 **DRINK** 2007 $ 18

ȲȲȲȲ **Shiraz 2001** Light to medium-bodied; elegant, spicy, cool-grown style; cherry fruit, lingering acidity. **RATING** 88 **DRINK** 2009 $ 20
Sparkling Shiraz 2001 Very powerful, traditional style; sweetness balancing phenolics. **RATING** 87 **DRINK** 2007 $ 30

ȲȲȲȲ **Blanc de Blanc 2000** **RATING** 85 **DRINK** Now $ 25

Galli Estate ★★★★☆

1507 Melton Highway, Rockbank, Vic 3335 **REGION** Sunbury
T (03) 9747 1444 **F** (03) 9747 1481 **OPEN** 7 days 11–5
WINEMAKER Stephen Phillips **EST.** 1997 **CASES** 12 000
PRODUCT RANGE ($14–36 R) Semillon, Sauvignon Blanc Semillon, Pinot Grigio, Chardonnay, La Vigna, Pinot Noir, Shiraz, Cabernet Sauvignon Franc Merlot, Sangiovese, Nebbiolo, Cabernet Sauvignon.
SUMMARY Galli Estate may be a newcomer to the scene, but it is a substantial one. Lorenzo and Pam Galli have planted 38 hectares of vineyard, the lion's share to cabernet sauvignon and shiraz, but with between 1.5–2.5 hectares of semillon, sauvignon blanc, pinot grigio, chardonnay, sangiovese and pinot noir. A large underground cellar has been constructed; already 50 metres long, it is to be extended in the future. A cellar-door sales, bistro and administration centre were completed in March 2002, with former Coldstream Hills winemaker Stephen Phillips now in charge. The quality is as high as the prices are low.

ȲȲȲȲȲ **Rockbank Shiraz 2002** Attractive combination of red cherry, raspberry and spicy blackberry fruit; soft tannins, subtle oak. **RATING** 91 **DRINK** 2012 $ 22
Rockbank Chardonnay 2003 Neatly balanced barrel ferment inputs into a mix of cashew, melon, stone fruit and citrus; long finish. **RATING** 90 **DRINK** 2008 $ 18

ȲȲȲȲ **Rockbank Pinot Noir 2003** Excellent colour; complex damson plum fruit flavours; medium-bodied, and the finish needs to soften. **RATING** 89 **DRINK** 2007 $ 18
Rockbank Sauvignon Blanc Semillon 2003 Clean; driven by sauvignon blanc varietal fruit, the semillon contributing to the structure; overall gentle mix of tropical flavours. **RATING** 88 **DRINK** Now $ 17.95
Rockbank Cabernet Sauvignon 2002 Olive, earth, blackberry and blackcurrant aromas and flavours; cool region, cool vintage, but has done well. **RATING** 88 **DRINK** 2010 $ 22
Rockbank Pinot Grigio 2003 Pink tinge is varietal; distinct aromas of peach and peach kernel, the flavours rich, the texture rounded; no alcohol heat. **RATING** 87 **DRINK** Now $ 19.95

Gapsted Wines

★★★★

Great Alpine Road, Gapsted, Vic 3737 **REGION** Alpine Valleys
T (03) 5751 1383 **F** (03) 5751 1368 **OPEN** 7 days 10–5
WINEMAKER Michael Cope-Williams, Shayne Cunningham **EST.** 1997 **CASES** 14 000
PRODUCT RANGE ($14–30 CD) Ballerina Canopy range of Riesling, Sauvignon Blanc, Chardonnay, Shiraz, Durif, Merlot, Cabernet Franc, Cabernet Sauvignon; Tutu Chardonnay Verdelho, Muscato, Dolcetto Syrah, Merlot Cabernet; Limited Release Pinot Grigio, Late Harvest Riesling, Malbec, Barbera, Tempranillo, Petit Manseng and Saperavi.
SUMMARY Gapsted is the premier brand of the Victorian Alps Wine Co, the latter primarily a contract-crush facility which processes grapes for 48 growers in the King and Alpine Valleys. The estate plantings total 10 hectares of shiraz, cabernet sauvignon, petit verdot and merlot, but the Gapsted wines come both from these estate plantings and from contract-grown fruit. All incorporate the 'Ballerina Canopy' tag, a reference to the open nature of this particular training method which is ideally suited to these regions. Exports to New Zealand, Japan and Germany.

ᵀᵀᵀᵀᵧ **Ballerina Canopy Cabernet Sauvignon 2000** Attractive medium-bodied cassis/berry, touches of chocolate and mocha; balanced, ripe tannins; stylish multi-trophy and gold medal winner. Excellent value. **RATING** 92 **DRINK** 2010 $ 23
Ballerina Canopy Cabernet Franc 2001 Cedary, spicy, gently savoury; an excellent example of this notoriously difficult variety. **RATING** 90 **DRINK** 2008 $ 23

ᵀᵀᵀᵀ **Limited Release Petit Manseng 2003** Very interesting wine; distinct lemon and fruit salad; plenty of presence; carries the touch of sweetness very well. **RATING** 89 **DRINK** Now $ 17
Limited Release Saperavi 2001 Has retained colour and developed in quite an elegant, fruit-driven mould; pleasing tannins to finish. **RATING** 89 **DRINK** 2011 $ 25
Ballerina Canopy Durif 2001 Typically deep colour and concentration of flavour and structure. It seems impossible to keep this variety down. **RATING** 88 **DRINK** 2012 $ 30
Limited Release Tempranillo 2001 Light to medium-bodied mix of spice and red berry fruits; good mouthfeel and fine tannins; should flower with years in bottle. **RATING** 87 **DRINK** 2009 $ 25

ᵀᵀᵀᵧ **Ballerina Canopy Shiraz 2000 RATING** 86 **DRINK** 2008 $ 23
Tutu Chardonnay Verdelho 2002 RATING 85 **DRINK** Now $ 14
Tutu Merlot Cabernet 2000 RATING 85 **DRINK** 2007 $ 14
Limited Release Barbera 2002 RATING 85 **DRINK** 2007 $ 25
Limited Release Late Harvest Riesling 2000 RATING 85 **DRINK** 2007 $ 17
Tutu Tempranillo 2003 RATING 84 **DRINK** Now $ 14

Garbin Estate

★★★☆

209 Toodyay Road, Middle Swan, WA 6056 **REGION** Swan Valley
T (08) 9274 1747 **F** (08) 9274 1747 **OPEN** 7 days 10.30–5.30
WINEMAKER Peter Garbin, Peter Grimwood **EST.** 1956 **CASES** 4000
PRODUCT RANGE ($14–25 CD) Chenin Blanc, Semillon, Chardonnay, Unwooded Chardonnay, Estate Shiraz, Basket Pressed Shiraz, Merlot, Cabernet Merlot, Liqueur Muscat, Liqueur Shiraz, Ruby Port.
SUMMARY Peter Garbin, winemaker by weekend and design draftsman by week, decided in 1990 that he would significantly upgrade the bulk fortified winemaking business commenced by his father in 1956. The 11-hectare vineyards have been replanted, the winery re-equipped, and the first of the new generation wines produced in 1994. The wines have since received significant critical acclaim, both locally and nationally. Exports to Hong Kong; otherwise sold direct from the winery.

ᵀᵀᵀᵀ **Merlot 2002** Cedar, cigar box and spice; red fruit at the core expressing clear varietal character. **RATING** 88 **DRINK** 2010 $ 19
Basket Pressed Shiraz 2002 Supple, soft, medium-bodied, blackberry, spice and earth; subtle oak, soft tannins. **RATING** 87 **DRINK** 2010 $ 23

ᵀᵀᵀᵧ **Chardonnay 2003 RATING** 84 **DRINK** Now $ 19

Garden Gully Vineyards ★★★★

Western Highway, Great Western, Vic 3377 **REGION** Grampians
T (03) 5356 2400 **F** (03) 5356 2400 **OPEN** By appointment
WINEMAKER Warren Randall **EST.** 1987 **CASES** 2000
PRODUCT RANGE ($13–27 CD) Riesling, Shiraz, Sparkling Shiraz, Tokay.
SUMMARY Given the skills and local knowledge of the syndicate which owns Garden Gully, it is not surprising that the wines are typically good: an attractive stone cellar-door sales area is an additional reason to stop and pay a visit. Shiraz produced from the 100-year-old vines adjoining the cellar door is especially good. The 4 hectares of shiraz is complemented by 3 hectares of riesling, providing another good wine.

Garlands ★★★★

Marmion Street off Mount Barker Hill Road, Mount Barker, WA 6324 **REGION** Frankland
T (08) 9851 2737 **F** (08) 9851 2686 **OPEN** Thurs–Sun and public holidays 10–4, or by appointment
WINEMAKER Michael Garland **EST.** 1996 **CASES** 3500
PRODUCT RANGE ($13–25 CD) Riesling, Reserve Chardonnay, Shiraz, Merlot, Saros; Barker Hill White and Red.
SUMMARY Garlands is a partnership between Michael and Julie Garland and their vigneron neighbours, Craig and Caroline Drummond. Michael Garland has come to grape growing and winemaking with a varied background in biological research, computer sales and retail clothing; he is now enrolled at Charles Sturt University for his degree in oenology, but already has significant practical experience behind him. A tiny but highly-functional winery was erected prior to the 2000 vintage, the earlier wines being made elsewhere. The winery has a capacity of 150 tonnes, and will continue contract-making for other small producers in the region as well as making the wine from the 6 hectares of estate vineyards planted to cabernet franc, sauvignon blanc, chardonnay, riesling, shiraz and cabernet sauvignon. Cabernet Franc is the winery specialty, but the quality of the wines has taken a giant leap forward. Exports to the UK.

ŸŸŸŸŸ **Merlot 2002** Fresh, supple red fruits; gentle tannins and extract; a hint of vanilla oak.
RATING 90 **DRINK** 2011 $ 18

ŸŸŸŸ **Chardonnay 2002** Complex, some bottle development; flavoursome, shortens slightly notwithstanding a hint of sweetness. **RATING** 87 **DRINK** Now $ 18

Gartelmann Hunter Estate ★★★★

Lovedale Road, Lovedale, NSW 2321 **REGION** Lower Hunter Valley
T (02) 4930 7113 **F** (02) 4930 7114 **OPEN** 7 days 10–5
WINEMAKER Monarch Winemaking Services (Contract) **EST.** 1970 **CASES** 10 000
PRODUCT RANGE ($13–30 CD) Benjamin Semillon, Reserve Semillon, Chenin Blanc, Chardonnay, Semillon Chenin Blanc, Vintage Brut, Sparkling Shiraz, Botrytis Chenin Blanc, Diedrich Shiraz, Wilhelm Shiraz, Merlot.
SUMMARY In 1996 Jan and Jorg Gartelmann purchased what was previously the George Hunter Estate, established by Sydney restaurateur Oliver Shaul in 1970. They acquired 16 hectares of mature vineyards, producing a limited amount of wine under the Gartelmann label in 1997 and moving to full production in 1998. Diedrich Shiraz is the flagship, consistently good. Exports to the UK, Germany and Canada.

ŸŸŸŸŸ **Semillon 2001** Still very fresh and and youthful; developing slowly, but very, very well.
RATING 92 **DRINK** 2010 $ 18
Wilhelm Shiraz 2002 Fine, elegant medium-bodied wine with dark fruits and ripe tannins; subtle oak. Screwcap. **RATING** 90 **DRINK** 2012 $ 20

ŸŸŸŸ **Reserve Semillon 2002** A fresh, estery, aromatic bouquet, excellent intensity, drive, line and length; mineral, talc and citrus. **RATING** 89 **DRINK** 2012 $ 25
Diedrich Shiraz 2002 Sweet, ripe plum and cherry fruit; clever oak handling; gentle tannins. **RATING** 89 **DRINK** 2009 $ 26
Botrytis Affected Semillon Chenin Blanc 2003 Not particularly complex, but excellent sugar/acid balance contributing to considerable length. **RATING** 89 **DRINK** 2008 $ 24

Vintage Brut 2000 Aromatic; full of character thanks to zesty fruit; good length, dry finish. **RATING** 88 **DRINK** 2007 $ 22

Reserve Semillon 2003 Very pale straw; crisp, tight and pure; balance, length and acidity; simply needs time. **RATING** 87 **DRINK** 2013 $ 25

ŶŶŶ **Benjamin Semillon 2003** **RATING** 85 **DRINK** 2010 $ 19

Shiraz 2001 **RATING** 85 **DRINK** Now $ 26

Sparkling Shiraz 2002 **RATING** 85 **DRINK** Now $ 26

Diedrich Shiraz 2001 **RATING** 84 **DRINK** 2007 $ 26

ŶŶŶ **Chenin Blanc 2003** **RATING** 82 $ 17

Gartner Family Vineyards NR

Sydney Road, Coonawarra, SA 5263 **REGION** Coonawarra
T (08) 8736 5011 **F** (08) 8736 5006 **OPEN** 7 days 10–4
WINEMAKER Peter Douglas (former) **EST.** 1997 **CASES** 15 000
PRODUCT RANGE ($14–28 CD) Limestone Coast Semillon Chardonnay, Padthaway Chardonnay, Padthaway Shiraz, Limestone Coast Shiraz Merlot, Coonawarra Cabernet Sauvignon.
SUMMARY After what seemed to be a spectacular and major entry into the Australian wine scene, the Gartner Family empire collapsed in 2003, with Ferrier Hodgeson appointed as receivers. The winery has been purchased by Grayton Tranter, but the longer term outcome is most uncertain. All that is known is that the ill luck which has followed Peter Douglas continues, as he has resigned as winemaker.

🐦 Gawler River Grove NR

PO Box 280, Virginia, SA 5120 (postal) **REGION** Adelaide Plains
T 0438 506 097 **F** (08) 8380 9787 **OPEN** Not
WINEMAKER Steve Black (Contract) **EST.** 2001 **CASES** 200
PRODUCT RANGE ($10.95–15 ML) Chardonnay, Grenache.
SUMMARY The vineyards at Gawler River Grove go back to the late 1940s, with 7.7 hectares of grenache bush vines; 5.8 hectares of chardonnay and 1.5 hectares of shiraz have been added since then. It was not until 2003 that a small amount of chardonnay was vinified for the Gawler River Grove label, grenache following in 2004.

Gecko Valley NR

Bailiff Road, via 700 Glenlyon Road, Gladstone, Qld 4680 **REGION** Queensland Coastal
T (07) 4979 0400 **F** (07) 4979 0500 **OPEN** 7 days 10–5
WINEMAKER Bruce Humphery-Smith (Contract) **EST.** 1997 **CASES** 1000
PRODUCT RANGE ($12.50–18.50 CD) Lightly Oaked Chardonnay, Special Reserve Chardonnay, Special Reserve Verdelho, Lazy Lizard White, Lazy Lizard Red, Special Reserve Shiraz, Liqueur Shiraz, Liqueur Mead.
SUMMARY Gecko Valley extends the viticultural map of Queensland yet further, situated little more than 50 kilometres off the Tropic of Capricorn in an area better known for beef farming and mineral activities. The 3-hectare vineyard (1 hectare each of chardonnay, verdelho and shiraz) was established by Tony (an engineer) and Coleen McCray (an accountant) after taking consultancy advice from Garry Crittenden. The coastal belt between Gladstone and Rockhampton has a unique climate, with lower rainfall than either the more northern or more southern coastal strips. The climate is hot, but the vineyard is only 1 kilometre from the tempering influence of the sea. It has been planted on free-draining, shallow soil, so excessive vigour is not a problem. The retention of Bruce Humphery-Smith underlines the serious aspirations of the McCrays to make 100 per cent central Queensland wines of real quality, the levels of sweetness in some being imposed by the strong palate preferences of the all-important cellar-door trade.

Geebin Wines NR

3729 Channel Highway, Birchs Bay, Tas 7162 **REGION** Southern Tasmania
T (03) 6267 4750 **F** (03) 6267 5090 **OPEN** 7 days 10–5
WINEMAKER Andrew Hood (Contract) **EST.** 1983 **CASES** 100

PRODUCT RANGE ($22–25 CD) Riesling, Chardonnay, Cabernet Sauvignon.
SUMMARY Although production is minuscule, quality has been consistently high. The Riesling is well made, but the interesting wine from this far southern vineyard is Cabernet Sauvignon — clearly, the vineyard enjoys favourable ripening conditions. With 0.9 hectare of vineyards. Geebin claims to be the smallest commercial producer in Australia, but isn't: Scarp Valley and (temporarily) Jollymont are smaller. The vineyard, incidentally, was once called Milnathort.

Gehrig Estate ★★★☆

Cnr Murray Valley Highway and Howlong Road, Barnawartha, Vic 3688 **REGION** Rutherglen
T (02) 6026 7296 **F** (02) 6026 7424 **OPEN** Mon–Sat 9–5, Sun 10–5
WINEMAKER Brian Gehrig **EST.** 1858 **CASES** 5000
PRODUCT RANGE ($13–32 CD) Chenin Blanc, Chardonnay, Autumn Riesling, Shiraz, Shiraz Cabernet, Durif, fortifieds.
SUMMARY An historic winery and adjacent house are superb legacies of the nineteenth century. Progressive modernisation of the winemaking facilities and operations has seen the quality of the white wines improve significantly, while the red wines now receive a percentage of new oak. Another recent innovation has been the introduction of the Gourmet Courtyard, serving lunch on weekends, public holidays and Victorian school holidays.

Gembrook Hill ★★★★☆

Launching Place Road, Gembrook, Vic 3783 **REGION** Yarra Valley
T (03) 5968 1622 **F** (03) 5968 1699 **OPEN** By appointment
WINEMAKER Timo Mayer **EST.** 1983 **CASES** 2000
PRODUCT RANGE ($21–35 R) Sauvignon Blanc, Chardonnay, Pinot Noir, Warrawong Pinot Noir, Mayer Vineyard Pinot Noir.
SUMMARY The 6-hectare Gembrook Hill Vineyard is situated on rich, red volcanic soils 2 kilometres north of Gembrook in the coolest part of the Yarra Valley. The vines are not irrigated, with consequent natural vigour control, and naturally low yields. Harvest usually spans mid-April, 3 weeks later than the traditional northern parts of the valley, and the style is consistently elegant. Exports to Denmark.

ᵀᵀᵀᵀᵞ **Pinot Noir 2002** Attractive savoury/plummy wine; good focus and very good length; markedly different from the Mayer Vineyard Pinot in style. **RATING** 93 **DRINK** 2009 $ 35
Mayer Vineyard Pinot Noir 2002 Deep colour, good hue; very intense aromas and flavours; dark plum and spice; sweet core and savoury fringes. **RATING** 93 **DRINK** 2011 $ 21
Chardonnay 2002 Intense melon, grapefruit, nectarine and cashew; fruit-driven with the concentration of the vintage evident. **RATING** 92 **DRINK** 2010 $ 30

ᵀᵀᵀᵞ **Sauvignon Blanc 2002 RATING** 86 **DRINK** Now $ 30

Gemtree Vineyards ★★★★★

PO Box 164, McLaren Vale, SA 5171 **REGION** McLaren Vale
T (08) 8323 8199 **F** (08) 8323 7889 **OPEN** Not
WINEMAKER Mike Brown **EST.** 1992 **CASES** 6000
PRODUCT RANGE ($16–37.50 R) Citrine Chardonnay, Uncut Shiraz, Paragon Shiraz, Tatty Road (Cabernet blend), Bloodstone Tempranillo.
SUMMARY The Buttery family, headed by Paul and Jill and with the active involvement of Melissa as viticulturist for Gemtree Vineyards, has been actively involved as grape growers in McLaren Vale since 1980, when they purchased their first vineyard. Today the family owns a little over 130 hectares of vines, the oldest block of 25 hectares on Tatachilla Road at McLaren Vale, planted in 1970. Recent releases have been especially good. Exports to the US, Canada, the UK, The Netherlands, Switzerland and Singapore.

ᵀᵀᵀᵀᵀ **Paragon Shiraz 2001** Spotlessly clean; rich, lush black fruits in a plum/prune/blackberry spectrum; soft tannins; totally slurpy. **RATING** 94 **DRINK** 2012 $ 40

ᵀᵀᵀᵀᵞ **Uncut Shiraz 2002** Clean, supple and round; medium-bodied, fruit-driven by blackberry and chocolate; sweet, ripe tannins. **RATING** 91 **DRINK** 2012 $ 25
Tatty Road 2002 A potent, vibrant mix of dark fruits from raspberries to blackberries; fruit-driven, fine tannins. Screwcap. **RATING** 90 **DRINK** 2015 $ 18

ℙℙℙℙ **Bloodstone Tempranillo 2002** Nice balance, texture and structure; has real finesse; cedar and spice undertones building varietal character. **RATING** 89 **DRINK** 2010 $ 25

ℙℙℙℙ **Citrine Chardonnay 2003** **RATING** 86 **DRINK** Now $ 16

🍇 Gentle Annie ★★★★☆

455 Nalinga Road, Dookie, Vic 3646 **REGION** Central Victorian Zone
T 0408 028 201 **F** (03) 9670 8085 **OPEN** By appointment
WINEMAKER David Hodgson, Tony Lacy **EST.** 1997 **CASES** 8000
PRODUCT RANGE ($14–25 ML) Sauvignon Blanc, Verdelho, Shiraz, Shiraz Cabernet Sauvignon, Cabernet Sauvignon.
SUMMARY Gentle Annie was established by Melbourne businessman Tony Cotter, together with wife Anne and five daughters assisting with sales and marketing. The name Gentle Annie was that of an early settler renowned for her beauty and gentle temperament. The vineyard is a substantial one, with 4 hectares of verdelho, 41 hectares of shiraz and 23 hectares of cabernet sauvignon planted on old volcanic ferrosol soils, similar to the red Cambrian loam at Heathcote. The winemaking team is headed by David Hodgson, who also heads up the Oenology faculty at Dookie College. Gentle Annie has hitherto sold the major part of its grape production, winning the Brown Brothers Grower of the Year title for the last two vintages. Other sales are to Southcorp. The increasing production of Gentle Annie wines has a substantial export component, likely to grow in the future. In the meantime, the very impressive wines are available by mail order and through <www.gentle-annie.com.au>.

ℙℙℙℙℙ **Shiraz 2002** Potent blackberry, prune and plum; rich in the mouth; ripe tannins; typical Central Victorian style. **RATING** 92 **DRINK** 2017 $ 25
Verdelho 2003 Floral, tangy and aromatic; a mix of citrus and apple; exceptional varietal example. **RATING** 90 **DRINK** Now $ 18
Shiraz Cabernet 2002 Big, chewy mid-palate of blackberry, chocolate and prune; the finish, however, is not extractive. **RATING** 90 **DRINK** 2015 $ 25
Cabernet Sauvignon 2002 Generous, fleshy ripe blackcurrant fruit and a touch of regional mint; medium-bodied, balanced tannins. **RATING** 90 **DRINK** 2013 $ 25

Geoff Hardy Wines ★★★★☆

c/- Pertaringa Wines, Cnr Hunt & Rifle Range Roads, McLaren Vale, SA 5171 **REGION** Adelaide Hills
T (08) 8323 8125 **F** (08) 8323 7766 **OPEN** At Pertaringa, Mon–Fri 9–5, weekends and public holidays 11–5
WINEMAKER Geoff Hardy, Ben Riggs **EST.** 1993 **CASES** 3000
PRODUCT RANGE ($28 CD) K1 range of Chardonnay, Pinot Noir, Shiraz, Cabernet; Wirrega Vineyard Petit Verdot.
SUMMARY Geoff Hardy wines come from 20 hectares of vines, with a large percentage of the grape production being sold to other makers. The new premium K1 range is impressive in both quality and value. Retail distribution through South Australia, New South Wales, Victoria and Queensland; exports to Germany, Denmark, Canada and Hong Kong.

ℙℙℙℙℙ **K1 Adelaide Hills Shiraz 2001** Complex spicy oaky aromas; plenty of plum fruit; impressively long, lingering savoury finish. **RATING** 94 **DRINK** 2016 $ 28

ℙℙℙℙℙ **K1 Adelaide Hills Chardonnay 2002** Extremely potent, complex, funky barrel-ferment aromas; the palate no less rich and powerful with ripe stone fruit and fig flavour; striking wine. **RATING** 92 **DRINK** 2007 $ 28

ℙℙℙℙ **K1 Adelaide Hills Cabernet Sauvignon 2001** Solid blackcurrant fruit with splashes of chocolate and spice; ripe tannins, subtle oak, good wine. **RATING** 88 **DRINK** 2011 $ 28
K1 Adelaide Hills Pinot Noir 2002 Jammy fruit aromas repeating on entry to the mouth; then an unexpected burst of exotic spicy flavours on the back palate and quite long finish. **RATING** 87 **DRINK** Now $ 28

Geoff Merrill Wines

★★★★

291 Pimpala Road, Woodcroft, SA 5162 **REGION** McLaren Vale
T (08) 8381 6877 **F** (08) 8322 2244 **OPEN** Mon–Fri 10–5, Weekends 12–5
WINEMAKER Geoff Merrill, Scott Heidrich **EST.** 1980 **CASES** 70 000
PRODUCT RANGE ($18–150 R) A change in brand structure has resulted in the Geoff Merrill Wines having Henley Shiraz at the top; the Reserve range representing the ultra-premium wines, the Regional range and the Varietal range; Mount Hurtle wines are sold exclusively through Vintage Cellars/Liquorland.
SUMMARY If Geoff Merrill ever loses his impish sense of humour or his zest for life, high and not-so-high, we shall all be the poorer. He is seeking to lift the profile of his wines on the domestic market; in 1998 the product range was rearranged into three tiers: premium (in fact simply varietal); reserve, the latter being the older (and best) wines, reflecting the desire for elegance and subtlety of this otherwise exuberant winemaker; and at the top, Henley Shiraz. As well as national retail distribution, significant exports to the UK, Switzerland, Belgium, Denmark and Malaysia.

ŸŸŸŸŸ **Henley Shiraz 1997** Seamless plum and dark chocolate fruit, spicy French oak and fine tannins; very long palate and finish; 200 cases made; 32 months new French oak. **RATING** 94 **DRINK** 2020 $150

ŸŸŸŸŸ **McLaren Vale Shiraz 2001** Supple and smooth; very attractive red and black fruits; subtle oak, good length. **RATING** 91 **DRINK** 2011 $22
McLaren Vale Grenache Rose 2003 Fresh cherry/cherry stone aromas, with a dash of strawberry on the palate; perfectly balanced finish; excellent example of style. **RATING** 90 **DRINK** Now $18
McLaren Vale Reserve Shiraz 1998 Savoury bottle-developed aromas; complex, multi-layered dark fruits, chocolate and oak flavours; soft ripe tannins. Good balance and length. **RATING** 90 **DRINK** 2013 $46
Coonawarra Reserve Cabernet Sauvignon 1998 Bottle-developed regional/varietal cedary, earthy aromas; palate of well above average length and intensity; lingering finish and aftertaste. **RATING** 90 **DRINK** 2015 $35

ŸŸŸŸ **McLaren Vale Sauvignon Blanc 2003** An aromatic mix of tropical fruit, snow pea, spice and mineral; excellent intensity, length and balance. **RATING** 89 **DRINK** Now $18
Chardonnay 2002 Medium-bodied, fruit-driven; melon and stone fruit; good balance. **RATING** 87 **DRINK** Now $18

ŸŸŸŸ **Chardonnay 2001** **RATING** 86 **DRINK** Now $18
Cabernet Sauvignon 2000 **RATING** 86 **DRINK** 2010 $22.50
Cabernet Shiraz 2001 **RATING** 86 **DRINK** 2007 $18
Reserve Chardonnay 1999 **RATING** 85 **DRINK** Now $25
Shiraz Grenache Mourvedre 2000 **RATING** 85 **DRINK** 2007 $18
McLaren Vale Shiraz 2000 **RATING** 84 **DRINK** 2008 $22

Geoff Weaver

★★★★★

2 Gilpin Lane, Mitcham, SA 5062 (postal) **REGION** Adelaide Hills
T (08) 8272 2105 **F** (08) 8271 0177 **OPEN** Not
WINEMAKER Geoff Weaver **EST.** 1982 **CASES** 3500
PRODUCT RANGE ($18–35 ML) Riesling, Sauvignon Blanc, Chardonnay, Pinot Noir, Cabernet Merlot.
SUMMARY This is now the full-time business of former Hardy Group chief winemaker Geoff Weaver. He draws upon a little over 11 hectares of vineyard established between 1982 and 1988; for the time being, at least, the physical winemaking is carried out by Geoff Weaver at Petaluma. He produces invariably immaculate Riesling and Sauvignon Blanc, and one of the longest-lived Chardonnays to be found in Australia, which has intense grapefruit and melon flavour. The beauty of the labels ranks supreme with that of Pipers Brook. The wines are exported to the US, the UK and Singapore.

ŸŸŸŸŸ **Lenswood Chardonnay 2001** Bright straw-green; super-fine, elegant, intense and very long citrussy/tangy palate. **RATING** 95 **DRINK** 2010 $35

Lenswood Riesling 2003 The bouquet is pure crystalline fragrance, the palate in the same mode. Zippy, lively and crisp, with flecks of chalk and slate through the fruit core of lime and apple; has immaculate balance and length. **RATING** 94 **DRINK** 2010 $ 22

ŦŦŦŦ **Lenswood Sauvignon Blanc 2003** Very fragrant gooseberry and passionfruit; delicate and fresh, though faintly reduced. **RATING** 91 **DRINK** Now $ 22

Ghost Rock Vineyard ★★★

PO Box 311, Devonport, Tas 7310 **REGION** Northern Tasmania
T (03) 6423 1246 **OPEN** Due to open 2004
WINEMAKER Tamar Ridge (Contract) **EST.** 2001 **CASES** 500
PRODUCT RANGE ($15–20 R) Sauvignon Blanc, Unwooded Chardonnay, Chardonnay, Pinot Noir.
SUMMARY Cate and Colin Arnold purchased the former Patrick Creek Vineyard (itself planted in 1989) in August 2001. They run a printing and design business in Devonport, and were looking for a suitable site to establish a vineyard, when the opportunity to buy Patrick Creek came up. The 1-hectare vineyard comprises half chardonnay and a quarter each of pinot noir and sauvignon blanc, planted on a northeasterly aspect on a sheltered slope.

ŦŦŦŦ **Rubicon Pinot Noir 2002** Noir Rich, ripe dark plum; lots of flesh and mouthfeel; development potential. **RATING** 89 **DRINK** 2009 $ 20

ŦŦŦŦ **Unwooded Chardonnay 2001** **RATING** 86 **DRINK** 2007 $ 16
Sauvignon Blanc 2003 **RATING** 85 **DRINK** Now $ 20
Chardonnay 2002 **RATING** 85 **DRINK** 2007 $ 15

Giaconda ★★★★★

McClay Road, Beechworth, Vic 3747 **REGION** Beechworth
T (03) 5727 0246 **F** (03) 5727 0246 **OPEN** By appointment
WINEMAKER Rick Kinzbrunner **EST.** 1985 **CASES** 2000
PRODUCT RANGE ($50–90 R) Aeolia, Nantua Les Deux, Chardonnay, Pinot Noir, Warner Vineyard Shiraz, Cabernet Sauvignon.
SUMMARY Wines which have a super-cult status and which, given the tiny production, are extremely difficult to find, sold chiefly through restaurants and mail order. All have a cosmopolitan edge befitting Rick Kinzbrunner's international winemaking experience. The Chardonnay and Pinot Noir are made in contrasting styles: the Chardonnay tight and reserved, the Pinot Noir more variable, but usually opulent and ripe. The rating is based on extensive tastings over the years, and recent tastings in restaurants and masterclasses. Exports to the UK and the US.

Giant Steps ★★★☆

10–12 Briarty Road, Gruyere, Vic 3770 **REGION** Yarra Valley
T (03) 5964 9555 **F** (03) 5964 9551 **OPEN** By appointment
WINEMAKER Phil Sexton, Allison Sexton **EST.** 1998 **CASES** 10 000
PRODUCT RANGE ($14.95–39.95 R) Giant Steps Chardonnay, Pinot Noir, Merlot; First Steps Chardonnay; Sexton Harry's Monster (Petit Verdot, Cabernet Sauvignon, Cabernet Franc, Merlot blend).
SUMMARY Phil Sexton made his first fortune as a pioneer micro-brewer, and invested a substantial part of that fortune in establishing the ultra-premium Margaret River winery, Devil's Lair. Late in 1996 he sold Devil's Lair to Southcorp, which had purchased Coldstream Hills earlier that year. Two years later, whether or not coincidentally, Phil and Allison Sexton purchased a hillside property less than a kilometre away from Coldstream Hills and sharing the same geological structure and aspect. The name Giant Steps comes in part from their love of jazz and the 1960 release of John Coltrane's album under that name, and partly reflecting the rise and fall of the property across a series of ridges ranging from 120 metres (400 feet) to 360 metres (1200 feet) level. They have established a striking and substantial vineyard comprising almost 34 hectares, predominantly planted to clonal selections of pinot noir and chardonnay, but with significant quantities of cabernet sauvignon and merlot, plus small plantings of cabernet franc and petit verdot. The wines are distributed nationally through Tucker Seabrook and imported into the US by Old Bridge Cellars.

ŸŸŸŸŸ **Chardonnay 2002** Intense, compact stone fruit and melon; some cashew; good acidity, long finish. Screwcap-guaranteed. **RATING** 91 **DRINK** 2010 $ 23.50

ŸŸŸŸ **Pinot Noir 2002** Clear varietal character in a dusty/spicy/sappy medium-bodied frame; not over-much flesh. **RATING** 87 **DRINK** 2007 $ 23.50

ŸŸŸŸ **Merlot 2002 RATING** 86 **DRINK** 2007 $ 27.50

Gibraltar Rock ★★★

Woodlands Road, Porongurup, WA 6324 **REGION** Porongurup
T (08) 9481 2856 **F** (08) 9481 2857 **OPEN** Wed–Sun 10–5
WINEMAKER Michael Garland (Contract) **EST.** 1979 **CASES** 400
PRODUCT RANGE ($16–22 CD) Riesling, Shiraz.
SUMMARY A once-tiny Riesling specialist in the wilds of the Porongurups forced to change its name from Narang because Lindemans felt it could be confused with its (now defunct) Nyrang Shiraz brand; truly a strange world. This beautifully sited vineyard and its long-lived Riesling were acquired by Perth orthopaedic surgeon Dr Peter Honey prior to the 2001 vintage. The vineyard now has 26 hectares of riesling, sauvignon blanc, chardonnay, pinot noir, merlot, shiraz and cabernet franc, and most of the grapes are sold to Houghton under a 10-year contract. Dr Honey intends to slowly increase production from the older vines under the Gibraltar Rock label.

ŸŸŸŸ **Shiraz 2002 RATING** 85 **DRINK** 2009 $ 25

Gibson's Barossa Vale Wines ★★★★

Willows Road, Light Pass, SA 5355 **REGION** Barossa Valley
T (08) 8562 3193 **F** (08) 8562 4490 **OPEN** Fri–Mon and public holidays 11–5
WINEMAKER Rob Gibson **EST.** 1996 **CASES** 3500
PRODUCT RANGE ($20–70 R) Shiraz, Old Vine Shiraz, Loose End Collection Shiraz, Merlot, Reserve Merlot, The Blend (Shiraz Mourvedre Grenache).
SUMMARY Rob Gibson spent much of his working life as a senior viticulturist for Penfolds. While at Penfolds he was involved in research tracing the characters that particular parcels of grapes give to a wine, which left him with a passion for identifying and protecting what is left of the original vineyard plantings in wine regions around Australia. His future plans are to release tiny quantities of wines from other regions, drawing upon old vineyards; this led to the acquisition of an additional 8 hectares of old shiraz, mourvedre and grenache, plus some of the oldest chardonnay vines in the Barossa (recent arrivals in comparison to shiraz, but planted in 1982). A carefully designed and built cellar door has also opened. These days his work as a viticultural consultant takes him all over Australia, and indeed all over the world, so his research contacts are maintained. Exports to the UK and Hong Kong.

ŸŸŸŸŸ **Old Vine Collection Shiraz 2001** Complex wine; black and red fruits, spice and game; vanilla oak and creamy tannins. **RATING** 90 **DRINK** 2014 $ 60
Reserve Merlot 2001 Excellent structure, mouthfeel and length; spicy, savoury edges to the fruit are strongly varietal; fine tannins. **RATING** 90 **DRINK** 2011 $ 28

ŸŸŸŸ **The Blend 2001** Nicely rounded and a gently fleshy array of juicy, red, sweet red fruits; good balance and finish. **RATING** 89 **DRINK** 2007 $ 19.50
Shiraz 2001 A complex mix of black fruits, spice, game and vanilla; less concentrated than the Old Vine Collection Shiraz. **RATING** 88 **DRINK** 2011 $ 25

Gidgee Estate Wines NR

441 Weeroona Drive, Wamboin, NSW 2620 **REGION** Canberra District
T (02) 6236 9506 **F** (02) 6236 9070 **OPEN** Weekends 12–4
WINEMAKER Andrew McEwin (Contract) **EST.** 1996 **CASES** 500
PRODUCT RANGE ($15–16 CD) Janette Murray Riesling, Chardonnay, Botrytis Riesling, Ensemble (Cabernet blend).
SUMMARY Brett and Cheryl Lane purchased the 1-hectare vineyard in 1996; it had been planted to riesling, chardonnay, cabernet sauvignon, cabernet franc and merlot over a 10-year period prior to its acquisition, but had been allowed to run down and needed to be rehabilitated. The Lanes intend to double the vineyard size over the next 2 years and have retained Andrew McEwin as contract winemaker.

Gilberts

★★★★★

RMB 438 Albany Highway, Kendenup via Mount Barker, WA 6323 **REGION** Mount Barker
T (08) 9851 4028 **F** (08) 9851 4021 **OPEN** 7 days 10–5
WINEMAKER Plantagenet (Contract) **EST.** 1980 **CASES** 4000
PRODUCT RANGE ($14–25 CD) Riesling, Alira Riesling Semillon, Chardonnay, Mount Barker Shiraz,
Three Devils Shiraz, Reserve Shiraz, Shiraz Cabernet, Cabernet Shiraz.
SUMMARY A part-time occupation for sheep and beef farmers Jim and Beverly Gilbert but a very
successful one. The now mature vineyard, coupled with contract-winemaking at Plantagenet, has
produced small quantities of high-quality Riesling and Chardonnay. The rating is for the Riesling
which won the trophy for Best Wine of Show at the Qantas West Australian Wines Show in both 2000
and 2001. The wines sell out quickly each year, with retail distribution through New South Wales,
Victoria, ACT and Western Australia, and exports to the US, the UK, Singapore and The Netherlands.
A restaurant and function area opened in April 2003, and further plantings are planned.

ŶŶŶŶŶ **Reserve Shiraz 2001** Excellent colour; intense, luscious black cherry and blackberry mid-
palate fruit, then very good tannins on the long finish. **RATING** 94 **DRINK** 2016 $ 27

ŶŶŶŶŶ **Riesling 2003** Powerful, intense, ripe apple and lime; flows strongly and evenly.
Screwcap. **RATING** 93 **DRINK** 2013 $ 20
Three Devils Shiraz 2002 Fragrant, spicy red fruits; juicy black cherry, plum and
blackberry flavours on the medium-bodied but long palate. **RATING** 91 **DRINK** 2012 $ 17.90
Shiraz Cabernet 2002 Fresh, tangy, spicy redcurrant and blackcurrant mix; good length
and mouthfeel. **RATING** 90 **DRINK** 2009 $ 19

ŶŶŶŶ **Mount Barker Shiraz 2001** Elegant, lively red berry fruit; nice touch of pepper; slightly
dry finish. **RATING** 89 **DRINK** 2010 $ 25

ŶŶŶŶ **Alira Riesling Semillon 2003** **RATING** 84 **DRINK** Now $ 16

Gilead Estate

★★★

1868 Wanneroo Road, Neerabup, WA 6031 (postal) **REGION** Swan District
T (08) 9407 5076 **F** (08) 9407 5187 **OPEN** Not
WINEMAKER Gerry Gauntlett **EST.** 1995 **CASES** 400
PRODUCT RANGE ($9.20–13.50 ML) Shiraz, Classic Dry Red, Cabernet Merlot.
SUMMARY A retirement — but nonetheless serious — venture for Judy and Gerry Gauntlett, who
planted 1.2 hectares on the Tuart sands of Wanneroo in 1990. The name comes from the Balm of
Gilead which, in Biblical times, was produced from trees on the hills northeast of Galilee, had healing
and had purifying qualities. The tiny production is mainly sold by mail order, with occasional tasting
days.

ŶŶŶŶ **Shiraz 2001** Plum, black cherry and a touch of vanilla; good texture; particularly well
priced. **RATING** 87 **DRINK** 2011 $ 13.50

ŶŶŶ **Cabernet Merlot 2001** **RATING** 82 $ 13.50

Gilgai Winery

NR

Tingha Road, Gilgai, NSW 2360 **REGION** Northern Slopes Zone
T (02) 6723 1204 **OPEN** Mon–Sat 10–6, Sun 12–6
WINEMAKER Keith Whish **EST.** 1968 **CASES** 550
PRODUCT RANGE Pinot Noir, Malbec, fortifieds.
SUMMARY Inverell medical practitioner Dr Keith Whish has been quietly producing wines from his 6-
hectare vineyard for almost 30 years. All of the production is sold through the cellar door. No tastings
for a decade or more.

🐞 Gin Gin Wines

NR

Gin Gin Historical Village, Mulgrave Street, Gin Gin, Qld 4671 **REGION** Queensland Coastal
T (07) 4157 3099 **F** (07) 4157 3088 **OPEN** 7 days 10–5
WINEMAKER Lyla McLaren **EST.** 2002

PRODUCT RANGE A range of varietally denominated table wines reflecting the plantings.

SUMMARY The 2.5-hectare vineyard of Lyla and John McLaren may not be large, but it is planted to a Joseph's Coat of varieties: sauvignon blanc, gewurztraminer, semillon, chardonnay, colombard, verdelho, pinot noir, merlot, grenache, cabernet sauvignon, malbec, shiraz, petit verdot, sangiovese and tempranillo. Similarly, the range of facilities available at the cellar door all encompassing, offering wine tourists everything they could wish for.

Gisborne Peak Wines ★★★☆

69 Short Road, Gisborne, Vic 3437 **REGION** Macedon Ranges
T (03) 5428 2228 **F** (03) 5428 4816 **OPEN** 7 days 11–5
WINEMAKER John Ellis (Contract) **EST.** 1978 **CASES** 1000
PRODUCT RANGE ($18–30 CD) Mawarra Estate Semillon, Duet (Chardonnay Semillon), Chardonnay, Pinot Noir.

SUMMARY Bob Nixon began the development of Mawarra Estate way back in 1978, planting his dream vineyard row-by-row, then acre-by-acre. The early years were difficult, but he persevered, and has now established chardonnay, semillon and pinot noir. Once the vineyard was in full bearing, a cellar door was always part of the scheme, but he just happens to be married to Barbara Nixon, founder of Victoria Winery Tours, and who has been in and out of cellar doors around Australia with greater frequency than any other living person. So it is that the tasting room has 8-foot wide shaded verandahs, plenty of windows and sweeping views of the Chardonnay Bowl and Semillon Flats. Deli-style foods are offered, all pre-packaged, featuring deli meats, cheese, antipasto and biscuits. Exports to the US.

ŢŢŢŢ Mawarra Mt Gisborne Estate Semillon 2000 RATING 85 **DRINK** Now $18

Glaetzer Wines ★★★★

34 Barossa Valley Way, Tanunda, SA 5352 **REGION** Barossa Valley
T (08) 8563 0288 **F** (08) 8563 0218 **OPEN** Mon–Sat 10.30–4.30, public holidays 1–4.30
WINEMAKER Colin Glaetzer, Ben Glaetzer **EST.** 1996 **CASES** 5000
PRODUCT RANGE ($19.99–54.99 R) Bush Vine Semillon, Semillon Ratafia, Grenache Mourvedre; Sparkling Pinot Noir, The Bishop Shiraz, Shiraz, Cabernet Sauvignon Malbec, Wallace (Shiraz Cabernet Grenache), Sparkling Shiraz.

SUMMARY Colin (recently installed as a Baron of the Barossa) and Ben Glaetzer are almost as well known in South Australian wine circles as Wolf Blass winemaker John Glaetzer, and, needless to say, they are all closely related. Glaetzer Wines purchases its grapes from third and fourth-generation Barossa Valley growers and makes an array of traditional Barossa styles. The Shiraz comes predominantly from vines 80 years or more old. National retail distribution; exports to the US, Canada, the UK, Germany, Greece, The Netherlands, New Zealand, Malaysia, Singapore and Fiji.

ŢŢŢŢŢ Barossa Valley Shiraz 1999 Elegant, refined wine; very good balance of blackberry/plum fruit with vanilla oak; lingering, fine-grained tannins. 80-year-old vines. **RATING** 92 **DRINK** 2014 $54.99
Bishop Barossa Valley Shiraz 1999 Fine, cedar and mocha overtones to spicy/plummy fruit; medium-bodied; good extract and length. **RATING** 90 **DRINK** 2012 $34.99

ŢŢŢŢ Wallace 2002 Fragrant, fresh red fruit-driven; light to medium-bodied; minimal tannins and oak. **RATING** 88 **DRINK** 2007 $19.99

Glastonbury Estate Wines ★★★

Shop 4, 104 Memorial Drive, Eumundi, Qld 4562 **REGION** Queensland Coastal
T (07) 5444 8557 **F** (07) 5442 8745 **OPEN** Tues 12–5, Wed 9–8, Thurs 12–8, Fri 12–5, Sat 9–8, Sun 12–5
WINEMAKER Peter Scudamore-Smith MW (Consultant) **EST.** 2001 **CASES** 4000
PRODUCT RANGE ($13–29 ML) Beach Series Unwooded Chardonnay, Shiraz Cabernet, Tickled Pink Rose, Blush; Emotions Cabernet Sauvignon.

SUMMARY Glastonbury Estate is situated in the hills of Glastonbury, high up in the Sunshine Coast hinterland, 50 minutes from Noosa. It is the vision of managing director Steve Davoren, who (in typical Queensland tradition) has established a combined wine and tourism venture. Six and a half hectares of chardonnay, merlot and cabernet sauvignon have been established on terraces cut into the hillsides, with further plantings underway. Peter Scudamore-Smith MW is the consultant winemaker, and the wines have already had significant success in wine competitions in Queensland. A large lodge comfortably sleeping three couples has been built, while Glastonbury Estate is intended to become one of the first developments in Queensland to offer building sites amongst the vines, with further details available from <www.glastonburyvineyard.com.au>.

ŶŶŶŶ   **Emotions Cabernet Sauvignon 2001** Very savoury/earthy/briary, short on red fruit flavours, but not length; fine tannins, good acidity; Italian food-style wine. **RATING** 87 **DRINK** 2011 $29

ŶŶŶ   **Beach Series Tickled Pink Rose 2003** **RATING** 83 $14

🐚 Gledswood Homestead and Winery   NR

900 Camden Valley Way, Catherine Fields, NSW 2171 **REGION** Sydney Basin
T (02) 9606 5111 **OPEN** 7 days 10–5
WINEMAKER Contract **EST.** 2000
SUMMARY The Gledswood Homestead and Winery complex is one of the most historically important properties in Australia, with the collection of buildings dating back to 1810, and the homestead from around 1820. While the owners live in the homestead, the homestead and all its ancillary buildings are devoted to a wide range of tourist activities, supported by the restaurant which is open 7 days.

Glenalbyn   ★★★

84 Halls Road, Kingower, Vic 3517 **REGION** Bendigo
T (03) 5438 8255 **F** (03) 5438 8255 **OPEN** 10.30–4.30 most days
WINEMAKER Lee (Leila) Gillespie **EST.** 1997 **CASES** 500
PRODUCT RANGE ($16–25 CD) Sauvignon Blanc, Pinot Noir, Cabernet Sauvignon.
SUMMARY When Leila Gillespie's great-grandfather applied for his land title in 1856, he had already established a vineyard on the property (in 1853). A survey plan of 1857 shows the cultivation paddocks, one marked the Grape Paddock, and a few of the original grape vines have survived in the garden which abuts the National Trust and Heritage homestead. In 1986 Leila and John Gillespie decided on a modest diversification of their sheep, wool and cereal crop farm, and began the establishment of 4 hectares of vineyards. Since 1997 Leila Gillespie has made the wine on a self-taught basis, with Cabernet Sauvignon, and more recently Pinot Noir and Sauvignon Blanc. In 2003 she commemorated 150 years of family ownership of the property; ironically, the 2003 drought meant that no grapes were picked. The 1998 vintage [Cabernet Sauvignon], tasted in February 2004, had developed even better than I had ever imagined it would, the tannins now merged with the dense, sweet fruit.

ŶŶŶŶ   **Cabernet Sauvignon 2001** **RATING** 86 **DRINK** Now $25
Cabernet Sauvignon 2002 **RATING** 85 **DRINK** Now $25
Cabernet Sauvignon 2000 **RATING** 85 **DRINK** Now $25
Pinot Noir 2001 **RATING** 84 **DRINK** Now $20

GlenAyr   ★★★☆

Back Tea Tree Road, Richmond, Tas 7025 **REGION** Southern Tasmania
T (03) 6260 2388 **F** (03) 6260 2691 **OPEN** Mon–Fri 8–5
WINEMAKER Andrew Hood **EST.** 1975 **CASES** 500
PRODUCT RANGE ($21–25 CD) Riesling, Chardonnay, Pinot Noir, Cabernet Shiraz Merlot; Tolpuddle Vineyards Chardonnay and Pinot Noir.
SUMMARY The substantial and now fully mature Tolpuddle Vineyard, which provides the grapes which go to make the GlenAyr wines, managed by Warren Schasser, who is completing a Bachelor of Applied Science (viticulture) degree at Charles Sturt University. The major part of the grape production continues to be sold to Domaine Chandon and Hardys, with most going to make premium still table wine, and a lesser amount to premium sparkling.

ŶŶŶŶŶ   **Tolpuddle Vineyards Pinot Noir 2002** Good hue; elegant, very pure plum and black cherry fruit; lime, length and concentration; still evolving. **RATING** 90 **DRINK** 2010 $25

ŶŶŶŶ   **Chardonnay 2002** **RATING** 84 **DRINK** 2008 $21

ŶŶŶ   **Pinot Noir 2002** **RATING** 83 $25

🍃 Glenburnie Vineyard NR

Black Range Road, Tumbarumba, NSW 2653 **REGION** Tumbarumba
T (02) 6948 2570 **F** (02) 6948 2570 **OPEN** 7 days 10–5
WINEMAKER Cofield Wines (Contract) **EST.** 1992 **CASES** 800
PRODUCT RANGE ($15–20 CD) Black Range label with Riesling, Sauvignon Blanc, Chardonnay, Sparkling Pinot Chardonnay, Pinot Noir.
SUMMARY Robert Parkes has established 12 hectares of vineyard planted to riesling, sauvignon blanc, chardonnay and pinot noir, the production is marketed under the Black Range Wines. The cellar door offers barbecue facilities, and accommodation is also available.

🍃 Glen Creek Wines NR

Glen Creek Road, Barjarg, Vic 3722 **REGION** Upper Goulburn
T (03) 5776 4271 **F** (03) 9873 5088 **OPEN** By appointment
WINEMAKER MasterWineMakers (Contract) **EST.** 2001
PRODUCT RANGE Pinot Gris, Chardonnay, Pinot Noir, Shiraz, Merlot, Cabernet Sauvignon.
SUMMARY Geoff Alford commenced the establishment of the vineyard in 1995 in Mount Strathbogie at Barjarg around 30 kilometres northwest of Mansfield, with the planting of 500 chardonnay vines. The estate has since grown to 6 hectares, with the addition of pinot gris, merlot, cabernet sauvignon and nebbiolo, while other local vineyards contribute shiraz, pinot noir and additional cabernet sauvignon. There is a complementary planting of olives. Part of the wine is made on-site, part off-site by MasterWineMakers. The wines are available by mail order, with limited retail distribution.

Glendonbrook ★★★

Lot 2 Park Street, East Gresford, NSW 2311 **REGION** Upper Hunter Valley
T (02) 4938 9666 **F** (02) 4938 9766 **OPEN** Mon–Fri 9–5, weekends and public holidays 10.30–4.30
WINEMAKER Geoff Broadfield **EST.** 2000 **CASES** 12 000
PRODUCT RANGE ($18.40–22.50 CD) Semillon, Semillon Chardonnay, Verdelho, Chardonnay, Shiraz, Shiraz Cabernet Merlot, Merlot.
SUMMARY Highly successful Sydney businessman Tom Smith and wife Terese purchased the Bingleburra homestead at East Gresford in the mid-1990s. The 600-hectare property raises beef cattle, but in 1997 the decision was taken to plant 12.5 hectares of vines (8.3 hectares shiraz, 4.2 hectares verdelho), and this in turn led to the construction shortly prior to the 2001 vintage of a $2 million, 300-tonne capacity winery, lifting their total investment in the wine industry to $3 million. All of the winemaking equipment is new, and the Smiths employed the highly experienced Geoff Broadfield as winemaker (with 20 Hunter Valley vintages under his belt). The estate-grown grapes are supplemented by contract-grown grapes, and the winery has sufficient capacity to also offer contract winemaking facilities for others. It marks a major return to the Gresford area where Dr Henry Lindeman established his Cawarra vineyards in the mid-1800s.

♥♥♥♥ **Reserve Chardonnay 2002** Peach, melon and citrus with grilled nut barrel ferment inputs; good lingering finish. **RATING** 88 **DRINK** Now $ 23

♥♥♥♥ **Merlot 2002** **RATING** 86 **DRINK** 2007 $ 23
Semillon 2002 **RATING** 85 **DRINK** Now $ 20
Unwooded Chardonnay 2002 **RATING** 84 **DRINK** Now $ 16.50
Cabernet Sauvignon 2002 **RATING** 84 **DRINK** Now $ 23

♥♥♥ **Verdelho 2003** **RATING** 83 $ 20

🍃 Glen Eldon Wines ★★★★

Glen Eldon, O'Herbig Road, Springton, SA 5235 (postal) **REGION** Eden and Barossa Valleys
T (08) 8568 2996 **F** (08) 8568 1833 **OPEN** Not
WINEMAKER Richard Sheedy **EST.** 1997 **CASES** 4000
PRODUCT RANGE ($14.50–23.50 ML) Eden Valley Riesling, Dry Bore Shiraz, Cabernet Sauvignon.
SUMMARY The Sheedy family — brothers Richard and Andrew, and wives Mary and Sue — have established their base at the Glen Eldon property given its name over 100 years ago, and which is today the home of Richard and Mary. It is here that the riesling is planted, while the shiraz and

cabernet sauvignon come from their vineyards in the Barossa Valley. Australian distribution has been established, as have exports to the UK, the US and Canada.

♀♀♀♀♀ Riesling 2003 Intense, pure Eden Valley lime juice aromas follows through impressively on the palate. Screwcap. **RATING** 95 **DRINK** 2013 $16

♀♀♀♀ Dry Bore Shiraz 2000 Complex, tangy blackberry, spice and mocha; lively, lingering finish; sweet fruit. **RATING** 89 **DRINK** 2012 $24
Cabernet Sauvignon 2001 Pleasant, medium-bodied, well balanced and structured; sweet fruit and fine tannins. **RATING** 88 **DRINK** 2011 $24

♀♀♀♀ Dry Bore Shiraz 2001 Aromatic red and black fruits, spice and a touch of game; zippy finish. **RATING** 86 **DRINK** 2010 $24

Glen Erin Vineyard Retreat   NR

Rochford Road, Lancefield, Vic 3435 **REGION** Macedon Ranges
T (03) 5429 1041 **F** (03) 5429 2053 **OPEN** Weekends, public holidays 10–6
WINEMAKER Brian Scales, John Ellis **EST.** 1993 **CASES** 1000
PRODUCT RANGE ($17–38 CD) Gewurztraminer, Deep Creek Sauvignon Blanc Semillon, Chardonnay, Pinot Noir, Mystic Park Sparkling Macedon, Deep Creek Shiraz Cabernet.
SUMMARY Brian Scales acquired the former Lancefield Winery and renamed it Glen Erin. Wines are contract-made from Macedon grapes and elsewhere and sold only through the cellar door and restaurant; the conference and function facilities are supported by 24 accommodation rooms.

♀♀♀♀♀ Mystic Park Chardonnay Pinot NV Full-on, big style, but has finesse, too; excellent balance and length. **RATING** 92 **DRINK** 2007 $30

Glenfinlass   NR

Elysian Farm, Parkes Road, Wellington, NSW 2820 **REGION** Central Ranges Zone
T (02) 6845 2011 **F** (02) 6845 3329 **OPEN** Sat 9–5, or by appointment
WINEMAKER Brian G Holmes **EST.** 1971 **CASES** 500
PRODUCT RANGE ($15–25 CD) Sauvignon Blanc, Drought Drop (Shiraz, Cabernet Sauvignon, Sauvignon Blanc).
SUMMARY The weekend and holiday hobby of Wellington solicitor Brian Holmes, who has wisely decided to leave it at that. I have not tasted the wines for many years, but the last wines I did taste were competently made. Wines are in short supply owing to drought (1998), frost (1999) and flooding (2000), promptly followed by 3 more years of drought.

Glengariff Estate Winery   NR

3234 Mount Mee Road, Dayboro Valley, Qld 4521 **REGION** Queensland Coastal
T (07) 3425 1299 **F** (07) 3425 1299 **OPEN** Fri–Sun 10–3
WINEMAKER Contract **EST.** 1999 **CASES** 350
PRODUCT RANGE ($19.50–23.90 CD) Honorah's Semillon Chardonnay, Honorah's Chardonnay, Sparkling Celebrations, Wild Vine Red, Honorah's Shiraz Cabernet Merlot, Denny's Port.
SUMMARY The word historic is as much overused as the word passionate, but this is an historic property with a quite remarkable story. The twice-married Honorah Mullins, first to a Mr Doyle and later to a Mr Mullins, moved with her husband from County Cork, Ireland to Australia in 1875. In 1876 they established the family dairy farm, now Glengariff Estate. At the age of 90 Honorah Mullins was still milking a herd of 40 cows, and when 111 she continued to take her morning walk with one of her sons, Dennis Doyle. When she died on 1 May 1926, one day before her 115th birthday, she had lived through the reign of six English monarchs, from George III to George V. Tracey Wrightson, the great, great granddaughter of Honorah Mullins, together with husband Andrew and children, now own and run the 100-hectare Glengariff Estate. It operates as a tourist attraction, with a restaurant and wedding function venue and (since 1999) as a grape grower and wine producer.

Glenguin ★★★★

Milbrodale Road, Broke, NSW 2330 **REGION** Lower Hunter Valley
T (02) 6579 1009 **F** (02) 6579 1009 **OPEN** 7 days at Boutique Wine Centre, Broke Road, Pokolbin
WINEMAKER Robin Tedder MW **EST.** 1993 **CASES** 9000
PRODUCT RANGE ($18–75 R) The Old Broke Block Semillon, Christina Semillon, River Terrace Vineyard Chardonnay, Griffith Vineyard Botrytised Semillon, Shiraz, Stonybroke Shiraz, School House Block Shiraz, Aristea Shiraz, Orange Vineyard Merlot; Maestro Pinot Grigio, Sangiovese Cabernet.
SUMMARY Glenguin's vineyard has been established along the banks of the Wollombi Brook by Robin (an MW), Rita and Andrew Tedder, Robin and Andrew being the grandsons of Air Chief Marshal Tedder, made Baron of Glenguin by King George VI in recognition of his wartime deeds. There are now two distinct ranges, with the Glenguin wines coming solely from the 19 hectares of estate plantings at Wollombi. The Maestro label is the polar opposite, matching grape varieties and site climates in regions as diverse as Orange and the Adelaide Hills. Exports to the UK, Germany and New Zealand.

♥♥♥♥♥ **Maestro Pinot Grigio 2003** Voluminous pear, spice and apple aromas, repeated on the abundantly flavoured, varietally driven palate. Grigios don't come much better. Screwcap. **RATING** 92 **DRINK** Now $ 23
Maestro Sangiovese 2002 Black cherry and spice fruit; very convincing texture and structure; fine but warm tannins; 93 per cent Sangiovese, 7 per cent Cabernet Sauvignon; 100 per cent Orange-sourced. **RATING** 90 **DRINK** 2010 $ 27

♥♥♥♥ **Aristea Shiraz 2000** Firm, slightly savoury black fruits offset by almost sweet tannins and clever oak handling. **RATING** 89 **DRINK** 2010 $ 75
Maestro Sangiovese Cabernet 2002 Savour, spicy, lemony; strongly varietal; a tweak of sweetness and of tannins on the finish. Appealing. Screwcap. From Orange. **RATING** 88 **DRINK** 2010 $ 27
Individual Vineyard Schoolhouse Block Shiraz 2001 Complex briar, earth, dark chocolate and berry aromas; savoury palate and finish. **RATING** 87 **DRINK** 2008 $ 30

♥♥♥♥ **Stonybroke Shiraz 2001** **RATING** 86 **DRINK** 2007 $ 20
The Old Broke Block Semillon 2003 **RATING** 85 **DRINK** 2008 $ 18

Glen Isla Estate ★★★★☆

107 Glen Isla Road, Bickley, WA 6076 (postal) **REGION** Perth Hills
T (08) 9293 5293 **F** (08) 9293 5293 **OPEN** By appointment
WINEMAKER John Griffiths (Contract) **EST.** 1998 **CASES** 350
PRODUCT RANGE ($16 ML) Shiraz, Merlot; Pinot Noir Methode Champenoise.
SUMMARY Jim Winterhalder has established 0.84 hectares each of merlot and pinot noir, and 2.38 hectares of shiraz, on slopes which straddle Piesse Brook, variously facing west, east and north. The wine is made by the highly-skilled John Griffiths, and, apart from a couple of retail outlets, is sold by mail order.

♥♥♥♥♥ **Shiraz 2002** Bright colour; a very attractive and supple array of raspberry, red cherry and blackberry fruit; good acidity and length. **RATING** 90 **DRINK** 2009 $ 16

Gloucester Ridge Vineyard ★★★★

Lot 7489 Burma Road, Pemberton, WA 6260 **REGION** Pemberton
T (08) 9776 1035 **F** (08) 9776 1390 **OPEN** 7 days 10–5 (until late Saturday)
WINEMAKER Brenden Smith **EST.** 1985 **CASES** 6000
PRODUCT RANGE ($10–25 CD) Sauvignon Blanc, Back Block White, Unwooded Chardonnay, Reserve Chardonnay, Chimere (Sparkling), Late Harvest Riesling, Seduction (Rose), Shiraz, Merlot, Cabernet Merlot, Back Block Red, Cabernet Sauvignon; Port.
SUMMARY Gloucester Ridge is the only vineyard located within the Pemberton town boundary, within easy walking distance. It is owned and operated by Don and Sue Hancock. Retail distribution in Queensland, New South Wales, Victoria and WA.

Gnadenfrei Estate

NR

Seppeltsfield Road, Marananga via Nuriootpa, SA 5355 **REGION** Barossa Valley
T (08) 8562 2522 **F** (08) 8562 3470 **OPEN** Tues–Sun 10–5.30
WINEMAKER Malcolm Seppelt **EST.** 1979 **CASES** 1500
PRODUCT RANGE ($12–40 CD) Riesling, Semillon, Traminer Riesling, Shiraz Grenache, St Michael's Shiraz, Tawny Port, Sparkling.
SUMMARY A strictly cellar-door operation, which relies on a variety of sources for its wines but has a core of 2 hectares of estate shiraz and 1 hectare of grenache. A restaurant presided over by Joylene Seppelt is open for morning teas, lunches and afternoon teas. Small quantities of the wines make their way to Pennsylvania, US.

Gold Dust Wines

NR

Southpark, Tallwood Road, Millthorpe, NSW 2798 **REGION** Orange
T (02) 6366 5168 **F** 902) 6361 9165 **OPEN** By appointment
WINEMAKER Contract **EST.** 1993 **CASES** 700
PRODUCT RANGE ($12–14.50 ML) Riesling, Chardonnay, Late Harvest Riesling.
SUMMARY John and Jacqui Corrie have established 3 hectares each of riesling and chardonnay, electing to sell two thirds of the production, and have the remainder contract-made, since 2001 by Jon Reynolds. Most of the wine is sold by mail order.

Golden Grape Estate

NR

Oakey Creek Road, Pokolbin, NSW 2321 **REGION** Lower Hunter Valley
T (02) 4998 7588 **F** (02) 4998 7730 **OPEN** 7 days 10–5
WINEMAKER Neil McGuigan (Consultant) **EST.** 1985
PRODUCT RANGE ($14.95–29.90 CD) Premier Semillon, Gewurztraminer, Sauvignon Blanc, Semillon Verdelho, Happy Valley Chardonnay, Five Star (light fruity), Frizzante Rose, Mount Leonard (Cabernet Sauvignon), Domaine Springton (Shiraz), Classic Red, fortifieds.
SUMMARY German-owned and unashamedly directed at the tourist, with a restaurant, barbecue and picnic areas, wine museum and separate tasting room for bus tours. The substantial range of wines are of diverse origins and style. The operation now has over 42 hectares of Hunter Valley plantings.

Golden Grove Estate

Sundown Road, Ballandean, Qld 4382 **REGION** Granite Belt
T (07) 4684 1291 **F** (07) 4684 1247 **OPEN** 7 days 9–5
WINEMAKER Sam Costanzo **EST.** 1993 **CASES** 10 000
PRODUCT RANGE ($10–15 CD) Accommodation Creek Classic White and Classic Dry Red, Muscadean, Rose, Shiraz, Cabernet Merlot, Liqueur Muscat.
SUMMARY Golden Grove Estate was established by Mario and Sebastiana Costanzo in 1946, producing stone fruits and table grapes for the fresh fruit market. The first wine grapes (shiraz) were planted in 1972, but it was not until 1985, when ownership passed to son Sam Costanzo and wife Grace, that the use of the property started to change. In 1993 chardonnay and merlot joined the shiraz, followed by cabernet sauvignon, sauvignon blanc and semillon. Wine quality has steadily improved, with many medals in regional shows awarded up to 2002, leading to national (though limited) retail distribution.

Golden Gully Wines

NR

5900 Midwestern Highway, Mandurama, NSW 2792 **REGION** Orange
T (02) 6367 5148 **F** (02) 6367 4148 **OPEN** Weekends 10–4, or by appointment
WINEMAKER Jon Reynolds (Contract) **EST.** 1994 **CASES** 1300
PRODUCT RANGE ($18–19 CD) Shiraz, Cabernet Merlot, Cabernet Sauvignon.
SUMMARY Kevin and Julie Bate have progressively established over 5 hectares of vineyard (2 hectares cabernet sauvignon, 1.6 hectares shiraz, 0.5 hectare merlot and 0.5 hectare each of semillon and sauvignon blanc). The first commercial crop came in 2001, but tiny makes in 1999 (Cabernet Shiraz) and 2000 (Cabernet Sauvignon) have both won bronze medals at the Bathurst Cool Climate Wine Show.

Golden Mile Wines

NR

47 Whitewood Drive, Upper Stuart, SA 5156 (postal) **REGION** Riverland
T (08) 8370 8041 **F** (08) 8370 8984 **OPEN** Not
WINEMAKER Tim Mader, Jane Mader **EST.** 2000
PRODUCT RANGE Big River, Aged Vine Shiraz, Merlot.
SUMMARY Tim and Jane Mader have set up what, by Riverland standards, is a micro-boutique, based on 8 hectares of merlot and shiraz at Barmera. Part of the production is sold, and part vinified for the Big River and Aged Vine Shiraz labels. The wine is sold chiefly by mail order.

Golders Vineyard

Bridport Road, Pipers Brook, Tas 7254 **REGION** Northern Tasmania
T (03) 6395 4142 **F** (03) 6395 4142 **OPEN** By appointment
WINEMAKER Richard Crabtree **EST.** 1991 **CASES** 450
PRODUCT RANGE ($23–40 R) Chardonnay, Pinot Noir, Reserve Pinot Noir.
SUMMARY The initial plantings of 1.5 hectares of pinot noir have been supplemented by a hectare of chardonnay. The quality of the Pinot Noir has been good from the initial vintage in 1995, hitting a high spot in 2000 and 2001.

Pinot Noir 2003 Plum, spice, briar, forest aromas and flavours on a light to medium-bodied, well-balanced palate. **RATING** 89 **DRINK** 2007 $ 23

Chardonnay 2003 **RATING** 84 **DRINK** Now $ 23

Goona Warra Vineyard

Sunbury Road, Sunbury, Vic 3429 **REGION** Sunbury
T (03) 9740 7766 **F** (03) 9744 7648 **OPEN** 7 days 10–5
WINEMAKER John Barnier, Mark Matthews **EST.** 1863 **CASES** 3000
PRODUCT RANGE ($18.50–33.50 CD) Semillon Sauvignon Blanc, Chardonnay, Black Cygnet Chardonnay (unwooded), Pinot Noir, Shiraz, Black Cygnet Cabernet Shiraz, Cabernet Franc, Cabernet Merlot.
SUMMARY An historic stone winery, established under this name by a nineteenth-century Victorian premier. A brief interlude as part of The Wine Investment Fund in 2001 is over, the Barniers having bought back the farm. Excellent tasting facilities; an outstanding venue for weddings and receptions; Sunday lunch also served. Situated 30 minutes drive from Melbourne (10 minutes north of Tullamarine Airport). Exports to the UK.

Pinot Noir 2002 Excellent mix of ripe plum and pinot fruit with more savoury/sous bois characters reflecting the vintage well. Screwcap a plus. **RATING** 93 **DRINK** 2008 $ 27
Cabernet Franc 2001 Strong colour; quite complex; more structure and flavour than the variety usually provides; blackberry, bitter chocolate and spice. **RATING** 91 **DRINK** 2010 $ 25

Chardonnay 2003 Medium-bodied stone fruit and melon; controlled barrel ferment inputs. **RATING** 87 **DRINK** Now $ 22

Semillon Sauvignon Blanc 2003 Subdued bouquet and primary fruit; texture and flavour complexity aided by a hint of oak. **RATING** 86 **DRINK** Now $ 18.50
Shiraz 2001 **RATING** 85 **DRINK** 2009 $ 33.50

Goorambath

103 Hooper Road, Goorambat, Vic 3725 **REGION** Glenrowan
T (03) 5764 1380 **F** (03) 5764 1320 **OPEN** By appointment
WINEMAKER David Hodgson **EST.** 1997 **CASES** 600
PRODUCT RANGE ($15–25 CD) Verdelho, Shiraz.
SUMMARY Lyn and Geoff Bath have had a long association with the Victorian wine industry. Since 1982 Geoff Bath has been senior lecturer in viticulture with the University of Melbourne at Dookie Campus; he and wife Lyn also owned (in conjunction with two other couples) a vineyard at Whitlands for 18 years. In July 2000 they sold their interest in that vineyard to focus on their small

vineyard at Goorambat, hence the clever name. Planting had begun in 1998 with 1 hectare of shiraz, subsequently joined by 1 hectare of verdelho, 0.5 hectare of orange muscat and 0.2 hectare of tannat.

ȲȲȲȲȲ **Shiraz 2001** Deep colour; rich, full and powerful; licorice, spice, blackberry and leather. Gold medal Victorian Wines Show 2002. **RATING** 94 **DRINK** 2021 $ 25

ȲȲȲȲȲ **Shiraz 2002** Deep, inky purple; ultra-powerful, rich and concentrated blackberry/black chocolate; balanced tannins, but a monster. **RATING** 92 **DRINK** 2017 $ 25

ȲȲȲȲ **Verdelho 2003** An abundance of fruit salad flavours; good balance; nearly rises above its station. Screwcap. **RATING** 87 **DRINK** Now $ 16

🐚 Gordon Sunter Wines NR

PO Box 12, Tanunda, SA 5352 **REGION** Barossa Valley
T (08) 8563 2349 **OPEN** Not
WINEMAKER Stuart Blackwell **EST.** 1982
PRODUCT RANGE A range of varietally denominated table wines reflecting the plantings.
SUMMARY Gordon Sunter Wines has lived a shadowy existence for over 20 years, as the part-time private label of St Hallett winemaker Stuart Blackwell. The deliberately low profile is not hard to understand.

🐚 Goulburn Terrace NR

340 High Street, Nagambie, Vic 3608 **REGION** Goulburn Valley
T (03) 5794 2828 **F** (03) 5794 1854 **OPEN** Weekends 10–5
WINEMAKER Dr Mike Boudry, Greta Moon **EST.** 1993
PRODUCT RANGE ($22 ML) Chardonnay, Shiraz, Cabernet.
SUMMARY Dr Mike Boudry and Greta Moon have established their 8-hectare vineyard on the west bank of the Goulburn River, around 8 kilometres south of Lake Nagambie. Planting began in 1993; chardonnay, marsanne, roussanne, shiraz and mataro have been established on the alluvial soils 10 000 years old, adjacent to the river, while the cabernet sauvignon has been planted on a gravelly rise based on 400 million year old Devonian rocks. The wines are made in small volumes, with open fermentation and hand plunging of the reds; all are basket pressed. The wines are sold direct from the vineyard by mail order, and at the cellar door in High Street, Nagambie, as well as being stocked by a number of local and Melbourne restaurants.

🐚 Goulburn Valley Estate Wines ★★☆

340 Trotter Road, Mooroopna North, Vic 3629 **REGION** Goulburn Valley
T (03) 5829 0278 **F** (03) 5829 0014 **OPEN** By appointment
WINEMAKER Rocky Scarpari **EST.** 2001
PRODUCT RANGE Sauvignon Blanc, Chardonnay, Shiraz, Merlot, Cabernet Sauvignon.
SUMMARY Rocky Scarpari heads Goulburn Valley Estate Wines, the wine being under the direction of the vastly experienced Lee Clarnette. Goulburn Valley Estate has a nominal 1.2 hectares of vines, the major part of its substantial production coming from growers in the Mooroopna area. The wines are sold under the Goulburn Shed brand, with exports to Hong Kong and Malaysia, and limited cellar door and mail order sales.

ȲȲȲ **Shiraz 2002 RATING** 82

Goundrey ★★★☆

Muir Highway, Mount Barker, WA 6324 **REGION** Mount Barker
T (08) 9892 1777 **F** (08) 9851 1997 **OPEN** 7 days 10–4.30
WINEMAKER David Martin, Michael Perkins, Stephen Craig **EST.** 1976 **CASES** 300 000
PRODUCT RANGE ($15.30–34 R) Windy Hill range of Chardonnay, Pinot Noir; Goundrey Homestead range of Riesling, Chenin Blanc, Classic White, Unwooded Chardonnay, Shiraz Cabernet, Cabernet Merlot; Reserve range of Riesling, Chardonnay, Pinot Noir, Shiraz, Cabernet Sauvignon; second label is Fox River with Chenin Semillon Verdelho, Chardonnay, Pinot Noir, Shiraz, Shiraz Cabernet; also Langton Sauvignon Blanc Semillon.

SUMMARY Jack Bendat acquired Goundrey when it was on its knees; through significant expenditure on land, vineyards and winery capacity, it became the House that Jack Built. In late 2002 it was acquired by Vincorp, Canada's largest wine producer, for a price widely said to be more than $30 million, a sum which would have provided Bendat with a very satisfactory return on his investment. One suspects it will be more of the same with Vincorp, which will continue to expand the empire. National distribution; exports to the US, Canada, Asia, the UK and Europe.

ṪṪṪṪṪ **Reserve Riesling 2003** Elegant, flowery but complex; apple, mineral and herb; a long dry finish; some toasty notes starting to appear. Screwcap. **RATING** 94 **DRINK** 2013 $ 17.85
Reserve Chardonnay 2001 Complex, stylish barrel ferment and fruit marriage; has considerable fruit depth, the oak in support. Best for years. Gold Sheraton Wine Awards 2003. **RATING** 94 **DRINK** 2008 $ 30

ṪṪṪṪṪ **Fox River Chardonnay 2002** Lovely wine; supple, smooth nectarine and melon fruit; gentle oak. **RATING** 90 **DRINK** 2007 $ 15

ṪṪṪṪ **Offspring Shiraz 2002** Supple, medium-bodied; blackberry, blackcurrant and spice; fruit-driven. Screwcap. **RATING** 89 **DRINK** 2010 $ 19.99
Reserve Shiraz 2001 Powerful, cool-grown array of aromas and flavours from red berry to herb, leaf and spice; slightly nippy tannins. **RATING** 88 **DRINK** 2013 $ 33.99
Langton Cabernet Shiraz 2001 Fresh, clean red and black fruits; medium-bodied, well balanced, easy style; soft tannins. Good value. **RATING** 87 **DRINK** 2010 $ 14.99

ṪṪṪṪ **Offspring Chardonnay 2002** Light to medium-bodied; well-balanced peach and nectarine; fruit-driven. Screwcap. **RATING** 86 **DRINK** Now $ 19.99
Homestead Shiraz 2002 **RATING** 86 **DRINK** 2007 $ 14.99
Offspring Cabernet Sauvignon 2002 Light to medium-bodied; nice blackcurrant/black fruits; direct, no frills style. Screwcap. **RATING** 86 **DRINK** 2009 $ 19.99
Reserve Chardonnay 2002 **RATING** 85 **DRINK** Now $ 30
Homestead Cabernet Merlot 2002 **RATING** 85 **DRINK** Now $ 17

ṪṪṪ **Classic White 2003** **RATING** 83 $ 14.95
Homestead Shiraz 2001 **RATING** 83 $ 14.99
Chenin Blanc 2003 **RATING** 82 $ 14.95

Governor Robe Selection
NR

Waterhouse Range Vineyards, Lot 11, Old Naracoorte Road, Robe, SA 5276
REGION Limestone Coast Zone
T (08) 8768 2083 **F** (08) 8768 2190 **OPEN** By appointment
WINEMAKER Cape Jaffa Wines (Contract) **EST.** 1998 **CASES** 750
PRODUCT RANGE ($17–30 R) Chardonnay, Shiraz, Cabernet Sauvignon.
SUMMARY Brothers Bill and Mick Quinlan-Watson, supported by a group of investors, began the development of Waterhouse Range Vineyards Pty Ltd in 1995, planting 15 hectares of vines that year, with further plantings over the following few years lifting the total area under vine to just under 60 hectares. The majority of the grapes are sold, with a lesser amount retained and contract-made at Cape Jaffa winery. The unusual name comes from the third Governor of South Australia, Frederick Holt Robe, who in 1845 selected the site for a port and personally put in the first survey peg at Robe. Next door is the Customs House which is a National Trust building, and which is depicted on the label.

Governor's Choice Winery
NR

Berghofer Road, Westbrook via Toowoomba, Qld 4350 **REGION** Queensland Zone
T (07) 4630 6101 **F** (07) 4630 6701 **OPEN** 7 days 9–5
WINEMAKER James Yates **EST.** 1999 **CASES** 1500
PRODUCT RANGE ($14–30 CD) Premium Semillon, Estate White, Verdelho, Chardonnay, Shiraz, Cabernet Shiraz, Cabernet Malbec, Cabernet Sauvignon, Tawny Port, White Port, Vintage Red Port.
SUMMARY This is a part winery, part premium guesthouse accommodation venture situated 18 kilometres from the town of Toowoomba. Three hectares of estate plantings produce chardonnay, shiraz, verdelho, cabernet sauvignon and malbec, made on-site and sold through the cellar door or to guests using the accommodation.

Gowrie Mountain Estate

NR

2 Warrego Highway, Kingsthorpe, Qld 4400 **REGION** Darling Downs
T (07) 4630 0566 **F** (07) 4630 0366 **OPEN** 7 days 10–5
WINEMAKER Peter Howland, Rod McPherson (Contract) **EST.** 1998 **CASES** 6000
PRODUCT RANGE ($14–18 CD) Semillon, Verdelho, Chardonnay, Reserve Shiraz, Family Reserve Shiraz, Gamay, Tempranillo, Cabernet Shiraz, Cabernet Sauvignon.
SUMMARY Situated northeast of Toowoomba, in the heart of the Darling Downs, this is a substantial new entrant, having already established 32 hectares to mainstream varieties, and to the new breed in the form of tempranillo (4 hectares) and gamay (2 hectares). Part of the production goes to Peter Howland in the Hunter Valley which makes the red wines, and part to Preston Peak, where the white wines and Tempranillo are made. An underground barrel and bottled wine storage area has been completed, with a sales, restaurant and general tourist facility planned. All of the Newberry family members, headed by father Ron, are involved in the venture.

Gracedale Hills Estate

NR

770 Healesville-Kooweerup Road, Healesville, Vic 3777 **REGION** Yarra Valley
T (03) 5967 3403 **F** (03) 5967 3581 **OPEN** Not
WINEMAKER Gary Mills **EST.** 1996 **CASES** 1300
PRODUCT RANGE Chardonnay, Shiraz.
SUMMARY Dr Richard Gutch has established 2 hectares of chardonnay and 2 hectares of shiraz at a time when most would be retiring from active business, but it represents the culmination of a life-long love of fine wine, and Richard Gutch has no hard feelings towards me when I encouraged him in the mid-1990s to plant vines on the north-facing slopes of his property. Here, too, the grapes have been sold to others, but he is now retaining sufficient to make around 1300 cases a year.

🌿 Grace Devlin Wines

★★★☆

53 Siddles Road, Redesdale, Vic 3444 **REGION** Heathcote
T (03) 5425 3101 **OPEN** By appointment
WINEMAKER Brian Paterson, Lee Paterson **EST.** 1998 **CASES** 200
PRODUCT RANGE ($20–30 R) Merlot, Cabernet Sauvignon.
SUMMARY Brian and Lee Paterson have 2 hectares of cabernet sauvignon and 0.5 hectare of merlot at Redesdale. It is one of the most southerly vineyards in the Heathcote region, and most of the vines are over 12 years old. (The property was previously known as Mount Lofty, after a local landmark, but was changed because of understandable confustion with Mount Lofty in the Adelaide Hills.) The name Grace Devlin comes from the middle names of Brian Paterson's grandmother, mother and daughters. Although production is as yet small, it is available in no less than 11 local outlets, notably the Woodend Bottle Shop, the Lake House at Daylesford, the Emeu Inn at Heathcote, the Redesdale Hotel and the Cosmopolitan Hotel and Restaurant at Trentham.

 Cabernet Sauvignon 2002 Plenty of depth and flesh to clean blackcurrant and blackberry fruit; ripe tannins. **RATING** 89 **DRINK** 2012

Gralaine Vineyard

NR

65 Feehan's Road, Mount Duneed, Vic 3216 (postal) **REGION** Geelong
T 0429 009 973 **F** (03) 9886 7377 **OPEN** Available 7 days 10–5 at Hanging Rock Winery, 88 Jim Road, Newham
WINEMAKER John Ellis (Contract) **EST.** 1983
PRODUCT RANGE ($26 CD) Merlot.
SUMMARY Graeme and Elaine Carroll have gradually established 4 hectares of low-yielding merlot (with a few cabernet sauvignon vines). There are no cellar-door sales, but the wine can be tasted at Hanging Rock Winery, where it is contract-made by John Ellis.

Gralyn Estate

Caves Road, Wilyabrup, WA 6280 **REGION** Margaret River
T (08) 9755 6245 **F** (08) 9755 6136 **OPEN** 7 days 10.30–4.30
WINEMAKER Graham Hutton, Merilyn Hutton, Bradley Hutton **EST.** 1975 **CASES** 2500
PRODUCT RANGE ($20–90 CD) Premium Dry White (Semillon), Late Harvest Riesling, Old Vine Shiraz, Late Harvest Cabernet, Shiraz Cabernet, Unoaked Cabernet, Cabernet Sauvignon, and an extensive range of fortifieds including Liqueur Riesling, White Port, Vintage Port and Ruby Port.
SUMMARY The move from primarily fortified wine to table wine production has been completed, and brought considerable success. The red wines are made in a distinctively different style from most of those from the Margaret River region, with an opulence (in part from American oak) which is reminiscent of some of the bigger wines from McLaren Vale. The age of the vines (30 years) and the site are also significant factors. Exports to the US, Denmark and Singapore.

▼▼▼▼▽ **Cabernet Sauvignon 2002** Strong varietal character; very good structure, balance and length; blackcurrant and a touch of chocolate; controlled oak. **RATING** 93 **DRINK** 2017 **$** 90
Old Vine Shiraz 2002 Less oak than in prior vintages; solid blackberry fruit; fine, savoury tannins to close. **RATING** 91 **DRINK** 2012 **$** 60
Shiraz Cabernet 2002 A rich mix of blackcurrant and blackberry fruit; oak obvious throughout; extract good. **RATING** 90 **DRINK** 2015 **$** 90

▼▼▼▼ **Premium Dry White 2003** Complex aromas and flavours, with lots of weight and richness, giving the impression of a background hint of oak, even though unwooded. **RATING** 88 **DRINK** 2007 **$** 20

Grampians Estate

NR

Mafeking Road, Willaura, Vic 3379 **REGION** Grampians
T (03) 5354 6245 **F** (03) 5354 6257 **OPEN** By appointment
WINEMAKER Simon Clayfield **EST.** 1989 **CASES** 1000
PRODUCT RANGE ($15.50–22 R) Mafeking Unwooded Chardonnay, Mafeking Gold Chardonnay, Mafeking Shiraz.
SUMMARY Ten years ago local farmers and graziers Sarah and Tom Guthrie decided to diversify their activities, while continuing to run their fat lamb and wool production. So they planted a little over 1.5 hectares each of shiraz and chardonnay, and opened the Thermopylae Host Farm business. This offers two farm-stay buildings, a five-bedroom shearer's cottage which sleeps 12, and a five-room miner's cottage which sleeps ten. They also secured the services of immensely experienced local winemaker Simon Clayfield to produce the Grampians Estate wines. These are sold to those who stay on the farm, which is able to offer an unusually wide range of activities; the wines are also available by direct mail order and at one or two local hotels including the Kookaburra Rest at Halls Gap.

Grancari Estate Wines

50 Northumberland Road, Onkaparinga Hills, SA 5162 **REGION** McLaren Vale
T (08) 8382 4465 **F** (08) 8382 4465 **OPEN** By appointment
WINEMAKER Michael Brown, Kevin O'Brien (Contract) **EST.** 1999 **CASES** 800
PRODUCT RANGE ($19.50–34 CD) Shiraz, Old Vine Grenache, Grenache Shiraz, Old Vine Merlot.
SUMMARY In 1983 Rino and Greta Ozzella purchased a small vineyard in McLaren Vale which had been planted in the early 1940s to a little under 3 hectares of grenache. The grapes were sold to other winemakers, and in 1993 the Ozzellas purchased two properties at Loxton in the Riverland. After 3 years developing the vineyards there, the Ozzellas sold the blocks and returned to McLaren Vale, planting a further 2.5 hectares of shiraz on a westerly slope facing the sea, and took the decision to establish their own brand. At the same time they began the conversion to organic, which has now been certified (in conversion). The wines are contract-made by Kevin O'Brien at Kangarilla Road.

▼▼▼▼▽ **Shiraz 2002** Clean; a lush array of black fruits and regional chocolate; well-handled oak and extract. **RATING** 90 **DRINK** 2012 **$** 34

▼▼▼▽ **Grenache Shiraz 2003** Fresh, sweet, juicy plummy/red berry fruit; avoids being jammy, but drink now. **RATING** 86 **DRINK** 2009 **$** 23

🐝 Grandview Vineyard ★★★☆

59 Devlyns Road, Birchs Bay, Tas 7162 **REGION** Southern Tasmania
T (03) 6267 4749 **F** (03) 6267 4779 **OPEN** 7 days 10–5
WINEMAKER Andrew Hood (Contract) **EST.** 1996 **CASES** 350
PRODUCT RANGE ($22–30 R) Gewurztraminer, Sauvignon Blanc, Chardonnay, Pinot Noir, Gamay.
SUMMARY Ryan Hartshorn has acquired the vineyard formerly burdened by the impossible name 2 Bud Spur. Hartshorn is moving the vineyard towards organic, and it is anticipated that 2005 will be in the conversion phase. It is a pocket handkerchief mix of varieties: 0.35 hectares gewurztraminer, 0.7 hectare chardonnay, 0.6 hectare pinot noir, 0.3 hectare sauvignon blanc and 0.05 hectare gamay.

�♀♀ **Pinot Noir 2003** Spotlessly clean; light to medium-bodied black cherry and plum; fine tannins; an elegant style, will benefit from cellaring. **RATING** 89 **DRINK** 2008 $ 25
Chardonnay 2002 Funky wild yeast/feral/solids style. Will divide opinion. **RATING** 88 **DRINK** 2009 $ 25

♀♀♀♀ **Gamay 2003** Bright cherry, light and cheerful; summer drinking. **RATING** 86 **DRINK** Now $ 30

♀♀♀ **Gewurztraminer 2003** **RATING** 83 $ 22

♀♀♀ **Sauvignon Blanc 2002** **RATING** 79 $ 22

Granite Hills ★★★★★

1481 Burke and Wills Track, Baynton, Kyneton, Vic 3444 **REGION** Macedon Ranges
T (03) 5423 7264 **F** (03) 5423 7288 **OPEN** Mon–Sat 10–6, Sun 12–6
WINEMAKER Llew Knight, Ian Gunter **EST.** 1970 **CASES** 7000
PRODUCT RANGE ($15–50 CD) Riesling, Chardonnay, Mica Chardonnay, Pinot Noir, Shiraz, Merlot, Cabernet Sauvignon, Reserve Cabernet, Sparkling.
SUMMARY Granite Hills is one of the enduring classics, pioneering the successful growing of riesling and shiraz in an uncompromisingly cool climate. It is based on 11 hectares of riesling, chardonnay, shiraz, cabernet sauvignon, merlot and pinot noir (the last used in its sparkling wine). After a quiet period in the 1990s, has been reinvigorated, its original two icons once again to the fore. The Rieslings age superbly, and the shiraz is at the forefront of the cool-climate school in Australia. Exports to the US and the UK.

♀♀♀♀♀ **Knight Riesling 2003** Glorious young riesling, intense and very long. Great combination citrus and acidity. **RATING** 95 **DRINK** 2013 $ 20

♀♀♀♀♀ **Knight Chardonnay 2002** Highly aromatic; fresh, zippy fruit; little or no oak evident. **RATING** 90 **DRINK** Now $ 18

♀♀♀♀ **Knight Cabernet Sauvignon 2001** Elegant, light to medium-bodied; red fruits and mint; low tannins, but not green. **RATING** 87 **DRINK** 2007 $ 26

♀♀♀♀ **Knight Brut 1998** **RATING** 85 **DRINK** Now $ 35
Knight Pinot Noir 2001 **RATING** 84 **DRINK** Now $ 24
Knight Pinot Noir 2000 **RATING** 84 **DRINK** 2007 $ 24
Knight Cabernet Sauvignon 2000 **RATING** 84 **DRINK** Now $ 26

Granite Ridge Wines ★★★

Sundown Road, Ballandean, Qld 4382 **REGION** Granite Belt
T (07) 4684 1263 **F** (07) 4684 1250 **OPEN** 7 days 9–5
WINEMAKER Dennis Ferguson, Juliane Ferguson **EST.** 1995 **CASES** 2000
PRODUCT RANGE ($10–20 CD) Goldies Unwooded Chardonnay, Bilby White, First Oak Chardonnay, Citrine Semillon (sweet), il Bello Rosso (Sparkling red), Topaz, Granite Garnet, Granite Rock Shiraz, Fergies Hill Merlot, The Ridge Merlot Cabernet Sauvignon, Millennium Cabernet Merlot, Bilby Red, Granite Grange Cabernet Sauvignon, Granite Amber Liqueur Muscat, Pops Port, Surrender Cream Liqueur.
SUMMARY Formerly known as Denlana Ferguson Estate Wines, Granite Ridge had considerable success in the mid-1990s, with both the 1995 and 1996 Cabernet Sauvignon being judged

Queensland's Best Cabernet (though quite by whom I am not sure); continues to be run by Dennis Ferguson. Its Goldies Unwooded Chardonnay was the first Queensland wine to be chosen as the official Parliamentary Wine of the Queensland Government. Most of the production comes from its 5-hectare vineyard planted to pinot gris, chardonnay, verdelho, merlot, shiraz, petit verdot, tempranillo and cabernet sauvignon.

ᵀᵀᵀ♀ **Merlot Cabernet Sauvignon 2001** RATING 86 DRINK 2007 $18

Grant Burge ★★★★

Barossa Vines, Krondorf Road, Tanunda, SA 5352 REGION Barossa Valley
T (08) 8563 3700 F (08) 8563 2807 OPEN 7 days 10–5
WINEMAKER Grant Burge EST. 1988 CASES 200 000
PRODUCT RANGE ($11.60–100 R) Has a core series of vineyard-designated varietal wines coupled with bin number special releases. Top-of-the-range reds are Meshach Shiraz, The Holy Trinity (Grenache Shiraz Mourvedre) and Shadrach Cabernet Sauvignon. The budget-priced Barossa Vines range joined the band in late 1999, Miamba Shiraz in 2001.
SUMMARY As one might expect, this very experienced industry veteran makes consistently good, full-flavoured and smooth wines chosen from the pick of the crop of his extensive vineyard holdings, which total an impressive 200 hectares; the immaculately restored/rebuilt stone cellar-door sales buildings are another attraction. The provocatively named The Holy Trinity (a Grenache Shiraz Mourvedre blend) joins Shadrach and Meshach at the top of the range. In 1999 Grant Burge repurchased the farm from Mildara Blass by acquiring the Krondorf winery (not the brand) in which he made his first fortune. He has renamed it Barossa Vines and, taking advantage of the great views it offers, has opened a cellar door offering casual food, featuring local produce wherever possible. Exports to the UK, Europe, the US, Canada and Asia.

ᵀᵀᵀᵀᵀ **Meshach Shiraz 1999** Fragrant black fruit aromas; excellent mouthfeel and balance; silky tannins and perfect oak. Fully deserves its multiple trophies and golds. RATING 95 DRINK 2014 $100

ᵀᵀᵀᵀ♀ **Filsell Shiraz 2002** Stacked full of blackberry and plum fruit, supple and rich; ripe tannins and good oak support. RATING 93 DRINK 2017 $29.80
Meshach Shiraz 2000 Continues the new Meschach style with more emphasis on fruit than oak; supple blackberry with a touch of chocolate; very fine tannins and good length. RATING 92 DRINK 2015 $100
RGSM1 Grenache Shiraz Mourvedre 1999 Fine and elegant; complex, savoury, spicy aromas; light to medium-bodied, with distinct Rhône overtones; good finish. RATING 92 DRINK 2009 $44.70
Filsell Shiraz 2001 Deeply coloured; archetypal Burge/Barossa dark berry and vanilla aromas, the palate with interesting and attractive savoury edges, possibly varying fruit ripeness. RATING 90 DRINK 2011 $29.80
Balthazar Shiraz Viognier 2002 Very good colour; juicy red berry flavours lifted by Viognier; medium-bodied, long, but not over-much structure. RATING 90 DRINK 2008 $36.40
Shadrach Cabernet Sauvignon 1999 Perfumed aromas; medium-bodied and finely balanced, with cedary oak and carefully modulated tannins. RATING 90 DRINK 2009 $39.95

ᵀᵀᵀᵀ **Miamba Shiraz 2002** Solid, rich, honest blackberry, plum and dark chocolate; good balance; good vintage. RATING 89 DRINK 2010 $19.85
Summers Eden Valley Chardonnay 2002 Smooth, medium-bodied, well integrated melon/stone fruit and oak; harmonious and balanced. RATING 88 DRINK 2007 $20
Barossa Vines Semillon Sauvignon Blanc 2003 Excellent depth of flavour and richness; ripe tropical notes, but not phenolic. Good value. RATING 87 DRINK Now $11.60
Lily Farm Frontignac 2003 As appealing as ever; juicy, tropical berry fruit; excellent intensity and clever balance of sugar and acidity. Dead-set Asian, and excellent value. RATING 87 DRINK Now $12
The Holy Trinity Grenache Shiraz Mourvedre 2000 Light to medium-bodied, with some minty edges; shows typical vintage character even with these old vines. RATING 87 DRINK 2007 $36.40

Barossa Vines Cabernet Sauvignon Merlot 2002 Honest wine; quite good varietal definition; a light to medium-bodied mix of red and black berries; minimal tannins. **RATING** 87 **DRINK** 2009 $ 15

Cameron Vale Cabernet Sauvignon 2001 Blackcurrant fruit with some savoury aspects partially offset by sweetening oak; balanced tannins. **RATING** 87 **DRINK** 2010 $ 24

♥♥♥♡ **The Holy Trinity Grenache Shiraz Mourvedre 2001** Pleasant, gently sweet, medium-bodied and well-balanced wine, with a high price tag. **RATING** 86 **DRINK** Now $ 36.40

Hillcott Merlot 2002 RATING 86 **DRINK** 2008 $ 18

Kraft Vineyard Sauvignon Blanc 2003 RATING 85 **DRINK** Now $ 15

Barossa Vines Shiraz 2002 RATING 85 **DRINK** 2007 $ 15

Pinot Noir Chardonnay NV RATING 85 **DRINK** Now $ 19.50

Barossa Vines Chardonnay 2003 RATING 84 **DRINK** Now $ 11.60

♥♥♥ **Zerk Semillon 2002 RATING** 83 $ 17

Barossa Vines Semillon 2003 RATING 82 $ 9.95

🦘 Great Lakes Wines   NR

115 Herivals Road, Wootton, NSW 2423 **REGION** Northern Rivers Zone
T (02) 4997 7255 **F** (02) 4997 7450 **OPEN** 7 days 10–5
WINEMAKER David Hook (Contract), Steve Attkins **EST.** 1990
PRODUCT RANGE A range of varietally denominated table wines reflecting the plantings.
SUMMARY Great Lakes Wines is situated south of the Hastings River region but well north of Newcastle. Robyn Piper and Steve Attkins have 4 hectares of semillon, chardonnay, verdelho, cabernet sauvignon, shiraz and chambourcin planted, and make the wine on-site with David Hook overseeing proceedings. The wines are sold by mail order and through the cellar door, which offers light meals, barbecue and picnic facilities.

Greenock Creek Wines   NR

Radford Road, Seppeltsfield, SA 5360 **REGION** Barossa Valley
T (08) 8562 8103 **F** (08) 8562 8259 **OPEN** Wed–Mon 11–5 when wine available
WINEMAKER Michael Waugh **EST.** 1978 **CASES** 2500
PRODUCT RANGE ($25–160 CD) Alices Shiraz, Apricot Block Shiraz, Seven Acre Shiraz, Creek Block Shiraz, Roennfeldt Road Shiraz, Cornerstone Grenache, Cabernet Sauvignon, Roennfeldt Road Cabernet Sauvignon.
SUMMARY Michael and Annabelle Waugh are disciples of Rocky O'Callaghan of Rockford Wines and have deliberately accumulated a series of old dryland, low-yielding Barossa vineyards, aiming to produce wines of unusual depth of flavour and character. They have handsomely succeeded in this aim, achieving icon status and stratospheric prices in the US, making the opinions of Australian scribes irrelevant. They also offer superior accommodation in the ancient but beautifully restored two-bedroom cottage 'Miriam's'; Michael Waugh is a skilled stonemason.

Green Valley Vineyard   ★★★★

3137 Sebbes Road, Forest Grove, WA 6286 **REGION** Margaret River
T (08) 9757 7510 **F** (08) 9757 7510 **OPEN** 7 days 10–6
WINEMAKER Moss Wood (Contract) **EST.** 1980 **CASES** 3500
PRODUCT RANGE ($17.50–30 CD) Riesling, Chardonnay, Gelignite Block Shiraz, Cabernet Sauvignon.
SUMMARY Owners Ed and Eleanore Green commenced the development of Green Valley Vineyard in 1980. It is still a part-time operation, with the wines made by contract, but production has grown steadily from the 7.7 hectares of vines, and the Cabernet Sauvignon has been a consistent medal winner. Exports to Singapore and the US.

♥♥♥♥♡ **Chardonnay 2002** Complex, toasty barrel ferment inputs to intense melon fruit; powerful impact and length. **RATING** 91 **DRINK** 2009 $ 34.50

🐚 Gregory's Wines

NR

1 Lizard Park Drive, Kilkerran, SA 5573 **REGION** The Peninsulas Zone
T (08) 8834 1258 **F** (08) 8834 1287 **OPEN** Mon–Fri 9–5
WINEMAKER Stephen John (Contract) **EST.** 2000
PRODUCT RANGE A range of varietally denominated table wines reflecting the plantings.
SUMMARY Rod and Toni Gregory have established 11 hectares of vineyard near Kilkerran, on the western side of the York Peninsula. The plantings comprise chardonnay, viognier, shiraz and cabernet sauvignon, and are chiefly sold through the cellar door and by mail order. The site has facilities to cater for concerts or festivals, and tours by arrangement.

Grevillea Estate

 ★★★☆

Buckajo Road, Bega, NSW 2550 **REGION** South Coast Zone
T (02) 6492 3006 **F** (02) 6492 5330 **OPEN** Sept–May Mon–Fri 9–5, weekends 10–5; June–Aug 7 days 10–4
WINEMAKER Nicola Collins **EST.** 1980 **CASES** 2000
PRODUCT RANGE ($16–30 CD) Daisy Hill Riesling, Rose Hill Gewurztraminer, Traminer Riesling, Lunatic Hill Sauvignon Blanc, Unoaked Chardonnay, Peak Hill Chardonnay, Kirby Reserve Chardonnay, Rougon, Grosse's Creek Merlot, Edmund Kirby Cabernet Sauvignon, Wetlands Cabernet Shiraz, Wetland Cabernet Sauvignon, Kirby Reserve Cabernet Sauvignon, Old Tawny Port.
SUMMARY A tourist-oriented winery which successfully sells all of its surprisingly large production through the cellar door and to local restaurants. The consistency and quality of the wines has improved out of sight; a further label redesign has also lifted the appeal.

ΨΨΨΨ **Kirby Family Reserve Alice Botrytis Gewurztraminer 2002** Developed gold; a complex wine with some gewurz varietal character still there; spicy peach flavours; well made. **RATING** 88 **DRINK** Now $ 18
Kirby Family Reserve Cabernet Sauvignon Cabernet Franc Merlot 2003 Sweeter mid-palate fruit than the Cabernet Sauvignon; good balance and length. **RATING** 87 **DRINK** 2010 $ 30

ΨΨΨ▽ **Kirby (JK) Family Reserve Cabernet Sauvignon 2003** As with all of the current releases, well made; light to medium-bodied savoury style; dips slightly on the mid-palate, but gains length on the finish. **RATING** 86 **DRINK** 2008 $ 25
Wetlands Cabernet Shiraz 2003 Savoury, spicy, earthy; light to medium-bodied, not forced; minimal tannins and oak but good finish and aftertaste. **RATING** 86 **DRINK** 2008 $ 20
Rose Hill Gewurztraminer 2001 RATING 85 **DRINK** Now $ 17
Lunatic Hill Sauvignon Blanc 2002 RATING 85 **DRINK** Now $ 17

Grey Sands

 ★★★★

Cnr Kerrisons Road and Frankford Highway, Glengarry, Tas 7275 **REGION** Northern Tasmania
T (03) 6396 1167 **F** (03) 6396 1153 **OPEN** Last Sunday of each month 10–5, or by appointment
WINEMAKER Bob Richter **EST.** 1989 **CASES** 450
PRODUCT RANGE ($26–35 CD) Pinot Gris, Merlot, Shiraz.
SUMMARY Bob and Rita Richter began the slow establishment of Grey Sands in 1988, slowly increasing the plantings over the ensuing 10 years to the present total of 2.5 hectares. The ultra-high density of 8900 vines per hectare partially reflects the experience gained by the Richters during a 3-year stay in England, during which time they visited many vineyards across Europe, and partially Bob Richter's graduate diploma in wine from Roseworthy Agricultural College.

ΨΨΨΨ▽ **Merlot 2001** Good flavour, structure and texture; medium-bodied, supple blackcurrant and raspberry fruit, fine tannins. **RATING** 90 **DRINK** 2010 $ 30

ΨΨΨΨ **Pinot Gris 2003** Pink tinged; bracing herbal, mineral style; touches of green apple and citrus. **RATING** 87 **DRINK** Now $ 26

Grosset ★★★★★

King Street, Auburn, SA 5451 **REGION** Clare Valley
T (08) 8849 2175 **F** (08) 8849 2292 **OPEN** Wed–Sun 10–5 from 1st week of September for approx 6 weeks
WINEMAKER Jeffrey Grosset **EST.** 1981 **CASES** 9000
PRODUCT RANGE ($30–58 CD) Watervale Riesling, Polish Hill Riesling, Semillon Sauvignon Blanc, Piccadilly Chardonnay, Gaia (Cabernet blend), Pinot Noir.
SUMMARY Jeffrey Grosset served part of his apprenticeship at the vast Lindeman Karadoc winery, moving from the largest to one of the smallest when he established Grosset Wines in its old stone winery. He now crafts the wines with the utmost care from grapes grown to the most exacting standards; all need a certain amount of time in bottle to achieve their ultimate potential, not the least the Rieslings and Gaia, among Australia's best examples of their kind. At a Riesling Summit held in Hamburg in the latter part of 1998, Grosset was voted Riesling Winemaker of the Year. He is also a passionate advocate of the use of screwcaps on all wines, red and white. Exports to the US, Europe and Asia mean a continuous shortage of the wines in all markets.

ŸŸŸŸŸ **Polish Hill Riesling 2003** Intense, fine and long, with great mid-palate flavour, beautiful acidity and fantastic mouthfeel. **RATING** 97 **DRINK** 2015 $ 39
Semillon Sauvignon Blanc 2003 Spotless, semillon-dominant aromas; long, lingering and precise palate; subtle passionfruit and gooseberry. Will hold its fruit for many years. **RATING** 95 **DRINK** 2010 $ 29.50
Watervale Riesling 2003 Intense aromas with more lime juice than usual; the palate follows the bouquet, with more weight and richness, particularly to the tropical/lime back palate. Dry finish. **RATING** 94 **DRINK** 2013 $ 33
Piccadilly Chardonnay 2002 Light straw-green; intense and complex yet fine aromas and flavours; stone fruit and subtle barrel ferment; long finish. **RATING** 94 **DRINK** 2010 $ 49.50
Gaia 2001 Pristine blackcurrant fruit aromas; supple, silky mouthfeel, and a long, clean finish. Screwcap. **RATING** 94 **DRINK** 2021 $ 58

ŸŸŸŸŸ **Pinot Noir 2002** Fragrant, spicy plum and black cherry; strong mid-palate; good line and length. **RATING** 92 **DRINK** 2008 $ 59.50

Grove Estate ★★★★

Murringo Road, Young, NSW 2594 **REGION** Hilltops
T (02) 6382 6999 **F** (02) 6382 4527 **OPEN** Weekends 10–5, or by appointment
WINEMAKER Monarch Winemaking Services (Contract) **EST.** 1989 **CASES** 3000
PRODUCT RANGE ($14–21 CD) Kingsvale Riesling, Hilltops Semillon, Murringo Way Chardonnay, The Cellar Block Shiraz, Hilltops Zinfandel, Basazi Barbera Sangiovese Zinfandel, The Partners Cabernet Sauvignon, Ignatius Zin.
SUMMARY A partnership of Brian Mullany, John Kirkwood and Mark Flanders has established a 30-hectare vineyard planted to semillon, chardonnay, merlot, shiraz, cabernet sauvignon and zinfandel. Some of the grapes are sold (principally to Southcorp), but an increasing amount of very good and interesting wine is contract-made by Monarch Winemaking Services for the Grove Estate label. Exports to the UK.

ŸŸŸŸŸ **The Partner's Reserve Cabernet Sauvignon 2001** Complex structure and texture, more oak maturation but similar blackberry/blackcurrant fruit; fine tannins. **RATING** 94 **DRINK** 2016 $ 25

ŸŸŸŸŸ **The Partners Cabernet Sauvignon 2001** Generously proportioned blackberry and blackcurrant fruit; excellent balance and mouthfeel. **RATING** 90 **DRINK** 2011 $ 19

ŸŸŸŸ **Murringo Way Chardonnay 2001** Aromatic peach and stone fruit; good length and acidity; entirely fruit-driven. **RATING** 89 **DRINK** 2007 $ 15
Basazi 2003 Bright colour; exotic, plush array of fruit aromas and flavours; brushes of chocolate, blackberry, prune and spice. Great value. Zinfandel, Sangiovese and Barbera. **RATING** 89 **DRINK** 2011 $ 16

The Cellar Block Shiraz 2001 Nice texture and mouthfeel; gentle mix of black fruits, chocolate and mocha; ripe, fine tannins. **RATING** 88 **DRINK** 2010 **$** 19
Hilltops Semillon 2002 Generous, ripe fruit ranging into tropical spectrum; masses of flavour; less sweet than the '03. **RATING** 87 **DRINK** Now **$** 15
Hilltops Zinfandel 2002 Good example of cool-grown Zinfandel; mix of cherry, spice and a touch of mint. **RATING** 87 **DRINK** 2009 **$** 17

🍷🍷🍷🍷 **Hilltops Semillon 2003** **RATING** 85 **DRINK** 2007 **$** 15

Grove Hill

★★★★

120 Old Norton Summit Road, Norton Summit, SA 5136 **REGION** Adelaide Hills
T (08) 8390 1437 **F** (08) 8390 1437 **OPEN** Sunday 11–5, or by appointment
WINEMAKER Neville Falkenberg (Contract) **EST.** 1978 **CASES** 500
PRODUCT RANGE ($22–40 CD) Chardonnay, Reserve Chardonnay, Sparkling Marguerite, Pinot Noir.
SUMMARY Grove Hill is a heritage property established in 1846 with the original homestead and outbuildings and held by the same family since that time.

Growlers Gully

★★★☆

354 Shaws Road, Merton, Vic 3715 **REGION** Upper Goulburn
T (03) 5778 9615 **F** (03) 5778 9615 **OPEN** Weekends and public holidays 10–5, or by appointment
WINEMAKER MasterWineMakers (Contract) **EST.** 1997 **CASES** 380
PRODUCT RANGE ($18–25 CD) Chardonnay, Shiraz, Cabernet Sauvignon.
SUMMARY Les and Wendy Oates began the establishment of the Growlers Gully vineyard in 1997, extending it in 1998 to a total of 4 hectares of shiraz and 1 hectare of cabernet sauvignon. It sits at an elevation of 375 metres with fertile brown clay loam soil. Very competent contract winemaking by MasterWineMakers has led to richly flavoured and coloured wine. A rammed earth cellar-door sales outlet opened in early 2002, with the ambition of ultimately offering light meals and the option to visitors of using the barbecue facilities on-site.

Guichen Bay Vineyards

★★★☆

PO Box 582, Newport, NSW 2106 **REGION** Mount Benson
T (02) 9997 6677 **F** (02) 9997 6177 **OPEN** Not
WINEMAKER Contract **EST.** 2003 **CASES** 200
PRODUCT RANGE ($16.50 ML) Force Ten Sauvignon Blanc, Shiraz.
SUMMARY Guichen Bay Vineyards is one of the three adjacent vineyards known collectively as the Mount Benson Community Vineyards. Between 1997 and 2001 120 hectares of vines were planted to chardonnay, sauvignon blanc, shiraz, merlot and cabernet sauvignon. While the major part of the production is sold under long-term contracts, the three owners have obtained a producers license under the Guichen Bay Vineyards label, and with the approval of the major grape purchasers, a small quantity of grapes are held back to be made into wine by local contract winemakers and released under the Guichen Bay Vineyards label. The town of Robe is situated on Guichen Bay, hence the name. The two wines released in 2004 were Sauvignon Blanc and Shiraz, but in 2005 it will be expanded to 600–700 cases including additional varieties.

🍷🍷🍷🍷 **Force Ten Sauvignon Blanc 2003** Aromatic tropical gooseberry bouquet; a clean, crisp and fresh palate, albeit with less fruit than the bouquet promises. **RATING** 88 **DRINK** Now **$** 16.50

Haan Wines

★★★★☆

Siegersdorf Road, Tanunda, SA 5352 **REGION** Barossa Valley
T (08) 8562 4590 **F** (08) 8562 4590 **OPEN** Not
WINEMAKER James Irvine (Contract) **EST.** 1993 **CASES** 4000
PRODUCT RANGE ($21–50 ML) Semillon, Viognier, Viognier Prestige, Viognier Ratafia, Chanticleer Sparkling Rose, Wilhelmus (red blend), Shiraz Prestige, Merlot Prestige.
SUMMARY Hans and Fransien Haan established their business in 1993 when they acquired a 16-hectare vineyard near Tanunda (since extended to 36.7 hectares). The primary focus was on

Merlot and in particular on the luxury Merlot Prestige, and they understandably chose James Irvine as their contract-winemaker, who has in fact produced sumptuous red wines across the range. There are no cellar-door sales; the wines distributed in eastern Australia through Australian Prestige Wines and exported to the UK, the US, Canada, Switzerland, Germany, Malaysia, Singapore, Hong Kong and Japan.

♥♥♥♥♥ **Wilhelmus 2001** Laden with red and blackcurrant, mulberry, soft tannins and spicy French oak, supple and elegant. **RATING** 94 **DRINK** 2015 $39.50

♥♥♥♥♥ **Viognier Prestige 2003** Intense, but finer than the varietal version; powerful, concentrated honeysuckle, fig and peach. One hundred dozen made. **RATING** 93 **DRINK** 2007 $45
Viognier 2003 Strong varietal fruit; yellow peach, apricot, fruit pastille and honeysuckle; almost too much of a good thing. **RATING** 90 **DRINK** Now $24.95
Merlot Prestige 2001 Abundant dark fruits on both bouquet and palate; good structure and density, but not as expressively varietal as prior vintages from Haan. **RATING** 90 **DRINK** 2011 $35

♥♥♥♥ **Viognier Ratafia NV** **RATING** 86 **DRINK** Now $24.95
Chanticleer Sparkling Rose NV **RATING** 86 **DRINK** Now $25

Hackersley ★★★★☆

Ferguson Road, Dardanup, WA 6236 **REGION** Geographe
T (08) 9384 6247 **F** (08) 9383 3364 **OPEN** Fri–Sun 10–4
WINEMAKER Tony Davis (Contract) **EST.** 1997 **CASES** 1000
PRODUCT RANGE ($15–27 CD) Semillon, Sauvignon Blanc Semillon, Verdelho, Shiraz, Merlot, Cabernet Sauvignon.
SUMMARY Hackersley is a partnership between the Ovens, Stacey and Hewitt families, friends since their university days, and with (so they say) the misguided belief that growing and making their own wine would be cheaper than buying it. They found what they describe as a 'little piece of paradise in the Ferguson Valley just south of Dardanup', and in September 1998 they planted a little under 8 hectares, extended in August 2000 to 9.5 hectares of the mainstream varieties, interestingly turning their back on chardonnay. Most of the crop is sold to Houghton; however, a small quantity of immaculately packaged Semillon Sauvignon Blanc, Shiraz and Cabernet has been made for release under the Hackersley label.

♥♥♥♥♥ **Merlot 2002** Lovely raspberry and blackcurrant fruit in abundance, the palate very smooth, the tannins fine. A supremely elegant wine. **RATING** 94 **DRINK** 2010 $24

♥♥♥♥ **Sauvignon Blanc 2003** Herbal, faintly smoky, aromas; light bodied with touches of passionfruit and asparagus. **RATING** 87 **DRINK** Now $17

🐚 Hahndorf Hill Winery ★★★☆

Lot 10 Plains Road, Hahndorf, SA 5245 **REGION** Adelaide Hills
T (08) 8388 7512 **F** (08) 8388 7618 **OPEN** Weekends and public holidays 10–5
WINEMAKER Geoff Weaver (Consultant) **EST.** 2002 **CASES** 1500
PRODUCT RANGE ($17.50–27 CD) Chardonnay, Trollinger Rose, Shiraz, Lemberger.
SUMMARY Larry Jacobs and Marc Dobson, both originally from South Africa, purchased Hahndorf Hill Winery in January 2002. Jacobs had given up a career in intensive care medicine in 1988 when he purchased an abandoned property in Stellenbosch and proceeded to establish one of Cape Town's best-known sauvignon blanc producers, Mulderbosch. When Mulderbosch was purchased at the end of 1996, the pair migrated to Australia and eventually found their way to Hahndorf Hill. In 1997 a winery with a precious 50-tonne licence was built on the property, and has now been converted to a cellar door. A new winery, using the same 50-tonne licence, but upgraded to deal with the ultra-strict effluent disposal requirements of the Adelaide Hills is to be constructed in time for the 2005 vintage. Trollinger and lemberger had been planted by the prior owners; both are exceedingly rare German varieties.

♥♥♥♥ **Chardonnay 2002** Extremely delicate citrus and stone fruit; notwithstanding the fruit delicacy, has soaked up the French oak in which the wine was fermented and matured. **RATING** 88 **DRINK** 2008 $27

♥♥♥♥ **Trollinger Rose 2003** **RATING** 85 **DRINK** Now $17.50

Haig

NR

Square Mile Road, Mount Gambier, SA 5290 **REGION** Mount Gambier
T (08) 8725 5414 **F** (08) 8725 5414 **OPEN** 7 days 11–5
WINEMAKER Martin Slocombe (Contract) **EST.** 1982 **CASES** 1000
PRODUCT RANGE ($16–19 CD) Chardonnay, Late Harvest Chardonnay, Pinot Noir, Cabernet Sauvignon.
SUMMARY The 4 hectares of estate vineyards are planted on the rich volcanic soils near the slopes of the famous Blue Lake of Mount Gambier. I have neither seen nor tasted the wines.

Hainault

★★★

255 Walnut Road, Bickley, WA 6076 **REGION** Perth Hills
T (08) 9293 8339 **OPEN** Weekends and public holidays 11–5, or by appointment
WINEMAKER Tony Davis (Contract) **EST.** 1980 **CASES** 1800
PRODUCT RANGE ($15–23 CD) Gewurztraminer, Talus (Sparkling Pinot Noir), Shiraz, Cabernet Sauvignon.
SUMMARY Lyn and Michael Sykes became the owners of Hainault in 2002, after Bill Mackey and wife Vicki headed off elsewhere. The 11 hectares of close-planted vines are hand-pruned and hand-picked, and the pinot noir is very sensibly used to make a sparkling wine, rather than a table wine. The plans are to open a restaurant when the necessary bureaucratic regulations have been dealt with.

Hamelin Bay

★★★★

McDonald Road, Karridale, WA 6288 **REGION** Margaret River
T (08) 9758 6779 **F** (08) 9758 6779 **OPEN** 7 days 10–5
WINEMAKER Julian Scott **EST.** 1992 **CASES** 10 000
PRODUCT RANGE ($17–43 R) Sauvignon Blanc, Semillon Sauvignon Blanc, Chardonnay, Five Ashes Reserve Chardonnay, Rampant White and Red, Five Ashes Reserve Shiraz, Cabernet Merlot, Cabernet Sauvignon.
SUMMARY The 25-hectare Hamelin Bay vineyard was established by the Drake-Brockman family. The initial releases were contract-made, but a winery with cellar-door sales facility was opened in 2000. In the meantime, production has increased from 5000 to 15 000 cases. Exports to the UK, Canada, Luxembourg and Singapore.

♈♈♈♈♈ **Rampant White 2003** Flowery, citrussy aromatics; long, clean, fresh and crisp; dry finish. Classic example. **RATING** 90 **DRINK** 2007 $17

Hamiltons Bluff

★★★

Longs Corner Road, Canowindra, NSW 2804 **REGION** Cowra
T (02) 6344 2079 **F** (02) 6344 2165 **OPEN** Weekends and holidays 10–4, Mon–Fri by appointment
WINEMAKER Contract **EST.** 1995 **CASES** 2000
PRODUCT RANGE ($14–25 CD) Canowindra Grossi Unwooded Chardonnay, Cowra Chardonnay, Reserve Chardonnay, Chairman's Reserve Chardonnay, Methode Champenoise, Sangiovese, Shiraz.
SUMMARY Hamiltons Bluff is owned and operated by the Andrews family, which planted 45 hectares of vines in 1995; 1998 produced the first crop, and three different Chardonnays were contract-made by Andrew Margan. The Cowra Chardonnay and Canowindra Grossi Chardonnay received medals at the 1998 Cowra Wine Show. Cellar-door sales opened in early 1999, heralding a new stage of development for the Cowra region. Exports to the US.

♈♈♈♈ **Reserve Chardonnay 2001** Developed green-gold; complex and mouthfilling mix of peachy fruit and oak; shortens slightly; drink soon. **RATING** 88 **DRINK** Now $19

♈♈♈♈ **Sangiovese 2002** Spice, tobacco and cherry; an almost lemony/citrussy tang to the finish; light to medium-bodied. Clear varietal character. **RATING** 86 **DRINK** 2007 $19
Sangiovese 2000 RATING 85 **DRINK** Now $19
Sangiovese 2001 RATING 84 **DRINK** Now $19
Methode Champenoise 1999 RATING 84 **DRINK** Now $11

♈♈♈ **Chardonnay 2002 RATING** 83 $14.50
Shiraz 2002 RATING 82 $19

Hamilton's Ewell Vineyards ★★★☆

Siegersdorf Vineyard, Barossa Valley Way, Tanunda, SA 5352 **REGION** Barossa Valley
T (08) 8231 0088 **F** (08) 8231 0355 **OPEN** Mon–Fri 10–5, Weekends 11–5
WINEMAKER Robert Hamilton, John Davey **EST.** 1837 **CASES** 13 000
PRODUCT RANGE ($16–38 R) Limestone Quarry Chardonnay, Railway Chardonnay, Railway Shiraz,
Fuller's Barn Shiraz, Stonegarden Grenache Shiraz, Ewell Cabernet Sauvignon.
SUMMARY Mark Hamilton, an Adelaide lawyer by profession, is a sixth generation direct descendent
of Richard Hamilton, who arrived in South Australia in 1838 (a year after the State was proclaimed)
and made his first wine in 1841. Hamilton's Ewell Vineyards remained in the family until 1979, when
it was acquired by Mildara Blass, much to Mark Hamilton's dismay. Since 1991 he has set about
building yet another Hamilton wine business by a series of astute vineyard acquisitions, and buying
back the name Hamilton's Ewell from Mildara. Most of the grapes are sold, but there is scope to very
significantly increase production in the years ahead. Exports to the US, Canada, Hong Kong and the
UK.

♟♟♟♟ **Sturt River Cabernet Shiraz 2002** Altogether surprising depth of blackcurrant and
blackberry fruit, even within the excellence of the Riverland Sunraysia vintage. Round and
supple; soft tannins; good value. **RATING** 87 **DRINK** Now $ 14

♟♟♟♟ **Stonegarden Eden Valley Riesling 2003** **RATING** 86 **DRINK** 2010 $ 18
Ewell Cabernet Sauvignon 2001 **RATING** 86 **DRINK** 2008 $ 28

♟♟♟ **Sturt River Chardonnay 2003** **RATING** 83 $ 14

Hanging Rock Winery ★★★★

88 Jim Road, Newham, Vic 3442 **REGION** Macedon Ranges
T (03) 5427 0542 **F** (03) 5427 0310 **OPEN** 7 days 10–5
WINEMAKER John Ellis **EST.** 1982 **CASES** 40 000
PRODUCT RANGE ($12–55 CD) The wines are offered in four tiers: at the bottom the Rock range of
Riesling, Chardonnay, Red (Shiraz blend), Merlot; next up the scale Victoria Chardonnay, Verdelho,
S (sweet white); then the trio of Central Highlands Pinot Noir, Victoria Shiraz, Victoria Cabernet
Merlot; at the top Jim Jim Sauvignon Blanc, Heathcote Shiraz, Macedon Cuvee, Gralaine Merlot.
SUMMARY The Macedon area has proved very marginal in spots, and the Hanging Rock vineyards,
with their lovely vista towards the Rock, are no exception. John Ellis has thus elected to source
additional grapes from various parts of Victoria to produce an interesting and diverse style of wines.
The low-priced Rock series, with its bold packaging, has replaced the Picnic wines. Exports to the
UK, Denmark, Sweden, Canada, New Zealand, Hong Kong, Singapore, Philippines, Malaysia and
Japan.

♟♟♟♟♟ **Heathcote Shiraz 2002** Dense and opaque; massively concentrated and focused; sweet,
spicy blackberry fruit. Handles the oak and alcohol with ease. **RATING** 95 **DRINK** 2022 $ 55
Heathcote Shiraz 2001 Blackberry and black cherry flavours swirl in a rich and opulent,
but not extractive, wine, which easily carries its 14 degrees alcohol. Another fine example
of this icon wine. **RATING** 94 **DRINK** 2021 $ 55

♟♟♟♟♟ **The Jim Jim Pinot Gris 2003** Fine, clear-cut apple aromas; lovely line and length; touch of
citrus; very good indeed. **RATING** 93 **DRINK** 2007 $ 25
The Jim Jim Gewurztraminer 2003 Delicate rose-petal aromas; crisp, lively and long; low
phenolics **RATING** 91 **DRINK** 2007 $ 25

♟♟♟♟ **Strathbogie Ranges Chardonnay 2002** Light to medium-bodied; gently sweet melon
fruit; good balance and length, just a lick of oak. Screwcap. **RATING** 89 **DRINK** 2007 $ 20
The Jim Jim Sauvignon Blanc 2003 Moderately intense; ranges through herb to tropical;
good length. **RATING** 88 **DRINK** Now $ 27
Yin Barum Merlot Cabernet Franc 2002 Medium-bodied; appealing, sweet raspberry,
redcurrant and blackcurrant fruit; fine tannins, subtle oak. Drink soon. **RATING** 88
DRINK 2008 $ 24
Amaroo Farm Shiraz Mourvedre 2002 Very good colour; nicely made; red and black
fruits given structure by the Mourvedre and some vanilla oak. From the Big Rivers region.
RATING 87 **DRINK** Now $ 16

ŢŢŢŶ **Gralaine Merlot 2000** Light to medium-bodied; clean, fresh, lively red fruits; extremely youthful. From Mount Duneed, Geelong. **RATING** 86 **DRINK** 2010 $ 26
The Jim Jim Gewurztraminer 2002 RATING 84 **DRINK** Now $ 25

Hanging Tree Wines   NR

Lot 2 O'Connors Road, Pokolbin, NSW 2325 **REGION** Lower Hunter Valley
T (02) 4998 6601 **F** (02) 4998 6602 **OPEN** By appointment
WINEMAKER Andrew Thomas (Contract) **EST.** 2003 **CASES** 1250
PRODUCT RANGE ($18–32 CD) Semillon, Unwooded Chardonnay, Shiraz, Cabernet Sauvignon.
SUMMARY Hanging Tree Wines is the former Van De Scheur Estate. A little under 3 hectares of semillon, chardonnay, shiraz and cabernet sauvignon provide the grapes for the wines which are contract-made by the highly skilled Andrew Thomas.

ŢŢŢŶ **Semillon 2003 RATING** 85 **DRINK** 2009 $ 21

Hankin Estate   ★★★☆

2 Johnsons Lane, Northwood via Seymour, Vic 3660 **REGION** Goulburn Valley
T (03) 5792 2396 **F** (03) 9353 2927 **OPEN** Weekends and public holidays 10–5
WINEMAKER Dr Max Hankin **EST.** 1975 **CASES** 1700
PRODUCT RANGE ($8–28 CD) Semillon, Verdelho, Rose, Shiraz, Merlot, Merlot Cabernet Franc Malbec, Cabernets Malbec, Cabernet Sauvignon Merlot.
SUMMARY Hankin Estate is now the principal occupation of Dr Max Hankin, who has retired from full-time medical practice. He has to contend with phylloxera, which decimated the original plantings, but has successfully replanted most of the vineyard.

ŢŢŢŢ **Shiraz 2000** Smooth, supple and well balanced; red fruits and integrated oak. **RATING** 89 **DRINK** 2010 $ 20

Hansen Hilltops   NR

Barwang Ridge, 1 Barwang Road, via Young, NSW 2594 **REGION** Hilltops
T (02) 6382 6363 **F** (02) 6382 6363 **OPEN** 7 days 11–6
WINEMAKER (Contract) **EST.** 1979 **CASES** 2000
PRODUCT RANGE ($15.50–18 CD) Riesling, Chardonnay Semillon, Cabernet Sauvignon.
SUMMARY The vineyard has 5 hectares of vines, 1 hectare each of riesling, chardonnay, shiraz, cabernet sauvignon, and a further hectare roughly split between semillon, merlot and malbec. The plantings date back to 1979, but the first wines were not made until the late 1990s. Peter Hansen points out there are only two vineyards at Barwang, both part of the original Barwang sheep station, McWilliam's and his. Perhaps a little cheekily, he goes on to point out that the difference is that his wines are produced solely from non-irrigated vines which are hand-picked and hand-pruned, and, into the bargain, are 10 years older than McWilliam's.

Hanson-Tarrahill Vineyard   ★★★

49 Cleveland Avenue, Lower Plenty, Vic 3093 (postal) **REGION** Yarra Valley
T (03) 9439 7425 **F** (03) 9439 4217 **OPEN** Not
WINEMAKER Dr Ian Hanson **EST.** 1983 **CASES** 900
PRODUCT RANGE ($22–25 R) Pinot Noir, Arundel (Cabernet blend), Tarra's Block Cabernets, LP (Cabernet blend), Cabernet Sauvignon.
SUMMARY Dental surgeon Ian Hanson planted his first vines in the late 1960s, close to the junction of the Yarra and Plenty Rivers; in 1983 those plantings were extended (with 3000 vines), and in 1988 the Tarrahill property at Yarra Glen was established with a further 4 hectares. Hanson is the name which appears most prominently on the newly designed labels; Tarrahill Vineyard is in much smaller type.

ŢŢŢŢŶ **Pinot Noir 2000** Earthy, spicy, savoury, foresty aromas in a savoury spectrum; good structure, balance and mouthfeel; long finish. **RATING** 90 **DRINK** Now $ 22

ŸŸŸŸ **Cabernet Sauvignon 2001 RATING** 86 **DRINK** 2016 $ 25

ŸŸŸ **LP 2002 RATING** 83 $ 83

ŸŸŸ **Tarra's Block Cabernets 2000 RATING** 77 $ 22

Happs ★★★☆

571 Commonage Road, Dunsborough, WA 6281 **REGION** Margaret River
T (08) 9755 3300 **F** (08) 9755 3846 **OPEN** 7 days 10–5
WINEMAKER Erl Happ, Mark Warren, Anne-Coralie Fleury **EST.** 1978 **CASES** 18 000
PRODUCT RANGE ($14–45 CD) Dry table wines are Semillon Chardonnay, Marrimee (Semillon Chenin Blanc), Viognier, Marsanne, PF White (Preservative Free), Verdelho, Chardonnay, PF Red (Preservative Free); Three Hills super-premium range of Shiraz, Charles Andreas (Cabernet blend), Grenache, Merlot, Nebbiolo, Malbec and Cabernet Franc.
SUMMARY Former schoolteacher turned potter and winemaker Erl Happ is an iconoclast and compulsive experimenter. Many of the styles he makes are very unconventional, the future likely to be even more so: the Karridale vineyard planted in 1994 has no less than 28 different varieties established. Merlot has been a winery specialty for a decade. Limited retail distributed through New South Wales, Victoria and Queensland and, more recently, exports to the US.

ŸŸŸŸ **Three Hills Nebbiolo 2001 RATING** 84 **DRINK** 2010 $ 28

Harbord Wines ★★★☆

PO Box 41, Stockwell, SA 5355 **REGION** Barossa Valley
T (08) 8562 2598 **F** (08) 8562 2598 **OPEN** Not
WINEMAKER Roger Harbord **EST.** 2003 **CASES** 1000
PRODUCT RANGE ($18–22 ML) Chardonnay, Shiraz.
SUMMARY Roger Harbord is a well-known and no less respected Barossa winemaker, with over 20 years' experience, the last ten as chief winemaker for Cellarmaster Wines, Normans and Ewinexchange. He has commenced his own virtual winery as a complementary activity; the grapes are contract-grown, and he leases winery space and equipment to make and mature the wines.

ŸŸŸŸ **Shiraz 2001** Tangy/savoury/earthy/spicy aromas and flavours; good balance, texture and length. **RATING** 89 **DRINK** 2011 $ 22
Chardonnay 2003 Quite complex and rich; peachy fruit runs through to citrussy acidity to close; plenty of depth. **RATING** 87 **DRINK** Now $ 18

Harcourt Valley Vineyards ★★★★

3339 Calder Highway, Harcourt, Vic 3453 **REGION** Bendigo
T (03) 5474 2223 **F** (03) 5474 2293 **OPEN** 7 days 11–5, 11–6 (Daylight savings)
WINEMAKER John Livingstone **EST.** 1976 **CASES** 1000
PRODUCT RANGE ($14–35 CD) Riesling, Chardonnay, Barbara's Shiraz, Pressings, Barbara's Reserve Shiraz, Cabernet Sauvignon.
SUMMARY John Livingstone (the winemaker) and wife Barbara (the viticulturist) acquired the 4-hectare vineyard many years ago. Shiraz remains the specialty (Riesling and Cabernet Sauvignon are also made) with a rich, full-bodied style typical of the region.

ŸŸŸŸŸ **Barbara's Shiraz Pressings 2001** Deep red-purple; softly plushy texture and tannins; mix of spice, mocha, chocolate, vanilla and dark plum. **RATING** 90 **DRINK** 2011 $ 45

ŸŸŸŸ **Barbara's Shiraz 2002** Blackberry, licorice, anise and a hint of game; slightly angular palate; hint of brett, but lots of character. **RATING** 89 **DRINK** 2012 $ 25
Cabernet Sauvignon 2001 Very sweet, ripe blackberry/plum/cassis; fruit-driven, ripe tannins. **RATING** 88 **DRINK** 2012 $ 25

ŸŸŸ **Chardonnay 2003 RATING** 83 $ 20

Hardys Reynella ★★★★★

Reynell Road, Reynella, SA 5161 **REGION** McLaren Vale
T (08) 8392 2222 **F** (08) 8392 2202 **OPEN** Mon–Fri 10–4, Sat 10–3.30, Sun 11–3.30, closed public holidays
WINEMAKER Peter Dawson, Paul Lapsley, Stephen Pannell, Ed Carr, Tom Newton **EST.** 1853
CASES 16 000
PRODUCT RANGE ($6.99–134.99 R) At the bottom comes the R&R range of all major varietals and blends; then Nottage Hill; Siegersdorf Riesling and Chardonnay; No Preservative Added range; next Chateau Reynella and Sir James premium varietals; then Eileen Hardy Chardonnay, Shiraz and Thomas Hardy Cabernet Sauvignon; Sir James and Arras; also superior-quality brandies and ports including Australia's finest Vintage Port.
SUMMARY The 1992 merger of Thomas Hardy and the Berri Renmano group may well have had some of the elements of a forced marriage at the time it took place, but the merged group prospered mightily over the next 10 years. So successful was it that a further marriage followed in early 2003, Constellation Wines of the US the groom, and BRL Hardy the bride. It has created the largest wine group in the world, but does mean that the inevitable has happened: ownership and control of one of Australia's most dynamic and biggest companies has migrated to the US, even with senior BRL Hardy executives appointed to the top positions in the Constellation wine group.

ŸŸŸŸŸ **Eileen Hardy Chardonnay 2001** Refined and elegant; stone fruit, melon and citrus fruit is interwoven with classy oak; good length. **RATING** 94 **DRINK** 2011 $ 39.99
Eileen Hardy Shiraz 2000 Dense, lush and luscious but not over the top; ripe black cherry and blackberry fruit; well integrated and balanced oak. **RATING** 94 **DRINK** 2016 $ 89.99
Sir James Vintage 1999 Gently nutty/bready malolactic and yeast lees aromas flow into a delicate yet complex palate, cashew and citrus providing counterparts on the long, intense finish. **RATING** 94 **DRINK** Now $ 25.99

ŸŸŸŸ♡ **Chateau Reynella Chardonnay 2002** Distinctly complex wild yeast barrel ferment/malolactic ferment style; melon and citrus fruit comes through intact on the lively, long palate. **RATING** 93 **DRINK** 2009
Thomas Hardy Cabernet Sauvignon 1999 Inky red-purple; massively powerful, dense blackberry fruit; long persistent tannins. One hundred per cent Margaret River. **RATING** 93 **DRINK** 2019 $ 89.99
Padthaway Unwooded Chardonnay 2002 Elegant wine; opens quietly; builds length and intensity on fruit-driven citrus palate. **RATING** 91 **DRINK** 2007 $ 15.99

ŸŸŸ♡ **Siegersdorf Riesling 2003** **RATING** 86 **DRINK** Now $ 10.99
Oomoo Shiraz 2002 **RATING** 86 **DRINK** 2007 $ 14
Sir James Sparkling Shiraz NV **RATING** 86 **DRINK** Now $ 25.99
Oomoo Shiraz 2001 **RATING** 85 **DRINK** Now $ 14
Padthaway Cabernet Sauvignon 2002 **RATING** 85 **DRINK** 2011 $ 19.99

ŸŸŸ **Nottage Hill Cabernet Sauvignon Shiraz 2001** **RATING** 83 $ 8.99
Omni NV **RATING** 81 $ 9.99

Hardys Tintara ★★★★★

202 Main Road, McLaren Vale, SA 5171 **REGION** McLaren Vale
T (08) 8392 4124 **F** (08) 8392 4155 **OPEN** 7 days 10–4.30
WINEMAKER Simon White, Robert Mann **EST.** 1876 **CASES** 45 000
PRODUCT RANGE ($15.99–48.99 R) Limited Release Shiraz, Grenache; Tintara Cellars Chardonnay, Shiraz and Cabernet Sauvignon.
SUMMARY Hardys Tintara is run as a separate winemaking entity, although all the Hardys wines are offered at cellar door. The Limited Release wines are first class; the Tintara Cellars appeal on the grounds of price. The rating is a compromise between the two ranges.

ŸŸŸŸŸ **Limited Release Shiraz 2000** Proclaims its class and region of origin instantaneously; an intense mix of black fruits, dark chocolate and licorice; excellent tannin and oak management; the vintage was not meant to be this good. **RATING** 95 **DRINK** 2020 $ 48.99

ŸŸŸ♡ **Cellars Cabernet Sauvignon 2000** **RATING** 84 **DRINK** 2007 $ 16

Hare's Chase

PO Box 46, Melrose Park, SA 5039 **REGION** Barossa Valley
T (08) 8277 3506 **F** (08) 8277 3543 **OPEN** Not
WINEMAKER Peter Taylor **EST.** 1998 **CASES** 2500
PRODUCT RANGE ($33–56 ML) Shiraz, Merlot.
SUMMARY Hare's Chase is the creation of two families who own the 100-year-old vineyard situated in the Marananga Valley subregion of the Barossa Valley. The simple, functional winery sits at the top of a rocky hill in the centre of the vineyard, which has some of the best red soil available for dry-grown viticulture. The winemaking arm of the partnership is provided by Peter Taylor, a senior red winemaker with Penfolds for over 20 years.

ΥΥΥΥ **Shiraz 2002** Has finesse and elegance, but — surprisingly — seems to lack the fruit concentration of the very best wines of the vintage; blackberry and spice; good balance and length; controlled oak. **RATING** 92 **DRINK** 2015 $ 56

Harewood Estate

Scotsdale Road, Denmark, WA 6333 **REGION** Denmark
T (08) 9840 9078 **F** (08) 9840 9053 **OPEN** 7 days 10–4
WINEMAKER James Kellie **EST.** 1988 **CASES** 4000
PRODUCT RANGE ($29.50 CD) Chardonnay, Pinot Noir, Block C Pinot Noir.
SUMMARY In July 2003 James Kellie, who for many years was a winemaker with Howard Park, and who was responsible for the contract making of Harewood Wines since 1998, purchased the estate with his father and sister as partners in the business. Events moved quickly thereafter, with the construction of a 300-tonne winery, offering both contract winemaking services for the Great Southern region, and the ability to expand the Harewood range to include subregional wines that showcase the region, hence the already much-expanded production.

ΥΥΥΥΥ **Chardonnay 2002** Stylish, fruit-driven nectarine, melon and citrus; builds through to an intense finish. **RATING** 93 **DRINK** 2012 $ 19.50

ΥΥΥΥ **Pinot Noir 2002** Light cherry and plum, and a touch of spice; struggles for authority. **RATING** 87 **DRINK** 2007 $ 29.50

Harmans Ridge Estate   NR

Cnr Bussell Highway and Harmans Mill Road, Wilyabrup, WA 6284 **REGION** Margaret River
T (08) 9755 7444 **F** (08) 755 7400 **OPEN** Wed–Mon 10–4
WINEMAKER Paul Green **EST.** 1999 **CASES** 20 000
PRODUCT RANGE ($14.95 CD) Riesling, Sauvignon Blanc, Semillon Sauvignon Blanc, Classic Dry White, Marsanne, Chardonnay, Rose, Pinot Noir, Grenache, Shiraz, Cabernet Merlot, Cabernet Sauvignon.
SUMMARY Harmans Ridge Estate, with a crush capacity of 1600 tonnes, is primarily a contract winery for larger producers in the Margaret River region which do not have their own winery/winemaker. It does however have 2 hectares of shiraz, and does make wines under the Harmans Ridge Estate label from grapes grown in Margaret River. A cellar door opened in mid-2003. The wines are sold in Western Australia, and exported to the US, Japan and Spain.

Harris Estate   NR

Paracombe Road, Paracombe, SA 5132 **REGION** Adelaide Hills
T (08) 8380 5353 **F** (08) 8380 5353 **OPEN** By appointment
WINEMAKER Trevor Harris **EST.** 1994 **CASES** 1000
PRODUCT RANGE Shiraz, Cabernet Sauvignon.
SUMMARY Trevor and Sue Harris have established 2.5 hectares of chardonnay, shiraz and cabernet sauvignon at Paracombe in the Adelaide Hills. The wines are distributed by The Wine Group, Victoria, and Jonathan Tolley, South Australia, and by mail order.

Hartley Estate ★★★

260 Chittering Valley Road, Lower Chittering, WA 6084 **REGION** Perth Hills
T (08) 9481 4288 **F** (08) 9481 4291 **OPEN** By appointment
WINEMAKER Steve Hagan (Contract) **EST.** 1999 **CASES** 1700
PRODUCT RANGE ($12.95–20 R) Shiraz, Cabernet Merlot, Cabernet Sauvignon.
SUMMARY Bernie and Erin Stephens purchased the property now named Hartley Estate without any forethought. While driving the Chittering Valley one Sunday with his daughter Angela, and reminiscing about the times he had spent there with his father Hartley, Stephen saw a For Sale sign on a property, and later that day the contract for sale was signed. Planting of 17 hectares of vines began, and after a tiny initial vintage in 2002, Cabernet and Sauvignon and Shiraz were made in commercial quantities in 2003. They form part of the Generations Series, recognising the involvement of three generations of the family: the founders, their children and the grandchildren born to three of the daughters in 2003. The major part of the crop goes to the Western Range wines, the remainder under the Hartley Estate label.

♥♥♥♡ **Cabernet Merlot 2003** Fresh, red and blackcurrant fruit; light-bodied; splashes of oak.
RATING 86 **DRINK** 2008 $13.90

Hartz Barn Wines ★★★☆

1 Truro Road, Moculta, Barossa Valley, SA 5353 **REGION** Eden Valley
T (08) 8563 9002 **F** (08) 8563 9002 **OPEN** By appointment
WINEMAKER David Barnett **EST.** 1997 **CASES** 1300
PRODUCT RANGE ($25–30 CD) General Store Shiraz, Mail Box Merlot, Carriages Cabernet Sauvignon.
SUMMARY Hartz Barn Wines was formed in 1997 by Penny Hart (operations director), David Barnett (winemaker/director), Katrina Barnett (marketing director) and Matthew Barnett (viticulture/cellar director), which may suggest the operation is rather larger than it in fact is. The business name and label have an unexpectedly complex background, too, involving elements from all the partners. The 'z' was added to Hart to reflect early German settler heritage in the Barossa Valley; Barn is a shortened version of Barnett; the HBW symbol within the heart has dual heritage, including the sheep branding iron that David Barnett's father, Henry William Barnett, used in New Zealand. The grapes come from the estate vineyards planted to riesling, lagrein, merlot, shiraz and cabernet sauvignon. Exports to the US, Canada and New Zealand.

♥♥♥♥♡ **Barossa Carriages Cabernet Sauvignon 2002** Ripe, deep, dense blackcurrant and
blackberry fruit; ripe tannins, subtle oak; long finish. **RATING** 90 **DRINK** 2012 $25

♥♥♥♡ **Barossa General Store Shiraz 2002 RATING** 86 **DRINK** 2008 $25
Barossa Mail Box Merlot 2002 RATING 86 **DRINK** 2007 $25

Hartzview Wine Centre NR

70 Dillons Road, Gardners Bay, Tas 7112 **REGION** Southern Tasmania
T (03) 6295 1623 **F** (03) 6295 1723 **OPEN** 7 days 9–5
WINEMAKER Andrew Hood (Contract), Robert Patterson **EST.** 1988 **CASES** 2000
PRODUCT RANGE ($18 CD) Chardonnay, Pinot Noir; also a range of Pig and Whistle Hill fruit wines.
SUMMARY A combined wine centre, offering wines from a number of local Huon Valley wineries, and also newly erected and very comfortable accommodation for six people in a separate, self-contained house. Hartzview table wines (produced from 3 hectares of estate plantings) are much to be preferred to the self-produced Pig and Whistle Hill fruit wines.

Harvey River Bridge Estate ★★★☆

Third Street, Harvey, WA 6220 **REGION** Geographe
T (08) 9729 2199 **F** (08) 9729 2298 **OPEN** 7 days 10–4
WINEMAKER Greg Jones **EST.** 2000 **CASES** 35 000
PRODUCT RANGE ($12–22 CD) The products come under five labels which, in ascending order of price and quality are Stone Gully (cask), Magellan, Harvey River Bridge Estate, Joseph River Estate and H on the Fringe, all being varietally based and identified.

SUMMARY This is a highly focused business which is a division of parent company Harvey Fresh (1994) Ltd, a producer of fruit juice and dairy products exported to more than 12 countries. It has ten contract growers throughout the Geographe region, the wines being made in a company-owned winery and juice factory. Despite its relative infancy, exports to the US, Japan, Malaysia, Singapore, Germany and Ireland have already commenced, while a wide range of marketing activities (including a wine club and website — www.harveyfresh.com.au) are utilised for the domestic market.

ȚȚȚȚ **Joseph River Estate Shiraz 2001** Complex, spice, blackberry, chocolate and mocha flavours; good tannin structure and mouthfeel; excellent value. **RATING** 90 **DRINK** 2011 $ 20

ȚȚȚȚ **Joseph River Estate Shiraz 2002** Clean; excellent black cherry and spice varietal character; deft oak and fine tannins; has line and elegance. **RATING** 89 **DRINK** 2012 $ 20
Billy Goat Hill Cabernet Merlot 2002 Complex smoky oak; tangy and lively, with flecks of olive; oak comes again, as do the tannins, on the finish. **RATING** 89 **DRINK** 2011 $ 15
Sauvignon Blanc 2003 Clean, fresh gooseberry fruit, with a lively, minerally finish. **RATING** 88 **DRINK** Now $ 16
Joseph River Estate Sauvignon Blanc 2003 Very powerful, in-your-face style; tropical gooseberry fruit. **RATING** 87 **DRINK** Now $ 19
Shiraz 2002 Abundant black cherry, spice, leather and chocolate fruit supported by balanced tannins. Medium-bodied. **RATING** 87 **DRINK** 2010 $ 16
Joseph River Estate Cabernet Sauvignon 2002 A slightly dusty bouquet, possibly cork affected, does not take away from the depth and power of the cassis/blackberry fruit on the palate. **RATING** 87 **DRINK** 2011 $ 20
Cabernet Shiraz Merlot 2001 Light to medium-bodied; an elegant mix of red and black fruits; appealing, slippery tannins. **RATING** 87 **DRINK** 2009 $ 16

ȚȚȚȚ **Billy Goat Hill Sauvignon Blanc 2002** **RATING** 86 **DRINK** Now $ 15
Chardonnay 2002 **RATING** 86 **DRINK** Now $ 16
Cabernet Sauvignon 2002 **RATING** 86 **DRINK** 2009 $ 16
Chardonnay 2003 **RATING** 85 **DRINK** Now $ 16
Joseph River Estate Cabernet Sauvignon 2001 **RATING** 85 **DRINK** 2008 $ 20
Joseph River Estate Sauvignon Blanc 2002 **RATING** 84 **DRINK** Now $ 19
Sauvignon Blanc Semillon 2003 **RATING** 84 **DRINK** 2007 $ 16

ȚȚȚ **Sauvignon Blanc 2002** **RATING** 83 $ 16
Cabernet Merlot 2002 **RATING** 82 $ 16
Cabernet Shiraz Merlot 2002 **RATING** 81 $ 16

Haselgrove ★★★★

Sand Road, McLaren Vale, SA 5171 **REGION** McLaren Vale
T (08) 8323 8706 **F** (08) 8323 8049 **OPEN** Mon–Fri 9–5, weekends 10–5
WINEMAKER Adrian Lockhart **EST.** 1981 **CASES** 60 000
PRODUCT RANGE ($10–45 R) The wines are sold in three ascending price tiers: at the bottom the Sovereign range; next the McLaren Vale series; and at the top the 'H' series of Adelaide Hills Viognier, Adelaide Hills Chardonnay, McLaren Vale Shiraz and Wrattonbully Cabernet Sauvignon.
SUMMARY Haselgrove has been through a tumultuous period following its acquisition by Barrington Estates, and the subsequent collapse of Barrington. The underlying winemaking operations of Haselgrove have continued, and respected former Hunter winemaker Adrian Lockhart (Young Winemaker of the Year 2001) as senior winemaker. Domestic retail distribution is exclusive to the Vintage Cellars, Liquorland and Theo's wine chains of Coles Myer; also limited on-premise distribution. Exports to the UK, Denmark, Sweden, Norway, Asia and Japan.

ȚȚȚȚ **'H' McLaren Vale Shiraz 2002** Deeply coloured; powerful black fruits and regional dark chocolate; persistent tannins; demands patience. **RATING** 89 **DRINK** 2017 $ 67
'H' Adelaide Hills Chardonnay 2003 Clean, fresh, lively light to medium-bodied; citrus, stone fruit, subtle oak; excellent length and finish. **RATING** 88 **DRINK** Now $ 25
'H' Adelaide Hills Viognier 2003 Clear-cut peach/honeysuckle/fruit pastille aromas; the palate is more delicate; crisp, crunchy, lingering acidity. **RATING** 88 **DRINK** Now

ȚȚȚȚ **'H' Wrattonbully Cabernet Sauvignon 2002** **RATING** 85 **DRINK** 2007 $ 50

Hastwell & Lightfoot

Foggo Road, McLaren Vale, SA 5171 (postal) **REGION** McLaren Vale
T (08) 8323 8692 **F** (08) 8323 8098 **OPEN** By appointment
WINEMAKER Goe DiFabio (Contract) **EST.** 1990 **CASES** 2000
PRODUCT RANGE ($17.50–25R) Viognier, Chardonnay, Shiraz, Tempranillo, Cabernet Franc, Cabernet Sauvignon.
SUMMARY Hastwell & Lightfoot is an offshoot of a rather larger grape growing business, with the majority of the grapes from the 16 hectares of vineyard being sold to others; the vineyard was planted in 1988 and the first grapes produced in 1990. Incidentally, the labels are once seen, never forgotten. Exports to the US, Germany, Singapore and New Zealand.

TTTTT **Tempranillo 2002** Very good colour; clean, pure dark fruits; excellent texture and structure, particularly the acidity. One of the best Tempranillos yet from Australia. **RATING** 92 **DRINK** 2010 **$** 22
Cabernet Sauvignon 2001 Tightly woven blackcurrant, bitter chocolate and briary fruit; sweet, fine ripe tannins on a stylish finish. **RATING** 90 **DRINK** 2011 **$** 22

TTTT **Viognier 2003** Clean and fresh, picking up character on the rich palate, although more from alcohol than from fruit flavour. **RATING** 87 **DRINK** Now **$** 25

TTTT **Shiraz 2001** **RATING** 86 **DRINK** 2007 **$** 22

Hawkers Gate

Lot 31 Foggo Road, McLaren Flat, SA 5171 **REGION** McLaren Vale
T 0403 809 990 **F** (08) 8323 9981 **OPEN** By appointment
WINEMAKER James Hastwell **EST.** 2000 **CASES** 300
PRODUCT RANGE ($16 ML) Chardonnay, Shiraz.
SUMMARY James Hastwell (son of Mark and Wendy Hastwell of Hastwell & Lightfoot Wines) decided he would become a winemaker when he was 9 years old, and duly obtained his wine science degree from the University of Adelaide, working each vintage during his degree course at Haselgrove Wines and later Kay Bros. It is a long way from Hawkers Gate, which takes its name from the gate at the border of Australia's dog fence between South Australia and New South Wales, 250 kilometres north of Broken Hill. A small on-site winery in Foggo Road was completed in time for the 2003 vintage; as well as giving greater control over the making of the Hawkers Gate wines, it acts as a barrel storage facility for Hastwell & Lightfoot wines. A few rows of saperavi have been planted. Exports to the US.

TTTT **Shiraz 2001** **RATING** 86 **DRINK** Now **$** 16
Chardonnay 2001 **RATING** 84 **DRINK** Now **$** 14

Hawley Vineyard

Hawley Beach, Hawley, Tas 7307 **REGION** Northern Tasmania
T (03) 6428 6221 **F** (03) 6428 6844 **OPEN** 7 days
WINEMAKER Julian Alcorso (Contract) **EST.** 1988 **CASES** 1000
PRODUCT RANGE ($18–25 R) Rubicon Chardonnay, Unwooded Chardonnay, Rubicon Pinot Noir.
SUMMARY Hawley Vineyard overlooks Hawley Beach and thence northeast to Bass Strait. It is established on an historic 200-hectare farming property, with Hawley House offering dining and accommodation in a grand style. There are no other vineyards in what is a unique winegrowing region, and few hoteliers-cum-viticulturists as flamboyant as owner Simon Houghton. Limited distribution in Sydney. Rating is on the basis of previous tastings.

Hay Shed Hill Wines

RMB 398, Harmans Mill Road, Wilyabrup, WA 6280 **REGION** Margaret River
T (08) 9755 6234 **F** (08) 9755 6305 **OPEN** 7 days 10.30–5
WINEMAKER Simon Keall **EST.** 1987 **CASES** 17 000
PRODUCT RANGE ($15–45 CD) Semillon, Sauvignon Blanc, Sauvignon Blanc Semillon, Chardonnay, Pinot Noir, Shiraz, Cabernet Franc, Cabernet Merlot, Cabernet Sauvignon; Pitchfork White, Pitchfork Pink (Rose), Pitchfork Red.

SUMMARY When erected in 1987, the winery was a landmark in the Margaret River region, and over the ensuing years the 'sold out' sign was often displayed. Quality wobbled in the lead-up to its ill-fated acquisition by Barrington Estate in 2000, but in November 2002 it joined Alexandra Bridge and Chestnut Grove as part of Mike Calneggia's Australian Wine Holdings Limited group, and a more settled future seems highly likely.

ŸŸŸŸ♀ Shiraz 2001 Powerful, ripe blackberry fruit, balanced oak. Not too tannic. **RATING** 91 **DRINK** 2014 $35

ŸŸŸŸ Pitchfork Shiraz Cabernet 2002 Leafy, spicy, minty, savoury style with good balance and length. **RATING** 88 **DRINK** 2010 $16

Hayward's Whitehead Creek   NR

80 Hall Lane, Seymour, Vic 3660 **REGION** Goulburn Valley
T (03) 5792 3050 **F** (03) 5792 3030 **OPEN** Mon–Sat 9–6, Sun 10–6
WINEMAKER Sid Hayward, David Hayward **EST.** 1975 **CASES** 50
PRODUCT RANGE ($8.50–15.50 CD) Riesling, Shiraz, Shiraz Merlot Cabernet Franc, Cabernet Sauvignon.
SUMMARY The 4.5 hectares of low-yielding, 25-year-old vines, make powerful wines in a somewhat rustic mode, perhaps, but at low prices. Production has decreased significantly, most of the grapes being sold.

🐌 Hazyblur Wines   NR

Lot 5, Angle Vale Road, Virginia, SA 5120 **REGION** Adelaide Plains
T (08) 8380 9307 **F** (08) 8380 8743 **OPEN** By appointment
WINEMAKER Ross Trimboli **EST.** 1998 **CASES** 2000
PRODUCT RANGE ($17.50–52 ML) Adelaide Hills Pinot Noir, Adelaide Plains Shiraz, Baroota Shiraz, Barossa Valley Shiraz, McLaren Vale Shiraz, Late Picked Shiraz, Grenache, Cabernet Sauvignon.
SUMMARY Robyne and Ross Trimboli hit the jackpot with their 2000 vintage red wines, sourced from various regions in South Australia, including one described by Robert Parker as 'Barotta, the most northerly region in South Australia' (it is in fact Baroota, and is not the most northerly) with Parker points ranging between 91 and 95. One of the wines included a Late Harvest Shiraz, tipping the scales at 17° alcohol, and contract-grown on Kangaroo Island. It is here that the Trimbolis have established their own 4.7-hectare vineyard, planted principally to cabernet sauvignon (2.4 hectares) and shiraz (1.6 hectares), the first vintage coming in 2004. Needless to say, almost all of the wine is exported to the US, with lesser amounts to Canada, the importer being the one and only Dan Phillips aka The Grateful Palate.

Healesville Ridge

458 Maroondah Highway, Healesville, Vic 3777 **REGION** Yarra Valley
T (03) 5962 4440 **F** (03) 5962 1186 **OPEN** 7 days 10–6 summer, weekends 10–6 winter
WINEMAKER Rob Dolan, Kate Goodman (Contract) **EST.** 1998 **CASES** 6000
PRODUCT RANGE ($18–24 CD) Sauvignon Blanc, Pinot Noir, Cabernet Sauvignon.
SUMMARY Planting on the 20-hectare property began in December 1998, and was completed in the spring of 1999. In all 13.6 hectares of vines have been established, including pinot noir (4.6 hectares), cabernet sauvignon (2.6 hectares), chardonnay (2.1 hectares), sauvignon blanc and shiraz (2 hectares each) and merlot (0.4 hectare). Situated 2.5 kilometres northeast of Healesville, it is one of the highest sites in the southern end of the Yarra Valley, the southern boundary of the sloping hillside being the Grace Burn, which was the vineyard name before it was recently purchased by James Bate of Patterson Lakes Estate, and renamed the vineyard Healesville Ridge.

🐌 Heartland Vineyard

PO Box 78, Greta, NSW 2334 **REGION** Lower Hunter Valley
T (02) 4938 6272 **F** (02) 4938 6004 **OPEN** Not
WINEMAKER David Hook **EST.** 1998 **CASES** 1500
PRODUCT RANGE ($10–17 ML) Semillon, Verdelho, Shiraz.

SUMMARY Duncan and Libby Thomson, cardiac surgeon and cardiac scrub nurse respectively, say Heartland Vineyard is the result of a seachange that got a little out of hand. 'After looking one weekend at some property in the Hunter Valley to escape the Sydney ratrace we stumbled upon the beautiful 90 acres that has become our vineyard.' Two hectares of shiraz and semillon were planted in 1998, and in 1999 the couple moved to the Hunter when a job for a cardiac surgeon became available in Newcastle. They have built a rammed earth house on the property, and extended the plantings to a total of a little over 5 hectares, with an exotic mix of shiraz, semillon, merlot, barbera, verdelho and viognier. The choice of name needs no comment.

ŸŸŸŸŸ **Semillon 2002** Abundance of clear-cut herb and soft citrus varietal character; good balance in relatively early-drinking style. **RATING** 90 **DRINK** 2007 $13.50

ŸŸŸŸ **Shiraz 2002 RATING** 86 **DRINK** 2008 $17
Verdelho 2003 RATING 84 **DRINK** Now $13.50

Heartland Wines ★★★☆

Level 1, 205 Greenhill Road, Eastwood, SA 5063 **REGION** Limestone Coast, Langhorne Creek
T (08) 8357 9344 **F** (08) 8357 9388 **OPEN** Not
WINEMAKER Ben Glaetzer **EST.** 2001 **CASES** 36 000
PRODUCT RANGE ($16–28 R) Viognier Pinot Gris, Director's Cut Shiraz, Amon-Ra Shiraz, Wirrega Limestone Coast Shiraz, Wirrega Limestone Coast Cabernet Merlot, Cabernet Sauvignon.
SUMMARY This is a joint venture between four industry veterans: winemakers Ben Glaetzer and Scott Collett, viticulturist Geoff Hardy and wine industry management specialist Grant Tilbrook. It draws upon grapes grown in the Limestone Coast, Barossa Valley and McLaren Vale, predominantly from vineyards owned by the partners. Its sights are firmly set on exports with impressive results. Two years ago, the plan was to increase production from 10 000 cases to 20 000, challenging enough, but in fact production has reached 36 000 cases, with the introduction of Chardonnay, Viognier, Rose, Sangiovese and Cabernet Sauvignon to complement the existing releases. The wines are principally contract-made at Barossa Vintners, but there are no local or cellar-door sales facilities. Red wine quality is admirable.

ŸŸŸŸŸ **Limestone Coast Shiraz 2002** Excellent concentration and focus; blackberry and dark plum fruit; plenty of tannin support. **RATING** 93 **DRINK** 2017 $16
Director's Cut Shiraz 2002 Even more dense than the varietal wine; massive and heroic, with the kitchen sink thrown at it. **RATING** 92 **DRINK** 2022 $28
Limestone Coast Cabernet Sauvignon 2002 Lush blackcurrant/cassis fruit has blotted up the oak; soft tannins. **RATING** 92 **DRINK** 2015 $16

ŸŸŸŸ **Limestone Coast Viognier Pinot Gris 2003** Strange bed fellows with a mix of citrus, fruit pastille and pear. **RATING** 87 **DRINK** Now $18

ŸŸŸŸ **Limestone Coast Petit Verdot 2002 RATING** 86 **DRINK** 2012 $16

ŸŸŸ **Semillon 2002 RATING** 83
Verdelho 2003 RATING 82

Heathcote Winery ★★★★

183–185 High Street, Heathcote, Vic 3523 **REGION** Heathcote
T (03) 5433 2595 **F** (03) 5433 3081 **OPEN** 7 days 11–5
WINEMAKER Jonathan Mepham **EST.** 1978 **CASES** 5000
PRODUCT RANGE ($14.50–40.50 CD) Cellar-door Thomas Craven range of MCV (Marsanne Chardonnay Viognier), Viognier, Chardonnay and Shiraz; premium range of Chardonnay, Cane Cut (Chenin Blanc), Violet (Rose style), Slaughterhouse Paddock Shiraz, Mail Coach Viognier and Mail Coach Shiraz; super-premium Curagee Viognier and Shiraz.
SUMMARY The Heathcote Winery is back in business with a vengeance. The wines are being produced predominantly from the 26 hectares of estate vineyard, and some from local and other growers under long-term contracts, and the tasting room facilities restored and upgraded. Exports to the UK.

ŸŸŸŸŸ **Curagee Shiraz 2002** Densely coloured; a rich explosion of blackberry, licorice, spice and dark chocolate, with that touch of viognier lift; considerable extract and length, good balance. **RATING** 94 **DRINK** 2022 $40.50

ŶŶŶŶŸ **Mail Coach Shiraz 2002** A rich and concentrated array of dark fruits with a tweak of viognier; will reach its peak before the Curagee, but is an excellent wine. From nine vineyard blocks. **RATING** 91 **DRINK** 2017 $ 24

ŶŶŶŶ **Chardonnay 2002** A complex and powerful wine; stone fruit, cashew and French oak; heats up a little with 14.5 degrees alcohol. **RATING** 89 **DRINK** Now $ 14.50
Slaughterhouse Paddock Shiraz 2002 Quite fragrant; rich, sweet, red and black fruits on the medium-bodied palate; blackberry, raspberry and plum. **RATING** 89 **DRINK** 2012 $ 32
Mail Coach Viognier 2003 Rich, round and smooth; has soaked up the oak; some dried fruit/pastille flavours, and, once again, alcohol certainly evident. **RATING** 88 **DRINK** 2007 $ 20

Heathfield Ridge Wines ★★★

PO Box 94, Kensington Park, SA 5068 **REGION** Limestone Coast Zone
T (08) 8363 5800 **F** (08) 8363 1980 **OPEN** Not
WINEMAKER Irvine Consultancy (Contract) **EST.** 1997 **CASES** 20 000
PRODUCT RANGE ($10.50–45 ML) Super-premium range of Jennifer Reserve Shiraz, Patrick Reserve Cabernet; premium range of Sauvignon Blanc, Reserve Chardonnay, Shiraz, Merlot, Cabernet Sauvignon; Wonambi Wines range of Chardonnay Sauvignon Blanc, Chardonnay, Shiraz and Caves Road range of Chardonnay Sauvignon Blanc, Chardonnay, Shiraz.
SUMMARY This is a different incarnation of Heathfield Ridge to that which appeared in my 2002 Wine Companion. The Heathfield Ridge Winery is now operated by Orlando Wyndham under what is described as a strategic alliance, and the Heathfield Ridge wines are no longer made at the winery, which is now called Russet Ridge. However, the Tidswell family have retained ownership of the two large vineyards, totalling 114 hectares, the lion's share planted to shiraz and cabernet sauvignon, with smaller plantings of merlot, chardonnay and sauvignon blanc. Part of the grape production is retained by the owners and vinified under the Heathfield Ridge label by the Irvine Consultancy group, the remainder sold to Russet Ridge.

ŶŶŶŶ **Jennifer Shiraz 1999** Complex; somewhat oak dominated, but a nice medium-bodied wine. **RATING** 87 **DRINK** 2010 $ 37

ŶŶŶ **Merlot 2000 RATING** 83 $ 19

ŶŶŸ **Caves Road Shiraz 2001 RATING** 76 $ 12

Heathvale ★★★☆

Saw Pit Gully Road, via Keyneton, SA 5353 **REGION** Eden Valley
T (08) 8564 8248 **F** (08) 8564 8248 **OPEN** By appointment
WINEMAKER Jim Irvine (Contract) **EST.** 1987 **CASES** 1250
PRODUCT RANGE ($20–30 ML) Chardonnay, Shiraz.
SUMMARY The origins of Heathvale go back to 1865, when William Heath purchased a 60-hectare property, establishing a fruit orchard and 8 hectares of vineyard. The wine was made in the cellar of the house which stands on the property today, and is occupied by current owners Trevor and Faye March. Heath's vines disappeared in the early 1900s, but the March's now have 3 hectares each of shiraz and cabernet sauvignon, and 2 hectares each of chardonnay and riesling in production. Trevor March is a trained viticulturist and is completing his studies for a Master of Viticulture degree at the Waite Campus of the University of Adelaide, and is a TAFE lecturer. Exports to the UK, Germany and the US.

ŶŶŶŶŸ **Shiraz 2002** Clean, medium-bodied; blackberry and lots of dark chocolate; fine, ripe tannins; positive oak. **RATING** 90 **DRINK** 2008 $ 30

ŶŶŶŶ **Chardonnay 2003** Fragrant fruit-driven style; lively citrus and stone fruit; good length. **RATING** 89 **DRINK** 2007 $ 20

Heggies Vineyard ★★★★

Heggies Range Road, Eden Valley, SA 5235 **REGION** Eden Valley
T (08) 8565 3203 **F** (08) 8565 3380 **OPEN** At Yalumba
WINEMAKER Peter Gambetta **EST.** 1971 **CASES** 13 000
PRODUCT RANGE ($18–23.95 CD) Riesling, Viognier, Chardonnay, Pinot Noir, Merlot.
SUMMARY Heggies was the second of the high-altitude (570 metres) vineyards established by S Smith & Sons (Yalumba), with plantings on the 120-hectare former grazing property commencing in 1973, now reaching 62 hectares. The once simple view of Heggies as a better white than red wine producer has become more complicated, with the pendulum swinging backwards and forwards according to vintage. Plantings of both chardonnay and viognier were increased in 2002. Exports to all major markets.

ΨΨΨΨΨ **Museum Reserve Eden Valley Riesling 1998** Glorious colour; complex, developed lime and toast; still shows primary fruit on the palate; delicate, gentle lime. Screwcap. **RATING** 93 **DRINK** 2008 $ 26.95

ΨΨΨΨ **Viognier 2002** Powerful honeysuckle and orange blossom varietal aromas; luscious and weighty palate with more of the same. **RATING** 89 **DRINK** Now $ 26.95
Chardonnay 2002 Full melon and stone fruit complexed by honey and cashew; subtle oak, long finish. **RATING** 88 **DRINK** Now $ 24.95
Merlot 2000 Good varietal character and structure; olive, blackberry and spice are on the austere side, but are convincing and stylish. **RATING** 87 **DRINK** 2008 $ 24.95

ΨΨΨΨ **Riesling 2003** **RATING** 85 **DRINK** 2007 $ 16.95

Helen's Hill Estate NR

PO Box 778, Lilydale, Vic 3140 **REGION** Yarra Valley
T (03) 9739 1573 **F** (03) 9739 0350 **OPEN** Not
WINEMAKER MasterWineMakers (Contract) **EST.** 1997
PRODUCT RANGE ($22.50–25 ML) Chardonnay, Pinot Noir.
SUMMARY Helen's Hill Estate is named in memory of the previous owner of the property Helen Fraser, and has 41 hectares. Allan Nalder, Roma and Lewis Nalder and Andrew and Robyn McIntosh, with backgrounds in banking and finance, grazing and medicine respectively are the five partners in the venture. A small planting of pinot noir and chardonnay dating from the mid-1980s is retained for the Helen's Hill Estate wines, but most of the output is sold to others, including Southcorp. The plantings now cover chardonnay, pinot noir, shiraz, merlot and cabernet sauvignon.

Helm ★★★☆

Butt's Road, Murrumbateman, NSW 2582 **REGION** Canberra District
T (02) 6227 5953 **F** (02) 6227 0207 **OPEN** Thurs–Mon 10–5
WINEMAKER Ken Helm **EST.** 1973 **CASES** 3000
PRODUCT RANGE ($20–25 CD) Riesling Classic Dry, Cowra Riesling Classic Dry, Gewurztraminer, Traminer Riesling, Unwooded Chardonnay, Chardonnay, Reserve Merlot, Cabernet Merlot, Cabernet Shiraz, Helm Reserve Blend.
SUMMARY Ken Helm is well-known as one of the more stormy petrels of the wine industry and is an energetic promoter of his wines and of the Canberra district generally. His wines have been consistent bronze medal winners, with silvers and the occasional gold dotted here and there. The wines have limited retail distribution in New South Wales, ACT and Victoria. The rating is for the reliable Riesling.

ΨΨΨΨ **Riesling 2003** Clean, intense citrus and mineral aromas, swelling into powerful tropical fruit on the palate. **RATING** 90 **DRINK** 2015 $ 20

ΨΨΨΨ **Late Harvest Riesling 2003** A creditable effort; nicely balanced spatlese style; lemony, with gentle acidity. **RATING** 87 **DRINK** 2008 $ 28

ΨΨΨΨ **Merlot 2001** Savoury olive and herb aromas and flavours; strongly varietal; light to medium-bodied. **RATING** 86 **DRINK** 2008 $ 20

ΨΨΨ **Cabernet Sauvignon 2001** **RATING** 83 $ 25

ΨΨΨ **Unwooded Chardonnay 2003** **RATING** 79 $ 20

🐚 Henderson Hardie

NR

PO Box 554, Wangaratta, Vic 3676 **REGION** King Valley
T (03) 5722 1850 **F** (03) 5721 5577 **OPEN** Not
WINEMAKER Howard Anderson (Contract) **EST.** 2000
PRODUCT RANGE Gewurztraminer, Chardonnay, Pinot Gris, Pinot Noir; also sparkling.
SUMMARY Gayle and Jim Hardie have established 12 hectares of gewurztraminer, chardonnay, pinot gris, pinot noir and pinot meunier in their Whitlands vineyard. Jim Hardie has had a long and high-profile career in viticulture and in viticultural research and the choice of the varieties planted in this high altitude vineyard reflects that knowledge. Howard Anderson, too, has many years under his belt as a winemaker in various parts of Victoria.

Henke

NR

175 Henke Lane, Yarck, Vic 3719 **REGION** Upper Goulburn
T (03) 5797 6277 **F** (03) 5797 6277 **OPEN** By appointment
WINEMAKER Tim Miller, Caroline Miller **EST.** 1974 **CASES** 250
PRODUCT RANGE ($23 CD) Shiraz, Shiraz Cabernet.
SUMMARY Produces tiny quantities of deep-coloured, full-flavoured, minty red wines known only to a chosen few. Usually a range of back vintages up to 5 years of age are available at the cellar door.

Henkell Wines

NR

Melba Highway, Dixons Creek, Vic 3775 **REGION** Yarra Valley
T (03) 9417 4144 **OPEN** Thurs and Sun 11–5, Fri–Sat 11–9
WINEMAKER Contract **EST.** 1988 **CASES** 500
PRODUCT RANGE ($18.60–24.80 CD) The wines come in two fundamentally different ranges: the cheapest (around $12) are from southeast Australia; the Yarra Valley varietal wines (Sauvignon Blanc, Chardonnay, Pinot Noir, Shiraz, Cabernet Merlot, Cabernet Sauvignon) at around $15.
SUMMARY Hans Henkell started with a 57-variety Heinz mix in the vineyard, but has now rationalised it to a total of 25 hectares of sauvignon blanc, chardonnay, pinot noir, shiraz and cabernet sauvignon. Most of the grapes are sold, with small amounts contract-made each year. And yes, Hans Henkell is part of the family. Dinner concerts are held regularly throughout the summer months; bookings essential. A city cellar door, for case sales only, is open by appointment at 53 Victoria Parade, Collingwood, phone (03) 8415 1910.

Henley Park Wines

NR

6 Swan Street, Henley Brook, WA 6055 **REGION** Swan Valley
T (08) 9296 4328 **F** (08) 9296 1313 **OPEN** Tues–Sun 10–5
WINEMAKER Claus Petersen, Lisbet Petersen **EST.** 1935 **CASES** 5000
PRODUCT RANGE ($9.95–15.95 CD) Semillon, Chenin Blanc, Classic White, Chardonnay, Muscat Gordo Blanco (late picked), Mousse Rose Brut (Methode Champenoise), Pinot Noir, Merlot, Shiraz, Cabernet Sauvignon, Shiraz Cabernet Merlot, Vintage Port, Old Tawny.
SUMMARY Henley Park, like so many Swan Valley wineries, was founded by a Yugoslav family, but it is now jointly owned by Danish and Malaysian interests, a multicultural mix if ever there was one. Majority owner and winemaker Claus Petersen arrived in 1986 and had his moment of glory in 1990 when Henley Park was the Most Successful Exhibitor at the Mount Barker Wine Show. Much of the production is sold through the cellar door (and exported to Denmark and Japan).

Henry's Drive

★★★★

PMB 182, Naracoorte, SA 5271 **REGION** Padthaway
T (08) 8765 6057 **F** (08) 8765 6090 **OPEN** Not
WINEMAKER Sparky Marquis, Sarah Marquis **EST.** 1998 **CASES** 8000
PRODUCT RANGE ($25–45 ML) Sparkling Shiraz, Shiraz, Reserve Shiraz, Cabernet Sauvignon, Reserve Cabernet Sauvignon.
SUMMARY The Longbottom families have been farming in Padthaway since the 1940s, a diverse operation from sheep and cattle to growing crops and onions. In 1992 a decision was made to further diversify and plant a few vines. Now with almost 300 hectares the vineyard is established consisting

mainly of shiraz and cabernet sauvignon and other varieties such as chardonnay, merlot, verdelho and sauvignon blanc. Henry's Drive is owned and operated by Brian and Kay Longbottom. Exports to the US, Canada, South-East Asia, the UK, Japan, Germany and Switzerland.

** YYYY** **Parson's Flat Padthaway Shiraz Cabernet 2002** Abundant black fruits and chocolate; good oak handling, well balanced. **RATING** 90 **DRINK** 2012

YYYY **Padthaway Cabernet Sauvignon 2002** **RATING** 84 **DRINK** Now

Henschke ★★★★★

Henschke Road, Keyneton, SA 5353 **REGION** Eden Valley
T (08) 8564 8223 **F** (08) 8564 8294 **OPEN** Mon–Fri 9–4.30, Sat 9–12, public holidays 10–3
WINEMAKER Stephen Henschke **EST.** 1868 **CASES** 40 000
PRODUCT RANGE ($12.80–288 CD) A cross-hatch of varietal wines with catchy names coming either from the Eden Valley or the Adelaide Hills, much estate-grown. The icon wines are Keyneton Estate, Mount Edelstone, Cyril Henschke Cabernet Sauvignon, Hill of Grace, Abbott's Prayer Cabernet Merlot.
SUMMARY Regarded as the best medium-sized red wine producer in Australia and has gone from strength to strength over the past two decades under the guidance of Stephen and Prue Henschke. The red wines fully capitalise on the very old, low-yielding, high-quality vines and are superbly made with sensitive but positive use of new small oak: Hill of Grace is second only to Penfolds Grange as Australia's red wine icon. Exports to the UK, Europe, Asia and the US.

YYYYY **Hill Of Grace 1999** Dense colour; powerful, classic thoroughbred texture and focus; black fruits; silky, smooth tannins and finish. No brett. **RATING** 96 **DRINK** 2019 **$** 288
Johann's Garden Grenache Shiraz Mourvedre 2002 Berries, herbs, spices and tobacco aromas, the supple, smooth and elegant palate flowing effortlessly across the tongue. **RATING** 95 **DRINK** 2010 **$** 34
Lenswood Croft Chardonnay 2002 Elegant, fragrant fig, melon and citrus; cashew/creamy bolt-ons to the long palate. **RATING** 94 **DRINK** 2010 **$** 37.60

YYYYY **Abbott's Prayer 2001** Fine and fragrant; seamless, rounded red berry fruits and cedary oak; fine tannins. **RATING** 93 **DRINK** 2011 **$** 59
Julius Eden Valley Riesling 2003 Regional lime and lemon plus passionfruit and spice; intense and elegant. **RATING** 92 **DRINK** 2013 **$** 23.50
Mount Edelstone 2001 Fresh and clean, light to medium-bodied red cherry/berry fruit; supple and smooth. **RATING** 91 **DRINK** 2014 **$** 62

YYYY **Sauvignon Blanc Semillon 2003** Fresh and clean; tropical overtones; even flow and mouthfeel. **RATING** 89 **DRINK** 2007 **$** 20.90
Henry's Seven 2002 In a tangy, herby, savoury, earthy spectrum; minimal oak; stylish. Screwcap. **RATING** 89 **DRINK** 2009 **$** 27.50
Lenswood Green's Hill Riesling 2003 Big, Four Square wine with solid lime and some tropical aromas and flavours. **RATING** 88 **DRINK** 2007 **$** 24.80
Coralinga Sauvignon Blanc 2003 Herb, citrus, asparagus and capsicum aromas; lacks intensity, but has pleasant varietal fruit. **RATING** 87 **DRINK** Now **$** 21.90
Tilly's Vineyard 2002 Well balanced and smooth; fruit salad flavours. **RATING** 87 **DRINK** Now **$** 12.80

YYYY **Lenswood Giles Pinot Noir 2002** **RATING** 86 **DRINK** 2007 **$** 39.70
Keyneton Estate Shiraz Cabernet Malbec 2001 **RATING** 85 **DRINK** 2008 **$** 32

Henty Brook Estate NR

Box 49, Dardanup, WA 6236 **REGION** Geographe
T (08) 9728 1459 **F** (08) 9728 1459 **OPEN** Weekends 10–4, Mon–Fri by appointment
WINEMAKER James Pennington (Contract) **EST.** 1994 **CASES** 400
PRODUCT RANGE ($10–15 CD) Sauvignon Blanc Semillon, Shiraz.
SUMMARY One hectare each of shiraz and sauvignon blanc and 0.5 hectare of semillon were planted in the spring of 1994. James Pennington is the contract-winemaker.

Heritage Estate ★★★☆

Granite Belt Drive, Cottonvale, Qld 4375 **REGION** Granite Belt
T (07) 4685 2197 **F** (07) 4685 2112 **OPEN** 7 days 9–5
WINEMAKER Paola Andrea Cabezas Rhymer **EST.** 1992 **CASES** 5000
PRODUCT RANGE ($12.50–35 CD) Semillon, Dry White, Semillon Chardonnay, Harvest Blend, Chardonnay, Club Red, Shiraz, Roswal Shiraz, Merlot, Cabernet Merlot, fortified and flavoured wines.
SUMMARY Bryce and Paddy Kassulke operate very successful winery, with many awards in recent years. It also showcases its wines through its cellar door at Mount Tamborine (corner Bartle Road and The Shelf Road, phone (07) 5545 3144) in an old church converted into a tasting and sales area, with views over the Gold Coast hinterland, also incorporating a restaurant, barbecue area and art gallery. The estate plantings, established in 1993, comprise chardonnay (2.5 hectares), merlot (1 hectare), shiraz (0.4 hectare) and cabernet sauvignon (0.1 hectare). The quality of the wines has been consistently good, in the top ten of the now innumerable Queensland wineries.

▼▼▼▼ **Private Reserve Merlot 2002** Light to medium-bodied; savoury/olive spectrum; fine tannins; good varietal character. **RATING** 88 **DRINK** 2007 $ 25
Chardonnay Semillon NV Comes together remarkably well; a blend of 2003 and 2002 Chardonnay and 2003 Semillon; good balance and length; subtle oak. **RATING** 87 **DRINK** Now $ 15.50
Botrytis Chardonnay 2003 Very strong botrytis; complex wine with lots of character; balancing acidity. **RATING** 87 **DRINK** 2008 $ 35

▼▼▼▽ **Reserve Semillon 2003** **RATING** 86 **DRINK** 2008
Private Reserve Chardonnay 2002 **RATING** 86 **DRINK** Now $ 19.50
Private Reserve Shiraz 2002 **RATING** 86 **DRINK** 2008 $ 22.50
Liqueur Muscat NV **RATING** 86 **DRINK** Now $ 12.50
Premium Oak Chardonnay 2002 **RATING** 85 **DRINK** Now $ 22.50
Unwooded Chardonnay 2002 **RATING** 84 **DRINK** Now $ 17.50

Heritage Farm Wines NR

RMB 1005 Murray Valley Highway, Cobram, Vic 3655 **REGION** Goulburn Valley
T (03) 5872 2376 **F** (03) 5872 2376 **OPEN** 7 days 9–5
WINEMAKER Roy Armfield **EST.** 1987 **CASES** 2000
PRODUCT RANGE ($5–12 CD) Riesling, Traminer Riesling, Moselle, Chardonnay are varietal releases; there are a considerable number of generic releases and fortified wines on sale at cellar door.
SUMMARY Heritage Farm claims to be the only vineyard and orchard in Australia still using horsepower, with Clydesdales used for most of the general farm work. The winery and cellar-door area also boasts a large range of restored horse-drawn farm machinery and a bottle collection. All of the wines are sold by mailing list and through the cellar door.

Heritage Wines ★★★★★

106a Seppeltsfield Road, Marananga, SA 5355 **REGION** Barossa Valley
T (08) 8562 2880 **F** (08) 8562 2692 **OPEN** 7 days 11–5
WINEMAKER Stephen Hoff **EST.** 1984 **CASES** 6000
PRODUCT RANGE ($14–34 CD) Semillon, Barossa Shiraz, Rossco's Shiraz, Cabernet Malbec, Cabernet Sauvignon, 10 Year Old Tokay.
SUMMARY A little-known winery which deserves a far wider audience, for Stephen Hoff is apt to produce some startlingly good wines. At various times the Chardonnay, Riesling (from old Clare Valley vines) and Rossco's Shiraz (now the flag-bearer) have all excelled, at other times not. Exports to the UK and the US.

▼▼▼▼▼ **Steve Hoff Barossa Shiraz 2002** Dense black cherry, plum and licorice; great depth, but not the least extractive. **RATING** 94 **DRINK** 2017 $ 24
Steve Hoff Cabernet Sauvignon 2002 Rich blackcurrant, blackberry and chocolate on a sumptuous palate; fine tannins. **RATING** 94 **DRINK** 2017 $ 24

▼▼▼▽ **Steve Hoff Barossa Semillon 2003** **RATING** 86 **DRINK** 2007 $ 14

Hermes Morrison Wines

NR

253 Swan Ponds Road, Woodstock, NSW 2793 **REGION** Central Ranges Zone
T (02) 6345 0153 **F** (02) 6345 0153 **OPEN** 7 days 10–5 summer, winter weekends and public holidays
WINEMAKER Jill Lindsay (Contract) **EST.** 1990 **CASES** 180
PRODUCT RANGE ($11–13 CD) Riesling, Semillon, Sauvignon Blanc, Chardonnay, Pinot Noir, Shiraz
Cabernet.
SUMMARY The Morrison family established their Hermes Poll Dorset Stud in 1972, which continues
but has now been joined by Hermes Morrison wines. The cellar door has been established by the side
of a large lake fed by cold, clear water welling up from subterranean caves, and a 10-minute walk
takes you to the summit of Mount Palatine, one of the highest peaks in the shire and with a
spectacular view of the Canobolas Mountains 80 kilometres away.

Herons Rise Vineyard

NR

Saddle Road, Kettering, Tas 7155 **REGION** Southern Tasmania
T (03) 6267 4339 **F** (03) 6267 4245 **OPEN** By appointment
WINEMAKER Andrew Hood **EST.** 1984 **CASES** 250
PRODUCT RANGE ($17.50–20 CD) Muller Thurgau Riesling, Pinot Noir.
SUMMARY Sue and Gerry White run a small stone country guesthouse in the D'Entrecasteaux
Channel area and basically sell the wines produced from the surrounding hectare of vineyard to those
staying at the two self-contained cottages. The Pinot Noir is strongly recommended. The postal
address for bookings is PO Box 271, Kettering, Tas 7155.

Hesperos Wines

PO Box 882, Margaret River, WA 6285 **REGION** Margaret River
T (08) 9757 6565 **F** (08) 9757 6565 **OPEN** Not
WINEMAKER Jurg Muggli **EST.** 1993 **CASES** 2000
PRODUCT RANGE ($14.50–19.50 CD) Sauvignon Blanc, Syrah.
SUMMARY Hesperos is the venture of Jurg Muggli and Sandra Hancock. It supplies Jurg Muggli's
winemaking skills to Xanadu, where Muggli has been resident winemaker for many years. It also has
a 30-hectare property near Witchcliffe between Cape Mentelle and Devil's Lair, with the potential of
15 hectares of vineyard, planting commenced in the winter of 1999. In the meantime the Hesperos
wines are made from purchased grapes; Shiraz and Sauvignon Blanc have been produced in each
vintage. Exports to Japan, Switzerland and Germany.

Hewitson

★★★★★

The Old Dairy Cold Stores, 66 London Road, Mile End, SA 5031 **REGION** Warehouse
T (08) 8443 6466 **F** (08) 8443 6866 **OPEN** By appointment
WINEMAKER Dean Hewitson **EST.** 1996 **CASES** 15 000
PRODUCT RANGE ($19–44 R) Eden Valley Riesling, L'Oizeau McLaren Vale Shiraz, Old Garden
Mourvedre, Ned & Henry's Barossa Shiraz, Miss Harry, Dry Grown and Ancient.
SUMMARY Dean Hewitson was a Petaluma winemaker for 10 years, and during that time managed to
do three vintages in France and one in Oregon as well as undertaking his Masters at UC Davis,
California. It is hardly surprising that the Hewitson wines are immaculately made from a technical
viewpoint. However, he has also managed to source 30-year-old riesling from the Eden Valley and
70-year-old shiraz from McLaren Vale, following on with a Barossa Valley Mourvedre produced from
145-year-old vines at Rowland Flat, and a Barossa Valley Shiraz and Grenache, coming from 60-
year-old vines at Tanunda. The vineyards are now under long-term contracts to Dean Hewitson.
Exports to the UK, Denmark, Finland, the US, Canada, Hong Kong and Singapore.

♟♟♟♟♟ **Ned & Henry's Shiraz 2002** Rich blackberry, licorice and spice fruit provides velvety
mouthfeel to a delicious and seductive wine. Great value. Screwcap. **RATING** 94
DRINK 2016 **$** 25
L'Oizeau Shiraz 2001 Complex, spicy blackberry fruit and oak aromas; a super-elegant,
graceful palate of black fruits, dark chocolate and fine tannins. **RATING** 94 **DRINK** 2016 **$** 36
Old Garden Mourvedre 2001 Potent, arresting rosemary and spice on the bouquet; bitter
chocolate and black cherry fruit; lingering finish, fine tannins. **RATING** 94 **DRINK** 2021 **$** 35

ΨΨΨΨ **Old Garden Mourvedre 2002** Intense earthy/bitter chocolate savoury varietal aromas and flavours; long palate, ripe tannins; carries its 15.5 degrees alcohol well. **RATING** 92 **DRINK** 2017 $ 35

ΨΨΨΨ **Eden Valley Riesling 2003** Mineral slate and talc aromas; tight, lime-accented mid-palate, slatey finish. **RATING** 89 **DRINK** 2009 $ 19
Miss Harry Dry Grown and Ancient 2002 A bright and lively cascade of red fruit flavours. Screwcap to keep it fresh. **RATING** 87 **DRINK** Now $ 19

🐝 Heytesbury Ridge ★★★☆

1170 Cooriemungle Road, Timboon, Vic 3268 **REGION** Geelong
T (03) 5598 7394 **F** (03) 5598 7396 **OPEN** 7 days 11–5 by appointment
WINEMAKER David Newton **EST.** 1998 **CASES** 700
PRODUCT RANGE ($15–20 CD) Sauvignon Blanc, Pinot Grigio, Chardonnay, Pinot Noir, Rose.
SUMMARY David and Dot Newton say that after milking cows for 18 years, they decided to investigate the possibility of planting a northeast-facing block of land which they owned but which was separate to the dairy farm. Their self-diagnosed mid-life crisis also stemmed from a lifelong interest in wine as consumers, and they decided to take the plunge. Two hectares of chardonnay and pinot noir were planted in December 1998, and another 2 hectares of pinot gris, pinot noir and sauvignon blanc the following year. The first two vintages were made at a Colac winery, but (having done a short winemaking course at Melbourne University Dookie Campus) the Newtons completed a small winery and made the 2003 vintage on-site. They have targetted the active, year-round tourism opportunities of the Great Ocean Road, and the Twelve Apostles in particular. Venturing inland the rainforest and waterfall in the Otway Ranges are a great summer destination. Another important part of the business is the 4.5-star rated bed and breakfast accommodation on the property.

ΨΨΨΨ **Pinot Noir 2003** Quite intense dark plum and black cherry fruit providing clear varietal character; good length; very well made. **RATING** 90 **DRINK** 2007 $ 20

ΨΨΨ **Chardonnay 2003** Clean, crisp, crunchy, Chablish-like; well-made. **RATING** 86 **DRINK** Now $ 20
Pinot Grigio 2003 A pinkish tinge from the skins; crisp, flinty acidity; long finish. **RATING** 86 **DRINK** 2007 $ 15

Hickinbotham NR

Nepean Highway (near Wallaces Road), Dromana, Vic 3936 **REGION** Mornington Peninsula
T (03) 5981 0355 **F** (03) 5981 0355 **OPEN** 7 days
WINEMAKER Andrew Hickinbotham **EST.** 1981 **CASES** 3000
PRODUCT RANGE ($16–32 CD) Chardonnay with Aligote, Taminga, Sparkling Pinot Rose, Pinot Noir, Shiraz, Coffee Rock Merlot, Cabernet Merlot; Jackals Run (named after the Hickinbotham's children Jake and Cal) Chardonnay, Shiraz Cabernet Grenache; fruit wines.
SUMMARY After a peripatetic period and a hiatus in winemaking, Hickinbotham established a permanent vineyard and winery base at Dromana. It now makes only Mornington Peninsula wines, drawing in part on 5 hectares of estate vineyards, and in part on contract-grown fruit. The wines are principally sold through the cellar door and mail order.

ΨΨΨ **Family Reserve Pinot Noir 2002** **RATING** 85 **DRINK** Now $ 32

Hidden Creek NR

Eukey Road, Ballandean, Qld 4382 **REGION** Granite Belt
T (07) 4684 1383 **F** (07) 4684 1355 **OPEN** Mon–Fri 11–3, weekends 10–4
WINEMAKER Jim Barnes **EST.** 1997 **CASES** 1400
PRODUCT RANGE ($11–22 CD) A full range of white and red table wines (including a Nebbiolo), and a Fortified Muscat made from vines planted at Hidden Creek in 1945.
SUMMARY A beautifully located vineyard and winery on a 1000-metre high ridge overlooking the Ballandean township and the Severn River valley, separated from Girraween National Park by Doctors Creek. The granite boulder-strewn hills mean that the 70-hectare property will only provide a little over 6 hectares of vineyard, in turn divided into six different blocks.

Hidden River Estate ★★★☆

Mullineaux Road, Pemberton, WA 6260 **REGION** Pemberton
T (08) 9776 1437 **F** (08) 9776 0189 **OPEN** 7 days 9–4
WINEMAKER Brenden Smith, Phil Goldring **EST.** 1994 **CASES** 2500
PRODUCT RANGE ($14.50–30 CD) Three Feathers Classic Dry White, Unwooded Chardonnay, Wooded Chardonnay, Sparkle Arse (Methode Champenoise), Late Picked Riesling, Pinot Noir, Authentic Basket Press Shiraz, Cabernet Sauvignon, Aged Cell Door Tawny Port, The Muskateer.
SUMMARY Phil and Sandy Goldring spent 10 years operating farm chalets in the Pemberton area before selling the business and retiring to become grape growers, with the intention of selling the grapes to others. However, they found old habits hard to kick, so opened a cellar-door sales and café/restaurant. It is a successful business with a very strong marketing push, a 1901 Kalgoorlie tram (the streetcar named Desire) having been purchased, renovated and installed on-site to provide more seating for the award-winning restaurant. I hope the Goldrings did not pay much for the tram.

TTTTY **Premium Wooded Chardonnay 2001** Complex bottle-developed and barrel-ferment aromas and flavours; strong peachy fruit; plenty happening. **RATING** 90 **DRINK** 2008 $22

TTTT **Pinot Noir 2002** Light-bodied; cherry and strawberry aromas and flavours, then a savoury, stem and leaf finish. **RATING** 87 **DRINK** 2008 $24

TTTY **Cabernet Sauvignon 2001 RATING** 86 **DRINK** 2007 $22
River Bed White 2003 RATING 85 **DRINK** 2007 $14.50
Basket Press Shiraz 2002 RATING 85 **DRINK** 2008 $24

TTT **Unwooded Chardonnay 2003 RATING** 83 $14.50
Three Feathers Classic Dry White 2003 RATING 83 $14.50

Highbank NR

Riddoch Highway, Coonawarra, SA 5263 **REGION** Coonawarra
T (08) 8736 3311 **F** (08) 8736 3122 **OPEN** By appointment
WINEMAKER Dennis Vice, Trevor Mast **EST.** 1986 **CASES** 1000
PRODUCT RANGE ($40 CD) Chardonnay, Basket Pressed Cabernet Blend, Basket Pressed Cabernet Sauvignon.
SUMMARY Mount Gambier lecturer in viticulture Dennis Vice makes a tiny quantity of smooth, melon-accented Chardonnay and stylish Coonawarra Cabernet blend of good quality which are sold through local restaurants and the cellar door, with limited Melbourne distribution. Intermittent exports to various countries.

Higher Plane Wines ★★★★

Location 1077, Wintarru Rise via Warner Glen Road, Forrest Grove, WA 6286 (postal)
REGION Margaret River
T (08) 9336 7855 **F** (08) 9336 7866 **OPEN** Not
WINEMAKER Keith Mugford (Contract) **EST.** 1997 **CASES** 1600
PRODUCT RANGE ($20–28 ML) Chardonnay, Pinot Noir, Merlot, Cabernet Merlot.
SUMMARY Plastic and hand-surgeon Dr Craig Smith, and wife Cathie, left nothing to chance in planning and establishing Higher Plane. As a prelude Cathie obtained a Master of Business in wine marketing from Edith Cowan University, and Craig began the wine marketing course at the University of Adelaide. Having read and consulted widely, the Smiths wrote to every real estate agent within the Margaret River region listing the criteria which had to be met for their proposed vineyard. Details of over 100 properties were faxed to the Smiths, before hearing about the property they have in fact purchased. Its eastern and northern boundaries adjoin Devil's Lair with similar gravelly, loamy, sandy soil. The wines are sold through an active mailing list with copious information, and limited retail distribution through Perth, New South Wales and Queensland.

TTTTY **Chardonnay 2002** Spotlessly clean, delicate stone fruit; nicely balanced and integrated oak. **RATING** 90 **DRINK** 2008 $28

TTTT **Merlot 2002** Powerful, vibrant fruit; dark berries, nice varietal twist of olive; fine-grained, persistent tannins. **RATING** 89 **DRINK** 2010 $25

TTTY **Pinot Noir 2002 RATING** 84 **DRINK** Now $20

Highland Heritage Estate

Mitchell Highway, Orange, NSW 2800 **REGION** Orange
T (02) 6361 3612 **F** (02) 6361 3613 **OPEN** Mon–Fri 9–3, weekends 9–5
WINEMAKER John Hordern, Rex D'Aquino **EST.** 1984 **CASES** 3500
PRODUCT RANGE ($10–30 CD) Under the Mount Canobolas label: Chardonnay, Sauvignon Blanc, Pinot Noir; Gosling Creek Chardonnay; and the newly released Wellwood Estate label.
SUMMARY The estate plantings have increased from 4 hectares to over 15 hectares, with plantings in 1995 and 1997 now in full production. The tasting facility is unusual: a converted railway carriage overlooking the vineyard.

High Valley Wines ★★★

137 Cassilis Road, Mudgee, NSW 2850 **REGION** Mudgee
T (02) 6375 0292 **F** (02) 6375 0228 **OPEN** 7 days 10–5
WINEMAKER Simon Gilbert, Ian MacRae, David Lowe **EST.** 1995 **CASES** 2000
PRODUCT RANGE ($13–23 CD) Chardonnay, Premium Chardonnay, Rose, Shiraz, Reserve Shiraz, Cabernet Sauvignon.
SUMMARY The Francis family, headed by Ro and Grosvenor Francis, have operated a sheep, wheat and cattle property at Dunedoo for several generations. Concurrently with handing over the property to their sons in 1995, Ro and Grosvenor subdivided and retained a 40-hectare block on which they have since established 11 hectares of shiraz, 6 hectares of cabernet sauvignon and 5 hectares of chardonnay. A grape supply agreement was entered into with Rothbury Estate, but a decision was taken to retain a portion of the grapes and develop the High Valley Wines label in 1998. While the property is only open by appointment, it does feature a gas and wood-fired working pottery, vineyard tours and farm tours.

ΨΨΨΨ **Premium Chardonnay 2003** Elegant; subtle oak infusion into a mix of cashew and melon. **RATING** 89 **DRINK** 2007 $ 23
Chardonnay 2003 Light to medium-bodied; subtle but complex touches of oak and malolactic fermentation inputs. **RATING** 87 **DRINK** 2007 $ 23

ΨΨΨΨ **Mudgee Chardonnay 1999 RATING** 86 **DRINK** Now $ 13
Rose 2003 RATING 86 **DRINK** Now $ 15
Chardonnay 2002 RATING 85 **DRINK** Now $ 23
Dunedoo Premium Chardonnay 2000 RATING 85 **DRINK** Now $ 17
Shiraz 2001 RATING 85 **DRINK** 2008 $ 19

ΨΨΨ **Shiraz 2002 RATING** 81 $ 19
Cabernet Sauvignon 2002 RATING 80 $ 18

Highway Wines NR

612 Great Northern Highway, Herne Hill, WA 6056 **REGION** Swan Valley
T (08) 9296 4354 **OPEN** Mon–Sat 8.30–6
WINEMAKER Tony Bakranich **EST.** 1954 **CASES** 4000
PRODUCT RANGE ($7–18 CD) Some white table wines, and many fortifieds, offered both in bottles and flagons.
SUMMARY A survivor of another era, when literally dozens of such wineries plied their business in the Swan Valley. It still enjoys a strong local trade, selling much of its wine in fill-your-own-containers, and two-litre flagons, with lesser quantities sold by the bottle.

🐂 Hillbillé

Blackwood Valley Estate, Balingup Road, Nannup, WA 6275 **REGION** Blackwood Valley
T (08) 9218 8199 **F** (08) 9218 8099 **OPEN** Weekends and holidays 10–4
WINEMAKER David Watson, Stuart Watson (Contract) **EST.** 1998 **CASES** 2500
PRODUCT RANGE ($18 ML) Chardonnay, Rose, Shiraz, Reserve Shiraz, Merlot, Merlot Shiraz.
SUMMARY Gary Bettridge began the establishment of 19 hectares of shiraz, cabernet sauvignon, merlot, chardonnay and semillon in 1998. It is situated in the Blackwood Valley between Balingup and Nannup, which the RAC describes as 'the most scenic drive in the southwest of Western Australia'. A

significant part of the grape production is sold to Goundrey, Vasse Felix, Plantagenet and Evans & Tate, but as from the 2003 vintage part has been vinified by the Watsons at Woodlands Wines.

ȲȲȲȲ **Merlot Shiraz 2003** A lively mix of fresh red fruits and more savoury notes; plenty of fruit intensity; very good mouthfeel. **RATING** 92 **DRINK** 2013 $18

Shiraz 2003 Deep, dense, dark black fruits; hints of spice and game; a rich and ample palate, not extractive. **RATING** 91 **DRINK** 2013 $18

ȲȲȲȲ **Merlot 2003** Abundant sweet, red berry fruit; oak prominent, and yet to integrate. **RATING** 88 **DRINK** 2010 $18

Chardonnay 2003 A very soft cashew and tropical mix; overall impression of sweetness. **RATING** 87 **DRINK** Now $18

Rose 2003 Particularly well-made; strawberry and cherry; just a little sweetness on the finish. **RATING** 87 **DRINK** Now $18

Hillbrook ★★★☆

639 Doust Road, Geary's Gap via Bungendore, NSW 2621 **REGION** Canberra District
T (02) 6236 9455 **F** (02) 6236 9455 **OPEN** Weekends and public holidays 10–5
WINEMAKER Contract **EST.** 1994 **CASES** 2000
PRODUCT RANGE ($19–25 CD) Riesling, Chardonnay, Pinot Noir, Merlot, Tawny Port.
SUMMARY Adolf and Levina Zanzert began the establishment of 8.5 hectares of vines at Geary's Gap in 1994. The wines have good retail distribution in the ACT, Bungendore and Cooma, and are also available through the cellar door and mailing list.

ȲȲȲȲ **Merlot 2002** Fresh, fragrant and elegant; light to medium-bodied red fruits and fine tannins. Good varietal character. **RATING** 87 **DRINK** 2010

Hillbrook Wines NR

Cnr Hillbrook and Wheatley Coast Roads, Quinninup, WA 6258 **REGION** Pemberton
T (08) 9776 7202 **F** (08) 9776 7202 **OPEN** By appointment
WINEMAKER Castle Rock Estate (Contract) **EST.** 1996 **CASES** 350
PRODUCT RANGE ($8.50–13.50 ML) Sauvignon Blanc, Merlot.
SUMMARY Brian Ede and partner Anne Walsh have established 1 hectare of sauvignon blanc and 3 hectares of merlot, and have the wines made for them by Robert Diletti at Castle Rock Estate. They are sold through the cellar door and via a mailing list, and — increasingly — by word of mouth.

Hillcrest Vineyards ★★★★☆

31 Phillip Road, Woori Yallock, Vic 3139 **REGION** Yarra Valley
T (03) 5964 6689 **F** (03) 5961 5547 **OPEN** By appointment
WINEMAKER Phillip Jones (Contract) **EST.** 1971 **CASES** 250
PRODUCT RANGE ($30–45 ML) Chardonnay, Pinot Noir, Cabernet Sauvignon.
SUMMARY David and Tanya Bryant may or may not realise it, but my association with Hillcrest goes back to 1985, when Coldstream Hills first started purchasing grapes from the then-owners Graeme and Joy Sweet. Although there was never a written contract, that arrangement continued until Hillcrest was sold, by which time the tiny amount of grapes coming from it was of no particular significance to Coldstream Hills. But the Sweets had stood by Coldstream Hills in the years of acute grape shortages, and we reciprocated further down the track. To say I am pleased that Hillcrest is in tender care, and receiving the attention it deserves, is putting it mildly. Tiny quantities of the 2001 Pinot Noir ($39) and 2002 Chardonay ($35) (both outstanding) are still available from the cellar door. Hillcrest declassified its 2002 vintage reds which are available from the winery as cleanskins at $19 per bottle.

🐚 Hillside Estate Wines NR

Marrowbone Road, Pokolbin, NSW 2320 **REGION** Lower Hunter Valley
T (02) 4991 4370 **F** (02) 4991 4371 **OPEN** By appointment
WINEMAKER Trevor Drayton (Contract) **EST.** 1995
PRODUCT RANGE ($10–14 ML) Verdelho, Chardonnay, Shiraz.

SUMMARY Rena and former noted journalist Ed Barnum have a substantial vineyard of 46 hectares planted to chardonnay, verdelho, traminer, shiraz and cabernet sauvignon, which is substantially more than a quiet retirement hobby. The wines are contract-made by district veteran Trevor Drayton.

Hill Smith Estate ★★★★

Flaxmans Valley Road, Eden Valley, SA 5235 **REGION** Eden Valley
T (08) 8561 3200 **F** (08) 8561 3393 **OPEN** At Yalumba
WINEMAKER Louisa Rose **EST.** 1979 **CASES** 5000
PRODUCT RANGE ($18.95 CD) Sauvignon Blanc.
SUMMARY Part of the Yalumba stable, drawing upon its own estate plantings including 15 hectares of sauvignon blanc. Over the years has produced some excellent wines, but the style (and perhaps quality) does seem to vary significantly with vintage, and the winery rating is a compromise between the best and the least. Exports to all major markets.

♥♥♥♥♥ Sauvignon Blanc 2003 Clean (no sweaty armpits), the middle palate laden with ripe tropical and gooseberry fruit, and — almost against the odds — doesn't cloy on the finish.
RATING 92 **DRINK** Now $18.95

Hills of Plenty NR

370 Yan Yean Road, Yarrambat, Vic 3091 **REGION** Yarra Valley
T (03) 9436 2264 **F** (03) 9436 2264 **OPEN** Last Sun of each month 11–6, or by appointment
WINEMAKER Karen Coulston **EST.** 1998 **CASES** 400
PRODUCT RANGE ($16.50–20 CD) Riesling, Sauvignon Blanc, Chardonnay, Olivia Kane, Pinot Noir, Shiraz, Cabernet Sauvignon.
SUMMARY Hills of Plenty has been established just outside the Melbourne metropolitan area, a few minutes drive north of Greensborough. There is a tiny 0.2-hectare vineyard of riesling, chardonnay and cabernet sauvignon around the winery, but most of the fruit is purchased from other regions, notably Geelong, Gippsland and Swan Hill. The tiny production means that the cellar door only opens once a month, but it is turned into a festive occasion with live music, and picnics or barbecues welcome.

Hillstowe ★★★★

104 Main Road, Hahndorf, SA 5245 **REGION** Adelaide Hills
T (08) 8388 1400 **F** (08) 8388 1411 **OPEN** 7 days 10–5
WINEMAKER Justin McNamee **EST.** 1980 **CASES** 12 000
PRODUCT RANGE ($16–46 R) A range of vineyard and varietal-designated wines of ascending price and quality, being Sauvignon Blanc, Scrub Block Pinot Gris, Buxton Chardonnay, Buxton Cabernet Merlot; and at the top end Adelaide Hills Udy's Mill Chardonnay, Udy's Mill Pinot Noir, Mary's Hundred Shiraz, The Pinch Row Lenswood Merlot.
SUMMARY Rapid-fire changes of ownership from founder Chris Lawrie to Banksia Wines then to Lion Nathan should (theoretically) not impact on the quality and style of the high quality Hillstowe wines. Its principal vineyard, Udy's Mill at Lenswood, has 17 hectares planted, supplementing McLaren Vale grapes coming from the Buxton Vineyard. The wines are exported to the UK, Canada, the US, Europe and Asia.

Hills View Vineyards ★★★☆

11 Main Avenue, Frewville, SA 5063 **REGION** McLaren Vale
T (08) 8338 0666 **F** (08) 8338 0666 **OPEN** Not
WINEMAKER Brett Howard **EST.** 1998 **CASES** 12 000
PRODUCT RANGE ($10–30 R) Three ranges of wines produced: Blewitt Springs Semillon, Chardonnay, Shiraz and Cabernet Sauvignon; Howard Fleurieu Semillon and Coonawarra Shiraz; Hills View Chardonnay Verdelho, Shiraz Cabernet and Cabernet Merlot.
SUMMARY District veteran Brett Howard, with 20 years winemaking experience, is now the winemaker for Hills View Vineyards, producing the Hills View Vineyards range of wines, the Blewitt Springs range and Howard label, a Fleurieu Semillon and a Coonawarra Shiraz released only in the best vintages.

ＹＹＹＹＹ **Blewitt Springs Chardonnay 2003** Fine, elegant and fresh; good length and balance; citrus/melon/nectarine fruit-driven. **RATING** 90 **DRINK** 2007 $ 22

ＹＹＹＹ **Blewitt Springs Shiraz 2001** Very ripe prune, blackberry and chocolate; a dense, fat, chewy 14.5 degrees alcohol; modern McLaren Vale style. **RATING** 89 **DRINK** 2011 $ 22

ＹＹＹＹ **Blewitt Springs Cabernet Sauvignon 2001** **RATING** 86 **DRINK** 2010 $ 22
Blewitt Springs Malbec 2001 **RATING** 86 **DRINK** 2009 $ 22

Hillwood Vineyard   NR

55 Innocent Street, Kings Meadows, Tas 7249 (postal) **REGION** Northern Tasmania
T 0418 500 672 **OPEN** Not
WINEMAKER Geoff Carr
PRODUCT RANGE Sauvignon Blanc, Pinot Gris, Chardonnay, Pinot Noir, Cabernet.
SUMMARY Geoff Carr, the owner, viticulturist and winemaker, has established his vineyard on the east bank of the Tamar River, looking out over the river. He supplements his estate-grown grapes by purchasing some chardonnay and pinot gris from local growers.

Hochkirch Wines   NR

Hamilton Highway, Tarrington, Vic 3301 **REGION** Henty
T (03) 5573 5200 **F** (03) 5573 5200 **OPEN** 11–5 by appointment
WINEMAKER John Nagorcka **EST.** 1997 **CASES** 1500
PRODUCT RANGE ($11–24 ML) Riesling, Semillon, Pinot Noir, Shiraz, Cabernet Sauvignon.
SUMMARY Jennifer and John Nagorcka have developed Hochkirch in response to the very cool climate with growing season temperatures similar to Burgundy. A high density planting pattern was implemented, with a low fruiting wire to take advantage of soil warmth in the growing season, and the focus was placed on pinot noir (4.5 hectares), with lesser quantities of riesling, cabernet sauvignon, semillon and shiraz. The vines are not irrigated and no synthetic fungicides, pesticides or fertilisers are used; currently the Nagorckas are trialling biodynamic practice. Wines with considerable complexity and interest are the result, the Pinot Noir having received critical acclaim in a number of quarters.

Hoffmann's   ★★★☆

Ingoldby Road, McLaren Flat, SA 5171 **REGION** McLaren Vale
T (08) 8383 0232 **F** (08) 8383 0232 **OPEN** 7 days 11–5
WINEMAKER Nick Holmes (Consultant) **EST.** 1996 **CASES** 2500
PRODUCT RANGE ($16–21 CD) Chardonnay, Shiraz, Cabernet Sauvignon.
SUMMARY Peter and Anthea Hoffmann have been growing grapes at their property in Ingoldby Road since 1978, and Peter Hoffmann has worked at various wineries in McLaren Vale since 1979. Both he and Anthea have undertaken courses at the Regency TAFE Institute in Adelaide, and (in Peter Hoffmann's words) 'in 1996 we decided that we knew a little about winemaking and opened a small cellar door'. Exports to the UK, Germany, Canada and Malaysia.

ＹＹＹＹＹ **Shiraz 2002** Medium-bodied; licorice, prune and dark chocolate; ripe tannins; good texture and length. **RATING** 90 **DRINK** 2015 $ 21

ＹＹＹＹ **Cabernet Sauvignon 2002** Solid black fruits, earth and chocolate; good balance and length. **RATING** 88 **DRINK** 2012 $ 21

ＹＹＹＹ **Chardonnay 2003** **RATING** 84 **DRINK** Now $ 16

ＹＹＹ **Merlot 2002** **RATING** 81 $ 16

🐌 Holley Hill   ★★★☆

136 Ronalds Road, Willung South, Vic 3847 **REGION** Gippsland
T (03) 5198 2205 **F** (03) 5198 2205 **OPEN** Thurs–Sun and public holidays 10–6
WINEMAKER David Packham **EST.** 1998 **CASES** 300
PRODUCT RANGE ($12–25 CD) Sauvignon Blanc, Chardonnay, Pinot Rose, Shiraz, Cabernet Merlot.

SUMMARY David Packham has used his background as a Master of Applied Science, formerly a research scientist with the CSIRO, and more recently with the Bureau of Meteorology, to plan the establishment of Holley Hill. He served his apprenticeship at another winery for 2 years before acquiring the then two-year-old Holley Hill vineyard, planted to 0.5 hectare each of chardonnay, sauvignon blanc and pinot noir. A large hay shed on the property was converted to a winery, and the cellar door opened in November 2002. The sweet Pinot Rose is particularly (and successfully) directed at the local community.

ŸŸŸŸ   **Shiraz 2002** Deeply coloured; youthful spice, black cherry and plum; firm but not extractive. Full of promise. Great debut. **RATING** 89 **DRINK** 2012 $18

ŸŸŸ̈   **Rose 2003** **RATING** 85 **DRINK** Now $13

Hollick   ★★★★

Riddoch Highway, Coonawarra, SA 5263 **REGION** Coonawarra
T (08) 8737 2318 **F** (08) 8737 2952 **OPEN** 7 days 9–5
WINEMAKER Ian Hollick, David Norman **EST.** 1983 **CASES** 50 000
PRODUCT RANGE ($16–59 R) A very disciplined array of products with Riesling, Sauvignon, Sauvignon Blanc Semillon, Wilgha Vineyard Unoaked Chardonnay, Pinot Noir, Tempranillo and Shiraz Cabernet Sauvignon at the lower end of the price range; Reserve Chardonnay, Cabernet Sauvignon Merlot, Pinot Noir Chardonnay, Sparkling Merlot in the middle; Wilgha Shiraz, Neilson's Block Merlot and Ravenswood, the deluxe Ravenswood Cabernet Sauvignon at the top.
SUMMARY Winner of many trophies (including the most famous of all, the Jimmy Watson), its wines are well crafted and competitively priced, although sometimes a little on the light side. A $1 million cellar door and restaurant complex opened in June 2002. National distribution in all States; exports to Europe and Asia.

ŸŸŸŸ̈   **Ravenswood Cabernet Sauvignon 2000** Sweeter fruit with more cassis than the '01; fine and elegant. **RATING** 93 **DRINK** 2014 $59
        Ravenswood Cabernet Sauvignon 2001 Blackcurrant, earth and blackberry; medium-bodied, supple, smooth and long; good tannins. **RATING** 92 **DRINK** 2015 $59
        Sauvignon Blanc Semillon 2003 Attractive lemon/lemon rind aromas and flavours; lingering mouthfeel and acidity. **RATING** 90 **DRINK** 2008 $17
        Neilson's Block Merlot 2001 Appealing medium-bodied style; clean, fresh, small red berry fruits and gently ripe tannins; good mouthfeel and balance. **RATING** 90 **DRINK** 2008 $55

ŸŸŸŸ   **Wilgha Vineyard Unoaked Chardonnay 2003** Pleasing stone fruit and citrus; extra flavour on the mid-palate makes this a good example of its style. **RATING** 87 **DRINK** Now $16
        Pinot Noir 2003 Youthful colour; a subdued bouquet, then a light to medium-bodied palate with plum and black cherry fruit; balance good but varietal character lacking. **RATING** 87 **DRINK** Now $20

ŸŸŸ̈   **Neilson's Block Merlot 2002** **RATING** 86 **DRINK** 2009 $55
        Coonawarra Sparkling Merlot 2001 **RATING** 86 **DRINK** 2007 $29.80
        Riesling 2003 **RATING** 85 **DRINK** 2007 $18
        Reserve Chardonnay 2002 **RATING** 85 **DRINK** Now $22

Hollyclare   NR

940 Milbrodale Road, Broke, NSW 2330 **REGION** Lower Hunter Valley
T (02) 6579 1193 **F** (02) 6579 1269 **OPEN** Weekends 10–5 by appointment
WINEMAKER Tamburlaine (Contract) **EST.** 1987 **CASES** 2000
PRODUCT RANGE Semillon, Unwooded Semillon, Chardonnay, Chardonnay Semillon, Shiraz.
SUMMARY John Holdsworth established the Hollyclare Vineyard (now totalling 3 hectares each of chardonnay, semillon, shiraz and 1 hectare of aleatico) 10 years ago, but the Hollyclare label is a relatively new one on the market. While the wines are made under contract at Tamburlaine, Hollyclare has its own dedicated wine tanks and all of the wines are estate-grown.

Holly Folly

NR

649 Campersic Road, Baskerville, WA 6056 **REGION** Swan Valley
T (08) 9296 2043 **F** (08) 9296 2043 **OPEN** By appointment
WINEMAKER Peter Hollingworth **EST.** 1995 **CASES** 400
PRODUCT RANGE ($5–15 ML) Dry White, Verdelho (Barrel Fermented and Barrel Aged), Marsanne, Methode Champenoise, Light Red, Merlot.
SUMMARY Peter Hollingworth clearly has a sense of humour and a sense of perspective. He began the establishment of the 11.5 hectares of vineyards (planted to chenin blanc, chardonnay, viognier, marsanne, verdelho, petit verdot, grenache and merlot) in 1995, but it was not until 2000 that the necessary producers licence was obtained, and in October of that year he embarked upon the limited release of the 400-case production, destined mainly for friends and acquaintances. Most of the grapes are sold to other producers.

Holm Oak

★★★★

RSD 256 Rowella, West Tamar, Tas 7270 **REGION** Northern Tasmania
T (03) 6394 7577 **F** (03) 6394 7350 **OPEN** 7 days 10–5
WINEMAKER Nick Butler, Julian Alcorso **EST.** 1983 **CASES** 3000
PRODUCT RANGE ($16–25 R) Riesling, Chardonnay, Reserve Chardonnay, Tyrian Rose Pinot Noir, Cabernet Sauvignon.
SUMMARY The Butler family produces tremendously rich and strongly flavoured red wines from the vineyard situated on the banks of the Tamar River, and which takes its name from the grove of oak trees planted around the turn of the century and originally intended for the making of tennis racquets. The white wines, too, led by Riesling, have also impressed over the past few years.

♟♟♟ **Riesling 2003 RATING** 83 **$** 22

Home Hill

★★★☆

38 Nairn Street, Ranelagh, Tas 7109 **REGION** Southern Tasmania
T (03) 6264 1200 **F** (03) 6264 1069 **OPEN** 7 days 10–5
WINEMAKER Peter Dunbaven **EST.** 1994 **CASES** 2500
PRODUCT RANGE ($19–35 CD) Sauvignon Blanc, Sylvaner, Unwooded Chardonnay, Kelly's Reserve Chardonnay, Kelly's Reserve Sticky, Kelly Cuvee, Pinot Noir, Kelly's Reserve Pinot Noir.
SUMMARY Terry and Rosemary Bennett planted their first half hectare of vines in 1994 on gentle slopes in the beautiful Huon Valley. The plantings were quickly extended to 3 hectares, with another hectare planted in 1999. A 70-seat restaurant is open for lunch Wednesday to Sunday and dinner on Saturday.

♟♟♟♟ **Kelly's Reserve Chardonnay 2003** Supple and elegant; crisp melon fruit; good line and length. **RATING** 88 **DRINK** 2007 **$** 23
Sylvaner 2003 Authentic blossom, herb and spice varietal aromas; moderately intense; good line and length. **RATING** 87 **DRINK** 2007 **$** 19

♟♟♟♟ **Pinot Noir 2002 RATING** 86 **DRINK** 2008 **$** 35
Unoaked Chardonnay 2003 RATING 85 **DRINK** Now **$** 19

Honeytree Estate

★★★☆

16 Gillards Road, Pokolbin, NSW 2321 **REGION** Lower Hunter Valley
T (02) 4998 7693 **F** (02) 4998 7693 **OPEN** Wed–Fri 11–4, weekends 10–5
WINEMAKER Contract **EST.** 1970 **CASES** 3600
PRODUCT RANGE ($15–25 CD) Semillon, Clairette, Dessert Semillon, Shiraz, Cabernet Sauvignon.
SUMMARY The Honeytree Estate vineyard was first planted in 1970, and for a period of time wines were produced under the Honeytree Estate label. It then disappeared but the vineyard has since been revived by Dutch-born Henk Strengers and family. Its 10 hectares of vines are of shiraz, cabernet sauvignon, semillon and a little clairette, known in the Hunter Valley as blanquette, and a variety which has been in existence there for well over a century. Jancis Robinson comments that the wine 'tends to be very high in alcohol, a little low in acid and to oxidise dangerously fast', but in a sign of the times the first Honeytree Clairette sold out so quickly (in 4 weeks) that 2.2 hectares of vineyard has been grafted over to additional clairette. Exports to The Netherlands.

YYYY **Semillon 2003** Lemon blossom and Aspro Clear aromas and flavours; good mid-palate length and balance; oh, for a screwcap. **RATING** 89 **DRINK** 2008 $ 15

Clairette 2003 A light, crisp bouquet, then a delicately balanced palate with some fruit and low level residual sweetness before a dry aftertaste. **RATING** 87 **DRINK** Now $ 20

YYYY **Cabernet Sauvignon 2002 RATING** 86 **DRINK** 2012 $ 25
Shiraz 2002 RATING 85 **DRINK** 2007 $ 20

Hope Estate ★★★

Cobcroft Road, Broke, NSW 2330 **REGION** Lower Hunter Valley
T (02) 6579 1161 **F** (02) 6579 1373 **OPEN** 7 days 10–4
WINEMAKER Josh Steele **EST.** 1996 **CASES** 30 000
PRODUCT RANGE ($15–20 CD) Semillon, Verdelho, Chardonnay, Shiraz, Merlot.
SUMMARY Pharmacist Michael Hope has come a long way since acquiring his first vineyard in the Hunter Valley in 1994. The Hunter Valley empire now encompasses three substantial vineyards and the former Saxonvale Winery, acquired in 1996, renamed Hope Estate, and refurbished at a cost of over $1 million. That, however, proved to be only the first step, for Hope has acquired most of the assets of the former public-listed Vincorp, including its Donnybrook Vineyard in Western Australia, and a $6 million acquisition of the Virgin Hills brand, its original 14-hectare vineyard, another nearby 32-hectare vineyard at Glenhope, a lease of the historic winery, and the acquisition of all Virgin Hills stocks. Exports to the US, the UK, Japan, Singapore and Hong Kong.

YYY **Shiraz 2001 RATING** 82 $ 20

Hoppers Hill Vineyards NR

Googodery Road, Cumnock, NSW 2867 **REGION** Central Ranges Zone
T (02) 6367 7270 **OPEN** By appointment
WINEMAKER Robert Gilmore **EST.** 1990
PRODUCT RANGE Chardonnay, Sauvignon Blanc, Dry White, Cabernet Franc Merlot, Cabernet Sauvignon.
SUMMARY The Gilmores planted their vineyard in 1980, using organic growing methods and using no preservatives or filtration in the winery, which was established in 1990. Not surprisingly, the wines cannot be judged or assessed against normal standards, but may have appeal in a niche market.

Horndale NR

Fraser Avenue, Happy Valley, SA 5159 **REGION** McLaren Vale
T (08) 8387 0033 **F** (08) 8387 0033 **OPEN** Mon–Sat 9–5, Sun and public holidays 10–5.30
WINEMAKER Phil Albrecht **EST.** 1896
PRODUCT RANGE ($8.90–17.90 CD) A comprehensive range of low-priced wines in two brackets, the cheaper Field River label of white and red table wines, and the slightly more expensive red wines under the Old Horndale label. Also a large range of fortified wines offered in various configurations from bottles up to 21-litre containers.
SUMMARY Established in 1896 and has remained continuously in production in one way or another since that time, but there have been a number of changes of ownership and direction, and the wines are only available from the cellar door and mail order. A personal connection is the Horndale Brandy my father used to buy 60 years ago, although it no longer appears on the extensive price list.

Horseshoe Vineyard NR

Horseshoe Road, Horseshoe Valley via Denman, NSW 2328 **REGION** Upper Hunter Valley
T (02) 6547 3528 **OPEN** Weekends 9–5
WINEMAKER John Hordern **EST.** 1986
PRODUCT RANGE ($13–18 CD) Classic Hunter Semillon, Chardonnay Semillon, Chardonnay, Pinot Noir.
SUMMARY Fell by the wayside after its wonderful start in 1986, with rich, full-flavoured, barrel-fermented Semillons and Chardonnays. These days John Hordern's main occupation seems to be as a highly successful contract winemaker, particularly for Penmara.

ΥΥΥ **Semillon 2003** RATING 83

ΥΥΥ **Shiraz 1999** RATING 79

🐚 Horvat Estate ★★☆

2444 Burke Street, Landsborough, Vic 3384 **REGION** Pyrenees
T (03) 5356 9296 **F** (03) 5356 9264 **OPEN** 7 days 10–5
WINEMAKER Andrew Horvat, Gabriel Horvat **EST.** 1995 **CASES** 1000
PRODUCT RANGE ($14–25 CD) Limited Edition (Chardonnay Sauvignon Blanc Semillon), Animate Series Chardonnay, Shiraz, Cabernet Sauvignon, Fortified Dessert Wine.
SUMMARY The Horvat family (including Janet, Andrew and Gabriel) began the development of their 7-hectare vineyard of shiraz in 1995, supplementing production with contract-grown grapes. The wine is made on-site using traditional methods and ideas, deriving in part from the family's Croatian background.

ΥΥΥΥ **Shiraz 2002** Blackberry, earth and spice aromas; youthful, juicy berry, fruit-driven palate; not over-extracted. **RATING** 87 **DRINK** 2012 $ 25

ΥΥΥ **Animated Series Chardonnay 2002** RATING 83 $ 20
Authentic Fortified Dessert Wine NV RATING 82 $ 14
Tri Blanc 2001 RATING 81 $ 20

Houghton ★★★★★

Dale Road, Middle Swan, WA 6056 **REGION** Swan Valley
T (08) 9274 5100 **F** (08) 9274 5372 **OPEN** 7 days 10–5
WINEMAKER Robert Bowen, Ross Pamment, Simon Osicka **EST.** 1836 **CASES** 280 000
PRODUCT RANGE ($6.99–180 R) Semillon Sauvignon Blanc, Chardonnay Verdelho, White Burgundy, Show Reserve White Burgundy, Chardonnay, Late Picked Verdelho, Cabernet Shiraz Merlot; Crofters Semillon Sauvignon Blanc, Chardonnay, Shiraz, Cabernet Merlot; finally, the super-premiums Jack Mann (Cabernet blend) and Gladstones Shiraz.
SUMMARY The five-star rating was once partially justified by Houghton White Burgundy, one of Australia's largest-selling white wines — almost entirely consumed within days of purchase — but which is superlative with 7 or so years bottle age. The Jack Mann red, Gladstones Shiraz, Houghton Reserve Shiraz, the Margaret River reds and Frankland Riesling are all of the highest quality, and simply serve to reinforce the rating. To borrow a phrase of the late Jack Mann, 'There are no bad wines here'.

ΥΥΥΥΥ **Frankland Shiraz 2000** Intermingling dark cherry, spice and plum aromas; the palate adds a dash of licorice, with excellent texture, depth and mouthfeel aided by fine tannins. **RATING** 96 **DRINK** 2010 $ 28.99
Gladstones Cabernet Sauvignon 1999 Flooded with redcurrant, blackcurrant and raspberry fruit on both bouquet and palate; great texture; fine tannins and sure oak handling. Gold medals 2001, 2002 and 2003 Qantas Wine Show of Western Australia. **RATING** 96 **DRINK** 2014 $ 59.99
Pemberton Chardonnay 2002 A complex, pleasantly funky bouquet; a nicely weighted and balanced palate, with a perfectly glorious, dry finish. **RATING** 95 **DRINK** 2012 $ 28.99

ΥΥΥΥΥ **Regional Riesling 2003** Fine, elegant and minerally; good intensity, length and drive. **RATING** 93 **DRINK** 2010 $ 21.99
Crofters Shiraz 2001 An infusion of soft, toasted oak through plum and spice fruit; the long palate has abundant sweet blackberry fruit, savoury, rippling tannins and well-handled oak. **RATING** 93 **DRINK** 2016 $ 24.99
Crofters Pinot Noir 2002 First up release of pinot noir, 55 per cent Pemberton, 45 per cent Manjimup. Complex, powerful dark plum plus splashes of spice and game; positive tannins, long lived style. **RATING** 90 **DRINK** 2010 $ 26.50

ᵀᵀᵀᵀ **White Burgundy 2003** Clean and fresh; lively palate, nice touches of passionfruit/stone fruit. **RATING** 89 **DRINK** 2008 $ 11.99
Semillon Sauvignon Blanc 2003 A faintly funky, powerful and complex wine, full of character. **RATING** 87 **DRINK** Now $ 11.99

ᵀᵀᵀ♀ **Rockwall Cabernet Sauvignon 2001** **RATING** 86 **DRINK** 2008 $ 12.99
Pemberton Sauvignon Blanc 2003 **RATING** 84 **DRINK** Now $ 21.99

House of Certain Views ★★★★☆

1238 Milbrodale Road, Broke, NSW 2330 **REGION** Lower Hunter Valley
T (02) 6579 1317 **F** (02) 6579 1317 **OPEN** Not
WINEMAKER Andrew Margan **EST.** 2001 **CASES** 1500
PRODUCT RANGE ($20–35 R) Coonabarabran Sauvignon Blanc, Orange Viognier, Coonabarabran Chardonnay, Orange Shiraz, Mt Kaputar Merlot, Broke Fordwich Barbera, Coonabarabran Cabernet Sauvignon.
SUMMARY A stand-alone business owned by Andrew and Lisa Margan, with a fascinating portfolio of wines based on exclusive or fairly new wine growing regions on the western side of the Great Dividing Range. The selection of the vineyard sites (via contract growers) involves a careful correlation of latitude, altitude, soil type and variety — the French catch it all in the single word terroir. The packaging of the wines, incidentally, is brilliant. Exports to Hong Kong, Canada and the UK.

ᵀᵀᵀᵀᵀ **Coonabarabran Cabernet Sauvignon 2001** Fragrant cassis, herb and blackcurrant aromas; lovely cabernet expression on the palate, with good texture, structure and balance. **RATING** 94 **DRINK** 2015 $ 35

ᵀᵀᵀᵀ **Orange Shiraz 2000** Red berries, spice, mint and leaf aromas and flavours; fine tannins; lingering finish. **RATING** 88 **DRINK** 2010 $ 30

Howard Park (Denmark) ★★★★☆

Scotsdale Road, Denmark, WA 6333 **REGION** Denmark
T (08) 9848 2345 **F** (08) 9848 2064 **OPEN** 7 days 10–4
WINEMAKER Michael Kerrigan, Andy Browning, Matt Burton **EST.** 1986 **CASES** 100 000
PRODUCT RANGE ($17–70 R) Limited quantities of Howard Park Riesling, Howard Park Cabernet Sauvignon Merlot, Scotsdale Shiraz, Scotsdale Cabernet Sauvignon, all at the ultra-premium end; the MadFish Bay range of Premium White, Sauvignon Blanc Semillon, Chardonnay, Premium Red, Rose, Pinot Noir, Shiraz, Cabernet Sauvignon Merlot Cabernet Franc.
SUMMARY All of the Howard Park wines are made here at the new, large winery. However, there are three groups of wines: those sourced from either Great Southern or Margaret River; the icon Howard Park Riesling and Cabernet Sauvignon Merlot; and the multi-regional MadFish range. Thus the Leston wines come from Margaret River, the Scotsdale from Great Southern. All are very impressive: MadFish rising well above its price point. Exports to all major markets.

ᵀᵀᵀᵀ♀ **Riesling 2003** Lime blossom aromas; long, supple lime/lemon/citrus flavours; no problem whatsoever with acidity. **RATING** 93 **DRINK** 2013 $ 25

ᵀᵀᵀᵀ **Sauvignon Blanc 2003** Trembles on the brink of reduction; lots of tropical fruit flavours; balancing acidity. **RATING** 88 **DRINK** Now $ 25

ᵀᵀᵀ♀ **Scotsdale Pinot Noir 2002** **RATING** 85 **DRINK** Now $ 35

Howard Park (Margaret River) ★★★★★

Miamup Road, Cowaramup, WA 6284 **REGION** Margaret River
T (08) 9848 2345 **F** (08) 9848 2064 **OPEN** 7 days 10–5
WINEMAKER Michael Kerrigan, Andy Browning, Matt Burton **EST.** 1986 **CASES** 100 000
PRODUCT RANGE ($17–75 R) Limited quantities of Howard Park Riesling, Howard Park Cabernet Sauvignon Merlot, Scotsdale Shiraz, Scotsdale Cabernet Sauvignon, all at the ultra-premium end; the MadFish Bay range of Premium White, Sauvignon Blanc Semillon, Chardonnay, Premium Red, Rose, Pinot Noir, Shiraz, Cabernet Sauvignon Merlot Cabernet Franc.

SUMMARY In the wake of its acquisition by the Burch family, and the construction of a large, state-of-the-art winery at Denmark, a capacious cellar door (incorporating Feng Shui principles) has been opened in the Margaret River, where there are also significant estate plantings. The Margaret River flagships are the Leston Shiraz and Leston Cabernet Sauvignon, but the Margaret River vineyards routinely contribute to all of the wines in the range, from MadFish at the bottom, to the icon Cabernet Sauvignon Merlot at the top. Exports to all major markets.

ⓘⓘⓘⓘⓘ **Chardonnay 2002** Extremely stylish, elegant and long; melon, stone fruit and grapefruit; perfect balance/integration of oak. **RATING** 94 **DRINK** 2010 $ 35

MadFish Chardonnay 2002 Pure chardonnay fruit expression; melon, nectarine and citrus; touches of fig and cashew/oak; great length. Outstanding value. Screwcap. **RATING** 94 **DRINK** 2007 $ 18

ⓘⓘⓘⓘⓘ **MadFish Premium White 2003** Tangy, zesty lemon rind, herb and citrus; lively and long; seemingly early-picked chardonnay. **RATING** 91 **DRINK** 2007 $ 15.50

MadFish Shiraz 2002 Vivid colour; highly fragrant, vibrantly fresh and fruity, but has good structure. As with all the MadFish wines, screwcap. **RATING** 90 **DRINK** 2009 $ 18

ⓘⓘⓘⓘ **MadFish Premium Red 2002** Cedary, earthy berry/blackberry fruit with savoury touches of mint and leaf. Classic Bordeaux blend. **RATING** 88 **DRINK** 2008 $ 15.50

🍇 Howards Lane Vineyard   NR

Howards Lane, Welby, Mittagong, NSW 2575 **REGION** Southern Highlands
T (02) 4872 1971 **F** (02) 4872 1971 **OPEN** 7 days 10–5
WINEMAKER Michelle Crockett (Contract) **EST.** 1994 **CASES** 650
PRODUCT RANGE ($18–26 ML) Chardonnay, Light Red, Fitzroy Red, Cabernet Sauvignon.
SUMMARY Tony and Mary Betteridge have developed the plantings over a 10-year period, establishing the Corrie Vineyard first, and recently the McCourt Vineyard. The cellar door, open daily, has light meals and picnic facilities. As at 2004 four vintages of chardonnay were on offer from the 2000 to 2003 vintages respectively.

🍇 HPR Wines   NR

260 Old Moorooduc Road, Tuerong, Vic 3933 (postal) **REGION** Mornington Peninsula
T (03) 5974 2097 **F** (03) 5974 3099 **OPEN** Not
WINEMAKER Hugh Robinson **EST.** 1988 **CASES** 250
PRODUCT RANGE ($35 R) Pinot Noir.
SUMMARY Hugh Robinson is a Mornington Peninsula veteran, with no less than 22 hectares of sauvignon blanc, semillon, chardonnay, pinot gris, pinot noir, merlot and shiraz. The major part of the production is sold as grapes to other makers, with the remainder made by Hugh Robinson on-site. Retail distribution through Rutherglen Wine and Spirit, or by mail order.

🍇 Hudson's Peak Wines   NR

92 Hillsborough Road, Hillsborough, NSW 2320 **REGION** Lower Hunter Valley
T 0409 660 883 **F** (02) 4930 0759 **OPEN** 7 days 10–5
WINEMAKER John Cassegrain (Contract) **EST.** 1998
PRODUCT RANGE ($10–18 ML) The wines sold in Australia are all under the Hudson's Peak label, including Semillon, Chardonnay Semillon, Verdelho, Chardonnay, Shiraz, Cabernet Merlot; those exported under the Longboat label.
SUMMARY Hudson's Peak Wines come from a historic property, first gazetted in 1829, and taken up by Beresford Hudson, who gave his name both to a nearby mountain top and (now) this substantial wine venture. The 53-hectare property includes 18 hectares of vines, almost half to shiraz, the remainder split between semillon, chardonnay, verdelho and merlot. Part of the production is sold as grapes, and part contract-made by John Cassegrain.

Hugh Hamilton

★★★★☆

McMurtrie Road, McLaren Vale, SA 5171 **REGION** McLaren Vale
T (08) 8323 8689 **F** (08) 8323 9488 **OPEN** Mon–Fri 10–5.30, weekends and public holidays 11–5.30
WINEMAKER Hugh Hamilton **EST.** 1991 **CASES** 6000
PRODUCT RANGE ($17.50–42 CD) An entertaining range of varietals linked with brands such as Menage a Trois, The Rascal, The Villain, Jekyll & Hyde, etc.
SUMMARY Hugh Hamilton is the most recent member of the famous Hamilton winemaking family to enter the business with a label of his own. Production comes in part from 18.2 hectares of estate plantings, supplemented by contract-grown material. Recent plantings go beyond the mainstream to sangiovese, tempranillo, petit verdot and saperavi. Limited retail distribution in most States; full information from <www.hamiltonwines.com.au>.

TTTTT **The Rascal Shiraz 2002** Dense, inky colour; deep blackberry/plum aromas and luscious, not jammy, fruit; fine, spicy ripe tannins. **RATING** 94 **DRINK** 2017 $ 24.50
The Villain Cabernet Sauvignon 2002 Lots of depth; a range of blackcurrant, blackberry and chocolate; good tannins. **RATING** 94 **DRINK** 2017 $ 24.50

TTTTY **The Loose Cannon Viognier 2003** Lots of varietal flavour; apricot, pear, musk, pastille and spice; all achieved without phenolics. **RATING** 90 **DRINK** Now $ 22.50

TTTT **The Madam Sparkling Merlot 2002** Lots of spicy, chocolate and cinnamon fruit; rich but not overdosed nor phenolic. Big surprise. **RATING** 88 **DRINK** 2007 $ 19.50
The Scallywag Unwooded Chardonnay 2003 Elegant; quite intense citrus and melon fruit; well above the average unwooded style. **RATING** 87 **DRINK** Now $ 17.50

TTT **The Trickster Verdelho 2003 RATING** 83 $ 18.50

Hugo

★★★☆

Elliott Road, McLaren Flat, SA 5171 **REGION** McLaren Vale
T (08) 8383 0098 **F** (08) 8383 0446 **OPEN** Mon–Fri 9–5, Sat 12–5, Sun 10.30–5
WINEMAKER John Hugo **EST.** 1982 **CASES** 12 000
PRODUCT RANGE ($15–38 R) Sauvignon Blanc, Unwooded Chardonnay, Chardonnay, Reserve Shiraz, Shiraz, Shiraz Grenache, Cabernet Sauvignon.
SUMMARY A winery which came from relative obscurity to prominence in the late 1980s with some lovely ripe, sweet reds which, while strongly American-oak-influenced, were quite outstanding. Has picked up the pace again after a dull period in the mid-1990s. There are 32 hectares of estate plantings, with part of the grape production sold to others. The wines are exported to the US, Canada, the UK, Germany and Singapore. The rating is on the basis of previous tastings.

TTTTY **Reserve Shiraz 2001** Medium-bodied, indeed bordering on elegant; smooth blackberry and dark cherry fruit, supple tannins, good length. **RATING** 92 **DRINK** 2011 $ 38

TTTT **Chardonnay 2003** Melon and nectarine fruit fused with subtle French oak. Screwcap. **RATING** 87 **DRINK** Now $ 19

TTTY **Cabernet Sauvignon 2001 RATING** 86 **DRINK** 2008 $ 21.50
Shiraz 2001 RATING 85 **DRINK** 2008 $ 20
Unwooded Chardonnay 2003 RATING 84 **DRINK** Now $ 14.99

Hundred Tree Hill

★★★

c/- Redbank Winery, 1 Sallys Lane, Redbank, Vic 3478 **REGION** Pyrenees
T (03) 5467 7255 **F** (03) 5467 7248 **OPEN** Mon–Sat 9–5, Sun 10–5
WINEMAKER Huw Robb, Scott Hutton, Sasha Robb **EST.** 1973 **CASES** 8000
PRODUCT RANGE ($14.50–25 ML) Sauvignon Blanc, Chardonnay, Pinot Noir, Shiraz, Cabernet
SUMMARY The next generation of the Robb family (Emily, Huw and Sasha) have established their own vineyard, with 6 hectares each of shiraz, cabernet sauvignon and cabernet franc, plus 2 hectares of pinot noir. Hundred Tree Hill was so named to commemorate the hundred trees which went into the building of the Hundred Tree Homestead. For the time being, the focus is on export sales, but the Robbs intend to diversify into the domestic market in the near future. Exports to Germany and the Philippines.

ΨΨΨΨ **Cabernet 2000** Has good depth and substance; ripe blackcurrant, some mocha; ripe tannins. **RATING** 88 **DRINK** 2011 $ 17.60

Cabernet 1999 Cedary, spicy/earthy bottle development; light to medium-bodied, but good length and fine tannins. **RATING** 87 **DRINK** 2008 $ 17.60

ΨΨΨΨ **Shiraz 1999 RATING** 86 **DRINK** Now $ 17.60

Shiraz 2001 RATING 85 **DRINK** Now $ 17.60

Hungerford Hill ★★★★

1 Broke Road, Pokolbin, NSW 2321 **REGION** Lower Hunter Valley
T 1800 187 666 **F** (02) 4998 7375 **OPEN** 7 days 10–5
WINEMAKER Phillip John **EST.** 1967 **CASES** 20 000
PRODUCT RANGE ($10–22.40 CD) A kaleidoscopic array of over 30 varietal wines from seven regions (six NSW, one SA) at many different price points, all identified by variety/varietal blend.
SUMMARY Hungerford Hill, sold by Southcorp to Cassegrain Wines in 2002, has emerged with its home base at the impressive winery on the corner of Allandale and Broke Roads, previously known as One Broke Road. The development of the One Broke Road complex proved wildly uneconomic, and the rationalisation process has resulted in Hungerford Hill being the principal tenant (under the direction of Phillip John), but also with significant contract winemaking by Andrew Thomas for other Hunter Valley brands. Restaurant One and Café One continue under the direction of Giles Marx. Exports to Hong Kong, Malaysia, China and New Zealand.

ΨΨΨΨΨ **Clare Valley Riesling 2003** Intense, focused, herb, citrus and mineral aromas and flavours. Remarkable length. **RATING** 94 **DRINK** 2013 $ 20

ΨΨΨΨΨ **Orange Merlot 2002** Savoury, earthy, olive aromas; light to medium-bodied; good length and finish; fine tannin structure. Strongly varietal throughout. Blue Gold medal Sydney International Wine Competition Now. **RATING** 90 **DRINK** 2010 $ 16.50

ΨΨΨΨ **Tumbarumba Pinot Noir 2002** Complex, smoky oak infusion on bouquet and palate; in the savoury spectrum with some stylish austerity; excellent length. **RATING** 89 **DRINK** 2008 $ 27

Pinot Noir 2002 Youthful colour; complex forest, spice and plum aromas; a tangy, savoury, almost lemony palate; good length. Eighty-five per cent pinot; the remaining 15 per cent (unstated) might well be white. No oak, but extended lees contact. Very clever indeed **RATING** 89 **DRINK** 2007 $ 18

Tumbarumba Chardonnay 2002 Still very crisp, youthful and light-bodied; tight grapefruit flavours; subtle oak. **RATING** 87 **DRINK** Now $ 16.50

ΨΨΨΨ **Hunter Valley Shiraz 2002 RATING** 84 **DRINK** 2008 $ 24

🍃 Hunter Park NR

PO Box 815, Muswellbrook, NSW 2333 **REGION** Upper Hunter Valley
T (02) 6541 4000 **F** (02) 6543 2456 **OPEN** Not
WINEMAKER Contract **EST.** 1977
PRODUCT RANGE A range of varietally denominated table wines reflecting the plantings.
SUMMARY The origins of Hunter Park go back more than 25 years; the business is based on 80 hectares of sauvignon blanc, chardonnay, merlot, cabernet sauvignon and cabernet franc managed by Andrew Dibley. The wines are not widely distributed in Australia (although they are available by mail order) but exports have been established to the UK, Germany and the US.

Hunting Lodge Estate ★★☆

703 Mt Kilcoy Road, Mount Kilcoy, Qld 4515 **REGION** South Burnett
T (07) 5498 1243 **F** (07) 5498 1243 **OPEN** 7 days 10–5
WINEMAKER Brian Wilson **EST.** 1999 **CASES** 3300
PRODUCT RANGE ($14–25 CD) Mauritius Traminer Riesling, Serengeti Oaked Chardonnay, Kalahari Unoaked Chardonnay, Simpson Red, Zambezi Cabernet Merlot, Cape Cabernet Sauvignon, Hunters Cabernet Sauvignon, Nairobi Tawny Port, Estate Tawny Port.

SUMMARY Yet another new player in the rapidly expanding Queensland wine industry, established in 1999 with plantings of 1 hectare each of verdelho, merlot and cabernet sauvignon. However, is offering a range of wines ranging from 1997 to 1999, including 'our famous Nairobi Port'; the names of the table wines all crosslink both to hunting and South Africa whence, one imagines, the owners originated. For good measure, there is a personal museum of hunting trophies.

▼▼▼♈ **Verdelho 2003** RATING 84 DRINK Now $ 20

▼▼♈ **Reserve Shiraz 2003** RATING 79 $ 25

Huntington Estate ★★★★★

Cassilis Road, Mudgee, NSW 2850 **REGION** Mudgee
T (02) 6373 3825 **F** (02) 6373 3730 **OPEN** Mon–Fri 9–5, Sat 10–5, Sun 10–3
WINEMAKER Susie Roberts **EST.** 1969 **CASES** 20 000
PRODUCT RANGE ($12.50–29.50 CD) Semillon, Semillon Chardonnay, Chardonnay, Rose Dry, Rose, Sweet White Blend, Rose Sweet Fruity Style, Rose Pinot Noir Dry; red wines are released under bin numbers (FB = full-bodied, MB = medium-bodied) comprising Shiraz, Dry Red Shiraz Cabernet, Cabernet Sauvignon.
SUMMARY The remarkable Roberts family members have a passion for wine which is equalled only by their passion for music, with the Huntington Music Festival a major annual event. The red wines of Huntington Estate are outstanding and sell for relatively low prices. The wines are seldom exported; almost all are sold via the cellar door and mailing list.

▼▼▼▼▼ **Special Reserve Shiraz 1993** Bin FB29. Excellent colour; still full of sweet red cherry and plum fruit; smooth tannins; excellent length. **RATING** 95 **DRINK** 2013 $ 30.50

▼▼▼▼♈ **Special Reserve Shiraz 1999** Bin FB33. Complex, powerful, long, multi-layered big impact style. Great character. **RATING** 93 **DRINK** 2019 $ 30.50
Shiraz 2000 Bin FB24. Clean but complex black fruit and vanilla aromas, then attractive ripe but not jammy blackberry/cherry/raspberry fruit, plus fine tannins. **RATING** 92 **DRINK** 2012 $ 17.50
Special Reserve Cabernet Sauvignon 2001 Bin FB24. Fragrant blackcurrant aromas; medium-bodied, sweet cassis fruit; excellent tannin structure/mouthfeel. **RATING** 92 **DRINK** 2018 $ 29.50
Special Reserve Shiraz 2001 Bin FB19. Ripe, deep plum/black cherry fruit; ripe tannins, balance and style. **RATING** 91 **DRINK** 2011 $ 29.50
Shiraz 2001 Bin FB36. Complex; obvious oak, and also greater tannins levels than the Bin FB19; dark fruits; long cellaring. **RATING** 90 **DRINK** 2016 $ 17.50
Shiraz 2000 Bin FB22. Big, ripe, luscious, plush blackberry, plum and mint; ripe tannins and oak. **RATING** 90 **DRINK** 2020 $ 17.50

▼▼▼▼ **Cabernet Sauvignon 2001** Bin FB26. More complex than the Bin FB24, but darts here, there and everywhere. **RATING** 87 **DRINK** 2010 $ 17.50

▼▼▼♈ **Semillon 2003** RATING 85 DRINK 2009 $ 12.50
Semillon 2002 RATING 85 DRINK 2007 $ 12.50
Chardonnay 2002 RATING 84 DRINK Now $ 17.50
Semillon Chardonnay 2002 RATING 84 DRINK Now $ 12.50

Huntleigh Vineyards ★★★☆

38 Tunnecliffes Lane, Heathcote, Vic 3523 **REGION** Heathcote
T (03) 5433 2795 **F** (03) 5433 2795 **OPEN** 7 days 10–5.30
WINEMAKER Leigh Hunt **EST.** 1975 **CASES** 500
PRODUCT RANGE ($15–23 CD) Traminer, Shiraz, Cabernet Sauvignon.
SUMMARY The wines are all made at the winery by former stockbroker Leigh Hunt from 5 hectares of estate-grown grapes, the last-tasted Cabernet Sauvignon (1998) being of exemplary quality.

Hunt's Foxhaven Estate

NR

Canal Rocks Road, Yallingup, WA 6282 **REGION** Margaret River
T (08) 9755 2232 **F** (08) 9255 2249 **OPEN** Weekends, holidays 11–5, or by appointment
WINEMAKER David Hunt **EST.** 1978 **CASES** 1000
PRODUCT RANGE ($12–22 CD) Riesling (dry and sweet), Semillon, Canal Rocks White, Yallingup
Classic, Noble Riesling, Hunting Pink, Cabernet Sauvignon.
SUMMARY A low profile operation, based on 4.5 hectares of vines progressively established, the oldest
being 25-year-old riesling. It seems that some of the grapes are sold, some swapped for semillon and
sauvignon blanc. All of the wine is sold through the cellar door and by mail order.

Hurley Vineyard

101 Balnarring Road, Balnarring, Vic 3926 **REGION** Mornington Peninsula
T (03) 5931 3000 **F** (03) 5931 3200 **OPEN** First weekend of each month or by appointment
WINEMAKER Kevin Bell **EST.** 1998 **CASES** 500
PRODUCT RANGE ($33 ML) Pinot Noir.
SUMMARY It's never as easy as it seems. While Kevin Bell carries on an active practice as a Queens
Counsel in fields as diverse as industrial, constitutional and native title law, and his wife Tricia Byrnes
has a busy legal life as a family law specialist in a small Melbourne law firm, they have done most of
the hard work in establishing Hurley Vineyard themselves, with family and friends. Most
conspicuously, Kevin Bell is a fifth-year part-time student in the applied science (wine science)
degree at Charles Sturt University, and has drawn on Matt White for consultancy advice, and
occasionally from Phillip Jones of Bass Phillip, and Domaine Fourrier and Gevrey Chambertin. The
2001 release was a dream start for the business.

ŶŶŶŶŶ **Pinot Noir 2001** Very rich and complex spicy plummy fruit with a savoury twist; excellent
length and persistence. A singularly impressive first-up effort. **RATING** 93 **DRINK** 2008
$33

Hutton Vale Vineyard

NR

'Hutton Vale', Stone Jar Road, Angaston, SA 5353 **REGION** Eden Valley
T (08) 8564 8270 **F** (08) 8564 8385 **OPEN** By appointment
WINEMAKER David Powell, Chris Ringland **EST.** 1960 **CASES** 500
PRODUCT RANGE ($19–59 ML) Riesling, Shiraz, Grenache Mataro.
SUMMARY John Howard Angas (who arrived in South Australia in 1843, aged 19, charged with the
responsibility of looking after the affairs of his father, George Fife Angas) named part of the family
estate Hutton Vale. It is here that John Angas, John Howard's great-great-grandson, and wife Jan
tend a little over 26 hectares of vines and produce (or, at least, Jan does) a range of jams, chutneys
and preserves. Almost all of the grapes are sold, a tiny quantity being made by the Who's Who of the
Barossa Valley, notably David Powell of Torbreck and Chris Ringland of Rockford. Most of the wine is
sold by mail order, and what is left is exported. I haven't tasted the wines, but I'm prepared to wager
they are of outstanding quality.

Ibis Wines

239 Kearneys Drive, Orange, NSW 2800 **REGION** Orange
T (02) 6362 3257 **F** (02) 6362 5779 **OPEN** Weekends and public holidays 11–5, or by appointment
WINEMAKER Phil Stevenson **EST.** 1988 **CASES** 900
PRODUCT RANGE ($14–25 CD) Riesling, Chardonnay, Cabernet Franc, Cabernet Sauvignon; Habitat
Sauvignon Blanc, Pinot Gris, Pagan, Pinot Noir, Merlot; Kanjara Shiraz.
SUMMARY Ibis Wines is located just north of Orange (near the botanic gardens) on what was once a
family orchard. Planting of the vineyard commenced in 1988, and after interim winemaking
arrangements a new winery was completed on the property in 1998. The grapes are sourced from the
home vineyards at an altitude of 800 metres, from the Habitat Vineyard at 1100 metres on Mount
Canobolas (pinot noir and merlot) and from the Kanjara Vineyard (shiraz). Wine quality has shown
steady improvement over the past couple of years.

ŶŶŶŶŶ **Habitat Pinot Gris 2003** Lively and fresh; excellent pear, apple and lemon varietal fruit;
immaculate balance and length. **RATING** 90 **DRINK** Now $20

ŸŸŸŸ **Unwooded Chardonnay 2001** Clean, crisp, very youthful; nectarine and citrus. Long, bright, but balanced, acidity. **RATING** 87 **DRINK** Now $16

Kanjara Shiraz 2001 Earth, spice and savoury black fruits; good texture and balance; savoury tannins to close. **RATING** 87 **DRINK** 2009 $25

Cabernet Franc 1999 Another surprise; savoury dark chocolate and blackcurrant fruit; rich mouthfeel; excellent for the variety. **RATING** 87 **DRINK** 2008 $18

ŸŸŸŸ **Habitat Sauvignon Blanc 2003** Pale straw-green; very lemony, sharp fruit; sherbet lemon tingle. Only 11.5 degrees alcohol. **RATING** 86 **DRINK** Now $18

Habitat Sauvignon Blanc 2002 Aromatic gooseberry, passionfruit, tropical flavours; fraction sweet overall. Polar opposite to the '03. **RATING** 86 **DRINK** Now $18

Cabernet Sauvignon 1998 Hanging in there pretty well; sweet cassis, berry and mint. **RATING** 86 **DRINK** 2007 $18

Riesling 2002 **RATING** 85 **DRINK** Now $16

Habitat Pinot Noir 2000 **RATING** 84 **DRINK** Now $18

ŸŸŸ **Habitat Merlot 2000** **RATING** 83 $16

🐏 Idlewild Wines   NR

South Western Highway, Harvey, WA 6220 **REGION** Geographe
T (08) 9729 2258 **F** (08) 9729 2258 **OPEN** 7 days 10–5
WINEMAKER Contract **EST.** 2001
PRODUCT RANGE Semillon, Chenin Blanc, Chardonnay, Merlot, Cabernet Sauvignon.
SUMMARY Carol and Peter Jackson have planted 4.2 hectares of chenin blanc, semillon, chardonnay, cabernet sauvignon and merlot, using contract-winemaking services for the wines. Sales are by mail order and through the cellar door.

Ilnam Estate   ★★★

750 Carool Road, Carool, NSW 2486 **REGION** Northern Rivers Zone
T (07) 5590 7703 **F** (07) 5590 7922 **OPEN** Wed–Mon 10–5
WINEMAKER Mark Quinn **EST.** 1998 **CASES** 3000
PRODUCT RANGE ($8–33 CD) Blue Series of Semillon, Butterfly Kiss (Rose style), Shiraz, Cabernet Sauvignon; Maroon Series of JMQ Chardonnay, Carool Chardonnay, Dryland Merlot, Dryland Cabernet Sauvignon.
SUMMARY This is the first vineyard and winery to be established in the Tweed Valley, 30 minutes from the Gold Coast. Two hectares each of chardonnay, cabernet sauvignon and shiraz, plus a small planting of chambourcin provide the basis for the estate-grown Carool wines. In addition, Ilnam Estate has a number of growers in the Stanthorpe area who supply grapes to complete the two series of wine. Ione, Lachlan, Nathan, Andrew and Mark Quinn are all involved in the family business.

ŸŸŸŸ **Carool Cabernet Sauvignon 2002** Savoury, earthy, leafy, briary style of Cabernet; not much sweet fruit, but has been well made. **RATING** 86 **DRINK** 2009 $30

Immerse   ★★★

1548 Melba Highway, Yarra Glen, Vic 3775 **REGION** Yarra Valley
T (03) 5965 2444 **F** (03) 5965 2460 **OPEN** Thurs–Mon 11–5
WINEMAKER Contract **EST.** 1989 **CASES** 800
PRODUCT RANGE ($22–26 CD) Sauvignon Blanc, Chardonnay, Pinot Noir, Shiraz.
SUMMARY Steve and Helen Miles have purchased the restaurant, accommodation and function complex previous known as Lovey's. A spa-based health farm has eight rooms, with a full range of services. I have to say that the name chosen both for the facility and for the wines is as far left of centre as it is possible to go. As previously, a substantial portion of the grapes produced are sold to other makers in the Yarra Valley, the 6.9-hectare vineyards having been rehabilitated.

ΨΨΨΨ **Sauvignon Blanc 2003** Clean, crisp, light passionfruit and blossom; good length and finish. **RATING** 87 **DRINK** Now $ 22

ΨΨΨΫ **Chardonnay 2002** **RATING** 85 **DRINK** Now $ 24

ΨΨΨ **Shiraz 2001** **RATING** 83 $ 26

Inchiquin Wines ★★★☆

PO Box 865, Clare, SA 5453 **REGION** Clare Valley
T (08) 8843 4210 **OPEN** Not
WINEMAKER Stephen McInerney **EST.** 1998 **CASES** 1000
PRODUCT RANGE ($12–17 ML) Riesling, Shiraz Cabernet.
SUMMARY Stephen McInerney learnt his trade on the winery floor on various parts of the world: his first experience came in 1985 at Jim Barry Wines where he spent a number of years before moving to Pikes. In the intervening period he worked as a Flying Winemaker in France, Oregon, Spain and Argentina. He is now assistant winemaker at the large, new Kirribilly Winery in the Clare Valley. He established Inchiquin Wines with his partner Kate Strachan, herself with great industry credentials, primarily as the viticulturist for Taylor's (previously Southcorp), which has the largest vineyards in the Clare Valley. The wines, incidentally, are made by Stephen McInerney at Pikes. Exports to Ireland.

Indigo Ridge ★★★☆

Icely Road, Orange, NSW 2800 **REGION** Orange
T (02) 6362 1851 **F** (02) 6362 1851 **OPEN** First and second weekend of the month 12–5, or by appointment
WINEMAKER Contract **EST.** 1995 **CASES** 600
PRODUCT RANGE ($18–29 ML) Sauvignon Blanc, Cabernet Merlot, Cabernet Sauvignon, Ophir Gold.
SUMMARY Indigo Ridge has 4.5 hectares of vineyard planted to cabernet sauvignon, sauvignon blanc and merlot. Production is still very small, and all of the wines are sold through the cellar door and by mail order, with limited on and off-premise distribution in Orange and Sydney.

ΨΨΨΨ **Sauvignon Blanc 2003** Clean, light to medium-bodied, good mouthfeel; gentle gooseberry/tropical fruit; well balanced. **RATING** 88 **DRINK** Now $ 21
Cabernet Sauvignon 2002 Light to medium-bodied; cedar, blackcurrant and a whisk of chocolate; picks up with nice sweet tannins on the finish. **RATING** 87 **DRINK** 2010 $ 30

Inghams Skilly Ridge Wines NR

Gillentown Road, Sevenhill via Clare, SA 5453 **REGION** Clare Valley
T (08) 8843 4330 **F** (08) 8843 4330 **OPEN** Weekends 10–5
WINEMAKER Clark Ingham, David O'Leary (Contract) **EST.** 1994 **CASES** 3000
PRODUCT RANGE ($16–24 CD) Riesling, Shiraz, Tempranillo, Merlot, Cabernet Sauvignon Merlot, Cabernet Sauvignon.
SUMMARY Clark Ingham has established a substantial vineyard of shiraz (8 hectares), cabernet sauvignon (7 hectares), chardonnay (4 hectares), riesling (3 hectares), merlot (2 hectares) and tempranillo and semillon (1 hectare each). Part of the production is made by contract winemaker David O'Leary (with input from Clark Ingham), with the remaining grape production sold.

Ingoldby ★★★☆

Ingoldby Road, McLaren Flat, SA 5171 **REGION** McLaren Vale
T (08) 8383 0005 **F** (08) 8383 0790 **OPEN** 7 days 10–4
WINEMAKER Charles Hargrave **EST.** 1983 **CASES** 170 000
PRODUCT RANGE ($15 R) Sauvignon Blanc, Semillon Sauvignon Blanc, Rose, Shiraz, Reserve Shiraz, Cabernet Sauvignon.
SUMMARY A sister operation to Andrew Garrett, also within the Beringer Blass wine group, with many of the wines now not having a sole McLaren Vale source but instead being drawn from regions across southeastern Australia. Over the past few years, winemaker Charles Hargrave has produced some excellent wines which provide great value for money.

ⓎⓎⓎⓎⓎ **Reserve Shiraz 2001** Rich, ripe, supple mouthfilling dark chocolate, blackberry and plum; good structure and length; deft oak. Multiple gold medal winner. **RATING** 91
DRINK 2021 $ 43

Injidup Point

NR

Caves Road, Wilyabrup, WA 6280 **REGION** Margaret River
T 0408 955 770 **F** (08) 9386 8352 **OPEN** By appointment
WINEMAKER Belinda Gould, Michael Standish **EST.** 1993 **CASES** 1000
PRODUCT RANGE ($15–20 ML) Sauvignon Blanc, Semillon Sauvignon Blanc, Shiraz, Cabernets Merlot.
SUMMARY The development of the substantial Indijup Point vineyard began in 1993; the plantings now comprise 5 hectares of cabernet sauvignon, 3 hectares each of shiraz and cabernet franc, 2 hectares of merlot and 1 hectare each of sauvignon blanc, pinot noir and semillon. Most of the grapes are sold to other makers, with a small amount reserved for mail order sale and other local distribution. An extensive native garden surrounds the property, which has views to the adjacent Leeuwin Naturaliste National Park.

Inneslake Vineyards

The Ruins Way, Inneslake, Port Macquarie, NSW 2444 **REGION** Hastings River
T (02) 6581 1332 **F** (02) 6581 0391 **OPEN** Mon–Fri 10–4, weekends 10–5
WINEMAKER John Cassegrain (Contract), Nick Charley **EST.** 1988 **CASES** 1000
PRODUCT RANGE ($11–18 CD) Semillon, Chardonnay, Summer White, Pinot Noir, Shiraz, Cabernet Merlot, Cabernet Sauvignon, Inneslake Mist, Tawny Port.
SUMMARY The property upon which the Iinneslake (formerly Charley Brothers) vineyard is established has been in the family's ownership since the turn of the last century but in fact had been planted to vines by a Major Innes in the 1840s. After carrying on logging and fruit growing at various times, the Charley family planted vines in 1988 with the encouragement of John Cassegrain. Around 7.5 hectares of vines have been established.

Innisfail Vineyards

Cross Street, Batesford, Vic 3221 **REGION** Geelong
T (03) 5276 1258 **F** (03) 5276 1258 **OPEN** By appointment
WINEMAKER Nick Farr **EST.** 1980 **CASES** 2000
PRODUCT RANGE ($15–25 ML) Riesling, Chardonnay, Pinot Noir, Cabernet Sauvignon Merlot.
SUMMARY This 6-hectare estate-based producer released its first wines way back in 1988, but has had a very low profile, notwithstanding the quality of its early wines. Nick Farr, son of Gary Farr of Bannockburn, is now the winemaker and the profile has increased, as has the quality of the wines.

International Vintners Australia

11 Biralee Road, Regency Park, SA 5010 (postal) **REGION** Yarra Valley
T (08) 8440 6300 **F** (08) 8244 5553 **OPEN** Not
WINEMAKER Mark Jamieson **EST.** 1995 **CASES** 100 000
PRODUCT RANGE ($10–52 R) The company's brands comprise Yarra Glen (for the Yarra Valley-sourced varietals), Springwood Park (premium South Australian varietals) and the lower-priced Kelly's Promise range. The Ironwood and Andrew Garrett labels are sold in export markets.
SUMMARY International Vintners arose from the ashes in 2001 when it provided the capital necessary to sustain the former Andrew Garrett business. The brands have extensive distribution in Australia and in overseas markets.

Ironbark Ridge Vineyard

NR

Middle Road Mail Service 825, Purga, Qld 4306 **REGION** Queensland Coastal
T (07) 5464 6787 **F** (07) 5464 6858 **OPEN** Tues–Sun and public holidays 10–5
WINEMAKER Contract **EST.** 1984 **CASES** 250
PRODUCT RANGE ($15–28 ML) Chardonnay, Reserve Chardonnay, Shiraz, Vintage Port, Sweet Red, Liqueur Chardonnay.

SUMMARY Ipswich is situated on the coastal side of the Great Dividing Range, and the high summer humidity and rainfall will inevitably provide challenges for viticulture here. On the evidence of the ''98 Chardonnay, Ironbark Ridge is capable of producing Chardonnay equal to the best from Queensland.

🐦 Iron Gate Estate ★★★

Oakey Creek Road, Pokolbin, NSW 2320 **REGION** Lower Hunter Valley
T (02) 4998 6570 **F** (02) 4998 6571 **OPEN** 7 days 10–4
WINEMAKER Carig Perry, Roger Lilliott **EST.** 2001 **CASES** 5000
PRODUCT RANGE ($16–30 CD) Semillon, Oaked Semillon, Verdelho, Unwooded Chardonnay, Chardonnay, Milenio, Sweet Semillon, Shiraz, Shiraz AO, Reserve Shiraz, Shiraz Cabernet Sauvignon, Cabernet Sauvignon, Sweet Shiraz.
SUMMARY Iron Gate Estate would not be out of place in the Napa Valley, which favours bold architectural statements made without regard to cost. No expense has been spared in equipping the winery, and lavish cellar door facilities. The business, headed by Roger Lilliott, plans to sell all of its wine through an active members club (with three levels, each carrying a larger discount) and through local and Newcastle region restaurants, bypassing normal retail trade altogether. The wines are made from 8 hectares of estate plantings of semillon, verdelho, chardonnay, cabernet sauvignon and shiraz, and include such exotic offerings as a sweet shiraz and a chardonnay made in the style of a fino sherry.

ŸŸŸŸŸ **Semillon 2001** Light and bright, still in its primary phase; lingering herb and lemon flavours. **RATING** 90 **DRINK** 2011 $16

ŸŸŸŸ **Semillon 2000** Like the 2001, still in its youth, albeit with the first signs of toast to the lemon and mineral base; good length. **RATING** 89 **DRINK** 2010 $16
Oaked Semillon 2001 Very subtle oak influence; shows earlier picking than the unwooded version, a slightly curious decision. **RATING** 87 **DRINK** 2010 $17

ŸŸŸŸ **Milenio 2001 RATING** 86 **DRINK** Now $17
Sweet Semillon 2003 RATING 84 **DRINK** Now $18

ŸŸŸ **Verdelho 2001 RATING** 83 $18.50
Shiraz 2002 RATING 83 $22
Unwooded Chardonnay 2001 RATING 82 $18.50
Chardonnay 2002 RATING 81 $19.50
Cabernet Sauvignon 2002 RATING 81 $25

ŸŸŸ **Shiraz Cabernet 2002 RATING** 79 $25

Iron Pot Bay Wines ★★★

766 Deviot Road, Deviot, Tas 7275 **REGION** Northern Tasmania
T (03) 6394 7320 **F** (03) 6394 7346 **OPEN** Thurs–Sun 11–5 Sept–May, June–Aug by appointment
WINEMAKER Andrew Pirie **EST.** 1988 **CASES** 2600
PRODUCT RANGE ($18–27 CD) Riesling, Traminer, Semillon Sauvignon Blanc, Pinot Grigio, Unwooded Chardonnay, Late Picked Riesling, Kyra Vintage Sparkling.
SUMMARY Iron Pot Bay is now part of the syndicate which has established Rosevears Estate, with its large, state-of-the-art winery erected on the banks of the Tamar. The vineyard takes its name from a bay on the Tamar River and is strongly maritime-influenced, producing delicate but intensely flavoured unwooded white wines.

ŸŸŸŸ **Unwooded Chardonnay 2003 RATING** 85 **DRINK** Now $20
Pinot Grigio 2003 RATING 84 **DRINK** 2007 $21

Ironwood Estate NR

RMB 1288 Porongurup, WA 6234 **REGION** Porongurup
T (08) 9853 1126 **F** (08) 9853 1172 **OPEN** By appointment
WINEMAKER Dianne Miller, Bill Crappsley (Consultant) **EST.** 1996 **CASES** 1600
PRODUCT RANGE ($13–20 CD) Riesling, Chardonnay, Reserve Chardonnay, Late Harvest, Rocky Rose, Shiraz, Merlot, Cabernet Merlot, Cabernet Sauvignon.

SUMMARY Ironwood Estate was established in 1996 when the first wines were made from purchased grapes. In the same year chardonnay, shiraz and cabernet sauvignon were planted on a northern slope of the Porongurup Range. The twin peaks of the Porongurups rise above the vineyard and provide the basis for the label design. The first estate-grown grapes were vinified at the new Porongurup Winery, erected for the 1999 vintage and which is co-owned with Jingalla, Chatsfield and Montgomery's Hill. Unfortunately samples of Reserve Chardonnay sent for tasting did not arrive.

Irvine ★★★☆

PO Box 308, Angaston, SA 5353 **REGION** Eden Valley
T (08) 8564 1046 **F** (08) 8564 1314 **OPEN** Not
WINEMAKER James Irvine, Joanne Irvine **EST.** 1980 **CASES** 6000
PRODUCT RANGE ($15–120 R) Under the cheaper Eden Crest label: Chardonnay, Pinot Gris, Merlot, Merlot Cabernet, Zinfandel Merlot, Meslier Brut; under the premium James Irvine label: The Baroness, Merlot Brut and (at the top of the tree) Grand Merlot.
SUMMARY Industry veteran Jim Irvine, who has successfully guided the destiny of so many South Australian wineries, quietly introduced his own label in 1991, although the vineyard from which the wines are sourced was commenced in 1983 and now comprises a patchwork quilt of a little over 12 hectares of vines. The flagship is the rich Grand Merlot. Much of the production is exported to the UK, Germany, Switzerland, the US, Japan, Taiwan, New Zealand, Hong Kong, the Philippines and Singapore. The top wines were not submitted for this edition.

♥♥♥♀ **The Baroness NV** A blend of three vintages ('99 to '01); merlot, cabernet franc and cabernet sauvignon; 50 per cent Eden and 50 per cent Barossa Valley. As complex as one might imagine, but simply too much oak. **RATING** 86 **DRINK** Now $35
Springhill Merlot 2001 RATING 84 **DRINK** Now $17

Irymple Estate Winery NR

2086 Karadoc Avenue, Irymple, Vic 3498 **REGION** Murray Darling
T (03) 5024 5759 **F** (03) 5024 5759 **OPEN** Not
WINEMAKER Contract **EST.** 1999 **CASES** 1500
PRODUCT RANGE ($5.50 R) Chardonnay, Shiraz.
SUMMARY Irymple is a paradox. On the one hand, it is estate-based, with only 2 hectares each of chardonnay and shiraz, and less than 1 hectare of merlot and cabernet sauvignon. On the other hand, the contract-made wines are sold in the old-fashioned way at distinctly old-fashioned prices: on last advice, in the case of the Chardonnay either cleanskin at under $5 a bottle; labelled at a little over $5 a bottle; or in a 10-litre cask costing $21.30. The Shiraz is offered only cleanskin or labelled, but at the same price as the Chardonnay. Wine quality is appropriate to the price.

Island Brook Estate ★★★★

817 Bussell Highway, Metricup, WA 6280 **REGION** Margaret River
T (08) 9755 7501 **F** (08) 9755 7008 **OPEN** 7 days 10–5
WINEMAKER Mark Lane **EST.** 1985 **CASES** 2000
PRODUCT RANGE ($13–70 CD) Semillon, Verdelho, Chardonnay, Jakes White, Jakes Red, Red Truck Red, Merlot, Cabernet Sauvignon, Reserve Cabernet Sauvignon.
SUMMARY Linda and Peter Jenkins purchased Island Brook from Ken and Judy Brook in early 2001, and have undertaken major renovations, including extensive vineyard re-trellising, before opening their cellar door in November 2001, followed by luxurious accommodation set among 45 acres of forest.

♥♥♥♥♀ **Reserve Cabernet Sauvignon 2001** Attractive cassis and blackcurrant fruit plus a dash of chocolate; fine, ripe tannins; good oak. **RATING** 92 **DRINK** 2016 $70

♥♥♥♥ **Jakes Red 2002** Densely coloured; massive, full-bodied blackberry and dark chocolate; show stopper style. **RATING** 88 **DRINK** 2013 $19

Ivanhoe Wines

Marrowbone Road, Pokolbin, NSW 2320 **REGION** Lower Hunter Valley
T (02) 4998 7325 **F** (02) 4998 7848 **OPEN** 7 days 10–5
WINEMAKER Stephen Drayton, Tracy Drayton **EST.** 1995 **CASES** 7000
PRODUCT RANGE ($15–40 CD) Various varietal wines under the Ivanhoe and Stephen Drayton Signature Series, including Semillon, Verdelho, Chardonnay, Late Picked Gewurztraminer, Chambourcin, Shiraz, Cabernet Sauvignon.
SUMMARY Stephen Drayton is the son of the late Reg Drayton and, with wife Tracy, is the third branch of the family to be actively involved in winemaking in the Hunter Valley. The property on which the vineyard is situated has been called Ivanhoe for over 140 years, and 25 hectares of 30-year-old vines provide high-quality fruit for the label. The plans are to build a replica of the old homestead (burnt down, along with much of the winery, in the 1968 bushfires) to operate as a sales area.

ΥΥΥΥ **Estate Semillon 2003** **RATING** 85 **DRINK** 2010 $16
     Estate Verdelho 2003 **RATING** 84 **DRINK** Now $18.50
     Premium Reserve Shiraz 2001 **RATING** 84 **DRINK** Now $40

ΥΥΥ **Stephen Drayton Shiraz 2001** **RATING** 83 $18.50
     Pressings Shiraz 2001 **RATING** 83 $24

Jackson's Hill Vineyard

Mount View Road, Mount View, NSW 2321 **REGION** Lower Hunter Valley
T 1300 720 098 **F** 1300 130 220 **OPEN** By appointment
WINEMAKER Mike Winborne **EST.** 1983 **CASES** 1600
PRODUCT RANGE ($14–20 CD) Semillon, Shiraz, Cabernet Franc, Cabernet Sauvignon.
SUMMARY One of the low profile operations on the spectacularly scenic Mount View Road, making small quantities of estate-grown (3 hectares) wine sold exclusively through the cellar door.

Jadran

445 Reservoir Road, Orange Grove, WA 6109 **REGION** Perth Hills
T (08) 9459 1110 **OPEN** Mon–Sat 10–8, Sun 11–5
WINEMAKER Steve Radojkovich **EST.** 1967
PRODUCT RANGE ($6–12 CD) Riesling, Hermitage, generic red and white table wines, sparkling, fortifieds.
SUMMARY A quite substantial operation which basically services local clientele, occasionally producing wines of quite surprising quality from a variety of fruit sources.

ΥΥΥΥ **Grove Verdelho 2002** Tangy, citrussy edges; nice mouthfeel; relatively dry finish.
     RATING 88 **DRINK** 2007

ΥΥΥΥ **Chardonnay 2002** **RATING** 84 **DRINK** Now

James Estate

951 Bylong Valley Way, Baerami via Denman, NSW 2333 **REGION** Upper Hunter Valley
T (02) 6547 5168 **F** (02) 6547 5164 **OPEN** 7 days 10–4.30
WINEMAKER Peter Orr **EST.** 1971 **CASES** 75 000
PRODUCT RANGE ($10–20 R) Two Reserves (Chardonnay, Shiraz) head the portfolio; next the Estate range of varietals, with the $10 per bottle Sundara range at the bottom.
SUMMARY David James (chief executive and principal shareholder of James Estate) laid the base for what is now a very substantial wine business with the acquisition of the former Serenella Estate in 1997. Having secured the funds to significantly expand the James Estate production, and the recruitment of former McWilliam's Mount Pleasant and Allandale winemaker Peter Orr, the business was already on the road to success. However, the demise of Hill International Wines, the owner of Basedow, Fern Hill and Marienberg Wines in South Australia presented James Estate with an opportunity to take four well-established brands along with a major distribution company. In the outcome Australian Beverage Distributors distributes the four major brands in all States, exports being handled by James Estate's own office in the US (opened 3 years ago) and in the UK (opened 1 year ago).

Jamiesons Run

★★★★★

Penola–Naracoorte Road, Coonawarra, SA 5263 **REGION** Coonawarra
T (08) 8736 3380 **F** (08) 8736 3307 **OPEN** Mon–Fri 9–4.30, weekends 10–4
WINEMAKER Andrew Hales **EST.** 1955 **CASES** 160 000
PRODUCT RANGE ($13–50 R) Jamiesons Run Chardonnay, McShane's Block Shiraz, Coonawarra Red, Coonawarra Merlot, Coonawarra Reserve, Alexander Block Cabernet, O'Dea's Block Cabernet Sauvignon. Also made are Mildara Coonawarra Cabernet Sauvignon, Robertson's Well Shiraz and Cabernet Sauvignon, Jimmy Watson Chardonnay and Cabernet Shiraz and Greg Norman Estates Yarra Valley Chardonnay and Limestone Coast Cabernet Merlot.
SUMMARY Once the prized possession of a stand-alone Mildara, which spawned a child called Jamiesons Run to fill the need for a cost-effective second label. Now the name Mildara is very nearly part of ancient wine history, and the child has usurped the parent. Worldwide distribution via Beringer Blass.

▼▼▼▼▼ **Winemakers Reserve Cabernet Sauvignon 2000** Still in the first flush of life; perfectly ripened cassis/blackcurrant cabernet varietal characters supported by fine, ripe tannins and perfectly integrated oak. Classic wine. Multi-trophy winner. **RATING** 96 **DRINK** 2020 $ 55
Limestone Coast Chardonnay 2003 Lively, long, citrus, nectarine and melon fruit on a light to medium-bodied palate; sure oak handling. Trophy winner Limestone Coast Wine Show 2003. **RATING** 94 **DRINK** 2007 $ 15
McShane's Block Shiraz 2001 Blackberry, spice and mint aromas; an unexpectedly rich, but not jammy, palate; blackberry and dark chocolate; fine-grained tannins. **RATING** 94 **DRINK** 2015 $ 39
Alexander Block Coonawarra Cabernet Sauvignon 2001 Potent and powerful; pristine earthy, blackcurrant cabernet in classic regional style; uncompromising; needs many years. **RATING** 94 **DRINK** 2025 $ 35

▼▼▼▼ **Robertson's Well Shiraz 2000** Leathery, earthy, savoury aromas moving more to blackberry on the palate; good depth. **RATING** 89 **DRINK** 2010 $ 23
Red Terra Reserve Cabernet Sauvignon 2001 A potent wine with lots of tannins surrounding its earthy, cedary, blackberry flavours; needs time to settle down. **RATING** 88 **DRINK** 2015 $ 23

▼▼▼▽ **Red Terra Reserve Shiraz 2001** **RATING** 86 **DRINK** 2011 $ 22
Rothwell Coonawarra Cabernet Sauvignon 2001 **RATING** 84 **DRINK** 2011
Robertson's Well Cabernet Sauvignon 2000 **RATING** 84 **DRINK** Now $ 23

▼▼▼ **South Australian Chardonnay 2002** **RATING** 83 $ 14

Jane Brook Estate

★★★☆

229 Toodyay Road, Middle Swan, WA 6056 **REGION** Swan Valley
T (08) 9274 1432 **F** (08) 9274 1211 **OPEN** Mon–Fri 10–5, weekends and public holidays 12–5
WINEMAKER Julie White, David Atkinson **EST.** 1972 **CASES** 20 000
PRODUCT RANGE ($13.50–35 CD) Ferguson Valley Pemberton Semillon, Semillon Sauvignon Blanc, James Vineyard Verdelho, Plain Jane Chenin Chardonnay, James Vineyard Chardonnay, Atkinson Shiraz, Back Block Shiraz, Plain Jane Shiraz, Mountjoy Cabernet Merlot, Elizabeth Jane Methode Champenoise, Plain Jane Methode Champenoise, Benjamin David Methode Champenoise Shiraz; fortifieds.
SUMMARY An attractive winery which relies in part on substantial cellar-door trade and in part on varying export markets, with much work having been invested in the Japanese market in recent years. It has established a vineyard in the Margaret River and also is now sourcing fruit from Pemberton, Ferguson Valley and Arthur River. The appointment of Julie White as chief winemaker has led to a distinct improvement in wine quality and consistency. Exports to the UK, France, the US, Korea, Singapore and Japan.

▼▼▼▼ **Back Block Shiraz 2002** Fresh black cherry, raspberry and blackberry fruit; elegant and unforced; minimal oak. **RATING** 88 **DRINK** 2007 $ 20.50
Atkinson Family Reserve Shiraz 2001 Earthy/savoury bottle-developed aromas; has unexpected length, which creeps up on retasting. Also Swan Valley origin. **RATING** 88 **DRINK** 2008 $ 29.50

Mountjoy Cabernet Merlot 2001 Clean, medium-bodied; small black fruits; gently sweet; fine definition and tannins. No region of origin. **RATING** 88 **DRINK** 2009 $ 20.50

James Vineyard Chardonnay 2002 Remarkably delicate and fresh melon and nectarine fruit; minimal oak. Unlikely style from the heat of the Swan Valley. **RATING** 87 **DRINK** Now $ 18.50

Plain Jane Shiraz 2003 Excellent early-drinking red, uncomplicated but fresh; flavoursome and dry. **RATING** 87 **DRINK** Now $ 13.50

Elizabeth Jane Methode Champenoise NV Intensely flowery and aromatic; fresh, light, crispy fruity; not complex. Perth Hills. **RATING** 87 **DRINK** Now $ 25.50

TTTT **Pemberton Swan Valley Sauvignon Blanc 2003** **RATING** 86 **DRINK** Now $ 18.50
Sauvignon Blanc Semillon 2003 **RATING** 86 **DRINK** Now $ 18.50
Merlot 2002 **RATING** 85 **DRINK** 2007 $ 20.50
James Vineyard Verdelho 2003 **RATING** 84 **DRINK** 2007 $ 18.50

Jansz ★★★★★

1216b Pipers Brook Road, Pipers Brook Tas 7254 **REGION** Northern Tasmania
T (03) 6382 7066 **F** (03) 6382 7088 **OPEN** 7 days 10–5
WINEMAKER Natalie Fryar **EST.** 1985 **CASES** 15 000
PRODUCT RANGE ($18–40 CD) Premium, Non-Vintage Cuvee and Premium Late Disgorged.
SUMMARY Jansz is part of the S Smith & Son/Yalumba group, and was one of the early sparkling wine labels in Tasmania, stemming from a short-lived relationship between Heemskerk and Louis Roederer. Its 15 hectares of chardonnay, 12 hectares of pinot noir and 3 hectares of pinot meunier correspond almost exactly to the blend composition of the Jansz wines. It is the only Tasmanian winery entirely devoted to the production of sparkling wine, which is of high quality.

TTTTT **Jansz 1999** Strong yellow-green; stone fruit and citrus; good depth, balance and mouthfeel; fresh yet complex. **RATING** 96 **DRINK** 2010 $ 32.95
Late Disgorged 1996 Light green-gold; intense and complex, yet still very fresh; citrus, stone fruit and just a touch of toast. **RATING** 94 **DRINK** Now $ 39

TTTT **Cuvee NV** Clean, lively and fresh, hints of brioche; brightly-accented citrussy fruit. **RATING** 88 **DRINK** Now $ 21.95

🐚 Jarrah Ridge Winery ★★★

PO Box 1078, Wangara, WA 6065 **REGION** Perth Hills
T 1800 800 047 **F** (08) 9409 8010 **OPEN** Not
WINEMAKER Rob Marshall (Contract) **EST.** 1998 **CASES** 6500
PRODUCT RANGE ($10.60–14.20 ML) Mt Gould Classic White, Balladonia Chenin Blanc, Balladonia Wooded Chenin Blanc, Milly Milly Shiraz, Milly Milly Wooded Shiraz.
SUMMARY Syd and Julie Pond have established a 13.5-hectare vineyard, 5 hectares of shiraz, the most important grape, the remainder divided between chenin blanc, chardonnay (3 hectares each), cabernet sauvignon, verdelho and viognier (1 hectare each) and merlot (2 hectares). Children Michael and Lisa are also involved in the business, with the experienced Rob Marshall as contract winemaker. Most of the wines have a degree of sweetness which will doubtless appeal to the cellar door and restaurant customers.

TTTT **Mt Gould Classic White 2002** Nicely balanced mix of tropical and herb fruit; subtle oak use. **RATING** 87 **DRINK** Now $ 10.60

TTTT **Mt Gould Classic White 2001** **RATING** 85 **DRINK** Now $ 10.60
Milly Milly Wooded Shiraz 2001 **RATING** 84 **DRINK** 2007 $ 14.20

TTT **Balladonna Wooded Chenin Blanc 2001** **RATING** 83 $ 12.80
Balladonna Chenin Blanc 2001 **RATING** 82 $ 11.80
Milly Milly Shiraz 2001 **RATING** 82 $ 11.80

TTT **Milly Milly Shiraz 2002** **RATING** 79 $ 11.80

Jarretts of Orange ★★★☆

Annangrove Park, Cargo Road, Orange, NSW 2800 (postal) **REGION** Orange
T (02) 6364 3118 **F** (02) 6364 3048 **OPEN** Not
WINEMAKER Mark Davidson, Chris Derrez **EST.** 1995 **CASES** 2000
PRODUCT RANGE ($15–18 R) Sauvignon Blanc, Marsanne, Chardonnay, Shiraz, Cabernet Merlot.
SUMMARY Justin and Pip Jarrett have established a very substantial vineyard, planted to chardonnay (38.5 hectares), cabernet sauvignon (29 hectares), shiraz (26 hectares), sauvignon blanc (19 hectares), merlot (12 hectares), pinot noir (7 hectares), riesling (4 hectares), marsanne (2 hectares), cabernet franc (1.5 hectares) and verdelho (1 hectare), amounting to 140 hectares in total. As well as managing this vineyard, they provide management and development services to growers of another 120 hectares in the region. Most of the grapes are sold, with a limited amount produced for local distribution and by mail order, with exports to the US pending. The wines are modestly priced.

ﾵﾵﾵﾵ **Marsanne 2002** Glowing green-yellow; floral jasmine aromas; considerable intensity, length and varietal character. **RATING** 90 **DRINK** Now

ﾵﾵﾵﾵ **Sauvignon Blanc 2003** Solid herb, grass, mineral and slate aromas and flavours; crisp acidity on a long finish. **RATING** 89 **DRINK** 2007 $ 15
Chardonnay 2002 Clean, light to medium-bodied; well-balanced stone fruit and subtle oak. **RATING** 87 **DRINK** Now
Shiraz 2002 Cool-grown spicy/minty edges to red fruits; subtle oak. **RATING** 87 **DRINK** 2008 $ 18

ﾵﾵﾵﾵ **Cabernet Merlot 2003** **RATING** 86 **DRINK** 2007 $ 16

Jarvis Estate ★★★

Lot 13, Wirring Road, Margaret River, WA 6285 **REGION** Margaret River
T (08) 9758 7526 **F** (08) 9758 8017 **OPEN** By appointment
WINEMAKER Mike Lemos (Contract) **EST.** 1995 **CASES** 3000
PRODUCT RANGE ($25–38 ML) Chardonnay, Shiraz, Cabernet Franc, Cabernet Sauvignon.
SUMMARY Matt and Jackie Jarvis carefully researched the Margaret River region, and in particular the Bramley locality, before purchasing their property, where they now live. It is planted to 3 hectares of cabernet sauvignon, 1.8 hectares each of shiraz and merlot, 1.4 hectares of chardonnay and 0.4 hectare of cabernet franc. The first vintage was 2002, the wines made under contract by well-known local winemakers. Not surprisingly, some show young vine character, but have been well made. Exports to Taiwan, Greece and Ireland have already commenced, and retail distribution in Victoria (DC Fine Wines) likewise.

ﾵﾵﾵﾵ **Shiraz 2002** Dark, ripe black fruit/plum/blackberry; plenty of depth and richness, but not over-extracted; fine tannins. **RATING** 89 **DRINK** 2010 $ 24

ﾵﾵﾵﾵ **Cabernet Franc 2002** **RATING** 86 **DRINK** 2008 $ 38
Chardonnay 2002 **RATING** 85 **DRINK** Now $ 24
Cabernet Sauvignon 2002 **RATING** 85 **DRINK** 2009 $ 24

Jasper Hill ★★★★★

Drummonds Lane, Heathcote, Vic 3523 **REGION** Heathcote
T (03) 5433 2528 **F** (03) 5433 3143 **OPEN** By appointment
WINEMAKER Ron Laughton, heading a team of four **EST.** 1975 **CASES** 3500
PRODUCT RANGE ($24.50–82 ML) Georgia's Paddock Riesling, Georgia's Paddock Semillon, Georgia's Paddock Shiraz, Georgia's Paddock Nebbiolo, Emily's Paddock Shiraz Cabernet Franc.
SUMMARY The red wines of Jasper Hill are highly regarded and much sought after, invariably selling out at cellar door and through the mailing list within a short time after release. These are wonderful wines in admittedly Leviathan mould, reflecting the very low yields and the care and attention given to them by Ron Laughton. The oak is not overdone, the fruit flavours showing Central Victoria at its best. There has been comment (and some criticism) in recent years about the alcohol level of the wines. Laughton responds by saying he picks the grapes when he judges them to be at optimum ripeness, and is in no way chasing high alcohol, whether to suit the US market or otherwise. I believe he is correct, and that the power of the fruit carries the alcohol.

Jasper Valley

NR

RMB 880 Croziers Road, Berry, NSW 2535 **REGION** Shoalhaven Coast
T (02) 4464 1596 **F** (02) 4464 1595 **OPEN** 7 days 9.30–5.30
WINEMAKER Contract **EST.** 1976 **CASES** 1500
PRODUCT RANGE ($6.50–18 CD) Traminer Riesling, Verdelho, Chardonnay, lambrusco, Shiraz, Shiraz
Cabernet, Summer Red, Cabernet Sauvignon, Black Eagle Tawny Port; also non-alcoholic fruit
wines.
SUMMARY A strongly tourist-oriented winery with most of its wine purchased as cleanskins from
other makers, but with 2 hectares of estate shiraz planted in 1976 by former owner Sidney Mitchell
the oldest vines in the region. Features around 1 hectare of lawns, barbecue facilities, and sweeping
views.

Jeanneret Wines

Jeanneret Road, Sevenhill, SA 5453 **REGION** Clare Valley
T (08) 8843 4308 **F** (08) 8843 4251 **OPEN** Mon–Fri 11–5, weekends and public holidays 10–5
WINEMAKER Ben Jeanneret **EST.** 1992 **CASES** 8000
PRODUCT RANGE ($18–55 CD) Riesling, Semillon Sauvignon Blanc, Chardonnay, Sparkling Grenache,
Grenache Shiraz, Shiraz, Denis Reserve Shiraz, Cabenets, Cabernet Sauvignon.
SUMMARY Jeanneret's fully self-contained winery has a most attractive outdoor tasting area and
equally attractive picnic facilities situated on the edge of a small lake surrounded by bushland. While
it did not open the business until October 1994, its first wine was in fact made in 1992 (Shiraz) and it
has already established a loyal following. National wholesale distribution; exports to the US, Canada,
the UK, Japan, Malaysia and Switzerland.

ŸŸŸŸŸ **Shiraz 2002** Abundant blackberry and blood plum fruit; rich but quite controlled full-
bodied style; good oak and tannin management. **RATING** 94 **DRINK** 2017 $ 22

ŸŸŸŸŸ **Cabernets 2001** Generous, lush but not jammy array of complex red and black fruit
flavours; smooth finish. **RATING** 93 **DRINK** 2016 $ 20
Riesling 2003 Citrus rind aromas; a powerful, intense and robust palate, with a citrussy,
lingering finish. **RATING** 92 **DRINK** 2013 $ 18

ŸŸŸŸ **Grenache Shiraz 2002** Confronting, jammy confection style of grenache — one of the
many faces of the variety. **RATING** 87 **DRINK** 2007 $ 17

Jeir Creek

NR

Gooda Creek Road, Murrumbateman, NSW 2582 **REGION** Canberra District
T (02) 6227 5999 **F** (02) 6227 5900 **OPEN** Fri–Sun, holidays 10–5
WINEMAKER Rob Howell **EST.** 1984 **CASES** 4000
PRODUCT RANGE ($18–28 CD) Riesling, Sauvignon Blanc, Chardonnay, Botrytis Semillon Sauvignon
Blanc, Pinot Noir, Shiraz, Cabernet Merlot, Muscat.
SUMMARY Rob Howell came to part-time winemaking through a love of drinking fine wine and is
intent on improving both the quality and consistency of his wines. It is now a substantial (and still
growing) business, with the vineyard plantings increased to 11 hectares by the establishment of more
cabernet sauvignon, shiraz and merlot.

Jenke Vineyards

Barossa Valley Way, Rowland Flat, SA 5352 **REGION** Barossa Valley
T (08) 8524 4154 **F** (08) 8524 5044 **OPEN** 7 days 11–5
WINEMAKER Kym Jenke **EST.** 1989 **CASES** 8000
PRODUCT RANGE ($15–40 CD) Semillon, Chardonnay, Sparkling Shiraz, Shiraz, Grenache,
Mourvedre, Merlot, Cabernet Franc, Cabernet Sauvignon.
SUMMARY The Jenkes have been vignerons in the Barossa since 1854 and have over 45 hectares of
vineyards; a small part of the production is now made and marketed through a charming restored
stone cottage cellar door. Wholesale distribution in Victoria and New South Wales; exports to
Singapore, Switzerland and New Zealand.

Jester Hill Wines

NR

292 Mount Stirling Road, Glen Aplin, Qld 4381 **REGION** Granite Belt
T (07) 4683 4380 **F** (02) 6622 3190 **OPEN** Fri–Mon 9–5
WINEMAKER Mark Ravenscroft (Contract) **EST.** 1993 **CASES** 1600
PRODUCT RANGE ($12.50–20 CD) Classic White, Chardonnay, Sparkling Shiraz, Summer Red, Shiraz, Cabernet Sauvignon, Fortified Shiraz.
SUMMARY A family-run vineyard situated in the pretty valley of Glen Aplin in the Granite Belt. The owners, John and Genevieve Ashwell, aim to concentrate on small quantities of premium quality wines reflecting the full-bodied style of the region. Believing that good wine is made in the vineyard, John and Genevieve spent the first 7 years establishing healthy, strong vines on well-drained soil.

Jim Barry Wines

Craig's Hill Road, Clare, SA 5453 **REGION** Clare Valley
T (08) 8842 2261 **F** (08) 8842 3752 **OPEN** Mon–Fri 9–5, weekends, holidays 9–4
WINEMAKER Mark Barry **EST.** 1959 **CASES** 60 000
PRODUCT RANGE ($12–130 CD) Watervale Riesling, Lodge Hill Riesling, Cellar Door Semillon, Clare Valley Chardonnay, Unwooded Chardonnay, Lavender Hill, Sparkling Pinot Chardonnay, Noble Riesling, Lodge Hill Shiraz, Shiraz Cabernet Sauvignon, McCrae Wood Shiraz, The Armagh (Shiraz), McCrae Wood Cabernet Sauvignon, Clare Valley Cabernet Sauvignon, Cabernet Sauvignon Shiraz, Cover Drive (Clare Valley and Coonawarra Cabernet Sauvignon).
SUMMARY The Armagh and the McCrae Wood range continue to stand out as the very best wines from Jim Barry, exceptionally concentrated and full-flavoured. The remainder are seldom less than adequate but do vary somewhat from one vintage to the next, with major success in 2001 and 2002. Has an exceptional viticultural resource base of 247 hectares of mature Clare Valley vineyards. Exports to the UK, much of Europe, North America, Japan and South-East Asia.

▼▼▼▼▼ **McRae Wood Shiraz 2001** Excellent hue; luscious, ripe raspberry, cherry, plum and mint; seductive mouthfeel. **RATING** 94 **DRINK** 2016 $35
The Armagh 2001 Deep colour; powerful, concentrated and chewy blackberry, licorice, leather, mocha and earth; right in the style slot. **RATING** 94 **DRINK** 2021 $130

▼▼▼▼▽ **Lodge Hill Shiraz 2002** Opaque colour; powerful blackberry, black olive and earth aromas; layer upon layer of black fruit flavours, but not extractive. **RATING** 93 **DRINK** 2017 $18

▼▼▼▼ **Lodge Hill Riesling 2003** Classic mineral herb and spice aromas; riper fruit flavours come through on the palate. **RATING** 89 **DRINK** 2008 $19.95
The Cover Drive Cabernet Sauvignon 2001 Clearly defined cassis and mulberry varietal aromas; a medium-bodied, supple palate with ripe tannins. A blend of estate-grown Clare Valley and Coonawarra cabernet sauvignon. **RATING** 88 **DRINK** 2011 $18
McRae Wood Shiraz 2000 Rich black fruits and abundant creamy/chewy vanillin oak on both bouquet and palate; the fruit needs time to express itself better. **RATING** 87 **DRINK** 2010 $35
The Family Vineyards Shiraz Cabernet 2001 Medium-bodied; black fruits with a touch of dark chocolate; good structure. Offered in both screwcap and cork. **RATING** 87 **DRINK** 2008 $14.95

▼▼▼▽ **Watervale Riesling Florita Vineyard 2003** **RATING** 86 **DRINK** Now $15
The Cover Drive Cabernet Sauvignon 2002 **RATING** 86 **DRINK** 2010 $18

Jimbour Wines

Jimbour Station, Jimbour, Qld 4406 **REGION** Queensland Zone
T (07) 4663 6221 **F** (07) 4663 6194 **OPEN** 7 days 10–4.30
WINEMAKER Peter Scudamore-Smith MW **EST.** 2000 **CASES** 7000
PRODUCT RANGE ($13–26 CD) Jimbour, Jimbour Station and Chinamans Wall range of Verdelho, Chardonnay, Shiraz, Merlot, Cabernet Sauvignon.

SUMMARY Jimbour Station was one of the first properties opened in the Darling Downs, the heritage-listed homestead built in 1876. The property has been owned by the Russell family since 1923, which has diversified by establishing a 20-hectare vineyard and opening a cellar door on the property. Its already substantial production, made under the direction of the well-known Master of Wine Peter Scudamore-Smith, is an indication of its intention to become one of Queensland's major wine producers. The impressive quality of the wines is such that this is no idle hope. Exports to Canada, Germany, Japan, the US and Korea.

ΥΥΥΥΥ **Jimbour Station Ludwig Leichhardt Reserve Merlot 2002** A complex mix of small berry black fruits and more savoury character; excellent varietal definition, texture, structure, line and length. A real eye opener. **RATING** 93 **DRINK** 2012 $26

Jimbour Station Ludwig Leichhardt Reserve Chardonnay 2002 A powerful, rich and concentrated bouquet and palate; plenty of French oak, but balanced by the power of the fruit. Quality wine by any standards. **RATING** 91 **DRINK** Now $26

ΥΥΥΥ **Jimbour Station Chardonnay 2002** Clear-cut yellow peach varietal character; plenty of weight, but not phenolic; subtle oak. **RATING** 88 **DRINK** Now $15

Jimbour Station Cabernet Sauvignon 2001 Clean, light to medium-bodied cassis/berry fruit; nice structure, but a slightly twitchy finish; plenty going for it. **RATING** 87 **DRINK** 2009 $19

Jimbour Station Living History Pinot Chardonnay NV Attractive strawberry-accented fruit; not sweet; another surprise performer. **RATING** 87 **DRINK** Now $25

ΥΥΥΥ **Jimbour Station Shiraz 2001 RATING** 85 **DRINK** 2007 $19

ΥΥΥ **Jimbour Station Linkeith Sunrise White 2003 RATING** 83 $13

Jindalee Estate ★★★★

265 Ballan Road, Moorabool, North Geelong, Vic 3221 **REGION** Geelong
T (03) 5276 1280 **F** (03) 5276 1537 **OPEN** 7 days 10–5
WINEMAKER Andrew Byers, Chris Sargeant **EST.** 1997 **CASES** 500 000
PRODUCT RANGE ($8.95–19.50 CD) Chardonnay, Shiraz, Merlot, Cabernet Sauvignon; under the Fettlers Rest label are Gewurztraminer, Chardonnay, Pinot Noir, Shiraz, Cabernet Shiraz.
SUMMARY Jindalee made its debut with the 1997 vintage. It is part of the Littore Group, which currently has 550 hectares of premium-wine grapes in wine production and under development in the Riverland. Corporate offices are now at the former Idyll Vineyard, acquired by Jindalee in late 1997. Here 14 hectares of estate vineyards have been re-trellised and upgraded, and produce the Fettlers Rest range. The Jindalee Estate Chardonnay can offer spectacular value, as it did in 2001. Exports to the UK, Sweden, the US and Canada.

ΥΥΥΥΥ **Fettlers Rest Chardonnay 2002** Strongly funky/feral aromas ex-barrel fermentation; palate more conventional, but still slightly feral. Some will love this wine. **RATING** 90 **DRINK** 2007 $18

Fettlers Rest Pinot Noir 2002 Scented spicy/sappy/leafy/aromas; red berry fruit on entry to the mouth, savoury finish. **RATING** 90 **DRINK** 2007 $19.50

ΥΥΥΥ **Cabernet Sauvignon 2002 RATING** 86 **DRINK** 2007 $9.90

Merlot 2002 RATING 85 **DRINK** Now $9

Chardonnay 2003 RATING 84 **DRINK** Now $9.90

Shiraz 2002 RATING 84 **DRINK** Now $9.90

Jingalla ★★★☆

RMB 1316 Bolganup Dam Road, Porongurup, WA 6324 **REGION** Porongurup
T (08) 9853 1023 **F** (08) 9853 1023 **OPEN** 7 days 10.30–5
WINEMAKER Diane Miller, Gary Baldwin (Consultant) **EST.** 1979 **CASES** 5000
PRODUCT RANGE ($13–25 CD) Great Southern White, Riesling, Riesling Reserve, Semillon Sauvignon Blanc, Verdelho, Late Harvest, Botrytis Riesling Verdelho, Shiraz, Shiraz Reserve, CabRouge, Cabernets Merlot, Cabernet Sauvignon, Tawny Port, Liqueur Muscat.
SUMMARY Jingalla is a family business, owned and run by Geoff and Nita Clarke and Barry and Shelley Coad, the latter the ever-energetic wine marketer of the business. The 8 hectares of hillside

vineyards are low-yielding, with the white wines succeeding best, but it also produces some lovely red wines. A partner in the new Porongurup Winery, which means it no longer has to rely on contract winemaking. National distribution.

ᵀᵀᵀᵀ **Sauvignon Blanc Verdelho 2003** RATING 86 DRINK Now $ 14

ᵀᵀᵀ **Shiraz 2001** RATING 83 $ 25

Jinglers Creek Vineyard ★★★

288 Relbia Road, Relbia, Tas 7258 (postal) **REGION** Northern Tasmania
T (03) 6344 3966 **F** (03) 6344 3966 **OPEN** Thurs–Sun 11–5
WINEMAKER Graham Wiltshire **EST.** 1998 **CASES** 900
PRODUCT RANGE ($18–25 R) Pinot Gris, Chardonnay, Pinot Noir.
SUMMARY One of the newer arrivals on the Tasmanian scene, with 2 hectares of pinot noir, pinot gris and chardonnay. Winemaking is done by industry veteran Graham Wiltshire, who knows more about growing grapes and making wine in Tasmania than any other active winemaker.

ᵀᵀᵀᵀ **Pinot Noir 2002** RATING 86 DRINK 2007 $ 22

Jinks Creek Winery ★★★★

Tonimbuk Road, Tonimbuk, Vic 3815 **REGION** Gippsland
T (03) 5629 8502 **F** (03) 5629 8551 **OPEN** By appointment
WINEMAKER Andrew Clarke **EST.** 1981 **CASES** 1000
PRODUCT RANGE ($22.50–35 CD) Sauvignon Blanc, Pinot Noir, Heathcote Shiraz, Longford Shiraz, Yarra Valley Shiraz.
SUMMARY Jinks Creek Winery is situated between Gembrook and Bunyip, bordering the evocatively named Bunyip State Park. While the winery was not built until 1992, planting of the 3.64-hectare vineyard started back in 1981 and all of the wines are estate-grown. The 'sold out' sign goes up each year, small wonder in vintages such as 2000 and 2002. Exports to the US and Singapore.

ᵀᵀᵀᵀᵀ **Longford Gippsland Shiraz 2002** Deeply coloured; licorice, spice, blackberry and chocolate ooze from every pore; excellent structure and texture. **RATING** 94 **DRINK** 2012 $ 28

ᵀᵀᵀᵀᵀ **Gippsland Pinot Noir 2002** Very complex dark plum and spice aromas, carrying through to the rich and potent palate, with a touch of game. Eight clones, and bottled unfiltered. **RATING** 91 **DRINK** 2007 $ 28
Heathcote Shiraz 2002 Deep red-purple; ripe blackberry, prune and licorice aromas, followed by brooding fruit on the palate; doesn't show its 14.7° alcohol and not extractive. **RATING** 90 **DRINK** 2015 $ 35
Yarra Valley Shiraz 2002 Complex spicy aromas, with hints of game; black plum/blackberry/spice fruit; firm finish. Not for the brett police. **RATING** 90 **DRINK** 2010 $ 28

ᵀᵀᵀᵀ **Chardonnay 2003** RATING 86 DRINK 2008 $ 28

ᵀᵀᵀ **Sauvignon Blanc 2003** RATING 83 DRINK Now $ 22.50

Jinnunger Vineyard ★★★☆

RMB 8601A Nanarup Road, Lower Kalgan, Albany, WA 6330 **REGION** Albany
T (08) 9846 4374 **F** (08) 9846 4474 **OPEN** By appointment
WINEMAKER Robert Diletti (Contract) **EST.** 1996 **CASES** 800
PRODUCT RANGE ($15–20 CD) Unoaked Chardonnay, Chardonnay, Pinot Noir.
SUMMARY Jinnunger Vineyard has been established by Colin Sanderson and Dierdre Coombe, both research scientists. They have planted 1 hectare each of chardonnay and pinot noir, and while they expect to increase the plantings, they will always run a small, hand-tended vineyard, ideally situated on a north-facing slope of Mount Mason close to the Southern Ocean. It is situated 18 kilometres east of Albany, and the name comes from the local Aboriginal (Nyungah) language meaning 'good views': the property looks out over the Porongorup and Stirling Ranges. The website is well worth a visit — <www.jinnunger.com.au>.

ŢŢŢŢŢ **Chardonnay 2002** Fleshy but not coarse; long, mouthfilling stone fruit, melon and a dash of citrus which has eaten up the new French oak. Stylish. **RATING** 92 **DRINK** 2009 $18

ŢŢŢŢ **Pinot Noir 2001** Slightly dusty oak in the background of a spicy/savoury/stemmy style, which has excellent length and all the signs of good winemaking. **RATING** 87 **DRINK** 2007 $20

ŢŢŢŢ **Unoaked Chardonnay 2003** **RATING** 85 **DRINK** Now $15

Joadja Vineyards ★★★☆

Joadja Road, Berrima, NSW 2577 **REGION** Southern Highlands
T (02) 4878 5236 **F** (02) 4878 5236 **OPEN** 7 days 10–5
WINEMAKER Kim Moginie **EST.** 1983 **CASES** 2000
PRODUCT RANGE ($15–35 CD) Classic Dry White, Sauvignon Blanc, Chardonnay, Botrytis Autumn Riesling, Cabernet Sangiovese, Cabernet Malbec, Cabernet Merlot, Mandemar, Christopher Tawny Port, Brambelini Liqueur.
SUMMARY The strikingly labelled Joadja Vineyards wines, first made in 1990, are principally drawn from 7 hectares of estate vineyards situated in the cool hills adjacent to Berrima. Mature vines and greater experience of this emerging region appears to have solved some of the early difficulties in securing full ripeness.

John Gehrig Wines ★★☆

Oxley-Milawa Road, Oxley, Vic 3678 **REGION** King Valley
T (03) 5727 3395 **F** (03) 5727 3699 **OPEN** 7 days 9–5
WINEMAKER John Gehrig **EST.** 1976 **CASES** 5600
PRODUCT RANGE ($9–25 CD) Riesling, Oxley Dry White, Chenin Blanc, Chardonnay, Pinot Victoria, Late Harvest Riesling, Pinot Noir Brut, Oxley Rose, Pinot Noir, King River Red, Border Blend, Merlot, Cabernet Merlot, fortifieds.
SUMMARY Honest, if seldom exciting, wines; the occasional Chardonnay, Pinot Noir, Merlot and Cabernet Merlot have, however, risen above their station.

John Kosovich Wines ★★★★

Cnr Memorial Ave & Great Northern Highway, Baskerville, WA 6056 **REGION** Swan Valley
T (08) 9296 4356 **F** (08) 9296 4356 **OPEN** 7 days 10–5.30
WINEMAKER John Kosovich **EST.** 1922 **CASES** 11 000
PRODUCT RANGE ($15–75 CD) Chenin Blanc, Verdelho, Unwooded Chardonnay, Chardonnay, Bronze Wing Chardonnay, Sparkling Burgundy, Late Pick Verdelho, Autumn Harvest, Shiraz, Bronze Wing Shiraz, Bronze Wing Merlot, Cabernet Sauvignon, Liqueur Muscat, Liqueur Verdelho, Liqueur Shiraz, Vintage Port.
SUMMARY The name change from Westfield to John Kosovich Wines does not signify any change in either philosophy or direction for this much admired producer of a surprisingly elegant and complex Chardonnay; the other wines are more variable, but from time to time has made attractive Verdelho and excellent Cabernet Sauvignon. The year 1998 saw the first release of wines partly or wholly coming from the family's new planting at Pemberton, those being Swan/Pemberton blends released under the Bronze Wing label. Limited retail distribution in Perth, Melbourne and Brisbane, exports to Singapore.

ŢŢŢŢŢ **Liqueur Muscat NV** Dark tawny-brown; an intense raisiny rancio bouquet then unctuously rich and sweet raisins-in-brandy palate. **RATING** 95 **DRINK** Now $55

Johnston Oakbank ★★★★☆

18 Oakwood Road, Oakbank, SA 5243 **REGION** Adelaide Hills
T (08) 8388 4263 **F** (08) 8388 4278 **OPEN** Mon–Fri 8–5
WINEMAKER David O'Leary (Contract), Geoff Johnston **EST.** 1843 **CASES** 4000
PRODUCT RANGE ($17–25 CD) Sauvignon Blanc, Chardonnay, Pinot Noir, Shiraz, Merlot.
SUMMARY The origins of this business, owned by the Johnston Group, date back to 1839, making it the oldest known family-owned business in South Australia. The vineyard at Oakbank is substantial, with 7 hectares each of sauvignon blanc and pinot noir, 6 hectares of shiraz, 5 hectares of chardonnay

and 4 hectares of merlot. The wines have retail distribution in South Australia (David Porter), Victoria (Fesq & Co.) and New South Wales (Nelson).

ҮҮҮҮҮ **Sauvignon Blanc 2003** An aromatic mix of herb, asparagus and gooseberry; stylish, tight palate; excellent lemony acidity. **RATING** 91 **DRINK** Now $ 17.95

Pinot Noir 2002 Complex all-spice, nutmeg, plum and forest flavours; striking palate, left of centre. **RATING** 90 **DRINK** 2007 $ 20.50

ҮҮҮҮ **Shiraz 2001** Spicy, raspberry cherry; medium-bodied; fine tannins and judicious oak. **RATING** 89 **DRINK** 2011 $ 20

🐝 John Wade Wines

NR

PO Box 23, Denmark, WA 6633 **REGION** Denmark
T (08) 9848 2462 **F** (08) 9848 2087 **OPEN** By appointment
WINEMAKER John Wade, Stephanie Wade, Alex Wade **EST.** 2000 **CASES** 1500
PRODUCT RANGE ($18–34 CD) Riesling, Chardonnay, Merlot Cabernet Franc, Cabernet Sauvignon Merlot Cabernet Franc.
SUMMARY John Wade is arguably the most experienced winemaker in Western Australia, with over 20 years' experience following his role as chief winemaker at Wynns Coonawarra Estate. He is best known for his involvement with Plantagenet and then Howard Park, and, having sold his interest in Howard Park, has become a consultant winemaker to a substantial number of producers; his own label is a relatively small part of his total wine business. The wines are chiefly sold through premium retail outlets and restaurants.

Jollymont

★★★★

145 Pullens Road, Woodbridge, Tas 7162 (postal) **REGION** Southern Tasmania
T (03) 6267 4594 **F** (03) 6267 4594 **OPEN** Not
WINEMAKER Andrew Hood (Contract) **EST.** 1988 **CASES** 40
PRODUCT RANGE ($32–34 R) Pinot Noir.
SUMMARY However briefly, Jollymont displaced Scarp Valley as the smallest producer in Australia, its 1998 vintage (the first) producing 10 cases, the next 20; it now produces 40. The vines are not irrigated, nor will they be, and Peter and Heather Kreet do not intend to sell any wine younger than 3–4 years old. Their aim is to produce wines of maximum intensity and complexity.

Jones Winery & Vineyard

★★★★

Jones Road, Rutherglen, Vic 3685 **REGION** Rutherglen
T (02) 6032 8496 **F** (02) 6032 8495 **OPEN** Thurs–Sun and public holidays 10–5
WINEMAKER Mandy Jones **EST.** 1864 **CASES** 600
PRODUCT RANGE ($18–40 CD) There are two labels; Jones The Winemaker is used for wines produced from contract-grown grapes (Sauvignon Blanc, Annie's White Marsanne, Chardonnay and Pinot Noir), while the Jones Winery & Vineyard label is used for wines made from estate-grown grapes (Shiraz and fortifieds).
SUMMARY Late in 1998 the winery was purchased from Les Jones by Leanne Schoen and Mandy and Arthur Jones (nieces and nephew of Les). The cellar-door sales area is situated in a building from the 1860s, still with the original bark ceiling and walls made from handmade bricks fired on-site; it was completely renovated in 2002/03.

🐝 Journeys End Vineyards

★★★★★

248 Flinders Street, Adelaide, SA 5000 (postal) **REGION** Warehouse
T 0409 011 633 **OPEN** Not
WINEMAKER Ben Riggs (Contract) **EST.** 2001 **CASES** 3000
PRODUCT RANGE ($15–40 R) Friends & Thieves Semillon, Made in the Vineyard Verdelho, Footprints on Maslin Chardonnay, Last Bunch Grenache, Hard Days Work Merlot, Three Brothers Reunion Shiraz, Beginnings Shiraz, Ascent Shiraz, The Arrival Shiraz.
SUMMARY A particularly interesting business in the virtual winery category which, while focused on McLaren Vale shiraz, also has contracts for other varieties in the Adelaide Hills and Langhorne Creek. The shiraz comes in four levels, and, for good measure, uses five different clones of shiraz to

amplify the complexity which comes from having contract grape growers in many different parts of McLaren Vale. The wines are distributed through a limited number of fine wine retailers, particularly in Melbourne, and are also available online from the website <www.journeysendvineyards.com.au>. Exports to the US, the UK, Germany, Canada and Singapore.

ŸŸŸŸŸ **Beginning Shiraz 2002** A wonderful wine; endlessly complex in terms of both flavour and structure; black fruits, dark chocolate, spice, tannins and oak all seamlessly interwoven; carries 15 degrees alcohol with ease. **RATING** 96 **DRINK** 2022 $25

ŸŸŸŸŸ **Ascent Shiraz 2001** A complex, medium to full-bodied array of red and black fruits; excellent use of French oak; overall supple mouthfeel. **RATING** 93 **DRINK** 2016 $30

ŸŸŸŸ **Three Brothers Reunion Shiraz 2002** Aromatic, spicy, juicy berry; fresh and crisp; early-drinking style. **RATING** 87 **DRINK** 2008 $15

Juniper Estate ★★★★★

Harmans Road South, Cowaramup, WA 6284 **REGION** Margaret River
T (08) 9755 9000 **F** (08) 9755 9100 **OPEN** 7 days 10–5
WINEMAKER Mark Messenger **EST.** 1973 **CASES** 10 000
PRODUCT RANGE ($16–32 CD) Under the Juniper Crossing label, Semillon Sauvignon Blanc, Chenin Blanc, Chardonnay, Late Harvest Riesling, Shiraz, Cabernet Merlot, Cabernet Sauvignon; Juniper Estate Riesling, Semillon, Shiraz, Cabernet Sauvignon; Wright's White Port.
SUMMARY This is the reincarnation of Wrights, which was sold by founders Henry and Maureen Wright in 1998. The 10-hectare vineyard has been retrellised, and the last 1.5 hectares of plantable land has seen the key plantings of shiraz and cabernet sauvignon increase a little. A major building program was completed in February 2000, giving Juniper Estate a new 250-tonne capacity winery, barrel hall and cellar-door facility. The Juniper family is a famous one in the Margaret River region, its strong artistic bent evident in the immaculate packaging and background material. Juniper Crossing wines use a mix of estate-grown and contract-purchased grapes from other Margaret River vineyards. The Juniper Estate releases are made only from the 28-year-old estate plantings. Exports to the US, the UK, Singapore and Denmark.

ŸŸŸŸŸ **Semillon 2002** A complex, intense and satisfying wine in true White Bordeaux style; the barrel-ferment component judged to perfection. Great length. **RATING** 94 **DRINK** 2010 $22

ŸŸŸŸŸ **Crossing Semillon Sauvignon Blanc 2003** Intense, crisp, minerally; good drive, and a particularly long finish. Semillon dominant. **RATING** 90 **DRINK** 2010 $15

ŸŸŸŸ **Crossing Chardonnay 2002** Clean, grapefruit and stone fruit aromas and flavours; stylish, fruit-driven, oak merely a backdrop. **RATING** 89 **DRINK** 2007 $18

🐚 Jupiter Creek Winery NR

10 Queen Street, Thebarton, SA 5031 (postal) **REGION** Adelaide Hills
T (08) 8354 3744 **F** (08) 8354 3822 **OPEN** Not
WINEMAKER Paul Lindner (Contract) **EST.** 1999
PRODUCT RANGE A range of varietally denominated table, sparkling and fortified wines reflecting the plantings.
SUMMARY Jupiter Creek has 8.9 hectares of vineyard under the control of viticulturist Michael Clarken at Echunga. The varieties planted are sauvignon blanc, grenache, cabernet sauvignon, merlot and shiraz; the wines are contract-made.

JYT Wines ★★★

De Beyers Road, Pokolbin, NSW 2320 **REGION** Lower Hunter Valley
T (02) 4998 7528 **F** (02) 4998 7370 **OPEN** 7 days 10–5
WINEMAKER Jay Tulloch, Julie Tulloch **EST.** 1996 **CASES** 2000
PRODUCT RANGE ($15–16.50 CD) Semillon, Verdelho, Chardonnay, Pink.
SUMMARY When Jay Tulloch left JY Tulloch and Sons in 1996, it appeared to mark the end of a 100-year, multi-generational association. However, when Southcorp decided to break up the Tulloch

business, selling the brand and the winery separately, a partnership was formed which now has Angove's, Inglewood Vineyards (Two Rivers) and Jay Tulloch all involved in one way or another. In parallel, Jay and wife Julie have established 0.6 hectare each of semillon, chardonnay, verdelho, shiraz and sangiovese. The wines are now sold through the new Tulloch cellar-door facility.

ŸŸŸŸ **Verdelho 2003** RATING 85 DRINK Now $ 15
Semillon 2003 RATING 84 DRINK 2008 $ 15
Shiraz 2000 RATING 84 DRINK 2010

🐝 Kabminye Wines ★★★☆

Krondorf Road, Tanunda, SA 5352 REGION Barossa Valley
T (08) 8563 0889 F (08) 8563 3828 OPEN 7 days 11–5
WINEMAKER Contract EST. 2001 CASES 2100
PRODUCT RANGE ($13.50–37.50 CD) Three Posts Eden Valley Riesling, Semillon, Frontignan Blanc, Ilona Cabernet Sauvignon Granaccia Rose, Schliebs Block (red blend), Irma Adeline (predominantly Shiraz, Mataro and Grenache), Barossa Shiraz, Hubert Shiraz.
SUMMARY Rick and Ingrid Glastonbury have established a combined café (serving traditional Barossa Valley lunches all day), peripheral art gallery and cellar door, with a surrounding 1.5 hectares of vineyard. Architect Rick Glastonbury has been a home winemaker for 30 years, but almost all of the wines under the Kabminye label are contract-made from purchased grapes.

ŸŸŸŸŸ **Hubert Shiraz 2001** Distinctly finer, tighter and longer than the standard Shiraz; French oak well integrated, although obvious. RATING 92 DRINK 2011 $ 37.50

ŸŸŸŸ **Irma Adeline 2001** Highly aromatic; sweet spicy/juicy berry flavours; good length, even though little tannin support. Blend of Shiraz, Mourvedre, Grenache, Marsanne, Roussanne and Ugni Blanc. RATING 89 DRINK 2009 $ 21.50
Three Posts Eden Valley Riesling 2003 Clean; apple, citrus and some lime; shortens fractionally. RATING 87 DRINK 2007 $ 19.50
Barossa Shiraz 2001 Ripe blackberry and vanilla flavours; soft tannins and moderate depth. American oak. RATING 87 DRINK 2009 $ 24
Schliebs Block 2002 Fragrant cedar, tobacco, leaf and spice aromas and flavours; light to medium-bodied; a blend of Mourvedre, Carignan, Cinsaut and Black Frontignac. RATING 87 DRINK 2007 $ 26

Kaesler Wines ★★★★★

Barossa Valley Way, Nuriootpa, SA 5355 REGION Barossa Valley
T (08) 8562 4488 F (08) 8562 4499 OPEN Mon–Sat 10–5, Sunday and public holidays 11.30–4
WINEMAKER Reid Bosward EST. 1990 CASES 12 000
PRODUCT RANGE ($9.50–155 CD) Riesling, Home Block Semillon, Old Vine Semillon, Prestige Semillon, Stonehorse Late Harvest, Reid's Rasp, Stonehorse Gilt-Finish, Stonehorse Shiraz, Old Vine Shiraz, Old Bastard Shiraz, Old Vine Grenache, Single Wire Merlot, Cabernet Sauvignon, Tawny Port, Cottage Block Fortified White.
SUMMARY The Kaesler name dates back to 1845, when the first members of the family settled in the Barossa Valley. The Kaesler vineyards date back to 1893, but the Kaesler ownership ended in 1968. After several changes, the present, much expanded, Kaesler Wines was acquired by a Swiss banking family, in conjunction with former Flying Winemaker Reid Bosward and wife Bindy. Bosward's vast experience in making wine in many different climates shows through in the wines, which now come from 24 hectares of estate vineyards which, as well as the 1893 shiraz, grenache and mourvedre, have grenache and mourvedre that was planted in the 1930s. A new winery was completed in time for the 2002 vintage. Exports to the US, Canada, Switzerland, Denmark, Sweden, Japan, Hong Kong and New Zealand.

ŸŸŸŸŸ **Old Vine Shiraz 2001** Great colour; excellent richness and depth to the blackberry/black plum fruit; deft tannin and oak management. RATING 94 DRINK 2016 $ 55

ŸŸŸŸŸ **Old Vine Semillon 2003** Very much new-generation winemaking approach; apple, mineral and citrus; crunchy acidity; benchmark Semillon for the Barossa. 11 degrees alcohol. RATING 92 DRINK 2010 $ 16.50
Avignon Shiraz Grenache Mourvedre 2002 Sweet, juicy berry aromas and flavours, led by Grenache; long and lingering. RATING 91 DRINK 2010 $ 30

Stonehorse Grenache Shiraz Mourvedre 2002 More powerful, with darker fruit/berry flavours than the Avignon; considerable structure and length. **RATING** 90 **DRINK** 2012 $17.50

ŸŸŸŸ **Old Vine Riesling 2003** Plenty of quite sweet citrus and apple aroma and flavour; softer style, quicker developing. **RATING** 88 **DRINK** Now $15
Stonehorse Shiraz 2002 Deeply coloured; rather closed, with solid black fruit flavours in a medium-bodied frame; a touch of Viognier; still at odds with itself. **RATING** 88 **DRINK** 2012 $30

Kalari Wines

NR

120 Carro Park Road, Cowra, NSW 2794 **REGION** Cowra
T (02) 6342 1465 **F** (02) 6342 1465 **OPEN** Weekends and public holidays 9–5
WINEMAKER Jill Lindsay, Jon Reynolds (Contract) **EST.** 1995 **CASES** 1200
PRODUCT RANGE ($14–25 CD) Semillon, Verdelho, Chardonnay, Late Picked Verdelho, Shiraz, Fortelho (fortified Verdelho).
SUMMARY Kalari Vineyards is yet another of the new brands to appear in the Cowra region. Fourteen and a half hectares of vines have been established, with a Verdelho, Chardonnay and Shiraz being included in the initial release.

Kalleske Wines

★★★★★

Vinegrove Road, Greenock, SA 5360 **REGION** Barossa Valley
T 0409 339 599 **F** (08) 8562 8118 **OPEN** Not
WINEMAKER Troy Kalleske **EST.** 1999 **CASES** 2000
PRODUCT RANGE ($17.50–100 ML) Semillon, Greenock Shiraz, Old Vine Shiraz, Grenache, Old Vine Grenache, Liqueur Shiraz.
SUMMARY The Kalleske family has been growing grapes on a mixed farming property in Greenock for over 100 years; John and Lorraine Kalleske, fifth-generation grape growers, currently manage the property. The 40-hectare vineyard is principally planted to shiraz, grenache, cabernet and semillon, the vines varying between 100 years old and only 5 years old, with an average age of about 50 years. No chemical fertilisers or pesticides are used, and some of the vineyard blocks are fully certified organic. Prior to 1999 all grapes were sold to large wineries in the region, but following a trial vintage in 1999 (2 tonnes of Shiraz were vinified) the decision was taken to establish a small winery on the estate, with open fermenters, a basket press, stainless steel tanks and an insulated barrel store. The quality and density of the 2002 wines is awesome, directly reflecting the old vines and open-fermentation techniques employed. Very definitely a winery to watch as its production increases to 4000 cases in 2004 and beyond.

ŸŸŸŸŸ **Greenock Shiraz 2002** Densely coloured; a gloriously rich, yet compact, array of blackberry, plum, dark chocolate, mocha and vanilla; lingering tannins. Carries 15.5 degrees alcohol remarkably well. **RATING** 96 **DRINK** 2022 $38
Old Vine Grenache 2002 Concentrated, imperious mix of black fruits, exotic, tangy spices and sweet American oak. Far more structure than most. **RATING** 94 **DRINK** 2012 $38

Kamberra

★★★★

Cnr Northbourne Avenue and Fleminton Road, Lyneham, ACT 2602 **REGION** Canberra District
T (02) 6262 2333 **F** (02) 6262 2300 **OPEN** 7 days 10–5
WINEMAKER Alex McKay, Ed Carr, Glenn James, Stephen Pannell **EST.** 2000 **CASES** 18 000
PRODUCT RANGE ($15–25 R) The wines come in two ranges: at the bottom, the Meeting Place label of Riesling, Sauvignon Blanc, Chardonnay, Pinot Noir Chardonnay, Shiraz, Cabernet Sauvignon; the premium range, under the Kamberra label, of Riesling, Chardonnay, Pinot Noir Chardonnay, Shiraz, Cabernet Sauvignon.
SUMMARY Kamberra is part of the BRL Hardy group, established in 2000 with the planting of 40 hectares of vines and a new winery within the Australian Capital Territory, only a few hundred metres away from the showground facilities where the national wine show is held every year. The two 100 per cent estate-grown wines are Riesling and Shiraz, but most of the wines have a Kamberra component.

ŸŸŸŸ **Meeting Place Chardonnay 2002** **RATING** 85 **DRINK** Now $15

Kancoona Valley Wines

NR

123 Morgan's Creek Road, Kancoona South, Vic 3691 **REGION** Alpine Valleys
T (02) 6028 9419 **F** (02) 6028 9051 **OPEN** Thurs–Sun 10–5, or by appointment
WINEMAKER Joseph Birti **EST.** 1989
PRODUCT RANGE ($20 CD) Pinot Noir, Pinot Noir Preservative Free, Cabernet Sauvignon, Cabernet
Sauvignon Preservative Free.
SUMMARY Joseph and Lena Birti began planting their vineyard in 1989. It is situated in a natural
amphitheatre 12 kilometres from the Kiewa River, halfway between Myrtleford and Mount Beauty.
Thermal breezes rising from the Kiewa River valley help protect the vines from fungal disease, and
the Birtis do not use any pesticides. They made their first wines in 1999, and from the word go have
offered preservative-free alternatives.

Kangarilla Road Vineyard & Winery

Kangarilla Road, McLaren Vale, SA 5171 **REGION** McLaren Vale
T (08) 8383 0533 **F** (08) 8383 0044 **OPEN** Mon–Fri 9–5, weekends 11–5
WINEMAKER Kevin O'Brien **EST.** 1975 **CASES** 25 000
PRODUCT RANGE ($12–28 CD) Chardonnay, Viognier, Zinfandel, Shiraz, Cabernet Sauvignon, Tawny
Port, Vintage Port.
SUMMARY Kangarilla Road Vineyard & Winery was formerly known as Stevens Cambrai. Long-time
industry identity Kevin O'Brien and wife Helen purchased the property in July 1997, and have now
fully established the strikingly labelled Kangarilla Road brand in place of Cambrai. Exports to the
US, the UK, Singapore and Indonesia.

▼▼▼▼ **Cabernet Sauvignon 2001** Clean, fresh, sweet raspberry and blackcurrant aromas and
flavours; light to medium-bodied, and not over-extracted. Good value. **RATING** 88
DRINK 2010 $19

▼▼▼ **Chardonnay 2003 RATING** 82 $15

Kangaroo Island Vines

c/- 413 Payneham Road, Felixstow, SA 5070 **REGION** Kangaroo Island
T (08) 8365 3411 **F** (08) 8336 2462 **OPEN** Not
WINEMAKER Caj Amadio **EST.** 1990 **CASES** 600
PRODUCT RANGE ($20–25 ML) Island Sting (honey liqueur), Kate's Block Shiraz, The Barque Mars
Shiraz, Florance Cabernet Merlot, Special Reserve Cabernet Merlot.
SUMMARY Kangaroo Island is another venture of Caj and Genny Amadio, with the wines being sold
through the Chain of Ponds cellar door. The Amadios have been the focal point of the development
of vineyards on Kangaroo Island, producing the wines not only from their own tiny planting of
450 vines on quarter of an acre, but also by buying grapes from other vignerons on the island. The
tiny quantities of wine so far produced, particularly the excellent Special Reserve Cabernet
Merlot, strongly support the notion that Kangaroo Island has an excellent climate for Bordeaux-
style reds.

▼▼▼▼ **Florance Cabernet Merlot 2000 RATING** 87 **DRINK** 2010 $19.95

Kangderaar Vineyard

NR

Wehla–Kingower Road, Rheola, Vic 3517 **REGION** Bendigo
T (03) 5438 8292 **F** (03) 5438 8292 **OPEN** Mon–Sat 9–5, Sun 10–5
WINEMAKER James Nealy **EST.** 1980 **CASES** 800
PRODUCT RANGE Riesling Traminer, Sauvignon Blanc, Chardonnay, Carmine, Cabernet Merlot,
Rheola Gold (White Port), Vintage Port (Touriga).
SUMMARY The 4.5-hectare vineyard is situated at Rheola, near the Melville Caves, said to have been
the hideout of the bushranger Captain Melville in the 1850s, and surrounded by the Kooyoora State
Park. It is owned by James and Christine Nealy.

Kara Kara Vineyard

Sunraysia Highway, St Arnaud, Vic 3478 (10 km sth of St Arnaud) **REGION** Pyrenees
T (03) 5496 3294 **F** (03) 5496 3294 **OPEN** Mon–Fri 10.30–6, weekends 9–6
WINEMAKER John Ellis (Contract), Steve Zsigmond **EST.** 1977 **CASES** 2500
PRODUCT RANGE ($20–29 CD) Sauvignon Blanc, Chardonnay, Shiraz, Cabernet Sauvignon.
SUMMARY Hungarian-born Steve Zsigmond comes from a long line of vignerons and sees Kara Kara as the eventual retirement occupation for himself and wife Marlene. He is a graduate of the Adelaide University Roseworthy campus wine marketing course, and worked for Yalumba and Negociants as a sales manager in Adelaide and Perth. He looks after sales and marketing from the Melbourne premises of Kara Kara, and the wine is contract-made by John Ellis, with consistent results. Draws upon 9 hectares of estate plantings.

Karina Vineyard

35 Harrisons Road, Dromana, Vic 3936 **REGION** Mornington Peninsula
T (03) 5981 0137 **F** (03) 5981 0137 **OPEN** Weekends 11–5, 7 days in January
WINEMAKER Gerard Terpstra **EST.** 1984 **CASES** 2000
PRODUCT RANGE ($12–19 CD) Riesling, Sauvignon Blanc, Chardonnay, Pinot Noir, Cabernet Merlot.
SUMMARY A typical Mornington Peninsula vineyard, situated in the Dromana/Red Hill area on rising, north-facing slopes, just 3 kilometres from the shores of Port Phillip Bay, immaculately tended and with picturesque garden surrounds. Fragrant Riesling and cashew-accented Chardonnay are usually its best wines. Exports to Japan.

Karl Seppelt

Ross Dewells Road, Springton, SA 5235 **REGION** Eden Valley
T (08) 8568 2378 **F** (08) 8568 2799 **OPEN** 7 days 10–5
WINEMAKER Karl Seppelt **EST.** 1981 **CASES** 5000
PRODUCT RANGE ($14–20 CD) Rhine Riesling, Chardonnay, Chardonnay Brut, Brut Sauvage, Sparkling Shiraz, Shiraz, Merlot, Cabernet Sauvignon, Flor Fino Sherry, Vintage Port, Tawny Port, Liqueur Muscat.
SUMMARY After experimenting with various label designs and names, Karl Seppelt (former marketing director of Seppelt) has decided to discontinue the brand name Grand Cru (although retaining it as a business name) and henceforth market the wines from his estate vineyards under his own name. They are now made at a small winery constructed on the property. The quality is consistent across the range, and the wines are exported to Canada and Germany.

Karri Grove Estate

PO Box 432, Margaret River, WA 6285 **REGION** Margaret River
T (08) 9757 6281 **F** (08) 9757 6353 **OPEN** Not
WINEMAKER Flying Fish Cove (white), David O'Leary (red) (both Contract) **EST.** 1991 **CASES** 3000
PRODUCT RANGE ($14–18 ML) Sauvignon Blanc Semillon, Verdelho, Shiraz, Merlot, Cabernet Sauvignon.
SUMMARY Karri Grove Estate is loosely associated with Flinders Bay, from which it purchases most of its grapes. The white wines are made at Flying Fish Cove in the Margaret River region but the grapes for the red wines are transported to South Australia, where they are contract-made by David O'Leary. Distribution is via wholesale distributors in New South Wales (Young and Rashleigh), Victoria (Sullivan Wine Agencies) and Queensland (Premier Small Vineyards). There is also limited availability by mail order.

Karriview

Cnr Scotsdale and Roberts Roads, Denmark, WA 6333 **REGION** Denmark
T (08) 9840 9381 **F** (08) 9855 1549 **OPEN** Fri–Sun 11–4, school and public holidays 7 days 11–4
WINEMAKER Elizabeth Smith **EST.** 1986 **CASES** 550
PRODUCT RANGE ($25–32 R) Chardonnay, Pinot Noir.

SUMMARY One and a half hectares each of immaculately tended pinot noir and chardonnay on ultra-close spacing produce tiny quantities of two wines of at times remarkable intensity, quality and style. Available only from the winery, but worth the effort. There is some vintage variation; the winery rating is based upon the successes, not the disappointments. Typically, back vintages are available; with age, the Pinot Noir acquires strong foresty characters which are quite Burgundian.

Katnook Estate ★★★★

Riddoch Highway, Coonawarra, SA 5263 **REGION** Coonawarra
T (08) 8737 2394 **F** (08) 8737 2397 **OPEN** Mon–Fri 9–4.30, Sat 10–4.30, Sun 12–4.30
WINEMAKER Wayne Stehbens **EST.** 1979 **CASES** 100 000
PRODUCT RANGE ($17–100 R) Under the premium Katnook label: Riesling, Sauvignon Blanc, Chardonnay, Chardonnay Brut, Shiraz, Merlot, Cabernet Sauvignon, Odyssey (super-premium Cabernet), Prodigy (super-premium Shiraz); under the Riddoch label: Sauvignon Blanc, Chardonnay, Sparkling Shiraz, Shiraz, Cabernet Shiraz, Cabernet Merlot, Cabernet Sauvignon.
SUMMARY Still one of the largest contract grape growers and suppliers in Coonawarra, selling more than half of its grape production to others. The historic stone woolshed in which the second vintage in Coonawarra (1896) was made and which has served Katnook since 1980 is being restored. Together the 1997 launch of the flagship Odyssey and the 2000 follow-up with Prodigy Shiraz point the way for a higher profile for the winemaking side of the venture. In a surprise (and not widely publicised) move, Freixenet, the Spanish cava producer, has recently acquired 60 per cent of Katnook. Exports to the UK, Europe, Asia and the US.

ᵀᵀᵀᵀ **Prodigy Shiraz 2000** Spicy, cedary, blackberry aromas and flavours; very typical, fine-grained tannins attesting to cask and bottle age. **RATING** 93 **DRINK** 2015 $ 100
Sauvignon Blanc 2003 Intense, classic redcurrant/gooseberry fruit aromas; the palate is polished and fine, not quite as powerful as the bouquet suggests, but very good nonetheless. **RATING** 91 **DRINK** 2008 $ 27
Cabernet Sauvignon 2001 Complex cedar, earth, bramble and blackcurrant with a twist of cassis; medium-bodied; good length and savoury tannins. **RATING** 90 **DRINK** 2011 $ 34

ᵀᵀᵀᵀ **Chardonnay 2002** Fine, elegant style; barrel-ferment, malolactic-ferment inputs evident; cashew and melon; shortens slightly. **RATING** 89 **DRINK** 2007 $ 32
Riddoch Sauvignon Blanc 2003 Quite powerful, mouthfilling gooseberry fruit; touches of herb and grass. Showing more early in its life than its big brother. **RATING** 88 **DRINK** Now $ 17
Riesling 2003 Apple blossom aromatics, quite delicate and fine; should develop very well given time. **RATING** 87 **DRINK** 2013 $ 19
Riddoch Cabernet Merlot 2002 Light to medium-bodied; well balanced and constructed; blackcurrant fruit, gentle oak and tannins. **RATING** 87 **DRINK** 2008 $ 20

ᵀᵀᵀᵀ **Merlot 2001** **RATING** 86 **DRINK** 2009 $ 34
Riddoch Sparkling Shiraz 2001 **RATING** 85 **DRINK** 2007 $ 22
Riddoch Cabernet Sauvignon 2001 **RATING** 84 **DRINK** Now

ᵀᵀᵀ **Riddoch Cabernet Shiraz 2001** **RATING** 81 $ 20

Kay Bros Amery ★★★★

Kay Road, McLaren Vale, SA 5171 **REGION** McLaren Vale
T (08) 8323 8211 **F** (08) 8323 9199 **OPEN** Mon–Fri 9–5, weekends and public holidays 12–5
WINEMAKER Colin Kay **EST.** 1890 **CASES** 10 000
PRODUCT RANGE ($20–45 CD) Shiraz, Block 6 Shiraz, Hillside Shiraz, Shiraz Mourvedre Grenache, Merlot, Cabernet Sauvignon; Founders Very Old Tawny Solera, Liqueur Muscat.
SUMMARY A traditional winery with a rich history and nearly 20 hectares of priceless old vines; while the white wines have been variable, the red wines and fortified wines can be very good. Of particular interest is Block 6 Shiraz, made from 100-year-old vines; both vines and wine are going from strength to strength. Exports to New Zealand, Singapore, the US and Canada.

Keith Tulloch Wine   ★★★★★

Lilywood Farm, O'Connors Road, Pokolbin, NSW 2320 **REGION** Lower Hunter Valley
T (02) 4990 7867 **F** (02) 4990 7171 **OPEN** Not
WINEMAKER Keith Tulloch **EST.** 1997 **CASES** 6500
PRODUCT RANGE ($16–44 R) Under the Keith Tulloch label: Semillon, Chardonnay, Botrytis Semillon,
Kester Shiraz, Merlot, Forres Blend (Cabernet Sauvignon, Petit Verdot, Merlot); Perdiem label has
Verdelho, Chardonnay, Shiraz, Cabernet Sauvignon.
SUMMARY Keith Tulloch is, of course, a member of the Tulloch family which has played such a leading
role in the Hunter Valley for over a century. Formerly a winemaker at Lindemans and then Rothbury
Estate, he is responsible for the production of Evans Family Wines as well as developing his own label
since 1997. Currently, moves are underway to centralise all of the winemaking at Hunter Ridge Winery,
where he will be permanently based. I cannot remember being more impressed with an initial release of
wines than with those under the Keith Tulloch label. The only problem is the small scale of their
production, like that of Jeffrey Grosset in his early days. There is the same almost obsessive attention to
detail, the same almost ascetic intellectual approach, the same refusal to accept anything but the best.

ΨΨΨΨΨ **Semillon 2003** Herb, spice and lanolin aromas with much more flavour and texture (a
        touch is barrel-fermented) than usual. Lemon, lemongrass and crunchy acidity to close.
        Trophy 2003 Hunter Valley Wine Show Best Current Vintage Dry White Wine. **RATING** 96
        DRINK 2015 $ 28

ΨΨΨΨΨ **Chardonnay 2003** Complex, sophisticated aromas; à la mode funk; similarly complex
        palate, layered and long. Screwcap. **RATING** 90 **DRINK** 2009 $ 28
        Merlot 2003 Clean, fresh, lively savoury/olive notes around the core of red fruits; fine,
        supple tannins. **RATING** 90 **DRINK** 2010 $ 24
        Botrytis Semillon 2001 Luscious caramelised peach, cumquat and honey mix; soft
        acidity, but doesn't cloy. **RATING** 90 **DRINK** 2007 $ 32

ΨΨΨΨ **Shiraz Viognier 2002** Elegant and fragrant; light-bodied, but balanced and long.
        RATING 89 **DRINK** 2009 $ 28

Kellermeister/Trevor Jones   ★★★☆

Barossa Valley Highway, Lyndoch, SA 5351 **REGION** Barossa Valley
T (08) 8524 4303 **F** (08) 8524 4880 **OPEN** 7 days 9–6
WINEMAKER Trevor Jones **EST.** 1996 **CASES** 25 000
PRODUCT RANGE ($10–75 CD) Kellermeister Sauvignon Blanc Semillon, Semillon, Colombard, Blue
Moon Chardonnay, Frontignac Auslese, sparkling, Red Cebo, Black Sash Shiraz, Shiraz Merlot,
Merlot, Cabernet Sauvignon, Ports and liqueurs. Under the Trevor Jones label: Riesling, Dry Grown
Shiraz, Wild Witch Shiraz, Boots Grenache, SAFM Shiraz Cabernet, Cabernet Merlot.
SUMMARY Trevor Jones is an industry veteran, with vast experience in handling fruit from the
Barossa Valley, Eden Valley and Adelaide Hills. He has finally taken the step of introducing his own
strikingly designed label, using grapes purchased from various contract growers, with the first wines
going on sale in 1996. Exports to the US (very successful) and Japan.

Kells Creek Vineyards   ★★★

Kells Creek Road, Mittagong, NSW 2575 **REGION** Southern New South Wales Zone
T (02) 4878 5096 **F** (02) 4878 5097 **OPEN** Wed–Sun 10–4, public holidays 10–5, or by appointment
WINEMAKER Eric Priebee **EST.** 2001
PRODUCT RANGE ($13–25 CD) Riesling, Sauvignon Blanc, Chardonnay, Chloe's Red (Pinot Noir);
Swifts Lane Maddie's White and Maddie's Red (on-premise only); also Littledale Estates range.
SUMMARY Kells Creek is one of the newer businesses to open in the rapidly expanding Southern
Highlands region. It has been established by Eric Priebee and wife Gaby Barfield, drawing principally
on other vineyards established in the Southern Highlands region around Mittagong, Moss Vale and
Aylmerton. The one wine not to come from the Southern Highlands is a 2000 Pinot Noir, made before
the establishment of Kells Creek, but of excellent quality. Kells Creek itself has 1 hectare of riesling
planted, and operates an energetic marketing program under the direction of industry veteran Douglas
Hamilton. In 2003 a joint venture was made with Littledale Estates of the Hunter Valley; Kells Creek
will make the wines on behalf of the partners and market them under the Littledale Estates Brand.

Kellybrook

Fulford Road, Wonga Park, Vic 3115 **REGION** Yarra Valley
T (03) 9722 1304 **F** (03) 9722 2092 **OPEN** Mon 11–5, Tues–Sat 9–6, Sun 11–6
WINEMAKER Darren Kelly, Philip Kelly **EST.** 1960 **CASES** 3000
PRODUCT RANGE ($15–45 CD) Riesling, Gewurztraminer, Chardonnay, Pinot Noir, Shiraz, Cabernet Merlot, Brut Pinot Noir Chardonnay, Champagne Cider, Apple Brandy, Liqueur Muscat, Old Vintage Tawny Port.
SUMMARY The 8-hectare vineyard is situated at Wonga Park at the entrance to the principal wine-growing areas of the Yarra Valley, replete with picnic area and a full-scale restaurant. As well as table wine, a very competent producer of both cider and apple brandy (in Calvados style). Retail distribution through Victoria, New South Wales and Queensland; exports to the UK and Denmark.

TTTTY **Chardonnay 2002** Clean, elegant; stone fruit and citrus; fruit-driven, good length. **RATING** 90 **DRINK** 2010 $ 27

TTTY **Cabernet Merlot 2002** Clean, fresh, light to medium-bodied redcurrant/blackcurrant fruit; minimal tannins. **RATING** 86 **DRINK** 2012 $ 27

Kelly's Creek

★★★★

RSD 226a Lower Whitehills Road, Relbia, Tas 7258 **REGION** Northern Tasmania
T (03) 6234 9696 **F** (03) 6231 6222 **OPEN** Not
WINEMAKER Andrew Hood (Contract) **EST.** 1992 **CASES** 650
PRODUCT RANGE ($15–18 R) Riesling, Chardonnay, Pinot Noir, Cabernet Sauvignon.
SUMMARY Kelly's Creek draws on 1 hectare of riesling and 0.2 hectare each of chardonnay, pinot noir and cabernet sauvignon. Its majority owner is Darryl Johnson, who runs the vineyard, with help from Guy Wagner, who describes himself as 'merely a marketing minion'. Small quantities of Riesling are made for Kelly's Creek; all vintages have had success at the Tasmanian Wines Show.

Kelman Vineyards

★★★

Cnr Oakey Creek and Mount View Roads, Pokolbin, NSW 2320 **REGION** Lower Hunter Valley
T (02) 4991 5456 **F** (02) 4991 7555 **OPEN** 7 days 10–5
WINEMAKER Simon Gilbert (Contract) **EST.** 1999 **CASES** 3000
PRODUCT RANGE ($14.50–20 CD) Orchard Block Semillon, Pond Block Chardonnay, Lakeview Lane Shiraz.
SUMMARY Kelman Vineyards is a California-type development on the outskirts of Cessnock. A 40-hectare property has been subdivided into 80 residential development lots, but with 8 hectares of vines wending between the lots under common ownership. In a sign of the times, part of the chardonnay has already been grafted across to shiraz before coming into full production, and the vineyard has the potential to ultimately produce 8000 cases a year. In the meantime, each owner will receive 12 cases a year of the wines produced by the vineyard, with the balance being available for sale via mail order (phone 02 4991 5456 for details) and through a single Sydney retail outlet. The Chardonnay is a nice, fresh wine, with light melon fruit, free of the dreaded oak chips.

TTTY **Orchard Block Semillon 2003** **RATING** 84 **DRINK** 2008 $ 19.50

Kelso

NR

Princes Highway, Narrawong, Vic 3285 **REGION** Henty
T (03) 5529 2334 **OPEN** By appointment
WINEMAKER Contract
PRODUCT RANGE Riesling, Cabernet Sauvignon.
SUMMARY Howard and Glenda Simmonds have established their vineyard 11 kilometres east of Portland, and produce Riesling and Cabernet Sauvignon.

🐚 Kelvedon

PO Box 126, Swansea, Tas 7190 **REGION** Southern Tasmania
T (03) 6257 8283 **F** (03) 6257 8179 **OPEN** Not
WINEMAKER Julian Alcorso (Contract) **EST.** 1998 **CASES** 250
PRODUCT RANGE ($25 ML) Pinot Noir.
SUMMARY Jack and Gill Cotton began the development of Kelvedon by planting 1 hectare of pinot noir in 1998. The plantings were extended in 2000/01 by an additional 5 hectares, half to pinot noir and half to chardonnay; all of the production from this is under contract to Hardys. Their first vintage of Pinot Noir from the initial hectare was in the excellent vintage of 2002, and fully reflected the potential of that year.

ᵀᵀᵀᵀ♀ Estate Pinot Noir 2002 Supple, ripe, bordering on voluptuous — but not jammy — black cherry and plum; silky, smooth finish. Screwcap. **RATING** 93 **DRINK** 2008 **$** 25

Kenilworth Bluff Wines ★★☆

Lot 13 Bluff Road, Kenilworth, Qld 4574 **REGION** Queensland Coastal
T (07) 5472 3723 **OPEN** Fri–Sun 10–4, and by appointment
WINEMAKER Bruce Humphery-Smith (Contract) **EST.** 1993
PRODUCT RANGE ($13–16 CD) Semillon, Chardonnay, Shiraz, Merlot, Cabernet Sauvignon.
SUMMARY Brian and Colleen Marsh modestly describe themselves as 'little more than hobbyists' but also admit that 'our wines show tremendous promise'. They began planting the vineyards in 1993 in a hidden valley at the foot of Kenilworth Bluff, and now have 4 hectares (shiraz, cabernet sauvignon, merlot, semillon, chardonnay) coming into bearing. Presently the wines are made off-site by Bruce Humphery-Smith, but one day the Marshes hope it will be feasible to establish an on-site winery.

ᵀᵀᵀ Bluff Semillon 2002 RATING 83 **$** 15

Kennedys Keilor Valley NR

Lot 3 Overnewton Road, Keilor, Vic 3036 **REGION** Sunbury
T (03) 9311 6246 **F** (03) 9331 6246 **OPEN** By appointment
WINEMAKER Peter Dredge **EST.** 1994 **CASES** 300
PRODUCT RANGE Chardonnay.
SUMMARY A small Chardonnay specialist, producing its only wine from 1.8 hectares of estate vineyards; half is sold as grapes, half is contract-made and sold by mailing list and word of mouth.

Kevin Sobels Wines NR

Cnr Broke and Halls Roads, Pokolbin, NSW 2321 **REGION** Lower Hunter Valley
T (02) 4998 7766 **F** (02) 4998 7475 **OPEN** 7 days (no fixed hours)
WINEMAKER Kevin Sobels **EST.** 1992 **CASES** 9000
PRODUCT RANGE ($15–25 CD) Gewurztraminer, Semillon, Verdelho, Chardonnay, Sparkling Burgundy, Traminer (Sticky), Rose, Pinot Noir, Shiraz, Cabernet Shiraz, Oak Aged Port.
SUMMARY Veteran winemaker Kevin Sobels has found yet another home, drawing upon 8 hectares of vineyards (originally planted by the Ross Jones family) to produce wines sold almost entirely through the cellar door and by mail order, with limited retail representation. The cellar door offers light meals and picnic and barbecue facilities.

Kies Family Wines

Barossa Valley Way, Lyndoch, SA 5381 **REGION** Barossa Valley
T (08) 8524 4110 **F** (08) 8524 4110 **OPEN** 7 days 9.30–4.30
WINEMAKER Jim Irvine **EST.** 1969 **CASES** 2500
PRODUCT RANGE ($14–42 CD) Riesling, Unwooded Semillon, Wooded Semillon, White Barossa (sweet), Heysen Gold (sweet), Sparkling Heysen Gold (sweet sparkling), Gravel Road Sparkling Grenache Shiraz, Monkey Nut Tree Sparkling Merlot, Boutique Red, Klauber Block Shiraz, Dedication Shiraz, Lyndoch Creek Merlot, Chaff Mill Cabernet Sauvignon, Bastardo (Rose style port), Tawny Port, White Muscat.

SUMMARY The Kies family has been resident in the Barossa Valley since 1857, with the present generation of winemakers being the fifth, their children the sixth. Until 1969 the family sold almost all the grapes to others, but in that year they launched their own brand, Karrawirra. The co-existence of Killawarra forced a name change in 1983 to Redgum Vineyard, and this business was in turn subsequently sold. Later still, Kies Family Wines opened for business, drawing upon vineyards up to 100 years old which had remained in the family throughout the changes, and offering a wide range of wines through the 1880 vintage cellar door. Exports to the UK, the US, Canada and Singapore.

Kilgour Estate

NR

85 McAdams Lane, Bellarine, Vic 3223 **REGION** Geelong
T (03) 5251 2223 **F** (03) 5251 2223 **OPEN** Wed–Sun 10.30–6, 7 days in Jan
WINEMAKER Karen Coulstone (Consultant) **EST.** 1989 **CASES** 4000
PRODUCT RANGE Pinot Gris, Chardonnay, Pinot Noir, Cabernet Sauvignon, sparkling.
SUMMARY Kilgour Estate has 7 hectares of vines, and the wines are contract-made. Fruit-driven Pinot Noir and Chardonnay are winery specialties, the Pinot Noir having won at least one gold medal. The beautifully situated cellar door has a restaurant and barbecue facilities.

Kilikanoon

Penna Lane, Penwortham, SA 5453 **REGION** Clare Valley
T (08) 8843 4377 **F** (08) 8843 4377 **OPEN** Weekends and public holidays 11–5
WINEMAKER Kevin Mitchell **EST.** 1997 **CASES** 15 000
PRODUCT RANGE ($17–40 CD) Morts Block Riesling, Barrel Fermented Semillon, Sparkling Pinot Chardonnay, Second Fiddle Grenache Rose, Oracle Shiraz, Covenant Shiraz, Siblings (Shiraz Grenache), Prodigal Grenache, Blocks Road Cabernet Sauvignon, Reserve Muscat.
SUMMARY Kilikanoon has 20 hectares of estate vineyards at Leasingham and Penwortham. It had the once-in-a-lifetime experience of winning 5 of the 6 trophies awarded at the 2002 Clare Valley Wine Show, spanning Riesling, Shiraz and Cabernet, and including Best Wine of Show. Hardly surprising, then, that production has risen sharply. Wholesale distribution in South Australia, Victoria and Western Australia; exports to the US, Canada, the UK, Singapore and Hong Kong.

ỸỸỸỸỸ **Oracle Shiraz 2001** The maximum possible amount of lusciously sweet red and black fruits, vanilla oak and soft tannins have been crammed into the bottle. **RATING** 94 **DRINK** 2017 $ 40

ỸỸỸỸỸ **Mort's Block Reserve Riesling 2003** Powerful, compact, lime and herb; concentrated and lingering; built for the long haul. **RATING** 93 **DRINK** 2015 $ 28
Blacket's Vineyard Eden Valley Riesling 2003 Intense lime, herb and spice; rich and powerful, but not heavy; ready now. Screwcap. **RATING** 93 **DRINK** 2008 $ 20
Covenant Shiraz 2001 Ultra-typical Clare; inky black fruits; strong spice and tannin background; powerful wine. **RATING** 93 **DRINK** 2016 $ 40
Morts Block Riesling 2003 Powerful herb and dried flower aromas; good depth and length, with some of the riper fruit flavours of the vintage on the palate. **RATING** 91 **DRINK** 2010 $ 20
Blocks Road Cabernet Sauvignon 2001 Strongly minty/leafy overtones to the bouquet are balanced by black fruits, a dash of chocolate and oak on the well-balanced palate. **RATING** 91 **DRINK** 2011 $ 28
McLaren Vale Parable Shiraz 2001 A very typical chocolate envelope wraps around supple black fruits; medium-bodied, subtle oak. **RATING** 90 **DRINK** 2010
Prodigal Grenache 2001 Shows good varietal character throughout; a complex mix of red fruits and savoury nuances; good structure and length. **RATING** 90 **DRINK** 2008 $ 25
Medley Grenache Shiraz Mourvedre 2001 Blackberry, plum, prune and spice; lingering, tangy finish; excellent structure and tannins. **RATING** 90 **DRINK** 2008 $ 25

ỸỸỸỸ **Second Fiddle Grenache Rose 2003** **RATING** 85 **DRINK** Now $ 18

🐚 Killara Park Estate ★★★☆

Suite 1230, 1 Queens Road, Melbourne, Vic 3004 (postal) **REGION** Yarra Valley
T (03) 9863 7505 **F** (03) 9863 7510 **OPEN** Not
WINEMAKER MasterWineMakers, Rob Dolan (Contract) **EST.** 1997 **CASES** 3500
PRODUCT RANGE ($16–20 ML) Chardonnay, Pinot Noir, Shiraz, Merlot.
SUMMARY The striking label design hints at the involvement of the Palazzo family owners in winemaking in Lombardia (Italy) since the 16th century. It also tells you that this is a highly focused, modern, wine-producing company. With just over 60 hectares of vineyards established since 1997, Killara Park is one of the larger grape suppliers in the Yarra Valley, capable of producing fruit of high quality from its steeply sloping vineyards. Around 90 per cent of the grapes are sold to companies such as Coldstream Hills and McWilliam's, but 10 per cent is now being vinified for the label, which will be sold only by mail order and through the Killara Park website <www.killarapark.com.au>.

▼▼▼▼ **Pinot Noir 2002** Light strawberry/cherry aromas; light entry, yet deceptive length and aftertaste. **RATING** 88 **DRINK** 2008 $16
Chardonnay 2002 Round and smooth, yet quite complex, showing development and barrel-ferment inputs; ripe melon/peach. **RATING** 87 **DRINK** 2007 $16
Merlot 2002 Light to medium-bodied; savoury/earthy/tangy varietal character; good length and structure. **RATING** 87 **DRINK** 2008 $14

▼▼▼▽ **Shiraz 2001 RATING** 84 **DRINK** 2007 $20

▼▼▼ **Merlot 2001 RATING** 83 $14

Killawarra ★★★

Tanunda Road, Nuriootpa, SA 5355 **REGION** Barossa Valley
T (08) 8560 9389 **F** (08) 8562 1669 **OPEN** Not
WINEMAKER Steve Goodwin **EST.** 1975
PRODUCT RANGE ($9.95–16.60 R) Only sparkling wines: Brut, Brut Cremant, Premier Brut, Killawarra 'K' series Vintage Pinot Noir Chardonnay and Sparkling Shiraz Cabernet.
SUMMARY Purely a Southcorp brand dedicated to sparkling wine, without any particular presence in terms of either vineyards or winery, but increasingly styled in a mode different from the Seaview or Seppelt wines. As one would expect, the wines are competitively priced, and what is more, have performed well in national wine shows.

▼▼▼▽ **Reserve Pinot Chardonnay 1999 RATING** 86 **DRINK** Now $16.60
Non Vintage Brut NV RATING 84 **DRINK** Now $10.65

Killerby ★★★★

Caves Road, Wilyabrup, WA 6280 **REGION** Margaret River
T 1800 655 722 **F** 1800 679 578 **OPEN** Not
WINEMAKER Mark Matthews **EST.** 1973 **CASES** 15 000
PRODUCT RANGE ($19–30 CD) Semillon, Semillon Sauvignon Blanc, Sauvignon Blanc, Chardonnay, Shiraz, Cabernet Sauvignon and budget-priced April Class (Traminer Semillon Chardonnay).
SUMMARY Has moved from Geographe to the Margaret River following the acquisition of a long-established vineyard on Caves Road with 23-year-old chardonnay vines. It continues to own its substantial and mature vineyards in Geographe, where the wines are still made. Exports to the US and Denmark.

Kimbarra Wines ★★★★

422 Barkly Street, Ararat, Vic 3377 **REGION** Grampians
T (03) 5352 2238 **F** (03) 5342 1950 **OPEN** Mon–Fri 9–5
WINEMAKER Peter Leeke, Ian McKenzie **EST.** 1990 **CASES** 1000
PRODUCT RANGE ($14–22 CD) Riesling, Shiraz, Cabernet Sauvignon.
SUMMARY Peter and David Leeke have established 12 hectares of riesling, shiraz and cabernet sauvignon, the three varieties which have proved best suited to the Grampians region. The particularly well made wines deserve a wider audience.

Kimber Wines

NR

Chalk Hill Road, McLaren Vale, SA 5171 **REGION** McLaren Vale
T (08) 8323 9773 **F** (08) 8323 9773 **OPEN** 7 days, Dec–Apr 9–6, or by appointment
WINEMAKER Reg Wilkinson **EST.** 1996 **CASES** 300
PRODUCT RANGE ($14–22 CD) Unwooded Chardonnay, Cabernet Sauvignon.
SUMMARY Kimber Wines is primarily a grape grower, selling its production from 2.5 hectares each of chardonnay and cabernet sauvignon, and 0.6 hectare of petit verdot to other, larger producers. A very small amount of its grapes are retained and vinified under the Kimber Wines label, typically selling out within a few months of release through the cellar door (hence the restricted opening hours). An added attraction is pick-your-own fruit (peaches, apricots and plums) during the summer months.

King River Estate

★★★

RMB 9300, Wangaratta, Vic 3677 **REGION** King Valley
T (03) 5729 3689 **F** (03) 5729 3688 **OPEN** Weekends, or by appointment
WINEMAKER Trevor Knaggs **EST.** 1996 **CASES** 2500
PRODUCT RANGE ($18–22 CD) Verdelho, Chardonnay, Nancy Shiraz, Merlot, Cabernet Sauvignon.
SUMMARY Trevor Knaggs, with the assistance of his father Collin (sic) began the establishment of King River Estate in 1990, making the first wines in 1996. The initial plantings were of 3.3 hectares each of chardonnay and cabernet sauvignon, followed by 8 hectares of merlot and 3 hectares of shiraz. More recent plantings have extended the varietal range with verdelho, viognier, barbera and sangiovese, lifting the total plantings to a substantial 18 hectares. Home-stay accommodation is available in the farm-style guesthouse. Needless to say, bookings are essential.

Kings of Kangaroo Ground

NR

15 Graham Road, Kangaroo Ground, Vic 3097 **REGION** Yarra Valley
T (03) 9712 0666 **F** (03) 9712 0566 **OPEN** Mon–Sat 10–6, Sun 12–6
WINEMAKER Ken King, Geoff Anson, Neil Johannesen **EST.** 1990 **CASES** 600
PRODUCT RANGE ($16–45 CD) Chardonnay, Pinot Noir, Multi-vintage Pinot Noir, Shiraz, Yarra Valley Cabernet Merlot, Cabernet Sauvignon.
SUMMARY Ken King's involvement in wine began back in 1984, as an amateur member of the Eltham and District Winemakers Guild. Around that time, the Guild was asked to manage a tiny (0.3 of an acre) experimental vineyard planted on the rich volcanic soil of Kangaroo Ground. In 1988 Ken King purchased a little under 3 hectares of similar land, which he describes as 'chocolate cake', and established 1 hectare of chardonnay and 0.6 hectare of pinot noir in 1990. Up until 2000, the grapes were sold to Diamond Valley, but each year King retained sufficient grapes to produce a barrel or two of Pinot Noir per vintage. He began experimenting with multi-vintage blends of pinot with up to 5 years of continuous ageing in French barriques. The wines have been well received at amateur wine shows, and the planned cellar door has now opened.

▼▼▼ **Ground Pinot Noir 2002 RATING** 83 **$** 26

Kingsley

NR

6 Kingsley Court, Portland, Vic 3305 **REGION** Henty
T (03) 5523 1864 **F** (03) 5523 1644 **OPEN** 7 days 1–4
WINEMAKER Contract **EST.** 1983 **CASES** 500
PRODUCT RANGE ($14–16 CD) Riesling, Chardonnay, Botrytis Riesling, Cabernet Sauvignon.
SUMMARY Only a small part of the 10 hectares is made into wine under contract; the remainder is sold as grapes. Older vintages are sometimes available at the cellar door, and tasting is strongly recommended, as there appears to be significant vintage variation.

🐌 Kingsley Grove

NR

49 Stuart Valley Drive, Kingaroy, Qld 4610 (postal) **REGION** South Burnett
T (07) 4163 6433 **F** (07) 4162 2201 **OPEN** Not
WINEMAKER Michael Berry, Patricia Berry **EST.** 1998
PRODUCT RANGE ($12.50–14.50 ML) Semillon, Cloud View Verdelho, Jimmy's Block Chardonnay,

Kingsley White, Grove Rose, Hilltop Shiraz, Merlot, Chambourcin, Long Row Sangiovese, Estate Cabernet Shiraz, Cabernet Sauvignon.

SUMMARY Michael and Patricia Berry have established a substantial vineyard of 8.7 hectares near Kingaroy. It is planted to verdelho, chardonnay, semillon, shiraz, merlot, sangiovese, chambourcin and cabernet sauvignon, and the wines are made on-site in a winery built in 2001 and extended in 2003. Michael Berry has undertaken viticulture studies at Melbourne University. The wines are sold by mail order and via the internet, <www.kingsleygrove.com>.

Kingston Estate ★★★☆

Sturt Highway, Kingston-on-Murray, SA 5331 **REGION** Riverland
T (08) 8130 4500 **F** (08) 8130 4511 **OPEN** By appointment
WINEMAKER Bill Moularadellis **EST.** 1979 **CASES** 100 000
PRODUCT RANGE ($8–21 R) A substantial range of branded varietal wines spanning price points from $8 to $20. At the top comes the Echelon range, for the best Chardonnay, Shiraz, Cabernet Sauvignon and Petit Verdot made each year (irrespective of origin); then comes the Empiric Selection of experimental varieties (such as Arneis, Viognier, Petit Verdot, Durif and Tempranillo).
SUMMARY Kingston Estate is a substantial and successful Riverland winery, crushing 10 000 tonnes a year and exporting 80 per cent of its production. It is only in recent years that it has turned its attention to the domestic market, with national distribution. It has also set up long-term purchase contracts with growers in the Clare Valley, the Adelaide Hills, Langhorne Creek and Mount Benson, and embarked on a program of expanding its varietal range.

🍷🍷🍷🍷🍷 **Echelon Shiraz 2001** Ripe plum and blackberry fruit; exceptionally smooth and supple, immaculately handled extract and oak. **RATING** 95 **DRINK** 2012 $ 18

🍷🍷🍷🍷🍷 **Empiric Selection Petit Verdot 2000** Holding colour very well; blackcurrant, plum and spice; sweet, fine tannins; considerable power and depth. Winner of 6 gold medals. **RATING** 90 **DRINK** 2008 $ 18

🍷🍷🍷🍷 **Empiric Selection Arneis 2003** Pear/pear skin aromas and flavours; particular acidity enlivens the long palate. Screwcap. **RATING** 89 **DRINK** 2008 $ 19
Empiric Selection Viognier 2003 Aromatic and clean, almost flowery; nice peach and spice mid-palate; good value. Screwcap. **RATING** 88 **DRINK** 2007 $ 19
Sauvignon Blanc 2002 A clean, dry, minerally bouquet leads into a well-structured palate with a mix of citrus and mineral. From the Adelaide Hills. **RATING** 87 **DRINK** Now $ 13.50
Echelon Chardonnay 2002 Generous, soft and sweet peachy fruit; fruit-driven, ready to roll. **RATING** 87 **DRINK** Now $ 21
Echelon Cabernet Sauvignon 2001 Pleasant light to medium-bodied wine; cassis, raspberry and redcurrant; fresh, but not in the class of the Echelon Shiraz. **RATING** 87 **DRINK** 2009 $ 21
Empiric Selection Durif 2000 Prune, blackberry and dark chocolate aromas and flavours; good depth; fine tannins and a touch of cedar. **RATING** 87 **DRINK** 2007 $ 18

🍷🍷🍷🍷 **Outback Chase Coonawarra Shiraz 2001** **RATING** 86 **DRINK** Now $ 9.99
Sarantos Soft Press Merlot 2002 **RATING** 86 **DRINK** Now $ 12.95
Ashwood Grove Cabernet Sauvignon 2002 **RATING** 86 **DRINK** Now
Cabernet Sauvignon 2002 **RATING** 86 **DRINK** 2010 $ 13
Outback Chase Coonawarra Cabernet Sauvignon 2002 **RATING** 86 **DRINK** 2007 $ 9.99
Empiric Selection Barbera 2003 **RATING** 86 **DRINK** Now $ 19
Ashwood Grove Cabernet Sauvignon 2002 **RATING** 86 **DRINK** 2007 $ 13.99
Sarantos Soft Press Sauvignon Blanc 2003 **RATING** 85 **DRINK** Now $ 12.95
Outback Chase Chardonnay 2002 **RATING** 85 **DRINK** Now $ 9.99
Merlot 2002 **RATING** 85 **DRINK** Now $ 13
Petit Verdot 2001 **RATING** 85 **DRINK** Now $ 14
Empiric Selection Tempranillo 2002 **RATING** 85 **DRINK** Now $ 18
Empiric Selection Viognier 2001 **RATING** 84 **DRINK** Now $ 19

🍷🍷🍷 **Shiraz 2002** **RATING** 83 $ 13
Sarantos Soft Press Australian Sparkling NV **RATING** 83 $ 12.95
Ashwood Grove Shiraz 2002 **RATING** 82 $ 13.99

Kingtree Wines

NR

Kingtree Road, Wellington Mills via Dardanup, WA 6326 **REGION** Geographe
T (08) 9728 3050 **F** (08) 9728 3113 **OPEN** 7 days 12–5.30
WINEMAKER Contract **EST.** 1991 **CASES** 1000
PRODUCT RANGE ($16–20 CD) Riesling, Sauvignon Blanc, Gerrasse White, Cabernet Merlot.
SUMMARY Kingtree Wines, with 2.5 hectares of estate plantings, is part of the Kingtree Lodge development, a four and a half-star luxury retreat in dense jarrah forest.

Kinloch Wines

 ★★☆

Kainui, Wairere Road, Booroolite, Vic 3723 **REGION** Upper Goulburn
T (03) 5777 3447 **F** (03) 5777 3449 **OPEN** 7 days 10–4
WINEMAKER Al Fencaros (Contract) **EST.** 1996
PRODUCT RANGE ($20–35 CD) Chardonnay, Pinot Noir, Pinot Meunier; Kainui Estate Unwooded Chardonnay, Kainui Estate Chardonnay.
SUMMARY Susan and Malcolm Kinloch began the development of their vineyard in 1996, at an altitude of 400 metres on the northern slopes of the Great Dividing Range, 15 minutes' drive from Mansfield. One of the unusual varieties in the portfolio is Pinot Meunier. The grapes are hand-picked and taken to the Yarra Valley for contract making.

▼▼▼   Chardonnay 2001 RATING 82

Kinvarra Estate

NR

RMB 5141, New Norfolk, Tas 7140 **REGION** Southern Tasmania
T (03) 6286 1333 **F** (03) 6286 2026 **OPEN** Not
WINEMAKER Andrew Hood **EST.** 1990 **CASES** 90
PRODUCT RANGE ($13.50–15 ML) Riesling, Pinot Noir.
SUMMARY Kinvarra is the part-time occupation of David and Sue Bevan; their wonderful 1827 homestead is depicted on the label. There is only 1 hectare of vines, half riesling and half pinot noir, and most of the crop is sold to Wellington Wines.

Kirkham Estate

NR

3 Argyle Street, Camden, NSW 2570 **REGION** Sydney Basin
T (02) 4655 7722 **F** (02) 4655 7722 **OPEN** 7 days 11–5
WINEMAKER Stan Aliprandi **EST.** 1993 **CASES** 3000
PRODUCT RANGE ($6–15.50 CD) Estate range of Traminer Riesling, Semillon, Semillon Chardonnay, Chardonnay, Sparkling Pinot Noir White, Sparkling Pinot Noir Pink, Old Gold Botrytis Semillon, White Lambrusco, lambrusco, Pinot Noir, Shiraz, Merlot, Cabernet Sauvignon, Port; Camden Vale range of Semillon Chardonnay, Classic Dry White, Classic Dry Red, Cabernet Shiraz.
SUMMARY Kirkham Estate is one of six or so wine producers near Camden; it's a far cry from the 18 producers of the mid-19th century, but still indicative of the growth of vineyards and winemakers everywhere. It is the venture of Leif Karlsson and Stan Aliprandi, the latter a former Riverina winemaker with an interesting career going back over 30 years. It draws upon 9 hectares of vineyards, planted to chardonnay, semillon, verdelho, petit verdot, shiraz, merlot, pinot noir and cabernet sauvignon, supplemented, it would seem, by grapes (and wines) purchased elsewhere.

Kirrihill Estates

 ★★★★

Wendouree Road, Clare, SA 5453 **REGION** Clare Valley
T (08) 8842 4087 **F** (08) 8842 4089 **OPEN** 7 days 10–4
WINEMAKER Richard Rowe, David Mavor **EST.** 1998 **CASES** 25 000
PRODUCT RANGE ($14.50–20 CD) Clare Valley Riesling, Clare Valley Semillon, Adelaide Hills Sauvignon Blanc, Adelaide Hills Chardonnay, Clare Valley Grenache Shiraz Mourvedre, Clare Valley Shiraz, Langhorne Creek Shiraz, Clare Valley Cabernet Sauvignon; Companions Riesling, Shiraz.
SUMMARY One of the larger vineyard and winery developments over the past 5 years, with a 7000-tonne, $10 million winery designed for modular expansion to 20 000 tonnes, currently storing

3 million litres of wine. It is associated with the Kirribilly Wine Group, which has developed and now manages 1300 hectares of vineyards through the Clare Valley, Adelaide Hills and Langhorne Creek. Small parcels of its managed vineyards are taken for the Kirrihill Estates wine range, with a Cabernet Sauvignon from each of the Clare and Langhorne Creek, plus a Sauvignon Blanc from the Adelaide Hills to complete the range. Richard Rowe, the chief winemaker, was responsible for many years for the Leasingham Classic Clare range, while assistant David Mavor worked both in France and for Tyrrell's in the Hunter Valley. The quality of the wines is thus no surprise.

ᵀᵀᵀᵀᵀ **Companions Riesling 2002** Lime blossom and herb aromas; crisp, lively and minerally in the mouth; clever touch of residual sugar; good length; a fine wine representing great value. **RATING** 92 **DRINK** 2012 $ 15

ᵀᵀᵀᵀ **Clare Valley Shiraz 2001** Medium-bodied, smooth and supple blackberry fruit; balanced tannins and oak. Easily accessible. Three gold medals: Melbourne, Griffith and Rutherglen. **RATING** 89 **DRINK** 2008 $ 24
Cabernet Sauvignon 2001 Blackberry, cassis and mint fruit, which is powerful but left of centre. **RATING** 88 **DRINK** 2010 $ 22

ᵀᵀᵀᵀ **Clare Valley Riesling 2003** **RATING** 86 **DRINK** 2008 $ 19
Companions Shiraz 2001 **RATING** 86 **DRINK** 2008 $ 15
Langhorne Creek Cabernet Sauvignon 2001 **RATING** 85 **DRINK** 2010 $ 22

Kirwan's Bridge Wines   NR

Lobb's Lane/Kirwan's Bridge Road, Nagambie, Vic 3608 **REGION** Nagambie Lakes
T (03) 5794 1777 **F** (03) 5794 1993 **OPEN** 7 days 10–5
WINEMAKER Anna Hubbard **EST.** 1997 **CASES** 1500
PRODUCT RANGE ($15–35 CD) Riesling, Marsanne, Shiraz, Merlot.
SUMMARY A major development, with over 35 hectares planted: a major emphasis on the Rhône varietals (7.9 hectares marsanne, 2.7 hectares viognier, 1.3 hectares of roussanne; and 11.2 hectares shiraz, 2.7 hectares mourvedre and 2.5 hectares grenache). A side bet on 4.8 hectares cabernet sauvignon, 2.4 hectares merlot and 1.3 hectares riesling rounds off the planting. The cellar door complex includes a restaurant (open for lunch and dinner Thursday to Sunday — dinner bookings essential), conference facility and art gallery. A protracted family inheritance dispute has severely impacted on the business.

Knappstein Lenswood Vineyards   ★★★★☆

Crofts Road, Lenswood, SA 5240 **REGION** Adelaide Hills
T (08) 8389 8111 **F** (08) 8389 8555 **OPEN** By appointment
WINEMAKER Tim Knappstein **EST.** 1981 **CASES** 10 000
PRODUCT RANGE ($22–51 R) Semillon, Sauvignon Blanc, Chardonnay, Pinot Noir, The Palatine.
SUMMARY Knappstein Lenswood Vineyards is now the sole (and full-time) occupation of Tim and Annie Knappstein, Tim Knappstein having retired from the winery which bears his name in the Clare Valley, and having sold most of the Clare vineyards to Petaluma (along with the wine business). With 25.5 hectares of close-planted, vertically trained vineyards maintained to his exacting standards, the business will undoubtedly add to the reputation of the Adelaide Hills as an ultra-premium area. Complex Chardonnay, intense Sauvignon Blanc and broodingly powerful yet stylish Pinot Noir are trailblazers. The wines are exported to the UK, the US, Canada, Japan, Belgium, Switzerland, Germany, Japan and Singapore.

ᵀᵀᵀᵀᵀ **Sauvignon Blanc 2003** Quite intense and long; mineral, capsicum and redcurrant; good balance. **RATING** 91 **DRINK** Now $ 23
Chardonnay 2001 Glowing yellow-green; complex, rich yellow peach and nectarine fruit offset by integrated barrel-ferment oak; long finish, good acidity. **RATING** 91 **DRINK** 2009 $ 24
Pinot Noir 2002 Ultra-complex spice, forest, plum and black cherry aromas; rich and powerful black plum fruit and velvety mouthfeel; in the take-no-prisoners end of the spectrum. **RATING** 91 **DRINK** 2009 $ 45

ᵀᵀᵀᵀ **Gewurztraminer 2003** **RATING** 85 **DRINK** 2011 $ 22

Knappstein Wines ★★★★

2 Pioneer Avenue, Clare, SA 5453 **REGION** Clare Valley
T (08) 8842 2600 **F** (08) 8842 3831 **OPEN** Mon–Fri 9–5, Sat 11–5, Sun and public holidays 11–4
WINEMAKER Andrew Hardy **EST.** 1976 **CASES** 45 000
PRODUCT RANGE ($11–42 R) Hand Picked Riesling, Dry Style Gewurztraminer, Semillon Sauvignon Blanc, Chardonnay, Shiraz, Chainsaw Shiraz, Enterprise Shiraz, Cabernet Merlot, Enterprise Cabernet Sauvignon.
SUMMARY Very much part of the Petaluma empire, with Andrew Hardy now a veteran of the region. The 90 hectares of mature estate vineyards in prime locations supply grapes both for the Knappstein brand and for wider Petaluma use. Exports to the UK, Canada, Japan and New Zealand.

ŸŸŸŸŸ **Enterprise Cabernet Sauvignon 2000** Medium-bodied; black fruits, herbs and touches of mocha and caramel on a complex palate. **RATING** 90 **DRINK** 2013 $42

ŸŸŸŸ **Hand Picked Riesling 2003** Solid, powerful, compact; rich, ripe fruit. **RATING** 89 **DRINK** 2007 $19
Enterprise Shiraz 2000 A neatly balanced offering of blackberry, cherry, mint and chocolate; soft tannins, nice oak. **RATING** 89 **DRINK** 2010 $42
Gewurztraminer 2003 Intense nutmeg spice aromas and flavours; unusual in the context of the Clare Valley; interesting. **RATING** 88 **DRINK** 2007 $19
Shiraz 2001 A complex mix of savoury, earthy, spicy red and black cherry aromas moving more to blackberry on the palate; fine tannins. **RATING** 88 **DRINK** 2011 $21
Semillon Sauvignon Blanc 2003 Synergistic, nicely balanced blend of gooseberry and a citrussy finish. **RATING** 87 **DRINK** Now $19

ŸŸŸŸ **Clare Valley Chardonnay 2002** **RATING** 84 **DRINK** Now $19

Knights Vines ★★☆

655 Henry Lawson Drive, Mudgee, NSW 2850 **REGION** Mudgee
T (02) 6373 3954 **F** (02) 6373 3750 **OPEN** Wed–Fri and Sun 10–4, Sat 10–5
WINEMAKER Peter Knights **EST.** 1985 **CASES** 1350
PRODUCT RANGE ($12–20 CD) Riesling, Sauvignon Blanc, Shiraz, Merlin Rouge, Merlot, Cabernet Sauvignon, Round Table Tawny, Lancelot's Liqueur.
SUMMARY Sometimes called Knights Vines, although the wines are marketed under the Eurunderee Flats label. There are 5 hectares of vineyards producing white wines of variable quality, and rather better dry red table wines. Exports to Hong Kong.

ŸŸŸ **Cabernet Sauvignon 2002** **RATING** 83 $18
Shiraz 2002 **RATING** 82 $20
Shiraz 2001 **RATING** 82 $20
Merlot 2002 **RATING** 82 $16

Knots Wines ★★★★

A8 Shurans Lane, Heathcote, Vic 3552 **REGION** Heathcote
T (03) 5441 5429 **F** (03) 5441 5429 **OPEN** Select weekends, or by appointment
WINEMAKER Lindsay Ross **EST.** 2001 **CASES** 750
PRODUCT RANGE ($20–25 ML) Drummers Plait Semillon Sauvignon Blanc, Carrick Bend Chardonnay, Rose Lashing Rose, Sheep Shank Shiraz, Larks Head Cabernet Merlot, Capstan Cabernet Sauvignon.
SUMMARY This is the venture of erstwhile Balgownie winemaker Lindsay Ross and wife Noeline, and is part of a broader business known as Winedrops; Winedrops acts as a wine production and distribution network for the Bendigo wine industry. The Knots wines are sourced from a number of long-established Heathcote and Bendigo vineyards, providing 0.5 hectare each of semillon and chardonnay, and 4 hectares each of shiraz and cabernets. The viticultural accent is on low-cropping vineyards with concentrated flavours, the winemaking emphasis on flavour, finesse and varietal expression.

Knowland Estate

NR

Mount Vincent Road, Running Stream, NSW 2850 **REGION** Mudgee
T (02) 6358 8420 **F** (02) 6358 8423 **OPEN** By appointment
WINEMAKER Peter Knowland **EST.** 1990 **CASES** 250
PRODUCT RANGE ($12.50–18 CD) Mt Vincent Semillon, Mt Vincent Sauvignon Blanc, Orange Pinot Noir, Mt Vincent Pinot Noir.
SUMMARY The former Mount Vincent Winery, at an altitude of 1080 metres, which sells much of its grape production from the 4 hectares of vineyards to other makers.

Koltz

NR

5 Adams Road, Blewitt Springs, SA 5171 (postal) **REGION** McLaren Vale
T (08) 8383 0023 **F** (08) 8383 0023 **OPEN** Not
WINEMAKER Mark Day **EST.** 1994 **CASES** 2000
PRODUCT RANGE ($20–25 ML) Shiraz, Mourvedre Shiraz Grenache, DogDay Shiraz, The Carbine (Shiraz Cabernet Sauvignon).
SUMMARY Mark Day and Anna Koltunow released their first wine in 1995, using grapes from the Bottin Vineyard in McLaren Vale. Mark Day had worked as winemaker at Maxwell Wines and Wirra Wirra in McLaren Vale, and has been a Flying Winemaker for six consecutive vintages in Europe. Day and Koltunow have decided to specialise in Shiraz and Shiraz blends from the McLaren Vale region, but have added sangiovese and mourvedre to the mix since the 2002 vintage. The wines are exported to England and the US, and can be ordered by mail.

Kominos Wines

NR

New England Highway, Severnlea, Qld 4352 **REGION** Granite Belt
T (07) 4683 4311 **F** (07) 4683 4291 **OPEN** 7 days 9–5
WINEMAKER Tony Comino **EST.** 1976 **CASES** 4000
PRODUCT RANGE ($12–20 CD) Semillon, Sauvignon Blanc, Sauvignon Semillon, Chenin Blanc Semillon Sauvignon Blanc, Chardonnay, Vin Doux, Nouvelle, Shiraz, Shiraz Cabernet, Merlot, Cabernet Franc, Cabernet Sauvignon.
SUMMARY Tony Comino is a dedicated viticulturist and winemaker and, together with his father, he has battled hard to prevent ACI obtaining a monopoly on glass production in Australia, foreseeing many of the things which have in fact occurred. However, Kominos keeps a very low profile, selling all of its wine through the cellar door and by mailing list.

Kongwak Hills Winery

NR

1030 Korumburra–Wonthaggi Road, Kongwak, Vic 3951 **REGION** Gippsland
T (03) 5657 3267 **F** (03) 5657 3267 **OPEN** Weekends and public holidays 10–5
WINEMAKER Peter Kimmer **EST.** 1989 **CASES** 600
PRODUCT RANGE ($10–25 CD) Riesling, Pinot Noir, Shiraz, Cabernet Malbec.
SUMMARY Peter and Jenny Kimmer started the development of their vineyard in 1989 and now have 0.5 hectare each of cabernet sauvignon, shiraz and pinot noir, together with lesser quantities of malbec, merlot and riesling. Most of the wines are sold at the cellar door, with limited distribution in Melbourne through Woods Wines Pty Ltd of Fitzroy.

Koonara

★★★☆

Skinner Road, Coonawarra, SA 5263 **REGION** Coonawarra
T (08) 8736 3267 **F** (08) 8736 3020 **OPEN** By appointment
WINEMAKER Dru Resckke, Peter Douglas (Consultant) **EST.** 1988
PRODUCT RANGE ($24–29 CD) Ezra's Gift Shiraz, Ambriel's Gift Cabernet Sauvignon.
SUMMARY Koonara is a sister, or, more appropriately, brother company to Reschke Wines. The latter is run by Burke Reschke, Koonara by his brother Dru. Both are sons of Trevor Reschke, who planted the first vines on the Koonara property in 1988. The initial planting was of cabernet sauvignon, followed by shiraz in 1993 and additional cabernet sauvignon in 1998. Peter Douglas, formerly Wynn's chief winemaker before moving overseas for some years, has returned to the district and is consultant winemaker for Koonara.

ŸŸŸŸ **Ezra's Gift Shiraz 2000** Slightly blurred bouquet; more focus in the mouth; fresh raspberry/redcurrant fruit; fine tannins. **RATING** 87 **DRINK** 2010 $ 24
Ambriel's Gift Cabernet Sauvignon 2002 Very ripe fruit ranging through plum, blackcurrant and blackberry; elements of spice. **RATING** 87 **DRINK** 2008 $ 29

Kooroomba Vineyards

168 FM Bells Road, Mount Alford via Boonah, Qld 4310 **REGION** Queensland Zone
T (07) 5463 0022 **F** (07) 5463 0441 **OPEN** Wed–Sun and public holidays 10–5
WINEMAKER Ballandean Estate (Contract) **EST.** 1998 **CASES** 2000
PRODUCT RANGE ($15–22 CD) Verdelho Marsanne, Alba, Chardonnay, Shiraz, Cabernet Merlot, Cabernet Sauvignon.
SUMMARY Kooroomba Vineyards is little more than 1 hour's drive from the Brisbane CBD, offering cellar-door wine tasting and sales, a vineyard restaurant, and a lavender farm. The 7.5 hectare vineyard is planted to verdelho, marsanne, merlot, shiraz and cabernet sauvignon, with chardonnay purchased from contract growers.

Kooyong ★★★★

PO Box 153, Red Hill South, Vic 3937 (postal) **REGION** Mornington Peninsula
T (03) 5989 7355 **F** (03) 5989 7677 **OPEN** Not
WINEMAKER Sandro Mosele **EST.** 1996 **CASES** 5000
PRODUCT RANGE ($36–45 R) Chardonnay, Pinot Noir.
SUMMARY Kooyong, owned by Giorgio and Dianne Gjergia, is one of the larger new entrants on the Mornington Peninsula scene, releasing its first wines in June 2001. Thirty-four hectares of vines are in bearing, 0.75 pinot noir, and 0.3 chardonnay. Winemaker Sandro Mosele is a graduate of Charles Sturt University, having previously gained a science degree. He has worked at Rochford and learnt from Sergio Carlei, of the Green Vineyards, and makes the wine at an on-site winery which also provides contract wine-making services for others. Production will increase to 10 000 cases from the first vintage (1999) of 1000 cases. The wines are distributed through Negociants Australia, and the quality is impressive. Exports to the US, the UK and Singapore.

ŸŸŸŸŸ **Chardonnay 2001** Appealing light green-gold colour; at once complex yet understated, with beautiful balance and integration of all the flavour components. **RATING** 91 **DRINK** 2007 $ 37

ŸŸŸŸ **Pinot Noir 2001** Shows clear varietal fruit throughout, with a complex mix of sappy/savoury/slightly stemmy components in an authentic but slightly austere mode. **RATING** 89 **DRINK** 2007 $ 40

Kopparossa Wines

PO Box 922, Naracoorte, SA 5271 **REGION** Wrattonbully
T 1800 620 936 **F** (08) 8762 0937 **OPEN** Not
WINEMAKER Gavin Hogg, Mike Press **EST.** 1996 **CASES** 5000
PRODUCT RANGE ($15–27 CD) Coonawarra range of Chardonnay, Shiraz, Cabernet Sauvignon Merlot; Limestone Coast (Wrattonbully) range of Shiraz, Merlot, Cabernet Sauvignon.
SUMMARY Kopparossa has undergone several transformations since its establishment in 1996, but the partnership of Gavin Hogg and Mike Press, with more than 60 years winemaking and grape-growing experience between them, has continued throughout. The business is now based on two estate vineyards, one in the Adelaide Hills, the other in Coonawarra, plus contract-grown grapes from Wrattonbully. The Adelaide Hills property, developed by the Press family and known as Kenton Valley, has 24 hectares of pinot noir, merlot, shiraz, cabernet sauvignon and chardonnay planted throughout 1998 and 1999. The Coonawarra vineyard is (at first sight controversially, but the vineyard is in fact on Stentiford Road) called Stentiford and is, quite literally, Gavin and Julie Hogg's back yard. It was planted between 1992 and 1993 with cabernet sauvignon, merlot and chardonnay.

ŸŸŸŸ **Coonawarra Cabernet Merlot 2000** **RATING** 85 **DRINK** 2007 $ 27

🍃 Kouark Vineyard ★★★☆

300 Thomspon Road, Drouin South, Vic 3818 **REGION** Gippsland
T (03) 5627 6337 **F** (03) 5627 6337 **OPEN** Weekends 12–5
WINEMAKER Phil Gray **EST.** 1997 **CASES** 1000
PRODUCT RANGE ($16–22 CD) Light Oaked Chardonnay, Oaked Chardonnay, Pinot Noir, Shiraz, Cabernet Sauvignon.
SUMMARY Dairy farmers Phil and Jane Gray decided to diversify with the establishment of a 4-hectare vineyard on part of their farm: 1.3 hectares each of chardonnay and pinot noir, and 0.7 hectare each of shiraz and cabernet sauvignon (and a few pinot gris vines) have been planted on a northeasterly slope, bordered on the east by a 2.4-hectare lake. As well as their general farming background, they have undertaken various Charles Sturt University grape and wine production courses, and similar short courses from other education facilities. A simple but appropriately equipped winery has been established on-site, and the wines are sold through a number of local stores and cafés. The name, incidentally, is believed to be the word for kookaburra in the language of the local Kurnai tribe.

🍷🍷🍷🍷 **Pinot Noir 2001** Savoury, spicy, stemmy aromas, moving to sweet plum and black cherry fruit on palate; fine tannins. **RATING** 88 **DRINK** Now $ 22
Shiraz 2001 Fruit-driven plum, prune and licorice; soft tannins; subtle oak handling throughout. **RATING** 87 **DRINK** 2010 $ 22

Kraanwood ★★★

8 Woodies Place, Richmond, Tas 7025 **REGION** Southern Tasmania
T (03) 6260 2540 **OPEN** Not
WINEMAKER Frank van der Kraan **EST.** 1994 **CASES** 150
PRODUCT RANGE ($16–25 ML) Schonburger, Montage, Unwooded Chardonnay, Pinot Noir.
SUMMARY Frank van der Kraan and wife Barbara established their 0.5-hectare vineyard between 1994 and 1995, with approximately equal plantings of pinot noir, chardonnay and cabernet sauvignon. Frank van der Kraan also manages the 1-hectare Pembroke Vineyard, and procures from it small quantities of schonburger, chardonnay, riesling and sauvignon blanc.

🍷🍷🍷 **Pinot Noir 2002 RATING** 83 $ 25

Kreglinger Estate NR

Limestone Coast Road, Mount Benson, SA 5265 (postal) **REGION** Mount Benson
T (08) 8768 5080 **F** (08) 8768 5083 **OPEN** Not
WINEMAKER Steve Grimley, Andrew Lanauze, Ralph Fowler **EST.** 2000 **CASES** 85 000
PRODUCT RANGE Riesling, Sauvignon Blanc, Pinot Gris, Shiraz, Merlot, Cabernet Sauvignon.
SUMMARY This is by far the largest and most important development in the Mount Benson region. It is ultimately owned by a privately held Belgian company, G & C Kreglinger, established in 1797. Kreglinger Australia was established in 1893 as an agribusiness export company specialising in sheep skins. In early 2002 Kreglinger Australia acquired Pipers Brook Vineyard; the separate brands of each venture are being maintained. The Mount Benson side commenced in 2000 with the development of a 160-hectare vineyard and a 2000-tonne winery, primarily aimed at the export market.

Krinklewood ★★★

712 Wollombi Road, Broke, NSW 2330 **REGION** Lower Hunter Valley
T (02) 9969 1311 **F** (02) 9968 3435 **OPEN** Weekends, long weekends, and by appointment
WINEMAKER Contract **EST.** 1981 **CASES** 5000
PRODUCT RANGE ($16–22 ML) Semillon, Verdelho, Chardonnay, Francesca Rose, Botrytis Semillon.
SUMMARY Rod and Suzanne Windrim first ventured to the Hunter Valley in 1981, establishing Krinklewood Cottage at Pokolbin and a 1-hectare vineyard. In 1996 they sold that property and moved to the Broke Fordwich region, where they planted 17.5 hectares with Dr Richard Smart as their viticultural consultant. They struck gold with their first vintage in 2000. Leading restaurant listings of the imaginatively packaged wines have followed.

🍷🍷🍷🍸 **Semillon 2003 RATING** 86 **DRINK** 2013 $ 18
Verdelho 2003 RATING 85 **DRINK** Now $ 18

Kulkunbulla ★★★★

Brokenback Estate, Lot 1 Broke Road, Pokolbin, NSW 2320 **REGION** Lower Hunter Valley
T (02) 4998 7140 **F** (02) 4998 7142 **OPEN** By appointment
WINEMAKER Rhys Eather, Gavin Lennard **EST.** 1996 **CASES** 5000
PRODUCT RANGE ($14–40 CD) Hunter Valley Semillon, Orion's Gate Semillon, The Glandore Semillon, Hunter Valley Chardonnay, Nullarbor Chardonnay, Orion's Gate Chardonnay, The Brokenback Chardonnay, Botrytis Semillon, Shiraz, Hilltops Shiraz, Petit Verdot, Cabernet Merlot.
SUMMARY Kulkunbulla is owned by a relatively small Sydney-based company headed by Gavin Lennard. It has purchased part of the Brokenback Estate in the Hunter Valley, formerly owned by Rothbury. For the time being, all Kulkunbulla's wines are sold by mail order, through a sophisticated brochure entitled Vinsight. Retail distribution in Victoria and Queensland.

ΤΤΤΤΤ **The Brokenback Chardonnay 2003** Complex, funky aromas; a powerful, complex palate follows the bouquet; full kit of winemaking tricks. **RATING** 91 **DRINK** 2008 $ 35
The Glandore Semillon 2003 Has more weight than the varietal version; lemon, mineral and lanolin run through an even palate. **RATING** 90 **DRINK** 2013 $ 27.50

ΤΤΤΤ **Hunter Valley Semillon 2003** Crisp, light and clean; mineral, spice, lemon and herbs. **RATING** 89 **DRINK** 2010 $ 20
Hunter Valley Chardonnay 2003 Glowing yellow-green; bosomy peach and butterscotch; soft; some alcohol sweetness. **RATING** 88 **DRINK** Now $ 25

🐌 Kurrajong Downs NR

Casino Road, via Tenterfield, NSW 2372 **REGION** Northern Slopes Zone
T (02) 6736 4590 **F** (02) 6736 1983 **OPEN** Thurs–Mon 10–4
WINEMAKER Mark Ravenscroft, Phillipa Hamblyn **EST.** 2000 **CASES** 2100
PRODUCT RANGE ($13–24 CD) Louisa Mary Semillon, Louisa Mary White, Timbarra Gold Chardonnay, Old Racecourse Taminga, Four Vineyards Sweet Red, Four Vineyards Red, All Nations Pinot Noir, Reserve Pinot Noir, Reserve Merlot, The Forge Merlot Cabernet Sauvignon, The Forge Cabernet Sauvignon Shiraz.
SUMMARY Jonus Rhodes arrived at Tenterfield in 1858, lured by the gold he mined for the next 40 years, until his death in 1898. He was evidently successful, for the family now runs a 2800-hectare cattle grazing property on which Lynton and Sue Rhodes have planted a little over 4 hectares of vineyard at an altitude of 850 metres. Development of the vineyard started in the spring of 1996, and encouraged further planting the following year. A substantial cellar door, restaurant and function centre have been established overlooking the vineyard (open from 10 am-4 pm Monday to Thursday, and for dinner on Friday and Saturday evening, with a capacity of over 100 people).

🐌 Kurtz Family Vineyards NR

PO Box 460, Nuriootpa, SA 5355 **REGION** Barossa Valley
T 0418 810 982 **F** (08) 8564 8278 **OPEN** Not
WINEMAKER John Zilm (Contract) **EST.** 1996
PRODUCT RANGE A range of varietally denominated table wines under the Boundary Row and Lunar Block labels.
SUMMARY The Kurtz family has 20 hectares of vineyard at Light Pass, planted to semillon, chardonnay, grenache, cabernet sauvignon, merlot, shiraz, cabernet franc, mourvedre and petit verdot. The wines are distributed in Victoria through Woods Wines, with exports to the US and Hong Kong. They are also available by mail order.

Kyeema Estate ★★★☆

43 Shumack Street, Weetangera, ACT 2614 (postal) **REGION** Canberra District
T (02) 6254 7557 (ah) **F** (02) 6254 7536 **OPEN** Not
WINEMAKER Andrew McEwin **EST.** 1986 **CASES** 1200
PRODUCT RANGE ($8–27.50 ML) Chardonnay, Shiraz, Reserve Shiraz, Merlot, Cabernet Merlot; lower-priced Blue Gum Chardonnay, Shiraz Merlot Cabernet Sauvignon

SUMMARY Part-time winemaker, part-time wine critic (with *Winewise* magazine) Andrew McEwin produces wines full of flavour and character; every wine released under the Kyeema Estate label has won a show award of some description. Limited retail distribution.

Kyneton Ridge Estate ★★★★☆

90 Blackhill School Road, Kyneton, Vic 3444 **REGION** Macedon Ranges
T (03) 5422 7377 **F** (03) 5422 3747 **OPEN** By appointment
WINEMAKER John Boucher **EST.** 1997 **CASES** 300
PRODUCT RANGE ($30 CD) Pinot Noir.
SUMMARY Kyneton Ridge Estate has been established by a family team of winemakers, with winemaking roots going back four generations in the case of John and Ann Boucher. Together with Pauline Russell they found what they believe is a perfect pinot noir site near Kyneton. They planted 2.5 hectares of pinot noir in 1997. 1.5 hectares of chardonnay and 0.5 hectare of shiraz were added in 2002.

ΥΥΥΥ⅋ **Pinot Noir 2002** Extraordinary colour, concentration and richness on entry into the mouth; almost inevitably, dips slightly thereafter. **RATING** 92 **DRINK** 2008 $ 30

Laanecoorie NR

4834 Bendigo/Maryborough Road, Betley, Vic 3472 **REGION** Bendigo
T (03) 5468 7260 **F** (03) 5468 7388 **OPEN** Weekends, and by appointment
WINEMAKER John Ellis (Contract) **EST.** 1982 **CASES** 1000
PRODUCT RANGE ($20 R) A single Bordeaux-blend dry red of Cabernet Franc, Cabernet Sauvignon and Merlot in roughly equal proportions.
SUMMARY John McQuilten's 7.5-hectare vineyard produces grapes of high quality, and competent contract winemaking by John Ellis at Hanging Rock has done the rest.

Labyrinth NR

PO Box 7372, Shepparton, Vic 3632 **REGION** Yarra Valley
T (03) 5831 2793 **F** (03) 5831 2982 **OPEN** Not
WINEMAKER Ariki Hill **EST.** 2000 **CASES** 850
PRODUCT RANGE ($36–62 R) Valley Farm Pinot Noir, Viggers Vineyard Pinot Noir, Bien Nacido Vineyard Pinot Noir.
SUMMARY Ariki Hill is running a unique wine business, the name Labyrinth being well chosen. While it is a Pinot Noir-only specialist, one is produced in the southern hemisphere (from the Yarra Valley) and one from the northern hemisphere (Santa Barbara, California) each year. Moreover, the wines come from individual vineyards, the Bien Nacido Vineyard having the deserved reputation as one of the best sources of pinot noir in California. Ariki Hill uses leased space in California and at Goulburn Valley Estate to make the wines, and also has active consultancy work in California.

La Cantina King Valley NR

RMB 9460 Honey's Lane, King Valley, Vic 3678 **REGION** King Valley
T (03) 5729 3615 **F** (03) 5729 3613 **OPEN** 7 days 10–5 (10–6 daylight savings)
WINEMAKER Gino Corsini **EST.** 1996 **CASES** 1500
PRODUCT RANGE ($10–14 CD) Riesling, Chardonnay, Dry Red, Shiraz, Barbera, Dolcetto, Nebbiolo, Sangiovese, Merlot, Cabernet Sauvignon.
SUMMARY Gino and Peter Corsini have 22 hectares of riesling, chardonnay, shiraz, merlot and cabernet sauvignon, selling most but making a small amount on-site in a winery 'made of Glenrowan granite stone in traditional Tuscan style'. The wines are made without the use of sulphur dioxide; in other words, they are organic.

Ladbroke Grove ★★★★☆

Riddoch Highway, Coonawarra, SA 5263 **REGION** Coonawarra
T (08) 8737 3777 **F** (08) 8737 3268 **OPEN** Wed–Sun 10–5
WINEMAKER Contract **EST.** 1982 **CASES** 5000

PRODUCT RANGE ($14–42 CD) Riesling, Sauvignon Blanc, Chardonnay Limited Release, Sparkling Cabernet Sauvignon, Township Block Shiraz, Wrattonbully Cabernet Merlot, Coonawarra Cabernet Sauvignon Reserve.

SUMMARY Having been established in 1982, Ladbroke Grove is a relatively old Coonawarra brand. However, while the vineyards remained, winemaking and marketing lapsed until the business was purchased by John Cox and Marie Valenzuela, who have quietly gone about the re-establishment and rejuvenation of the label, and were rewarded by a string of wine show results in 2002 and 2003. It has extensive grape sources, including the Killian vineyard, planted in 1990 to cabernet sauvignon (6 hectares), merlot (2.4 hectares) and chardonnay (1.6 hectares). It also leases a little over 1 hectare of dry-grown shiraz planted in 1965 in the centre of the Coonawarra township. In the spring of 2002 it began the development of a further vineyard at the northern end of Coonawarra; it has been planted to 6 hectares of cabernet sauvignon, 4.5 hectares of shiraz and 1.6 hectares each of viognier, riesling and merlot.

ŸŸŸŸŸ **Killian Vineyard Cabernet Sauvignon 2001** Luscious, ripe cassis and blackberry fruit; soft tannins on a very long finish. Multiple trophy winner at the Limestone Coast Wine Show 2003. **RATING** 96 **DRINK** 2018 $42

ŸŸŸŸŸ **Township Block Shiraz 2001** Supple, smooth black cherry and plum fruit; fine, ripe tannins. **RATING** 93 **DRINK** 2012 $23

ŸŸŸŸ **Reserve Shiraz 2001 RATING** 86 **DRINK** 2010 $35
Shiraz Viognier 2001 RATING 85 **DRINK** 2011 $26

Lake Barrington Estate ★★★

1133–1136 West Kentish Road, West Kentish, Tas 7306 **REGION** Northern Tasmania
T (03) 6491 1249 **F** (03) 6334 2892 **OPEN** Wed–Sun 10–5 (Nov–Apr)
WINEMAKER Steve Lubiana (Sparkling), Andrew Hood (Table) (both Contract) **EST.** 1986 **CASES** 500
PRODUCT RANGE ($18–35 CD) Riesling, Chardonnay, Pinot Noir, Alexandra (sparkling).
SUMMARY Lake Barrington Estate is owned by the vivacious and energetic Maree Taylor and takes its name from the adjacent Lake Barrington, 30 kilometres south of Devonport. There are picnic facilities at the 3-hectare vineyard, and, needless to say, the scenery is very beautiful.

ŸŸŸŸ **Chardonnay 2002 RATING** 86 **DRINK** 2007 $24

Lake Breeze Wines ★★★☆

Step Road, Langhorne Creek, SA 5255 **REGION** Langhorne Creek
T (08) 8537 3017 **F** (08) 8537 3267 **OPEN** 7 days 10–5
WINEMAKER Greg Follett **EST.** 1987 **CASES** 12 000
PRODUCT RANGE ($15–40 CD) Chardonnay, Winemakers Selection Shiraz, Grenache, Cabernet Sauvignon, Bernoota (Cabernet Shiraz).
SUMMARY The Folletts have been farmers at Langhorne Creek since 1880, grape growers since the 1930s. Since 1987 a small proportion of their grapes has been made into wine, and a cellar-door sales facility was opened in early 1991. The quality of the releases has been exemplary; the red wines are particularly appealing. Retail distribution in Victoria, New South Wales, Queensland and Western Australia is now augmented by exports to the US, Canada, the UK and Switzerland.

ŸŸŸŸ **Chardonnay 2002** Clean, clear stone fruit; a touch of well-integrated French oak adds complexity. **RATING** 88 **DRINK** Now $15

🐌 Lake Charlotte Wines NR

4750 Ballup Road, Wooroloo, WA 6558 **REGION** Perth Hills
T (08) 9573 1219 **F** (08) 9573 1616 **OPEN** Weekends and public holidays 10–5
WINEMAKER Jim Elson (Contract) **EST.** 2001
PRODUCT RANGE ($15–18 CD) Verdelho, Shiraz, Cabernet Sauvignon.
SUMMARY There is no doubt the Perth Hills is a very pretty wine region, its twisting roads and multiple sub-valleys reminding me in some ways of the Clare Valley. It also has the great advantage of being an easy drive from Perth. Peter and Edwina Carter have set up their cellar door in an idyllic setting on the edge of Lake Charlotte, with a typical wide open verandah under a low-sloping roof. They have 2.5 hectares of verdelho, cabernet sauvignon, shiraz and merlot, and their wines are contract-made by long-term Perth Hills winemaker Jim Elson.

Lake Cooper Estate NR

1608 Midland Highway, Corop, Vic 316 **REGION** Heathcote
T (03) 9397 7781 **F** (03) 9397 8502 **OPEN** Not
WINEMAKER Peter Kelliher, Donald Risstrom **EST.** 1998 **CASES** 600
PRODUCT RANGE ($25–30 R) Shiraz, Shiraz Merlot, Shiraz Cabernet Sauvignon, Cabernet Sauvignon.
SUMMARY Lake Cooper Estate is another new and substantial venture in the burgeoning Heathcote region. Planting began in 1998 with 12 hectares of shiraz, and has since been extended to 18 hectares of shiraz, 10 hectares cabernet sauvignon and small plantings of merlot and chardonnay; additional small blocks of more exotic varieties will follow. Owners Gerry and Geraldine McHarg completed an on-site winery in 2003 (till then, the wine was made elsewhere by Peter Kelliher) and a cellar door is due to open in late 2004/early 2005. In the meantime the wines can be ordered by mail or phone. Both vineyard and winery are set on the side of Mount Camel Range, with panoramic views of Lake Cooper, Greens Lake and the Corop township.

Lake George Winery ★★☆

Federal Highway, Collector, NSW 2581 **REGION** Canberra District
T (02) 4848 0039 **F** (02) 4848 0039 **OPEN** By appointment
WINEMAKER Angus Campbell **EST.** 1971 **CASES** 750
PRODUCT RANGE ($25–48 CD) Semillon, Chardonnay, Botrytis Semillon, Pinot Noir, Merlot, Barrel Select Merlot, Cabernet Sauvignon.
SUMMARY Dr Edgar Riek was an inquisitive, iconoclastic winemaker who was not content with his role as Godfather and founder of the Canberra District, forever experimenting and innovating. His fortified wines, vintaged in northeastern Victoria but matured at Lake George, were very good. However, he sold the winery to Angus Campbell several years ago, and after a period of consulting, has no further involvement.

Lake Moodemere Vineyard NR

McDonalds Road, Rutherglen, Vic 3685 **REGION** Rutherglen
T (02) 6032 9449 **F** (02) 6032 9449 **OPEN** Weekends and public holidays 10–5, Mon, Thurs, Fri 10–3.30
WINEMAKER Michael Chambers **EST.** 1995 **CASES** 30
PRODUCT RANGE ($12–25 CD) Riesling, Chardonnay, Late Harvest Biancone, Shiraz, Cabernet Sauvignon, Moodemere Muscat.
SUMMARY Michael, Belinda, Peter and Helen Chambers are all members of the famous Chambers family of Rutherglen. They have 30 hectares of vineyards (tended by Peter), and Lake Moodemere Homestead is in its 14th year as a bed and breakfast facility.

Lake's Folly ★★★★★

Broke Road, Pokolbin, NSW 2320 **REGION** Lower Hunter Valley
T (02) 4998 7507 **F** (02) 4998 7322 **OPEN** Mon–Sat 10–4
WINEMAKER Rodney Kempe **EST.** 1963 **CASES** 4500
PRODUCT RANGE ($40 CD) Simplicity itself: Chardonnay and Cabernets.
SUMMARY The first of the weekend wineries to produce wines for commercial sale, long revered for its Cabernet Sauvignon and thereafter its Chardonnay. Very properly, terroir and climate produce a distinct regional influence and thus a distinctive wine style. Some find this attractive, others are less tolerant. The winery continues to enjoy an incredibly loyal clientele, with much of each year's wine selling out quickly by mail order. Lake's Folly no longer has any connection with the Lake family, having been acquired some years ago by Perth businessman Peter Fogarty. Mr Fogarty's family company has previously established the Millbrook Winery in the Perth Hills, so is no stranger to the joys and agonies of running a small winery.

Lambert Vineyards NR

810 Norton Road, Wamboin, NSW 2620 **REGION** Southern New South Wales Zone
T (02) 6238 3414 **F** (02) 6238 3639 **OPEN** Weekends and public holidays 10–5, or by appointment
WINEMAKER Steve Lambert **EST.** 1998

PRODUCT RANGE Riesling, Traminer, Pinot Gris, Chardonnay, Pinot Noir, Shiraz, Merlot, Cabernet Sauvignon.

SUMMARY Ruth and Steve Lambert have established 8 hectares of riesling, chardonnay, pinot gris, pinot noir, cabernet sauvignon, merlot and shiraz. Steve Lambert makes the wines on-site; they are sold by mail order and through the cellar door, which offers light meals, barbecue and picnic facilities.

Lamont Wines ★★★★☆

85 Bisdee Road, Millendon, WA 6056 **REGION** Swan Valley
T (08) 9296 4485 **F** (08) 9296 1663 **OPEN** Wed–Sun 10–5
WINEMAKER Keith Mugford (Consultant) **EST.** 1978 **CASES** 12 000
PRODUCT RANGE ($10–25 CD) Riesling, Barrel Fermented Semillon, Quartet, Semillon Sauvignon Blanc, Chenin Blanc, Verdelho, Barrel Fermented Chardonnay, Methode Champenoise, Sweet White, Late Picked, Light Red Cabernet, Shiraz, Cabernet Merlot, Cabernet Sauvignon, Family Reserve; fortifieds, including Amontillado and Reserve Sherry (Oloroso style).

SUMMARY Corin Lamont is the daughter of the late Jack Mann, and, with the recent involvement of Keith Mugford as consultant, oversees the making of wines in a style which would have pleased her father. Lamont also boasts a superb restaurant run by grand-daughter Kate Lamont, with a gallery for the sale and promotion of local arts. The wines are going from strength to strength, utilising both estate-grown and contract-grown (from southern regions) grapes. Exports to the US.

♥♥♥♥♀ **Riesling 2003** Clean and crisp; light but intense passionfruit and lime juice flavours; clean lingering finish. **RATING** 93 **DRINK** 2013 $18
Verdelho 2003 Lively, fresh and zingy, with a touch of citrus drizzled over fruit salad; good balance and length. **RATING** 90 **DRINK** 2007 $16

♥♥♥♥ **Shiraz 2001** Medium-bodied; blackberry and black pepper; good oak balance and length. A Swan Valley/Donnybrook blend. **RATING** 89 **DRINK** 2011 $25
Barrel Fermented Chardonnay 2002 Ripe stone fruit and peach flavours drive the palate rather than the barrel fermentation in French oak. Soft and appealing. **RATING** 87 **DRINK** Now $22

♥♥♥♀ **Semillon Sauvignon Blanc 2003 RATING** 84 **DRINK** Now $20

♥♥♥ **Quartet 2003 RATING** 83 $14

🐚 Lancefield Winery NR

Scrubby Camp Road, Emu Flat, Lancefield, Vic 3435 **REGION** Macedon Ranges
T (03) 5433 5292 **F** (03) 5433 5114 **OPEN** By appointment
WINEMAKER Rod Schmidt **EST.** 1985 **CASES** 1000
PRODUCT RANGE ($14–33 CD) Unoaked Chardonnay, Chardonnay, Chardonnay Brut, Pinot Noir, Cabernet Shiraz.

SUMMARY Lancefield Winery was established by Andrew Pattison, with plantings of 1 hectare each of chardonnay and shiraz, and 0.5 hectare each of gewurztraminer, pinot noir and cabernets/merlot. With Rod Schmidt in charge from June 2004, it is in the course of developing its own labels, the other brands having moved across to Pattison's newly established Burke and Wills Winery.

🐚 Landsborough Valley Estate

850 Landsborough–Elmhurst Road, Landsborough, Vic 3385 **REGION** Pyrenees
T (03) 5356 9390 **F** (03) 5356 9130 **OPEN** By appointment
WINEMAKER Wal Henning **EST.** 1996 **CASES** 3000
PRODUCT RANGE ($18–50 R) Mornington Chardonnay, Shiraz, Geoff Oliver Classic Shiraz, Cabernet Merlot, Geoff Oliver Classic Cabernet.

SUMMARY LVE (for short) has its origins stretching as far back as 1963, when civil engineering contractor Wal Henning was engaged to undertake work at Chateau Remy (now Blue Pyrenees). He was so impressed with the potential of the region for viticulture that he began an aerial search for sites with his close friend Geoff Oliver. Their first choice, at the head of the Malakoff Gap on the Elmhurst–Lansborough Road, was not available, so ultimately they chose a site which is now Taltarni, developing 40 hectares. Taltarni was then sold, and the pair (with Geoff's brother Max) moved on to establish Warrenmang Vineyard. When it, too, was sold, the pair were left without a vineyard, but in 1996 they were finally able to purchase the property they had identified 33 years previously, which is now partly given over to LVE and partly to the giant Glen Kara vineyard. They have established 20 hectares of vineyard on LVE, the lion's share to shiraz, with lesser amounts of cabernet sauvignon, pinot noir, chardonnay and riesling.

▼▼▼▼▽ **Cabernet Merlot 2001** Medium-bodied; very good texture and length; black fruits, bitter chocolate, ripe tannins and subtle oak. **RATING** 92 **DRINK** 2016 $ 32
Geoff Oliver Classic Cabernet 2002 Strong varietal expression; blackcurrant, with touches of leaf and olive; subtle oak. **RATING** 90 **DRINK** 2012 $ 40

▼▼▼▼ **Geoff Oliver Classic Shiraz 2002** Fragrant, savoury, spicy aromas; medium-bodied; blackberry fruit, fine tannins; elegant. **RATING** 89 **DRINK** 2010 $ 40
Mornington Chardonnay 2001 Gentle stone fruit and citrus flavours; obvious cool-climate growing; little or no oak evident. **RATING** 88 **DRINK** 2007 $ 18

▼▼▼▽ **Shiraz 2002** **RATING** 85 **DRINK** 2007 $ 22

Langanook Wines ★★★☆

91 McKittericks Road, Sutton Grange, Vic 3448 **REGION** Bendigo
T (03) 5474 8250 **OPEN** Weekends and public holidays 11–5, or by appointment
WINEMAKER Matt Hunter **EST.** 1985 **CASES** 750
PRODUCT RANGE ($16.50–33.50 CD) Chardonnay, Syrah, Cabernet Sauvignon, Reserve Cabernet Sauvignon Blend.
SUMMARY The Langanook vineyard was established back in 1985 (the first wines coming much later), at an altitude of 450 metres on the granite slopes of Mount Alexander. The climate is much cooler than in other parts of Bendigo, with a heat summation on a par with the Yarra Valley. The 20-tonne winery allows minimal handling of the wines. Exports to Belgium and Canada.

▼▼▼▼▽ **Syrah 2002** Voluptuously ripe black plum, prune, blackberry, spice and licorice; fragrant and flavoursome. Fifteen per cent Heathcote. **RATING** 91 **DRINK** 2014 $ 28

▼▼▼▽ **Chardonnay Viognier 2002** Driven by its exotic fruit salad and substantial alcohol mix; subtle oak. **RATING** 86 **DRINK** Now $ 19

Langbrook Estate Vineyard NR

65 Summerhill Road, Yarra Junction, Vic 3797 **REGION** Yarra Valley
T (03) 5967 1320 **F** (03) 5967 1182 **OPEN** By appointment
WINEMAKER MasterWineMakers (Contract) **EST.** 1996 **CASES** 360
PRODUCT RANGE ($18–20 CD) Sauvignon Blanc, Cabernet Merlot.
SUMMARY Langbrook Estate has 9 hectares of pinot noir, 5 hectares of sauvignon blanc, 4 hectares each of chardonnay and merlot and 1 hectare of cabernet sauvgnon planted, which will provide the base for a substantial output in future years. A bed and breakfast cottage and studio joins the many wine-linked bed and breakfast operations in the Yarra Valley.

🦡 Langleyvale Vineyard NR

43 Blackhill School Road, Kyneton, Vic 3444 **REGION** Macedon Ranges
T 0417 359 106 **F** (03) 9576 2966 **OPEN** From November 2004
WINEMAKER Richard Beniac **EST.** 2000 **CASES** 250
PRODUCT RANGE Merlot.
SUMMARY Richard Beniac purchased his property at Macedon after completing a part-time university viticulture course; he conducted soil tests and collected weather data before deciding to take on the challenge of cool-climate viticulture. The first plantings were 2.6 hectares of merlot, followed by 0.6 hectare each of shiraz and cabernet franc. Merlot was the first wine produced in 2004, to be followed in 2006/07 by Shiraz and Cabernet Franc.

Langmeil Winery

Cnr Para and Langmeil Roads, Tanunda, SA 5352 **REGION** Barossa Valley
T (08) 8563 2595 **F** (08) 8563 3622 **OPEN** 7 days 11–4.30
WINEMAKER Paul Lindner **EST.** 1996 **CASES** 15 000
PRODUCT RANGE ($12.50–55 CD) Eden Valley Riesling, White Frontignac, Semillon, Chardonnay, Bella Rouge Cabernet Sauvignon (Rose style), Valley Floor Shiraz, The Freedom Shiraz, Three Gardens Shiraz Grenache Mourvedre, The Fifth Wave Grenache, Cabernet Sauvignon, Liqueur Shiraz, Barossa Tawny.
SUMMARY Vines were first planted at Langmeil in the 1840s, and the first winery on the site, known as Paradale Wines, opened in 1932. In 1996 cousins Carl and Richard Lindner, along with brother-in-law Chris Bitter, formed a partnership to acquire and refurbish the winery and its 5-hectare vineyard, which is planted to shiraz, including 2 hectares planted in 1846. This vineyard has now been supplemented by another vineyard acquired in 1998, taking total plantings to 14.5 hectares and including cabernet sauvignon and grenache. Distribution in New South Wales and Victoria; exports to the US, Canada, France, Russia, Holland, Malaysia, Hong Kong and New Zealand.

TTTTT **The Freedom Shiraz 2001** Dense red-purple; mouthfilling, dense black plum, blackberry, prune, anise; ripe tannins; oak in pure support role. **RATING** 91 **DRINK** 2016 $ 70

TTTT **Jackman's Cabernet Sauvignon 2001** Ripe, juicy red berry and cassis fruit; supple and rich; soft tannins and gentle oak. From 40-year-old vines. **RATING** 89 **DRINK** 2008 $ 50
The Fifth Wave Grenache 2001 Strong colour; a mix of plum jam, mocha and vanilla, followed by savoury, slightly dry tannins to hold the voluptuous fruit in check. **RATING** 88 **DRINK** 2008 $ 35

Lark Hill

★★★★

521 Bungendore Road, Bungendore, NSW 2621 **REGION** Canberra District
T (02) 6238 1393 **F** (02) 6238 1393 **OPEN** Wed–Mon 10–5
WINEMAKER Dr David Carpenter, Sue Carpenter **EST.** 1978 **CASES** 4000
PRODUCT RANGE ($14–45 CD) Riesling, Sauvignon Blanc, Chardonnay, Late Harvest (dessert wine), Pinot Noir, Exaltation Pinot Noir, Shiraz, Exaltation Merlot, Cabernet Merlot, Exaltation Cabernet.
SUMMARY The Lark Hill vineyard is situated at an altitude of 860 metres, level with the observation deck on Black Mountain Tower, and offers splendid views of the Lake George Escarpment. Right from the outset, the Carpenters have made wines of real quality, style and elegance; they have defied all the odds (and conventional thinking) with the quality of their Pinot Noirs, so the high quality of the other wines comes as no surprise. Exports to the UK.

TTTT **Riesling 2003** Clean, mineral and spice aromas; passionfruit and lime on the fractionally sweet palate. **RATING** 89 **DRINK** 2008 $ 19.80·

Lashmar

★★★★

c/- 24 Lindsay Terrace, Belair, SA 5052 **REGION** Warehouse
T (08) 8278 3669 **F** (08) 8278 3998 **OPEN** Not
WINEMAKER Colin Cooter **EST.** 1996 **CASES** 1000
PRODUCT RANGE ($20–34 R) Viognier; Three Valleys Shiraz; Sisters Shiraz, Merlot and Cabernet Sauvignon; Kangaroo Island Cabernet Sauvignon.
SUMMARY Colin and Bronwyn Cooter (who are also part of the Lengs & Cooter business) are the driving force behind Antechamber Bay Wines. The wines are in fact labelled and branded Lashmar; the Kangaroo Island Cabernet Sauvignon comes from vines planted in 1991 on the Lashmar family property situated on the extreme eastern end of Kangaroo Island overlooking Antechamber Bay. The first commercial wines were made in 1999 and released in October 2000. To give the business added volume, the Three Valleys and Sisters wines (coming from other regions) are made. Exports to the US, Canada and Asia.

TTTTT **Sister's Blend McLaren Vale Cabernet Shiraz Merlot 2001** Ample, rich, supple fruits but the inevitable touch of regional chocolate; ripe tannins and lingering, long finish.
RATING 91 **DRINK** 2014 $ 20

Three Valleys Shiraz 2001 A generous wine; attractive mix of blackberry, plum, dark chocolate and mocha; good balance and extract. McLaren Vale, Clare and Eden Valleys. **RATING** 90 **DRINK** 2011 $ 24

▼▼▼▼ **McLaren Vale Viognier 2002** Generously proportioned; well-handled oak adds to the texture and structure inherent in the variety; some warmth ex the 14.5 degrees alcohol. Screwcap. **RATING** 89 **DRINK** Now $ 26

Kangaroo Island Cabernet 2001 Dark fruits with lots of lingering milky tannins, partly from French oak; not particularly well focused. **RATING** 87 **DRINK** 2009 $ 30

Latara   NR

Cnr McDonalds and Deaseys Roads, Pokolbin, NSW 2320 **REGION** Lower Hunter Valley
T (02) 4998 7320 **OPEN** Sat 9–5, Sun 9–4
WINEMAKER Iain Riggs (Contract) **EST.** 1979 **CASES** 250
PRODUCT RANGE ($9.50–11 CD) Semillon.
SUMMARY The bulk of the grapes produced on the 6-hectare Latara vineyard, which was planted in 1979, are sold to Brokenwood. A small quantity is vinified for Latara and sold under its label. As one would expect, the wines are very competently made, and are of show medal standard.

🍇 Laurance of Margaret River   ★★☆

Lot 549 Caves Road, Wilyabrup, WA 6280 **REGION** Margaret River
T (08) 9755 6276 **F** (08) 9755 6276 **OPEN** Not
WINEMAKER Bruce Dukes (Consultant) **EST.** 2001 **CASES** 4600
PRODUCT RANGE ($27 R) White, Rose, Red.
SUMMARY While this is a family business, it is Dianne Laurance who is the driving force. Her husband Bruce Carr and son Brendon Carr (plus wife Kerrianne) are involved: Brendon is vineyard manager, living on the property with his wife and child. The 40-hectare property had 21 hectares planted when it was purchased, and since its acquisition it has been turned into a showplace, with a rose garden to put that of Voyager Estate to shame. While the wine is made off-site by consultant winemaker Bruce Dukes, a substantial wine storage facility has been built on-site. But it is the tenpin-sized bottles with ceramic-baked labels which will gain the most attention, and the bottles doubtless have secondary uses as lamp stands.

▼▼▼ **Rose 2002 RATING** 83 $ 27

Laurel Bank   ★★★

130 Black Snake Lane, Granton, Tas 7030 **REGION** Southern Tasmania
T (03) 6263 5977 **F** (03) 6263 3117 **OPEN** By appointment
WINEMAKER Andrew Hood (Contract) **EST.** 1987 **CASES** 1200
PRODUCT RANGE ($18–23 R) Sauvignon Blanc, Pinot Noir, Cabernet Sauvignon Merlot.
SUMMARY Laurel (hence Laurel Bank) and Kerry Carland began planting their 3-hectare vineyard in 1986. They delayed the first release of their wines for some years and (by virtue of the number of entries they were able to make) won the trophy for Most Successful Exhibitor at the 1995 Royal Hobart Wine Show. Things have settled down since; wine quality is solid and reliable.

▼▼▼▼ **Riesling 2003 RATING** 84 **DRINK** 2007 $ 18

▼▼▼ **Pinot Noir 2002 RATING** 83 $ 22

Lauren Brook   ★★★★

Eedle Terrace, Bridgetown, WA 6255 **REGION** Blackwood Valley
T (08) 9761 2676 **F** (08) 9761 1879 **OPEN** Fri–Wed 11–4.30
WINEMAKER Stephen Bullied **EST.** 1993 **CASES** 500
PRODUCT RANGE ($17–35 CD) Chardonnay, Bridgetown Classic, Shiraz, Cabernet Sauvignon.
SUMMARY Lauren Brook is established on the banks of the beautiful Blackwood River, and is the only commercial winery in the Bridgetown subregion of Mount Barker. An 80-year-old barn on the property has been renovated to contain a micro-winery and a small gallery. There is 1 hectare of estate chardonnay, supplemented by grapes purchased locally.

Lawrence Victor Estate ★★★★

Arthur Street, Penola, SA 5277 **REGION** Coonawarra
T (08) 8737 3572 **F** (08) 8737 3582 **OPEN** 7 days 10–5
WINEMAKER Contract **EST.** 1994 **CASES** 2000
PRODUCT RANGE ($21–25 CD) Shiraz, Cabernet Sauvignon.
SUMMARY Lawrence Victor Estate is part of a large South Australian company principally engaged in
the harvesting and transportation of softwood plantation logging. The company was established by
Lawrence Victor Dohnt in 1932, and the estate has been named in his honour by the third generation
of the family. Although a small part of the group's activities, the plantings (principally contracted to
Southcorp) are substantial, with 11 hectares of shiraz and 20 hectares of cabernet sauvignon
established between 1994 and 1999. An additional 12 hectares of cabernet sauvignon and 6 hectares
of pinot noir were planted in 2000.

Lawson's Hill ★★☆

Henry Lawson Drive, Eurunderee, Mudgee, NSW 2850 **REGION** Mudgee
T (02) 6373 3953 **F** (02) 6373 3948 **OPEN** Mon, Thurs, Fri, Sat 10–4.30, Sun 10–4
WINEMAKER Various Contract and Jose Grace **EST.** 1985 **CASES** 3500
PRODUCT RANGE ($11–39 CD) Chardonnay, Verdelho, Sauvignon Blanc, Riesling, Traminer Riesling,
Louisa Rose, Cabernet Merlot, Pinot Noir Gamay, Reserve Dryland Cabernet Sauvignon, Port.
SUMMARY Former music director and arranger (for musical acts in Sydney clubs) Jose Grace and wife
June run a strongly tourist-oriented operation situated next door to the Henry Lawson Memorial,
offering a kaleidoscopic array of wines, produced from 8 hectares of vineyard, and made under contract.

ΨΨΨΨ **Chardonnay 2002 RATING** 84 **DRINK** Now $18
Sauvignon Blanc Marsanne Chardonnay 2002 RATING 84 **DRINK** Now $16

ΨΨΨ **Verdelho 2002 RATING** 82 $16

ΨΨΨ **Pinot Noir 2002 RATING** 79 $16

Lazy River Estate NR

29R Old Dubbo Road, Dubbo, NSW 2830 **REGION** Western Plains Zone
T (02) 6882 2111 **F** (02) 6882 2111 **OPEN** By appointment
WINEMAKER Contract **EST.** 1997 **CASES** 1400
PRODUCT RANGE ($15–35 ML) Hippo Beach Semillon, Squatters Chair Chardonnay, Hippo Beach
Shiraz, Squatters Chair Petit Verdot, Squatters Chair Cabernet Sauvignon.
SUMMARY The Scott family have planted 3 hectares each of chardonnay and semillon, 1 hectare of
merlot, and 1.5 hectares each of petit verdot and cabernet sauvignon. It is situated a little under
3 kilometres from the end of the main street of Dubbo, and a cellar door is planned; until that time
visits are by appointment only. The wines are made at Briar Ridge.

Leabrook Estate ★★★★★

24 Tusmore Avenue, Leabrook, SA 5068 (postal) **REGION** Adelaide Hills
T (08) 8331 7150 **F** (08) 8364 1520 **OPEN** By appointment
WINEMAKER Colin Best **EST.** 1998 **CASES** 4500
PRODUCT RANGE ($17–30 ML) Sauvignon Blanc, Chardonnay, Charleston Rose, Pinot Noir, Reserve
Pinot Noir, Cabernet Merlot, Cabernet Franc, Shiraz, Three Regions Shiraz.
SUMMARY With a background as an engineer, and having dabbled in home winemaking for 30 years,
Colin Best took the plunge and moved into commercial-scale winemaking in 1998. His wines are now
to be found in a who's who of restaurant wine lists, and some of the best independent wine retailers
on the east coast. Best says, 'I consider that my success is primarily due to the quality of my grapes,
since they have been planted on a 1.2 x 1.2 metre spacing and very low yields.' I won't argue with that,
and he has also done a fine job in converting the grapes into wine. A cellar door is planned for the
near future.

ΨΨΨΨΨ **Cabernet Franc 2002** Aromatic and scented; light to medium-bodied; vibrant spicy/tangy
fruit and persistent finish and aftertaste; gossamer tannins. Reminiscent of Chinon.
RATING 94 **DRINK** 2008 $24

ΥΥΥΥ♀ **Cabernet Merlot 2002** Richly endowed with classic cassis and blackcurrant fruit; medium-bodied, and excellent balance of French oak; long finish. **RATING** 93 **DRINK** 2012 $22

Three Region Shiraz 2002 Powerful, tightly focused blackberry and spice; tannins give good structure; needs cellaring. Adelaide Hills, Langhorne Creek, Adelaide Plains. **RATING** 90 **DRINK** 2015 $30

ΥΥΥΥ **Pinot Noir 2002** Savoury, spicy, gamey, foresty aromas and flavours; fine tannins and good length. **RATING** 88 **DRINK** 2007 $24

Leasingham
★★★★★

7 Dominic Street, Clare, SA 5453 **REGION** Clare Valley
T (08) 8842 2555 **F** (08) 8842 3293 **OPEN** Mon–Fri 8.30–5.30, weekends 10–4
WINEMAKER Kerri Thompson **EST.** 1893 **CASES** 70 000
PRODUCT RANGE ($12.99–55.95 R) Classic Clare Riesling, Shiraz, Sparkling Shiraz and Cabernet Sauvignon at the top end; mid-range Bin 7 Riesling, Bin 37 Chardonnay, Bin 23 Semillon, Bin 56 Cabernet Malbec, Bin 61 Shiraz; finally, low-priced Hutt Creek Riesling, Sauvignon Blanc, Shiraz Cabernet; also Bastion Shiraz Cabernet.
SUMMARY Successive big-company ownerships and various peregrinations in labelling and branding have not resulted in any permanent loss of identity or quality. With a core of high-quality, aged vineyards to draw on, Leasingham is in fact going from strength to strength under BRL Hardy's direction. The stentorian red wines take no prisoners, compacting densely rich fruit and layer upon layer of oak into every long-lived bottle; the Bin 7 Riesling often excels.

ΥΥΥΥΥ **Show Reserve Limited Release Shiraz 1995** Abundant, layered blackberry/licorice fruit; not jammy; excellent extract of tannins and oak. A re-release with 7 gold medals. **RATING** 94 **DRINK** 2015 $34.95

ΥΥΥΥ♀ **Bin 7 Riesling 2003** A clean and precisely chiselled bouquet leads into a palate with considerable intensity and length; lime/citrus with a flinty underlay. Generous but not heavy. **RATING** 93 **DRINK** 2013 $16

Bin 61 Shiraz 2001 Clean, direct blackberry; flecks of licorice and chocolate; typically mouthfilling and generous; positive oak, soft tannins. **RATING** 91 **DRINK** 2016 $21.99

Leconfield
★★★★☆

Riddoch Highway, Coonawarra, SA 5263 **REGION** Coonawarra
T (08) 8737 2326 **F** (08) 8737 2385 **OPEN** 7 days 10–5
WINEMAKER Paul Gordon, Tim Bailey (Assistant) **EST.** 1974 **CASES** 15 000
PRODUCT RANGE ($17.95–29.95 CD) Old Vines Riesling, Chardonnay, Noble Riesling, Shiraz, Merlot, Petit Verdot, Cabernet Sauvignon.
SUMMARY A distinguished estate with a proud, even if relatively short, history. Long renowned for its Cabernet Sauvignon, its repertoire has steadily grown, with the emphasis on single varietal wines. The style overall is fruit rather than oak-driven. Exports to Canada, the US, Asia, the UK and Europe.

ΥΥΥΥ♀ **Old Vines Riesling 2003** Very floral lime blossom aromas; fine, crisp, intense and long; strongly regional. **RATING** 93 **DRINK** 2013 $19.95

Cabernet Sauvignon 2001 Medium-bodied; cassis/blackcurrant; attractive oak sweetness and mouthfeel. **RATING** 93 **DRINK** 2011 $29.95

Merlot 2002 Powerful, concentrated and complex dark berry and mulberry fruit; ripe tannins, balanced oak; Australian merlot, rather than classic. **RATING** 91 **DRINK** 2015 $27.95

Chardonnay 2003 Well balanced and integrated barrel-ferment inputs to the melon and cashew fruit; excellent acidity on the finish. Screwcap. **RATING** 90 **DRINK** 2008 $18.95

ΥΥΥΥ **Shiraz 2002** Clean, red berry fruits; smooth, medium-bodied; oak well balanced and integrated. **RATING** 88 **DRINK** 2010 $27.95

LedaSwan ★★★

179 Memorial Avenue, Baskerville, WA 6065 **REGION** Swan Valley
T (08) 9296 0216 **OPEN** 7 days 11–4.30
WINEMAKER Duncan Harris **EST.** 1998 **CASES** 250
PRODUCT RANGE ($16–23 CD) Chenin Blanc, Verdelho, Shiraz, Organic Shiraz, Pedro Ximinez, Muscat a Petits Grains.
SUMMARY LedaSwan claims to be the smallest winery in the Swan Valley. It uses organically grown grapes, partly coming from its own vineyard, and partly contract-grown, although the intention is to move to 100 per cent estate-grown in the future, utilising the 2 hectares of estate vineyards. Duncan Harris moved from the coast to Baskerville in 1998, and retired from engineering in 2001 to become a full-time vintner, winning several awards. Tours of the underground cellar are offered.

ΥΥΥΥ **Shiraz 2001** Clean, fresh, red cherry and plum; light to medium-bodied; no frills or pretensions; simply a nice wine. **RATING** 87 **DRINK** 2008 $ 19

Leeuwin Estate ★★★★★

Stevens Road, Margaret River, WA 6285 **REGION** Margaret River
T (08) 9759 0000 **F** (08) 9759 0001 **OPEN** 7 days 10–4.30, Saturday evening dinner
WINEMAKER Bob Cartwright, Paul Atwood **EST.** 1974 **CASES** 60 000
PRODUCT RANGE ($21–76 CD) Art Series Riesling, Sauvignon Blanc, Chardonnay, Pinot Noir, Shiraz, Cabernet Sauvignon; Brut; Prelude Vineyards Classic Dry White, Chardonnay, Cabernet Merlot and Siblings Sauvignon Blanc Semillon, Shiraz are lower-priced alternatives.
SUMMARY Leeuwin Estate's Chardonnay is, in my opinion, Australia's finest example, based on the wines of the last 20 vintages, and it is this wine alone which demands a five-star rating for the winery. The Cabernet Sauvignon can be an excellent wine with great style and character in warmer vintages, and Shiraz has made an auspicious debut. Almost inevitably, the other wines in the portfolio are not in the same Olympian class, although the Prelude Chardonnay and Sauvignon Blanc are impressive at their lower price level. Exports to all major markets.

ΥΥΥΥΥ **Art Series Chardonnay 2001** Classic Leeuwin, classic Margaret River; intense stone fruit and grapefruit aromas, then a gloriously textured and multi-faceted palate; outstanding balance and length. **RATING** 97 **DRINK** 2016 $ 76
Art Series Chardonnay 2000 A fine, focused, elegant wine, slowly unfolding as it ages in bottle, building on the long and seamless fusion of nectarine, grapefruit and oak. **RATING** 95 **DRINK** 2015 $ 76

ΥΥΥΥ♀ **Art Series Shiraz 2002** Excellent colour; blackberry, raspberry, cherry and spice; plenty of texture and weight; subtle oak, good length. **RATING** 93 **DRINK** 2012 $ 34
Prelude Vineyards Chardonnay 2002 Fragrant, fresh, lively and long; driven by its nectarine/grapefruit flavours; subtle oak. **RATING** 92 **DRINK** 2010 $ 30
Art Series Riesling 2003 Passionfruit aromas; light, delicate and fresh; good length. **RATING** 90 **DRINK** 2009 $ 22
Art Series Shiraz 2001 Medium-bodied; fresh blackberry and spice and the finest possible tannins; finesse, not power. **RATING** 90 **DRINK** 2009 $ 34

ΥΥΥΥ **Art Series Sauvignon Blanc 2003** Clean, delicate passionfruit-accented fruit; finely structured and balanced. **RATING** 89 **DRINK** Now $ 31
Siblings Sauvignon Blanc Semillon 2003 Spotlessly clean and fresh; lemon and mineral; lively finish. **RATING** 88 **DRINK** Now $ 21
Prelude Vineyards Cabernet Merlot 2001 Leafy, minty redcurrant and raspberry; firm but fine tannins. **RATING** 87 **DRINK** 2011 $ 30

ΥΥΥ♀ **Art Series Cabernet Sauvignon 2000** **RATING** 86 **DRINK** 2010 $ 54

Leland Estate ★★★★

PO Lenswood, SA 5240 **REGION** Adelaide Hills
T (08) 8389 6928 **OPEN** Not
WINEMAKER Robb Cootes **EST.** 1986 **CASES** 1200

PRODUCT RANGE ($14–17 CD) Sauvignon Blanc, Pinot Noir, Adele (sparkling).
SUMMARY Former Yalumba senior winemaker Robb Cootes, with a Master of Science degree, deliberately opted out of mainstream life when he established Leland Estate, living in a split-level, one-roomed house built from timber salvaged from trees killed in the Ash Wednesday bushfires. The Sauvignon Blanc is usually good. Retail distribution in Victoria, New South Wales and Queensland via Prime Wines; exports to the US, Canada and Japan.

Le 'Mins Winery   NR

40 Lemins Road, Waurn Ponds, Vic 3216 (postal) **REGION** Geelong
T (03) 5241 8168 **OPEN** Not
WINEMAKER Steve Jones **EST.** 1994 **CASES** 80
PRODUCT RANGE ($10 R) Pinot Noir.
SUMMARY Steve Jones presides over 0.5 hectare of pinot noir planted in 1998 to the MV6 clone, and 0.25 hectare of the same variety planted 4 years earlier to Burgundy clone 114. The tiny production is made for Le 'Mins at Prince Albert Vineyard, and the wine is basically sold by word of mouth.

Lengs & Cooter

24 Lindsay Terrace, Belair, SA 5042 **REGION** Warehouse
T (08) 8278 3998 **F** (08) 8278 3998 **OPEN** Not
WINEMAKER Contract **EST.** 1993 **CASES** 8000
PRODUCT RANGE ($16–45 ML) Watervale Riesling, Clare Valley Semillon, Adelaide Hills Pinot Noir, Clare Valley Old Vines Shiraz, Reserve Shiraz, Victor (Grenache Shiraz), Swinton Cabernet Sauvignon.
SUMMARY Carel Lengs and Colin Cooter began making wine as a hobby in the early 1980s. Each had (and has) a full-time occupation outside the wine industry, and it was all strictly for fun. One thing has led to another, and although they still possess neither vineyards nor what might truly be described as a winery, the wines graduated to big boy status, winning gold medals at national wine shows and receiving critical acclaim from writers across Australia. Exports to the UK, Canada, Singapore and Malaysia.

ΨΨΨΨΨ **Reserve McLaren Vale Shiraz 2001** Rich, velvety black fruits, dark chocolate and spice; textured by fine, integrated tannins; excellent finish. **RATING** 94 **DRINK** 2016 $ 45

ΨΨΨΨ **Clare Valley Old Vines Shiraz 2001** Bright colour; fresh raspberry and blackberry fruit; supple and smooth; fine tannins; only an eyelash behind the Reserve Shiraz. **RATING** 93 **DRINK** 2016 $ 25
The Victor 2002 Lovely rich sweet raspberry, cherry and blackberry mix; fine ripe tannins. Screwcap. **RATING** 92 **DRINK** 2010 $ 18
Adelaide Hills Pinot Noir 2002 A massively built wine like some others from the region; rich, ripe satsuma plum and spice; worth cellaring. Screwcap. **RATING** 90 **DRINK** 2010 $ 18

ΨΨΨΨ **Swinton Cabernet Sauvignon 2001** Quite aromatic and scented; tangy, almost lemony, flavours, unusual but not unpleasant. **RATING** 87 **DRINK** 2009 $ 21

ΨΨΨ **Watervale Riesling 2003** Slate, herb and lime; solid, rich and a trifle Four Square. Screwcap. **RATING** 86 **DRINK** 2009 $ 17

ΨΨΨ **Sparkling Red NV RATING** 83 $ 10

Lenton Brae Wines

Wilyabrup Valley, Margaret River, WA 6285 **REGION** Margaret River
T (08) 9755 6255 **F** (08) 9755 6268 **OPEN** 7 days 10–6
WINEMAKER Edward Tomlinson **EST.** 1983
PRODUCT RANGE ($15–34 CD) Semillon Sauvignon Blanc, Chardonnay, Late Harvest Semillon, Lae Harvest Sauvignon Blanc, Shiraz, Late Harvest Shiraz, Cabernet Sauvignon (Reserve Red), Cabernet Merlot.
SUMMARY Former architect, town planner and political wine activist Bruce Tomlinson built a strikingly beautiful winery but would not stand for criticism of his wines or politics. Son Edward is more relaxed, and is in fact making wines which require no criticism. Retail distribution through all States, and exports to the UK, Singapore, the US and Canada.

ΥΥΥΫ **Semillon Sauvignon Blanc 2003** A chameleon wine which changes constantly in the glass, showing some reduced characters one moment, the next not. The constant is excellent texture, structure and acidity. **RATING** 93 **DRINK** 2007 $ 19

Cabernet Merlot 2002 Insistent varietal fruit aromas; firmly framed and focused around bright blackcurrant and raspberry fruit. **RATING** 92 **DRINK** 2012 $ 20

Margaret River Chardonnay 2002 Elegant style; excellent length and balance, driven by stone fruit/grapefruit flavours; will develop. **RATING** 90 **DRINK** 2009 $ 34

ΥΥΥΥ **Margaret River 2001** Suave opening of cassis, berry and mint, moving through punchy tannins on the finish; needs time to sort itself out. **RATING** 89 **DRINK** 2016 $ 34

Leo Buring ★★★★★

Tanunda Road, Nuriootpa, SA 5355 **REGION** Barossa Valley
T (08) 8560 9408 **F** (08) 8563 2804 **OPEN** Not
WINEMAKER Oliver Crawford **EST.** 1931
PRODUCT RANGE ($17.95–34.15 R) A Riesling-only product range, headed by Leonay, with a changing bin number (for 2002 DWF18), and Eden Valley Riesling and Clare Valley Riesling in support.
SUMMARY Earns its high rating by virtue of being Australia's foremost producer of Rieslings over a 35-year period, with a rich legacy left by former winemaker John Vickery. After veering away from its core business with other varietal wines, has now been refocused as a specialist Riesling producer.

ΥΥΥΫ **Eden Valley Riesling 2003** Spice, herb, mineral and citrus; a very long and even palate; ripe lemon and citrus flavours. Good balance. **RATING** 92 **DRINK** 2013 $ 18.60

Leonay Riesling 2003 Clean but closed; mineral and faint blossom aromas; tightly wound-up palate; lingering minerally acidity. **RATING** 91 **DRINK** 2013 $ 34.15

ΥΥΥΥ **Clare Valley Riesling 2003** Firm slate and herb aromas; attractive passionfruit and lime on entry to the mouth; softens on the finish. **RATING** 88 **DRINK** 2007 $ 18.60

Lerida Estate ★★★

The Vineyards, Old Federal Highway, Lake George, NSW 2581 **REGION** Canberra District
T (02) 4848 0231 **F** (02) 4848 0232 **OPEN** 7 days 11–4.30, or by appointment
WINEMAKER Jeff Aston, Greg Gallagher **EST.** 1999 **CASES** 1500
PRODUCT RANGE ($15–30 CD) Unoaked Chardonnay, Chardonnay, Pinot Noir, Cowra Merlot, Merlot Cabernet Franc, Langhorne Creek Cabernet Sauvignon.
SUMMARY Lerida Estate continues the planting of vineyards along the escarpment sloping down to Lake George. It is immediately to the south of the Lake George vineyard established by Edgar Riek 30 years ago. Inspired by Edgar Riek's success with pinot noir, Lerida founder Jim Lumbers has planted 6 hectares of pinot noir, together with 1 hectare each of chardonnay and merlot, and 0.5 hectare of pinot gris. The only Lerida wine so far released has been an unwooded Chardonnay; the other wines come from elsewhere. The intention is to ultimately rely entirely on estate-grown grapes for the Lerida label, with a second label (Gryphon) for wines made from purchased grapes. An open-air winery was put in place for the 2000 and 2001 vintages, and a Glen Murcott-designed tasting, barrel and function room has been erected on-site.

ΥΥΥΫ **Lake George Pinot Noir 2002** **RATING** 86 **DRINK** 2007 $ 30

Lake George Shiraz 2002 **RATING** 85 **DRINK** 2008 $ 21

Lake George Chardonnay 2002 **RATING** 84 **DRINK** Now $ 19.50

Lethbridge Wines

74 Burrows Road, Lethbridge, Vic 3222 **REGION** Geelong
T (03) 5281 7221 **F** (03) 5281 7221 **OPEN** Fri–Sun and public holidays 10.30–5, or by appointment
WINEMAKER Ray Nadeson, Maree Collis **EST.** 1996 **CASES** 1500
PRODUCT RANGE ($20–38 CD) Sauvignon Blanc Semillon, Pinot Gris, Pinot Noir, Old Vine Shiraz, Merlot, Old Vine Malbec, Redenberg Cabernet.
SUMMARY Lethbridge was founded by three scientists: Ray Nadeson, Maree Collis and Adrian Thomas. In Ray Nadeson's words, 'Our belief is that the best wines express the unique character of

special places. With this in mind our philosophy is to practise organic principles in the vineyard, complemented by traditional winemaking techniques, to allow the unique character of the site to be expressed in our fruit and captured in our wine.' As well as understanding the importance of terroir, the partners have built a unique load-bearing straw-bale winery, designed to recreate the controlled environment of cellars and caves in Europe. Winemaking is no less ecologically sound: hand picking, indigenous yeast fermentations, small open fermenters, pigeage (treading the grapes) and minimal handling of the wine throughout the maturation process are all part and parcel of the highly successful Lethbridge approach.

ﾔﾔﾔﾔ **Pinot Noir 2002** Tangy, savoury, herbal, foresty aromas; fires on the palate; long and intense dark plum and fine tannins. **RATING** 91 **DRINK** 2008 $ 32

ﾔﾔﾔﾔ **Gold Cap Shiraz 2001** Light to medium-bodied; spicy, savoury red fruits; minimal tannins. **RATING** 88 **DRINK** 2009 $ 38
Sauvignon Blanc Semillon 2003 Clean, fresh and crisp bouquet; gentle fruit salad flavours, with rather more sweetness than expected. **RATING** 87 **DRINK** Now $ 20
Rebenberg Cabernet Sauvignon 2001 A spicy, dusty, minty blackcurrant mix; light to medium-bodied; fine tannins. **RATING** 87 **DRINK** 2011 $ 32

🍇 Leura Park Estate ★★★★☆

1400 Portarlington Road, Curlewis, Vic 3222 **REGION** Geelong
T (03) 5253 3180 **F** (03) 5251 1262 **OPEN** Weekends 11–5
WINEMAKER Steve Webber (Contract) **EST.** 1995 **CASES** 600
PRODUCT RANGE ($18.50–25.80 CD) Sauvignon Blanc, 25 d'Gris, Chardonnay, Pinot Noir.
SUMMARY Stephen and Lisa Cross gained fame as restaurateurs in the 1990s, first at Touche and then at the outstanding Saltwater at Noosa Heads. They have established a very substantial vineyard, with 8 hectares of chardonnay and 3+ hectares each of pinot gris, pinot noir and sauvignon blanc, with 1 hectare of shiraz yet to come into bearing. Ninety per cent of the production is sold to De Bortoli, where the truly excellent wines for release under the Leura Park label are made. Certain to be one of the star turns of the year.

ﾔﾔﾔﾔﾔ **Chardonnay 2001** Superfine and elegant; delicate stone fruit flavours; lovely line and length. **RATING** 95 **DRINK** 2010 $ 25.80

ﾔﾔﾔﾔ **Chardonnay 2002** Complex, intense barrel-ferment and bottle-developed characters; lots of personality; a touch of funk works very well; lingering grapefruit finish. **RATING** 93 **DRINK** 2007 $ 25.80
Sauvignon Blanc 2002 Spotless, crisp, minerally aromas; good length and mouthfeel; delicious gooseberry, lime and passionfruit flavours. **RATING** 90 **DRINK** Now $ 18.50
25 d'Gris Pinot Gris 2002 Wonderfully fragrant peach skin aromas; concentrated palate fruit with some alcohol sweetness (14.4 degrees), but impressive. **RATING** 90 **DRINK** Now $ 28

ﾔﾔﾔﾔ **Pinot Noir 2003** Good colour; an ample mix of strawberry and cherry fruit, with a hint of spice and plenty of varietal character. A surprise performer, possibly pointing the way to the future. **RATING** 89 **DRINK** 2008 $ 25.80
Pinot Noir 2001 Light to medium-bodied; cherry/spicy/savoury aromas and flavours; subtle oak, but not intense. **RATING** 88 **DRINK** Now $ 25.80

Leven Valley Vineyard NR

321 Raymond Road, Gunns Plains, Tas 7315 **REGION** Northern Tasmania
T (03) 6429 1186 **F** (03) 6429 1369 **OPEN** 7 days 9–5
WINEMAKER Richard Richardson (Contract) **EST.** 1997 **CASES** 800
PRODUCT RANGE ($18 CD) Chardonnay, Pinot Noir.
SUMMARY John and Wendy Weatherly have acquired the former Moonrakers Vineyard from Stephen and Diana Usher, and have changed the name, but otherwise left well alone. The vineyard consists of 0.5 hectare each of chardonnay and pinot noir on a north-facing slope above the picturesque valley of Gunns Plains. The deep loam over limestone soil holds much promise.

Liebich Wein

Steingarten Road, Rowland Flat, SA 5352 **REGION** Barossa Valley
T (08) 8524 4543 **F** (08) 8524 4543 **OPEN** Weekends 11–5, Mon–Fri 11–5, appointments advisable
WINEMAKER Ron Liebich **EST.** 1992 **CASES** 3000
PRODUCT RANGE ($13.50–40 CD) Riesling of the Valleys (Barossa and Clare Valley Riesling), Riesling Traminer, Unwooded Chardonnay, Fortified Semillon, Pinot Noir Blend, Leveret Shiraz, The Darkie Shiraz, The Potter's Merlot, The Lofty Cabernet Sauvignon, Crackerjack Cabernet, Tawny Port, Benno Port, Vintage Port, Muscat; bulk port constitutes major sales.
SUMMARY Liebich Wein is Barossa Deutsch for 'Love I wine'. The Liebich family have been grape growers and winemakers at Rowland Flat since 1919, CW 'Darky' Liebich was one of the great local characters. His nephew, Ron Liebich, commenced making wine in 1969, but it was not until 1992 that he and his wife Janet began selling wine under the Liebich Wein label. Exports to the US, the UK and Germany.

ΨΨΨΨΨ **Leveret Shiraz 2002** Very rich, concentrated and appropriately ripe fruit; exotic spices and bitter chocolate; good tannins. **RATING** 94 **DRINK** 2017 **$** 23

ΨΨΨΨΨ **The Darkie Shiraz 2002** Dense, impenetrable colour; layer upon layer of black fruits and spices; what cricketers would call a 'sandshoe crusher'; the US, here I come. 15.7 degrees alcohol. **RATING** 92 **DRINK** 2022 **$** 40
Crackerjack Cabernet 2002 A very rich mix of dark chocolate, blackcurrant and blackberry; abundant milky tannins need to integrate. **RATING** 90 **DRINK** 2017 **$** 23

ΨΨΨΨ **The Potter's Merlot 2002** Dense, dark red; masses of ripe blackcurrant and plum, but little obvious varietal character. **RATING** 89 **DRINK** 2012 **$** 24
The Lofty Cabernet Sauvignon 2002 A long, intense palate with lingering savoury tannins on the finish; very different from the Crackerjack. **RATING** 88 **DRINK** 2012 **$** 32

ΨΨΨ **Pinot Noir Merlot 2003** **RATING** 83 **$** 12

Lighthouse Peak

NR

Tumbarumba–Khancoban Road, Bringenbrong, NSW 3707 **REGION** Tumbarumba
T 0500 524 444 **F** 0500 524 445 **OPEN** Not
WINEMAKER Kerry Potocky-Pacay **EST.** 1996
PRODUCT RANGE A range of varietally denominated table wines reflecting the plantings.
SUMMARY Ian Tayles has established a 2-hectare vineyard on the historic Tumbarumba–Khancoban Road. It is planted to sauvignon blanc, chardonnay, verdelho, pinot noir, cabernet sauvignon and merlot, and the wines are sold by mail order.

Lilac Hill Estate

★★★

55 Benara Road, Caversham, WA 6055 **REGION** Swan Valley
T (08) 9378 9945 **F** (08) 9378 9946 **OPEN** Tues–Sun 10.30–5.00
WINEMAKER Stephen Murfit **EST.** 1998 **CASES** 15 000
PRODUCT RANGE ($14–22 CD) Chenin Blanc, Semillon, Semillon Sauvignon Blanc, Verdelho, Chardonnay Verdelho, Chardonnay, Late Picked Frontignan, Zinfandel, Shiraz, Merlot, Cabernet Merlot, White Port, Old Tawny Port; Reserve Semillon, Shiraz.
SUMMARY Lilac Hill Estate is part of the renaissance which is sweeping the Swan Valley. Just when it seemed it would die a lingering death, supported only by Houghton, Sandalford and the remnants of the once Yugoslav-dominated cellar-door trade, wine tourism has changed the entire scene. Thus Lilac Hill Estate, drawing in part upon 4 hectares of estate vineyards, has already built a substantial business, relying on cellar-door trade and limited retail distribution. Considerable contract winemaking on-site fleshes out the business even further.

ΨΨΨΨΨ **Verdelho 2003** Very generous, rich, tropical fruit showing strong varietal character; while full, is not phenolic. **RATING** 91 **DRINK** Now **$** 16

ΨΨΨΨ **Two Seasons Reserve Merlot 2002** A pleasant, light mix of raspberry, cherry and more savoury, spicy notes. **RATING** 86 **DRINK** 2007 **$** 20
Late Picked Frontignan Muscat 2003 **RATING** 86 **DRINK** Now **$** 16
Semillon Sauvignon Blanc 2003 **RATING** 85 **DRINK** Now **$** 16

Chenin Blanc 2003 RATING 84 DRINK Now $14
Reserve Shiraz 2002 RATING 84 DRINK 2009 $20

TTT **Cape White 2003** RATING 83 $14

🍇 Lillian ★★★★

Glauders Road, Pemberton, WA 6260 (postal) **REGION** Pemberton
T (08) 9776 0193 **F** (08) 9776 0193 **OPEN** Not
WINEMAKER John Brocksopp **EST.** 1993 **CASES** 400
PRODUCT RANGE ($24 R) Marsanne, Shiraz Mataro.
SUMMARY The long-serving (and continuing consultant) viticulturist to Leeuwin Estate, John Brocksopp began the establishment of his 3-hectare vineyard planted to the Rhône trio of marsanne (1 hectare), roussanne (0.25 hectare) and viognier (0.25 hectare) and the south of France trio of shiraz (1.3 hectares), mourvedre (0.2 hectare) and graciano (0.2 hectare) in 1993, hastening slowly until their first tiny vintage in 1998. The varietal mix may seem à la mode, but it in fact comes from John Brocksopp's early experience working for Seppelt at Barooga in New South Wales, and before that in his formative years in the Barossa Valley. The wines are sold by mail order and word of mouth, but are also exported to the UK through Domaine Direct.

TTTTT **Marsanne 2002** Particularly elegant and finely balanced wine; touches of citrus and honeysuckle; long, clean finish with no heat. **RATING** 90 **DRINK** 2007 $24

TTTT **Shiraz Mataro 2000** Light to medium-bodied; good structure and balance; savoury, spicy black fruits and gentle tannins on the finish. **RATING** 88 **DRINK** 2010 $24

🍇 Lilliput Wines NR

Withers Road, Springhurst, Vic 3602 **REGION** Rutherglen
T (03) 5726 5055 **F** (03) 5726 5056 **OPEN** By appointment
WINEMAKER P Hellema **EST.** 2002
PRODUCT RANGE Shiraz, Cabernet Merlot.
SUMMARY The Hellema family has established its vineyard at Springhurst, with 6 hectares of cabernet sauvignon, merlot, shiraz and petit verdot. The as yet tiny production is sold by mail order and through the cellar door when open.

Lillydale Estate ★★★★★

45 Davross Court, Seville, Vic 3139 **REGION** Yarra Valley
T (03) 5964 2016 **F** (03) 5964 3009 **OPEN** 7 days 11–5
WINEMAKER Jim Brayne, Max McWilliam **EST.** 1975
PRODUCT RANGE ($14–23.50 R) Gewurztraminer, Sauvignon Blanc, Chardonnay, Pinot Noir, Shiraz, Cabernet Merlot.
SUMMARY Acquired by McWilliam's Wines in 1994 and Max McWilliam is in charge of the business. With a number of other major developments, notably Coonawarra and Barwang, on its plate, McWilliam's has adopted a softly, softly approach to Lillydale Estate; a winery restaurant opened in February 1997.

TTTTT **Shiraz 2002** Excellent cool-grown shiraz; intense black cherry, pepper, raspberry and spice; subtle vanilla oak; fine, ripe tannins. **RATING** 94 **DRINK** 2012 $23

TTTTT **Chardonnay 2002** Appealing citrus, melon and stone fruit flavours on the palate; excellent mouthfeel and intensity through to a long finish. **RATING** 93 **DRINK** 2009 $23
Pinot Noir 2002 Intense, spicy, savoury edges to the core of black fruits; very good structure and length. **RATING** 91 **DRINK** 2007 $23
Chardonnay 2003 Fine, elegant, understated; clean, tangy, citrus and melon; long finish; minimal oak. Screwcap. **RATING** 90 **DRINK** 2010 $19.50

TTTT **Pinot Noir 2003** Bright colour; ripe, spicy/plummy fruit; some fine tannins to close. Screwcap. **RATING** 89 **DRINK** 2009 $23
Gewurztraminer 2003 Delicate rose petal and lychee aromas and flavours; long, lingering acidity. Screwcap. **RATING** 88 **DRINK** 2007 $20

Lillypilly Estate ★★★★

Lillypilly Road, Leeton, NSW 2705 **REGION** Riverina
T (02) 6953 4069 **F** (02) 6953 4980 **OPEN** Mon–Sat 10–5.30, Sun by appointment
WINEMAKER Robert Fiumara **EST.** 1982 **CASES** 10 000
PRODUCT RANGE ($12.50–16.50 CD) Semillon, Sauvignon Blanc, Chardonnay, Tramillon®
(Traminer Semillon), Spatlese Lexia, Noble Riesling, Noble Muscat of Alexandria, Noble Harvest,
Red Velvet® (medium sweet red), Shiraz, Petit Verdot, Cabernet Sauvignon, Tawny Port, VP
(fortified Shiraz).
SUMMARY Apart from occasional vintage ports, the best wines by far are the botrytised white wines,
with the Noble Muscat of Alexandria unique to the winery; these wines have both style and intensity
of flavour, and can age well. The rating is strongly influenced by the very good botrytis wines. Exports
to the US and Canada.

ŸŸŸŸŸ **Noble Blend 2000** Glowing gold; luscious, peachy complexity offset by lingering, fine
acidity. Top example from the region. **RATING** 94 **DRINK** 2007 $ 15.50

ŸŸŸŸŸ **Noble Sauvignon Blanc 2002** Extremely complex aromas ranging through spice,
mandarin, lemon rind and cumquat; good length and acidity. **RATING** 92 **DRINK** 2010
$ 14.50

ŸŸŸŸ **Cabernet Sauvignon 2002** Light to medium-bodied with positive varietal character and
good length, all typical of an outstanding vintage. **RATING** 87 **DRINK** Now $ 16.50

ŸŸŸŸ **Tramillon® 2003 RATING** 84 **DRINK** Now $ 13.95

ŸŸŸ **Lexia 2002 RATING** 83 $ 13.95
Shiraz 2002 RATING 82 $ 16.50

Lilyvale Wines ★★☆

Riverton Road, via Texas, Qld 4385 **REGION** Granite Belt
T (07) 4653 5280 **F** (07) 4653 5287 **OPEN** 7 days 10–4 by appointment
WINEMAKER John Hordern, Peter Scudamore-Smith (Contract) **EST.** 1997 **CASES** 4000
PRODUCT RANGE ($15–16 R) Silver Downs Semillon, Inca's Lily Verdelho, Texas Gold Late Harvest
Semillon, The Texan Shiraz, The Royce Merlot.
SUMMARY Yet another new but substantial winery in Queensland. It has established 5 hectares
each of shiraz and chardonnay, 3 hectares of cabernet sauvignon, around 2.5 hectares each of
semillon and verdelho, and 1.5 hectares of merlot. The vineyard is situated near the Dumaresq
River, on the border between Queensland and New South Wales. Part of the wine is made under
the direction of Peter Scudamore-Smith MW, and part goes all the way to New South Wales'
Upper Hunter, where John Hordern is winemaker. Exports to the US, Canada, Singapore and
Japan.

ŸŸŸŸ **The Spur Cabernet Sauvignon 2002 RATING** 86 **DRINK** 2009 $ 16
The Royce Merlot 2002 RATING 85 **DRINK** Now $ 16

ŸŸŸ **The Texan Shiraz 2002 RATING** 83 $ 16
Texas Gold 2003 RATING 83 $ 16
Watson's Crossing Chardonnay 2003 RATING 80 $ 15

Limb Vineyards NR

PO Box 145, Greenock, SA 5360 **REGION** Barossa Valley
T 0419 846 549 **F** (08) 8347 7484 **OPEN** Not
WINEMAKER Contract **EST.** 1997
PRODUCT RANGE Shiraz Mourvedre, Cabernet.
SUMMARY Julie Limb manages the business, based on 15 hectares of cabernet sauvignon, shiraz and
mourvedre. The wines are contract-made, the principal market being the US; they are available by
mail order within Australia.

Lindemans (Coonawarra)

Main Penola–Naracoorte Road, Coonawarra, SA 5263 **REGION** Coonawarra
T (02) 4998 7684 **F** (02) 4998 7682 **OPEN** Not
WINEMAKER Greg Clayfield **EST.** 1908
PRODUCT RANGE ($15–49.95 R) Pyrus (Cabernet blend), Limestone Ridge (Shiraz Cabernet), and St George (Cabernet Sauvignon). Also the remnants of the Rouge Homme brand.
SUMMARY Lindemans is clearly the strongest brand other than Penfolds (and perhaps Rosemount) in the Southcorp Group, with some great vineyards and a great history. The Coonawarra vineyards are of ever-increasing significance because of the move towards regional identity in the all-important export markets, which has led to the emergence of a new range of regional/varietal labels. Whether the fullest potential of the vineyards (from a viticultural viewpoint) is being realised has been a matter of debate, but there are distinct signs of change for the better. Worldwide distribution.

ᵀᵀᵀᵀᵀ **Limestone Ridge 2000** Attractive blackberry and blackcurrant; good texture and balance; combines richness and elegance. **RATING** 94 **DRINK** 2015 $49

ᵀᵀᵀᵀ♀ **St George 2000** Supple, smooth, medium-bodied; sweet cassis/blackberry fruit, gentle oak and fine tannins. **RATING** 92 **DRINK** 2014 $49

Pyrus 2000 Ripe fruit flavours and aromas; supple; excellent balance and texture. **RATING** 92 **DRINK** 2012 $49

Lindemans (Hunter Valley)

McDonalds Road, Pokolbin, NSW 2320 **REGION** Lower Hunter Valley
T (02) 4998 7684 **F** (02) 4998 7324 **OPEN** 7 days 10–5
WINEMAKER Wayne Falkenberg, Greg Clayfield **EST.** 1843
PRODUCT RANGE ($19.90–80 CD) Hunter Valley Semillon, Chardonnay, Shiraz; Ben Ean Shiraz, Steven Shiraz.
SUMMARY One way or another, I have intersected with the Hunter Valley in general and Lindemans in particular for over 45 years. The wines are no longer made in the Lower Hunter, and the once mighty Semillon is a mere shadow of its former self. However, the refurbished historic Ben Ean winery (while no longer making wine) is a must-see for the wine tourist.

ᵀᵀᵀᵀ♀ **Hunter River Classic Release Semillon 1995** Reserve Bin 8645. Excellent green-gold; smooth, honeyed wine, still with crisp acidity; good length. **RATING** 92 **DRINK** 2009 $24.99

Lindemans (Karadoc) ★★★

Edey Road, Karadoc via Red Cliffs, Vic 3496 **REGION** Murray Darling
T (03) 5051 3333 **F** (03) 5051 3390 **OPEN** 7 days 10–4.30
WINEMAKER Greg Clayfield, Wayne Falkenberg **EST.** 1974 **CASES** 8 million
PRODUCT RANGE ($6.95–10.15 CD) Bin 23 Riesling, Bin 65 Chardonnay (one of the largest selling Chardonnay brands in the world), Bin 95 Sauvignon Blanc, Bin 99 Pinot Noir, Bin 45 Cabernet Sauvignon, Bin 50 Shiraz, Bin 40 Merlot are the most important; Cawarra range is at a lower price.
SUMMARY Now the production centre for all of the Lindemans and Leo Buring wines, with the exception of special lines made in the Coonawarra and Hunter wineries. The very large winery allows all-important economies of scale, and is the major processing centre for the beverage wine sector (casks, flagons and low-priced bottles) of the Southcorp empire. Its achievement in making several million cases of Bin 65 Chardonnay a year is extraordinary given the quality and consistency of the wines. Worldwide distribution.

ᵀᵀᵀᵀ **Bin 50 Shiraz 2002** Clearly expressed bright plum and blackberry fruit; quite silky; excellent value. **RATING** 87 **DRINK** Now $10.15

Cawarra Merlot 2002 User-friendly in every way, with plenty of sweet, juicy, soft red fruit flavours, and minimal tannins. A reflection of the excellent 2002 vintage in the Riverland. **RATING** 87 **DRINK** Now $7.80

Bin 45 Cabernet Sauvignon 2002 Well above average in its price range; smooth red and black fruits; fine, soft tannins; good length. **RATING** 87 **DRINK** Now $10.15

ΨΨΨΫ Bin 65 Chardonnay 2003 RATING 86 DRINK Now $ 10.15
Bin 75 Riesling 2003 RATING 85 DRINK 2007 $ 9.90
Cawarra Shiraz Cabernet 2002 RATING 84 DRINK Now $ 6.95
Cawarra Cabernet Merlot 2002 RATING 84 DRINK Now $ 6.95

ΨΨΨ Bin 25 Sparkling 2002 RATING 83 $ 10.15
Cawarra Semillon Chardonnay 2003 RATING 81 $ 6.95

ΨΨΫ Cawarra Semillon Chardonnay 2002 RATING 79 $ 6.95
Cawarra Colombard Semillon 2002 RATING 78 $ 6.95

Lindemans (Padthaway) ★★★★

Naracoorte Road, Padthaway, SA 5271 REGION Padthaway
T (02) 4998 7684 F (02) 4998 7682 OPEN Not
WINEMAKER Greg Clayfield EST. 1908
PRODUCT RANGE ($11–29.90 R) Reserve Padthaway Chardonnay, Reserve Cabernet Merlot, plus the Limestone Coast varietal range.
SUMMARY Lindemans Padthaway Chardonnay is one of the better premium Chardonnays on the market in Australia, with an exceptional capacity to age. However, all of the wines under the Padthaway label offer consistent quality and value for money.

ΨΨΨΨ **Padthaway Merlot 2000** Light to medium-bodied; clear varietal expression through spice, olive, berry and cedar; excellent texture and structure. RATING 89 DRINK Now $ 14.40
Padthaway Reserve Cabernet Sauvignon 2000 Clear-cut and bright varietal fruit comes through strongly on both bouquet and palate, with cassis/blackcurrant running through to a creditably long finish. RATING 88 DRINK 2009 $ 14.40
Padthaway Chardonnay 2003 Refined style; citrus stone fruit and melon; dry finish and minimal oak. RATING 87 DRINK 2007 $ 14.40
Padthaway Reserve Shiraz 2002 Fully reflects the vintage, with concentrated, almost essency, black fruits running through a very ripe, generous palate. RATING 87 DRINK 2008 $ 14.90

ΨΨΨΫ **Reserve Pinot Chardonnay 1999** RATING 86 DRINK Now $ 14.95

Lindenderry at Red Hill ★★★★

142 Arthurs Seat Road, Red Hill, Vic 3937 REGION Mornington Peninsula
T (03) 5989 2933 F (03) 5989 2936 OPEN 7 days 11–5
WINEMAKER Lindsay McCall (Contract) EST. 1999 CASES 1500
PRODUCT RANGE ($19–35 CD) Chardonnay, Pinot Blanc, Pinot Noir, Lindenwarrah Merlot.
SUMMARY Lindenderry at Red Hill is a sister operation to Lancemore Hill in the Macedon Ranges and Lindenwarrah at Milawa. It offers a five-star country house hotel, conference facilities, a function area, day spa, à la carte restaurant situated on 16 hectares of park-like gardens, but also includes a little over 3 hectares of vineyards, equally planted to pinot noir and chardonnay 10 years ago. The wines are made by Lindsay McCall of Paringa Estate fame, using similar techniques to those he uses for his estate wines.

Lindrum ★★★

c/- Level 29, Chifley Tower, 2 Chifley Square, Sydney, NSW 2000 (postal) REGION Langhorne Creek
T (02) 9375 2185 F (02) 9375 2121 OPEN Not
WINEMAKER Michael Potts (Contract) EST. 2001 CASES 12 000
PRODUCT RANGE ($17–99 ML) Premium range of Clara Semillon Chardonnay, Horace Cabernet Shiraz; Reserve range of Verdelho, Chardonnay, Shiraz, Cabernet Sauvignon.
SUMMARY The Lindrum story is a fascinating one; few Australians will not have heard of Walter Lindrum, who reigned as World Professional Billiards and Snooker Champion for over 30 years. What few would know is that his great-grandfather, Frederick Wilhelm von Lindrum, was a renowned vigneron in Norwood, South Australia, and also became Australia's first professional

billiards champion, beating the English champion, John Roberts, in 1869. The wines are made from purchased grapes by contract winemaker Michael Potts at Potts' Bleasdale Winery; an active website <www.lindrum.com> helps the marketing effort, which is otherwise through retail sources.

▼▼▼▽ **Horace Shiraz 2001** RATING 85 DRINK 2008 $ 26

Lirralirra Estate   ★★★☆

Paynes Road, Lilydale, Vic 3140 REGION Yarra Valley
T (03) 9735 0224 F (03) 9735 0224 OPEN Weekends and holidays 10–6, Jan 7 days
WINEMAKER Alan Smith EST. 1981 CASES 300
PRODUCT RANGE ($17–30 CD) Sauvignon Blanc, Reserve Sauvignon Blanc, Fume Blanc, Semillon Sauvignon Blanc, Reserve Pinot Noir, Cabernets.
SUMMARY Alan Smith started Lirralirra with the intention of specialising in a Sauternes-style blend of botrytised semillon and sauvignon blanc. It seemed a good idea — in a sense it still does, on paper — but it simply didn't work. He has had to change direction to a more conventional mix, but has done so with dignity and humour.

▼▼▼▼▽ **Pinot Noir 2002** Complex foresty/plummy/spicy aromas; rich, ripe plummy fruit and complementary tannins. Future guaranteed by the screwcap. RATING 90 DRINK 2009 $ 23

▼▼▼▼ **Yarra Valley Cabernets 2000** RATING 85 DRINK 2010 $ 23

� Little Brampton Wines   ★★★☆

PO Box 61, Clare, SA 5453 REGION Clare Valley
T (08) 8843 4201 F (08) 8843 4244 OPEN Not
WINEMAKER Contract EST. 2001 CASES 800
PRODUCT RANGE ($19–24 ML) Riesling, Cabernet Sauvignon.
SUMMARY Alan and Pamela Schwarz have established 10 hectares of vineyard, with 4 hectares each of shiraz and cabernet sauvignon and 2 hectares of riesling. It is one of the newest wineries in the Clare Valley region.

▼▼▼▼▽ **Riesling 2003** Powerful but smooth, full of citrus/tropical fruit; early maturing. RATING 91 DRINK 2008 $ 19

▼▼▼▼ **Cabernet Sauvignon 2001** RATING 85 DRINK 2007 $ 24

� Little Bridge   ★★★★

PO Box 499, Bungendore, NSW 2621 REGION Canberra District
T (02) 6251 5242 F (02) 6251 4379 OPEN Not
WINEMAKER Greg Gallagher, Sue Carpenter, David Carpenter (all Contract), John Leyshon EST. 1996
CASES 1000
PRODUCT RANGE ($14–20 ML) Riesling, Unwooded Chardonnay, Chardonnay, Pinot Noir, Merlot, Cabernet Sauvignon.
SUMMARY Little Bridge Vineyard is a partnership between John and Val Leyshon, and Rowland and Madeleine Clark. The labels, with photographs of a rocky coastline, stem from the fact that the partners were friends long before they decided to go into the wine business, every year having a fishing holiday on a secluded part of the NSW south coast at a property owned by Rowland Clark's family. The establishment date of 1996 was when the business partnership was formed, and after a false start in 1997 with the planting of the first vines, 2 hectares of chardonnay, pinot noir, riesling and merlot were planted on Rowland Clark's property at Butmaroo, near Bungendore, at a height of 860 metres above sea level. A further 2.5 hectares are being planted in the spring of 2004. Greg Gallagher, at Jeir Creek Winery, makes the white wines; the pinot noir is made by Sue and David Carpenter at Lark Hill Winery, in each case with John Leyshon in close attendance. The quality of the first releases is all one could hope for.

▼▼▼▼▽ **Cabernet Sauvignon 2002** Excellent cassis/blackcurrant varietal character; medium-bodied, with gently ripe tannins; balanced oak. RATING 91 DRINK 2012 $ 18

▼▼▼▼ **Riesling 2003** Aromatic lime, herb and spice; limey mid-palate, minerally finish. Screwcap. RATING 89 DRINK 2010 $ 17

Pinot Noir 2003 Light to medium-bodied; clear varietal character in spicy/savoury spectrum; good length and finish. **RATING** 88 **DRINK** 2008 $ 20

Unwooded Chardonnay 2003 Tangy citrus and stone fruit; bright acidity; good length, well above average. Screwcap. **RATING** 87 **DRINK** 2009 $ 14

Chardonnay 2003 Subtle oak; light to medium-bodied; peach and stone fruit; well balanced. **RATING** 87 **DRINK** 2009 $ 15

Merlot 2002 Well-made; small red fruit berries; subtle oak; neatly balanced. **RATING** 87 **DRINK** 2009 $ 19

🐦 Little River Estate   NR

c/- 147 Rankins Road, Kensington, Vic 3031 (postal) **REGION** Upper Goulburn
T 0418 381 722 **OPEN** Not
WINEMAKER Philip Challen, Oscar Rosa, Nick Arena **EST.** 1986 **CASES** 250
PRODUCT RANGE ($20–25 R) Challen Chardonnay, Little River Blend (Cabernet blend).
SUMMARY Philip (a chef and hotelier) and Christine Challen began the establishment of their vineyard in 1986 with the planting of 0.5 hectare of cabernet sauvignon. Two hectares of chardonnay (and a few vines of pinot noir) followed several years later. Vineyard practice and soil management are based on organic principles and produces low yields, notwithstanding the fairly old vines. While made in small quantities, they are available in virtually every hotel, restaurant and liquor store in the region, and in a considerable number of outlets in Melbourne.

Little River Wines   NR

Cnr West Swan and Forest Roads, Henley Brook, WA 6055 **REGION** Swan Valley
T (08) 9296 4462 **F** (08) 9296 1022 **OPEN** 7 days 10–5
WINEMAKER Bruno de Tastes **EST.** 1934 **CASES** 3000
PRODUCT RANGE ($15–28 CD) Chenin Blanc, Viognier, Chardonnay, Brut de Brut, Vin Doux Late Harvest, Noble Classic, Florial Dry Rose, Old Vines Shiraz, Cabernet Sauvignon Merlot.
SUMMARY Following several quick changes of ownership (and of consultant winemakers), the former Glenalwyn now has as its winemaker the eponymously named Count Bruno de Tastes. The wines come from 4 hectares of estate vineyards. Exports to Hong Kong and Malaysia.

Little Valley   ★★★★

RMB 6047 One Chain Road, Merricks North, Vic 3926 **REGION** Mornington Peninsula
T (03) 5989 7564 **F** (03) 5989 7564 **OPEN** By appointment
WINEMAKER Richard McIntyre (Contract) **EST.** 1998 **CASES** 300
PRODUCT RANGE ($18–20 ML) Chardonnay, Pinot Noir.
SUMMARY Wesley College teacher Sue Taylor and part-time Anglican minister and husband Brian have planted 0.8 hectare each of chardonnay and pinot noir on their Little Valley property, simultaneously building their house on the property. They have Ian MacRae as consultant viticulturist, and Rick McIntyre (of Moorooduc Estate) makes the wines. Unfortunately, the 2002 vintage was so small that there will be no 2002 Chardonnay and less than 40 dozen bottles of Pinot Noir from the vintage. It is just as well the Mornington Peninsula is such a beautiful place, the Little Valley property itself a prime example of that beauty, providing a return which is not measured in dollars and cents.

Little Wine Company   ★★★★

824 Milbrodale Road, Broke, NSW 2330 **REGION** Lower Hunter Valley
T (02) 6579 1111 **F** (02) 6579 1440 **OPEN** Fri–Mon 10–4.30, Wed 12.30–4
WINEMAKER Ian Little, Suzanne Little **EST.** 1984 **CASES** 15 000
PRODUCT RANGE ($15–24 R) The Olivine range of Viognier, Sangiovese Rose, Sangiovese, Shiraz Viognier, Merlot; and the Canberra District-sourced Talga range of Chardonnay and Shiraz.
SUMMARY A name change to The Little Wine Company, and the narrowed focus on the two brands, coupled with yet another change of address, may cause momentary confusion. The Talga wines come from a vineyard planted between 1980 and 1996 at an altitude of nearly 700 metres on the slopes of the Gundaroo Valley near Canberra. The bottom line, however, is a quality-oriented business with exports to the US and Canada complementing domestic sales.

🍷🍷🍷🍷🍸 **Olivine Gewurztraminer 2003** Classic spice and rose petal aromas; very well made; flavour without phenolics. **RATING** 90 **DRINK** 2007 $ 19

Talga Shiraz 2001 Clean red and black fruits; spicy, savoury notes; medium-bodied, but complex flavours; good tannins and length. **RATING** 90 **DRINK** 2011 $ 23

🍷🍷🍷🍷 **Olivine Viognier 2003** Unlikely origins of Big Rivers and Hunter, but over-delivers big-time; sweet pastille fruit, good balance and length. No hard phenolics. **RATING** 89 **DRINK** 2007 $ 19

🍷🍷🍷🍸 **Olivine Sangiovese Rose 2003** **RATING** 86 **DRINK** Now $ 19

Olivine Sangiovese 2002 **RATING** 85 **DRINK** Now $ 19

Llangibby Estate ★★★

Old Mount Barker Road, Echunga, SA 5153 (postal) **REGION** Adelaide Hills
T (08) 8338 5529 **F** (08) 8338 7118 **OPEN** Not
WINEMAKER Ben Riggs (Contract) **EST.** 1998 **CASES** 600
PRODUCT RANGE ($10–17 ML) Sauvignon Blanc, Pinot Noir, Pinot Shiraz (Hermitage), Shiraz Cabernet, Tempranillo.
SUMMARY Chris Addams Williams and John Williamson have established a substantial vineyard cresting a ridge close to Echunga, at a height of 360 metres. The varietal choice is eclectic, the lion's share to a little over 5 hectares each of shiraz and cabernet sauvignon, then 1.95 hectares of tempranillo, 1.4 hectares of sauvignon blanc, and a tiny planting of pinot noir. Until 2002 this was used to provide a Pinot Hermitage blend, but from that year both a varietal Tempranillo and a Pinot Noir have joined the product range alongside Sauvignon Blanc and Shiraz Cabernet. Exports to the UK.

🍷🍷🍷🍸 **Tempranillo 2002** **RATING** 86 **DRINK** 2007 $ 29.95

🍷🍷🍷 **Sauvignon Blanc 2003** **RATING** 82 $ 19

🍃 Loch Luna NR

Morgan Road, Overland Corner, SA 5345 **REGION** Riverland
T (08) 8588 7210 **F** (08) 8588 7210 **OPEN** By appointment most days 1–5
WINEMAKER Grant Semmens (Contract) **EST.** 1999
PRODUCT RANGE ($13–18 CD) Verdelho, Shiraz, Cabernet Sauvignon.
SUMMARY Raymond Neindorf and Louise Spangler run a small eco-business taking full advantage of the national heritage-listed wetlands reserves; Loch Luna Eco-Stay is part of the world network of biosphere reserves. A cottage for two to three people is 300 metres from the homestead/cellar door. The wines come from 10 hectares of vineyards, and are made (by contract) in limited quantities. Further details are available at <www.riverland.net.au/~lochluna>.

🍃 Lochmoore ★★★☆

PO Box 430, Trafalgar, Vic 3824 **REGION** Gippsland
T 0402 216 622 **OPEN** Not
WINEMAKER Harry Friend (Contract) **EST.** 1997
PRODUCT RANGE ($16–18 ML) Chardonnay, Pinot Noir.
SUMMARY The 2 hectares of chardonnay and pinot noir at Lochmoore are tended by one of the most highly qualified viticulturists one is ever likely to meet. Sue Hasthorpe grew up in Trafalgar, obtained a Bachelor of Science (Hons) and Doctor of Philosophy in Physiology at the University of Melbourne, then worked and travelled as a medical research scientist in Australia, the UK, the US and Europe, including a year at the Pasteur Institute in Paris. After returning to Australia she studied viticulture via the University of Melbourne Dookie College Campus by distance education. If this were not enough, she is now doing a Masters of Agribusiness at the University of Melbourne. The wines are sold through a number of local restaurants and shops, and by mail order. The bargain-priced Chardonnay has been made with typical sensitivity by Harry Friend.

🍷🍷🍷🍷 **Chardonnay 2002** Gently complex, seamless, interwoven ripe peach, cashew and oak; soft finish. **RATING** 87 **DRINK** Now $ 16

Logan Wines ★★★

1320 Castelreagh Highway, Mudgee NSW **REGION** Orange
T (02) 9958 6844 **F** (02) 9958 1258 **OPEN** Not
WINEMAKER Peter Logan **EST.** 1997 **CASES** 20 000
PRODUCT RANGE ($15–27 R) Sauvignon Blanc, Chardonnay, Reserve Chardonnay, Weemala
Chardonnay, Shiraz, Weemala Shiraz, Weemala Merlot, Cabernet Merlot.
SUMMARY Logan wines is a family operation, founded by businessman Mal Logan, assisted by three
of his children: Peter, who just happens to be an oenology graduate from the University of Adelaide,
Greg (advertising) and Kylie (office administrator). Retail distribution in all States; exports to the
UK, Canada, Mexico, Germany and Sweden.

ŸŸŸŸ **Sauvignon Blanc 2003** Complex array of tropical, peach and mango; soft but
flavoursome. **RATING** 87 **DRINK** Now $18.95

ŸŸŸŸ **Apple Tree Flat Semillon Sauvignon Blanc 2003** Not intense but well made and
balanced; gentle herbaceous/citrus mix; good value. **RATING** 86 **DRINK** Now $9.95
Apple Tree Flat Chardonnay 2001 Gentle melon and fig; subtle oak; easy mouthfeel and
good finish; good value. **RATING** 86 **DRINK** Now $9.95
Hannah Rose 2003 **RATING** 84 **DRINK** Now $17.95
Apple Tree Flat Shiraz 2001 **RATING** 84 **DRINK** Now $9.95

ŸŸŸ **Apple Tree Flat Merlot 2002** **RATING** 82 $9.95

London Lodge Estate NR

Muswellbrook Road, Gungal, NSW 2333 **REGION** Upper Hunter Valley
T (02) 6547 6122 **F** (02) 6547 6122 **OPEN** 7 days 10–9
WINEMAKER Gary Reed (Contract) **EST.** 1988
SUMMARY The 16-hectare vineyard of Stephen and Joanne Horner is planted to chardonnay, pinot
noir, shiraz and cabernet sauvignon, and sold through a cellar door (and restaurant) with a full array
of tourist attractions, including arts and crafts.

Long Gully Estate ★★★☆

Long Gully Road, Healesville, Vic 3777 **REGION** Yarra Valley
T (03) 9510 5798 **F** (03) 9510 9859 **OPEN** 7 days 11–5
WINEMAKER Daniel Stocker **EST.** 1982 **CASES** 150 000
PRODUCT RANGE ($15–30 CD) Premium range of Riesling, Sauvignon Blanc, Chardonnay, Reserve Ice
Riesling, Pinot Noir, Shiraz, Reserve Merlot, Irma's Cabernet; Victoria Collection of Spatlese Riesling,
Sauvignon Blanc Semillon Chardonnay, Chardonnay, Bunyarra Rose, Pinot Noir, Cabernet Sauvignon.
SUMMARY One of the larger (but by no means largest) of the Yarra Valley producers which have
successfully established a number of export markets over recent years. Wine quality has risen,
doubtless due to a core of mature vineyards; it is able to offer a range of wines with 2–3 years bottle
age. Recent vineyard extensions underline the commercial success of Long Gully. Exports to the UK,
Switzerland and Singapore.

ŸŸŸŸŸ **Chardonnay 2001** Light to medium-bodied, clean and elegant; melon and nectarine
backed by subtle oak and malolactic influences; developing well. **RATING** 90 **DRINK** 2008
$22
Reserve Ice Riesling 2002 Good lime juice concentration and length; upper-end auslese
sweetness; good balance. **RATING** 90 **DRINK** 2009 $23

ŸŸŸŸ **Irma's Cabernet Sauvignon 2000** Savoury, earthy style with a core of medium-bodied
blackcurrant fruit. **RATING** 88 **DRINK** 2010 $24
Pinot Noir 2002 Clean, fresh and surprisingly delicate for the vintage; strawberry and
cherry fruit; early drinking. **RATING** 87 **DRINK** Now $22

ŸŸŸŸ **Semillon 2002** **RATING** 85 **DRINK** 2007 $18
Shiraz 2000 **RATING** 84 **DRINK** 2009 $22

ŸŸŸ **Victoria Collection Cabernet 2001** **RATING** 83 $15

Longleat Estate

105 Old Weir Road, Murchison, Vic 3610 **REGION** Goulburn Valley
T (03) 5826 2294 **F** (03) 5826 2510 **OPEN** Fri–Mon and public holidays 10–5, or by appointment
WINEMAKER Guido Vazzoler **EST.** 1975 **CASES** 4000
PRODUCT RANGE ($12.50–19.90 CD) River's Edge Riesling, Founder's Reserve Semillon, Semillon Sauvignon Blanc, Murchison Mill Shiraz, Old Weir Road Shiraz, Campbell's Bend Cabernet Sauvignon.
SUMMARY Sandra and Guido Vazzoler acquired the long-established Longleat Estate vineyard in 2003. The wines are estate-grown; there is limited distribution through Tasman Liquor Traders, supported by cellar-door sales, mail order and www.longleatwines.com.

ŦŦŦŦŸ **Campbell's Bend Cabernet Sauvignon 2002** Nice core of sweet blackcurrant fruit, bordering on cassis; fine, ripe tannins; nice oak. **RATING** 91 **DRINK** 2014 $ 20
Murchison Mill Shiraz 2002 Complex; blackberry, spice and raspberry plus touches of mocha and vanilla; subtle finish. **RATING** 90 **DRINK** 2012 $ 20

Long Point Vineyard

6 Cooinda Place, Lake Cathie, NSW 2445 **REGION** Hastings River
T (02) 6585 4598 **F** (02) 6584 8915 **OPEN** Thurs–Sun and public holidays 10–6, or by appointment
WINEMAKER Graeme Davies **EST.** 1995 **CASES** 600
PRODUCT RANGE ($13–20 CD) Traminer, Chardonnay, Shiraz, Duet Cabernet Sauvignon Chambourcin. Also ginger beer, mead and orange liqueur.
SUMMARY In turning their dream into reality, Graeme (an educational psychologist) and Helen (chartered accountant) Davies took no chances. After becoming interested in wine as consumers through wine appreciation courses, the Davies moved from Brisbane so that 36-year-old Graeme could begin his study for a postgraduate diploma in wine from Roseworthy. Late in 1993 they purchased a 5-hectare property near Lake Cathie, progressively establishing 2 hectares of chardonnay, shiraz, chambourcin, cabernet sauvignon and frontignac. As well as having a full-time job at Cassegrain and establishing the vineyard, Graeme Davies self-built the house, which was designed by Helen and has a pyramid-shaped roof and an underground cellar. All of the wines are made on-site.

Longview Vineyard

Pound Road, Macclesfield, SA 5153 **REGION** Adelaide Hills
T (08) 8388 9694 **F** (08) 8388 9693 **OPEN** Sunday 11–5, or by appointment
WINEMAKER Shaw & Smith, Kangarilla Road (Contract) **EST.** 1995 **CASES** 5300
PRODUCT RANGE ($20–27 ML) Iron Knob Riesling, My Fat Goose Semillon Sauvignon Blanc, Beau Sea Viognier, Blue Cow Unwooded Chardonnay, Yakka Shiraz, Epitome Red, Black Crow Nebbiolo, The Mob Zinfandel, Devil's Elbow Cabernet.
SUMMARY In a strange twist of fate, Longview Vineyard came to be through the success of Two Dogs, the lemon-flavoured alcohol drink created by Duncan MacGillivray and sold in 1995 to the Pernod Ricard Groupe (also the owners of Orlando). Over 60 hectares have been planted, with shiraz and cabernet sauvignon accounting for a little over half, plus significant plantings of chardonnay and merlot, and smaller plantings of viognier, semillon, riesling, sauvignon blanc, zinfandel and nebbiolo. The majority of the production is sold to Southcorp, but $1.2 million has been invested in establishing a cellar door and function area, barrel rooms and an overall administration centre for the Group activities. All of the buildings enjoy a spectacular view over the Coorong and Lake Alexandrina.

ŦŦŦŦŸ **Single Vineyard Yakka Shiraz 2002** Medium-bodied; smooth blackberry and spice; good French oak and fine tannins through a long finish. **RATING** 91 **DRINK** 2012 $ 22
Single Vineyard Devil's Elbow Cabernet Sauvignon 2002 Earthy, spicy overtones to a core of blackcurrant fruit; savoury and long; lingering tannins. **RATING** 91 **DRINK** 2017 $ 22
Single Vineyard Iron Knob Riesling 2003 Delicate apple blossom aromas; a mix of crisp apple and citrus flavours; fresh finish. **RATING** 90 **DRINK** 2008 $ 16
Single Vineyard Yakka Shiraz 2001 Medium-bodied; gently savoury; sweet blackberry and plum fruit; fine, ripe tannins and good oak handling. **RATING** 90 **DRINK** 2010 $ 22

ŦŦŦŦ **Single Vineyard My Fat Goose Semillon Sauvignon Blanc 2003** Quite complex fruit aromas and flavours; the barest touch of oak; herbs and sweet lemon flavours. **RATING** 89 **DRINK** 2007 $ 15
Single Vineyard Blue Cow Chardonnay 2003 While unoaked, has particularly good length to the white peach fruit flavours; lingering finish. **RATING** 89 **DRINK** Now $ 16
Single Vineyard Whippet Sauvignon Blanc 2003 Spotlessly clean and crisp; mineral, gooseberry herbaceous flavours; good length. **RATING** 88 **DRINK** Now $ 17.50

ŦŦŦŸ **Single Vineyard Beau Sea Viognier 2003 RATING** 86 **DRINK** 2007 $ 19.60
Single Vineyard Devil's Elbow Cabernet Sauvignon 2001 RATING 86 **DRINK** 2008 $ 22
Single Vineyard The Mob Zinfandel 2002 Exotic spice, prune jam aromas; so ripe and jammy in the mouth it seems sweet — painfully so, indeed. Some may love it. **RATING** 86 **DRINK** 2007 $ 29
Single Vineyard Black Crow Nebbiolo 2002 Typically pale colour; very, very savoury varietal flavours; fine tannins; at the opposite end of the universe from the Zinfandel. **RATING** 86 **DRINK** 2008 $ 22

Lost Lake ★★★

Lot 3 Vasse Highway, Pemberton, WA 6260 **REGION** Pemberton
T (08) 9776 1251 **F** (08) 9776 1919 **OPEN** Wed–Sun 10–4
WINEMAKER Justin Hearn, Melanie Bowater **EST.** 1990 **CASES** 5000
PRODUCT RANGE ($14–20 CD) Semillon, Sauvignon Blanc, Semillon Chardonnay, Chardonnay, Pinot Noir, Shiraz, Shiraz Merlot, Cabernet Shiraz.
SUMMARY Previously known as Eastbrook Estate, its origins go back to 1990 and to the acquisition of an 80-hectare farming property which was subdivided into three portions: 16 hectares, now known as Picardy, were acquired by Dr Bill Pannell; 18 hectares became the base for Lost Lake; and the remainder was sold. The initial plantings in 1990 were of pinot noir and chardonnay, followed by shiraz, sauvignon blanc, merlot and cabernet sauvignon between 1996 and 1998 — 9 hectares are now planted. A jarrah pole and cedar winery with a crush capacity of 300 tonnes was built in 1995, together with a restaurant which seats 150 people; it is open 6 days a week for lunch and for dinner on Friday and Saturday nights. In 1999 the business was acquired by four Perth investors. Exports to the UK.

ŦŦŦŦŸ **Chardonnay 2001** Appealing cashew and melon, bottle-developed, multi-layered flavours; mouthfilling and supple. **RATING** 90 **DRINK** 2008 $ 18

ŦŦŦŸ **Pinot Noir 2001 RATING** 86 **DRINK** Now $ 18
Semillon Chardonnay 2002 RATING 85 **DRINK** Now $ 14
Cabernet Shiraz 2001 RATING 84 **DRINK** Now $ 16

ŦŦŦ **Sauvignon Blanc 2001 RATING** 83 $ 16

Lost Valley Winery ★★★☆

Strath Creek, Vic 3658 (postal) **REGION** Upper Goulburn
T (03) 9592 3531 **F** (03) 9592 6396 **OPEN** Not
WINEMAKER Alex White (Contract) **EST.** 1995 **CASES** 2500
PRODUCT RANGE ($30–32 R) Shiraz, Merlot, Cortese.
SUMMARY Dr Robert Ippaso planted the Lost Valley vineyard at an elevation of 450 metres on the slopes of Mount Tallarook, with 1.5 hectares of shiraz, merlot and cortese. The cortese is the only such planting in Australia. It pays homage to Dr Ippaso's birthplace: Savoie, in the Franco-Italian Alps, where cortese flourishes. Exports to the UK and Canada.

ŦŦŦŦ **Merlot 2002** Striking wine with some late-picked fruit characters; sweet red fruits on entry, then veering to savoury on the long finish. **RATING** 89 **DRINK** 2008 $ 32
Cortese 2003 Still water-white; spotlessly clean mineral, apple and pear, but you have to look to find the constituents. **RATING** 87 **DRINK** 2007 $ 30

Louee ★★★☆

Cox's Creek Road, Rylstone, NSW 2849 **REGION** Upper Goulburn
T (02) 8923 5373 **F** (02) 8923 5362 **OPEN** 7 days 9–5
WINEMAKER David Lowe, Jane Wilson (Contract) **EST.** 1998 **CASES** 1500
PRODUCT RANGE ($15–18 ML) Nullo Mountain Riesling, Cox's Crown Verdelho, Tongbong Chardonnay, Nullo Late Picked Riesling, Rumkers Peak Shiraz.
SUMMARY Jointly owned by Rod James and Tony Maxwell. While a relative newcomer on the scene, Louee promises to be a substantial operation. Its home vineyard at Rylstone has over 32 hectares of plantings, led by cabernet sauvignon, shiraz, petit verdot and merlot, with chardonnay, cabernet franc and verdelho making up the balance. The second vineyard is on Nullo Mountain, bordered by the Wollemi National Park, at an altitude of 1100 metres, high by any standards. Here the cool-climate varieties of riesling, sauvignon blanc, pinot noir, pinot gris and nebbiolo have been planted, 4 hectares in all. With the involvement of ex-McWilliam's senior marketing man David Boyce, and contract winemaking by the very experienced David Lowe and Jane Wilson team, the venture promises to be very successful.

▼▼▼▼ **Nullo Mountain Riesling 2003** Clean, tight bouquet, touch of mineral; good mouthfeel, focus and length; citrus blossom flavours. **RATING** 88 **DRINK** Now $18

▼▼▼▽ **Rumkers Peak Shiraz 2002 RATING** 86 **DRINK** 2009 $18
Cox's Crown Verdelho 2003 RATING 84 **DRINK** Now $15

Louis-Laval Wines NR

160 Cobcroft Road, Broke, NSW 2330 **REGION** Lower Hunter Valley
T (02) 6579 1105 **F** (02) 6579 1105 **OPEN** By appointment
WINEMAKER Roy Meyer **EST.** 1987 **CASES** 1200
PRODUCT RANGE ($25 CD) Shiraz, Cabernet Sauvignon.
SUMMARY It is ironic that the winery name should have eponymous associations with Alfa Laval, the giant Swiss food and wine machinery firm. Roy Meyer runs an organic vineyard (using only sulphur and copper sprays) and is proud of the fact that the winery has no refrigeration and no stainless steel. The wines produced from the 2.5-hectare vineyard are fermented in open barrels or cement tanks, and maturation is handled entirely in oak.

Lovegrove Vineyard and Winery ★★★☆

1420 Heidelberg–Kinglake Road, Cottles Bridge, Vic 3099 **REGION** Yarra Valley
T (03) 9718 1569 **F** (03) 9718 1028 **OPEN** Weekends and public holidays 11–6, Mon–Fri by appointment
WINEMAKER Stephen Bennett **EST.** 1983 **CASES** 1500
PRODUCT RANGE ($15–32 CD) Sauvignon Blanc, Chardonnay, Quest Chardonnay, Paradis, Petillant Methode Champenoise, Pinot Noir, Merlot, Cabernet Merlot.
SUMMARY Lovegrove is a long-established winery in the Diamond Valley subregion, and while production is limited, it offers the visitor much to enjoy, with picturesque gardens overlooking the Kinglake Ranges; antipasto, soup and cheese lunch; barbecue and picnic tables; and live music on the second Sunday of the month. Art exhibitions are also staged, and the winery caters for private functions. The wines are produced from 4 hectares of estate plantings which are now fully mature, and a range of vintages is available.

Lowe Family Wines ★★★☆

Tinja Lane, Mudgee, NSW 2850 **REGION** Mudgee
T (02) 6372 0800 **F** (02) 6372 0811 **OPEN** Fri–Mon 10–5, or by appointment
WINEMAKER David Lowe, Jane Wilson **EST.** 1987 **CASES** 6000
PRODUCT RANGE ($10–28 CD) Semillon, Chardonnay, Botrytis Semillon, Shiraz, Merlot, Orange Red (Cabernet blend); also Tinja Chardonnay, Merlot Rose, Sangiovese, Zinfandel.
SUMMARY Former Rothbury winemaker David Lowe and Jane Wilson make the Lowe Family Wines at two locations, principally at their purpose-built winery at Mudgee, but also with a shopfront in the Hunter Valley via the former Peppers Creek. Exports to the UK, Germany and Canada.

ῙῙῙῙ **Chardonnay 2000** Fruit-driven; nectarine and peach flavours; good length and freshness for its age. **RATING** 88 **DRINK** 2007 $ 23
Shiraz 2002 Pleasing medium body; black cherry and a touch of plum; smooth tannins, well-handled oak. **RATING** 88 **DRINK** 2012 $ 28
Tinja 2003 Spice, tobacco and black cherry; good texture in light to medium-bodied context; convincing tangy varietal character. **RATING** 87 **DRINK** 2009 $ 18

ῙῙῙῚ **Orange Red 1999** **RATING** 85 **DRINK** 2008 $ 28

ῙῙῙ **Rockpool Semillon 1996** **RATING** 83 $ 21
Mudgee Merlot 2002 **RATING** 83 $ 25

Lowe Family Wines (Hunter Valley)

Cnr Broke Road and Ekerts Lane, Pokolbin, NSW 2321 **REGION** Lower Hunter Valley
T (02) 4998 7121 **F** (02) 4998 7121 **OPEN** Wed–Mon 10–5
WINEMAKER David Lowe, Jane Wilson **EST.** 1987 **CASES** 2500
PRODUCT RANGE ($15–25 CD) Semillon, Chardonnay, Shiraz, Merlot, Orange Red (Cabernet blend), Yacht Club Port; also Peppers Creek wines (Hunter Valley) Rose, Merlot and Shiraz.
SUMMARY The former Peppers Creek winery has been acquired by David Lowe and Jane Wilson, and is now the Hunter Valley base for Lowe Family Wines. For the time being the Peppers Creek brand is being maintained.

ῙῙῙ **Hunter Valley Semillon 2003** **RATING** 82 $ 21

Loxley Vineyard NR

362 Pastoria East Road, Pipers Creek near Kyneton, Vic 3444 **REGION** Macedon Ranges
T (03) 9616 6598 **F** (03) 9614 2249 **OPEN** Not
WINEMAKER Alison Cash, John Ellis, Llew Knight (Contract) **EST.** 1999 **CASES** 1200
PRODUCT RANGE ($20 CD) Riesling, sparkling, Pinot Noir, Merlot; second label Chases Lane.
SUMMARY A partnership is developing a vineyard/resort/entertainment complex at Loxley. Seventeen hectares of vineyard have been planted, and contract winemaking arranged through John Ellis and Llew Knight. Wines will be produced under two labels, as part of the crop is being sold to John Ellis of Hanging Rock. The first commercial release (2003 Pinot Noir) will be in 2004, through the cellar door, by mail order and at selected restaurants.

Lucas Estate

Donges Road, Severnlea, Qld 4352 **REGION** Granite Belt
T (07) 4683 6365 **F** (07) 4683 6356 **OPEN** 7 days 10–5
WINEMAKER Peter Lucas, Jim Barnes **EST.** 1999 **CASES** 300
PRODUCT RANGE ($16–20 CD) Chardonnay, Chardoux, Shiraz, Merlot, Cabernet Shiraz, Cabernet Sauvignon, Liquer Muscat.
SUMMARY Louise Samuel and husband Colin Sellars purchased Lucas Estate in 2003. Prior owner Peter Lucas remains involved with the winemaking of the wines, drawing upon 2.5 hectares of estate plantings.

ῙῙῙῙ **Merlot 2002** Blackcurrant and hints of spice and licorice; plenty of mouthfeel; good structure. **RATING** 87 **DRINK** 2010 $ 19.50

🐌 Lucy's Run

1274 Wine Country Drive, Rothbury, NSW 2335 **REGION** Lower Hunter Valley
T (02) 4938 3594 **F** (02) 4938 3592 **OPEN** 7 days 10–5
WINEMAKER David Hook (Contract) **EST.** 1998 **CASES** 1000
PRODUCT RANGE ($15–20 CD) Verdelho, Sweet Dessert Verdelho, Shiraz, Merlot.
SUMMARY The Lucy's Run business has a variety of offerings of wine, cold pressed extra virgin olive oil and self-catering farm accommodation. The wines are made from 4 hectares of verdelho, merlot and shiraz, the 2002 Merlot winning a gold medal at the 2003 Hunter Valley Wine Show. The feisty label design, incidentally, is the work of local artist Paula Rengger, who doubles up as the chef at Shakey Tables Restaurant, itself the deserving winner of numerous recent awards.

Lyre Bird Hill ★★★

370 Inverloch Road, Koonwarra, Vic 3954 **REGION** Gippsland
T (03) 5664 3204 **F** (03) 5664 3206 **OPEN** Weekends and public holidays 10–5, or by appointment
WINEMAKER Owen Schmidt **EST.** 1986 **CASES** 2000
PRODUCT RANGE ($15–30 CD) Riesling, Riesling Cellar Reserve, Traminer, Sauvignon Blanc, Bowers Bouquet (white blend), Chardonnay, Shiraz Rose, Pinot Noir, Pinot Noir Cellar Reserve, Shiraz, Cabernet Sauvignon, Salut! (Cabernet Sauvignon Shiraz Merlot), Rhapsody (sparkling), Phantasy (sparkling), Golden Nectar (dessert).
SUMMARY Former Melbourne professionals Owen and Robyn Schmidt make small quantities of estate-grown wine (the vineyard is 2.4 hectares in size), and offer accommodation for three couples (RACV four-star rating) in their spacious guesthouse and self-contained cottage. Various weather-related viticulture problems have seen the Schmidts supplement their estate-grown intake with grapes from contract growers in Gippsland and the Yarra Valley, and also provide contract winemaking services.

Mabrook Estate ★★☆

258 Inlet Road, Bulga, NSW 2330 **REGION** Lower Hunter Valley
T (02) 9971 9994 **F** (02) 9971 9924 **OPEN** Weekends 10–4
WINEMAKER Larissa Kalt, Tony Kalt **EST.** 1996 **CASES** 800
PRODUCT RANGE ($10–18 CD) Semillon, Apricot Paddock Semillon, Verdelho, Wombat Creek Verdelho, Honey Paddock Shiraz; Conspiracy Merlot, Cabernet Merlot, Cabernet Sauvignon, Port.
SUMMARY The Swiss-born Kalt family began the establishment of Mabrook Estate in 1996, planting 3 hectares of semillon, 2 hectares of shiraz and 1 hectare of verdelho. Parents Mona and Tony Kalt decided to use organic growing methods from the word go, and the vineyard is now certified organic by NASAA (National Association Sustainable Agriculture Australia). Daughter Larissa, having obtained an Honours degree in Medical Science at the University of Sydney, decided to pursue winemaking by working as a 'lab rat' and cellar hand at a local winery, and visited Switzerland and Italy to observe small-scale family winemaking in those countries. The red wines are all very light in structure and extract, which may be intentional.

ŸŸŸŸ **Conspiracy Port NV** RATING 84 **DRINK** Now $10

ŸŸŸ **Honey Paddock Shiraz 2001** RATING 83 $11
Conspiracy Merlot 2002 RATING 83 $14
Conspiracy Cabernet Sauvignon 2002 RATING 83 $11

McAlister Vineyards NR

Golden Beach Road, Longford, Vic 3851 **REGION** Gippsland
T (03) 5149 7229 **F** (03) 5149 7229 **OPEN** By appointment
WINEMAKER Peter Edwards **EST.** 1975 **CASES** 550
PRODUCT RANGE A single wine, The McAlister, which is a blend of Cabernet Sauvignon, Cabernet Franc and Merlot.
SUMMARY The McAlister Vineyards actively shun publicity or exposure; on the basis of prior tastings, this is a pity. Exports to the US and the UK.

Macaw Creek Wines ★★★☆

Macaw Creek Road, Riverton, SA 5412 **REGION** Mount Lofty Ranges Zone
T (08) 8847 2237 **F** (08) 8847 2237 **OPEN** Sun and public holidays 11–4
WINEMAKER Rodney Hooper **EST.** 1992 **CASES** 4000
PRODUCT RANGE ($13–30 CD) Riesling, Sauvignon Blanc Semillon, Pedro Ximinez (sweet white), Yoolang Preservative Free Shiraz, Shiraz, Reserve Shiraz Cabernet, Grenache Shiraz, Tawny Port.
SUMMARY The property on which Macaw Creek Wines is established has been owned by the Hooper family since the 1850s, but development of the estate vineyards did not begin until 1995; 10 hectares have been planted since that time, with a further 20 hectares planted in the winter/spring of 1999. Rodney and Miriam Hooper established the Macaw Creek brand previously (in 1992), with wines made from grapes from other regions, including the Preservative-Free Yoolang Cabernet Shiraz. Rodney Hooper is a highly qualified and skilled winemaker with experience in many parts of Australia and in Germany, France and the US. Exports to the US, Canada and Malaysia.

ΥΥΥΥΥ **Reserve Shiraz Cabernet 2002** Rich, juicy blackberry and raspberry mix; supple and smooth; great length. **RATING** 91 **DRINK** 2007 $ 30

ΥΥΥΥ **Riesling 2002** Overall, quite firm and robust; mineral and citrus pick up the pace on the back palate and finish. Screwcap. **RATING** 89 **DRINK** 2010 $ 14

Yoolang Preservative Free Shiraz 2002 Great colour; smooth, medium-bodied, with no hint of oxidation. Black fruits and dark chocolate; soft finish. Very strange decision to use cork, not screwcap. Best preservative-free wine in Australia. **RATING** 89 **DRINK** Now $ 15.50

Shiraz 2001 Quite fragrant; spicy, savoury red and black fruits; light to medium-bodied; silky texture, fine tannins. **RATING** 89 **DRINK** 2008 $ 15

Grenache Shiraz 2002 Very smooth and supple; light to medium-bodied; spicy/savoury edges to the sweet berry mid-palate fruit. Very good value. **RATING** 89 **DRINK** 2007 $ 13

Semillon Sauvignon Blanc 2002 Powerful herb and citrus, some minerality; even flow, well-balanced; good value. Screwcap. **RATING** 88 **DRINK** 2009 $ 13

McGee Wines   NR

1710 Wattlevale Road, Nagambie, Vic 3608 **REGION** Nagambie Lakes
T (03) 5794 1530 **F** (03) 5794 1530 **OPEN** By appointment
WINEMAKER Don Lewis (Contract) **EST.** 1995 **CASES** 750
PRODUCT RANGE ($15.95 R) Chardonnay, Shiraz, Cabernet Sauvignon.
SUMMARY Andrew McGee and partner Kerry Smith (the latter the viticulturist) have established 12 hectares of vines on the banks of the Goulburn River, the majority planted to shiraz, with lesser quantities of grenache, viognier and mourvedre. Currently, 95 per cent of the production is sold to Mitchelton, where the McGee wines are presently made, but the plan is for the partners to make the wine themselves in the future, and to increase production. The wines are distributed through Woods Wines, 35 Greeves Street, Fitzroy, Vic 3065.

🐌 McGlashan's Wallington Estate   NR

225 Swan Bay Road, Wallington, Vic 3221 **REGION** Geelong
T (03) 5250 5760 **F** (03) 5250 5760 **OPEN** By appointment
WINEMAKER Robin Brockett (Contract) **EST.** 1996 **CASES** 1000
PRODUCT RANGE ($18–25 CD) Chardonnay, Pinot Noir, Shiraz.
SUMMARY Russell and Jan McGlashan began the establishment of their 10-hectare vineyard in 1996. Chardonnay (5 hectares) and pinot noir (3 hectares) make up the bulk of the plantings, with the remainder shiraz, and the wines are made by Robin Brockett at Scotchmans Hill. Local restaurants around Geelong and the Bellarine Peninsula take much of the wine, but cellar-door sales are available by appointment.

McGuigan Wines   ★★★★

Cnr Broke and McDonald Roads, Pokolbin, NSW 2321 **REGION** Lower Hunter Valley
T (02) 4998 7700 **F** (02) 4998 7401 **OPEN** 7 days 9.30–5
WINEMAKER Peter Hall **EST.** 1992 **CASES** 400 000
PRODUCT RANGE ($9.30–49.50 CD) The wines are sold in several price brackets: the Black Label range; the Bin range; Vineyard Selection; Shareholder range; Superior range; Personal Reserve range; and Genus 4. All are varietally donominated; also Howcroft Estate.
SUMMARY A publicly listed company, which is the ultimate logical expression of Brian McGuigan's marketing drive and vision, and which is on a par with that of Wolf Blass in his heyday. Highly successful in its chosen niche market notwithstanding some labels which are garish. Has been particularly active in export markets, notably the US and more recently China. The overall size of the company has been quadrupled by the acquisition of Simeon Wines; the production figure is no indication of the volume of wine made. Yaldara and Miranda are now also part of the empire.

ΥΥΥΥΥ **Bin 8000 Sauvignon Blanc 2003** Aromatic, truly remarkable varietal aromas and flavours given its geographic origin (Hunter Valley); tangy gooseberry, apple and passionfruit. Screwcap. **RATING** 92 **DRINK** Now $ 13.50

Genus 4 Old Vine Shiraz 2002 Medium-bodied but intense red and black fruits; oak and tannins in the back seat; long finish, has style. **RATING** 90 **DRINK** 2012 $ 21.99

ΨΨΨΨ **Bin 9000 Semillon 2003** Yet another surprise (and top gold National Wine Show) from McGuigan; lively, fresh, lemony tang; great back palate and finish. **RATING** 89 **DRINK** 2013 $ 13.50
Personal Reserve Hunter Valley Chardonnay 2003 Extremely complex charry barrel-ferment inputs throughout, saved by a tight, dry finish from going completely over the top. **RATING** 89 **DRINK** Now $ 26

ΨΨΨΨ **Bin 6000 Verdelho 2003** **RATING** 86 **DRINK** Now $ 13.50
Earth's Portrait Limestone Coast Shiraz 2002 **RATING** 86 **DRINK** 2012 $ 18
Personal Reserve Hunter Valley Shiraz 2002 **RATING** 86 **DRINK** 2007 $ 49.50
Earth's Portrait Barossa Valley Merlot 2002 **RATING** 86 **DRINK** 2010 $ 18
Bin 4000 Cabernet Sauvignon 2002 **RATING** 85 **DRINK** 2008 $ 13.50

ΨΨΨ **Earth's Portrait Adelaide Plains Sauvignon Blanc 2003** **RATING** 83 $ 18
Bin 3000 Merlot 2002 **RATING** 83 $ 13.50
Bin 2000 Shiraz 2002 **RATING** 80 $ 13.99

McIvor Creek   NR

Costerfield Road, Heathcote, Vic 3523 **REGION** Heathcote
T (03) 5433 4000 **F** (03) 5433 3456 **OPEN** 7 days 10–5.30
WINEMAKER Peter Turley **EST.** 1973 **CASES** 1000
PRODUCT RANGE ($12.50–27.50 CD) Chardonnay, Marsanne, Shiraz, Cabernet Shiraz, Fine Old Tawny Port.
SUMMARY The beautifully situated McIvor Creek winery is well worth a visit and does offer wines in diverse styles; the red wines are the most regional. Peter Turley has 5 hectares of cabernet sauvignon together with 2.5 hectares of cabernet franc and merlot, and supplements his intake with grapes from other growers.

🍃 McIvor Estate   ★★★★

80 Tooborac–Baynton Road, Tooborac, Vic 3522 **REGION** Heathcote
T (03) 5433 5266 **F** (03) 5433 5358 **OPEN** Weekends and public holidays 10–5, or by appointment
WINEMAKER Adrian Munari (Contract) **EST.** 1997 **CASES** 1200
PRODUCT RANGE ($22 ML) Marsanne, Shiraz, Sangiovese, Cabernet Merlot.
SUMMARY McIvor Estate is situated at the base of the Tooborac Hills, at the southern end of the Heathcote wine region, 5 kilometres southwest of the Tooborac township towards Lancefield. Five and a half hectares of vines have been planted to marsanne, roussanne, shiraz, cabernet sauvignon, merlot, nebbiolo and sangiovese; there are also a little under 7 hectares of olive trees of various sorts. The quality of the early releases is very encouraging, with the Marsanne (incorporating a dash of Roussanne) and Sangiovese adding a dimension to the more typical reds from the Heathcote region. Competent contract winemaking also plays a part.

ΨΨΨΨΨ **Reserve Heathcote Sangiovese 2002** Good colour; high-toned, exuberant red cherry, spice, tobacco and leaf; intense, long and lingering palate; full of interest; one of the best Sangioveses to date from Australia. **RATING** 91 **DRINK** 2010 $ 22
Marsanne 2001 Pale straw-green; a very similar style to the '02, but with slightly more intensity and bottle development; interesting wine; slow developing. **RATING** 90 **DRINK** 2010 $ 22

ΨΨΨΨ **Marsanne 2002** Pale straw-green; very clever use of subtle French oak to add a dimension to the structure, not so much to the flavour; green melon fruit is delicate, but lingering. **RATING** 89 **DRINK** 2010 $ 22
Cabernet Merlot 2002 Clean, fresh red and blackcurrant fruit; touches of spice and mint; fine tannins, brisk acidity. **RATING** 87 **DRINK** 2009 $ 22

🐏 McKellar Ridge Wines NR

40 Rohan Rivett Crescent, McKellar, ACT 2617 (postal) **REGION** Canberra District
T (02) 6258 1556 **F** (02) 6258 9770 **OPEN** Not
WINEMAKER Brian Johnston **EST.** 2000 **CASES** 300
PRODUCT RANGE ($17–19 ML) Unoaked Semillon Chardonnay, Cabernet Sauvignon.
SUMMARY Dr Brian Johnston and wife Janet are the partners in McKellar Ridge Wines. He is
studying wine science at Charles Sturt University, and in the interim is making the wines at Jeir
Creek under the guidance of Rob Howell, Bryan Martin and Greg Gallagher.

McLaren Vale III Associates ★★★★

130 Main Road, McLaren Vale, SA 5171 **REGION** McLaren Vale
T 1800 501 513 **F** (08) 8323 7422 **OPEN** Mon–Fri 9–5, tasting by appointment
WINEMAKER Brian Light **EST.** 1999 **CASES** 14 000
PRODUCT RANGE ($17.90–40 R) Chenin Blanc, Barrel Fermented Semillon, Three-D Sauvignon Blanc
Semillon Chenin Blanc Chardonnay, Chardonnay, Sparkling Chardonnay Pinot, The Third Degree
(Merlot Cabernet Shiraz), Shiraz, Squid Ink Reserve Shiraz, Three Score & 10 Grenache, Merlot
Elite.
SUMMARY The three associates in question all have a decade or more of wine industry experience:
Mary Greer is managing partner, Reginald Wymond chairing partner, and Christopher Fox partner.
The partnership owns 34 hectares of vines spanning two vineyards, one owned by Mary and John
Greer, the other by Reg and Sue Wymond. The label was first introduced in 1999, the aim being to
produce affordable quality wine. Exports to the US, Canada and Germany.

ΨΨΨΨ **Squid Ink Reserve Shiraz 2001** Medium-bodied; soft, earthy varietal fruit with
pronounced vanilla oak; mainstream style. **RATING** 87 **DRINK** 2010 $ 40

ΨΨΨΨ **Barrel Fermented Semillon 2002 RATING** 86 **DRINK** Now $ 17.90

ΨΨΨ **Associates Merlot 2002 RATING** 83 $ 22.90

🐏 McLean's Farm Wines NR

PO Box 403, Tanunda, SA 5352 **REGION** Barossa Valley
T (08) 8564 3340 **F** (08) 8564 3340 **OPEN** Not
WINEMAKER Bob McLean **EST.** 2001 **CASES** 3000
PRODUCT RANGE ($14.99–29 R) Barossa Shiraz, Schubert McLean Shiraz Cabernet South Australian,
Reserve Shiraz Cabernet Barossa.
SUMMARY At various times known as the Jolly Green Giant and Sir Lunchalot, Bob McLean has come
perilously close to being a marketing legend in his own lifetime, moving from Orlando to Petaluma
and then (for longer and more importantly) to St Hallett. He is now free to do his own thing, starting
with what he terms as 'The Virtual Winery', in partnership with long-term friends Dean and Rod
Schubert (the latter a notable Australian artist). Most of the production is exported to the UK, but
wines are now coming onto the Australian market. Around the corner lies barr-eden, a very real
vineyard and winery in the course of establishment on top of Mengler's Hill, at an altitude of 520
metres.

McLeish Estate ★★★☆

Lot 3 De Beyers Road, Pokolbin, NSW 2320 **REGION** Lower Hunter Valley
T (02) 4998 7754 **F** (02) 4998 7754 **OPEN** 7 days 10–5, or by appointment
WINEMAKER Andrew Thomas **EST.** 1985 **CASES** 3000
PRODUCT RANGE ($14–35 CD) Semillon, Semillon Chardonnay, Verdelho, Verdelho Chardonnay,
Chardonnay, Botrytis Semillon, Shiraz, Reserve Shiraz, Merlot, Cabernet Sauvignon.
SUMMARY Bob and Maryanne McLeish commenced the establishment of their vineyard in 1985, and
have progressively planted over 10 hectares. They have now moved to opening up their cellar door to
the public, having accumulated a number of gold medals for their wines.

ΨΨΨΨΨ **Reserve Chardonnay 2003** Abundant, sweet peach/stone fruit; smooth texture; well
integrated French oak. **RATING** 91 **DRINK** Now $ 25

ŶŶŶŶ **Semillon Chardonnay 2003** Clean and crisp, citrus-tinged; good length and balance. **RATING** 87 **DRINK** 2008 $14

ŶŶŶŶ **Reserve Shiraz 2002** Light to medium-bodied; fresh red and black fruits, then slightly spiky acidity; all over the place. **RATING** 86 **DRINK** 2008 $35
Verdelho 2003 RATING 85 **DRINK** Now $16

ŶŶŶ **Semillon 2003 RATING** 83 $15

McPherson Wines ★★★

PO Box 529, Artarmon, NSW 1570 **REGION** Nagambie Lakes
T (02) 9436 1644 **F** (02) 9436 3144 **OPEN** Not
WINEMAKER Andrew Dean, Andrew McPherson **EST.** 1993 **CASES** 300 000
PRODUCT RANGE ($7.50–17.99 R) Murray Darling range of Semillon Chardonnay, Verdelho, Chardonnay, Shiraz, Shiraz Cabernet, Merlot, Cabernet Merlot, Cabernet Sauvignon; Goulburn Valley Reserve Chardonnay and Reserve Shiraz.
SUMMARY McPherson Wines is little known in Australia but is, by any standards, a substantial business. Its wines are almost entirely produced for the export market, with sales in Australia through the Woolworths group, including Safeway and First Estate. The wines are made at various locations from contract-grown grapes, and represent good value at their price point. For the record, McPherson Wines is a joint venture between Andrew McPherson and Alister Purbrick of Tahbilk. Both have had a lifetime of experience in the industry. Exports to the US, Canada, the UK, New Zealand, Europe and Asia.

ŶŶŶŶŶ **Reserve Goulburn Valley Shiraz 2002** Good focus, depth and balance; blackberry and plum fruit; gently savoury tannins, good oak. **RATING** 90 **DRINK** 2010 $17.99

ŶŶŶŶ **Reserve Goulburn Valley Chardonnay 2002 RATING** 86 **DRINK** Now $17.99
Semillon Chardonnay 2003 Lively and fresh; some lemony tang from the Semillon component; nice balance and length. **RATING** 86 **DRINK** Now $8.99
Murray Darling Shiraz Cabernet 2003 Nice, fresh, juicy, bright fruit; clean finish. **RATING** 86 **DRINK** Now $8.50
Reserve Goulburn Valley Chardonnay 2003 RATING 85 **DRINK** Now $17.99
Cabernet Sauvignon 2003 RATING 85 **DRINK** Now $8.50
Verdelho 2003 RATING 84 **DRINK** Now $7.50

ŶŶŶ **Murray Darling Shiraz 2002 RATING** 83 $8.50
Merlot 2003 RATING 83 $8.50

Macquariedale Estate NR

170 Sweetwater Road, Rothbury, NSW 2335 **REGION** Lower Hunter Valley
T (02) 6574 7012 **F** (02) 6574 7013 **OPEN** By appointment
WINEMAKER Ross McDonald **EST.** 1993 **CASES** 5000
PRODUCT RANGE ($14–24 ML) Old Vine Semillon, Premium Blend Semillon Chardonnay, Four Winds Chardonnay, Macqblush (Rose), Thomas Shiraz, Matthew Merlot, Cabernet Sauvignon.
SUMMARY Macquariedale is an acorn to oak story, beginning with a small hobby vineyard in Branxton many years ago, and now extending to three vineyards around the Lower Hunter with a total 15 hectares of semillon, chardonnay, shiraz, merlot and cabernet sauvignon. This has led to Ross McDonald and his family leaving a busy Sydney life for that of a full-time grape grower and winemaker. The wines are sold by mailing list, through the Boutique Wine Centre in Pokolbin or via the 30 or so restaurants that list the wines. Those restaurants have included such icons as Banc and Bathers Pavilion. Limited exports to the US, Canada, Singapore and Japan.

McVitty Grove ★★★

Wombeyan Caves Road, Mittagong, NSW 2575 **REGION** Southern Highlands
T (02) 4878 5044 **F** (02) 4878 5524 **OPEN** 7 days 10–5
WINEMAKER Madew Wines (Contract) **EST.** 1998 **CASES** 1000
PRODUCT RANGE ($12.50–22.50 R) Pinot Gris, Cut Arm (dessert), Endymion (sparkling), Fire Engine Red (Pinot Noir), Pinot Noir.

SUMMARY Notwithstanding his 20-year career in finance, Mark Phillips also had 6 years of tertiary study in horticulture when he and wife Jane began the search for a Southern Highlands site suited to premium grape growing and olive cultivation. In 1998 their search culminated in the acquisition of 42 hectares of farm land on the Wombeyan Caves Road, just out of Mittagong. They have now established 5.5 hectares of pinot noir and pinot gris on deep, fertile soils at the front of the property. In addition, a 1.5-hectare olive grove has been planted; it provides the backdrop for the cellar door and café which opened in April 2004.

♥♥♥♡ **Pinot Gris 2003** RATING 85 DRINK Now $20

McWilliam's ★★★★

Jack McWilliam Road, Hanwood, NSW 2680 REGION Riverina
T (02) 6963 0001 F (02) 6963 0002 OPEN Mon–Sat 9–5
WINEMAKER Jim Brayne, Simon Crook EST. 1916
PRODUCT RANGE ($6–80 R) A disciplined and easy-to-follow product range (all varietally identified) commencing with Hillside casks; Inheritance Range; Hanwood; Charles King; JJ McWilliam (first released 1996); Winemaker's Reserve Chardonnay and Cabernet Shiraz; and Regional Collection Limited Release. Also superb fortified wines, including MCW11 Liqueur Muscat and 10-Year-Old Hanwood Tawny Port, heading a much larger range of Sherries, which still form an important part of the business.
SUMMARY The best wines to emanate from the Hanwood winery are from other regions, notably the Barwang Vineyard at Hilltops in New South Wales, and Coonawarra and Eden Valley; as McWilliam's viticultural resources have expanded, so have they been able to produce regional blends from across southeastern Australia under the Hanwood label; in the last few years, these have been startlingly good. Exports to many countries via a major distribution joint venture with Gallo.

♥♥♥♥♡ **Eden Valley Riesling 2003** Intense and long; a seamless blend of mineral and lime juice; perfect balance. Screwcap. RATING 93 DRINK 2015 $18.50
Margaret River Semillon Sauvignon Blanc 2003 Spotlessly clean; ripe citrus and herbs; long and lingering gently sweet fruit; dry finish. RATING 90 DRINK 2007 $18
Barossa Shiraz 2002 Fragrant, supple black plum and blackberry; elegant and long, fine tannins. RATING 90 DRINK 2010 $18.50

♥♥♥♥ **Hanwood Shiraz 2002** Fresh and lively, driven by blackberry, plum and cherry fruit, and just enough oak and tannin. Its screwcap will underwrite cellaring if you are so inclined. Smashing value. RATING 89 DRINK 2007 $12
JJ McWilliam Riverina Botrytis Semillon 2001 Very sweet and rich; unctuous honey, citrus and peach; needs time. RATING 89 DRINK 2008 $23
Clare Valley Riesling 2003 Powerful and compact; rich tropical fruit on entry, but doesn't carry through. RATING 88 DRINK 2008 $18
Hanwood Semillon Chardonnay 2002 Neat wine; driven by citrus fruit and a whisper of oak; good length. RATING 88 DRINK Now $11.50

♥♥♥♡ **Coonawarra Shiraz 2001** RATING 86 DRINK 2009 $18.50
Hanwood Sauvignon Blanc 2003 RATING 85 DRINK Now $12
Hanwood Merlot 2002 RATING 85 DRINK Now $12

♥♥♥ **Coonawarra Cabernet Sauvignon 2001** RATING 83 $18.50

McWilliam's Mount Pleasant ★★★★★

Marrowbone Road, Pokolbin, NSW 2320 REGION Lower Hunter Valley
T (02) 4998 7505 F (02) 4998 7761 OPEN 7 days 10–5
WINEMAKER Phillip Ryan, Andrew Leembruggen EST. 1921
PRODUCT RANGE ($10–45 R) The base range is led by Mount Pleasant Elizabeth Semillon, with a range of other white and red varietals; then individual vineyard wines: Rosehill Shiraz, Old Paddock & Old Hill Shiraz, Lovedale Semillon; then Maurice O'Shea Chardonnay, Shiraz; finally, Museum releases of Elizabeth, Lovedale Semillon.

SUMMARY McWilliam's Elizabeth and the glorious Lovedale Semillon are generally commercially available with 4–5 years of bottle age; they are undervalued treasures with a consistently superb show record. The three individual vineyard wines, together with the Maurice O'Shea memorial wines, add to the lustre of this proud name. Exports to many countries, the most important being the UK, the US, Germany and New Zealand.

ŸŸŸŸŸ **Maurice O'Shea Shiraz 2000** Lusciously rich blackberry and spice; perfect oak integration; long finish. Best since O'Shea death in 1956. **RATING** 97 **DRINK** 2020 $ 45
Lovedale Semillon 1998 Clean toast and lemon-accented bouquet lead into an immaculately balanced palate with the first signs of honey and other mature flavours starting to emerge, then the lemony acidity on a great finish. Top 100 2003 **RATING** 96 **DRINK** 2020 $ 44
Museum Elizabeth Semillon 1996 Complex and intense, the fresh acidity in perfect balance and providing great length. **RATING** 95 **DRINK** 2011 $ 30
Museum Elizabeth Semillon 1995 Aromatic citrus and honey aromas and flavours; excellent length, life and tingling acidity. Just flexing its muscles. **RATING** 94 **DRINK** 2010 $ 28

ŸŸŸŸŸ **Early Release Elizabeth Semillon 2001** Intense varietal aromas are already building complexity, and the palate, too, has lots of herb and lemon fruit, the honey to come later. Great length and style. **RATING** 93 **DRINK** 2011 $ 16
Elizabeth Semillon 2000 The bouquet is still developing in that in-between phase; the palate is smooth and supple; ripe lemon, soft acidity. Overall, in transition. **RATING** 90 **DRINK** 2010 $ 18

ŸŸŸŸ **Maurice O'Shea Chardonnay 2002** Obvious toasty barrel-ferment inputs on the bouquet; the palate has a mix of lighter, almost minerally notes, with cashew and nectarine. **RATING** 89 **DRINK** 2007 $ 38
Verdelho 2003 Lively citrussy overtones to fruit salad flavours; well balanced, and excellent length. Impressive. **RATING** 89 **DRINK** Now $ 16.50
Verdelho 2001 Abundant flavour and depth; soft fruit salad; clean, relatively dry finish. Good varietal example. **RATING** 87 **DRINK** Now $ 16.50

ŸŸŸŸ **Philip Shiraz 1999** **RATING** 85 **DRINK** 2007 $ 18

Madew Wines   ★★★☆

Westering, Federal Highway, Lake George, NSW 2581 **REGION** Canberra District
T (02) 4848 0026 **F** (02) 4848 0026 **OPEN** Weekends, public holidays 11–5
WINEMAKER David Madew **EST.** 1984 **CASES** 2500
PRODUCT RANGE ($13–30 CD) Riesling, Belle Riesling, Reserve Riesling, Semillon, Pinot Gris, Belle Pinot Gris, Chardonnay, Phoenix (Botrytis Chardonnay), Dry Red, Merlot, Cabernets.
SUMMARY Madew Wines bowed to the urban pressure of Queanbeyan and purchased the Westering Vineyard from Captain G P Hood some years ago. Plantings there have now increased to 9.5 hectares, with 1 hectare each of shiraz and pinot gris coming into bearing. Madew's restaurant, grapefoodwine, which is open Friday to Saturday for lunch and dinner and Sunday for breakfast and lunch, won the Best Restaurant in a Winery award in 2001, and also hosts monthly music concerts. At the time of going to press, was being offered for sale.

🐦 Madigan Vineyard   NR

Lot 1 Wilderness Road, Rothbury, NSW 2320 **REGION** Lower Hunter Valley
T (02) 4998 7815 **F** (02) 4998 7116 **OPEN** Weekends 10–5
WINEMAKER Monarch Winemaking Services (Contract) **EST.** 1996
PRODUCT RANGE A range of varietally denominated table wines reflecting the plantings.
SUMMARY Bob and Ann Rich have 3 hectares of chardonnay, verdelho and shiraz at Rothbury, with the infinitely experienced Keith Holder as viticulturist, and Monarch Winemaking Services equally competently looking after winemaking. Virtually all the wine is sold by mailing list and through the cellar door.

Maglieri of McLaren Vale ★★★☆

Douglas Gully Road, McLaren Flat, SA 5171 **REGION** McLaren Vale
T (08) 8383 0177 **F** (08) 8383 0735 **OPEN** Mon–Sat 9–4, Sun 12–4
WINEMAKER Charles Hargrave **EST.** 1972 **CASES** 14 000
PRODUCT RANGE ($5.50–40 R) Produces a range of Italian-derived styles for specialty markets within Australia, and is increasingly known for the quality of its varietal table wines, spearheaded by Semillon, Chardonnay, Merlot, Cabernet Sauvignon and Shiraz, the last released in two guises: as a simple varietal, and the top-end Steve Maglieri. Usually, several vintages available at any one time.
SUMMARY Was one of the better-kept secrets among the wine cognoscenti, but not among the many customers, who drink thousands of cases of white and red Lambrusco every year, an example of niche marketing at its profitable best. It was a formula which proved irresistible to Beringer Blass, which acquired Maglieri in 1999. Its dry red wines are invariably generously proportioned and full of character, the Shiraz particularly so.

 TTTTY **Sangiovese 2002** Brilliant red-purple; vibrant cherry and spice aromas and flavours; good mouthfeel. **RATING** 90 **DRINK** 2010 $ 23

TTTT **Cabernet Sauvignon 2001** Ripe blackcurrant, blackberry and dark chocolate aromas and flavours; nice tannins and oak. **RATING** 89 **DRINK** 2011 $ 19
Nebbiolo 2002 Powerful, quite austere black fruits, earth and bitter chocolate; savoury tannins. **RATING** 89 **DRINK** 2008 $ 23
Barbera 2002 Vibrant, low pH style with juicy plummy fruit and a lingering finish. **RATING** 88 **DRINK** 2007 $ 23

TTTY **Shiraz 2001 RATING** 84 **DRINK** Now $ 19

Main Ridge Estate ★★★★★

80 William Road, Red Hill, Vic 3937 **REGION** Mornington Peninsula
T (03) 5989 2686 **F** (03) 5931 0000 **OPEN** Mon–Fri 12–4, weekends 12–5
WINEMAKER Nat White **EST.** 1975 **CASES** 1000
PRODUCT RANGE ($45–50 CD) Chardonnay, The Acre Pinot Noir, Half Acre Pinot Noir.
SUMMARY Nat White gives meticulous attention to every aspect of his viticulture and winemaking, doing annual battle with one of the coolest sites on the peninsula. The same attention to detail extends to the winery and the winemaking. Incidentally, despite such minuscule production, domestic sales through the cellar door and by mail order, and exports to the UK and Singapore.

TTTTT **Chardonnay 2002** Ultra-complex and powerful; rich butterscotch, cashew and stone fruit; layer upon layer of flavour. **RATING** 94 **DRINK** 2012 $ 45

Maiolo Wines ★★★☆

Bussell Highway, Carbunup River, WA 6282 **REGION** Margaret River
T (08) 9755 1060 **F** (08) 9755 1060 **OPEN** 7 days 10–5
WINEMAKER Charles Maiolo **EST.** 1999 **CASES** 3000
PRODUCT RANGE ($14.50–26 CD) Semillon Sauvignon Blanc, Chardonnay, Pinot Noir, Shiraz, Cabernet Sauvignon.
SUMMARY Charles Maiolo has established a 28-hectare vineyard planted to semillon, sauvignon blanc, chardonnay, pinot noir, shiraz, merlot and cabernet sauvignon. He has a wine science degree from Charles Sturt University, and presides over a winery with a capacity of 250 to 300 tonnes. As the vines are still coming into bearing, production will increase from the present level of around 50 tonnes to over 200 tonnes, with the option of selling surplus grapes. The red wines, in particular, show great promise, with Shiraz and Cabernet Sauvignon to the fore. The white wines have a constant thread of reduction and are less appealing. The wines are distributed in Western Australia and New South Wales.

Majella ★★★★★

Lynn Road, Coonawarra, SA 5263 **REGION** Coonawarra
T (08) 8736 3055 **F** (08) 8736 3057 **OPEN** 7 days 10–4.30
WINEMAKER Bruce Gregory **EST.** 1969 **CASES** 12 000

PRODUCT RANGE ($16–72 CD) Riesling, Sparkling Shiraz, Shiraz, The Malleea Shiraz Cabernet, Cabernet Sauvignon.

SUMMARY Majella is one of the more important contract grape growers in Coonawarra, with 61 hectares of vineyard, principally shiraz and cabernet sauvignon, and with a little riesling and merlot in production and now fully mature. Common gossip has it that part finds its way into the Wynns John Riddoch Cabernet Sauvignon and Michael Shiraz, or their equivalent within the Southcorp Group. The Malleea is one of Coonawarra's best wines. Production under the Majella label has increased substantially over the past few years, rising from 2000 to 12 000 cases, with exports to the US, Canada, Singapore, Malaysia and Hong Kong.

ŸŸŸŸŸ **The Malleea 2000** Young red wine is seldom as exuberantly joyful as this; fragrant cassis and cedar swirls from the glass; an exceptionally supple palate with a flawless, seamless marriage of fruit, oak and tannin. RATING 96 DRINK 2020 $72

Cabernet Sauvignon 2001 Spotlessly clean, perfectly articulated cassis and blackcurrant fruit; long palate with pure fruit, the oak merely in support, as are tannins. RATING 95 DRINK 2016 $33

ŸŸŸŸŸ **The Malleea 2001** Oozing blackcurrant and blackberry; juicy mouthfeel with cascading sweet fruit and totally ripe tannins. RATING 93 DRINK 2016 $72

Shiraz 2001 Aromatic, lively, fresh raspberry, cherry and herb aromas and flavours; fine tannins, subtle oak. RATING 90 DRINK 2011 $33

Malcolm Creek Vineyard ★★★★

Bonython Road, Kersbrook, SA 5231 REGION Adelaide Hills
T (08) 8389 3235 F (08) 8389 3235 OPEN Weekends and public holidays 11–5, or by appointment
WINEMAKER Reg Tolley EST. 1982 CASES 700
PRODUCT RANGE ($16–20 CD) Chardonnay, Cabernet Sauvignon.
SUMMARY Malcolm Creek is the retirement venture of Reg Tolley, and keeps a low profile. However, the wines are invariably well made and develop gracefully; they are worth seeking out, and are usually available with some extra bottle age at a very modest price. Exports to the UK.

ŸŸŸŸŸ **Chardonnay 2002** As ever, sophisticated but restrained winemaking; melon fruit and a touch of cashew; excellent balance and length. RATING 92 DRINK 2009 $16

ŸŸŸŸ **Cabernet Sauvignon 2001** Offers a mix of black fruits, earth and cedar; persistent tannins. RATING 87 DRINK 2010 $20

🍇 Mandalay Estate NR

Mandalay Road, Mumballup, WA 6010 REGION Geographe
T (08) 9372 2006 F (08) 9384 5962 OPEN Weekends and public holidays 10–5
WINEMAKER Contract EST. 1997
PRODUCT RANGE ($14–16 CD) Chardonnay, Shiraz, Shiraz Cabernet, Zinfandel, Cabernet Sauvignon.
SUMMARY Terry and Bernice O'Connell have established 4 hectares of chardonnay, shiraz, cabernet sauvignon and zinfandel on their 40-hectare property, previously owned by Bunnings Tree Farms and hence abounding with tree stumps. The tasting room has been established in an old plant shed on the property, and the wines are sold through the cellar door and by mail order.

Mandurang Valley Wines NR

77 Fadersons Lane, Mandurang, Vic 3551 REGION Bendigo
T (03) 5439 5367 F (03) 5439 3850 OPEN Weekends and holidays 11–5
WINEMAKER Wes Vine EST. 1994 CASES 2000
PRODUCT RANGE ($13–18 CD) Riesling, Pinot Noir, Shiraz, Cabernet Sauvignon.
SUMMARY Wes and Pamela Vine have slowly built Mandurang Valley Wines, utilising 2.5 hectares of estate vines and a further 6 hectares of estate-grown grapes. As from Easter 2001 they have been offering café lunches to complement the outdoor seating and barbecue facilities already in existence. The wines are chiefly sold through the cellar door and by mailing list, with limited Melbourne distribution through Bacchus Wines, Armadale.

Mann

NR

105 Memorial Avenue, Baskerville, WA 6056 **REGION** Swan Valley
T (08) 9296 4348 **F** (08) 9296 4348 **OPEN** Weekends 10–5, and by appointment from 1 Aug until sold out
WINEMAKER Dorham Mann **EST.** 1988 **CASES** 600
PRODUCT RANGE ($18–30 CD) Methode Champenoise Cygne Blanc, Methode Champenoise
(Cabernet).
SUMMARY Industry veteran Dorham Mann has established a one-wine label for what must be
Australia's most unusual wine: a dry, only faintly pink, sparkling wine made exclusively from
cabernet sauvignon and cygne blanc grown on the 2.5-hectare estate surrounding the cellar door.
Dorham Mann explains, 'Our family has made and enjoyed the style for more than 30 years, although
just in a private capacity until recently.'

Mansfield Wines

★★★

204 Eurunderee Lane, Mudgee, NSW 2850 **REGION** Mudgee
T (02) 6373 3871 **F** (02) 6373 3708 **OPEN** Thurs–Tues and public holidays 10–5, or by appointment
WINEMAKER Bob Heslop **EST.** 1975 **CASES** 2000
PRODUCT RANGE ($8–32 CD) Sauvignon Blanc, Frontignac, Chardonnay, Spectabilis White (semi-
sweet), Sparkling Muscat, Spectabilis Red, Shiraz, Touriga, Zinfandel, Cabernet Sauvignon Merlot,
Cabernet Sauvignon, and a selection of fortified wines.
SUMMARY Mansfield Wines has moved with the times, moving the emphasis from fortified wines to
table wines (though still offering some fortifieds) and expanding the product range to take in cutting-
edge varietal reds such as Touriga and Zinfandel.

ŸŸŸŸ **Cabernet Sauvignon 2002 RATING** 86 **DRINK** 2007 $16
Touriga 2002 Spicy, cedary, dusky fruit flavours; prune and blackberry; good tannins.
Interesting use of a Port varietal. **RATING** 86 **DRINK** 2008 $18
Semillon 2003 RATING 85 **DRINK** 2009 $13
Cabernet 2002 RATING 84 **DRINK** 2010 $16

Mantons Creek Vineyard

★★★★

Tucks Road, Main Ridge, Vic 3928 **REGION** Mornington Peninsula
T (03) 5989 6264 **F** (03) 5989 6348 **OPEN** 7 days 11–5
WINEMAKER Alex White (Contract) **EST.** 1994 **CASES** 4500
PRODUCT RANGE ($22–45 CD) Gewurztraminer, Sauvignon Blanc, Pinot Gris, Chardonnay,
Tempranillo, Pinot Noir, Sparkling.
SUMMARY The 19-hectare property was originally an orchard, herb farm and horse stud. After the
vineyard was established, the grapes were sold to other wineries in the region until 1998, when the
first Mantons Creek wines were made from the 10-hectare vineyard planted in 1994. A purpose-built
cellar door, restaurant and 4-bedroom accommodation unit was opened in December 1998; the
property was purchased by Dr Michael Ablett, a retired cardiologist, and his wife Judy in March
2001. Exports to Hong Kong and Japan.

ŸŸŸŸŸ **Chardonnay 2000** Fresh, aromatic nectarine and citrus fruit aromas; a lovely, fruit-driven
palate, long and supple; perfect balance. **RATING** 94 **DRINK** 2007 $22

ŸŸŸŸŸ **Tempranillo 2001** Spicy, vibrant fruit aromas; tangy, quasi-citrussy flavours, long and
piercing. One of the best Australian Tempranillos by far to so far pass my lips. **RATING** 90
DRINK 2008 $45

ŸŸŸŸ **Jessica Sauvignon Blanc 2002** Notwithstanding the screwcap closure, shows some bottle
development, with a mix of acacia, honey, gooseberry and tropical fruit; quite fleshy.
RATING 89 **DRINK** Now $30
Sauvignon Blanc 2003 Spotlessly clean; light, minerally, with a subtle twist of
tropical/juicy fruit. **RATING** 88 **DRINK** 2008 $30
Jessica Tempranillo 2002 Spicy, tangy, almost citrussy flavours, with clear varietal
expression à la Rioja; light to medium-bodied. **RATING** 88 **DRINK** 2007 $50
Vintage Brut 2001 Bright, fresh, lemony, lively and zesty. **RATING** 87 **DRINK** Now $28
Trio 2000 Interesting sweet, dried tropical fruit mix, then a moderately dry finish. Late-
harvested Sauvignon Blanc, Gewurztraminer and Muscat. **RATING** 87 **DRINK** Now $18

ΨΨΨΨ   **Pinot Noir 2001** RATING 86 DRINK Now $ 30
     Pinot Noir Pinot Meunier Pinot Gris 2001 RATING 86 DRINK Now $ 28
     Pinot Gris 2000 RATING 85 DRINK Now $ 22
     Pinot Meunier 2001 RATING 85 DRINK Now $ 30
     Uno 2001 RATING 85 DRINK Now $ 18
     Muscat 2003 RATING 85 DRINK Now $ 25
     Gewurztraminer 2003 RATING 84 DRINK Now $ 45

🦉 Marandoo Estate

NR

Ground Floor, 62 Greenhill Road, Wayville, SA 5034 (postal) **REGION** Langhorne Creek
T (08) 8373 9977 **F** (08) 8373 9988 **OPEN** Not
WINEMAKER Michael Potts (Contract) **EST.** 1990
PRODUCT RANGE ($21 ML) Chardonnay, Shiraz Cabernet; Marandoo Run Cabernet Sauvignon.
SUMMARY Marandoo Estate (and Marandoo Run) are the visible but very small part of a very large and complex vineyard-owning, vineyard management and grape-growing group that has 1100 hectares of vineyards under management around Australia, extending from Langhorne Creek to Padthaway, Margaret River, the Barossa Valley, the Canberra District and Young.

Margan Family

1238 Milbrodale Road, Broke, NSW 2330 **REGION** Lower Hunter Valley
T (02) 6579 1317 **F** (02) 6579 1317 **OPEN** 7 days 10–5
WINEMAKER Andrew Margan **EST.** 1997 **CASES** 30 000
PRODUCT RANGE ($13–27 CD) Semillon, Verdelho, Chardonnay, Botrytis Semillon, Shiraz, Shiraz Saignee, Merlot, Cabernet Sauvignon.
SUMMARY Andrew Margan followed in his father's footsteps by entering the wine industry 20 years ago and has covered a great deal of territory since, working as a Flying Winemaker in Europe, then for Tyrrell's, first as a winemaker, then as marketing manager. His wife Lisa, too, has had many years of experience in restaurants and marketing. They now have 46 hectares of fully yielding vines at their 50-hectare Ceres Hill homestead property at Broke, and they lease the nearby Vere Vineyard of 13 hectares. The first stage of a 700-tonne on-site winery was completed in 1998, the first wines having been made elsewhere in 1997. Wine quality (and the packaging) is consistently good. Café Beltree is open for light meals and coffee. Exports to the UK, the US, Canada and The Netherlands.

ΨΨΨΨΨ   **Beltree Semillon 2003** Fragrant and pure herb and lemon aromas; wonderful intensity, line and length; lingering finish. **RATING** 94 **DRINK** 2015 $ 13

ΨΨΨΨΨ   **Chardonnay 2002** Medium bodied; complex yet smooth, with well integrated oak and melon/peach fruit; good length and balance. **RATING** 91 **DRINK** Now $ 20

ΨΨΨΨ   **Shiraz 2002** Traditional blackberry, earth and bitter chocolate aromas and flavours; balanced oak and tannins; begs for time. **RATING** 89 **DRINK** 2012 $ 19.50
     Semillon 2003 Powerful and complex herb and mineral aromas; plenty of weight and authority to the palate. **RATING** 88 **DRINK** 2013 $ 17
     Cabernet Sauvignon 2002 Blackberry, sweet leather and vanilla, smooth and supple, the oak still integrating, but well made. **RATING** 88 **DRINK** 2012 $ 19.50
     Merlot 2002 Complex, distinctly savoury flavours; lingering, olive-tinged tannins and a touch of oak. **RATING** 87 **DRINK** 2010 $ 19.50

ΨΨΨ   **Verdelho 2003** RATING 83 DRINK Now $ 17

Marienberg

2 Chalk Hill Road, McLaren Vale, SA 5171 **REGION** McLaren Vale
T (08) 8323 9666 **F** (08) 8323 9600 **OPEN** 7 days 10–5
WINEMAKER Peter Orr **EST.** 1966 **CASES** 25 000
PRODUCT RANGE ($13–39 CD) The wines are in two tiers: the lower are Cottage Classic varietals; at the top are the Reserve Chardonnay, Shiraz and Cabernet Sauvignon.
SUMMARY Another long-established business (founded by Australia's first female owner/vigneron, Ursula Pridham) acquired by James Estate in 2003.

Marinda Park Vineyard ★★★★

238 Myers Road, Balnarring, Vic 3926 **REGION** Mornington Peninsula
T (03) 5989 7613 **F** (03) 5989 7613 **OPEN** Thurs–Mon 11–5, 7 days in January
WINEMAKER Sandro Mosele (Contract) **EST.** 1999 **CASES** 2100
PRODUCT RANGE ($19–26 CD) Sauvignon Blanc, Henk's Dry White, Chardonnay, Rose, Pinot Noir, Merlot.
SUMMARY Mark and Belinda Rodman have established 10 hectares of chardonnay, sauvignon blanc, pinot noir and merlot on their vineyard on the outskirts of Balnarring. They operate the business in conjunction with American partners Norm and Fanny Winton, who are involved in the sale and distribution of the wines in the US and Singapore. The wines are principally sold overseas, but are available locally by mail order, and have been sold through the cellar door at the small French Provincial-style café since October 2003. Exports to the US and Singapore.

ΥΥΥΥΥ **Chardonnay 2002** Complex, appealing, funky aromas; intense citrus and stone fruit with some bottle development starting. **RATING** 93 **DRINK** 2008 $ 24
Pinot Noir 2002 Complex, slightly dusty/stalky/spicy/smoky aromas; focused plum and black cherry fruits take control on the palate. **RATING** 91 **DRINK** 2007 $ 26
Chardonnay 2003 Fine but intense grapefruit and stone fruit mix; fruit-driven; good length. **RATING** 90 **DRINK** 2007 $ 24
Chardonnay 2001 Complex, rich, bottle-developed, full-bodied peaches and cream style; utterly seductive. **RATING** 90 **DRINK** Now $ 24
Second Label Pinot Noir 2003 Vivid, light purple-red; ripe, primary plum and black cherry fruit; good fruit depth; will build complexity. **RATING** 90 **DRINK** 2007

ΥΥΥΥ **Sauvignon Blanc 2003** Smooth tropical/gooseberry/passionfruit aromas and flavours; clean, quite soft finish. Agglomerate cork a worry. **RATING** 88 **DRINK** Now $ 19
Rose 2003 Bright colour; appealing cherry and strawberry mix; good intensity and balance. **RATING** 87 **DRINK** Now $ 19

ΥΥΥΥ **Pinot Noir 2001** **RATING** 84 **DRINK** Now $ 26

ΥΥΥ **Merlot 2002** **RATING** 79 $ 26
Merlot 2001 **RATING** 79 $ 26

Mariners Rest ★★★

Jamakarri Farm, Roberts Road, Denmark, WA 6333 **REGION** Denmark
T (08) 9840 9324 **F** (08) 9840 9321 **OPEN** 7 days 11–5
WINEMAKER Brenden Smith **EST.** 1996 **CASES** 750
PRODUCT RANGE ($15–22.50 R) Chardonnay, Southern White, Autumn Gold, Autumn Red, Southern Red, Pinot Noir, Nelson's Blood (Tawny Port).
SUMMARY Mariners Rest is the reincarnation of the now defunct Golden Rise winery. A new 2.5-hectare vineyard was planted in the spring of 1997, and a slightly odd selection of replacement wines are being marketed.

ΥΥΥΥ **Unwooded Chardonnay 2003** **RATING** 86 **DRINK** Now $ 20

Maritime Estate ★★★★

Tucks Road, Red Hill, Vic 3937 **REGION** Mornington Peninsula
T (03) 9848 2926 **F** (03) 9848 2926 **OPEN** Weekends and public holidays 11–5, 7 days 27 Dec–26 Jan
WINEMAKER Clare Halloran **EST.** 1988 **CASES** 2000
PRODUCT RANGE ($16–28 CD) Pinot Gris, Unwooded Chardonnay, Chardonnay, Pinot Noir.
SUMMARY John and Linda Ruljancich and Kevin Ruljancich have enjoyed great success since their first vintage in 1994, no doubt due in part to skilled contract winemaking, but also to the situation of their vineyard, looking across the hills and valleys of the Red Hill subregion. The JDR Chardonnay and PJR Pinot Noir reviewed in the 2004 *Wine Companion* have improved significantly with additional bottle age, the Chardonnay winning both gold medals and a trophy. However, the 2002 vintage was, to use John Ruljancich's words, 'virtually non-existent'.

Marius Wines

PO Box 45, Willunga, SA 5172 **REGION** McLaren Vale
T 0402 344 340 **F** (08) 8557 1034 **OPEN** Not
WINEMAKER Mark Day **EST.** 1994 **CASES** 500
PRODUCT RANGE ($25 R) Shiraz.
SUMMARY Roger Pike says he has loved wine for over 30 years; that for 15 years he has had the desire to add a little bit to the world of wine; and that 8 years ago he decided to do something about it, so he ripped up the front paddock and planted 1.6 hectares of shiraz in 1994. He sold the grapes from the 1997–99 vintages, but when the 1998 vintage became a single-vineyard wine (made by the purchaser of the grapes) selling in the US at $40, the temptation to have his own wine became irresistible. The wines are available by mail order and via www.mariuswines.com.au.

ŸŸŸŸŸ **Shiraz 2002** Intense, focused and concentrated; almost a vinous black hole in space; has soaked up the oak and gone to sleep; patience. **RATING** 91 **DRINK** 2015 $25

Markwood Estate

NR

Morris Lane, Markwood, Vic 3678 **REGION** King Valley
T (03) 5727 0361 **F** (03) 5727 0361 **OPEN** 7 days 9–5
WINEMAKER Rick Morris **EST.** 1971 **CASES** 200
PRODUCT RANGE ($15–30 CD) Riesling, Cabernet Sauvignon, White Port, Old Tawny Port.
SUMMARY A member of the famous Morris family, Rick Morris shuns publicity and relies virtually exclusively on cellar-door sales for what is a small output. Of a range of table and fortified wines tasted some years ago, the Old Tawny Port (a cross between Port and Muscat, showing more of the character of the latter than the former) and a White Port (seemingly made from Muscadelle) were the best.

🐦 Maroochy Springs

NR

80 Musavale Road, Erwah Vale near Eumundi, Qld 4562 **REGION** Queensland Coastal
T (07) 5442 8777 **F** (07) 5442 8745 **OPEN** 7 days 12–6
WINEMAKER Kevin Watson (Contract) **EST.** 2001
PRODUCT RANGE ($18 CD) Chambourcin; White Chambourcin, Verdelho.
SUMMARY Jack and Margaret Connolly have established yet another winery in the Queensland Coastal region. It is situated in the beautiful Erwah Valley at the foothills of the Blackall Range, 30 minutes' drive from Noosa and only 6 kilometres west of Eumundi. The usual range of general tourist facilities and attractions, including an air-conditioned cellar door and a barbecue/picnic area.

🐦 Marquis Phillips

NR

2 Riviera Court, Pasadena, SA 5042 (postal) **REGION** Fleurieu/Limestone Coast Zone
T (08) 8357 4560 **F** (08) 8357 4234 **OPEN** Not
WINEMAKER Sparky Marquis, Sarah Marquis, Kim Johnston **EST.** 1998
PRODUCT RANGE A range of varietally denominated table wines reflecting the plantings.
SUMMARY Marquis Phillips is the export-oriented brand created by the high-profile Sparky and Sarah Marquis winemaking duo. Their very large production is directed to the Canadian, German, Singapore and the US markets, but is nominally available by mail order.

Marribrook

Albany Highway, Kendenup, WA 6323 **REGION** Mount Barker
T (08) 9851 4651 **F** (08) 9851 4652 **OPEN** Wed–Sun and public holidays 10.30–4.30
WINEMAKER Gavin Berry, Richard Robson **EST.** 1990 **CASES** 2000
PRODUCT RANGE ($14–25 CD) Semillon Sauvignon Blanc, Stirling White (Semillon), Botanica Chardonnay, Reserve Chardonnay, Marsanne, Marsanne Oaked, Marri Gold (Marsanne), Cabernet Malbec Merlot.
SUMMARY The Brooks family purchased the former Marron View 5.6-hectare vineyard from Kim Hart in 1994 and renamed the venture Marribrook Wines. Those wines are now made by Gavin Berry at Plantagenet, having been made at Alkoomi up to 1994. The Brooks have purchased an

additional property on the Albany Highway north of Mount Barker and immediately south of Gilberts. Cellar-door sales have moved to this location, and a dedicated cellar-door sales building encompassing a small restaurant and gallery was completed in 2000, with great views out to the Stirling Range. Retail distribution in Western Australia and Victoria; exports to Singapore.

ＹＹＹＹＹ **Cabernet Malbec Merlot 2001** Attractive blackcurrant, blackberry and licorice fruit drives a long palate; ripe tannins. **RATING** 90 **DRINK** 2011 $19

Marschall Groom Cellars   NR

28 Langmeil Road, Tanunda, SA 5352 (postal) **REGION** Barossa Valley
T (08) 8563 1101 **F** (08) 8563 1102 **OPEN** Not
WINEMAKER Daryl Groom **EST.** 1997
PRODUCT RANGE A range of varietally denominated table wines reflecting the plantings.
SUMMARY This is a family venture involving Daryl Groom, former Penfolds but now long-term Geyser Peak winemaker in California, Jeannette and David Marschall. It is an export-focused business, the principal markets being Sweden and the US.

Marsh Estate   NR

Deasy's Road, Pokolbin, NSW 2321 **REGION** Lower Hunter Valley
T (02) 4998 7587 **F** (02) 4998 7884 **OPEN** Mon–Fri 10–4.30, weekends 10–5
WINEMAKER Andrew Marsh **EST.** 1971 **CASES** 7000
PRODUCT RANGE ($18–25 CD) Semillon, Private Bin Semillon, Chardonnay (oaked and unoaked), Semillon Sauternes, Shiraz (Private Bin, Vat S and Vat R), Cabernet Sauvignon, Cremant Brut.
SUMMARY Through sheer consistency, value for money and unrelenting hard work, the Marsh family (who purchased the former Quentin Estate in 1978) has built up a sufficiently loyal cellar-door and mailing list clientele to allow all of the considerable production to be sold direct. Wine style is always direct, with oak playing a minimal role and prolonged cellaring paying handsome dividends. No recent tastings, but Marsh Estate has moved ahead with production rising to 7000 cases and Andrew Marsh succeeding Peter Marsh as winemaker.

Martins Hill Wines   ★★☆

Sydney Road, Mudgee, NSW 2850 **REGION** Mudgee
T (02) 6373 1248 **F** (02) 6373 1248 **OPEN** Not
WINEMAKER Pieter Van Gent (Contract) **EST.** 1985 **CASES** 600
PRODUCT RANGE ($12–15 ML) Sauvignon Blanc, Dolce Vita, Pinot Noir, Alfresco Red, Cabernet Sauvignon.
SUMMARY Janette Kenworthy and Michael Sweeny are committed organic grape growers and are members of the Organic Vignerons Association. It is a tiny operation at the moment, with 0.5 hectare each of sauvignon blanc and pinot noir, 1 hectare of cabernet sauvignon and 1.5 hectares of shiraz in production. While there is no cellar door (only a mailing list), organic vineyard tours and talks can be arranged by appointment.

ＹＹＹＹ **Sauvignon Blanc 2003 RATING** 84 **DRINK** Now $13

ＹＹＹ **Pinot Noir 2002 RATING** 81 $15

Marybrook Vineyards   NR

Vasse–Yallingup Road, Marybrook, WA 6280 **REGION** Margaret River
T (08) 9755 1143 **F** (08) 9755 1112 **OPEN** Fri–Mon 10–5, 7 days 10–5 school holidays
WINEMAKER Aub House **EST.** 1986 **CASES** 2000
PRODUCT RANGE ($11–26.50 CD) Verdelho, Chardonnay, Classic White, Nectosia (sweet), Grenache, Cabernet, Cabernet Franc, Temptation (sweet red), Ruby Jetty Port, Liqueur Muscat.
SUMMARY Marybrook Vineyards is owned by Aub and Jan House. Eight hectares of vineyards are in production, with back vintages often available.

Mary Byrnes Wine   NR

Rees Road, Ballandean, Qld 4382 **REGION** Granite Belt
T (07) 4684 1111 **F** (07) 4684 1312 **OPEN** Weekends and public holidays 10–5, or by appointment
WINEMAKER Mary Byrnes **EST.** 1991 **CASES** 2000
PRODUCT RANGE ($15–22 CD) Viognier, Marsanne, Chardonnay, Rose, Sweet Ayla Red, Shiraz, Liqueur Muscat.
SUMMARY Mary Byrnes, who has a wine science degree, acquired her property in 1991, subsequently planting 4 hectares of shiraz and 1 hectare each of marsanne, viognier, roussane and mourvedre, topping the planting off with 0.5 hectare of grenache and 0.5 hectare of black hamburg muscat. She has deliberately grown the vines without irrigation, thereby limiting yield and (in her words) ensuring a distinctive regional quality and flavour. The wines are sold via mail order and the cellar door.

ꙮ Maslin Old Dunsborough Wines   NR

90 Naturaliste Terrace, Dunsborough, WA 6281 **REGION** Margaret River
T (08) 9755 3578 **F** (08) 9755 3578 **OPEN** Weekends, or by appointment
WINEMAKER Robert Maslin **EST.** 1999
PRODUCT RANGE Dry White, Pinot Noir, Cabernet Sauvignon.
SUMMARY Yet another new entrant in the Margaret River region, established by Robert and Leonie Maslin. They have planted semillon, sauvignon blanc, chenin blanc, pinot noir, merlot and cabernet sauvignon, and Robert Maslin makes the wines on-site. Accommodation is available, and the cellar door offers barbecue facilities.

ꙮ Massena Vineyards   NR

PO Box 54, Tanunda, SA 5352 **REGION** Barossa Valley
T (08) 8564 3037 **F** (08) 8564 3037 **OPEN** Not
WINEMAKER Dan Standish, Jaysen Collins **EST.** 2000
PRODUCT RANGE A range of varietally denominated table wines reflecting the plantings.
SUMMARY Massena Vineyards draws upon 2 hectares of grenache, shiraz, mourvedre, durif and tinta amarella at Nuriootpa. It is an export-oriented business, selling to the US, Denmark and England. The wines can, however, be purchased by mail order.

Massoni   ★★★☆

PO Box 298, Newport, Vic 3015 **REGION** Pyrenees/Mornington Peninsula
T 1300 131 175 **F** 1300 131 185 **OPEN** Not
WINEMAKER Jill Marshall **EST.** 1984 **CASES** 10 000
PRODUCT RANGE ($13–80 R) Riesling, Chardonnay, Lectus Cuvee, Pinot Noir, Shiraz, Cabernet Merlot; Homes Chardonnay, Pinot Noir, Shiraz, Cabernet Merlot.
SUMMARY At the time of writing, it was uncertain whether Massoni would become a brand under the Warrenmang vehicle, or continue as a separate entity. In any event, the tasting notes (and the individual brand names) will be unaffected by the ultimate outcome. Exports to the US.

▼▼▼▼▽ **Massoni Shiraz 2002** Redolent with luscious black fruits and spice; mouthfilling; impressive length and finish. Pyrenees. **RATING** 93 **DRINK** 2017 $ 35
Estate Shiraz 2001 A complex array of blackberry, cedar, chocolate and vanilla; long, fine tannins; excellent wine. **RATING** 93 **DRINK** 2016 $ 60
Cabernet Sauvignon 2000 Good blackcurrant, cedar and earth varietal character; fine tannins run through a long finish. **RATING** 91 **DRINK** 2015 $ 33

▼▼▼▼ **Massoni Riesling 2003** Firm, mineral and spice aromas; lemony minerally flavours; fine-boned. From the Henty region. **RATING** 89 **DRINK** 2010
Bazzani Chardonnay 2003 Nice wine; lots of melon and peach fruit; round, and carries its 14.2 degrees alcohol surprisingly well. **RATING** 89 **DRINK** Now $ 13
Massoni Chardonnay 2001 Complex, powerful, rich and ripe; peach, butter and cashew. Mornington Peninsula. **RATING** 89 **DRINK** Now $ 30
Massoni Pinot Noir 2000 Holding hue well; light to medium-bodied; complex spice, game and forest floor; lingering acidity. **RATING** 89 **DRINK** 2007 $ 35

Massoni Cabernet Merlot 2001 Cedar, mint, leaf and spice; red and black berries; good tannin management to round off the fruit. Pyrenees. **RATING** 89 **DRINK** 2011 $35

Massoni Pinot Noir 2001 Spicy, savoury, strawberry/cherry/plum; fine and persistent finish. Mornington Peninsula. **RATING** 88 **DRINK** 2007 $35

Black Puma Shiraz 2001 Big, ultra-ripe style; some prune jam characters, but plenty happening. **RATING** 88 **DRINK** 2011 $80

Massoni Cuvee NV Lively, lemony, zesty; fresh apple, citrus and pear. Mornington Peninsula. **RATING** 88 **DRINK** Now $30

Massoni Chardonnay 2000 Complex barrel-ferment/bottle-developed/malolactic aromas and flavours; needs more fruit drive. **RATING** 87 **DRINK** Now $30

ⵀⵀⵀⵖ   **Massoni Shiraz 2001** **RATING** 86 **DRINK** Now $35
Homes Chardonnay 2001 **RATING** 86 **DRINK** Now $18
Homes Cabernet Merlot 2001 **RATING** 86 **DRINK** 2007 $20
Bazzani Cabernet Shiraz Dolcetto 2001 **RATING** 85 **DRINK** 2007 $18

ⵀⵀⵀ   **Homes Pinot Noir 2001** **RATING** 83 $20

Matilda's Estate ★★★☆

RMB 654 Hamilton Road, Denmark, WA 6333 **REGION** Denmark
T (08) 9848 1951 **F** (08) 9848 1957 **OPEN** 7 days 10–5
WINEMAKER Brenden Smith, Dave Cleary **EST.** 1990 **CASES** 5000
PRODUCT RANGE ($13–25 CD) Semillon Sauvignon Blanc, Unwooded Chardonnay, Sparkling White, Sparkling Red, Late Picked Riesling, Autumn Amethyst (light red), Pinot Noir, Cabernet Sauvignon Shiraz, Cabernet Sauvignon Cabernet Franc, Tawny Port Muscat blend.
SUMMARY In September 2002 the founders of Matilda's Meadow (as it was then known), Don Turnbull and Pamela Meldrum, sold the business to former citizen of the world, Steve Hall. It is a thriving business based on 6 hectares of estate plantings, with a restaurant offering morning and afternoon tea, lunch Tuesday to Sunday and dinner Thursday to Saturday.

ⵀⵀⵀⵀ   **Cabernet Merlot 2002** Spicy, leafy, minty overtones to raspberry/redcurrant/cassis fruit; a lively, fresh finish. **RATING** 87 **DRINK** 2008 $18

ⵀⵀⵀⵖ   **Fossil Series Unwooded Chardonnay 2003** Clean, crisp melon fruit; an appealing, albeit simple wine. **RATING** 86 **DRINK** 2007 $20
Fossil Series Semillon Sauvignon Blanc 2003 **RATING** 85 **DRINK** Now $17.50

Mawson Ridge NR

24–28 Main Road, Hahndorf, SA 5066 **REGION** Adelaide Hills
T (08) 8338 0828 **F** (08) 8338 0828 **OPEN** Summer Tues–Sat 11–5, Winter Wed–Sat 11–5, Sun 12–5
WINEMAKER Michael Scarpantoni (Contract) **EST.** 1998 **CASES** 400
PRODUCT RANGE ($13–20 CD) Sauvignon Blanc, Pinot Gris, Unoaked Chardonnay, Chardonnay, Pinot Noir, Stringybark Cutter Merlot Cabernets, Flinder's Reef Cabernet Sauvignon; the lower-priced range of Blend One (Barossa Cabernet Shiraz), Blend Two (McLaren Vale Grenache Shiraz), Blend Three (Clare Valley Grenache Cabernet).
SUMMARY You might be forgiven for thinking the winery name carries the cool-climate association a little bit too far. In fact, Sir Douglas Mawson, also a conservationist and forester, arrived in the Lenswood region in the early 1930s, harvesting the native stringybarks for hardwood and replanting the cleared land with pine trees. A hut that Mawson built on the property still stands today on Mawson Road, which the vineyard fronts. Here Raymond and Madeline Marin have established 5.5 hectares of vines, having added 2 hectares of pinot gris in 2002, with contract winemaking by Michael Scarpantoni.

Maximilian's Vineyard NR

Main Road, Verdun, SA 5245 **REGION** Adelaide Hills
T (08) 8388 7777 **F** (08) 8388 1371 **OPEN** Wed–Mon 11–5
WINEMAKER Contract **EST.** 1994 **CASES** 2000
PRODUCT RANGE ($18–26 CD) Unwooded Chardonnay, Chardonnay, Methode Champenoise, Two Up Cabernet, Headstand Cabernet, Cabernet Sauvignon.

SUMMARY Maximilian and Louise Hruska opened Maximilian's Restaurant in 1976, accommodated in a homestead built in 1851. Two hectares of chardonnay and 6 hectares of cabernet sauvignon were planted in 1994, and surround the restaurant. The Cabernet Sauvignon is made by Grant Burge, the Chardonnay at Scarpantoni Estate under the direction of the Hruskas' eldest son, Paul. Since graduating from Roseworthy, Paul Hruska has completed vintages in Burgundy, Spain, Margaret River and the Clare Valley, and when he finally decides to come home, an on-site winery will be developed.

Maxwell Wines ★★★★★

Olivers Road, McLaren Vale, SA 5171 **REGION** McLaren Vale
T (08) 8323 8200 **F** (08) 8323 8900 **OPEN** 7 days 10–5
WINEMAKER Mark Maxwell, Adam Hooper **EST.** 1979 **CASES** 10 000
PRODUCT RANGE ($12–65 CD) Under the Maxwell Wines brand, Old Vines Semillon, Verdelho, Frontignac Spatlese, Chardonnay, Cabernet Merlot; Ellen Street Shiraz, Four Roads Shiraz, Lime Cave Cabernet Sauvignon; and Honey Mead, Spiced Mead, Liqueur Mead, Old Tawny Port, Liqueur Muscat.
SUMMARY Maxwell Wines has come a long way since opening for business in 1979 using an amazing array of Heath Robinson equipment in cramped surroundings. A state-of-the-art and much larger winery was built on a new site in time for the 1997 vintage; this was appropriate for a brand which has produced some excellent white and red wines in recent years. Exports to the US, Canada, the UK, Switzerland, Austria, Germany, Belgium, Hong Kong, Singapore, Thailand and New Zealand.

ŸŸŸŸŸ **Reserve Lime Cave Cabernet Sauvignon 2001** Layer upon layer of blackcurrant and bitter chocolate fruit; perfectly balanced oak. **RATING** 94 **DRINK** 2016 $ 60

ŸŸŸŸŸ **Lime Cave Cabernet Sauvignon 2001** A sweet, rich mix of blackcurrant and dark chocolate; velvety, rich and round. McLaren Vale at its best. **RATING** 93 **DRINK** 2021 $ 28
Lime Cave Cabernet Sauvignon 2002 Very good colour; blackcurrant, blackberry, chocolate and sweet earth; good length, lingering savoury tannins. **RATING** 92 **DRINK** 2017 $ 28

ŸŸŸŸ **Ellen Street Shiraz 2001** Very ripe plum, prune and blackberry aromas; hyper-rich, ripe, luscious mouthfilling fruit; slightly old-fashioned McLaren Vale style. **RATING** 89 **DRINK** 2014 $ 30

Maygars Hill Winery ★★★★☆

53 Longwood–Mansfield Road, Longwood, Vic 3665 **REGION** Strathbogie Ranges
T (03) 5798 5417 **F** (03) 5798 5457 **OPEN** By appointment
WINEMAKER Sam Plunkett (Contract) **EST.** 1997 **CASES** 900
PRODUCT RANGE ($12–32 CD) The Abbey Semillon, Shiraz, Cabernet Sauvignon, Reserve Cabernet Sauvignon.
SUMMARY The 8-hectare property known as Maygars Hill was purchased by Jenny Houghton in 1994. The plan, now a reality, was to establish on-site bed and breakfast accommodation, and to plant a small vineyard, which now comprises 1.6 hectares of shiraz and 0.8 hectare of cabernet sauvignon. The name comes from Lieutenant Colonel Maygar, who fought with outstanding bravery in the Boer War in South Africa in 1901, where he was awarded the Victoria Cross. In World War I he rose to command of the 8th Light Horse Regiment, winning yet further medals for bravery, before his death on 1 November 1917.

ŸŸŸŸŸ **Cabernet Sauvignon 2002** Very expressive and attractive cassis, blackcurrant fruit; excellent balance, texture and length. Trophy winner 2003 Victorian Wines Show. **RATING** 94 **DRINK** 2012 $ 22

M. Chapoutier Australia ★★★☆

PO Box 437, Robe, SA 5276 **REGION** Mount Benson
T (08) 8768 5076 **F** (08) 8768 5073 **OPEN** Not
WINEMAKER Olivier Antoine, Nigel Squire **EST.** 1998 **CASES** 4000
PRODUCT RANGE ($23 R) Shiraz, Cabernet Sauvignon.
SUMMARY This is one of several winemaking ventures the famous Rhône Valley firm of M. Chapoutier is establishing in Australia. The large biodynamic vineyard is made up of 16.5 hectares of shiraz, 10 hectares of cabernet sauvignon, 4 hectares each of marsanne and viognier, with 2 hectares of

sauvignon blanc in the course of establishment. For the time being the wines are made at nearby Cape Jaffa; exports to Europe, Asia, the US, New Zealand, Kong Kong, Japan, Singapore and Indonesia.

ȲȲȲȲ **Syrah 2001** A complex of spice, game and black cherry fruit; funky aspects do not detract. **RATING** 88 **DRINK** 2011 $ 23

Meadowbank Estate ★★★★

699 Richmond Road, Cambridge, Tas 7170 **REGION** Southern Tasmania
T (03) 6248 4484 **F** (03) 6248 4485 **OPEN** 7 days 10–5
WINEMAKER Andrew Hood (Contract) **EST.** 1974 **CASES** 7000
PRODUCT RANGE ($25–42 CD) Riesling, Sauvignon Blanc, Unwooded Chardonnay, Grace Elizabeth Chardonnay, Mardi (sparkling), Pinot Noir, Henry James Pinot Noir, Cabernet Sauvignon.
SUMMARY Now an important part of the Ellis family business on what was once (but is no more) a large grazing property on the banks of the Derwent. Increased plantings are being established under contract to BRL Hardy, and a splendid new winery has been built to handle the increased production, with wine quality consistently excellent. The winery has expansive entertainment and function facilities, capable of handling up to 1000 people, and offering an arts and music program throughout the year, plus a large restaurant that is open 7 days.

ȲȲȲȲȲ **Mardi 2002** Onion skin-pink; an attractive mix of strawberry, stone fruit and citrus; long palate; good balance and finish. Includes 20 per cent pinot meunier. **RATING** 92 **DRINK** Now $ 38
Grace Elizabeth Chardonnay 2002 Elegant, fine, subtle; restrained citrus and French oak; fractionally short. **RATING** 90 **DRINK** 2007 $ 31
Pinot Gris 2003 Pale blush colour; aromatic apple and pear bouquet; very good flavour and balance; much more character than most. **RATING** 90 **DRINK** 2007 $ 28
Henry James Pinot Noir 2002 Stacked with flavour in the dark fruit spectrum; extractive or simply low yield? Very long. **RATING** 90 **DRINK** 2011 $ 42

ȲȲȲȲ **Chardonnay 2003** Lively, fresh, long nectarine and ripe citrus; lingering finish. Screwcap. **RATING** 89 **DRINK** 2008 $ 25
Riesling 2003 Apple blossom and lime; nice balance and mouthfeel to lime/lemon fruit; lighter style. **RATING** 88 **DRINK** 2011 $ 25
Pinot Noir 2002 Very ripe, rich plum aromas and flavours; will build complexity. **RATING** 88 **DRINK** 2007 $ 28
Sauvignon Blanc 2003 Clean, fresh, clear varietal character; mix of mineral and gooseberry; very delicate. **RATING** 87 **DRINK** Now $ 27.50

ȲȲȲȲ **Grace Elizabeth Chardonnay 2003** **RATING** 85 **DRINK** 2007 $ 31
Unwooded Chardonnay 2002 **RATING** 84 **DRINK** Now $ 25

ȲȲȲ **Unwooded Chardonnay 2003** **RATING** 83 $ 25
Pinot Noir 2003 **RATING** 83 $ 28
Cabernet 2002 **RATING** 83 $ 29

Meerea Park ★★★★

Lot 3 Palmers Lane, Pokolbin, NSW 2320 **REGION** Lower Hunter Valley
T (02) 4998 7474 **F** (02) 4930 7100 **OPEN** At The Boutique Wine Centre, Broke Road, Pokolbin 9–5
WINEMAKER Rhys Eather **EST.** 1991 **CASES** 10 000
PRODUCT RANGE ($18.50–60 R) Epoch Semillon, Terracotta Semillon, Alexander Munro Semillon, Lindsay Hill Viognier, Lindsay Hill Verdelho, Chardonnay, Alexander Munro Chardonnay, Late Harvest Viognier, The Aunts Shiraz, Alexander Munro Shiraz, Terracotta Shiraz, Shiraz Viognier, Cabernet Merlot.
SUMMARY All of the wines are produced from grapes purchased from growers, primarily in the Pokolbin, Broke Fordwich and Upper Hunter regions, but also from as far afield as Orange and Young. It is the brainchild of Rhys Eather, a great-grandson of Alexander Munro, a leading vigneron in the mid-19th century; he makes the wine at the former Little's Winery on Palmer's Lane in Pokolbin. Retail distribution through the principal States, and exports to the UK, The Netherlands, Germany, the US, Canada and the Philippines.

ΥΥΥΥ **Terracotta Semillon 1999** Tight, fine and long; lemon, herbs and spices; much better balance than the Alexander Munro; destined to be a classic. **RATING** 93 **DRINK** 2009 $ 30
Terracotta Shiraz 2001 A complex array of leather, briar, earth, licorice and — ultimately — black fruit aromas. Very powerful tannins tremble on the brink but don't go over the top, and do contribute to the savoury/spicy/leathery regional flavours. A Hunter Valley answer to McLaren Vale. Has 4 per cent Viognier co-fermented with the Shiraz. **RATING** 92 **DRINK** 2016 $ 60
Alexander Munro Semillon 2000 Intense, clean citrus/lemon/herb; still at the start of its life, but plenty there. **RATING** 91 **DRINK** 2010 $ 25

ΥΥΥΥ **Epoch Semillon 2002** Rich and ripe, citrus moving into tropical aromas; some botrytis? A rich, full-bodied palate likewise a function of the year. **RATING** 88 **DRINK** 2007 $ 18.50
Alexander Munro Shiraz 2001 Complex regional earth, leather and game; abundant flavour and aftertaste, but the line is fractured. **RATING** 88 **DRINK** 2011 $ 50
Alexander Munro Semillon 1999 Still zesty and lively; penetrating, lingering acidity seems unlikely to ever soften to the point of comfort. **RATING** 87 **DRINK** 2014 $ 25
Cabernet Merlot 2001 Blackcurrant, spice, earth and mint aromas are followed by a palate which opens with sweet, red fruits, then moves to fine but pervasive tannins (added?) on the palate. A blend of Hilltops and Orange grapes. **RATING** 87 **DRINK** 2010 $ 22

ΥΥΥΥ **Lindsay Hill Viognier 2003** **RATING** 84 **DRINK** Now $ 22

ΥΥΥ **Alexander Munro Chardonnay 2002** **RATING** 80 $ 25

Melaleuca Grove ★★★

8 Melaleuca Court, Rowville, Vic 3178 (postal) **REGION** Upper Goulburn
T (03) 9752 7928 **F** (03) 9752 7928 **OPEN** Not
WINEMAKER Jeff Wright **EST.** 1999 **CASES** 1000
PRODUCT RANGE ($16 ML) Yea Valley Chardonnay, Shiraz, Merlot, Cabernet Sauvignon; Yarra Valley Chardonnay.
SUMMARY Jeff and Anne Wright are both honours graduates in biochemistry who have succumbed to the lure of winemaking after lengthy careers elsewhere; in the case of Jeff, 20 years in research and hospital science. He commenced his winemaking apprenticeship in 1997 at Green Vineyards, backed up by further vintage work in 1999 and 2000 at Bianchet and Yarra Valley Hills, both in the Yarra Valley. At the same time he began the external Bachelor of Applied Science (Wine Science) course at Charles Sturt University, while continuing to work in biochemistry in the public hospital system. They purchase grapes from various cool-climate regions, including Yea and the Yarra Valley. They are available through selected Melbourne retailers and restaurants, and by mailing list.

ΥΥΥΥ **Yea Valley Shiraz 2000** Savoury/earthy/spicy black fruit aromas; while only medium-bodied, lingers long in the mouth; good aftertaste. **RATING** 89 **DRINK** 2010 $ 18

ΥΥΥΥ **Yea Valley Chardonnay 2002** **RATING** 86 **DRINK** 2007 $ 18
Sauvignon Blanc 2003 **RATING** 85 **DRINK** Now $ 16

🌿 Melange Wines NR

Farm 1291 Harward Road, Griffith, NSW 2680 **REGION** Riverina
T (02) 6962 7783 **F** (02) 6962 7783 **OPEN** 7 days 10–5
WINEMAKER Angelo D'Aquino **EST.** 2000
PRODUCT RANGE A range of varietally denominated table wines reflecting the plantings.
SUMMARY Melange Wines is a relative newcomer in the Riverina region, although Angelo D'Aquino comes from a family with considerable viticultural experience. There are 25 hectares of sauvignon blanc, semillon, chardonnay, verdelho, trebbiano, muscat gordo blanco, shiraz and durif planted. The cellar door offers light meals and winery tours plus tutored tastings.

🐾 Mengler View Wines   NR

Magnolia Road, Tanunda, SA 5352 **REGION** Barossa Valley
T (08) 8563 2217 **F** (08) 8563 2408 **OPEN** By appointment
WINEMAKER Bob Mitchell **EST.** 1995
PRODUCT RANGE A range of varietally denominated table wines reflecting the plantings.
SUMMARY Bob Mitchell has 2 hectares of cabernet sauvignon, merlot and shiraz, and makes the
wines. While available through the cellar door and by mail order, they are principally directed to the
US market.

🐾 Merli   NR

19 One Chain Road, Merricks North, Vic 3926 **REGION** Mornington Peninsula
T (03) 5989 7435 **F** (03) 9380 2555 **OPEN** By appointment
WINEMAKER Ennio Merli, David Merli **EST.** 2000
PRODUCT RANGE Chardonnay, Pinot Noir, Shiraz, Cabernet Merlot.
SUMMARY Ennio, David and Jonathan Merli have established 4 hectares of chardonnay, pinot noir,
shiraz, cabernet sauvignon and merlot at Merricks North. The relatively small production is made
on-site, and sold by mail order and through the cellar door.

Mermerus Vineyard   ★★★★

60 Soho Road, Drysdale, Vic 3222 **REGION** Geelong
T (03) 5253 2718 **F** (03) 5226 1683 **OPEN** First Sunday of each month and every Sunday in January
WINEMAKER Paul Champion **EST.** 2000 **CASES** 600
PRODUCT RANGE ($16–20 CD) Chardonnay, Pinot Noir, Pope's Eye Pinot Noir, Shiraz.
SUMMARY Commencing in 1996, Paul Champion has established 1.5 hectares of pinot noir, 1 hectare
of chardonnay and 0.2 hectare of riesling at Mermerus, making the wine on-site at the winery, which
was built in 2000, and also acting as contract winemaker for small growers in the region. The first
commercial wines were made in the following year, and are sold through the cellar door, by mailing
list and at selected restaurants.

ΨΨΨΨ **Pinot Noir 2002** Aromatic, ripe plum aromas; very powerful and concentrated; should
live for many years. **RATING** 91 **DRINK** 2010 $ 20

ΨΨΨΨ **Chardonnay 2002** Rich yellow peach and nectarine fruit with some toasty bottle-
developed characters; full-bodied style, good value. **RATING** 89 **DRINK** 2007 $ 16

Merrebee Estate   NR

Lot 3339 St Werburghs Road, Mount Barker, WA 6234 **REGION** Mount Barker
T (08) 9851 2424 **F** (08) 9851 2425 **OPEN** By appointment
WINEMAKER Brenden Smith (Contract) **EST.** 1986 **CASES** 500
PRODUCT RANGE ($15–25 CD) Riesling, Chardonnay, Mount Barker Chardonnay, Shiraz; Giles Point
Sauvignon Blanc Chardonnay and Unwooded Chardonnay.
SUMMARY Planting of the Merrebee Estate vineyards commenced in 1986 and has now reached a
little under 9 hectares. The wines are available from selected retailers in Western Australia and from
Rathdowne Cellars, Melbourne, and Ultimo Wine Centre, Sydney; exports to the UK, the US and
Canada.

Merricks Creek Wines   ★★★★★

44 Merricks Road, cnr Yal Yal Road, Merricks, Vic 3916 **REGION** Mornington Peninsula
T (03) 5989 8868 **F** (03) 9827 2220 **OPEN** By appointment
WINEMAKER Nick Farr, Peter Parker **EST.** 1998 **CASES** 330
PRODUCT RANGE ($22–45 CD) Sparkling Pinot Noir, Pinot Noir Young Vines, Pinot Noir Merricks,
Pinot Noir Close Planted, Pinot Noir Nick Farr.
SUMMARY Peter and Georgina Parker retained Gary Farr (of Bannockburn) as viticultural consultant
before they commenced establishment of their 2-hectare pinot noir vineyard. They say, 'He has been
an extraordinarily helpful and stern taskmaster from day one. He advised on clonal selection, trellis

design and planting density, and visits the vineyard regularly to monitor canopy management.' (Son Nick Farr completes the circle as contract winemaker.) The vineyard is planted to a sophisticated and rare collection of new pinot noir clones, and is being planted at the ultra-high density of 500 mm spacing on 1-metre high trellising. Virtually no wine was made in 2002, and the 2003 vintage will come on to the market late in 2004.

Merricks Estate ★★★☆

Thompsons Lane, Merricks, Vic 3916 **REGION** Mornington Peninsula
T (03) 5989 8416 **F** (03) 9613 4242 **OPEN** First weekend of each month, each weekend in Jan and public holiday weekends 12–5
WINEMAKER Paul Evans **EST.** 1977 **CASES** 2000
PRODUCT RANGE ($25–27 CD) Chardonnay, Pinot Noir, Shiraz, Cabernet Sauvignon.
SUMMARY Melbourne solicitor George Kefford, together with wife Jacquie, runs Merricks Estate as a weekend and holiday enterprise. Right from the outset it has produced distinctive, spicy, cool-climate Shiraz which has accumulated an impressive array of show trophies and gold medals.

ΨΨΨΨΨ **Pinot Noir 2001** Holding hue well; opens with spicy, savoury aromas, then plenty of smooth, sweet plummy/cherry fruit on the palate; good length. **RATING** 90 **DRINK** 2007 $ 27

ΨΨΨΨ **Chardonnay 2000** Bottle-developed complexity; nutty cashew and melon and a touch of honey; nice spicy finish and acidity. **RATING** 88 **DRINK** Now $ 25

ΨΨΨΨ **Shiraz 1999 RATING** 86 **DRINK** Now $ 25
Cabernet Sauvignon 1998 RATING 86 **DRINK** 2007 $ 25

Merum ★★★★★

Hillbrook Road, Quinninup, WA 6258 **REGION** Pemberton
T (08) 9776 6011 **F** (08) 9776 6022 **OPEN** By appointment
WINEMAKER Jan Davies (Contract) **EST.** 1996 **CASES** 1000
PRODUCT RANGE ($20–28 ML) Semillon, Shiraz.
SUMMARY Merum was founded by the late Maria Melsom (formerly winemaker at Driftwood Estate) and Michael Melsom (former vineyard manager for Voyager Estate, both in the Margaret River region). The 6.3 hectares of vineyard (3.3 shiraz, 2 semillon, 1 chardonnay) was planted in 1996, with the first wine made in 1999. The quality of the wines so far released has been truly excellent.

ΨΨΨΨΨ **Semillon 2003** Complex and mouthfilling, but perfect balance and texture give great finesse; some tropical notes, then gentle, lemony acidity. Screwcap. **RATING** 94 **DRINK** 2010 $ 22

ΨΨΨΨΨ **Semillon 2002** The bouquet is complex, rich, stylish and tangy, the palate bursting with flavour, helped by the clever blending in of 10 per cent Chardonnay. **RATING** 90 **DRINK** 2010 $ 22
Shiraz 2002 Obvious cool-climate spice, bramble and blackberry mix; good control of extract and oak. **RATING** 90 **DRINK** 2011 $ 28

Metcalfe Valley ★★☆

283 Metcalfe–Malmsbury Road, Metcalfe, Vic 3448 **REGION** Macedon Ranges
T (03) 5423 2035 **OPEN** By appointment
WINEMAKER Ian Pattison **EST.** 1994 **CASES** 500
PRODUCT RANGE ($25 R) Shiraz, Cabernet Sauvignon.
SUMMARY Ian Pattison, with a PhD in metallurgy, and a Diploma in horticultural science and viticulture from Melbourne University/Dookie College, purchased Metcalfe Valley from the Frederiksens in 2003. With a little under 5 hectares of shiraz (2–10 years old), and 2 hectares of sauvignon blanc (planted 2003), production will increase significantly.

ΨΨΨΨ **Cabernet Sauvignon 2002 RATING** 85 **DRINK** 2010 $ 25

ΨΨΨ **Shiraz 2002 RATING** 82 $ 25

Metier Wines

Tarraford Vineyard, 440 Healesville Road, Yarra Glen, Vic 3775 (postal) **REGION** Yarra Valley
T 0419 678 918 **F** (03) 5962 2194 **OPEN** Not
WINEMAKER Martin Williams MW **EST.** 1995 **CASES** 2000
PRODUCT RANGE ($18–37.50 R) Tarraford Vineyard Chardonnay, Schoolhouse Vineyard Chardonnay, Tarraford Vineyard Pinot Noir, Schoolhouse Vineyard Pinot Noir, Manytrees Vineyard Shiraz Viognier; new lower-priced Milkwood range.
SUMMARY Metier is the French word for craft, trade or profession; the business is that of Yarra Valley-based winemaker Martin Williams MW, who has notched up an array of degrees and winemaking stints in France, California and Australia which are, not to put too fine a point on it, extraordinary. The focus of Metier is to produce individual-vineyard wines, initially based on grapes from the Tarraford and Schoolhouse Vineyards, both in the Yarra Valley. The quality of the Viognier, Pinot Noir, Shiraz and Chardonnay is extremely high. Exports to the UK, the US and Hong Kong.

▼▼▼▼▼ **Tarraford Vineyard Chardonnay 2000** Still youthful, developing slowly: melon and citrus aromas have a subtle oak infusion; the lovely mouthfeel is provided by a gently creamy centre to the surrounding melon and citrus fruit. **RATING** 95 **DRINK** 2009 $ 32

▼▼▼▼▽ **Schoolhouse Vineyard Pinot Noir 2001** Good colour; fine cherry, plum and mint flavours; clean and supple, has great length. **RATING** 92 **DRINK** 2008 $ 37.50
Tarraford Vineyard Pinot Noir 2001 Complex plum, earth, and a hint of game on the bouquet; similarly complex palate; the strength is in the finish and aftertaste. **RATING** 91 **DRINK** 2007 $ 37.50

▼▼▼▼ **Manytrees Vineyard Shiraz Viognier 2001** Fresh, fragrant; light to medium-bodied spicy, savoury flavours; minimal tannins. **RATING** 88 **DRINK** 2007 $ 37.50

▼▼▼▽ **Milkwood Sauvignon Blanc 2003** **RATING** 86 **DRINK** Now $ 18
Milkwood Chardonnay 2002 **RATING** 86 **DRINK** Now $ 19.95

Meure's Wines

16 Fleurtys Lane, Birchs Bay, Tas 7162 **REGION** Southern Tasmania
T (03) 6267 4483 **F** (03) 6267 4483 **OPEN** By appointment
WINEMAKER Louise Brightman **EST.** 1991 **CASES** 500
PRODUCT RANGE ($30–40 ML) Sauvignon Blanc, Pinot Gris, Chardonnay, Pinot Noir.
SUMMARY Dirk Meure has established 1 hectare of vineyard on the shores of D'Entrecasteaux Channel, overlooking Bruny Island. The Huon Valley is the southernmost wine region in Australia, and it was here that Dirk Meure's parents settled on their arrival from The Netherlands in 1950. He says he has been heavily influenced by his mentors, Steve and Monique Lubiana. The philosophy is to produce low yields from balanced vines and to interfere as little as possible in the winemaking and maturation process.

▼▼▼▼▼ **d'Meure Pinot Noir 2001** Excellent depth and varietal definition; ripe but not overripe blood plum fruit; supple mouthfeel, good length and fine tannins. **RATING** 94 **DRINK** 2008 $ 39

▼▼▼▼ **d'Meure Chardonnay 2001** Complex, funky wild yeast aromas; a long palate, again walking on the wild side. **RATING** 87 **DRINK** 2007 $ 29

Miceli ★★★★

60 Main Creek Road, Arthurs Seat, Vic 3936 **REGION** Mornington Peninsula
T (03) 5989 2755 **F** (03) 5989 2755 **OPEN** First weekend each month 12–5, public holidays, and also every weekend and by appointment in Jan
WINEMAKER Anthony Miceli **EST.** 1991 **CASES** 3000
PRODUCT RANGE ($20–40 CD) Iolanda's Pinot Grigio, Unwooded Chardonnay, Olivia's Chardonnay, Michael Methode Champenoise, Rose Methode Champenoise, Pinot Noir, Lucy's Choice Pinot Noir.
SUMMARY This may be a part-time labour of love for general practitioner Dr Anthony Miceli, but this hasn't prevented him taking the whole venture very seriously. He acquired the property in 1989

specifically for the purpose of establishing a vineyard, carrying out the first plantings of 1.8 hectares in November 1991, followed by a further hectare of pinot gris in 1997. Between 1991 and 1997 Dr Miceli enrolled in and thereafter graduated from the Wine Science course at Charles Sturt University, and thus manages both vineyard and winery. Retail distribution through fine wine outlets and restaurants in Melbourne.

ŸŸŸŸŸ **Michael Methode Champenoise 2001** Very fragrant; tangy, citrussy lemon peel and apple aromas; fresh and zippy on the palate; penetrating acidity, long finish. **RATING** 90 **DRINK** Now $ 40

ŸŸŸŸ **Rose Methode Champenoise 2001** Lively and fresh, with distinct strawberry nuances; balanced and long. Pinot Noir the major component. **RATING** 89 **DRINK** Now $ 40

Michael Unwin Wines ★★★★☆

2 Racecourse Road, Beaufort, Vic 3373 **REGION** Grampians
T (03) 5349 2021 **F** (03) 5349 2032 **OPEN** 7 days 10–6
WINEMAKER Michael Unwin **EST.** 2000 **CASES** 1000
PRODUCT RANGE ($8.90–40 R) Acrobat Collection range of Riesling, Chardonnay, Botrytis Riesling, Shiraz, Cabernet Sauvignon; Wine Station Chardonnay, Muscat of Alexandria; Tattooed Lady Shiraz and Cabernet Sauvignon.
SUMMARY Michael Unwin Wines was established at Ararat, Victoria by winemaker Michael Unwin and wife and business partner Catherine Clark. His track record as a winemaker is extensive, spanning 16 years and including extended winemaking experience in France, New Zealand and Australia, finding time in between to obtain a postgraduate degree in oenology and viticulture at Lincoln University, Canterbury, New Zealand. He carries on a multi-faceted business, including contract winemaking and consulting; the winemaking takes place in a converted textile factory.

Michelini Wines ★★★

Great Alpine Road, Myrtleford, Vic 3737 **REGION** Alpine Valleys
T (03) 5751 1990 **F** (03) 5751 1410 **OPEN** 7 days 10–5
WINEMAKER Greg O'Keefe **EST.** 1982 **CASES** 5000
PRODUCT RANGE ($10–20 CD) Riesling, Unwooded Chardonnay, Chardonnay, Fizz White and Red, Pinot Noir, Marzemino, Shiraz, Merlot, Cabernet Sauvignon, Fragolino; Devils Creek Chardonnay and Merlot.
SUMMARY The Michelini family are among the best-known grape growers in the Buckland Valley of northeast Victoria. Having migrated from Italy in 1949, the Michelinis originally grew tobacco, diversifying into vineyards in 1982. A little over 42 hectares of vineyard have been established on terra rossa soil at an altitude of 300 metres, mostly with frontage to the Buckland River. The major part of the production is sold (to Orlando and others), but since 1996 an on-site winery has permitted the Michelinis to vinify part of their production. The winery in fact has capacity to handle 1000 tonnes of fruit, thereby eliminating the problem of moving grapes out of a declared phylloxera area.

ŸŸŸŸ **Riesling 2002** Firm, clean, bright lemon, citrus and herb; plenty of mid-palate flavour. **RATING** 88 **DRINK** 2007 $ 13.50
Chardonnay 2001 Considerable French oak impact on the sweet stone fruit and spice flavours. **RATING** 88 **DRINK** Now $ 17.50

ŸŸŸŸ **Fragolino NV** Made from fragola grapes, fragola being the Italian word for strawberry. And, indeed, the wine tastes exactly of strawberries, more so than many strawberry wines. Off-dry. **RATING** 86 **DRINK** Now $ 20
Merlot 2001 **RATING** 86 **DRINK** 2007 $ 18.50
Marzemino 2001 **RATING** 85 **DRINK** Now $ 19
Devils Creek Fizz Pinot Chardonnay NV **RATING** 84 **DRINK** Now $ 20

ŸŸŸ **Fragolino Blush 2003** **RATING** 83 $ 20
Fizz Sparkling Merlot NV **RATING** 83 $ 20
Devils Creek Chardonnay 2003 **RATING** 82 $ 10
Devils Creek Merlot 2002 **RATING** 81 $ 10

Middlebrook Estate

RSD 43 Sand Road, McLaren Vale, SA 5171 **REGION** McLaren Vale
T (08) 8383 0600 **F** (08) 8383 0557 **OPEN** Mon–Fri 10.30–4, weekends 11.30–4.30
WINEMAKER Joseph Cogno, Michael Petrucci **EST.** 1947 **CASES** 65 000
PRODUCT RANGE ($14–20 CD) At the top come Middlebrook Pinot Chardonnay, Unwooded Semillon, Sauvignon Blanc, Chardonnay, Frontignac, Shiraz and Cabernet Sauvignon; then cheaper wines under the Cogno label.
SUMMARY After a brief period of ownership by industry veteran Bill Clappis (who renovated and reopened the winery), ownership has now passed to the Cogno family, which has been winemaking at Cobbity, near Camden, New South Wales, since 1964. Through Middlebrook the family has become one of the largest producers of Lambrusco in Australia: it is available Australia-wide through Liquorland stores. Many other wines (18 in all) are produced under the Cogno Brothers label, and the Middlebrook cask hall has been given over to production of the Medlow chocolate range. The top wines are still sold under the Middlebrook label.

🍷🍷🍷🍷 **Joseph Cogno Shiraz Grenache 2001** Attractive, bright blackberry, raspberry and chocolate fruit; fine tannin and oak inputs; good length and finish. **RATING** 90 **DRINK** 2011 $ 20

🍷🍷🍷🍷 **Vineyard Selection Cabernet Sauvignon 2000** Gently sweet blackcurrant fruit; supple tannins; an ever-present touch of regional chocolate. **RATING** 87 **DRINK** 2010 $ 22

🍷🍷🍷🍷 **Vineyard Selection Shiraz 2000 RATING** 86 **DRINK** 2009 $ 22
Vineyard Selection Chardonnay 2000 RATING 84 **DRINK** Now $ 15.50

🐖 Middlesex 31 NR

PO Box 367, Manjimup, WA 6258 **REGION** Manjimup
T (08) 9771 2499 **F** (08) 9771 2499 **OPEN** Not
WINEMAKER Brenden Smith, Dave Cleary, Mark Aitken **EST.** 1990 **CASES** 1000
PRODUCT RANGE ($12.40–24 ML) Verdelho, Chardonnay, Pinot Noir, Shiraz.
SUMMARY Dr John Rosser (a local GP who runs the Manjimup Medical Centre) and Rosemary Davies have planted 6.5 hectares of vines, predominantly to shiraz, chardonnay and verdelho, with a little patch of pinot noir. There is a tempting range of back vintage wines available at tempting prices. Also back vintages of Chardonnay, Shiraz and Pinot Noir.

Middleton Wines

Flagstaff Hill Road, Middleton, SA 5213 **REGION** Currency Creek
T (08) 8555 4136 **F** (08) 8555 4108 **OPEN** Fri–Sun 11–5
WINEMAKER Nigel Catt **EST.** 1979 **CASES** 3000
PRODUCT RANGE ($14–15 CD) Riesling, Semillon, Chardonnay, Merlot, Shiraz, Cabernet Sauvignon.
SUMMARY The Bland family has acquired Middleton Wines and has changed the entire focus of the business. Previously, all of the production from the 20 hectares of estate plantings was sold either as grapes or as bulk wine; now much is made into wine at the on-site winery.

🍷🍷🍷🍷 **Currency Creek Shiraz 1999** Very similar to the 2001 Alexandre's; great length and lingering finish, almost like high quality Pinot Noir. **RATING** 89 **DRINK** 2010 $ 15
Alexandre's Currency Creek Shiraz 2001 Pale colour, but has considerable (and unexpected) length; savoury notes; fine, ripe, lingering tannins. **RATING** 88 **DRINK** 2010 $ 15

🍷🍷🍷🍷 **Currency Creek Cabernet Plus Merlot 2000 RATING** 86 **DRINK** 2007 $ 15
Alexandre's Currency Creek Cabernet Sauvignon 2001 RATING 86 **DRINK** 2009 $ 15
Currency Creek Cabernet Sauvignon 2000 RATING 86 **DRINK** 2007 $ 15
Currency Creek Semillon 2000 RATING 84 **DRINK** Now $ 14

🍷🍷🍷 **Currency Creek Sauvignon Blanc 2000 RATING** 81 $ 14

Mildara (Murray Darling) ★★★

Wentworth Road, Merbein, Vic 3505 **REGION** Murray Darling
T (03) 5021 9332 **F** (03) 5021 1300 **OPEN** Mon–Fri 9–5, weekends 10–4
WINEMAKER David Tierney **EST.** 1888 **CASES** 12 000
PRODUCT RANGE ($10.50–27.50 R) Under the Mildara label, Chardonnay, Shiraz, Coonawarra Cabernet Sauvignon; Half Mile Creek Verdelho, Chardonnay, Shiraz, Cabernet Merlot; Mount Helen Chardonnay, Cabernet Sauvignon Merlot; Church Hill Chardonnay, Cabernet Shiraz; also makes fine sherries (Chestnut Teal, George and Supreme) and superb Pot Still Brandy.
SUMMARY A somewhat antiquated Merbein facility remains the overall group production centre, although all of its premium wines are sourced from and made at Coonawarra.

Milford Vineyard ★★★★★

Tasman Highway, Cambridge, Tas 7170 **REGION** Southern Tasmania
T (03) 6248 5029 **F** (03) 6248 5076 **OPEN** Not
WINEMAKER Andrew Hood (Contract) **EST.** 1984 **CASES** 200
PRODUCT RANGE ($22 R) Pinot Noir.
SUMMARY Given the tiny production, Milford is understandably not open to the public; the excellent Pinot Noir is quickly sold by word of mouth. The 150-hectare grazing property (the oldest Southdown sheep stud in Australia) has been in Charlie Lewis's family since 1830. Only 15 minutes from Hobart, and with an absolute water frontage to the tidal estuary of the Coal River, it is a striking site. The vineyard is established on a patch of 1.5 metre-deep sand over a clay base with lots of lime impregnation.

Milimani Estate NR

92 The Forest Road, Bungendore, NSW 2621 **REGION** Canberra District
T (02) 6238 1421 **F** (02) 6238 1424 **OPEN** Weekends and public holidays 10–5
WINEMAKER Lark Hill (Contract) **EST.** 1989 **CASES** 1400
PRODUCT RANGE ($15.40–19 R) Sauvignon Blanc, Chardonnay, Pinot Noir, Cabernet Franc Merlot.
SUMMARY The Preston family (Mary, David and Rosemary) have established a 3-hectare vineyard at Bungendore planted to sauvignon blanc, chardonnay, pinot noir, merlot and cabernet franc. Contract winemaking at Lark Hill guarantees the quality of the wine.

Millbrook Estate ★★☆

Lot 18/19 Mount View Road, Millfield, NSW 2325 **REGION** Lower Hunter Valley
T (02) 4998 1155 **F** (02) 4998 1155 **OPEN** 7 days 10–5
WINEMAKER John Lyons **EST.** 1996 **CASES** 600
PRODUCT RANGE ($9–18 CD) Wollombi Brook Sauvignon Blanc, Illa-Langi Chardonnay Semillon, Unwooded Chardonnay, Old Mill Chardonnay, Sparkling Chardonnay, Sparkling Pinot Noir Chardonnay, Hunter Valley Rose, Shiraz, Ruby Port.
SUMMARY The 2.6 hectares of Millbrook Estate vineyards produces between 400 cases (in a dry year) and 800 cases (in a good year). Interestingly, the vineyard is situated on a geological fault line, and is in fact an uplifted ancient creek bed. The wines are sold only through the cellar door and through the vineyard cottage operated by the Lyons family.

Millbrook Winery ★★★★☆

Old Chestnut Lane, Jarrahdale, WA 6124 **REGION** Perth Hills
T (08) 9525 5796 **F** (08) 9525 5672 **OPEN** 7 days 10–5, lunches Wed–Sun 12–3
WINEMAKER Tony Davis **EST.** 1996 **CASES** 10 000
PRODUCT RANGE ($16.50–35 CD) Sauvignon Blanc, Chardonnay, Viognier, Shiraz, Cabernet Sauvignon Merlot; under the Barking Owl label, Semillon Sauvignon Blanc, Viognier, Chardonnay, Late Harvest, Grenache Rose, Shiraz, Cabernet Sauvignon Merlot, Cabernet Plus.
SUMMARY The strikingly situated Millbrook Winery, opened in December 2001, is owned by the highly successful Perth-based entrepreneur Peter Fogarty and wife Lee. They also own Lake's Folly in the Hunter Valley, and have made a major commitment to the quality end of Australian wine. Millbrook draws on 7.5 hectares of vineyards in the Perth Hills, planted to sauvignon blanc, semillon,

chardonnay, viognier, cabernet sauvignon, merlot, shiraz and petit verdot. It also purchases grapes from the Perth Hills and Geographe regions. The wines under both the Millbrook and the Barking Owl label are of consistently high quality. The wines are distributed by WA Vintners in Western Australia and Fesq & Co. in New South Wales; exports to the US and Germany.

ŶŶŶŶŶ **Chardonnay 2002** Highly skilled winemaking; perfectly integrated and balanced fruit and oak; elegance and power. **RATING** 93 **DRINK** 2008 $ 28

Cabernet Merlot 2001 Fragrant, sweet red berry fruits; fine texture and tannins; good length. **RATING** 92 **DRINK** 2011 $ 32

Shiraz 2001 Spicy blackberry fruit has an extra edge of fragrance from the viognier component; medium-bodied but vibrant, with very good balance and acidity. **RATING** 91 **DRINK** 2011 $ 32

Barking Owl Semillon Sauvignon Blanc 2003 Very good length and intensity; a mix of passionfruit, gooseberry and ripe apple flavours; crisp finish. **RATING** 90 **DRINK** Now $ 16.50

ŶŶŶŶ **Sauvignon Blanc 2003** Well made; not much varietal character, but has good balance and length. **RATING** 87 **DRINK** Now $ 20

ŶŶŶŶ **Barking Owl Cabernet Sauvignon Merlot 2002 RATING** 86 **DRINK** 2007 $ 18
Viognier 2002 RATING 85 **DRINK** 2007 $ 35

ŶŶŶ **Estate Chardonnay 2002 RATING** 82 $ 28

Millers Samphire   NR

Watts Gully Road, cnr Robertson Road, Kersbrook, SA 5231 **REGION** Adelaide Hills
T (08) 8389 3183 **F** (03) 8389 3183 **OPEN** 7 days 9–5 by appointment
WINEMAKER Tom Miller **EST.** 1982 **CASES** 80
PRODUCT RANGE ($9 CD) Riesling.
SUMMARY Next after Scarp Valley, one of the smallest wineries in Australia offering wine for sale; pottery also helps. Tom Miller has one of the more interesting and diverse CVs, with an early interest in matters alcoholic leading to the premature but happy death of a laboratory rat at Adelaide University and his enforced switch from biochemistry to mechanical engineering. The Riesling is a high-flavoured wine with crushed herb and lime aromas and flavours.

Millfield   ★★☆

Lot 341, Mount View Road, Millfield, NSW 2325 **REGION** Lower Hunter Valley
T (02) 4998 1571 **F** (02) 4998 0172 **OPEN** Weekends 10–4
WINEMAKER David Lowe **EST.** 1997 **CASES** 500
PRODUCT RANGE ($20–26 CD) Semillon, Chardonnay, Rose, Shiraz.
SUMMARY Situated on the picturesque Mount View Road, Millfield made its market debut in June 2000. The neatly labelled and packaged wines have won gold medals and trophies right from the first vintage in 1998, and praise from winewriters and critics both in Australia and the UK. The wines are sold both through the cellar door and by mailing list, and through a limited number of fine wine retail outlets and top quality restaurants. Exports to the UK through Corney & Barrow.

ŶŶŶ **Semillon 2000 RATING** 83 $ 20
Semillon 2003 RATING 80 $ 20

Millinup Estate   ★★★★

RMB 1280 Porongurup Road, Porongurup, WA 6324 **REGION** Porongurup
T (08) 9853 1105 **F** (08) 9853 1105 **OPEN** Weekends 10–5, or by appointment
WINEMAKER Mike Garland (Red), Diane Miller (White) **EST.** 1989 **CASES** 250
PRODUCT RANGE ($16–18 CD) Twin Peaks Riesling, Old Cottage Riesling, Cabernet Sauvignon Cabernet Franc Merlot.
SUMMARY The Millinup Estate vineyard was planted in 1978, when it was called Point Creek. Owners Peter and Lesley Thorn purchased it in 1989, renaming it and having the limited production (from 0.5 hectare of riesling, supplemented by purchased red grapes) vinified at Garlands and the Porongurup winery.

Minot Vineyard ★★★

PO Box 683, Margaret River, WA 6285 **REGION** Margaret River
T (08) 9757 3579 **F** (08) 9757 2361 **OPEN** By appointment 10–5
WINEMAKER Harmans Estate (Contract) **EST.** 1986 **CASES** 1500
PRODUCT RANGE ($14–30 CD) Semillon, Semillon Sauvignon Blanc, Cabernet Sauvignon.
SUMMARY Minot, which takes its name from a small chateau in the Loire Valley in France, is the husband and wife venture of the Miles family. It produces three wines from the 4.5-hectare plantings of semillon, sauvignon blanc and cabernet sauvignon.

ΥΥΥΥ **Cabernet Sauvignon 2001** **RATING** 86 **DRINK** 2010 $ 29

Mintaro Wines ★★★☆

Leasingham Road, Mintaro, SA 5415 **REGION** Clare Valley
T (08) 8843 9150 **F** (08) 8843 9050 **OPEN** 7 days 10–4.30
WINEMAKER Peter Houldsworth **EST.** 1984 **CASES** 5000
PRODUCT RANGE ($16–24 CD) Riesling, Late Picked Riesling, Anastasia's Sparkling Cabernet Grenache, Shiraz, Belles Femmes et Grand Vin Premium Shiraz, Leckie Window Premium Cabernet Sauvignon; Monarch of Mintaro Riesling, Semillon Chardonnay, Shiraz, Cabernet Franc, Cabernet Sauvignon.
SUMMARY Has produced some very good Riesling over the years, developing well in bottle. The red wines are formidable: massive in body and extract, built for the long haul.

Minto Wines NR

'Minto', Faraday via Castlemaine, Vic 3450 **REGION** Bendigo
T (03) 5473 3278 **OPEN** By appointment
WINEMAKER Alan Elliot **EST.** 1998 **CASES** 130
PRODUCT RANGE ($17–20 CD) Chardonnay, Cabernet Sauvignon.
SUMMARY Alan and Heather Elliot have established a substantial business, anchored around 8 hectares of chardonnay, pinot noir, shiraz and cabernet sauvignon, supplemented by contract-grown grapes. It is still early in the development of the business, and sales are only by mail order and through the cellar door, which is housed in the former Faraday school.

Miramar ★★★

Henry Lawson Drive, Mudgee, NSW 2850 **REGION** Mudgee
T (02) 6373 3874 **F** (02) 6373 3854 **OPEN** 7 days 9–5
WINEMAKER Ian MacRae **EST.** 1977 **CASES** 8000
PRODUCT RANGE ($11–33 CD) Riesling, Semillon, Fume Blanc, Chardonnay, Eurunderee Rose, Shiraz, Cabernet Sauvignon; Doux Blanc (sweet white), Encore and Encore Rouge (sparkling).
SUMMARY Industry veteran Ian MacRae has demonstrated his skill with every type of wine over the decades, ranging from Rose to Chardonnay to full-bodied reds. All have shone under the Miramar label at one time or another, although the Ides of March are pointing more to the reds than the white these days. A substantial part of the production from the 35 hectares of estate vineyard is sold to others, the best being retained for Miramar's own use. From 2002, all wines, including reds, have been sealed with Stelvin. As at March 2003 Miramar was on the market, but the MacRaes will continue to own and run the separate Eljamar business.

ΥΥΥΥ **Chardonnay 2002** Complex, smoky barrel-ferment influences run through a rich yellow peach/stone fruit-flavoured palate; a hint of sweetness. **RATING** 89 **DRINK** 2008 $ 15

ΥΥΥΥ **Cabernet Sauvignon 2002** **RATING** 86 **DRINK** 2012 $ 20

ΥΥΥ **Sauvignon Blanc 2002** **RATING** 83 $ 13
Shiraz 2002 **RATING** 81 $ 19
Riesling 2003 **RATING** 80 $ 12

Miranda Wines

★★★☆

57 Jondaryan Avenue, Griffith, NSW 2680 **REGION** Riverina
T (02) 6960 3000 **F** (02) 6962 6944 **OPEN** 7 days 9–5
WINEMAKER Sam F Miranda, Garry Wall, Hope Golding, Luis E Simian **EST.** 1939 **CASES** 2.5 million
PRODUCT RANGE ($6–24.85 R) Golden Botrytis; Mirool Creek range of Semillon Sauvignon Blanc, Chardonnay, Brut Reserve, Red Brut, Shiraz, Merlot, Durif, Cabernet Shiraz; Somerton Semillon Chardonnay, Unoaked Chardonnay, Shiraz Cabernet Merlot, Merlot; also lower-priced Christy's Land and assorted varietals, generics, sparkling and ports.
SUMMARY In 2003 Miranda Wines was purchased by the McGuigan/Simeon group, which will, however, presumably keep the brand portfolio largely intact, perhaps investing more in the most successful brands and markets.

ΨΨΨΨΨ **Golden Botrytis 2002** Already deep gold in colour; luscious honey/honeycomb/apricot/peach flavours; as always, good balancing acidity. **RATING** 92 **DRINK** 2007 $15

ΨΨΨΨ **High Country Sauvignon Blanc 2003** Strongly varietal, aromatic and potent bouquet; no reduction; the palate is less intense, but has length. **RATING** 89 **DRINK** Now
Cabernet Sauvignon 2002 Another tribute to the 2002 vintage; clean, supple, cassis-accented; gentle oak. **RATING** 89 **DRINK** 2007
High Country Merlot 2003 Well made; attractive small red berry fruits; light to medium-bodied; gently savoury tannins. **RATING** 88 **DRINK** 2007
Family Reserve Barossa Old Vine Shiraz 2000 Very sweet, slightly jammy fruit; light to medium-bodied; appealing finish. **RATING** 87 **DRINK** 2008 $24.85
High Country Cabernet Sauvignon 2001 Struck it very lucky in some wine shows; cedary/earthy/savoury flavours. **RATING** 87 **DRINK** 2008

ΨΨΨΨ **High Country Chardonnay 2003 RATING** 86 **DRINK** Now
High Country Shiraz 2001 RATING 86 **DRINK** 2008
High Country Riesling 2003 RATING 85 **DRINK** Now $12.95
Mirool Creek Chardonnay 2003 RATING 85 **DRINK** Now
Somerton Merlot 2003 RATING 84 **DRINK** Now

ΨΨΨ **Mirool Creek Semillon Sauvignon Blanc 2003 RATING** 83
Somerton Semillon Chardonnay 2003 RATING 83
Somerton Chardonnay 2003 RATING 82 $6.99
White Shiraz 2003 RATING 82
Firefly Shiraz 2002 RATING 82
Family Reserve Barossa Chardonnay 2000 RATING 80

ΨΨΨ **Firefly Chardonnay 2002 RATING** 78

Mr Riggs Wine Company

★★★★★

PO Box 584, McLaren Vale, SA 5171 **REGION** McLaren Vale
T (08) 8556 4460 **F** (08) 8556 4462 **OPEN** Not
WINEMAKER Ben Riggs **EST.** 2001 **CASES** 1000
PRODUCT RANGE ($25–45 R) Adelaide Hills Viognier, Tempranillo, McLaren Vale Shiraz, Adelaide Hills Shiraz Viognier, Tempranillo.
SUMMARY After 14 years as winemaker at Wirra Wirra, and another six at various Australian wineries, as well as numerous northern hemisphere vintages, Ben Riggs has decided to establish his own business. His major activity is as consultant winemaker to Penny's Hill, Pertaringa, Coriole and Geoff Hardy, and he keeps his hand in by consulting for Cazal Viel in the south of France and for UK-based distributor Western Wines. His domestic winemaking will also include sourcing grapes for and making commercial batches of wine for wholesale and retail entities in Australia, adopting a 'grape to plate' approach. He also makes wine on his own behalf for the Mr Riggs label, initially buying select parcels of grapes from old vines in McLaren Vale, and in due course also utilising grapes from his own vineyard at Piebald Gully, where he has recently planted 4 hectares of shiraz, 1.5 hectares of viognier and 1 hectare of petit verdot. Exports to the US, the UK, Denmark and Malyasia.

🍷🍷🍷🍷🍷 **Shiraz 2002** Concentrated, opulent blackberry fruit encased in a delicious wrapping of dark chocolate; has chewed up the French oak in which it was aged; fine ripe tannins; power with finesse. **RATING** 95 **DRINK** 2022 $45

🍷🍷🍷🍷🍷 **Tempranillo 2002** Complex; distinct spice, cedar and leather fragrance; a light to medium-bodied, almost silky, palate, lively and tangy; fresh finish. **RATING** 90 **DRINK** 2008 $25

🍷🍷🍷🍷 **Viognier 2003 RATING** 86 **DRINK** 2007 $25

Mistletoe Wines ★★★☆

771 Hermitage Road, Pokolbin, NSW 2320 **REGION** Lower Hunter Valley
T (02) 4998 7770 **F** (02) 4998 7792 **OPEN** 7 days 10–6
WINEMAKER John Cassegrain (Contract), Nick Paterson (Consultant) **EST.** 1989 **CASES** 3000
PRODUCT RANGE ($16.50–23 CD) Semillon, Silvereye Semillon, Chardonnay, Reserve Chardonnay, The Rose, Shiraz, Reserve Shiraz, Mistela.
SUMMARY Mistletoe Wines, owned by Ken and Gwen Sloan, can trace its history back to 1909, when a substantial vineyard was planted on what was then called Mistletoe Farm. The Mistletoe Farm brand made a brief appearance in the late 1970s but then disappeared. It has now been revived under the Mistletoe Wines label by the Sloans, with contract winemaking providing consistent results. No retail distribution, but worldwide delivery service available ex winery. The art gallery features works by local artists.

🍷🍷🍷🍷 **Reserve Semillon 2003** Fragrant herb and lanolin aromas; good weight and length; lemony acidity. Strangely, cork-finished. **RATING** 90 **DRINK** 2009 $19

🍷🍷🍷🍷 **Reserve Semillon 2002** Has developed well over the past 12 months; still fresh, with a faint touch of spritz; good mouthfeel and length. **RATING** 89 **DRINK** 2008 $19
Reserve Shiraz 2002 Regional spicy/earthy/savoury aromas; sweet raspberry/blackberry fruit on a pleasant palate. **RATING** 89 **DRINK** 2010 $23
Semillon 2000 Still tight and delicate; lemon and herb; will continue to improve if the cork holds. **RATING** 88 **DRINK** 2010 $16.50
Shiraz 2002 Opens quietly on the bouquet and palate, but then builds through to a long, lingering finish; good balance and mouthfeel. **RATING** 88 **DRINK** 2009 $20
Gold Dessert Semillon 2003 Very sweet tropical/peachy fruit; has swallowed up the French oak ex barrel ferment; should develop very well. **RATING** 87 **DRINK** 2008 $16.50

🍷🍷🍷🍷 **Silvereye Semillon 2003** Fresh and clean; distinct sweetness on the finish makes it ideal for cellar door. Screwcap. **RATING** 86 **DRINK** Now $16.50
Semillon 2003 RATING 85 **DRINK** 2007 $16.50
Reserve Chardonnay 2003 RATING 85 **DRINK** Now $23
The Rose 2003 RATING 84 **DRINK** Now $16.50

🍷🍷🍷 **Shiraz 2001 RATING** 83 $20
Mistela NV RATING 83 $21
Reserve Semillon 2001 RATING 82 $19

Mitchell ★★★★

Hughes Park Road, Sevenhill via Clare, SA 5453 **REGION** Clare Valley
T (08) 8843 4258 **F** (08) 8843 4340 **OPEN** 7 days 10–4
WINEMAKER Andrew Mitchell **EST.** 1975 **CASES** 30 000
PRODUCT RANGE ($20–25 CD) Watervale Riesling, The Growers Semillon, Noble Semillon, Sparkling Peppertree, The Growers Grenache, Peppertree Vineyard Shiraz, Sevenhill Cabernet Sauvignon.
SUMMARY For years this was one of the stalwarts of the Clare Valley, producing long-lived Rieslings and Cabernet Sauvignons in classic regional style; has now extended the range with very creditable Semillon and Shiraz. A lovely old stone apple shed provides the cellar door and upper section of the compact winery. Production has increased by 50 per cent over the past few years, and as well as national retail distribution, the wines are exported to the US.

▼▼▼▼▽ **Watervale Riesling 2003** Potent mineral citrus and spice aromas; abundant flavour and richness in the ripe style of the vintage; good length. **RATING** 92 **DRINK** 2010 $ 20
Peppertree Vineyard Shiraz 2002 Deeply coloured, the wine is flooded with blackberry, licorice, and a touch of tar; excellent length and mouthfeel. Screwcap. **RATING** 92 **DRINK** 2017 $ 25
The Growers Semillon 2002 Complex wine; excellent use of a touch of French oak; flows seamlessly; sweet, citrussy fruit. Screwcap. **RATING** 91 **DRINK** 2007 $ 20

▼▼▼▼ **Sevenhill Vineyard Cabernet Sauvignon 2001** Smooth, medium-bodied; flows well; blackcurrant, fine tannins; good oak support. **RATING** 89 **DRINK** 2011 $ 25
Sevenhill Vineyard Cabernet Sauvignon 2000 Savoury, soft, earthy, with a core of sweet blackcurrant; nice texture. **RATING** 89 **DRINK** 2010 $ 25
Noble Semillon 2001 Brightly coloured; clean, well-balanced lemony/tropical fruit and acidity; not much botrytis, more late harvest. Screwcap. **RATING** 88 **DRINK** 2010 $ 25

▼▼▼▽ **The Growers Grenache 2001** **RATING** 86 **DRINK** 2007 $ 20

Mitchelton   ★★★★

Mitchellstown via Nagambie, Vic 3608 **REGION** Nagambie Lakes
T (03) 5736 2222 **F** (03) 5736 2266 **OPEN** 7 days 10–5
WINEMAKER Don Lewis, Toby Barlow **EST.** 1969 **CASES** 200 000
PRODUCT RANGE ($10–50 CD) Top-of-the-range is Print Shiraz; then come Chardonnay, Viognier, Airstrip Marsanne Roussanne Viognier, Shiraz, Crescent Shiraz Mourvedre Grenache, Cabernet Sauvignon; next, Blackwood Park range of Riesling, Late Harvested Riesling, Botrytis Riesling; Preece range of Sauvignon Blanc, Chardonnay, Sparkling Chardonnay Pinot Noir, Shiraz, Merlot, Cabernet Sauvignon; and finally Thomas Mitchell range of Marsanne, Chardonnay, Shiraz, Cabernet Sauvignon Shiraz.
SUMMARY Acquired by Petaluma in 1994, having already put the runs on the board in no uncertain fashion with the gifted winemaker Don Lewis. Boasts an impressive array of wines across a broad spectrum of style and price, but each carefully aimed at a market niche. Exports to the UK, the US and New Zealand.

▼▼▼▼▽ **Print Shiraz 1999** A supple, medium-bodied palate of blackberry and black cherry; deft oak handling, and lovely fine tannins. Very stylish. **RATING** 93 **DRINK** 2009 $ 49
Airstrip Marsanne Roussanne Viognier 2002 Solid, complex, multi-faceted peach and rose petal; hints of nutty oak; striking, sweet fruit. **RATING** 92 **DRINK** 2007 $ 24.95
Print Shiraz 2001 Smooth and supple; rich blackberry/cherry fruit; good line and length; fine tannins and controlled oak. **RATING** 92 **DRINK** 2011 $ 50
Preece Sauvignon Blanc 2003 Strongly varietal herb, gooseberry and asparagus aromas, and an equally flavoursome palate. **RATING** 91 **DRINK** Now $ 14.95

▼▼▼▼ **Classic Release Marsanne 1998** Glowing yellow-green; very rich honeysuckle, toast and nutty/spicy back palate. Disconcertingly fragile cork. **RATING** 89 **DRINK** Now $ 32
Blackwood Park Cabernet Sauvignon 1999 Clean, nicely ripened and weighted blackcurrant fruit; fine, ripe tannins, long finish. Top value. **RATING** 89 **DRINK** 2007 $ 17
Blackwood Park Riesling 2003 Floral and spice aromas and flavours; light-bodied; nicely balanced. **RATING** 88 **DRINK** 2008 $ 17
Parish Shiraz 2002 Very ripe red and black fruits; licorice, chocolate and prune; entirely fruit-driven. **RATING** 88 **DRINK** 2012 $ 30
Central Victorian Shiraz 2001 Medium-bodied; harmonious red and black fruit flavours on the neatly balanced mid-palate. **RATING** 88 **DRINK** 2011 $ 19.99
Central Victorian Shiraz 2002 Quite complex texture and structure in medium-bodied mode; a mix of sweet and more savoury/spicy fruits. **RATING** 87 **DRINK** 2009 $ 20
Blackwood Park Botrytis Riesling 2002 Fresh, lemony/citrussy aromas and flavours; user-friendly style. **RATING** 87 **DRINK** Now $ 17

▼▼▼▽ **Preece Chardonnay 2003** **RATING** 86 **DRINK** Now $ 14.95
Roussanne 2003 **RATING** 86 **DRINK** 2007 $ 25
Viognier 2003 **RATING** 86 **DRINK** Now $ 19
Crescent Shiraz Mourvedre Grenache 2001 **RATING** 86 **DRINK** 2008 $ 24.95

Preece Merlot 2002 RATING 86 DRINK 2007 $ 14
Preece Chardonnay 2002 RATING 85 DRINK Now $ 14.95
Blackwood Park Merlot 2002 RATING 85 DRINK 2007 $ 17
Blackwood Park Merlot 2001 RATING 85 DRINK Now $ 17
Blackwood Park Cabernet Sauvignon 2001 RATING 85 DRINK 2008 $ 17

ŸŸŸ **Blackwood Park Chardonnay 2002** RATING 81 $ 17

Mitolo Wines   ★★★★★

34 Barossa Valley Way, Tanunda, SA 5352 (postal) REGION McLaren Vale
T (08) 8282 9000 F (08) 8380 8312 OPEN Not
WINEMAKER Ben Glaetzer EST. 1999 CASES 4000
PRODUCT RANGE ($27–66 R) Jester Tarlton Shiraz, G.A.M. McLaren Vale Shiraz, Reiver Shiraz Barossa Valley, Savitar Shiraz McLaren Vale, Serpico McLaren Vale Cabernet Sauvignon.
SUMMARY Frank Mitolo began making wine in 1995 as a hobby, and soon progressed to undertaking formal studies in winemaking. His interest grew year by year, but it was not until 2000 that he took the plunge into the commercial end of the business, retaining Ben Glaetzer to make the wines for him. Since that time, a remarkably good series of wines have been released. Imitation being the sincerest form of flattery, part of the complicated story behind each label name is pure Torbreck, but Mitolo then adds a Latin proverb or saying to the label name. A natty little loosely tied explanation/translation booklet tied to the neck of each bottle would be useful.

ŸŸŸŸŸ **Reiver Barossa Shiraz 2002** A focused, supple and smooth array of black and red fruits; ripe tannins; great balance and length; quality oak, beautifully made. RATING 95 DRINK 2022 $ 55
G.A.M. McLaren Vale Shiraz 2002 Supple and perfectly balanced; medium-bodied black fruits, dark chocolate and spice; sweet fruit on the finish; very stylish wine. RATING 94 DRINK 2017 $ 55

ŸŸŸŸŸ **Jester Tarlton Shiraz 2002** A complex mix of blackberry, spice, earth and dark chocolate; savoury tannins to finish; very different style. Screwcap. RATING 90 DRINK 2012 $ 27

Molly Morgan Vineyard   ★★★★

Talga Road, Lovedale, NSW 2321 REGION Lower Hunter Valley
T (02) 9816 4088 F (02) 9816 2680 OPEN By appointment
WINEMAKER John Baruzzi (Consultant) EST. 1963 CASES 5500
PRODUCT RANGE ($18–35 ML) Joe's Block Semillon, Old Vines Semillon, Semillon Sauvignon Blanc, Chardonnay, Shiraz.
SUMMARY Molly Morgan has been acquired by Andrew and Hady Simon, who established the Camperdown Cellars Group in 1971 (which became the largest retailer in Australia) before passing on to other pursuits. They have been recently joined by their former general manager (at Camperdown Cellars) Grant Breen. The property is planted to 5.5 hectares of 25-year-old unirrigated semillon, which goes to make the Old Vines Semillon, 0.8 hectare for Joe's Block Semillon, 2.5 hectares of chardonnay and 1.2 hectares of shiraz. The wines are contract-made (as has always been the case, in fact, but to a high standard). Exports to the US, Canada, Ireland, China and Japan.

ŸŸŸŸŸ **Old Vines Semillon 2002** Clean; powerful and concentrated; sturdy structure; abundant mid-palate and long finish. RATING 91 DRINK 2010 $ 22

ŸŸŸŸ **Woodpecker Wooded Semillon 2003** Crisp, clean and lemony; the faintest touch of spicy oak; if you have to oak Semillon, this is how to do it. RATING 89 DRINK 2008 $ 24
Rosella's Rest Semillon Sauvignon Blanc 2003 Interesting influence from Sauvignon Blanc; white peach and nectarine; good length and balance; off centre. RATING 89 DRINK 2007 $ 22
Partner's Reserve Chardonnay 2003 Strong yellow clingstone peach and equally strong barrel-ferment inputs; flaunts its wares; consistent, showy style. RATING 89 DRINK Now $ 35
Partner's Reserve Shiraz 2002 Medium-bodied, nice blackberry/plum fruit; slightly dusty oak; needs time to sort itself out. RATING 88 DRINK 2012 $ 35

ΨΨΨΨ   **Joe's Block White 2003** RATING 86 DRINK Now $ 22
        Shiraz 2002 RATING 86 DRINK 2007 $ 25
        Red Mistress Sparkling Shiraz NV RATING 86 DRINK 2007 $ 23
        Partner's Reserve Botrytis Semillon 2003 RATING 85 DRINK 2007 $ 24

ΨΨΨ   **Fair Lady Sparkling NV** RATING 83 $ 20

Monahan Estate ★★★★

Lot 1 Wilderness Road, Rothbury, NSW 2320 REGION Lower Hunter Valley
T (02) 4930 9070 F (02) 4930 7679 OPEN Thurs–Sun 10–5
WINEMAKER Monarch Winemaking Services (Contract) EST. 1997 CASES 2000
PRODUCT RANGE ($13–17 CD) Semillon, Old Bridge Semillon, Old Bridge Unwooded Chardonnay.
SUMMARY Having become partners with founder Matthew Monahan in 1999, John and Patricia Graham now own the estate outright. It is bordered by Black Creek in the Lovedale district, an area noted for its high-quality semillon; the old bridge adjoining the property is displayed on the wine label; the wines themselves have been consistent silver and bronze medal winners at the Hunter Valley Wine Show.

ΨΨΨΨ   **Old Bridge Semillon 2002** Very similar to the '03, but has greater length. RATING 90
        DRINK 2009

ΨΨΨΨ   **Old Bridge Semillon 2003** Spotlessly clean and fresh; good balance of ripe
        lemon/vanillin flavours; subliminal hint of fruit sweetness. RATING 89 DRINK 2009

Monbulk Winery ★★☆

Macclesfield Road, Monbulk, Vic 3793 REGION Yarra Valley
T (03) 9756 6965 F (03) 9756 6965 OPEN Weekends and public holidays 12–5, or by appointment
WINEMAKER Paul Jabornik EST. 1984 CASES 800
PRODUCT RANGE ($11.90–16.50 CD) Chardonnay, Riesling, Pinot Noir, Shiraz, Cabernet Sauvignon; also fruit wines, including kiwifruit, strawberry, blackberry, raspberry and plum.
SUMMARY Originally concentrated on kiwifruit wines but now extending to table wines; the very cool Monbulk subregion should be capable of producing wines of distinctive style, but the table wines are (unfortunately) not of the same standard as the kiwifruit wines, which are quite delicious.

Monichino Wines ★★☆

1820 Berrys Road, Katunga, Vic 3640 REGION Goulburn Valley
T (03) 5864 6452 F (03) 5864 6538 OPEN Mon–Sat 9–5, Sun 10–5
WINEMAKER Carlo Monichino, Terry Monichino EST. 1962 CASES 16 000
PRODUCT RANGE ($12–25 CD) Riesling, Semillon Sauvignon Blanc, Sauvignon Blanc, Chardonnay, Botrytis Semillon, Orange Muscat, Golden Lexia, Rose Petals Spatlese, Rosso Dolce, Shiraz, Merlot, Carlo's Pressings, Cabernet Sauvignon; various ports and fortifieds; bulk sales also available.
SUMMARY A winery which has quietly made some clean, fresh wines in which the fruit character is carefully preserved, and has shown a deft touch with its Botrytis Semillon.

ΨΨΨΨ   **Sangiovese 2002** RATING 84 DRINK Now $ 18

ΨΨΨ   **Riesling 2002** RATING 82 $ 12

Montalto Vineyards

33 Shoreham Road, Red Hill South, Vic 3937 REGION Mornington Peninsula
T (03) 5989 8412 F (03) 5989 8417 OPEN 7 days 12–5
WINEMAKER Robin Brockett EST. 1998 CASES 3500
PRODUCT RANGE ($18.50–28 CD) Riesling, Chardonnay, Rose, Pinot Noir; second label Pennon Riesling, Semillon Sauvignon Blanc, Chardonnay, Cuvee One, Rose, Pinot Noir, Shiraz.
SUMMARY John Mitchell and family established Montalto Vineyards in 1998, although the core of the vineyard goes back to 1986. There are 3 hectares of chardonnay and 5.6 hectares of pinot noir, with

0.5 hectare each of semillon, riesling and pinot meunier. Intensive vineyard work opens up the canopy, with yields ranging between 1.5 and 2.5 tonnes per acre, and the majority of the fruit hand-harvested. Wines are released under two labels, the flagship Montalto and Pennon, the latter effectively a lower-priced, second label. The high-quality restaurant, open daily for lunch and on Friday and Saturday evenings, also features guest chefs and cooking classes. A new star in the peninsula sky.

ŸŸŸŸŸ **Chardonnay 2002** Stylish but intense; great complexity and concentration; stone fruit and creamy/nutty influences ex barrel fermentation. **RATING** 95 **DRINK** 2010 $ 27

ŸŸŸŸŸ **Riesling 2003** Clean and fresh; attractive mineral/apple/citrus flavours; good line and length. **RATING** 91 **DRINK** 2010 $ 23
Pennon Pinot Noir 2002 Vivid deep colour; hyper-ripe black plum and morello cherry; subtle oak. Will build. **RATING** 91 **DRINK** 2007 $ 23
Pennon Chardonnay 2002 Clean, fresh, citrussy; fruit-driven, with excellent balance and length. **RATING** 90 **DRINK** 2008 $ 18.50

ŸŸŸŸ **Pennon Semillon Sauvignon Blanc 2003** Crystal-clean and clear; nicely made and balanced; has good length. Mornington/Margaret River. Screwcap. **RATING** 89 **DRINK** 2007 $ 18.50
Pennon Rose 2003 Clean, firm and crisp; not too sweet, almost lemony. **RATING** 87 **DRINK** Now $ 18.50

Montara
★★★☆

Chalambar Road, Ararat, Vic 3377 **REGION** Grampians
T (03) 5352 3868 **F** (03) 5352 4968 **OPEN** Mon–Sat 10–5, Sun 12–4
WINEMAKER Mike McRae **EST.** 1970
PRODUCT RANGE ($13.50–27 CD) Riesling, Chardonnay, Pinot Noir, Shiraz, Merlot, Cabernet Sauvignon, Shiraz Port; 'M' range of Chardonnay, Pinot Noir Shiraz.
SUMMARY Achieved considerable attention for its Pinot Noirs during the 1980s, but other regions (and other makers) have come along since. It continues to produce wines of distinctive style, and smart new label designs do help. Limited national distribution; exports to the UK, Switzerland, Canada and Hong Kong.

Montgomery's Hill
★★★★☆

Hassell Highway, Upper Kalgan, Albany, WA 6330 **REGION** Albany
T (08) 9844 3715 **F** (08) 9844 1104 **OPEN** 7 days 11–5
WINEMAKER Robert Lee (Porongurup Winery), John Wade (Consultant) **EST.** 1996 **CASES** 2000
PRODUCT RANGE ($12.50–22.50 R) Sauvignon Blanc, Chardonnay, Unwooded Chardonnay, Cabernet Franc, Cabernets.
SUMMARY Montgomery's Hill is 16 kilometres northeast of Albany on a north-facing slope on the banks of the Kalgan River. The vineyard is situated on an area which was previously an apple orchard and is a diversification for the third generation of the Montgomery family, which owns the property. Chardonnay, cabernet sauvignon and cabernet franc were planted in 1996, followed by sauvignon blanc, shiraz and merlot in 1997. Since 1999, Montgomery's Hill has been made at the new Porongurup Winery.

ŸŸŸŸŸ **Chardonnay 2002** Light to medium-bodied; excellent fruit/oak balance and integration; long, lingering grapefruit and melon plus a splash of cashew. Altogether stylish. **RATING** 94 **DRINK** 2012 $ 18.50

ŸŸŸŸŸ **Cabernet Sauvignon 2001** An attractive mix of blackberry, dark chocolate and mint aromas; good phenological ripeness; oak and tannins neatly balanced. **RATING** 90 **DRINK** 2011 $ 18.50

ŸŸŸŸ **Sauvignon Blanc 2003** **RATING** 86 **DRINK** Now $ 15.50

ŸŸŸ **Unwooded Chardonnay 2003** **RATING** 83 $ 16.50
Kalgan Sunset Red 2003 **RATING** 83 $ 12.50

Monument Vineyard ★★★☆

Cnr Escort Way and Manildra Road, Cudal, NSW 2864 **REGION** Central Ranges Zone
T (02) 6364 2294 **F** (02) 6364 2069 **OPEN** By appointment
WINEMAKER Alison Eisermann **EST.** 1998 **CASES** 1000
PRODUCT RANGE ($12–18 CD) Riesling, Semillon Sauvignon Blanc, Pinot Gris, Marsanne, Rose, Pinot Noir, Shiraz, Hospital Hill Shiraz, Sangiovese, Cabernet Sauvignon Shiraz Merlot, Cabernet Sauvignon.
SUMMARY In the early 1990s, five mature-age students at Charles Sturt University, successful in their own professions, decided to form a partnership to develop a substantial vineyard and winery on a scale that they could not individually afford, but could do so collectively. After a lengthy search, a large property at Cudal was identified, with ideal terra rossa basalt-derived soil over a limestone base. The property now has 110 hectares under vine, as a result of planting in the spring of 1998 and 1999.

♥♥♥♥ **Shiraz 2002** Very ripe black fruits ranging from blackberry into plum; plush, sweetly rounded mouthfeel; minimal oak. 50 per cent Cudal, 50 per cent Orange. **RATING** 87 **DRINK** 2010 $16
Hospital Hill Reserve Shiraz Viognier 2002 A fragrant lift to the bouquet; palate shows 12 per cent viognier component quite clearly; almost juicy flavours and fine tannins. **RATING** 87 **DRINK** 2009 $18
Sangiovese 2002 Much greater depth than most examples of the variety; sweet raspberry and redcurrant fruit; faintly sweet finish. Real promise. **RATING** 87 **DRINK** Now $18

Moonbark Estate Vineyard NR

Lot 11 Moonambel–Natte Yallock Road, Moonambel, Vic 3478 (postal) **REGION** Pyrenees
T 0439 952 263 **F** (03) 9870 6116 **OPEN** Not
WINEMAKER Kim Hart (Contract) **EST.** 1998 **CASES** 300
PRODUCT RANGE ($18 R) Shiraz.
SUMMARY Rod Chivers and his family have been slowly establishing their vineyard over the past 6 years, with 0.5 hectare of shiraz in bearing. A further hectare-plus of cabernet sauvignon and merlot are due to be planted over the next few years on the red clay and quartz soils typical of the region. The wines are made at Warrenmang Estate by Kim Hart, and are sold through local restaurants and retailers.

Moondah Brook ★★★★☆

c/- Houghton, Dale Road, Middle Swan, WA 6056 **REGION** Swan Valley
T (08) 9274 5372 **F** (08) 9274 5372 **OPEN** Not
WINEMAKER Robert Bowen, Ross Pamment **EST.** 1968 **CASES** 80 000
PRODUCT RANGE ($12.99–15.99 R) Chardonnay, Chenin Blanc, Verdelho, Sauvignon Blanc, Shiraz, Cabernet Sauvignon, Maritime (sparkling); also occasional Show Reserve releases of Chenin Blanc and Verdelho.
SUMMARY Part of the BRL Hardy wine group which has its own special character as it draws part of its fruit from the large Gingin vineyard, 70 kilometres north of the Swan Valley, and part from the Margaret River and Great Southern. In recent times it has exceeded even its own reputation for reliability with some quite lovely wines: in particular honeyed, aged Chenin Blanc and finely structured Cabernet Sauvignon.

♥♥♥♥ **Shiraz 2001** Generously proportioned and structured wine; dark chocolate, plum, blackberry; savoury tannins. **RATING** 89 **DRINK** 2010 $14.50

Moondarra ★★★☆

Browns Road, Moondarra, Vic 3825 (postal) **REGION** Gippsland
T (03) 9598 3049 **F** (03) 9598 0677 **OPEN** Not
WINEMAKER Neil Prentice **EST.** 1991
PRODUCT RANGE ($20–100) Holly's Garden Whitlands Pinot Gris, Samba Side Pinot Noir, Conception Pinot Noir, Holly's Garden Whitlands Pinot Noir.
SUMMARY In 1991 Neil Prentice and family established their Moondarra Vineyard in Gippsland, planted to 1.5 hectares of 11 low-yielding clones of pinot noir, to which they have recently added

0.25 hectare each of nebbiolo and piccolit. The vines are not irrigated, and vineyard management is predicated on the minimum use of any sprays, with the aim of ultimately moving to biodynamic/pagan farming methods. The winemaking techniques are strongly influenced by the practices of controversial Lebanese-born Burgundy consultant Guy Accad, with 10 days of pre-fermentation maceration and whole bunches added prior to fermentation. The wines are distributed in Melbourne and Sydney by Select Vineyards, and are exported the US, Japan and Singapore.

▼▼▼▼♈ **Conception Pinot Noir 2001** Light to medium-bodied; foresty; fairly austere, but has balance and length; overall elegance. **RATING** 90 **DRINK** 2008 $100

▼▼▼▼ **Holly's Garden Whitlands Pinot Gris 2002** Has considerable persistence; crisp acidity set against a touch of sweetness from 15.5 degrees alcohol; strangely, doesn't burn. Screwcap. **RATING** 89 **DRINK** 2008 $20

▼▼▼♈ **Holly's Garden Whitlands Pinot Noir 2002** **RATING** 85 **DRINK** 2007 $30

Moorebank Vineyard

NR

Palmers Lane, Pokolbin, NSW 2320 **REGION** Lower Hunter Valley
T (02) 4998 7610 **F** (02) 4998 7367 **OPEN** Fri–Mon 10–5, or by appointment
WINEMAKER Iain Riggs (Contract) **EST.** 1977 **CASES** 2000
PRODUCT RANGE ($21.50–29.50 CD) Gewurztraminer, Summar Semillon, Charlton Chardonnay, Trueman Traminer Late Harvest, The Son's Sparkling Merlot, Merlot, now sold in the narrow 500-ml Italian glass bottle known as Bellissima.
SUMMARY Ian Burgess and Debra Moore own a mature 6-hectare vineyard planted to chardonnay, semillon, gewurztraminer and merlot, with a small cellar-door operation offering immaculately packaged wines in avant-garde style. The peachy Chardonnay has been a medal winner at Hunter Valley Wine Shows.

Moores Hill Estate

 ★★★

3343 West Tamar Highway, Sidmouth, Tas 7270 **REGION** Northern Tasmania
T (03) 6394 7649 **F** (03) 6394 7649 **OPEN** Oct–June Wed–Sun 10–5, Mon–Tues by appointment for group bookings
WINEMAKER Julian Alcorso (Contract) **EST.** 1997 **CASES** 3000
PRODUCT RANGE ($16–23 CD) Riesling, Chardonnay, Unwooded Chardonnay, Pinot Noir, Cabernet Merlot.
SUMMARY Karen and Rod Thorpe, the latter with a background in catering, together with Bob Harness, have established their vineyard on the gentle slopes of the west Tamar Valley. They have planted 4.9 hectares of riesling, chardonnay, pinot noir, merlot and cabernet sauvignon, with additional newly planted riesling. It represents a full circle for the Thorpes, because when they purchased the property a little over 20 years ago there was an old vineyard which they pulled out. A wine-tasting and sales area made from Tasmanian timber opened at the end of 2002.

▼▼▼▼ **Riesling 2003** Big, rich, complex; some faint touches of reduction which will dissipate with age. **RATING** 89 **DRINK** 2012 $18

▼▼▼♈ **Pinot Noir 2002** **RATING** 86 **DRINK** 2007 $23
Unwooded Chardonnay 2003 **RATING** 84 **DRINK** Now $16
Chardonnay 2002 **RATING** 84 **DRINK** 2007 $18

Moorilla Estate

 ★★★★★

655 Main Road, Berriedale, Tas 7011 **REGION** Southern Tasmania
T (03) 6277 9900 **F** (03) 6249 4093 **OPEN** 7 days 10–5
WINEMAKER Michael Glover **EST.** 1958 **CASES** 16 000
PRODUCT RANGE ($19.50–95 CD) Varietals under the basic Moorilla label; Reserve range, the 2000 Merlot still under the Winter Collection label; the white label range, it would seem, has been phased out.
SUMMARY Moorilla Estate is an icon in the Tasmanian wine industry and is thriving. Wine quality continues to be unimpeachable, while the opening of the museum in the marvellous Alcorso house

designed by Sir Roy Grounds adds even more attraction for visitors to the estate, a mere 15–20 minutes from Hobart. Five-star self-contained chalets are available, with a restaurant open for lunch 7 days a week. Exports to Hong Kong and Denmark.

ŸŸŸŸŸ **Riesling 2003** Fragrant and floral; fresh, lively passionfruit and lime; perfect balance and length. **RATING** 94 **DRINK** 2008 $ 23

ŸŸŸŸŸ **White Label Pinot Noir 2002** Complex, ripe, potent black fruit/plum aromas and flavours; mouthfilling and compelling. **RATING** 93 **DRINK** 2010 $ 35
Claudio's Reserve Pinot Noir 2002 Deep colour; laden with concentrated, ripe satsuma plum and blackberry fruit; seems far riper than its 12.8 degrees alcohol suggest. **RATING** 93 **DRINK** 2009 $ 95
Gewurztraminer 2003 Strongly varietal, rich and intense lychee; big mouthfeel. **RATING** 92 **DRINK** 2007 $ 29
Black Label Chardonnay 2001 A complex amalgam of nutty oak and tangy fruit aromas; excellent balance and mouthfeel; complex cashew and oak, controlled acidity. **RATING** 92 **DRINK** 2011 $ 19.50
Reserve Chardonnay 2002 Long and intense; nectarine, citrus and creamy ML influences offset by lingering acidity. **RATING** 91 **DRINK** 2010 $ 38.50
Winter Collection Reserve Merlot 2000 Very powerful, concentrated blackcurrant and strong, savoury tannins. Confrontational style, for long ageing. **RATING** 91 **DRINK** 2020 $ 39
Black Label Pinot Noir 2002 Tightly structured and quite distinctive; dark plum, spice and a twist of acidity, still to loosen up. **RATING** 90 **DRINK** 2007 $ 24

ŸŸŸŸ **Reserve Cabernet Sauvignon 2000** Dense colour; leafy, savoury undertones to black fruits, powerful but very austere; will age. **RATING** 89 **DRINK** 2010 $ 45
Brut 2000 Fresh green apple aromas; crisp, lively; good length and balance. **RATING** 87 **DRINK** 2007 $ 29.50

ŸŸŸŸ **Reserve Chardonnay 2002** **RATING** 86 **DRINK** 2008 $ 38.50
Black Label Chardonnay 2002 **RATING** 84 **DRINK** 2007 $ 19.50
Black Label Pinot Noir 2003 **RATING** 84 **DRINK** Now $ 24

ŸŸŸ **Black Label Sauvignon Blanc 2003** **RATING** 83 $ 21.50
White Label Chardonnay 2002 **RATING** 83 $ 26.50
Unoaked Chardonnay 2003 **RATING** 82 $ 21.50

Moorooduc Estate ★★★★★

501 Derril Road, Moorooduc, Vic 3936 **REGION** Mornington Peninsula
T (03) 5971 8506 **F** (03) 5971 8550 **OPEN** Weekends 11–5, 7 days in January
WINEMAKER Dr Richard McIntyre **EST.** 1983 **CASES** 2500
PRODUCT RANGE ($23–60 R) Pinot Gris, Chardonnay, The Moorooduc Chardonnay, Devil Bend Creek Chardonnay, Pinot Noir, The Moorooduc Pinot Noir, Devil Bend Pinot Noir, Shiraz, Robinson Vineyard Shiraz, Cabernet.
SUMMARY Dr Richard McIntyre regularly produces one of the richest and most complex Chardonnays in the region, with melon/fig/peach fruit set against sumptuous spicy oak, and that hallmark soft nutty/creamy/regional texture. As well as retail distribution, the wines are exported through Trembath and Taylor.

ŸŸŸŸŸ **Chardonnay 2002** Greater complexity and power than The Moorooduc; wild yeast/barrel-ferment inputs; superb length and finish. **RATING** 94 **DRINK** 2009 $ 30.90

ŸŸŸŸŸ **The Moorooduc Chardonnay 2002** Almost satin-smooth; cashew, melon and fig; very even, long and fleshy. **RATING** 93 **DRINK** 2010 $ 60

ŸŸŸŸ **Devil Bend Creek Chardonnay 2002** Typical Mornington style; cashew, malolactic and barrel ferment; light to medium-bodied melon and fig fruit. **RATING** 89 **DRINK** Now $ 23.15

🐌 Morambro Creek Wines ★★★☆

Riddoch Highway, Padthaway, SA 5271 (postal) **REGION** Padthaway
T (08) 8765 6043 **F** (08) 8765 6011 **OPEN** Not
WINEMAKER Nicola Honeysett **EST.** 1994 **CASES** 6000
PRODUCT RANGE ($16–20 R) Chardonnay, Shiraz, Cabernet Sauvignon.
SUMMARY The Bryson family has been involved in agriculture for more than a century, moving to Padthaway in 1955 as farmers and graziers. In the early 1990s they began the establishment of 125 hectares of vines, planted principally to chardonnay, shiraz and cabernet sauvignon, but with further plantings planned for the near future. The wines have been consistent winners of bronze and silver medals at Australian wine shows since their release.

🍷🍷🍷🍷 **Shiraz 2002** Deep, plushy blackberry fruit; rich and mouthfilling; best of the four vintages so far released. **RATING** 90 **DRINK** 2012 $ 20

🍷🍷🍷🍷 **Shiraz 1999** Deeply coloured; concentrated black fruits, with some savoury notes; good length; carries the 15.3 degrees alcohol, though not without a struggle. **RATING** 88 **DRINK** 2014 $ 20
Cabernet Sauvignon 2000 Clean blackcurrant/cassis fruit with ample depth and length; good structure. **RATING** 88 **DRINK** 2012 $ 20

🍷🍷🍷🍷 **Shiraz 2000** **RATING** 86 **DRINK** 2009 $ 20
Cabernet Sauvignon 2001 **RATING** 86 **DRINK** 2013 $ 20
Shiraz 2001 **RATING** 84 **DRINK** 2010 $ 20
Cabernet Sauvignon 2002 **RATING** 84 **DRINK** 2012 $ 20

🍷🍷🍷 **Cabernet Sauvignon 1999** **RATING** 82 $ 20

Morgan Simpson ★★★☆

PO Box 39, Kensington Park, SA 5068 **REGION** McLaren Vale
T 0417 843 118 **F** (08) 8364 3645 **OPEN** Not
WINEMAKER Richard Simpson **EST.** 1998 **CASES** 1200
PRODUCT RANGE ($14.50–17.50 R) Chardonnay, Stone Hill Shiraz, Row 42 Cabernet Sauvignon.
SUMMARY Morgan Simpson was founded by South Australian businessman George Morgan (since retired) and winemaker Richard Simpson, who is a wine science graduate from Charles Sturt University. The grapes are sourced from the Clos Robert Vineyard (where the wine is made) established by Robert Allen Simpson in 1972. The aim was — and is — to provide drinkable wines at a reasonable price. It succeeds.

🍷🍷🍷🍷 **Stone Hill Shiraz 2002** Blackberry, plum, spice, earth and chocolate; good balance and length; not extractive. **RATING** 89 **DRINK** 2010 $ 17.50
Chardonnay 2002 Typical restrained, balanced and utterly reliable medium-bodied, easy-access style. **RATING** 87 **DRINK** Now $ 14.50

🍷🍷🍷🍷 **Row 42 Cabernet Sauvignon 2002** **RATING** 86 **DRINK** 2010 $ 17.50

Morgan Vineyards ★★★★

30 Davross Court, Seville, Vic 3139 **REGION** Yarra Valley
T (03) 5964 4807 **OPEN** Mon–Fri 11–4, weekends and public holidays 11–5
WINEMAKER Roger Morgan **EST.** 1987 **CASES** 1000
PRODUCT RANGE ($19–25 CD) Chardonnay, Pinot Noir, Merlot, Cabernet Merlot, Cabernet Sauvignon.
SUMMARY Roger and wife Ally Morgan have brought Morgan Vineyards along slowly. In 1987 they purchased a small 1.6-hectare vineyard of cabernet sauvignon and pinot noir which had been planted in 1971. They extended the plantings in 1989 with more pinot, again in 1991 (more cabernet sauvignon plus merlot) and finally in 1995 (chardonnay), bringing the total area under vine to 5.66 hectares. In 1997 Roger Morgan completed all the academic requirements of the wine science degree course at Charles Sturt University, and finally embarked on making the wines under the Morgan Vineyards label. An on-site winery and elegant tasting room have been established, Roger Morgan's aim being to build a reputation for making elegant wines at reasonable prices.

ΨΨΨΨ **Cabernet Sauvignon 2001** Healthy colour; sweet cassis/blackcurrant fruit; fine, stylish tannins; good length. **RATING** 90 **DRINK** 2010 **$** 25

ΨΨΨΨ **Chardonnay 2003** Delicate but intense; typical Yarra length and lingering finish; driven by fresh grapefruit and nectarine flavours. **RATING** 88 **DRINK** 2007 **$** 24
Pinot Noir 2002 A mix of spice, forest floor and plum; good length, though lighter than many from 2002; good texture. **RATING** 88 **DRINK** Now **$** 28

Morialta Vineyard   NR

195 Norton Summit Road, Norton Summit, SA 5136 **REGION** Adelaide Hills
T (08) 8390 1061 **F** (08) 8390 1585 **OPEN** By appointment
WINEMAKER Jeffrey Grosset (Contract) **EST.** 1989 **CASES** 500
PRODUCT RANGE ($15–23 R) Sauvignon Blanc, Unwooded Chardonnay, Chardonnay, Rose, Pinot Noir.
SUMMARY Morialta Vineyard was planted in 1989 on a site first planted to vines in the 1860s by John Baker, who named his property Morialta Farm. The Bunya pine depicted on the label is one of the few surviving trees from that era, and indeed one of the few surviving trees of that genus. The 20-hectare property has 11 hectares under vine, planted to chardonnay, pinot noir, cabernet sauvignon, sauvignon blanc, shiraz and merlot. Most of the grapes are sold to Southcorp. Given the age of the vineyard and contract winemaking by Jeffrey Grosset, it is not surprising that the wines have done well in the Adelaide Hills Wine Show. They are sold through selected restaurants in Adelaide as well as by mail order.

Morningside Wines

711 Middle Tea Tree Road, Tea Tree, Tas 7017 **REGION** Southern Tasmania
T (03) 6268 1748 **F** (03) 6268 1748 **OPEN** By appointment
WINEMAKER Peter Bosworth **EST.** 1980 **CASES** 500
PRODUCT RANGE ($19–34 ML) Riesling, Chardonnay, Pinot Noir, Cabernet Sauvignon.
SUMMARY The name 'Morningside' was given to the old property on which the vineyard stands because it gets the morning sun first — the property on the other side of the valley was known as 'Eveningside' — and, in accordance with the observation of the early settlers, the Morningside grapes achieve full maturity with good colour and varietal flavour. Production is as yet tiny, but will increase as the 2.9-hectare vineyard matures, and as recent additions of clonally selected pinot noir (including 8104, 115 and 777) come into bearing. Retail distribution through Sutherland Cellars, Melbourne and the Tasmanian Wine Centre.

ΨΨΨΨ **Pinot Noir 2002** Very complex, with lots of dark berry fruit and concentration; long carry, but slightly hard finish. **RATING** 88 **DRINK** 2009 **$** 34

ΨΨΨ **Chardonnay 2002** **RATING** 83 **$** 23
Riesling 2003 **RATING** 81 **$** 20

Morning Star Estate

1 Sunnyside Road, Mount Eliza, Vic 3930 **REGION** Mornington Peninsula
T (03) 9787 7760 **F** (03) 9787 7160 **OPEN** 7 days 10–5
WINEMAKER Sandro Mosele (Contract) **EST.** 1992 **CASES** 4000
PRODUCT RANGE ($12–34 CD) Chardonnay, Pinot Noir, Shiraz, Merlot Cabernet, Cabernet Sauvignon (Coonawarra); Sunnyside range of Sauvignon Blanc, Pinot Gris, Chardonnay, Pinot Noir, Cabernet Sauvignon.
SUMMARY In 1992 Judy Barrett purchased this historic property, the house built in 1867, and (with her family) spent the next 10 years repairing years of neglect. Over the same timeframe, 10 hectares each of pinot gris, chardonnay and pinot noir were planted. The wines — all sold through the estate's accommodation, conference and function centre and cellar door — are made by Sandro Mosele at Kooyong Estate. Most of the grapes are sold; the remainder go to make the Morning Star wines.

ΨΨΨΨΨ **Pinot Noir 2002** Deeply coloured; intense damson plum aromas; concentrated and focused, silky smooth; wholly arresting wine. **RATING** 95 **DRINK** 2007 **$** 28

ΨΨΨΨ **Chardonnay 2002** Complex, funky, wild yeast barrel-ferment aromas; a lighter mid-palate, then a slightly grippy finish. Has attitude. **RATING** 89 **DRINK** 2008 $28

ΨΨΨΨ **Sauvignon Blanc 2002** **RATING** 86 **DRINK** Now $24

ΨΨΨ **Shiraz 2001** **RATING** 83 $30

Morning Sun Vineyard NR

337 Main Creek Road, Main Ridge, Vic 3928 **REGION** Mornington Peninsula
T (03) 5989 6571 **OPEN** By appointment
WINEMAKER Rod Bourchier (Contract) **EST.** 1995
PRODUCT RANGE Semillon, Chardonnay, Pinot Gris, Pinot Noir.
SUMMARY Mario Toniolo has managed the development of 6 hectares of vineyard in the Main Ridge area of Red Hill. The varieties planted are semillon, chardonnay, pinot gris, pinot noir and barbera, and the wines are made on-site under the direction of contract winemaker Rod Bourchier. Sales are by mail order and through the cellar door, with the option of meals by special arrangement.

Mornington Estate ★★★☆

c/- Dromana Estate, Harrison's Road and Bittern–Dromana Road, Dromana, Vic 3936
REGION Mornington Peninsula
T (03) 5987 3800 **F** (03) 5981 0714 **OPEN** at Dromana Estate 7 days 11–4
WINEMAKER Gary Crittenden, Rollo Crittenden **EST.** 1989 **CASES** 8000
PRODUCT RANGE ($17–21.50 CD) Sauvignon Blanc, Chardonnay, Pinot Noir, Shiraz.
SUMMARY As with so many Mornington Peninsula vineyards, a high degree of viticultural expertise, care and attention are needed to get to first base. With a little over 20 hectares in production, it is one of the larger vineyards on the peninsula and is an important part of the publicly-listed Dromana Estate group. The majority of the grapes are sold to others.

ΨΨΨΨ **Sauvignon Blanc 2003** A clean opening; crisp, chalky, minerally finish; asparagus and herb along the way. **RATING** 87 **DRINK** Now $18

Morris ★★★★★

Mia Mia Road, Rutherglen, Vic 3685 **REGION** Rutherglen
T (02) 6026 7303 **F** (02) 6026 7445 **OPEN** Mon–Sat 9–5, Sun 10–5
WINEMAKER David Morris **EST.** 1859 **CASES** 100 000
PRODUCT RANGE ($13.99–69.95 R) Table wines include Chardonnay, Sparkling Shiraz Durif, Shiraz, Rutherglen Durif, Rutherglen Blue Imperial Cinsaut, Cabernet Sauvignon; then fortified wines: Black Label Liqueur Muscat, Liqueur Muscat, Premium Liqueur Muscat, Liqueur Tokay, Premium Liqueur Tokay, Premium Amontillado, Black Label Tawny Port, Old Tawny Port; tiny quantities of Show Reserve are released from time to time, mainly ex winery.
SUMMARY One of the greatest of the fortified winemakers, ranking with Chambers Rosewood. If you wish to test that view, try the Old Premium Muscat and Old Premium Tokay, which are absolute bargains given their age and quality and which give rise to the winery rating. The Durif table wine is a winery specialty, the others dependable; the white wines are all made by owner Orlando.

ΨΨΨΨΨ **Old Premium Rare Rutherglen Tokay NV** Deep, aged olive-brown; super intense, with a resplendent array of spices, cake and tea leaf surrounded by smoky rancio which cuts the richness and provides a lingering, intense but pleasingly dry aftertaste. **RATING** 97 **DRINK** Now $69.95

Old Premium Rare Rutherglen Muscat NV Deep olive-brown; dense spice, plum pudding and raisin aromas; utterly exceptional intensity and length; altogether in another dimension; while based upon some very old wine, is as fresh as a daisy. **RATING** 97 **DRINK** Now $69.95

Cellar Reserve Grand Rutherglen Tokay NV Very rich, very complex tea leaf, spice and Christmas cake aromas, some honey and butterscotch lurking; floods the mouth, intense and long, with a pronounced rancio cut, yet not sharp or volatile. **RATING** 95 **DRINK** Now $30

Cellar Reserve Grand Rutherglen Muscat NV Full olive-brown, green rim. A powerful and intense bouquet, rancio, spice and raisin; while less unctuous than some of its peers, the palate has outstanding texture, intensity and length. **RATING** 94 **DRINK** Now $30

ɪɪɪɪɪ **Classic Rutherglen Liqueur Tokay NV** Olive-brown; a very complex, classic mix of tea leaf, honey, butterscotch and some fish oil flavours is supported by excellent texture and balance. **RATING** 93 **DRINK** Now $16.99

Classic Rutherglen Liqueur Muscat NV A multiplicity of flavours, centred around raisin muscat fruit, but with a spicy jab of rancio to liven up the finish. **RATING** 92 **DRINK** Now $16.99

Durif 2000 Rich and slurpy sweet licorice and black plum; far less tannic than usual. **RATING** 91 **DRINK** 2010 $20

ɪɪɪɪ **Rutherglen Shiraz 2001 RATING** 84 **DRINK** 2007 $15

Morrisons Riverview Winery   NR

Lot 2, Merool Lane, Moama, NSW 2731 **REGION** Perricoota
T(03) 5480 0126 **F**(03) 5480 7144 **OPEN** 7 days 10–5
WINEMAKER John Ellis **EST.** 1996 **CASES** 2500
PRODUCT RANGE ($14–25 CD) Semillon, Sauvignon Blanc, Sauvignon Blanc Semillon, Pink Fronti, Adonis (late harvest Sauvignon Blanc), Shiraz, Cabernet Sauvignon Shiraz, Cabernet Sauvignon, Isaac White Port, Muscat; Chardonnay coming next vintage.
SUMMARY Alistair and Leslie Morrison purchased this historic piece of land in 1995. Plantings began in 1996 with shiraz and cabernet sauvignon, followed in 1997 by sauvignon blanc and frontignac, and grenache in 1998, totalling 6 hectares. The cellar door and restaurant opened in spring 2000, serving light lunches, platters, picnic baskets, coffee and gourmet cakes; wines are sold by the glass, bottle or box and tastings are free of charge.

Mortimers of Orange   NR

'Chestnut Garth', 786 Burrendong Way, Orange, NSW 2800 **REGION** Orange
T(02) 6365 8689 **F**(02) 6365 8689 **OPEN** 7 days 10–4
WINEMAKER Simon Gilbert, Jim Chatto (Contract) **EST.** 1996 **CASES** 2250
PRODUCT RANGE ($21–25 R) Chardonnay, with Pinot Noir, Shiraz and Cabernet Sauvignon due for the 2003 release.
SUMMARY Peter and Julie Mortimer began the establishment of their vineyard (named after a quiet street in the Humberside village of Burton Pidsea in the UK) in 1996. They now have just over 4 hectares of chardonnay, shiraz, cabernet sauvignon, merlot and pinot noir.

Moss Brothers   ★★★★

Caves Road, Wilyabrup, WA 6280 **REGION** Margaret River
T(08) 9755 6270 **F**(08) 9755 6298 **OPEN** 7 days 10–5
WINEMAKER David Moss **EST.** 1984 **CASES** 20 000
PRODUCT RANGE ($14–40 CD) Semillon, Sauvignon Blanc, Jane Moss Semillon Sauvignon Blanc, Verdelho, Oaked Chardonnay, Non Wooded Chardonnay, Moses Rock White, Jane Moss Pinot Noir, Shiraz, Cabernet Merlot, Cellar Door Red, Moses Rock Red (the last two unusual blends, Moses Rock including Merlot, Pinot Noir, Grenache and Cabernet Franc); Drummond Hill range of Semillon, Sauvignon Blanc, Unwooded Chardonnay.
SUMMARY Established by long-term viticulturist Jeff Moss and his family, notably sons Peter and David and Roseworthy graduate daughter Jane. A 100-tonne rammed-earth winery was constructed in 1992 and draws upon both estate-grown and purchased grapes. Wine quality has improved dramatically, in first the white wines, and more recently the reds. National wholesale distribution; exports to the US, Canada, Europe, Singapore and Hong Kong.

ɪɪɪɪɪ **Jane Moss Semillon Sauvignon Blanc 2003** Aromatic and intense bouquet; herbs, tropical fruit and gooseberry; good balance and length. **RATING** 90 **DRINK** 2007 $20

Jane Moss Semillon Sauvignon Blanc 2002 None of the reduced aromas evident in the sister sauvignon blanc; tight lemon, asparagus, grass and mineral flavours; plenty of presence and grip. **RATING** 90 **DRINK** Now $20

ŸŸŸŸ **Verdelho 2003** A particularly good example of the variety; potent, powerful and rich; concentrated fruit salad flavours; good balance. **RATING** 88 **DRINK** Now $ 20
Cabernet Sauvignon Merlot 2001 Classic savoury/gravelly Margaret River style with persistent tannins; needing patience to resolve. **RATING** 88 **DRINK** 2014 $ 40
Semillon 2003 A pungent, powerful, confrontational wine; gooseberry and asparagus; more akin to Sauvignon Blanc; demands food. **RATING** 87 **DRINK** Now $ 20

ŸŸŸŸ **Drummond Hill Sauvignon Blanc 2003** Powerful, herbaceous and dry; good length, touches of mineral. **RATING** 86 **DRINK** Now $ 16
Shiraz 2001 RATING 86 **DRINK** 2009 $ 35
Shiraz 2002 RATING 85 **DRINK** 2012 $ 35
Jane Moss Pinot Noir 2001 RATING 84 **DRINK** Now $ 20

ŸŸŸ **Sauvignon Blanc 2003 RATING** 82 $ 20

ŸŸŸ **Cabernet Sauvignon Merlot 2000 RATING** 79 $ 40

Moss Wood   ★★★★☆

Metricup Road, Wilyabrup, WA 6280 **REGION** Margaret River
T (08) 9755 6266 **F** (08) 9755 6303 **OPEN** By appointment
WINEMAKER Keith Mugford **EST.** 1969 **CASES** 11 000
PRODUCT RANGE ($22–77 R) Semillon, Chardonnay, Lefroy Brook Vineyard Chardonnay, Pinot Noir, Lefroy Brook Pinot Noir, Cabernet Sauvignon, Glenmore Vineyard Cabernet Sauvignon, Amy's Vineyard Cabernet Sauvignon; Ribbon Vale Semillon Sauvignon Blanc, Merlot, Cabernet Sauvignon Merlot Cabernet Franc.
SUMMARY Widely regarded as one of the best wineries in the region, capable of producing glorious Semillon (the best outside the Hunter Valley) in both oaked and unoaked forms, unctuous Chardonnay and elegant, gently herbaceous, superfine Cabernet Sauvignon which lives for many years. In 2002 Moss Wood acquired the Ribbon Vale Estate, which is now merged within its own business, the Ribbon Vale wines now being treated as vineyard-designated within the Moss Wood umbrella. Exports to all major markets.

ŸŸŸŸŸ **Ribbon Vale Vineyard Cabernet Merlot 2001** Elegant, with great structure and mouthfeel; blackcurrant, cedar and spice; lovely tannins on the finish. Screwcap. **RATING** 93 **DRINK** 2016 $ 29.50
Semillon 2003 Screwcap-closed, without a hint of reduction; focused in that typical Margaret River style, with power and weight from 14 degrees alcohol. A long life ahead. **RATING** 91 **DRINK** 2010 $ 28.50
Lefroy Brook Vineyard Chardonnay 2002 Pale straw-green; aromatic citrus and stone fruit; long, lingering finish. **RATING** 90 **DRINK** 2008 $ 34.50
Cabernet Sauvignon 2000 Fine, elegant, medium-bodied mix of cassis, cedar and mocha; long, fine finish. **RATING** 90 **DRINK** 2015 $ 82

ŸŸŸŸ **Chardonnay 2002** Mouthfilling, round, nectarine and peach; viscosity from alcohol. **RATING** 89 **DRINK** 2007 $ 49

ŸŸŸŸ **Amy's Vineyard Cabernet Sauvignon 2002 RATING** 86 **DRINK** 2011 $ 35
Pinot Noir 2001 RATING 85 **DRINK** 2007 $ 45

Mountadam   ★★★☆

High Eden Road, Eden Valley, SA 5235 **REGION** Eden Valley
T (08) 8564 1900 **F** (08) 8564 1999 **OPEN** 7 days 11–4
WINEMAKER Andrew Ewart, Tim Heath **EST.** 1972 **CASES** 25 000
PRODUCT RANGE ($13–52 CD) Under the premium Mountadam label are Riesling, Chardonnay, Pinot Noir Chardonnay, Pinot Noir, The Red (50 per cent Merlot, 50 per cent Cabernet), Merlot, Cabernet Sauvignon; under the David Wynn label are Chardonnay, Shiraz, Patriarch Shiraz; under organically grown Eden Ridge label are Sauvignon Blanc, Cabernet Sauvignon; also Ratafia Chardonnay and Pinot Noir.

SUMMARY One of the leading small wineries, founded by David Wynn and run by winemaker son Adam Wynn, initially offering only the Mountadam range at relatively high prices. The subsequent development of the three ranges of wines has been very successful, judged from both a winemaking and a wine marketing viewpoint. Mountadam has built up an extensive export network over many years, with the US, Canada, Hong Kong, Japan and the UK being the major markets, but also extending across the breadth of Europe and most Asian markets. Acquired by Cape Mentelle in 2000.

ŸŸŸŸ **Patriarch Shiraz 2000** Spicy red berry fruits, crisp rather than luscious; controlled oak. **RATING** 89 **DRINK** 2009 $ 42

Eden Valley Riesling 2003 Powerful; early hints of kerosene and spice; pleasant balance. **RATING** 88 **DRINK** 2009 $ 24

The Red 2001 A complex wine, rich and big; slightly gamey undertones to the very ripe 'dead fruit' of the palate. **RATING** 88 **DRINK** 2012 $ 42

Eden Valley DW Shiraz 2001 Fully ripe style; touches of prune and black plum; good oak balance and length. **RATING** 87 **DRINK** 2011 $ 38

ŸŸŸŸ **Eden Valley Chardonnay 2000** **RATING** 86 **DRINK** Now $ 34

Barossa Cabernet Merlot 2002 Quite rich blackcurrant and dark chocolate fruit, with pronounced, lingering tannins. Significantly, the best of the three new Barossa releases. **RATING** 86 **DRINK** 2012 $ 18.50

Eden Valley Pinot Noir 2001 **RATING** 85 **DRINK** Now $ 42

Barossa Unoaked Chardonnay 2003 **RATING** 84 **DRINK** Now $ 16.50

ŸŸŸ **Barossa Unoaked Chardonnay 2002** **RATING** 83 $ 16.50

Eden Valley Chardonnay 2001 **RATING** 83 $ 34

Mount Alexander Vineyard

NR

Calder Highway, North Harcourt, Vic 3453 **REGION** Bendigo
T (03) 5474 2262 **F** (03) 5474 2553 **OPEN** 7 days 10–5.30
WINEMAKER Keith Walkden **EST.** 1984 **CASES** 6000
PRODUCT RANGE ($10–14 CD) A wide range of various table wines, sparklings, fortifieds, meads and liqueurs.
SUMMARY A substantial operation, with 17 hectares planted to all the right varieties.

Mount Anakie Wines

★★☆

130 Staughton Vale Road, Anakie, Vic 3221 **REGION** Geelong
T (03) 5284 1256 **F** (03) 5284 1405 **OPEN** 7 days 11–5
WINEMAKER Otto Zambelli **EST.** 1968 **CASES** 6000
PRODUCT RANGE ($15–34 CD) Biancone, Riesling, Lexia, Semillon, Chardonnay, Vic Classic Rose, Shiraz, Cabernet Shiraz, Cabernet Sauvignon, Tawny Port.
SUMMARY Also known as Zambelli Estate, this operation once produced some excellent wines (under its various ownerships and winemakers), all distinguished by their depth and intensity of flavour. No recent tastings; prior to that, the wines tasted were but a shadow of their former quality. The level of activity seems relatively low.

Mount Avoca Winery

★★★☆

Moates Lane, Avoca, Vic 3467 **REGION** Pyrenees
T (03) 5465 3282 **F** (03) 5465 3544 **OPEN** Mon–Fri 9–5, weekends 10–5
WINEMAKER Matthew Barry **EST.** 1970 **CASES** 15 000
PRODUCT RANGE ($15–30 CD) Sauvignon Blanc, Semillon Sauvignon Blanc, Chardonnay, Merlot, Shiraz, Cabernet Sauvignon.
SUMMARY A substantial winery which has long been one of the stalwarts of the Pyrenees region, and is steadily growing, with 23.7 hectares of vineyards. There has been a significant refinement in the style and flavour of the red wines over the past few years. I suspect a lot of worthwhile work has gone into barrel selection and maintenance. In July 2003, after a short period as part of the ill-fated Barrington Estates group, it was sold back to Matthew Barry by the Barrington administrator. Exports to Asia.

ŸŸŸŸŸ **Semillon Sauvignon Blanc 2003** A surprise packet; very attractive citrus-tinged aromas; good mouthfeel and balance. **RATING** 91 **DRINK** 2008 $ 15

Sauvignon Blanc 2003 A quiet bouquet belies the intensity and power of the palate; ripe, layered varietal character. **RATING** 90 **DRINK** Now $ 17

ŶŶŶŶ **Shiraz 2001** Medium-bodied; blackberry and chocolate plus a nice touch of vanilla oak. **RATING** 88 **DRINK** 2010 $ 20
Cabernet Sauvignon 2000 Clean, ripe red and black fruits; soft, ripe tannins and sweet oak. **RATING** 88 **DRINK** 2010 $ 20

ŶŶŶŶ **Chardonnay 2001 RATING** 86 **DRINK** 2007 $ 20
Merlot 2000 RATING 86 **DRINK** 2009 $ 20
Sparkling Shiraz NV RATING 85 **DRINK** Now $ 25

Mount Beckworth ★★★

RMB 915 Learmonth Road, Tourello via Ballarat, Vic 3363 **REGION** Ballarat
T (03) 5343 4207 **F** (03) 5343 4207 **OPEN** Weekends 10–6, and by appointment
WINEMAKER Paul Lesock **EST.** 1984 **CASES** 1000
PRODUCT RANGE ($16–20 CD) Unwooded Chardonnay, Chardonnay, Pinot Noir, Shiraz, Cabernet Merlot.
SUMMARY The 4-hectare Mount Beckworth vineyard was planted in 1984/85, but it was not until 1995 that the full range of wines under the Mount Beckworth label appeared. Until that time much of the production was sold to Seppelt Great Western for sparkling wine use. It is owned and managed by Paul Lesock, who studied viticulture at Charles Sturt University, and his wife Jane. The wines usually reflect the very cool climate. Limited Victorian retail distribution.

ŶŶŶŶ **Shiraz 2002** Very spicy/minty/menthol aromas and flavours; a hint of game, too; ultra-cool region and similarly cool vintage. **RATING** 87 **DRINK** 2008 $ 20

ŶŶŶŶ **Unwooded Chardonnay 2003 RATING** 86 **DRINK** 2008 $ 16
Cabernet Merlot 2002 RATING 84 **DRINK** 2008 $ 16

🐌 Mt Billy ★★★☆

18 Victoria Street, Victor Harbor, SA 5211 (postal) **REGION** Southern Fleurieu
T (08) 8552 7200 **F** (08) 8552 8333 **OPEN** Not
WINEMAKER Contract **EST.** 2000 **CASES** 1700
PRODUCT RANGE ($15–42 ML) Valleys Riesling, Chardonnay Pinot Meunier, Barossa Shiraz Rose, Harmony (Shiraz blend), Antiquity Shiraz.
SUMMARY John Edwards became a resident dentist at Victor Harbor in 1983, having been an avid wine collector (and consumer) since 1973. John and wife Pauline purchased a 3.75-hectare property in the hills behind Victor Harbor, and the sheep and goats ultimately gave way to plantings of 1.2 hectares each of chardonnay and pinot meunier. The original intention was to sell the grapes, but low yields quickly persuaded Edwards that making and selling a bottle-fermented sparkling wine was the way to go. Additionally, in 1999, 1 tonne each of grenache and shiraz were purchased in the Barossa Valley, and David Powell of Torbreck agreed to make the wine. Mt Billy was born.

ŶŶŶŶ **Harmony 2001** Black fruits, bitter chocolate and subtle oak; not the least bit jammy; well proportioned and well named. **RATING** 88 **DRINK** 2008 $ 23
Antiquity Shiraz 2001 Traditional Barossa style, with ripe black cherry and plum fruit supported by soft tannins and a hint of vanilla oak. **RATING** 87 **DRINK** 2011 $ 23

ŶŶŶŶ **Chardonnay Pinot Meunier NV RATING** 86 **DRINK** Now $ 26
Valleys Riesling 2002 RATING 84 **DRINK** 2008 $ 15

Mount Broke Wines ★★★

Adams Peak Road, Broke, NSW 2330 **REGION** Lower Hunter Valley
T (02) 6579 1314 **F** (02) 6579 1314 **OPEN** 7 days 11–4
WINEMAKER Contract **EST.** 1997 **CASES** 1250
PRODUCT RANGE ($13.75–30 CD) Quince Tree Paddock Semillon, Harrowby Verdelho, Adam's Peak Chardonnay, River Bank Shiraz, Black Pine Ridge Merlot, Quince Tree Paddock Barbera, Harrowby Cabernet Merlot.

SUMMARY Phil and Jo McNamara began planting their 9.6-hectare vineyard, on the west side of Wollombi Brook, to shiraz, merlot, verdelho, barbera, semillon, chardonnay and cabernet sauvignon in 1997. It is early days, but they have already established a wine club and have opened The Cow Café, with wine tasting and wine function capacity; it is open as a restaurant Friday evenings.

ΥΥΥΥ **River Bank Shiraz 2002** A medium-bodied blend of blackberry, plum and earth; sweet mid-palate, then a lingering, savoury finish. Screwcap. **RATING** 88 **DRINK** 2009 $ 25

ΥΥΥΥ **Quince Tree Paddock Barbera 2003** Light to medium-bodied; a mix of earthy, spicy, savoury aromas and flavours; daunting price. **RATING** 86 **DRINK** 2009 $ 30
Harrowby Cabernet Merlot 2002 **RATING** 85 **DRINK** Now $ 19
Quince Tree Paddock Semillon 2003 **RATING** 84 **DRINK** 2013 $ 13.75

ΥΥΥ **River Bank Verdelho 2003** **RATING** 83 $ 13.75

🐦 Mount Buninyong Winery   NR

Platts Road, Scotsburn, Vic 3352 **REGION** Ballarat
T (03) 5341 8360 **F** (03) 5341 2442 **OPEN** 7 days
WINEMAKER Peter Armstrong **EST.** 1993
PRODUCT RANGE Table, sparkling, organic and fortified wines.
SUMMARY Mount Buninyong Winery is the venture of Peter and Jan Armstrong, assisted by son and daughter-in-law Malcolm and Sandra Armstrong. It is situated just to the south of Ballarat, with 4 hectares of riesling, chardonnay, pinot noir and cabernet sauvignon established near Scotsburn. A range of table, fortified, sparkling and organic wines are made under the Mount Buninyong, Ballarat Wines and Ballarat Regional Wines labels. The cellar door has barbecue and picnic facilities.

🐦 Mount Burrumboot Estate   ★★★★☆

3332 Heathcote–Rochester Road, Colbinabbin, Vic 3559 **REGION** Heathcote
T (03) 5432 9238 **F** (03) 5432 9238 **OPEN** Weekends and public holidays 11–5, or by appointment
WINEMAKER Cathy Branson **EST.** 1999 **CASES** 500
PRODUCT RANGE ($15–28 CD) Verdelho, Shiraz, Reserve Shiraz, Merlot.
SUMMARY 'Mount Burrumboot Estate was born in 1999, when Andrew and Cathy Branson planted vines on the Home Block of the Branson family farm "Donore" on the slopes of Mount Burrumboot, on the Mount Camel Range, above Colbinabbin. Originally the vineyard was just another diversification of an already diverse farming enterprise. However, the wine bug soon bit Andrew and Cathy, and so a winery was established. The first wine was made in 2001 by contract — however, the 2002 vintage saw the first wine made by Cathy in the machinery shed, surrounded by headers and tractors. Very primitive, and the appearance of the new 50-tonne winery in August 2002 was greeted with great enthusiasm!' And then you taste the wines. Amazing.

ΥΥΥΥΥ **Shiraz 2002** Dense purple-red; blackberry, licorice, anise in abundance, the palate extended by intense, savoury tannins. **RATING** 90 **DRINK** 2017 $ 25
Merlot 2002 Deep purple-red; clean, rich, fully ripe; a lovely medium-bodied red wine; not especially varietal, but who cares. **RATING** 90 **DRINK** 2010 $ 25

Mount Cathedral Vineyards   ★★☆

125 Knafl Road, Taggerty, Vic 3714 **REGION** Upper Goulburn
T 0409 354 069 **F** (03) 9354 0994 **OPEN** By appointment
WINEMAKER Oscar Rosa, Nick Arena **EST.** 1995 **CASES** 400
PRODUCT RANGE ($20–35 ML) Chardonnay, Merlot, Cabernet Sauvignon Merlot.
SUMMARY The Rosa and Arena families established Mount Cathedral Vineyards in 1995, the vines being planted at an elevation of 300 metres on the north face of Mount Cathedral. The first plantings were of 1.2 hectares of merlot and 0.8 hectare of chardonnay, followed by 2.5 hectares of cabernet sauvignon and 0.5 hectare of cabernet franc in 1996. Oscar Rosa, chief winemaker, completed a Bachelor of Wine Science course at Charles Sturt University in 2002. He gained practical experience working at Yering Station during 1998 and 1999.

ΥΥΥ **Chardonnay 2002** **RATING** 81 $ 20

Mount Charlie Winery ★★★

228 Mount Charlie Road, Riddells Creek, Vic 3431 **REGION** Macedon Ranges
T (03) 5428 6946 **F** (03) 5428 6946 **OPEN** Weekends by appointment
WINEMAKER Trefor Morgan **EST.** 1991 **CASES** 1000
PRODUCT RANGE ($20–22 CD) Sauvignon Blanc, Chardonnay, Red (Shiraz Merlot Cabernet blend).
SUMMARY Mount Charlie's wines are sold principally by mail order and through selected restaurants. A futures program encourages mailing list sales with a discount of over 25 per cent on the ultimate release price. Owner/winemaker Trefor Morgan is perhaps better known as a Professor of Physiology at Melbourne University.

TTTY **Red 2002 RATING** 85 **DRINK** 2007 $ 22

TTT **Chardonnay 2002 RATING** 81 $ 20

Mount Coghill Vineyard ★★★★

Clunes–Learmonth Road, Coghills Creek, Vic 3364 **REGION** Ballarat
T (03) 5343 4329 **OPEN** Weekends 10–5
WINEMAKER Norman Latta **EST.** 1993 **CASES** 200
PRODUCT RANGE ($12–20 CD) Chardonnay, Pinot Noir.
SUMMARY Ian and Margaret Pym began the development of their tiny vineyard in 1995 with the planting of 1280 pinot noir rootlings, adding 450 chardonnay rootlings the next year. The first harvest, in 2000, produced 0.5 tonne of pinot noir and 0.3 tonne of chardonnay (sold), but when production leapt to 4 tonnes of pinot noir and 1.5 tonnes of chardonnay in 2001, the decision was taken to have the wine made and released under the Mount Coghill Vineyard label.

TTTTY **Chardonnay 2002** Pale straw-green; fine, tangy, grapefruit-accented; long finish; well made. **RATING** 90 **DRINK** 2009 $ 20

Mount Delancey Winery NR

60 De Lancey Road, Wandin North, Vic 3139 **REGION** Yarra Valley
T (03) 5964 4964 **OPEN** Weekends 10–5.30, or by appointment
WINEMAKER Jordan Metlikovec **EST.** 1985 **CASES** 200
PRODUCT RANGE ($10–20 CD) Chardonnay, Pinot Noir, Cabernet Sauvignon; also fruit wines.
SUMMARY Jordan Metlikovec makes a tiny quantity of wine and fruit wine from a mixed planting of 1 hectare which includes chardonnay, pinot noir and cabernet sauvignon, also purchasing approximately 2 tonnes of grapes from other small Yarra Valley vineyards and berry growers.

Mount Duneed NR

Feehan's Road, Mount Duneed, Vic 3216 **REGION** Geelong
T (03) 5264 1281 **F** (03) 5264 1281 **OPEN** Public holidays and weekends 11–5, or by appointment
WINEMAKER Ken Campbell, John Darling **EST.** 1970 **CASES** 1000
PRODUCT RANGE ($10–18 CD) Semillon, Sauvignon Blanc, Riesling, Botrytis Semillon, Malbec, Cabernet Malbec, Cabernet Sauvignon.
SUMMARY Rather idiosyncratic wines are the order of the day, some of which can develop surprisingly well in bottle; the Botrytis Noble Rot Semillon has, from time to time, been of very high quality. A significant part of the production from the 7.5 hectares of vineyards is sold to others.

Mount Eliza Estate ★★★☆

Cnr Sunnyside Road and Nepean Highway, Mt Eliza, Vic 3930 **REGION** Mornington Peninsula
T (03) 9787 0663 **F** (03) 9708 8355 **OPEN** 7 days 11–5
WINEMAKER Scott Ireland (Contract) **EST.** 1997 **CASES** 8500
PRODUCT RANGE ($16–35 CD) Riesling, Sauvignon Blanc, Chardonnay, Pinot Noir, Magnus Maximus Pinot Noir, Shiraz, Astrid Elizabeth Pinot Noir Chardonnay.
SUMMARY Robert and Jenny Thurley planted the 7.84-hectare vineyard at Mount Eliza Estate in 1997; the varieties are riesling, chardonnay, sauvignon blanc, shiraz, pinot noir and cabernet

sauvignon. Son James, presently studying viticulture, has worked at the vineyard since day one under the direction of viticulturist Graeme Harrip, making the business a family affair. The cellar door, which has great views across Port Phillip Bay to the Melbourne city skyline, was opened in November 2000. The contract winemaker is Scott Ireland, of Provenance, who has had many years experience in making wines from the Port Phillip Zone.

Mount Eyre Vineyard ★★★☆

1325 Broke Road, Broke, NSW 2330 **REGION** Lower Hunter Valley
T 0438 683 973 **F** (02) 9744 3508 **OPEN** By appointment
WINEMAKER C P Lin **EST.** 1996 **CASES** 9000
PRODUCT RANGE ($14–35 CD) Released under three labels: the Mount Eyre range of Semillon, Semillon Chardonnay, Unwooded Chardonnay; Three Ponds Semillon, Chardonnay, Shiraz; and Neptune (sparkling Semillon).
SUMMARY Mount Eyre draws on two vineyards, the first a 24-hectare estate at Broke, planted to semillon, chardonnay, shiraz, chambourcin, cabernet franc and cabernet sauvignon; the second, Holman Estate, in Gillards Road, Pokolbin, with 4 hectares of shiraz and 1.8 hectares of merlot. C P Lin is the newly appointed winemaker, surely the only blind Chinese winemaker in the world. For good measure, having completed the Hunter vintage he crosses back to Mountford Winery, near Christchurch, New Zealand to work with pinot noir each year. Most amazingly of all, he has translated the *Oxford Companion to Wine* into Braille. The wines are exported to Canada, Thailand, Germany and the Maldives.

▼▼▼▼♈ **Three Ponds Semillon 2001** Glowing yellow-green; honey and lightly browned toast, then lingering, lemony acidity; developing nicely, without fuss. **RATING** 91 **DRINK** 2008 $ 20
Three Ponds Shiraz 2001 Strongly regional; traditional spicy/earthy style entirely driven by shiraz varietal character; a long savoury palate; fine black fruits and finish. **RATING** 91 **DRINK** 2010 $ 35
Three Ponds Shiraz 2002 Plum and blackberry fruit; hints of earth and spice; particularly good tannin structure. **RATING** 90 **DRINK** 2010 $ 35

▼▼▼▼ **Cabernet Franc 2002** Clean, fresh and lively red berry fruit on a light to medium-bodied palate; good finish; impressive for a difficult variety. **RATING** 87 **DRINK** 2008 $ 15

▼▼▼♈ **Neptune Sparkling Semillon 2001** **RATING** 86 **DRINK** 2007 $ 30
Rose 2002 **RATING** 85 **DRINK** Now $ 15
Three Ponds Chardonnay 2001 **RATING** 84 **DRINK** Now $ 20

Mountford ★★★★

Bamess Road, West Pemberton, WA 6260 **REGION** Pemberton
T (08) 9776 1345 **F** (08) 9776 1345 **OPEN** Mon–Fri 10–4, weekends 10–5
WINEMAKER Andrew Mountford, Saxon Mountford **EST.** 1987 **CASES** 3000
PRODUCT RANGE ($14.50–28.50 CD) Sauvignon Blanc, Unwooded Chardonnay, Reserve Chardonnay, Pinot Noir, Merlot, Cabernet Merlot, Vintage Port, sparkling.
SUMMARY English-born and trained Andrew Mountford and wife Sue migrated to Australia in 1983, first endeavouring to set up a winery at Mudgee and thereafter moving to Pemberton, with far greater success. Their strikingly packaged wines are produced from 6 hectares of permanently netted, dry-grown vineyards.

Mount Gisborne Wines ★★★☆

83 Waterson Road, Gisborne, Vic 3437 **REGION** Macedon Ranges
T (03) 5428 2834 **F** (03) 5428 2834 **OPEN** Weekends 10–5
WINEMAKER Stuart Anderson **EST.** 1986 **CASES** 1500
PRODUCT RANGE ($14–25 CD) Chardonnay, Pinot Noir.
SUMMARY Mount Gisborne Wines is very much a weekend and holiday occupation for proprietor David Ell, who makes the wines from the 7-hectare vineyard under the watchful and skilled eye of industry veteran Stuart Anderson, now living in semi-retirement high in the Macedon Hills.

Mount Horrocks ★★★★☆

The Old Railway Station, Curling Street, Auburn, SA 5451 **REGION** Clare Valley
T (08) 8849 2243 **F** (08) 8849 2265 **OPEN** Weekends and public holidays 10–5
WINEMAKER Stephanie Toole **EST.** 1982 **CASES** 4500
PRODUCT RANGE ($24.95–38 CD) Watervale Riesling, Semillon, Chardonnay, Cordon Cut Riesling, Shiraz, Cabernet Merlot.
SUMMARY Mount Horrocks has well and truly established its own identity in recent years, aided by positive marketing and, equally importantly, wine quality which has resulted in both show success and critical acclaim. Exports to the UK, the US, Belgium, Switzerland, The Netherlands, Italy and Japan. Lunches available on weekends.

ᵀᵀᵀᵀᵀ **Semillon 2002** Barrel-fermented and 8 months' oak maturation; the wine has eaten the oak; fascinating, one of the best examples of this style. **RATING** 94 **DRINK** 2010 $ 27

ᵀᵀᵀᵀ♈ **Cabernet Merlot 2001** Not star-bright in colour; a complex array of red and black berry fruits, herbs and spice aromas; good mouthfeel and structure; restrained oak, and the red fruits come up progressively. **RATING** 90 **DRINK** 2016 $ 38

ᵀᵀᵀᵀ **Watervale Riesling 2003** A clean but very closed bouquet; more flavour, quite ripe, emerges on the palate; demands time. **RATING** 89 **DRINK** 2018 $ 28
Shiraz 2001 A subdued bouquet, but flowers on the palate; damson plum, licorice and blackberry flavours; soft tannins. Screwcap. **RATING** 89 **DRINK** 2011 $ 38
Cordon Cut Riesling 2003 Dried fruit aromas and flavours; predominantly citrus, but also stone fruit; lusciously sweet. **RATING** 89 **DRINK** 2007 $ 32.75

ᵀᵀᵀ♈ **Chardonnay 2002 RATING** 86 **DRINK** Now $ 24.95

Mount Ida ★★★★

Northern Highway, Heathcote, Vic 3253 **REGION** Heathcote
T (03) 8626 3340 **OPEN** Not
WINEMAKER Matt Steel **EST.** 1978 **CASES** 2000
PRODUCT RANGE ($36 R) Shiraz.
SUMMARY Established by the famous artist Leonard French and Dr James Munro but purchased by Tisdall after the 1987 bushfires and thereafter by Beringer Blass when it acquired Tisdall. Up to the time of the fires, wonderfully smooth, rich red wines with almost voluptuous sweet, minty fruit were the hallmark. After a brief period during which the name was used as a simple brand (with various wines released), has returned to a single estate-grown wine.

ᵀᵀᵀᵀ **Shiraz 2001** Pleasant medium-bodied wine; gently ripe black fruits; soft tannins. **RATING** 89 **DRINK** 2010 $ 27

Mountilford NR

Mount Vincent Road, Ilford, NSW 2850 **REGION** Mudgee
T (02) 6358 8544 **F** (02) 6358 8544 **OPEN** 7 days 10–4
WINEMAKER Don Cumming **EST.** 1985 **CASES** 1800
PRODUCT RANGE ($12–22 CD) Riesling, Highland White, Windamere, Sylvaner, Chardonnay, Pinot Noir, Pinot Shiraz, Cabernet Shiraz, Jubilation Cabernet Shiraz, Sir Alexander Port, Lady Alex.
SUMMARY Surprisingly large cellar-door operation which has grown significantly over the past few years, utilising 7 hectares of estate vineyards. Roughly half the production is sold to other winemakers. I have not, however, had the opportunity to taste the wines.

Mt Jagged Wines NR

Main Victor Harbor Road, Mt Jagged, SA 5211 **REGION** Southern Fleurieu
T (08) 8554 9532 **F** (08) 8224 0727 **OPEN** Weekends and holidays 10–5, or by appointment
WINEMAKER Mike Farmilo (Contract) **EST.** 1989 **CASES** 7000
PRODUCT RANGE ($14–18 CD) Semillon, Unwooded Chardonnay, Shiraz, Merlot Cabernet Sauvignon.
SUMMARY Jerry White immigrated to Australia in 1970, and after a successful business career, purchased 100 hectares at Mt Jagged in 1988. The land is located on the main road to Victor

Harbor, which he believed would generate ample cellar-door sales demand. However, being the first to plant in the region, he also decided to plant 28 hectares, thus producing sufficient grapes to supply large companies, and he duly entered into a contract with Penfolds, with semillon, chardonnay, merlot, cabernet sauvignon and shiraz all being sold. It was not until 1996 that the first Mt Jagged wine appeared, and by 2001 more and more fruit was being diverted to the Mt Jagged label, with exports to the US in place, and retail distribution in New South Wales, Queensland and Victoria through Irvine's Fine Wines. The cool, maritime environment was described by John Gladstones as 'what appears to be the best climate in mainland South Australia for making table wines'.

Mount Langi Ghiran Vineyards ★★★★☆

Warrak Road, Buangor, Vic 3375 **REGION** Grampians
T (03) 5354 3207 **F** (03) 5354 3277 **OPEN** Mon–Fri 9–5, weekends 12–5
WINEMAKER Trevor Mast, Dan Buckle **EST.** 1969 **CASES** 45 000
PRODUCT RANGE ($20–55 CD) Riesling, Pinot Gris, Botrytis Riesling, Cliff Edge Shiraz; under Langi label, Shiraz and Cabernet Merlot.
SUMMARY A maker of outstanding cool-climate peppery Shiraz, crammed with flavour and vinosity, and very good Cabernet Sauvignon. The Shiraz points the way for cool-climate examples of the variety, for weight, texture and fruit richness all accompany the vibrant pepper-spice aroma and flavour. The business was acquired by the Rathbone family group in November 2002, and hence will be integrated with the Yering Station product range, a synergistic mix with no overlap. Trevor Mast will continue to run the Langi Ghiran operation, which has an export network throughout the UK, the US, Canada, New Zealand, Asia and Europe.

ŸŸŸŸŸ **Pinot Gris 2003** Authentic array of pear, apple, spice and musk aromas; great palate flavour and weight; top-class Pinot Gris. Screwcap. **RATING** 92 **DRINK** 2007 $ 22
Riesling 2003 Moderately intense lemon and apple; supple and smooth, excellent length and balance. **RATING** 91 **DRINK** 2010 $ 20

ŸŸŸŸ **Cliff Edge Shiraz 2001** Minty, savoury red berry fruits; minimal oak; gentle tannins. **RATING** 87 **DRINK** 2009 $ 28

Mt Lofty Ranges Vineyard ★★★★

Harris Road, Lenswood, SA 5240 **REGION** Adelaide Hills
T (08) 8389 8339 **F** (08) 8389 8349 **OPEN** Weekends 11–5, or by appointment
WINEMAKER Nepenthe (Contract) **EST.** 1992 **CASES** 1000
PRODUCT RANGE ($16–25 CD) Five Vines Riesling, Sauvignon Blanc, Chardonnay, Old Pump Shed Pinot Noir.
SUMMARY Mt Lofty Ranges Vineyard is owned by Alan Herath and Jan Reed, who have been involved from the outset in planting, training and nurturing the 4.6-hectare vineyard. Both had professional careers but are now full-time vignerons. Skilled winemaking by Peter Leske at Nepenthe has already brought rewards and recognition to the vineyard. Victorian distribution through Colonial Wines; elsewhere direct from the winery.

ŸŸŸŸŸ **Ranges Vineyard Old Pump Shed Pinot Noir 2002** Finely crafted; plum, cherry and strawberry fruit aromas; tight, fine tannins; excellent texture and structure. **RATING** 93 **DRINK** 2009 $ 25
Ranges Vineyard Five Vines Riesling 2003 Fragrant apple blossom and passionfruit aromas; fine, feathery, delicate and crisp; good balance. **RATING** 91 **DRINK** 2012 $ 16

ŸŸŸŸ **Ranges Vineyard Chardonnay 2002** Light colour; delicate, grapefruit-dominated palate, long and very crisp; minimal oak. Will develop. **RATING** 89 **DRINK** 2010 $ 16

ŸŸŸŸ **Ranges Vineyard Sauvignon Blanc 2003** **RATING** 86 **DRINK** Now $ 18

Mount Majura Vineyard

RMB 314 Majura Road, Majura, ACT 2609 **REGION** Canberra District
T (02) 6262 3070 **F** (02) 6262 4288 **OPEN** Sun 10–5
WINEMAKER Dr Frank van de Loo **EST.** 1988 **CASES** 2000

PRODUCT RANGE ($12–25 ML) Riesling, Pinot Gris, Chardonnay, Woolshed Creek White and Red, Pinot Noir, Cabernet Franc Merlot.

SUMMARY The first vines were planted in 1988 by Dinny Killen on a site on her family property which had been especially recommended by Dr Edgar Riek; its attractions were red soil of volcanic origin over limestone, with the reasonably steep east and northeast slopes providing an element of frost protection. The 1-hectare vineyard was planted to pinot noir, chardonnay and merlot in equal quantities; the pinot noir grapes were sold to Lark Hill and used in their award-winning Pinot Noir, while the chardonnay and merlot were made for Mount Majura by Lark Hill; both wines have enjoyed show success. The syndicate which purchased the property in 1999 has extended the plantings, and Dr Frank van de Loo makes the wines in leased space at Brindabella Hills. He is at the planning stage of an on-site winery and cellar door.

ŸŸŸŸ **Chardonnay 2002** At once complex yet balanced; melon, fig, cashew and barrel ferment; harmonious. **RATING** 89 **DRINK** 2007 $ 20

Pinot Noir 2002 Light spice, plum and forest aromas; good varietal flavour in lighter mode; nice mouthfeel. **RATING** 88 **DRINK** 2011 $ 25

Riesling 2003 Powerful, ripe, slightly old fashioned; abundant tropical fruit. **RATING** 87 **DRINK** 2009 $ 16

Pinot Gris 2003 Clean, crisp, well made; surprising length and freshness. **RATING** 87 **DRINK** Now $ 16

Shiraz 2002 Finely tempered black plum/blackberry/black cherry fruit; not yet complex. **RATING** 87 **DRINK** 2011 $ 25

ŸŸŸŸ **Merlot 2002 RATING** 84 **DRINK** 2007 $ 15

Cabernet Franc Merlot 2000 RATING 84 **DRINK** Now $ 17

ŸŸŸ **Cabernet Franc Merlot 2001 RATING** 83 $ 17

Mount Markey   NR

Swifts Creek–Omeo Road, Cassilis, Vic 3896 **REGION** Gippsland
T (03) 5159 4264 **F** (03) 5159 4599 **OPEN** Wed–Mon 10–5
WINEMAKER Howard Reddish **EST.** 1991 **CASES** 750
PRODUCT RANGE ($13.50–18 CD) Morning Star Classic Dry White, Pinot Gris, Mountain Maid Chardonnay, The Howitt Pinot Noir, Cassilis Valley Dry Red, Lone Hand Cabernet Sauvignon; also honey meads, fruit wines.
SUMMARY Howard and Christine Reddish have established two vineyards, one of 2 hectares surrounding the winery, the other of 3 hectares on the slopes of Mount Markey, at an altitude of nearly 500 metres. The winery is appropriately built on the site of the Cassilis Wine Palace, which served the local goldmining families for almost 70 years until the gold ran out in the 1940s. A sheltered barbecue spot is among the many attractions for the general and wine tourist.

Mount Mary   ★★★★★

Coldstream West Road, Lilydale, Vic 3140 **REGION** Yarra Valley
T (03) 9739 1761 **F** (03) 9739 0137 **OPEN** Not
WINEMAKER Dr John Middleton **EST.** 1971 **CASES** 3000
PRODUCT RANGE ($32–60 ML) Chardonnay, Triolet (Sauvignon Blanc, Semillon, Muscadelle), Pinot Noir, Cabernets Quintet (Bordeaux blend).
SUMMARY Superbly refined, elegant and intense Cabernets and usually outstanding and long-lived Pinot Noirs fully justify Mount Mary's exalted reputation. The Triolet blend is very good, more recent vintages of Chardonnay even better. Limited quantities of the wines are sold through the wholesale/retail distribution system in Victoria, New South Wales, Queensland and South Australia.

Mount Moliagul

Clay Gully Lane, Moliagul, Vic 3472 **REGION** Bendigo
T (03) 9809 2113 **OPEN** By appointment, call 0427 221 641
WINEMAKER Terry Flora **EST.** 1991 **CASES** 500
PRODUCT RANGE ($15–30 ML) Unwooded Chardonnay, Pinot Noir, Shiraz, Shiraz Cabernet Sauvignon Merlot, Cabernet Sauvignon. Cerise (muscat), Fortified Riesling.

SUMMARY Terry and Bozenka Flora began the establishment of their tiny vineyard in 1991, gradually planting 0.5 hectare each of shiraz and cabernet sauvignon, and 0.2 hectare of chardonnay. Terry Flora has completed two winemaking courses, one with Winery Supplies and the other at Dookie College, and has learnt his craft very well. Has an outstanding 2003 Shiraz in the pipeline.

ΨΨΨΨ **Shiraz 2002** Dense inky purple; saturated blackberry and plum fruit; great depth and richness; not extractive. **RATING** 93 **DRINK** 2018 $ 30

ΨΨΨΨ **Cabernet Sauvignon 2002** Attractive mix of redcurrant and blackcurrant fruit; as yet, straight-line texture. **RATING** 87 **DRINK** 2012 $ 25

Mount Panorama Winery NR

117 Mountain Straight, Mount Panorama, Bathurst, NSW 2795 **REGION** Southern New South Wales Zone
T (02) 6331 5368 **OPEN** 7 days 10.30–5
WINEMAKER Desmond McMahon **EST.** 1991 **CASES** 600
PRODUCT RANGE ($10–18 CD) Riesling, Chardonnay, Shiraz, Honey Wine.
SUMMARY For all the obvious reasons, Mount Panorama Winery makes full use of its setting on Mountain Straight after the 'Hell Corner' on the inside of the famous motor racing circuit. All the winemaking is done on-site, from picking and using the hand-operated basket press through to bottling, labelling, etc. They are gradually extending both the size and scope of the cellar-door facilities to take advantage of the tourist opportunities of the site.

Mount Prior Vineyard

Gooramadda Road, Rutherglen, Vic 3685 **REGION** Rutherglen
T (02) 6026 5591 **F** (02) 6026 5590 **OPEN** 7 days 9–5
WINEMAKER Brian Devitt **EST.** 1860 **CASES** 10 000
PRODUCT RANGE ($17–40 CD) Dry white, sweet white, dry red, fortified and sparkling wines.
SUMMARY A full-scale tourist facility, with yet more in the pipeline: full accommodation packages at the historic Mount Prior House; a restaurant operating weekends under the direction of Trish Hennessy (for groups of six or more), with four consecutive *Age Good Food Guide* awards to its credit; picnic and barbecue facilities; and a California-style gift shop. The wines are basically sold through the cellar door and an active mailing list. The already substantial 112 hectares of vineyards were expanded by a further 5 hectares of durif planted in 1998, a mark both of the success of Mount Prior and of the interest in Durif.

ΨΨΨΨ **Reserve Port Museum Release NV** Christmas cake and spice aromas and flavours show the obvious wood age; chocolate, spice and biscuit. **RATING** 88 **DRINK** 2003 $ 40

ΨΨΨΨ **Director's Selection Muscat (375 ml) NV** Clean spirit, raisin and honey aromas; greater density than the price suggests, showing some older material with fresh, predominantly younger components; excellent value. **RATING** 86 **DRINK** Now $ 13

🐚 Mt Samaria Vineyard

RMB 1626 Midland Highway, Lima South, Vic 3673 **REGION** Goulburn Valley
T (03) 5768 2550 **OPEN** By appointment
WINEMAKER Various **EST.** 1992 **CASES** 400
PRODUCT RANGE ($15–17 CD) Pinot Gris, Shiraz, Cabernet Shiraz.
SUMMARY The 3-hectare Mt Samaria Vineyard, with shiraz (1.7 hectares) and tempranillo (0.8 hectare) having the lion's share, accompanied by a little cabernet and pinot gris, is owned and operated by Judy and Roger Cowan. Plantings took place over an 8-year period, and in the early days the grapes were sold to Delatite, the Cowans venturing into wine production only in 1999. Michael Reid at Auldstone makes part of the shiraz, and Roger Cowan (who has completed a short winemaking course at Dookie College) makes another portion, together with Cabernet Shiraz. The production sells out each year, most of the sales at the annual tastings at the winery and in Melbourne in May. Apart from a few local restaurants and the Tatong Farmers Market, the wine is sold by mail order.

ᵀᵀᵀᵀ **Shiraz 2002** Attractive earthy/spicy/leathery varietal character; light to medium-bodied; good length. **RATING** 88 **DRINK** 2009 $ 15

Cabernet Shiraz 2002 Well made; red and black fruits merge with sweet oak; soft tannins; good balance. **RATING** 88 **DRINK** 2010 $ 17

Mt Surmon Wines ★★★★

Scarlatties Cellar Door Gallery, Basham Road, Stanley Flat, SA 5453 **REGION** Clare Valley
T (08) 8842 1250 **F** (08) 8842 4064 **OPEN** Fri–Sun 10–5, or by appointment
WINEMAKER Neil Paulett (Contract) **EST.** 1995 **CASES** 500
PRODUCT RANGE ($16–19 CD) Riesling, Pinot Gris, Chardonnay, Sparkling Riesling, Shiraz, Cabernet Merlot, Cabernet Sauvignon.
SUMMARY The Surmon family has established just under 20 hectares of vineyard, half to shiraz, the remainder to cabernet sauvignon, nebbiolo, chardonnay, pinot gris and viognier. Most of the grapes are sold to other wineries (some on a swap basis for riesling and merlot), but small quantities are made by Neil Paulett and are sold through Scarlatties Cellar Door Gallery and a few local hotels. The first wines were made in 1999 (Cabernet Merlot and Shiraz), with white wines added in subsequent vintages.

ᵀᵀᵀᵀᵀ **Cabernet Sauvignon 2002** Ultra-concentrated blackberry and dark chocolate fruit; touches of herb and licorice; great value and a cellaring special, but oh, what a label. **RATING** 90 **DRINK** 2017 $ 19

🦘 Mount Torrens Vineyards NR

PO Box 1679, Mount Torrens, SA 5244 **REGION** Adelaide Hills
T (08) 8389 4229 **F** (08) 8389 4229 **OPEN** Not
WINEMAKER David Powell (Contract) **EST.** 1996
PRODUCT RANGE Shiraz Viognier under the Solstice and Mount Torrens Vineyards labels.
SUMMARY Mount Torrens Vineyards has 3 hectares of shiraz and viognier, with a distinguished team of Mark Whisson as viticulturist and David Powell as contract winemaker. The wines are available by mail order, but are chiefly exported to England and the US.

Mount Trio Vineyard ★★★★☆

Cnr Castle Rock and Porongurup Roads, Porongurup, WA 6324 **REGION** Porongurup
T (08) 9853 1136 **F** (08) 9853 1120 **OPEN** By appointment
WINEMAKER Gavin Berry **EST.** 1989 **CASES** 5000
PRODUCT RANGE ($14.50–22.50 R) Riesling, Sauvignon Blanc, Chardonnay, Pinot Noir, Shiraz, Cabernet Merlot, Liqueur Muscat.
SUMMARY Mount Trio was established by Gavin Berry and Gill Graham shortly after they moved to the Mount Barker district in late 1988. Gavin Berry was assistant winemaker to John Wade, and Gill managed the cellar-door sales. Gavin is now senior winemaker and managing director of Plantagenet, and Gill is the mother of two young children. In the meantime they have slowly built up the Mount Trio business, based in part upon estate plantings of 2 hectares of pinot noir and 0.5 hectare of chardonnay and in part on purchased grapes. An additional 6 hectares was planted in the spring of 1999, duly bringing production to its planned 5000-case level.

ᵀᵀᵀᵀᵀ **Riesling 2003** Crisp, firm mineral and herb; a tight palate, with hints of passionfruit. **RATING** 90 **DRINK** 2008 $ 16.50

Cabernet Merlot 2001 Elegant, medium-bodied wine with appropriately savoury edges to the black fruits; good length and finish. **RATING** 90 **DRINK** 2011 $ 17.50

ᵀᵀᵀᵀ **Sauvignon Blanc 2003** Moderately intense; spotlessly clean, with clearly expressed varietal fruit and good length. **RATING** 87 **DRINK** Now $ 14.90

Pinot Noir 2002 Savoury, dark plum and spice; plenty of upfront flavour, but fades slightly on the finish. **RATING** 87 **DRINK** Now $ 18

Mount View Estate ★★★☆

Mount View Road, Mount View, NSW 2325 **REGION** Lower Hunter Valley
T (02) 4990 3307 **F** (02) 4991 1289 **OPEN** 7 days 10–5
WINEMAKER Andrew Thomas (Consultant) **EST.** 1971 **CASES** 3100
PRODUCT RANGE ($12–40 CD) Reserve Semillon, Verdelho, Chardonnay, Merlot and Cabernet Sauvignon; Shiraz and Basalt Hill Shiraz Pinot; also fortifieds.
SUMMARY The Tulloch family no longer owns nor has any interest in Mount View Estate following its sudden sale in 2000, but winemaking has passed to the capable hands of former Tyrrell's winemaker Andrew Thomas. The 30-year-old vines are paying big dividends.

ŶŶŶŶŶ **Reserve Merlot 2002** Considerable depth and style; blackcurrant and redcurrant fruit; very good tannin and oak extract; they simply don't come better than this in the Hunter Valley. **RATING** 92 **DRINK** 2012 $ 24

ŶŶŶŶ **Reserve Cabernet Sauvignon 2002** Elegant savoury/chocolatey overtones to the medium-bodied palate; good length; from McLaren Vale. **RATING** 89 **DRINK** 2012 $ 20
Reserve Chardonnay 2003 Nicely balanced and integrated fruit and oak; a fleshy style for early drinking. **RATING** 88 **DRINK** 2007 $ 18

ŶŶŶŶ **Reserve Semillon 2003** **RATING** 86 **DRINK** 2010 $ 18

ŶŶŶ **Reserve Verdelho 2003** **RATING** 83 $ 16

Mountview Wines NR

Mount Stirling Road, Glen Aplin, Qld 4381 **REGION** Granite Belt
T (07) 4683 4316 **F** (07) 4683 4111 **OPEN** Fri–Sun 9.30–4.30, 7 days during school and public holidays
WINEMAKER Jim Barnes **EST.** 1990 **CASES** 1250
PRODUCT RANGE ($10–18 CD) Sauvignon Blanc Semillon, Classic Dry White, Emu Swamp Sweet White, Mount Stirling Bubbles (red and white), Cerise (rose), Shiraz, Merlot, Cabernet Merlot, Port.
SUMMARY Mountview Wines has changed hands and is now owned by Pauline Stewart. I have no reason to suppose the quality of the Shiraz (in particular) has diminished.

Mount William Winery ★★★☆

Mount William Road, Tantaraboo, Vic 3764 **REGION** Macedon Ranges
T (03) 5429 1595 **F** (03) 5429 1998 **OPEN** By appointment
WINEMAKER Murray Cousins, John Ellis (both Contract) **EST.** 1987 **CASES** 1500
PRODUCT RANGE ($15–38 CD) Bedbur's Riesling, Stuart's Block Semillon, Chardonnay Semillon, Chardonnay, Macedon Blanc de Blanc, Louise Clare (sparkling red), Pinot Noir, Cabernets.
SUMMARY Adrienne and Murray Cousins established 7.5 hectares of vineyards between 1987 and 1999, planted to pinot noir, cabernet franc, merlot and chardonnay. The wines are made under contract (at Hanging Rock) and are sold through a stone tasting room cellar-door facility which was completed in 1992, and through a number of fine wine retailers around Melbourne.

ŶŶŶŶŶ **Blanc de Blanc 1999** Tight, fine and elegant; very good balance and length; lingering acidity and aftertaste. Trophy Macedon Wine Show. **RATING** 94 **DRINK** 2007 $ 33

ŶŶŶ **Chardonnay 2000** **RATING** 83 $ 26
Pinot Noir 2000 **RATING** 83 $ 25

Mudgee Wines NR

Henry Lawson Drive, Mudgee, NSW 2850 **REGION** Mudgee
T (02) 6372 2258 **OPEN** Thurs–Mon 10–5, holidays 7 days
WINEMAKER David Conway **EST.** 1963 **CASES** 600
PRODUCT RANGE ($9–15 CD) Chardonnay, Gewurztraminer, Trebbiano, Riesling, Rose, Shiraz, Pinot Noir, Cabernet Sauvignon.
SUMMARY Following the acquisition of Mudgee Wines by the Conway family, the organic winemaking practices of the former owner Jennifer Meek have been discontinued, with conventional viticultural and winemaking practices now adopted.

Mulcra Estate Wines ★★★☆

13 Newton Avenue, Irymple, Vic 3498 (postal) **REGION** Murray Darling
T (03) 5024 5683 **F** (03) 5024 5683 **OPEN** Not
WINEMAKER Glen Olsen **EST.** 2002 **CASES** 1000
PRODUCT RANGE ($25 ML) Windmill Chardonnay Reserve, Windmill Petit Verdot Reserve.
SUMMARY Samuel and Anna Andriske were part of a wave of Germans who left their homeland in the 1840s to escape poverty, wars and religious differences. The majority settled in the Barossa Valley, but one group was brought to Geelong by its then mayor. Grape growing was part of a mixed farming business for the Andriskes, but in the wake of phylloxera, the third generation (Charles Andriske) moved to Mildura. His sons established Mulcra Estate in 1933, selling grapes to Mildara and also producing table grapes. Finally, the fifth generation, Marlene Andriske and son Mark, have taken the move from grape growing to winemaking, with 3 hectares of chardonnay, supplemented by grapes purchased from a local grower.

ΨΨΨΨ **Windmill Reserve Petit Verdot 2002** Unexpectedly rich and sweet black fruits, with plenty of structure and balanced tannins. **RATING** 88 **DRINK** 2010 $25

ΨΨΨΨ **Windmill Reserve Chardonnay 2002 RATING** 85 **DRINK** Now $25

Mulligan Wongara Vineyard ★★★

603 Grenfell Road, Cowra, NSW 2794 **REGION** Cowra
T (02) 6342 9334 **F** (02) 6342 9334 **OPEN** Sat, public holidays (Sun if a public holiday weekend) 10–4
WINEMAKER Nick Millichip (Consultant) **EST.** 1993 **CASES** 2000
PRODUCT RANGE ($15–20 CD) Chardonnay, Unwooded Chardonnay, Shiraz, Reserve Shiraz, Cabernet Sauvignon.
SUMMARY Andrew and Emma Mulligan began the establishment of their 16-hectare vineyard in 1993. Plantings now comprise chardonnay (14 hectares), shiraz (2.5 hectares), cabernet (3.5 hectares) and sangiovese (1 hectare); a significant part of the grapes are sold to others, the wines being made under contract at Cabonne. A striking tower cellar door and cellar are now open, and the wines are sold direct to Sydney restaurants and retailers.

ΨΨΨΨ **Chardonnay 2001 RATING** 86 **DRINK** 2007

Mulyan ★★★☆

North Logan Road, Cowra, NSW 2794 **REGION** Cowra
T (02) 6342 1289 **F** (02) 6341 1015 **OPEN** Sat–Mon and public holidays 10–5, or by appointment Mon–Fri (phone (02) 6342 1336)
WINEMAKER Simon Gilbert (Contract) **EST.** 1994 **CASES** 2000
PRODUCT RANGE ($11–25 CD) Chardonnay, Shiraz; Bushrangers Bounty Chardonnay, Shiraz.
SUMMARY Mulyan is a 1350-hectare grazing property purchased by the Fagan family in 1886 from Dr William Redfern, a leading 19th-century figure in Australian history. The current-generation owners, Peter and Jenni Fagan, began the establishment of 45 hectares of shiraz in 1994, and intend increasing the vineyard area to 100 hectares. Presently there are 29 hectares of shiraz and 15 hectares of chardonnay, with an experimental plot of sangiovese. The label features a statue of the Roman God Mercury which has stood in the Mulyan homestead garden since being brought out from Italy in 1912 by Peter Fagan's grandmother. The wines have limited Sydney retail distribution and are also available through the Quarry Cellars in Cowra.

ΨΨΨΨ **Cowra Shiraz 2001** Much more structure and depth than the Bushrangers version; darker fruit flavours, and savoury tannins. **RATING** 88 **DRINK** 2011 $25
Bushrangers Bounty Shiraz 2001 Light to medium-bodied; attractive cherry and raspberry fruit; early drinking. **RATING** 87 **DRINK** 2007 $15

Munari Wines ★★★★☆

1129 Northern Highway, Heathcote, Vic 3523 **REGION** Bendigo
T (03) 5433 3366 **F** (03) 5433 3095 **OPEN** 7 days 10–5
WINEMAKER Adrian Munari, Deborah Munari **EST.** 1993 **CASES** 2000
PRODUCT RANGE ($20–40 CD) Viognier, Chardonnay, Shiraz, Schoolhouse Red, Shiraz, Merlot, Malbec, Cabernet Sauvignon Cabernet Franc.

SUMMARY Adrian and Deborah Munari made a singularly impressive entry into the winemaking scene, with both their initial vintages winning an impressive array of show medals, and have carried on in similar vein since then. With a little under 8 hectares of estate vines, production will be limited, but the wines are well worth seeking out. Exports to the US and Korea.

ΨΨΨΨΫ **Cabernet Sauvignon 2002** Medium-bodied in typical elegant style; blackcurrant and mulberry; fine tannins, good length. **RATING** 92 **DRINK** 2012 $35

Schoolhouse Red 2002 Strong, deep colour; complex, rich and opulent, but not jammy; ripe tannins; Shiraz, Viognier and Cabernet Sauvignon. **RATING** 92 **DRINK** 2015 $35

The Bendigo Shiraz 2002 Elegant, medium-bodied; lovely black cherry and blackberry fruit; smooth, silky, supple. **RATING** 91 **DRINK** 2010 $20

Lady's Pass Shiraz 2002 Very complex licorice, black cherry, leather and spice aromas; intense flavours track the bouquet; well-handled oak and extract. **RATING** 90 **DRINK** Now $40

ΨΨΨΨ **The Last Chardonnay 2002** Rich, full, powerful stone fruit; grip and length. **RATING** 89 **DRINK** 2007 $25

One Off Viognier 2002 Undoubted varietal character; rich fruit pastille, apricot and dried apple; no phenolics. **RATING** 89 **DRINK** Now $25

Mundoonen

NR

Yass River Road, Yass, NSW 2582 **REGION** Canberra District
T (02) 6227 1353 **F** (02) 6227 1453 **OPEN** By appointment
WINEMAKER Terry O'Donnell **EST.** 2003 **CASES** 900
PRODUCT RANGE ($15–20 CD) Riesling, Late Harvest Riesling, Cabernet Sauvignon.
SUMMARY Jenny and Terry O'Donnell are new arrivals in the Canberra District region, releasing their first wines in August 2003. The estate winery is situated beside the Yass River behind one of the oldest settlers cottages in the Yass River Valley, dating back to 1858. Estate plantings of shiraz and viognier are supplemented by contract-grown riesling, sauvignon blanc and cabernet sauvignon. The barrel shed has been created by refurbishing and insulating a 140-year-old building on the property.

Mundrakoona Estate

NR

Sir Charles Moses Lane, Old Hume Highway, Woodlands via Mittagong, NSW 2575
REGION Southern New South Wales Zone
T (02) 4872 1311 **F** (02) 4872 1322 **OPEN** Weekends and public holidays 9–6
WINEMAKER Anton Balog **EST.** 1997 **CASES** 1800
PRODUCT RANGE ($18–32 CD) Riesling, Sauvignon Blanc, Reserve Chardonnay, Nouveau Rouge, Reserve Cabernet Sauvignon Merlot.
SUMMARY During 1998 and 1999 Anton Balog progressively planted 3.2 hectares of pinot noir, sauvignon blanc and tempranillo at an altitude of 680 metres. He is using wild yeast ferments, hand-plunging and other 'natural' winemaking techniques with the aim of producing Burgundian-style Pinot and Chardonnay and Bordeaux-style Sauvignon Blanc and Cabernet Sauvignon. For the foreseeable future, estate production will be supplemented by grapes grown from local Southern Highlands vineyards.

Murdoch Hill

★★★☆

Mappinga Road, Woodside, SA 5244 **REGION** Adelaide Hills
T (08) 8389 7081 **F** (08) 8389 7991 **OPEN** By appointment
WINEMAKER Brian Light (Contract) **EST.** 1998 **CASES** 1500
PRODUCT RANGE ($15–18 R) Sauvignon Blanc, Chardonnay, Cabernet Sauvignon.
SUMMARY A little over 21 hectares of vines have been established on the undulating, gum-studded countryside of the Erinka property, owned by the Downer family, 4 kilometres east of Oakbank. In descending order of importance, the varieties established are sauvignon blanc, shiraz, cabernet sauvignon and chardonnay. The wines are distributed by Australian Prestige Wines in Melbourne and Sydney.

ΨΨΨΨ **Sauvignon Blanc 2003** Floral passionfruit aromas; lemon tingle flavours, crisp, tangy finish. **RATING** 88 **DRINK** Now $17

Murdock ★★★★

Riddoch Highway, Coonawarra, SA 5263 **REGION** Coonawarra
T (08) 8737 3700 **F** (08) 8737 2107 **OPEN** Not
WINEMAKER Peter Bissell (Contract) **EST.** 1998 **CASES** 2000
PRODUCT RANGE ($20–42 CD) Riesling, Merlot, Cabernet Sauvignon.
SUMMARY The Murdock family has established 10.4 hectares of cabernet sauvignon, 2 hectares of shiraz, 1 hectare of merlot, and 0.5 hectare each of chardonnay and riesling, and produces small quantities of an outstanding Cabernet Sauvignon, contract-made by Peter Bissell at Balnaves. The labels, incidentally, are ultra-minimalist; no flood of propaganda here.

ȚȚȚȚȚ **Cabernet Sauvignon 2001** Inky purple; a massive wine with huge extract; abundant black fruits and tannins. **RATING** 93 **DRINK** 2020 $42

ȚȚȚȚ **Merlot 2001** Strong colour; clean, ripe redcurrant and raspberry; touches of spice, fine tannins and controlled oak. **RATING** 89 **DRINK** 2011 $24
Riesling 2002 Delicate floral blossom aromas, then a crisp, elegant and fresh palate; typical Coonawarra; the blossom will intensify with age. **RATING** 88 **DRINK** 2010 $20

🍇 Murdup Wines ★★★

Southern Ports Highway, Mount Benson, SA 5275 **REGION** Mount Benson
T (08) 8768 6190 **F** (08) 8768 6190 **OPEN** 7 days 10–4
WINEMAKER Ralph Fowler (Contract) **EST.** 1996 **CASES** 950
PRODUCT RANGE ($17–25 CD) Sauvignon Blanc, Shiraz, Cabernet Sauvignon.
SUMMARY Andy and Melinda Murdock purchased their property in 1996; when first settled as a grazing property in the 1860s it was called Murdup, and the Murdocks have adopted that name. Beginning in 1997, they have established 10 hectares of vineyard, the lion's share going to cabernet sauvignon and shiraz. Further plantings of shiraz and sauvignon blanc are in the pipeline.

ȚȚȚȚ **Shiraz 2002** Inky, impenetrable colour; extremely concentrated dark fruits/blackberries, but not too tannic. **RATING** 89 **DRINK** 2017 $25

ȚȚȚ **Cabernet Sauvignon 2002** **RATING** 83 $20
Sauvignon Blanc 2003 **RATING** 82 $17

🍇 Murray Estate NR

Tocumwal–Barooga Road, Yarrawonga, Vic 3730 **REGION** Murray Darling
T (03) 5745 8345 **F** (03) 5745 8346 **OPEN** Weekends 11–5
WINEMAKER John Weinert **EST.** 1997
PRODUCT RANGE ($10–16 CD) Riesling, Chenin Blanc, Brut Reserve, Shiraz, Barrel Fermented Shiraz, A Bit of Old Tawny, Fine Old Muscat.
SUMMARY John and Sue Weinert were involved from the ground up in planting their 2.6-hectare vineyard to riesling, chenin blanc, merlot, shiraz and cabernet sauvignon. They make the wines on-site, selling these through the cellar door and by mail order.

🍇 Murrin Bridge Wines NR

PO Box 16, Lake Cargelligo, NSW 2672 **REGION** Riverina
T (02) 6898 2264 **F** (02) 6898 2263 **OPEN** Not
WINEMAKER Dom Piromalli (Contract) **EST.** 1999 **CASES** 3500
PRODUCT RANGE ($11 ML) Chardonnay, Shiraz.
SUMMARY The Murrin Bridge Vineyard arose out of a program set up by the Aboriginal and Torres Strait Islander Commission (ATSIC) in 1999 with five members of the Murrin Bridge Aboriginal community, who had received training for a diploma in viticulture from the TAFE college at Griffith. Plantings began with 2 hectares of shiraz in 1999, followed by a further 8 hectares in 2000, and a yet further extension in 2002 with shiraz, semillon and chardonnay. Very attractive wine bottle stands are hand-made from local hardwoods gathered from the paddocks and banks of the Lachlan River.

Murrindindi ★★★★☆

Cummins Lane, Murrindindi, Vic 3717 **REGION** Upper Goulburn
T (03) 5797 8448 **F** (03) 5797 8448 **OPEN** Mon–Wed 9–4, Thurs–Sun 9–8.30 at Marmalades Café, Yea
WINEMAKER Alan Cuthbertson **EST.** 1979 **CASES** 1500
PRODUCT RANGE ($20 R) Chardonnay, Shiraz, Merlot, Cabernets Merlot, Cabernet Sauvignon.
SUMMARY Situated in an unequivocally cool climate, which means that special care has to be taken with the viticulture to produce ripe fruit flavours. In more recent vintages, Murrindindi has succeeded handsomely in so doing. Limited Sydney and Melbourne distribution through Wine Source.

🍷🍷🍷🍷🍷 **Cabernet 2002** Concentrated and intense black and red fruits, cedar and spice; nice oak. **RATING** 91 **DRINK** 2014 $ 20
Chardonnay 2001 Bright yellow-green; excellent balance and integration of fruit and oak; gently sweet melon, good length. **RATING** 90 **DRINK** 2007 $ 20

🍷🍷🍷🍷 **Shiraz 2002** Gently spicy, savoury edges; unforced, light to medium-bodied; good balance, fine tannins. **RATING** 89 **DRINK** 2008 $ 20
Merlot 2001 Savoury earthy, briary, olive flavours; builds on second taste. **RATING** 88 **DRINK** 2009 $ 20
Cabernet Sauvignon 2001 Savoury blackcurrant aromas; as with the Merlot, creeps up on you; initially light, spicy, herbal, then intensifies on the finish. **RATING** 88 **DRINK** 2010 $ 20

Murrumbateman Winery NR

Barton Highway, Murrumbateman, NSW 2582 **REGION** Canberra District
T (02) 6227 5584 **OPEN** Thurs–Sun 10–5
WINEMAKER Duncan Leslie **EST.** 1972 **CASES** 1500
PRODUCT RANGE ($14–30 CD) Riesling, Sauvignon Blanc, Verdelho, Sally's Sweet White, Rose, Shiraz, Cabernet Merlot, Mead, Fortifieds and Sparkling.
SUMMARY Revived after a change of ownership, the Murrumbateman Winery draws upon 4.5 hectares of vineyards, and also incorporates an à la carte restaurant and function room, together with picnic and barbecue areas.

Myrtaceae ★★★★☆

53 Main Creek Road, Red Hill, Vic 3937 **REGION** Mornington Peninsula
T (03) 5989 2045 **F** (03) 5989 2845 **OPEN** First weekend of each month and public holidays
WINEMAKER Julie Trueman **EST.** 1985 **CASES** 200
PRODUCT RANGE ($18–26 CD) Chardonnay, Cabernet Sauvignon.
SUMMARY The development of the Myrtaceae vineyard began in 1985 with the planting of 0.7 hectare of cabernet sauvignon, cabernet franc and merlot intended for a Bordeaux-style red blend. Between 1988 and 1996 the grapes were sold, but it became evident that these late-ripening varieties were not well suited to the site, and between then and 2000 the vineyard was converted to 0.5 hectare each of pinot noir and chardonnay. The remaining vintages of Cabernet Sauvignon in the cellar will be sold progressively, and in the future the releases will be solely of Pinot Noir and Chardonnay. The viticulturist is John Trueman, and the winemaker is his wife Julie Trueman; they are also the proprietors. Part of the property is devoted to the Land for Wildlife Scheme, with an extensive garden in the course of development, and a cellar-door sales area and courtyard opened in January 2003.

🍷🍷🍷🍷🍷 **Chardonnay 2002** Tangy, lively, grapefruit and citrus; long finish; perfect acidity. **RATING** 93 **DRINK** 2007 $ 27
Pinot Noir 2002 Elegant but intense; that finer structure and tighter acidity of the Main Ridge subregion; savoury, dark fruits. **RATING** 90 **DRINK** 2008 $ 27

Naked Range Wines

125 Rifle Range Road, Smiths Gully, Vic 3760 **REGION** Yarra Valley
T (03) 9710 1575 **F** (03) 9710 1655 **OPEN** By appointment
WINEMAKER Robert Dolan (Contract), Kate Goodman **EST.** 1996 **CASES** 2500
PRODUCT RANGE ($19–22 CD) Naked Range of Sauvignon Blanc, Chardonnay, Pinot Noir, Merlot, Cabernet Merlot, Cabernet Sauvignon.

SUMMARY Mike Jansz began the establishment of the Jansz Estate vineyard in 1996 at Smiths Gully, in the Diamond Valley subregion of the Yarra Valley. He has established 7 hectares of vineyard, one-third planted to sauvignon blanc, a small patch to pinot noir and the remainder to cabernet sauvignon (predominant), merlot and cabernet franc. The wines are made at the Punt Road winery by former Yarra Ridge winemaker Rob Dolan, and marketed under the striking Naked Range label, one calculated to give the US BATF cardiac arrest if ever the wines were to be exported there. Limited retail distribution in all States, and exports to the UK, Korea, Indonesia and Vietnam supplement cellar door and mail list sales.

ΨΨΨΨ **Sauvignon Blanc 2003 RATING** 85 **DRINK** Now $ 20.90
Pinot Noir 2003 RATING 84 **DRINK** Now $ 24.20

Nandroya Estate

NR

262 Sandfly Road, Margate, Tas 7054 **REGION** Southern Tasmania
T (03) 6267 2377 **OPEN** By appointment
WINEMAKER Andrew Hood (Contract) **EST.** 1995 **CASES** 400
PRODUCT RANGE ($20–25 CD) Sauvignon Blanc, Pinot Noir.
SUMMARY John Rees and family have established 0.75 hectare each of sauvignon blanc and pinot noir, the wines being sold through the cellar door and to one or two local restaurants. The Reeses regard it as a holiday and retirement project and modestly wonder whether they deserve inclusion in this work. They certainly do, for wineries of this size are an indispensable part of the Tasmanian fabric.

Narkoojee

★★★★

170 Francis Road, Glengarry, Vic 3854 **REGION** Gippsland
T (03) 5192 4257 **F** (03) 5192 4257 **OPEN** 10–4 by appointment
WINEMAKER Harry Friend, Axel Friend **EST.** 1981 **CASES** 1500
PRODUCT RANGE ($15–35 CD) Lily Grace Chardonnay, Reserve Chardonnay, The Rose, Pinot Noir, Myrtle Point Shiraz, Yorkie's Gully, Cabernet Sauvignon.
SUMMARY Narkoojee Vineyard is within easy reach of the old goldmining town of Walhalla, and looks out over the Strzelecki Ranges. The wines are produced from a little over 10 hectares of estate vineyards, with chardonnay accounting for half the total. Harry Friend was an amateur winemaker of note before turning to commercial winemaking with Narkoojee. His skills showing through with all the wines, none more so than the Chardonnay. Small amounts are exported; much is sold through the cellar door and the mailing list.

ΨΨΨΨΨ **Reserve Chardonnay 2002** Interesting aromas with hints of tobacco; complex, rich and mouthfilling; fig, peach, cream and cashew. **RATING** 94 **DRINK** 2007 $ 32

ΨΨΨΨ **Lily Grace Chardonnay 2002** Stone fruit and fig; some nutty/creamy notes; good balance, but fractionally short. **RATING** 89 **DRINK** Now $ 32
Cabernet Sauvignon 2001 A clean, medium-bodied mix of red and black fruits; particularly good length and finish. **RATING** 88 **DRINK** 2011 $ 28
Trafalgar Chardonnay 2002 Clean, gentle, light to medium-bodied; stone fruit/peach-driven; good acidity. **RATING** 87 **DRINK** Now $ 18

ΨΨΨΨ **The Athelstan Merlot 2001 RATING** 85 **DRINK** Now $ 35
Pinot Noir 2002 RATING 84 **DRINK** Now $ 30

Nashdale Wines

NR

Borenore Lane, Nashdale, NSW 2800 **REGION** Orange
T (02) 6365 2463 **F** (02) 6361 4495 **OPEN** Weekends 2–6
WINEMAKER Mark Davidson (Contract) **EST.** 1990 **CASES** 1000
PRODUCT RANGE ($10–25 CD) Riesling, Sauvignon Blanc, Chardonnay, Pinot Noir, Cabernet Sauvignon.
SUMMARY Orange solicitor Edward Fardell commenced establishing the 10-hectare Nashdale Vineyard in 1990. At an elevation of 1000 metres, it offers panoramic views of Mount Canobolas and the Lidster Valley, with a restaurant/café open on weekends.

Nassau Estate ★★★☆

Fish Fossil Drive, Canowindra, NSW 2804 **REGION** Cowra
T (02) 9267 4785 **F** (02) 9267 3844 **OPEN** Not
WINEMAKER Andrew Margan (Contract) **EST.** 1996 **CASES** 1500
PRODUCT RANGE ($19–23 R) Semillon, Chardonnay, Shiraz, Cabernet Sauvignon.
SUMMARY The Curran family established its 110-hectare vineyard adjacent to the Belubula River at Canowindra in 1996. The vineyard was named in honour of forebear Joseph Barbeler, who had been involved in a similar endeavour 140 years earlier in the Duchy of Nassau on the river Rhine near Frankfurt. A significant proportion of the grapes are contracted for sale to one of Australia's largest wineries, with selected amounts retained and contract-made for the Nassau Estate label by Andrew Margan.

Nazaaray NR

266 Meakins Road, Flinders, Vic 3929 **REGION** Mornington Peninsula
T (03) 9585 1138 **F** (03) 9585 1140 **OPEN** By appointment
WINEMAKER Paramdeep Ghumman **EST.** 1996 **CASES** 350
PRODUCT RANGE ($16–33 ML) Pinot Gris, Chardonnay, Pinot Noir.
SUMMARY Paramdeep Ghumman is, as far as I am aware, the only Indian-born winery proprietor and winemaker in Australia. He and his wife migrated from India 22 years ago, and purchased the Nazaaray vineyard property in 1991. An initial trial planting of 400 vines in 1996 was gradually expanded to the present level of 1.6 hectares of pinot noir, 0.4 hectare of pinot gris and 0.15 hectare of chardonnay. Notwithstanding the micro-size of the estate, all of the wines are made and bottled on-site, and both the 2001 ad 2002 Pinot Noirs were awarded bronze medals at the Cool Climate Wine Show.

Neagles Rock Vineyards ★★★★★

Lots 1 and 2 Main North Road, Clare, SA 5453 **REGION** Clare Valley
T (08) 8843 4020 **F** (08) 8843 4021 **OPEN** 7 days 10–5
WINEMAKER Neil Pike (Consultant), Steve Wiblin **EST.** 1997 **CASES** 6000
PRODUCT RANGE ($18–21 CD) Riesling, Semillon Sauvignon Blanc, Shiraz, Grenache, Grenache Shiraz, Sangiovese, Cabernet Sauvignon.
SUMMARY Owner-partners Jane Willson and Steve Wiblin have taken the plunge in a major way, simultaneously raising a young family, resuscitating two old vineyards, and — for good measure — stripping a dilapidated house to the barest of bones and turning it into a first-rate, airy restaurant-cum-cellar door (which I wholeheartedly recommend, from personal experience). They bring 35 years of industry experience to Neagles Rock. Jane Willson held a senior marketing position with Southcorp before heading up Negociants Australia's Sales and Marketing team in a 15-year career which brought her unqualified respect. Steve Wiblin's 20-year career spanned Guinness to Grange, public companies to small ones, marketing to finance. In 2003 Neagles Rock purchased the vineyards and winery of Duncan Estate, bringing its estate plantings to 25 hectares, two thirds planted prior to 1980. Exports to the US and Singapore.

▼▼▼▼▼ **Grenache Shiraz 2002** Light to medium-bodied; very supple, and lovely spicy overtones to the flavours. Fine tannins. **RATING** 94 **DRINK** 2009 $18

▼▼▼▼▽ **Cabernet Sauvignon 2002** Abundant blackcurrant/blackberry/mulberry fruit sweeps through the length of the palate; ripe tannins, nice oak. Great value. **RATING** 93 **DRINK** 2017 $21
Barrel Nurtured Semillon 2003 Complex and (relatively speaking) rich; ripe fruit flavours; dash of French oak; all work well. **RATING** 91 **DRINK** Now $17
Shiraz 2002 Medium-bodied, but with a complex web of black fruits, spice, mocha and ripe tannins; good length and finish. **RATING** 90 **DRINK** 2010 $21

▼▼▼▼. **Sangiovese 2002** Highly spicy black cherry; striking wine; lingering tannins. Made for Italian food. **RATING** 88 **DRINK** 2009 $21

Needham Estate Wines

NR

Ingoldby Road, McLaren Flat, SA 5171 **REGION** McLaren Vale
T (08) 8383 0301 **F** (08) 8383 0301 **OPEN** Not
WINEMAKER Contract **EST.** 1997 **CASES** 2800
PRODUCT RANGE ($17–25 R) Albertus Shiraz, White House Shiraz.
SUMMARY Clive Needham has two vineyards; the first, of 4 hectares, is newly planted and came into
full production in 2001. The second has less than 0.5 hectare of 100-year-old shiraz vines, which go
to produce the White House Shiraz, with an annual production of only 120 cases.

Neighbours Vineyards

NR

75 Fullarton Road, Kent Town, SA 5067 (postal) **REGION** McLaren Vale
T (08) 8331 8656 **F** (08) 8331 8443 **OPEN** Not
WINEMAKER Chester Osborn **EST.** 1995 **CASES** 800
PRODUCT RANGE ($26 ML) Shiraz.
SUMMARY Esteemed (and, dare I say, now senior) journalist Bob Mayne planted 1.6 hectares of Shiraz
in McLaren Vale in 1995, without any clear objective in mind, and certainly not planning on
venturing into winemaking. However, one thing leads to another, and in 1998 he formed Neighbours
Vineyards Pty Ltd, its 14 shareholders all being McLaren Vale grape growers.

Nelson Touch

NR

Hamilton Road, Denmark, WA 6333 **REGION** Denmark
T (08) 9385 3552 **F** (08) 9286 2060 **OPEN** Not
WINEMAKER Michael Staniforth (Contract) **EST.** 1990 **CASES** 2000
PRODUCT RANGE ($20–25 R) Sauvignon Blanc, Pinot Noir, Cabernet Merlot.
SUMMARY Barbara and Brett Nelson began the development of their vineyard back in 1990, and until
1999, they sold all of the grapes to other wineries, including Howard Park. While Howard Park
continues to receive some grapes, the lion's share of the plantings of the 1.5 hectares each of
sauvignon blanc, pinot noir and cabernet sauvignon, plus 0.5 hectare of merlot, is now used for the
Nelson Touch label. The name comes from the saying that Admiral Nelson had the 'Nelson touch'
when he defeated the French, because everything he did turned to naval gold.

Nepenthe Vineyards

★★★★★

Jones Road, Balhannah, SA 5242 **REGION** Adelaide Hills
T (08) 8431 7588 **F** (08) 8431 7688 **OPEN** 7 days 10–4
WINEMAKER Peter Leske, Louise Brightman **EST.** 1994 **CASES** 60000
PRODUCT RANGE ($12.99–50 R) Riesling, Semillon, Sauvignon Blanc, Tryst White, Unwooded
Chardonnay, Chardonnay, Pinot Gris, Pinot Noir, Tryst Red, Zinfandel, Tempranillo, The Rogue, The
Fugue (Cabernet Merlot).
SUMMARY The Tweddell family has established a little over 160 hectares of close-planted vineyards at
Lenswood since 1994, with an exotic array of varieties reflected in the wines. In late 1996 it obtained
the second licence to build a winery in the Adelaide Hills, Petaluma being the only other successful
applicant, back in 1978. A large winery has been constructed, with Peter Leske in charge of
winemaking. Nepenthe has quickly established itself as one of the most exciting new wineries in
Australia. Distribution through most States, and exports to the UK, the US, Canada, Switzerland,
Belgium, Italy, Austria, Denmark, Japan and Hong Kong.

ΨΨΨΨΨ **Adelaide Hills Riesling 2003** Passionfruit blossom aromatics; elegant, delicate but
focused palate, with great length, line and finish. Lovely wine. **RATING** 94 **DRINK** 2010 $ 20

ΨΨΨΨΨ **Pinot Gris 2002** Gris Pink tinges; spice, musk and peach fruit; has elegance along with
the abundant flavour. First class example of the style. **RATING** 93 **DRINK** Now $ 20
Alta Semillon Sauvignon Blanc 2003 Lots of aroma and flavour; passionfruit, citrus and
gooseberry; good balance and aftertaste. **RATING** 92 **DRINK** Now $ 18
The Rogue 2002 Cedary, earthy, spicy, savoury surrounds to blackcurrant fruit; good
tannins and length; stylish, Bordeaux-like. **RATING** 92 **DRINK** 2012 $ 17

Adelaide Hills Sauvignon Blanc 2003 A lively mix of gooseberry, citrus and a distinct splash of fruit spice/cinnamon (not oak); long finish. **RATING** 91 **DRINK** Now $ 20.99

Pinot Gris 2003 Pale blush colour; aromatic musk, apple and spice fruit; clear varietal definition. **RATING** 90 **DRINK** Now $ 20

ƳƳƳƳ **Pinot Noir 2002** Aromatic, ripe plum, spice and oak; very powerful; still in compartments. **RATING** 89 **DRINK** 2008 $ 28

Hungry Ground Cabernet Sauvignon 2001 Light to medium-bodied, minty/leafy/berry aromas and flavours; not over-extracted. **RATING** 88 **DRINK** 2008 $ 29.99

Lenswood Zinfandel 2002 Yes it is 'strongly varietal in a cool climate spicy mode', but the price is hot. **RATING** 88 **DRINK** 2009 $ 50

ƳƳƳƳ **Tryst Cabernet Tempranillo Zinfandel 2002** **RATING** 84 **DRINK** Now $ 14

ƳƳƳ **Tempranillo 2002** **RATING** 82 $ 25

⚘ New England Estate

NR

Delungra, NSW 2403 **REGION** Northern Slopes Zone
T (02) 6724 8508 **F** (02) 6724 8507 **OPEN** 7 days 10–5
WINEMAKER John Cassegrain (Contract) **EST.** 1997
PRODUCT RANGE A range of varietally denominated table wines reflecting the plantings.
SUMMARY New England Estate is situated 33 kilometres west of Inverell; Ross Thomas has established a very substantial vineyard of 36 hectares planted to chardonnay, cabernet sauvignon, merlot and shiraz. The wines are sold by mail order and through the cellar door, which has barbecue and picnic facilities. There is also a museum, and accommodation is available.

New Era Vineyard

NR

PO Box 239, Woodside, SA 5244 **REGION** Adelaide Hills
T (08) 8389 7562 **F** (08) 8389 7562 **OPEN** Not
WINEMAKER Paracombe (Contract) **EST.** 1988
PRODUCT RANGE Gold Cabernet Sauvignon.
SUMMARY Patricia Wark's 12.5-hectare vineyard, planted to chardonnay, cabernet sauvignon, merlot and shiraz, is under long-term contract to Wolf Blass, providing the grapes for Wolf Blass Adelaide Hills Cabernet Merlot. A tiny proportion of cabernet sauvignon is retained and contract-made at Paracombe.

New Glory

NR

931 Murray Valley Highway, Echuca, Vic 3564 **REGION** Goulburn Valley
T (03) 5480 7090 **F** (03) 5480 7096 **OPEN** 7 days 10–5
WINEMAKER Pat Colombo **EST.** 2000 **CASES** 16 000
PRODUCT RANGE ($7–20 CD) Chardonnay Sauvignon Blanc, Chardonnay, Echuca Rose, Romance, Sparking Chardonnay Sauvignon Blanc, Sparkling Shiraz, Sangiovese Merlot Petit Verdot, Shiraz Durif, Cabernet Sauvignon.
SUMMARY New Glory is the reincarnation of Echuca Estate Wines, which had New Glory Vineyard as its largest supplier amongst a matrix of contributing growers. The operation now has substantial plantings of shiraz, cabernet sauvignon, durif, petit verdot, sangiovese and mourvedre, the only white variety being verdelho.

Next Generation Wines

Grants Gully Road, Clarendon, SA 5157 **REGION** Adelaide Hills
T (08) 8383 5555 **F** (08) 8383 5551 **OPEN** Mon–Sat 9–5
WINEMAKER Natasha Mooney **EST.** 2001 **CASES** 400 000
PRODUCT RANGE ($11–18 R) The wines have four levels. The Fifth Element is the flagship range of Barossa Valley Shiraz and Eden Valley Riesling. Next comes The Collection series, from the Adelaide Hills and Margaret River, then Vin Five range from southeastern Australia. The fourth level is the budget-priced Stockman's Post range of Australian Dry Red and Dry White.

SUMMARY The trendily named Next Generation was the brainchild of wine industry professionals Sam Atkins and David Cumming, who have many years' experience between them working for some of Australia's largest companies. The appointment of Natasha Mooney, previously chief winemaker at Barossa Valley Estate, added significantly to the venture. In 2002 the business was acquired by Xanadu Wines, which has now commenced domestic distribution to supplement the original business base established in the UK under the Phoenix brand.

ȲȲȲȲ **NXG The Collection Margaret River Cabernet Sauvignon 2001** Savoury, earthy framework for blackcurrant fruit; well balanced, long finish. **RATING** 87 **DRINK** 2008 $18

ȲȲȲȲ **NXG The Collection Adelaide Hills Chardonnay 2000 RATING** 86 **DRINK** Now $17

ȲȲȲ **NXG Vin Five Shiraz 2001 RATING** 83 $11
NXG Vin Five Cabernet Sauvignon 2001 RATING 82 $11

ȲȲȲ **NXG Vin Five Chardonnay 2002 RATING** 79 $11

Nicholson River   ★★★☆

Liddells Road, Nicholson, Vic 3882 **REGION** Gippsland
T (03) 5156 8241 **F** (03) 5156 8433 **OPEN** 7 days 10–4 by appointment
WINEMAKER Ken Eckersley **EST.** 1978 **CASES** 3000
PRODUCT RANGE ($15–35 CD) 'Dry Gold Wines' include Semillon, Semillon Sauvignon Blanc, Chardonnay, Montview Chardonnay; 'Sweet Gold Wines' include Gippsland Chardonnay, Late Picked Semillon; 'Red Wines' include Pinot Noir, Gippsland Pinot Noir, Montview Pinot Noir, Cabernet Merlot and The Nicholson (Merlot Shiraz).
SUMMARY The fierce commitment to quality in the face of the temperamental Gippsland climate and the frustratingly small production has been handsomely repaid by some massive Chardonnays and quixotic red wines (from 9 hectares of estate plantings), mostly sold through the cellar door; a little is exported to the UK, Thailand and the US. Ken Eckersley does not refer to his Chardonnays as white wines but as gold wines, and lists them accordingly in his newsletter.

ȲȲȲȲȲ **Merlot 2001** Bramble, briar and olive; attractive red fruits at the centre; good control of extract. **RATING** 90 **DRINK** 2009 $27
The Nicholson 2000 Medium-bodied; clean, ripe blackberry/blackcurrant/ briar/spice flavours; lingering fine, savoury tannins. **RATING** 90 **DRINK** 2012 $27
Late Pick Chardonnay 2001 Intense and long palate, showing some botrytis complexity; balanced acidity. **RATING** 90 **DRINK** 2008 $15

ȲȲȲȲ **Pinot Noir 2001** Cherry and plum with a savoury twist; comes alive on the back palate and finish, like the proverbial peacock's tail. **RATING** 89 **DRINK** 2008 $35
Late Pick Semillon 2001 Richer and more powerful than the Chardonnay, but less complex and graceful. **RATING** 88 **DRINK** 2007 $15
Semillon Sauvignon Blanc 2002 Big, rich, bold, mouthfilling Nicholson River style; virtually unique these days. **RATING** 87 **DRINK** 2007 $22

ȲȲȲȲ **Chardonnay 2001 RATING** 86 **DRINK** 2007 $35
Cabernet Merlot 2001 RATING 85 **DRINK** 2010 $22

🐌 Nick Haselgrove Wines   NR

Range Road, Willunga Hill, SA 5172 **REGION** McLaren Vale
T (08) 8556 7340 **F** (08) 8556 7340 **OPEN** By appointment
WINEMAKER Nick Haselgrove **EST.** 1993
PRODUCT RANGE Shiraz.
SUMMARY This is the personal winemaking venture of Nick Haselgrove, utilising 10 hectares of shiraz to produce wines under the Nick Haselgrove and Blackbilly labels.

Nightingale Wines   ★★★☆

1239 Milbrodale Road, Broke, NSW 2330 **REGION** Lower Hunter Valley
T (02) 6579 1499 **F** (02) 6579 1477 **OPEN** 7 days 10–4
WINEMAKER Michael Caban, Nigel Robinson **EST.** 1997 **CASES** 10 000

PRODUCT RANGE ($18–25 CD) Semillon, Verdelho, Unwooded Chardonnay, Chardonnay, sparkling, Botrytis Semillon, Shiraz, Merlot, Cabernet Sauvignon, Port; Night Owl Selection Unwooded Chardonnay and Shiraz Cabernet Merlot.

SUMMARY Paul and Gail Nightingale have wasted no time since establishing their business in 1997. They have planted 3 hectares each of verdelho and merlot, 2 hectares of shiraz, 1.5 hectares each of chardonnay and cabernet sauvignon and 1 hectare of chambourcin. The wines are contract-made, and are sold only through the cellar door and an actively promoted wine club, and to selected local restaurants. Exports to the UK, Malaysia, Singapore and Canada.

ΤΤΤΤΤ **Semillon 2003** A touch of CO_2 will help the wine age; intense, long and incisive varietal fruit, precisely focused. Gold medal Hunter Valley Wine Show 2003. **RATING** 94
DRINK 2013 $ 22

ΤΤΤ **Cabernet Sauvignon 2002 RATING** 80 $ 21

🐾 Nillahcootie Estate ★★★★

RMB 1637, Lima South, Vic 3673 **REGION** Goulburn Valley
T (03) 5768 2666 **F** (03) 5768 2678 **OPEN** By appointment
WINEMAKER Sam Plunkett (Contract) **EST.** 1988 **CASES** 700
PRODUCT RANGE ($15–19 R) Chardonnay, Sparkling Shiraz, Shiraz, Lightning Ridge Shiraz, Shiraz Cabernet, Maggies Paddock (Merlot Cabernet Sauvignon).
SUMMARY Karen Davy and Michael White decided to diversify their primary business of beef cattle production on their 280-hectare property in 1988. Between then and 2001 they planted a little over 7 hectares of grapes, initially content to sell the production to other local wineries, but in 2001 they retained a small proportion of the grapes for their own label; the following year they increased this to the equivalent of 700 cases. In 2001 they purchased a 20-hectare property overlooking Lake Nillahcootie. They have renovated a homestead (available for rent) and commenced construction of the cellar door, due for completion by September 2004. The wines are sold in several Melbourne outlets (St Kilda Cellars and South Melbourne Cellars) and through restaurants and retailers in the region.

ΤΤΤΤΥ **Strathbogie Ranges Chardonnay 2003** A complex bouquet suggesting a touch of oak (there is none); plenty of depth, flavour and character to the ripe, luscious stone fruit palate. Impressive value. **RATING** 90 **DRINK** 2007 $ 16
Shiraz Cabernet 2002 Plenty of power and structure; savoury blackberry fruit builds all the way through to the finish. **RATING** 90 **DRINK** 2015 $ 15

ΤΤΤΤ **Shiraz 2002** Fresh, lively, supple red fruits in youthful, cool-grown style; a touch of vanilla oak adds interest. **RATING** 88 **DRINK** 2010 $ 15

🐾 Nirvana Estate NR

339 Sandy Creek Road, Kilcoy, Qld 4515 **REGION** Queensland Coastal
T (07) 5498 1055 **F** (07) 5498 1099 **OPEN** Tues–Sun and public holidays 10–5
WINEMAKER Contract **EST.** 1996
PRODUCT RANGE A range of varietally denominated table wines reflecting the plantings.
SUMMARY Julie Doolan has 5.3 hectares planted to sauvignon blanc, semillon, chardonnay, cabernet sauvignon, merlot and shiraz, contract-made off-site. The cellar door offers light meals, and can cater for concerts or festivals.

Noon Winery NR

Rifle Range Road, McLaren Vale, SA 5171 **REGION** McLaren Vale
T (08) 8323 8290 **F** (08) 8323 8290 **OPEN** Weekends 10–5 from November (while stock is available)
WINEMAKER Drew Noon MW **EST.** 1976 **CASES** 2500
PRODUCT RANGE ($15–25 CD) One Night (Rose), Solaire (Reserve Grenache), Eclipse (Grenache Shiraz), Reserve Shiraz, Reserve Cabernet, Vintage Port.
SUMMARY Drew Noon has returned to McLaren Vale and purchased Noon's from his parents (though father David still keeps an eye on things), after having spent many years as a consultant oenologist and viticulturist in Victoria, and thereafter as winemaker at Cassegrain. Some spectacular and unusual wines have followed, such as the 17.9 degrees alcohol Solaire Grenache, styled like an Italian

Amarone. Low prices mean each year's release sells out in 4–5 weeks. In 1998 Drew Noon gained the coveted Master of Wine (MW) award. Exports to the UK, the US, Canada, Germany, Switzerland, Belgium, Singapore, Japan and New Zealand.

Noosa Valley Winery NR

855 Noosa–Eumundi Road, Doonan, Qld 4562 **REGION** Queensland Coastal
T (07) 5449 1675 **F** (07) 5449 1679 **OPEN** Wed–Sat 11–5
WINEMAKER Robinsons (Contract) **EST.** 1999
PRODUCT RANGE ($14 CD) Chambourcin.
SUMMARY Irish-born George and Sue Mullins came to Australia over 30 years ago, but it was not until 1999 that they purchased the property and opened a bed and breakfast business. The potential for wine became obvious, and 550 chambourcin vines were planted in 2000 at the front of the 5-hectare property, giving rise to the first vintage in 2003. The cellar door also acts as a satellite cellar door for Robinsons wines, the contract winemaker.

No Regrets Vineyard NR

40 Dillons Hill Road, Glaziers Bay, Tas 7109 **REGION** Southern Tasmania
T (03) 6295 1509 **F** (03) 6295 1509 **OPEN** By appointment, also at Salamanca Market, Hobart, most Saturdays
WINEMAKER Andrew Hood (Contract), Eric Phillips **EST.** 2000 **CASES** 160
PRODUCT RANGE ($20–30 CD) Riesling, Gewurztraminer, Chardonnay, Miss Otis (sparkling), Pinot Noir.
SUMMARY Having sold Elsewhere Vineyard, Eric and Jette Phillips have turned around and planted another vineyard almost next door, called No Regrets. This is their 'retirement' vineyard, because they will be producing only one wine from the 1 hectare of pinot noir newly planted. The first vintage came in 2003; in the meantime they are selling residual stock from their days at Elsewhere Vineyard.

Normanby Wines ★★★

Rose-Lea Vineyard, Dunns Avenue, Harrisville, Qld 4307 **REGION** Queensland Zone
T (07) 5467 1214 **OPEN** 7 days winter 10–5, summer 10–7
WINEMAKER Kevin Watson, Andrew Hickinbotham (Contract) **EST.** 1999 **CASES** 800
PRODUCT RANGE ($14–18 CD) Verdelho, Rose, Veraz (Shiraz Verdelho), Shiraz, Port.
SUMMARY Normanby Wines fills in more of the Queensland viticultural jigsaw puzzle, situated approximately 50 kilometres due south of Ipswich. The vineyard comprises 1 hectare each of verdelho and shiraz, and 0.2 hectare each of chambourcin, durif and grenache. In a commendable display of courage, Normanby describes its 2002 Shiraz as 'a territorial Shiraz showing the unique quality and flavours of this region, which will soon be recognised as one of Australia's best'.

 Rose 2002 Light cherry fruit, slightly off-dry, but well enough balanced; summer style.
RATING 87 **DRINK** Now $ 16

 Verdelho 2003 RATING 84 **DRINK** Now $ 15
Country Shiraz 2002 RATING 84 **DRINK** Now $ 18

ТТТ **View Verdelho 2002 RATING** 83 $ 16
Veraz 2002 RATING 83 $ 16

Normans ★★★☆

Grant's Gully Road, Clarendon, SA 5157 **REGION** Adelaide Hills
T (08) 8383 5555 **F** (08) 8383 5551 **OPEN** Mon–Sat 9–4
WINEMAKER Natasha Mooney, Joel Tilbrook **EST.** 1853 **CASES** 80 000
PRODUCT RANGE ($9–40 R) The wines come in four ascending levels of price and quality: at the bottom, Lone Gum; then Encounter Bay; then Old Vine; Chais Clarendon at the top.
SUMMARY Following the acquisition of the Normans winery and brands by Xanadu Wines in October 2001, the two businesses have now been integrated from an administration and sales and marketing viewpoint. However, the production from the two wineries continues to be regionally focused and the individual brands remain intact. While the business now trades under the combined banner of

Xandadu Normans, some of the McLaren Vale and Adelaide Hills brands, notably Chais Clarendon at the top, continue.

ҰҰҰҰ️ **Chais Clarendon Shiraz 2001** Plush blackberry, plum, red berry and spice mix; smooth, supple and stylish; deft oak. **RATING** 91 **DRINK** 2011 $40

ҰҰҰҰ **Old Vine Cabernet Sauvignon 1999** Potent, powerful blackcurrant and blackberry fruit; lingering tannins, needing time. Fourteen per cent shiraz and cabernet franc in the blend. **RATING** 89 **DRINK** 2014 $25
Encounter Bay Shiraz 2001 Pleasant, medium-bodied; gentle berry fruit; supple and smooth. **RATING** 87 **DRINK** 2008 $14

ҰҰҰҰ️ **Chais Clarendon Cabernet Sauvignon 1999** **RATING** 86 **DRINK** 2009 $40

ҰҰҰ **Encounter Bay Classic Dry White 2002** **RATING** 83 $12

🦊 Norse Wines   NR

24 Damascus Road, Gin Gin, Qld 4671 **REGION** Queensland Coastal
T (07) 4157 3636 **F** (07) 4157 3637 **OPEN** 7 days 10–5
WINEMAKER Thomas Janstrom, Peter Janstrom **EST.** 1998
PRODUCT RANGE A range of varietally denominated table wines reflecting the plantings.
SUMMARY Peter and Dianna Janstrom have established their 2-hectare vineyard at Gin Gin, 37 kilometres due west of Bundaberg. Here they have chardonnay, verdelho, shiraz, cabernet sauvignon and touriga nationale, producing both table and fortified wines. The cellar door offers all the usual tourist facilities.

🦊 Norton Estate   ★★★☆

Plush Hannan Road, Lower Norton, Vic 3400 **REGION** Central Victorian Zone
T (03) 5384 8235 **F** (03) 8384 8235 **OPEN** 7 days 10–4
WINEMAKER Michael Unwin (Contract), Chris Spence, Peter Spence **EST.** 1997 **CASES** 600
PRODUCT RANGE ($17.50–27.50 CD) Sauvignon Blanc, Shiraz, Cabernet Sauvignon.
SUMMARY Donald Spence worked for the Victorian Department of Forests for 36 years before retiring in 1992. In 1996 he, wife Wendy and sons Christopher and Peter purchased a farm at Lower Norton, and instead of following the regional wool, meat and wheat farming, trusted their instincts in planting vines on the lateritic buckshot soil. The vineyard is 6 kilometres northwest of the Grampians GI, and will have to be content with the Central Victorian Zone until a sufficient number of others follow suit and plant on the 1000 or so hectares of suitable soil in the Lower Norton area. The Spences have planted 2.5 hectares of shiraz, 1.43 hectares of cabernet sauvignon and 0.4 hectare of sauvignon blanc, intending to double the plantings once the Wimmera Irrigation System comes on stream.

ҰҰҰҰ **Shiraz 2001** Pleasant, light to medium-bodied; black cherry/blackberry fruit; good flow, fine tannins. **RATING** 88 **DRINK** 2009 $24.95
Cabernet Sauvignon 2001 Ripe blackcurrant fruit; slightly simple, but unforced and flows well. **RATING** 87 **DRINK** 2008 $24.95

ҰҰҰ **Sauvignon Blanc 2003** **RATING** 83 $17.50

Nugan Estate   ★★★☆

60 Banna Avenue, Griffith, NSW 2680 **REGION** Riverina
T (02) 6962 1822 **F** (02) 6962 6392 **OPEN** Mon–Fri 9–5
WINEMAKER Daren Owers **EST.** 1999 **CASES** 400 000
PRODUCT RANGE ($8.99–29.95 R) Under the Nugan Estate label are individual vineyard varietals (Riesling, Sauvignon Blanc, Chardonnay, Durif, Cabernet Sauvignon); a large number of varietals under the cheaper Cookoothama brand.
SUMMARY Nugan Estate has arrived on the scene like a whirlwind. It is an offshoot of the Nugan group, a family company established over 60 years ago in Griffith as a broad-based agricultural business. It is headed by Michelle Nugan, inter alia the recipient of an Export Hero Award 2000. Nine years ago the company began developing vineyards, and it is now a veritable giant, with 310

hectares at Darlington Point, 52 hectares at Hanwood and 120 hectares at Hillston (all in New South Wales), 100 hectares in the King Valley, Victoria, and 10 hectares in McLaren Vale. In addition, it has contracts in place to buy 1000 tonnes of grapes per year from Coonawarra. It sells part of the production as grapes, part as bulk wine and part under the Cookoothama and Nugan Estate labels. Exports to the US, Canada, Ireland, Norway, Denmark, Sweden and New Zealand.

ΥΥΥΥΥ **Cookoothama Riesling 2003** Very complex, rich and full; distinct fruit sweetness. RATING 91 DRINK 2008
Cookoothama Botrytis Semillon 2002 Complex; very sweet brulée style; tropical glazed fruits, good acidity. RATING 90 DRINK Now $21.45

ΥΥΥΥ **Manuka Grove Vineyard Durif 2002** Dense, deep; compact and rich dark fruits; nice touches of cedar and spice; ideally suited to the region. RATING 88 DRINK 2007 $24
Frasca's Lane Vineyard Sauvignon Blanc 2002 Clean, quite ripe gooseberry and passionfruit; nice mouthfeel. RATING 87 DRINK Now $19.95
Cookoothama Pigeage Merlot 2002 Considerable fruit depth; blackcurrant with savoury notes; slightly short finish. RATING 87 DRINK 2008 $26.95
Alcira Vineyard Coonawarra Shiraz 2002 Smoky, earthy, dusty overtones to red fruit; a touch of lift; fine tannins. RATING 87 DRINK 2006 $23.95

ΥΥΥΥ **Cookoothama Shiraz 2002** RATING 86 DRINK 2007 $15.95
Alcira Vineyard Cabernet Sauvignon 2001 RATING 86 DRINK Now $22.95
Cookoothama Sauvignon Blanc 2003 RATING 85 DRINK Now $15.95
Frasca's Lane Vineyard Chardonnay 2002 RATING 85 DRINK Now $18.95
Cookoothama Chardonnay 2002 RATING 84 DRINK Now $16
Family 3rd Generation Chardonnay 2002 RATING 84 DRINK Now

ΥΥΥ **Family 3rd Generation Cabernet Sauvignon 2002** RATING 82
Talinga Park Cabernet Merlot 2002 RATING 80 $8.99

ΥΥΥ **Talinga Park Chardonnay 2001** RATING 79 $8.99

Nuggetty Vineyard ★★★☆

280 Maldon–Shelbourne Road, Nuggetty, Vic 3463 REGION Bendigo
T (03) 5475 1347 F (03) 5475 1647 OPEN Weekends and public holidays 10–4, or by appointment
WINEMAKER Greg Dedman, Jackie Dedman EST. 1993 CASES 1000
PRODUCT RANGE ($15–30 CD) Semillon, Shiraz, Cabernet Sauvignon.
SUMMARY The family-owned vineyard was established in 1994 by Greg and Jackie Dedman. Greg (a Charles Sturt University graduate) is also chief winemaker at Blue Pyrenees Estate, while Jackie (having spent 18 months at Bowen Estate between March 1997 and August 1998) has simultaneously undertaken the wine marketing degree at Charles Sturt University and the winemaking degree at the University of Adelaide. They share the vineyard and winery tasks, which include 6.5 hectares of estate plantings (semillon, shiraz and cabernet sauvignon). Mailing list and cellar-door sales are available while stocks last.

ΥΥΥΥΥ **Shiraz 2001** Rich, medium to full-bodied; appealing array of black fruits and licorice; good tannin structure; nice oak. RATING 91 DRINK 2011 $25

ΥΥΥΥ **Cabernet Sauvignon 2001** RATING 86 DRINK 2010 $25
Barrel Fermented Semillon 2001 RATING 84 DRINK Now $15

Nursery Ridge Estate ★★★

Calder Highway, Red Cliffs, Vic 3496 REGION Murray Darling
T (03) 5024 3311 F (03) 5024 3311 OPEN By appointment
WINEMAKER Donna Stephens EST. 1999 CASES 1100
PRODUCT RANGE ($14–16 R) Sparkling Shiraz, Cassia Street Shiraz, Shiraz Cabernet, Petit Verdot, Cottrell's Hill Cabernet Sauvignon, Parb's Cabernet Sauvignon.
SUMMARY The estate takes its name from the fact that it is situated on the site of the original vine nursery at Red Cliffs. It is a family-owned and operated affair, with shiraz, cabernet sauvignon, chardonnay and petit verdot in production, and viognier planted in 2001. A cellar door and new winery site on the Calder Highway, Red Cliffs, opened in 2001. The well-priced wines are usually well

made, with greater richness and depth of fruit flavour than most other wines from the region, although I didn't know what to make of the incredibly dense and powerful 2001 Petit Verdot. Production is planned to rise from 60 tonnes to a total of 250 tonnes.

Oak Dale Wines

NR

40 Titford Road, Tresco, Vic 3583 **REGION** Swan Hill
T (03) 5037 2911 **F** (03) 5037 2911 **OPEN** By appointment
WINEMAKER Robert Zagar (Contract) **EST.** 2000
PRODUCT RANGE Mourvedre (Mataro) and fortified wines.
SUMMARY Glen and Anne Cook have established 6.3 hectares of mourvedre, muscat and sultana; the latter two are especially suited to the fortified wines made for them, while the mourvedre is dual purpose. The relatively small amount of wine made is sold locally, by mail order and through the cellar door.

Oakover Estate

14 Yukich Close, Middle Swan, WA 6056 **REGION** Swan Valley
T (08) 9274 0777 **F** (08) 9274 0788 **OPEN** 7 days 11–5
WINEMAKER Julie White (Contract) **EST.** 1990 **CASES** 3500
PRODUCT RANGE ($16.50–22.50 CD) Verdelho, Chenin Blanc, S.V. Classic (Chardonnay Chenin Blanc), Chardonnay, Shiraz, Cabernet Sauvignon.
SUMMARY Owned by the Yukich family, part of the long-established Dalmatian Coast/Croatian cultural group in the Swan Valley, with its roots going back to the early 1900s. However, Oakover Estate is very much part of the new wave in the area, with a very large vineyard holding of 64 hectares, planted predominantly to chardonnay, shiraz, chenin blanc and verdelho. Part of the production is sold to others, and the talented Julie White is contract winemaker for the 3500 cases sold through the cellar door and the large, new café/restaurant and function centre situated in the heart of the vineyard.

Oakridge

864 Maroondah Highway, Coldstream, Vic 3770 **REGION** Yarra Valley
T (03) 9739 1920 **F** (03) 9739 1923 **OPEN** 7 days 10–5
WINEMAKER David Bicknell **EST.** 1978
PRODUCT RANGE ($18.99–30.50 CD) Sauvignon Blanc, Chardonnay, sparkling, Rose, Pinot Noir, Shiraz, Merlot, Cabernet Merlot, Cabernet Sauvignon.
SUMMARY The 1997 capital raising by Oakridge Vineyards Limited led to the opening of a new winery on a prominent Maroondah Highway site in 1998. In 2001 the then struggling company was acquired by Evans & Tate. The appointment of David Bicknell (formerly for many years at De Bortoli) has revitalised the winemaking. Exports to the US, Canada, Switzerland and the Philippines.

TTTTT **Chardonnay 2002** Fine, elegant, intense racy style; grapefruit and melon flavours, subtle oak. Screwcap. **RATING** 93 **DRINK** 2010 $24
Pinot Noir 2002 The bouquet is slightly muffled, but will open. Complex spicy/stemmy flavours with considerable length, line and intensity coming through on the palate. Screwcap. **RATING** 91 **DRINK** 2010 $24
Shiraz 2002 Fragrant red and black fruits from cherry to blackberry; fine tannins; elegant, cool climate wine. **RATING** 91 **DRINK** 2012 $25.50
Sauvignon Blanc 2003 Crisp, lively mix of gooseberry, asparagus and passionfruit; penetrating lemony acidity; long finish. **RATING** 90 **DRINK** 2006 $18.99
Sauvignon Blanc 2002 Clean, clearly articulated varietal blossom aromas; fresh, light, lively mineral and gooseberry palate. Screwcap. **RATING** 90 **DRINK** Now $18.99
Cabernet Sauvignon 2001 Bright, fresh, casis/blackcurrant fruit; fine tannins and subtle oak; delicious. **RATING** 90 **DRINK** 2010 $30.50

TTTT **Cabernet Merlot 2001** A solid mix of blackcurrant, cassis and olive; builds on the long finish. **RATING** 88 **DRINK** 2010 $18.99

TTTT **Rose 2003** Lively, fresh, zesty and not sweet; nice summer wine. **RATING** 86 **DRINK** Now $18

Oakvale ★★★☆

Broke Road, Pokolbin, NSW 2320 **REGION** Lower Hunter Valley
T (02) 4998 7088 **F** (02) 4998 7077 **OPEN** 7 days 10–5
WINEMAKER Cameron Webster **EST.** 1893 **CASES** 17 000
PRODUCT RANGE ($17–30 CD) Gold Rock range of Semillon Chardonnay, Verdelho, Chardonnay, Shiraz; Reserve range of Elliott's Well Semillon, Peach Tree Chardonnay, Peppercorn Shiraz
SUMMARY All of the literature and promotional material emphasises the fact that Oakvale has been family-owned since 1893. What it does not mention is that three quite unrelated families have been the owners: first, and for much of the time, the Elliott family; then former Sydney solicitor Barry Shields; and then, since 1999, Richard and Mary Owens, who also own the separately run Milbrovale winery at Broke. Be that as it may, the original slab hut homestead of the Elliott family, which is now a museum, and the atmospheric Oakvale winery, are in the 'must visit' category. The winery complex offers a delicatessen, coffee shop, a book shop and has picnic and playground facilities. Live entertainment each weekend between 11 am and 3 pm. Exports to the UK, Ireland and the US.

ΥΥΥΥ **Elliott's Well Semillon 2001** Very complex, with some bottle-developed characters, and the suggestion of some botrytis; strays into tropical territory on the palate. Drink sooner rather than later. **RATING** 89 **DRINK** Now $ 25
Peppercorn Shiraz 2002 Light to medium-bodied; red and black fruits; supple and unforced; good regional typicity. **RATING** 87 **DRINK** 2010 $ 30

ΥΥΥ? **Sparkling Shiraz 1999** **RATING** 86 **DRINK** 2008 $ 39
Gold Rock Shiraz 2002 **RATING** 85 **DRINK** 2007 $ 19.50

ΥΥΥ **Gold Rock Verdelho 2003** **RATING** 83 $ 19.50

Observatory Hill Vineyard NR

107 Centauri Drive, Mount Rumney, Tas 7170 (postal) **REGION** Southern Tasmania
T (03) 6238 5380 **OPEN** Not
WINEMAKER Andrew Hood (Contract) **EST.** 1991 **CASES** 50
PRODUCT RANGE ($22–23 ML) Chardonnay, Cabernet Sauvignon.
SUMMARY Chris and Glenn Richardson have developed their vineyard slowly since acquiring the property in 1990. In 1991 50 vines were planted, another 300 were planted in 1992, and further plantings over the intervening years lifted the total to 1.2 hectares in 2002. Whatever wine is not sold by mail order is sometimes available at the nearby Mornington Inn.

Occam's Razor ★★★★

c/- Jasper Hill, Drummonds Lane, Heathcote, Vic 3523 (postal) **REGION** Heathcote
T (03) 5433 2528 **F** (03) 5433 3143 **OPEN** Not
WINEMAKER Emily Laughton **EST.** 2001 **CASES** 400
PRODUCT RANGE ($36 R) Shiraz.
SUMMARY Emily Laughton has decided to follow in her parents' footsteps after first seeing the world and having a range of casual jobs. Having grown up at Jasper Hill, winemaking was far from strange, but she decided to find her own way, buying grapes from a small vineyard owned by Jasper Hill employee Andrew Conforti and his wife Melissa. She then made the wine 'with guidance and inspiration from my father, and with assistance from winemaker Mario Marson'. The name comes from William of Ockham (also spelt Occam) (1285–1349), a theologian and philosopher responsible for many sayings, including that appearing on the back label of the wine: 'what can be done with fewer is done in vain with more'. Only 400 cases are made, and the wine is being exclusively distributed in fine restaurants across Australia.

Oddfellows Wines ★★★★

PO Box 88, Langhorne Creek, SA 5255 **REGION** Langhorne Creek
T (08) 8537 3326 **F** (08) 8537 3319 **OPEN** Not
WINEMAKER Greg Follett **EST.** 1997 **CASES** 2300
PRODUCT RANGE ($18–29 ML) Shiraz, Shiraz Cabernet.

SUMMARY An export-oriented business buying its grapes from a range of Langhorne Creek grape growers. Exports to Singapore, China, the US, Canada and Belgium are supplemented by direct sales in Australia.

ŸŸŸŸ♀ **Langhorne Creek Shiraz Cabernet 2001** Very much richer, more concentrated and sturdy than the 2002; abundant blackberry and plum fruit; good tannins. A more predictable gold medal winner (Perth 2003). **RATING** 93 **DRINK** 2016 $ 28
Langhorne Creek Shiraz Cabernet 2002 Fragrant, highly aromatic red fruits; fresh flavours; elegant, light to medium-bodied style. Not your average gold medal winner (Adelaide 2003). **RATING** 90 **DRINK** 2010 $ 28

Old Caves

NR

New England Highway, Stanthorpe, Qld 4380 **REGION** Granite Belt
T (07) 4681 1494 **F** (07) 4681 2722 **OPEN** Mon–Sat 9–5, Sun 10–4
WINEMAKER David Zanatta **EST.** 1980 **CASES** 3000
PRODUCT RANGE ($12–19.50 CD) Chardonnay, Light Red, Zinfandel, Merlot, Cabernet Merlot and a range of generic wines in both bottle and flagon, including fortifieds.
SUMMARY Old Caves is a family business run by David, his wife Shirley and their three sons, Tony, Jeremy and Nathan, drawing on 5 hectares of estate vineyards. The wines are sold locally, through the cellar door and by mail order.

Old Kent River

★★★★☆

Turpin Road, Rocky Gully, WA 6397 **REGION** Frankland River
T (08) 9855 1589 **F** (08) 9855 1660 **OPEN** At South Coast Highway, Kent River Wed–Sun 9–5 (extended hours during tourist season)
WINEMAKER Alkoomi (Contract), Michael Staniford **EST.** 1985 **CASES** 3000
PRODUCT RANGE ($19.50–65 CD) Sauvignon Blanc, Chardonnay, Pinot Noir, Reserve Pinot Noir, Shiraz, Diamontina (Sparkling).
SUMMARY Mark and Debbie Noack have done it tough all of their relatively young lives, but have earned respect from their neighbours and from the other producers to whom they sell more than half the production from the 16.5-hectare vineyard they have established on their sheep property. More importantly still, the quality of their wines goes from strength to strength. Exports to Canada, the UK, The Netherlands, Hong Kong and Japan.

Old Loddon Wines

★★★

5 Serpentine Road, Bridgewater, Vic 3516 **REGION** Bendigo
T (03) 5437 3197 **F** (03) 5438 3502 **OPEN** Weekends 11–5, Mon–Fri by appointment
WINEMAKER Graeme Leith **EST.** 1995 **CASES** 5000
PRODUCT RANGE ($15–16 CD) Merlot, Merlot Franc, Franc, Cabernet Blend, Cabernet Sauvignon.
SUMMARY Russell and Jill Burdett began planting 3 hectares of cabernet franc, merlot, cabernet sauvignon and shiraz on the banks of the Loddon River at Bridgewater in 1987. Until 1995, all of the grapes were sold to other makers (including Passing Clouds), but in that year the Burdetts began to vinify part of the production. They have steadily increased their own wine production since that time with the assistance of their daughters Brooke and Lisa. All of the wine is sold through the cellar door and by mailing list.

ŸŸŸŸ **Franc 2002** As with all the Old Loddon wines, picked very ripe, but works much better here; black fruits/dark plums; sweet but not jammy. **RATING** 88 **DRINK** 2010 $ 16

ŸŸŸ♀ **Cabernet Sauvignon 2002** **RATING** 86 **DRINK** 2008 $ 15
Merlot 2002 **RATING** 84 **DRINK** 2007 $ 16

Old Station Vineyard

★★★☆

St Vincent Street, Watervale, SA 5452 **REGION** Clare Valley
T 0414 441 925 **F** (02) 9144 1925 **OPEN** Not
WINEMAKER David O'Leary, Nick Walker (Contract) **EST.** 1926 **CASES** 2000
PRODUCT RANGE ($12–20 ML) Watervale Riesling, Watervale Free Run Rose, Grenache Shiraz, Shiraz.

SUMMARY When Bill and Noel Ireland decided to retire from the Sydney retail scene in 1996 to go all the way up (or down) the production stream and become grape growers and winemakers, they did not muck around. In 1995 they had purchased a 6-hectare, 70-year-old vineyard at Watervale and formed a significantly larger joint venture in the Margaret River region, which has given birth to Flinders Bay wines. In its first year of shows the Old Station Vineyard wines won two gold, three silver and 8 bronze medals, a reflection of the strength of old vines and the skills of O'Leary and Walker. Now, I just wonder what Bill Ireland feels about retailers who slash and burn the theoretical retail price of his wines.

O'Leary Walker Wines ★★★★★

Main Road, Leasingham, SA 5452 (PO Box 49, Watervale, SA 5452) **REGION** Clare Valley
T (08) 8843 0022 **F** (08) 8843 0156 **OPEN** Not
WINEMAKER David O'Leary, Nick Walker **EST.** 2001 **CASES** 14 000
PRODUCT RANGE ($19–21 R) Riesling, Semillon, Sauvignon Blanc, Chardonnay, Pinot Noir, Shiraz and Cabernet Merlot variously from the Clare and Eden Valleys, Adelaide Hills and McLaren Vale.
SUMMARY David O'Leary and Nick Walker have more than 30 years' combined experience as winemakers working for some of the biggest Australian wine groups. They have taken the plunge, and have backed themselves to establish their own winery and brand. Their main vineyard is at Watervale in the Clare Valley, with over 36 hectares of riesling, shiraz, cabernet sauvignon, merlot and semillon. In the Adelaide Hills they have established 14 hectares of chardonnay, cabernet sauvignon, pinot noir, shiraz, sauvignon blanc and merlot. Winemaking skills are not in doubt, and nor is the quality of the vineyards. Wine prices are highly competitive. Exports to the US, Canada, the UK, Indonesia and Singapore.

ŸŸŸŸŸ **Watervale Riesling 2003** Firm, focused, herb, citrus and slate aromas, then a generous but not flabby palate, with excellent balance, mouthfeel and length. Right in the slot.
RATING 94 **DRINK** 2013 $ 19.50

ŸŸŸŸŸ **Clare Valley McLaren Vale Shiraz 2002** Blackberry, licorice and spice; fine texture; good tannin/oak management. **RATING** 93 **DRINK** 2012 $ 20.95
Polish Hill River Riesling 2003 Light green-yellow; passionfruit, lime and mineral run through a wine of depth and power. **RATING** 92 **DRINK** 2010 $ 19.50
Clare Valley Adelaide Hills Cabernet Merlot 2002 Brimming with ripe fruit, the sweetness neatly offset by hints of olive and supple tannins. **RATING** 91 **DRINK** 2012 $ 19.50

ŸŸŸŸ **Adelaide Hills Pinot Noir 2002** Lots of character and power; rich, full, spicy fruit, verging on plum pudding. For robust game dishes. **RATING** 89 **DRINK** 2008 $ 20.95
Adelaide Hills Chardonnay 2002 Light and delicate, with minerally overtones; delicate oak a plus. **RATING** 87 **DRINK** Now $ 20.95

ŸŸŸ **Adelaide Hills Sauvignon Blanc 2003** **RATING** 83 $ 19.50

Olive Farm NR

77 Great Eastern Highway, South Guildford, WA 6055 **REGION** Swan Valley
T (08) 9277 2989 **F** (08) 9277 6828 **OPEN** Wed–Sun 10–5.30 cellar sales, 11.30–2.30 café
WINEMAKER Ian Yurisich **EST.** 1829 **CASES** 3500
PRODUCT RANGE ($11.50–35 CD) Traminer, Sauvignon Blanc Semillon, Chenin Blanc, Classic White, Verdelho, Unwooded Chardonnay, Chardonnay, Sauterne Style, Pinot Noir, Shiraz, Merlot, Cabernet Shiraz Merlot, Cabernet Sauvignon, fortifieds, sparkling.
SUMMARY The oldest winery in Australia in use today, and arguably the least communicative. The ultra-low profile in no way inhibits flourishing cellar-door sales. The wines come from 14 hectares of estate plantings of 11 different varieties.

Oliverhill NR

Seaview Road, McLaren Vale, SA 5171 **REGION** McLaren Vale
T (08) 8323 8922 **F** (08) 8323 8916 **OPEN** By appointment
WINEMAKER Stuart Miller **EST.** 1973 **CASES** 3000
PRODUCT RANGE ($18–25 CD) Jimmy Section Shiraz, Bradey Block Grenache, Cabernet Sauvignon.

SUMMARY Stuart and Linda Miller purchased the property in a thoroughly run-down state in 1993, and gradually restored the vineyard and winery. The wines are sold through the cellar door, and via the online retailer auswine.com.au; small exports to the US and Canada.

Olivers Taranga Vineyards ★★★☆

Olivers Road, McLaren Vale, SA 5171 **REGION** McLaren Vale
T (08) 8323 8498 **F** (08) 8323 7498 **OPEN** By appointment
WINEMAKER Corrina Rayment **EST.** 1839 **CASES** 3000
PRODUCT RANGE ($20–40 CD) Shiraz, HJ Reserve Shiraz, Corrinas Cabernet Sauvignon Shiraz.
SUMMARY 1839 was the year in which William and Elizabeth Oliver arrived from Scotland to settle at McLaren Vale. Six generations later, members of the family are still living on the Whitehill and Taranga farms, 2 kilometres north of McLaren Vale. The Taranga property has 12 varieties planted on 92 hectares; historically, grapes from the property have been sold to up to five different wineries, but since 1994 some of the old vine shiraz has been made under the Oliver's Taranga label. From the 2000 vintage, the wine has been made by Corrina Rayment (the Oliver family's first winemaker and a sixth-generation family member). Exports to Belgium, Canada, Singapore, Germany, New Zealand, Switzerland, Thailand and the US.

ΥΥΥΥΥ **Shiraz 2002** Dense colour; strongly regional, opulent blackberry, plum and chocolate mid-palate; tightens up nicely with tannins on the finish. **RATING** 90 **DRINK** Now $ 20

ΥΥΥΥ **HJ Reserve Shiraz 2001** **RATING** 85 **DRINK** 2010 $ 45

🐚 Olsen ★★☆

RMB 252 Osmington Road, Osmington, WA 6285 **REGION** Margaret River
T (08) 9757 4536 **F** (08) 9757 4114 **OPEN** By appointment
WINEMAKER Bernard Abbott **EST.** 1986 **CASES** 2500
PRODUCT RANGE ($14–25 ML) Verdelho, Chardonnay, Shiraz, Merlot, Cabernet Sauvignon.
SUMMARY Steve and AnnMarie Olsen have planted 3.25 hectares of cabernet sauvignon, and 2 hectares each of semillon and chardonnay, which they tend with the help of their four children. It was the desire to raise their children in a healthy, country environment that prompted the move to establish the vineyard, coupled with a longstanding dream to make their own wine. The wines are sold through a wide range of restaurants and specialist retailers in most States, distributed direct ex the vineyard.

ΥΥΥΥ **Cabernet Sauvignon 2001** **RATING** 84 **DRINK** 2007 $ 25

ΥΥΥ **Cabernet Sauvignon 2002** **RATING** 82 $ 25

Olssens of Watervale ★★★

Sollys Hill Road, Watervale, SA 5452 **REGION** Clare Valley
T (08) 8843 0065 **F** (08) 8843 0065 **OPEN** Thurs–Sun and public holidays 11–5, or by appointment
WINEMAKER Contract **EST.** 1994 **CASES** 1000
PRODUCT RANGE ($19–26 CD) Riesling, Semillon, Botrytised Riesling, Merlot, Shiraz, Cabernet Sauvignon Cabernet Franc Merlot.
SUMMARY Kevin and Helen Olssen first visited the Clare Valley in December 1986. Within two weeks they and their family decided to sell their Adelaide home and purchased a property in a small, isolated valley 3 kilometres north of the township of Watervale. Between 1987 and 1993 production from the 5-hectare vineyard was sold to other makers, but in 1993 the decision was taken to produce wine under the Olssen label.

ΥΥΥΥ **Cabernet Sauvignon Cabernet Franc Merlot 2001** Very ripe but not bulky fruit; touches of mint around redcurrant; minimal tannins. **RATING** 87 **DRINK** 2008 $ 20

ΥΥΥΥ **Shiraz 2002** **RATING** 86 **DRINK** 2007 $ 25

🐚 Orange Country Wines NR

Underwood Road, Borenore, NSW 2800 **REGION** Orange
T (02) 6365 2221 **F** (02) 6365 2227 **OPEN** 7 days 10–5
WINEMAKER Don MacLennan, David MacLennan **EST.** 1999

PRODUCT RANGE Semillon, Sauvignon Blanc, Chardonnay, Pinot Noir, Shiraz, Cabernet Sauvignon.
SUMMARY Don and David MacLennan have planted sauvignon blanc, semillon, chardonnay, pinot noir, cabernet sauvignon and shiraz, and are making the wines on-site in a winery constructed with sawdust blocks and ironbark posts. The wines are sold by mail order and through the cellar door (9 kilometres from the town of Orange), which also offers local crafts and paintings.

🍇 Orange Mountain Wines ★★★

Cnr Forbes Road and Radnedge Lane, Orange, NSW 2800 **REGION** Orange
T (02) 6365 2626 **OPEN** Weekends and public holidays 9–5
WINEMAKER Terry Dolle **EST.** 1997 **CASES** 500
PRODUCT RANGE ($18–22 ML) Sauvignon Blanc, Manildra Viognier, Pinot Noir, Manildra Shiraz Viognier, Manildra Cabernet Sauvignon.
SUMMARY Terry Dolle has a total of 6 hectares of vineyards, part at Manildra (established 1997) and the remainder at Orange (in 2001). The Manildra climate is distinctly warmer than that of Orange, and the plantings reflect the climatic difference, with pinot noir and sauvignon blanc at Orange, and shiraz, cabernet sauvignon, merlot and viognier at Manildra.

🍷🍷🍷🍷 **Pinot Noir 2002** The spicy strawberry flavours are at the savoury end of the spectrum, but the wine has length and balance, and fine texture. **RATING** 87 **DRINK** Now $ 18

🍷🍷🍷🍷 **Manildra Viognier 2003** **RATING** 85 **DRINK** Now $ 22

🍷🍷🍷 **Sauvignon Blanc 2003** **RATING** 83 $ 18
Sauvignon Blanc 2002 **RATING** 83 $ 18
Manildra Cabernet Sauvignon 2001 **RATING** 83 $ 18
Manildra Shiraz Viognier 2002 **RATING** 82 $ 18

Orani Vineyard NR

Arthur Highway, Sorell, Tas 7172 **REGION** Southern Tasmania
T (03) 6225 0330 **F** (03) 6225 0330 **OPEN** Weekends and public holidays 9.30–6.30
WINEMAKER Julian Alcorso (Contract) **EST.** 1986
PRODUCT RANGE ($24–25 R) Riesling, Chardonnay, Pinot Noir.
SUMMARY The first commercial release from Orani was of a 1992 Pinot Noir, with Chardonnay and Riesling following in the years thereafter. Since that time Orani has continued to do well with its Pinot Noirs, including a ripe, plummy, highly flavoured wine from the 1999 vintage. Owned by Tony and Angela McDermott, the latter the President of the Royal Hobart Wine Show. All of the wines are released with some years' bottle age.

🍇 Oranje Tractor Wine/Lincoln & Gomm Wines ★★★☆

Lot 6 Link Road, Albany, WA 6330 **REGION** Great Southern
T (08) 9842 5175 **F** (08) 9842 5179 **OPEN** By appointment
WINEMAKER Rob Diletti (Contract) **EST.** 1998 **CASES** 600
PRODUCT RANGE ($12.50–20.50 ML) Riesling, Sauvignon Blanc, Late Harvest Riesling, Cabernet Merlot.
SUMMARY The seemingly complicated name tells part of the story of the vineyard owned by Murray Gomm and Pamela Lincoln. Murray Gomm was born on the property next door, but moved to Perth to work in the physical education and health promotion field. It was here he met nutritionist Pamela Lincoln, who completed the wine science degree at Charles Sturt University in 2000, before being awarded a Churchill Fellowship to study organic grape and wine production in the US and Europe. When the partners began the establishment of their 3-hectare vineyard, they went down the organic path route with the aid of an ancient 1964 vintage Fiat tractor, which is orange. Spelt with a 'j' it becomes the Dutch word for orange and was intended to pay a compliment to the international stream of WWOOFers who have come to work on the property. WWOOFers are not dogs, but 'Willing Workers on Organic Farms' who, along with free-ranging chickens and guinea fowl, keep the vineyard healthy. The wines are made by Rob Diletti, and a significant proportion is consumed by the WWOOFers, but there is the Tractor Seat Wine Club and the mailing list for others who wish to gain access.

🍷🍷🍷🍷 **Oranje Tractor Riesling 2003** Excellent varietal character; clear, crisp citrus and lemon; good balance; long, dry finish. **RATING** 90 **DRINK** 2010 $ 14.50

ΨΨΨΨ **Oranje Tractor Sauvignon Blanc 2003** Clean, crisp and firm; mineral and herb; good length and finish. **RATING** 87 **DRINK** Now $ 17.50

ΨΨΨ♡ **Oranje Tractor Cabernet Merlot 2002 RATING** 85 **DRINK** 2008 $ 20.50

🐌 O'Regan Creek Vineyard and Winery NR

969 Pialba–Burrum Heads Road, Hervey Bay, Qld 4655 (postal) **REGION** Queensland Coastal
T (07) 4128 7636 **OPEN** Not
WINEMAKER John Fuerst, Cathy Fuerst **EST.** 1998
PRODUCT RANGE A range of varietally denominated table wines reflecting the plantings.
SUMMARY John and Kathy Fuerst have established their vineyard right on the Queensland coast, planting cabernet sauvignon, shiraz, chambourcin (doubtless suited to the climate) and zinfandel.

Orlando ★★★★☆

Jacob's Creek Visitor Centre, Barossa Valley Way, Rowland Flat, SA 5352 **REGION** Barossa Valley
T (08) 8521 3000 **F** (08) 8521 3003 **OPEN** 7 days 10–5
WINEMAKER Philip Laffer, Bernard Hicken, Sam Kurtz **EST.** 1847
PRODUCT RANGE ($8.95–59.95 R) The table wines are sold in four ranges: first the national and international best-selling Jacob's Creek Semillon Sauvignon Blanc, Semillon Chardonnay, Chardonnay, Riesling, Shiraz Cabernet, Grenache Shiraz and special Limited Releases; then the Gramp's range of Chardonnay, Botrytis Semillon, Grenache, Cabernet Merlot; next the Saint range, St Helga Eden Valley Riesling, St Hilary Padthaway Chardonnay, St Hugo Coonawarra Cabernet Sauvignon; finally the premium range of Steingarten Riesling, Jacaranda Ridge Cabernet Sauvignon and Lawsons Padthaway Shiraz; sparkling wines under the Trilogy and Carrington labels.
SUMMARY Jacob's Creek is one of the largest-selling brands in the world and is almost exclusively responsible for driving the fortunes of this French-owned (by Pernod Ricard) company. A colossus in the export game, chiefly to the UK and Europe, but also to the US and Asia. Wine quality across the full spectrum from Jacob's Creek upwards has been exemplary, driven by the production skills of Philip Laffer. The global success of the basic Jacob's Creek range has had the perverse effect of prejudicing many critics and wine writers who fail (it seems) to objectively look behind the label and taste what is in fact in the glass.

ΨΨΨΨ♡ **Centenary Hill Shiraz 1997** Smooth, satiny, long and seamless integration of fruit and oak; lovely mature wine. **RATING** 93 **DRINK** 2007 $ 54
St Hugo Cabernet Sauvignon 2000 Excellent varietal delineation; cassis, mulberry and blackcurrant married with attractive oak and fine tannins; elegant. **RATING** 93 **DRINK** 2015 $ 37.99
Lawson's Padthaway Shiraz 1998 Excellent colour and depth; generous, mouth-coating black fruits, spice and well integrated oak; built to stay. **RATING** 92 **DRINK** 2018 $ 60
St Helga Eden Valley Riesling 2003 Pure, fine, clean floral aromas; elegant, quite delicate lime and passionfruit flavours. **RATING** 91 **DRINK** 2013 $ 14
Barossa Special Vintage Riesling 2003 Very subdued, tight mineral/spice bouquet, the palate firm but not phenolic; purpose-built for ageing. Nostalgic cellar-door release only version. **RATING** 91 **DRINK** 2013 $ 26
Jacob's Creek Reserve Riesling 2003 Fine mineral and herb aromas; attractive citrus and passionfruit flavours; good value. **RATING** 90 **DRINK** 2010 $ 14.95
Jacob's Creek Reserve Chardonnay 2002 A complex bouquet supports the sustained, pure varietal citrus and stone fruit flavours of the palate; developing slowly and with grace. **RATING** 90 **DRINK** 2007 $ 14.95
Botrytis Noble Late Harvest 2001 Complex, but elegant and fresh; marmalade and honey; very good acidity, length and balance. **RATING** 90 **DRINK** Now $ 16

ΨΨΨΨ **Jacob's Creek Riesling 2003** Abundant citrus and tropical fruit; well balanced; subliminal sweetness. Great value, as ever. **RATING** 89 **DRINK** 2007 $ 8.95
St Helga Eden Valley Riesling 2002 Aromas of light toast and lime; a fresh and vibrant palate; lime and mineral. **RATING** 89 **DRINK** 2012 $ 14
St Hilary Padthaway Chardonnay 2002 Super-elegant and refined; crisp stone fruit; fades slightly on finish. **RATING** 89 **DRINK** 2007 $ 18

Gramp's Barossa Grenache 2002 Spicy, smoky raspberry fruit supported by plenty of structure; overall, very appealing style. **RATING** 89 **DRINK** Now $ 15.99

Jacob's Creek Chardonnay 2003 Scented, aromatic and fresh citrus/lime aromas; faintest touch of sweetness. **RATING** 87 **DRINK** Now $ 8.95

Jacob's Creek Limited Release Chardonnay 2002 Distinctly tangy/lemony/citrussy, the palate with considerable length, but not complex. **RATING** 87 **DRINK** 2007 $ 30.95

Jacob's Creek Shiraz 2002 Reflects the 2002 vintage; far more depth to the fruit than normal years; good length, too. **RATING** 87 **DRINK** Now $ 8.95

Gramps Cabernet Merlot 2001 Rich, opulent blackcurrant and cedary oak; abundant tannins; full power. **RATING** 87 **DRINK** 2011 $ 15.99

Jacob's Creek Chardonnay Pinot NV Totally unexpected finesse and delicacy; the citrus and spice palate has good balance and length, presumably the reason why it claimed a double gold medal from the San Francisco Wine Fair. **RATING** 87 **DRINK** Now $ 9.95

Trilogy Brut NV A touch of yeasty/creamy autoloysis; clean, fresh, lingering tangy/citrussy fruit. Bottle-fermented. **RATING** 87 **DRINK** Now $ 14

▼▼▼▽ **Jacob's Creek Semillon Sauvignon Blanc 2003** **RATING** 86 **DRINK** Now $ 8.95
Gramp's Barossa Chardonnay 2002 **RATING** 86 **DRINK** Now $ 15.99
Jacob's Creek Reserve Shiraz 2001 **RATING** 86 **DRINK** 2008 $ 14.95
Jacob's Creek Reserve Cabernet Sauvignon 2001 **RATING** 86 **DRINK** 2008 $ 14.95
St Hugo Cabernet Sauvignon 2001 **RATING** 86 **DRINK** 2011 $ 37.99
Trilogy 2001 Clean, fresh red and black currant fruit; only light to medium-bodied, but long in the mouth and finish. Cool-climate components obvious. Value. **RATING** 86 **DRINK** 2010 $ 13.99
Trilogy White 2003 **RATING** 85 **DRINK** Now $ 14

▼▼▼ **Jacob's Creek Merlot 2002** **RATING** 83 $ 8.95
Carrington Vintage Brut 2003 **RATING** 83 $ 5.99
Jacob's Creek Shiraz 2001 **RATING** 82 $ 8.95

Osborns ★★★★

166 Foxeys Road, Merricks North, Vic 3926 **REGION** Mornington Peninsula
T (03) 5989 7417 **F** (03) 5989 7510 **OPEN** Weekends Oct–June, and by appointment
WINEMAKER Richard McIntyre (Consultant), Frank Osborn **EST.** 1988 **CASES** 1500
PRODUCT RANGE ($18–32 CD) Chardonnay, Rose, Pinot Noir, Pinot Noir Reserve, Merlot, Cabernet Merlot, Cabernet Sauvignon.
SUMMARY Frank and Pamela Osborn are now Mornington Peninsula veterans, having purchased the vineyard land in Ellerina Road in 1988 and (with help from son Guy) planted the vineyard over the following 4 years. The first release of wines in 1997 offered six vintages each of Chardonnay and Pinot Noir and five vintages of Cabernet Sauvignon, quite a debut. Part of the production from the 5.5 hectares of vineyards is sold to others, but increasing amounts are made and marketed under the Osborns label.

▼▼▼▼▽ **Chardonnay 2002** Silky smooth, seamless and focused; quite delicate but intense grapefruit/stone fruit mix; subtle oak. Screwcap. **RATING** 92 **DRINK** 2008 $ 23

▼▼▼▼ **Merlot 2001** Aromatic, spicy and savoury, with an almost citrussy tang to the lively finish. Screwcap. **RATING** 88 **DRINK** 2007 $ 23

🍃 Oscar's Leap NR

Lot 125 Caves Road, Wilyabrup, WA 6280 **REGION** Margaret River
T (08) 9755 6688 **F** (08) 9755 6788 **OPEN** 7 days 10–5
WINEMAKER Flying Fish Cove (Contract) **EST.** 1998
PRODUCT RANGE Sauvignon Blanc Semillon, Shiraz, Merlot, Cabernets.
SUMMARY Damon Eastaugh has established a substantial vineyard of 17.5 hectares, planted to sauvignon blanc, semillon, merlot, shiraz, cabernet franc and cabernet sauvignon. The wines are made at Flying Fish Cove, which has had outstanding success in making wines for a number of producers in the Margaret River region. The wines are sold by mail order and through the cellar door, which has picnic facilities in a garden setting, and a gallery.

O'Shea & Murphy Rosebery Hill Vineyard ★★★

Rosebery Hill, Pastoria Road, Pipers Creek, Vic 3444 **REGION** Macedon Ranges
T (03) 5423 5253 **F** (03) 5424 5253 **OPEN** By appointment
WINEMAKER Barry Murphy, John O'Shea **EST.** 1984 **CASES** 1500
PRODUCT RANGE ($15–20 R) Shiraz, Cabernet Sauvignon Cabernet Franc Merlot.
SUMMARY Planting of the 8-hectare vineyard on a north-facing slope of red basalt soil which runs at the 550 metre elevation line began in 1984; it is believed the hill was the site of a volcanic eruption 7 million years ago. The vines were established without the aid of irrigation (and remain unirrigated), and produced the first small crop in 1990. No grapes were produced between 1993 and 1995 owing to mildew: Murphy and O'Shea say, 'We tried to produce fruit with no sprays at all, and learned the hard way.' Part of the current production is made for the O'Shea & Murphy Rosebery Hill label, and part is sold to others, all of whom attest to the quality of the fruit.

TTTT **Rosebery Hill Macedon Shiraz 2001** Cherry/cherry pip; fine, light to medium-bodied, with very obvious cool-grown conditions; will hopefully flesh out with time in bottle. **RATING** 87 **DRINK** 2010 $ 20
Cabernet Sauvignon Cabernet Franc Merlot 2000 Super-fine, super-elegant, light-bodied Chinon (Loire Valley) style. **RATING** 87 **DRINK** 2007 $ 20

TTTY **Cabernet Sauvignon Cabernet Franc Merlot 2001** **RATING** 86 **DRINK** 2009 $ 20
Pipers Creek Macedon Shiraz 2000 **RATING** 84 **DRINK** Now $ 20

TTY **Chardonnay 2002** **RATING** 78 $ 20

🐀 Otway Estate ★★★

20 Hoveys Road, Barongarook, Vic 3249 **REGION** Geelong
T (03) 5233 8400 **F** (03) 5233 8343 **OPEN** Mon–Fri 11–4.30, weekends 10–5
WINEMAKER Ian Deacon **EST.** 1983 **CASES** 3500
PRODUCT RANGE ($15–20 CD) Semillon Sauvignon, Unwooded Chardonnay, Chardonnay, Pinot Noir; Yahoo Creek range of Sauvignon Blanc, Chardonnay, Pinot Noir, Shiraz, Cabernet Merlot.
SUMMARY While the history of Otway Estate dates back to 1983, when the first vines were planted by Stuart and Eileen Walker, the current group of nine family and friends, including winemaker Ian Deacon, have substantially expanded the scope of the business. There are now 6 hectares of vineyard, planted primarily to chardonnay (3 hectares) and pinot noir (2 hectares) with small patches of riesling, semillon, sauvignon blanc and cabernet making up the remainder. The wines made from these plantings are sold under the Otway Estate label; wines made from contract-grown grapes in the region are marketed under the Yahoo Creek label. These are aimed at cafés and brasseries, with significant distribution around the general region. In late 2000 three luxury self-contained cottages were built in the bush surrounding the vineyard, adding a further dimension to the business.

TTTY **Semillon Sauvignon Blanc 2003** **RATING** 86 **DRINK** Now $ 15

TTT **Pinot Noir 2002** **RATING** 82 $ 15
Shiraz 2002 **RATING** 82 $ 15

🐀 Outram Estate ★★★☆

PO Box 621, Broadway, NSW 2007 **REGION** Lower Hunter Valley
T (02) 9481 7576 **F** (02) 9481 7879 **OPEN** Not
WINEMAKER Peter Howland (Contract) **EST.** 1995 **CASES** 1150
PRODUCT RANGE ($19.99 R) Fordwich Verdelho, Limited Release Merlot.
SUMMARY Dr Geoff Cutter says his inspiration to start Outram Estate came from Max Lake, a visit to St Emilion/Pomerol in Bordeaux, and my account of the establishment of Coldstream Hills, which he read in one of my books. His aim is to produce quality, not quantity, and with Peter Howland in charge of winemaking, there is no reason why he should not do so. He has 5 hectares of merlot on rich red volcanic basalt, and 13 hectares of verdelho and chardonnay on the sandy grey alluvial soils of the Wollombi Creek. The wines are distributed by Pacific Wine Connections, and exported to the UK, Fiji, Taiwan and the US. They are also available by mail order.

🍷🍷🍷🍷 **Limited Release Merlot 2003** Supple, medium-bodied, sweet red berry fruit; similarly sweet oak; utterly seductive style. **RATING** 89 **DRINK** 2009 **$** 19.99

Fordwich Verdelho 2000 Complex; 10 per cent barrel ferment in American oak, the toasty characters from bottle age and oak. Overall viscosity and fruit sweetness. **RATING** 87 **DRINK** Now **$** 19.99

Oyster Cove Vineyard

NR

134 Manuka Road, Oyster Cove, Tas 7054 **REGION** Southern Tasmania
T (03) 6267 4512 **F** (03) 6267 4635 **OPEN** By appointment
WINEMAKER Andrew Hood (Contract) **EST.** 1994 **CASES** 100
PRODUCT RANGE ($15–20 CD) Chardonnay, Pinot Noir.
SUMMARY The striking label of Oyster Cove, with a yacht reflected in mirror-calm water, is wholly appropriate, for Jean and Rod Ledingham have been quietly growing tiny quantities of grapes from their 1 hectare of chardonnay and pinot noir since 1994.

Padthaway Estate

★★★★

Riddoch Highway, Padthaway, SA 5271 **REGION** Padthaway
T (08) 8734 3148 **F** (08) 8734 3188 **OPEN** 7 days 10–4
WINEMAKER Ulrich Grey-Smith **EST.** 1980 **CASES** 6000
PRODUCT RANGE ($15–25 R) Unwooded Chardonnay, Chardonnay, Eliza Pinot Chardonnay, Elgin Merlot, Cabernet Sauvignon.
SUMMARY For many years, until the opening of Stonehaven, this was the only functioning winery in Padthaway, set in the superb grounds of the estate in a large and gracious old stone woolshed; the homestead is in the Relais et Chateaux mould, offering luxurious accommodation and fine food. Sparkling wines are the specialty of the estate. Padthaway Estate also acts as a tasting centre for other Padthaway-region wines. National retail distribution; exports to the UK.

🍷🍷🍷🍷🍷 **Cabernet Sauvignon 2001** Cedary/smoky overtones to cassis fruit; restrained cabernet varietal character; altogether elegant; very good finish. **RATING** 91 **DRINK** 2011 **$** 18.95

Chardonnay 2002 Rich melon and citrus offset by creamy cashew notes; deft oak, good length. **RATING** 90 **DRINK** 2007 **$** 18.95

🍷🍷🍷🍷 **Elgin Merlot 2001** **RATING** 84 **DRINK** 2007 **$** 19

Palandri Wines

★★★

Bussell Highway, Cowaramup, WA 6284 **REGION** Margaret River
T (08) 9755 5711 **F** (08) 9755 5722 **OPEN** Wed–Mon 10–4
WINEMAKER Tony Carapetis **EST.** 1999 **CASES** 240 000
PRODUCT RANGE ($12–35 R) Baldivis Estate Classic Dry White and Cabernet Shiraz are the entry-point wines. Under the mid-priced Aurora label are Semillon Sauvignon Blanc, Semillon Chardonnay, Chardonnay, Shiraz, Merlot, Cabernet Shiraz; the flagship Palandri range consists of Riesling, Semillon, Sauvignon Blanc, Chardonnay, Shiraz, Cabernet Merlot, Cabernet Sauvignon.
SUMMARY A state-of-the-art winery completed just prior to the 2000 vintage now has a capacity of 2500 tonnes. The vineyards which are scheduled to supply Palandri Wines with 50 per cent of its intake are situated in the Frankland River subregion of the Great Southern: 150 hectares of vines were planted at Frankland River in September 1999. The major varieties are shiraz, merlot, cabernet sauvignon, riesling, chardonnay and sauvignon blanc. A further 60 hectares were planted in early September 2000, making this the largest single vineyard developed in Western Australia to this point. A second block has been purchased south of the Frankland River vineyard, and a further 140 hectares are being developed there. There is a school of thought (particularly in Perth) which suggests that Palandri may have been overly ambitious in its pursuit of rapid growth.

🍷🍷🍷🍷 **Chardonnay 2002** Fresh, lively and fruit-driven; citrus-accented; medium body and clean finish. A blend of Margaret River and Great Southern. **RATING** 88 **DRINK** Now **$** 19.95

Aurora Shiraz 2001 Good colour; fruit-driven; supple, round mouthfeel; plummy fruit, fine tannins. **RATING** 87 **DRINK** 2008 **$** 14.95

Margaret River Cabernet Sauvignon 2002 Powerful, dense, concentrated, lush blackcurrant; slightly over the top; should improve with age. **RATING** 87 **DRINK** 2010 $24.95

ŢŢŢ Baldivis Estate Classic Dry White 2003 **RATING** 83 $11.95
Baldivis Estate Merlot 2002 **RATING** 83 $12
Margaret River Cabernet Merlot 2002 **RATING** 83 $24.95
Baldivis Estate Cabernet Merlot 2002 **RATING** 83 $11.95

Palmara ★★★☆

1314 Richmond Road, Richmond, Tas 7025 **REGION** Southern Tasmania
T (03) 6260 2462 **F** (03) 6260 2462 **OPEN** Sept–May 7 days 12–6
WINEMAKER Allan Bird **EST.** 1985 **CASES** 300
PRODUCT RANGE ($12.50–32.50 CD) Montage, Chardonnay, Exotica (Siegerrebe), Pinot Noir, Cabernet Sauvignon.
SUMMARY Allan Bird makes the Palmara wines in tiny quantities. (The vineyard is slightly less than 1 hectare in total.) The Pinot Noir has performed consistently well since 1990. The Exotica Siegerrebe blend is unchallenged as Australia's most exotic and unusual wine, with pungent jujube/lanolin aromas and flavours.

🐌 Palmers Wines NR

Lot 152 Palmers Lane, Pokolbin, NSW 2321 **REGION** Lower Hunter Valley
T (02) 4998 7452 **F** (02) 9949 9884 **OPEN** Weekends 10–5, or by appointment
WINEMAKER Contract **EST.** 1986 **CASES** 1100
PRODUCT RANGE ($14–17 CD) Rose Palmer Verdelho, Willie Palmer Chardonnay, George Palmer Shiraz.
SUMMARY The name of the vineyard and that of the lane on which it is established came from Henry Palmer, who arrived in 1862. Three generations of the family continued to work the 40-hectare property as a mixed farming enterprise, but when the last (William) died in the 1970s, the property was to all intents and purposes abandoned. Purchased in 1986, the new owners set about rebuilding the original Palmer homestead, which now serves as the cellar door, and establishing 2.6 hectares of vineyard (chardonnay, verdelho, semillon and shiraz). Some of the grapes are sold to other winemakers, and the remainder are contract-made under the Palmers Wines brand.

Palmer Wines ★★★☆

Caves Road, Wilyabrup, WA 6280 **REGION** Margaret River
T (08) 9756 7388 **F** (08) 9756 7399 **OPEN** 7 days 10–5
WINEMAKER Bruce Dukes **EST.** 1977 **CASES** 6000
PRODUCT RANGE ($14–42 R) Sauvignon Blanc, Semillon Sauvignon Blanc, Chardonnay, Shiraz, Merlot, Shiraz Cabernet, Cabernet Sauvignon.
SUMMARY Stephen and Helen Palmer planted their first hectare of vines way back in 1977, but a series of events (including a cyclone and grasshopper plagues) caused them to lose interest and instead turn to thoroughbred horses. But with encouragement from Dr Michael Peterkin of Pierro, and after a gap of almost 10 years, they again turned to viticulture, and now have 15 hectares planted to the classic varieties. The cellar door opened in April 2002.

ŢŢŢŢŢ Sauvignon Blanc Semillon 2003 Spotlessly clean, with the varieties welded seamlessly; good length and balance; a hint of sweetness adds to the appeal. **RATING** 90 **DRINK** 2007 $14

ŢŢŢŢ Sauvignon Blanc 2003 Elegant, fragrant, clear and clean varietal character in a light-bodied mode. **RATING** 89 **DRINK** Now $14
Cabernet Sauvignon 2001 Blackcurrant, with some olive and earth nuances; overall, in austere Margaret River style. **RATING** 88 **DRINK** 2009 $16.25
Merlot 2000 Savoury olive and earth aromas and flavours; fine but persistent tannins. **RATING** 87 **DRINK** 2008 $23.75

Pankhurst ★★★★

Old Woodgrove, Woodgrove Road, Hall, NSW 2618 **REGION** Canberra District
T (02) 6230 2592 **F** (02) 6230 2592 **OPEN** Weekends, public holidays, or by appointment
WINEMAKER Dr David Carpenter, Sue Carpenter, Dr Roger Harris (Contract) **EST.** 1986 **CASES** 4000
PRODUCT RANGE ($15–25 CD) Sauvignon Blanc Semillon, Chardonnay, Late Harvest Semillon, Pinot Noir, Cabernet Merlot, Cabernet Sauvignon.
SUMMARY Agricultural scientist and consultant Allan Pankhurst and wife Christine (with a degree in pharmaceutical science) have established a 5.7-hectare, split canopy vineyard. Tastings of the first wines produced showed considerable promise. In recent years Pankhurst has shared success with Lark Hill in the production of surprisingly good Pinot Noir — surprising given the climatic limitations. Says Christine Pankhurst, 'the result of good viticulture here and great winemaking at Lark Hill', and she may well be right.

ΨΨΨΨ **Chardonnay 2002** Intense and quite complex; well-balanced barrel-ferment inputs to long, nectarine and citrus palate. Screwcap. **RATING** 91 **DRINK** 2007 $ 18

ΨΨΨΨ **Pinot Noir 2002** Light, elegant, savoury, woodsy style belies its 13.9 degrees alcohol; fine tannins add length. **RATING** 87 **DRINK** Now $ 25

ΨΨΨΨ **Cabernet Merlot 2002 RATING** 84 **DRINK** 2007 $ 18

Panorama ★★★★☆

1848 Cygnet Coast Road, Cradoc, Tas 7109 **REGION** Southern Tasmania
T (03) 6266 3409 **F** (03) 6266 3482 **OPEN** Wed–Mon days 10–5
WINEMAKER Michael Vishacki **EST.** 1974 **CASES** 210
PRODUCT RANGE ($10–37 CD) Sauvignon Blanc, Chardonnay, Reserve Chardonnay, Late Harvest, Rose, Pinot Noir, Reserve Pinot Noir, Cabernet Sauvignon, Ruby Port, Cherry Port, Pear Liqueur.
SUMMARY Michael and Sharon Vishacki purchased Panorama from Steve Ferencz in 1997, and have since spent considerable sums building a brand new winery, an attractive cellar-door sales outlet, and in trebling the vineyard size.

Panton Hill Winery NR

145 Manuka Road, Panton Hill, Vic 3759 **REGION** Yarra Valley
T (03) 9719 7342 **F** (03) 9719 7362 **OPEN** Weekends and public holidays 11–5, or by appointment
WINEMAKER Dr Teunis A P Kwak **EST.** 1988 **CASES** 400
PRODUCT RANGE ($18–28 CD) Chardonnay, Pinot Noir, Cabernet Franc, Sparkling Cabernet Franc, Cabernet Sauvignon Merlot, fortifieds.
SUMMARY Melbourne academic Dr Teunis Kwak has a 4-hectare fully mature vineyard, part planted in 1976, the remainder in 1988. Part of the production is sold to others, and part is retained for the Panton Hill label. The vineyard is a picturesque one, established on a fairly steep hillside, and there is a large stone hall available for functions.

Paperbark Vines NR

PO Box 2553, Kent Town, SA 5071 **REGION** Warehouse
T (08) 8431 3675 **F** (08) 8431 3674 **OPEN** Not
WINEMAKER Contract **EST.** 2000
PRODUCT RANGE Chardonnay, Shiraz, Cabernet Sauvignon.
SUMMARY Paperbark Vines is a virtual winery owned by Mark Cohen of Malesco Imports and Export Pty Ltd. Chardonnay, Cabernet Sauvignon and Shiraz are made under the Paperbark Vines label, and sold only into Malaysia, Singapore, Thailand and the US.

Paracombe Wines ★★★★☆

Main Road, Paracombe, SA 5132 (postal) **REGION** Adelaide Hills
T (08) 8380 5058 **F** (08) 8380 5488 **OPEN** Not
WINEMAKER Paul Drogemuller **EST.** 1983 **CASES** 4500

PRODUCT RANGE ($21–69 ML) Holland Creek Riesling, Semillon, Sauvignon Blanc, Chardonnay, Shiraz, Somerville Shiraz Limited Release, The Reuben, Cabernet Franc, Cabernet Sauvignon.
SUMMARY The Drogemuller family have established 12 hectares of vineyards at Paracombe, reviving a famous name in South Australian wine history. The wines are stylish and consistent, and are sold by mail order and through retailers in South Australia. Exports to the US, Malaysia, Japan, the UK, Switzerland and Sweden.

▼▼▼▼▼ **The Reuben 2001** Highly aromatic and spicy; delicious medium-bodied wine, entirely fruit-driven by its cocktail of Cabernet Sauvignon, Malbec, Merlot, Cabernet Franc and Shiraz. **RATING** 94 **DRINK** 2016 $ 25

▼▼▼▼▽ **Chardonnay 2002** Abundant flavour and concentration; ripe melon and stone fruit; excellent length. **RATING** 92 **DRINK** 2008 $ 25
Somerville Shiraz 2000 Very ripe, luscious plum/plum jam; concentrated and rich; out on its own. **RATING** 90 **DRINK** 2016 $ 69

▼▼▼▼ **Holland Creek Riesling 2003** Clean and crisp; apple blossom aromas; passionfruit on the palate. **RATING** 89 **DRINK** 2010 $ 21
Shiraz 2002 Smoky, spicy, leafy, savoury envelope around red fruits; light to medium-bodied; fine tannins. **RATING** 89 **DRINK** 2010 $ 27
Cabernet Sauvignon 2001 Subtly sweet Ribena/minty edges to blackcurrant fruit; light and elegant. **RATING** 89 **DRINK** 2011 $ 27
Sauvignon Blanc 2003 Clean, nicely balanced; core of tropical/gooseberry fruit. **RATING** 88 **DRINK** Now $ 21
Cabernet Franc 2002 Spice, cedar, tobacco and leaf aromas and flavours; strongly varietal; idiosyncratic. **RATING** 87 **DRINK** 2009 $ 27

🐚 Paradigm Hill ★★★☆

26 Merricks Road, Merricks, Vic 3916 **REGION** Mornington Peninsula
T 0438 114 480 **F** (03) 5989 2191 **OPEN** By appointment
WINEMAKER George Mihaly **EST.** 1999 **CASES** 1000
PRODUCT RANGE ($24–38 CD) Riesling, Pinot Gris, the Oracle Pinot Noir.
SUMMARY Dr George Mihaly (with a background in medical research and thereafter in the biotechnology and pharmaceutical industry) and wife Ruth (a former chef and caterer) have realised a 30-year dream of establishing their own vineyard and winery, altogether abandoning their previous careers to do so. George Mihaly brought with him all of the necessary scientific qualifications, and built on those by making the 2001 Merricks Creek wines, moving to home base at Paradigm Hill for the 2002 vintage, all along receiving guidance and advice from Nat White from Main Ridge Estate. The vineyard, under Ruth's control and with advice from Shane Strange, is planted to 2.1 hectares of pinot noir, 1 hectare of shiraz, 0.9 hectare of riesling and 0.4 hectare of pinot gris.

▼▼▼▼▽ **Pinot Gris 2003** Plenty of intensity and length; apple and spice; long, convincing finish. **RATING** 90 **DRINK** Now $ 34

▼▼▼▼ **The Oracle Pinot Noir 2003** Plum jam and spice aromas; ripe fruit, bordering 14 degrees alcohol; woodsy/briary finish. **RATING** 88 **DRINK** 2008

▼▼▼▽ **Riesling 2003** **RATING** 86 **DRINK** Now $ 24

Paradise Enough ★★★☆

Stewarts Road, Kongwak, Vic 3951 **REGION** Gippsland
T (03) 5657 4241 **F** (03) 5657 4229 **OPEN** Thurs–Mon 10–5
WINEMAKER John Bell, Sue Armstrong **EST.** 1987 **CASES** 600
PRODUCT RANGE ($17–25 CD) Chardonnay, Reserve Chardonnay, Pinot Noir, Cabernet Merlot, Pinot Chardonnay.
SUMMARY John Bell and Sue Armstrong planted a small vineyard on their substantial dairy and beef property in 1987 and have since expanded the planting to 4.4 hectares. A small family operation, wines are available from cellar door, mailing list and local restaurants, with exports to the UK.

Paringa Estate

44 Paringa Road, Red Hill South, Vic 3937 **REGION** Mornington Peninsula
T (03) 5989 2669 **F** (03) 5931 0135 **OPEN** 7 days 11–5
WINEMAKER Lindsay McCall **EST.** 1985 **CASES** 5000
PRODUCT RANGE ($15–52 CD) Peninsula range of Chardonnay, Pinot Noir, Shiraz; Estate range of White Pinot, Riesling, Pinot Gris, Chardonnay, Pinot Noir, Shiraz; Sparkling Shiraz, Cabernet Sauvignon.
SUMMARY No longer a rising star, but a star shining more brightly in the Mornington Peninsula firmament than any other. As recent vintages have emphasised, the Red Hill district of the Mornington Peninsula region is sensitive to growing season conditions, and Paringa shines most brightly in the warmer years. The restaurant is open 7 days 10–3.

ŸŸŸŸŸ Peninsula Pinot Noir 2002 Pure, vibrant and focused fruit aromas, the red fruit palate the hallmark length and texture of Paringa, finishing with silky fine tannins. **RATING** 94 **DRINK** 2008 $ 24.95

Parish Hill Wines NR

Parish Hill Road, Uraidla, SA 5142 (postal) **REGION** Adelaide Hills
T (08) 8390 3927 **F** (08) 8390 0394 **OPEN** Not
WINEMAKER Andrew Cottell **EST.** 1998 **CASES** 500
PRODUCT RANGE ($25 ML) Arneis, Pinot Noir, Nebbiolo.
SUMMARY Andrew Cottell and Joy Carlisle only have a tiny 1.6-hectare vineyard on a steep, sunny, exposed slope adjacent to their house and micro on-site winery (which has approval for a total crush of 15 tonnes), but have taken the venture very seriously. Andrew Cottell studied wine science and viticulture at Charles Sturt University, where he was introduced to the Italian varieties; this led to the planting of 0.2 hectare of arneis and 0.5 hectare of nebbiolo. The other two varieties are new French clones selected by Professor Bernard at Dijon University. An attempt to use an organic spray program in 2002 failed, and while they adopt integrated pest management, soft environmental practices and beneficial insects, they have retreated to the safer ground of conventional vineyard management for the time being at least.

Parker Coonawarra Estate

Riddoch Highway, Coonawarra, SA 5263 **REGION** Coonawarra
T (08) 8737 3525 **F** (08) 8737 3527 **OPEN** 7 days 10–4
WINEMAKER Andrew Pirie, Peter Bissell (Contract) **EST.** 1985 **CASES** 5000
PRODUCT RANGE ($38–80 R) Terra Rossa Merlot, Terra Rossa First Growth, Terra Rossa Cabernet Sauvignon.
SUMMARY While always a high-profile brand, Parker Coonawarra Estate became headline news in March 2003 with the abrupt disappearance of Andrew Pirie from Pipers Brook Vineyards (which he had founded) and his equally rapid reappearance as chief executive of Parker Coonawarra Estate, responsible for every aspect of the business. The estate is now a 50/50 joint venture between the Parker family and interests associated with James Fairfax, the prior connection with Pepper Tree wines having been severed. While Andrew Pirie has ultimate winemaking responsibility, the wines are in fact contract-made by Pete Bissell at Balnaves. Acquired by the Rathbone family in May 2004. Exports to the US, the UK, Switzerland, Germany, Taiwan, Hong Kong, Singapore, Malaysia, Indonesia and Japan.

ŸŸŸŸŸ First Growth 2001 Rich, multi-layered cassis, blackcurrant fruit, oak and tannins, all seamlessly woven into a full-bodied, classic Coonawarra Cabernet. **RATING** 94 **DRINK** 2016 $ 66.90

ŸŸŸŸŸ Terra Rossa Cabernet Sauvignon 2001 Powerful, concentrated and rich; abundant blackcurrant and cassis fruit; powerful tannin structure. Hands off. **RATING** 93 **DRINK** 2021 $ 38

Terra Rossa Merlot 2001 A complex, seamless flow of red fruits, oak and tannins; medium to full-bodied, and perhaps more a very good red wine than a varietal Merlot. **RATING** 90 **DRINK** 2011 $ 39.50

Park Wines

NR

RMB 6291 Sanatorium Road, Allan's Flat, Yackandandah, Vic 3691 **REGION** Alpine Valleys
T (02) 6027 1564 **F** (02) 6027 1561 **OPEN** Weekends and public holidays 10–5
WINEMAKER Rod Park, Julia Park **EST.** 1995
PRODUCT RANGE ($16–17 CD) Chardonnay, Cabernet Sauvignon.
SUMMARY Rod and Julia Park have a 6-hectare vineyard of riesling, chardonnay, merlot, cabernet franc and cabernet sauvignon, set in the beautiful hill country of the Ovens Valley. Part of the vineyard is still coming into bearing, and the business is still in its infancy.

Parri Estate

★★★☆

Sneyd Road, Mount Jagged, SA 5210 **REGION** Southern Fleurieu
T (08) 8554 9595 **F** (08) 8554 9505 **OPEN** Not
WINEMAKER Linda Domas **EST.** 1998 **CASES** 2100
PRODUCT RANGE Semillon, Viognier Chardonnay, Pinot Noir, Shiraz.
SUMMARY Alice, Peter and John Phillips have established a substantial business with a clear marketing plan, and an obvious commitment to quality. Thirty-3 hectares of chardonnay, viognier, sauvignon blanc, semillon, pinot noir, cabernet sauvignon and shiraz have been planted using modern trellis and irrigation systems. The protected valley in which the vines are planted has a creek which flows throughout the year, and which has been rejuvenated by the planting of 3000 trees. Distribution in Victoria and New South Wales is underway, with exports to Japan, Denmark and Canada. The Parri Estate letterhead, indeed, has a Japanese business address in Tokyo. The quality of the first wines from young vines promises much for the future.

ΨΨΨΨ **Viognier Chardonnay 2003** Perhaps a marriage of convience; quite aromatic peach blossom and honeysuckle; soft, fruity entry; crisp acidity. **RATING** 88 **DRINK** Now $28
Semillon 2003 Clean, clear, crisp lemon and grass aromas and flavours; well balanced; medium-term development. **RATING** 87 **DRINK** 2008 $15
Shiraz 2001 Excellent colour; light to medium-bodied; attractive red fruits; oak quite evident. **RATING** 87 **DRINK** 2008 $25

ΨΨΨΨ **Unfiltered Pinot Noir 2002** **RATING** 84 **DRINK** Now $32

Passing Clouds

★★★★☆

RMB 440 Kurting Road, Kingower, Vic 3517 **REGION** Bendigo
T (03) 5438 8257 **F** (03) 5438 8246 **OPEN** Weekends 12–5, Mon–Fri by appointment
WINEMAKER Graeme Leith **EST.** 1974 **CASES** 4000
PRODUCT RANGE ($14–40 CD) Red wine specialist; principal wines include Pinot Noir, Grenache, Merlot, Graeme's Blend (Shiraz Cabernet), Angel Blend (Cabernet), Cabernets; Chardonnay and Sauvignon Blanc from the Goulburn Valley. Also available: Three Wise Men Pinot Noir.
SUMMARY Graeme Leith is one of the great personalities of the industry, with a superb sense of humour, and he makes lovely regional reds with cassis, berry and mint fruit. His smiling, bearded face adorned the front cover of many of the Victorian Tourist Bureau's excellent tourist publications for several years. Exports to the US.

ΨΨΨΨΨ **Angel Blend 2002** Powerful but already rounded and balanced; medium-bodied with sweetly ripe, but not jammy, fruit. **RATING** 93 **DRINK** 2015 $30
Graeme's Blend Shiraz Cabernet 2002 Deep colour; dense, mouthfilling blackberry, plum and blackcurrant; ripe tannins, very good balance. **RATING** 92 **DRINK** 2012 $25
Shiraz 2002 Clean, medium-bodied; seamlessly balanced and integrated blackberry fruit, oak and tannins. **RATING** 91 **DRINK** 2012 $40
Yarra Valley Pinot Noir 2002 Complex, mouthfilling style; sweeter and softer fruit than many from the vintage; multi-spice and plum flavours. **RATING** 90 **DRINK** Now $20

Pasut Family Wines

NR

Block 445 Calder Highway, Sunnycliffs, Vic 3496 **REGION** Murray Darling
T (03) 5024 2361 **OPEN** By appointment
WINEMAKER Stuart Kilmister (Contract) **EST.** 2000

PRODUCT RANGE An eclectic range of intriguingly named alternative varietals.
SUMMARY Denis and Pauline Pasut have 10 hectares of vineyards at Sunnycliffs, with a very interesting range of varietals planted: pinot gris, sangiovese, barbera, fragola, nebbiolo and vermentino, all of which are (with the qualified exception of pinot gris) grapes grown chiefly in Italy. If the varieties planted are exotic, the brands are more so: Pasut, Pinkbits, Fatbelly and Alpino Misto.

Paternoster   NR

17 Paternoster Road, Emerald, Vic 3782 **REGION** Yarra Valley
T (03) 5968 3197 **F** (03) 5968 3197 **OPEN** Weekends 11–6
WINEMAKER Philip Hession **EST.** 1985 **CASES** 700
PRODUCT RANGE ($15–120 CD) Lily, Chardonnay, Jack of Hearts Chardonnay, Rosemary, Pinot Noir, Pinot Noir Reserve, Jack of Hearts Pinot Noir, Queen Jane Pinot Noir, Jack of Hearts Shiraz, Cabernets, Jack of Hearts Cabernets, Tawny Port.
SUMMARY The densely planted, non-irrigated vines (at a density of 5000 vines to the hectare) cascade down a steep hillside at Emerald in one of the coolest parts of the Yarra Valley. Pinot Noir is the specialty of the winery, which produces intensely flavoured wines with a strong eucalypt mint overlay reminiscent of the wines of Delatite. No recent tastings; there also seems to be some dispute as to whether or not Paternoster falls within the Yarra Valley.

🐦 Paterson's Tumblong Vineyard   ★★★☆

474 Old Hume Highway Road, Tumblong, NSW 2729 **REGION** Gundagai
T (02) 6944 9227 **F** (02) 9880 9176 **OPEN** Weekends 9–5
WINEMAKER Celine Rousseau (Contract) **EST.** 1997 **CASES** 700
PRODUCT RANGE ($18 CD) Shiraz, Cabernet Sauvignon.
SUMMARY The Paterson family began the development of the 12-hectare vineyard in 1996. It is a powerful team: Robert Paterson (M.Ec [Sydney], PMD [Harvard]) was a Senior Vice President of Coca Cola, and his wife Rhondda was a teacher, before both turned to cattle farming in the early 1980s and grape growing in the mid-1990s. Son Stuart Paterson has a PhD in Chemical Engineering from the University of New South Wales, and has recently completed most of the core subjects in viticulture and wine science at Charles Sturt University; his wife Rainny is an architect. Most of the grapes grown elsewhere in Gundagai are sold to major wine companies for blended wines; Paterson's is one of the few estate-based operations.

▼▼▼▼ **Shiraz 2002** Fully ripe, luscious black cherry and blackberry, still fruit-driven; complexity to come. **RATING** 88 **DRINK** 2009 $18
Gundagai Cabernet Sauvignon 2001 Ripe blackberry fruit with earthy notes, and a touch of bitter chocolate; ripe tannins. **RATING** 87 **DRINK** 2009 $18

▼▼▼▽ **Gundagai Cabernet Sauvignon 2002 RATING** 86 **DRINK** Now $18

Patrick's Vineyard   ★★★★★

Croziers Road, Cobaw via Mount Macedon, Vic 3441 (postal) **REGION** Macedon Ranges
T 0419 598 401 **F** (03) 9521 6266 **OPEN** Not
WINEMAKER Alan Cooper (Contract) **EST.** 1996 **CASES** 350
PRODUCT RANGE ($17 ML) Patrick's Pinot.
SUMMARY Noell and John McNamara and Judy Doyle planted 2 hectares of pinot noir over the 1996 and 1997 planting seasons. The vineyard stands high on the southern slopes of the Cobaw Ranges, with an 1862 settler's cottage still standing and marking the first land use in the region. At an altitude of 600 metres, even pinot ripens very late in the season, typically at the end of April or early May, but in the right years, when the canopy has turned entirely from green to yellow-gold, the results can be impressive.

▼▼▼▼▼ **Pinot Noir 2002** An intense, stylish and complex mix of dark berries, plums and multi spices; excellent oak; long, lingering finish. **RATING** 94 **DRINK** 2009 $17

🐦 Patrick T Winemaking Services NR

Cnr Ravenswood Lane and Riddoch Highway, Coonawarra, SA 5263 **REGION** Coonawarra
T (08) 8737 3687 **F** (08) 8737 3689 **OPEN** 7 days 10–4.30
WINEMAKER Pat Tocaciu **EST.** 1996 **CASES** 2500
PRODUCT RANGE ($20–49 CD) The Caves Riesling, The Caves Shiraz, Home Block Cabernet
Sauvignon.
SUMMARY Patrick Tocaciu is a district veteran, coming to Patrick T Winemaking Services via the
former Heathfield Ridge Winery and (previously) Hollick Wines. He and his partners have almost 44
hectares of vines at Wrattonbully, and another 2 hectares of cabernet sauvignon in Coonawarra. The
Wrattonbully plantings cover all the major varieties, while the Coonawarra plantings give rise to the
Home Block Cabernet Sauvignon.

Patritti Wines

13–23 Clacton Road, Dover Gardens, SA 5048 **REGION** Adelaide Zone
T (08) 8296 8261 **F** (08) 8296 5088 **OPEN** Mon–Sat 9–6
WINEMAKER G Patritti, J Patritti **EST.** 1926 **CASES** 100 000
PRODUCT RANGE ($3.70–25 CD) A kaleidoscopic array of table, sparkling, fortified and flavoured
wines (and spirits) offered in bottle and flagon. The table wines are sold under the Blewitt Springs
Estate, Patritti and Billabong Wines brands; the upper tier being the Dover Private Bin Wines.
SUMMARY A traditional, family-owned business offering wines at modest prices, but with impressive
vineyard holdings of 10 hectares of shiraz in Blewitt Springs and 6 hectares of grenache at Aldinga
North.

🐦 Patterson Lakes Estate ★★★★

Riverend Road, Bangholme, Vic 3175 (postal) **REGION** Port Phillip Zone
T (03) 9773 1034 **F** (03) 9772 5634 **OPEN** Not
WINEMAKER Bill Christophersen **EST.** 1998 **CASES** 1500
PRODUCT RANGE Pinot Noir, Shiraz; others in the near future.
SUMMARY Former property developer James Bate has followed in the footsteps of the late Sid
Hamilton (who established Leconfield in Coonawarra when he was 80) by starting Patterson Lakes
Estate not long before he turned 80. The original planting was of 3 hectares of shiraz, with a further 3
hectares more of shiraz, 0.8 hectare each of viognier and tempranillo, a patch of cabernet franc/petit
verdot/merlot for a Bordeaux blend, and small amounts of mourvedre, cinsaut and grenache to go
with the shiraz. A small winery was completed in time for the 2004 vintage. Sullivan Wine Agencies
handles the domestic distribution, and exports to the US have also been established.

ŸŸŸŸ♀ **Hildesheim Vineyard Pinot Noir 2002** Spicy, sappy, savoury aromas are strongly varietal;
light to medium-bodied; fine spice plum and briar; silky feel and length; stylish.
RATING 90 **DRINK** Now $15

ŸŸŸŸ **Hildesheim Vineyard Shiraz 2002** Supple, smooth, light to medium-bodied mix of spice,
black cherry, raspberry and blackberry; the elegance doesn't even hint at the 14 degrees
alcohol. **RATING** 89 **DRINK** 2008 $17

Pattersons ★★★★

St Werburghs Road, Mount Barker, WA 6234 **REGION** Mount Barker
T (08) 9851 2063 **F** (08) 9851 2063 **OPEN** Sat–Wed 10–5, or by appointment
WINEMAKER Plantagenet (Contract) **EST.** 1982 **CASES** 500
PRODUCT RANGE ($15–29 CD) Chardonnay, Unwooded Chardonnay, Pattersons Curse Chardonnay,
Sparkling Shiraz, Pinot Noir, Shiraz, Pattersons Curse Shiraz.
SUMMARY Schoolteachers Sue and Arthur Patterson have grown chardonnay, shiraz and pinot noir
and grazed cattle as a weekend relaxation for a decade. The cellar door is in a recently completed and
very beautiful rammed-earth house, and a number of vintages are on sale at any one time. Good
Chardonnay and Shiraz have been complemented by the occasional spectacular Pinot Noir.

Paul Conti Wines ★★★☆

529 Wanneroo Road, Woodvale, WA 6026 **REGION** Greater Perth Zone
T (08) 9409 9160 **F** (08) 9309 1634 **OPEN** Mon–Sat 9.30–5.30, Sun by appointment
WINEMAKER Paul Conti, Jason Conti **EST.** 1948 **CASES** 7000
PRODUCT RANGE ($12–30 CD) The Tuarts Chenin Blanc, Unwooded Chardonnay, The Tuarts Chardonnay, Tuart Grove Chardonnay, Lorenzo Sparkling Chenin Blanc, Nero Sparkling Shiraz, Late Harvest Muscat Fronti, Medici Ridge Pinot Noir, Old Vine Grenache Shiraz, Medici Ridge Shiraz, Mariginiup Shiraz, Medici Ridge Merlot, The Tuarts Cabernet Sauvignon, White Port, Reserve Port, Reserve Muscat.
SUMMARY Third-generation winemaker Jason Conti has now assumed day-to-day control of winemaking, although father Paul (who succeeded his father in 1968) remains interested and involved in the business. Over the years Paul Conti challenged and redefined industry perceptions and standards; the challenge for Jason Conti (which he shows every sign of meeting) will be to achieve the same degree of success in a relentlessly and increasingly competitive market environment. Exports to the UK, Switzerland, Denmark, Singapore, Malaysia and Japan.

ȲȲȲȲȲ **Mariginiup Shiraz 2001** Clean black cherry and raspberry fruit; medium-bodied; fine, ripe tannins; subtle oak. **RATING** 90 **DRINK** 2011 $ 28

ȲȲȲȲ **The Tuarts Chardonnay 2003** Melon and stone fruit, with a whisk of oak, builds to a strong, focused finish. **RATING** 88 **DRINK** 2007 $ 19.99

ȲȲȲȲ **Lorenza Sparkling Chenin Blanc NV RATING** 86 **DRINK** 2007 $ 18
The Tuarts Chenin Blanc 2003 RATING 85 **DRINK** Now $ 14.99
Late Harvest Muscat Fronti 2003 RATING 84 **DRINK** Now $ 14.99

Paulett ★★★★

Polish Hill Road, Polish Hill River, SA 5453 **REGION** Clare Valley
T (08) 8843 4328 **F** (08) 8843 4202 **OPEN** 7 days 10–5
WINEMAKER Neil Paulett **EST.** 1983 **CASES** 12 500
PRODUCT RANGE ($15–30 CD) Polish Hill River Riesling, Stone Cutting Unwooded Chardonnay, Late Harvest Riesling, Trillians Sparkling Riesling, Clare Blue Sparkling Shiraz, Shiraz, Andreas Shiraz, Stone Cutting Shiraz Cabernet Malbec, Cabernet Merlot.
SUMMARY The Paulett story is a saga of Australian perseverance, commencing with the 1982 purchase of a property with 1 hectare of vines and a house, promptly destroyed by the terrible Ash Wednesday bushfires of the following year. Son Matthew has joined Neil and Alison Paulett as a partner in the business, responsible for viticulture and the plantings now total 25 hectares on a much-expanded property holding of 147 hectares. The winery and the cellar door have wonderful views over the Polish Hill River region, the memories of the bushfires long gone. Exports to the UK and New Zealand.

ȲȲȲȲ **Andreas Shiraz 2001** Very rich, ripe and complex; medium to full-bodied blackberry, chocolate and mocha; ripe tannins. **RATING** 92 **DRINK** 2015
Polish Hill River Riesling 2003 Powerful, rich, luscious citrus and tropical fruit; no need to cellar, but has screwcap. **RATING** 90 **DRINK** Now $ 18
Polish Hill River Shiraz 2001 Well balanced, medium-bodied; supple blackberry, mulberry and spice fruit; fine tannins, subtle oak. **RATING** 90 **DRINK** 2011 $ 22

ȲȲȲȲ **Polish Hill River Cabernet Merlot 2001** Light to medium-bodied; easy style, not a lot of structure, just gently sweet fruit. **RATING** 87 **DRINK** 2008 $ 20

Paul Osicka ★★★★

Majors Creek Vineyard at Graytown, Vic 3608 **REGION** Heathcote
T (03) 5794 9235 **F** (03) 5794 9288 **OPEN** Mon–Sat 10–5, Sun 12–5
WINEMAKER Paul Osicka **EST.** 1955
PRODUCT RANGE ($14–25 CD) Chardonnay, Riesling, Cabernet Sauvignon, Shiraz.
SUMMARY A low-profile producer but reliable, particularly when it comes to its smooth but rich Shiraz. The wines are distributed in Melbourne and Sydney by Australian Prestige Wines, with exports to the UK, Hong Kong and Japan.

Paxton Wines ★★★★

Sand Road, McLaren Vale, SA 5171 (postal) **REGION** McLaren Vale
T (08) 8323 8645 **F** (08) 8323 8903 **OPEN** Not
WINEMAKER Contract **EST.** 1997 **CASES** 1500
PRODUCT RANGE ($25–40 R) Shiraz.
SUMMARY David Paxton is one of Australia's best known viticulturists and consultants. He founded Paxton Vineyards in McLaren Vale with his family in 1979, and has since been involved in various capacities in the establishment and management of vineyards in the Adelaide Hills, Coonawarra, Clare Valley, Yarra Valley, Margaret River and Great Southern. The family vineyards in McLaren Vale remain the centre of attention, and are still contract-growers for others. However, as a means of promoting the quality of the grapes produced by the vineyards, Paxton Wines has ventured into small-scale winemaking (via contract) with an initial release of Shiraz. There are plans to increase the range in the future, but the volume of production of each wine will remain small. Exports to the US, Canada and Singapore.

ㅜㅜㅜㅜ **McLaren Vale Shiraz 2002** Supple, smooth, focused blackberry, spice, mocha and chocolate flavours; fine tannins. Top vintage. **RATING** 92 **DRINK** 2015 $ 33

ㅜㅜㅜㅜ **Chardonnay 2003** Elegant, fresh, lively fruit-driven, nectarine and citrus. Screwcap. **RATING** 88 **DRINK** 2007 $ 25.60

🐌 Peacetree Estate NR

Harmans South Road, Wilyabrup, WA 6280 **REGION** Margaret River
T (08) 9755 5170 **F** (08) 9755 9275 **OPEN** 7 days 10–6
WINEMAKER Paul Green (Contract) **EST.** 1995 **CASES** 1250
PRODUCT RANGE ($13–30 CD) Semillon Sauvignon Blanc, Sauvignon Blanc, Cabernet Merlot, Cabernet Sauvignon, Reserve Cabernet Sauvignon.
SUMMARY Three generations of the Tucker family were involved in the first plantings at Peacetree Estate in 1995; however, it was of olive trees, not vines. The latter followed quickly thereafter with sauvignon blanc and cabernet sauvignon, and for the first two vintages the grapes were sold to Hay Shed Hill, in the third year to Palandri. In 2001 the Tuckers decided to take the plunge and have the wine bottled under the Peacetree Estate label, opening the cellar-door sales in December 2002, selling out of the 2001 vintage within 5 months. A little semillon and merlot is also grown and made.

Peacock Hill Vineyard ★★★

Cnr Branxton Road & Palmers Lane, Pokolbin, NSW 2320 **REGION** Lower Hunter Valley
T (02) 4998 7661 **F** (02) 4998 7661 **OPEN** Thurs–Mon, public and school holidays 10–5, or by appointment
WINEMAKER Bill Sneddon, Rod Russell **EST.** 1969 **CASES** 1500
PRODUCT RANGE ($23–36 CD) Top Block Chardonnay, Fond Memories, Jaan Shiraz, Faith Cabernet Sauvignon.
SUMMARY The Peacock Hill Vineyard was first planted in 1969 as part of the Rothbury Estate, originally being owned by a separate syndicate but then moving under the direct control and ownership of Rothbury. After several further changes of ownership as Rothbury sold many of its vineyards, George Tsiros and Silvi Laumets acquired the 8-hectare property in October 1995. Since that time they have rejuvenated the vineyard and built a small but attractive accommodation lodge for two people, and have a tennis court and petanque rink for their exclusive enjoyment. Over the years, Peacock Hill has been a consistent medal winner in local wine shows.

ㅜㅜㅜㅜ **Top Block Chardonnay 2003** Aromatic, tangy citrus and stone fruit; elegant and tight, yet flavoursome and long. **RATING** 92 **DRINK** 2008 $ 35

ㅜㅜㅜ **Jaan Shiraz 2002 RATING** 83 $ 30
Faith Cabernet Sauvignon 2002 RATING 81 $ 30

Pearson Vineyards
NR

Main North Road, Penwortham, SA 5453 **REGION** Clare Valley
T (08) 8843 4234 **F** (08) 8843 4141 **OPEN** Mon–Fri 11–5, weekends 10–5
WINEMAKER Jim Pearson **EST.** 1993 **CASES** 800
PRODUCT RANGE ($13–18 CD) Riesling, Late Harvest Riesling, Cabernet Franc, Cabernet Sauvignon.
SUMMARY Jim Pearson makes the Pearson Vineyard wines at Mintaro Cellars. The 1.5-hectare estate vineyards surround the beautiful little stone house which acts as a cellar door and which appears on the cover of my book, *The Wines, The History, The Vignerons of the Clare Valley*.

Peel Estate
★★★★

Fletcher Road, Baldivis, WA 6171 **REGION** Peel
T (08) 9524 1221 **F** (08) 9524 1625 **OPEN** 7 days 10–5
WINEMAKER Will Nairn **EST.** 1974 **CASES** 7000
PRODUCT RANGE ($14–55 R) Wood-Matured Chenin Blanc, Premium White, Verdelho, Chardonnay, Pichet Premium Red, Shiraz, Zinfandel, Cabernet Sauvignon.
SUMMARY The winery rating is given for its Shiraz, a wine of considerable finesse and with a remarkably consistent track record. Every year Will Nairn holds a Great Shiraz Tasting for 6-year-old Australian Shirazs, and pits Peel Estate (in a blind tasting attended by 60 or so people) against Australia's best. It is never disgraced. The white wines are workmanlike, the wood-matured Chenin Blanc another winery specialty, although not achieving the excellence of the Shiraz. At 5 years of age it will typically show well, with black cherry and chocolate flavours, a strong dash of American oak, and surprising youth. Exports to the UK, Malaysia and Hong Kong.

Peerick Vineyard
★★★★

Wild Dog Track, Moonambel, Vic 3478 **REGION** Pyrenees
T (03) 5467 2207 **F** (03) 5467 2207 **OPEN** Weekends and public holidays 11–4
WINEMAKER Contract **EST.** 1990 **CASES** 2500
PRODUCT RANGE ($12–32 CD) Sauvignon Blanc, Semillon Sauvignon Blanc, Viognier, Pinot Noir, Shiraz, Merlot, Cabernet Sauvignon.
SUMMARY Peerick is the venture of Chris Jessup and wife Meryl. They have mildly trimmed their Joseph's coat vineyard by increasing the plantings to 5.6 hectares and eliminating the malbec and semillon, but still manage to grow cabernet sauvignon, shiraz, cabernet franc, merlot, sauvignon blanc, and viognier. Quality has improved year by year as the vines have approached maturity. Exports to New Zealand.

ᵀᵀᵀᵀ **Viognier 2003** Highly perfumed musk and spice bouquet; the palate tightens up with good acidity; impressive. Screwcap. **RATING** 91 **DRINK** Now $ 23.75

ᵀᵀᵀᵀ **Shiraz 2001** A light to medium-bodied mix of savoury/spicy notes on black fruits; controlled extract and tannins. **RATING** 89 **DRINK** 2008 $ 28.50
Merlot 2001 An attractive wine with similar structure to the Shiraz; a blend of savoury and sweet dark fruits; fine, ripe tannins. **RATING** 89 **DRINK** 2008 $ 23.75
Cabernet Sauvignon 2001 Blackcurrant and blackberry with an earthy, savoury twist throughout the palate which gives a certain austerity, though authentic varietal character; fine tannins. **RATING** 88 **DRINK** 2010 $ 30.50

Pegeric Vineyard
NR

PO Box 227, Woodend, Vic 3442 **REGION** Macedon Ranges
T (03) 9354 4961 **F** (03) 9354 4961 **OPEN** Not
WINEMAKER Llew Knight, Ian Gunter, Chris Cormack **EST.** 1991 **CASES** 100
PRODUCT RANGE ($85–95 ML) Pinot Noir, Tumbetin.
SUMMARY Owner and viticulturist Chris Cormack accumulated an oenological degree and experience in every facet of the wine industry here and overseas before beginning the establishment of the close-planted, non-irrigated, low-yielding Pegeric Vineyard at an altitude of 640 metres on red volcanic basalt soil. As a separate exercise, Chris Cormack has also made several vintages of a cross-regional blend of Cabernet Shiraz named Tumbetin.

Pembroke

NR

Richmond Road, Cambridge, Tas 7170 **REGION** Southern Tasmania
T (03) 6248 5139 **F** (03) 6234 5481 **OPEN** By appointment
WINEMAKER Andrew Hood (Contract) **EST.** 1980 **CASES** 200
PRODUCT RANGE ($24 ML) Pinot Noir.
SUMMARY The 1-hectare Pembroke vineyard was established in 1980 by the McKay and Hawker
families and is still owned by them. It is predominantly planted to pinot noir, with tiny quantities of
chardonnay, riesling and sauvignon blanc.

Penbro Estate

★★★★

Cnr Melba Highway and Murrindindi Road, Glenburn, Vic 3717 **REGION** Upper Goulburn
T (03) 9215 2229 **F** (03) 9215 2346 **OPEN** By appointment, cellar door at Glenburn pub
WINEMAKER MasterWineMakers (Contract) **EST.** 1997 **CASES** 3500
PRODUCT RANGE ($14.50–21.60 CD) Chardonnay, Unwooded Chardonnay, Pinot Noir, Shiraz, Merlot,
Cabernet Sauvignon.
SUMMARY Since 1997 the Bertalli family has established 40 hectares of chardonnay, pinot noir,
merlot, cabernet sauvignon and shiraz. The wines have won several silver and bronze medals at the
Victorian Wines Show. Part of the grape production is sold, part vinified for the Penbro brand.
Distribution in Victoria by The Wine Group.

ŸŸŸŸŸ **Pinot Noir 2002** Fragrant cherry blossom and spice; delicate, fine cherry and strawberry
varietal fruit; good length. Can it be repeated? **RATING** 91 **DRINK** 2008 $ 21.60
Cabernets 2003 Medium-bodied, supple, smooth and elegant; sophisticated
winemaking; black fruits, dark chocolate and subtle tannins. **RATING** 90 **DRINK** 2012
$ 21.50

ŸŸŸŸ **Chardonnay 2002** Smooth, medium-bodied; nectarine, melon, peach and creamy
cashew. **RATING** 89 **DRINK** 2007 $ 19.95
Merlot 2002 Ultra-savoury/earthy/olivaceous style; nice spicy tannins and oak. **RATING** 88
DRINK 2009 $ 21.50
Unwooded Chardonnay 2003 Light to medium-bodied; clean melon, nectarine and
citrus; good length. **RATING** 87 **DRINK** Now $ 18.45

ŸŸŸŸ **Shiraz 2002** Fresh, lively, minty, cherry, berry; elegant, light-bodied; drink soon.
RATING 86 **DRINK** 2007 $ 21.50

Pendarves Estate

★★★

110 Old North Road, Belford, NSW 2335 **REGION** Lower Hunter Valley
T (02) 6574 7222 **F** (02) 9970 6152 **OPEN** Weekends 11–5, Mon–Fri by appointment
WINEMAKER Greg Silkman (Contract) **EST.** 1986 **CASES** 12 000
PRODUCT RANGE ($18–25 CD) An unusual portfolio of Sauvignon Blanc, Verdelho, Unoaked
Chardonnay, Chardonnay, Pinot Noir, Chambourcin, Shiraz, Merlot Malbec Cabernet.
SUMMARY The perpetual-motion general practitioner and founder of the Australian Medical Friends
of Wine, Dr Philip Norrie, is a born communicator and marketer as well as a wine historian of note.
He also happens to be a passionate advocate of the virtues of verdelho, inspired in part by the high
regard held for that variety by vignerons around the turn of the century. His ambassadorship for the
cause of wine and health in both Australia and overseas has led to the development of a joint venture
for the production and export distribution of a large volume brand 'The Wine Doctor', and to the
establishment of export markets in Singapore, the UK, Germany, China, India, Russia and Malaysia
(as well as national distribution).

ŸŸŸŸ **Verdelho 2000** Light straw-green; good length and mouthfeel, still fresh, balancing
acidity will sustain further bottle development. Impressive. **RATING** 87 **DRINK** Now $ 18
Shiraz 2001 A mix of berry and earthy regional aromas; solid plum and blackberry palate,
savoury nuances. **RATING** 87 **DRINK** 2011 $ 25

ŸŸŸŸ **Chardonnay 2000** **RATING** 86 **DRINK** Now $ 20
Verdelho 2001 **RATING** 85 **DRINK** Now $ 18
Pinot Noir 2001 **RATING** 85 **DRINK** 2010 $ 20

> Sauvignon Blanc Semillon 2002 **RATING** 84 **DRINK** Now $ 18
> Unoaked Chardonnay 2001 **RATING** 84 **DRINK** Now $ 18

ȲȲȲ Merlot Malbec 2001 **RATING** 83 $ 25
Chambourcin 2001 **RATING** 80 $ 20

Penfolds ★★★★★

Tanunda Road, Nuriootpa, SA 5355 **REGION** Barossa Valley
T (08) 8568 9290 **F** (08) 8568 9493 **OPEN** Mon–Fri 10–5, weekends and public holidays 11–5
WINEMAKER Peter Gago **EST.** 1844 **CASES** 1.4 million
PRODUCT RANGE ($6.50–400 CD) At the bottom is the Rawsons Retreat; next Koonunga Hill, then Thomas Hyland; next the bin range of Bin 28 Kalimna Shiraz, Bin 128 Coonawarra Shiraz, Bin 138 Old Vine Shiraz Grenache Mourvedre, Bin 407 Cabernet Sauvignon, Bin 389 Cabernet Shiraz and Bin 707 Cabernet Sauvignon. The premium wines are Eden Valley Reserve Riesling, Adelaide Hills Chardonnay, Reserve Bin Chardonnay and Yattarna; and finally the top three red wines of St Henri Shiraz, RWT Shiraz and Grange. A range of tawny ports culminates in Great Grandfather.
SUMMARY Senior among the numerous wine companies or stand-alone brands in Southcorp Wines and undoubtedly one of the top wine companies in the world in terms of quality, product range and exports. The consistency of the quality of the red wines and their value for money is recognised worldwide, and — headed by the development of the ultra-premium Yattarna Chardonnay — it has steadily raised the quality of its white wines.

ȲȲȲȲȲ Yattarna Chardonnay 2000 Penetrating stone fruit and citrus aromas flowing through to a palate with excellent attack, line and length, the French oak seamlessly integrated throughout. **RATING** 96 **DRINK** 2010 $ 100
Grange 1999 Concentrated blackberry and licorice fruit, the oak perfectly integrated. A powerful, masculine style, a touch more austere than the '98. **RATING** 95 **DRINK** 2029 $ 400

ȲȲȲȲȳ Reserve Bin Aged Release Clare Valley Riesling 1998 Ultra-classic toast and kerosene; abundant mid-palate gentle lime juice flavours, are perfectly balanced by quite soft acidity on the finish. **RATING** 93 **DRINK** 2008 $ 20
St Henri Shiraz 1999 Bramble, briar and spice aromas; then a palate with bitter chocolate, licorice and blackberry joining the background components of the bouquet; very well-handled tannins; Penfolds is on top of this aspect of the game. **RATING** 93 **DRINK** 2015 $ 60
Old Vine Barossa Valley Bin 138 Shiraz Mourvedre Grenache 2002 A smooth and even flow of aromas of dark plum, the palate following the bouquet; very well balanced, great potential. **RATING** 93 **DRINK** 2011 $ 25
Bin 707 Cabernet Sauvignon 2001 Abundant red and black fruit aromas on the bouquet, the oak still integrating; blackcurrant and blackberry fruit are matched by mouth-coating tannins. **RATING** 93 **DRINK** 2025 $ 140
Bin 389 Cabernet Shiraz 2001 Spicy blackcurrant, cassis and redcurrant fruits; supple, ripe tannins; very well-handled oak. **RATING** 93 **DRINK** 2021 $ 40
Eden Valley Reserve Riesling 2002 Notwithstanding the screwcap, complexity already building, with strong mineral, slate, spice and citrus flavours moving through to a spicy, low pH finish. **RATING** 92 **DRINK** 2012 $ 24.99
Bin 128 Coonawarra Shiraz 2001 Vibrant, almost essency, blackberry and raspberry fruit; intense; finishes with savoury tannins. **RATING** 92 **DRINK** 2016 $ 25
Bin 407 Cabernet Sauvignon 2001 Scented spice and blackcurrant aromas; mouthfilling blackcurrant and chocolate fruit; balanced tannins. **RATING** 92 **DRINK** 2016 $ 30

ȲȲȲȲ Eden Valley Reserve Riesling 2003 Spicy/minerally; flecks of blossom and crushed herb; youthful, fresh, tightly focused; lime juice in the background. Screwcap. **RATING** 89 **DRINK** 2009 $ 24.99
Kalimna Bin 28 Shiraz 2001 Exotic prune, plum and licorice fruits on a powerful palate, finishing with forbidding tannins. **RATING** 89 **DRINK** 2016 $ 25
Reserve Bin Fleurieu Semillon 1999 Complex aromas; a big, full-bodied, oaked style saved by its acidity. **RATING** 87 **DRINK** 2007 $ 19

ΥΥΥΥ Koonunga Hill Semillon Chardonnay 2002 RATING 86 DRINK Now $13.90
Rawsons Retreat Merlot 2002 RATING 86 DRINK Now $9.99
Rawson's Retreat Shiraz Cabernet 2003 RATING 85 DRINK 2007 $9.99
Rawson's Retreat Cabernet Sauvignon 2003 RATING 85 DRINK 2007 $9.99

ΥΥΥ Minchinbury Sparkling NV RATING 82 $6.50

Penfolds Magill Estate ★★★★☆

78 Penfold Road, Magill, SA 5072 REGION Adelaide Zone
T (08) 8301 5569 F (08) 8301 5588 OPEN 7 days 10.30–4.30
WINEMAKER Peter Gago EST. 1844
PRODUCT RANGE ($65 CD) Magill Estate Shiraz.
SUMMARY The birthplace of Penfolds, established by Dr Christopher Rawson Penfold in 1844, his
house still part of the immaculately maintained property. It includes 6 hectares of precious shiraz
used to make Magill Estate; the original and subsequent winery buildings, most still in operation or
in museum condition; the Penfolds corporate headquarters; and the much-acclaimed Magill
Restaurant, with panoramic views back to the city, a great wine list and fine dining. All this a
20-minute drive from Adelaide's CBD.

Penley Estate ★★★☆

McLeans Road, Coonawarra, SA 5263 REGION Coonawarra
T (08) 8736 3211 F (08) 8736 3124 OPEN 7 days 10–4
WINEMAKER Kym Tolley EST. 1988 CASES 30 000
PRODUCT RANGE ($19.50–75 CD) Chardonnay, Hyland Shiraz, Special Select Shiraz, Ausvetia Shiraz,
Shiraz Cabernet Sauvignon, Merlot, Reserve Cabernet Sauvignon, Phoenix Cabernet Sauvignon.
SUMMARY Owner winemaker Kym Tolley describes himself as a fifth-generation winemaker, the
family tree involving both the Penfolds and the Tolleys. He worked 17 years in the industry before
establishing Penley Estate and has made every post a winner since, producing a succession of rich,
complex, full-bodied red wines and stylish Chardonnays. Now ranks among the best wineries in
Coonawarra, drawing upon 91 precious hectares of estate plantings. Exports to the US, Europe and
Asia.

ΥΥΥΥΥ Ausvetia Shiraz 2001 Medium to full-bodied; ripe blackberry fruit with touches of spice
and oak; ripe tannins in support. RATING 90 DRINK 2016 $75.30

ΥΥΥΥ Chardonnay 2002 In typical tightly wound regional style; citrussy/lemony; nice length
and carry; not complex but fresh and appealing. RATING 89 DRINK 2007 $19.50
Shiraz Cabernet Sauvignon 2001 Solid, sweet, ripe blackberry and cherry fruit; slightly
simple overall. RATING 88 DRINK 2011 $29.70
Hyland Shiraz 2002 Medium-bodied; a smooth mix of red and black fruits; simple
structure. RATING 87 DRINK 2008 $20.50
Merlot 2002 Spicy, light to medium-bodied; savoury/leafy/olivaceous varietal characters.
RATING 87 DRINK 2008 $30.99

ΥΥΥΥ Phoenix Cabernet Sauvignon 2002 RATING 86 DRINK 2010 $24

Penmara ★★★

Bridge Street, Muswellbrook, NSW 2333 REGION Upper Hunter Valley
T (02) 9362 5157 F (02) 9362 5157 OPEN Not
WINEMAKER John Horden EST. 2000 CASES 30 000
PRODUCT RANGE The wines are made in three levels: at the bottom the Five Families range; next in the
ladder the Reserve range; and finally the Individual Vineyard range made only in exceptional
vintages. The varieties offered including Semillon, Verdelho, Shiraz, Merlot, Cabernet Sauvignon.
SUMMARY Penmara was formed with the banner '5 Vineyards: 1 Vision'. In fact a sixth vineyard
has already joined the group, the vineyards pooling most of their grapes, with a central
processing facility, and marketing focused exclusively on exports. The members are Lilyvale
Vineyards, in the Northern Slopes region near Tenterfield; Tangaratta Vineyards at Tamworth;
Birnam Wood, Rothbury Ridge and Martindale Vineyards in the Hunter Valley; and Highland

Heritage at Orange. In all these vineyards give Penmara access to 128 hectares of shiraz, chardonnay, cabernet sauvignon, semillon, verdelho and merlot. Exports to the US, Canada, Singapore and Japan.

Penna Lane Wines ★★★★☆

Lot 51, Penna Lane, Penwortham via Clare, SA 5453 **REGION** Clare Valley
T (08) 8843 4364 **F** (08) 8843 4349 **OPEN** Thurs–Sun and public holidays 11–5, or by appointment
WINEMAKER Contract **EST.** 1998 **CASES** 3000
PRODUCT RANGE ($17–35 CD) Riesling, Semillon, Shiraz, The Willsmore Reserve Shiraz, Cabernet Sauvignon.
SUMMARY Ray and Lynette Klavin, then living and working near Waikerie in the Riverland, purchased their 14-hectare property in the Skilly Hills in 1993. It was covered with rubbish, Salvation Jane, a derelict dairy and a tumbledown piggery, and every weekend they travelled from Waikerie to clean up the property, initially living in a tent and thereafter moving into the dairy which had more recently been used as a shearing shed. Planting began in 1996, and in 1997 the family moved to the region, Lynette to take up a teaching position and Ray to work at Knappstein Wines. Ray had enrolled at Roseworthy in 1991, and met Stephen Stafford-Brookes, another mature-age student, and both graduated from Roseworthy in 1993, having already formed a winemaking joint venture for Penna Lane. Picnic and barbecue facilities are available at the cellar door, and light lunches are served. Exports to the US.

ΨΨΨΨΨ **The Willsmore Shiraz 2002** Dense colour; dense and concentrated but a supple mix of blackberry and dark chocolate; ripe tannins, good oak, good balance. **RATING** 94 **DRINK** 2020 $35

ΨΨΨΨΨ **Shiraz 2002** Very powerful and complex blackberry and licorice; a hint of game; strong structure. **RATING** 91 **DRINK** 2015 $22
Riesling 2003 Fragrant lime juice aromas and flavours; has depth. Screwcap, but relatively quick-developing. Good length. **RATING** 90 **DRINK** 2007 $19
Cabernet Sauvignon 2002 Very complex, intense savoury blackberry fruit; lingering tannins provide sustained length. **RATING** 90 **DRINK** 2015 $22

ΨΨΨΨ **Semillon 2003** Typically powerful and long, more to Margaret River than Hunter in style; sweet citrus fruit, almost tropical. **RATING** 89 **DRINK** 2008 $17

🐛 Pennyfield Wines ★★★

Pennyfield Road, Berri, SA 5343 **REGION** Riverland
T (08) 8582 3595 **F** (08) 8582 3205 **OPEN** Not
WINEMAKER David Smallacombe **EST.** 2000 **CASES** 3500
PRODUCT RANGE ($13–20 ML) There are two varietal product ranges: the flagship Pennyfield Chardonnay, Shiraz, Cabernet Sauvignon; and the second label Cragg's Creek Chardonnay, Rose, Shiraz Cabernet. Other varietals including Petit Verdot and Viognier are in the pipeline.
SUMMARY Pennyfield Wines is named in memory of the pioneering family which originally developed the property part of which is now owned by the Efrosinis family. Pennyfield draws on 17.7 hectares of estate vineyards (principally planted to cabernet sauvignon and shiraz) but is also supplied with chardonnay, merlot, petit verdot, touriga and viognier by four local growers. It is also part of a new association in the course of formation, Riverland Boutique Wines Incorporated, which has 24 members with, or soon to be with, producers licences.

ΨΨΨΨ **Basket Pressed Petit Verdot 2002** Strong colour; dense and powerful black fruits; licorice and dark chocolate; abundant structure, but not extractive. Deserves its string of medals. **RATING** 90 **DRINK** 2012 $20

ΨΨΨΨ **Basket Pressed Shiraz 2002** Clean, fresh red and black fruits; medium-bodied; good tannins and length. **RATING** 87 **DRINK** 2008 $20
Basket Pressed Shiraz 2001 Appealing, sweet red berry fruit; soft mouthfeel from ripe tannins and well-judged oak. **RATING** 87 **DRINK** 2009 $20
Basket Pressed Cabernet Sauvignon 2001 Smooth, supple red and blackcurrant fruit; fine tannins. Very similar in style to the shiraz. **RATING** 87 **DRINK** 2010 $20

ㅜㅜㅜㅜ **Chardonnay 2003** Clean, rich, full-bodied peachy fruit; 14 degrees alcohol gives the impression of sweetness. **RATING** 86 **DRINK** Now $ 17
Basket Pressed Cabernet Sauvignon 2002 Strongly savoury earthy/briary aromas, but more sweet fruit on the palate. **RATING** 86 **DRINK** 2007 $ 20
Chardonnay 2002 **RATING** 85 **DRINK** Now $ 17
Cragg's Creek Shiraz Cabernet 2002 **RATING** 85 **DRINK** 2007 $ 20
Liqueur Chardonnay Viognier NV **RATING** 85 **DRINK** Now $ 20
Basket Pressed Merlot 2002 **RATING** 84 **DRINK** 2007 $ 20

ㅜㅜㅜ **Cragg's Creek Rose 2003** **RATING** 83 $ 13
Cragg's Creek Chardonnay 2002 **RATING** 82 $ 13

Penny's Hill ★★★★

Main Road, McLaren Vale, SA 5171 **REGION** McLaren Vale
T (08) 8556 4460 **F** (08) 8556 4462 **OPEN** 7 days 10–5
WINEMAKER Ben Riggs (Contract) **EST.** 1988 **CASES** 7000
PRODUCT RANGE ($15–75 R) Goss Corner Semillon, Chardonnay, Nobilis Botrytis Semillon, Shiraz, Footprint Shiraz, Grenache, Malpas Road Merlot, Specialized Shiraz Cabernet Merlot, Fortified Shiraz.
SUMMARY Penny's Hill is owned by Adelaide advertising agency businessman Tony Parkinson and wife Susie. The Penny's Hill vineyard is 43.5 hectares and, unusually for McLaren Vale, is close-planted with a thin vertical trellis/thin vertical canopy, the work of consultant viticulturist David Paxton. The innovative red dot packaging was the inspiration of Tony Parkinson, recalling the red dot sold sign on pictures in an art gallery and now giving rise to the Red Dot Art Galley opening at Penny's Hill. Exports to the US, Canada, the UK, Switzerland, Denmark and Singapore.

ㅜㅜㅜㅜㅜ **Specialized 2002** Powerful, rich and complex blackberry/bitter chocolate aromas and flavours; good tannin structure. **RATING** 90 **DRINK** 2012 $ 27
Malpas Road Merlot 2002 Cool vintage gives excellent varietal expression; small, red berry fruits at the centre, then a lingering, savoury (but not green) finish. **RATING** 90 **DRINK** 2010 $ 20

ㅜㅜㅜㅜ **Footprint McLaren Vale Shiraz 2001** Attractive blackberry and blackcurrant fruit with earthy overtones; ripe tannins; good extract and oak. **RATING** 89 **DRINK** 2011 $ 40
Grenache 2002 Plenty of depth and structure in medium-bodied mode; sweet, juicy grenache varietal character, plus a coat of regional chocolate. **RATING** 89 **DRINK** 2007 $ 25
Chardonnay 2002 Ripe melon into tropical fruit; has soaked up the oak; full flavoured, drink-now style. **RATING** 87 **DRINK** Now $ 20.50
Shiraz 2001 Pleasant, easy, light to medium-bodied; sweet fruit, splashes of chocolate and vanilla. **RATING** 87 **DRINK** 2009 $ 29

ㅜㅜㅜㅜ **Goss Corner Semillon 2002** **RATING** 85 **DRINK** Now $ 19

Pennyweight Winery ★★★

Pennyweight Lane, Beechworth, Vic 3747 **REGION** Beechworth
T (03) 5728 1747 **F** (03) 5728 1704 **OPEN** 7 days 10–5
WINEMAKER Stephen Newton Morris **EST.** 1982 **CASES** 1000
PRODUCT RANGE ($16–30 CD) Beechworth Riesling, Semillon Sauvignon Blanc, Gamay, Beechworth Pinot Noir, Beechworth Shiraz, Beechworth Cabernet; also important is the range of Oloroso, Fino and Amontillado sherries and a range of ports from Old Tawny, Ruby, Gold and Muscat.
SUMMARY Pennyweight was established by Stephen Morris, great-grandson of GF Morris, founder of Morris Wines. The 4 hectares of vines are not irrigated and are organically grown. The business is run by Stephen, together with his wife Elizabeth and assisted by their three sons; Elizabeth Morris says, 'It's a perfect world', suggesting Pennyweight is more than happy with its lot in life.

ㅜㅜㅜㅜ **Semillon Sauvignon Blanc 2003** Light to medium-bodied; clean; not much varietal character but nice mouthfeel and balance; gently ripe. **RATING** 87 **DRINK** 2008 $ 20

ㅜㅜㅜ **Cabernet Sauvignon Cabernet Franc Merlot 2001** **RATING** 83 $ 25

Peos Estate ★★★

Graphite Road, Manjimup, WA 6258 **REGION** Manjimup
T (08) 9772 1378 **F** (08) 9772 1372 **OPEN** 7 days 10–4
WINEMAKER Larry Cherubino **EST.** 1996 **CASES** 3000
PRODUCT RANGE ($15–30 CD) Unwooded Chardonnay, Four Aces Shiraz, Manjin Shiraz, Cabernet Sauvignon.
SUMMARY The Peos family has farmed the West Manjimup district for 50 years, the third generation of four brothers commencing the development of a substantial vineyard in 1996. In all, little over 33 hectares of vines, with shiraz (10 hectares), merlot (7 hectares), chardonnay (6.5 hectares), cabernet sauvignon (4 hectares) and pinot noir, sauvignon blanc and verdelho (2 hectares each). Exports to Denmark.

ΨΨΨΨ **Four Aces Shiraz 2002** Fragrant, spicy, raspberry and blackberry aromas and flavours; fine tannins, balanced oak. **RATING** 89 **DRINK** 2010 $ 30

ΨΨΨΨ **Cabernet Sauvignon 2002 RATING** 86 **DRINK** 2009 $ 25

Pepper Tree Wines ★★★☆

Halls Road, Pokolbin, NSW 2321 **REGION** Lower Hunter Valley
T (02) 4998 7539 **F** (02) 4998 7746 **OPEN** Mon–Fri 9–5, weekends 9.30–5
WINEMAKER Chris Cameron **EST.** 1993 **CASES** 60 000
PRODUCT RANGE ($16–70 CD) Gewurztraminer, Sauvignon Blanc, Unwooded Chardonnay, Chardonnay, Frost Hollow, Shiraz, Mulberry Row, Merlot, Cabernet Merlot Franc; Reserve range of Semillon, Sauvignon Blanc, Verduzzo, Verdelho, Viognier, Chardonnay, Shiraz, Coonawarra Merlot, Cabernet Franc, Malbec, Coonawarra Cabernet Sauvignon; fortifieds.
SUMMARY The Pepper Tree winery is situated in the complex which also contains The Convent guesthouse and Roberts Restaurant. In October 2002 it was acquired by a company controlled by Dr John Davis, who owns 50 per cent of Briar Ridge and has substantial vineyard interests throughout NSW and SA. Pepper Tree has made a determined, and quite successful, effort to establish its reputation as one of Australia's leading producers of Merlot. Exports to the US, the UK, Switzerland, Singapore and Indonesia.

ΨΨΨΨΨ **Wrattonbully Reserve Cabernet Sauvignon 2002** Lush cassis and blackcurrant; good tannin support; balanced oak. **RATING** 92 **DRINK** 2012 $ 30
Reserve Semillon 2003 Herb and lanolin aromas; a long, tight palate with lingering, minerally acidity. **RATING** 90 **DRINK** 2008 $ 21

ΨΨΨΨ **Reserve Shiraz 2002** Medium-bodied, a range of sweet, red berry damson plum and mint aromas, all attesting to the cool climate of Orange. **RATING** 88 **DRINK** 2010 $ 30
Reserve Semillon 2002 Water white, but surprisingly aromatic lime blossom; crisp, clean, linear; demands time. **RATING** 87 **DRINK** 2013 $ 21

ΨΨΨΨ **Reserve Verduzzo 2003 RATING** 85 **DRINK** Now $ 22
Silenus Grande Reserve Methode Champenoise 2003 RATING 85 **DRINK** 2007 $ 30

ΨΨΨ **Reserve Viognier 2003 RATING** 83 $ 22
Reserve Shiraz 2001 RATING 83 $ 30
Reserve Verdelho 2003 RATING 81 $ 20

Peppin Ridge NR

Peppin Drive, Bonnie Doon, Vic 3720 **REGION** Upper Goulburn
T (03) 5778 7430 **F** (03) 5778 7430 **OPEN** 7 days 11–5
WINEMAKER Don Adams **EST.** 1997 **CASES** 400
PRODUCT RANGE ($15–23 CD) Verdelho, Marsanne, Shiraz, Syrah Marsanne, Syrah Durif, Merlot.
SUMMARY Peppin Ridge is planted on the shores of Lake Eildon; the land forms part of a vast station property established in 1850, and now partly under Lake Eildon. The property in question was then acquired by the Peppin family who developed the Peppin Merino sheep, said to be the cornerstone of the Australian wool industry. The plantings of marsanne, verdelho, shiraz and merlot cover 4 hectares, and the wine is made on-site. The initial releases of the red wines had exaggerated, pervasive aromas and flavours of menthol and eucalypt, of a kind and to a degree not previously encountered by me.

Perrini Estate

NR

Bower Road, Meadows, SA 5201 **REGION** Adelaide Hills
T (08) 8388 3210 **F** (08) 8388 3210 **OPEN** Wed–Sun and public holidays 10–5
WINEMAKER Antonio Perrini **EST.** 1997 **CASES** 3500
PRODUCT RANGE ($13–21.50 CD) Semillon Sauvignon Blanc, Unwooded Chardonnay, Shiraz, Merlot, Sangiovese, Cabernet Sauvignon, Tony's Blend, Tawny Port.
SUMMARY Perrini Estate is very much a family affair; Tony and Connie Perrini had spent their working life in the retail food business, and Tony purchased the land in 1988 as a hobby farm and retirement home (or so Tony told Connie). In 1990 Tony planted his first few grapevines, began to read everything he could about making wine, and thereafter obtained vintage experience at a local winery. Next came highly successful entries into amateur winemaker competitions, and that was that. Together the family established the 6 hectares of vineyard and built the winery and cellar door, culminating in the first commercial releases of the 1997 vintage, and steadily increasing production thereafter. Exports to Singapore.

Pertaringa

Cnr Hunt & Rifle Range Roads, McLaren Vale, SA 5171 **REGION** McLaren Vale
T (08) 8323 8125 **F** (08) 8323 7766 **OPEN** Mon–Fri 9–5, weekends and public holidays 11–5
WINEMAKER Geoff Hardy, Ben Riggs **EST.** 1980 **CASES** 10 000
PRODUCT RANGE ($15–30 CD) Bonfire Block Semillon, Scarecrow Sauvignon Blanc, The Full Fronti, The Final Front, Two Gentlemens Grenache, Undercover Shiraz, Over the Top Shiraz, Understudy Cabernet, Rifle and Hunt Cabernet.
SUMMARY The Pertaringa wines are made from part of the grapes grown by leading viticulturists Geoff Hardy and Ian Leask. The Pertaringa vineyard of 31 hectares was acquired in 1980 and rejuvenated; establishment of the ultra-cool Kuitpo vineyard in the Adelaide Hills began in 1987 and now supplies leading makers such as Southcorp and Petaluma. Retail distribution through South Australia, New South Wales, Victoria and Queensland; exports to Germany, Switzerland, Denmark, Hong Kong, Malaysia, Canada and the US.

ΨΨΨΨΨ **Undercover Shiraz 2002** Archetypal yet restrained McLaren Vale style; a melange of black fruits and dark chocolate; silky tannins, good mouthfeel. **RATING** 92 **DRINK** 2012 $ 18
Understudy Cabernet Sauvignon 2002 Attractive black and redcurrant fruit; excellent tannin structure and length; subtle oak. **RATING** 90 **DRINK** 2012 $ 18
Rifle and Hunter Cabernet Sauvignon 2001 Elegant medium-bodied wine; black and redcurrant fruits, fine tannins and subtle oak; good texture and structure. **RATING** 90 **DRINK** 2011 $ 30

ΨΨΨΨ **Bonfire Block Semillon 2002** A powerful bouquet; auto-suggestion of smoke; curiously, less intensity on the palate than the bouquet suggests, but well balanced and avoids phenolics. **RATING** 87 **DRINK** 2007 $ 20
The Final Fronti 2003 Highly aromatic and grapey; well done off-dry style; serve with ice blocks and/or soda in summer. **RATING** 87 **DRINK** Now $ 15
Two Gentlemen's Grenache 2001 Light to medium-bodied, user-friendly and food-friendly; gently spicy/savoury. **RATING** 87 **DRINK** Now $ 20

ΨΨΨΨ **Scarecrow Sauvignon Blanc 2003** **RATING** 85 **DRINK** Now $ 17.50
Over The Top Shiraz 2001 **RATING** 84 **DRINK** 2009 $ 30

Peschar's

NR

179 Wambo Road, Bulga, NSW 2330 **REGION** Lower Hunter Valley
T (02) 4927 1588 **F** (02) 4927 1589 **OPEN** Not
WINEMAKER Tyrrell's (Contract) **EST.** 1995 **CASES** 8000
PRODUCT RANGE ($14–18.50 ML) Chardonnay, Shiraz, Cabernet Merlot.
SUMMARY In 1995 John and Mary Peschar purchased the historic Meerea Park property which had been in the ownership of the Eather family, the name of which continues to be used by the Eathers for a quite separate winemaking operation. The property acquired by the Peschars is situated at the foot of the Wollemi National Park which rises steeply behind the vineyard, the

latter being planted on sandy alluvial soils. There are 16 hectares of chardonnay, the wine being contract-made by Tyrrell's. While the focus is on Chardonnay, the Peschars have sourced 6 hectares of vines in the Limestone Coast Zone of South Australia for the production of Shiraz and Cabernet Merlot.

Petaluma ★★★★★

Spring Gully Road, Piccadilly, SA 5151 **REGION** Adelaide Hills
T (08) 8339 4122 **F** (08) 8339 5253 **OPEN** At Bridgewater Mill
WINEMAKER Brian Croser **EST.** 1976 **CASES** 30 000
PRODUCT RANGE ($18–120 R) Riesling, Viognier, Chardonnay, Coonawarra (Cabernet Merlot), Coonawarra Merlot, Shiraz Viognier, Croser (Sparkling); Second label Sharefarmers White and Red. Bridgewater Mill is another label — see separate entry.
SUMMARY The Petaluma empire comprises Knappstein Wines, Mitchelton, Stonier and Smithbrook. In late 2001 the Petaluma group was acquired by New Zealand brewer Lion Nathan, but left Brian Croser in place. Croser has never compromised his fierce commitment to quality, and doubtless never will. The Riesling is almost monotonously good; the Chardonnay is a category leader, the Merlot another marvellously succulent wine to buy without hesitation. Exports to the UK, the US and New Zealand.

ΤΤΤΤΤ **Piccadilly Vineyard Chardonnay 2001** Elegant in the extreme; all the components beautifully proportioned and weighted around a core of melon and stone fruit. **RATING** 95 **DRINK** 2009 $40

Tiers Chardonnay 2001 Finely tuned and structured; seamlessly balanced and integrated winemaker inputs; melon, fig and cashew, all the components balanced. **RATING** 95 **DRINK** 2011 $120

ΤΤΤΤΥ **Hanlin Hill Riesling 2003** The screwcap version definitely has more aromatic lift than the cork-finished wine; light, but very long citrus and mineral flavours, acidity adding length. **RATING** 93 **DRINK** 2023 $24

B+V Viognier 2002 Complex yet delicate rose petal, pastille, spice varietal aromas and flavours. **RATING** 93 **DRINK** Now $36

Coonawarra Merlot 2001 Powerfully constructed and textured, but clear varietal character; red fruits/raspberry then fine-grained, slightly savoury, tannins. **RATING** 93 **DRINK** 2016 $50

Shiraz 2001 Clean blackberry and cherry aromas; a refined, medium-bodied palate; good texture, structure and oak handling; lingering fine tannins. **RATING** 92 **DRINK** 2011 $45

Coonawarra 2001 A medium-bodied array of blackcurrant, redcurrant and raspberry fruit; soft, faintly furry tannins. **RATING** 92 **DRINK** 2015 $60

Croser 2000 Typically fine and discreet; mineral-accented; very tight and focused; needs more bottle age. **RATING** 91 **DRINK** 2009 $40

Sharefarmers Red 2000 Round mouthfeel and quite generous; cedar, cigar, prune, blackberry and ripe tannins. **RATING** 90 **DRINK** 2010 $18

ΤΤΤΤ **B+V Viognier 2003** A quiet bouquet; only comes out of its shell on the back palate and finish with pastille fruit flavours and the texture coming through. **RATING** 89 **DRINK** Now $35

🐌 Peter Howland Wines ★★★★★

2/14 Portside Crescent, Wickham, NSW 2293 **REGION** Warehouse
T (02) 4920 2622 **F** (02) 4920 2699 **OPEN** By appointment
WINEMAKER Peter Howland **EST.** 2001 **CASES** 4000
PRODUCT RANGE ($30–35 ML) Maxwell Vineyard Hunter Valley Chardonnay, Langley Vineyard Donnybrook Shiraz, Parsons Vineyard Frankland River Shiraz, Pine Lodge Vineyard Mount Barker Shiraz.
SUMMARY Peter Howland graduated from Adelaide University in 1997 with a first-class Honours degree in oenology. He has worked in regions as diverse as the Hunter Valley, Margaret River, Hastings Valley, Macedon Ranges and Puglia in Italy. Newcastle may seem a strange place for a winery cellar door, but this is in fact where his insulated and refrigerated barrel shed is located. He

ferments his wines at Serenella Estate, where he also acts as contract winemaker for Outram Estate in the Hunter Valley and Gowrie Mountain Estate in Toowoomba, Queensland. Factor in the three individual vineyard Shirazs made from the Langley Vineyard in Donnybrook, the Parsons Vineyard in Frankland River and the Pine Lodge Vineyard at Mount Barker (all three in Western Australia) with a Chardonnay from the Maxwell Vineyard in the Hunter Valley and a Shiraz from the 50-year-old vines of the Bainton Vineyard in the Broke Fordwich subregion of the Hunter Valley, and the full dimension of the virtual winery becomes clear. If he maintains the quality of the initial releases — and there seems no reason why not — this will quickly become a very well-known label.

TTTTT **Parsons Vineyard Frankland River Shiraz 2002** Vivid purple; complex black fruits with touches of spice and herb; considerable length, and great structure. **RATING** 94 **DRINK** 2012 $ 33

TTTT? **Langley Vineyard Donnybrook Shiraz 2002** Deeply coloured; complex dark plum, black cherry and spice drive a full flavoured but elegant wine; the oak and extract have been well controlled, the tannins soft. **RATING** 93 **DRINK** 2010 $ 30

TTTT **Pine Lodge Vineyard Mount Barker Shiraz 2002** Very complex, with some Rhône-like spice/pepper/game; very powerful array of flavours on the palate, with just the faintest touch of gamey bitterness. **RATING** 89 **DRINK** 2010 $ 35

Peter Lehmann   ★★★★

Para Road, Tanunda, SA 5352 **REGION** Barossa Valley
T (08) 8563 2100 **F** (08) 8563 3402 **OPEN** Mon–Fri 9.30–5, weekends and public holidays 10.30–4.30
WINEMAKER Andrew Wigan, Peter Scholz, Leonie Lange, Ian Hongell **EST.** 1979 **CASES** 200 000
PRODUCT RANGE ($12–75 CD) Blue Eden Riesling, Barossa Semillon, Chenin Blanc, Semillon Chardonnay, Chardonnay, Noble Semillon, Seven Surveys Grenache Shiraz Mourvedre, Shiraz, Shiraz Grenache, Cabernet Franc, Cabernet Sauvignon, Clancy's Red. Premium wines are Eden Valley Reserve Riesling, Reserve Semillon, Mentor, Stonewell Shiraz, Eight Songs Shiraz, Black Queen Sparkling Shiraz.
SUMMARY After one of the more emotional and intense takeover battles in the latter part of 2003, Peter Lehmann fought off the unwanted suit of Allied Domeq, and is now effectively controlled by the Swiss/Californian Hess Group. The takeover should reinforce the core business, and protect the interests both of employees, but also Peter Lehmann's beloved Barossa Valley grape growers. Exports to the UK through its own subsidiary; also to New Zealand, Europe, Asia, the South Pacific and the US.

TTTTT **Eden Valley Reserve Riesling 1998** The bouquet is literally jam-packed with apple, lime, mineral and toast, the palate similarly rich and flooded with flavour; great balance and complexity. Top 100 2003. **RATING** 95 **DRINK** 2008 $ 24

TTTT? **Eight Songs Shiraz 2000** Earthy, spicy, savoury aromas, then lively, juicy berry flavours; quite tangy; fine tannins. **RATING** 90 **DRINK** 2010 $ 55
Vintage Port 1996 Spice, blackberry, licorice and chocolate; rich and sweet in traditional Aus style; has breed though. **RATING** 90 **DRINK** 2016

TTTT **GSM Grenache Shiraz Mourvedre 2002** An attractive mix of sweet raspberry, redcurrant and plum; light to medium-bodied and fruit-driven. **RATING** 87 **DRINK** Now $ 16

TTT? **Riesling 2003** **RATING** 86 **DRINK** Now $ 12
Clancy's 2002 **RATING** 86 **DRINK** 2009 $ 13
Chardonnay 2002 **RATING** 85 **DRINK** Now $ 15
Barossa Merlot 2001 **RATING** 85 **DRINK** Now $ 20

TTT **Semillon Chardonnay 2002** **RATING** 83 $ 12
Chenin Blanc 2002 **RATING** 83 $ 12
Shiraz Grenache 2003 **RATING** 82 $ 12

Peterson Champagne House   NR

Cnr Broke and Branxton Roads, Pokolbin, NSW 2320 **REGION** Lower Hunter Valley
T (02) 4998 7881 **F** (02) 4998 7882 **OPEN** 7 days 9–5
WINEMAKER Contract **EST.** 1994 **CASES** 7000
PRODUCT RANGE ($17–39 CD) Chardonnay, Shiraz; Sparkling wines including Peterson House
Gateway, Botrytis Semillon, Semillon Pinot Noir, Chardonnay Pinot Noir, Pinot Chardonnay
Meunier, Shiraz, Merlot, Chambourcin, Cabernet Sauvignon.
SUMMARY Prominently and provocatively situated on the corner of Broke and Branxton Roads as one
enters the main vineyard and winery district in the Lower Hunter Valley. It is an extension of the
Peterson family empire and, no doubt, very deliberately aimed at the tourist. While the dreaded word
'Champagne' has been retained in the business name, the wine labels now simply say Peterson
House, which is a big step in the right direction. Almost all of the wine is sold through the cellar door
and through the wine club mailing list.

Petersons   ★★★★

Mount View Road, Mount View, NSW 2325 **REGION** Lower Hunter Valley
T (02) 4990 1704 **F** (02) 4991 1344 **OPEN** Mon–Sat 9–5, Sun 10–5
WINEMAKER Colin Peterson, Gary Reed **EST.** 1971 **CASES** 15 000
PRODUCT RANGE ($19–70 CD) Semillon, Shirley Semillon, Show Reserve Semillon, Verdelho, Chardonnay,
Cuvee Chardonnay, Samantha Sparkling, Botrytis Semillon, Pinot Noir, Shiraz, Back Block Shiraz, Ian's
Selection Shiraz, Cabernet Sauvignon, Back Block Cabernet Sauvignon, Muscat, Vintage Port.
SUMMARY Ian and Shirley Peterson were among the early followers in the footsteps of Max Lake,
contributing to the Hunter Valley renaissance which has continued to this day. Grape growers since
1971 and winemakers since 1981, the second generation of the family, headed by Colin Peterson, now
manages the business. It has been significantly expanded to include 16 hectares at Mount View, a 42-
hectare vineyard in Mudgee (Glenesk), and an 8-hectare vineyard near Armidale (Palmerston). In
2002 the winery won 9 gold medals and 3 trophies, mainly at lesser shows.

TTTTT **Glenesk Shiraz 2001** Complex herb, spice, licorice and black fruits; good structure and
length; has vivacity. Top gold 2003 Mudgee Wine Show. **RATING** 94 **DRINK** 2011 $70

TTTTY **Old Block Shiraz 2001** Ripe plum and blackberry fruit; some licorice; generous, soft and
plush. **RATING** 93 **DRINK** 2011 $38

TTTT **Mudgee Chardonnay 2002** Complex barrel-ferment aromas and flavours; rich, high
alcohol style. **RATING** 87 **DRINK** Now $21.50
Strikes Shiraz 2001 Dark chocolate and blackberry fruit; ripe style, with lots of mid-
palate fruit. **RATING** 87 **DRINK** 2009 $38

TTTY **Mudgee Verdelho 2002** **RATING** 85 **DRINK** Now $19.50
Chardonnay 2002 **RATING** 84 **DRINK** Now $26

Petrene Estate   NR

Muirillup Road, Northcliffe, WA 6262 **REGION** Pemberton
T (08) 9776 7145 **F** (08) 9776 7145 **OPEN** Weekends and holidays 10.30–4
WINEMAKER Contract **EST.** 1994
PRODUCT RANGE Sauvignon Blanc, Chardonnay, Pinot Noir.
SUMMARY Peter Hooker and Irene Wilson have established 2 hectares of chardonnay, sauvignon
blanc and pinot noir, the tiny production being contract-made.

Pettavel   ★★★★

65 Pettavel Road, Waurn Ponds, Vic 3216 **REGION** Geelong
T (03) 5266 1120 **F** (03) 5266 1140 **OPEN** 7 days 10–5.30
WINEMAKER Peter Flewellyn **EST.** 2000 **CASES** 20 000
PRODUCT RANGE ($14–40 CD) Evening Star range with Riesling, Sauvignon Blanc Semillon,
Chardonnay, Cabernet Sauvignon Merlot; Platina range of Chardonnay, Pinot Noir, Petit Verdot,
Cabernet Sauvignon; Emigre Shiraz.

SUMMARY This is a major new landmark in the Geelong region. Mike and wife Sandi Fitzpatrick sold their large Riverland winery and vineyards, and moved to Geelong where, in 1990, they began developing vineyards at Sutherlands Creek. Here they have been joined by daughter Robyn (who overseas management of the business) and son Reece (who coordinates the viticultural resources). A striking and substantial winery was opened in time for the 2002 vintage, prior to which time the wines were contract-made at Mount Langi Ghiran. The development also includes a modern tasting area adjacent to a restaurant which is open 7 days a week for lunch. The size of the development is such that it can accommodate private functions and corporate events for up to 180 seated guests. The quality of the initial releases is thoroughly impressive. Exports to the UK, Canada, Sweden and China.

ŶŶŶŶŶ **Platina Merlot Petit Verdot 2002** Fascinating wine, with a gloriously long but fine palate, the Merlot doing most of the work but with a twist from the Petit Verdot. **RATING** 94 **DRINK** 2015 $ 25

ŶŶŶŶŷ **Platina Cabernet Sauvignon Cabernet Franc 2001** Still bright purple-red; spotlessly clean cassis, blackcurrant, mulberry and raspberry flavours; very fine tannins. **RATING** 92 $ 25
Evening Star Chardonnay 2002 Stone fruit, melon and citrus; plenty of structure, but not phenolic; excellent value. **RATING** 90 **DRINK** 2007 $ 16

ŶŶŶŶ **Platina Pinot Noir 2002** Savoury/spicy/gamey aromas; incredibly powerful, intense and very tannic; could go anywhere. **RATING** 89 **DRINK** 2015 $ 25
Evening Star Riesling 2003 Floral, spicy style; apple, citrus and pear flavours. **RATING** 87 **DRINK** 2008 $ 14

ŶŶŶŷ **Southern Emigre Shiraz 2002** **RATING** 86 **DRINK** 2008 $ 40
Evening Star Sauvignon Blanc Semillon 2003 **RATING** 85 **DRINK** 2007 $ 14
Evening Star Cabernet Merlot 2001 **RATING** 85 **DRINK** Now $ 16

Pewsey Vale ★★★★★

PO Box 10, Angaston, SA 5353 **REGION** Eden Valley
T (08) 8561 3200 **F** (08) 8561 3393 **OPEN** At Yalumba
WINEMAKER Louisa Rose **EST.** 1961 **CASES** 18 000
PRODUCT RANGE ($13.50–26.95 CD) Riesling, The Contour Riesling.
SUMMARY Pewsey Vale was a famous vineyard established in 1847 by Joseph Gilbert, and it was appropriate that when S Smith & Son (Yalumba) began the renaissance of the high Adelaide Hills plantings in 1961, they should do so by purchasing Pewsey Vale and establishing 40 hectares of riesling and 2 hectares each of gewurztraminer and pinot gris. After a dip in form, Pewsey Vale has emphatically bounced back to its very best. The Riesling has also finally benefitted from being the first wine to be bottled with a Stelvin screwcap in 1977. While public reaction forced the abandonment of the initiative for almost 20 years, Yalumba/Pewsey Vale never lost faith in the technical advantages of the closure. Exports to all major markets.

ŶŶŶŶŶ **Museum Release The Contours Riesling 1999** Super-intense and fragrant; herbs, spice and a hint of kerosene; pungent, penetrating grapefruit, lime and herb; great acidity and length. Screwcap, of course. **RATING** 96 **DRINK** 2009 $ 26.95
The Contours Eden Valley Riesling 1998 Brassy coloured, it has potent bottle-developed kerosene aromas, the equally potent palate with long, toasty bottle-developed flavours, tightened by citrussy acidity. **RATING** 96 **DRINK** 2013 $ 24.95

ŶŶŶŶ **Riesling 2003** Fine, moderately intense, flowery aromatics; gentle lime and tropical fruit flavours. **RATING** 89 **DRINK** 2008 $ 16.95

Pfeiffer ★★★☆

167 Distillery Road, Wahgunyah, Vic 3687 **REGION** Rutherglen
T (02) 6033 2805 **F** (02) 6033 3158 **OPEN** Mon–Sat 9–5, Sun 10–5
WINEMAKER Christopher Pfeiffer, Je230.n Pfeiffer **EST.** 1984 **CASES** 20 000
PRODUCT RANGE ($11.50–46.50 R) Pfeiffer varietal table and fortified wines sold through the cellar door only; Vintage Reserve range, the Carlyle varietal wines and Classic Rutherglen Muscat sold through retail and export.

SUMMARY Ex-Lindeman fortified winemaker Chris Pfeiffer occupies one of the historic wineries (built 1880) which abound in northeast Victoria and which is worth a visit on this score alone. The fortified wines are good, and the table wines have improved considerably over recent vintages, drawing upon 32 hectares of estate plantings. The winery offers barbecue facilities, children's playground, gourmet picnic hampers, and dinners (by arrangement). Exports to the UK, Canada, Singapore and Taiwan (under the Carlyle label).

ɥɥɥɥ̽ **Carlyle Riesling 2003** Elegant and racy passionfruit, lime and apple; clean and lingering. **RATING** 93 **DRINK** 2010 $14.99
Christopher's Vintage Port 2001 Complex, spicy/briary fruit; strongly varietal; excellent use of spirit; true Vintage Port, not too sweet. Touriga. **RATING** 92 **DRINK** 2011 $22.50

ɥɥɥɥ **Riesling 2003** Discreet apple and lime blossom; mineral backbone; clean, good length. Upper King Valley and Strathbogie Ranges. **RATING** 89 **DRINK** 2010 $15
Classic Rutherglen Muscat NV Fresh, grapey/spirity bouquet has crystal clear varietal character; the palate is at the lighter end of the spectrum, but has, like the bouquet, clearly defined and engaging varietal character. **RATING** 89 **DRINK** Now $22.50
Auslese Tokay 2003 Clean, oozing sweet grapey fruit juice flavours balanced by lingering acidity. **RATING** 89 **DRINK** 2007 $15
Pale Dry Flor Fino NV Powerful Fino style; nice cut of rancio; slightly less alcohol might lead to more finesse. **RATING** 88 **DRINK** Now $22.50
Cabernet Sauvignon 2000 Leafy/earthy/savoury/chocolatey overtones to blackcurrant fruit; long finish and aftertaste. **RATING** 87 **DRINK** 2010 $17.90
Old Distillery Classic Rutherglen Tokay NV A fruity, grapey bouquet with some spice, and a hint of vanillin oak. Relatively light in the mouth, fruity, not as focused as the other wines in its peer group. **RATING** 87 **DRINK** Now $22.50

ɥɥɥ̽ **Rutherglen Tawny NV** **RATING** 85 **DRINK** Now $16.50
Marsanne 2002 **RATING** 84 **DRINK** Now $15
Gamay 2003 **RATING** 84 **DRINK** Now $15.50

ɥɥɥ **Merlot 1999** **RATING** 83 $30

Pfitzner ★★★★

PO Box 1098, North Adelaide, SA 5006 **REGION** Adelaide Hills
T (08) 8390 0188 **F** (08) 8390 0188 **OPEN** Not
WINEMAKER Petaluma (Contract) **EST.** 1996 **CASES** 1500
PRODUCT RANGE ($16.50–19.95 R) Sauvignon Blanc, Chardonnay, Pinot Noir, Merlot.
SUMMARY The subtitle to the Pfitzner name is Eric's Vineyard. The late Eric Pfitzner purchased and aggregated a number of small, subdivided farmlets to protect the beauty of the Piccadilly Valley from ugly rural development. His three sons inherited the vision, with a little under 6 hectares of vineyard planted principally to chardonnay and pinot noir, plus small amounts of sauvignon blanc and merlot. Half the total property has been planted, the remainder preserving the natural eucalypt forest. The wines are made by Petaluma, and roughly half the production is sold in the UK. The remainder is sold through single retail outlets in Adelaide, Sydney, Melbourne and Perth.

ɥɥɥɥ **Eric's Vineyard Pinot Noir 2001** Plum, spice and forest aromas and flavours; good balance and length, but slightly tough overall. **RATING** 89 **DRINK** Now $19.95

Phaedrus Estate ★★★★

220 Mornington-Tyabb Road, Moorooduc, Vic 3933 **REGION** Mornington Peninsula
T 903) 5978 8134 **F** (03) 5978 8134 **OPEN** Weekends and public holidays 11–5
WINEMAKER Ewan Campbell, Maitena Zantvoort **EST.** 1997 **CASES** 900
PRODUCT RANGE ($18–25 R) Pinot Gris, Chardonnay, Pinot Noir, Shiraz.
SUMMARY Ewan Campbell and Maitena Zantvoort established Phaedrus Estate in 1997. At that time both had already had winemaking experience with large wine companies, and were at the point of finishing their wine science degrees at Adelaide University. They decided they wished to (in their words) 'produce ultra-premium wine with distinctive and unique varietal flavours, which offer

serious (and lighthearted) wine drinkers an alternative to mainstream commercial styles'. Campbell and Zantvoort believe that quality wines are made in the process involving both art and science, and I don't have any argument with that.

ＹＹＹＹ **Pinot Noir 2002** Very ripe, complex dark plum and spice; powerful, intense and long. Screwcap will underwrite future development. **RATING** 91 **DRINK** 2012 $ 20
Chardonnay 2002 Complex, tangy characters ex-bottle development, cool vintage and low yield; intense, fruit-driven; lingering finish. Screwcap. **RATING** 90 **DRINK** 2010 $ 18

ＹＹＹＹ **Shiraz 2001** Spicy black fruits in full-on cool climate style; lingering finish. **RATING** 87 **DRINK** 2008 $ 20

ＹＹＹＹ **Pinot Gris 2003** **RATING** 86 **DRINK** Now $ 18

Phillip Island Vineyard ★★★★

Berrys Beach Road, Phillip Island, Vic **REGION** Gippsland
T (03) 5956 8465 **F** (03) 5956 8465 **OPEN** 7 days 11–7 (Nov–March) 11–5 (April–Oct)
WINEMAKER David Lance, James Lance **EST.** 1993 **CASES** 3500
PRODUCT RANGE ($18–50 CD) Sea Spray (Sparkling), Sauvignon Blanc, Cape Woolamai Semillon Sauvignon Blanc, Summerland (Chardonnay), Newhaven (Riesling Traminer), Botrytis Chardonnay, Pinot Noir, The Nobbies (Pinot Noir), Merlot, Berry's Beach (Cabernet Sauvignon), Western Port, Pyramid Rock (Shiraz).
SUMMARY 1997 marked the first harvest from the 2.5 hectares of the Phillip Island vineyard, which is totally enclosed in the permanent silon net which acts both as a windbreak and protection against birds. The quality of the wines across the board make it clear; this is definitely not a tourist trap cellar door, rather a serious producer of quality wine. Exports to South-East Asia.

ＹＹＹＹＹ **Gippsland Pinot Noir 2002** Very distinguished and fine Pinot; beautiful texture and line; silky/spicy fruit. **RATING** 95 **DRINK** 2010 $ 50

ＹＹＹＹＹ **Gippsland Chardonnay 2001** Youthful green-gold; super-fine style; nectarine and melon; subtle oak, long finish. **RATING** 92 **DRINK** 2008 $ 28

ＹＹＹＹ **Cabernet Sauvignon 2001** Earth, leaf, spice and blackcurrant on a light to medium-bodied palate; subtle oak. **RATING** 88 **DRINK** 2011 $ 28
Newhaven Riesling 2003 Solidly constructed and weighted; a hint of sweetness to the finish; Yarra Valley origin. **RATING** 87 **DRINK** Now $ 18

ＹＹＹＹ **Berrys Beach Cabernet Sauvignon 2002** **RATING** 86 **DRINK** 2007 $ 22

ＹＹＹ **The Nobbies 2001** **RATING** 82 $ 27.40

Phillips Brook Estate ★★★★★

Lot 2, Redmond-Hay River Road, Redmond, WA 6332 (postal) **REGION** Albany
T (08) 9845 3124 **F** (08) 9845 3126 **OPEN** Not
WINEMAKER Rob Diletti (Contract) **EST.** 1975 **CASES** 400
PRODUCT RANGE ($15–20 R) Riesling, Cabernet Sauvignon.
SUMMARY Bronwen and David Newbury first became viticulturists near the thoroughly unlikely town of Bourke, in western New South Wales. They were involved with Dr Richard Smart in setting up the First Light vineyard, with the aim of making the first wine in the world each calendar year. Whatever marketing appeal the idea may have had, the wine was never going to be great, so in May 2001 they moved back to Western Australian and the Great Southern region. The name comes from the adjoining Phillips Brook Nature Reserve, and the permanent creek in their property which they assume is the Phillips Brook. 2.2 hectares of riesling and 2.4 hectares of cabernet sauvignon had been planted in 1975, but thoroughly neglected in the intervening years. The Newburys have rehabilitated the old plantings, and have added 4.9 hectares of chardonnay, 1.15 hectares of merlot, 0.83 hectare of cabernet franc and 0.71 hectare of sauvignon blanc (complementing a single row of old vines).

ＹＹＹＹ **Great Southern Riesling 2003** Clean, fresh, citrus aromas; the palate comes alive with penetrating, tingling lime juice flavours. **RATING** 92 **DRINK** 2013 $ 17

Phillips Estate ★★★

Lot 964a Channybearup Road, Pemberton, WA 6230 **REGION** Pemberton
T (08) 9776 0381 **F** (08) 9776 0381 **OPEN** 7 days 10.30–4
WINEMAKER Phillip Wilkinson **EST.** 1996 **CASES** 5000
PRODUCT RANGE ($13–30 CD) Riesling, Sauvignon Blanc, Pinot Noir, Arista Shiraz, Cabernet Merlot, Cabernet Sauvignon.
SUMMARY Phillip Wilkinson has developed 4.5 hectares of vines framed by an old-growth Karri forest on one side and a large lake on the other. As well as the expected varieties, he has planted 1 hectare of zinfandel; so far as I know, it is the only example of this variety in the Pemberton region. Sophisticated winemaking techniques are used at the fermentation stage, but fining and filtration are either not used at all, or employed to a minimum degree. Exports to the UK.

ŸŸŸŸ **Pinot Noir 2002** Complex; plum, spice and forest; good mouthfeel and length. **RATING** 88 **DRINK** 2007 $25

ŸŸŸŸ **Shiraz 2002** **RATING** 84 **DRINK** Now $20

🐌 Pialligo Estate NR

18 Kallaroo Road, Pialligo, ACT 2609 **REGION** Canberra District
T (02) 6247 6060 **F** (02) 6262 6074 **OPEN** Thurs–Sun and public holidays 10–5
WINEMAKER Andrew McEwin, Greg Gallagher (Contract) **EST.** 1999 **CASES** 1000
PRODUCT RANGE ($15–22 CD) Riesling, Unwooded Chardonay, Rose, Shiraz, Sangiovese, Merlot.
SUMMARY Sally Milner and John Nutt began the establishment of their 4-hectare vineyard (1.5 hectares of merlot, 1 hectare of riesling and 0.5 hectare each of shiraz, cabernet sauvignon and sangiovese) in 1999. The cellar-door sales and café opened July 2002, with views of Mount Ainslie, Mount Pleasant, Duntroon, the Telstra Tower, Parliament House and the Brindabella Ranges beyond. The property, which has a 1-kilometre frontage to the Molonglo River, also includes an olive grove, yet is only 5 minutes drive from the centre of Canberra. Experienced contract-winemaking should underwrite the quality of the wines.

Piano Gully NR

Piano Gully Road, Manjimup, WA 6258 **REGION** Manjimup
T (08) 9772 3140 **F** (08) 9316 0336 **OPEN** By appointment
WINEMAKER Ashley Lewkowski **EST.** 1987 **CASES** 4000
PRODUCT RANGE ($15–24 ML) Chardonnay Sauvignon Blanc, Chardonnay, Pinot Noir, Cabernet Sauvignon Shiraz, Cabernet Sauvignon.
SUMMARY The 5-hectare vineyard was established in 1987 on rich Karri loam, 10 kilometres south of Manjimup, with the first wine made from the 1991 vintage. A change of ownership and winemaker has seen a dramatic lift in wine quality. For the record, the name of the road (and hence the winery) commemorates the shipping of a piano from England by one of the first settlers in the region. The horse and cart carrying the piano on the last leg of the long journey were within sight of their destination when the piano fell from the cart and was destroyed. Prior tastings showed the skills of contract winemaker Michael Staniford.

Picardy ★★★★★

Cnr Vasse Highway and Eastbrook Road, Pemberton, WA 6260 **REGION** Pemberton
T (08) 9776 0036 **F** (08) 9776 0245 **OPEN** By appointment
WINEMAKER Bill Pannell, Dan Pannell **EST.** 1993 **CASES** 5000
PRODUCT RANGE ($25–60 CD) Chardonnay, Pinot Noir, Tete de Cuvee Pinot Noir, Shiraz, Merlot Cabernet, Merlimont.
SUMMARY Picardy is owned by Dr Bill Pannell and his wife Sandra, who were the founders of Moss Wood winery in the Margaret River region (in 1969). Picardy reflects Bill Pannell's view that the Pemberton area will prove to be one of the best regions in Australia for Pinot Noir and Chardonnay, but it is perhaps significant that the wines to be released include a Shiraz, and a Bordeaux-blend of 50 per cent Merlot, 25 per cent Cabernet Franc and 25 per cent Cabernet Sauvignon. Time will tell whether Pemberton has more Burgundy, Rhône or Bordeaux in its veins. Picardy has lost no time in setting up national distribution, and exports to the US, Japan, Indonesia, Hong Kong and France.

ŸŸŸŸŸ **Shiraz 2002** Complex licorice, anise, spice, black plum and blackberry aromas and flavours flood the mouth. **RATING** 94 **DRINK** 2012 $ 25

ŸŸŸŸŸ **Chardonnay 2002** Complex cashew and toast barrel ferment and malolactic ferment inputs into the aromas and flavours; light to medium-bodied; supple, smooth melon and stone fruit through to a clean finish. **RATING** 93 **DRINK** 2007 $ 30
Pinot Noir 2002 Very fine and elegant in foresty/savoury spectrum; lovely gossamer/silk tannins and mouthfeel. Understated. **RATING** 91 **DRINK** 2007 $ 30
Merlimont 2001 A complex amalgam of savoury/briary notes and black fruit aromas; intense blackcurrant in the mouthfeel; spice and cedar in the background. Merlot Cabernet Sauvignon Cabernet Franc blend. **RATING** 90 **DRINK** 2011 $ 35

ŸŸŸŸŸ **Merlot Cabernet 2000** **RATING** 85 **DRINK** Now $ 25

Piccadilly Fields

NR

185 Piccadilly Road, Piccadilly, SA 5151 **REGION** Adelaide Hills
T (08) 8370 8800 **F** (08) 8232 5395 **OPEN** Not
WINEMAKER Sam Virgara **EST.** 1989 **CASES** 2000
PRODUCT RANGE Chardonnay, Merlot Cabernet Franc Cabernet Sauvignon.
SUMMARY Piccadilly Fields has only a passing resemblance to its original state. The Virgara family has joined with a syndicate of investors which jointly own 176 hectares of vineyards through various parts of the Adelaide Hills, producing up to 1000 tonnes per year. The lions share is sold as grapes to other winemakers, a token 30 or so tonnes held for the Piccadilly Fields label.

Pierro

★★★★★

Caves Road, Wilyabrup via Cowaramup, WA 6284 **REGION** Margaret River
T (08) 9755 6220 **F** (08) 9755 6308 **OPEN** 7 days 10–5
WINEMAKER Dr Michael Peterkin **EST.** 1979 **CASES** 7500
PRODUCT RANGE ($25–65 CD) Chardonnay, Semillon Sauvignon Blanc LTC, Cabernet Sauvignon Merlot.
SUMMARY Dr Michael Peterkin is another of the legion of Margaret River medical practitioners who, for good measure, married into the Cullen family. Pierro is renowned for its stylish white wines, which often exhibit tremendous complexity. The Chardonnay can be monumental in its weight and complexity. The wines are exported to the UK, the US, Japan and Indonesia.

ŸŸŸŸŸ **Chardonnay 2002** Fine, melon and cashew; long and intense; more refined and tight than the usual Pierro blockbuster. **RATING** 94 **DRINK** 2012 $ 65

ŸŸŸŸŸ **Semillon Sauvignon Blanc LTC 2003** Crisp, grassy herbal aromas; excellent mouthfeel, balance and length; touch of tropical fruit. **RATING** 93 **DRINK** 2009 $ 25
Cabernet Sauvignon Merlot 2001 Stylish and elegant, spare, slightly savoury frame, but a core of delicious red and blackcurrant fruit; fine tannins. **RATING** 93 **DRINK** 2011 $ 60

🦀 Pier 10

NR

10 Shoreham Road, Shoreham, Vic 3916 **REGION** Mornington Peninsula
T (03) 5989 8848 **F** (03) 5989 8848 **OPEN** Wed–Sun 11–5, 7 days Dec–Mar
WINEMAKER Kevin McCarthy (Contract) **EST.** 1996
PRODUCT RANGE ($20–35 CD) Pinot Gris, Reserve Pinot Gris, Chardonnay, White Pinot, Pinot Noir.
SUMMARY Eric Baker and Sue McKenzie began the development of Pier 10 with the aim of creating first-up a lifestyle, thereafter a potential retirement business. Both took part in setting up the vineyard while continuing to work in Melbourne before handing over viticultural management of the 3.2 hectares to Mark Danaher. The varieties planted are chardonnay, pinot gris and pinot noir and with ultra-competent winemaking, the sold-out sign goes up regularly. The cellar door offers light meals and barbecue and picnic facilities.

Piesse Brook

NR

226 Aldersyde Road, Bickley, WA 6076 **REGION** Perth Hills
T (08) 9293 3309 **F** (08) 9293 3309 **OPEN** Sat 1–5, Sun, public holidays 10–5 and by appointment
WINEMAKER Di Bray, Ray Boyanich (Michael Davies, Consultant) **EST.** 1974 **CASES** 1200
PRODUCT RANGE ($10–17.50 CD) Chardonnay, Shiraz, Brian Murphy Reserve Shiraz, Merlot, Cabernet Sauvignon, Cabernet Merlot, Cabernet Shiraz, Cabernova (early-drinking style).
SUMMARY Surprisingly good red wines made in tiny quantities, and which have received consistent accolades over the years. The first Chardonnay was made in 1993; a trophy winning Shiraz was produced in 1995. Now has 4 hectares of chardonnay, shiraz, merlot and cabernet sauvignon under vine. Exports to the UK.

Pieter van Gent

Black Springs Road, Mudgee, NSW 2850 **REGION** Mudgee
T (02) 6373 3807 **F** (02) 6373 3910 **OPEN** Mon–Sat 9–5, Sun 11–4
WINEMAKER Pieter van Gent, Philip van Gent **EST.** 1978 **CASES** 10 000
PRODUCT RANGE ($11.50–24 CD) The dry wines are Verdelho, Chardonnay, Muller Thurgau, Matador Shiraz, Alba Crest Cabernet Merlot, Conquistador Cabernet Sauvignon; the Flower of Florence, Angelic White, Sundance White and Sundance Soft Red all have varying degrees of sweetness; fortified wines are the specialty, including Pipeclay Port, Mudgee White Port, Cornelius Port, Mudgee Oloroso, Mistella, Pipeclay Vermouth, Liqueur Muscat.
SUMMARY Many years ago Pieter van Gent worked for Lindemans, before joining Craigmoor then moving to his own winery in 1979. Here, he and his family have forged a strong following, initially for his fortified wines, but now also for the table wines. Visits to Duyfken Studio (Goldsmith Sabine van Gent's jewelry) available, as is accommodation at the Bushman's Cottage.

ŸŸŸŸ **Verdelho 2003** **RATING** 84 **DRINK** Now $ 15
      Matador Shiraz 2002 **RATING** 84 **DRINK** 2007 $ 16.50

ŸŸŸ **Chardonnay 2001** **RATING** 83 $ 15

ŸŸŸ **Conquistador Cabernet Sauvignon 2002** **RATING** 79 $ 15.50

Piggs Peake

697 Hermitage Road, Pokolbin, NSW 2320 **REGION** Lower Hunter Valley
T (02) 6574 7000 **F** (02) 6574 7070 **OPEN** 7 days 10–5, 10–6 during daylight savings
WINEMAKER Steve Langham **EST.** 1998 **CASES** 1500
PRODUCT RANGE ($24–40 CD) Sows Ear Semillon, Wiggly Tail Marsanne, Silk Purse Verdelho, Littel Pig Verdelho, Hogshead Chardonnay, I Swine.
SUMMARY The derivation of the name remains a mystery to me, and if it is a local landmark, I have not heard of it. Certain it is that it is one of the newer wineries to be constructed in the Hunter Valley, sourcing most of its grapes from other growers to complement the hectare of estate shiraz. The arrival of Steve Langham (having previously worked four vintages at Allandale) has seen a very marked increase in quality. Listings at a number of Sydney's best restaurants has followed.

ŸŸŸŸŸ **Sows Ear Semillon 2003** Potent, intense aromas with a hint of lanolin; extremely intense, crushed herb/grass and mineral palate. Low pH. Pity about the cork finish. **RATING** 93 **DRINK** 2018 $ 26

ŸŸŸŸ **Silk Purse Verdelho NV** Well above average richness and mouthfeel; tropical fruit salad, the alcohol adding a touch of sweetness. **RATING** 88 **DRINK** Now $ 24
      Wiggly Tail Marsanne 2003 Some floral blossom aromas; good intensity, length and persistence; varietal character lacking. **RATING** 87 **DRINK** Now $ 24

Pike & Joyce

Mawson Road, Lenswood, SA 5240 (postal) **REGION** Adelaide Hills
T (08) 8843 4370 **F** (08) 8843 4353 **OPEN** Not
WINEMAKER Neil Pike, John Trotter **EST.** 1998 **CASES** 2500
PRODUCT RANGE ($19–28 ML) Sauvignon Blanc, Pinot Gris, Chardonnay, Pinot Noir.

SUMMARY As the name suggests, this is a partnership between the Pike family (of Clare Valley fame) and the Joyce family, related to Andrew Pike's wife Cathy. The Joyce family have been orchardists at Lenswood for over 100 years, but also have extensive operations in the Riverland. Together with Andrew Pike (formerly chief viticulturist for the Southcorp group) they have established 18.5 hectares of vines, with the lion's share of the plantings going to pinot noir, sauvignon blanc and chardonnay, followed by merlot, pinot gris and semillon. The wines are made at Pikes Clare winery and are distributed nationally by Tucker Seabrook, with exports to the UK, the US and Singapore.

ŸŸŸŸŸ **Chardonnay 2002** Complex, rich, powerful barrel ferment inputs on bouquet and palate; stone fruit comes through on the finish. **RATING** 90 **DRINK** Now $ 28

Pinot Noir 2002 Very complex earthy/savoury/woodsy berry aromas and flavours; long, lingering finish with a nice twist of acidity. **RATING** 90 **DRINK** 2008 $ 28

ŸŸŸŸ **Sauvignon Blanc 2003** Faintly feral/funky aromas, but has good tropical fruit and length. **RATING** 87 **DRINK** Now $ 19

Pikes ★★★★

Polish Hill River Road, Sevenhill, SA 5453 **REGION** Clare Valley
T (08) 8843 4370 **F** (08) 8843 4353 **OPEN** 7 days 10–4
WINEMAKER Neil Pike, John Trotter **EST.** 1984 **CASES** 35 000
PRODUCT RANGE ($15–55 CD) Riesling, Sauvignon Blanc Semillon, Viognier, Chardonnay, Shiraz, Shiraz Grenache Mourvedre, Premio Sangiovese, Merlot, Cabernet Sauvignon; Luccio white and red.
SUMMARY Owned by the Pike brothers, one of whom (Andrew) was for many years the senior viticulturist with Southcorp, the other (Neil) a former winemaker at Mitchell. Pikes now has its own winery, with Neil Pike presiding. Generously constructed and flavoured wines are the order of the day. The wines are exported to the UK, Switzerland, Ireland, Germany, Belgium, The Netherlands, Denmark, Cyprus, Finland, Japan, Hong Kong, Malaysia, Singapore, New Zealand, the US and Canada.

ŸŸŸŸŸ **Riesling 2003** Generous, mouthfilling, ripe lime juice flavours; excellent early-drinking style. **RATING** 91 **DRINK** 2008 $ 20

Cabernet Sauvignon 2001 Powerful, rich blackcurrant, blackberry and bitter chocolate; lingering but fine tannins. **RATING** 90 **DRINK** 2016 $ 22

ŸŸŸŸ **Shiraz 2001** Powerful blackberry fruit; touches of earth and dark chocolate; well-integrated oak. **RATING** 89 **DRINK** 2011 $ 22

Merlot 2001 Medium-bodied; strong savoury/leafy/earthy/olive aromas and flavours; on the austere side, but strongly varietal. **RATING** 88 **DRINK** 2010 $ 22

Chardonnay 2002 Very well made; nutty, creamy overtones to gentle melon fruit; subtle oak. **RATING** 87 **DRINK** Now $ 20

ŸŸŸŸ **Shiraz Grenache Mourvedre 2001** **RATING** 85 **DRINK** Now $ 20
Luccio (Red) 2001 **RATING** 84 **DRINK** Now $ 15

Pinelli ★★★

30 Bennett Street, Caversham, WA 6055 **REGION** Swan Valley
T (08) 9279 6818 **F** (08) 9377 4259 **OPEN** Mon–Fri 9–5.30, weekends 10–5
WINEMAKER Robert Pinelli, Daniel Pinelli **EST.** 1979 **CASES** 10 000
PRODUCT RANGE ($10–14 CD) Chenin Blanc, Verdelho, Classic Dry White, Unwooded Chardonnay, Late Harvest Verdelho, Scarlet (medium sweet red), Shiraz, Cabernet Merlot, Cabernet Sauvignon, Tawny Port.
SUMMARY Dominic Pinelli and son Robert — the latter a Roseworthy Agricultural College graduate — sell 75 per cent of their production in flagons but are seeking to place more emphasis on bottled-wine sales in the wake of recent show successes with Chenin Blanc.

ŸŸŸŸ **Unwooded Chardonnay 2003** **RATING** 86 **DRINK** Now $ 12

Pinnacle Wines ★★★★

50 Pinnacle Road, Orange, NSW 2800 **REGION** Orange
T (02) 6365 3316 **OPEN** By appointment
WINEMAKER David Lowe, Jane Wilson (Contract) **EST.** 1999 **CASES** 400

PRODUCT RANGE ($22 ML) Pinot Gris.

SUMMARY Peter Gibson began the establishment of Pinnacle Wines with the planting of 2 hectares of pinot gris in 1999 on the slopes of Mount Canobolas at an elevation of around 1000 metres. The vineyard is close to Brangayne of Orange, and Peter Gibson says that Brangayne's success played a considerable part in his decision to plant the vineyard. Just over 1 hectare of viognier and 1.6 hectares of pinot noir (using the new Burgundy clones 777, 115 and 114 in conjunction with MV6), plus a little riesling, has brought the total to 4 hectares.

YYYY **Pinot Gris 2003** Clean, nicely focused and balanced, sweet apple, then fresh lemony acidity on the finish. Screwcap. **RATING** 88 **DRINK** 2007 $ 22

Pipers Brook Vineyard ★★★★★

1216 Pipers Brook Road, Pipers Brook, Tas 7254 **REGION** Northern Tasmania
T (03) 6382 7527 **F** (03) 6382 7226 **OPEN** 7 days 10–5
WINEMAKER Rene Bezemer **EST.** 1974 **CASES** 90 000
PRODUCT RANGE ($17.75–69.29 CD) The basic Estate varietals of Riesling, Gewurztraminer, Pinot Gris, Chardonnay, Pinot Noir; next Reserve Chardonnay and Pinot Noir; then Single Site Upper Slopes Riesling, Summit Chardonnay and The Lyre Pinot Noir; Opimian (Cabernet blend). Also the second label Ninth Island range of varietals and the Wavecrest range.
SUMMARY The Pipers Brook Tasmanian empire has over 220 hectares of vineyard supporting the Pipers Brook and Ninth Island labels, with the major focus, of course, being on Pipers Brook. As ever, fastidious viticulture and winemaking, immaculate packaging and enterprising marketing constitute a potent and effective blend. Pipers Brook operates two cellar-door outlets, one at headquarters, and one at Strathlyn (phone 03 6330 2388). In 2001 it became yet another company to fall prey to a takeover, in this instance by Belgian-owned sheepskin business Kreglinger, which has also established a large winery and vineyard at Mount Benson in South Australia. The wines are exported to the UK, Europe, the US, Japan, Canada and Singapore, and are distributed throughout Australia by S Smith & Son. In a seismic and utterly unexpected eruption in February 2003, Andrew Pirie's services were abruptly terminated.

YYYYY **Pirie Cuvee 1998** Bright, light straw with excellent mousse; a very fine, tight and elegant bouquet with aromas of pear and brioche; an intense, crisp and tight palate, long and lingering, and with great finesse. **RATING** 95 **DRINK** 2007 $ 54.95
The Summit Chardonnay 2000 Developed straw; a complex mix of barrel ferment, bottle development and malolactic aromas, the palate much more focused; citrus melon fruit; excellent line and lingering finish. **RATING** 94 **DRINK** 2008 $ 55

YYYYY **Cuvee Clarke Reserve 2003** Complex array of mandarin, peach and nectarine fruit; perfect balance; lingering finish. **RATING** 92 **DRINK** 2009 $ 30.50
Ninth Island Pinot Noir 2003 Nice texture and weight; plum, soft spice and a touch of stem; good length. **RATING** 91 **DRINK** 2007 $ 23
Reserve Pinot Noir 2002 Powerful, concentrated dark plum with savoury/chocolatey/earthy notes; destined to be long-lived. **RATING** 91 **DRINK** 2010 $ 49.90
Estate Pinot Noir 2002 Interesting aromas, quite spicy and oaky; more fruit comes through on the plum and spice palate. **RATING** 90 **DRINK** 2009 $ 37

YYYY **Reserve Chardonnay 2000** Melon, fig and cashew aromas from barrel and malolactic fermentation inputs; also adding to texture and complexity. **RATING** 89 **DRINK** 2007 $ 45.65
Estate Riesling 2003 Spotlessly clean and lively; good focus and balance; apple/citrus. **RATING** 88 **DRINK** 2012 $ 27.89
Estate Pinot Gris 2003 Varietal musk aromas; clean, firm, crisp palate; subtle touch of barrel ferment; good balance/finish. **RATING** 88 **DRINK** 2007 $ 28
Ninth Island Pinot Grigio 2003 A challenging and interesting mix of gritty, minerally, flinty flavours alongside pear and apple; fractionally hot finish. **RATING** 87 **DRINK** Now $ 21

YYYY **Riesling 2003** **RATING** 86 **DRINK** 2012 $ 27.90
Estate Gewurztraminer 2003 **RATING** 86 **DRINK** 2008 $ 27.89
Ninth Island Sauvignon Blanc 2003 **RATING** 86 **DRINK** Now $ 21

YYY **Ninth Island Chardonnay 2003** **RATING** 83 $ 22.80
Estate Chardonnay 2002 **RATING** 83 $ 34.65

Piromit Wines

NR

113 Hanwood Avenue, Hanwood, NSW 2680 **REGION** Riverina
T (02) 6963 0200 **F** (02) 6963 0277 **OPEN** Mon–Fri 9–5
WINEMAKER Dom Piromalli, Pat Mittiga **EST.** 1998 **CASES** 60 000
PRODUCT RANGE ($8–17 CD) Semillon, Old Briggie Semillon Chardonnay, Colombard Chardonnay, Chardonnay, Botrytis Semillon, Shiraz, Old Briggie Shiraz Cabernet, Cabernet Merlot, Cabernet Sauvignon.
SUMMARY I simply cannot resist quoting directly from the background information kindly supplied to me. 'Piromit Wines is a relatively new boutique winery situated in Hanwood, New South Wales. The winery complex, which crushed 1000 tonnes this season (2000), was built for the 1999 vintage on a 14-acre site which was until recently used as a drive-in. Previous to this, wines were made on our 100-acre vineyard. The winery site is being developed into an innovative tourist attraction complete with an Italian restaurant and landscaped formal gardens.' It is safe to say this extends the concept of a boutique winery into new territory, but then it is a big country. It is a family business run by Pat Mittiga, Dom Piromalli and Paul Hudson.

Pirramimma

Johnston Road, McLaren Vale, SA 5171 **REGION** McLaren Vale
T (08) 8323 8205 **F** (08) 8323 9224 **OPEN** Mon–Fri 9–5, Sat 11–5, Sun, public holidays 11.30–4
WINEMAKER Geoff Johnston, Simon Parker **EST.** 1892 **CASES** 40 000
PRODUCT RANGE ($13–26.50 R) Adelaide Hills Semillon, McLaren Vale Semillon, Stock's Hill Semillon Sauvignon Blanc, Stocks Hill Semillon Chardonnay, Hillsview Chardonnay, Late Harvest Riesling, Stock's Hill Shiraz, Merlot, Petit Verdot, Hillsview Cabernet Merlot, Cabernet Sauvignon, Ports.
SUMMARY An operation with large vineyard holdings of very high quality and a winery which devotes much of its considerable capacity to contract-processing of fruit for others. In terms of the brand, has been a consistent under-performer during the 1990s. The marketing of the brand does scant justice to the very considerable resources available to it, notably its gold medal-winning Petit Verdot and fine, elegant Chardonnay. Exports to the US, Canada, the UK, Germany, Switzerland, Malaysia, Singapore, Japan and New Zealand.

🍷🍷🍷🍷🍷 **Reserve Shiraz 2001** Brimming with dark berry and bitter chocolate fruit; great mouthfeel, fine tannins, integrated oak. **RATING** 93 **DRINK** 2016 $ 26.50
Old Bush Vine Grenache 2002 Excellent colour; lush red and black fruits in a web of fine, cedary tannins — simply delicious. Best of all, has a screwcap. **RATING** 93 **DRINK** 2007 $ 18
Reserve Cabernet Sauvignon 2001 Deep colour; classic cassis/blackcurrant; dash of regional chocolate; ripe, lingering tannins. **RATING** 92 **DRINK** 2014 $ 26.50
Reserve Petit Verdot 2001 Complex, savoury, herb aromas; supple, medium-bodied, black fruits and lingering fine tannins. **RATING** 91 **DRINK** 2011 $ 26.50

🍷🍷🍷🍷 **Stock's Hill Semillon Sauvignon Blanc 2003** Slate and mineral dominant, with herb and grass aromas and flavours in the background. **RATING** 87 **DRINK** Now $ 13

🍷🍷🍷🍷 **Stock's Hill Shiraz 2001** **RATING** 86 **DRINK** 2008 $ 15
Chardonnay Unoaked 2001 **RATING** 84 **DRINK** Now $ 14.50
Stock's Hill Cabernet Sauvignon 2000 **RATING** 84 **DRINK** Now $ 15

Pizzini

King Valley Road, Wangaratta, Vic 3768 **REGION** King Valley
T (03) 5729 8278 **F** (03) 5729 8495 **OPEN** 7 days 12–5
WINEMAKER Alfred Pizzini, Joel Pizzini, Mark Walpole **EST.** 1980 **CASES** 12 000
PRODUCT RANGE ($14–40 CD) Bianco, Riesling, Sauvignon Blanc, Arneis, Chardonnay, Verduzzo, Rosetta, Shiraz, Merlot, Sangiovese, Nebbiolo, Shiraz Cabernet, Cabernet, .
SUMMARY Fred and Katrina Pizzini have been grape growers in the King Valley for over 20 years with 66 hectares of vineyard. Grape growing (rather than winemaking) still continues to be the major focus of activity, but their move into winemaking has been particularly successful, and I can personally vouch for their Italian cooking skills. It is not surprising, then, that their wines should span both Italian and traditional varieties. Exports to Hong Kong and China.

Plantagenet

Albany Highway, Mount Barker, WA 6324 **REGION** Mount Barker
T (08) 9851 2150 **F** (08) 9851 1839 **OPEN** 7 days 9–5
WINEMAKER Gavin Berry, Richard Robson **EST.** 1974 **CASES** 130 000
PRODUCT RANGE ($11–38 CD) Riesling, Omrah Sauvignon Blanc, Omrah Chardonnay (unoaked), Mount Barker Chardonnay, Fronti, Fine White, Fine Red, Eros, Pinot Noir, Shiraz, Henry II, Cabernet Sauvignon, Mount Barker Brut; Breakaway Fine White and Fine Red; Hazard Hill Semillon Sauvignon Blanc, Late Harvest Riesling, Shiraz Grenache; Rocky Horror Vineyard Merlot, Cabernet Franc.
SUMMARY The senior winery in the Mount Barker region which is making superb wines across the full spectrum of variety and style — highly aromatic Riesling, tangy citrus-tinged Chardonnay, glorious Rhône-style Shiraz and ultra-stylish Cabernet Sauvignon. The five-star rating is driven by the superb 2001 vintage wines. Exports to the US, Canada, the UK, Germany, The Netherlands, Denmark, Switzerland, Singapore, Malaysia, New Zealand, Japan and Hong Kong.

ΥΥΥΥΥ **Mount Barker Shiraz 2001** Oozes blackberry, black cherry and spice aromas, the palate at once plush yet elegant, perfectly proportioned and weighted, finishing with fine, ripe tannins. **RATING** 95 **DRINK** 2016 $ 38
Rocky Horror Vineyard Merlot 2001 Impressive colour, bouquet, palate and finish all signal a merlot in heroic style, with layers of blackcurrant, olive and substantial, but balanced, tannins. **RATING** 95 **DRINK** 2016 $ 38
Mount Barker Cabernet Sauvignon 2001 Powerful blackberry and earth aromas, the palate much finer and more elegant; impressive length and balance. **RATING** 94 **DRINK** 2016 $ 30

ΥΥΥΥΥ **Chenin Blanc Off the Rack 2003** Lusciously sweet peach and apricot flavours; barest hint of French oak; great Loire Valley style. **RATING** 92 **DRINK** 2010 $ 25
Rocky Horror Vineyard Cabernet Franc 2001 Strong colour; attractive cedary/spicy/berry aromas; medium-bodied, supple and round; blackcurrant and ripe tannins; utterly exceptional for cabernet franc. **RATING** 92 **DRINK** 2016 $ 28
Mount Barker Pinot Noir 2001 Stylish and elegant wine; savoury flavours but silky mouthfeel; line and length; best for years. **RATING** 90 **DRINK** 2007 $ 23

ΥΥΥΥ **Mount Barker Riesling 2003** Very pale, almost water-white; very tight and youthful mineral, slate and acid flavours; simply not ready. **RATING** 87 **DRINK** 2013 $ 18

ΥΥΥΥ **Omrah Sauvignon Blanc 2003** **RATING** 86 **DRINK** Now $ 17
Mount Barker Pinot Noir 2002 **RATING** 85 **DRINK** Now $ 23
Hazard Hill Semillon Sauvignon Blanc 2003 **RATING** 84 **DRINK** Now $ 11

ΥΥΥ **Hazard Hill Shiraz Grenache 2002** **RATING** 83 $ 12

Platt's NR

Murray Valley Highway, Browns Plains via Rutherglen, Vic 3685 **REGION** Rutherglen
T (02) 6032 9381 **F** (02) 6372 1055 **OPEN** 7 days 9–5
WINEMAKER Barry Platt **EST.** 1983 **CASES** 4000
PRODUCT RANGE ($9–12 CD) Chardonnay, Semillon, Gewurztraminer, Cabernet Sauvignon.
SUMMARY District veteran Barry Platt has moved the cellar door to the historic (but now renovated) Fairfield Winery, built in 1895. The 8 hectares of estate vineyards in Mudgee are supplemented by purchased grapes from other Mudgee growers, and the business has grown substantially. Platt's elects not to enter the Mudgee Wine Show, and it is many years since I have tasted the wines.

Platypus Lane Wines ★★★

PO Box 1140, Midland, WA 6936 **REGION** Swan District
T (08) 9250 1655 **F** (08) 9274 3045 **OPEN** Not
WINEMAKER Brenden Smith (Contract) **EST.** 1996
PRODUCT RANGE Chardonnay, Shiraz, Muscat.
SUMMARY Platypus Lane, with a small core of 2.5 hectares of chardonnay, shiraz and muscat, gained considerable publicity for owner Ian Gibson when its Shiraz won the inaugural John Gladstones Trophy at the Qantas Western Australian Wines Show for the wine showing greatest regional and

varietal typicity. Much of the credit can no doubt go to contract-winemaker Brendan Smith, who handles significant quantities of grapes brought in from other producers as well as from the core vineyards. The wines are distributed in Australia through National Liquor, and are exported to the UK and the US.

ȲȲȲȲ **Unwooded Chardonnay 2003** RATING 85 DRINK Now

Plunkett ★★★☆

Cnr Hume Highway and Lambing Gully Road, Avenel, Vic 3664 REGION Strathbogie Ranges
T (03) 5796 2150 F (03) 5796 2147 OPEN 7 days 11–5 (cellar door), Thurs–Mon 11–5 (restaurant)
WINEMAKER Sam Plunkett, Victor Nash EST. 1980 CASES 15 000
PRODUCT RANGE ($16–35 CD) The top-of-the-range wines are released under the Strathbogie Ranges label with Riesling, Chardonnay, Shiraz, Merlot, Cabernet Merlot, Tawny Port; standard wines under the Blackwood Ridge brand of Gewurztraminer, Sauvignon Blanc, Unwooded Chardonnay, Pinot Noir, Shiraz.
SUMMARY The Plunkett family first planted grapes way back in 1968, establishing 3 acres with 25 experimental varieties. Commercial plantings commenced in 1980, with 100 hectares now under vine, and more coming. While holding a vigneron's licence since 1985, the Plunketts did not commence serious marketing of the wines until 1992 and have now settled down into producing an array of wines which are pleasant and well-priced, the Reserves in another quality and price league. Wholesale distribution to all States; exports to the US, Canada, the UK, Germany, Malaysia, Indonesia, Vietnam and Hong Kong.

ȲȲȲȲȲ **Strathbogie Ranges Reserve Shiraz 2002** Powerful blackberry, licorice and spice; the aggressive tannins should soften. RATING 90 DRINK 2012 $ 35

ȲȲȲȲ **Strathbogie Ranges Cabernet Merlot 2002** An exotic and lively mix of spice, anise, redcurrant and blackcurrant; some tannins to close. RATING 89 DRINK 2010 $ 19
Blackwood Ridge Pinot Noir 2003 Rich, round, sweet dark plum and spice fruit; tending towards dry red style, but still a surprise packet. RATING 88 DRINK Now $ 17
Blackwood Ridge Unwooded Chardonnay 2003 Bright grapefruit and nectarine; lively and fresh, crisp finish. RATING 87 DRINK Now $ 16
Strathbogie Ranges Chardonnay 2003 Light to medium-bodied; delicate barrel ferment and malolactic ferment inputs; cashew and melon, but not intense. RATING 87 DRINK 2007 $ 19

ȲȲȲȲ **Strathbogie Ranges Reserve Merlot 2002** RATING 85 DRINK 2012 $ 35

ȲȲȲ **Blackwood Ridge Shiraz 2001** RATING 81 $ 17

Poet's Corner ★★★★☆

Craigmoor Road, Mudgee, NSW 2850 REGION Mudgee
T (02) 6372 2208 F (02) 6372 4464 OPEN Mon–Sat 10–4.30, Sun and public holidays 10–4
WINEMAKER James Manners EST. 1858 CASES 150 000
PRODUCT RANGE ($9.99–25 R) Semillon Sauvignon Blanc Chardonnay, Unwooded Chardonnay, Shiraz Cabernet Sauvignon Cabernet Franc; PC range of Chardonnay, Merlot, Pinot Chardonnay; Henry Lawson range of Semillon, Chardonnay, Shiraz, Cabernet Sauvignon; also home to the Craigmoor and Montrose labels.
SUMMARY Poet's Corner is located in one of the oldest wineries in Australia to remain in more or less continuous production: Craigmoor (as it was previously known) was built by Adam Roth in 1858/1860, whose grandson Jack Roth ran the winery until the early 1960s. It is the public face for Poet's Corner, Montrose and Craigmoor wines, all of which are made at the more modern Montrose winery (which is not open to the public).

ȲȲȲȲȲ **Montrose Stony Creek Chardonnay 2002** Classy wine; subtle barrel ferment/malo inputs; creamy, also minerally; elegant. RATING 94 DRINK 2007 $ 14.99

ȲȲȲȲȲ **Henry Lawson Semillon 2002** Aromatic lemongrass bouquet; intense palate, a touch of passionfruit and a crisp finish. Value. RATING 92 DRINK 2010 $ 13
Montrose Sangiovese 2002 Clearly articulated savoury/spicy varietal black fruits; lingering tannins; convincing example. RATING 90 DRINK 2009 $ 25

ΨΨΨΨ **Montrose Black Shiraz 2001** Driven by fully ripe dark plum and blackberry fruit; soft tannins, good length. **RATING** 88 **DRINK** 2009 $ 24.99

ΨΨΨΨ **PC Merlot 2002** Outstanding value; sweet red fruits, fresh and lively. Highly likely to have been made using micro-oxygenation techniques. No regional claim. Great now, great value. **RATING** 86 **DRINK** Now $ 9.99

ΨΨΨ **PC Merlot 2001 RATING** 80 $ 9.99

Pokolbin Estate ★★☆

McDonalds Road, Pokolbin, NSW 2321 **REGION** Lower Hunter Valley
T (02) 4998 7524 **F** (02) 4998 7765 **OPEN** 7 days 10–6
WINEMAKER Contract **EST.** 1980 **CASES** 2500
PRODUCT RANGE ($14.50–48 CD) Riesling, Semillon, Chardonnay, Show Reserve Chardonnay, Late Harvest Riesling, Shiraz; Verdelho Solera, Tawny and Vintage Port.
SUMMARY An unusual outlet, offering its own-label wines made under contract by Trevor Drayton, together with other Hunter Valley wines; also cheap varietal 'cleanskins'. Wine quality under the Pokolbin Estate label has been very modest, although the 1997 Hunter Riesling (perversely, true Riesling, not Semillon) won a silver medal and was the top-pointed wine in its class at the 1997 Hunter Valley Wine Show.

ΨΨΨΨ **Shiraz 2001 RATING** 84 **DRINK** 2011 $ 32

ΨΨΨ **Reserve Shiraz 2001 RATING** 81 $ 48

Polin & Polin Wines ★★★☆

Wyameta, Bell's Lane, Denman, NSW 2328 **REGION** Upper Hunter Valley
T (02) 6547 2955 **F** (02) 9969 9665 **OPEN** Not
WINEMAKER Peter Orr (Contract) **EST.** 1997 **CASES** 1200
PRODUCT RANGE ($18 ML) Limb of Addy Shiraz.
SUMMARY The 6-hectare vineyard was established by Lexie and Michael Polin (and family) in 1997. It is not named for them, as one might expect, but to honour Peter and Thomas Polin who migrated from Ireland in 1860, operating a general store in Coonamble. Limb of Addy has a distinctly Irish twist to it, but is in fact a hill immediately to the east of the vineyard. The 6 hectares of shiraz will grow to 8 hectares in the near future.

ΨΨΨΨ **Limb of Addy Shiraz 2002** Red fruits and a touch of regional earth; light to medium-bodied; controlled tannins and good balance. **RATING** 87 **DRINK** 2010 $ 18
Limb of Addy Shiraz 2001 An elegant, medium-bodied wine, carefully made and crafted; pleasant red fruit flavours, though not concentrated. **RATING** 87 **DRINK** 2007 $ 18

Politini Wines ★★★

65 Upper King River Road, Cheshunt, Vic 3678 **REGION** King Valley
T (03) 5729 8277 **F** (03) 5729 8373 **OPEN** Weekends and public holidays 11–5, or by appointment
WINEMAKER Warren Proft **EST.** 1989 **CASES** 2200
PRODUCT RANGE ($14.50–21 ML) Sauvignon Blanc, Chardonnay, Shiraz, Merlot, Cabernet Sauvignon.
SUMMARY The Politini family have been grapegrowers in the King Valley supplying major local wineries since 1989, selling to Brown Brothers, Miranda and the Victorian Alps Winery. In 2000 they decided to withhold 20 tonnes per year for the purposes of the Politini Wines label, and have established sales outlets at a number of high class Melbourne restaurants and clubs. The wines are also available through mail order and the cellar door on long weekends and public holidays.

ΨΨΨΨ **Merlot 2000 RATING** 85 **DRINK** Now $ 19.50
Chardonnay 2000 RATING 84 **DRINK** Now $ 17.50

Polleters ★★★★

Polleters Road, Moonambel, Vic 3478 (postal) **REGION** Pyrenees
T (03) 9569 5030 **OPEN** Weekends 10–5
WINEMAKER Mark Summerfield **EST.** 1994 **CASES** 450
PRODUCT RANGE ($17.50–25 ML) Shiraz, Shiraz Merlot, Shiraz Cabernet, Merlot, Morgans Choice, Cabernet Franc.
SUMMARY Pauline and Peter Bicknell purchased the 60-hectare property on which their vineyard now stands in 1993, at which time it had been part of a larger grazing property. The first vines were planted in spring 1994, and there are now 2 hectares each of shiraz and cabernet sauvignon, 1.25 hectares of cabernet franc and 0.75 hectare of merlot. In the first few years the grapes were sold, but as from 2001 part of the production has been taken to produce the impressively rich and powerful wines. The grapes are hand-picked, fermented in open vats with hand plunging, and matured for 18 months in American oak.

TTTTY **Shiraz 2002** Ripe, lush, densely concentrated array of black fruits; splashes of spice, chocolate and mocha; fine tannins. **RATING** 91 **DRINK** 2015 $ 25
Morgans Choice 2002 Ultra-ripe array of black fruits, spice and chocolate; the tannins persistent but balanced; good length. **RATING** 90 **DRINK** 2012 $ 25

TTTY **Merlot 2002** Olive, spice, briar, chocolate, blackcurrant and mint; a strange though intense jumble. **RATING** 87 **DRINK** 2011 $ 25

Pondalowie Vineyards ★★★★☆

6 Main Street, Bridgewater-on-Loddon, Vic 3516 **REGION** Bendigo
T (03) 5437 3332 **F** (03) 5437 3332 **OPEN** Weekends and public holidays 12–5, or by appointment
WINEMAKER Dominic Morris, Krystina Morris **EST.** 1997 **CASES** 1500
PRODUCT RANGE ($20–32 ML) MT Unwooded Tempranillo, Shiraz Viognier, The Gladstone (Shiraz Cabernet).
SUMMARY Dominic and Krystina Morris both have a strong winemaking background, gained from working in Australia, Portugal and France. Dominic has worked alternate vintages in Australia and Portugal since 1995, and Krystina has worked there, at St Hallett, Boar's Rock and currently for Portavin wine bottlers. They have established 5.5 hectares of shiraz, 2 hectares each of tempranillo and cabernet sauvignon, and a little viognier, malbec and touriga. The wines have been eagerly sought in the UK market, leaving only a small amount to be sold through trendy Melbourne bars and bistros, with a few country outlets thrown in for good measure.

TTTTT **Shiraz Viognier 2002** Luscious, complex blend of blackberry, licorice, spice and chocolate; excellent texture; sweet tannins. **RATING** 94 **DRINK** 2012 $ 32

TTTTY **Cabernet Malbec 2002** Sweet dark fruits with spice/hay seed malbec influence obvious; fine-grained tannins to close. **RATING** 91 **DRINK** 2012 $ 32
MT Unoaked Tempranillo 2003 Brilliant colour; aromatic, perfumed, sweet fruit aromas and flavours; very fine, soft tannins. Impressive. **RATING** 90 **DRINK** 2008 $ 22

TTTT **Shiraz Cabernet 2002** Fresh raspberry and blackcurrant fruits; light to medium-bodied; minimal oak and fine tannins. Stylish. **RATING** 89 **DRINK** 2010 $ 20
Malbec Shiraz 2001 Clear malbec varietal input with a mix of poached berry and spice flavours; light to medium-bodied, and not over-extractive nor over-oaked. **RATING** 88 **DRINK** 2007 $ 30
The Gladstone Shiraz Cabernet 2001 Like each of the Pondalowie wines, very well made and balanced, the extract not forced. Vine age should bring greater depth and intensity. **RATING** 87 **DRINK** 2008 $ 20

TTTY **Shiraz 2001** **RATING** 86 **DRINK** 2007 $ 26

Pontville Station ★★★★

948 Midland Highway, Pontville, Tas 7030 **REGION** Southern Tasmania
T (03) 6268 1635 **OPEN** Not
WINEMAKER Peter Rundle **EST.** 1990 **CASES** 90

PRODUCT RANGE ($17–25 ML) Dessert Riesling, Pinot Noir.

SUMMARY Peter and Jane Rundle have a tiny vineyard of 0.5 hectare, mainly planted to pinot noir. Because the vineyard has been established in a frost-prone site, they have from time-to-time purchased small quantities of grapes from other growers, but in February 2002 were able to make the first commercial vineyard release, hot on the heels of winning a silver medal with each wine at the 2002 Tasmanian Wines Show, the Pinot Noir in one of the strongest Pinot classes ever seen in Australia, and the Dessert Riesling coming second in its class. No further news, however.

Poole's Rock   ★★★★

De Beyers Road, Pokolbin, NSW 2321 REGION Lower Hunter Valley
T (02) 9563 2500 F (02) 9563 2555 OPEN 7 days 10–5
WINEMAKER Patrick Auld EST. 1988 CASES 42 000
PRODUCT RANGE ($14.95–32.95 R) Chardonnay, Shiraz; Firestick Chardonnay and Shiraz Cabernet Sauvignon (from Langhorne Creek).

SUMMARY Sydney merchant banker David Clarke has had a long involvement with the wine industry. The 18-hectare Poole's Rock vineyard, planted purely to chardonnay, is his personal venture, the resource initially bolstered by the acquisition of the larger, adjoining Simon Whitlam Vineyard. However, the purchase of the 74-hectare Glen Elgin Estate upon which the 2500-tonne former Tulloch winery is situated, takes Poole's Rock (and its associated brand Cockfighter's Ghost) into another dimension. The wine has retail distribution throughout Australia and is exported to Europe, the US and Canada, New Zealand and Asia.

ΨΨΨΨΨ **Shiraz 2000** Medium-bodied; good regional expression of the variety; spicy, earthy, savoury notes to the ripe core of fruit; ripe tannins, good length. RATING 91 DRINK 2010 $25

Chardonnay 2000 Round, soft, smooth peach and a touch of honey; good balancing acidity. Three gold medals in 2003. RATING 90 DRINK Now $23.50

ΨΨΨΨ **Chardonnay 2002** RATING 84 DRINK Now $23.50

Pooley Wines   ★★★☆

Cooinda Vale Vineyard, Barton Vale Road, Campania, Tas 7026 REGION Southern Tasmania
T (03) 6224 3591 F (03) 6224 3591 OPEN Tues–Sun 10–5
WINEMAKER Mat Pooley, Andrew Hood (Contract) EST. 1985 CASES 1500
PRODUCT RANGE ($18–40 CD) Coal River Riesling, Coal River Chardonnay, Nellie's Nest Pinot Noir, Cooinda Vale Pinot Noir, Coal River Pinot Noir; Reserve range of Coal River Pinot Gris, Family Reserve Pinot Noir, Family Reserve Cabernet Merlot.

SUMMARY Three generations of the Pooley family have been involved in the development of the Cooinda Vale Estate; it was indeed under the Cooinda Vale label that the winery was previously known. After a tentative start on a small scale, plantings have now reached 8 hectares on a property which covers both sides of the Coal River in a region which is substantially warmer and drier than most people realise. The wines have limited retail distribution in Victoria (Sutherland Fine Wines) and of course in Tasmania. Limited exports to the UK and the US.

ΨΨΨΨΨ **Coal River Chardonnay 2002** Highly aromatic, exotic aromas of wild flowers/acacia/lychee; the palate expands and lengthens on finish with Tasmanian acidity. RATING 90 DRINK 2010 $22

ΨΨΨΨ **Nellie's Nest Pinot Noir 2002** Very complex and stylish; some stem, but good fruit and oak handling; has finesse. RATING 89 DRINK 2008 $18

Coal River Chardonnay 2001 Light to medium-bodied; smooth and subtle stone fruit/melon/citrus; fruit-driven. RATING 87 DRINK 2007 $22

ΨΨΨΨ **Coal River Riesling 2003** RATING 86 DRINK 2009 $20

Coal River Pinot Noir 2002 RATING 85 DRINK Now $26

ΨΨΨ **Pinot Gris 2003** RATING 83 $22

Poplar Bend

NR

RMB 8655 Main Creek Road, Main Ridge, Vic 3928 **REGION** Mornington Peninsula
T (03) 5989 6046 **F** (03) 5989 6460 **OPEN** Weekends and public holidays 10–5, also by appointment
WINEMAKER David Briggs **EST.** 1988 **CASES** 350
PRODUCT RANGE ($16–28 CD) Pineau Chloe, Cabernet Chloe, Sparkling Chloe, Pinot Noir, Cellar
Reserve Pinot Noir, Cabernet Shiraz.
SUMMARY Poplar Bend was the child of Melbourne journalist, author and raconteur Keith Dunstan
and wife, Marie, who moved into full-scale retirement in 1997, selling Poplar Bend to David Briggs.
The changes are few; the label still depicts Chloe in all her glory, which could be calculated to send
the worthy inhabitants of the Bureau of Alcohol, Tobacco and Firearms (of the US) into a state of
cataleptic shock.

Port Phillip Estate

261 Red Hill Road, Red Hill, Vic 3937 **REGION** Mornington Peninsula
T (03) 5989 2708 **F** (03) 5989 3017 **OPEN** Weekends and public holidays 11–5
WINEMAKER Lindsay McCall, Sandro Mosele (Contract) **EST.** 1987 **CASES** 4000
PRODUCT RANGE ($18–30 CD) Sauvignon Blanc, Chardonnay, Pinot Noir, Reserve Pinot Noir, Shiraz,
Reserve Shiraz.
SUMMARY Established by leading Melbourne QC Jeffrey Sher, who, after some prevarication, sold the
estate to Giorgio and Dianne Gjergja in February 2000. The Gjergjas are rightly more than content
with the quality and style of the wines; the main changes are enhanced cellar-door facilities and
redesigned labels.

TTTTT **Pinot Noir 2001** The bouquet is fresh and bright, with spicy/sappy red fruits, the long and
lingering palate with delicious strawberry and plum flavours; great elegance. **RATING** 95
DRINK 2008 $ 30
Pinot Noir 2002 Intensely focused ripe, plum fruit; exceptional length and line; should
develop superbly. **RATING** 94 **DRINK** 2010 $ 30

TTTTY **Chardonnay 2002** Complex, funky, with some wild yeast/barrel ferment inputs to the
bouquet; long, intense palate; stone fruit just carries the oak. **RATING** 91 **DRINK** 2007 $ 20

TTTY **Sauvignon Blanc 2003** **RATING** 86 **DRINK** Now $ 20

Portree

★★★★

72 Powells Track via Mount William Road, Lancefield, Vic 3455 **REGION** Macedon Ranges
T (03) 5429 1422 **F** (03) 5429 2205 **OPEN** Weekends and public holidays 11–5
WINEMAKER Ken Murchison **EST.** 1983 **CASES** 1000
PRODUCT RANGE ($15–38 CD) Chardonnay, Aged Release Chardonnay, Macedon (Blanc de Blanc,
cellar door only), Pinot Noir, Damask (Cabernet Franc Rose), Quarry Red (Cabernet Franc Merlot).
SUMMARY Owner Ken Murchison selected his 5-hectare Macedon vineyard after studying viticulture
at Charles Sturt University and being strongly influenced by Dr Andrew Pirie's doctoral thesis. All of
the wines show distinct cool-climate characteristics, the Quarry Red having clear similarities to the
wines of Chinon in the Loire Valley. However, it is with Chardonnay that Portree has done best and
which is its principal wine (in terms of volume). As from the 1998 vintage the wines have been made
at an on-site winery.

TTTTY **Pinot Noir 2002** Youthful, bright and fresh; quite silky; considerable potential. **RATING** 90
DRINK 2007 $ 25

Port Stephens Winery

NR

69 Nelson Bay Road, Bobs Farm, NSW 2316 **REGION** Northern Rivers Zone
T (02) 4982 6411 **F** (02) 4982 6766 **OPEN** 7 days 10–5
WINEMAKER Contract **EST.** 1984 **CASES** 3500
PRODUCT RANGE ($13.50–21.50 CD) Sauvignon Blanc, Unwooded Chardonnay, Tri-Blend, Tomaree
White, Golden Sands, Tomaree Red, Reserve Shiraz, Cabernet Merlot, Reserve Cabernet Sauvignon,
Sparkling and fortifieds.

SUMMARY Planting of the quite substantial Port Stephens Wines vineyard began in 1984, and there are now 4 hectares of vines in production. The wines are made under contract-made in the Hunter Valley but are sold through the attractive, Boutique Wine Centre on-site, recently extended to offer over 100 wines from 30 wineries as far afield as Manjimup in Western Australia.

🐾 Possums Vineyard ★★★★☆

31 Thornber Street, Unley Park, SA 5061 (postal) **REGION** McLaren Vale
T (08) 8272 3406 **F** (08) 8272 3406 **OPEN** Not
WINEMAKER Brian Light (Consultant) **EST.** 2000 **CASES** 3000
PRODUCT RANGE ($14–18.40 ML) Shiraz, Cabernet Sauvignon.
SUMMARY Possums Vineyard is owned by the very distinguished wine scientist and researcher Dr John Possingham, and Carol Summers. They have 17.2 hectares of cabernet sauvignon, 15 hectares of shiraz, 14.2 hectares of chardonnay and 0.4 hectare of grenache established in two vineyards, one at Blewitt Springs, the other at Willunga. They regards themselves as grapegrowers, rather than winemakers, with the bulk of the grapes sold to Beringer Blass and d'Arenberg. However, with the advent of Boar's Rock Winery, and the contract-making facilities it offers, they have embarked on making wines under the Possums Vineyard label, using Brian Light as a consultant. Their major focus is on export markets, with distribution in the US through Epicurean Wines, and also in the UK, Belgium and Canada. In Australia the wines are available only by mail order.

🍷🍷🍷🍷 **Shiraz 2002** Dense red-purple; complex, high-toned blackberry, prune, plum and chocolate rounded up by ripe tannins. **RATING** 92 **DRINK** 2012 $18.40

Pothana ★★★★☆

Pothana Lane, Belford, NSW 2335 **REGION** Lower Hunter Valley
T (02) 6574 7164 **F** (02) 6574 7209 **OPEN** By appointment
WINEMAKER David Hook **EST.** 1984 **CASES** 5000
PRODUCT RANGE ($16–30 ML) Pothana Semillon, Chardonnay, Shiraz; also The Gorge range of Mosto (Semillon), Semillon, Semillon Sauvignon Blanc, Verdelho, Pinot Grigio, Unwooded Chardonnay, Chardonnay, Pinot Noir, Shiraz. All are estate-grown; the Pothana range is produced in tiny quantities (250 cases) and then only in the best vintages.
SUMMARY With over 20 years experience, David Hook worked as a winemaker for Tyrrell's and Lake's Folly, also doing the full Flying Winemaker bit, with jobs in Bordeaux, the Rhône Valley, Spain, the US and Georgia. He and his family began the establishment of the vineyard (in 1984) and the winery (in 1990). The wines are available by mailing list, but have distribution by Grapelink in NSW and Victoria, Queensland and Tasmania by Prime Wines.

🍷🍷🍷🍷🍷 **Belford Semillon 2003** Classic restraint and classic length; slate, mineral, green pea; very good, lingering acidity. **RATING** 94 **DRINK** 2013 $22
Belford Semillon 2002 Of near-identical style and quality to the '03. **RATING** 94 **DRINK** 2013 $22

🍷🍷🍷🍷 **Belford Shiraz 2002** Abundant, rich, plum and blackberry fruit; medium to full-bodied; excellent flesh and structure. **RATING** 92 **DRINK** 2012 $30
Belford Chardonnay 2003 Fine, elegant, understated style; peach, some fig; minimal oak; good length. **RATING** 90 **DRINK** 2007 $30

🍷🍷🍷🍷 **The Gorge Unwooded Chardonnay 2003** Plenty of ripe stone fruit flavour, offering more than the usual boring stuff. **RATING** 87 **DRINK** Now $16
The Gorge Chardonnay 2003 Unoaked style; clean, fresh, light to medium-bodied melon/stone fruit. Good value. Screwcap. **RATING** 87 **DRINK** Now $16

🍷🍷🍷🍷 **The Gorge Verdelho 2003** **RATING** 86 **DRINK** Now $16
The Gorge Shiraz 2002 **RATING** 86 **DRINK** 2008 $16

Potters Clay Vineyards ★★★

Main Road, Willunga, SA 5172 **REGION** McLaren Vale
T (08) 8556 2799 **F** (08) 8556 2922 **OPEN** Not
WINEMAKER John Bruschi **EST.** 1994 **CASES** 900

PRODUCT RANGE ($15.90–16.90 R) Chardonnay, Shiraz, Merlot Cabernet Franc.

SUMMARY John and Donna Bruschi are second generation grape growers who assumed full ownership of the 16-hectare Potters Clay Vineyard in 1994 with the aim of establishing their own winery and label. In 1999 construction of stage one of a two-stage boutique winery was completed. Stage one is a winery production facility, stage two (at some future date) is to be the cellar door, restaurant and garden/picnic area. At least this is in the correct order; all too often it is the cellar door and restaurant which come first. The clever packaging and high-quality promotional literature should do much to enhance sales.

Preston Peak ★★★

31 Preston Peak Lane, Toowoomba, Qld 4352 **REGION** Granite Belt
T (07) 4630 9499 **F** (07) 4630 9499 **OPEN** Wed–Sun 10–5
WINEMAKER Philippa Hambleton, Rod MacPherson **EST.** 1994 **CASES** 3000
PRODUCT RANGE ($9–24 CD) Leaf Series range of Semillon, Sauvignon Blanc, Verdelho, Chardonnay, Shiraz, Merlot, Cabernet Merlot; Wild Flower White, Rose and sparkling, Red; Venus, Reserve Chardonnay, Reserve Shiraz, Cabernet Merlot; sparkling and fortified.
SUMMARY Dentist owners Ashley Smith and Kym Thumpkin have a substantial tourism business. The large, modern cellar door can accommodate functions of up to 150 people, and is often used for weddings and other events. It is situated less than 10 minutes drive from the Toowoomba city centre, with views of Table Top Mountain, the Lockyer Valley and the Darling Downs. There is no charge for tastings, but bookings for groups of more than 20 people are appreciated.

ŸŸŸŸ **Leaf Series Cabernet Sauvignon Petit Verdot 2002** Attractive sweet berry fruit supported by gentle tannins; minimal oak influence. **RATING** 87 **DRINK** 2009 $ 19

ŸŸŸŸ **Reserve Shiraz 2001** **RATING** 86 **DRINK** 2007 $ 24

ŸŸŸ **Leaf Series Verdelho 2003** **RATING** 83 $ 17

❧ Pretty Sally Estate ★★★★

PO Box 549, Kilmore East, Vic 3764 **REGION** Central Victorian Zone
T + 1 650 851 8662 **F** + 1 650 851 1868 **OPEN** Not
WINEMAKER John Ellis (Contract) **EST.** 1996 **CASES** 900
PRODUCT RANGE ($37.90–48.50 R) Sauvignon Blanc, Shiraz, Cabernet Sauvignon.
SUMMARY The McKay, Davies and Cornew families have joined to create the Pretty Sally business. It is based on estate plantings of 11.7 hectares of shiraz, 23.8 hectares of cabernet sauvignon and a splash of sauvignon blanc. The vineyard is still coming into production, the first commercial vintage being made in 2001. The wines are made by the veteran John Ellis and are chiefly exported to the US, where Pretty Sally has a permanent office.

ŸŸŸŸŸ **Sauvignon Blanc 2002** Intensely focused and long; lemon, gooseberry and passionfruit; very good acidity; fresh finish. **RATING** 90 **DRINK** Now $ 37.90

ŸŸŸŸ **Cabernet Sauvignon 2001** **RATING** 86 **DRINK** 2008 $ 47

Preveli Wines ★★★★☆

Bessell Road, Rosa Brook, Margaret River, WA 6285 **REGION** Margaret River
T (08) 9757 2374 **F** (08) 9757 2790 **OPEN** Mon–Sat 10.30–8.30, Sun 12–6
WINEMAKER Andrew Gamen Jnr, Frank Kittler, Mike Lemmes (Contract) **EST.** 1995 **CASES** 8000
PRODUCT RANGE ($9.95–31.95 CD) Semillon, Reserve Semillon, Reserve Semillon Sauvignon Blanc, Chardonnay, Late Harvest Semillon, Shiraz, Merlot, Shiraz Cabernet Sauvignon, Cabernet Sauvignon.
SUMMARY Andrew and Greg Home have turned a small business into a substantial one, with 15 hectares of vineyards at Rosabrook (supplemented by contracts with local growers), and winemaking spread between a number of contract makers. The wines are of impressive quality, and have retail distribution in NSW (Irvines Fine Wines) and in Perth; the Prevelly Liquor Store (owned by the Homes) is the main local outlet.

ŸŸŸŸŸ **Chardonnay 2003** Harmonious fusion of barrel ferment and malolactic influences; excellent balance of creamy and more citrussy/stone fruit/grapefruit flavours. **RATING** 93 **DRINK** 2009 $ 22.95

Merlot 2001 At the big end of the Merlot spectrum; a forceful and focused mix of black fruits, olives and spices; lingering tannins. **RATING** 92 **DRINK** 2016 **$** 31.95

Cabernet Sauvignon 2001 Good colour; rich, ripe blackcurrant/cassis/mulberry fruit, touches of mocha and spice; fine, ripe tannins. **RATING** 91 **DRINK** 2016 **$** 29.95

Reserve Semillon 2002 Complex and long; intense lemony/grassy fruit interwoven with subtle barrel-ferment French oak; good food style. **RATING** 90 **DRINK** 2008 **$** 21.95

ŢŢŢŢ **Semillon Sauvignon Blanc 2003** Sauvignon Blanc makes a big impact; typical regional, fractionally fuzzy ripeness; gooseberry/tropical fruit over the Semillon base. **RATING** 87 **DRINK** 2007 **$** 15.95

ŢŢŢŢ **Shiraz 2002 RATING** 86 **DRINK** 2010 **$** 31.95

Primo Estate

★★★★☆

Old Port Wakefield Road, Virginia, SA 5120 **REGION** Adelaide Plains
T (08) 8380 9442 **F** (08) 8380 9696 **OPEN** June–Aug Mon–Sat 10–4, Sep–May Mon–Fri 10–4
WINEMAKER Joseph Grilli **EST.** 1979 **CASES** 20 000
PRODUCT RANGE ($14–50 CD) La Biondina Colombard, Il Briccone Shiraz Sangiovese; under the Joseph label are d'Elena Pinot Grigio, La Magia Botrytis, Angel Gully Shiraz, Moda Amarone Cabernet Merlot, The Fronti, Sparkling Red.
SUMMARY Roseworthy dux Joe Grilli has risen way above the constraints of the hot Adelaide Plains to produce an innovative and always excellent range of wines. The biennial release of the Joseph Sparkling Red (in its tall Italian glass bottle) is eagerly awaited, the wine immediately selling out. Also unusual and highly regarded are the vintage-dated extra virgin olive oils. However, the core lies with the zingy, fresh Colombard, the velvet-smooth Adelaide Shiraz and the distinguished, complex Joseph Cabernet Merlot. National distribution through Negociants; exports to the UK, Asia, and Europe.

ŢŢŢŢŢ **La Biondina Colombard 2003** Fragrant; lots of ripe fruit offset by cleansing acidity on a lingering finish. **RATING** 91 **DRINK** Now **$** 14

Joseph Moda Amarone Cabernet Merlot 2001 Typical cedary, savoury aromas, then a fine boned and structured palate; cedar, dark chocolate and spices; not as fleshy as some years. Will develop. **RATING** 91 **DRINK** 2016 **$** 50

ŢŢŢŢ **Joseph Angel Gully Shiraz 2001** Strong colour; pronounced, fleshy varietal licorice and blackberry aromas, the palate generous, based on almost chewy, but not hard, tannins, rather than on vibrant fruit **RATING** 89 **DRINK** 2011 **$** 50

Joseph La Magia Botrytis 2002 Fragrant, pristine varietal aromas reflecting 85 per cent riesling, 15 per cent gewurztraminer. Well balanced; still to build complexity. **RATING** 89 **DRINK** 2008 **$** 26

Joseph d'Elena Pinot Grigio 2003 Apple/apple blossom/pear aromas then a crisp, minerally palate, not particularly intense, but long. **RATING** 87 **DRINK** Now **$** 29

Il Briccone Shiraz Sangiovese 2002 Light to medium-bodied; distinctive lemony/savoury twist ex the sangiovese. **RATING** 87 **DRINK** 2007 **$** 19

Prince Albert

★★★★

100 Lemins Road, Waurn Ponds, Vic 3216 **REGION** Geelong
T (03) 5241 8091 **F** (03) 5241 8091 **OPEN** By appointment
WINEMAKER Bruce Hyett **EST.** 1975 **CASES** 100
PRODUCT RANGE ($24.20 ML) Pinot Noir.
SUMMARY Australia's true Pinot Noir specialist (it has only ever made the one wine), which also made much of the early running with the variety: the wines always show good varietal character and have rebounded after a dull patch in the second half of the 1980s. In 1998 the vineyard and winery was certified organic by OVAA Inc. Apart from the mailing list, the wine is sold through fine wine retailers in Sydney and Melbourne, with a little finding its way to the UK. The impact of the drought resulted in a radically decreased production of the 2002 and 2003 vintages.

🍇 Prince of Orange ★★★☆

'Cimbria', The Escort Way, Borenore, NSW 2800 **REGION** Orange
T (02) 6365 2396 **F** (02) 6365 2396 **OPEN** Sat 11–5, or by appointment
WINEMAKER Greg Silkman, Jim Chatto (Contract) **EST.** 1996 **CASES** 1200
PRODUCT RANGE ($17–23 ML) Sauvignon Blanc, Mistelle Blanc (Dessert), Cabernet Rose, Reserve Cabernet Sauvignon.
SUMMARY Harald and Coral Brodersen purchased the 40-hectare Cimbria property in 1990, and having established the supporting infrastructure of dams, fencing and an incomplete residence, planted 3 hectares of sauvignon blanc and 2 hectares of cabernet sauvignon in 1996. In 2001 0.75 hectare each of merlot and shiraz were added, with viognier and semillon rootlings waiting in a nursery until drought-breaking rains arrive. The Brodersens produce around 45 tonnes of grapes each year, using a little under 20 tonnes for the Prince of Orange label, and selling the remainder to supplement small earnings from sheep grazing and off-farm income. The name, the label design, and the branding were respectively inspired by the link between Thomas Livingstone Mitchell, Surveyor General of New South Wales, who served in the British army during the Peninsula Wars against Napoleon alongside Willem, Prince of Orange, who was aide-de-camp to the Duke of Wellington. It was Mitchell who named the town Orange in honour of his friend, who had by then been crowned King Willem II of The Netherlands.

ŶŶŶŶ **Sauvignon Blanc 2003** Clean, fresh, clear varietal citrus and gooseberry fruit; good acidity to close. **RATING** 87 **DRINK** Now $ 17.50

ŶŶŶŶ **Reserve Cabernet Sauvignon 2002** Aromatic, typically cool grown style; long, savoury, fine tannins on finish; needed a touch more ripeness. **RATING** 86 **DRINK** 2009 $ 23
Rose 2003 **RATING** 85 **DRINK** Now $ 17.50

🍇 Printhie Wines NR

'Printhie', Molong, NSW 2866 **REGION** Orange
T (02) 6366 8463 **F** (02) 6366 9243 **OPEN** By appointment
WINEMAKER Andrew Margan (Contract) **EST.** 1996
PRODUCT RANGE A range of varietally denominated table wines reflecting the plantings.
SUMMARY Jim and Ruth Swift have planted 32 hectares of viognier, cabernet sauvignon, merlot and shiraz, and employed Andrew Margan as their contract winemaker. The wine is distributed by Partners In Wine, and is also available through the cellar door and by mail order.

Provenance Wines ★★★★★

870 Steiglitz Road, Sutherlands Creek, Vic 3331 **REGION** Geelong
T (03) 5272 2362 **F** (03) 5272 1551 **OPEN** By appointment
WINEMAKER Scott Ireland **EST.** 1995 **CASES** 2000
PRODUCT RANGE ($23.50–30 R) Pinot Gris, Chardonnay, Pinot Noir, Shiraz.
SUMMARY A joint venture between Pam and Richard Austin of Austin's Barrabool wines on the one hand, and Scott Ireland on the other, has resulted in the building of a new winery on land owned by the Austins at Sutherlands Creek, and leased to winemaker Scott Ireland. Here he will make the Provenance wines, the Austin's Barrabool wines, and also provide contract winemaking services for several small companies within the region.

ŶŶŶŶŶ **Geelong Shiraz 2002** Very complex spicy/licorice/game Côte Rôtie-style; fine, supple tannins and texture. **RATING** 94 **DRINK** 2012 $ 30

ŶŶŶŶ **Geelong Pinot Noir 2002** Exotic, ripe plum and a touch of prune; powers through to a long finish. Despite the bouquet, does not go over the top. **RATING** 93 **DRINK** 2008 $ 30
Geelong Pinot Gris 2003 Stylish, full-flavoured apple/pear/peach skin and the barest hint of oak. Not phenolic; outstanding for variety. **RATING** 92 **DRINK** Now $ 26.95
Geelong Chardonnay 2002 Complex, rich, multi-layered, mouthfilling; ripe stone fruit and an intriguing hint of herb. **RATING** 91 **DRINK** 2007 $ 23.50

Providence Vineyards ★★★★★

236 Lalla Road, Lalla, Tas 7267 **REGION** Northern Tasmania
T (03) 6395 1290 **F** (03) 6395 2088 **OPEN** 7 days 10–5
WINEMAKER Andrew Hood (Contract) **EST.** 1956 **CASES** 800
PRODUCT RANGE ($19–32 CD) Riesling, Semillon, Monet Chardonnay, Botrytis Semillon, Pinot Noir, Monet Pinot Noir; in exceptional years may be released under the Miguet label.
SUMMARY Providence incorporates the pioneer vineyard of Frenchman Jean Miguet, now owned by the Bryce family, which purchased it in 1980. The original 1.3-hectare vineyard has been expanded to a little over 3 hectares, as well as grafting over unsuitable grenache and cabernet (left from the original plantings) to chardonnay and pinot noir and semillon. Miguet in fact called the vineyard 'La Provence', reminding him of the part of France from whence he came, but after 40 years the French authorities forced a name change to Providence.

ΨΨΨΨΨ **Miguet Reserve Chardonnay 2000** Rich, full, complex and ripe stone fruit, honey and oak flavours seamlessly welded; very good length. **RATING** 94 **DRINK** 2007 $ 25.50
Monet Reserve Chardonnay 1998 Ageing superbly; graceful and elegant, still quite youthful; less complex than the '00 Miguet, but equally good. **RATING** 94 **DRINK** 2008 $ 20
Miguet Reserve Pinot Noir 2002 Classic tangy, smoky, sous bois aromas; plum and hints of sour cherries; long, lingering finish. Stylish. **RATING** 94 **DRINK** 2009 $ 32

ΨΨΨΨΨ **Miguet Reserve Pinot Noir 2001** Right in the slot for the Providence Reserve style; smoky, savoury, sous bois; focused, tight and fine; silky texture. **RATING** 93 **DRINK** 2008 $ 32
Monet Reserve Pinot Noir 1998 A fragrant, savoury/spicy wine; altogether elegant and fine; at its peak. **RATING** 93 **DRINK** 2008 $ 22

ΨΨΨΨ **Riesling 2003 RATING** 84 **DRINK** 2009 $ 19

Puddleduck Vineyard ★★★☆

992 Richmond Road, Richmond, Tas 7024 (postal) **REGION** Southern Tasmania
T (03) 6260 2301 **F** (03) 6260 2301 **OPEN** Not
WINEMAKER Andrew Hood (Contract) **EST.** 1997 **CASES** 500
PRODUCT RANGE ($20–25 ML) Sauvignon Blanc, Pinot Noir.
SUMMARY The cutely-named Puddleduck Vineyard is owned and run by Darren and Jackie Brown, who have spent a lifetime working in the Tasmanian wine industry. Darren's career began with Moorilla Estate mowing lawns (aged 16), eventually ending up as assistant winemaker to Julian Alcorso, and also as vineyard manager. With the changing of the guard at Moorilla and the departure of Julian Alcorso, Darren left to become vineyard manager of both Craigow and 572 Richmond Road in the Coal Valley. Jackie continued to work at the cellar door and restaurant of Moorilla, moving to Craigow when its cellar door opened, and thereafter working in the restaurant and cellar door at Coal Valley Vineyard (formerly Treehouse). In the meantime, they had purchased a house with a block of land suitable for viticulture, and have so far planted 0.6 hectare of pinot noir and 0.4 hectare of sauvignon blanc, but in the meantime are sourcing grapes from other vineyards in the region (particularly those managed by Darren) until they have sufficient vineyards of their own.

ΨΨΨΨ **Pinot Noir 2003** Very fragrant and lively; light to medium-bodied; strawberry/cherry/plum fruit; crisp, almost lemony, acidity. **RATING** 89 **DRINK** 2007 $ 25

ΨΨΨΨ **Sauvignon Blanc 2003 RATING** 86 **DRINK** Now $ 20

Punters Corner ★★★★★

Cnr Riddoch Highway and Racecourse Road, Coonawarra, SA 5263 **REGION** Coonawarra
T (08) 8737 2007 **F** (08) 8737 3138 **OPEN** 7 days 10–5
WINEMAKER Peter Bissell (Contract) **EST.** 1988 **CASES** 8500
PRODUCT RANGE ($20–59.50 CD) Chardonnay, Shiraz, Spartacus Reserve Shiraz, Cabernet Merlot, Cabernet Sauvignon, Cabernet.

SUMMARY The quaintly named Punters Corner started off life in 1975 as James Haselgrove but in 1992 was acquired by a group of investors who quite evidently had few delusions about the uncertainties of viticulture and winemaking, even in a district as distinguished as Coonawarra. The arrival of Peter Bissell as winemaker at Balnaves paid immediate (and continuing) dividends. Sophisticated packaging and label design add to the appeal of the wines. National retail distribution; exports to the UK, Belgium, Denmark, Hong Kong, China, Malaysia, Singapore and Japan.

▼▼▼▼▼ **Cabernet Sauvignon 2001** Excellent colour; rich cassis/blackberry fruit; very good balance, extract and length. **RATING** 95 **DRINK** 2016 $ 27.50

▼▼▼▼▽ **Triple Crown 2001** Smooth, supple and elegant; a medium-bodied array of gently sweet red and black fruits; good length and finish. **RATING** 92 **DRINK** 2011 $ 24
Single Vineyard Coonawarra Chardonnay 2002 Obvious barrel-ferment oak still to integrate on the bouquet; more fruit on the nectarine and citrus palate; long and lingering. **RATING** 90 **DRINK** 2008 $ 26

▼▼▼▼ **Shiraz 2001** Medium-bodied; red berry, mint, earth and spice; good texture and length. **RATING** 88 **DRINK** 2009 $ 20

Punt Road ★★★★

10 St Huberts Road, Coldstream, Vic 3770 **REGION** Yarra Valley
T (03) 9739 0666 **F** (03) 9739 0633 **OPEN** 7 days 10–5
WINEMAKER Kate Goodman **EST.** 2000 **CASES** 6000
PRODUCT RANGE ($20–26 R) Sauvignon Blanc, Pinot Gris, Chardonnay, Late Harvest Semillon, Pinot Noir, Shiraz, Merlot, Cabernet Sauvignon.
SUMMARY Punt Road was originally known as The Yarra Hill, a name abandoned because of the proliferation of wineries with the word 'Yarra' as part of their name. The situation of the vineyard and winery (opposite St Huberts) remains unchanged, centred on a large, new winery which produces the Punt Road wines, as well as undertaking substantial contract winemaking for others. The Punt Road wines are made from the best parcels of fruit grown on 100 hectares of vineyards owned by members of the Punt Road syndicate, and represent the tip of the iceberg.

▼▼▼▼▽ **Pinot Noir 2002** Aromatic spice, plum and strawberry; good length and fine tannin structure. **RATING** 92 **DRINK** 2007 $ 25
Chardonnay 2003 Fine, elegant stone fruit/melon/citrus; understated harmony. **RATING** 90 **DRINK** 2008 $ 26

▼▼▼▼ **Chardonnay 2002** Quite sophisticated barrel ferment and malo inputs; creamy, nutty flavours and texture. **RATING** 89 **DRINK** 2007 $ 26
Shiraz 2002 Distinctly fragrant and spicy overtones to plum/black cherry fruit; light to medium-bodied, but has considerable length. **RATING** 89 **DRINK** 2011 $ 25
Late Harvest Semillon (500 ml) 2002 Quite intense mandarin/cumquat fruit; good acidity; subtle oak. **RATING** 88 **DRINK** 2008 $ 26
Sauvignon Blanc 2003 Clean mineral and herb; delicate, but not short of varietal fruit. **RATING** 87 **DRINK** Now $ 20

▼▼▼▽ **Pinot Noir 2003** **RATING** 86 **DRINK** Now $ 25

🐌 Purple Patch Wines NR

101 Main Avenue, Merbein, Vic 3505 **REGION** Murray Darling
T (03) 5025 3558 **F** (03) 5025 2253 **OPEN** By appointment
WINEMAKER Brian Davey **EST.** 2001
PRODUCT RANGE Shiraz, Cabernet Merlot.
SUMMARY The neatly named Purple Patch Wines has been established by Brian Davey with a 2.5 hectare planting of cabernet sauvignon, merlot and shiraz. The wines are made on-site by Brian Davey with assistance from a contract winemaker. The small production is principally sold by mail order.

Pycnantha Hill Estate ★★★★

Benbournie Road, Clare, SA 5453 (postal) **REGION** Clare Valley
T (08) 8842 2137 **F** (08) 8842 2137 **OPEN** Not
WINEMAKER Jim Howarth **EST.** 1997 **CASES** 1000
PRODUCT RANGE ($15–22.50 R) Riesling, Chardonnay, Shiraz, Reserve Shiraz, Sangiovese, Cabernet
Merlot.
SUMMARY The Howarth family progressively established 2.4 hectares of vineyard from 1987, making
its first commercial vintage 10 years later in 1997. *Acacia pycnantha* is the botanic name for the
golden wattle which grows wild over the hills of the Howarth farm, and they say it was 'a natural
choice to name our vineyards Pycnantha Hill'. I am not too sure that marketing gurus would agree,
but there we go. Moreover, the quality of the wines should speak for itself.

ŸŸŸŸŸ **Riesling 2003** Slate, mineral, herb and citrus aromas; powers through to a long finish
with minerally acidity. **RATING** 90 **DRINK** 2013 $ 15
Shiraz 2002 An attractive mix of black fruits, spice and dark chocolate; soft, plush
tannins; good balance. **RATING** 90 **DRINK** 2012 $ 15

ŸŸŸŸ **Chardonnay 2002** **RATING** 86 **DRINK** 2007 $ 16
Sangiovese 2003 **RATING** 86 **DRINK** Now $ 15
Cabernet Merlot 2002 **RATING** 85 **DRINK** 2009 $ 15

🐚 Pyramid Hill Wines ★★★☆

194 Martindale Road, Denman, NSW 2328 **REGION** Upper Hunter Valley
T (02) 6547 2755 **F** (02) 6547 2735 **OPEN** By appointment
WINEMAKER James Chatto (Contract) **EST.** 2002 **CASES** 3000
PRODUCT RANGE ($16.95–21.95 R) Semillon, Verdelho, Unwooded Chardonnay, Chardonnay, Shiraz,
Merlot.
SUMMARY Pyramid Hill is a partnership between the Adler and Hilder families. Richard Hilder is a
veteran viticulturist who oversaw the establishment of many of the Rosemount vineyards. Nicholas
Adler and Caroline Sherwood made their mark in the international film industry before moving to
Pyramid Hill in 1997 with their four young children. Seventy-2 hectares of chardonnay, semillon,
verdelho, shiraz, merlot, cabernet sauvignon and ruby cabernet have been established with a
computer-controlled irrigation system backed up by a network of radio-linked weather and soil
moisture sensors which constantly relay data detailing the amount of available moisture at different
soil depths to a central computer, thus avoiding excess irrigation as well as preventing vine-stress.
Most of the grapes are sold to leading makers (guess who), but a small amount has been vinified
under the Pyramid Hill label, with cautious expansion in the years ahead. The wines are very
competently contract-made at Monarch Winemaking Services by James Chatto.

ŸŸŸŸŸ **Semillon 2003** Tangy citrus, lemon, herb aromas; fresh and bracing; good balance and
length. **RATING** 90 **DRINK** 2013 $ 16.95

ŸŸŸŸ **Semillon 2002** Aromatic herb and passionfruit; lively; good mouthfeel and balance.
RATING 87 **DRINK** 2009 $ 16.95
Merlot 2002 Clear varietal character, with good texture and length; fine grained tannins;
particularly good given the challenging vintage. **RATING** 87 **DRINK** 2009 $ 21.95

ŸŸŸŸ **Shiraz 2002** **RATING** 86 **DRINK** 2008 $ 21.95
Chardonnay 2002 **RATING** 85 **DRINK** Now $ 19.95

ŸŸŸ **Unwooded Chardonnay 2002** **RATING** 83 $ 16.95
Verdelho 2003 **RATING** 83 $ 16.95
Verdelho 2002 **RATING** 82 $ 16.95

🐚 Pyramids Road Wines NR

Pyramids Road, Wyberba, Qld 4382 **REGION** Granite Belt
T (07) 4684 5151 **F** (07) 4684 5151 **OPEN** Weekends and public holidays 10–4.30
WINEMAKER Warren Smith **EST.** 1999 **CASES** 300
PRODUCT RANGE ($15–30 CD) Semillon, Verdelho, Shiraz, Merlot, Mourvedre, Cabernet Sauvignon.

SUMMARY Warren Smith, and partner Sue, moved to the Granite Belt region in 1999. With encouragement and assistance from the team at Ballandean Estate, the first vines were planted in November 1999, the first vintage following in 2002. Current vineyard area is just 1.5 hectares; further plantings are planned but will not exceed 4 hectares. The 2002 Shiraz won the Trophy for Best Queensland Shiraz at the 2003 Australian Small Winemakers Show. All wines are made on-site and the production area can be viewed from the cellar door.

Pyrenees Ridge Vineyard ★★★★☆

532 Caralulup Road, Lamplough via Avoca, Vic 3467 **REGION** Pyrenees
T (03) 5465 3710 **F** (03) 5465 3320 **OPEN** Thurs–Mon and public holidays 10–5
WINEMAKER Graeme Jukes **EST.** 1998 **CASES** 1500
PRODUCT RANGE ($19–40 R) Shiraz, Reserve Shiraz, Cabernet Shiraz, Cabernet Sauvignon, Vintage Port.
SUMMARY Notwithstanding the quite extensive winemaking experience (and formal training) of Graeme Jukes, this started life as a small scale, winemaking in the raw, version of the French garagiste winemaking approach. Together with wife Sally-Ann, Graeme Jukes has planted 2 hectares each of cabernet sauvignon and shiraz; the grape intake is supplemented by purchases from other growers within the region. The success of the wines has been such that the winery size will be doubled, another 1.5 hectares of estate plantings will be completed, and contract purchases increased. Contract winemaking for others will also be expanded. Australian Prestige Wines distributes limited quantities of the wine in Melbourne, with a tiny percentage going overseas; the rest is sold by mail order and through the cellar door. Exports to the US.

ŸŸŸŸŸ **Reserve Shiraz 2002** Very complex, concentrated and powerful blackberry, plum, prune and spice; quite gamey; might excite the attention of the brett police. **RATING** 92 **DRINK** 2017 $ 40
Cabernet Sauvignon 2002 Rich, velvety black fruits; good oak and acid balance; cleansing acidity to add length to the finish. **RATING** 90 **DRINK** 2017 $ 25

Queen Adelaide ★★☆

Sturt Highway, Waikerie, SA 5330 **REGION** Barossa Valley
T (08) 8541 2588 **F** (08) 8541 3877 **OPEN** Not
WINEMAKER Various **EST.** 1858
PRODUCT RANGE ($6.50–7.45 R) Rhine Riesling, Chenin Blanc, Semillon Chardonnay, Chardonnay, Spatlese Lexia, Sauvignon Blanc, Regency Red, Shiraz, Grenache Pinot Noir, Cabernet Sauvignon.
SUMMARY The famous brand established by Woodley Wines and some years ago subsumed into the Seppelt and now Southcorp Group. It is a pure brand, without any particular home either in terms of winemaking or fruit sources, but is hugely successful; Queen Adelaide Chardonnay is and has for some time been the largest-selling bottled white wine in Australia. The move away from agglomerate to Stelvin closures has ended the glue-taint problems of prior years. The 2002 releases had synethetic corks, inappropriate for anything other than immediate consumption.

ŸŸŸŸ **Cabernet Sauvignon 2002** **RATING** 84 **DRINK** Now $ 7.45

ŸŸŸ **Riesling 2002** **RATING** 83 $ 7.45
Chardonnay 2003 **RATING** 83 $ 7.45
Classic Dry White 2003 **RATING** 81 $ 6.50

ŸŸŸ **Chardonnay 2002** **RATING** 79 $ 7.45
Shiraz 2002 **RATING** 79 $ 7.45
Semillon Chardonnay 2002 **RATING** 74 $ 7.45

Racecourse Lane Wines ★★★

PO Box 215, Balgowlah, NSW 2093 **REGION** Lower Hunter Valley
T 0418 242 490 **F** (02) 9949 7185 **OPEN** Not
WINEMAKER David Fatches **EST.** 1998 **CASES** 600
PRODUCT RANGE ($19 ML) Semillon, Verdelho, Shiraz.
SUMMARY Mike and Helen McGorman purchased the 15-hectare property now known as Racecourse Lane Wines in 1998. They have established 1.6 hectares of shiraz and 0.8 hectare each of semillon,

verdelho and sangiovese. Consultancy viticultural advice from Brian Hubbard, and winemaking by David Fatches, a long-term Hunter Valley winemaker (who also makes wine in France each year) has paid dividends. The wines are sold only through mail order and to a handful of top restaurants, including the Rockpool in Sydney.

ΥΥΥ   **Semillon 2003** RATING 86 DRINK 2011 $ 19
         Verdelho 2003 RATING 84 DRINK Now $ 19

Raleigh Winery   NR

Queen Street, Raleigh, NSW 2454 **REGION** Northern Rivers Zone
T (02) 6655 4388 **F** (02) 6655 4265 **OPEN** 7 days 10–5
WINEMAKER Lavinia Dingle **EST.** 1982 **CASES** 500
PRODUCT RANGE ($15 CD) Fox Gully Dry White (Semillon Chardonnay), Late Harvest, Rouge (Rose), Riverbank Red (Shiraz Cabernet), port.
SUMMARY Raleigh Winery lays claim to being Australia's most easterly vineyard. The vineyard was initiated in 1982 and was purchased by Lavinia and Neil Dingle in 1989, with the wine produced in part from 1 hectare of vines planted to no less than six varieties. The wines have won bronze medals at the Griffith Wine Show.

Ralph Fowler Wines

Limestone Coast Road, Mount Benson, SA 5275 **REGION** Mount Benson
T (08) 8768 5000 **F** (08) 8768 5008 **OPEN** 7 days 10–5
WINEMAKER Ralph Fowler **EST.** 1999 **CASES** 6000
PRODUCT RANGE ($15–30 CD) Sauvignon Blanc, Viognier, Botrytis Semillon, Shiraz Viognier, Cabernet Sauvignon; second label Frog Island Chardonnay, Sparkling Red, Pinot Noir, Shiraz, Cabernet Sauvignon.
SUMMARY Established in February 1999 by the Fowler family, headed by well-known winemaker Ralph Fowler, with wife Deborah and children Sarah (currently studying Wine Science) and James are all involved in the 40-hectare vineyard property at Mount Benson. Ralph Fowler began his winemaking career at Tyrrell's moving to the position of chief winemaker before moving to Hungerford Hill, and then the Hamilton/Leconfield group. He thus brings great experience to the venture, and has interestingly planted two varieties to provide the flagship wines: shiraz and viognier. Exports to the US, Germany, Austria, Malaysia, China and Singapore.

ΥΥΥΥ   **Shiraz Viognier 2002** Complex licorice, spice and blackberry fruit; smooth, velvety texture. RATING 91 DRINK 2012 $ 25

ΥΥΥΥ   **Limestone Coast Cabernet Sauvignon 2001** Blackcurrant, olive and cedar; fine tannins, good oak. RATING 89 DRINK 2011 $ 25

ΥΥΥΥ   **Mount Benson Sauvignon Blanc 2003** RATING 85 DRINK Now $ 18
         Mount Benson Viognier 2003 RATING 85 DRINK Now $ 30
         Limestone Coast Shiraz 2000 RATING 85 DRINK 2007 $ 30

Ramsay's Vin Rose

30 St Helier Road, The Gurdies, Vic 3984 **REGION** Gippsland
T (03) 5997 6531 **F** (03) 5997 6158 **OPEN** Wed–Mon 12–5
WINEMAKER Dianne Ramsay, Roger Cutler **EST.** 1995 **CASES** 400
PRODUCT RANGE ($8–25 CD) Riesling, Chardonnay, Rose (dry), Satin Rose (sweet), Merlot, Cabernet Sauvignon.
SUMMARY The slightly curious name (which looks decidedly strange in conjunction with Riesling and Cabernet Sauvignon) stems from the original intention of Alan and Dianne Ramsay to grow roses on a commercial scale on their property. Frank Cutler at Western Port Winery persuaded them to plant wine grapes instead, establishing the first 2 hectares of vines in 1995. They opened their micro-winery in 1999, and have four two-bedroom self-contained units set around their 800-bush rose garden. The pinot noir and chardonnay are sold to Diamond Valley, so for the time being the range of wines released is limited to Riesling, a Cabernet Franc based Rose and Cabernet Sauvignon, with a Merlot maturing in barrel. Ultimately, the Ramsay's hope to use all of the estate grapes for their wines.

ŸŸŸŸŸ **Cabernet Sauvignon 2001** Excellent varietal character in a medium-bodied mode; cassis/blackcurrant; good balance, structure and finish; deserves its show success. **RATING** 92 **DRINK** 2011 $ 25

ŸŸŸ **Chardonnay 2003 RATING** 83 $ 20

Random Valley Organic Wines   NR

PO Box 11, Karridale, WA 6288 **REGION** Margaret River
T (08) 9758 6707 **F** (08) 9758 6707 **OPEN** Not
WINEMAKER Saxon Mountford **EST.** 1995 **CASES** 3000
PRODUCT RANGE ($18.50–21 R) Sauvignon Blanc, Semillon Sauvignon Blanc, Shiraz.
SUMMARY The Little family has established 7 hectares of sauvignon blanc, semillon, shiraz and cabernet sauvignon, with a no-holds-barred organic grapegrowing program. No chemical-based fertilizers, pesticides or herbicides are used in the vineyard, building humus and biological activity in the soil. Given that the 7 hectares under vine produce 50 tonnes per year, it is evident that the approach has worked well. The wines are sold through mail order and the website <www.randomvalley.com>.

Raven Wines   NR

PO Box 482, Stanthorpe, Qld 4380 **REGION** Granite Belt
T (07) 4681 0717 **F** (07) 4681 0717 **OPEN** Not
WINEMAKER Mark Ravenscroft **EST.** 2002
PRODUCT RANGE A limited range of varietally denominated table wines.
SUMMARY Mark Ravenscroft is the winemaker at Robert Channon Wines, and makes a small amount of wine under his own label for sale by mail order.

Raydon Estate   ★★★★

Lake Plains Road, Langhorne Creek, SA 5255 **REGION** Langhorne Creek
T (08) 8537 3158 **F** (08) 8537 3158 **OPEN** 7 days 11–5, at Bremer Restaurant, Langhorne Creek.
WINEMAKER Wayne Dutschke (Contract) **EST.** 1999 **CASES** 1000
PRODUCT RANGE ($19 ML) Tails South Shiraz, Tails South Cabernet Sauvignon.
SUMMARY The establishment date of any winery business can have a wide number of meanings. In this instance it is the date of the first vintage, but Colleen and Joe Borrett planted 8 hectares each of shiraz and cabernet sauvignon many years ago, selling the majority of the grapes to Bleasdale and Southcorp. A small parcel of shiraz not under contract gave them the opportunity to move into the winemaking business, now extended with a little cabernet sauvignon. Exports to Malaysia and the US.

ŸŸŸŸŸ **Tails South Cabernet Sauvignon 2001** Sweet blackcurrant, cassis and touches of chocolate; medium-bodied, well balanced; fine tannins; carries alcohol. **RATING** 90 **DRINK** 2011 $ 19

ŸŸŸŸ **Tails South Shiraz 2000** Medium-bodied, with spicy red fruits and good length; similar toast and vanilla; finer tannins. **RATING** 89 **DRINK** 2009 $ 19
Tails South Shiraz 2001 Clean, fragrant spice and red fruit aromas and flavours; toast and vanilla, then savoury, slightly grippy tannins. **RATING** 88 **DRINK** 2010 $ 19

ŸŸŸŸ **Tails South Cabernet Sauvignon 2000 RATING** 86 **DRINK** 2009 $ 19

Ray-Monde   ★★★☆

250 Dalrymple Road, Sunbury, Vic 3429 **REGION** Sunbury
T (03) 5428 2657 **F** (03) 5428 3390 **OPEN** Sundays or by appointment
WINEMAKER John Lakey **EST.** 1988 **CASES** 700
PRODUCT RANGE ($25–30 CD) Rubina (Rose), Pinot Noir.
SUMMARY The Lakey family has established 5 hectares of pinot noir on their 230-hectare grazing property at an altitude of 400 metres. Initially the grapes were sold to Domaine Chandon, but in 1994 son John Lakey (who had gained experience at Tarrawarra, Rochford, Virgin Hills, Coonawarra plus a vintage in Burgundy) commenced making the wine — and very competently.

Reads

NR

Evans Lane, Oxley, Vic 3678 **REGION** King Valley
T (03) 5727 3386 **F** (03) 5727 3386 **OPEN** Mon–Sat 9–5, Sun 10–6
WINEMAKER Kenneth Read **EST.** 1972 **CASES** 1900
PRODUCT RANGE ($7.50–13 CD) Riesling, Chardonnay, Sauvignon Blanc, Crouchen, Cabernet Shiraz,
Cabernet Sauvignon, port.
SUMMARY Limited tastings have not impressed, but there may be a jewel lurking somewhere, such as
the medal-winning though long-gone 1990 Sauvignon Blanc. No tastings for some time.

Redbank Winery

★★★★

1 Sally's Lane, Redbank, Vic 3467 **REGION** Pyrenees
T (03) 5467 7255 **F** (03) 5467 7248 **OPEN** Mon–Sat 9–5, Sun 10–5
WINEMAKER Neill Robb **EST.** 1973 **CASES** 58 000
PRODUCT RANGE ($10.90–59 CD) The range centres on a series of evocatively named red wines, with
Sally's Paddock the flagship; then Rising Chardonnay, Sunday Morning Pinot Gris, Frenchman's
Pinot Noir, Fighting Flat Shiraz and Percydale Cabernet Merlot. Long Paddock and Billa Bridge are
cheaper, larger-volume second labels.
SUMMARY Neill Robb makes very concentrated wines, full of character; the levels of volatile acidity
can sometimes be intrusive but are probably of more concern to technical tasters than to the general
public. Sally's Paddock is the star, a single vineyard block with an esoteric mix of Cabernet, Shiraz
and Malbec and which over the years has produced many great wines.

ŸŸŸŸŸ **Sally's Paddock 2001** Clean, with some lifted aromatics; a mix of minty cassis, blackberry
and chocolate fruit; fine tannins, good balance. **RATING** 90 **DRINK** 2016 $ 59

ŸŸŸŸ **Sunday Morning Pinot Gris 2003** **RATING** 86 **DRINK** Now $ 21

ŸŸŸ **The Long Paddock Sauvignon Blanc 2003** **RATING** 82 $ 12

Red Clay Estate

★★☆

269 Henry Lawson Drive, Mudgee, NSW 2850 **REGION** Mudgee
T (02) 6372 4569 **F** (02) 6372 4596 **OPEN** Jan–Sept 7 days 10–5, Oct–Dec Mon–Fri 10–5,
or by appointment
WINEMAKER Ken Heslop **EST.** 1997
PRODUCT RANGE Cabernet Merlot.
SUMMARY Ken Heslop and Annette Bailey are among the recent arrivals in Mudgee, with a 2.5-
hectare vineyard planted to a diverse range of varieties. The wines are exclusively sold through the
cellar door and by mail order.

ŸŸŸŸ **Cabernet Sauvignon 2002** **RATING** 84 **DRINK** 2010

ŸŸŸ **Merlot 2002** **RATING** 81

Red Earth Estate Vineyard

★★★

18L Camp Road, Dubbo, NSW 2830 **REGION** Western Plains Zone
T (02) 6885 6676 **F** (02) 6882 8297 **OPEN** 7 days 10–4, or by appointment
WINEMAKER Ken Borchardt **EST.** 2000 **CASES** 5000
PRODUCT RANGE ($10–16.50 CD) Riesling, Verdelho, Unwooded Chardonnay, Cuvee, Shiraz,
Unwooded Cabernet Sauvignon, Cabernet Sauvignon.
SUMMARY Ken and Christine Borchardt look set to be the focal point of wine growing and making in
the future Macquarie Valley region of the Western Plains Zone. They have planted 1.3 hectares each
of riesling, verdelho, frontignac, grenache, shiraz and cabernet sauvignon at the winery, with a
further planting each of shiraz, cabernet franc and cabernet sauvignon on another site. The winery
has a maximum capacity of 14 000 cases, and the Borchardts are offering contract winemaking
facilities in addition to making and marketing their own brand.

ŸŸŸŸ **Merlot 2003** **RATING** 85 **DRINK** Now $ 10
Chardonnay 2003 **RATING** 84 **DRINK** Now $ 10

Red Edge ★★★★

Golden Gully Road, Heathcote, Vic 3523 **REGION** Heathcote
T (03) 9337 5695 **F** (03) 9337 7550 **OPEN** By appointment
WINEMAKER Peter Dredge, Judy Dredge **EST.** 1971 **CASES** 1000
PRODUCT RANGE ($25–40 ML) Shiraz, Jackson's Vineyard Shiraz, Cabernet Sauvignon.
SUMMARY Red Edge is a relatively new name on the scene, but the vineyard dates back to 1971, at the renaissance of the Victorian wine industry. In the early 1980s it produced the wonderful wines of Flynn & Williams and has now been rehabilitated by Peter and Judy Dredge, producing two quite lovely wines in their inaugural vintage and have continued that form in succeeding vintages. They now have a little over 15 hectares under vine, and Red Edge has become a full-time occupation for Peter Dredge. Exports to the US and the UK.

ŸŸŸŸŸ **Shiraz 2002** Youthful purple; assertive oak on the bouquet, but strong blackberry, licorice, spice and plum fruit sustains the long, well-balanced palate. **RATING** 90 **DRINK** 2017 $40

ŸŸŸŸ **Cabernet Sauvignon 2002** Ultra-ripe, juicy, jammy aromas; very juicy sweet fruit offset by tannins. 14.8 degrees alcohol; a little over the top. **RATING** 89 **DRINK** 2017 $40
Jackson's Vineyard Shiraz 2002 Highly fragrant and aromatic raspberry and cherry aromas; fresh, vibrant juicy fruit and low tannins. Eighty-five per cent young vine shiraz and mourvedre and a touch of riesling. **RATING** 88 **DRINK** 2009 $25

❧ Redesdale Estate Wines ★★★★★

North Redesdale Road, Redesdale, Vic 3444 **REGION** Heathcote
T (03) 5425 3236 **F** (03) 5425 3122 **OPEN** Nov–April weekends 11–4, or by appointment
WINEMAKER Tobias Ansted (Contract) **EST.** 1982 **CASES** 1000
PRODUCT RANGE ($25–35 CD) Shiraz, Cabernets.
SUMMARY Planting of the Redesdale Estate vines began in 1982 on the northeast slopes of a 25-hectare grazing property, fronting on one side to the Campaspe River. The rocky quartz and granite soil meant the vines had to struggle for existence, and when Peter Williams and wife Suzanne Arnall-Williams purchased the property in 1988 the vineyard was in a state of disrepair. They have not only rejuvenated the vineyard, but also planted an olive grove, and more recently still erected a self-contained two-storey cottage surrounded by a garden which is part of the Victorian Open Garden Scheme (and cross-linked to a villa in Tuscany). It was not until 1999 that the Williams' decided to retain part of the crop for their own wine, culminating in 2002 with the first full make from the vineyard under the Redesdale Estate label. The purchase of new French oak and the retention of Tobias Ansted of Balgownie can only add to the already impressive quality of the wines.

ŸŸŸŸŸ **Shiraz 2002** Intense raspberry and blackberry fruit with fine tannins throughout; excellent mouthfeel, length and aftertaste. **RATING** 94 **DRINK** 2017 $32

ŸŸŸŸŸ **Cabernets 2002** Luscious cassis/blackcurrant fruit carries its 14.5 degrees alcohol without any fuss at all; long, supple finish. **RATING** 93 **DRINK** 2017 $32
Shiraz 2001 Strong colour; excellent regional style; supple, round, smooth and sweet black fruits (cherry, berry); savoury tannins to close. **RATING** 90 **DRINK** 2011 $32
Cabernets 2001 A good wine; simply a notch down from the '02. **RATING** 90 **DRINK** 2015 $32

Redgate ★★★☆

Boodjidup Road, Margaret River, WA 6285 **REGION** Margaret River
T (08) 9757 6488 **F** (08) 9757 6308 **OPEN** 7 days 10–5
WINEMAKER Andrew Forsell **EST.** 1977 **CASES** 14 000
PRODUCT RANGE ($15.50–36 CD) OFS Semillon, Sauvignon Blanc Reserve, Sauvignon Blanc Semillon, Chenin, Chardonnay, Pinot Noir, Shiraz, Cabernet Franc, Cabernet Sauvignon Franc Merlot, Bin 588 (Cabernet blend), Cabernet Sauvignon, WWW Ullinger Reserve, Anastasia's Delight (Fortified Semillon), White Port.
SUMMARY Twenty hectares of vineyard provide the base for a substantial winery, which probably has a lower profile than it deserves. The wines have limited distribution in the eastern States, and export

markets in Singapore, Hong Kong, Canada, Japan, Denmark, Germany, Switzerland, the US and the UK have been established.

ΤΤΤΤΥ **OFS Semillon 2003** Herb and wild flower aromas; smooth palate, crisp finish. **RATING** 90 **DRINK** 2010 $ 19

ΤΤΤΤ **Cabernet Sauvignon Cabernet Franc Merlot 2001** Fragrant herb, spice and olive aromas; has length and fine, savoury tannins; slightly austere style; no bad thing. **RATING** 89 **DRINK** 2009 $ 30
Cabernet Franc 2001 Fragrant, light to medium-bodied; red berries with a twist of savoury spice. Margaret River succeeds with the variety where others fail. **RATING** 88 **DRINK** 2011 $ 36
Sauvignon Blanc Semillon 2003 Crisp, quite concentrated and focused; mineral, lemon and red apple; good acidity. **RATING** 87 **DRINK** 2008 $ 15.50

ΤΤΤΥ **Shiraz 2001** **RATING** 84 **DRINK** 2009 $ 22

ΤΤΥ **Sauvignon Blanc Reserve 2003** **RATING** 78 $ 19

Red Hill Estate ★★★★★

53 Redhill-Shoreham Road, Red Hill South, Vic 3937 **REGION** Mornington Peninsula
T (03) 5989 2838 **F** (03) 5989 2855 **OPEN** 7 days 11–5
WINEMAKER Michael Kyberd **EST.** 1989 **CASES** 30 000
PRODUCT RANGE ($14–30 CD) Particular emphasis on Methode Champenoise, but also producing Pinot Grigio, Sauvignon Blanc, Chardonnay, Botrytis, Pinot Noir, Shiraz, Cabernet Merlot, Liqueur Muscat; Bimaris range of Sauvignon Blanc, Chardonnay, Rose, Pinot Noir; Classic Release Chardonnay, Pinot Noir.
SUMMARY Red Hill has three vineyard sites: Range Road of a little over 31 hectares, Red Hill Estate (the home vineyard) of 10 hectares, and The Briars of 2 hectares. Taken together, the vineyards make Red Hill Estate one of the largest producers of Mornington Peninsula wines. The business was established by Sir Peter Derham and family, but majority ownership now rests with a group of investors headed by Tony Palazzo, who has had a lifelong involvement in all aspects of the industry; the Derhams continue to hold a stake in the business. The tasting room and ever-busy restaurant have a superb view across the vineyard to Westernport Bay and Phillip Island. Production continues to surge, and the winery goes from strength to strength. Exports to the US, Canada, the UK and Sweden.

ΤΤΤΤΤ **Classic Release Chardonnay 2001** Stone fruit, melon and citrus; great length and intensity; lingering aftertaste; subtle oak. **RATING** 94 **DRINK** 2008 $ 30

ΤΤΤΤΥ **Pinot Noir 2002** Complex, intense yet elegant; long, lingering plum, spice and forest flavours; good aftertaste. **RATING** 92 **DRINK** 2009 $ 20
Shiraz 2002 Cool-grown but ripe spice, licorice, blackberry and redcurrant mix; good length; fine-grained tannins. **RATING** 90 **DRINK** 2012 $ 25
Blanc de Blanc 2001 Crisp, limey, citrussy; bright, brisk and fresh. **RATING** 90 **DRINK** 2007 $ 26

ΤΤΤΤ **Pinot Grigio 2003** Blush pink; floral strawberry and apple aromas; intense, well balanced and lingering acidity. **RATING** 89 **DRINK** Now $ 22
Bimaris Cabernet Shiraz Merlot 2002 Sweet cassis/raspberry aromas and flavours before a gently savoury/leafy bite to close. **RATING** 88 **DRINK** 2012 $ 14
Cabernet Merlot 2001 Savoury, earthy, leafy black fruits; some oak sweetening. **RATING** 87 **DRINK** 2009 $ 25

Redman ★★★

Riddoch Highway, Coonawarra, SA 5253 **REGION** Coonawarra
T (08) 8736 3331 **F** (08) 8736 3013 **OPEN** Mon–Fri 9–5, weekends 10–4
WINEMAKER Bruce Redman, Malcolm Redman **EST.** 1966 **CASES** 11 000
PRODUCT RANGE ($16.99–27.99 R) Shiraz, Cabernet Sauvignon Merlot, Cabernet Sauvignon.
SUMMARY After a prolonged period of mediocrity, the Redman wines are showing sporadic signs of improvement, partly through the introduction of modest amounts of new oak, even if principally

American. It would be nice to say the wines now reflect the full potential of the vineyard, but there is still some way to go.

ΥΥΥΥ   **Cabernet Sauvignon 2001** Medium-bodied, with plenty of cassis/blackcurrant fruit; more structure than usual; ample tannins and oak. **RATING** 88 **DRINK** 2011 $ 27.95

ΥΥΥϘ   **Shiraz 1999 RATING** 84 **DRINK** Now $ 16.99

Red Mud   NR

PO Box 237, Paringa, SA 5340 **REGION** Riverland
T (08) 8595 8042 **F** (08) 8595 8042 **OPEN** Not
WINEMAKER Mike Farmilo **EST.** 2002
PRODUCT RANGE Shiraz.
SUMMARY The Red Mud wines come from large plantings of shiraz, chardonnay, petit verdot and cabernet sauvignon near Nelwood, 20 miles east of Renmark near the South Australian border. The grapegrowers who are shareholders in the company have been growing grapes for up to three generations in the Riverland.

Red Rock Winery   NR

Red Rock Reserve Road, Alvie, Vic 3249 **REGION** Western Victoria Zone
T (03) 5234 8382 **F** (03) 5234 8382 **OPEN** 7 days 10–5
WINEMAKER Rohan Little **EST.** 1981 **CASES** 5000
PRODUCT RANGE ($15–25 R) Semillon Sauvignon, Chardonnay, Pinot Noir, Shiraz, Cabernet Sauvignon Merlot.
SUMMARY The former Barongvale Estate, which has progressively established 10 hectares of sauvignon blanc, semillon, pinot noir, and shiraz; a part-time occupation for Rohan Little, with wines sold under both the Red Rock and Otway Vineyards labels. It takes its new name from the now dormant Red Rock Volcano which created the lakes and craters of the Western Districts when it last erupted 8000 years ago. The winery café opened in early 2002.

Red Tail Wines   NR

15 Pinnacle Place, Marlee, NSW 2429 **REGION** Northern Rivers Zone
T (02) 6550 5084 **F** (02) 6550 5084 **OPEN** By appointment
WINEMAKER Serenella Estate (Contract) **EST.** 1992 **CASES** 300
PRODUCT RANGE ($11–15.50 ML) Marlee White, Semillon, Colombard, Semillon Colombard, Merlot.
SUMMARY Warren and Sue Stiff have planted 0.5 hectare each of colombard, semillon and verdelho, and a 0.25-hectare of merlot, at their property situated in the Northern Rivers Zone, northwest of Taree. The vineyard takes its name from the red-tailed black cockatoo which inhabits the area; the very reasonably-priced wines are available by phone, fax or mail order.

Reedy Creek Vineyard   NR

Reedy Creek, via Tenterfield, NSW 2372 **REGION** Northern Slopes Zone
T (02) 6737 5221 **F** (02) 6737 5200 **OPEN** 7 days 9–5
WINEMAKER Contract **EST.** 1971 **CASES** 2800
PRODUCT RANGE ($13–17 CD) Bianco Alpino, Chardonnay, Unwooded Chardonnay, Rosso Alpino, Shiraz Mourvedre, Old Vine Shiraz, Merlot, Durif, Liqueur Muscat, Red Deer Port.
SUMMARY Like so many Italian settlers in the Australian countryside, the De Stefani family has been growing grapes and making wine for its own consumption for over 30 years at its Reedy Creek property near Tenterfield, in the far north of New South Wales. What is more, like their compatriots in the King Valley, the family's principal activity until 1993 was growing tobacco, but the continued rationalisation of the tobacco industry prompted the De Stefanis to turn a hobby into a commercial exercise. The vineyard has now been expanded to 6.1 hectares, and the first commercial vintage of Shiraz was made in 1995, with Chardonnay following in 1998. The wines are sold cellar door from the maturation cellar opened in 1997.

Rees Miller Estate ★★★☆

5355 Goulbourn Highway, Yea, Vic 3717 **REGION** Upper Goulburn
T (03) 5797 2101 **F** (03) 5797 3276 **OPEN** Weekends and public holidays 10–5
WINEMAKER David Miller **EST.** 1996 **CASES** 3000
PRODUCT RANGE ($22–45 CD) Meadows Hill Chardonnay, Pinot Noir, Wilhemina Pinot Noir, Shiraz, Eildon Shiraz, Thousand Hills Reserve Shiraz, Manytrees Shiraz Viognier, Sier's Field Reserve (cabernet blend)
SUMMARY Partners Sylke Rees and David Miller purchased the 64-hectare property in 1998, with 1 hectare of pinot noir (planted in 1996). Since extending the plantings with another block of pinot noir, 3 hectares of cabernet sauvignon, 1 hectare each of merlot and shiraz, and 0.5 hectare of cabernet franc, all of which came into production in 2002. They use integrated pest management (no insecticides) and deliberately irrigate sparingly, the upshot being yields of 2.5 tonnes per hectare (a ton to the acre in the old money). All of the wines are made on-site, and the production will be limited to a Pinot Noir, a Shiraz and an Australian Bordeaux-style red, some named after the original owners of the property, Daniel Joseph and Wilhemina Therese Sier.

TTTT **Wilhemina Pinot Noir 2002** Solid, ripe, black cherry and plum fruit; needs to build complexity, but should do so. **RATING** 87 **DRINK** 2011 $30
One Thousand Hills Shiraz 2002 High-toned herb, spice, blackberry and game aromas; the powerful palate is caught by grippy tannins on the finish; these will soften with time, but so may the fruit. **RATING** 87 **DRINK** 2014 $30

TTTY **Sier's Field Reserve 2002** **RATING** 85 **DRINK** 2008 $30

Reg Drayton Wines ★★★☆

Cnr Pokolbin Mountain & McDonalds Roads, Pokolbin, NSW 2321 **REGION** Lower Hunter Valley
T (02) 4998 7523 **F** (02) 4998 7523 **OPEN** 7 days 10–5
WINEMAKER Tish Cecchini, Robyn Drayton **EST.** 1989 **CASES** 5500
PRODUCT RANGE ($18–30 CD) Lambkin Semillon, Lambkin Verdelho, Pokolbin Hills Chardonnay, Pokolbin Hills Chardonnay Semillon, Pamela Robyn Sparkling Chardonnay, Botrytis Semillon, Rose, Three Sons Shiraz, Pokolbin Hills Shiraz, Pokolbin Hills Cabernet Shiraz, Hunter Classic Verdelho Liqueur, Tawny Port.
SUMMARY Reg and Pam Drayton were among the victims of the Seaview/Lord Howe Island air crash in October 1984, having established Reg Drayton Wines after selling their interest in the long-established Drayton Family Winery. Their daughter Robyn (a fifth-generation Drayton and billed as the Hunter's first female vigneron) and husband Craig continue the business, which draws chiefly upon the Pokolbin Hills Estate but also takes fruit from the historic Lambkin Estate vineyard.

Reilly's Wines ★★★★

Cnr Hill and Burra Streets, Mintaro, SA 5415 **REGION** Clare Valley
T (08) 8843 9013 **F** (08) 8843 9013 **OPEN** 7 days 10–5, restaurant open for dinner Mon–Sat
WINEMAKER Justin Ardill **EST.** 1994 **CASES** 10 000
PRODUCT RANGE ($17–45 CD) Watervale Riesling, Late Picked Watervale Riesling, Block 1919 Grenache Shiraz, Sparkling Dry Land Shiraz, Dry Land Shiraz, Dry Land Cabernet Sauvignon, Bin 8 Cabernet Sauvignon, flagship wine is Stolen Block Shiraz.
SUMMARY Cardiologist Justin and Julie Ardill are relative newcomers in the Clare Valley, with half a dozen or so vintages under their belt. An unusual sideline of Reilly's Cottage is the production of Extra Virgin Olive Oil; unusual in that it is made from wild olives found in the Mintaro district of the Clare Valley. The restaurant is open 7 days for lunch and Monday, Wednesday, Friday and Saturday for dinner. Exports to the US, Ireland, Malaysia and Singapore.

TTTTY **Watervale Riesling 2003** Voluminous, rich citrus and tropical fruit aromas; voluptuous mouthfeel replicating the bouquet. For immediate consumption. **RATING** 91 **DRINK** 2007 $19
Dry Land Cabernet Sauvignon 2001 Savoury, earthy, blackberry fruit, and a dusting of spice; ample length. **RATING** 90 **DRINK** 2011 $30

Late Picked Watervale Riesling 2002 Excellent style; achieves elegance and intensity, with overtones of the Rheingau; picked late but the fermentation stopped. Serve fully chilled. **RATING** 90 **DRINK** 2007 $ 17

▼▼▼▼ **Stolen Block Shiraz 2001** Big, blockbuster style; deep, multi-layered blackberry/anise fruit. **RATING** 89 **DRINK** 2011 $ 45

Old Bush Vine Grenache Shiraz 2002 Rich, glossy black fruits, spice and cake; good balance and mouthfeel. **RATING** 88 **DRINK** 2009 $ 22

▼▼▼▼ **Dry Land Shiraz 2001 RATING** 86 **DRINK** 2010 $ 29

Dry Land Sparkling Shiraz 2002 RATING 85 **DRINK** Now $ 29

🦡 Remo & Son's Vineyard

NR

58 Blaxland Ridge Road, Kurrajong, NSW 2758 **REGION** South Coast Zone
T (02) 4576 1539 **F** (02) 4576 0072 **OPEN** Weekends by appointment
WINEMAKER Remo Crisante **EST.** 1998
PRODUCT RANGE A range of varietally denominated table wines reflecting the plantings.
SUMMARY Remo and Mark Crisante have pushed the viticultural envelope that little bit further by planting 2 hectares of chardonnay, verdelho, merlot, cabernet sauvignon and traminer at Kurrajong, for long a holiday destination for Sydneysiders. The fact that Kurrajong is in the South Coast Zone may come as a surprise, since it is 100 kilometres also northwest of Sydney, but the zone boundaries have always been a matter of convenience, and had to be so drawn as to cover all of the State. A restaurant and accommodation are available on-site, pointing to the conference and function market.

Renewan Murray Gold Wines

★★★

Murray Valley Highway, Piangil, Vic 3597 **REGION** Swan Hill
T (03) 5030 5525 **F** (03) 5030 5695 **OPEN** 7 days 9–5
WINEMAKER John Ellis **EST.** 1989 **CASES** 220
PRODUCT RANGE Riesling, Shiraz, Durif, Cabernet Sauvignon Merlot.
SUMMARY In 1990 former senior executive at Nylex Corporation in Melbourne, Jim Lewis, and artist wife Marg, retired to what is now Renewan Vineyard, set on the banks of the Murray River. It is a small business, based on 2.5 hectares of estate plantings, and all of the production is sold by cellar door and mail order, with limited distribution to local hotels, bottle shops and restaurants.

▼▼▼▼ **Shiraz 2002** Dense purple-red; honest, full-flavoured wine reflecting the outstanding vintage; no frills, just fruit. **RATING** 87 **DRINK** 2007 $ 18

Durif 2002 While powerful, less intense than some Murray River-grown durif, but with more light and shade to the black fruits. **RATING** 87 **DRINK** 2008 $ 22

▼▼▼▼ **Cabernet Sauvignon 2002 RATING** 84 **DRINK** Now $ 17

▼▼▼ **Riesling 2003 RATING** 82 $ 14

Reschke Wines

★★★★☆

Level 1, 43 The Parade, Norwood, SA 5067 (postal) **REGION** Coonawarra
T (08) 8363 3343 **F** (08) 8363 3378 **OPEN** Not
WINEMAKER Peter Douglas (Contract) **EST.** 1998 **CASES** 6000
PRODUCT RANGE ($25–115 ML) Taikurri (Cabernet blend), Vitulus Cabernet Sauvignon, Bos Cabernet Sauvignon, Empyrean Cabernet Sauvignon.
SUMMARY It's not often that the first release from a new winery is priced at $100 per bottle (since increased to $115), but that is precisely what Reschke Wines achieved with its 1998 Cabernet Sauvignon. The family has been a landholder in the Coonawarra region for almost 100 years, with a large landholding which is partly terra rossa, part woodland. 15.5 hectares of merlot, 105 hectares of cabernet sauvignon, 0.5 hectare of cabernet franc and 2.5 hectares of shiraz are in production, with a further 26 hectares planted prior to the end of 2001, mostly to shiraz, and with a little petit verdot. Exports to the US, Canada, Singapore and Malaysia.

 TTTTY **Empyrean Cabernet Sauvignon 1998** Earth, cedar and cigar box aromas; long and intense; savoury tannins to the finish; evolving well. **RATING** 93 **DRINK** 2013 $100
Bos Cabernet Sauvignon 2002 Fragrant cassis and blackcurrant; very well balanced and integrated oak; fine and supple tannins. **RATING** 91 **DRINK** 2012 $35

TTTT **Vitulus Cabernet Sauvignon 2002** Voluminous dark fruits; blackcurrant and chocolate; lots of tannins; age-worthy. **RATING** 88 **DRINK** 2015 $25
Vitulus Cabernet Sauvignon 2001 Attractive red and blackcurrant fruit aromas; light to medium-bodied; clean, supple and fresh; totally appealing. The yield said to be restricted to just under 1 tonne per hectare by careful pruning. **RATING** 87 **DRINK** 2009 $25

Rex Vineyard

NR

Beaufort, WA 6315 **REGION** Central Western Australia Zone
T (08) 9384 3210 **F** (08) 9384 3210 **OPEN** Not
WINEMAKER Julie White (Contract) **EST.** 1991 **CASES** 500
PRODUCT RANGE Unwooded Chardonnay, Elvira Methode Champenoise, Cabernet Sauvignon Shiraz Merlot.
SUMMARY Peter and Gillian Rex have established 2 hectares of chardonnay, cabernet sauvignon, merlot and shiraz. Approximately half of each year's production is sold as grapes, the remainder contract-made by the highly-competent Julie White in the Swan Valley.

Reynell

★★★★★

Reynell Road, Reynella, SA 5161 **REGION** McLaren Vale
T (08) 8392 2222 **F** (08) 8392 2202 **OPEN** 7 days 10–4, except public holidays
WINEMAKER Paul Lapsley **EST.** 1838 **CASES** 16 000
PRODUCT RANGE ($21.99–50 R) Basket Pressed Shiraz, Basket Pressed Merlot, Basket Pressed Cabernet Sauvignon.
SUMMARY Reynell is the name under which all wines from the historic Reynella winery (once called Chateau Reynella) are released. What is more, the range of wines was compressed and taken into the super-premium category with the introduction of the Basket Pressed range in 1997.

TTTTT **Basket Pressed Shiraz 2000** While concentrated and focused, has elegance; well-balanced red fruits and subtle oak; fine tannins. Six trophies. **RATING** 94 **DRINK** 2015 $50

Reynolds Vineyards

★★★★☆

'Quondong', Cargo Road, Cudal, NSW 2864 (postal) **REGION** Orange
T (02) 6364 2330 **F** (02) 6364 2388 **OPEN** Not
WINEMAKER Jon Reynolds, Nic Millichip, Tom Cleland, Robert Black **EST.** 1994 **CASES** 250 000
PRODUCT RANGE ($12–29 CD) Moon Shadow Chardonnay, Marble Man Merlot, The Jezebel Cabernet Sauvignon (from Orange) at the top tier; then comes the Orange range of Chardonnay, Shiraz, Merlot, Cabernet Merlot, Cabernet Sauvignon; and finally the Little Boomey range (from the Central Ranges) of Sauvignon Blanc, Limited Release Chardonnay, Shiraz, Merlot, Cabernet Merlot, Cabernet Sauvignon.
SUMMARY It is ironic that a company with a 20 000-tonne winery, 900 hectares of vineyards at Molong near Orange, and a highly skilled winemaking team lead by Jon Reynolds should be fighting for its financial life. A tax scheme gone wrong is the main reason, and somewhere along the way, one can only assume the company will be restructured and recapitalised. The irony is even greater when the quality of the wines coming through fully reflects the great potential Reynolds Vineyards has. Exports to the US, the UK and Europe.

TTTTT **Moon Shadow Chardonnay 2001** Spotlessly clean; a sophisticated, subtle and harmonious blend of nectarine, fruit and oak; perfectly balanced. **RATING** 94 **DRINK** 2010 $22.99

TTTTY **Reserve Chardonnay 2002** Elegant, crisp, understated Chablis style; nectarine/citrus fruit; long palate and finish. **RATING** 93 **DRINK** 2009 $16.99
Little Boomey Sauvignon Blanc 2003 Tightly structured and intense tropical and gooseberry fruit; clean as a whistle; great value. **RATING** 90 **DRINK** Now $11.99
Moon Shadow Shiraz 2001 Red and black fruits plus spice, leather and mocha; fine, medium-bodied style. **RATING** 90 **DRINK** 2014 $22.99

Ribarits Estate Wines

NR

Sturt Highway, Trentham Cliffs, NSW 2738 (postal) **REGION** Murray Darling
T 0409 330 997 **F** (03) 5024 0332 **OPEN** Not
WINEMAKER Contract **EST.** 1998 **CASES** 4000
PRODUCT RANGE ($6.40–6.80 ML) Chardonnay, Shiraz, Merlot, Cabernet Sauvignon.
SUMMARY Adrian Ribarits has developed over 82 hectares of chardonnay, merlot, shiraz and cabernet sauvignon, primarily as a contract grape grower for Simeon Wines. A small part of the grape production is vinified for Ribarits Estate and sold by mail order at yesterday's prices, with various bronze medals to their credit.

Richard Hamilton

 ★★★★☆

Main Road, Willunga, SA 5172 **REGION** McLaren Vale
T (08) 8556 2288 **F** (08) 8556 2868 **OPEN** 7 days 10–5
WINEMAKER Paul Gordon, Tim Bailey (Assistant) **EST.** 1972 **CASES** 20 000
PRODUCT RANGE ($10.95–49.95 R) Slate Quarry Riesling, Synergy Semillon Sauvignon Blanc, Almond Grove Chardonnay, Colton Ruins GSM, Gumprs' Block Shiraz, Lot 148 Merlot, Synergy Cabernet Merlot, Hut Block Cabernet Sauvignon; Hamilton Reserve wines are Richard Hamilton Signature Chardonnay, Marion Vineyard Grenache Shiraz, Burton's Vineyard Grenache Shiraz, Centurion 100 Year Old Vines Shiraz, Egremont Reserve Merlot.
SUMMARY Hamilton has outstanding estate vineyards, some of great age, all fully mature. The arrival (in 2002) of former Rouge Homme winemaker Paul Gordon has allowed the full potential of those vineyards to be expressed. Exports to Europe, the US, Canada and Asia.

ŸŸŸŸŸ **Centurion Shiraz 2001** An intense and very long mix of blackberry, raspberry, black cherry and spice; subtle oak; altogether impressive. From 109-year-old vines. **RATING** 94 **DRINK** 2016 $49.95

ŸŸŸŸŸ **Marion Vineyard Grenache Shiraz 2001** Very good colour; a classic, rich and supple mix of juicy berry, licorice, dark chocolate and soft, ripe fine tannins. An historic patch of vines now in suburban Adelaide. **RATING** 92 **DRINK** 2014 $29.95

ŸŸŸŸ **Almond Grove Chardonnay 2003** Elegant, soft nectarine fruit aromas and flavours; subliminal oak; good length. Screwcap. **RATING** 89 **DRINK** 2007 $14.95
Signature Chardonnay 2003 Ripe, peachy fruit with plenty of depth; again controlled oak, but I prefer the Almond Grove. Screwcap. **RATING** 88 **DRINK** 2007 $24.95
Hamilton Burton's Vineyard Old Bush Vine Grenache Shiraz 2001 Opens with a mix of spicy, juicy berry fruits; then persistent tannins and regional chocolate flavours, not entirely balanced. **RATING** 87 **DRINK** 2009 $29.95

ŸŸŸ **Hamilton Slate Quarry Riesling 2003 RATING** 83 $14.95

Richfield Estate

NR

Bonshaw Road, Tenterfield, NSW 2372 **REGION** Northern Slopes Zone
T (07) 3832 0228 **F** (07) 3832 0225 **OPEN** 7 days 10–4
WINEMAKER John Cassegrain **EST.** 1997 **CASES** 15 000
PRODUCT RANGE ($10.90–14.90 R) The Estate Range comprises Semillon, Verdelho Semillon, Chardonnay, Shiraz, Merlot and Cabernet Merlot; the second label Classic Range is Semillon Chardonnay and Cabernet Shiraz.
SUMMARY Richfield is owned by Corporation Franco Asiatique, headquartered in Singapore. Bernard Forey is the majority shareholder of the company, and now lives in Brisbane. Denis Parsons, of Bald Mountain Vineyards, is a director and shareholder of the company, and is in charge of management of its operations, as it is only 20 minutes drive south of Bald Mountain. It is located in a picturesque section of Tenterfield Creek, just to the west of the town of Tenterfield. A substantial vineyard has been established comprising shiraz (11.1 hectares), cabernet sauvignon (4.3 hectares), merlot (3.7 hectares), ruby cabernet (3.1 hectares), semillon (2.9 hectares), chardonnay (2.6 hectares) and verdelho (1.3 hectares). The first vintage was made in 2000, and it is expected the bulk of Richfield's sales will come from the export markets of South-East Asia.

Richmond Estate

NR

99 Gadds Lane, North Richmond, NSW 2754 **REGION** Sydney Basin
T (02) 4573 1048 **OPEN** Weekends 11–6
WINEMAKER Tony Radanovic **EST.** 1967 **CASES** 600
PRODUCT RANGE ($15–35 CD) Chardonnay, Shiraz, Malbec, Cabernet Sauvignon.
SUMMARY While this is only the second time Richmond Estate has been listed in the *Wine Companion*, it was also featured in a number of books I wrote between 1979 and 1984, as then-proprietor Barry Bracken (a Sydney orthopaedic surgeon) was making excellent Shiraz and Cabernet Sauvignon. However, late in 1984 he sold the property, and it went through several owners before being purchased by Monica and Tony Radanovic in 1987. The Radanovics have restored the vineyard which had been run down in the years prior to their purchase, and while only 3 hectares are under vine, the vineyard is used by the University of Western Sydney as its field laboratory for undergraduate and wine production courses.

Richmond Grove

 ★★★☆

Para Road, Tanunda, SA 5352 **REGION** Barossa Valley
T (08) 8563 7300 **F** (08) 8563 2804 **OPEN** 7 days 10.30–4.30
WINEMAKER Steve Clarkson **EST.** 1983 **CASES** 150 000
PRODUCT RANGE ($12.50–18.99 R) Watervale Riesling, Barossa Riesling, Hunter Valley Semillon, Marlborough Sauvignon Blanc, Verdelho, McLaren Vale Chardonnay, French Cask Chardonnay, Chardonnay Pinot, Barossa Shiraz, Coonawarra Shiraz, Cabernet Merlot, Coonawarra Cabernet Sauvignon.
SUMMARY Richmond Grove now has two homes, including one in the Barossa Valley. It is owned by Orlando Wyndham and draws its grapes from diverse sources. The Richmond Grove Barossa Valley and Watervale Rieslings made by the team directed by John Vickery represent excellent value for money (for Riesling) year in, year out. If these were the only wines produced by Richmond Grove, it would have five-star rating. Exports to the UK.

▼▼▼▽ **Watervale Riesling 2003** Intense mineral herb and spice aromas; opens with the expected richness on the palate; fades fractionally on the finish. **RATING** 90 **DRINK** 2008 $16

▼▼▼▼ **Silver Series Riesling 2002** Classic slate and blossom aromas; feather light and crisp palate; blend of Barossa and Eden Valleys. **RATING** 89 **DRINK** 2012 $13.99
Silver Series Shiraz 2001 Blackberry, plum and raspberry; medium-bodied, supple and smooth; gentle tannins. Padthaway/Coonawarra. **RATING** 88 **DRINK** 2010 $12.50
Coonawarra Cabernet Sauvignon 2001 Sweet cassis/blackcurrant fruit; plenty of body; slightly assertive tannins. **RATING** 87 **DRINK** 2011 $18.99

▼▼▼▽ **Barossa Shiraz 2001 RATING** 86 **DRINK** 2008 $18.99
Barossa Riesling 2003 RATING 85 **DRINK** 2008 $14
Silver Series Riesling 2003 RATING 85 **DRINK** 2010 $13.99
French Cask Chardonnay 2002 RATING 84 **DRINK** Now $13.99

▼▼▼ **Chardonnay Pinot Noir NV RATING** 83 $13.99

Richmond Park Vineyard

★★★★

Logie Road, Richmond, Tas 7025 (postal) **REGION** Southern Tasmania
T (03) 6265 2949 **F** (03) 6265 3166 **OPEN** Not
WINEMAKER Andrew Hood (Contract) **EST.** 1989 **CASES** 250
PRODUCT RANGE ($15–22 ML) Chardonnay, Pinot Noir.
SUMMARY A small vineyard owned by Tony Park, which gives the clue to the clever name. It is 20 minutes drive from Hobart, and a particular (and uncommon) attraction for mail list clients is the availability of 375 ml bottles.

Rickety Gate

NR

PO Box 202, Denmark, WA 6333 **REGION** Denmark
T F (08) 9840 9503 **OPEN** Not
WINEMAKER John Wade (Contract) **EST.** 2000 **CASES** 1500
PRODUCT RANGE ($18–22.50 ML) Riesling, Chardonnay, Merlot.
SUMMARY The 3-hectare vineyard of Rickety Gate is situated on north-facing slopes of the Bennet Ranges, in an area specifically identified by Dr John Gladstones as highly suited to cool climate viticulture. The property was purchased by Russell and Linda Hubbard at the end of 1999, and after vineyard preparation work directed by veteran consultant viticulturist Ted Holland, 1.8 hectares of merlot, 0.8 hectare of riesling and 0.5 hectare of chardonnay and pinot noir were planted by September 2000. John Wade has been retained to make the wines at the small on-site winery on the property. The first release was in July 2003, and all of the wines are sold solely through their website <www.ricketygate.com.au>.

Ridgeback Wines

New Chum Gully Estate, Howards Road, Panton Hill, Vic 3759 **REGION** Yarra Valley
T (03) 9719 7687 **F** (03) 9719 7667 **OPEN** By appointment
WINEMAKER MasterWineMakers (Contract) **EST.** 2000 **CASES** 1200
PRODUCT RANGE ($23–25 ML) Chardonnay, Pinot Noir, Merlot, the Jana Cabernet Merlot, Cabernet Sauvignon.
SUMMARY Ron and Lynne Collings purchased their Panton Hill property in March 1990, clearing the land and making it ready for the first vine planting in 1992, now totalling a little over 4 hectares on the hillside slopes beneath their house, Ron Collings having completed the degree in wine growing at Charles Sturt University in 1997, with the Dean's Award for Academic Excellence. Most of the grapes were sold to Coldstream Hills, but Ron Collings made small batches of wine himself each year, which ultimately led to the decision to establish the Ridgeback label, with contract winemaking, although Collings is never far from the scene at vintage. The name, incidentally, is intended to reflect in part the rolling hillside of Panton Hill, and to salute the Collings' Rhodesian Ridgeback dogs, Jana being the most recent arrival. Exports to the UK.

Chardonnay 2002 Well-made; intense, well-focused and tight fusion of grapefruit and nectarine with barrel ferment and other inputs. **RATING** 91 **DRINK** 2009 $ 25
Pinot Noir 2002 Attractive plum, black cherry and spice; medium-bodied; lingering finish with a nice savoury twist. **RATING** 90 **DRINK** 2007 $ 23

The Jana Cabernet Merlot 2002 RATING 86 **DRINK** 2008 $ 25

Ridgeline

NR

PO Box 695, Healesville, Vic 3777 **REGION** Yarra Valley
T 0421 422 154 **OPEN** Not
WINEMAKER Mark Haisma **EST.** 2001 **CASES** 150
PRODUCT RANGE Pinot Noir, Shiraz, Merlot, Cabernet Sauvignon Merlot.
SUMMARY Mark Haisma has established 2 hectares of pinot noir, shiraz, cabernet sauvignon and merlot on a small hillside vineyard on Briarty Road; his neighbours include such well-known producers as Yarra Yering and Giant Steps, and two substantial vineyards, one owned by Coldstream Hills, the other by Malcolm Fell. The wines are available by mail, email and phone order.

Rigel Wines

PO Box 18062, Collins Street East, Melbourne, Vic 8004 **REGION** Mornington Peninsula
T 1300 131 081 **F** 1300 131 281 **OPEN** From early 2004 at the General Store, Merricks
WINEMAKER MasterWineMakers (Contract) **EST.** 1989 **CASES** 1500
PRODUCT RANGE ($16.95–38 ML) The wines come under three labels: under Rigel Mornington Peninsula Chardonnay, Pinot Noir and Shiraz; under Rigel Barooga Road Chardonnay, Shiraz, Merlot and Cabernet Sauvignon; and under Rigel XLV Sangiovese, Nebbiolo and Zinfandel.
SUMMARY Rigel Wine Company is owned by Dr Damian and Sue Ireland and Michael and Mary Calman; the Irelands own the Mornington Peninsula vineyard at Shoreham, which provides the grapes for the super-premium Rigel label. The second property is at Tocumwal and has 80 hectares

of vines with 6 kilometres of Murray River frontage. Most of the grapes are sold to other winemakers, but part of the production has been vinified for both the local and export markets. The 2003 and subsequent vintages were made by MasterWineMakers.

Rimfire Vineyards ★★★

Bismarck Street, MacLagan, Qld 4352 **REGION** Queensland Zone
T (07) 4692 1129 **F** (07) 4692 1260 **OPEN** 7 days 10–5
WINEMAKER Tony Connellan **EST.** 1991 **CASES** 6000
PRODUCT RANGE ($12–20 CD) Aleatico, Verdelho, Musque, Chardonnay, Marsanne Chardonnay, Pioneer White, Country Rose, Touriga Nacional, Ruby Cabernet, Sangiovese, Shiraz, Hogshead (Shiraz Cabernet), Colonial Cabernet; fortifieds.
SUMMARY The Connellan family (parents Margaret and Tony and children Michelle, Peter and Louise) began planting the 12-hectare, 14-variety Rimfire Vineyards in 1991 as a means of diversification of their very large (1500-hectare) cattle stud in the foothills of the Bunya Mountains, 45 minutes drive northeast of Toowoomba. Increasingly producing a kaleidoscopic array of all manner of wines, the majority without any regional claim of origin. The Black Bull Café is open daily 10–5, blackboard menu and wine by the glass. Annual Jazz on the Lawn concert each spring.

Rivendell ★★★☆

Lot 328 Wildwood Road, Yallingup, WA 6282 **REGION** Margaret River
T (08) 9755 2235 **F** (08) 9755 2301 **OPEN** 7 days 10–5
WINEMAKER Mark Standish, Michael Adderley **EST.** 1987 **CASES** 3000
PRODUCT RANGE ($12.50–20 CD) Semillon Sauvignon Blanc, Honeysuckle Late Harvest Semillon, Verdelho, Shiraz Cabernet.
SUMMARY With 4 hectares of vineyards in bearing, production for Rivendell is supplemented by contract-grown grapes. The cellar-door sales facility is in a garden setting, complete with restaurant. An unusual sideline is the sale of 50 types of preserves, jams and chutneys.

♼♼♼♼ **Semillon 2002** Elegant and fresh herb and mineral; not particularly intense, but nicely balanced. **RATING** 87 **DRINK** 2007 $ 20

RiverBank Estate ★★★

126 Hamersley Road, Caversham, WA 6055 **REGION** Swan Valley
T (08) 9377 1805 **F** (08) 9377 2168 **OPEN** 7 days 10–5
WINEMAKER Robert James Bond **EST.** 1993 **CASES** 5000
PRODUCT RANGE ($12–26 CD) Semillon, Verdelho, Chenin, Chenin Chardonnay, Unwooded Chardonnay, Chardonnay, Celebration White, Jailbird White, Classic Sweet White, Jailbird Red, Celebration Red, Padlock Paddock Shiraz, Padlock Paddock Merlot, Pinot Noir, Grenache Shiraz, Shiraz, Cabernet, Fortified Muscat, Fortified Shiraz.
SUMMARY Robert Bond, a graduate of Charles Sturt University and a Swan Valley viticulturist for 20 years, established RiverBank Estate in 1993. He draws upon 11 hectares of estate plantings and, in his words, 'The wines are unashamedly full-bodied, produced from ripe grapes in what is recognised as a hot grape growing region.' Wines extending back over many vintages are available at the cellar door. Bond conducts 8-week wine courses affiliated with the Wine Industry Association of WA. A large restaurant is also open 7 days 11–5, with provision for corporate events at special times.

♼♼♼♼ **Padlock Paddock Merlot 2001** Good mouthfeel, texture and balance; savoury, cedary flavours. **RATING** 87 **DRINK** 2008 $ 18
Chardonnay Brut NV Well-made; no frills; dry and well balanced. **RATING** 87 **DRINK** Now $ 25
Fortified Muscat NV Pungent grapey aromas; high-toned spirit; serve on the rocks. **RATING** 87 **DRINK** Now $ 26

♼♼♼♼ **Chenin Blanc 2002** **RATING** 85 **DRINK** Now $ 15
Celebration Red 2002 **RATING** 85 **DRINK** Now $ 12

♼♼♼ **Padlock Paddock Shiraz 2001** **RATING** 83 $ 20

Riverina Estate

700 Kidman Way, Griffith, NSW 2680 **REGION** Riverina
T (02) 6963 8300 **F** (02) 6962 4628 **OPEN** Mon–Fri 9–5, Sat 10–4
WINEMAKER Sam Trimboli, Moreno Chiappin, Roberto Delgado **EST.** 1969 **CASES** 750 000
PRODUCT RANGE ($5–35 CD) An extensive range of varietal wines with Warburn Estate, Ballingal Estate 3 Corners, Lizard Ridge and Kanga's Leap, Bushman's Gully, Kooba Estate, Kimberly Creek and Lombard Station all offering a kaleidoscopic range of varietals and varietal blends.
SUMMARY One of the large producers of the region, drawing upon 1100 hectares of estate plantings. While much of the wine is sold in bulk to other producers, selected parcels of the best of the grapes are made into table wines, with at one time spectacular success. Current tastings are more as one would expect. Exports to the US.

♥♥♥♥ **Warburn Estate Show Reserve Shiraz 2001** Densely coloured and ultra-potent blackberry, prune, licorice, oak and tannins. Finesse not on the agenda. **RATING** 89 **DRINK** 2013 $ 21.95

♥♥♥♡ **Warburn Estate Premium Reserve Shiraz 2002 RATING** 86 **DRINK** 2007 $ 13.99
1164 Family Reserve Shiraz 2000 RATING 85 **DRINK** Now $ 35

River Park

River Park Road, Cowra, NSW 2794 **REGION** Cowra
T (02) 6342 3596 **F** (02) 6341 3711 **OPEN** By appointment
WINEMAKER John Hordern (Contract) **EST.** 1994 **CASES** 800
PRODUCT RANGE ($13–14 CD) Chardonnay, Cabernet Sauvignon.
SUMMARY Bill and Chris Murphy began the establishment of River Park in 1994, planting 8 hectares of chardonnay and 7 hectares of cabernet sauvignon on the banks of the Lachlan River, on the outskirts of Cowra. Most of the grapes are sold to major wine companies, but a small amount is made under contract and is sold through many different local wine outlets.

♥♥♥ **Chardonnay 2002 RATING** 82 $ 13

♥♥♡ **Cabernet Sauvignon 2001 RATING** 78 $ 14

Riversands Vineyards NR

Whytes Road, St George, Qld 4487 **REGION** Queensland Zone
T (07) 4625 3643 **F** (07) 4625 5043 **OPEN** Mon–Sat 8–6, Sunday 9–4
WINEMAKER Ballandean Estate (Contract) **EST.** 1990 **CASES** 3500
PRODUCT RANGE ($12–20 CD) Beardmore's Dry White, Explorers Chardonnay, Major Mitchell White, Western Rivers Run (Shiraz Cabernet), Dr Seidel's Soft Red, Ellen Meacle Merlot, Stirlings Reserve, Golden Liqueur Muscat, Black Magic Port.
SUMMARY Riversands is situated on the banks of the Balonne River near St George in the southwest corner of Queensland. It is a mixed wine grape and table grape business, acquired by present owners Alison and David Blacket in 1996. The wines are very competently made under contract at Ballandean Estate and have already accumulated a number of silver and bronze medals. The Chardonnay is particularly meritorious.

RiverStone Wines NR

105 Skye Road, Coldstream, Vic 3770 **REGION** Yarra Valley
T (03) 5962 3947 **F** (03) 5962 6616 **OPEN** Thurs–Mon 10–6
WINEMAKER Punt Road (Contract) **EST.** 1995
PRODUCT RANGE ($22–24 CD) Sauvignon Blanc, Chardonnay, Pinot Noir, Shiraz, Cabernet Sauvignon.
SUMMARY Peter and Jenny Inglese began the establishment of 10 hectares of sauvignon blanc, chardonnay, pinot noir, shiraz and cabernet sauvignon in 1995, building a blue stone homestead and cellar door, incorporating 100-year-old reclaimed timber. The site has 360-degree views of the Yarra Valley and surrounding mountains, and antipasto platters are available for those who wish to stay a little longer and absorb the beauty of the Valley. The wines are available only through the cellar door and by mail order.

Robert Channon Wines ★★★★★

Bradley Lane, Stanthorpe, Qld 4380 **REGION** Granite Belt
T (07) 4683 3260 **F** (07) 4683 3109 **OPEN** 7 days 10–5 (closed January)
WINEMAKER Mark Ravenscroft **EST.** 1998 **CASES** 3500
PRODUCT RANGE ($13–29.50 CD) Verdelho, Singing Lake Chardonnay Verdelho, Chardonnay, Singing Lake Rose, Light Horse Red, Singing Lake Shiraz Cabernet Merlot, Merlot, Shiraz Cabernet Sauvignon, Casanova's Storm Vintage Port.
SUMMARY Peggy and Robert Channon have established 1.6 hectares each of chardonnay, merlot and cabernet sauvignon, 2.4 hectares of chardonnay and just under a hectare of shiraz under permanent bird protection netting. The initial cost of installing permanent netting is high, but in the long term is well worth it. While primarily aimed at excluding birds, it also protects the grapes against hail damage. Finally, there is no pressure to pick the grapes before they are fully ripe. The strategy has already provided rewards, with Verdelho of the highest quality and some very good Merlot and Shiraz Cabernet Sauvignon; these wines enjoyed exceptional show success.

YYYYY **Verdelho 2003** Aromatic, tangy fruit; works the same magic with the variety as Primo Estate does with Colombard; excellent length. **RATING** 94 **DRINK** Now $ 24.50

YYYYY **Reserve Merlot 2002** Excellent varietal character; olive, cedar, blackcurrant, earth and spice; good balance, texture and structure. **RATING** 92 **DRINK** 2010 $ 29.50

YYYY **Reserve Cabernet Sauvignon 2002** Light to medium-bodied; a mix of red and black fruits; belies its 14 degrees alcohol. **RATING** 88 **DRINK** 2009 $ 29.50
Reserve Chardonnay 2002 Light to medium-bodied; well made and balanced, with some oak push; good length. **RATING** 87 **DRINK** 2008 $ 24.50
Singing Lake Rose 2002 Well made; has resisted the sugar trap; fresh, fruity strawberry flavours and dry finish. **RATING** 87 **DRINK** Now $ 14.50

YYYY **Shiraz Cabernet Sauvignon 2002** **RATING** 84 **DRINK** 2008 $ 17.50

Roberts Estate ★★☆

Game Street, Merbein, Vic 3505 **REGION** Murray Darling
T (03) 5024 2944 **F** (03) 5024 2877 **OPEN** Not
WINEMAKER John Pezzaniti **EST.** 1998 **CASES** 100 000
PRODUCT RANGE ($8.95–9.95 R) Semillion Sauvignon Blanc, Chardonnay, Merlot, Shiraz, Cabernet Sauvignon; under the Denbeigh label Chardonnay, Semillon Chardonnay, Colombard Chardonnay, Cabernet Shiraz, Cabernet Merlot; and Commissioners Block Chardonnay and Cabernet Merlot.
SUMMARY A very large winery acting as a processing point for grapes grown up and down the Murray River. Over 10 000 tonnes are crushed each vintage; much of the wine is sold in bulk to others, but some is exported under the Denbeigh and Commissioners Block labels. Exports to 14 of Australia's major markets.

Robert Stein Vineyard ★★★☆

Pipeclay Lane, Mudgee, NSW 2850 **REGION** Mudgee
T (02) 6373 3991 **F** (02) 6373 3709 **OPEN** 7 days 10–4.30
WINEMAKER Robert Stein, Michael Slater **EST.** 1976 **CASES** 6500
PRODUCT RANGE ($12.50–27.50 CD) Gewurztraminer, Semillon, Semillon Riesling, Semillon Chardonnay, Unwooded Chardonnay, Chardonnay, Late Harvest Riesling Traminer, Cabernet Rose, Shiraz, Reserve Shiraz (dellar door only), Cabernet Sauvignon Shiraz, Cabernet Sauvignon and a range of muscats and ports.
SUMMARY The sweeping panorama from the winery is its own reward for cellar-door visitors. Right from the outset this has been a substantial operation but has managed to sell the greater part of its production direct from the winery by mail order and through the cellar door, with retail distribution in Sydney, Victoria and South Australia. Wine quality, once variable, albeit with top wines from time to time, has become much more consistent. Exports to the UK.

YYYYY **Reserve Shiraz 2002** Sumptuous, ripe blackberry, plum fruit on the mid-palate; slightly drying tannins need to soften; leave alone. **RATING** 90 **DRINK** 2015 $ 27.50

ΥΥΥΥ **Reserve Cabernet Sauvignon 2002** Pleasant medium-bodied blackcurrant and blackberry fruit; touches of mocha and vanilla; soft tannins. **RATING** 88 **DRINK** 2011 $ 27.50
Shiraz 2002 A nice touch of faintly charry oak; smooth, chocolate-accented fruit; controlled tannins. **RATING** 87 **DRINK** 2010 $ 17

ΥΥΥΥ **Chardonnay 2001** Clean, fine and delicate; stone fruit and minimal oak. Has barely moved down the development path; Peter Pan style. **RATING** 86 **DRINK** 2008 $ 14
Cabernet Sauvignon 2002 RATING 86 **DRINK** 2015 $ 17
Late Harvest Riesling Traminer 2003 RATING 86 **DRINK** 2007 $ 12.50
Traminer Riesling 2003 RATING 85 **DRINK** Now $ 12.50
Shiraz 2001 RATING 85 **DRINK** 2011 $ 17
Chardonnay 2003 RATING 84 **DRINK** Now $ 14

ΥΥΥ **Unwooded Chardonnay 2003 RATING** 83 $ 14
Cabernet Rose 2003 RATING 83 $ 12.50

Robinsons Family Vineyards ★★★

Curtin Road, Ballandean, Qld 4382 **REGION** Granite Belt
T (07) 4684 1216 **F** (07) 4684 1216 **OPEN** 7 days 10–5
WINEMAKER Craig Robinson **EST.** 1969 **CASES** 3000
PRODUCT RANGE ($14–22 CD) Unwooded Chardonnay, Chardonnay, Vintage Brut, Shiraz, Shiraz Cabernet, Cabernet Sauvignon, Lyra Liqueur.
SUMMARY One of the pioneers of the Granite Belt, with the second generation of the family Robinson now in control. One thing has not changed: the strongly held belief of the Robinsons that the Granite Belt should be regarded as a cool, rather than warm, climate. It is a tricky debate, because some climatic measurements point one way, others in the opposite direction. Embedded in all this are semantic arguments about the meaning of the words cool and warm. Sufficient to say that shiraz and (conspicuously) cabernet sauvignon are the most suitable red varieties for that region, semillon, verdelho and chardonnay the best white varieties.

Robinvale ★★★

Sea Lake Road, Robinvale, Vic 3549 **REGION** Murray Darling
T (03) 5026 3955 **F** (03) 5026 1123 **OPEN** Mon–Fri 9–6, Sun 1–6
WINEMAKER Bill Caracatsanoudis **EST.** 1976 **CASES** 10 000
PRODUCT RANGE ($7.50–28 CD) A unique offering of white, red and fortified wines, the majority estate-grown under the internationally recognised Bio-Dynamic Demeter Grade A requirements, the highest level. In addition, a number are Kosher wines, and all are certified free of any genetically modified organisms.
SUMMARY Robinvale was one of the first Australian wineries to be fully accredited with the Biodynamic Agricultural Association of Australia. Most, but not all, of the wines are produced from organically grown grapes, with certain of the wines made preservative-free. Production has grown dramatically, no doubt reflecting the interest in organic and biodynamic viticulture and winemaking. Exports to the UK, Japan, Belgium, Canada and the US.

ΥΥΥΥ **Demeter No Preservatives Cabernets 2003** Fresh blackcurrant fruit; good depth and structure; ripe tannins will help conservation, as will the screwcap. This is a very good preservative-free wine. **RATING** 88 **DRINK** Now $ 20
Organic Origins Cabernet Franc Cabernet Sauvignon Merlot Ruby Cabernet 2002 Light to medium-bodied; a clean array of black and red fruits; lingering but soft tannins. Nice wine. **RATING** 87 **DRINK** 2008 $ 19

ΥΥΥ **Organic Origins White 2002 RATING** 82 $ 19

Roche Wines ★★★☆

Broke Road, Pokolbin, NSW 2320 **REGION** Lower Hunter Valley
T (02) 4998 7600 **F** (02) 4998 7706 **OPEN** 7 days 10–5
WINEMAKER Sarah-Kate Dineen (Contract) **EST.** 1999 **CASES** 8500
PRODUCT RANGE ($19–45 R) Tallawanta range of Semillon, Unwooded Chardonnay, Chardonnay, Shiraz.

SUMMARY Roche Wines, with its production of 8500 cases from 7 hectares each of semillon and shiraz and 5 hectares of chardonnay, is but the tip of the iceberg of the massive investment made by Bill Roche in the Pokolbin subregion. He has transformed the old Hungerford Hill development on the corner of Broke and McDonalds Roads, and built a luxurious resort hotel with extensive gardens and an Irish pub on the old Tallawanta Vineyard, as well as resuscitating the vines on Tallawanta. The wines are all sold on-site through the various outlets in the overall development.

ᵀᵀᵀᵀ **Tallawanta Semillon 2003** Excellent focus, length and intensity; very highly commended (gold medal equivalent) at 2003 Hunter Valley Wine Show. **RATING** 92 **DRINK** 2013 $19

ᵀᵀᵀᵀ **Tallawanta Shiraz 2000** Smooth, ripe blackberry and plum fruit; controlled oak and tannins. **RATING** 87 **DRINK** 2010 $28

ᵀᵀᵀᵀ **Tallawanta Shiraz 2001** **RATING** 85 **DRINK** 2011

Rochford's Eyton
★★★★☆

Cnr Maroondah Highway and Hill Road, Coldstream, Vic 3370 **REGION** Yarra Valley
T (03) 5962 2119 **F** (03) 5962 5319 **OPEN** 7 days 10–5
WINEMAKER David Creed **EST.** 1993 **CASES** 14 000
PRODUCT RANGE ($18–40 R) The E range of (mainly) Yarra Valley wines: Arneis, Macedon Ranges Yarra Valley Riesling, Sauvignon Blanc; R Macedon Ranges Chardonnay, Pinot Noir, Pinot Gris; and V Victoria Pinot Noir, Shiraz, Merlot.
SUMMARY Following the acquisition of Eyton-on-Yarra by Helmut and Yvonne Konecsny, major changes have followed. Most obvious is the renaming of the winery and brand, slightly less so the move of the winemaking operations of Rochford to Rochford's Eyton. The label design is essentially the same, the use of simple letter subtly denoting the geographical origin of each of the three wine ranges.

ᵀᵀᵀᵀᵀ **E Yarra Valley Pinot Noir 2002** Complex and intense; savoury, forest floor edges to spice and dark plum fruit; long finish. **RATING** 94 **DRINK** 2010 $27

ᵀᵀᵀᵀᵀ **V Victoria Shiraz 2003** Good colour; powerful licorice, spice, blackberry and plum; plenty of depth and development potential. Three Central Victorian vineyards. **RATING** 93 **DRINK** 2013 $18
R Macedon Ranges Pinot Noir 2001 Fragrant, spicy, savoury bouquet; elegant but intense, with length and persistent aftertaste. **RATING** 91 **DRINK** Now $38
R Macedon Ranges Chardonnay 2002 Subtle nectarine/stone fruit aromas are complexed by oak and malolactic influences; delicate and graceful in the mouth. **RATING** 90 **DRINK** 2008 $27
E Yarra Valley Arneis 2003 Aromatic lemony/floral blossom aromas; considerable texture and structure; most distinctive examples so far from Australia. Contract-grown, despite the name. **RATING** 90 **DRINK** 2007 $22
E Yarra Valley Cabernet Sauvignon 2001 Abundant, strongly varietal, ripe blackcurrant fruit; the luscious palate is likewise fruit-driven. **RATING** 90 **DRINK** 2011 $27

ᵀᵀᵀᵀ **E Yarra Valley Chardonnay 2002** Complex barrel ferment/malolactic ferment and lees inputs make the winemaker's fingerprints a little too obvious, but certainly has character. **RATING** 89 **DRINK** 2007 $22
E Macedon Ranges Yarra Valley Riesling 2003 Aromatic bouquet, some spicy elements; good depth; pineapple and lime plus mineral; abundant character. **RATING** 88 **DRINK** 2013 $22
E Yarra Valley Sauvignon Blanc 2002 Clean, crisp, tight mineral aromas and flavours; austere, firm, classic seafood style. **RATING** 88 **DRINK** Now $22
R Macedon Ranges Pinot Gris 2003 Gris Pear, apple and some spice aromas reflected in the well-balanced palate. **RATING** 87 **DRINK** 2007 $27

ᵀᵀᵀᵀ **V Victoria Pinot Noir 2003** **RATING** 85 **DRINK** Now $18
E Yarra Valley Shiraz 2001 **RATING** 85 **DRINK** 2007 $27
V Victoria Merlot 2003 **RATING** 85 **DRINK** 2007 $18
R Macedon Ranges Pinot Noir 2002 **RATING** 84 **DRINK** Now $38
V Victoria Merlot 2002 **RATING** 84 **DRINK** Now $18

ᵀᵀᵀ **E Yarra Valley Sauvignon Blanc 2003** **RATING** 83 $22

RockBare Wines ★★★★

PO Box 63, Mt Torrens, SA 5244 **REGION** McLaren Vale
T (08) 8389 9584 **F** (08) 8389 9587 **OPEN** Not
WINEMAKER Tim Burvill **EST.** 2000 **CASES** 20 000
PRODUCT RANGE ($15–35 R) McLaren Vale Chardonnay, McLaren Vale Shiraz; then the higher priced
Elysian Fields range with Clare Valley Riesling, Adelaide Hills Chardonnay, Barossa Valley Shiraz.
SUMMARY A native of Western Australia, Tim Burvill moved to South Australia in 1993 to undertake
the winemaking course at the University of Adelaide Roseworthy Campus. Having completed an
honours degree in oenology, he was recruited by Southcorp, and quickly found himself in a senior
winemaking position, with responsibility for super-premium whites including Penfolds Yattarna.
Knowing full well the cost of setting up a winery, he makes the wines under lend-lease arrangements
with other wineries. They are distributed in Queensland, Victoria the ACT and New South Wales by
Wine Source, and in the other States by Red+White. Exports to the US and Canada.

TTTTT Shiraz 2002 Rich, ripe, luscious blackberry and plum; deft French oak. Excellent value.
   RATING 90 **DRINK** 2012 $15

Rockfield Estate ★★★★

Rosa Glen Road, Margaret River, WA 6285 **REGION** Margaret River
T (08) 9757 5006 **F** (08) 9757 5006 **OPEN** 7 days 10.30–5
WINEMAKER Mike Lemmes **EST.** 1997 **CASES** 8000
PRODUCT RANGE ($15–35 CD) Semillon, Semillon Sauvignon Blanc, Unwooded Chardonnay,
Chardonnay, Chardonnay Methode Champenoise, Autumn Harvest Semillon, Rosa (Rose), Shiraz,
Cabernet Merlot; Reserve Chardonnay, Cabernet Sauvignon.
SUMMARY Rockfield Estate Vineyard is very much a family affair. Dr Andrew Gaman wears the hats
of chief executive officer, assistant winemaker and co-marketing manager; wife Anne Gaman is a
director; Alex Gaman and Nick McPherson are viticulturists, Andrew Gaman Jr is also an assistant
winemaker and Anna Walter (nee Gaman) helps Dr Andrew Gaman with the marketing. The
Chapman Brook meanders through the property, the vines running from its banks up to the wooded
slopes above the valley floor, and the winery offers light refreshments and food from the café
throughout the day. Exports to the UK, Denmark, India, Thailand, Vietnam and Singapore.

TTTTT Reserve Cabernet Sauvignon 2001 Powerful, blackcurrant and dark chocolate fruit
   supported by ample, ripe tannins. Very good mouthfeel and balance; long finish.
   RATING 94 **DRINK** 2016 $35

TTTTT Reserve Chardonnay 2003 A complex amalgam of barrel ferment and malolactic inputs
   to a creamy palate with nice melon fruit; good balance and length; stylish regional
   example. Screwcap. **RATING** 92 **DRINK** 2011 $35

TTTT Semillon Sauvignon Blanc 2003 RATING 86 **DRINK** 2008 $15
   Unwooded Chardonnay 2003 RATING 84 **DRINK** 2007 $15

Rockford ★★★★

Krondorf Road, Tanunda, SA 5352 **REGION** Barossa Valley
T (08) 8563 2720 **F** (08) 8563 3787 **OPEN** Mon–Sat 11–5
WINEMAKER Robert O'Callaghan, Chris Ringland **EST.** 1984
PRODUCT RANGE ($12.50–53 CD) Eden Valley Riesling, Local Growers Semillon, White Frontignac,
Alicante Bouchet, RD Pinot Chardonnay, Moppa Springs (Grenache Shiraz Mataro), Rod & Spur
(Shiraz Cabernet), Basket Press Shiraz, Sparkling Black Shiraz, Rifle Range Cabernet Sauvignon,
Marion Tawny Port.
SUMMARY The wines are sold through Adelaide retailers only (and the cellar door) and are unknown
to most eastern Australian wine-drinkers, which is a great pity because these are some of the most
individual, spectacularly flavoured wines made in the Barossa today, with an emphasis on old, low-
yielding dryland vineyards. This South Australian slur on the palates of Victoria and NSW is
exacerbated by the fact that the wines are exported to Switzerland, the UK and New Zealand; it all
goes to show we need proper authority to protect our living treasures.

Rock House

NR

St Agnes Hill, Calder Highway, Kyneton, Vic 3444 (postal) **REGION** Macedon Ranges
T (03) 5422 2205 **F** (03) 9388 9355 **OPEN** Not
WINEMAKER Malcolm Stewart **EST.** 1990 **CASES** 350
PRODUCT RANGE ($11–16.50 ML) Riesling, Kyneton Assemblage (red blend).
SUMMARY Ray Lacey and partners have established 6 hectares of riesling, cabernet sauvignon and merlot. By far the greatest percentage of the production is sold as grapes, with 5 tonnes being used for the Rock House wines. There are no cellar-door sales; all of the wine is sold through local retail outlets and by mail order.

Rocklea Vineyard

NR

Londons Road, Lovedale, NSW 2325 (postal) **REGION** Lower Hunter Valley
T (02) 9980 7000 **F** (02) 9980 2833 **OPEN** Not
WINEMAKER Bill Sneddon (Contract) **EST.** 1989
PRODUCT RANGE A range of varietally denominated table wines reflecting the plantings.
SUMMARY Allan Brown has 10 hectares in the Lovedale area planted to semillon, chardonnay and shiraz. The wine is available by mail order, and limited amounts are exported.

Rocland Wines

NR

PO Box 679, Nuriootpa, SA 5355 **REGION** Barossa Valley
T (08) 8562 202 **F** (08) 8562 2182 **OPEN** Not
WINEMAKER Contract **EST.** 2000
PRODUCT RANGE Shiraz.
SUMMARY Rocland Wines is primarily a bulk winemaking facility for contract work, but Frank Rocca does have 6 hectares of shiraz which is used to make Rocland Wines, largely destined for the Canadian market.

Rodericks

NR

90 Goshnicks Road, Murgon, Qld 4605 **REGION** South Burnett
T (07) 4168 4768 **F** (07) 4168 4768 **OPEN** 7 days 10–5
WINEMAKER Colin Roderick, Robert Roderick **EST.** 1996
PRODUCT RANGE A range of varietally denominated table wines reflecting the plantings.
SUMMARY The Roderick family (Wendy, Colin and Robert) have a substantial 22-hectare vineyard planted to semillon, chardonnay, colombard, verdelho, cabernet sauvignon, merlot, malbec, shiraz, white muscat, muscat hamburg and tarrango, and make the wine on-site. The production is largely sold by mail order and through the cellar door, which offers the full gamut of facilities, including light meals.

Roehr

NR

Roehr Road, Ebenezer near Nuriootpa, SA 5355 **REGION** Barossa Valley
T (08) 8565 6242 **F** (08) 8565 6242 **OPEN** Not
WINEMAKER Contract **EST.** 1995 **CASES** 300
PRODUCT RANGE Elmor's Ebenezer Old Vine Shiraz.
SUMMARY Karl Wilhelm Roehr arrived in Australia in 1841, and was among the earliest settlers at Ebenezer in the northern end of the Barossa Valley. His great, great grandson Elmor Roehr is the custodian of 20 hectares of shiraz, grenache, mataro and chardonnay on a vineyard passed down through the generations. In 1995 he decided to venture into winemaking and produced a Shiraz from 80-year-old vines which typically crop at less than 1.5 tonnes to the acre. It is sold exclusively in Germany and the US.

Rogues Gallery

NR

PO Box 10295, Adelaide BC, SA 5000 **REGION** McLaren Vale
T 0413 263 713 **F** (08) 8410 0918 **OPEN** Not
WINEMAKER Contract **EST.** 1996
PRODUCT RANGE ($14.20–21.25 ML) Shiraz, Cabernet Sauvignon.

SUMMARY Stephen Inglis sources the material for the Rogues Gallery wines in various ways, part coming from 4 hectares of vineyards in the heart of McLaren Vale, 2.4 hectares at Blewitt Springs and 1.7 hectares on the Willunga Scarp. Less than 20 tonnes are crushed for the Rogues Gallery label, the remainder headed elsewhere. The wines are exported to Canada, the UK and the US, and have limited distribution in Victoria by Yarra Valley Wine Consultants; they are also available via mail order.

Rojo Wines NR

34 Breese Street, Brunswick, Vic 3056 **REGION** Port Phillip Zone
T (03) 9383 4681 **F** (03) 9386 5699 **OPEN** By appointment
WINEMAKER Graeme Rojo **EST.** 1999
PRODUCT RANGE Nebbiolo, Sangiovese, Dolcetto.
SUMMARY Graeme Rojo is a biochemistry graduate, who worked in marketing post-graduation, while home winemaking for over 20 years. In 1999 he finally moved to establish his own label while working as assistant winemaker at Brunswick Hill Wines. Here the focus is on nebbiolo, sangiovese and dolcetto.

Romavilla NR

Northern Road, Roma, Qld 4455 **REGION** Queensland Zone
T (07) 4622 1822 **F** (07) 4622 1822 **OPEN** Mon–Fri 8–5, Sat 9–12, 2–4
WINEMAKER David Wall, Richard Wall **EST.** 1863 **CASES** 3000
PRODUCT RANGE ($10–40 CD) An extensive range of varietal and generic table wines and fortified wine styles, including Madeira and Tawny Port, are on sale at the winery; the Very Old Tawny Port is made from a blend of material ranging in age from 10 to 25 years.
SUMMARY An amazing historic relic, seemingly untouched since its nineteenth-century heyday, producing conventional table wines but still providing some extraordinary fortifieds, including a truly stylish Madeira made from Riesling and Syrian (the latter variety originating in Persia). David Wall has now been joined by son Richard in the business, which will hopefully ensure continuity for this important part of Australian wine history. Exports to Hong Kong and Canada.

Rosabrook Estate ★★★★☆

Rosa Brook Road, Margaret River, WA 6285 **REGION** Margaret River
T (08) 9757 2286 **F** (08) 9757 3634 **OPEN** 7 days 10–4
WINEMAKER Simon Keall **EST.** 1980 **CASES** 4000
PRODUCT RANGE ($15–22 CD) Semillon Sauvignon Blanc, Chardonnay, Autumn Harvest Riesling, Botrytis Riesling, Shiraz, Cabernet Merlot.
SUMMARY The 14-hectare Rosabrook Estate vineyards have been established progressively since 1980, with seven varieties planted. The cellar-door facility is housed in what was Margaret River's first commercial abattoir, built in the early 1930s, with a new winery constructed in 1993. Its abortive acquisition by Palandri Wines should not divert attention from the quality of the wines.

ΨΨΨΨΨ **Semillon Sauvignon Blanc 2002** Highly fragrant and aromatic; intense fruit ranging through passionfruit, lemon and gooseberry. **RATING** 95 **DRINK** 2008

Rosebrook Estate ★★☆

1090 Maitlandvale Road, Rosebrook, NSW 2320 **REGION** Lower Hunter Valley
T (02) 4930 1114 **F** (02) 4930 1690 **OPEN** By appointment
WINEMAKER Graeme Levick **EST.** 2000 **CASES** 1200
PRODUCT RANGE ($12–20 CD) Verdelho, Unwooded Chardonnay, Chardonnay, Shiraz, Muscat.
SUMMARY Graeme and Tania Levick run Rosebrook Estate and Hunter River Retreat as parallel operations. These include self-contained cottages, horse-riding, tennis, canoeing, swimming, bush walking, fishing, riverside picnic area, recreation room and minibus for winery tours and transport to functions or events in the area. Somewhere in the middle of all of this they have established 2.5 hectares each of chardonnay and verdelho, purchasing shiraz and muscat to complete the product range.

ΨΨΨ **Chardonnay 2002** **RATING** 83 **$** 18.50

Rosemount Estate (Hunter Valley) ★★★★

Rosemount Road, Denman, NSW 2328 **REGION** Upper Hunter Valley
T (02) 6549 6450 **F** (02) 6549 6499 **OPEN** 7 days 10–4
WINEMAKER Andrew Koerner **EST.** 1969
PRODUCT RANGE ($8.50–75 CD) A very large range of wines which in almost all instances are varietally identified, sometimes with the conjunction of vineyards at the top end of the range, and which in the case of the lower-priced volume varietals increasingly come from all parts of southeast Australia. Roxburgh Chardonnay is the white flag-bearer; Mountain Blue Shiraz Cabernet the real leader. The regional range encompasses Coonawarra, Orange and Mudgee (Hill of Gold).
SUMMARY Rosemount Estate achieved a miraculous balancing act maintaining wine quality while presiding over an ever-expanding empire and dramatically-increasing production. The wines were consistently of excellent value; all had real character and individuality; not a few were startlingly good. The outcome was the merger with Southcorp in March 2001; what seemed to be a powerful and synergistic merger turned out to be little short of a disaster, Southcorp losing more than its market capitalisation and more than half of its most effective and talented employees. A rebuilding process has begun under the direction of chief executive officer John Ballard, but no one is expecting any quick fix to the endemic problems facing Southcorp in Australia, the UK and the US.

ΨΨΨΨΨ **Mountain Blue Shiraz Cabernet 2000** Striking purple-red; abundant blackberry, dark plum and chocolate in an opulently rich and flavoursome palate. **RATING** 94 **DRINK** 2015 $52.40
Rose Label Orange Vineyard Merlot 2001 Excellent varietal character in both flavour (red fruits with a hint of spice) and structure (very fine tannins). **RATING** 94 **DRINK** 2010 $27

ΨΨΨΨ **Show Reserve Semillon 2002** Toasty notes starting to appear on bouquet; good balance and flavour; forward style. **RATING** 89 **DRINK** 2007 $23.95
Hill of Gold Mudgee Chardonnay 2002 The moderately intense, fruit-driven bouquet has nectarine and peach varietal fruit, the medium-bodied palate with clearly articulated melon and stone fruit varietal character. Clean finish. **RATING** 89 **DRINK** 2008 $17.90
Diamond Label Shiraz 2002 Solid blackberry and plum; good texture and structure; some real tannin inputs. **RATING** 88 **DRINK** 2007 $15.50
Diamond Label Sauvignon Blanc 2003 Subdued bouquet; plenty of varietal fruit on palate through passionfruit/tropical spectrum. **RATING** 87 **DRINK** Now $15.85
Grenache Shiraz 2002 Abundant juicy raspberry fruit; svelte mouthfeel; drink today. **RATING** 87 **DRINK** Now $11.75
Hill of Gold Mudgee Cabernet Sauvignon 2001 Savoury and blackberry aromas; the medium-bodied palate neatly balances blackberry fruit and a touch of oak, finishing with modest tannins. An easy drinking style. **RATING** 87 **DRINK** Now $17.90
Diamond Label Cabernet Sauvignon 2001 Sweet blackcurrant fruit; round, supple mouthfeel; easy-access style. **RATING** 87 **DRINK** 2009 $15.85

ΨΨΨΨ **Diamond Label Riesling 2002** **RATING** 86 **DRINK** 2007 $15.85
Diamond Label Semillon 2002 **RATING** 86 **DRINK** Now $15.85
Diamond Label Merlot 2002 **RATING** 86 **DRINK** Now $15.85
Sangiovese 2003 **RATING** 86 **DRINK** 2008 $13.99
Chardonnay 2002 **RATING** 85 **DRINK** Now $15.85

ΨΨΨ **Traminer Riesling 2003** **RATING** 83 $11.75
Jigsaw Shiraz Grenache 2003 **RATING** 83 $8.50
Jigsaw Chardonnay Verdelho Sauvignon Blanc 2002 **RATING** 82 $8.50
Jigsaw Shiraz Grenache 2002 **RATING** 82 $8.50

Rosemount Estate (McLaren Vale) ★★★★★

Ingoldby Road, McLaren Vale, SA 5171 **REGION** McLaren Vale
T (08) 8383 0001 **F** (08) 8383 0456 **OPEN** Mon–Sat 10–5, Sun and public holidays 11–4
WINEMAKER Charles Whish **EST.** 1888
PRODUCT RANGE ($19–60.90 CD) Balmoral Syrah, Show Reserve Shiraz, GSM (Grenache Shiraz Mourvedre), Traditional (Cabernet blend).

SUMMARY The specialist red wine arm of Rosemount Estate, responsible for its prestigious Balmoral Syrah, Show Reserve Shiraz and GSM, as well as most of the other McLaren Vale-based Rosemount brands. These wines come in large measure from 325 hectares of estate plantings.

ΥΥΥΥΥ **Balmoral Syrah 2000** Laden with rich blackberry, bitter chocolate and licorice fruit; oak and tannin management exemplary; particularly outstanding given the vintage. **RATING** 95 **DRINK** 2015 $ 60.90

ΥΥΥΥΥ **Balmoral Syrah 2001** Voluminous, lush dark fruit aromas; powerful, deep blackberry palate with substantial tannins. **RATING** 92 **DRINK** 2016 $ 60.90
Traditional 2001 Appealing array of red and black fruits, the oak restrained; supple and round, nicely balanced. Winner of the Jimmy Watson Trophy 2002. **RATING** 92 **DRINK** 2011 $ 28.75

ΥΥΥΥ **Show Reserve Shiraz 2001** Rich and ripe black fruits and splashes of chocolate; tannins tremble on the brink of dominance. **RATING** 88 **DRINK** 2013 $ 19

Rosenvale Wines ★★★★☆

Lot 385 Railway Terrace, Nuriootpa, SA 5355 **REGION** Barossa Valley
T 0407 390 788 **F** (08) 8565 7206 **OPEN** By appointment
WINEMAKER James Rosenzweig, Mark Jamieson **EST.** 2000 **CASES** 1700
PRODUCT RANGE ($14.50–31 ML) Semillon, Chardonnay, Shiraz, Shiraz Cabernet Sauvignon, Cabernet Sauvignon.
SUMMARY The Rosenzweig family has 80 hectares of vineyards, some old and some new, planted to riesling, semillon, semillon, pinot noir, grenache, shiraz and cabernet sauvignon. Most of the grapes are sold to other producers, but since 1999 select parcels have been retained and vinified for release under the Rosenvale label. The red wines from 2002 are great, and the white wines have also improved. Exports to Singapore.

ΥΥΥΥΥ **Shiraz 2002** Saturated colour, aromas and flavours; gloriously mouthfilling, satiny and smooth black fruits; excellent finish. **RATING** 94 **DRINK** 2022 $ 28

ΥΥΥΥΥ **Cabernet Sauvignon 2002** Great colour; totally delicious cassis and blackcurrant fruit; soft but lingering tannins; excellent French oak handling. **RATING** 93 **DRINK** 2017 $ 28

ΥΥΥΥ **Barrel Fermented Chardonnay 2002** Well above average; gently ripe melon and fig fruit; excellent oak balance and integration. **RATING** 88 **DRINK** 2007 $ 14.50

ΥΥΥΥ **Semillon 2003** **RATING** 86 **DRINK** Now $ 14.50

Rosevears Estate ★★★☆

1a Waldhorn Drive, Rosevears, Tas 7277 **REGION** Northern Tasmania
T (03) 6330 1800 **F** (03) 6330 1810 **OPEN** 7 days 10–4
WINEMAKER Andrew Pirie **EST.** 1999 **CASES** 8000
PRODUCT RANGE ($20.30–71 CD) Riesling, Traminer, Sauvignon Blanc, Pinot Gris, Unwooded Chardonnay, Chardonnay, Reserve Chardonnay, Sparkling Brut, Sparkling Rose Brut, Rose, Pinot Noir, Reserve Pinot Noir, Cabernet Merlot, Cabernet Sauvignon; Notley Gorge range of Riesling, Chardonnay, Pinot Noir, Cabernet Merlot and Cabernet Sauvignon.
SUMMARY The multi-million dollar Rosevears Estate winery and restaurant complex was opened by the Tasmanian premier in November 1999. Built on a steep hillside overlooking the Tamar River, it is certain to make a lasting and important contribution to the Tasmanian wine industry. It is owned by a syndicate of investors headed by Dr Mike Beamish and incorporates both Notley Gorge and Ironpot Bay. Spacious, high quality accommodation units with a splendid view over the Tamar River were opened in September 2003.

ΥΥΥΥΥ **Merlot 2001** Complex, intense and long; clearly defined, savoury varietal character; forest and black fruits; lingering finish. **RATING** 91 **DRINK** 2011 $ 35.50

ΥΥΥΥ **Unwooded Chardonnay 2003** Clean, pure fruit aromas, citrus and nectarine; has excellent length and finish thanks to natural acidity. **RATING** 89 **DRINK** 2008 $ 23.70

ΥΥΥΥ **Riesling 2003** **RATING** 86 **DRINK** 2010 $ 29

Sauvignon Blanc 2003 RATING 85 DRINK Now $ 25
Gewurztraminer 2003 RATING 84 DRINK Now $ 22
Pinot Noir 2002 RATING 84 DRINK 2008 $ 40

Rosily Vineyard ★★★★

Yelveton Road, Wilyabrup, WA 6284 REGION Margaret River
T (08) 9755 6336 F (08) 9221 3309 OPEN By appointment
WINEMAKER Mike Lemmes, Dan Pannell (Consultant) EST. 1994 CASES 6800
PRODUCT RANGE ($16–20 ML) Semillon, Semillon Sauvignon Blanc, Sauvignon Blanc, Chardonnay,
Shiraz, Cabernet Merlot, Cabernet Sauvignon.
SUMMARY The partnership of Mike and Barb Scott and Ken and Dot Allan acquired the Rosily
Vineyard site in 1994. Under the direction of consultant Dan Pannell (of the Pannell family) 12
hectares of vineyard were planted over the next 3 years: first up sauvignon blanc, semillon,
chardonnay and cabernet sauvignon, and thereafter merlot, shiraz and a little grenache and cabernet
franc. The first crops were sold to other makers in the region, but in 1999 Rosily built a winery with a
120-tonne capacity, and is now moving to fully utilise that capacity.

ȚȚȚȚ Sauvignon Blanc 2003 Clear, clean-cut varietal aromas; delicate palate; distinctly
         lemony tang; good balance and length. RATING 90 DRINK Now $ 18

ȚȚȚȚ Semillon Sauvignon Blanc 2003 Clean, fresh, neatly judged blend; good balance and
         structure; herb, ripe fruit and subtle French oak. The screwcap will insure cellaring.
         RATING 89 DRINK 2008 $ 20
         Cabernet Sauvignon 2001 A clear, clean bouquet with blackcurrant and redcurrant
         aromas plus a touch of French oak. The medium-bodied palate focuses on pristine fruit,
         the texture and structure through tannins and faintly earthy varietal notes. RATING 89
         DRINK 2011 $ 20
         Shiraz 2001 A clean, fragrant, cherry/red fruit bouquet; the light to medium-bodied
         palate providing more of the same; fine tannins give an overall savoury, restrained caste to
         a wine of some elegance. RATING 88 DRINK 2009 $ 20

ȚȚȚȚ Cabernet Merlot 2001 Light but bright red-purple; fragrant berry, leaf and mint aromas
         flow into a light to medium-bodied palate, with pleasant fruit, and fine tannins; lacks
         concentration. RATING 85 DRINK 2008 $ 20

Rosnay Organic Wines ★★☆

Rivers Road, Canowindra, NSW 2804 REGION Cowra
T (02) 6344 3215 F (02) 6344 3229 OPEN By appointment
WINEMAKER Various contract EST. 2002 CASES 3000
PRODUCT RANGE ($16.99–21.99 R) Chardonnay Semillon, Shiraz.
SUMMARY Rosnay Organic Wines is, to put it mildly, an interesting business venture, with the
Statham and Gardner families at its centre. Thirty-6 hectares of vineyard has been established on the
140-hectare property, part of which has been divided into 12 blocks ranging from 8 to 10 hectares,
along with ten housing blocks of 5000 square metres, with all the requisite building approvals and
services provided. The viticulture is organic, and the management company provides active growers
or absentee investors with a range of specialist organic farming machinery and contract
management. Winemaking is split between John Cassegrain of Cassegrain Wines, Kevin Karstrom of
Botobolar and Rodney Hooper, each one of whom has expertise in organic grape growing and
organic winemaking.

ȚȚȚȚ Unwooded Chardonnay Semillon 2003 RATING 84 DRINK Now $ 16.99

ȚȚȚ   Shiraz 2002 RATING 83 $ 19.99

Ross Estate Wines ★★★

Barossa Valley Way, Lyndoch, SA 5351 REGION Barossa Valley
T (08) 8524 4033 F (08) 8524 4533 OPEN Mon–Sat 10–5, Sun 1–5
WINEMAKER Rod Chapman EST. 1999 CASES 10 000

PRODUCT RANGE ($13–26 CD) Riesling, Semillon, Sauvignon Blanc, Chardonnay, Beekeeper's Blend (Late Harvest), Shiraz, Tempranillo Graciano (bi-annual cellar-door release only), Old Vine Grenache, Merlot, Lynedoch (Cabernet Sauvignon Cabernet Franc Merlot), Cabernet Sauvignon.
SUMMARY Darius and Pauline Ross laid the foundation for Ross Estate Wines when they purchased 43 hectares of vines which included two blocks of 75 and 90-year-old grenache. Also included were blocks of 30-year-old riesling and semillon, and 13-year-old merlot. The remaining vines were removed and planted with chardonnay, sauvignon blanc, cabernet sauvignon, cabernet franc and shiraz, which are now 7 years old. A winery was built in time for the 1998 vintage, and a tasting room was opened in 1999. The immensely experienced Rod Chapman, with 39 vintages under his belt including 18 years as red winemaker with Southcorp/Penfolds, is in charge of winemaking. Exports to the US, Asia and Europe.

ΥΥΥΥ **Northridge Shiraz 2001 RATING** 85 **DRINK** 2007 $20

Ross Hill Vineyard ★★★

62 Griffin Road, via Ammerdown, Orange, NSW 2800 **REGION** Orange
T (02) 6360 0175 **F** (02) 6363 1674 **OPEN** By appointment
WINEMAKER David Lowe, Stephen Doyle (Contract) **EST.** 1994 **CASES** 2500
PRODUCT RANGE ($15–24 CD) Sauvignon Blanc, Chardonnay, Rose, Mick's Lot Shiraz, Merlot, Isabelle Merlot Cabernet, Cabernet Sauvignon.
SUMMARY Peter and Terri Robson began planting 12 hectares of vines in 1994. Chardonnay, sauvignon blanc, merlot, cabernet sauvignon, shiraz and cabernet franc have been established on north-facing, gentle slopes at an elevation of 800 metres. No insecticides are used in the vineyard, the grapes are hand-picked and the vines hand-pruned. Ross Hill also has an olive grove with Italian oil varieties, and the Spanish variety manzanilla which is also a popular table olive. Exports to the UK.

ΥΥΥΥ **Merlot 2002** Spicy savoury aromatic nuances; subtle oak, good structure. **RATING** 88
DRINK 2010 $24
Cabernet Sauvignon 2002 Medium-bodied; plenty of flesh and extract; blackcurrant, blackberry; gentle oak. **RATING** 87 **DRINK** 2010 $24

ΥΥΥΥ **Mick's Lot Shiraz 2002 RATING** 85 **DRINK** 2007 $24
Chardonnay 2002 RATING 84 **DRINK** Now $18
Cabernet Sauvignon 2001 RATING 84 **DRINK** Now $24

ΥΥΥ **Sauvignon Blanc 2002 RATING** 83 **DRINK** Now $15
Rose 2003 RATING 83 $15

Rothbury Ridge NR

Talga Road, Rothbury, NSW 2320 **REGION** Lower Hunter Valley
T (02) 4930 7122 **F** (02) 4930 7198 **OPEN** Mon–Sat 9–5, Sun 10–5
WINEMAKER Peter Jorgensen **EST.** 1998 **CASES** 10 000
PRODUCT RANGE ($15–55 CD) Stanleigh Park Reserve Semillon, Winemakers Semillon, Anne Chardonnay Semillon, Mary Unwooded Chardonnay (Chablis Style), Steven Chardonnay, Mount Royal Reserve Durif, Edgar Chambourcin, Mount Royal Reserve Chambourcin, James Shiraz, Rose Chambourcin Traditional Methode Champenoise.
SUMMARY Rothbury Ridge has an extraordinarily eclectic choice of varieties planted, with between 1.2 hectares and 2.4 hectares each of chardonnay, semillon, verdelho, chambourcin, durif, shiraz and cabernet sauvignon. It is owned by a public company (not listed on the Stock Exchange) with an imposing array of directors, and actively markets its wines through a wine club.

Rotherhythe NR

Hendersons Lane, Gravelly Beach, Exeter, Tas 7251 **REGION** Northern Tasmania
T (03) 6394 4869 **OPEN** By appointment
WINEMAKER Steven Hyde **EST.** 1976 **CASES** 1600
PRODUCT RANGE ($16–26.95 CD) Chardonnay, Pinot Noir, Cabernet Sauvignon, Pinot Chardonnay.

SUMMARY At the 1996 Tasmanian Wines Show Rotherhythe swept all before it, winning trophies galore. Ironically, two days later Dr Steven Hyde sold the vineyard, although he has retained all of the existing wine stocks and will remain involved in the winemaking for some time to come. In both 1997 and again in 1998 Rotherhythe was awarded the trophy for Most Successful Exhibitor at the Tasmanian Wines Show. Since then the pace has slowed, with most of the grapes sold, one imagines at a substantial price.

Rothvale Vineyard ★★★★

Deasy's Road, Pokolbin NSW 2321 **REGION** Lower Hunter Valley
T (02) 4998 7290 **F** (02) 4998 7926 **OPEN** 7 days 10–5
WINEMAKER Max Patton, Luke Patton **EST.** 1978 **CASES** 8000
PRODUCT RANGE ($14–28 CD) Vat 8 Semillon, Barrel Fermented Semillon, Sirens Lair Semillon, Semillon Muscat, Angus Semillon Chardonnay, Unwooded Chardonnay, Reserve Chardonnay A (American Oak), Reserve Chardonnay F (French Oak), Annie's Dry Red, Tilda's Shiraz, Luke's Shiraz, Sirens Lair Shiraz, Cabernet Sauvignon.
SUMMARY Owned and operated by the Patton family, headed by Max Patton who has the fascinating academic qualifications of BVSc, MSc London, BA Hons Canterbury, the scientific part of which has no doubt come in useful for his winemaking. The wines are sold only through the cellar door and direct to an imposing list of restaurants in the Hunter Valley and Sydney. Rothvale also has four vineyard cottages available for bed and breakfast accommodation. The wines have already accumulated an impressive array of medals, and are of commendably consistent style and quality. Exports to the UK and the US.

Roundstone Winery & Vineyard ★★★☆

54 Willow Bend Drive, Yarra Glen, Vic 3775 **REGION** Yarra Valley
T (03) 9730 1181 **F** (03) 9730 1151 **OPEN** Thurs–Sun and public holidays 10–5, or by appointment
WINEMAKER John Derwin, Rob Dolan and Kate Goodman (Consultants) **EST.** 1998 **CASES** 2000
PRODUCT RANGE ($16–35 CD) Viognier, Chardonnay, Charmed Chardonnay, Roses, Gamay, Pinot Noir, Rubies Pinot Noir, Merlot, Shiraz Viognier, Lightening Hill Cabernets.
SUMMARY John and Lynne Derwin have moved quickly since establishing Roundstone, planting 8 hectares of vineyard (half to pinot noir with a mix of the best clones) building a small winery, and opening a cellar door and restaurant situated on the side of a dam. The Derwins tend the vineyard, enlist the aid of friends to pick the grapes, John makes the wine in conjunction with advice from Rob Dolan and Kate Goodman, Lynne is the chef and sommelier. Her pride and joy is a shearers' stove, which was used at the Yarra Glen Grand Hotel for 100 years before being abandoned, and which is now at the centre of the kitchen. The restaurant opened in December 2001, and has established itself as one of the best winery restaurants in the valley.

TTTTY **Rubies Pinot Noir 2002** Significantly more complex than the varietal, though still in the lighter-bodied end of the spectrum; has good length and persistence. **RATING** 90 **DRINK** 2008 $ 27

TTTT **Viognier 2003** Shows varietal character in gentle fashion; pastille flavours; supple mouthfeel. **RATING** 88 **DRINK** Now $ 27
Gamay 2003 Very interesting wine; plum, prune and spice in thoroughly authentic varietal mode; good balance and length. **RATING** 88 **DRINK** Now $ 18
Pinot Noir 2002 Lively, fresh, tangy black cherry, plum and spice; light to medium-bodied; best now. **RATING** 88 **DRINK** Now $ 20
Chardonnay 2003 Gentle handling and winemaker inputs; soft melon and cashew; well balanced. As with the previous vintage, preferred to the more expensive Charmed. **RATING** 87 **DRINK** Now $ 20

TTTY **Charmed Chardonnay 2003** **RATING** 86 **DRINK** 2007 $ 27
Roses 2003 Well above average length and intensity for a Rose; balanced sweetness and acidity. **RATING** 86 **DRINK** Now $ 16
Lightning Hill Cabernets 2002 **RATING** 86 **DRINK** 2007 $ 23
Shiraz Viognier 2002 **RATING** 85 **DRINK** Now $ 23

Rumbalara

NR

Fletcher Road, Fletcher, Qld 4381 **REGION** Granite Belt
T (07) 4684 1206 **F** (07) 4684 1299 **OPEN** 7 days 9–5
WINEMAKER Wayne Beecham (Contract) **EST.** 1974 **CASES** 1500
PRODUCT RANGE ($11.50–19.50 CD) Barrel Fermented Semillon, Granitegolde, Light Shiraz, Cabernet
Sauvignon, Pinot Noir, Cabernet Shiraz and a range of Fortified wines, Cider and Vermouth.
SUMMARY Has produced some of the Granite Belt's finest honeyed Semillon and silky, red berry
Cabernet Sauvignon, but quality does vary. The winery incorporates a spacious restaurant, and there
are also barbecue and picnic facilities. No recent tastings, but the change of owners in 2003 will
hopefully see more activity.

Rumball Sparkling Wines

NR

55 Charles Street, Norwood, SA 5067 **REGION** Adelaide Zone
T (08) 8332 2761 **F** (08) 8364 0188 **OPEN** Mon–Fri 9–5
WINEMAKER Peter Rumball **EST.** 1988 **CASES** 10 000
PRODUCT RANGE ($14–21 R) Vintage Brut, Sparkling Merlot, Sparkling Shiraz (also available in half
bottles, magnums and jeroboams).
SUMMARY Peter Rumball has been making and selling sparkling wine for as long as I can remember,
but has led a somewhat peripatetic life, starting in the Clare Valley but now operating one of the 12
Methode Champenoise lines in Australia, situated in the Adelaide suburb of Norwood. The grapes
are purchased and the wines made under the supervision of Peter Rumball. His particular specialty
has always been Sparkling Shiraz, and was so long before it became 'flavour of the month'. National
retail distribution through Tucker Seabrook, and exports to the UK, the US and Japan.

Rusden Wines

NR

Magnolia Road, Tanunda, SA 5352 (postal) **REGION** Barossa Valley
T (08) 8563 2976 **F** (08) 8563 0885 **OPEN** Not
WINEMAKER Christian Canute **EST.** 1998 **CASES** 1800
PRODUCT RANGE Christine's Vineyard Grenache, Ripper Creek Cabernet Shiraz, Chookshed
Zinfandel, Driftsand Grenache Mataro Shiraz, Black Guts Shiraz, Boundaries Cabernet.
SUMMARY The Canute family (Dennis, Christine and Christian) have been long-term grape growers
with 14 hectares of sauvignon blanc, chenin blanc, grenache, cabernet sauvignon, merlot, shiraz,
mourvedre and zinfandel. While only part of the production is vinified under the Rusden label,
exports have been established to the US, the UK, Germany, France and New Zealand.

Russet Ridge

 ★★★☆

Cnr Caves Road and Riddoch Highway, Naracoorte, SA 5271 **REGION** Wrattonbully
T (08) 8762 0114 **F** (08) 8762 0341 **OPEN** Thurs–Mon 11–4.30
WINEMAKER Philip Laffer, Sam Kurtz **EST.** 2000 **CASES** 35 000
PRODUCT RANGE ($17 R) Coonawarra Chardonnay, Coonawarra Cabernet Shiraz Merlot.
SUMMARY This is the former Heathfield Ridge winery, built in 1998 as a contract crush and
winemaking facility for multiple clients, but purchased by Orlando in 2000. It is the only winery in
the large Wrattonbully region, and also receives Orlando's Coonawarra and Padthaway grapes, and
other Limestone Coast fruit.

Rutherglen Estates

 ★★★☆

Cnr Great Northern Road and Murray Valley Highway, Rutherglen, Vic 3685 **REGION** Rutherglen
T (02) 6032 8516 **F** (02) 6032 8517 **OPEN** Not
WINEMAKER Nick Butler, David Valentine **EST.** 2000 **CASES** 25 000
PRODUCT RANGE ($12–16 R) Chardonnay Marsanne, Shiraz, Shiraz Mourvedre, Durif, Sangiovese.
SUMMARY The Rutherglen Estates brand is an offshoot of a far larger contract crush and make business,
with a winery capacity of 4000 tonnes (roughly equivalent to 280 000 cases). Rutherglen is in a
declared phylloxera region, which means all of the grapes grown within that region have to be vinified
within it, itself a guarantee of business for ventures such as Rutherglen Estates. It also means that some
of the best available material can be allocated for the brand, with an interesting mix of varieties.

Ryland River

NR

RMB 8945 Main Creek Road, Main Ridge, Vic 3928 **REGION** Mornington Peninsula
T (03) 5989 6098 **F** (03) 9899 0184 **OPEN** Weekends and public holidays 10–5, or by appointment
WINEMAKER John W Bray **EST.** 1986 **CASES** 2000
PRODUCT RANGE ($15–30 CD) Semillon Sauvignon Blanc, Chardonnay, Cabernet Sauvignon, Jack's
Delight Tawny Port and Muscat.
SUMMARY John Bray has been operating Ryland River at Main Ridge on the Mornington Peninsula
for a number of years, but not without a degree of controversy over the distinction between Ryland
River wines produced from Mornington Peninsula grapes and those produced from grapes
purchased from other regions. A large lake with catch-your-own trout and a cheese house are general
tourist attractions.

Rymill Coonawarra

 ★★★★☆

The Riddoch Run Vineyards, Riddoch Highway, Coonawarra, SA 5263 **REGION** Coonawarra
T (08) 8736 5001 **F** (08) 8736 5040 **OPEN** 7 days 10–5
WINEMAKER John Innes **EST.** 1970 **CASES** 50 000
PRODUCT RANGE ($14–30 CD) Sauvignon Blanc, Chardonnay, Pinot Noir Chardonnay, The Bees
Knees Sparkling Red, June Traminer Late Harvest, Shiraz, MC2 (Merlot Cabernet Sauvignon
Cabernet Franc), Cabernet Sauvignon.
SUMMARY The Rymills are descendants of John Riddoch and have long owned some of the finest
Coonawarra soil, upon which they have grown grapes since 1970, with present plantings of 170
hectares. Peter Rymill made a small amount of Cabernet Sauvignon in 1987 but has long since
plunged headlong into commercial production, with winemaker John Innes presiding over the
striking winery portrayed on the label. Australian distribution is through Negociants Australia;
exports to all major markets in Europe and Asia.

ȲȲȲȲȲ **Sauvignon Blanc 2003** Powerful wine with clear varietal fruit; considerable length and
intensity; spotlessly clean. **RATING** 92 **DRINK** 2007 $ 17
Cabernet Sauvignon 2000 Good length and depth; classic blackcurrant fruit with a
regional earthy underlay; medium to full-bodied, with ripe tannins and good oak.
RATING 92 **DRINK** 2010 $ 28.50

ȲȲȲȲ **MC2 2001** Light to medium-bodied; blackcurrant, cassis, mint, leaf and earth; fine
savoury tannins. **RATING** 87 **DRINK** Now $ 19

Sabella Vineyards

 ★★★☆

PO Box 229, McLaren Vale, SA 5171 **REGION** McLaren Vale
T 0416 361 369 **F** (08) 8323 8270 **OPEN** Not
WINEMAKER Michael Petrucci **EST.** 1999 **CASES** 450
PRODUCT RANGE ($15–22 R) Sauvignon Blanc Semillon, Shiraz, Cabernet Sauvignon.
SUMMARY Giuseppe (Joe) Petrucci was born at Castellino in Campobasso in the Molise region of
Italy, where his family were farmers. His father migrated to Australia in 1960, the rest of the
family following him in 1966. In 1976 Joe and wife Rosa (and their children) moved to McLaren
Vale where they purchased their first vineyard in McMurtrie Road. Over the years their vineyards
have increased from 10 to 44 hectares, their grapes sold to Wirra Wirra, Kreglinger, Beringer
Blass, Rosemount, Middlebrook Estate and RockBare Estate. In 1999 they decided to keep some
grapes back for release under the Sabella label; Sabella drives from a pseudonym given to the
Petrucci name six generations ago. Son Michael just happens to be the winemaker at Middlebrook
which completes the circle. The wines are distributed by Unique Wines, Athol Park, South
Australia.

ȲȲȲȲ **Shiraz 2000** Light to medium-bodied; gently sweet red fruits; touches of vanilla and
chocolate. **RATING** 87 **DRINK** 2008 $ 22
Cabernet Sauvignon 2000 Very ripe blackcurrant fruit; good oak and tannin levels.
RATING 87 **DRINK** 2009 $ 22

Saddlers Creek

Marrowbone Road, Pokolbin, NSW 2320 **REGION** Lower Hunter Valley
T (02) 4991 1770 **F** (02) 4991 2482 **OPEN** 7 days 9–5
WINEMAKER John Johnstone **EST.** 1989 **CASES** 20 000
PRODUCT RANGE ($21–58 CD) Classic Hunter Semillon, Verdelho, Marrowbone Chardonnay, Reserve Chardonnay, Classical Gas (Methode Champenoise), Botrytis Semillon, Equus Shiraz, Equus McLaren Vale Shiraz, Single Vineyard Hunter Shiraz, Reserve Shiraz, Reserve Merlot, Bluegrass Cabernet Sauvignon, Langhorne Reserve Cabernet, Muscat Exclusif.
SUMMARY Made an impressive entrance to the district with consistently full flavoured and rich wines, and has continued on in much the same vein, with good wines across the spectrum. Limited retail distribution in New South Wales, Queensland and Victoria. Exports to Canada, New Zealand and Mauritius.

ᵀᵀᵀᵀᵀ **Bluegrass Cabernet Sauvignon 2001** Gentle cassis berry fruit and lots of sweet vanillin oak; works surprisingly well; very supple, harmonious texture. **RATING** 90 **DRINK** 2016 $ 28

ᵀᵀᵀᵀ **Reserve Shiraz 2000** Strongly regional savoury/earthy style; fine, lingering tannins give structure. **RATING** 89 **DRINK** 2011 $ 46
Reserve Chardonnay 2002 Clean melon and a touch of fig; light to medium-bodied; subtle French oak infusion; overall elegance. **RATING** 88 **DRINK** 2007 $ 35

ᵀᵀᵀᵀ **Classic Hunter Semillon 2003** **RATING** 86 **DRINK** 2010 $ 22
Single Vineyard Hunter Shiraz 2002 **RATING** 85 **DRINK** 2008 $ 50

ᵀᵀᵀ **Marrowbone Chardonnay 2001** **RATING** 82 $ 26

🐌 St Aidan

RMB 205 Ferguson Road, Dardanup, WA 6236 **REGION** Geographe
T (08) 9728 3007 **F** (08) 9728 3006 **OPEN** Weekends and public holidays 10–5, or by appointment
WINEMAKER Mark Messenger (Contract) **EST.** 1996 **CASES** 1000
PRODUCT RANGE ($14–17 ML) Chardonnay, Myra, Cabernet Sauvignon.
SUMMARY Phil and Mary Smith purchased their property at Dardanup in 1991, 20 minutes drive from the Bunbury hospitals for which Phil Smith works. They first ventured into Red Globe table grapes, planting 1 hectare in 1994/5, followed by a hectare of mandarins and oranges. With this experience, and with Mary completing a TAFE viticulture course, they extended their horizons by planting a hectare each of cabernet sauvignon and chardonnay in 1997. A little muscat followed in 2001. The wines are contract-made, and each vintage since the first in 2000 has been rewarded with medals, chiefly at the Qantas West Australian Wine Show.

ᵀᵀᵀᵀ **Chardonnay 2003** Moderate weight and complexity; lacks fruit intensity, but has positive oak. **RATING** 87 **DRINK** Now $ 15
Cabernet Sauvignon 2002 Elegant and fragrant; light-bodied, but with fresh raspberry/blackberry fruit, fine tannins, subtle oak. **RATING** 87 **DRINK** 2009 $ 17

St Anne's Vineyards

Cnr of Perricoota Road and 24 Lane, Moama, NSW 2731 **REGION** Perricoota
T (03) 5480 0099 **F** (03) 5480 0077 **OPEN** 7 days 9–5; also at Garrards Lane, Myrniong
WINEMAKER Richard McLean **EST.** 1972 **CASES** 20 000
PRODUCT RANGE ($14–25 CD) Predominantly wines made from grapes grown in the Perricoota region, and the occasionaly Riesling and Cabernet Sauvignon from the small Ballarat vineyard. Much of the cellar-door trade is based on a range of sweet and fortified wines, the latter available in flagons and in 13-litre and 23-litre 'Maturation Barrels'. The Port is available in large quantities to re-fill barrels.
SUMMARY St Anne's is by far the most active member of the newly registered (under the Geographic Indications Legislation) region in southern New South Wales. Richard McLean has established 80 hectares of estate vineyards, with another 120 hectares of grower vineyards to draw upon. Shiraz, cabernet sauvignon, grenache and mourvedre account for over 75 per cent of the plantings, but there is a spread of the usual white wines and few red exotics. The wines are all competently made. Most of

the St Anne's wines are sold through the two cellar-door operations, and in particular the Myrniong cellar door, which is surrounded by a somewhat scrappy vineyard, but which attracts considerable passing trade and wedding receptions.

🐌 Saint Derycke's Wood Winery   NR

Cnr Greenhills and Joadja Roads, Berrima, NSW 2576 **REGION** Southern Highlands
T (02) 4878 5439 **F** (02) 4878 5133 **OPEN** Weekends and public holidays 10–5, or by appointment
WINEMAKER Sean O'Regan **EST.** 1995
PRODUCT RANGE ($13–20 CD) Semillon Chardonnay, Marsanne, Unwooded Chardonnay, Lightly Oaked Chardonnay, Deuce (Sweet), Rose, Merlot, Cabernet Merlot, Cabernet Sauvignon, Drunk Monk Fine Old Tawny Port.
SUMMARY Sue and John Rappell own the intriguingly-named winery, one of the many newcomers to the Southern Highlands region. He has planted 6.5 hectares to riesling, chardonnay, marsanne, pinot noir, cabernet sauvignon, merlot, shiraz and cabernet franc and the wines are made on-site except, one would imagine, for the fortified wines. The wines are sold by mail order and through the cellar door on weekends when open; many local restaurants also list the wines.

St Gregory's   NR

Bringalbert South Road, Bringalbert South via Apsley, Vic 3319 **REGION** Henty
T (03) 5586 5225 **OPEN** By appointment
WINEMAKER Gregory Flynn **EST.** 1983
PRODUCT RANGE ($17.50 CD) Port.
SUMMARY Unique port-only operation selling its limited production direct to enthusiasts (by mailing list).

St Hallett   ★★★★☆

St Hallett's Road, Tanunda, SA 5352 **REGION** Barossa Valley
T (08) 8563 7000 **F** (08) 8563 7001 **OPEN** 7 days 10–5
WINEMAKER Stuart Blackwell, Di Ferguson, Matt Gant **EST.** 1944 **CASES** 100 000
PRODUCT RANGE ($11–75 CD) Poacher's Blend, Eden Valley Riesling, Semillon Sauvignon Blanc, Blackwell Semillon, God's Block Semillon, Black (Sparkling Shiraz), Touriga Rose, Gamekeeper's Reserve, Faith Shiraz, Blackwell Shiraz, Old Block Shiraz, Third Century Shiraz, Sangiovese, Touriga Nacional, Cabernet Shiraz, Cabernet Sauvignon, Pedro Ximenez.
SUMMARY Nothing succeeds like success, St Hallett merged with Tatachilla to form Banksia Wines, which was then acquired by New Zealand's thirsty Lion Nathan. St Hallett understandably continues to ride the Shiraz fashion wave, but all its wines are honest and well-priced. Exports to the UK, the US, Canada, Hong Kong and Japan.

TTTTY **Eden Valley Riesling 2003** A crystal clear and clean bouquet, followed by classic regional lime and lemon juice flavours; fluid and even in the mouth, and a long, lingering finish, appropriately dry and crisp. **RATING** 93 **DRINK** 2010 $ 16.50
Gamekeeper's Reserve 2002 Medium-bodied; quite complex juicy berry flavours; spicy finish. **RATING** 91 **DRINK** 2008 $ 13.95
Faith Shiraz 2002 Juicy red and blackberry fruits, a touch of licorice, fine tannins. Plenty happening. **RATING** 90 **DRINK** 2012 $ 21.50
GST 2002 Juicy red cherry and berry flavours plus a touch of cinnamon; medium-bodied and seductive. A cleverly labelled blend of grenache, shiraz and touriga. **RATING** 90 **DRINK** Now $ 19.95

TTTT **Poacher's Blend 2003** Abundant fruit flavour, augmented by clever touch of residual sugar; a blend of semillon, riesling, colombard and sauvignon blanc. **RATING** 89 **DRINK** Now $ 13.95
Blackwell Shiraz 2000 Clean, fresh, fruit-forward cherry/raspberry; smooth and supple. Excellent given the vintage. **RATING** 89 **DRINK** 2008 $ 29.95
Old Block Shiraz 2000 A powerful mix of blackcurrant and blackberry is on the plus side; there seems to be a slight hint of meatiness on the down side. **RATING** 87 **DRINK** 2010 $ 54

TTTY **Eden Valley Chardonnay 2002** **RATING** 86 **DRINK** Now $ 25

St Huberts

Maroondah Highway, Coldstream, Vic 3770 **REGION** Yarra Valley
T (03) 9739 1118 **F** (03) 9739 1096 **OPEN** Mon–Fri 9–5, weekends 10.30–5.30
WINEMAKER Matt Steel **EST.** 1966 **CASES** 15 000
PRODUCT RANGE ($19.50–43 R) Sauvignon Blanc, Roussane, Chardonnay, Pinot Chardonnay, Pinot Noir, Cabernet Merlot, Cabernet Sauvignon, Reserve Cabernet Sauvignon.
SUMMARY A once famous wine (in the context of the Yarra Valley) which seems to have lost of its focus since the merger of Mildara with Blass, and now part of Beringer Blass. However, the wines are reliable, and the cellar door — if somewhat humble — is well situated.

TTTTY **Roussanne 2002** Remarkably aromatic orange blossom bouquet; crisp and clean, has length and balance. **RATING** 90 **DRINK** Now $ 26

TTTT **Pinot Noir 2002** Curiously light given the vintage, with nice texture and length, but lacking mid-palate flesh. **RATING** 88 **DRINK** 2009 $ 27

TTTY **Chardonnay 2002** **RATING** 86 **DRINK** Now $ 23

St Ignatius Vineyard

Sunraysia Highway, Avoca, Vic 3467 **REGION** Pyrenees
T (03) 5465 3542 **F** (03) 5465 3542 **OPEN** 7 days 10–5
WINEMAKER Enrique Diaz **EST.** 1992 **CASES** 1000
PRODUCT RANGE ($20–35 CD) Hangmans Gully Chardonnay, Shiraz, Cabernet Sauvignon.
SUMMARY Silvia and husband Enrique Diaz began the establishment of their vineyard, winery and restaurant complex in 1992. They have established shiraz (the major planting at 3.2 hectares), chardonnay (1.6 hectares), cabernet sauvignon (1 hectare) and sauvignon blanc (0.4 hectare) in bearing, with merlot (1.6 hectares) and sangiovese (0.2 hectare) planted coming into production. The vineyard has already received three primary production awards, and all of the wine is made on-site by Enrique Diaz. Exports to the UK.

St Leonards ★★★☆

Wahgunyah, Vic 3687 **REGION** Rutherglen
T (02) 6033 1004 **F** (02) 6033 3636 **OPEN** Mon–Fri 9–5, Sat 10–5
WINEMAKER Peter Brown, Dan Crane **EST.** 1860
PRODUCT RANGE ($12–45 CD) Semillon, Chenin Blanc, Sauvignon Blanc, Sauvignon Blanc Semillon, Chardonnay, Orange Muscat, Wahgunyah Brut, Sparkling Shiraz, Kalara Rose, Pinot Noir, Shiraz, Wahgunyah Shiraz, Cabernet Franc, Heritage Cabernet Sauvignon, Heritage Release Tawny Port, Classic Rutherglen Muscat.
SUMMARY An old favourite, relaunched in late 1997 with a range of three premium wines cleverly marketed through a singularly attractive cellar door and bistro at the historic winery on the banks of the Murray. All Saints and St Leonards are now wholly owned by Peter Brown; the vast majority of the wines are sold through the cellar door and by mailing list.

TTTTY **Wahgunyah Shiraz 1998** Spice/anise aromas; sweetly ripe blackberry, plum, spice and mocha; appealing tannins and oak. **RATING** 90 **DRINK** 2008 $ 24.50

TTTT **Pinot Noir 2003** Sweet plum and black cherry; supple and smooth; a major surprise, probably from the King Valley/Alpine regions. **RATING** 87 **DRINK** 2008 $ 16

TTTY **Orange Muscat 2003** **RATING** 86 **DRINK** Now $ 19.50
Wahgunyah Shiraz 2002 **RATING** 86 **DRINK** 2010 $ 24.50

St Mary's NR

V & A Lane, via Coonawarra, SA 5277 **REGION** Limestone Coast Zone
T (08) 8736 6070 **F** (08) 8736 6045 **OPEN** 7 days 10–4
WINEMAKER Barry Mulligan **EST.** 1986 **CASES** 4000
PRODUCT RANGE ($12–22 CD) Shiraz, Merlot, Cabernet Sauvignon.

SUMMARY The Mulligan family has lived in the Penola/Coonawarra region since 1909. In 1937 a 250-hectare property 15 kms to the west of Penola, including an 80-hectare ridge of terra rossa over limestone, was purchased for grazing. The ridge was cleared; the remainder of the property was untouched and is now a private wildlife sanctuary. In 1986 Barry & Glenys Mulligan planted shiraz and cabernet sauvignon on the ridge, followed by merlot in the early 1990s. The first wines were made in 1990, and national distribution began in 1992, followed by exports in 1996. It remains a wholly estate-based operation.

St Matthias ★★★

113 Rosevears Drive, Rosevears, Tas 7277 **REGION** Northern Tasmania
T (03) 6330 1700 **F** (03) 6330 1975 **OPEN** 7 days 10–5
WINEMAKER Michael Glover **EST.** 1983 **CASES** 16 000
PRODUCT RANGE ($19.50–25.50 CD) Riesling, Pinot Gris, Chardonnay, Brut, Pinot Noir, St Matthias (cabernet blend).
SUMMARY After an uncomfortable period in the wilderness following the sale of the vineyard to Moorilla Estate, and the disposal of the wine made by the previous owners under the St Matthias label, Moorilla has re-introduced the label, and markets a full range of competitively priced wines which are in fact made at Moorilla Estate.

ŸŸŸŸ **Vintage Brut 2001** Fresh, crisp lemony; lively, good length and balance; restrained style.
RATING 87 **DRINK** 2008 $ 22.50
Brut NV Pale straw-green; fresh, crisp lemony; lively, good length and balance; in restrained style. **RATING** 87 **DRINK** Now $ 24

ŸŸŸŸ **Riesling 2003** **RATING** 86 **DRINK** 2010 $ 19.50

ŸŸŸ **Pinot Gris 2003** **RATING** 82 $ 19.50

🐦 St Michael's Vineyard NR

Pook Road, Toolleen, Vic 3521 **REGION** Heathcote
T (03) 5433 2580 **F** (03) 5433 2612 **OPEN** By appointment
WINEMAKER Mick Cann **EST.** 1994 **CASES** 550
PRODUCT RANGE ($12.25–31.25 ML) Semillon, Shiraz, Merlot, Personal Reserve Cabernet Sauvignon.
SUMMARY Owner/winemaker Mick Cann has established 5 hectares of vines on the famous deep red Cambrian clay loam on the east face of the Mount Camel Range. Planting began in 1994, continued in 1995, with a further extension in 2000. Shiraz (3 hectares), merlot (1.5 hectares) and petit verdot (0.25 hectare) are the main varieties, with a smattering of cabernet sauvignon and semillon. Part of the production is sold to David Anderson of Wild Duck Creek, the remainder made by Mick Cann, using open fermentation, hand plunging of skins and a basket press, a low technology but highly effective way of making high quality red wine. Not surprisingly, the 'sold out' sign appears soon after the wines are released.

🐦 St Petrox NR

352 Luskintyre Road, Luskintyre, NSW 2321 **REGION** Lower Hunter Valley
T (02) 4930 6120 **F** (02) 4930 6070 **OPEN** Not
WINEMAKER Peter Jorgensen **EST.** 2000 **CASES** 3000
PRODUCT RANGE Durif Chambourcin, Durif Shiraz, Chambourcin Shiraz, Cabernet Sauvignon.
SUMMARY Peter Jorgensen has established 4 hectares of vines, choosing to plant two varieties ignored by all others in the Hunter Valley, mondeuse and durif. If recognised at all, most people will associate mondeuse with Brown Brothers and northeast Victoria, but it is a rarely propagated yet interesting red varietal.

Salem Bridge Wines NR

Salem Bridge Road, Lower Hermitage, SA 5131 **REGION** Adelaide Hills
T (08) 8380 5240 **F** (08) 8380 5240 **OPEN** Not
WINEMAKER Barry Miller **EST.** 1989 **CASES** 300
PRODUCT RANGE Cabernet Franc.

SUMMARY Barry Miller acquired the 45-hectare Salem Bridge property in the Adelaide Hills of South Australia in 1988. A little under 2 hectares of cabernet franc were planted in 1989, and cabernet franc has been the only commercial release prior to 1999. However, a further 14 hectares have been planted to cabernet sauvignon, shiraz and merlot, with a Shiraz and Cabernet Sauvignon release in the pipeline. The core business is contract growing, with only 10 per cent of the production vinified for the Salem Bridge label. The wine is made off site by contract-winemaking, with input from Barry Miller.

Salena Estate   NR

Bookpurnong Road, Loxton, SA 5343 **REGION** Riverland
T (08) 8584 1333 **F** (08) 8584 1388 **OPEN** Mon–Fri 8.30–5
WINEMAKER Grant Semmens **EST.** 1998 **CASES** 130 000
PRODUCT RANGE ($13–31 CD) At the bottom is the Salena Estate range of Chardonnay, Shiraz, Merlot, Cabernet Sauvignon; next is Ellen Landing Shiraz, Petit Verdot, Cabernet Sauvignon; at the top is the Bookpurnong Hill range of Shiraz, Block 267 (blend of Cabernet Sauvignon, Petit Verdot, Merlot, Shiraz), Cabernet Sauvignon; Amore Fortified Chardonnay.
SUMMARY This business, established in 1998, encapsulates the hectic rate of growth across the entire Australian wine industry. Its 1998 crush was 300 tonnes, and by 2001 it was processing 7000 tonnes. This was in part produced from over 200 hectares of estate vineyards, supplemented by grapes purchased from other growers. It is the venture of Bob and Sylvia Franchitto, the estate being named after their daughter Salena. Export distribution to the US, the UK, Sweden, Malaysia, Hong Kong and Singapore has already been established to supplement local distribution; it is the export market which will take the lion's share.

Salitage   ★★★☆

Vasse Highway, Pemberton, WA 6260 **REGION** Pemberton
T (08) 9776 1771 **F** (08) 9776 1772 **OPEN** 7 days 10–4
WINEMAKER Patrick Coutts, Greg Kelly **EST.** 1989 **CASES** 20 000
PRODUCT RANGE ($17–35 R) Sauvignon Blanc, Chardonnay, Unwooded Chardonnay, Pinot Noir, Pemberton (Cabernet blend); Treehouse range Sauvignon Blanc, Chardonnay Verdelho, Pinot Noir, Shiraz, Cabernet Merlot.
SUMMARY Salitage is the showpiece of Pemberton. If it had failed to live up to expectations, it is a fair bet the same fate would have befallen the whole of the Pemberton region. The quality and style of Salitage did vary substantially, presumably in response to vintage conditions and yields, but since 1999 seemed to have found its way, with a succession of attractive wines. Key retail distribution in all States, and exports to New Zealand, Singapore, Japan, Hong Kong, Malaysia, Germany, Switzerland, Canada, Denmark, Holland, the UK and the US.

ㅜㅜㅜㅜ **Unwooded Chardonnay 2003 RATING** 86 **DRINK** Now $ 16
        Pinot Noir 2002 RATING 84 **DRINK** Now $ 34

Salomon Estates   ★★★★

PO Box 621, McLaren Vale, SA 5171 **REGION** Langhorne Creek
T 0419 864 155 **F** (08) 8323 7726 **OPEN** Not
WINEMAKER Bert Salomon **EST.** 1997
PRODUCT RANGE ($16.50–35 ML) Finniss River Shiraz, Bin 4 Baan Shiraz Petit Verdot, Norwood Cabernet Shiraz, Finniss River Cabernet Merlot.
SUMMARY Bert Salomon is an Austrian winemaker with a long-established family winery in the Kremstal region, not far from Vienna. He became acquainted with Australia during his time as head of the Austrian Wine Bureau, and was so taken by Adelaide that he moved his family there for the first few months each year, sending his young children to school and setting in place an Australian red winemaking venture. He has now retired from the Bureau, and is a full-time travelling winemaker, running the family winery in the northern hemisphere vintage, and overseeing the making of the Salomon Estates wines at Boar's Rock in the first half of the year.

ㅜㅜㅜㅜㅜ **Finniss River Cabernet Merlot 2001** A supple, smooth basket of red and black fruits; again, fine, silky tannins; excellent balance. **RATING** 91 **DRINK** 2013 $ 24.50
        Finniss River Shiraz 2001 Good structure and complexity; blackberry, spice and dark chocolate; well-handled oak; silky tannins and extract. **RATING** 90 **DRINK** 2011 $ 35

▼▼▼▼ **Bin 4 Baan Shiraz Petit Verdot 2002** The structure is stiffened by Petit Verdot; red and black fruits from the Shiraz; well balanced and integrated; fine, long finish. **RATING** 88 **DRINK** 2012 $ 24.50

Norwood Cabernet Shiraz 2001 A subdued bouquet but plenty of sweet raspberry/blackcurrant/dark chocolate fruit on the palate; soft tannins. **RATING** 87 **DRINK** 2010 $ 16.50

Saltram ★★★★

Salters Gully, Nuriootpa, SA 5355 **REGION** Barossa Valley
T (08) 8564 3355 **F** (08) 8564 2209 **OPEN** 7 days 10–5
WINEMAKER Nigel Dolan **EST.** 1859
PRODUCT RANGE ($10–65 R) At the top is No. 1 Shiraz; then Mamre Brook, now 100 per cent Barossa and comprising Chardonnay, Shiraz and Cabernet Sauvignon; Metala Black Label and White Label; and the Saltram Classic range sourced from southeast Australia; also Pepperjack range with Shiraz and Cabernet Sauvignon.
SUMMARY There is no doubt that Saltram has taken giant strides towards regaining the reputation it held 30 or so years ago. Under Nigel Dolan's stewardship, grape sourcing has come back to the Barossa Valley for the flagship wines, a fact of which he is rightly proud. The red wines, in particular, have enjoyed great show success over the past few years, with No. 1 Shiraz, Mamre Brook and Metala leading the charge.

▼▼▼▼▼ **No. 1 Reserve Shiraz 1999** An alluring, Joseph's Coat rainbow of aromas, the palate sumptuously rich, layered and textured. Dark chocolate, dark fruits and ripe tannins ripple harmoniously through the supple palate and finish. **RATING** 96 **DRINK** 2019 $ 65

Mamre Brook Cabernet Sauvignon 2001 Firm but vibrant cassis and blackcurrant flecked with touches of earth and herb; long finish; surprise packet. **RATING** 94 **DRINK** 2011 $ 26

▼▼▼▼▽ **No. 1 Reserve Shiraz 2000** Less density than normal, reflecting the vintage; blackberry fruit with savoury overtones of spice, earth and licorice; balanced oak and tannins. **RATING** 90 **DRINK** 2010 $ 65

▼▼▼▼ **Barossa Shiraz 2002** Good balance and length, reflecting the good vintage; plenty of ripe black cherry/blackberry fruit; subtle oak. **RATING** 88 **DRINK** 2009 $ 16

Mamre Brook Shiraz 2001 Solid blackberry fruit; slightly dusty tannins; plenty of overall presence. **RATING** 88 **DRINK** 2011 $ 26

Pepperjack Barossa Shiraz 2001 Blackberry, black cherry and plum; good structure; lingering tannins and neat oak. **RATING** 88 **DRINK** 2011 $ 23

Pepperjack Grenache Rose 2003 Vivid colour; crisp, fresh, vibrant raspberry; good style and length. Cheeky price. **RATING** 87 **DRINK** Now $ 22

▼▼▼▽ **Pepperjack Barossa Grenache Shiraz Mourvedre 2001** Light to medium-bodied; nicely balanced array of spice, plum jam and raspberry; fine, soft tannins. **RATING** 86 **DRINK** Now $ 22

Barossa Semillon Sauvignon Blanc 2003 **RATING** 84 **DRINK** Now $ 16

Barossa Chardonnay 2003 **RATING** 84 **DRINK** Now $ 16

🍎 Samson Hill Estate ★★★☆

360 Eltham-Yarra Glen Road, Kangaroo Ground, Vic 3097 **REGION** Yarra Valley
T (03) 9712 0715 **F** (03) 9712 0815 **OPEN** Thurs–Sun 11–8, or by appointment
WINEMAKER Steven Sampson, Pago Sampson **EST.** 1997 **CASES** 3000
PRODUCT RANGE ($16–35 CD) Verdelho, Sweet Verdelho, Rose, Pinot Noir, Reserve Pinot Noir, Shiraz.
SUMMARY In a region noted for its spectacular scenery, Samson Hill Estate has been established by Steven and Pago Sampson on one of the most spectacular sites of all. At the very top of Kangaroo Ground, it looks to the city of Melbourne (with the buildings clearly visible) thence to Kinglake and the Dandenongs, and then all the way to Mount Macedon. They have planted 3 hectares of pinot noir, 2 of verdelho and 0.5 hectare of shiraz, the verdelho firmly aimed at the cellar-door market. The cellar door offers casual dining and catering for all functions.

ȲȲȲȲ **Reserve Pinot Noir 2001** Strong colour; complex dark plum, spice and forest aromas; a rich palate, masses of dark, ripe plummy fruit; strongly varietal; a pinot with attitude. **RATING** 92 **DRINK** 2008 $28

ȲȲȲȲ **Shiraz 2002 RATING** 86 **DRINK** 2007 $25
Verdelho 2002 RATING 84 **DRINK** Now $19
Sweet Verdelho 2002 RATING 84 **DRINK** Now $19

Sandalford   ★★★★★

West Swan Road, Caversham, WA 6055 **REGION** Swan Valley/Margaret River
T (08) 9374 9374 **F** (08) 9274 2154 **OPEN** 7 days 10–5
WINEMAKER Paul Boulden **EST.** 1840 **CASES** 100 000
PRODUCT RANGE ($12.99–29.95 R) Two ranges: the premium varietals under the Sandalford label sourced from the Margaret River, and the second label Element.
SUMMARY Some years ago the upgrading of the winery and the appointment of Paul Boulden as chief winemaker resulted in far greater consistency in quality, and the proper utilisation of the excellent vineyard resources of Sandalford in Margaret River and Mount Barker. Things have continued on an even keel since. Exports to the UK, Switzerland, the US, Japan, Singapore and Hong Kong among a total of 35 destinations.

ȲȲȲȲȲ **Margaret River Cabernet Sauvignon 2002** Flooded with cassis/blackcurrant fruit balanced by quality oak; ripe, but also long and elegant. Trophy winner. **RATING** 95 **DRINK** 2015 $29
Riesling 2003 Clean, floral lime aromas; juicy lemon and passionfruit flavours, long and almost succulent; totally delicious. Eighty-five per cent Mount Barker. **RATING** 94 **DRINK** 2010 $24.95

ȲȲȲȲȲ **Shiraz 2002** Ripe, full, deep and powerful blackberry fruit supported by fine but persistent tannins; equal parts Frankland and Margaret River. **RATING** 91 **DRINK** 2017 $29.95

ȲȲȲȲ **Semillon Sauvignon Blanc 2003** After a slow start, comes alive on the palate with gooseberry and lemon sherbet; good length. **RATING** 89 **DRINK** 2012 $21.95
Merlot 2002 Tangy, savoury, complex red berry and olive fruit; fine tannins. Ten per cent cabernet. **RATING** 88 **DRINK** 2015 $29.95
Semillon 2003 Soft barrel-ferment characters throughout; good length to the fruit, although the oak type is not convincing. **RATING** 87 **DRINK** 2008 $24.95
Element Merlot 2003 Attractive, fresh red fruits; neatly balanced; best of the Element range. **RATING** 87 **DRINK** 2008 $12.99
Cabernet Merlot 2002 Medium-bodied; savoury, earthy berry flavours; scores mainly on length and persistence of palate. **RATING** 87 **DRINK** 2010 $21.95
Cabernet Sauvignon 2002 Red berry and leaf aromas; the palate builds considerable strength, the tannins a touch abrasive. Demands time. **RATING** 87 **DRINK** 2015 $29.95
Element Late Harvest 2003 RATING 87 **DRINK** 2007 $12.99

ȲȲȲȲ **Element Shiraz Cabernet 2002 RATING** 85 **DRINK** 2007 $12.99

ȲȲȲ **Element Chardonnay 2003 RATING** 83 $12.99
Element Classic White 2003 RATING 82 $12.99

Sandalyn Wilderness Estate   NR

Wilderness Road, Rothbury, NSW 2321 **REGION** Lower Hunter Valley
T (02) 4930 7611 **F** (02) 4930 7611 **OPEN** 7 days 10–5
WINEMAKER Adrian Sheridan (Contract) **EST.** 1988 **CASES** 6000
PRODUCT RANGE ($16–25 CD) Semillon, Verdelho, Semillon Verdelho, Chardonnay, Semillon Late Harvest, Pinot Noir, Conservatory Shiraz, sparkling.
SUMMARY Sandra and Lindsay Whaling preside over the picturesque cellar-door building of Sandalyn on the evocatively named Wilderness Road, where you will find a one-hole golf range and views to the Wattagan, Brokenback and Molly Morgan ranges. The estate has 8.85 hectares of vineyards. Exports to Ireland.

Sand Hills Vineyard

NR

Sandhills Road, Forbes, NSW 2871 **REGION** Central Ranges Zone
T (02) 6852 1437 **F** (02) 6852 4401 **OPEN** Mon–Sat 9–5, Sun 12–5
WINEMAKER Jill Lindsay, John Saleh **EST.** 1920 **CASES** 400
PRODUCT RANGE ($10–17 CD) Banderra The White, Colombard Semillon, Classic Dry White, Chardonnay, Banderra The Red, Vat 1 Dry Red, Dry Red, Pinot Noir, Shiraz Cabernet, Cabernet Shiraz, Lucien Tawny Port, Oloroso Cream Sherry.
SUMMARY Having purchased Sand Hills from long-term owner Jacques Genet, the Saleh family has replanted the vineyard to appropriate varieties, with over 6 hectares of premium varieties having been established. Winemaking is carried out by Jill Lindsay of Woodonga Hill.

Sandhurst Ridge

 ★★★★★

156 Forest Drive, Marong, Vic 3515 **REGION** Bendigo
T (03) 5435 2534 **F** (03) 5435 2548 **OPEN** Wed–Mon 12–5, or by appointment
WINEMAKER Paul Greblo, George Greblo **EST.** 1990 **CASES** 2500
PRODUCT RANGE ($30–36 CD) Sauvignon Blanc, Chardonnay, Shiraz, Reserve Shiraz, Merlot, Cabernet Sauvignon.
SUMMARY The four Greblo brothers, with combined experience in business, agriculture, science and construction and development began the establishment of Sandhurst Ridge in 1990 with the planting of the first 2 hectares of shiraz and cabernet sauvignon. Those plantings have now been increased to over 6 hectares, principally cabernet and shiraz, but with small amounts of merlot, sauvignon blanc and chardonnay. The fully equipped winery was completed in 1996 with a cellar capacity of 400 barriques. The winery rating is given for its red wines. Exports to the US.

ŸŸŸŸŸ **Reserve Shiraz 2002** Intense, concentrated blackberry fruit runs through the length of the full-bodied palate; very good tannin and American oak balance and integration. **RATING** 94 **DRINK** 2017 $ 36
Cabernet Sauvignon 2002 Ripe, opulent blackcurrant and cassis; good handling of French oak; ripe tannins, lingering finish. **RATING** 94 **DRINK** 2017 $ 30

ŸŸŸŸŸ **Shiraz 2002** Sweet, rich blackberry fruit and integrated vanillin oak; multi-layered flavours; good tannins. **RATING** 93 **DRINK** 2015 $ 30

ŸŸŸŸ **Fringe Shiraz 2002** Quite savoury and spicy red and black fruits; medium-bodied; well-handled oak and extract. Grapes from neighbouring growers. **RATING** 89 **DRINK** 2010 $ 30

ŸŸŸŸ **Merlot 2002 RATING** 86 **DRINK** 2008 $ 30

Sandstone

 ★★★☆

Cnr Johnson and Caves Road, Wilyabrup, WA 6280 **REGION** Margaret River
T (08) 9755 6271 **F** (08) 9755 6292 **OPEN** 7 days 11–4
WINEMAKER Mike Davies, Jan Davies **EST.** 1988 **CASES** 4000
PRODUCT RANGE ($12.50–31.50 CD) Semillon, Spindrift Semillon Sauvignon Blanc, Cabernet Sauvignon, Spindrift Cabernet Sauvignon.
SUMMARY The family operation of consultant-winemakers Mike and Jan Davies, who also operate very successful mobile bottling plants. It will eventually be estate-based following the planting of 9 hectares (semillon and cabernet sauvignon).

ŸŸŸŸŸ **Cabernet Sauvignon 1999** Abundant blackcurrant fruit aromas and flavours; excellent oak handling; balanced tannins. **RATING** 94 **DRINK** 2014 $ 31.50

ŸŸŸŸ **Semillon 2002** Rich, full-bodied and powerful; developed notwithstanding screwcap; toasty/nutty notes; food style. **RATING** 87 **DRINK** Now $ 19.50

ŸŸŸŸ **Cabernet Sauvignon 2000 RATING** 85 **DRINK** 2009 $ 31.50

Sandy Farm Vineyard   NR

RMB 3734 Sandy Farm Road, Denver via Daylesford, Vic 3641 **REGION** Macedon Ranges
T (03) 5348 7610 **OPEN** Weekends 10–5, or by appointment
WINEMAKER Peter Comisel **EST.** 1988 **CASES** 800
PRODUCT RANGE ($19–28 CD) Preservative Free Pinot Noir and Cabernet Merlot.
SUMMARY Peter Comisel and Dot Hollow have acquired Sandy Farm from founder Peter Covell.
There are 1.5 hectares of cabernet sauvignon, cabernet franc, merlot and 0.5 hectare of pinot noir,
with a small, basic winery in which they make preservative-free Cabernet Sauvignon, Merlot and
Pinot Noir, attracting a loyal local following.

Sanguine Estate   ★★★★☆

77 Shurans Lane, Heathcote, Vic 3523 (postal) **REGION** Heathcote
T (03) 9646 6661 **F** (03) 9646 1746 **OPEN** Not
WINEMAKER Mark Hunter, Peter Dredge (Contract) **EST.** 1997 **CASES** 450
PRODUCT RANGE ($40 R) Heathcote Shiraz.
SUMMARY The Hunter family, with parents Linda and Tony at the head, and their two children, Mark
and Jodi with their respective partners Melissa and Brett, began the establishment of the vineyard in
1997. From a starting base of 4 hectares of shiraz planted that year, it has now grown to 13.4 hectares
of shiraz, and 2 hectares of eight different varieties including chardonnay, viognier, merlot,
tempranillo, zinfandel, petit verdot, cabernet sauvignon, merlot and cabernet franc. Yet another
planting (in the spring of 2002) added another 7.3 hectares of shiraz. Low-yielding vines and the
magic of the Heathcote region have produced Shiraz of exceptional intensity, which as received rave
reviews in the US, and led to the 'sold out' sign being posted almost immediately upon release. With
the ever-expanding vineyard, Mark Hunter has become full-time vigneron, and Jodi Marsh part-
time marketer and business developer. For the foreseeable future the wines will continue to be
contract-made. Exports to the US.

TTTTT **Heathcote Shiraz 2002** Densely coloured; archetypal Heathcote, ultra-rich and plush;
blackberry, plum, licorice and ripe tannins; heroic style needing patience. **RATING** 90
DRINK 2017 $40

Saracen Estates   ★★★☆

Caves Road, Wilyabrup, WA 6280 **REGION** Margaret River
T (08) 9221 4955 **F** (08) 9221 4966 **OPEN** By appointment
WINEMAKER Bill Crappsley **EST.** 1998 **CASES** 30 000
PRODUCT RANGE ($16–25 R) Sauvignon Blanc, Classic Dry White, Chardonnay, Classic Dry Red,
Shiraz, Cabernet Sauvignon; budget-priced Emu Springs range of Chardonnay, Shiraz and Cabernet
Sauvignon.
SUMMARY The Cazzolli and Saraceni families have established 40 hectares of vines on their
80-hectare property at Metricup, with a restaurant and cellar door planned. The name not only
echoes one of the founding families, but also pays tribute to the Saracens, one of the most advanced
races in cultural and social terms at the time of the Crusades. The business has lost no time in
securing eastern States distribution, with exports to the UK, Singapore, Malaysia, Hong Kong, India
and Europe.

Sarsfield Estate   ★★★☆

345 Duncan Road, Sarsfield, Vic 3875 **REGION** Gippsland
T (03) 5156 8962 **F** (03) 5156 8970 **OPEN** By appointment
WINEMAKER Dr Suzanne Rutschmann **EST.** 1995 **CASES** 1000
PRODUCT RANGE ($18.50–22 CD) Pinot Noir, Cabernets Shiraz Merlot.
SUMMARY The property is owned by Suzanne Rutschmann, who has a PhD in Chemistry, a Diploma
in Horticulture and and a BSc (Wine Science) from Charles Sturt University, and by Swiss-born Peter
Albrecht, a civil and structural engineer who has also undertaken various courses in agriculture and
viticulture. For a part-time occupation, these are exceptionally impressive credentials. Their
2-hectare vineyard was planted between 1991 and 1998; the first vintage made at the winery was
1998, the grapes being sold to others in previous years. High quality packaging a plus.

ΤΤΤΤ **Pinot Noir 2002** Perceptively light savoury/foresty style; spicy flavours and good length. **RATING** 87 **DRINK** 2007 $ 18.50

ΤΤΤΥ **Cabernets Shiraz Merlot 2002** **RATING** 86 **DRINK** 2007 $ 18.50

Savaterre NR

PO Box 337, Beechworth, Vic 3747 **REGION** Beechworth
T (03) 5727 0551 **F** (03) 5727 0551 **OPEN** Not
WINEMAKER Keppell Smith **EST.** 1996
PRODUCT RANGE Chardonnay, QED Pinot Noir, Pinot Noir.
SUMMARY Keppell Smith embarked on a career in wine in 1996, studying winemaking at Charles Sturt University and (at a practical level) with Phillip Jones at Bass Phillip. He purchased the 40-hectare property on which Savaterre has been established at a height of 440 metres, and has close planted (7500 vines per hectare) 1 hectare each of chardonnay and pinot noir. Organic principles govern the viticulture, and the winemaking techniques look to the old world rather than the new. Smith's stated aim is to produce outstanding, individualistic wines far removed from the mainstream. Details of restaurants offering Savaterre are on the website <www.savaterre.com>.

Scarborough

Gillards Road, Pokolbin, NSW 2321 **REGION** Lower Hunter Valley
T (02) 4998 7563 **F** (02) 4998 7786 **OPEN** 7 days 9–5
WINEMAKER Ian Scarborough **EST.** 1985 **CASES** 14 000
PRODUCT RANGE ($19–25 CD) Semillon, Semillon Sauvignon Blanc, Chardonnay (Blue Label), Chardonnay (Traditional), Pinot Noir.
SUMMARY Ian Scarborough put his white winemaking skills beyond doubt during his years as a consultant, and has brought all of those skills to his own label. He makes two radically different styles of Chardonnay, the Blue Silver Label in a light, elegant, Chablis style for the export market and a much richer, strongly barrel-fermented wine (with a mustard/gold label) for the Australian market. However, the real excitement lies with the future and the portion of the old Lindemans Sunshine Vineyard which he has purchased (after it lay fallow for 30 years) and planted with semillon and (quixotically) pinot noir. The first vintage from the legendary Sunshine Vineyard was made in 2004; in the meantime, Ian Scarborough has kept his hand in with contract-grown semillon. Exports to the UK, the US, South-East Asia and Japan.

ΤΤΤΤΥ **Blue Label Chardonnay 2002** Elegant and aromatic; melon and a touch of citrus; shows Hunter Chardonnay at its best. Screwcap. **RATING** 93 **DRINK** 2007 $ 19
Shiraz 2002 Beautifully weighted and balanced; seductive plum, cherry and raspberry fruit; fine tannins on the finish. Screwcap. **RATING** 93 **DRINK** 2012 $ 25
Semillon Sauvignon Blanc 2003 Works very well indeed; driven by Semillon, the Sauvignon Blanc adding impact; interesting wine. **RATING** 91 **DRINK** 2008 $ 18
Semillon 2003 Powerful wine; lots of depth of fruit, reflecting the higher than average 12.5 degrees alcohol. Screwcap, but no need to wait. **RATING** 90 **DRINK** 2007 $ 19

ΤΤΤΤ **Traditional Chardonnay 2001** Bright green-gold; rich and quite developed, notwithstanding the screwcap; yellow peach fruit; higher alcohol. **RATING** 89 **DRINK** Now $ 21

ΤΤΤΥ **Pinot Noir 2001** **RATING** 86 **DRINK** 2007 $ 21

Scarpantoni Estate

Scarpantoni Drive, McLaren Flat, SA 5171 **REGION** McLaren Vale
T (08) 8383 0186 **F** (08) 8383 0490 **OPEN** Mon–Fri 9–5, weekends & public holidays 11–5
WINEMAKER Michael Scarpantoni, Filippo Scarpantoni **EST.** 1979 **CASES** 30 000
PRODUCT RANGE ($6–36 CD) Block 1 Riesling, Sauvignon Blanc, Unwooded Chardonnay, Chardonnay, Cellared Release Chardonnay, Fleurieu Brut, Black Tempest (sparkling), Botrytis Riesling, Fiori, Ceres (Rose), School Block (Shiraz Cabernet Merlot), Block 3 Shiraz, Showcroft (Shiraz Grenache Gamay), Blue Tongue Cabernet Sauvignon, Estate Reserve, Tawny Port, Vintage Port, V.P. Shiraz.

SUMMARY With 20 hectares of shiraz, 11 hectares of cabernet sauvignon, 3 hectares each of chardonnay and sauvignon blanc, 1 hectare each of merlot and gamay, and 0.5 hectare of petit verdot, Scarpantoni has come a long way since Domenico Scarpantoni purchased his first property of 5.6 hectares in 1958. At that time he was working for Thomas Hardy at its Tintara winery, and subsequently became vineyard manager for Seaview Wines, responsible for the contoured vineyards which were leading edge viticulture in the 1960s. In 1979 his two sons, Michael and Filippo, built the winery, which has now been extended to the point where all of the grapes from the estate plantings are used to make wine under the Scarpantoni label. As the vines have matured, quality has gone from strength to strength, with distribution in all States and exports to the US, the UK, Switzerland, The Netherlands, Germany and New Zealand.

ттттт **Reserve Shiraz Cabernet Sauvignon 2001** Smooth, supple blackberry and raspberry; fine-grained tannins; well-integrated new oak. Stylish wine. **RATING** 92 **DRINK** 2016 $ 36
Blanche Point Maslin Beach Vineyard 2001 Elegant, gently undulating red fruits drive the palate; very good mouthfeel and ripeness. **RATING** 92 **DRINK** 2011 $ 25
Block 3 Shiraz 2002 Intense, essencey, concentrated, saturated black fruits and dark chocolate; very typical of the vintage. **RATING** 91 **DRINK** 2017 $ 22

тттт **Ceres Rose 2003** Highly aromatic; very clever use of CO_2, spritz, residual sugar and balancing acidity. **RATING** 89 **DRINK** Now $ 14
Peddler Creek Shiraz 2002 Extraordinary, inky purple; massively concentrated, with lots of regional dark chocolate; inevitably somewhat extractive, but a massive bang for the dollar. **RATING** 89 **DRINK** 2012 $ 15
Cabernet Sauvignon 2002 Very ripe blackcurrant, chocolate and prune mix backed by ripe tannins and subtle oak. **RATING** 89 **DRINK** 2012 $ 22
School Block 2002 Fresh and lively berry, earth, spice and mint; fruit-driven style. **RATING** 87 **DRINK** 2008 $ 15
Black Tempest NV Strong licorice and dark chocolate aromas and flavours; mercifully not too sweet, the Achilles heel of many sparkling shirazs. **RATING** 87 **DRINK** 2010 $ 28

ттттт **Sauvignon Blanc 2003** **RATING** 85 **DRINK** Now $ 18
Unwooded Chardonnay 2003 **RATING** 84 **DRINK** Now $ 14

Scarp Valley Vineyard   NR

6 Robertson Road, Gooseberry Hill, WA 6076 **REGION** Perth Hills
T (08) 9454 5748 **OPEN** By appointment
WINEMAKER Contract **EST.** 1978 **CASES** 25
PRODUCT RANGE ($20 ML) Darling Range Hermitage.
SUMMARY Owner Robert Duncan presides over what has to be one of the smallest producers in Australia, with 0.25 acre of shiraz and 30 cabernet sauvignon vines producing a single cask of wine each year if the birds do not get the grapes first.

Schild Estate Wines   ★★★★

Cnr Barossa Valley Way and Lyndoch Valley Road, Lyndoch, SA 5351 **REGION** Barossa Valley
T (08) 8524 5560 **F** (08) 8524 4333 **OPEN** 7 days 10–5
WINEMAKER Daniel Eggleton, Contract **EST.** 1998 **CASES** 10 000
PRODUCT RANGE ($14–30 CD) Barossa Riesling, Eden Valley Riesling, Semillon, Semillon Sauvignon Blanc, Frontignac, Chardonnay, Shiraz, Merlot, Cabernet Sauvignon.
SUMMARY Ed Schild has been a Barossa Valley grape grower who first planted a small vineyard at Rowland Flat in 1952, steadily increasing his vineyard holdings over the past 50 years to their present level of 157 hectares. Currently only 10 per cent of the production from these vineyards (now managed by son Michael Schild) are used to produce Schild Estate Wines, but the plans are to steadily increase this percentage. The flagship wine will be made from 150-year-old shiraz vines on the Moorooroo Block. The cellar-door sales is situated in what was the ANZ Bank at Lyndoch, and provides the sort of ambience which can only be found in the Barossa Valley. Exports to Malaysia, Belgium, Germany, the UK, the US and Canada.

ттттт **Shiraz 2002** Deep, dense colour; typical of vintage, redolent with dark fruits and chocolate; supple, ripe tannins and nice oak. **RATING** 94 **DRINK** 2017 $ 24

YYYYY **Cabernet Sauvignon 2002** Complex blackcurrant, mint and blackberry fruit with savoury nuances; fine texture and structure. RATING 90 DRINK 2012 $ 24

YYYY **Barossa Valley Riesling 2003** Mainstream style, but flowers on the back palate and finish. RATING 89 DRINK 2007 $ 15
Limited Release Shiraz 2001 Savoury/earthy/chocolatey overtones; some spice and cedar; fine tannin structure. RATING 89 DRINK 2011 $ 30
Merlot 2002 Densely coloured; powerful, savoury olive, forest and briar aromas and flavours. RATING 89 DRINK 2012 $ 24

YYYY **Frontignac 2003** RATING 86 DRINK Now $ 14
Chardonnay 2002 RATING 84 DRINK Now $ 15

Schindler Northway Downs ★★★★☆

437 Stumpy Gully Road, Balnarring, Vic 3926 REGION Mornington Peninsula
T (03) 5983 1945 F (03) 9580 4262 OPEN First weekend each month
WINEMAKER Tammy Schindler-Hands EST. 1996 CASES 250
PRODUCT RANGE ($18–25 CD) Chardonnay, Pinot Noir.
SUMMARY Establishment of the vineyard by the Schindler family began in 1996 with the planting of the first 2 hectares of pinot noir and chardonnay. A further 4 hectares of pinot noir were planted on an ideal north-facing slope in 1999, and the first vintage followed in 2000. The cellar door was subsequently established, and opens on the first weekend of each month, offering Austrian food and live Austrian music on the Sunday.

YYYYY **Pinot Noir 2002** Shows all the concentration and power of the tiny yield of 2002; exotically and deliciously ripe; long finish. RATING 93 DRINK 2009 $ 25

🐾 Schubert Estate ★★★★★

Roennfeldt Road, Marananga, SA 5355 REGION Barossa Valley
T (08) 8562 3375 F (08) 8562 4338 OPEN By appointment
WINEMAKER Steve Schubert, Cecilia Schubert EST. 2000 CASES 100
PRODUCT RANGE ($38 ML) Goose Yard Block Shiraz.
SUMMARY Steve and Cecilia Schubert are primarily grapegrowers, with 14 hectares of shiraz and little over 1 hectare of semillon, and almost all the production is sold to Torbreck Vintners. They purchased the 25-hectare property from a relative in 1986, when it was in such a derelict state that there was no point in trying to save the old vines. Moreover, both were working in other areas, and it was some years before they began replanting at a little under 2 hectares per year. In 2000 they decided to keep enough grapes to make a barrique of wine for their own (and friends) consumption, and were sufficiently encouraged by the outcome to obtain the necessary licence and venture into the dizzy heights of two hogsheads a year. The wine is made on-site, with wild yeast, open fermentation, basket pressing and bottling without filtration. The 2002 wine is utterly exceptional; the challenge will be to keep the quality in the years ahead.

YYYYY **Goose Yard Block Shiraz 2002** Impenetrable colour; extraordinarily concentrated black fruits, dark chocolate, mocha and spice; almost viscous in texture, yet not extractive. Only 14 degrees alcohol. RATING 96 DRINK 2027 $ 38

Scorpo Wines ★★★★★

23 Old Bittern-Dromana Road, Merricks North, Vic 3926 REGION Mornington Peninsula
T (03) 5989 7697 F (03) 9813 3371 OPEN By appointment
WINEMAKER Paul Scorpo, Sandro Mosele EST. 1997 CASES 2000
PRODUCT RANGE ($28–36 CD) Pinot Gris, Chardonnay, Pinot Noir, Shiraz.
SUMMARY Paul Scorpo has a 25-year background as a horticulturist and landscape architect involved in major projects varying from private gardens to golf courses in Australia, Europe and South-East Asia. His wife Caroline and daughters Emma, Sarah and Clare, have a common love for food, wine and gardens, all of which led to the family buying a derelict apple and cherry orchard (originally planted in the early 1900s) on gentle rolling hills halfway between Port Phillip and Westernport Bay. It is part of a ridge system which climbs up to Red Hill, and offers north and

northeast facing slopes on red-brown, clay loam soils. Here they have established 2 hectares of pinot noir, 1.25 hectares of chardonnay, 0.75 hectare of pinot gris and 0.5 hectare of shiraz. The wines are made by Paul Scorpo and Sandro Mosele at Kooyong, and were first released in 2002. A cellar door, forming part of the original house on the property, is planned, with extensive ocean views from each side.

ŸŸŸŸŸ Pinot Noir 2002 Amazing, youthful purple; powerful and dense, but not extractive; plummy fruit; will be long-lived. **RATING** 94 **DRINK** 2015 $ 36

ŸŸŸŸŸ Chardonnay 2002 Complex aromas lead into an ultra-rich, concentrated sweet peach palate; crammed with character. **RATING** 92 **DRINK** 2007 $ 33

ŸŸŸŸ Pinot Gris 2003 Filled out by 14 degrees alcohol; definitely gris not grigio; quite soft, some lychee and musk. **RATING** 88 **DRINK** Now $ 28

Scotchmans Hill   ★★★★★

190 Scotchmans Road, Drysdale, Vic 3222 **REGION** Geelong
T (03) 5251 3176 **F** (03) 5253 1743 **OPEN** 7 days 10.30–5.30
WINEMAKER Robin Brockett **EST.** 1982 **CASES** 50 000
PRODUCT RANGE ($16.50–75 CD) Riesling, Sauvignon Blanc, Chardonnay, Sutton Vineyard Chardonnay, Pinot Noir, Norfolk Pinot Noir, Shiraz, Cabernet Sauvignon Merlot; Swan Bay range of Sauvignon Blanc Semillon, Chardonnay, Pinot Noir, Shiraz; The Hill range of Chardonnay Sauvignon Blanc, Cabernet Sauvignon.
SUMMARY Situated on the Bellarine Peninsula, southeast of Geelong, with a well-equipped winery and first class vineyards. It is a consistent performer with its Pinot Noir and has a strong following in both Melbourne and Sydney for its astutely priced, competently made wines. A doubling in production has seen the establishment of export markets to the UK, Holland, Switzerland, Hong Kong and Singapore. The second label of Spray Farm takes its name from a National Trust property with panoramic views of Port Phillip Bay and Melbourne, which has also been planted to vines by the Brown family and is run as a distinct vineyard and brand operation. The same four varieties are produced but at a lower price point across the range.

ŸŸŸŸŸ Chardonnay 2002 Complex barrel ferment/malolactic inputs; intense, tangy nectarine and grapefruit; fruit-driven, the oak eaten up. **RATING** 94 **DRINK** 2012 $ 28.50

ŸŸŸŸŸ Norfolk Vineyard Pinot Noir 2001 Spicy, savoury, foresty aromas; the flavours build and intensify through to a long finish and aftertaste. **RATING** 93 **DRINK** 2011 $ 73
Chardonnay 2001 Stylish, tangy, citrussy fruit; medium-bodied; good length and oak handling. **RATING** 91 **DRINK** Now $ 28.50
Pinot Noir 2002 Mint, strawberry and cherry make appealing fruit on entry to the mouth; tannin structure provides length to the finish. **RATING** 91 **DRINK** 2009 $ 29
Sutton Vineyard Chardonnay 2001 Oak and barrel ferment influences very evident; melon and cashew flavours; well balanced. **RATING** 90 **DRINK** 2010 $ 73
Shiraz 2002 Herbs, spices, licorice and red fruits; satiny tannins; crisp acidity. **RATING** 90 **DRINK** 2012 $ 29.50
Shiraz 2001 Very complex Côte Rôtie lookalike; black fruits, spice and game; sure to raise argument about brett. **RATING** 90 **DRINK** 2009 $ 29.50

ŸŸŸŸ Sauvignon Blanc 2003 Spicy, faintly cosmetic aromas; clean, crisp, citrussy; picks up pace on lingering finish. **RATING** 89 **DRINK** Now $ 23
Swan Bay Pinot Noir 2002 Spicy, tangy, foresty and lively; good line, length and positive varietal character. Shows the great vintage. **RATING** 89 **DRINK** Now $ 20
Swan Bay Sauvignon Blanc Semillon 2003 Mineral, herb and grass; good length and finish. **RATING** 87 **DRINK** Now $ 18.50
Swan Bay Pinot Noir 2003 Vividly coloured; very ripe black cherry fruit; plenty of flavour, but short finish. **RATING** 87 **DRINK** Now $ 20

ŸŸŸŸ Swan Bay Chardonnay 2003 **RATING** 86 **DRINK** 2007 $ 16.50
Swan Bay Sauvignon Blanc 2003 **RATING** 84 **DRINK** Now $ 17.50

Scotts Brook NR

Scotts Brook Road, Boyup Brook, WA 6244 **REGION** Blackwood Valley
T (08) 9765 3014 **F** (08) 9765 3015 **OPEN** Weekends, school holidays 10–5, or by appointment
WINEMAKER Contract **EST.** 1987 **CASES** 1000
PRODUCT RANGE ($10–20 CD) Riesling, Chardonnay, Cabernet Sauvignon.
SUMMARY The Scotts Brook winery at Boyup Brook (equidistant between the Margaret River and Great Southern regions) has been developed by local schoolteachers Brian Walker and wife Kerry — hence the opening hours during school holidays. There are 17 hectares of vineyards, but the majority of the production is sold to other winemakers, with limited quantities being made by contract.

Scotts Hill Vineyard NR

280 Lillicur Road, Amherst, Vic 3371 (postal) **REGION** Pyrenees
T (03) 5463 2468 **OPEN** Not
WINEMAKER Lester Scott, Pamela Scott **EST.** 2000
PRODUCT RANGE Pinot Noir, Shiraz, Bordeaux blends.
SUMMARY Lester and Pamela Scott have established 3 hectares of pinot noir, cabernet sauvignon, merlot, shiraz, cabernet franc and petit verdot at Amherst. They make the wine on-site, but are yet to establish a distribution system.

Scrubby Creek Wines NR

566 Crystal Creek Road, Alexandra, Vic 3714 **REGION** Upper Goulburn
T (03) 5772 2191 **F** (03) 5772 1048 **OPEN** 7 days 9–5
WINEMAKER MasterWineMakers (Contract) **EST.** 1995 **CASES** 400
PRODUCT RANGE ($22–30 CD) Chardonnay, Cabernet Sauvignon.
SUMMARY The Stastra and Napier families are next door neighbours, who have jointly planted 3.5 hectares of chardonnay, the wines being made by MasterWineMakers. As well as the cellar door and mail order sales route, the wines are exported to the UK and the US.

Seashell Wines NR

Ammon Road, Balingup, WA 6253 (postal) **REGION** Blackwood Valley
T (08) 9307 1469 **F** (08) 9307 1469 **OPEN** Not
WINEMAKER Stephen Bullied (Contract) **EST.** 1994 **CASES** 1500
PRODUCT RANGE ($13.50–16.50 ML) Semillon, Shiraz.
SUMMARY Dr Barry Wilson is a biologist and specialist of Australian marine shells and marine ecology, and a director of the Australian Wildlife Conservancy. He and his family planted the first 4 hectares of semillon and shiraz in 1993, subsequently extending the plantings to 6 hectares. Part of the proceeds of the sale of the wines is donated to various wildlife conservation activities, particularly the restoration of endangered species.

Sea Winds Vineyard NR

PO Box 511, Dromana, Vic 3936 **REGION** Mornington Peninsula
T (03) 5989 6204 **F** (03) 5989 6204 **OPEN** Not
WINEMAKER Kevin McCarthy (Contract) **EST.** 1990
PRODUCT RANGE Sauvignon Blanc, Chardonnay, Pinot Noir.
SUMMARY Douglas Schwebel has established 3 hectares of sauvignon blanc, chardonnay and pinot noir; the wines are contract-made, and sold by mail order.

Seldom Seen Vineyard

Cnr Gulgong and Hill End Roads, Mudgee, NSW 2850 **REGION** Mudgee
T (02) 6372 0839 **F** (02) 6372 2806 **OPEN** 7 days 9.30–5
WINEMAKER Barry Platt, Marcus Platt **EST.** 1987 **CASES** 3000

PRODUCT RANGE ($10–19 CD) Traminer, Unwooded Semillon, Semillon, Chardonnay Semillon, Unwooded Chardonnay, Chardonnay, Autumn Harvest (dessert), Cabernet Sauvignon Shiraz, Liqueur Muscat.

SUMMARY A substantial grape grower (with 18 hectares of vineyards) which reserves a proportion of its crop for making and release under its own label.

Seppelt ★★★★★

1 Seppeltsfield Road, Seppeltsfield via Nuriootpa, SA 5355 **REGION** Barossa Valley
T (08) 8568 6217 **F** (08) 8562 8333 **OPEN** Mon–Fri 10–5, weekends and public holidays 11–5
WINEMAKER James Godfrey **EST.** 1851
PRODUCT RANGE ($10–1050 CD) The great wines of Seppeltsfield are first and foremost Para Liqueur, Para Liqueur 21 year old, Vintage Tawny, Show Tawny Port DP90, Rutherglen Show Muscat, Rutherglen Show Tokay, Trafford DP30, Seppeltsfield Fino Sherry, Show Amontillado DP116, Show Fino DP117, Show Oloroso DP38, Seppelt Show Vintage Shiraz, Dorrien Cabernet Sauvignon. The 100 Year Old Para Liqueur Port is the $1050 a bottle (750 ml) jewel in the crown, the current vintage being the 1904.

SUMMARY A multi-million-dollar expansion and renovation program has seen the historic Seppeltsfield winery become the production centre for the Seppelt fortified and South Australian table wines, adding another dimension to what was already the most historic and beautiful major winery in Australia. It is now home to some of the world's unique fortified wines, nurtured and protected by the passionate James Godfrey. Worldwide distribution.

ŸŸŸŸŸ **100 Year Old Para Liqueur 1904** Impenetrable olive-brown; a deep, concentrated bouquet with wood, earth, briar and chocolate aromas intermingling. The palate is tremendously rich and chewy with dark chocolate, toffee and plum pudding flavours, followed by that omnipresent (and very necessary) acidity on the finish. **RATING** 97 **DRINK** Now $ 1050

Show Tawny Port DP90 NV Spice, butterscotch and more nutty characters, but it is the length of flavour and finish which is absolutely remarkable. Given its age, arguably the most undervalued wine on the Australian market today. **RATING** 97 **DRINK** Now

Rare Rutherglen Tokay DP59 NV Scented spice, toffee, caramel and tea leaf aromas intermingle with pronounced rancio. The super-elegant, intense, and long palate has a refined and controlled complexity, the flavours peeling off like layers of onion skin. Between 1990 and 2002 received 4 trophies and 48 gold medals in Australian wine shows. **RATING** 97 **DRINK** Now $ 65

Rare Rutherglen Muscat GR113 NV Deep mahogany-brown; olive rim; a mix of almond, smoke, spice, rose petal and raisin; a Joseph's coat of flavours; wonderful life and style, the finish lasting forever. **RATING** 96 **DRINK** Now $ 65

Show Oloroso Sherry DP38 NV Nutty rancio complexity, with just a hint of sweetness; finely balanced with a constant interplay between nutty, honeyed sweetness and drier, rancio characters. **RATING** 95 **DRINK** Now

Amontillado Sherry DP116 NV Enticing richness with brandysnap/biscuit aromas; great balance, with some sweetness on the mid-palate, then a long, dry, fresh finish. **RATING** 94 **DRINK** Now $ 19.95

Para Liqueur Port NV Complex, and richer and sweeter than DP90 with malt, butterscotch and strong rancio characters; complex structure and great power, yet paradoxically has an almost dry finish, and no biscuity aftertaste. **RATING** 94 **DRINK** Now

Grand Rutherglen Tokay DP57 NV Extremely fine aromas, with piercing complexity coupled with elegance, rancio running through the amalgam of tea leaf and honey; silky smooth yet textured toffee, honey, butterscotch and a whisper of tea leaf. Great length and balance **RATING** 94 **DRINK** Now $ 26.95

Grand Rutherglen Muscat DP63 NV Glowing olive-brown; intense but very supple, with spicy plum pudding and caramel flavours; a fine and lingering finish. **RATING** 94 **DRINK** Now $ 26.95

ŸŸŸŸŸ **Show Fino Sherry DP117 NV** Bright green-yellow; clean, vibrant, rancio aromas with some dried lemon skin lead into a fresh, bright palate, so bone-dry it almost disappears, but leaves a lingering, haunting aftertaste. **RATING** 93 **DRINK** Now $ 19.95

Rutherglen Tokay DP37 NV Pale, bright golden-brown; rich, tea leaf, honey and malt aromas; the palate with more complex structure and weight than the other wines in its class. Serve fully chilled in summer and at cellar temperature in winter. **RATING** 90 **DRINK** Now $16.95

Rutherglen Muscat DP33 NV Bright tawny-gold; fresh, floral fruit aromatics with splashes of spice; clean spirit. Lively, grapey/raisiny fruit perfectly balanced by acidity and the thrust of the spirit. **RATING** 90 **DRINK** Now $16.95

Seppelt Great Western ★★★★★

Moyston Road, Great Western via Ararat, Vic 3377 **REGION** Grampians
T (03) 5361 2222 **F** (03) 5361 2200 **OPEN** 7 days 10–5
WINEMAKER Arthur O'Connor, Stephen Goodwin **EST.** 1865
PRODUCT RANGE ($12–58.90 CD) Chalambar Shiraz and Harpers Range Cabernet Sauvignon are the entry point; next up the Premium Selection of Chardonnay, Shiraz and Cabernet Sauvignon; thence to the Winemaker's Selection of Jaluka Chardonnay and St Peters Great Western Shiraz. Occasional special releases from Seppelt's Drumborg Vineyard and Great Western Riesling. Sparkling wines (from the bottom up) comprise Fleur de Lys; Original Sparkling Shiraz; Salinger and Show Sparkling Shiraz.
SUMMARY Australia's best-known producer of sparkling wine, always immaculate in its given price range but also producing excellent Great Western-sourced table wines, especially long-lived Shiraz and Australia's best Sparkling Shirazs. The glitzy ever-changing labels have rightly been consigned to the rubbish bin, with a return to the classic feel of the 1960s, and the product range significantly rationalised.

ΤΤΤΤΤ **Drumborg Riesling 2003** The intensely fragrant bouquet is at once steely yet flowery; the fine lime and mineral flavours build progressively through a gloriously long palate. **RATING** 97 **DRINK** 2018 $27.75

St Peters Shiraz 1999 Complex and opulent blackberry, spice, licorice and plum, velvety mouthfeel, fully ripe tannins and balanced oak. **RATING** 95 **DRINK** 2014 $52.40

ΤΤΤΤႳ **Jaluka Chardonnay 2002** Complex barrel ferment inputs on bouquet; refined, elegant and tight melon, cashew and fig flavours. **RATING** 91 **DRINK** 2007 $26.40

Marsanne Roussanne 2003 Pear, apple, stone fruit and spice aromas; an array of softly ripe fruits supported by delicate oak. From the Glenlofty Vineyard. **RATING** 91 **DRINK** 2007 $27.75

Victorian Premium Reserve Chardonnay 2003 Finely tuned and focused; crisp nectarine fruit and subtle oak; scores on length. Screwcap. **RATING** 90 **DRINK** 2007 $16.99

Victorian Premium Reserve Shiraz 2002 Elegant, medium-bodied, fruit-driven style; a mix of blackberry, redcurrant, pepper and spice; fresh finish. **RATING** 90 **DRINK** 2010 $16.99

Victorian Premium Reserve Shiraz 2001 Big hitting style; lots of dark berry and dark chocolate fruit, and a touch of mint for good measure. **RATING** 90 **DRINK** 2011 $16.99

ΤΤΤΤ **Original Sparkling Shiraz 1999** Classic licorice, boot polish, blackberry and spice flavours; undoubtedly the best in its price range. **RATING** 89 **DRINK** 2009 $19.95

Fleur de Lys Chardonnay Pinot NV Spicy, nutty aromas, then a palate with abundant flavour and complexity, the slightly sweet dosage offset by pleasing acidity on the finish. **RATING** 88 **DRINK** Now $12.90

ΤΤΤႳ **Fleur de Lys Pinot Noir Chardonnay 2000** **RATING** 86 **DRINK** Now $12.90

Serafino Wines ★★★☆

McLarens on the Lake, Kangarilla Road, McLaren Vale, SA 5171 **REGION** McLaren Vale
T (08) 8323 0157 **F** (08) 8323 0158 **OPEN** Mon–Fri 10–5, weekends and public holidays 10–4.30
WINEMAKER Scott Rawlinson **EST.** 2000 **CASES** 17 000
PRODUCT RANGE ($12–20 CD) Serafino range of Semillon, Unwooded Chardonnay, Barrel Fermented Chardonnay, Shiraz, Cabernet Sauvignon; McLarens on the Lake range of Chardonnay, Reserve Chardonnay Pinot, Cabernet Shiraz Merlot, Old Tawny Port.

SUMMARY In wake of the sale of Maglieri Wines to Beringer Blass in 1998, Maglieri founder Steve Maglieri acquired the McLarens on the Lake complex which had originally been established by Andrew Garrett. The accommodation has been upgraded and a larger winery was commissioned prior to the 2002 vintage. The operation draws upon 40 hectares each of shiraz and cabernet sauvignon, 7 hectares of chardonnay, 2 hectares each of merlot, semillon, barbera, nebbiolo and sangiovese, and 1 hectare of grenache. Part of the grape production will be sold to others, the remainder to produce wines under the Serafino and McLarens on the Lake labels. Exports to the UK, the US, Asia, Italy and New Zealand.

TTTT **Shiraz 2001** Built in traditional, heroic style with lots of very big and ripe blackberry fruit accompanied by lashings of oak and heaps of tannins. RATING 89 DRINK 2016 $18

TTTT **McLaren Vale Barrel Fermented Chardonnay 2002** RATING 84 DRINK 2007

Serenella   ★★★☆

Lot 300 Hermitage Road, Pokolbin, NSW 2325 REGION Lower Hunter Valley
T (02) 4998 7992 F (02) 4998 7993 OPEN 7 days 9.30–5
WINEMAKER Letitia Cecchini EST. 1971 CASES 5000
PRODUCT RANGE ($18–25 CD) Estate range of Reserve Semillon, Reserve Verdelho, Reserve Chardonnay, Botrytis Semillon, Late Picked Verdelho, Liqueur Verdelho, Reserve Shiraz, Cabernet Sauvignon; Arlecchino Semillon, Arlecchino Rose.
SUMMARY The establishment date of 1971 is that of the original incarnation of Serenella, which is now James Estate. It was in that year that Giancarlo and Maria Cecchini, who had immigrated from Italy 21 years earlier established their first vineyard in the Upper Hunter. In 1997 the assets (but not the name) of Serenella Estate were sold, with a view to re-establishing the business in the Lower Hunter Valley. The following year they were able to buy a 43-hectare block of virgin land on Hermitage Road, Pokolbin, from Murray Tyrrell. The family lost no time in building a state-of-the-art winery, a restaurant (Arlecchino Trattoria), and a cellar-door sales and small function area, and planting 2.5 hectares of sangiovese. Daughter Tish Cecchini continues the senior winemaking role she had at the original Serenella Estate with help from assistant winemaker, Michael Hudson. The Serenella Estate range of wines are produced from Hunter Valley-grown grapes (the Semillon from a 40-year-old dryland vineyard) while the cheaper Arlecchino range is sourced variously from the Hunter Valley and Mudgee.

TTTT **Reserve Semillon 2003** Tight, some mineral on the bouquet; clean herb, lemon and mineral flavours; long finish, will build. RATING 90 DRINK 2013 $20
Reserve Botrytis Semillon 2002 Powerful, complex and intense fragrance; multi-flavoured range of preserved fruit; very luscious; needed a touch more acid. Riverina grapes. RATING 90 DRINK Now $25

TTTT **Reserve Shiraz 2002** RATING 86 DRINK 2008 $22
Verdelho 2003 RATING 84 DRINK Now $18

Serventy Organic Wines   ★★☆

Valley Home Vineyard, Rocky Road, Forest Grove, WA 6286 REGION Margaret River
T (08) 9757 7534 F (08) 9757 7534 OPEN Fri–Sun, holidays 10–4
WINEMAKER Frank Kittler EST. 1984 CASES 650
PRODUCT RANGE ($22–28 CD) Chardonnay, Solstice Rose, Pinot Noir, Shiraz.
SUMMARY Peter Serventy is nephew of the famous naturalist Vincent Serventy and son of ornithologist Dominic Serventy. It is hardly surprising, then, that Serventy should practise strict organic viticulture, using neither herbicides nor pesticides. The wines, too, are made with a minimum of sulphur dioxide, added late in the piece and never exceeding 30 parts per million.

Setanta Wines   ★★★★★

RSD 43 Williamstown Road, Forreston, SA 5233 (postal) REGION Adelaide Hills
T (08) 8380 5516 F (08) 8380 5516 OPEN Not
WINEMAKER Rod Chapman, Rebecca Wilson EST. 1997 CASES 1800
PRODUCT RANGE ($18–24 R) Speckled House Riesling, Emer Chardonnay, Cuchulain Shiraz, Black Sanglain Cabernet Sauvignon.

SUMMARY Setanta is a family-owned operation involving Sheilagh Sullivan, her husband Tony and brother Bernard; the latter is the viticulturist, while Tony and Sheilagh manage marketing, administration and so forth. Of Irish parentage (they are first generation Australians) they chose Setanta, Ireland's most famous mythological hero, as the brand name. The beautiful and striking labels tell the individual stories which in turn give rise to the names of each of the wines, immediately asking the question how much of *Lord of the Rings* was inspired by Celtic myth. The wines are distributed by Aria Wine Co into selected wine retailers in Adelaide and the eastern States capital cities. They are well worth tracking down, not only for the outstanding quality of the wine but for those marvellous labels. Superb, hand-sorted corks of the highest quality. Exports to the US and Ireland.

Settlers Ridge ★★★☆

54b Bussell Highway, Cowaramup, WA 6284 **REGION** Margaret River
T (08) 9755 5883 **F** (08) 9755 5883 **OPEN** 7 days 10–5
WINEMAKER Wayne Nobbs **EST.** 1994 **CASES** 3300
PRODUCT RANGE ($16–35 CD) Chenin Blanc, Sauvignon Blanc, Shiraz, Merlot, Sangiovese Novello, Cabernet Sauvignon, Lantana, Tawny Port.
SUMMARY Wayne and Kaye Nobbs have established what they say is the only vineyard in Western Australia with organic certification and the only producer in Australia with dual classification from NASAA (National Association for Sustainable Agriculture Australia) and OVAA (Organic Vignerons Association of Australia Inc.). They have 10 hectares of vineyard, including shiraz, cabernet sauvignon, merlot, sangiovese, malbec, chenin blanc and sauvignon blanc. Exports to Germany.

ΨΨΨΨΨ **Merlot 2001** Cedary, earthy varietal aromas; good structure and length; sweet tannins. Altogether impressive. **RATING** 92 **DRINK** 2008 $ 25
Cabernet Sauvignon 2001 Densely coloured; very concentrated, powerful, inky black fruits; a hint of game; lingering tannins. **RATING** 92 **DRINK** 2021 $ 29
Organic Shiraz 2001 Brightly coloured; clean, well made, medium-bodied; blackberry/black cherry and spice; fine tannins. **RATING** 90 **DRINK** 2011 $ 25

ΨΨΨΨ **Organic Shiraz 2002** Attractive, medium-bodied; spicy black cherry; good oak and extract. **RATING** 87 **DRINK** 2011 $ 25
Shiraz Cabernet 1997 Earthy/spicy fragrance and flavours; light to medium-bodied; ageing nicely. **RATING** 87 **DRINK** Now $ 35
Sangiovese Novello 2003 Very unusual aromas and flavours; Ribena and soda pop; cellar-door special. **RATING** 87 **DRINK** Now
Organic Port NV Very powerful, rich black fruits; striking licorice and blackberry; slightly funky fortifying spirit. **RATING** 87 **DRINK** 2010 $ 20

ΨΨΨΨ **Lantana Rose 2003** **RATING** 84 **DRINK** Now $ 18.50
Organic Shiraz 2000 **RATING** 84 **DRINK** Now $ 25

ΨΨΨ **Chenin Blanc 2003** **RATING** 83 $ 16
Sauvignon Blanc 2003 **RATING** 82 $ 17

Settlers Rise Montville ★★★☆

249 Western Avenue, Montville, Qld 4560 **REGION** Queensland Coastal
T (07) 5478 5558 **F** (07) 5478 5655 **OPEN** 7 days 10–5
WINEMAKER Peter Scudamore-Smith MW (Contract) **EST.** 1998 **CASES** 3000
PRODUCT RANGE ($15.50–27 CD) Queensland Classic, Blackall Range White, Verdelho, Chardonnay, Razorback Red, Reserve Shiraz, Shiraz Cabernet, Lake Baroon Cabernet Merlot, Tawny Port.
SUMMARY Settlers Rise is located in the beautiful highlands of the Blackall Range, 75 minutes drive north of Brisbane and 20 minutes from the Sunshine Coast. A little over a hectare of chardonnay, verdelho, shiraz and cabernet sauvignon have been planted at an elevation of 450 metres on the deep basalt soils of the property. First settled in 1887, Montville has gradually become a tourist destination, with a substantial local arts and crafts industry and a flourishing bed and breakfast and lodge accommodation infrastructure.

ΨΨΨΨ **Reserve Chardonnay 2002** An attractive mix of yellow peach and tropical fruit; well balanced and integrated oak; very impressive. **RATING** 90 **DRINK** Now $ 17.50

ŢŢŢŢ **Reserve Shiraz 2001** Clear varietal expression, similar to the Hunter Valley; an amalgam of blackberry, earth, chocolate and vanilla flavours; good balance. **RATING** 88 **DRINK** 2009 $27

Queensland Classic White 2003 A blend of Semillon, Sauvignon Blanc and Chardonnay; has length and intensity; nice lemon and herb crispness. **RATING** 87 **DRINK** Now $17.50

ŢŢŢŢ **Shiraz Cabernet NV** **RATING** 86 **DRINK** 2007 $19
Sparkling Shiraz NV **RATING** 85 **DRINK** 2007 $22

ŢŢŢ **Verdelho 2003** **RATING** 83 $17.50
Razorback Red 2003 **RATING** 83 $16.50
Blackall Range White 2002 **RATING** 82 $15.50

7 Acres Winery NR

374 Mons Road, Forest Glen, Buderim, Qld 4556 **REGION** Queensland Coastal
T (07) 5445 1198 **F** (07) 5445 1799 **OPEN** Mon–Fri 10–4, weekends 10–5
WINEMAKER Tom Weidmann **EST.** 1985 **CASES** 3000
PRODUCT RANGE ($10–30 CD) A kaleidoscopic array of fruit-based wines; table wines include White Moon, Red Moon, Chardonnay, Shiraz, Shiraz Cabernet Merlot, liqueurs are Limoncello, Almondo, Espresso; Old Buderim Ginger, Strawberry Port, Old Ned (spirit), Porto Rubino, Ruby Moon Port (Shiraz Durif Sangiovese).
SUMMARY When Swiss-trained winemaker Tom Weidmann bought the former Moonshine Valley Winery, which had originally been established to produce fruit wines, he changed not only the name but also the focus of the business. The 2004 vintage was Tom Weidmann's 23rd, and he seeks to make wines from single-vineyard sources, showing the grower and the place of the vineyard on the label. At the other extreme, there is also a range of ports and liqueurs for the general tourist, and the first sparkling wine from the Sunshine Coast, named Rose of Buderim.

Sevenhill Cellars ★★★★☆

College Road, Sevenhill, SA 5453 **REGION** Clare Valley
T (08) 8843 4222 **F** (08) 8843 4382 **OPEN** Mon–Fri 9–5, weekends 10–5
WINEMAKER Brother John May, Tim Eniel **EST.** 1851 **CASES** 35 000
PRODUCT RANGE ($10–30 CD) Riesling, Gewurztraminer, St Aloysius (Chenin Blanc Chardonnay Verdelho), College White, Verdelho, Botrytis Semillon, Shiraz, Merlot, STM (Shiraz Touriga Malbec), Shiraz Malbec, Grenache, Cabernet Sauvignon, Seven Brothers (Cabernet Shiraz), St Ignatius (Cabernet Sauvignon Merlot Malbec Cabernet Franc), fortifieds, sacramental wine.
SUMMARY One of the historical treasures of Australia; the oft-photographed stone wine cellars are the oldest in the Clare Valley, and winemaking is still carried out under the direction of the Jesuitical Manresa Society and in particular Brother John May. Quality is very good, particularly that of the powerful Shiraz, all the wines reflecting the estate-grown grapes from old vines. Extensive retail distribution throughout all States; exports to New Zealand, Switzerland and the UK.

ŢŢŢŢŢ **Riesling 2003** Aromas leap from the glass; a cascade of lime, passionfruit and tropical flavours run through the length of the palate. **RATING** 93 **DRINK** 2013 $19

St Ignatius 2001 Abundant, ripe blackcurrant/mulberry/blackberry fruit matched by ripe, persistent tannins. Forty per cent cabernet, 30 per cent merlot, 20 per cent malbec, 10 per cent cabernet franc. **RATING** 91 $24

Shiraz 2000 Highly scented, aromatic, juicy blackberry fruit in abundance. **RATING** 90 **DRINK** 2012 $19

Seven Mile Vineyard ★★☆

84 Coolangatta Road, Coolangatta, NSW 2535 **REGION** Shoalhaven Coast
T (02) 4448 5466 **F** (02) 9357 3141 **OPEN** Wed–Sun 10–6 (summer), Thurs–Sun 10–5 (winter)
WINEMAKER Eric Swarbrick **EST.** 1998 **CASES** 1500
PRODUCT RANGE ($15–18 CD) Verdelho, Chardonnay, Chambourcin, Petit Verdot, Cabernet Sauvignon.
SUMMARY The 1.8-hectare Seven Mile Vineyard was established by Joan and Eric Swarbrick in 1997, situated east of the town of Berry, and within the sound of the surf on the Seven Mile Beach. The

vineyard overlooks Coomonderry Swamp, one of the largest coastal wetlands in New South Wales. The first three vintages (including 2003) used chambourcin, verdelho and cabernet sauvignon from the estate plantings, the petit verdot due to come on-stream in 2004. In 2002 chardonnay juice was purchased from the adjacent Southern Highlands region, and is made and released in unoaked form. All of the wines are made on-site by Eric Swarbrick.

ΨΨΥ **Verdelho 2002** RATING 79 $18

Sevenoaks Wines ★★★

304 Doyles Creek Road, Jerrys Plains, NSW 2330 REGION Lower Hunter Valley
T (02) 6576 4285 F (02) 9586 3685 OPEN By appointment
WINEMAKER John Hordern (Contract) EST. 1997 CASES 1200
PRODUCT RANGE ($14–27 CD) Vino Estivo Sangiovese, Rows 1 to 26 Shiraz, Woodlands Shiraz.
SUMMARY Robert and Deborah Sharp established Sevenoaks Wines in 1997 with the original intention of selling the grapes to other winemakers. With only 2 hectares of shiraz, 1.5 hectares of sangiovese and 0.5 hectare of petit verdot, it was inevitable the wine from their grapes would be blended with many others, so in 2000 the Sharps changed course, retaining John Hordern as contract winemaker. The vineyard is part of a 68-hectare property which abuts the Wollemi National Park at the bottom of the slopes that rise to be Mount Woodlands. Exports to Singapore, Malaysia and China.

ΨΨΨΨ **Rows 1 to 26 Shiraz 2002** Light to medium-bodied; attractive, sweet cherry fruit, fine tannins, gentle oak. RATING 87 DRINK 2008 $23

ΨΨΨΥ **Woodlands Shiraz 2001** RATING 85 DRINK 2007 $19

Severn Brae Estate NR

Lot 2 Back Creek Road (Mount Tully Road), Severnlea, Qld 4352 REGION Granite Belt
T (07) 4683 5292 F (07) 3391 3821 OPEN Mon–Fri 12–3, weekends 10–5, or by appointment
WINEMAKER Bruce Humphery-Smith EST. 1987 CASES 1400
PRODUCT RANGE ($14–16 CD) Murray Grey White, Unwooded Chardonnay, Estate Chardonnay, Light Fruity Red, Merlot Sangiovese, Reserve Shiraz; Liqueur Muscat and Chardonnay.
SUMMARY Patrick and Bruce Humphery-Smith have established 5.5 hectares of chardonnay with relatively close spacing and trained on a high two-tier trellis. Two-thirds of the production is sold, one-third used for the Severn Brae label.

Seville Estate ★★★★★

65 Linwood Road, Seville, Vic 3139 REGION Yarra Valley
T (03) 5964 2622 F (03) 5964 2633 OPEN By appointment
WINEMAKER Iain Riggs EST. 1970 CASES 4000
PRODUCT RANGE ($25–60 CD) Chardonnay, Pinot Noir, Reserve Pinot Noir, Shiraz, Old Vine Reserve Shiraz, Old Vine Reserve Cabernet Sauvignon
SUMMARY The changes have come thick and fast for this long-established Yarra Valley producer. In February 1997 it was jointly acquired by Brokenwood and associated shareholders. Late in 2002 it was decided to move the business to Beechworth, but retain the brand, selling the winery and vineyard in the Yarra Valley, but with a grape supply agreement from the estate back to the vendors. Simultaneously, a shareholding group (closely associated with Brokenwood, but no longer including Brokenwood itself) was formed to finance the new venture. The wines are exported to the UK, the US, Malaysia and Singapore.

ΨΨΨΨΨ **Old Vine Reserve Shiraz 2001** Fragrant black cherry, spice and licorice aromas and flavours, with a dash of bitter chocolate; medium-bodied, fine and long. RATING 94 DRINK 2014 $60

ΨΨΨΨΥ **Chardonnay 2002** Sophisticated and integrated barrel ferment inputs to bouquet; supple melon and stone fruit flavours; excellent balance and length. RATING 93 DRINK 2008 $25
Shiraz 2001 Powerful, concentrated blackberry and spice; surprising tannins and structure add to the length. RATING 92 DRINK 2011 $27

Unfiltered Pinot Noir 2002 Not entirely bright; supple, fine and long; a light to medium-bodied mix of red fruits and integrated oak; lingering finish. **RATING** 90 **DRINK** 2007 $ 27
Reserve Old Vine Cabernet Sauvignon 2001 An elegant, medium-bodied fresh mix of redcurrant and blackcurrant, judicious oak and tannins. **RATING** 90 **DRINK** 2011 $ 35

ΨΨΨΨ **Shiraz 2002** Strongly spicy/herbal reflecting the cool vintage; a mix of red and black fruits; light to medium-bodied. **RATING** 89 **DRINK** 2008 $ 27

🍇 Seville Hill ★★★☆

8 Paynes Road, Seville, Vic 3139 **REGION** Yarra Valley
T (03) 5964 3284 **F** (03) 5964 2142 **OPEN** 7 days 10–6
WINEMAKER Dom Bucci, John D'Aloisio **EST.** 1991 **CASES** 1500
PRODUCT RANGE ($18–25 CD) Sauvignon Blanc, Chardonnay, Reserve Shiraz, Merlot, Cabernet Sauvignon.
SUMMARY John and Josie D'Aloisio have had a long-term involvement in the agricultural industry, which ultimately led to the establishment of the Seville Hill vineyard in 1991. There they have 2.4 hectares of cabernet sauvignon and 1.3 hectares each of merlot, shiraz and chardonnay. John D'Aloisio makes the wines with Dominic Bucci, a long-time Yarra resident and winemaker.

ΨΨΨΨ **Reserve Shiraz 2001** Bright colour; light to medium-bodied; attractive mix of red and black fruits drive the wine; not especially complex. **RATING** 88 **DRINK** 2009 $ 25
Chardonnay 2001 Bright light green; complex, obvious barrel-ferment aromas are good, but the oak flavours do not flatter the wine. **RATING** 87 **DRINK** Now $ 22

ΨΨΨ♡ **Merlot 2001 RATING** 85 **DRINK** Now $ 22
Cabernet Sauvignon 2001 RATING 84 **DRINK** Now $ 22

🍇 Sewards ★★★

Lot 2, Wildwood Road, Yallingup, WA 6282 **REGION** Margaret River
T 0413 567 693 **F** (08) 6267 8009 **OPEN** Not
WINEMAKER Michael Kelly (Contract) **EST.** 1995 **CASES** 625
PRODUCT RANGE ($13.50–18 ML) Sauvignon Blanc, Sauvignon Blanc Semillon, Shiraz, Cabernet Sauvignon.
SUMMARY The 10-hectare vineyard was established by Dr John McCarthy Seward in 1995, and is now run by family members. Most of the grapes are sold to Fermoy Estate, where the wines are contract-made. For the time being, sales are by mail order only, but a cellar door may be opened down the track.

ΨΨΨ♡ **Shiraz 2002 RATING** 84 **DRINK** 2007 $ 18

ΨΨΨ **Cabernet Sauvignon 2001 RATING** 83 $ 15.50
Shiraz 2001 RATING 80 $ 18

Shadowfax Vineyard and Winery ★★★★★

K Road, Werribee, Vic 3030 **REGION** Geelong
T (03) 9731 4420 **F** (03) 9731 4421 **OPEN** 7 days 11–5
WINEMAKER Matt Harrop **EST.** 2000 **CASES** 15 000
PRODUCT RANGE ($19–70 CD) Sauvignon Blanc, Pinot Gris, Viognier, Chardonnay, Pinot Noir, McLaren Vale Shiraz, Werribee Shiraz, Heathcote Shiraz, K Road Sangiovese Merlot Shiraz, Yarra Valley Cabernet Sauvignon.
SUMMARY Shadowfax is part of an awesome development at Werribee Park, a mere 20 minutes from Melbourne towards Geelong. The truly striking winery, designed by Wood Marsh architects, was erected in time for the 2000 vintage crush, adjacent to the extraordinary 60-room private home built in the 1880s by the Chirnside family and known as The Mansion. It was then the centrepiece of a 40 000-hectare pastoral empire, and the appropriately magnificent gardens were part of the reason why the property was acquired by Parks Victoria in the early 1970s. The mansion is now The Mansion Hotel, with 92 rooms and suites, with the emphasis on conference bookings during the week, and

general tourism on the weekend. The striking packaging of the wines, and the quality of the first releases, all underline the thoroughly serious nature of this quite amazing venture. Exports to the UK, the US, Japan, Singapore and New Zealand.

ŸŸŸŸŸ **Werribee Shiraz 2002** Dense, impenetrable colour; licorice/anise, dark plum and blackberry aromas; and a palate laden with black fruits, a touch of chocolate, and soft, dense tannins. **RATING** 95 **DRINK** 2017 $ 26
Chardonnay 2002 Brilliant colour; supple, smooth melon and cashew; great texture and mouthfeel; perfect acidity to close. **RATING** 94 **DRINK** 2009 $ 30

ŸŸŸŸŸ **Pinot Noir 2002** Clear and fresh plum/black cherry fruit in abundance on the palate; a little simple; should build with time. A blend of Beechworth, Yarra Ranges and Geelong fruit. **RATING** 93 **DRINK** 2012 $ 33
Viognier 2003 Ripe pastille, apricot and peach fruit; good length, mouthfeel and cleansing acidity. **RATING** 92 **DRINK** Now $ 20
One Eye Heathcote Shiraz 2001 A fragrant, elegant style, way to the left of the normal Heathcote blood and thunder; fine tannins and a long finish; counter-cultural restraint. **RATING** 90 **DRINK** 2011 $ 70
Pink Cliffs Heathcote Shiraz 2001 Powerful, black fruits and licorice; lush mid palate and considerable tannins running through to a long finish. **RATING** 90 **DRINK** 2016 $ 70

ŸŸŸŸ **Adelaide Hills Pinot Gris 2003** Spotlessly clean; apple/apple skin/pear aromas and flavours; good balance and mouthfeel; a touch of mineral on the finish. **RATING** 89 **DRINK** Now $ 24
Adelaide Hills Sauvignon Blanc 2003 Clean and firm; curiously neutral fruit, but the balance is good. **RATING** 87 **DRINK** Now $ 19

Shantell ★★★★

1974 Melba Highway, Dixons Creek, Vic 3775 **REGION** Yarra Valley
T (03) 5965 2264 **F** (03) 5965 2331 **OPEN** 7 days 10.30–5
WINEMAKER Shan Shanmugam, Turid Shanmugam **EST.** 1980 **CASES** 2500
PRODUCT RANGE ($15–32 CD) Semillon, Chardonnay, Glenlea Chardonnay, Pinot Noir, Shiraz, Cabernet Sauvignon, Sparkling.
SUMMARY The substantial and now fully mature Shantell vineyards provide the winery with a high-quality fruit source; part is sold to other Yarra Valley makers, the remainder vinified at Shantell. In January 1998 Shantell opened a new cellar door situated at 1974 Melba Highway, 50 metres along a service road from the highway proper. Chardonnay, Semillon and Cabernet Sauvignon are its benchmark wines, sturdily reliable, sometimes outstanding. An on-site café provides light lunches. Domestic and international distribution through Australian Prestige Wines.

Sharmans ★★★☆

Glenbothy, 175 Glenwood Road, Relbia, Tas 7258 **REGION** Northern Tasmania
T (03) 6343 0773 **F** (03) 6343 0773 **OPEN** Thurs–Sun 10–5, closed during winter
WINEMAKER Russell Cook, Rosevears Estate (Contract) **EST.** 1987 **CASES** 1000
PRODUCT RANGE ($16–23 CD) Riesling, Sauvignon Blanc, Unoaked Chardonnay, Chardonnay, Pinot Noir.
SUMMARY Mike Sharman has very probably pioneered one of the more interesting wine regions of Tasmania, not far south of Launceston but with a distinctly warmer climate than (say) Pipers Brook. Ideal north-facing slopes are home to a vineyard now approaching 3 hectares, most still to come into bearing. The few wines produced in sufficient quantity to be sold promise much for the future.

ŸŸŸŸ **Pinot Noir 2002** Supple, smooth plummy fruit; elegant style, good length. **RATING** 91 **DRINK** 2008 $ 23

ŸŸŸŸ **Sauvignon Blanc 2003** Floral, quasi Lantana aromas; powerful, crisp palate; unconventional. **RATING** 87 **DRINK** Now $ 17

ŸŸŸŸ **Chardonnay 2002 RATING** 85 **DRINK** 2007 $ 18
Riesling 2003 RATING 84 **DRINK** 2009 $ 16

🐌 Sharpe Wines of Orange NR

Fanning Lane, Emu Swamp, Orange, NSW 2800 **REGION** Orange
T (02) 6361 9046 **F** (02) 6361 1645 **OPEN** First weekend of the month, or by appointment
WINEMAKER Margot Sharpe, Rob Black **EST.** 1998 **CASES** 1000
PRODUCT RANGE ($15–25 ML) Chardonnay, Cabernet Rose, Single Barrel Cabernet Sauvignon, The Jack Demmery Cabernet Sauvignon.
SUMMARY When Margot and Tony Sharpe began the establishment of their 3-hectare vineyard predominantly planted to cabernet sauvignon, with lesser amounts of merlot and cabernet franc, the wheel turned in a somewhat wayward full circle. Sharpe Bros Cordials was established in 1868 by strict Methodists to give the working man something else to drink rather than the demon alcohol. Says Margot Sharpe: 'I do believe there might be some serious grave turning over the product.' The Rose and Single Barrel Cabernet Sauvignon were made by the Sharpes in a tiny winery established in small stables at the back of their house; The Jack Demmery Cabernet Sauvignon (named in honour of Margot Sharpe's late father, who died just as planting of the vineyard was completed) was made by Jon Reynolds.

Shaw & Smith

Lot 4 Jones Road, Balhannah, SA 5242 **REGION** Adelaide Hills
T (08) 8398 0500 **F** (08) 8398 0600 **OPEN** Weekends 10–4
WINEMAKER Martin Shaw **EST.** 1989 **CASES** 30 000
PRODUCT RANGE ($18–39 CD) Riesling, Sauvignon Blanc, Unoaked Chardonnay, Reserve Chardonnay, M3 Vineyard Chardonnay, Elixir Shiraz, Merlot; also Incognito range of Eden Valley Riesling, Adelaide Hills Chardonnay, Adelaide Hills Merlot.
SUMMARY Has progressively moved from a contract grape-grown base to estate production with the development of a 40-hectare vineyard at Balhannah in the Adelaide Hills, followed by the erection prior to the 2000 vintage of a state-of-the-art, beautifully designed and executed winery at Balhannah, ending the long period of tenancy at Petaluma. The wines have wide international distribution including the UK, Japan, the US, Canada, Hong Kong, Japan and Singapore.

🍷🍷🍷🍷🍷 **M3 Vineyard Chardonnay 2002** The bouquet shows complex but not aggressive barrel ferment inputs, the melon and cashew palate supple, smooth and long, the result of sophisticated craftsmanship. **RATING** 95 **DRINK** 2009 $37
Sauvignon Blanc 2003 Clean, fresh and crisp; no hint of reduction as in 2002; flows evenly through to a long finish, with excellent varietal fruit expression in a sweeter spectrum. **RATING** 94 **DRINK** Now $23
Shiraz 2002 Star anise, plum and blackberry aromas and flavours; fine, silky tannins; neatly balanced oak. **RATING** 94 **DRINK** 2012 $37
Adelaide Hills Merlot 2002 Spotlessly clean; intense, fruit-driven but complex; a web of small red fruits with nuances of spice and olive; very good mouthfeel. **RATING** 94 **DRINK** 2012 $30

🍷🍷🍷🍷🍷 **Unoaked Chardonnay 2003** Stone fruit and citrus; highly aromatic, clean, long and lingering; way above average for the category. **RATING** 90 **DRINK** 2009 $24

🐌 Shaw Vineyard Estate NR

PO Box 31, Murrumbateman, NSW 2582 **REGION** Canberra District
T 0412 633 542 **F** (02) 6227 5865 **OPEN** Not **EST.** 1999
SUMMARY Graeme and Michael Shaw have established a little over 30 hectares of vineyard, planted to semillon, riesling, shiraz, merlot and cabernet sauvignon. The lion's share of production is sold to BRL Hardy, with a small amount made for ultimate release under the Shaw Vineyard Estate label. It is hoped to construct a winery, cellar door and restaurant to open sometime in 2005, but this will depend on the Building Approval process and other such matters.

🐌 Shawwood Estate

Cnr Craigmoor Road and Henry Lawson Drive, Mudgee, NSW 2850 **REGION** Mudgee
T (02) 6372 0237 **F** (02) 6372 0238 **OPEN** Weekends and public holidays 10–4
WINEMAKER Craig Bishop **EST.** 1998 **CASES** 2500

PRODUCT RANGE ($12–19.50 ML) Verdelho, Unwooded Chardonnay, Chardonnay, Shiraz, Cabernet Shiraz, Cabernet Sauvignon.

SUMMARY Shawwood Estate has been established a mere 2.5 kilometres from the Mudgee GPO, on a slight rise on the northern side of Mudgee overlooking the township. A group of investors, including Charles Tym, Alison Bishop and Craig Bishop (the winemaker) have planted 3.3 hectares each of shiraz and cabernet sauvignon, and 1.7 hectares each of chardonnay and verdelho. The wines are made on-site by Craig Bishop, who is also responsible for the vineyard.

ŸŸŸŸ **Shiraz 2002** Solid, rich and powerful; blackberry, plum and bitter chocolate flavours; good structure. **RATING** 87 **DRINK** 2010 $ 15.80

ŸŸŸŸ **Cabernet Sauvignon 2002** **RATING** 86 **DRINK** 2012 $ 12

ŸŸŸ **Verdelho 2002** **RATING** 83 $ 15.80
Chardonnay 2003 **RATING** 82 $ 12
Verdelho 2003 **RATING** 81 $ 15.80

ŸŸŸ **Chardonnay 2002** **RATING** 79 $ 12

Sheep's Back ★★★★☆

PO Box 441, South Melbourne, Vic 3205 **REGION** Barossa Valley
T (03) 9696 7018 **F** (03) 9686 4015 **OPEN** Not
WINEMAKER Dean Hewitson **EST.** 2001 **CASES** 1000
PRODUCT RANGE ($40 R) Shiraz.
SUMMARY Sheep's Back is a joint venture between Neil Empson (with 30 years' experience as an exporter to Australia and elsewhere of Italian wines) and Dean Hewitson. They decided to produce a single estate-grown shiraz after an extensive search found a 6-hectare vineyard of 75-year-old vines. The wine is distributed in Australia by Trembath & Taylor, by Meadowbank Estates in the US and in Canada by Empson Canada.

ŸŸŸŸ **Shiraz 2001** Supple, smooth and rounded; the oak, tannins and fruit are balanced and integrated; blackberry and fine leather flavours. **RATING** 90 **DRINK** 2011 $ 37.50

Shelmerdine Vineyards ★★★★☆

PO Box 18152, Collins Street East, Melbourne, Vic 8001 **REGION** Yarra Valley
T (03) 9207 3090 **F** (03) 9207 3061 **OPEN** Not
WINEMAKER Kate Goodman (Contract) **EST.** 1989
PRODUCT RANGE ($19–26 ML) Yarra Valley Sauvignon Blanc, Heathcote Viognier, Yarra Valley Pinot Noir, Heathcote Shiraz, Yarra Valley Merlot, Heathcote Cabernet Sauvignon.
SUMMARY Stephen Shelmerdine has been a major figure in the wine industry for well over 20 years, like his family before him (who founded Mitchelton Winery), and has been honoured for his many services to the industry. The venture has 130 hectares of vineyards spread over three sites, Lusatia Park in the Yarra Valley and Merindoc Vineyard and Willoughby Bridge in the Heathcote region. Substantial quantities of the grapes produced are sold to others, with a small amount of high quality wines contract-made by Kate Goodman at the Punt Road Winery.

ŸŸŸŸ **Shiraz 2002** Deeply coloured; intense blackberry/black plum/spice/cherry fruit; very good texture; mixes power and finesse. **RATING** 93 **DRINK** 2012 $ 26
Sauvignon Blanc 2003 Spotlessly clean, fresh and lively aromas; tangy gooseberry and citrus flavours; good acidity and length. **RATING** 90 **DRINK** Now $ 20
Chardonnay 2002 Obvious barrel-ferment inputs; intense and long, with a faintly nutty finish and aftertaste. **RATING** 90 **DRINK** 2010 $ 24
Pinot Noir 2002 Quite savoury and restrained; shows its class with its drive through to the back palate, finish and aftertaste. **RATING** 90 **DRINK** 2008 $ 24.50

ŸŸŸŸ **Viognier 2002** **RATING** 85 **DRINK** Now $ 25

Sherwood Estate
★★★☆

1187 Gowings Hill Road, Sherwood, NSW 2440 **REGION** Hastings River
T (02) 6581 4900 **F** (02) 6581 4728 **OPEN** Fri–Sun and public holidays 11–4, or by appointment
WINEMAKER James Hilliard **EST.** 1998 **CASES** 750
PRODUCT RANGE ($16–25 CD) Semillon, Gazebo White (Semillon Chardonnay), Verdelho, Chardonnay, Sherwood Frost (Dessert Semillon), Middle Paddock Chambourcin, Gazebo Red (Cabernet Merlot), Cabernet Merlot.
SUMMARY John and Helen Ross began planting the Sherwood Estate vineyard in 1998 with 2 hectares of chambourcin. Subsequently, verdelho, chardonnay, cabernet franc, semillon and (most recently) sangiovese have been planted, with 10 hectares now under vine. The vineyard is situated in the Macleay Valley, 15 minutes west of Kempsey on the New South Wales North Coast, with a total of 43 hectares of undulating fertile soils, rich in limestone. The wines are also available from the Sherwood Wine Embassy, Pacific Highway, Port Macquarie, which is open 7 days.

Shingleback
★★★★

Cnr Little and California Roads, McLaren Vale, SA 5171 **REGION** McLaren Vale
T (08) 8370 3299 **F** (08) 8370 0088 **OPEN** By appointment
WINEMAKER John Davey **EST.** 1995 **CASES** 40 000
PRODUCT RANGE ($15–45 ML) Semillon, Chardonnay, Shiraz, D Block Reserve Shiraz, Cabernet Sauvignon.
SUMMARY Shingleback has 80 hectares of vineyards in McLaren Vale, with part of the grape production vinified under the Shingleback label. It is a specialist export business with exports to Germany, Switzerland and the US, but the wines are also available by mail order locally. The excellent 2002 vintage wines, in particular, have characters one more readily associates with cool climates; it will be interesting to see how much this was a vintage effect, how much it is due to vineyard site and aspect, and how much to the winery. Exports to the US and Switzerland.

ŢŢŢŢŢ **D Block Reserve Shiraz 2002** Spicy, tangy black cherry and spice; medium-bodied; good extract and oak control; has considerable length. **RATING** 92 **DRINK** 2012 $ 45
Cabernet Sauvignon 2002 Blackcurrant, cedar, olive and bitter chocolate; good texture and depth; ditto oak. **RATING** 91 **DRINK** 2017 $ 29
D Block Reserve Shiraz 2001 Complex black fruits sweeten up on the palate, supported by fine, ripe tannins; good length. **RATING** 90 **DRINK** 2011 $ 45

ŢŢŢŢ **Shiraz 2002** Solid, medium-bodied black fruits plus mocha and vanilla oak; plenty of focus. **RATING** 89 **DRINK** 2012 $ 29

ŢŢŢŢ **Shiraz 2001** **RATING** 84 **DRINK** Now $ 29

Shiralee Wines
NR

PO Box 260, Nuriootpa, SA 5355 **REGION** Barossa Valley
T (08) 8564 2799 **F** (08) 8564 2799 **OPEN** Not
WINEMAKER Bob Mitchell **EST.** 2001
PRODUCT RANGE A range of varietally denominated table wines reflecting the plantings.
SUMMARY Shiralee Wines is the venture of Graeme Ruwoldt and Bob Mitchell, with access to 25 hectares of chardonnay and shiraz in the Barossa Valley. Only part of the output is vinified for sale under the Shiralee brand; the major market is the US.

Shirvington
NR

PO Box 222, McLaren Vale, SA 5171 **REGION** McLaren Vale
T (08) 8383 0554 **F** (08) 8383 0556 **OPEN** Not
WINEMAKER Sarah Marquis, Sparky Marquis **EST.** 1996 **CASES** 2200
PRODUCT RANGE ($60–70 R) Shiraz, Cabernet Sauvignon.
SUMMARY The Shirvington family began the development of their McLaren Vale vineyards in 1996 under the direction of viticulturist Peter Bolte, and now have 35 hectares under vine, the majority to shiraz and cabernet sauvignon, and with small additional plantings of merlot, cabernet franc and verdelho. A substantial part of the production is sold as grapes, a part (the best) being reserved for the Shirvington wines which are made by the very well-known team of Sarah and Sparky Marquis.

Shottesbrooke

Bagshaws Road, McLaren Flat, SA 5171 **REGION** McLaren Vale
T (08) 8383 0002 **F** (08) 8383 0222 **OPEN** Mon–Fri 10–4.30, weekends and public holidays 11–5
WINEMAKER Nick Holmes, Hamish Maguire **EST.** 1984 **CASES** 10 000
PRODUCT RANGE ($14–35 CD) Sauvignon Blanc, Chardonnay, Merlette (Merlot Rose), Shiraz, Eliza Reserve Shiraz, Merlot, Cabernet Merlot Malbec, Cabernet Sauvignon, Punch Reserve Cabernet, Bernesh Bray Liqueur Tawny.
SUMMARY For many years now the full-time business of former Ryecroft winemaker Nick Holmes, drawing primarily on estate-grown grapes at his Myoponga vineyard. He has always stood out for the finesse and elegance of his wines compared with the Dam Buster, high alcolhol reds for which McLaren Vale has become famous (or infamous, depending on one's point of view). By quietly hanging in there, the wheel has started to turn full circle, with finesse and elegance much more appreciated. Exports to the UK, the US, Canada, Germany, The Netherlands and New Zealand supplement distribution through all Australian States.

ΥΥΥΥΥ **Punch Reserve Cabernet Sauvignon 2002** Significantly riper and slightly more concentrated than the standard release, but still not a blockbuster; blackberry, cassis and chocolate fruit; good oak. **RATING** 93 **DRINK** 2017 $ 35
Cabernet Sauvignon 2002 Elegant blackberry and blackcurrant mix; has effortless length. **RATING** 91 **DRINK** 2012 $ 18
Eliza Shiraz 2002 Clearly defined black cherry/raspberry fruit in typically elegant Shottesbrooke style; fine tannins. **RATING** 90 **DRINK** 2010 $ 35

ΥΥΥΥ **Fleurieu Sauvignon Blanc 2003** Light to medium intensity; fresh citrus/passionfruit/gooseberry, tending tropical; good mouthfeel; good value. Screwcap. **RATING** 89 **DRINK** Now $ 15
Merlot 2002 Earthy, spicy, savoury varietal character; medium-bodied, good length and texture; fruit-driven. **RATING** 89 **DRINK** 2010 $ 17
Chardonnay 2003 Super-refined, super-subtle and understated, but all the components are in balance. Screwcap. **RATING** 87 **DRINK** Now $ 15.50
Cabernet Sauvignon Merlot Malbec 2001 Fine, savoury, supple style with earthy notes and minimal oak. **RATING** 87 **DRINK** 2009 $ 18.50

ΥΥΥΥ **Bermesh Bray Liqueur Tawny NV** **RATING** 86 **DRINK** Now $ 30

ΥΥΥ **Merlette Free Run Merlot 2003** **RATING** 83 $ 14

Silk Hill

★★★★

324 Motor Road, Deviot, Tas 7275 **REGION** Northern Tasmania
T (03) 6394 7385 **F** (03) 6394 7392 **OPEN** Thurs–Sun 9–5
WINEMAKER Gavin Scott **EST.** 1990 **CASES** 300
PRODUCT RANGE ($16–20 CD) Pinot's Rose, Pinot Noir.
SUMMARY Pharmacist Gavin Scott has been a weekend and holiday viticulturist for many years, having established the Glengarry Vineyard, which he sold, and then establishing the 1.5-hectare Silk Hill (formerly Silkwood Vineyard) in 1989, planted exclusively to pinot noir. Growing and making Pinot Noir and fishing will keep him occupied when he sells his pharmacy business.

ΥΥΥΥΥ **Reserve Pinot Noir 2002** Rich; abundant damson plum and black cherry fruit; good length, not extractive. **RATING** 92 **DRINK** 2009

ΥΥΥΥ **Pinot Noir 2002** Plum, spice and oak; good mid-palate, some length. **RATING** 87 **DRINK** 2008

Silkwood Wines

★★★★

Lot 5204 Channybearup Road, Pemberton, WA 6260 **REGION** Pemberton
T (08) 9776 1584 **F** (08) 9776 0019 **OPEN** 7 days 11–4
WINEMAKER Contract **EST.** 1998 **CASES** 800
PRODUCT RANGE ($14–20 ML) Riesling, Sauvignon Blanc, Pinot Noir, Shiraz, Merlot, Cabernet Sauvignon.

SUMMARY Third-generation farmers Pam and John Allen returned from a short break running small businesses in Adelaide and Perth to purchase Silkwood in 1998. Plantings began with 3 hectares of shiraz and 2 hectares of sauvignon blanc in 1999, followed by a further 5.5 hectares of riesling, pinot noir, merlot and cabernet sauvignon in 2000. The vineyard is patrolled by a large flock of guinea fowl, eliminating most insect pests, and reducing the use of chemicals. The wines are sold direct ex the winery in case lots, with an internet order form for those wishing to use this medium. The plans are to extend the sales to restaurants and begin exports in the near future.

TTTT **Pinot Noir 2003** Plenty of varietal character; dark plum with touches of forest, game and spice. **RATING** 89 **DRINK** 2007 $ 20

Cabernet Merlot 2002 Quite fragrant red fruits; builds on the back palate through to the finish courtesy of ripe tannins. **RATING** 88 **DRINK** 2010 $18.75

Silverwood Wines ★★★★

Bittern-Dromana Road, Balnarring, Vic 3926 **REGION** Mornington Peninsula
T 0419 890 317 **F** (03) 9888 5303 **OPEN** Not
WINEMAKER Keith Bown, Paul Dennis **EST.** 1997 **CASES** 150
PRODUCT RANGE ($20.50–45 ML) Chardonnay, Rose, Pinot Noir, Reserve Pinot Noir.
SUMMARY Paul and Denise Dennis were inspired to establish Silverwood as a consequence of living in France for a year. They, with members of their family, did much of the establishment work on the vineyard, which is meticulously maintained. Most of the grapes are sold to other Mornington Peninsula wineries, but a small amount of attractive wines have been made under the Silverwood label.

TTTTY **Reserve Pinot Noir 2002** Intense plum and black cherry fruit, though 18 months in French oak was a little too long. **RATING** 90 **DRINK** 2008 $45

TTTT **Pinot Noir 2002** Strong, very ripe dark plum/spice aromas; concentrated and powerful in the mouth; not fined — perhaps a pity. **RATING** 89 **DRINK** 2010 $ 24.50

Chardonnay 2002 Very complex, with some slightly feral characters, but has good length and balance. **RATING** 88 **DRINK** 2008 $ 20.50

Simon Gilbert Wines ★★★☆

1220 Sydney Road, Mudgee, NSW 2850 (postal) **REGION** Mudgee
T (02) 9958 1322 **F** (02) 8920 1333 **OPEN** Not
WINEMAKER Simon Gilbert **EST.** 1993 **CASES** 35 000
PRODUCT RANGE ($15–45 R) Card Series Semillon Sauvignon Blanc, Verdelho, Chardonnay, Shiraz, Cabernet Merlot; next Family Selection Orange Pinot Noir, Mudgee Shiraz, McLaren Vale Grenache Shiraz Mourvedre, Mudgee Sangiovese, Central Ranges Cabernet Merlot; and at the top Wongalere McLaren Vale Shiraz, Abbaston Cabernet Sauvignon.
SUMMARY Courtesy of a public share issue, a large, state-of-the-art winery was constructed at Mudgee, with contract winemaking the core business. A series of problems, including the failure of some of the clients to pay for the wine made for them, has left the business in a financially precarious state, but a rescue plan was underway in March 2004. Simon Gilbert himself continues to work long and hard, producing good wines both for the Simon Gilbert label and for the better clients, and one can only hope that the future is more rewarding. Exports to the UK, Canada and Singapore.

Simon Hackett ★★★☆

Budgens Road, McLaren Vale, SA 5171 **REGION** McLaren Vale
T (08) 8323 7712 **F** (08) 8323 7713 **OPEN** Wed–Sun 11–5
WINEMAKER Simon Hackett **EST.** 1981 **CASES** 20 000
PRODUCT RANGE ($15–35 R) McLaren Vale Riesling, Barossa Valley Semillon, Barossa Valley Chardonnay, McLaren Vale Shiraz, McLaren Vale Anthony's Reserve Shiraz, McLaren Vale Old Vine Grenache, McLaren Vale Foggo Road Cabernet Sauvignon.
SUMMARY In 1998 Simon Hackett acquired the former Taranga winery in McLaren Vale, which has made his winemaking life a great deal easier. He also has 8 hectares of estate vines and has contract growers in McLaren Vale, the Adelaide Hills and the Barossa Valley, with another 32 hectares of vines.

Sinclair Wines

NR

Graphite Road, Glenoran, WA 6258 **REGION** Manjimup
T (08) 9421 1399 **F** (08) 9421 1191 **OPEN** By appointment
WINEMAKER Brenden Smith (Contract) **EST.** 1994 **CASES** 2500
PRODUCT RANGE ($15–25 CD) Sauvignon Blanc, Unwooded Chardonnay, Chardonnay, Chardonnay Manjimup, Rose of Glenoran, Cabernet Merlot Jezebel, Cabernet Sauvignon, Cabernet Sauvvignon Giovanni.
SUMMARY Sinclair Wines is the child of Darelle Sinclair, a science teacher, wine educator and graduate viticulturist from Charles Sturt University, and John Healy, a lawyer, traditional jazz musician and graduand wine marketing student of Adelaide University, Roseworthy Campus. Five hectares of estate plantings are in production.

Sirromet Wines

 ★★★★☆

850–938 Mount Cotton Road, Mount Cotton, Qld 4165 **REGION** Queensland Coastal
T (07) 3206 2999 **F** (07) 3206 0900 **OPEN** 7 days 10–5
WINEMAKER Adam Chapman, Alain Rousseau, Craig Stevenson **EST.** 1998 **CASES** 60 000
PRODUCT RANGE ($12–30 CD) Perfect Day range of Semillon Verdelho Chardonnay, Harvest White, Chardonnay, Rose, Harvest Red, Dolce, Telunapa, Shiraz Cabernet Merlot, Siren's Rock; Vineyard Selection range of Semillon, Sauvignon Blanc Semillon, Chardonnay, Pinot Chardonnay Sparkling, Teewah, Chambourcin, Shiraz, Petit Verdot, Cabernet Sauvignon, Seven Scenes range of Chardonnay, Pinot Chardonnay Sparkling, Merlot, Shiraz, Finito Muscat; and Private Bin at the top.
SUMMARY This is an unambiguously ambitious venture, with the professed aim of creating Queensland's premier winery. The Morris family, founders of Sirromet Wines, which owns Mount Cotton Estate, retained a leading architect to design the striking state-of-the-art winery with an 80 000-case production capacity; the State's foremost viticultural consultant to plant the three major vineyards which total 100 hectares; and the most skilled winemaker practising in Queensland, Adam Chapman, to make the wine. It has a 200-seat restaurant; a wine club offering all sorts of benefits to its members; and is firmly aimed at the domestic and international tourist market, taking advantage of its situation half way between Brisbane and the Gold Coast. The intention is to move to a predominantly estate-based operation as quickly as the vineyards (planted to 14 varieties) come into production. Both the consistency and quality of the wines released so far and their modest pricing bodes well for the future. Exports to the UK, Iceland, Canada and Japan.

ꔹꔹꔹꔹ **TM Queensland Chardonnay 2002** Funky, complex, rich and intense barrel ferment and other winemaker inputs; the fruit easily carries these inputs; thoroughly impressive. 100 cases made. **RATING** 92 **DRINK** 2007 $30
Seven Scenes Cabernet Sauvignon 2002 Immaculately crafted; blackcurrant and blackberry fruit plus fine, ripe tannins; very good balance and length. **RATING** 92 **DRINK** 2012 $22
Vineyard Selection Queensland Semillon 2002 Plenty of varietal character on both bouquet and palate; intensely flavoured, and building well. **RATING** 91 **DRINK** 2009 $12

ꔹꔹꔹꔹ **Perfect Day Shiraz Cabernet 2002** A mouthfilling, lush, but not jammy, basket of red fruits; soft, supple, ripe tannins; fruit-driven. **RATING** 89 **DRINK** 2007 $12
Seven Scenes Merlot 2002 Earthy/briary/foresty varietal aromas and flavours; strongly structured. **RATING** 89 **DRINK** 2010 $22
Vineyard Selection Cabernet Merlot 2002 Abundant black fruit aromas and flavours; at the bigger end of the spectrum, the cabernet influence obvious; good structure. Screwcap. **RATING** 89 **DRINK** 2012 $16
Seven Scenes Chardonnay 2002 Complex, oak-driven style; less might have been better. **RATING** 87 **DRINK** 2007 $22
Seven Scenes Merlot 2001 Fragrant and light-bodied, but strongly varietal throughout; a mix of blackcurrant, olive and fruitcake; subtle oak. **RATING** 87 **DRINK** 2008 $22
Vineyard Selection Petit Verdot 2002 Very ripe black fruits intermingle with dusty tannins and hints of cedar/cigar box; controlled tannins. **RATING** 87 **DRINK** 2008 $16

ꔹꔹꔹꔹ **Perfect Day Shiraz Mataro 2003** **RATING** 84 **DRINK** Now $12

ꔹꔹꔹ **Pinot Gris 2003** **RATING** 79 $16

Sittella Wines

100 Barrett Road, Herne Hill, WA 6056 **REGION** Swan Valley
T (08) 9296 2600 **F** (08) 9296 2600 **OPEN** Tues–Sun and public holidays 11–4
WINEMAKER John Griffiths, Matthew Bourness **EST.** 1998 **CASES** 5000
PRODUCT RANGE A range of varietal wines variously linked either to the Swan Valley or Margaret River.
SUMMARY ($11.95–22 CD) Perth couple Simon and Maaike Berns acquired a 7-hectare block (with 5 hectares of vines) at Herne Hill, making the first wine in February 1998 and opening the most attractive cellar-door facility later in the year. They also own the 10-hectare Wildberry Springs Estate vineyard in the Margaret River region, which commenced to provide grapes from the 1999 vintage.

ŸŸŸŸ **Satin 2002** Light to medium-bodied; fresh and lively aromatic bouquet; gently sweet juicy berry fruit; dry finish. A blend of Merlot, Cabernet Sauvignon and Shiraz. **RATING** 87 **DRINK** 2008 $ 15.95

ŸŸŸŸ **Cabernet Sauvignon 2001 RATING** 86 **DRINK** 2007 $ 17.95
Unwooded Chardonnay 2003 RATING 85 **DRINK** Now $ 15.50
Chenin Blanc 2003 RATING 85 **DRINK** Now $ 14.20
Shiraz 2002 RATING 84 **DRINK** Now $ 14.95

ŸŸŸ **Silk 2003 RATING** 83 $ 14.50

S Kidman Wines

Riddoch Highway, Coonawarra, SA 5263 **REGION** Coonawarra
T (08) 8736 5071 **F** (08) 8736 5070 **OPEN** 7 days 9–5
WINEMAKER John Innes (Contract) **EST.** 1984 **CASES** 8000
PRODUCT RANGE ($14–22 CD) Riesling, Sauvignon Blanc, Shiraz, Cabernet Sauvignon.
SUMMARY One of the district pioneers, with a 16-hectare estate vineyard which is now fully mature. Limited retail distribution in Melbourne and Adelaide and exports through Australian Prestige Wines.

ŸŸŸŸŸ **Coonawarra Riesling 2003** Highly aromatic apple blossom aromas; delicate but long and balanced palate; lovely wine. **RATING** 93 **DRINK** 2013 $ 15

ŸŸŸŸ **Coonawarra Sauvignon Blanc 2003 RATING** 84 **DRINK** Now $ 14

Skillogalee

Off Hughes Park Road, Sevenhill via Clare, SA 5453 **REGION** Clare Valley
T (08) 8843 4311 **F** (08) 8843 4343 **OPEN** 7 days 10–5
WINEMAKER Dave Palmer **EST.** 1970 **CASES** 7000
PRODUCT RANGE Riesling, Gewurztraminer, Chardonnay, Sparkling Riesling, Late Picked Riesling, Shiraz, The Cabernets, fortifieds.
SUMMARY ($12.50–35 CD) David and Diana Palmer purchased the small hillside stone winery from the George family at the end of the 1980s and have capitalised to the full on the exceptional fruit quality of the Skillogalee vineyards. The winery also has a well-patronised lunchtime restaurant. All of the wines are generous and full-flavoured, particularly the reds. In July 2002 the Palmers purchased next door neighbour Waninga Vineyards, with 30 hectares of 30-year-old vines, allowing a substantial increase in production without any change in quality or style. Exports to the UK, Switzerland, Hong Kong and the US.

ŸŸŸŸ **Riesling 2003** Clean, ripe citrus aromas; an intense and powerful palate with similar ripe citrus on the mid to back palate; considerable structure. **RATING** 90 **DRINK** 2013 $ 20.50

ŸŸŸŸ **Shiraz 2001** Complex spice, leather, black fruit and vanilla aromas; a juicy berry palate with pleasantly pronounced acidity. **RATING** 88 **DRINK** 2010 $ 29

ŸŸŸŸ **Gewurztraminer 2003 RATING** 86 **DRINK** 2007 $ 20.50

Small Gully Wines

NR

Roenfeldt Road, Greenock, SA 5355 (postal) **REGION** Barossa Valley
T 0411 690 047 **F** (08) 8376 4276 **OPEN** Not
WINEMAKER Stephen Black **EST.** 2000 **CASES** 2000
PRODUCT RANGE ($25–37 ML) Semillon, Shiraz, Gawler River Shiraz, Ringbark Red Shiraz Cabernet.
SUMMARY Stephen Black is producing a carefully positioned range of wines, from Barossa Valley Semillon ($7) and Gawler River Shiraz ($12) in cleanskin form progressing upwards to $25 for the Ringbark Red Shiraz Cabernet blend and $37 for the flagship product, Small Gully Shiraz. (Last available prices.)

Smithbrook

Smith Brook Road, Middlesex via Manjimup, WA 6258 **REGION** Manjimup
T (08) 9772 3557 **F** (08) 9772 3579 **OPEN** By appointment
WINEMAKER Michael Symons, Jonathan Farrington **EST.** 1988 **CASES** 15 000
PRODUCT RANGE ($17–35 ML) Sauvignon Blanc, Chardonnay, Merlot, The Yilgarn, Cabernet Sauvignon.
SUMMARY Smithbrook is a major player in the Manjimup region, with 60 hectares of vines in production. A majority interest was acquired by Petaluma in 1997 but will continue its role as a contract grower for other companies, as well as supplying Petaluma's needs and making relatively small amounts of wine under its own label. Perhaps the most significant change has been the removal of Pinot Noir from the current range of products, and the introduction of Merlot. National distribution through Negociants; exports to UK, New Zealand and Japan.

ŸŸŸŸ **Merlot 2001** Distinctly varietal spicy and olive overtones to the black fruit at its core; well balanced and impressive. **RATING** 90 **DRINK** 2010 $ 24

ŸŸŸŸ **The Yilgarn 2001** An expressive range of black fruits, still very youthful to the point of aggression. **RATING** 87 **DRINK** 2011 $ 24

ŸŸŸŸ **Sauvignon Blanc 2003 RATING** 86 **DRINK** Now $ 18
Pemberton Sauvignon Blanc 2002 RATING 85 **DRINK** Now $ 17.50

SmithLeigh Vineyard

★★★

53 Osborne Road, Lane Cove, NSW 2066 **REGION** Lower Hunter Valley
T 0418 484 565 **F** (02) 9420 2014 **OPEN** Not
WINEMAKER Andrew Margan (Contract) **EST.** 1997 **CASES** 3000
PRODUCT RANGE ($13–16 CD) Old Vine Hunter Semillon, Verdelho, Chardonnay, Shiraz.
SUMMARY As the name suggests, a partnership between Rod and Ivija Smith and John and Jan Leigh, which purchased part of the long-established Lindeman Cobcroft Road vineyard from Southcorp in 1996. A lot of work in the vineyard, and skilled contract winemaking by Andrew Margan has produced the right outcomes.

ŸŸŸŸ **Old Vine Reserve Semillon 2003** Already showing plenty of mid-palate, sweet citrus fruit; generous style. **RATING** 89 **DRINK** 2008 $ 13

ŸŸŸŸ **Semillon 2003 RATING** 84 **DRINK** 2010 $ 15

ŸŸŸ **Semillon 2002 RATING** 80 $ 15

Snowdon Wines

NR

Bawden road, Woodend, Vic 3442 **REGION** Macedon Ranges
T (03) 5423 5252 **F** (03) 5423 5272 **OPEN** 7 days 10–5
WINEMAKER Andrew Byers **EST.** 1987
PRODUCT RANGE Various price pointed ranges of varietal wines under brands such as Koala Blue, Olivia and under regional groupings.
SUMMARY The Neylon family has built up a wide ranging wine business; most of the wine is exported, the US being the principal market.

Snowy River Winery

NR

Rockwell Road, Berridale, NSW 2628 **REGION** Southern New South Wales Zone
T (02) 6456 5041 **F** (02) 6456 5005 **OPEN** Wed–Sun, 7 days during school holidays
WINEMAKER Manfred Plumecke **EST.** 1984 **CASES** 2500
PRODUCT RANGE ($10–20 CD) Snowy White, Alpine Dry White, Sauvignon Blanc Chardonnay, Sylvaner Muller Thurgau, Sieger Rebe [sic], Rhine Riesling Auslese, Noble Riesling, Snow Bruska, Snowy Port, Tawny Port.
SUMMARY An operation which relies entirely on the substantial tourist trade passing through or near Berridale on the way to the Snowy Mountains. The product range is, to put it mildly, eclectic; all the wines are said to be made on-site, and the grapes for all of the white varietals are estate-grown.

Somerset Hill Wines

★★★☆

891 McLeod Road, Denmark, WA 6333 **REGION** Denmark
T (08) 9840 9388 **F** (08) 9840 9394 **OPEN** 7 days 11–5
WINEMAKER James Kellie (Contract) **EST.** 1995 **CASES** 3000
PRODUCT RANGE ($12.80–30 CD) Semillon, Sauvignon Blanc, Semillon Sauvignon Blanc, Chardonnay (unwooded), Constellation (sparkling), Harmony (sweet white blend), Pinot Noir, Merlot.
SUMMARY Graham Upson commenced planting 11 hectares of pinot noir, chardonnay, semillon, merlot and sauvignon blanc in 1995, and Somerset Hill Wines duly opened its limestone cellar-door sales area with sweeping views out over the ocean. Limited retail distribution in Melbourne and Sydney, exports to Denmark, Europe and Greenland. At the time of going to print, was being offered for sale.

Sorrenberg

NR

Alma Road, Beechworth, Vic 3747 **REGION** Beechworth
T (03) 5728 2278 **F** (03) 5728 2278 **OPEN** Mon–Fri by appointment, most weekends 1–5 (by appointment)
WINEMAKER Barry Morey **EST.** 1986 **CASES** 1200
PRODUCT RANGE ($22–36 CD) Sauvignon Blanc Semillon, Chardonnay, Gamay, Cabernet Sauvignon, Havelock Hills Shiraz, Cabernet Merlot Franc.
SUMMARY Barry and Jan Morey made their first wines in 1989 from the 3-hectare vineyard situated on the outskirts of Beechworth. No recent tastings, but the wines have a good reputation and loyal clientele, selling out rapidly. The Gamay is a specialty, the Chardonnay likewise.

Southern Dreams

NR

10293 Deeside Coast Road, Northcliffe, WA 6262 **REGION** Pemberton
T (08) 9775 1027 **F** (08) 9389 9242 **OPEN** By appointment
WINEMAKER John Wade, Gordon Parker (Contract) **EST.** 1997
PRODUCT RANGE ($18–23 ML) Sauvignon Blanc, Shiraz, Cabernet Sauvignon Merlot.
SUMMARY John Akehurst and family have planted 12 hectares of sauvignon blanc, chardonnay, merlot, shiraz and cabernet sauvignon. Giant Karri, Marri and Jarrah trees surround the property, with the Shannon National Park on one side. The adjacent 10-hectare dam is home to a family of black swans, ducks and visiting pelicans. The vineyard is managed by Brian Roche and the wines are made by the highly-credentialled team of John Wade and Gordon Parker. So far, the wines are sold through the website <www.southerndreams.com.au>, mail order and, to a lesser degree, the cellar door.

Southern Grand Estate

NR

111 Goulburn Street, Sydney, NSW 2000 (postal) **REGION** Upper Hunter Valley
T (02) 9282 0987 **F** (02) 9211 8130 **OPEN** Not
WINEMAKER Jon Reynolds (Contract) **EST.** 1997
PRODUCT RANGE ($20–25 R) A wide range of table wines reflecting the Joseph's coat spread of plantings.
SUMMARY This is a large, export-oriented business, once known as Hollydeen. The estate vineyards comprise semillon (12.4 hectares), chardonnay (9 hectares), traminer (6 hectares), verdelho (5.6 hectares), sauvignon blanc (2 hectares), cabernet franc (8.8 hectares), cabernet sauvignon (7.8 hectares), pinot noir (4 hectares) and ruby cabernet (3.6 hectares).

🍃 Southern Highland Wines

NR

Oldbury Road, Sutton Forest, NSW 2577 **REGION** Southern Highlands
T (02) 4868 2300 **F** (02) 4868 1808 **OPEN** 7 days 10–5
WINEMAKER Eddy Rossi **EST.** 2003 **CASES** 10 000
PRODUCT RANGE ($20 ML) Riesling, Sauvignon Blanc, Novello Bianco, Chardonnay, Golden Vale
Botrytis, Shiraz, Chambourcin, Novello Rosso, Cabernet Sauvignon.
SUMMARY The venture is owned by its five directors, with 50 years of experience in the wine
industry and in commerce. John Gilbertson ran Ericsson in New Zealand and thereafter China
between 1983 and 2000. Darren Corradi and Eddy Rossi are respectively in charge of viticulture
and winemaking, both with lengthy careers in various Griffith wineries, the same training ground
for production director Frank Colloridi. New Zealand-born Simon Gilbertson graduated from
Lincoln University with a degree in agriculture, and after 13 years in corporate life, purchased
three vineyards in Hawke's Bay, New Zealand; he is de facto general manager and sales director.
Forty-one hectares of vines have been established, a veritable fruit salad of pinot gris, riesling,
gewurztraminer, sauvignon blanc, chardonnay, viognier, nebbiolo, sangiovese, pinot noir, shiraz
and cabernet sauvignon.

🍃 Spoehr Creek Wines

★★★

Greenhill Road, Balhannah, SA 5242 **REGION** Adelaide Hills
T (08) 8398 0884 **F** (08) 8398 0885 **OPEN** Weekends 11–5, or by appointment
WINEMAKER Stephen Black **EST.** 2001 **CASES** 2000
PRODUCT RANGE ($12–20 ML) Sauvignon Blanc, Viogner, Chardonnay, Rose, Pinot Noir, Merlot,
Shiraz, Sparkling Merlot, Fortified Gordo.
SUMMARY Philip Reid and Margie Ringwood purchased the previous Pibbin vineyard and winery
(excluding the brand name and stock) in March 2001. It is one of a handful of on-site wineries in the
Adelaide Hills; very few licences have been issued due to the desire to protect the quality of the
ground water as an important source for Adelaide's water supply. The vineyard is planted to merlot
(3 hectares), pinot noir (1.35 hectares), sauvignon blanc (1 hectare) and viogner (0.7 hectare), and
the grape intake is supplemented by purchases both from Adelaide Hills growers and from the
Riverland and Adelaide Plains for the Rose and planned Shiraz at lower price points. A much
expanded range of wines from 2003 will take the production to around 5000 cases, and will lead to
distribution in South Australia and the eastern States.

ŸŸŸŸ   **Merlot 2001** Clean, fresh, bright juicy red and black fruit flavours; ripe tannins; has
soaked up the oak in which it spent 20 months. **RATING** 89 **DRINK** 2010 $16
Pinot Noir 2001 Fresh cherry and strawberry aromas; a delicate palate, but has length and
bright finish; screwcap will protect the fruit freshness. **RATING** 87 **DRINK** Now $18

ŸŸŸŸ   **Chardonnay 2002 RATING** 85 **DRINK** Now $15
Rose 2002 RATING 84 **DRINK** Now $12

ŸŸŸ   **Viognier 2002 RATING** 82 $20

🍃 Springbrook Mountain Vineyard

NR

2824 Springbrook Road, Springbrook, Qld 4213 **REGION** Queensland Coastal
T (07) 5533 5300 **F** (07) 5533 5212 **OPEN** 7 days 10–4
WINEMAKER Bruce Humphery-Smith (Contract) **EST.** 2000 **CASES** 2000
PRODUCT RANGE ($13–20 CD) Purlingbrook, Mountain Dew, Verdelho, Unwooded Chardonnay,
Chardonnay, Rainforest Red, Queensland Red, Reserve Shiraz, Cabernet Sauvignon, liqueurs.
SUMMARY The 6-hectare Springbrook Mountain Vineyard has been established on a 32-hectare
property surrounded by rainforest on the Springbrook Plateau, part of the volcanic rim of Mount
Warning. It is also in the heart of a tourist wonderland, 45 minutes from Surfers Paradise and just
north of the New South Wales border. A 100-tonne on-site winery is to be constructed, plus a
chapel for weddings, nine chalets and ten permanent tents, all to come over the next 5 years. The
attention of Bruce Humphery-Smith as consultant winemaker suggests it's not all tourism,
however.

🦅 SpringLane ★★★☆

PO Box 390, Yarra Glen, Vic 3775 **REGION** Yarra Valley
T (03) 9730 1107 **F** (03) 9739 0135 **OPEN** Not
WINEMAKER Tom Carson (Contract) **EST.** 1998 **CASES** 1800
PRODUCT RANGE ($23.50–28.50 ML) Viognier, Pinot Rose, Merlot.
SUMMARY SpringLane is the separately owned wine business of Graeme Rathbone, brother of Doug Rathbone, who is the (corporate) owner of Yering Station. The wines are made at Yering Station from grapes grown on the SpringLane Vineyard established some years ago. There are 14 hectares in total, comprising merlot (4 hectares), pinot noir (3 hectares), shiraz, cabernet sauvignon and viognier (2 hectares each) and cabernet franc (1 hectare). Part of the production is sold to Yering Station, part used for the SpringLane label. They are sold by mail order and through specialty retail and restaurant outlets.

▼▼▼▼▽ **Viognier 2002** Complex, tangy multi-aromas and flavours; powerful and complex wine.
RATING 90 **DRINK** Now $ 28.50

▼▼▼▼ **Rose 2002** Very different from the '03, part stylistic and part vintage; more complex in many levels; there is significant bottle variation, however. **RATING** 88 **DRINK** Now $ 23.50
Rose 2003 Light salmon-pink; an admirably clean, fresh and crisp array of red fruits; good balance, not sweet. **RATING** 87 **DRINK** Now $ 23.50
Merlot 2001 Spice, earth, olive and small black fruits; light to medium-bodied and not forced by extract or oak; fine tannins to close. **RATING** 87 **DRINK** 2008 $ 28.50

Spring Ridge Wines   NR

880 Darbys Falls Road, Cowra, NSW 2794 **REGION** Cowra
T (02) 6341 3820 **F** (02) 6341 3820 **OPEN** By appointment
WINEMAKER Contract **EST.** 1997
PRODUCT RANGE ($13–16 ML) Semillon, Chardonnay, Shiraz.
SUMMARY Peter and Anne Jeffery have established 5 hectares of shiraz, 2.5 hectares each of chardonnay and semillon, 1.7 hectares of cabernet sauvignon and 1 hectare of merlot. They sell by far the greatest part of the grape production, having a small amount made under the Spring Ridge Wines label.

🦅 Springton Cellars   NR

14 Miller Street, Springton, SA 5235 **REGION** Southern Flinders Ranges
T (08) 8568 2220 **F** (08) 8346 9533 **OPEN** Weekends 12.30–6.30
WINEMAKER Chris Thomas **EST.** 1999
PRODUCT RANGE Old Gunyah Road Shiraz, Cabernet Sauvignon.
SUMMARY Dr Allen E. Gale has a CV of extraordinary length, specialising in allergy. Together with Chris Thomas he has established 1 hectare of vines at Wilmington in the Southern Flinders Ranges, a very promising area which is a newly-recognised region under the Geographic Indication legislation. The Cabernet Sauvignon and Shiraz are made off-site by Chris Thomas, and are chiefly sold from the cellar door and the adjoining Café C Restaurant together with hotels and restaurants throughout the mid and far north. For reasons not immediately clear, Old Gunyah Road Shiraz won the Upper Spencer Gulf 'Exporting to the World Award 2001/2002'.

Spring Vale Vineyards ★★★☆

130 Spring Vale Road, Cranbrook, Tas 7190 **REGION** Southern Tasmania
T (03) 6257 8208 **F** (03) 6257 8598 **OPEN** Mon–Fri 10–5, or by appointment
WINEMAKER Kristen Lyne **EST.** 1986 **CASES** 3000
PRODUCT RANGE ($13.50–35 CD) Gewurztraminer, Chardonnay, Salute (sparkling), Louisa (sweet), Pinot Gris, Pinot Noir; Baudin Chardonnay and Pinot Noir.
SUMMARY Rodney Lyne has progressively established 1.5 hectares each of pinot noir and chardonnay and then added 0.5 hectare each of gewurztraminer and pinot gris; the latter produced a first crop in 1998. Frost has caused havoc from time to time, not only financially destructive, but also frustrating, for Spring Vale can, and does, produce first-class wines when the frost stays away. Exports to the UK.

YYYY **Louisa 2003** Powerful, luscious and long, though not particularly complex; may build with time. **RATING** 89 **DRINK** 2009 $ 18

Chardonnay 2002 Lots of rich, ripe nectarine fruit, still building complexity. **RATING** 87 **DRINK** 2009 $ 18

Pinot Noir 2002 Quite complex tangy/sappy style; just a hint of mint detracts. **RATING** 87 **DRINK** 2008 $ 35

Salute 2000 Obvious straw tinge; generous mouthfeel; dried fruit and nuts; good balance, fractionally sweet. **RATING** 87 **DRINK** 2007 $ 30

YYYY **Gewurztraminer 2003** **RATING** 85 **DRINK** Now $ 21

YYY **Pinot Gris 2003** **RATING** 83 $ 21

Springviews Wine

Woodlands Road, Porongurup, WA 6324 **REGION** Porongurup
T (08) 9853 2088 **F** (08) 9853 2098 **OPEN** 7 days 10–5
WINEMAKER Howard Park (Contract) **EST.** 1994 **CASES** 400
PRODUCT RANGE ($15–20 CD) Riesling, Chardonnay, Cabernet Sauvignon.
SUMMARY Andy and Alice Colquhoun planted their 5-hectare vineyard (2 hectares each of chardonnay and cabernet sauvignon and 1 hectare of riesling) in 1994. The wine is contract-made and is sold through the cellar door and mailing list.

Stanley Brothers ★★★

Barossa Valley Way, Tanunda, SA 5352 **REGION** Barossa Valley
T (08) 8563 3375 **F** (08) 8563 3758 **OPEN** 7 days 9–5
WINEMAKER Lindsay Stanley **EST.** 1994 **CASES** 15 000
PRODUCT RANGE ($11–25 CD) Sylvaner, Semillon Riesling, Full Sister Semillon, Chardonnay, Premium Barossa Cuvee, John Hancock Shiraz, August Shiraz, Thoroughbred Cabernet Sauvignon, Black Sheep Shiraz Malbec Merlot, Choc-a-Bloc (chocolate port).
SUMMARY Former Anglesey winemaker and industry veteran Lindsay Stanley established his own business in the Barossa Valley when he purchased (and renamed) the former Kroemer Estate in late 1994. As one would expect, the wines are competently made, although usually very light-bodied. Twenty-one hectares of estate plantings have provided virtually all of the grapes for the business. Exports to Switzerland, France, Luxembourg, Japan, Hong Kong, Malaysia and the US.

YYYY **August Shiraz 2000** **RATING** 84 **DRINK** Now $ 25

Shiraz Malbec Merlot 2001 **RATING** 84 **DRINK** Now $ 15.50

Thoroughbred Cabernet Sauvignon 2000 **RATING** 84 **DRINK** 2007 $ 19.50

YYY **Full Sister Semillon 2002** **RATING** 83 $ 15.50

Stanton & Killeen Wines

Jacks Road, Murray Valley Highway, Rutherglen, Vic 3685 **REGION** Rutherglen
T (02) 6032 9457 **F** (02) 6032 8018 **OPEN** Mon–Sat 9–5, Sun 10–5
WINEMAKER Chris Killeen **EST.** 1875 **CASES** 15 000
PRODUCT RANGE ($11–100 CD) A red wine and fortified wine specialist, though offering Chardonnay, Riesling, White Frontignac, Auslese Tokay and Parkview Dry White as well as Parkview Dry Red, Moodemere Shiraz, Cabernet Franc Merlot, Cabernet Shiraz, Shiraz, Durif; fortifieds include Rutherglen White Port, Rutherglen Ruby Port, Rutherglen Muscat; Classic Rutherglen Tawny, Tokay and Muscat; Grand Rutherglen Muscat; Rare Rutherglen Muscat.
SUMMARY Chris Killeen has skilfully expanded the portfolio of Stanton & Killeen but without in any way compromising its reputation as a traditional maker of smooth, rich reds, some of Australia's best Vintage Ports, and attractive, fruity Muscats and Tokays. All in all, deserves far greater recognition. Exports to the UK.

YYYYY **Rare Rutherglen Muscat NV (375 ml)** Deep brown, olive-rimmed; has fantastic flair and style; in the mouth, there is still a core of fresh muscat fruit encased in a complex web of nutty, raisin-accented rancio, spirit the hidden scalpel. **RATING** 96 **DRINK** Now $ 100

Vintage Port 1999 Truly eclectic six-variety blend which all comes together on the finish and aftertaste; almost dry; very Portuguese in style. **RATING** 94 **DRINK** 2021 $ 27

Grand Rutherglen Muscat NV (500 ml) Full olive-brown; clear-cut rancio aligns with clean spirit and spicy/grapey fruit; excellent balance and structure, the tannins subliminal, but giving another dimension to the flavour; very long, fine finish. **RATING** 94 **DRINK** Now $ 75

ŶŶŶŶŶ **Classic Rutherglen Tokay NV (500 ml)** Light to medium golden-brown; great clarity and freshness, with honey and tea-leaf aromas; lively and vibrant with similar finesse and harmony to the Campbell wines. Finishes with excellent acidity and a clean, crisp aftertaste. **RATING** 92 **DRINK** Now $ 25

Classic Rutherglen Muscat NV (500 ml) Has a great display of grapey varietal fruit, skilfully combining younger and older material. Fine tannins give the wine extra structure and intensity. **RATING** 92 **DRINK** Now $ 25

Shiraz Durif 2002 Round, supple and rich; blackberry, spiced/strewed plum; but not jammy, gentle tannins. **RATING** 90 **DRINK** 2017 $ 17

Cabernet Sauvignon 2002 Interesting; the profile of cooler region cabernet; blackcurrant, touches of leaf and spice; neat oak. **RATING** 90 **DRINK** 2015 $ 18

Cabernet Sauvignon Cabernet Franc Merlot 2002 Deeply coloured; complex rich and powerful blackberry/blackcurrant; hint of bitter chocolate. **RATING** 90 **DRINK** 2012 $ 22

ŶŶŶŶ **Rutherglen Muscat NV (500 ml)** Bright tawny, with a faint crimson blush; high-toned spirit on the bouquet lifts rather than obscures the fruit; intense, raisiny yet fresh. **RATING** 89 **DRINK** Now $ 16.50

Stanton Estate   NR

135 North Isis Road, Childers, Qld 4660 **REGION** Queensland Zone
T (07) 4126 1255 **F** (07) 4126 1823 **OPEN** Weekends 10–5, or by appointment
WINEMAKER Symphony Hill (Contract) **EST.** 2000 **CASES** 500
PRODUCT RANGE ($14–30 CD) Organic range of Marsanne Verdelho, Verdelho, Marsanne, Cabernet Sauvignon Merlot; Chardonnay, Rose, Shiraz, Ruby Port.
SUMMARY Keith and Joy Stanton have established 2 hectares of verdelho, marsanne, cabernet sauvignon and merlot using organic growing methods, and are seeking organic certification, making Stanton Estate the only organically-grown wine in Queensland. The wines are also made to BFA standards, which permit the use of some SO_2, but within strictly controlled limits. The wines are contract-made by Symphony Hill Wine Pty Ltd, and sell out rapidly through the cellar door and Woodgate Restaurant.

Star Lane   NR

RMB 1167 Star Lane, Beechworth, Vic 3747 **REGION** Beechworth
T (03) 5728 7268 **OPEN** By appointment
WINEMAKER Keppell Smith (Contract) **EST.** 1996
PRODUCT RANGE Rose, Shiraz, Merlot.
SUMMARY Liz and Brett Barnes have established 4 hectares of shiraz and merlot (planted in 1996) with further plantings of riesling and chardonnay scheduled for late 2004. When Liz Barnes completed her winemaking course, she will take responsibility for winemaking from Keppell Smith (of Savaterre), but, even then, will continue to sell 70 per cent of their grape production.

Statford Park   NR

Farmgate at Statford Park, Pearson's Lane, Wildes Meadow, NSW 2577 **REGION** Southern Highlands
T (02) 4885 1101 **F** (02) 4885 1035 **OPEN** 7 days 10–5
WINEMAKER Contract **EST.** 2000 **CASES** 1000
PRODUCT RANGE ($13.25 R) Wildes Meadow range of Classic White Sauvignon Blanc, Chardonnay Blend, Classic Red Cabernet Hermitage (sic) and Classic Red Cabernet Merlot.
SUMMARY Statford Park is situated in the triangle bounded by Robertson 5 kilometres east, Burrawang 5 kilometres to the northwest and the site of Wildes Meadow some 6 kilometres

southwest. The Wildes Meadow Creek rises in the northeastern end of the valley, runs east-west through to Lake Fitzroy a few kilometres further west. In 1997/98 6500 vines were planted, the first wine release following in June 2001. The cellar door has an exotic array of lavender and other products.

Station Creek

NR

Edi Road, Cheshunt, Vic 3678 **REGION** King Valley
T (03) 5729 8265 **F** (03) 5729 8056 **OPEN** 7 days
WINEMAKER Warren Proft (Contract) **EST.** 1999 **CASES** 2000
PRODUCT RANGE ($10–25 CD) Sauvignon Blanc, Grand Cru Reserve, Sparkling Shiraz, Shiraz, Merlot, Cabernet Sauvignon.
SUMMARY David and Sharon Steer have established 5 hectares of vineyards at Cheshunt, planted to sauvignon blanc, cabernet sauvignon, merlot and shiraz. Sales are by mail order and through the cellar door, which offers light meals, crafts, a gallery and local produce.

Staughton Vale Vineyard

NR

20 Staughton Vale Road, Anakie, Vic 3221 **REGION** Geelong
T (03) 5284 1477 **F** (03) 5284 1229 **OPEN** Fri–Mon and public holidays 10–5, or by appointment
WINEMAKER Paul Chambers **EST.** 1986 **CASES** 2000
PRODUCT RANGE Riesling, Pinot Noir, Staughton (Merlot blend), Tawny Port, Liqueur Shiraz.
SUMMARY Paul Chambers has 6 hectares of closely-planted vines, with the accent on the classic Bordeaux mix of cabernet sauvignon, merlot, cabernet franc and petit verdot, although chardonnay and pinot noir are also planted. Weekend lunches available at the Staughton Cottage Restaurant.

Steels Creek Estate

★★★

1 Sewell Road, Steels Creek, Vic 3775 **REGION** Yarra Valley
T (03) 5965 2448 **F** (03) 5965 2448 **OPEN** Weekends and public holidays 10–6, or by appointment
WINEMAKER Simon Peirce **EST.** 1981 **CASES** 400
PRODUCT RANGE ($15–22 CD) Colombard, Chardonnay, Shiraz, Cabernet Sauvignon.
SUMMARY Established by brother and sister team Simon and Kerri Peirce. While only a tiny operation, with 1.7 hectares of vineyard planted at various times between 1981 and 1994, Steels Creek Estate has an on-site winery where the wines are made with assistance from consultants, but increasingly by Simon Peirce, who has completed his associate diploma in Applied Science (Winegrowing) at Charles Sturt University.

TTTT **Shiraz 2001** Spicy blackberry fruit; medium-bodied; good balance, and expands on the finish. **RATING** 89 **DRINK** 2009 $ 22

TTTY **Chardonnay 2001 RATING** 85 **DRINK** Now $ 15

Stefano Lubiana

★★★★

60 Rowbottoms Road, Granton, Tas 7030 **REGION** Southern Tasmania
T (03) 6263 7457 **F** (03) 6263 7430 **OPEN** Sun–Thurs 11–3 (closed some public holidays)
WINEMAKER Steve Lubiana **EST.** 1990 **CASES** 8000
PRODUCT RANGE ($23–47 CD) Riesling, Sauvignon Blanc, Pinot Grigio, Sur Lie Chardonnay, Chardonnay, NV Brut, Pinot Noir, Primavera Pinot Noir, Merlot.
SUMMARY The charming, self-effacing Steve Lubiana has moved from one extreme to the other, having run Lubiana Wines at Moorook in the South Australian Riverland for many years before moving to Granton to set up a substantial winery. The estate-produced Stefano Lubiana wines come from 14 hectares of beautifully located vineyards sloping down to the Derwent River. All the Lubiana wines are immaculately crafted. Exports to Denmark and Germany.

TTTTY **Chardonnay 2002** Fully ripened nectarine and stone fruit; fine acidity, good balance and perfect oak. **RATING** 93 **DRINK** 2007 $ 37

TTTT **Pinot Grigio 2003** Pinot Gris Good line, length and balance; delicate pear and a hint of musk; crisp finish. **RATING** 87 **DRINK** 2007 $ 25

🐚 Steler Estate Wines

NR

26 Belvedere Close, Pakenham Upper, Vic 3810 **REGION** Gippsland
T (03) 9796 5766 **F** (03) 9796 5695 **OPEN** By appointment
WINEMAKER Andrew Clarke (Contract) **EST.** 1996 **CASES** 150
PRODUCT RANGE ($25 CD) Merlot.
SUMMARY Croatian-born Tom Steler had a tough upbringing as an orphan in his native country, but he overcame many obstacles to obtain a degree in forestry before migrating to Australia in 1970. Shortly thereafter he met wife Suzanna, and together they established a successful UV coating and spray-painting business. They planted the first vines in 1996, intending simply to make wine for their own consumption, but further plantings in 1997 have resulted in a little less than a hectare of shiraz and merlot. In the first years of production, Sergio Carlei was the consultant/contract winemaker, but in 2004 the winemaking was transferred to the Steler Estate property, with Andrew Clarke of Jinks Creek Winery doing the honours.

Stellar Ridge Estate

★★★

Clews Road, Cowaramup, WA 6284 **REGION** Margaret River
T (08) 9755 5635 **F** (08) 9755 5636 **OPEN** 7 days 10–5
WINEMAKER Mark Lane **EST.** 1994 **CASES** 1500
PRODUCT RANGE ($16–25 CD) Sauvignon Blanc, Verdelho, Unwooded Chardonnay, Late Harvest Sauvignon Blanc, Shiraz, Cabernet Sauvignon; also estate-grown varietally identified olive oil (Pendolino, Leccino, Frantolo, WA Mission).
SUMMARY Colin and Helene Hellier acquired a 49-hectare grazing property at Cowaramup in 1993 which included 2.5 hectares of chardonnay and sauvignon blanc planted in 1987. A large dam was constructed in 1994, and the following year 11 hectares of new vineyards and 4 hectares of olive trees were planted; 1.6 hectares of zinfandel followed in 1996, bringing total plantings to 15.1 hectares. The majority of the 100-tonne grape production is sold to other local wineries, with 14 to 15 tonnes being retained for the Stellar Ridge label. The wines are sold exclusively through the cellar door and by mailing list. At the time of going to print, was being offered for sale.

♥♥♥♀ Verdelho 2002 RATING 84 **DRINK** Now $16

Stephen John Wines

★★★★

Government Road, Watervale, SA 5452 **REGION** Clare Valley
T (08) 8843 0105 **F** (08) 8843 0105 **OPEN** 7 days 11–5
WINEMAKER Stephen John **EST.** 1994 **CASES** 7500
PRODUCT RANGE ($15–40 CD) Watervale Riesling, Semillon Sauvignon Blanc, Blanc de Blanc, Traugott Cuvee Sparkling Burgundy, Pinot Noir, Clare Valley Shiraz, Estate Reserve Shiraz, Merlot, Estate Reserve Cabernet Sauvignon.
SUMMARY The John family is one of the best-known names in the Barossa Valley, with branches running Australia's best cooperage (AP John & Sons) and providing the chief winemaker of Lindemans (Philip John) and the former chief winemaker of Quelltaler (Stephen John). Stephen and Rita John have now formed their own family business in the Clare Valley, based on a 6-hectare vineyard overlooking the town of Watervale and supplemented by modest intake from a few local growers. The cellar-door sales area is housed in an 80-year-old stable which has been renovated and is full of rustic charm. The significantly increased production and good quality of the current releases has led to the appointment of distributors in each of the eastern States, and exports to the UK, the US, Malaysia and Singapore.

♥♥♥♥♥ Dry Grown Shiraz 2001 Excellent, pure shiraz fruit in red fruit spectrum; long, lingering fine tannins; elegant. **RATING** 94 **DRINK** 2015 $20

♥♥♥♥♀ Estate Reserve Shiraz 2000 Complex and powerful, more in black fruit/blackberry/black plum spectrum; luscious, yet only 13 degrees alcohol. **RATING** 93 **DRINK** 2017 $40

♥♥♥♥ Watervale Riesling 2003 Clean, generous citrus/lime/tropical fruit mix; good balance. **RATING** 89 **DRINK** 2008 $20

♥♥♥♀ Traugott Cuvee NV RATING 86 **DRINK** 2008 $20
Merlot 2002 RATING 85 **DRINK** 2010 $18

♥♥♥ Pinot Noir 2002 RATING 83 $15

Step Road Winery

★★☆

Davidson Road, Langhorne Creek, SA 5255 (postal) **REGION** Langhorne Creek
T (08) 8537 3342 **F** (08) 8537 3357 **OPEN** Not
WINEMAKER Rob Dundon **EST.** 1998 **CASES** 120 000
PRODUCT RANGE ($11.95–19.50 CD) The economy second label is Red Wing, with Chardonnay and Cabernet Sauvignon; under the Step Road Label Sauvignon Blanc (Adelaide Hills), Pinot Noir, Shiraz (McLaren Vale and Langhorne Creek), Sangiovese (Langhorne Creek) and Cabernet Sauvignon (McLaren Vale and Langhorne Creek).
SUMMARY Step Road has 30 hectares of vineyard in Langhorne Creek, and 40 hectares in the Adelaide Hills, supplementing the production from those vineyards with cabernet sauvignon and shiraz purchased from McLaren Vale. It is an autonomous business, but operationally part of the Beresford Wines group. The wines are distributed nationally by Red+White; exports to the UK, the US, Denmark and New Zealand.

ΨΨΨ **Adelaide Hills Pinot Noir 2001 RATING** 78 $ 17

Sterling Heights

NR

PO Box 115, Launceston, Tas 7250 **REGION** Northern Tasmania
T (03) 6376 1419 **OPEN** Not
WINEMAKER Moorilla Estate (Contract) **EST.** 1988 **CASES** 400
PRODUCT RANGE ($14–16 CD) Riesling, Chardonnay, Breton Rose, Pinot Noir.
SUMMARY Geoff and Jenny Wells have sold their 2-hectare vineyard at Winkleigh, which was the source for the Sterling Heights wines. They have retained the Sterling Heights brand, and will continue to sell the packaged wine they have in stock. A new planting at St Helens is in contemplation.

Stevens Brook Estate

★★★

620 High Street, Echuca, Vic 3564 **REGION** Perricoota
T (03) 5480 1916 **F** (03) 5480 2004 **OPEN** 7 days 10–5
WINEMAKER Mal Stewart, David Cowburn **EST.** 1995 **CASES** 5000
PRODUCT RANGE ($15–24 CD) Verdelho, Chardonnay, Portia Sparkling Shiraz, Sanchez (Chianti style), Shiraz, Sangiovese, Petit Verdot, Cabernet Sauvignon; Gerbera Series range of Lazy Lizard White, Pretty in Pink Spatlese, Brown Dog Red.
SUMMARY The Stevens Brook Estate vineyard was established in 1996, with the first commercial production in 1999. Initially the grapes were sold to Rosemount, Southcorp and others, but are now being diverted to the Stevens Brook Estate label. The yield is restricted to 3 to 4 tonnes per acre, roughly half the regional average. The winery was built in 1999 on a separate property on the Echuca side of the Murray River, with an ultimate capacity of 1500 tonnes. The winery itself is established on a 40-hectare site which will be fully planted, allowing significant growth in the volume of the Stevens Brook Estate brand. Just to complicate the picture a little further, but for good reasons, Bill Stevens has established the cellar door operation in the Port of Echuca district, the philosophy being to take the cellar door to the customer, rather than try to draw the customer to the vineyard.

ΨΨΨΨ **Shiraz 2003** Very good colour; rich, generous array of black fruits; good tannin management. **RATING** 87 **DRINK** 2008
Sangiovese 2003 Light to medium-bodied; aromatic, spicy, tangy; unexpected varietal authenticity. **RATING** 87 **DRINK** 2008

ΨΨΨΨ **Petit Verdot 2003** The extra degree of colour and flavour the variety provides under these conditions; however, short finish. **RATING** 86 **DRINK** 2008
Cabernet Sauvignon 2003 RATING 85 **DRINK** 2007
Verdelho 2003 RATING 84 **DRINK** Now

ΨΨΨ **Chardonnay 2003 RATING** 80

Sticks

★★★☆

St Huberts Road, Coldstream, Vic 3770 **REGION** Yarra Valley
T (03) 9739 0666 **F** (03) 9739 0633 **OPEN** 7 days 10–5
WINEMAKER Rob Dolan **EST.** 2000 **CASES** 20 000
PRODUCT RANGE ($16.99–19.50 R) Sauvignon Blanc, Sauvignon Blanc Semillon, Chardonnay, Pinot
Noir, Shiraz, Merlot, Cabernet Sauvignon.
SUMMARY Rob Dolan, the affable, towering (former) long-serving winemaker at Yarra Ridge, has
always had the nickname Sticks, doubtless recognising his long legs. Since leaving Yarra Ridge
several years ago, he has made wine first at Dominion and now at The Punt Road winery. But he has
also decided to produce his own range of wines, which he makes at The Yarra Hill, the grapes being
chosen from 100 hectares spread across three Yarra Valley vineyards. The wines are keenly priced,
the packaging excellent, and national distribution through Red+White should all contribute to rapid
growth for the brand. A new cellar door opened mid-2004.

♀♀♀♀♀ Chardonnay 2003 Classic Yarra Chardonnay; a long, elegant palate with sweet stone fruit
and melon, subtle oak. **RATING** 91 **DRINK** 2008 **$** 16.99

♀♀♀♀ Sauvignon Blanc 2003 Clean, fresh and crisp; asparagus, gooseberry and mineral.
RATING 87 **DRINK** Now **$** 16.99

Pinot Noir 2003 Pleasant plum and red cherry fruit; relatively crisp finish; no frills but it
is Pinot Noir. **RATING** 87 **DRINK** Now **$** 19.50

Stone Bridge Estate

NR

RMB 189 Holleys Road, Manjimup, WA 6258 **REGION** Manjimup
T (08) 9773 1371 **F** (08) 9773 1309 **OPEN** By appointment
WINEMAKER Syd Hooker, Kate Hooker **EST.** 1991 **CASES** 3000
PRODUCT RANGE ($20–30 R) Sauvignon Blanc Semillon, Methode Champenoise, Shiraz, Cabernet
Merlot Malbec.
SUMMARY Syd and Sue Hooker purchased the property on which Stone Bridge Estate is established in
1990, and planted the first vines that year. A subsequent planting in 1996 has increased the vineyard size
to 8 hectares, with shiraz (2 hectares) a total of 1.7 hectares of pinot noir and chardonnay, 1.6 hectares of
the four Bordeaux varieties, 1 hectare each of semillon, sauvignon blanc and sangiovese. The pinot noir
and chardonnay go to provide the Methode Champenoise, made (on-site, like all the other wines) by
daughter Kate, a graduate winemaker and viticulturist from the Lycee Viticole d'Avize in Champagne.

Stone Chimney Creek

NR

PO Box 401, Angaston, SA 5353 **REGION** Barossa Valley
T (08) 8565 3339 **F** (08) 8565 3339 **OPEN** Not
WINEMAKER Chris Ringland **EST.** 1989 **CASES** 100
PRODUCT RANGE ($535 R) Three Rivers Shiraz.
SUMMARY Another tiny production wine produced by ringmaster Chris Ringland, and effectively sold
only in the US through The Grateful Palate. Two hectares of old vine shiraz produce between 60 and
100 cases per year of wine at a breathtaking price. Chris Ringland politely explains that due to the
tiny production, he cannot routinely provide bottles for evaluation.

Stone Coast

18 North Terrace, Adelaide, SA 5000 (postal) **REGION** Wrattonbully
T (08) 8212 1801 **F** (08) 8212 4022 **OPEN** Not
WINEMAKER Steve Maglieri, Scott Rawlinson **EST.** 1997 **CASES** 900
PRODUCT RANGE ($25 R) The Struggle Shiraz, The Commitment Cabernet Sauvignon.
SUMMARY The development of the 33 hectares of cabernet sauvignon and 11 hectares of shiraz which
constitutes the vineyard was exceptionally difficult. It is situated on a terra rossa ridge top, but had
unusually thick limestone slabs running through it, which had caused others to bypass the property.
A 95-tonne bulldozer was hired to deep rip the limestone, but was unequal to the task, and ultimately
explosives had to be used to create sufficient inroads to allow planting. Fifteen per cent of the
production from the vineyard is used to make the wines under the direction of the immensely
experienced Steve Maglieri.

Stonehaven ★★★★

Riddoch Highway, Padthaway, SA 5271 **REGION** Padthaway
T (08) 8765 6140 **F** (08) 8765 6137 **OPEN** 7 days 10–4
WINEMAKER Susanne Bell, Adrienne Cross **EST.** 1998 **CASES** 200 000
PRODUCT RANGE ($12.50–26.99 R) Padthaway Unwooded Chardonnay, Cabernet Merlot, Chardonnay, Limestone Coast Chardonnay, Limestone Coast Viognier, Shiraz, Limestone Coast Shiraz, Padthaway Cabernet Sauvignon, Limited Release Chardonnay.
SUMMARY It is, to say the least, strange that it should have taken 30 years for a substantial winery to be built at Padthaway. However, when BRL Hardy took the decision, it was no half measure: $20 million has been invested in what is the largest greenfields winery built in Australia for more than 20 years. Exports to the US, Canada and the UK.

ΨΨΨΨΨ **Limestone Coast Shiraz 2001** Massively powerful, in-your-face style, loaded with blackberry, licorice and supporting tannins. Works infinitely better than the Limited Vineyard Release version. **RATING** 94 **DRINK** 2016 $ 15.99

ΨΨΨΨΨ **Limited Release Padthaway Chardonnay 2002** Oak makes a major statement throughout; good length and line; supple fruit. **RATING** 92 **DRINK** 2007 $ 26.99
Limestone Coast Cabernet Sauvignon 2002 Complex, rich, distinctly ripe spicy/blackberry/mulberry fruit ripples through to the finish. **RATING** 90 **DRINK** 2012 $ 17

ΨΨΨΨ **Limited Release Padthaway Shiraz 2001** Massively powerful and complex, with dark fruits and charry oak. **RATING** 89 **DRINK** 2011 $ 26.99
Stepping Stone Coonawarra Cabernet Sauvignon 2002 Medium-bodied; firm, direct, primary blackcurrant fruit; no oak frills; value. **RATING** 88 **DRINK** 2010 $ 12.50

ΨΨΨΨ **Stepping Stone Padthaway Chardonnay 2003 RATING** 86 **DRINK** 2007 $ 12.95
Limestone Coast Viognier 2003 RATING 86 **DRINK** Now $ 15.99
Limestone Coast Chardonnay 2002 RATING 85 **DRINK** Now $ 15.99

ΨΨΨ **Padthaway Viognier 2003 RATING** 83 $ 15.99

🐛 Stonehurst Wines Cedar Creek ★★★

Wollombi Road, Cedar Creek, NSW 2325 **REGION** Lower Hunter Valley
T (02) 4998 1576 **F** (02) 4998 0008 **OPEN** 7 days 10–5
WINEMAKER Contract **EST.** 1995 **CASES** 3500
PRODUCT RANGE ($15–25 ML) Semillon, Unwooded Chardonnay, Chardonnay, Sparkling Chardonnay, Late Harvest Semillon, Golden Dessert Semillon, Autumn Harvest Chambourcin, Shiraz Chambourcin, Chambourcin, Growers Reserve.
SUMMARY Stonehurst (subtitled Cedar Creek) has been established by Daryl and Phillipa Heslop on a historic 220-hectare property in the Wollombi Valley, underneath the Pokolbin Range. They have 6.5 hectares of vineyards, planted to chambourcin, semillon, chardonnay and shiraz; the wines are made at Monarch Winemaking Services, which underwrites quality. A substantial part of the business, however, is the six self-contained cottages on the property, which can be seen on their website <www.cedarcreekcottages.com.au>.

ΨΨΨΨ **Cedar Creek Golden Dessert Semillon 2002** Lusciously sweet, but with balancing acidity; not complex as yet; will build honey and peach. **RATING** 87 **DRINK** 2008 $ 25

Stonemont NR

421 Rochford Road, Rochford, Vic 3442 **REGION** Macedon Ranges
T (03) 5429 1540 **F** (03) 5429 1878 **OPEN** By appointment
WINEMAKER Contract **EST.** 1997 **CASES** 500
PRODUCT RANGE ($18 R) Chardonnay, Sparkling Macedon, Pinot Noir.
SUMMARY Ray and Gail Hicks began the establishment of their vineyard in 1993, extending plantings to a total of 1.5 hectares each of chardonnay and pinot noir in 1996. The tiny production of Chardonnay, Pinot Noir and Sparkling Macedon is contract-made by various Macedon Ranges winemakers, and the wines are sold by mail order and (by appointment) through the cellar door, which is situated in a heritage stone barn on the vineyard site.

Stone Ridge

NR

35 Limberlost Road, Glen Aplin, Qld 4381 **REGION** Granite Belt
T (07) 4683 4211 **F** (07) 4683 4211 **OPEN** 7 days 10–5
WINEMAKER Jim Lawrie, Anne Kennedy **EST.** 1981 **CASES** 2100
PRODUCT RANGE ($10–60 CD) Semillon, Marsanne, Viognier, Chardonnay, Pinot Noir, Shiraz, Cabernet Malbec, Cabernet Sauvignon; Mount Sterling Dry Red Shiraz.
SUMMARY Jim Lawrie and Anne Kennedy were among the new arrivals at the start of the expansion of the Granite Belt region. They have progressed from a tiny make of Shiraz in a microscopic winery to a very much larger business, with some particularly interesting varietal wines.

Stoney Rise

PO Box 12, Kings Meadows, Tas 7249 **REGION** Mount Benson
T 0419 540 770 **F** (03) 6343 2076 **OPEN** Not
WINEMAKER Joe Holyman **EST.** 2000 **CASES** 2500
PRODUCT RANGE ($16.99–20 ML) Sauvignon Blanc, Hey Hey Rose, Cotes du Robe Shiraz.
SUMMARY Matt Lowe and Joe Holyman met as 14-year-old school boys in Tasmania before they headed off in different directions, Joe Holyman to establish a record of the most number of catches by a wicket keeper on debut in first-class cricket, Matt Lowe to see the world. They came together once again at Roseworthy undertaking the marketing degree, leading to positions as sales representatives. Matt then trained to be a chef, while Joe set off for a series of vintages in Burgundy, Provence and the Douro Valley. Their paths crossed again when they both began working at Cape Jaffa Wines at Robe on the Limestone Coast, and to the establishment of their own brand as a side interest. Joe Holyman now works in Tasmania, but the brand continues. Exports to the US.

ŶŶŶŶ **Hey Hey Rose 2003** Fresh, lively strawberry and cherry; relatively dry finish. **RATING** 87
    DRINK Now $ 16.99
    Cotes du Robe Shiraz 2002 Battlestar Galactica style, very much the product of the vintage; saturated, essencey, red and black fruits; lots of puppy fat to lose. **RATING** 87
    DRINK 2016 $ 19.99

Stonier Wines

362 Frankston–Flinders Road, Merricks, Vic 3916 **REGION** Mornington Peninsula
T (03) 5989 8300 **F** (03) 5989 8709 **OPEN** 7 days 11–5
WINEMAKER Geraldine McFaul **EST.** 1978 **CASES** 25 000
PRODUCT RANGE ($18–55 CD) Sauvignon Blanc, Chardonnay, Reserve Chardonnay, Pinot Noir Chardonnay, Pinot Noir, Reserve Pinot Noir, Cabernet Sauvignon Cabernet Franc; KBS Chardonnay and Pinot Noir.
SUMMARY One of the most senior wineries on the Mornington Peninsula, now part of the Petaluma group which is in turn owned by Lion Nathan of New Zealand. Wine quality is assured, as is the elegant, restrained style of the majority of the wines. Exports to the UK, Canada, Belgium, Germany, Italy, The Netherlands, New Zealand, Malaysia, Hong Kong, Singapore and Japan.

ŶŶŶŶŶ **Chardonnay 2003** Complex, concentrated melange of stone fruit, melon, fig and cashew reflecting barrel ferment and malolactic ferment inputs; considerable length. **RATING** 91
    DRINK 2008 $ 23
    Reserve Chardonnay 2002 Elegant, fine restrained style showing strong malolactic creamy cashew influences; fruit slightly diminished, but should bounce back. **RATING** 91
    DRINK 2007 $ 39

ŶŶŶŶ **Pinot Noir 2003** Mainstream Mornington Peninsula Pinot Noir style; nice plummy fruit and subtle oak; slightly simple; needs a year or two. **RATING** 89 **DRINK** 2007 $ 23
    KBS Vineyard Pinot Noir 2000 Complex foresty, savoury, tobacco leaf; good texture and weight, but the mid-palate fruit isn't there. **RATING** 88
    Pinot Noir Chardonnay 2001 Stone fruit and melon; good length, but not complex; may develop under cork. **RATING** 87 **DRINK** Now $ 24.95

Stratherne Vale Estate

NR

Campbell Street, Caballing, WA 6312 **REGION** Central Western Australia Zone
T (08) 9881 2148 **F** (08) 9881 3129 **OPEN** Not
WINEMAKER Contract **EST.** 1980 **CASES** 600
PRODUCT RANGE A single red wine made from a blend of cabernet sauvignon, zinfandel, merlot and
shiraz.
SUMMARY Stratherne Vale Estate stretches the viticultural map of Australia yet further. It is situated
near Narrogin, which is north of the Great Southern region and south of the most generous extension
of the Darling Ranges. The closest viticultural region of note is at Wandering, to the northeast.

Strathewen Hills

1090 Strathewen Road, Strathewen, Vic 3099 **REGION** Yarra Valley
T (03) 9714 8464 **F** (03) 9714 8464 **OPEN** By appointment
WINEMAKER William Christophersen **EST.** 1991
PRODUCT RANGE ($20–75 R) Chardonnay, Pinot Noir, Merlot, Tribal Elder Shiraz, Merlot Cabernets.
SUMMARY Joan and William (who I have always called Bill) Christophersen began the slow process of
establishing Strathewen Hills in 1991. The vineyard was established with ultra-close spacing, with 3
hectares planted predominantly to pinot noir, chardonnay, shiraz, merlot and small amounts of
cabernet sauvignon, cabernet franc and a few bits and pieces, but frost caused persistent losses until
protective sprinklers were installed. Since then a series of high quality small volume wines have been
made.

ŸŸŸŸŸ **Tribal Elder Shiraz 2001** Spotlessly clean and impressively ripe black cherry, blackberry
and spice; excellent texture and structure; juicy black fruits and fine ripe tannins; oak in
support. **RATING** 94 **DRINK** 2011

ŸŸŸŸ **Pinot Noir 2002** Good colour; ripe, full plummy fruit, some spice; ripe tannins, though
trails off a little on the finish. **RATING** 89 **DRINK** 2007 $ 25
Strathewen Hills Merlot Cabernet Sauvignon 2001 Elegant, light to medium-bodied;
raspberry and blackberry fruit, fine tannins and good length. **RATING** 87 **DRINK** 2008

ŸŸŸŸ **Shiraz Cabernet 2002 RATING** 86 **DRINK** 2008 $ 20

Strathkellar

NR

Murray Valley Highway, Cobram, Vic 3644 **REGION** Goulburn Valley
T (03) 5873 5274 **F** (03) 5873 5270 **OPEN** 7 days 10–5
WINEMAKER Tahbilk (Contract) **EST.** 1990 **CASES** 2000
PRODUCT RANGE ($14–18 CD) Chenin Blanc, Chardonnay, Sparkling Brut Reserve, Sparkling Shiraz,
Late Picked Chenin Blanc, Sweet Muscatel, Shiraz, Grenache Shiraz Mataro, Muscat, Tokay, Putters
Port, Old Putters Port.
SUMMARY Dick Parkes planted his 6-hectare vineyard to chardonnay, shiraz and chenin blanc in
1990, and has the wine contract-made at Tahbilk by Alister Purbrick. The fact that the wines are
made at Tahbilk is a sure guarantee of quality, and the prices are modest.

Strath Valley Vineyard

NR

Strath Valley Road, Strath Creek, Vic 3658 **REGION** Upper Goulburn
T (03) 5784 9229 **F** (03) 5784 9381 **OPEN** Weekends 10–5, or by appointment
WINEMAKER Contract **EST.** 1994 **CASES** 1300
PRODUCT RANGE Sauvignon Blanc, Boundary Range Shiraz.
SUMMARY Chris and Robyn Steen have established 12.5 hectares of chardonnay, sauvignon blanc,
cabernet sauvignon and shiraz. By far the largest part of the production is sold as grapes, with around
1300 cases of Sauvignon Blanc and Shiraz being sold through the cellar door.

Straws Lane ★★★★

1282 Mount Macedon Road, Hesket, Vic 3442 **REGION** Macedon Ranges
T (03) 9654 9380 **F** (03) 9663 6300 **OPEN** Weekends and public holidays 10–4, or by appointment
WINEMAKER Stuart Anderson, John Ellis **EST.** 1987 **CASES** 1800
PRODUCT RANGE ($22–40 R) Gewurztraminer, Blanc de Noirs, Pinot Noir.
SUMMARY The Straws Lane vineyard was planted in 1987, but the Straws Lane label is a relatively
new arrival on the scene; after a highly successful 1995 vintage, adverse weather in 1996 and 1997
meant that little or no wine was made in those years, but the pace picked up again with subsequent
vintages. Stuart Anderson guides the making of the Pinot Noir, Hanging Rock Winery handles the
Gewurztraminer and the sparkling wine base, and Cope-Williams looks after the tiraging and
maturation of the sparkling wine. It's good to have co-operative neighbours. A tasting of some of the
oldest vintages of Pinot Noir in 2003 revealed wines with considerable finesse and varietal
character. The 2003 Pinot Noir and 2003 Mt Camel Heathcote Shiraz (tasted from barrel) look full
of promise.

♥♥♥♥ **Pinot Noir 2001** Rich, complex and ripe; multi-layered fruit; very slightly over-extracted.
RATING 90 **DRINK** 2008 $ 28

♥♥♥♥ **Gewurztraminer 2003 RATING** 85 **DRINK** Now $ 22

🍂 Stringybark NR

2060 Chittering Road, Chittering, WA 6084 **REGION** Perth Hills
T (08) 9571 8069 **F** (08) 9561 6547 **OPEN** Thurs–Sun 12–5
WINEMAKER Stephen Murfitt (Contract) **EST.** 1985
PRODUCT RANGE ($18–21 CD) Verdelho, Cabernet Shiraz.
SUMMARY Bruce and Mary Cussen have a vineyard dating back to 1985, but the development of the
cellar door and restaurant complex is far more recent. They have 2 hectares of verdelho, chardonnay
and cabernet sauvignon at Chittering, and have the wines contract-made by Stephen Murfitt at Lilac
Hill Estate. Their cellar door and country-style restaurant is open from noon to 5pm Thursday to
Sunday at prices which will not unduly hurt the pocket.

Stringy Brae ★★★☆

Sawmill Road, Sevenhill, SA 5453 **REGION** Clare Valley
T (08) 8843 4313 **F** (08) 8843 4319 **OPEN** Weekends and public holidays 11–5, Mon–Fri refer to road
sign
WINEMAKER Contract (Mitchell) **EST.** 1991 **CASES** 2500
PRODUCT RANGE ($18–65 CD) Riesling, Sparkling Riesling, Shiraz, Mote Hill Reserve Black Knight
Shiraz, Cabernet Sauvignon.
SUMMARY Donald and Sally Willson have established over 10 hectares of vineyards that since the
1996 vintage have produced all the grapes for their wines. (Previously grapes from Langhorne Creek
were used.) The Australian domestic market is serviced direct by mail order, but the wines are
exported to the UK.

♥♥♥♥ **Riesling 2003** Clean, tight slate and mineral aromas; reserved, faintly spritzy palate; time
needed. **RATING** 89 **DRINK** 2010 $ 18

♥♥♥♥ **Shiraz 2001** A tightly knit mix of red and black berry fruits; some savoury tannins; vanilla
oak. Screwcap. **RATING** 86 **DRINK** 2009 $ 20
Cabernet Sauvignon 2001 RATING 86 **DRINK** 2009 $ 20

Stuart Range ★★★

67 William Street, Kingaroy, Qld 4610 **REGION** South Burnett
T (07) 4162 3711 **F** (07) 4162 4811 **OPEN** 7 days 9–5
WINEMAKER Ross Whiteford **EST.** 1997 **CASES** 15 000
PRODUCT RANGE ($10–18 CD) Chardonnay, Shiraz Cabernet, Range White and Red, Blue Moon
Liqueur, Explorer Port; Goodger Chardonnay, Verdelho, Shiraz, Shiraz Cabernet Merlot.
SUMMARY Stuart Range is a prime example of the extent and pace of change in the Queensland wine

industry, coming from nowhere in 1997 to crushing just under 120 tonnes of grapes in its inaugural vintage in 1998. The grapes are supplied by up to seven growers in the South Burnett Valley with 52 hectares planted by 1996. A state-of-the-art winery has been established within an old butter factory building.

ŦŦŦŦ **Goodger Shiraz 2002** Light to medium-bodied; gently spicy earthy/leathery varietal fruit; Hunter-like length and balance in diminuendo. **RATING** 87 **DRINK** 2007 $18

ŦŦŦŢ **Chardonnay 2003 RATING** 85 **DRINK** Now $18
Goodger Cabernet Sauvignon Shiraz Merlot 2002 RATING 84 **DRINK** Now $16

ŦŦŦ **Chardonnay 2002 RATING** 83 $18
Range Red NV RATING 83 $10
Verdelho 2003 RATING 82 $16
Shiraz Cabernet 2002 RATING 82 $14
Range White NV RATING 80 $10

Studley Park Vineyard ★★★★

5 Garden Terrace, Kew, Vic 3101 (postal) **REGION** Port Phillip Zone
T (03) 9254 2777 **F** (03) 9254 2535 **OPEN** Not
WINEMAKER Llew Knight (Contract) **EST.** 1994 **CASES** 250
PRODUCT RANGE ($25 R) Cabernet Sauvignon.
SUMMARY Geoff Pryor's Studley Park Vineyard is one of Melbourne's best-kept secrets. It is situated on a bend of the Yarra River barely 4 kilometres from the Melbourne CBD on a 0.5-hectare block once planted to vines, but for a century used for market gardening. A spectacular aerial photograph shows how immediately across the river, and looking directly to the CBD, is the epicentre of Melbourne's light industrial development, while on the northern and eastern boundaries are suburban residential blocks. The vineyard is sheltered (and hidden) by groves of large elm and plane trees, although a glimpse of it can be seen from the Walmer Street footbridge which forms part of the main Yarra Trail. Because of zoning restrictions, cellar-door tastings and sales are not possible at the vineyard, and most sales take place directly over the internet from the website <www.studleypark.com>.

ŦŦŦŦ **Cabernet Sauvignon 2000** Fragrant, cedary, olive-accented black fruits; elegant and unforced; ageing slowly; fine-grained tannins. **RATING** 89 **DRINK** 2010 $25

Stumpy Gully ★★★☆

1247 Stumpy Gully Road, Moorooduc, Vic 3933 **REGION** Mornington Peninsula
T (03) 5978 8429 **F** (03) 5978 8419 **OPEN** Weekends 11–5
WINEMAKER Wendy Zantvoort, Maitena Zantvoort, Ewan Campbell **EST.** 1988 **CASES** 4000
PRODUCT RANGE ($16–35 CD) Riesling, Sauvignon Blanc, Marsanne, Pinot Grigio, Chardonnay, Botrytis Riesling, Pinot Noir, Sangiovese, Red Dog Red, Shiraz, Cabernet Sauvignon, Fortified Sauvignon Blanc; also Peninsula Panorama Chardonnay and Pinot Noir.
SUMMARY When Frank and Wendy Zantvoort began planting their first vineyard in 1989 there were no winemakers in the family; now there are three, plus two viticulturists. Mother Wendy was first to obtain her degree from Charles Sturt University, followed by daughter Maitena, who then married Ewan Campbell, another winemaker. Father Frank and son Michael look after the vineyards. The original vineyard has 9 hectares of vines, but in establishing the new 20-hectare Moorooduc vineyard (first harvest 2001) the Zantvoorts have deliberately gone against prevailing thinking, planting it solely to red varieties, predominately cabernet sauvignon, merlot and shiraz. They believe they have one of the warmest sites on the Peninsula, and that ripening will in fact present no problems. In all they now have ten varieties planted, producing a dozen different wines. Exports to the UK and The Netherlands.

ŦŦŦŦŢ **Sauvignon Blanc 2003** Pristine, razor-sharp, grassy varietal character; at once delicate, but intense and long. **RATING** 93 **DRINK** Now $18

ŦŦŦŦ **Pinot Noir 2002** Very ripe fruit style; forest floor, plum and prune all coalesce. **RATING** 89 **DRINK** 2007 $20
Red Dog Red 2003 A mix of ripe, black fruits and a dash of chocolate; good tannins; surprise performer. **RATING** 88 **DRINK** 2008 $20

Chardonnay 2003 Light citrus and melon fruit; slightly green tinges. **RATING** 87 **DRINK** 2007 $18

Pinot Grigio 2003 Apple and wet stone aromas; powdery palate then alcohol on the finish. **RATING** 87 **DRINK** Now $25

ΥΥΥΨ **Cabernet Sauvignon 2002 RATING** 85 **DRINK** 2008 $28

Suckfizzle & Stella Bella ★★★★★

PO Box 536, Margaret River, WA 6288 **REGION** Margaret River
T (08) 9757 6377 **F** (08) 9757 6022 **OPEN** Not
WINEMAKER Janice McDonald **EST.** 1997 **CASES** 20 000
PRODUCT RANGE ($14–45 CD) Suckfizzle range of Sauvignon Blanc, Semillon Sauvignon Blanc, Chardonnay, Tempranillo, Sangiovese Cabernet Merlot; Stella Bella Sauvignon Blanc Semillon, Cabernet Sauvignon. Also lower-priced Scuttlebutt range.
SUMMARY First things first. The back label explains: 'the name Suckfizzle has been snaffled from the 14th-century monk and medico turned writer Rabelais and his infamous character the great Lord Suckfizzle'. Suckfizzle is the joint venture of two well-known Margaret River winemakers who, in deference to their employers, do not identify themselves on any of the background material or the striking front and back labels of the wines. Exports to the UK, Belgium, Fiji, Hong Kong, Singapore and Canada.

ΥΥΥΥΥ **Suckfizzle Cabernet Sauvignon 2001** Masses of fully ripe blackcurrant fruit; exemplary oak and tannin management; lovely wine. **RATING** 95 **DRINK** 2016 $45

Stella Bella Sauvignon Blanc 2003 Still clear and clean; very good fruit balance and mouthfeel; long, lingering finish. **RATING** 94 **DRINK** Now $22

Suckfizzle Sauvignon Blanc Semillon 2002 Strong, toasty barrel-ferment aromas; fruit responds with zeal in a full array of tropical flavours. **RATING** 94 **DRINK** 2009 $45

Stella Bella Shiraz 2002 Black cherry and blackberry fruit; lovely texture caresses the mouth; fine and supple tannins; good oak. **RATING** 94 **DRINK** 2012 $26

ΥΥΥΥΨ **Stella Bella Chardonnay 2002** Delicate but complex wild yeast/barrel-ferment background inputs; stone fruit; oak downplayed, crisp acidity. **RATING** 90 **DRINK** 2008 $25

Stella Bella Tempranillo 2002 Very good colour; excellent texture and structure to the dark cherry and plum fruit; amazingly, from 10-year-old vines. **RATING** 90 **DRINK** 2010 $28

ΥΥΥΥ **Stella Bella Cabernet Sauvignon Merlot 2001** A savoury mix of black fruit, blackcurrant and bitter chocolate, finishing with persistent, dry but fine tannins. **RATING** 89 **DRINK** 2011 $26

ΥΥΥΨ **Stella Bella Semillon Sauvignon Blanc 2003 RATING** 86 **DRINK** Now $14

Summerfield ★★★★★

Main Road, Moonambel, Vic 3478 **REGION** Pyrenees
T (03) 5467 2264 **F** (03) 5467 2380 **OPEN** 7 days 9–5.30
WINEMAKER Ian Summerfield, Mark Summerfield **EST.** 1979 **CASES** 3500
PRODUCT RANGE ($15–50 CD) Sauvignon Blanc, Trebbiano, Shiraz, Reserve Shiraz, Shiraz Cabernet, Cabernet Merlot, Cabernet Sauvignon, Reserve Cabernet.
SUMMARY A specialist red wine producer, the particular forte of which is Shiraz. The red wines are consistently excellent, luscious and full-bodied and fruit-driven, but with a slice of vanillin oak to top them off. Exports to the US and the UK.

ΥΥΥΥΥ **Shiraz 2002** Opulently ripe and dense plum and prune; restrained vanilla oak; ripe, fleshy tannins. **RATING** 94 **DRINK** 2015 $28

ΥΥΥΥΨ **Reserve Cabernet 2002** Concentrated blackberry/cassis and a touch of chocolate; savoury tannins balance the sweet fruit. **RATING** 93 **DRINK** 2015 $50

ΥΥΥΥ **Tradition Cabernet Merlot 2002** Lusciously rich and ripe plum, prune, chocolate and blackcurrant threaten excessive sweetness, but the wine finishes dry. **RATING** 89 **DRINK** 2010 $28

🌿 Summerhill Wines   NR

64–65 Dandenong-Hastings Road, Somerville, Vic 3912 **REGION** Mornington Peninsula
T 0413 784 317 **OPEN** By appointment
WINEMAKER Robert Zagar **EST.** 1998
PRODUCT RANGE Pinot Noir, Shiraz; fortifieds.
SUMMARY Robert Zagar has established 4 hectares of pinot noir and shiraz, and (apparently with material from elsewhere) makes both table and fortified wines under the Summerhill, Coat of Arms, Brockville and Pattersons Estate labels. The wines are available by mail order; also exported to Malaysia.

Summit Estate

291 Granite Belt Drive, Thulimbah, Qld 4377 **REGION** Granite Belt
T (07) 4683 2011 **F** (07) 4683 2600 **OPEN** 7 days 9–5
WINEMAKER Paola Carberaz Rhymer **EST.** 1997 **CASES** 4000
PRODUCT RANGE ($9.90–29 CD) Semillon Chardonnay, Verdelho, Chardonnay, Reserve Chardonnay, Sweet White, Sweet Red, Sparkling Pinot Noir, Emily Rose, Reserve Pinot Noir, Shiraz, Shiraz Cabernet Sauvignon, Reserve Merlot, Tempranillo, Petit Verdot, Cabernet Merlot, Cabernet Sauvignon, Golden Gleam, Liqueur Muscat, Tawny Port.
SUMMARY Summit Estate is the public face of the Stanthorpe Wine Co, owned by a syndicate of ten professionals who work in Brisbane, but who share a love of wine. They operate the Stanthorpe Wine Centre, which offers wine education as well as selling wines from other makers in the region, and, of course, Summit Estate. The 17-hectare vineyard is planted to chardonnay, marsanne, pinot noir, shiraz, merlot, tempranillo, petit verdot and cabernet sauvignon, and they have set up a small, specialised winemaking facility.

🍷🍷🍷🍷 **Merlot Cabernet Shiraz 2002** A fragrant mix of dark berry and earth aromas; raspberry, redcurrant and blackcurrant fruits drive the palate; minimal oak and tannin influence. Gold and trophy in local Toowoomba derby. **RATING** 90 **DRINK** 2010 $ 24

🍷🍷🍷🍷 **Reserve Shiraz 2002** Strong red-purple; light to medium-bodied; dark cherry and plum fruit; good length; soft, persistent tannins. **RATING** 88 **DRINK** 2007 $ 29
Reserve Cabernet Merlot 2002 An attractive mix of red and black fruits, then a savoury/briary finish. **RATING** 87 **DRINK** 2008 $ 22

🍷🍷🍷 **Verdelho 2003 RATING** 83 $ 24

Surveyor's Hill Winery   NR

215 Brooklands Road, Wallaroo, NSW 2618 **REGION** Canberra District
T (02) 6230 2046 **F** (02) 6230 2048 **OPEN** Weekends and public holidays or by appointment
WINEMAKER Contract **EST.** 1986 **CASES** 1000
PRODUCT RANGE ($10–22 R) Riesling, Sauvignon Blanc, Pinot Noir, Rosado Touriga, Shiraz, Cabernet Merlot.
SUMMARY Surveyor's Hill has 10 hectares of vineyard, but most of the grapes are sold to BRL Hardy Kamberra, which vinifies the remainder for Surveyor's Hill — which should guarantee the quality of the wines sold. Also offers bed and breakfast accommodation.

🌿 Susannah Brook Wines   NR

43 Beryl Avenue, Millendon, WA 6056 **REGION** Swan District
T (08) 9296 4129 **OPEN** By appointment
WINEMAKER John Daniel **EST.** 1984
PRODUCT RANGE A range of varietally denominated table wines reflecting the plantings.
SUMMARY Susannah Brook is a small but long-established Swan Valley business, where John Daniel has 2 hectares of chenin blanc, chardonnay, verdelho, cabernet sauvignon, merlot, malbec, shiraz and muscat, making the range of table and fortified wines on-site. The small production is largely sold by mail order.

🐾 Sutherland Estate ★★★★

2010 Melba Highway, Dixons Creek, Vic 3775 **REGION** Yarra Valley
T 0402 052 287 **F** (03) 9762 1122 **OPEN** Thurs–Mon 10–5
WINEMAKER Alex White (Contract) **EST.** 2000 **CASES** 2000
PRODUCT RANGE ($16–28 CD) Chardonnay, Rose, Pinot Noir, Shiraz, Tempranillo, Cabernet Sauvignon.
SUMMARY The Phelan family (father Ron, mother Sheila, daughter Catherine and partner Angus Ridley) established Sutherland Estate in 2000 when they acquired a mature 2-hectare vineyard on the Melba Highway at Dixons Creek. Later that year they planted another 3.2 hectares, including a small amount of tempranillo. Both Catherine and Angus are in their fifth year of the part-time viticulture and oenology course at Charles Sturt University, and when a planned on-site winery is completed, they will take over winemaking responsibilities. A cellar-door complex, designed and built by Ron Phelan, is already open.

ΨΨΨΨ **DHV Pinot Noir 2001** Savoury but with plenty of spicy black fruits/plums; considerable tannin structure and support. **RATING** 89 **DRINK** 2008 **$** 28
DHV Shiraz 2001 Blackberry, raspberry and spice; medium-bodied and not forced; subtle oak, nice wine. **RATING** 89 **DRINK** 2010 **$** 28

Sutherland Smith Wines NR

Cnr Falkners Road & Murray Valley Highway, Rutherglen, Vic 3685 **REGION** Rutherglen
T (02) 6032 8177 **F** (02) 6032 8177 **OPEN** Weekends, public and Victorian school holidays 10–5, other Fridays 11–5 pm
WINEMAKER George Sutherland-Smith **EST.** 1993 **CASES** 1000
PRODUCT RANGE ($12.70–100 CD) Riesling, Josephine (Riesling Traminer), Chardonnay, George's Private Blend Shiraz Cabernet, George's Private Blend Merlot Cabernet Shiraz, Cabernet Shiraz, Cabernet Sauvignon, Port, Vintage Port.
SUMMARY George Sutherland-Smith, for decades managing director and winemaker at All Saints, has opened up his own small business at Rutherglen, making wine in the refurbished Emu Plains winery, originally constructed in the 1850s. He draws upon fruit grown in a leased vineyard at Glenrowan and also from grapes grown in the King Valley.

🐾 Sutton Grange Winery ★★☆

PO Box 181, East Kew, Vic 3102 **REGION** Bendigo
T (03) 5474 8277 **F** (03) 9859 5655 **OPEN** Not
WINEMAKER Gilles Lapalus **EST.** 1998 **CASES** 1600
PRODUCT RANGE ($14.95–17.95 R) Fairbank range of Rose, Syrah, Syrah Cabernet, Cabernet Sauvignon.
SUMMARY The 400-hectare Sutton Grange property is a thoroughbred stud acquired in 1996 by Peter Sidwell, a Melbourne-based business man with horse racing and breeding one of his activities. A lunch visit to the property by long-term friends Alec Epis and Stuart Anderson led to the decision to plant 12 hectares of syrah, merlot, cabernet sauvignon, viognier and sangiovese, and to the recruitment of French winemaker Gilles Lapalus, who just happens to be the partner of Stuart Anderson's daughter. The on-site winery, built from Western Australian limestone, was completed in time for the 2001 vintage, and a tasting room is due to open in spring 2004. The initial release is under the Fairbank label; a super-premium, limited release range under the Sutton Grange label is scheduled for late 2004.

ΨΨΨΨ **Fairbank Syrah 2001 RATING** 85 **DRINK** 2009 **$** 17.95
Fairbank Cabernet Sauvignon 2001 RATING 85 **DRINK** 2010 **$** 17.95

ΨΨΨ **Fairbank Shiraz Cabernet 2001 RATING** 83 **$** 14.95
Fairbank Rose 2002 RATING 81 **$** 14.95

🐾 Swallows Welcome NR

Wallis Road, East Witchcliffe, WA 6286 **REGION** Margaret River
T (08) 9757 6312 **F** (08) 9757 6312 **OPEN** 7 days by appointment
WINEMAKER Tim Negus **EST.** 1994
PRODUCT RANGE Merlot, Cabernets.

SUMMARY Tim Negus has established a 3-hectare vineyard planted cabernet sauvignon, merlot and cabernet franc and makes the wine on-site. The small production is sold by mail order and through the cellar door, which offers barbecue and garden facilities for the visitor (with the appropriate appointment).

Swanbrook Estate Wines

38 Swan Street, Henley Brook, WA 6055 **REGION** Swan Valley
T (08) 9296 3100 **F** (08) 9296 3099 **OPEN** 7 days 10–5
WINEMAKER Rob Marshall **EST.** 1998 **CASES** 10 000
PRODUCT RANGE ($12–40 CD) Semillon, Classic Dry White, Chenin (wood aged), Verdelho, Chardonnay, Classic Shiraz, Estate Shiraz, Cabernet Merlot.
SUMMARY This is the reincarnation of Evans & Tate's Gnangara Winery. It secures most of its grapes from contract growers in the Perth Hills and Swan Valley, but also has the 60-year-old block of shiraz around the winery. A little under 40 per cent of the annual crush is for the Swanbrook label, the remainder being contract winemaking for others. Owner John Andreou (a Perth restaurateur) has invested $2 million in upgrading and expanding the facilities, and former Evans & Tate winemaker Rob Marshall has continued at Swanbrook, providing valuable continuity.

Swan Valley Wines ★★★

261 Haddrill Road, Baskerville, WA 6065 **REGION** Swan Valley
T (08) 9296 1501 **F** (08) 9296 1733 **OPEN** Fri–Sun and public holidays 10–5
WINEMAKER Julie White (Contract) **EST.** 1999 **CASES** 3000
PRODUCT RANGE ($13.50–20 CD) Semillon, Chenin Blanc, Chardonnay, Grenache Blush, Grenache, Shiraz, Grenache, White Port, Tawny Port.
SUMMARY Peter and Paula Hoffman, together with sons Paul and Thomas, acquired their 6-hectare property in 1989. It had a long history of grape growing, and the prior owner had registered the name Swan Valley Wines back in 1983. In 1999 the family built a new winery to handle the grapes from 2.3 hectares of chenin blanc, 1.4 hectares of grenache, a little over 0.5 hectare each of semillon, malbec and cabernet sauvignon and a smaller amount of shiraz. South African-trained Julie White is contract winemaker. Exports to Japan.

ŸŸŸŸ **Shiraz 2003** Good colour; robust, powerful, deep blackberry fruit; fruit-driven; good tannin management. **RATING** 89 **DRINK** 2010 $16.50

ŸŸŸŸ **Grenache 2003** **RATING** 85 **DRINK** Now $15

ŸŸŸ **Chenin Blanc 2003** **RATING** 83 $14
White Grenache 2003 **RATING** 83 $14
Chardonnay 2003 **RATING** 82 $15

🍇 Sweet Water Hill Wines NR

17 Roberts Road, Anderleigh, Qld 4570 **REGION** Queensland Zone
T (07) 5485 7007 **F** (07) 5485 7007 **OPEN** 7 days 10–5
WINEMAKER Tony Totivan **EST.** 1999
PRODUCT RANGE A range of varietally denominated table wines reflecting the plantings.
SUMMARY Tony Totivan has established 5 hectares of semillon, chardonnay, cabernet sauvignon, shiraz, muscat hamburg and white muscat, and makes the wine on-site, with a range of table and fortified wines available. The cellar door offers light meals and the other usual facilities including picnic and barbecue.

Sylvan Springs Estates

RSD 405 Blythmans Road, McLaren Flat, SA 5171 (postal) **REGION** McLaren Vale
T (08) 8383 0500 **F** (08) 8383 0499 **OPEN** Not
WINEMAKER Brian Light (Consultant) **EST.** 1974 **CASES** 2000
PRODUCT RANGE ($12–17.60 ML) Chardonnay, Shiraz, Cabernet Sauvignon.
SUMMARY The Pridmore family has been involved in grape growing and winemaking in McLaren Vale for four generations spanning over 100 years. The pioneer was Cyril Pridmore who established

The Wattles Winery in 1896, purchasing Sylvan Park, one of the original homesteads in the area, in 1901. The original family land in the township of McLaren Vale was sold in 1978, but not before third generation Digby Pridmore had established new vineyards (in 1974) near Blewitt Springs. When he retired in 1990, his son David purchased the 45-hectare vineyard (planted to 11 different varieties) and, with sister Sally, ventured into winemaking in 1996, with Brian Light as consultant winemaker.

Symphonia Wines ★★★★☆

1699 Boggy Creek Road, Myrrhee, Vic 3732 **REGION** King Valley
T (03) 5729 7519 **F** (03) 5729 7519 **OPEN** By appointment
WINEMAKER Peter Read **EST.** 1998 **CASES** 1500
PRODUCT RANGE ($15–20 CD) Riesling, Pinot Grigio, Chardonnay Plus, Viognier Petit Manseng, Pinot Grigio, Pinot Chardonnay, Blanc de Blanc, Quintus (merlot, cabernet sauvignon, saperavi, tannat, tempranillo blend), Merlot, Merlot Plus, Tempranillo, Saperavi, Las Triadas.
SUMMARY Peter Read and his family are veterans of the King Valley, commencing the development of their vineyard in 1981 to supply Brown Brothers. As a result of extensive trips to both Western and Eastern Europe, Peter Read embarked on an ambitious project to trial a series of grape varieties little known in this country. The process of evaluation and experimentation continues, but since Symphonia released the first small quantities of wines in mid-1998 and it has built on that start. A number of the wines have great interest and no less merit.

▼▼▼▼▽ **Pinot Grigio 2003** Highly aromatic apple, pear, musk and spice. A delicate yet intense palate, more gris than grigio. Good acidity. Screwcap. **RATING** 90 **DRINK** 2007 $17.50
Quintus 2003 Clean; a kaleidoscopic array of fruit aromas and flavours built on a platform of persistent tannins. **RATING** 90 **DRINK** 2013 $20
Tannat 2003 Has all the expected colour and tannins, but also has balance and vinosity; nice raspberry and redcurrant flavours. **RATING** 90 **DRINK** 2010 $20

▼▼▼▼ **Viognier Petit Manseng 2003** Abundant peach and apricot flavours; powerful but not phenolic or hot. For the varietal voyeurs. **RATING** 89 **DRINK** Now $17.50
Tempranillo 2003 More depth and concentration than most examples of the variety; cherry and plum; soft, fine tannins. **RATING** 88 **DRINK** 2010 $15
Saperavi 2003 As befits the variety, dense, deep colour; potent black fruit aromas; powerful and dense in the mouth, but falters on the mid-palate. **RATING** 88 **DRINK** 2013 $20
Myrrhee Hills Cabernet Merlot 2002 Light to medium-bodied; a gentle mix of fresh blackberry and a slightly savoury finish. **RATING** 87 **DRINK** 2008
Las Triadas 2003 Fresh, lively array of red fruits; light to medium-bodied; fine tannins. Tempranillo, Cabernet Sauvignon, Merlot. **RATING** 87 **DRINK** 2010 $20

▼▼▼▽ **King Valley Merlot 2002** **RATING** 86 **DRINK** 2007 $17.50
Pinot Chardonnay 1999 **RATING** 86 **DRINK** 2007 $20

🐌 Symphony Hill Wines NR

2017 Eukey Road, Ballandean, Qld 4382 **REGION** Granite Belt
T (07) 4684 1388 **F** (07) 4684 1399 **OPEN** 7 days 10–5
WINEMAKER Blair Duncan **EST.** 1999 **CASES** 13 000
PRODUCT RANGE ($12–45 CD) Red Serenade, Estate Shiraz, Family Reserve Shiraz, Reserve Cabernet Sauvignon.
SUMMARY Ewen and Elissa Macpherson purchased what was then an old table grape and orchard property in 1996. In partnership with Ewen's parents, Bob and Jill Macpherson, they have developed 4 hectares of vineyards, while Ewen has completed his Bachelor of Applied Science in viticulture (in 2003). They have also secured the services of Blair Duncan as winemaker, who had a long career with Lindemans and Penfolds before moving to Arrowfield Wines in the Hunter Valley and now up to Queensland. The vineyard has been established using state-of-the-art technology, and it is not surprising that the 2002 Symphony Hill Reserve Cabernet Sauvignon should have won a gold medal at the 2003 Australian Small Winemakers Show (despite its name, a serious show with high judging standards). Symphony Hill's vineyard manager, Mike Hayes, has a degree in viticulture and is a third generation viticulturist in the Granite Belt region. Between he and Ewen Macpherson, a trial block of

50 varieties has been established, including such rarely encountered varieties as picpoul, tannat and mondeuse. The wines are sold by mail order, through the internet and from the cellar door which offers light meals and a full range of other facilities.

Tahbilk ★★★★

Goulburn Valley Highway, Tabilk, Vic 3608 **REGION** Nagambie Lakes
T (03) 5794 2555 **F** (03) 5794 2360 **OPEN** Mon–Sat 9–5, Sun 11–5
WINEMAKER Alister Purbrick, Neil Larson, Alan George **EST.** 1860 **CASES** 110 000
PRODUCT RANGE ($13.40–119.95 R) Riesling, Semillon, Sauvignon Blanc, Marsanne, Roussanne, Viognier, Verdelho, Chardonnay, Dulcet (sweet white), Brut Cuvee, Sparkling Lexia, Shiraz, 1933 Vines Reserve Shiraz, Cabernet Franc, Merlot, Malbec, Cabernet Merlot, Cabernet Sauvignon; 1860 Vines Shiraz is rare flagship, with a Reserve red released from each vintage; fortifieds.
SUMMARY A winery steeped in tradition (with high National Trust classification), which should be visited at least once by every wine-conscious Australian, and which makes wines — particularly red wines — utterly in keeping with that tradition. The essence of that heritage comes in the form of the tiny quantities of Shiraz made entirely from vines planted in 1860. As well as Australian national distribution through Tucker Seabrook, Tahbilk has agents in every principal wine market, including the UK, Europe, Asia and the US.

ΨΨΨΨ **Reserve Cabernet Sauvignon 1998** Excellent varietal character; strong blackcurrant aroma and flavour; great structure and finish; delicate French oak and controlled tannins. **RATING** 92 **DRINK** 2015 $ 69.95
1860 Vines Shiraz 1998 Powerful, yet restrained, long and intense; mix of black fruits, spice and ripe, fine tannins; echo of cedar. **RATING** 91 **DRINK** 2018 $ 119.50
Marsanne 2002 Lemon and honeysuckle flavours, and great balance of fruit and acidity, guaranteeing its future, however attractive it is now. **RATING** 90 **DRINK** 2012 $ 13.40
Marsanne 1998 Light gold; rich, toasty honeyed aromas and flavours; excellent balancing acidity. Re-release. **RATING** 90 **DRINK** 2007 $ 13.40
Reserve Shiraz 1998 Excellent mouthfeel; sweetly savoury mid to back-palate; fine, lingering tannins; French oak well integrated. **RATING** 90 **DRINK** 2015 $ 69.95

ΨΨΨΨ **Viognier 2003** Fragrant, with good varietal character; balanced, but fractionally short on the finish. **RATING** 89 **DRINK** 2007 $ 18.95

ΨΨΨΨ **Riesling 2003 RATING** 86 **DRINK** 2009 $ 15.95

Tait Wines ★★★☆

Yaldara Drive, Lyndoch, SA 5351 **REGION** Barossa Valley
T (08) 8524 5000 **F** (08) 8524 5220 **OPEN** Weekends and public holidays 11–5, or by appointment
WINEMAKER Bruno Tait **EST.** 1994 **CASES** 2000
PRODUCT RANGE ($15–30 CD) Chardonnay, Liquid Gold Fronti, Basket Pressed Shiraz, The Ball Buster (Shiraz Cabernet Merlot blend), Basket Pressed Cabernet Sauvignon.
SUMMARY The Tait family has been involved in the wine industry in the Barossa for over 100 years, making not wine but barrels. Their more recent venture into winemaking was immediately successful; retail distribution through single outlets in Melbourne, Adelaide and Sydney; exports to the US, Germany, Malaysia and Singapore.

Talijancich NR

26 Hyem Road, Herne Hill, WA 6056 **REGION** Swan Valley
T (08) 9296 4289 **F** (08) 9296 1762 **OPEN** Sun–Fri 11–5
WINEMAKER James Talijancich **EST.** 1932 **CASES** 10 000
PRODUCT RANGE ($17–135 CD) Verdelho, Voices Dry White, Grenache, Shiraz, Julian James White Liqueur, Julian James Red Liqueur, Liqueur Tokay 375 ml.
SUMMARY A former fortified wine specialist (with old Liqueur Tokay) now making a select range of table wines, with particular emphasis on Verdelho — on the third Saturday of August each year there is a tasting of fine 3-year-old Verdelho table wines from both Australia and overseas. Also runs an active wine club and exports to China, Japan and Hong Kong. Won the Wine Press Club Trophy at the 2003 Qantas Wine Show of Western Australia for most successful under 250-tonne producer.

Taliondal

NR

270 Old North Road, Pokolbin, NSW 2320 **REGION** Lower Hunter Valley
T (02) 9427 6812 **F** (02) 9427 6812 **OPEN** By appointment
WINEMAKER Frank Brady **EST.** 1974 **CASES** 240
PRODUCT RANGE ($8–15 ML) Cabernet Sauvignon.
SUMMARY The Brady Bunch, headed by Frank Brady, acquired Taliondal in 1974 as a family hideaway. Says Frank Brady, 'When in the Hunter do as the Hunter does', so 1 hectare of cabernet sauvignon was planted in 1974, and 1.5 hectares of traminer the following year. For many years the family was content to sell the grapes to local vignerons, but now take a small portion of the production and make wine on the property. The Cabernet Sauvignon has been a consistent medal-winner at Hunter shows.

Tallarook

★★★☆

2 Delaney's Road, Warranwood, Vic 3134 **REGION** Upper Goulburn
T (03) 9876 7022 **F** (03) 9876 7044 **OPEN** Not
WINEMAKER MasterWineMakers (Contract) **EST.** 1987 **CASES** 11 000
PRODUCT RANGE ($15–27.50 R) Chardonnay, Marsanne, Rose, Pinot Noir, Shiraz Viognier; second label of Terra Felix with Chardonnay, Merlot Cabernet and Shiraz.
SUMMARY Tallarook has been established on a property between Broadford and Seymour at an elevation of 200–300 metres. Fourteen hectares of vines have been planted since 1987, the three principal varieties being chardonnay, shiraz and pinot noir. The retainingof Martin Williams as winemaker in the 1998 vintage brought a substantial change in emphasis, and the subsequent release of an impressive Chardonnay. The business now has a permanent winery home at Warranwood (the former Yarra Valley Hills winery). The wines are mainly sold by mail order; also retail distribution in Melbourne and exports to the UK and Europe.

ŸŸŸŸ **Marsanne 2002** Talc, chalk, pear and apple aromas; crisp, firm and not the least phenolic; good varietal fruit. **RATING** 89 **DRINK** 2012 $ 27.50
Shiraz 2002 Light to medium-bodied; bright, brisk red cherry fruit; good length and lively finish. **RATING** 88 **DRINK** 2009 $ 27.50
Terra Felix Chardonnay 2002 Clean and crisp; citrus and stone fruit with a mineral spine and very subtle oak. Utterly belies its 14 degrees alcohol. **RATING** 87 **DRINK** 2007 $ 15
Pinot Noir 2002 Direct, simple cherry and plum flavours; still mono-dimensional. **RATING** 87 **DRINK** 2007 $ 25
Terra Felix Shiraz 2003 Strong purple-red; a medium-bodied mix of blackberry and dark plum fruit backed by fine tannins; fruit-driven. **RATING** 87 **DRINK** 2009 $ 15
Terra Felix Merlot Cabernet 2003 Youthful, bright purple-red; light to medium-bodied; attractive raspberry and redcurrant mix; clean finish; best soonest. **RATING** 87 **DRINK** 2007 $ 15

ŸŸŸŸ **Chardonnay 2002** **RATING** 86 **DRINK** 2007 $ 25
Terra Felix Shiraz 2002 **RATING** 86 **DRINK** 2009 $ 15
Rose 2003 **RATING** 85 **DRINK** Now $ 20.50

ŸŸŸ **Terra Felix Chardonnay 2003** **RATING** 83 $ 15

Tallavera Grove Vineyard and Winery

NR

Mount View Road, Mount View via Cessnock, NSW 2325 **REGION** Lower Hunter Valley
T (02) 4990 7535 **F** (02) 4990 5232 **OPEN** Thurs–Mon 10–5
WINEMAKER Chris Cameron **EST.** 2000 **CASES** 1800
PRODUCT RANGE ($11–20 CD) Semillon, Semillon Sauvignon Blanc, Verdelho, Chardonnay, Shiraz, Cabernet.
SUMMARY Tallavera Grove is one of the many wine interests of John Davis and family. The family is a 50 per cent owner of Briar Ridge, a major shareholder in the parent company of Peppertree Wines; a 12-hectare vineyard in Coonawarra; a 100-hectare vineyard at Wrattonbully (the Stonefields Vineyard); and a 36-hectare vineyard at Orange (Jokers Peak). The Mount View winery will eventually be equipped to handle between 200 and 300 tonnes of fruit from the various family vineyards, with wines from Jokers Peak and the Stonefields Vineyards, and from Coonawarra in 2005.

🍇 Tallis Wines

PO Box 10, Dookie, Vic 3646 **REGION** Central Victorian Zone
T (03) 5823 5383 **F** (03) 5828 6532 **OPEN** Not
WINEMAKER Richard Tallis, Gary Baldwin (Consultant) **EST.** 2000 **CASES** 750
PRODUCT RANGE ($15–18 ML) Viognier, Dookie Hills Shiraz, Dookie Hills Cabernet Sauvignon.
SUMMARY Richard, Mark and Alice Tallis have a substantial vineyard with 16 hectares of shiraz, 5 hectares of cabernet sauvignon, 2 hectares of viognier and 1 hectare of merlot. While most of the grapes are sold, they have embarked on winemaking with the aid of Gary Baldwin of Wine Net, and done so with considerable success. the philosophy of their viticulture and winemaking is to adopt a low-input and sustainable system; all environmentally harmful sprays are eliminated.

🍷🍷🍷🍷 **Dookie Hills Shiraz 2002** Plush, luscious, ripe black fruits; fruit and alcohol sweetness. Good wine, but might have been better still if picked earlier. **RATING** 88 **DRINK** 2012 $16

🍷🍷🍷🍷 **Dookie Hills Viognier 2003** **RATING** 86 **DRINK** Now $18

Tall Poppy Wines

PO Box 4147, Mildura, Vic 3502 **REGION** Murray Darling
T (03) 5022 7255 **F** (03) 5022 7250 **OPEN** 7 days 8.30–5
WINEMAKER Barossa Vintners (Contract) **EST.** 1997 **CASES** 20 000
PRODUCT RANGE ($10–15 R) Viognier, Unwooded Chardonnay, Chardonnay, Shiraz, Merlot, Petit Verdot, Sangiovese, Merlot Cabernet Sauvignon Shiraz, Cabernet Sauvignon.
SUMMARY Tall Poppy Wines is in its infancy as a wine brand, but with lofty ambitions. It owns 4.5 hectares each of shiraz and viognier, but is able to draw upon grapes sourced from 170 hectares of vineyards owned by its directors, with a volume potential of 300 000 to 400 000 cases aimed at the export market, the UK, Vietnam, Malaysia, Singapore, New Zealand and Phillipines.

🍷🍷🍷🍷 **Chardonnay 2002** **RATING** 84 **DRINK** Now $10

Taltarni

339 Taltarni Road, Moonambel, Vic 3478 **REGION** Pyrenees
T (03) 5459 7900 **F** (03) 5467 2306 **OPEN** 7 days 10–5
WINEMAKER Leigh Clarnette, Loic Le Calvez, Mark Laurence **EST.** 1972 **CASES** 80 000
PRODUCT RANGE ($12.40–50 R) Sauvignon Blanc, Fiddleback White, Brut, Brut Tache, Rose, Fiddleback Red, Shiraz, Cephas (Shiraz Cabernet), Merlot, Cabernet Merlot, Cabernet Sauvignon; Lalla Gully Sauvignon Blanc, Chardonnay.
SUMMARY After a hiatus of 2 years or so following the departure of long-serving winemaker and chief executive Dominique Portet, Taltarni has gathered new momentum and inspiration, with an executive and winemaking team headed by the multi-talented Peter Steer. Major changes in the approach to the vineyards; major upgrading of winery equipment and investment in new oak barrels; a long-term contract arrangement for the purchase of grapes from the Heathcote region; and the release of a new flagship wine, Cephas, are the visible signs of the repositioning of the business. It is still too early to say whether the portfolio of wines under Cephas will be (relative to their price) of similar quality, but there is every reason to guess that they will. Exports to all the major markets, including the UK, the US, Canada, Japan, Hong Kong, Switzerland, Sweden and extensively throughout South-East Asia and Western Europe.

🍷🍷🍷🍷🍷 **Lalla Gully Riesling 2003** Fragrant lemon blossom aromas; abundant flavour and depth; likewise balance and length. **RATING** 93 **DRINK** 2010
Cephas 2001 A complex array of aromas and flavours; black fruits, cedar and spice; excellent balance and mouthfeel. **RATING** 93 **DRINK** 2016 $49.70
Sauvignon Blanc 2003 Fragrant tropical blossom and gooseberry fruit; excellent length and style; Tasmanian contribution makes a major mark. **RATING** 92 **DRINK** Now $19.50

🍷🍷🍷🍷 **Lalla Gully Chardonnay 2000** Complex, but light-bodied, elegant style; cashew and melon; a 290-case mix of Pipers Brook and Pyrenees material. **RATING** 89 **DRINK** Now $25
Shiraz 2001 Clean, light to medium-bodied, with very good mouthfeel and balance; strikes a happy medium; the best for some years. **RATING** 89 **DRINK** 2011 $30.60

Cabernet Merlot 2001 A well-crafted, fruit-driven style; soft, sweet fruits; neatly balanced and, in common with all of the 2001 wines, good mouthfeel. Has a Riverland component. RATING 87 DRINK 2008 $19.50

Brut 2001 Fine, citrussy aromas and flavours; crisp and bright; the one-third contribution from Tasmania drives the wine. RATING 87 DRINK Now $21.50

♈♈♈♈ **Brut Tache 2001** RATING 86 DRINK Now $21.50

♈♈♈ **Fiddleback White 2002** RATING 83 $12.40
Rose 2003 RATING 82 $15.70

Talunga   NR

Adelaide to Mannum Road, Gumeracha, SA 5233 REGION Adelaide Hills
T (08) 8389 1222 F (08) 8389 1233 OPEN Wed–Sun and public holidays 10.30–5
WINEMAKER Vince Scaffidi EST. 1994 CASES 6000
PRODUCT RANGE ($14.50–29.50 CD) Sauvignon Blanc, Chardonnay, Pinot Noir, Shiraz, Terrace Block Grenache, Sangiovese, Sangiovese Merlot, High Block Cabernet Sauvignon; Scaffidi Nebbiolo.
SUMMARY Talunga owners Vince and Tina Scaffidi have a one-third share of the 62-hectare Gumeracha Vineyards, and it is from these vineyards that the Talunga wines are sourced. In November 2002 the 2001 Sangiovese won the trophy for Best Red Wine of Show at the Australian Alternative Varieties Wine Show.

Tamar Ridge   ★★★★★

Auburn Road, Kayena, Tas 7270 REGION Northern Tasmania
T (03) 6394 1111 F (03) 6394 1126 OPEN 7 days 10–5
WINEMAKER Michael Fogarty, Matt Lowe EST. 1994 CASES 35 000
PRODUCT RANGE ($15–38 CD) Riesling, Gewurztraminer, Sauvignon Blanc, Pinot Gris, Chardonnay, Josef Chromy Selection Botyrytis, TRV Tasmania (Sparkling), Josef Chromy Blanc de Noir, Pinot Noir, Cabernet Sauvignon, Cellar Release Cabernet Sauvignon; also lower-priced Devil's Corner range.
SUMMARY In April 2003 Gunns Limited, a large, publicly listed Tasmanian forestry and agribusiness entity purchased Tamar Ridge. With the retention of Dr Richard Smart as viticultural advisor, the largest expansion of Tasmanian plantings is underway, with 100 hectares to be planted each year for the next 5 years at Waterhouse, in the far northeastern corner of the State. This is the driest and warmest part of Tasmania, and Richard Smart is supremely confident that it will produce grapes of high quality. This will more than double the entire plantings in Tasmania and underwrite significant sales both domestically and in export markets. Exports to the US, Ireland, Denmark, Germany, Japan and Singapore.

♈♈♈♈♈ **Friends Chardonnay 2002** Some funky/feral barrel ferment notes supported by powerful, intense nectarine and grapefruit; smoky overtones. RATING 94 DRINK 2011
Pinot Noir 2002 Very deeply coloured, saturated dark plum aromas, and an immensely concentrated (but not over-extractive) palate, with layers of plum and black cherry.
RATING 94 DRINK 2010 $26
Josef Chromy Botrytis 2001 Very complex, intense botrytis; similarly complex and powerful palate; riesling and sauvignon blanc blend. RATING 94 DRINK 2009 $22

♈♈♈♈♈ **Riesling 2003** Expressive lime juice aromas; powerful, rich, strong structure; weighty and long. RATING 93 DRINK 2012 $19.95

♈♈♈♈ **Cellar Release Sauvignon Blanc 2003** Complex, but not swamped by oak; ripe gooseberry/tropical fruit; good balance. RATING 89 DRINK 2007 $21
Gewurztraminer 2003 Delicate herb and spice; some rose petal; nicely balanced and elegant. RATING 87 DRINK Now $19.95
Pinot Gris 2003 Good varietal fruit expression; apple, pear and musk; good finish.
RATING 87 DRINK 2007 $21

♈♈♈♈ **Devil's Corner Pinot Noir 2003** RATING 86 DRINK 2008 $18
Sauvignon Blanc 2003 RATING 84 DRINK Now $19

♈♈♈ **Devil's Corner Chardonnay 2003** RATING 83 $16

Tamborine Estate Wines

NR

32 Hartley Road, North Tamborine, Qld 4272 **REGION** Queensland Coastal
T (07) 5545 1711 **F** (07) 5545 3522 **OPEN** 7 days 10–4
WINEMAKER John Cassegrain **EST.** 1990 **CASES** 3000
PRODUCT RANGE ($15–29 CD) Traminer Riesling, Verdelho, Unwooded Chardonnay, Chardonnay, Reserve Chardonnay, Sparkling Pinot Noir Chardonnay, Sparkling Shiraz, Botrytis, Rose, Rosso Dolce, Reserve Black Shiraz, Shiraz Cabernet, Cabernet Merlot, White Fortified, Tawny Port.
SUMMARY Tamborine Estate is a joint venture between the well-known John Cassegrain (of Cassegrain Wines at Port Macquarie) and French-born entrepeneur Bernard Forey (owner of the large Richfield Vineyard at Tenterfield in northern New South Wales). They have acquired the former Mount Tamborine Winery and its 2.5 hectares of merlot, cabernet franc and malbec planted adjacent to the winery.

Tamburlaine

★★★

McDonalds Road, Pokolbin, NSW 2321 **REGION** Lower Hunter Valley
T (02) 4998 7570 **F** (02) 4998 7763 **OPEN** 7 days 9.30–5
WINEMAKER Mark Davidson, Michael McManus, Jeremy Gordon **EST.** 1966 **CASES** 70 000
PRODUCT RANGE ($18–24 CD) Orange Reserve range of Riesling, Sauvignon Blanc, Chardonnay; Hunter Reserve range of Semillon, Verdelho, Chardonnay, Syrah; Natural Selection range of Shiraz, Chambourcin, Cabernet Sauvignon; Botrytis, Muscat Aged Liqueur.
SUMMARY A thriving business which, notwithstanding the fact that it has doubled its already substantial production in recent years, sells over 90 per cent of its wine through the cellar door and by mailing list (with an active tasting club members' cellar program offering wines which are held and matured at Tamburlaine). Unashamedly and deliberately focused on the tourist trade (and, of course, its wine club members).

ŦŦŦŶ **Semillon 2003** RATING 86 DRINK 2008 $ 22
Verdelho 2003 RATING 85 DRINK Now $ 22

Taminick Cellars

★★★☆

Booth Road, Taminick, Vic 3675 **REGION** Glenrowan
T (03) 5766 2282 **F** (03) 5766 2151 **OPEN** Mon–Sat 9–5, Sun 10–5
WINEMAKER Peter Booth **EST.** 1904 **CASES** 4000
PRODUCT RANGE ($8–16 CD) Trebbiano, Chardonnay, Late Harvest Trebbiano, Shiraz, Cabernet Merlot, Cabernet Sauvignon, ports, muscat.
SUMMARY Traditional producer of massively flavoured and very long-lived red wines, most sold to long-term customers and through the cellar door.

ŦŦŦŦ **Premium Shiraz 2002** Blackberry, prune and dark chocolate aromas; powerful, ripe, fruit-flooded and driven; soft tannins. Carries its 14.3 degrees alcohol well. **RATING** 89 **DRINK** 2012 $ 16
Special Release Cabernet Sauvignon 2002 Densely coloured; a massive wine, with layer upon layer of black fruits, bitter chocolate, earth and tannins; regional, not varietal, but impressive. **RATING** 87 **DRINK** 2022 $ 16

Tangaratta Estate

NR

RMB 637 Old Winton Road, Tamworth, NSW 2340 **REGION** Northern Slopes Zone
T (02) 6761 5660 **F** (02) 6766 5383 **OPEN** Sun–Fri 10–5
WINEMAKER John Hordern (Contract) **EST.** 1999 **CASES** 23 000
PRODUCT RANGE ($12–20 CD) Verdelho, Dry White, Stoney Ridge Shiraz, Old Winton Reserve Shiraz, Old Winton Reserve Merlot, Cabernet Merlot.
SUMMARY Another recent entry into the Northern Slopes Zone, with a substantial 29-hectare vineyard planted to verdelho, cabernet sauvignon, merlot and shiraz. The wines are exported to Canada, Japan, Malaysia, Singapore and the US, and are also available by mail order and through the cellar door, which has light meals and barbecue facilities when open.

Tanglewood Downs

NR

Bulldog Creek Road, Merricks North, Vic 3926 **REGION** Mornington Peninsula
T (03) 5974 3325 **F** (03) 5974 4170 **OPEN** Sun–Mon 12–5
WINEMAKER Ken Bilham, Wendy Bilham **EST.** 1984 **CASES** 1200
PRODUCT RANGE ($25 CD) Riesling, Gewurztraminer, Chardonnay, Pinot Noir, Cabernet Sauvignon, Cabernet Franc Merlot.
SUMMARY One of the smaller and lower-profile wineries on the Mornington Peninsula, with Ken Bilham quietly doing his own thing on 2.5 hectares of estate plantings. Winery lunches and dinners are available by arrangement.

Tanglewood Vines

NR

RMB 383, Bridgetown, WA 6255 (postal) **REGION** Blackwood Valley
T (08) 9764 4051 **OPEN** Not
WINEMAKER Contract **EST.** 1999
PRODUCT RANGE Cabernet Sauvignon Merlot.
SUMMARY Tanglewood Vines has established 2.4 hectares of cabernet sauvignon and 2 hectares of merlot, with a planting of viognier in 2002. The wines were due to be come onto the market in 2004.

Tanjil Wines

11 Brigantine Court, Patterson Lakes, Vic 3197 (postal) **REGION** Gippsland
T (03) 9773 0378 **F** (03) 9773 0378 **OPEN** Not
WINEMAKER Robert Hewet, Olga Garot **EST.** 2001 **CASES** 1200
PRODUCT RANGE ($15 R) Pinot Grigio, Pinot Noir.
SUMMARY Robert Hewet and Olga Garot planted 3 hectares of pinot noir and 1 hectare of pinot grigio on a north-facing slope at an altitude of 200 metres between the Latrobe and Tanjil Valleys. The red brown loam over clay has good water retention, and the vines have not been nor will be irrigated, with an expected yield of only 5 tonnes per hectare. The 2002 vintage wines were made from purchased fruit; 2003 was the first estate-grown production of pinot noir.

▼▼▼▼ **Pinot Noir 2003** Good structure and length; a balanced mix of plum and more foresty/savoury notes. **RATING** 89 **DRINK** 2008 $15

Tannery Lane Vineyard

★★★

174 Tannery Lane, Mandurang, Vic 3551 **REGION** Bendigo
T (03) 5439 3227 **F** (03) 5439 4003 **OPEN** By appointment
WINEMAKER Lindsay Ross (Contract) **EST.** 1990 **CASES** 250
PRODUCT RANGE ($22–24 CD) Sangiovese, Shiraz.
SUMMARY In 1990 planting began of the present total of 2 hectares of shiraz, cabernet sauvignon, cabernet franc, sangiovese, merlot and nebbiolo. Their sangiovese was one of the first plantings of the variety in the Bendigo region. The micro-production is sold through the cellar door only and then only while stocks last, which typically is not for very long. Now owned by the Williams family.

Tantemaggie

NR

Mullineaux Road, Pemberton, WA 6260 **REGION** Pemberton
T (08) 9776 1164 **F** (08) 9776 1810 **OPEN** By appointment
WINEMAKER Contract **EST.** 1987 **CASES** 300
PRODUCT RANGE ($18–25 CD) Verdelho, Cabernet Sauvignon.
SUMMARY Tantemaggie was established by the Pottinger family with the help of a bequest from a deceased aunt named Maggie. It is part of a mixed farming operation, and by far the greatest part of the 28 hectares is under long-term contract to Houghton. The bulk of the plantings are cabernet sauvignon, verdelho and chardonnay, the former producing the light-bodied style favoured by the Pottingers.

🍇 Tapanappa

NR

PO Box 174, Crafers, SA 5152 **REGION** Wrattonbully
T 0418 818 223 **F** (08) 8370 8374 **OPEN** Not
WINEMAKER Brian Croser **EST.** 2003
PRODUCT RANGE Bordeaux-style blends of Cabernet Sauvignon, Merlot and Cabernet Franc.
SUMMARY Arguably the most interesting of all new wineries to be announced in Australia over the past few years. Its partners are Brian Croser of Petaluma, Jean-Michel Cazes of Chateau Lynch-Bages in Pauillac, and Societe Jacques Bollinger, the parent company of Champagne Bollinger. The core of the business is the Koppamurra vineyard acquired from Koppamurra Wines prior to the 2003 vintage; the 2003 vintage Cabernet Sauvignon Merlot and Cabernet Franc from the 2003 vintage will be released under the Tapanappa brand in early 2005. In the meantime, the vineyard has been entirely reworked onto vertical spur positioning, and given that it was planted in 1975 (one of the two original vineyards in the Koppamurra area), will undoubtedly produce fruit of great quality. By chance, Brian Croser made the 1980 Ashbourne Cabernet Sauvignon (from Koppamurra) on behalf of Geoff Weaver, and comments that it 'is still an intense ripe fruit wine of exquisite balance, finesse and complexity'. Tapanappa will in due course gain access to other grape varieties on other unique sites in Australia.

Tapestry

★★★★

Olivers Road, McLaren Vale, SA 5171 **REGION** McLaren Vale
T (08) 8323 9196 **F** (08) 8323 9746 **OPEN** 7 days 11–5
WINEMAKER Jon Ketley **EST.** 1971 **CASES** 10 000
PRODUCT RANGE ($10–36 CD) Riesling, Chardonnay, Spaetlese, Bin 338 Shiraz, Cabernet Shiraz, Cabernet Sauvignon, Muscat of Alexandria, Old Tawny Port.
SUMMARY After a relatively brief period of ownership by Brian Light the former Merrivale Winery was then acquired by the Gerard family in 1997, previously owners of Chapel Hill. It has 40 hectares of 30-year-old vineyards, 6.5 hectares in McLaren Vale and 33.5 hectares in Bakers Gully. Less than half the grapes are used for the Tapestry label.

🍷🍷🍷🍷 **Fifteen Barrels Cabernet Sauvignon 2001** A panoply of cedar, savoury blackcurrant aromas and flavours, with strong French oak contribution throughout. Flashy show style. **RATING** 93 **DRINK** 2016 $ 36

The Vincent Shiraz 2001 Rich, very complex; strong American oak infusion but seamless integration; not jammy; ripe tannins. **RATING** 92 **DRINK** 2016 $ 36

🍷🍷🍷 **McLaren Vale Chardonnay 2002 RATING** 86 **DRINK** 2007 $ 15

Tarrangower Estate

★★★

17 Baldry Street, Malmsbury, Vic 3446 **REGION** Macedon Ranges
T (03) 5423 2088 **F** (03) 5423 2088 **OPEN** Weekends 10–5, or by appointment
WINEMAKER Tom Gyorffy **EST.** 1993 **CASES** 200
PRODUCT RANGE ($20–38 CD) The Revolution Chardonnay, Coliban Cabernet Shiraz, Shiraz Cabernet.
SUMMARY Tarrangower Estate is situated on the northeastern edge of the township of Malmsbury, at the western end of the Macedon Ranges wine region. At an altitude of 470 metres, it is one of the warmest sites in the region. The varieties planted are chardonnay, shiraz, cabernet sauvignon and merlot. Tom Gyorffy is a Melbourne lawyer, but as a mature-age student he graduated with an associate degree in applied science (wine growing) from Charles Sturt University in 1997. His philosophy is to make 'natural wines' and to deliberately oxidise (hyper-oxidation) the chardonnay.

🍷🍷🍷🍷 **The Revolution Chardonnay 2001** Developed colour; ripe, yellow peach, minimal oak impact; manages to carry 14.8 degrees alcohol. **RATING** 88 **DRINK** Now $ 28

🍷🍷🍷 **Shiraz Cabernet 2001 RATING** 85 **DRINK** 2008 $ 28

🍷🍷🍷 **Coliban Cabernet Shiraz 2000 RATING** 83 $ 20

Tarrawarra Estate ★★★★☆

Healesville Road, Yarra Glen, Vic 3775 **REGION** Yarra Valley
T (03) 5962 3311 **F** (03) 5962 3887 **OPEN** 7 days 11–5
WINEMAKER Clare Halloran, Bruce Walker **EST.** 1983 **CASES** 25 000
PRODUCT RANGE ($20–50 R) Chardonnay and Pinot Noir; also Kidron Chardonnay and Shiraz (kosher).
SUMMARY Slowly developing Chardonnay of great structure and complexity is the winery specialty; robust Pinot Noir also needs time and evolves impressively if given it. The opening of the large on-site art gallery (and its attendant café/restaurant) in early 2004 adds another dimension to the tourism tapestry of the Yarra Valley. For the time being, the gallery is only open from Wednesday to Sunday, but as the *Michelin Guide* would have it, is definitely worth a detour. National retail distribution; exports to the UK, Switzerland, Belgium, Singapore, Italy and the US.

Tarrington Vineyards ★★★★★

Hamilton Highway, Tarrington, Vic 3301 **REGION** Henty
T (03) 5572 4509 **F** (03) 5572 4509 **OPEN** By appointment
WINEMAKER Tamara Irish **EST.** 1993 **CASES** 300
PRODUCT RANGE ($27.50–45 R) Chardonnay, Pinot Noir, Cuvee Emilie Pinot Noir.
SUMMARY The grape growing and winemaking practices of Burgundy permeate every aspect of Tarrington Vineyards. While its establishment began in 1993, there has been no hurry to bring the vineyard into production. Two varieties only have been planted: pinot noir and chardonnay, with a planting density varying between 3333 and 8170 vines per hectare. There are no less than nine clones in the 2 hectares of pinot noir, and four clones in the 1 hectare of chardonnay. The approach to making the Pinot Noir is common in Burgundy, while the unoaked Chardonnay is kept in tank on fine lees for 9 months, the traditional method of making Chablis. Everything about the operation speaks of a labour of love, with a high standard of packaging and presentation of all background material. The exemplary wines are to be found on a thoroughly impressive collection of Victoria's top restaurant wine lists.

🍷🍷🍷🍷🍷 **Chardonnay 2002** Not particularly aromatic, but incredibly long and intense; pear, stone fruit, apple and grapefruit flavours intermingle; great acidity. Unquestionably the finest unwooded Chardonnay in Australia. **RATING** 96 **DRINK** 2012 **$** 40

Pinot Noir 2002 Deeply coloured; exceptionally concentrated, powerful and long myriad of flavours; an exotic, spicy tang to the finish and lingering aftertaste; savoury, yet not the least bit green; wonderful acidity. **RATING** 96 **DRINK** 2012 **$** 35

Cuvee Emilie Pinot Noir 2001 Elegant yet powerful; the full Chambolle Musigny peacock's tail opens on the finish; very fine, long, savoury tannins; has years to develop even more personality. A single barrel made. **RATING** 94 **DRINK** 2009 **$** 45

Tarwin Ridge NR

Wintles Road, Leongatha South, Vic 3953 **REGION** Gippsland
T (03) 5664 3211 **F** (03) 5664 3211 **OPEN** Weekends and holidays 10–5
WINEMAKER Brian Anstee **EST.** 1983 **CASES** 700
PRODUCT RANGE ($16–27 CD) Sauvignon Blanc, White Merlot, Pinot Noir, Pinot Noir Premium, Cabernet Merlot.
SUMMARY For the time being Brian Anstee is making his wines at Nicholson River under the gaze of fellow social worker Ken Eckersley; the wines come from 2 hectares of estate pinot and 0.5 hectare each of cabernet and sauvignon blanc.

Tassell Park Wines ★★★☆

Treeton Road, Cowaramup, WA 6284 **REGION** Margaret River
T (08) 9755 5440 **F** (08) 9755 5442 **OPEN** 7 days 10–5
WINEMAKER Flying Fish Cove (Contract) **EST.** 2001 **CASES** 1000
PRODUCT RANGE ($16–25 CD) Chenin Blanc, Sauvignon Blanc, Sauvignon Blanc Semillon, Shiraz, Cabernet Sauvignon Merlot.

SUMMARY One of the light brigade of newcomers to the Margaret River region, where Ian and Tricia Tassell have 7 hectares of sauvignon blanc, chenin blanc, semillon, cabernet sauvignon, merlot, shiraz and petit verdot. Their wines are made at Flying Fish Cove which seems a particularly good move, winning a string of bronze medals. They are sold through the website <www.tassellparkwines.com>, by mail order and through the cellar door which offers light meals to take away.

ƳƳƳƳƳ **Shiraz 2002** Lovely black cherry and blackberry fruit; very good mouthfeel; supple tannins. **RATING** 90 **DRINK** 2010 $ 22

ƳƳƳƳ **Cabernet Sauvignon Merlot 2002** **RATING** 86 **DRINK** 2009 $ 25

Tatachilla ★★★★

151 Main Road, McLaren Vale, SA 5171 **REGION** McLaren Vale
T (08) 8323 8656 **F** (08) 8323 9096 **OPEN** Mon–Sat 10–5, Sunday and public holidays 11–5
WINEMAKER Michael Fragos, Justin McNamee **EST.** 1901 **CASES** 250 000
PRODUCT RANGE ($11.95–50 CD) Adelaide Hills Sauvignon Blanc, Growers (Chenin Blanc Semillon Sauvignon Blanc), Adelaide Hills Chardonnay, McLaren Vale Chardonnay, Padthaway Chardonnay, Sparkling Pinot Noir, Sparkling Malbec, Foundation Shiraz, McLaren Vale Shiraz, Adelaide Hills Merlot, McLaren Vale Merlot, Clarendon Merlot, Keystone (Grenache Shiraz), Partners (Cabernet Sauvignon Shiraz), McLaren Vale Cabernet Sauvignon, Padthaway Cabernet Sauvignon, 1901 Cabernet Sauvignon, Tawny Port; at the bottom is the lower-priced Breakneck Creek range varietals.
SUMMARY Tatachilla was reborn in 1995 but has an at-times tumultuous history going back to 1901. For most of the time between 1901 and 1961 the winery was owned by Penfolds but was closed in that year before being reopened in 1965 as the Southern Vales Co-operative. In the late 1980s it was purchased and renamed The Vales but did not flourish, and in 1993 it was purchased by local grower Vic Zerella and former Kaiser Stuhl chief executive Keith Smith. After extensive renovations, the winery was officially reopened in 1995 and won a number of tourist awards and accolades. The star turns are Keystone (Grenache Shiraz) and Foundation Shiraz, bursting with vibrant fruit. Became part of Banksia Wines in 2001, in turn acquired by Lion Nathan in 2002. Exports to the UK, the US and New Zealand.

ƳƳƳƳƳ **McLaren Vale Chardonnay 2002** Fragrant and elegant; grapefruit, melon and nectarine with a gently creamy texture; clever winemaking, great value. **RATING** 93 **DRINK** 2007 $ 16.50
McLaren Vale Cabernet Sauvignon 2001 An opulently rich bundle of blackcurrant and chocolate; soft tannins, good oak. **RATING** 90 **DRINK** 2011 $ 22.95

ƳƳƳƳ **McLaren Vale Shiraz 2001** In typical Tatachilla style, a huge wine, crammed with fruit; the tannins, at least, are not overplayed. **RATING** 89 **DRINK** 2016 $ 22
Lightly Oaked Chardonnay 2003 Cleverly crafted; delicate citrus and melon fruit with the barest touch of oak; long, clean finish. **RATING** 88 **DRINK** Now $ 14.90

ƳƳƳƳ **Foundation Shiraz 2001** **RATING** 86 **DRINK** 2012 $ 45
Adelaide Hills Chardonnay 2002 **RATING** 84 **DRINK** Now $ 19
Growers 2003 **RATING** 84 **DRINK** Now $ 12.95

Tatehams Wines ★★★☆

Main North Road, Auburn, SA 5451 **REGION** Clare Valley
T (08) 8849 2030 **F** (08) 8849 2260 **OPEN** Wed–Sun 10–5
WINEMAKER Mike Jeandupeux **EST.** 1998 **CASES** 500
PRODUCT RANGE ($15–28 CD) Riesling, Shiraz, Merlot, Sangiovese.
SUMMARY Mike and Isabel Jeandupeux left the French-speaking part of Switzerland in September 1997 to begin a new life in Australia. They now operate a restaurant and guesthouse at Auburn, in the southern end of the Clare Valley. The 1863 stone building, which originally operated as a general store and stables, has been completely refurbished, with several buildings offering a variety of upscale accommodation. The winemaking side of the business is effectively an add-on, with most of the wine sold through the restaurant and cellar door, but with a mailing list and limited distribution in Adelaide. The Riesling is particularly attractive.

Tatler Wines

★★★★

Lot 15 Lovedale Road, Lovedale, NSW 2321 **REGION** Lower Hunter Valley
T (02) 4930 9139 **F** (02) 4930 9145 **OPEN** 7 days 9.30–5.30
WINEMAKER Jim Chatto, Ross Pearson, Alasdair Sutherland, Jenny Bright (Contract) **EST.** 1998
CASES 2000
PRODUCT RANGE ($14–24 CD) Nigel's Semillon, Whisper's Chardonnay Semillon Sauvignon Blanc,
Pinot Grigio, Dimitri's Paddock Chardonnay, The Sticky, Rita's Rose, Pinot Noir Chardonnay,
Sparkling Shiraz, Archie's Paddock Shiraz.
SUMMARY Tatler Wines is a family-owned company headed by Theo and Spiro Isakidis, Sydney
hoteliers. The name comes through the Tatler Hotel on George Street, Sydney, where the Isakidis
family met Tony Brown and wife Deborah; the latter two now run the Hunter vineyard and cellar
door. It is a substantial one, with 21 hectares of estate vineyards planted to chardonnay, shiraz,
semillon, pinot gris, cabernet franc and sangiovese.

ŸŸŸŸŸ **Nigel's Semillon 2001** Delicious flavours as the wine moves smoothly through
adolescence to maturity; lemon and honey; lingering finish. **RATING** 93 **DRINK** 2011 $ 16
Whispers Semillon Sauvignon Blanc 2003 Spotlessly clean; a very long palate;
lingering, lemony flavours and acidity; a blend of Hunter Valley and Orange grapes.
RATING 90 **DRINK** 2007

ŸŸŸŸ **Archie's Paddock Shiraz 2001** Red berry/cherry/plum fruit drive the light to medium-
bodied, clean, palate. **RATING** 87 **DRINK** 2009 $ 20
The Sticky NV Quite intense lemony fruit and even more lemony acidity; be warned.
RATING 87 **DRINK** Now $ 18

ŸŸŸŸ **Dimitri's Paddock Chardonnay 2001** **RATING** 85 **DRINK** Now $ 18
Nigel's Semillon 2003 **RATING** 84 **DRINK** 2010 $ 16

Tawonga Vineyard

NR

2 Drummond Street, Tawonga, Vic 3697 **REGION** Alpine Valleys
T (03) 5754 4945 **F** (03) 5754 4945 **OPEN** By appointment
WINEMAKER John Adams **EST.** 1994 **CASES** 450
PRODUCT RANGE ($14.40–15.50 CD) Verdelho, Viognier, Shiraz, Merlot.
SUMMARY Diz and John Adams made their first wine in 1995, but it was not until 1998 that they
finally received their producer's license entitling them to sell the wine they had made. With a planned
maximum production of less than 1000 cases, Tawonga has been able to take advantage of the small
business tax exemption. In the meantime their handcrafted wines (virtually all of which have won
show medals) remain at a magically low prices.

Taylors

★★★★☆

Taylors Road, Auburn, SA 5451 **REGION** Clare Valley
T (08) 8849 2008 **F** (08) 8849 2240 **OPEN** Mon–Fri 9–5, Sat and public holidays 10–5, Sun 10–4
WINEMAKER Adam Eggins, Helen McCarthy **EST.** 1969 **CASES** 250 000
PRODUCT RANGE ($13–65 R) Ultra-premium St Andrews varietals head the portfolio; then the
regional blends in the Jarraman range; Taylors Estate core range of varietals are the heart of the
business; the budget-priced Promised Land range come at the bottom.
SUMMARY The family founded and owned Taylors continues to flourish and expand, with yet further
extensions to its vineyards, now totalling over 500 hectares, by far the largest holding in Clare Valley.
There have also been substantial changes on the winemaking front, both in terms of the winemaking
team and in terms of the wine style and quality, particularly through the outstanding St Andrews
range. Widespread national distribution, with exports to the UK, Ireland, New Zealand and Malaysia.

ŸŸŸŸŸ **St Andrews Cabernet Sauvignon 1998** Classic bottle-developed savoury, earthy edges to
blackcurrant fruit; a long, supple palate. **RATING** 93 **DRINK** 2013 $ 56.95
Clare Riesling 2003 Spotless apple and lime blossom aromas; a crisp and lively palate
with a strong mineral spine. Classic cellaring proposition. **RATING** 92 **DRINK** 2013 $ 17.50
Jaraman Riesling 2002 Fine, clean mineral aromas; delicate passionfruit, lime and
lemon flavours; good balance and length. Clare and Eden Valley blend. **RATING** 92
DRINK 2012 $ 29.95

Jaraman Chardonnay 2001 Stylish and supple; gently sweet stone fruit; subtle barrel ferment inputs; Clare and Adelaide Hills blend. A great success. **RATING** 92 **DRINK** 2010 $ 29.95

Jaraman Cabernet Sauvignon 2000 Fragrant cassis, cedar and earth aromas; carefully crafted; cedar, spice and blackberry; elegant, medium-bodied. **RATING** 90 **DRINK** 2015 $ 34.95

ŸŸŸŸ **St Andrews Chardonnay 2000** Rich, sweet peach, butterscotch and toast flavours; good acidity gives length; not an easy variety in the Clare Valley. **RATING** 88 **DRINK** Now $ 37.75

Pinot Noir 2002 The winemakers have really worked miracles with this, especially the line and length of the palate, and the finish. **RATING** 87 **DRINK** Now $ 17.95

Jaraman Shiraz 2001 Light to medium-bodied, savoury and quite oaky; nicely balanced but lacks the expected generosity. Clare Valley and McLaren Vale. Paradoxically, the least of the four releases. **RATING** 87 **DRINK** 2009 $ 34.95

Merlot 2003 Medium-bodied; sweet red and blackcurrant fruit; a consistent performer. **RATING** 87 **DRINK** 2008 $ 17.95

St Andrews Merlot 2001 Fine, savoury, woodsy, briary style; lingering tannins. Screwcap. Fully priced. **RATING** 87 **DRINK** 2009 $ 65

ŸŸŸŸ **Gewurztraminer 2002** **RATING** 84 **DRINK** Now $ 14

ŸŸŸ **Promised Land Unwooded Chardonnay 2003** **RATING** 83 $ 13
Chardonnay 2003 **RATING** 83 $ 17.95

🦎 Teakles Hill Wines   NR

PO Box 251, Woodside, SA 5244 **REGION** Adelaide Hills
T (08) 8389 9375 **F** (08) 8389 9375 **OPEN** Not
WINEMAKER Contract **EST.** 2001 **CASES** 1000
PRODUCT RANGE ($18–22 ML) Pinot Noir, Shiraz, Cabernet Sauvignon.
SUMMARY William Borchardt and James Bidstrup have established 4 hectares of vineyard, planted to pinot noir, cabernet sauvignon and shiraz. A small amount is made for sale under the Teakles Hill brand, sold by mail order.

Temple Bruer   ★★★★

Milang Road, Strathalbyn, SA 5255 **REGION** Langhorne Creek
T (08) 8537 0203 **F** (08) 8537 0131 **OPEN** Mon–Fri 9.30–4.30
WINEMAKER David Bruer **EST.** 1980 **CASES** 14 000
PRODUCT RANGE ($12.80–23.70 R) Riesling, Chenin Blanc, Sauvignon Blanc, Verdelho, Viognier, Botrytis Riesling, Cornucopia Grenache, Cabernet Merlot, Reserve Merlot, Shiraz Malbec, Sparkling Cabernet Merlot.
SUMMARY Always known for its eclectic range of wines, Temple Bruer (which also carries on a substantial business as a vine propagation nursery) has seen a sharp lift in wine quality. Clean, modern redesigned labels add to the appeal of a stimulatingly different range of red wines. Part of the production from the 24 hectares of estate vineyards is sold to others, the remainder being made under the Temple Bruer label. The vineyard is now certified organic. Exports to the US and Japan.

ŸŸŸŸŸ **Bin 621 Shiraz Blend 2002** Delicious raspberry and redcurrant fruit; fine tannins; good balance. Top Gold 2003 National Wine Show. **RATING** 94 **DRINK** 2010

Templer's Mill   ★★★☆

The University of Sydney, Leeds Parade, Orange, NSW 2800 **REGION** Orange
T (02) 6360 5570 **F** (02) 6362 7625 **OPEN** 7 days 11–4
WINEMAKER Reynolds Wines **EST.** 1997 **CASES** 1300
PRODUCT RANGE ($12.50–16 CD) Sauvignon Blanc, Chardonnay, Shiraz, Merlot, Cabernet Sauvignon.
SUMMARY Templer's Mill was one of Australia's first flour mills, providing flour for early gold fields at Ophir near Orange. this historic mill is now a ruin on Narrambla, an adjacent property to the University of Sydney's Orange Campus farm and birthplace of AB (Banjo) Paterson. The 19.4-hectare vineyard is planted to cabernet sauvignon, chardonnay, shiraz, sauvignon blanc and merlot (in

descending order of magnitude); part of the production is made under the Templer's Mill label, part sold as grapes, the operation overseen by viticulture lecturer Peter Hedberg.

ŸŸŸŸŸ **Chardonnay 2001** Very complex, powerful, full-bodied, ripe peachy fruit; lingering finish; not hot. **RATING** 91 **DRINK** Now $ 13.25

ŸŸŸŸ **Sauvignon Blanc 2002** Crisp, spotlessly clean; light passionfruit and gooseberry flavours. **RATING** 88 **DRINK** Now $ 12.50
Merlot 2001 Attractive sweet red berry fruits; nice, subtle savoury twist on the finish. **RATING** 88 **DRINK** 2009 $ 14.10
Cabernet Sauvignon 2000 Light to medium-bodied; savoury/herbal/earthy aromas and flavours in cool-grown style; just gets there, while the 2001 doesn't. **RATING** 87 **DRINK** 2009 $ 14.10

ŸŸŸŸ **Shiraz 2001** **RATING** 86 **DRINK** 2007 $ 14.10
Cabernet Sauvignon 2001 **RATING** 86 **DRINK** 2008 $ 14.10

Tempus Two Wines   ★★★☆

Broke Road, Pokolbin, NSW 2321 **REGION** Lower Hunter Valley
T (02) 4993 3999 **F** (02) 4993 3988 **OPEN** 7 days 9–5
WINEMAKER Sarah-Kate Dineen **EST.** 1997 **CASES** 50 000
PRODUCT RANGE ($14–30 CD) Varietal range of Eden Valley Riesling, Semillon Sauvignon Blanc, Verdelho, Cowra Chardonnay, Hunter Shiraz, Merlot, Cabernet Merlot; Pewter range of Sparkling Chardonnay, Botrytis Semillon, Pinot Gris, Wilde Chardonnay, Vine Vale Shiraz, Hunter Merlot, Hollydene Cabernet Sauvignon.
SUMMARY Tempus Two is the name for what was once Hermitage Road Wines, a piece of doggerel akin to that of Rouge Homme, except that it is not Franglais, but a mix of Latin (Tempus means time) and English. I should not be too critical, however; the change was forced on the winery by the EU Wine Agreement and the prohibition of the use of the word 'hermitage' on Australian wine labels. Nor should the fracas over the labels disguise the fact that some very attractive wines have appeared so far, and will do so in the future, no doubt, particularly given the arrival of Sarah-Kate Dineen as winemaker in the striking new winery on Broke Road. Exports to the UK.

ŸŸŸŸŸ **Pinot Gris 2003** Aromatic apple blossom bouquet; intense, lingering citrussy overtones to the palate; good balance and length. King Valley material. **RATING** 90 **DRINK** Now $ 25

ŸŸŸŸ **Vine Vale Barossa Shiraz 2002** Quite fragrant; fresh red and blackberry fruit on a medium-bodied palate; good length. **RATING** 88 **DRINK** 2010 $ 30
Botrytis Semillon 250 ml 2003 Extremely sweet canned pineapple flavours with some (but not quite enough) balancing acidity. **RATING** 87 **DRINK** 2008 $ 20

ŸŸŸŸ **Verdelho 2003** **RATING** 85 **DRINK** Now $ 14
Pewter Label Melange a Trois 2003 **RATING** 84 **DRINK** Now $ 25
Vine Vale Barossa Shiraz 2000 **RATING** 84 **DRINK** 2007 $ 30

ŸŸŸ **Tempus Two Hunter Shiraz 2002** **RATING** 81 $ 14

Ten Minutes by Tractor Wine Co   ★★★★☆

111 Roberts Road, Main Ridge, Vic 3928 **REGION** Mornington Peninsula
T (03) 5989 6084 **F** (03) 5989 6599 **OPEN** Weekends and holidays 11–5
WINEMAKER Richard McIntyre (Pinot Noir, Chardonnay), Alex White (Sauvignon Blanc, Pinot Gris)
EST. 1999 **CASES** 3000
PRODUCT RANGE ($18.50–45 CD) Sauvignon Blanc, Pinot Gris, Chardonnay, Sweet Allis, Pinot Noir, Pinot Noir Reserve; Judd Vineyard Chardonnay, Pinot Noir; McCutcheon Vineyard Chardonnay, Pinot Noir; Wallis Vineyard Chardonnay, Pinot Noir.
SUMMARY This has to be one of the cleverest pieces of marketing I have ever come across, the unforgettable name reinforced by superb graphics. But it also has a particularly clever business plan, and some excellent wines to support the business. The company belongs to the Judd, McCutcheon and Wallis families, each of which established a 6-hectare vineyard a decade ago, but decided to merge the operations in 1999, realising that each of the three properties are only 10 minutes by

tractor distant from each other. While most of the grapes were and are sold to other winemakers, in 2000 they began making limited quantities of wines under the 10X label (drawing on all three properties) and individual vineyard selection wines from each of the three properties. A number of Melbourne restaurants list the wines, and exports to Hong Kong, San Francisco, New York and London are being developed. The cellar door serves light lunches. At the time of going to press had just been sold to Martin Spedding.

Terrel Estate Wines   NR

Whitton Stock Route, Yenda, NSW 2681 **REGION** Riverina
T (02) 6968 1110 **F** (02) 6968 1120 **OPEN** By appointment
WINEMAKER Robert Guadagnini **EST.** 1994
PRODUCT RANGE A range of varietal and varietal blends under various brand labels.
SUMMARY Gonzalo Terrel Senior heads a very large operation, little known in the domestic market, but with 250 hectares of all of the major varietals and a few out of left field such as tempranillo. It is primarily a bulk processing facility, with much of the wine sold in bulk to other winemakers, part vinified under the Terrel Estate, Morning Mist, Pebblestone and Majestic brands.

T'Gallant

1385 Mornington-Flinders Road, Main Ridge, Vic 3928 **REGION** Mornington Peninsula
T (03) 5989 6565 **F** (03) 5989 6577 **OPEN** 7 days 10–5
WINEMAKER Kathleen Quealy, Kevin McCarthy **EST.** 1990 **CASES** 30 000
PRODUCT RANGE ($15–49 R) An ever-changing list of names (and avant-garde label designs) but with Unwooded Chardonnay and Pinot Gris at the centre. Labels include The T'Gallant Chardonnay, Pinot Grigio, Tribute Pinot Gris, Imogen Pinot Gris, Celia's White Pinot, Cape Schanck Pinot Grigio Chardonnay, Io Botrytis Pinot Gris, Triumph Late Harvest Pinot Gris, Holystone, Romeo, Batch #1 Pinot Noir, Cape Schanck Pinot Noir, Juno Lyncroft Pinot Noir; TGQ Moscato and Sangiovese.
SUMMARY Husband and wife consultant-winemakers Kathleen Quealy and Kevin McCarthy carved out an important niche market for the T'Gallant label, so much so that in April 2003, after protracted negotiations, it was acquired by Beringer Blass. The acquisition of a 15-hectare property, and the planting of 10 hectares of pinot gris gives the business a firm geographic base, as well as providing increased resources for its signature wine. The yearly parade of new (usually beautiful and striking, it is true) labels designed by Ken Cato do not make my life at all easy. No sooner is the database built up than it is discarded for next year's rash of labels. La Baracca Trattoria is open 7 days for lunch and for specially booked evening events. Exports to the UK and the US.

Pinot Grigio 2003 Lively, tangy, zesty and minerally; quite complex, fresh finish; low alcohol welcome. **RATING** 91 **DRINK** Now $ 21
Tribute Pinot Gris 2002 Firm, spicy, minerally aromas; spice and wild herb flavours; balanced acidity. **RATING** 90 **DRINK** Now $ 29

Unwooded Chardonnay 2002 Quite intense stone fruit and grapefruit aromas; the palate doesn't quite deliver, tending four-square. **RATING** 88 **DRINK** Now $ 22

Beechworth Pinot Noir 2002 RATING 86 **DRINK** Now $ 49
Cape Schanck Pinot Noir 2002 RATING 86 **DRINK** Now $ 17

Thalgara Estate   NR

De Beyers Road, Pokolbin, NSW 2321 **REGION** Lower Hunter Valley
T (02) 4998 7717 **F** (02) 4998 7774 **OPEN** 7 days 10–5
WINEMAKER Steve Lamb **EST.** 1985 **CASES** 3000
PRODUCT RANGE ($15–30 CD) Chardonnay, Show Reserve Chardonnay, Semillon Chardonnay, Shiraz, Show Reserve Shiraz, Shiraz Cabernet.
SUMMARY A low-profile winery which had its moment of glory at the 1997 Hunter Valley Wine Show when it won the Doug Seabrook Memorial Trophy for Best Dry Red of Show with its 1995 Show Reserve Shiraz.

The Blok Estate   NR

Riddoch Highway, Coonawarra, SA 5263 **REGION** Coonawarra
T (08) 8737 2734 **F** (08) 8737 2994 **OPEN** 7 days 10–4
WINEMAKER Contract **EST.** 1999 **CASES** 1200
PRODUCT RANGE ($16–28 CD) Riesling, Chardonnay, Pinot Chardonnay, Shiraz, Cabernet Sauvignon.
SUMMARY Di and John Blok have owned a tiny vineyard planted to cabernet sauvignon for the past 5 years. They have now decided to take the production from this and from contract-grown grapes elsewhere in Coonawarra for release under their own label. The cellar door is situated in an old stone home which has recently been renovated and surrounded by newly landscaped gardens.

The Carriages Vineyard   ★★☆

549 Kotta Road, Echuca, Vic 3564 **REGION** Goulburn Valley
T (03) 5483 7767 **F** (03) 5483 7767 **OPEN** By appointment
WINEMAKER Plunkett (Contract) **EST.** 1996 **CASES** 600
PRODUCT RANGE ($17–19 R) Merlot, Cabernet Merlot.
SUMMARY David and Lyndall Johnson began the development of The Carriages in 1996, planting 2.5 hectares of merlot and a little over 1.5 hectares of cabernet sauvignon, the latter subsequently increased by a further 2 hectares. The wines are made at Plunkett's, where David Johnson was previously employed. The name and the extremely innovative packaging stems from the fact that the Johnson's bought four old railway carriages which they have parked side-by-side and painstakingly rehabilitated, now providing them with their house. Each bottle is identified with a cardboard rail ticket, printed by the company which provides the tickets for the Puffing Billy railway in the Dandenongs, and which is strikingly similar to the tickets of bygone years. Vertically bisected with brown on the left side, and yellow on the right side, the ticket manages to show the brand name, the vintage, the variety, the number of standard drinks, the alcohol and the bottle number (which is in fact the ticket number, or vice versa). Finally, the ticket is fixed to the label with fine twine, so it can be removed either as a memento or for further orders.

▼▼▼   **Cabernet Sauvignon 2002 RATING** 81 $ 19

🍂 The Deanery Vineyards   ★★★☆

PO Box 1172, Balhannah, SA 5242 **REGION** Adelaide Hills
T (08) 8390 1948 **F** (08) 8390 0321 **OPEN** Not
WINEMAKER Duncan Dean (Sangiovese), Contract **EST.** 1995 **CASES** 450
PRODUCT RANGE ($16–19 ML) Quartz Block Sauvignon Blanc, Bull Paddock Shiraz, Three Generations Sangiovese.
SUMMARY The Dean family — Pat and Henry, and their sons Duncan, Nick and Alan — purchased a 30-hectare dairy farm at Balhannah in late 1994, and planted 6.5 hectares of chardonnay, sauvignon blanc and semillon in the spring of 1995, subsequently adding a 0.67-hectare block of shiraz. Pinot noir and a tiny block of sangiovese were also subsequently planted at a separate property at Piccadilly. A further 8 hectares are now being developed on a third property adjacent to the original Balhannah holding. Alan Dean, a Charles Sturt University-trained viticulturist and former Petaluma vineyard manager, is in charge of the vineyards, working alongside brother Duncan and with part-time help from the third generation. The primary aim of the business is contract grapegrowing, the purchasers including Petaluma, Tower Estate and Jeffrey Grosset.

▼▼▼▼▼   **Bull Paddock Shiraz 2001** Fragrant bouquet; excellent varietal expression and style; spicy red and black fruits, fine tannins and subtle oak. **RATING** 90 **DRINK** 2011 $ 16

▼▼▼▼   **Quartz Block Sauvignon Blanc 2003 RATING** 84 **DRINK** Now $ 19

▼▼▼   **Three Generations Sangiovese 2001 RATING** 83 $ 16

🍂 The Duke Vineyard   ★★☆

38 Paringa Road, Red Hill South, Vic 3937 **REGION** Mornington Peninsula
T (03) 5989 2407 **F** (03) 5989 2407 **OPEN** Weekends and public holidays 12–5
WINEMAKER Geoff Duke **EST.** 1989 **CASES** 500
PRODUCT RANGE ($20–30 ML) Chardonnay, Pinot Noir.

SUMMARY Geoff and Sue Duke run a tiny, low-key winery with a 1.6-hectare vineyard equally divided between chardonnay and pinot noir. Its establishment goes back to 1989, 1994 marking the first commercial Chardonnay and 1997 for the first Pinot Noir. The wines are made in an on-site micro-winery and back vintages are available; none of the wines are sold until they are 2 years old.

ꭎꭎꭎꭎ **Chardonnay 2000** RATING 85 DRINK Now $ 25
    Pinot Noir 2000 RATING 84 DRINK Now $ 30

ꭎꭎꭎ **Chardonnay 2001** RATING 82 $ 25

ꭎꭎꭎ **Pinot Noir 2001** RATING 79 $ 30

The Falls Vineyard   NR

RMB 2750 Longwood-Gobur Road, Longwood East, Vic 3665 **REGION** Strathbogie Ranges
T (03) 5798 5291 **F** (03) 5798 5437 **OPEN** 7 days 9–5
WINEMAKER Andrew Cameron **EST.** 1969 **CASES** 1000
PRODUCT RANGE ($10–16 CD) The Falls Riesling, The Falls Chardonnay, Longwood Shiraz, The Falls Shiraz, Longwood Reserve Shiraz.
SUMMARY The Falls Vineyard was planted by Andrew and Elly Cameron way back in 1969, as a minor diversification for their pastoral company. Two hectares of shiraz, originally established on a wide T-trellis, but now converted to vertical spur positioning, provides both the Longwood Shiraz and the Longwood Reserve Shiraz. The wines (showing pronounced cool climate characteristics) are made on-site, but are bottled at Mitchelton. With only 1000 cases per year, the wines are basically sold by word of mouth, and the cellar door is open only if you phone beforehand or take advantage of the bed and breakfast accommodation offered by the Camerons.

The Fleurieu   ★★★★

Main Road, McLaren Vale, SA 5171 **REGION** McLaren Vale
T (08) 8323 8999 **F** (08) 8323 9332 **OPEN** 7 days 9–5
WINEMAKER Mike Farmilo **EST.** 1994 **CASES** 3500
PRODUCT RANGE ($19–45 R) Shiraz, released under the Fleurieu and Stump Hill labels.
SUMMARY A specialist Shiraz producer, with 6.5 hectares of estate vineyards and contract winemaking by the former long-serving Seaview/Edwards & Chaffey winemaker Mike Farmilo. Exports to the UK, the US, Singapore, Hong Kong, Japan, the Philippines and Canada.

ꭎꭎꭎꭎꭎ **Stump Hill Shiraz 2001** Generous red and black fruits on entry, closing with substantial tannins. RATING 90 DRINK 2011 $ 20

ꭎꭎꭎꭎ **Stump Hill Shiraz 2000** Similar to the '01; ripe, quite dense black fruits and chocolate; the tannins have softened. RATING 89 DRINK 2010 $ 20

ꭎꭎꭎꭎ **Shiraz 2000** RATING 86 DRINK 2008 $ 35 $ 45

The Gap Vineyard   ★★★☆

Pomonal Road, Halls Gap, Vic 3381 **REGION** Grampians
T (03) 5356 4252 **F** (03) 5356 4646 **OPEN** Wed–Sun 10–5, 7 days school and public holidays
WINEMAKER Trevor Mast, Dan Buckle **EST.** 1969 **CASES** 1500
PRODUCT RANGE ($16–26 CD) Riesling, Chardonnay, Reserve Chardonnay, Rose, Reserve Shiraz, Shiraz Grenache, Cabernet Sauvignon, Cassel Port; Four Sisters Sauvignon Blanc Semillon and Shiraz; Billi Billi Creek Shiraz Grenache Cabernet
SUMMARY The Gap is the reincarnation of Boroka, a spectacularly situated vineyard 5 kilometres east of Halls Gap, with the slopes of the Mount William Range forming a backdrop. The vineyard was planted in 1969 but following its acquisition by Mount Langi Ghiran has been rehabilitated (including transplanted riesling vines), and extensive renovations have been made to the cellar-door sales area which offers estate-grown The Gap wines and a selection of Mount Langi Ghiran and Four Sisters wines. Exports to Germany.

ꭎꭎꭎꭎ **Gap Riesling 2003** Classic mineral, lime and spice aromas and flavours; considerable power and length. First vintage new plantings and transplanted 25-year-old vines. Screwcap. RATING 90 DRINK 2010 $ 18

Cabernet Sauvignon 2001 Attractive, ripe blackberry, chocolate and earth flavours; overall sweet fruit; good tannins and oak. **RATING** 90 **DRINK** 2012 $ 26

ᵀᵀᵀᵀ **Shiraz 2001** Medium-bodied plum and black cherry, with spicy/savoury tannins; more weight than the '02. **RATING** 87 **DRINK** 2009 $ 26

ᵀᵀᵀᵀ **Shiraz 2002 RATING** 85 **DRINK** 2007 $ 26
Billi Billi Creek Shiraz Grenache Cabernet 2001 RATING 85 **DRINK** 2007 $ 16

The Garden Vineyard   NR

174 Graydens Road, Moorooduc, Vic 3933 **REGION** Mornington Peninsula
T (03) 5978 8336 **F** (03) 5978 8343 **OPEN** Weekends Nov–Mar and first weekend of Oct and Apr–Jun 11–5, or by appointment (closed July, Aug, Sept)
WINEMAKER Richard McIntyre (Contract) **EST.** 1995 **CASES** 130
PRODUCT RANGE ($20–25 CD) Pinot Gris, Pinot Noir.
SUMMARY This captures the delights of the Mornington Peninsula in so many ways. As the name suggests, it is as much a garden as it is a vineyard; Di and Doug Johnson began the establishment of a walled garden 7 years ago, at much the same time as they decided to increase the existing 0.5 hectare of pinot noir (planted in 1989) with an additional hectare of pinot noir and 0.5 hectare of pinot gris. The entrance fee to the garden is $8, but there is no charge for wine tasting. Most visitors end up enjoying both.

The Grove Vineyard   NR

Cnr Metricup and Carter Roads, Wilyabrup, WA 6284 **REGION** Margaret River
T (08) 9755 7458 **F** (08) 9755 7458 **OPEN** 7 days 9–4
WINEMAKER Steven Hughes **EST.** 1995 **CASES** 1500
PRODUCT RANGE ($15–35 CD) Sauvignon Blanc Semillon, Wood Matured Verdelho, Chardonnay, Shiraz, Tempranillo Graciano, The Shed Red (Merlot), Cabernet Sauvignon; sparkling wines include Pinot Chardonnay, Rose, Cabernet Sauvignon, Merlot, Verdelho, Semillon and Shiraz.
SUMMARY Steve and Val Hughes gave their vineyard its name to acknowledge their former residence in a street called The Grove, which was in turn part of an olive grove near Perth planted by the monks from the New Norcia monastery north of Perth. They have planted a fruit salad vineyard, the major varieties being sauvignon blanc (2.65 hectares), chardonnay (1.5 hectares), cabernet sauvignon (1.88 hectares), with lesser but not insignificant plantings of semillon, pinot noir, shiraz, merlot, verdelho, tempranillo and graciano. They run a restaurant, provide accommodation, feature coffee roasting sales and tastings, a gourmet delicatessen, olive oil and, of course, cellar-door sales with a wide range of wines reflecting the fruit salad plantings.

The Gurdies   NR

St Helier Road, The Gurdies, Vic 3984 **REGION** Gippsland
T (03) 5997 6208 **F** (03) 5997 6511 **OPEN** 7 days 10–5, or by appointment
WINEMAKER Peter Kozik **EST.** 1991 **CASES** 1500
PRODUCT RANGE ($18–25 CD) Riesling, Gurdies Hill White (Chardonnay), Pinot Noir, Reserve Pinot Noir, Shiraz, Merlot, Cabernet Merlot, Gurdies Hill Red (Cabernet Sauvignon Shiraz), Cabernet Sauvignon.
SUMMARY The only winery in the southwest Gippsland region, established on the slopes of The Gurdies hills overlooking Westernport Bay and French Island. Plantings of the 3.5-hectare vineyard commenced in 1981, but no fruit was harvested until 1991 owing to bird attack. A winery has been partially completed, and it is intended to increase the vineyards to 8 hectares and ultimately build a restaurant on-site.

🍂 The Islander Estate Vineyards   NR

PO Box 621, McLaren Vale, SA 5171 **REGION** Fleurieu Zone
T (08) 8323 7724 **F** (08) 8323 7726 **OPEN** Not
WINEMAKER Jacques Lurton
PRODUCT RANGE Semillon, Shiraz Grenache Malbec.
SUMMARY This is the venture of Bordeaux born and trained winemaker Jacques Lurton, who is involved in wine ventures in both the northern and southern hemispheres, emulating the Australian

Flying Winemaker model. He has established 11 hectares of vineyard on Kangaroo Island, planted to semillon, grenache, malbec and shiraz. The wines are exported to the UK and the US.

The Lane ★★★★★

Ravenswood Lane, Hahndorf, SA 5245 **REGION** Adelaide Hills
T (08) 8388 1250 **F** (08) 8388 7233 **OPEN** Not
WINEMAKER Robert Mann, (red and white), Ed Carr (sparkling) at Hardys **EST.** 1993 **CASES** 35 000
PRODUCT RANGE ($20–50 R) The Gathering Sauvignon Semillon, Beginning Chardonnay, Reunion Shiraz, 19th Meeting Cabernet Sauvignon; Starvedog Lane Sauvignon Blanc, No Oak Chardonnay, sparkling, Shiraz Viognier, Shiraz, Merlot, Cabernet Merlot, Cabernet Sauvignon.
SUMMARY With their sales and marketing background, John and Helen Edwards opted for a major lifestyle change when they began the establishment of the first of the present 28.1 hectares of vineyards in 1993. Initially, part of the production was sold to BRL Hardy, but now some of the wine is made for release under The Lane label (until 2003, Ravenswood Lane). A joint venture with BRL Hardy is Starvedog Lane, producing wines from a patchwork of vineyards throughout the Adelaide Hills. Exports to the UK and Singapore.

ΥΥΥΥΥ **Starvedog Lane Chardonnay 2002** Complex bouquet; a lovely, elegant wine showing its cool-grown origins; line and length. **RATING** 94 **DRINK** 2009 $ 26.99

ΥΥΥΥΥ **19th Meeting Cabernet Sauvignon 2001** Clear cut and clean blackcurrant and spice fruit; fine-grained tannins, controlled oak. **RATING** 93 **DRINK** 2016 $ 49.99
Starvedog Lane Chardonnay Pinot Noir Pinot Meunier 1999 Floral citrus and spice aromas; surprisingly crisp and delicate, notwithstanding prolonged lees ageing. Adelaide Hills. **RATING** 92 **DRINK** 2007 $ 27
Starvedog Lane Merlot 2001 Pure varietal fruit on both bouquet and palate; olive savoury overtones; great flow and line. **RATING** 91 **DRINK** 2011 $ 27

ΥΥΥΥ **Starvedog Lane Sauvignon Blanc 2003** A minerally, faintly reductive bouquet; lively, long gooseberry and passionfruit palate. **RATING** 88 **DRINK** Now $ 20
Starvedog Lane No Oak Chardonnay 2003 Tangy, crisp and zesty; grapefruit and stone fruit; has real character. **RATING** 87 **DRINK** Now $ 20

🐝 The Lily Stirling Range NR

Lot 3004 Chester Pass Road, Stirling Range via Borden, WA 6338 **REGION** Great Southern
T (08) 9827 9205 **F** (08) 9827 9206 **OPEN** 7 days 10–5
WINEMAKER Pleun Hitzert **EST.** 1990
PRODUCT RANGE ($14.50–26.50 CD) Ellen Peak Chenin Blanc, Mondurup Peak Classic Dry White, Mondurup Peak Chardonnay, Mount Success Auslese Dessert Wine, Mount Trio Shiraz, The Abbey Liqueur Port; organic wines.
SUMMARY An interesting, indeed exotic tourism complex owned and run by two Dutch families, Hennie and Pleun Hitzert and Ron and Sue Terwijn. It features The Lily Railway Station restaurant on the reconstructed 1924 Gnowangerup Railway Station, and a windmill. This was completed in August 2003 with the help of a group of millwrights from Schiedam in The Netherlands; a 3-tonne grinding stone now produces stone-ground flour (available from The Lily and soon from outlets around Western Australia). Less exotic, perhaps, is the 3-hectare vineyard planted to chenin blanc, chardonnay, grenache, cabernet sauvignon and cabernet franc, which goes to make the wines, which are sold through the cellar door, by mail order and in the restaurant.

The Mews NR

84 Gibson Street, Kings Meadows, Tas 7249 **REGION** Northern Tasmania
T (03) 6344 2780 **F** (03) 6343 2076 **OPEN** Not
WINEMAKER Graham Wiltshire **EST.** 1984 **CASES** 300
PRODUCT RANGE Chardonnay.
SUMMARY Robin and Anne Holyman have established 0.4 hectare of pinot noir and 9.2 hectares of chardonnay at Kings Meadows, only 4 kilometres from the centre of Launceston. Most of the grapes are sold; industry veteran Graham Wiltshire acts as winemaker for the remainder, and the wines are sold by direct contact with the Holymans.

The Minya Winery

NR

Minya Lane, Connewarre, Vic 3227 **REGION** Geelong
T (03) 5264 1397 **F** (03) 5264 1097 **OPEN** Public holidays, or by appointment
WINEMAKER Susan Dans **EST.** 1974 **CASES** 1400
PRODUCT RANGE ($15.50–18 CD) Gewurztraminer, Chardonnay, Shiraz, Grenache, Cabernet Sauvignon Merlot.
SUMMARY Geoff Dans first planted vines on his family's dairy farm in 1974. There were further plantings in 1982 and 1988, lifting the total to 4 hectares. I have not tasted any of the wines, but the concerts staged in summer sound appealing. Grenache is a highly unusual variety for this neck of the woods.

The Natural Wine Company

217 Copley Road, Upper Swan, WA 6069 **REGION** Swan Valley
T (08) 9296 1436 **F** (08) 9296 1436 **OPEN** Wed–Sun and public holidays 10–5
WINEMAKER Colin Evans **EST.** 1998 **CASES** 1500
PRODUCT RANGE ($15 CD) Semillon, Chenin Semillon, Chenin Blanc, Verdelho, Unwooded Chardonnay, Chardonnay, Pinot Noir, Shiraz, Cabernet Sauvignon.
SUMMARY Owners Colin and Sandra Evans say the name of the business is intended to emphasise that no herbicides or systemic pesticides are used in the vineyard, which is situated on the western slopes of the Darling Range. Weed control is achieved through mulching, and Sandra does the vineyard work and helps with the night shift during vintage. She was also responsible for the koala emerging from the barrel on the label. The vineyard is within a short walk of Bells Rapids and close to the Walunga National Park.

The Oaks Vineyard and Winery

31 Melba Highway, Yering, Vic 3770 **REGION** Yarra Valley
T (03) 9739 0070 **F** (03) 9739 0577 **OPEN** Weekends 10.30–5, or by appointment
WINEMAKER Karen Coulston (Contract) **EST.** 2000 **CASES** 500
PRODUCT RANGE ($15–17.50 CD) Deschamps (Sauvignon Blanc Chardonnay Riesling), Chardonnay for Terri, Pinot Noir, Cabernet Sauvignon Merlot.
SUMMARY The Oaks has been established in what was originally a Presbyterian Manse, the change in use coming after a long period of neglect, and thus not incurring the wrath of the previous occupants. Owner Pauline Charlton spent 12 months restoring the Victorian homestead to its former glory prior to the opening. An on-site gallery features photographs by Pauline Charlton's daughter, Mackenzie, and fellow students of the Photography Studies College. The vineyard is close-planted, and the wine competently made by Karen Coulston.

TTTT **Chardonnay for Terri 2001** Light to medium-bodied, subtle and supple; melon and a touch of fig; good balance. **RATING** 89 **DRINK** 2008 $ 17.50
Cabernet Sauvingon Merlot 2001 Pleasant, well balanced, light to medium-bodied; fresh, gently ripe red fruits; no frills. **RATING** 87 **DRINK** 2009 $ 15

The Rothbury Estate

Broke Road, Pokolbin, NSW 2321 **REGION** Lower Hunter Valley
T (02) 4998 7363 **F** (02) 4993 3559 **OPEN** 7 days 9.30–4.30
WINEMAKER Neil McGuigan **EST.** 1968 **CASES** 82 500
PRODUCT RANGE ($8.90–23 R) At the top comes the Individual Vineyard range of Hunter Valley Semillon, Chardonnay and Shiraz; next the Hunter Valley range of varietals; and finally varietals from Mudgee and Cowra.
SUMMARY Rothbury celebrated its 30th birthday in 1998, albeit not quite in the fashion that founder and previous chief executive Len Evans would have wished. After a protracted and at times bitter takeover battle, it became part of the Beringer Blass empire. The style and quality of the wines is unashamedly commercial these days; by rights they should be better.

TTTTY **Old Liqueur Aleatico NV** Complex Christmas cake aromas and flavours; cask-aged rancio characters starting to develop; clean finish. Impressive. **RATING** 90 **DRINK** 2010 $ 16

ŸŸŸŸ **Black Label Semillon 2003** Intense, distinctive lanolin varietal aromas; powerful, herb-accented palate; depth and length. **RATING** 87 **DRINK** 2015 $ 20

ŸŸŸŸ **Neil McGuigan Series Semillon 2003** **RATING** 86 **DRINK** 2012 $ 18
Gerry Sissingh Semillon 2002 **RATING** 86 **DRINK** 2012 $ 23
Orange Sauvignon Blanc 2003 Spotlessly clean, crisp and correct; light-bodied, but good value. **RATING** 86 **DRINK** Now $ 12
Brokenback Chardonnay 2002 **RATING** 86 **DRINK** Now $ 22
Black Label Cabernet Sauvignon 2002 **RATING** 86 **DRINK** 2014
Brokenback Semillon 2003 **RATING** 85 **DRINK** 2009 $ 22
Brokenback Chardonnay 2001 **RATING** 85 **DRINK** Now $ 22
Gerry Sissingh Semillon 2003 **RATING** 84 **DRINK** 2010 $ 23
Hunter Valley Semillon 2003 **RATING** 84 **DRINK** 2008 $ 20
Brokenback Semillon 2002 **RATING** 84 **DRINK** Now $ 22
Cowra Chardonnay 2003 **RATING** 84 **DRINK** Now $ 12

ŸŸŸ **Black Label Semillon 2002** **RATING** 83 $ 20
Hunter Valley Verdelho 2003 **RATING** 83 $ 13
Futures Shiraz 2000 **RATING** 83 $ 33
Gerry Sissingh Hunter Valley Shiraz 2001 **RATING** 82 $ 27.50
Individual Vineyard Mudgee Shiraz 2001 **RATING** 82

The Settlement Wine Co. NR

Cnr Oliver's and Chalk Hill Roads, McLaren Vale, SA 5171 **REGION** McLaren Vale
T (08) 8323 7344 **F** (08) 8323 7355 **OPEN** 7 days 10–5
WINEMAKER Vincenzo Berlingieri **EST.** 1992 **CASES** 3500
PRODUCT RANGE ($16–20 CD) Langhorne Creek wines with Pinot Noir, Shiraz, Cabernet Franc, Cabernet Sauvignon Cabernet Franc, Sparkling Shiraz; McLaren Vale Shiraz.
SUMMARY Vincenzo Berlingieri, one of the great characters of the wine industry, arrived in Sydney with beard flowing and arms waving in the 1970s and successfully gained considerable publicity for his then McLaren Vale winery. Fortune did not follow marketing success for this research scientist, who had arrived to work in plant genetics at Melbourne University's Botany Department in 1964, armed with a doctorate in agricultural science from Perugia University, Italy. However, after various moves he is now in business again, with his children, Jason, John and Annika, sourcing most of the grapes from Langhorne Creek and McLaren Vale. Most of the business is in unlabelled cleanskin form at yesterday's prices, sold only through a mailing list/direct order system.

The Silos Estate NR

Princes Highway, Jaspers Brush, NSW 2535 **REGION** Shoalhaven Coast
T (02) 4448 6082 **F** (02) 4448 6246 **OPEN** 7 days 10–5
WINEMAKER Bevan Wilson **EST.** 1985 **CASES** 1000
PRODUCT RANGE ($10–25 CD) Traminer Riesling, Semillon, Unoaked Chardonnay, Chardonnay, Simply Savvy, Wileys Creek Brut, Diva (dessert), Coral Blush, Coral Crossing, Reserve Shiraz, Tawny Port, Liqueur Muscat.
SUMMARY Since 1995, Gaynor Sims and Kate Khoury, together with viticulturist Jovica Zecevic, have worked hard to improve the quality of the wine, starting with the 5 hectares of estate vineyards, but also in the winery. The winery continues to rely on the tourist trade, however, and the wines do not appear in normal retail channels.

The Vineyards Estate ★★☆

555 Hermitage Road, Pokolbin, NSW 2320 **REGION** Lower Hunter Valley
T (02) 4998 7822 **F** (02) 6574 7276 **OPEN** 7 days 10–5, Splash Restaurant Wed–Sun from 6.30 pm
WINEMAKER Greg Silkman (Contract) **EST.** 1993 **CASES** 500
PRODUCT RANGE ($22–23 CD) Edith Margaret Chardonnay, Vivian Laurie Merlot.
SUMMARY The major investment and principal business of The Vineyards Estate is the eight studio/suite guesthouse sitting among the 5 hectares of vines. There is also a high-quality restaurant (Splash)

offering the prospect of all-inclusive gourmet weekends for around $695 per couple. The estate wines are sold through the restaurant and guesthouse, with other local wines available in the restaurant.

TTT   **Chardonnay 1999** RATING 83 $ 22

The Warren Vineyard   NR

Conte Road, Pemberton, WA 6260 **REGION** Pemberton
T (08) 9776 1115 **F** (08) 9776 1115 **OPEN** 7 days 11–5
WINEMAKER Bernard Abbott **EST.** 1985 **CASES** 400
PRODUCT RANGE ($15–30 CD) Riesling, Cabernet Merlot, Cabernet Blanc.
SUMMARY The 1.5-hectare vineyard was established in 1985 and is one of the smallest in the Pemberton region, coming to public notice when its 1991 Cabernet Sauvignon won the award for the Best Red Table Wine from the Pemberton Region at the 1992 SGIO Western Australia Winemakers Exhibition. Bottle-aged Riesling has also had notable success, the 1994 winning the trophy for Best Aged White at the 1998 Qantas Wine Show of West Australia.

The Willows Vineyard

Light Pass Road, Light Pass, Barossa Valley, SA 5355 **REGION** Barossa Valley
T (08) 8562 1080 **F** (08) 8562 3447 **OPEN** 7 days 10.30–4.30
WINEMAKER Peter Scholz, Michael Scholz **EST.** 1989 **CASES** 6000
PRODUCT RANGE ($13.90–52 R) Riesling, Semillon, Shiraz, Cabernet Sauvignon. Flagship wine is Bonesetter Shiraz.
SUMMARY The Scholz family have been grape growers for generations, and have almost 40 hectares of vineyards, selling part and retaining part of the crop. Current-generation winemakers Peter and Michael Scholz could not resist the temptation to make smooth, well balanced and flavoursome wines under their own label. These are all marketed with some years' bottle age. Exports to the UK and New Zealand.

TTTTT   **Bonesetter Shiraz 2001** A very complex and concentrated range of black plum/blackberry and French oak aromas and flavours; ripe, dry tannins. Will be long-lived. First release of a super-premium wine from The Willows. **RATING** 93 **DRINK** 2021 $ 52

Thistle Hill   ★★★

McDonalds Road, Mudgee, NSW 2850 **REGION** Mudgee
T (02) 6373 3546 **F** (02) 6373 3540 **OPEN** Mon–Sat 9.30–5, Sun and public holidays 9.30–4
WINEMAKER Lesley Robertson, Ian MacRae, Robert Paul (Consultant) **EST.** 1976 **CASES** 4000
PRODUCT RANGE ($15–24 CD) Riesling, Semillon, Special Reserve Semillon, Chardonnay, Pinot Noir, Shiraz, Premium Shiraz, Cabernet Shiraz, Cabernet Sauvignon, Premium Cabernet Sauvignon, Liqueur Muscat.
SUMMARY The Robertson family has put the sudden death of husband and father Dave behind it. All of the 2003 and 2004 wines were made on-site with the help of consultant winemaker Robert Paul, the white wines being made (as previously) by Ian MacRae. Whatever additional assistance is needed is happily provided by the remaining wine community of Mudgee. The vineyard, incidentally, is registered by the National Association for Sustainable Agriculture Australia (NASAA), which means no weedicides, insecticides or synthetic fertilisers — the full organic system.

TTTT   **Premium Shiraz 2001** Very good colour; fresh red berry fruit; well balanced; fresh red fruit flavours run through to the finish; medium-bodied. **RATING** 88 **DRINK** 2009 $ 20.50
     Liqueur Muscat 1997 Light to medium-bodied; clear, spicy/grapey fruit; easy, early-drinking style. **RATING** 87 **DRINK** Now $ 15

TTTY   **Riesling 2003** RATING 85 DRINK 2009 $ 15
     Shiraz 2001 RATING 85 DRINK 2009 $ 21
     Premium Cabernet Sauvignon 2001 RATING 85 DRINK 2007 $ 24

TTT   **Pinot Noir 2001** RATING 83 $ 21
     Cabernet Sauvignon 2002 RATING 82 $ 21
     Cabernet Shiraz 2000 RATING 82 $ 21
     Pinot Noir 2002 RATING 81 $ 21

Thomas Wines

c/- The Small Winemakers Centre, McDonalds Road, Pokolbin, NSW 2321 **REGION** Lower Hunter Valley
T (02) 4991 6801 **F** (02) 4991 6801 **OPEN** 7 days 10–5
WINEMAKER Andrew Thomas **EST.** 1997 **CASES** 1500
PRODUCT RANGE ($20–32 R) Semillon, Shiraz.
SUMMARY Andrew Thomas came to the Hunter Valley from McLaren Vale, to join the winemaking team at Tyrrell's. After 13 years with Tyrrell's, he left to undertake contract work and to continue the development of his own winery label, a family affair run by himself and his wife Jo. The Semillon is sourced from a single vineyard owned by local grower Ken Bray, renowned for its quality, while the Shiraz is a blend of 60 per cent Hunter Valley shiraz and 40 per cent McLaren Vale shiraz. The wines are virtually exclusively available at The Small Winemakers Centre, although they can be found on restaurant lists throughout the Hunter Valley.

🐦 Thompson Estate

Harmans Road South, Wilyabrup, WA 6280 **REGION** Margaret River
T (08) 9386 1751 **F** (08) 9386 1708 **OPEN** Not
WINEMAKER Contract **EST.** 1998 **CASES** 2000
PRODUCT RANGE ($22–35 R) Chardonnay, Pinot Chardonnay, Pinot Noir, Cabernet Merlot, Cabernet Sauvignon.
SUMMARY Cardiologist Peter Thompson began the establishment of Thompson Estate in 1994, when the first vines were planted. He was inspired by his and his family's shareholdings in the Pierro and Fire Gully vineyards, and by visits to many of the world's premium wine regions. A total of 12 hectares has since been established, 4.8 hectares to cabernet sauvignon, cabernet franc and merlot, the remainder more or less equally divided between chardonnay and pinot noir. The plantings came into full production in 2004, with an ultimate maximum production of 5800 cases. The Thompsons have split the winemaking between specialist winemakers: chardonnay by Mike Peterkin of Pierro, Cabernet Merlot by Mark Messenger of Juniper Estate and previously of Cape Mentelle, Pinot Noir by Flying Fish Cove, and Pinot Chardonnay by Harold Osborne of Cloudy Bay.

ŶŶŶŶŶ **Chardonnay 2002** A mix of power and subtlety; stone fruit, cashew and oak seamlessly interwoven; both depth and length. **RATING** 93 **DRINK** 2010 $ 35
Cabernet Sauvignon 2002 Fresh, lively cassis berry offset by touches of earth and olive; typical Margaret River structure; needs time to soften. **RATING** 90 **DRINK** 2015 $ 35

ŶŶŶŶ **Semillon Sauvignon Blanc 2003** Well made; complex, layered style; restrained mineral, herb and spice notes; good balance and length. **RATING** 89 **DRINK** 2008 $ 22
Cabernet Merlot 2002 Plush cassis/currant fruit; oak and tannins in restraint; still very youthful, will build. **RATING** 88 **DRINK** 2012 $ 25
Pinot Noir 2002 Smooth and ripe black cherry and plum fruit; shows Margaret River is not impossible for the variety, although it is more a red wine than pinot. **RATING** 87 **DRINK** 2007 $ 25

ŶŶŶŶ **Chardonnay Pinot 2001** **RATING** 86 **DRINK** 2008 $ 35

🐦 Thomson Brook Wines NR

Lot 1 Thomson Road, Donnybrook, WA 6239 **REGION** Geographe
T (08) 9731 0590 **F** (08) 9731 0590 **OPEN** Wed–Sun and public holidays
WINEMAKER Terry Foster **EST.** 1993
PRODUCT RANGE A range of varietally denominated table wines reflecting the plantings.
SUMMARY Pam and Terry Foster have established 6 hectares of riesling, sauvignon blanc, semillon, chardonnay, verdelho, pinot noir, shiraz, merlot, cabernet sauvignon and barbera, and make the wine on-site. The principal sales outlet is the cellar door, supplemented by mail order; the cellar door offers barbecue facilities and local produce.

Thomson Vintners   NR

5 O'Loughlin Street, Waikerie, SA 5330 (postal) **REGION** Riverland
T (08) 8541 2168 **F** (08) 8541 3369 **OPEN** Mon–Fri 9–5
WINEMAKER Colin Glaetzer, Ben Glaetzer **EST.** 1996 **CASES** 50 000
PRODUCT RANGE ($9.95 R) Woolpunda range of Chardonnay, Shiraz, Merlot, Cabernet; also Larra Pinta Sparkling Burgundy.
SUMMARY Although the year of establishment is shown as 1996, Thomson Vintners have been grape growers in the Riverland since 1961, among the first to plant cabernet sauvignon, and also (much later on) among the first to introduce regulated deficit irrigation (to reduce yield and improve quality). Most of the 7000–8000 tonnes of grapes produced from the 480 hectares of vineyards are sold to major wine companies, but the long-term plan is to lift the amount used for the Thomson's Woolpunda label from its present level of about 8–9 per cent to 20 per cent. With the experienced winemaking team of Colin and Ben Glaetzer in charge, the under $10 price point for the wines is obviously attractive, and the wines are now distributed in most States, with exports to the UK, Canada, Germany, Denmark, China, Norway and Singapore.

Thornborough Estate   NR

PO Box 678, Virginia, SA 5120 **REGION** Adelaide Plains
T (08) 8235 0419 **OPEN** Not
WINEMAKER George Girgolas **EST.** 2000 **CASES** 2000
PRODUCT RANGE ($25–30 R) Shiraz.
SUMMARY George Girgolas has been a long-term grape grower near Virginia in the Adelaide Plains region, with 116 hectares of 38-year-old vines, the grapes all previously contract-sold to Yalumba. He was indeed Yalumba's Grower of the Year in 2000. Three years ago he and his family acquired the Thornborough property (5 kilometres from the vineyard), which includes a two-storey stone house built in 1827, and straddles the Gawler River. The plans are to convert Thornborough into a guesthouse.

Thorn-Clarke Wines   ★★★★

Milton Park, Gawler Park Road, Angaston, SA 5353 **REGION** Barossa Valley
T (08) 8564 3036 **F** (08) 8564 3255 **OPEN** Mon–Fri 9–5
WINEMAKER Derek Fitzgerald **EST.** 1997 **CASES** 20 000
PRODUCT RANGE ($15–40 CD) Sandpiper range of Eden Valley Riesling, Eden Valley Pinot Gris, Eden Valley Chardonnay, Barossa Shiraz, Barossa Cabernet Sauvignon; Shotfire Ridge Barossa Shiraz, William Randell Barossa Shiraz, Terra Ross Nebbiolo, Shotfire Ridge Barossa Quartage.
SUMMARY To say this is a substantial new venture is to put it mildly. Two hundred and sixty-four hectares of vineyard has been established, with shiraz (136 hectares), cabernet sauvignon (59 hectares) and merlot (28 hectares) being the principal plantings, supported by lesser amounts of petit verdot, cabernet franc, chardonnay, riesling and pinot gris. Is now one of the largest grape growers in the Barossa, with the 240 hectares total plantings spread across four vineyard sites. A significant part of the production is sold to others. The aim for the Thorn-Clarke wines is to over-deliver quality at each price point. Wine quality is very good, and sales promotion energetic. Exports to the UK, Switzerland and New Zealand.

▼▼▼▼▽ **Shotfire Ridge Barossa Valley Shiraz 2002** A rich and sumptuous, but not jammy, array of fruits and spices; fine tannins. **RATING** 92 **DRINK** 2015 $ 23
William Randell Barossa Valley Shiraz 2002 Blackberry, chocolate and vanilla; medium-bodied, hides 14.5 degrees alcohol; fine tannins. **RATING** 91 **DRINK** 2012 $ 40
SandPiper Eden Valley Riesling 2003 Rich, full, citrus aromas and flavours; round, smooth; attractive early drinking. **RATING** 90 **DRINK** 2008 $ 15
Shotfire Ridge Barossa Valley Quartage 2002 Bright, rich and sweet red and black fruits; good density and mouthfeel; soft tannins. **RATING** 90 **DRINK** 2010 $ 23

▼▼▼▼ **Sandpiper Eden Valley Pinot Gris 2003** Highly aromatic and intensely floral; spicy adjuncts to a long finish. Convincing varietal example. **RATING** 89 **DRINK** 2007 $ 15
Sandpiper Barossa Shiraz 2003 Interesting velvety texture is the main feature; soft black fruits; early-drinking style. **RATING** 87 **DRINK** Now $ 15

ΫΫΫΫ **Sandpiper Eden Valley Chardonnay 2003** RATING 86 DRINK Now $ 15
SandPiper Cabernet Sauvignon 2002 RATING 86 DRINK 2008 $ 15

Thornhill/The Berry Farm ★★★

Bessel Road, Margaret River, WA 6285 **REGION** Margaret River
T (08) 9757 5054 **F** (08) 9757 5116 **OPEN** 7 days 10–4.30
WINEMAKER Eion Lindsay **EST.** 1990 **CASES** 1000
PRODUCT RANGE ($11.50–25 CD) Under the Thornhill label, Classic Dry Semillon, Sauvignon Blanc, Rosette, Shiraz, Cabernet Sauvignon, Tickled Pink (Sparkling Cabernet Sauvignon), Still Tickled Pink (Light Cabernet Sauvignon). Under The Berry Farm label, a range of fruit-based wines, including Sparkling Strawberry and Plum Port.
SUMMARY Although I have not enjoyed the Thornhill table wines, the fruit wines under The Berry Farm label are extraordinarily good. The Sparkling Strawberry wine has intense strawberry flavour; the Plum Port likewise, carrying its 16 degrees alcohol with remarkable ease.

ΫΫΫΫ **Thornhill Cabernet Sauvignon 2001** RATING 86 DRINK 2010 $ 18
Thornhill Semillon Sauvignon Blanc 2003 RATING 85 DRINK Now $ 16.50

ΫΫΫ **Thornhill 2003** RATING 83 $ 15.50

3 Drops NR

5 Blount Close, Winthrop, WA 6150 (postal) **REGION** Great Southern
T (08) 9310 7198 **F** (08) 9310 7264 **OPEN** Not
WINEMAKER John Wade (Contract) **EST.** 1998
PRODUCT RANGE A range of varietally denominated table wines reflecting the plantings.
SUMMARY The name 3 Drops is not about the three owners (John Bradbury, Joanne Bradbury and Nichole Wallich), but was created to reflect wine, olive oil and water, all of which are found on the property, a substantial vineyard at Mount Barker. The 16 hectares are planted to riesling, sauvignon blanc, semillon, chardonnay, cabernet sauvignon, merlot, shiraz and cabernet franc, and the wines are contract-made by the team of John Wade and Robert Diletti. Australian Prestige Wines is the national distributor, and the wines are also available by mail order.

ΫΫΫΫ **Cabernet Sauvignon Cabernet Franc 2002** Excellent structure; sweetly ripe, gentle red berry fruits; balanced tannins and oak. **RATING** 89 **DRINK** 2012 $ 22
Sauvignon Blanc 2003 Attractive lemon citrus aromas moving to gooseberry and passionfruit on the palate; dry finish. **RATING** 87 **DRINK** Now $ 20

Three Moon Creek ★★★

Waratah Vineyard, Gladstone Road, Mungungo via Monto, Qld 4630 **REGION** Queensland Zone
T (07) 4166 5100 **F** (07) 4166 5200 **OPEN** Tues–Sun and public holidays 10–5
WINEMAKER Peter Scudamore-Smith MW (Contract) **EST.** 1998 **CASES** 1500
PRODUCT RANGE ($14–25 CD) White Blend, Waratah Estate Verdelho, Rose, Shiraz, Monal Merlot, The Gorge (fortified dessert wine); Gentle Annie Verdelho, Shiraz and Cabernet Sauvignon.
SUMMARY David Bray is one of the doyens of wine journalism in Brisbane, and, indeed, Australia. After decades of writing about wine he and wife Pamela have joined Max Lindsay (Pamela's brother) and partner Lynne Tucker in establishing the Waratah Vineyard and Winery joint venture at Mungungo, near Monto, at the top of the Burnett Valley. The wines are principally sourced from the Waratah Vineyard, with 3.2 hectares of vineyard planted to chardonnay, verdelho, semillon, marsanne, viognier, shiraz, merlot and petit verdot, an exotic mix if ever there was one, supplemented by grapes grown at Inglewood and Murgon. The wines are made by the energetic Peter Scudamore-Smith MW. The Gentle Annie range should not be confused with Gentle Annie Wines of Victoria.

ΫΫΫΫ **Gentle Annie Shiraz 2001** RATING 86 DRINK 2008 $ 24
Gentle Annie Verdelho 2003 RATING 85 DRINK Now $ 18
Gentle Annie Shiraz 2002 RATING 85 DRINK 2012 $ 24
Gentle Annie Cabernet Sauvignon 2002 RATING 85 DRINK 2008 $ 25

Three Wise Men

95 Hayseys Road, Narre Warren East, Vic 3804 (Woongarra Winery) **REGION** Port Phillip Zone
T (03) 5438 8257 **F** (03) 5438 8246 **OPEN** Thurs–Sun 9–5 by appointment
WINEMAKER Graeme Leith **EST.** 1994 **CASES** 800
PRODUCT RANGE ($15–45 CD) Pinot Noir, Reserve Pinot Noir, Shiraz.
SUMMARY The Three Wise Men are (or were) Graeme Leith (of Passing Clouds fame), Dr Bruce Jones (Woongarra vineyard owner and grape grower) and Dr Graham Ellender (a semi-retired dentist-turned-winemaker). The project came about after a trial batch was made in 1998 by Bruce Jones' consultant, Andrew Clarke. The 1999 and 2000 vintages were made at Graham Ellender's winery, but he thereafter retired from the venture as his own production grew, and there are now two wise men, Graham Leith as winemaker and Bruce Jones as grape grower. Each takes half of the resulting wine, and sells it through his own winery, Passing Clouds and Woongarra, respectively. The quality of the wines speaks for itself.

ΥΥΥΥ **Pinot Noir 2002** Powerful, intense, exotic oriental spice aromas; an array of spicy flavours and flecks of stemmy/green notes on the palate. **RATING** 91 **DRINK** 2010 $ 25

Thumm Estate Wines   NR

87 Kriedeman Road, Upper Coomera, Qld 4209 **REGION** Queensland Coastal
T (07) 5573 6990 **F** (07) 5573 4099 **OPEN** 7 days 9.30–5
WINEMAKER Robert Thumm **EST.** 2000 **CASES** 3000
PRODUCT RANGE ($14–22.50 CD) Riesling, Semillon, Sauvignon Blanc, Unwooded Chardonnay, Chardonnay, Shiraz, Cabernet Sauvignon.
SUMMARY Robert Thumm, born in 1950, eldest son of Hermann Thumm (founder of Chateau Yaldara in the Barossa Valley) gained his degree in oenology from the University of Geisenheim, Germany. In 1999, when the family business was sold, he and wife Janet decided to move to Queensland, establishing the new winery in a valley below the Tamborine Mountain Tourist Centre. Here they have planted cabernet sauvignon and petit verdot, but also have 1.5 hectares of riesling and 1.2 hectares of sauvignon blanc in production in the Adelaide Hills. The venture, and its associated wine club, is firmly aimed at the general tourist market.

Tilba Valley   NR

Lake Corunna Estate, 947 Old Highway, Narooma, NSW 2546 **REGION** South Coast Zone
T (02) 4473 7308 **F** (02) 4473 7484 **OPEN** Oct–April 7 days 10–5, May–Sept Wed–Sun 11–4 (closed August)
WINEMAKER Bevan Wilson **EST.** 1978 **CASES** 600
PRODUCT RANGE ($16–18 CD) Traminer Riesling, Semillon, Semillon Chardonnay, Chambourcin, Cabernet Shiraz.
SUMMARY A strongly tourist-oriented operation, serving a ploughman's lunch daily from noon to 2 pm. Has 8 hectares of estate vineyards.

Tim Adams

Warenda Road, Clare, SA 5453 **REGION** Clare Valley
T (08) 8842 2429 **F** (08) 8842 3550 **OPEN** Mon–Fri 10.30–5, weekends 11–5
WINEMAKER Tim Adams **EST.** 1986 **CASES** 35 000
PRODUCT RANGE ($16–60 CD) Riesling, Semillon, Botrytis Riesling, The Fergus (Grenache), Shiraz, Aberfeldy Shiraz, Cabernet, Tawny Port.
SUMMARY Tim and Pam Adams have built a first-class business since Tim Adams left his position as winemaker at Leasingham in 1985. Eleven hectares of estate vineyards increasingly provide the wine for the business, supplemented by grapes from local growers. Tim Adams has consistently produced wines of exceptional depth of flavour and he also makes significant quantities of wine under contract for others in the district. Exports to the UK, The Netherlands, Sweden, Canada, Singapore and the US.

ΥΥΥΥ **Semillon 2002** Lovely lemon, lime and tropical mix of aromas and flavours; great line, length and balance. **RATING** 93 **DRINK** 2010 $ 17
Aberfeldy Shiraz 2001 Complex, concentrated licorice, blackberry and prune aromas; the palate is laden with ripe fruit and vanilla oak in the background. **RATING** 92 **DRINK** 2015 $ 55

Riesling 2003 Classic, tight, minerally aromas; flavours of apple, quince and lime; intense, tight, discreet. **RATING** 91 **DRINK** 2013 $ 20

Shiraz 2002 Powerful array of black fruit flavours; controlled extract/tannins/oak. **RATING** 90 **DRINK** 2012 $ 26

♥♥♥♥ **The Fergus 2002** Light-bodied; quixotic blend which works quite well in the context of the overall style. Savoury. Screwcap. **RATING** 87 **DRINK** 2007 $ 23

Tim Gramp ★★★★

Mintaro/Leasingham Road, Watervale, SA 5452 **REGION** Clare Valley
T (08) 8344 4079 **F** (08) 8342 1379 **OPEN** Weekends and holidays 10.30–4.30
WINEMAKER Tim Gramp **EST.** 1990 **CASES** 6000
PRODUCT RANGE ($16.50–36.50 R) Watervale Riesling, McLaren Vale Shiraz, McLaren Vale Reserve Shiraz, McLaren Vale Grenache, Gilbert Valley Shiraz Cabernet, Watervale Cabernet Sauvignon.
SUMMARY Tim Gramp has quietly built up a very successful business with a limited product range, and — by keeping overheads to a minimum — provides good wines at modest prices. The operation is supported by 2 hectares of cabernet sauvignon around the cellar door. Exports to the UK, the US, Malaysia and New Zealand.

♥♥♥♥♡ **McLaren Vale Shiraz 2002** Deep colour; dense earthy/savoury/gamey aromas; the palate a deep well of blackberry, blackcurrant, chocolate and vanilla. **RATING** 92 **DRINK** 2017 $ 36.50

♥♥♥♥ **Watervale Riesling 2003** Clean, firm mineral and citrus aromas; plenty of depth and power, though stops a little short. **RATING** 89 **DRINK** 2008 $ 19.80

Watervale Cabernet Sauvignon 2002 High pH colour; earthy/savoury/austere end of the spectrum; medium-bodied, with a core of black fruits. **RATING** 87 **DRINK** 2009 $ 19.80

♥♥♥♡ **Grenache 2002 RATING** 86 **DRINK** 2007 $ 16.50

🍇 Timmins Wines NR

PO Box 1481, Lane Cove, NSW 1595 **REGION** Warehouse
T (02) 9480 4722 **F** (02) 9472 4733 **OPEN** Not
WINEMAKER John Timmins **EST.** 2001 **CASES** 400
PRODUCT RANGE ($25–30 ML) Hunter Valley Shiraz, Orange Cabernet Sauvignon.
SUMMARY Unusually, this is a micro-wine operation without its own vineyard. Pharmacist John Timmins completed his Bachelor of Applied Science (wine science) degree in 2003, and is using his qualifications to make wines in small volumes from grapes grown in the Hunter Valley and Orange regions. All of the wines are sold by mail order.

Tim Smith Wines ★★★★☆

PO Box 446, Tanunda, SA 5352 **REGION** Barossa Valley
T (08) 8563 0939 **OPEN** Not
WINEMAKER Tim Smith **EST.** 2001 **CASES** 500
PRODUCT RANGE ($23–29 R) Shiraz, Grenache Mataro Shiraz.
SUMMARY Tim Smith aspires to make wines in the mould of the great producers of Côte Rôtie and Chateauneuf du Pape, but using a new world approach. It is a business in its infancy, with only two wines, a Shiraz and a Grenache Shiraz Mourvedre blend.

♥♥♥♥♥ **Barossa Valley Shiraz 2002** Dense purple-red; a plush, lush cascade of sweet berry fruits, long and intense, tangy and lively; not the least heavy; ultra-sophisticated winemaking. **RATING** 94 **DRINK** 2017 $ 29

♥♥♥♥ **Grenache Shiraz Mourvedre 2002** Surprisingly light colour; light to medium-bodied; convincing, though slightly jammy varietal fruit; fine, ripe tannins. Total contrast to the Shiraz. **RATING** 88 **DRINK** 2007 $ 25

Tin Cows ★★★★

Tarrawarra Estate, Healesville Road, Yarra Glen, Vic 3775 **REGION** Yarra Valley
T (03) 5962 3311 **F** (03) 5962 3887 **OPEN** 7 days 11–5
WINEMAKER Clare Halloran, Bruce Walker **EST.** 1983 **CASES** 18 000
PRODUCT RANGE ($20 CD) Chardonnay, Pinot Noir, Shiraz, Merlot.
SUMMARY Tin Cows (formerly Tunnel Hill) is regarded by Tarrawarra as a separate business, drawing most of its grapes from the 21-hectare Tin Cows Vineyard adjacent to the Maroondah Highway. The wines are intended to be more accessible when young, and are significantly cheaper than the Tarrawarra wines.

Tinderbox Vineyard ★★★★☆

Tinderbox, Tas 7054 **REGION** Southern Tasmania
T (03) 6229 2994 **F** (03) 6229 2994 **OPEN** By appointment
WINEMAKER Andrew Hood (Contract) **EST.** 1994 **CASES** 185
PRODUCT RANGE ($30 CD) Pinot Noir.
SUMMARY Liz McGown is a Hobart nurse who has established her vineyard on the slope beneath her house, overlooking the entrance to the Derwent River and the D'Entrecasteaux Channel, doubling the size from 1 to 2 hectares in 2003. The attractive label was designed by Barry Tucker, who was so charmed by Liz McGown's request that he waived his usual (substantial) fee.

🍷🍷🍷🍷🍷 **Pinot Noir 2002** Stylish, smooth and supple, black cherry, a touch of sous bois; long finish; elegance, not power. **RATING** 91 **DRINK** 2010 $30

Tingle-Wood ★★★★☆

Glenrowan Road, Denmark, WA 6333 **REGION** Denmark
T (08) 9840 9218 **F** (08) 9840 9218 **OPEN** Thurs–Mon 9–5, 7 days during holidays
WINEMAKER Brenden Smith (Contract) **EST.** 1976 **CASES** 1000
PRODUCT RANGE ($15–18 CD) Yellow Tingle Riesling, Tree Top Walk (late harvest), Red Tingle Cabernet Sauvignon Shiraz.
SUMMARY An intermittent producer of Riesling of extraordinary quality, although birds and other disasters do intervene and prevent production in some years. The rating is given for the Riesling, which remains a sentimental favourite of mine. Exports to the UK.

Tinklers Vineyard ★★☆

Pokolbin Mountains Road, Pokolbin, NSW 2320 **REGION** Lower Hunter Valley
T (02) 4998 7435 **F** (02) 4998 7529 **OPEN** 7 days 10–4
WINEMAKER Ian Tinkler, Usher Tinkler **EST.** 1997 **CASES** 1500
PRODUCT RANGE ($11–25 CD) School Block Semillon, Flemings Semillon, Pokolbin Mountains Semillon Verdelho, Lucerne Paddock Verdelho, Mt Bright Chardonnay, Eruptions Sparkling Shiraz, Volcanic Ash (sweet white), Côte D'or Shiraz, Steep Hill Shiraz, Mt Bright Shiraz, U&I Shiraz, Mt Bright Merlot, Pokolbin Mountains Cabernet Merlot, Pokolbin Mountains Cabernet Sauvignon, Usher Gordon Muscat.
SUMMARY Brothers Ian and Usher Tinkler own a large (41.5-hectare) vineyard on the slopes of the Pokolbin Mountain Road; most of the production is sold, a small amount being contract-made for cellar-door sales. The names of the wines are, if nothing else, highly imaginative.

🍷🍷🍷 **School Block Semillon 2003** **RATING** 83 $15

Tinlins NR

Kangarilla Road, McLaren Flat, SA 5171 **REGION** McLaren Vale
T (08) 8323 8649 **F** (08) 8323 9747 **OPEN** 7 days 9–5
WINEMAKER Warren Randall **EST.** 1977 **CASES** 30 000
PRODUCT RANGE ($1.50–3.40 CD) Generic table, fortified and flavoured wines priced from $3.70 for table wines and $4.50 for fortified wines.
SUMMARY A very interesting operation run by former Seppelt sparkling winemaker Warren Randall. It draws upon 100 hectares of estate vineyards, and specialises in bulk wine sales to the major

Australian wine companies. A small proportion of the production is sold direct through the cellar door at mouthwateringly low prices to customers who provide their own containers and purchase by the litre. McLaren Vale's only bulk wine specialist.

Tinonee Vineyard   NR

Milbrodale Road, Broke, NSW 2330 **REGION** Lower Hunter Valley
T (02) 6579 1308 **F** (02) 9719 1833 **OPEN** Weekends and public holidays 11–4
WINEMAKER Andrew Margan, Ray Merger (Contract) **EST.** 1997 **CASES** 384
PRODUCT RANGE ($15–18 CD) Verdelho, Chardonnay, Shiraz, Durif, Merlot, Chambourcin.
SUMMARY Ian Craig has established 14 hectares of vineyards on a mix of red volcanic and river flat soils at Broke. Part are in production, with the remainder coming into bearing, ultimately capable of producing 5000 cases of wine per year.

Tin Shed Wines   ★★★★

PO Box 504, Tanunda, SA 5352 **REGION** Eden Valley
T (08) 8563 3669 **F** (08) 8563 3669 **OPEN** Not
WINEMAKER Andrew Wardlaw, Peter Clarke **EST.** 1998 **CASES** 3000
PRODUCT RANGE ($15–40) Riesling, Rose, Shiraz, Three Vines MSG (Mourvedre Shiraz Grenache).
SUMMARY Tin Shed proprietors Andrew Wardlaw and Peter Clarke weave all sorts of mystique in producing and marketing the Tin Shed wines. They say 'our wines are hand-made so we can only produce small volumes; this means we can take more care at each step of the winemaking process ... most bizarre of all we use our nose, palette (sic) and commonsense as opposed to the safe and reliable formula preached by our Unis and peers'. The Tin Shed newsletter continues with lots of gee-whizz, hay-seed jollity, making one fear the worst, when the reality is that the wines (even the Wild Bunch Riesling, wild-fermented without chemicals) are very good indeed. The retail stockists also tell you this is a quality producer: they include Ultimo Wines in Sydney; Burwood Cellars and Nicks in Melbourne; Melbourne Street Cellars, Edinburgh Cellars and East End in Adelaide; and Nedlands Hotel in Perth. Exports to the UK, the US, New Zealand and Japan.

🐚 Tintagel Wines   ★★★★★

71 The Avenue, Nedlands, WA 6009 (postal) **REGION** Margaret River
T (08) 9386 2420 **F** (08) 9386 2420 **OPEN** Not
WINEMAKER Mark Messenger (Contract) **EST.** 1993 **CASES** 1000
PRODUCT RANGE ($15–20 ML) Semillon, Shiraz.
SUMMARY The Westphal family began the establishment of their 8-hectare vineyard in 1993; there are now 2 hectares each of chardonnay, shiraz and cabernet sauvignon, and 1 hectare each of semillon and merlot. It is located just south of the township of Margaret River, rubbing shoulders with names such as Leeuwin Estate and Devil's Lair. Part of the crop is sold to other makers, part is vinified by Mark Messenger for the Tintagel Wines brand. It is sold via its website <www.tintagelwines.com.au>, and has established exports to Malaysia.

 Semillon 2001 Glowing yellow-green; developing beautifully into White Burgundy style; a mix of honey and lemon; very good acidity and persistence. **RATING** 94 **DRINK** 2008 $ 15

 Shiraz 2002 Above average richness and texture; raspberry and blackberry mix; good mouthfeel and a long, fine finish. **RATING** 93 **DRINK** 2012 $ 20

Tintilla Wines   NR

725 Hermitage Road, Pokolbin, NSW 2320 **REGION** Lower Hunter Valley
T (02) 6574 7093 **F** (02) 9767 6894 **OPEN** Weekends 10.30–6, Mon–Fri afternoons by appointment
WINEMAKER Greg Silkman, Monarch Winemaking Services (Contract) **EST.** 1993 **CASES** 4000
PRODUCT RANGE ($16.50–35 CD) Semillon, Rosato di Jupiter, Reserve Shiraz, James Shiraz, Saphira Sangiovese, Catherine de'M Sangiovese Merlot, Shiraz, Justine Merlot, Merlot, Fortified Semillon (White Port), Fortified Shiraz (Vintage Port).
SUMMARY The Lusby family have established a 7.5-hectare vineyard (including 1 hectare of sangiovese) on their northeast-facing vineyard, which has red clay and limestone soil. They have also planted an olive grove producing four different types of olives, which are cured and sold on the estate.

Tipperary Hill Estate

NR

Alma–Bowendale Road, Alma via Maryborough, Vic 3465 **REGION** Bendigo
T (03) 5461 3312 **F** (03) 5461 3312 **OPEN** Weekends 10–5, or by appointment
WINEMAKER Paul Flowers **EST.** 1986 **CASES** 500
PRODUCT RANGE ($16–24 CD) Pinot Shiraz, Cabernets, Tulkara.
SUMMARY All of the wine is sold through the cellar door and the on-site restaurant (open on Sundays). Says Paul Flowers, production depends 'on the frost, wind and birds', which perhaps explains why this is very much a part-time venture. Situated 7 kilometres west of the city of Maryborough, Tipperary Hill Estate is the only winery operating in the Central Goldfields Shire. Winemaker Paul Flowers built the rough-cut pine winery and the bluestone residential cottage next door with the help of friends.

Tizzana Winery

★★★

518 Tizzana Road, Ebenezer, NSW 2756 **REGION** Sydney Basin
T (02) 4579 1150 **F** (02) 4579 1216 **OPEN** Weekends, holidays 12–6, or by appointment
WINEMAKER Peter Auld **EST.** 1887 **CASES** 500
PRODUCT RANGE ($15–45 CD) Glenorie Semillon and Chardonnay; Shiraz, Cabernet Shiraz, Aleatico, Vintage Port, Old Sweet White.
SUMMARY Tizzana has been a weekend and holiday occupation for Peter Auld for many years now. It operates in one of the great historic wineries built (in 1887) by Australia's true renaissance man, Dr Thomas Fiaschi. The wines may not be great, but the ambience is. Moreover, the cabernet sauvignon and shiraz have been replanted on the same vineyard as that first planted by Fiaschi in 1885. Peter Auld has also developed Tizzana as a wine education centre.

TTTT **Aleatico di Tizzana 2003** Made in Vin Santo style, with 15.5 degrees alcohol; spicy, tangy and long; not at all sweet. **RATING** 87 **DRINK** Now $45

TTTY **Clarissa Cabernet Sauvignon Shiraz 2000** **RATING** 85 **DRINK** 2007 $25

Tobias Wines

★★★☆

PO Box 296, Angaston, SA 5353 **REGION** Eden Valley
T (08) 8565 3395 **F** (08) 8565 3379 **OPEN** Not
WINEMAKER Toby Hueppauff **EST.** 2000 **CASES** 2000
PRODUCT RANGE Riesling, Pinot Noir, Shiraz, Merlot.
SUMMARY When Toby and Treena Hueppauff sold their well-known Kaesler Wines property at Nuriootpa they wasted no time in purchasing another vineyard, with a little under 6 hectares of vines. They intend to sell most of the wine on the export market, with Riesling presently available, and Shiraz, Merlot and Pinot Noir being bottled in late 2004, when prices will be finalised.

TTTT **Eden Valley Riesling 2001** Rich, lime/tropical fruit aromas and flavours; a big wine, short on finesse, but long on flavour. **RATING** 87 **DRINK** Now

Tobin Wines

NR

34 Ricca Road, Ballandean, Qld 4382 **REGION** Granite Belt
T (07) 4684 1235 **F** (07) 4684 1235 **OPEN** By appointment
WINEMAKER Adrian Tobin, David Gianini, Mark Ravenscroft (Contract) **EST.** 1964 **CASES** 1000
PRODUCT RANGE ($2.60–18 CD) Semillon and Shiraz are the flagship wines; other varietals and blends also offered.
SUMMARY In the early 1900s the Ricca family planted table grapes, planting shiraz and semillon in 1964/65; these are said to be the oldest vinifera vines in the Granite Belt region. The Tobin family (headed by Adrian and Frances Tobin) purchased the vineyard in 2000 and have substantially increased plantings. There are now nearly 10 hectares planted to semillon, verdelho, chardonnay, sauvignon blanc, shiraz, merlot, cabernet sauvignon and tempranillo, with some remaining rows of table grapes. However, one thing has not changed — bulk wine made in traditional Italian style and sold in 15–203-litre drums at enticingly low prices.

Tokar Estate ★★★☆

6 Maddens Lane, Coldstream, Vic 3770 **REGION** Yarra Valley
T (03) 5964 9585 **F** (03) 9706 4033 **OPEN** Fri–Sun and long weekends 10–5
WINEMAKER Paul Evans **EST.** 1996 **CASES** 1500
PRODUCT RANGE ($19.50–25 CD) Pinot Noir, Shiraz, Tempranillo, Cabernet Sauvignon.
SUMMARY Leon Tokar is one of a number of new arrivals on Maddens Lane, having established over 5 hectares of pinot noir, 2.5 hectares of shiraz, and 2 hectares each of cabernet sauvignon and — interestingly — tempranillo. Part of the grape production is sold to Southcorp; the remainder is contract-made. A new cellar door, barrel room and restaurant were opened late 2002.

▼▼▼▼ **Shiraz 2001** Clean, light to medium-bodied; spicy black cherry/blackberry fruit; fine, supple tannins and good oak. **RATING** 89 **DRINK** 2011
Cabernet Sauvignon 2001 A fresh and clean mix of redcurrant and blackcurrant fruit; soft, supple mouthfeel; gentle oak. **RATING** 88 **DRINK** 2011 **$** 24
Pinot Noir 2001 Very ripe, rich dried fruit/spice aromas; more black plum in the mouth; alcohol heat. **RATING** 87 **DRINK** 2009 **$** 23.50

▼▼▼▽ **Rossetto 2003 RATING** 85 **DRINK** Now
Tempranillo 2001 RATING 85 **DRINK** 2007

Tollana ★★★★

Tanunda Road, Nuriootpa, SA 5355 **REGION** Barossa Valley
T (08) 8560 9408 **F** (08) 8562 2494 **OPEN** Not
WINEMAKER Oliver Crawford **EST.** 1888
PRODUCT RANGE ($13–22 R) Eden Valley Riesling, Adelaide Hills Sauvignon Blanc, Eden Valley Adelaide Hills Chardonnay, Botrytis Riesling, Shiraz Bin TR16, Cabernet Sauvignon Bin TR222.
SUMMARY As the Southcorp wine group moves to establish regional identity for its wines, Tollana is emphasising its Eden Valley base. Seemingly as a by-product of Penfolds development of Yattarna and related wines, the Tollana Chardonnay style has become more elegant, now standing comfortably alongside the flavoursome Riesling and Shiraz.

Tomboy Hill Vineyard NR

203 Sim Street, Ballarat, Vic 3350 (postal) **REGION** Ballarat
T (03) 5331 3785 **OPEN** Not
WINEMAKER Scott Ireland (Contract) **EST.** 1984
PRODUCT RANGE Chardonnay, Pinot Noir.
SUMMARY Ian Watson has established a micro-planting of chardonnay and pinot noir (0.2 hectare) sold under the Tomboy Hill Vineyard, Circa Eureka and Rebellion brands, strongly suggesting that production is boosted by contract-grown grapes.

Tombstone Estate NR

5R Basalt Road, Dubbo, NSW 2830 **REGION** Western Plains Zone
T (02) 6882 6624 **F** (02) 6882 6624 **OPEN** By appointment
WINEMAKER Rod Tilling **EST.** 1997
PRODUCT RANGE A range of varietal table wines plus fortifieds.
SUMMARY The ominously named Tombstone Estate has been established by Rod and Patty Tilling, who have planted 5 hectares of chardonnay, pinot noir, shiraz, cabernet sauvignon, sangiovese, barbera and muscat. Rod Tilling makes the wine on-site, with sales through local outlets, by mail order and through the cellar door, the last with barbecue and picnic facilities.

Toms Cap Vineyard NR

322 Lays Road, Carrajung Lower, Vic 3844 **REGION** Gippsland
T (03) 5194 2215 **F** (03) 5194 2369 **OPEN** Weekends by appointment
WINEMAKER Owen Schmidt (Contract) **EST.** 1994

PRODUCT RANGE ($14–24 CD) Sauvignon Blanc, Chardonnay, Botrytis Sauvignon Blanc, Cabernet Sauvignon.

SUMMARY Graham Morris began the development of the vineyard in 1992 on a 40-hectare property surrounded by the forests of the Strzlecki Ranges, the 90-mile beach at Woodside, and the Tarra Bulga National Park, one of the four major areas of cool temperature rainforest in Victoria. The vineyard has 2.4 hectares of cabernet sauvignon, chardonnay, sauvignon blanc and riesling. The property also has a three-bedroom family cottage, and two two-bedroom spa cottages. The wines are made at a nearby winery, Lyre Bird Hill.

Tom's Waterhole Wines

NR

Felton, Longs Corner Road, Canowindra, NSW 2804 **REGION** Cowra
T (02) 6344 1819 **F** (02) 6344 2172 **OPEN** Weekends and public holidays 10–4, or by appointment
WINEMAKER Graham Kerr **EST.** 1997 **CASES** 1500
PRODUCT RANGE ($8–15 CD) Waterhole Blend Dry White, Chardonnay, Waterhole Blend Dry Red, Cabernet Sauvignon, Humpers Port.
SUMMARY Graham Timms and Graham Kerr started the development of Tom's Waterhole Wines in 1997, progressively establishing 3 hectares of shiraz, 2 hectares of cabernet sauvignon, and 1 hectare of semillon, merlot, the planting program completed in 2001. A decision has been taken to bypass the use of irrigation, and the yields will be low, with an expectation that the small on-site winery will crush around 20 tonnes per year.

Toolangi Vineyards

2 Merriwee Crescent, Toorak, Vic 3142 (postal) **REGION** Yarra Valley
T (03) 9822 9488 **F** (03) 9804 3365 **OPEN** Not
WINEMAKER Contract **EST.** 1995 **CASES** 4000
PRODUCT RANGE ($20–55 R) Chardonnay, Estate Chardonnay, Reserve Chardonnay, Pinot Noir, Shiraz, Cabernet.
SUMMARY Garry and Julie Hounsell acquired their property in the Dixons Creek subregion of the Yarra Valley, adjoining the bottom edge of the Toolangi State Forest, in 1995. Plantings have taken place progressively since that year, with 13 hectares now in the ground. The primary accent is on pinot noir, chardonnay and cabernet, accounting for all but 1 hectare which is predominantly shiraz, and a few rows of merlot. As only half the vineyards are in bearing, production is supplemented by chardonnay and pinot noir contract-grown in the Coldstream subregion, cropped at two tonnes per acre. Winemaking is split between Tom Carson of Yering Station, Rick Kinzbrunner of Giaconda and Trevor Mast of Mount Langi Ghiran, as impressive a trio of contract winemakers as one could wish for. Exports to the UK.

ŸŸŸŸŸ **Reserve Chardonnay 2002** Very complex barrel-ferment inputs; distinct Burgundian twist; powerful, concentrated and complex; melon, fig and creamy/toasty overlays. **RATING** 95 **DRINK** 2012 $ 55

ŸŸŸŸŸ **Chardonnay 2002** Clean, clear-cut, intense melon and nectarine fruit; light to medium-bodied, fine and elegant; excellent oak. **RATING** 90 **DRINK** 2010 $ 30

ŸŸŸŸ **Black Label Chardonnay 2002** **RATING** 85 **DRINK** Now $ 20

Toolleen Vineyard

2004 Gibb Road, Toolleen, Vic 3551 (postal) **REGION** Heathcote
T (03) 5433 6397 **F** (03) 5433 6397 **OPEN** Not
WINEMAKER Dominique Portet (Contract) **EST.** 1996 **CASES** 1000
PRODUCT RANGE ($45–48 R) Shiraz, Cabernet Sauvignon.
SUMMARY Owned by Mr K C Huang and family Toolleen's 14.7 hectares of shiraz, cabernet sauvignon, merlot, cabernet franc and durif are planted on the western slope of Mount Camel, 18 kilometres north of Heathcote. The lower Cambrian red soils are now well recognised for their suitability for making full-bodied and strongly structured red wines. Eighty per cent of the wine is exported to Taiwan, Malaysia, Singapore, Hong Kong and the US.

ŸŸŸŸ♀ **Shiraz 2002** Dense, deep, black fruits, spice and licorice; fruit-driven, brisk finish; still to settle down in bottle. **RATING** 90 **DRINK** 2015 $45

Cabernet Sauvignon 2002 Lifted juicy berry aromatics; luscious cassis and blackcurrant fruit; like the Shiraz, needs time to settle down. **RATING** 90 **DRINK** 2015 $45

🌿 Toomah Wines   NR

'Seven Oaks', 635 Toomuc Valley Road, Pakenham, Vic 3810 **REGION** Port Phillip Zone
T (03) 5942 7583 **F** (03) 5942 7583 **OPEN** Weekends 11–6, or by appointment
WINEMAKER Matt Robinson **EST.** 1996 **CASES** 2000
PRODUCT RANGE ($20–30 ML) Sauvignon Blanc Chardonnay, Sauvignon Blanc, Pinot Noir, Cabernet Sauvignon, Cabernets.
SUMMARY Toomah Wines is owned and managed by Matt and Michelle Robinson; the 6.5 hectares of vineyards have been planted on Matt's parents' historically important 226-hectare grazing property. Once owned by the Kitchen family (of Lever and Kitchen fame), the property boasted the largest orchard in the southern hemisphere in its 1930s heyday. Matt Robinson has a Bachelor of Agricultural Science from Melbourne University, and is completing his Wine Science degree (by correspondence) from Charles Sturt University. Two historic buildings on the property are being restored, one serving as the winery, the other as cellar door.

Toorak Estate   NR

Toorak Road, Leeton, NSW 2705 **REGION** Riverina
T (02) 6953 2333 **F** (02) 6953 4454 **OPEN** Mon–Fri 10–5, Sat by appointment
WINEMAKER Robert Bruno **EST.** 1965 **CASES** 400 000
PRODUCT RANGE ($6–26 CD) At the top, Willandra Estate table wines; then Willandra Leeton; next Amesbury Estate ($6) plus sundry fortified wines.
SUMMARY A traditional, long-established Riverina producer with a strong Italian-based clientele around Australia. Production has been increasing significantly, utilising 150 hectares of estate plantings and grapes purchased from other growers. The prices are low; only the Botrytis Semillon is more than $15 a bottle.

Torbreck Vintners   ★★★★★

Roennfeldt Road, Marananga, SA 5352 **REGION** Barossa Valley
T (08) 8562 4155 **F** (08) 8562 4195 **OPEN** 7 days 10–6
WINEMAKER David Powell, Dan Standish **EST.** 1994 **CASES** 40 000
PRODUCT RANGE ($15.50–187.50 ML) VMR (Viognier Marsanne Roussanne), The Bothie (dessert), The Steading (Grenache Shiraz), The Struie (Shiraz), Juveniles (Grenache, Mourvedre, Shiraz), Descendant (Shiraz Viognier), The Factor (Shiraz), Run Rig; Woodcutter's Red.
SUMMARY Between 1994 and early 2002 Torbreck was in the headlines for all the right reasons, and in particular the quality, style and branding of its outstanding red wines. For the next 12 months it was in the headlines for all the wrong reasons, as the marriage breakup between David Powell and his wife led to a near-death experience for Torbreck. The outcome has been that the business is now owned by Jack Cowan and Colin Ryan, with David Powell continuing as chief winemaker and general manager. The hope and expectation is that he will be able to progressively build back part ownership of the business. It has great assets, including precious holdings of old, dry-grown vines and contacts second to none with external growers. The branding has always been of the highest order, and the wines have not lost their icon status.

ŸŸŸŸŸ **The Descendant 2002** Super-intense and powerful, but retains that touch of finesse which is the mark of Torbreck. Lush blackberry fruit with twists of licorice, earth and spice; lingering finish. **RATING** 96 **DRINK** 2022 $125

The Struie 2002 A cascade of black fruits and spices; medium-bodied but very long and intense; excellent tannin and oak management. **RATING** 94 **DRINK** 2017 $46

The Factor 2001 Dense red-purple; vanilla and cedar surround a rich core of black fruits; excellent extract and length; good oak. **RATING** 94 **DRINK** 2016 $125

The RunRig 2001 Rich, layered and complex black fruits, spice and licorice; excellent texture and structure. **RATING** 94 **DRINK** 2016 $187.50

ŸŸŸŸ **Woodcutter's Red 2002** Much more richness and depth than prior vintages; plum, a touch of prune; good acidity. **RATING** 89 **DRINK** 2007 $ 18.50

Marsanne Viognier Roussanne 2002 Varietally correct, but rather brutish, mouthfilling, confrontational wine; others will enjoy it more. **RATING** 88 **DRINK** Now $ 32.50

ŸŸŸ **Woodcutter's White 2002 RATING** 83 $ 15.50

Touchwood Wines

PO Box 91, Battery Point, Tas 7004 **REGION** Southern Tasmania
T (03) 6223 3996 **F** (03) 6223 2384 **OPEN** Not
WINEMAKER Moorilla Estate (Contract) **EST.** 1992 **CASES** 1500
PRODUCT RANGE ($27.50–30 R) Coal River Cuvee, Pinot Noir.
SUMMARY Peter and Tina Sexton planted 5 hectares of vineyard in the early 1990s; pinot noir and chardonnay are the principal varieties, with a small amount of cabernet sauvignon and merlot. Through on a north-facing hill, with heavy black soil over a calcareous lime base, it has never been an easy site, with frost claiming some vintages, and lack of heat others.

Tower Estate ★★★★☆

Cnr Broke and Hall Roads Pokolbin, NSW 2320 **REGION** Lower Hunter Valley
T (02) 4998 7989 **F** (02) 4998 7919 **OPEN** 7 days 10–5
WINEMAKER Dan Dineen **EST.** 1999 **CASES** 10 000
PRODUCT RANGE ($26–42 CD) Clare Valley Riesling, Hunter Valley Semillon, Adelaide Hills Sauvignon Blanc, Hunter Valley Verdelho, Hunter Valley Chardonnay, Adelaide Hills Chardonnay, Yarra Valley Pinot Noir, Hunter Valley Shiraz, Barossa Valley Shiraz, Orange Sangiovese, Orange Barbera, Orange Merlot, Coonawarra Cabernet Sauvignon, Hunter Valley Muscat.
SUMMARY Tower Estate is a joint venture headed by Len Evans, featuring a luxury conference centre and accommodation. It draws upon varieties and regions which have a particular synergy, coupled with the enormous knowledge of Len Evans and the winemaking skills of Dan Dineen. Exports to the UK, Denmark, France, the US, Canada and Japan.

ŸŸŸŸŸ **Clare Valley Riesling 2003** Some CO_2 obvious; moderately intense citrus and apple, with sweet mid-palate fruit followed by a dry finish; good line. **RATING** 93 **DRINK** 2009 $ 24

Hunter Valley Semillon 2003 A spotlessly clean and crisp bouquet, then a long, lingering and intense steely palate, with herbs lurking in the background. A prayer that the corks will allow it to achieve full maturity. **RATING** 93 **DRINK** 2018 $ 19

Hunter Valley Chardonnay 2002 Skilfully made; elegant, understated style; gentle melon, cashew and subtle oak. **RATING** 91 **DRINK** Now $ 26

Barossa Shiraz 2002 Rich black and red berry fruits; good oak integration; savoury notes from fine tannins. **RATING** 91 **DRINK** 2012 $ 40

Coonawarra Cabernet Sauvignon 2001 Spice, cedar and vanilla aromas; potent cassis/blackberry fruit and a long finish. **RATING** 90 **DRINK** 2016 $ 40

ŸŸŸŸ **Orange Sangiovese 2002** Very pure, linear expression; not particularly welcoming but authentic woodsy/leafy/savoury aromas and flavours. **RATING** 87 **DRINK** 2008 $ 27

ŸŸŸŸ **Orange Merlot 2002 RATING** 86 **DRINK** 2007 $ 32

ŸŸŸ **Hunter Valley Verdelho 2003 RATING** 83 $ 24

Towerhill Estate

Albany Highway, Mount Barker, WA 6324 **REGION** Mount Barker
T (08) 9851 1488 **F** (08) 9851 2982 **OPEN** Fri–Sun 10–5 (7 days during school holidays)
WINEMAKER Contract **EST.** 1993 **CASES** 750
PRODUCT RANGE ($13–19 CD) Classic Riesling, Unwooded Chardonnay, Sweet Riesling, Merlot, Cabernet Merlot.
SUMMARY The Williams family, headed by Alan and Diane, began the establishment of Towerhill Estate in 1993, planting chardonnay (1.5 hectares), cabernet sauvignon (2 hectares), riesling (1 hectare) and merlot (2 hectares). Commencing in 1996, the grapes were sold to other producers, but

since 1999 limited quantities have been made. These wines have had consistent show success at the Qantas Wine Show of Western Australia and sell out quickly through the cellar door and local outlets.

▼▼▼▼ **Riesling 2003** Tropical lime aromas; touch of botrytis; plenty of weight, good length, but very faintly phenolic. **RATING** 89 **DRINK** 2008 $ 15

Cabernet Sauvignon Merlot 2002 A complex array of fruit flavours, the texture smooth and silky; however, charry barrel-ferment oak intimidates the fruit on the finish. **RATING** 87 **DRINK** 2011 $ 19

Trafford Hill Vineyard   NR

Lot 1 Bower Road, Normanville, SA 5204 **REGION** Southern Fleurieu
T (08) 8558 3595 **OPEN** Thurs–Mon and holidays 10.30–5
WINEMAKER John Sanderson **EST.** 1996 **CASES** 500
PRODUCT RANGE ($8–19 CD) Riesling, Sparkling Shiraz, Family Reserve Red, Sam-Jack Tawny Port, Parsons Ghost Liqueur Tawny Port.
SUMMARY Irene and John Sanderson have established 2 hectares of vineyard at Normanville, on the coast of the Fleurieu Peninsula near to its southern extremity. Irene carries out all the viticulture, and John Sanderson makes the wine with help from district veteran Allan Dyson. Distribution is through local restaurants, mail order and the cellar door.

Train Trak   ★★★☆

957 Healesville–Yarra Glen Road, Yarra Glen, Vic 3775 **REGION** Yarra Valley
T (03) 9429 4744 **F** (03) 9427 1510 **OPEN** By appointment
WINEMAKER MasterWineMakers (Contract) **EST.** 1995 **CASES** 4000
PRODUCT RANGE ($22–26 R) Chardonnay, Rose, Pinot Noir, Shiraz, Cabernet Sauvignon.
SUMMARY The unusual name comes from the abandoned Yarra Glen to Healesville railway, which was built in 1889 and remained in use until 1980. Part of it passes by the Train Trak vineyard, although I do not know why Trak has been spelt as it has. A total of 18.5 hectares of vines have been established, the oldest (2.3 hectares of pinot noir, 1.1 hectares of chardonnay and 1 hectare of shiraz) dating back to 1995 and hence in bearing; the remaining 14.1 hectares are now coming into bearing.

▼▼▼▼ **Chardonnay 2003** Spotlessly clean, elegant melon and grapefruit; as yet slightly simple; should build complexity with time. **RATING** 89 **DRINK** 2007 $ 22

Pinot Noir 2002 Bright, fresh strawberry/cherry fruit and a crisp finish; likewise needs time. **RATING** 88 **DRINK** 2007 $ 26

Tranquil Vale   ★★★

325 Pywells Road, Luskintyre, NSW 2321 **REGION** Lower Hunter Valley
T (02) 4930 6100 **F** (02) 4930 6105 **OPEN** Thurs–Mon 10–4, or by appointment
WINEMAKER Andrew Margan, David Hook **EST.** 1996 **CASES** 2800
PRODUCT RANGE ($17–28 CD) Semillon, Chardonnay, Old Luskie (dessert), Shiraz, Cabernet Franc Shiraz.
SUMMARY Phil and Lucy Griffiths purchased the property sight-unseen from a description in an old copy of the *Australian Weekend* found in the High Commission Office in London. The vineyard they established is situated on the banks of the Hunter River, opposite Wyndham Estate, on relatively fertile, sandy, clay loam. Irrigation has been installed, and what is known as VSP trellising. Within the blink of an eye, they found themselves 'in the amusing position that people ask us our opinion!' The three luxury, self-contained cottages on-site offer the extras of a swimming pool, tennis court, gymnasium, etc, and sleep a family or two couples each. Finally, competent contract-winemaking has resulted in the production of good wines, some of which have already had show success.

▼▼▼▼ **Semillon 2000** Glowing yellow-green; faintly funky, complex bottle-developed aromas; a long palate held together by crunchy acidity. Aged re-release. **RATING** 89 **DRINK** Now $ 28

▼▼▼▽ **Semillon 2003** **RATING** 86 **DRINK** 2009 $ 28

Shiraz 2000 Quite complex spice, anise, game and black fruit aromas; light to medium-bodied, falling away slightly on the finish. **RATING** 86 **DRINK** Now $ 19

Cabernet Shiraz 2001 Sweet red berry fruits and a touch of mint; light to medium-bodied, soft tannins. **RATING** 86 **DRINK** 2007 $ 17

Shiraz 2002 **RATING** 85 **DRINK** 2007 $ 19
Shiraz 2001 **RATING** 85 **DRINK** Now $ 19
Old Luskie NV **RATING** 85 **DRINK** Now $ 17
Cabernet Shiraz 2002 **RATING** 84 **DRINK** Now $ 17
Methode Champenoise 2001 **RATING** 84 **DRINK** Now $ 25

Transylvania Winery
NR

Monaro Highway, Cooma, NSW 2630 **REGION** Southern New South Wales Zone
T (02) 6452 4374 **F** (02) 6452 6281 **OPEN** 7 days 9–5, restaurant 11–11, by appointment
WINEMAKER Peter Culici **EST.** 1989
PRODUCT RANGE Varietal table and fortified wines under the Culici's label.
SUMMARY Peter Culici operates Transylvania, drawing in part on a 2.4-hectare vineyard of sauvignon blanc, gewurztraminer, chardonnay, pinot noir, cabernet sauvignon, merlot and muscadelle. Both table and fortified wines are sold through the cellar door and the on-site restaurant.

Trappers Gully
NR

Lot 6 Boyup Road, Mount Barker, WA 6324 **REGION** Mount Barker
T (08) 9851 2565 **F** (08) 9851 2565 **OPEN** By appointment
WINEMAKER Clea Candy, Michael Garland (Consultant) **EST.** 1998 **CASES** 800
PRODUCT RANGE ($15–17 CD) Chenin Blanc, Sauvignon Blanc, Shiraz.
SUMMARY The Lester and Candy families, with fascinating and varied backgrounds, began the development of Trappers Gully in 1998. Clea Candy has the most directly relevant CV, as a qualified viticulturist and practised winemaker, and, according to the official history, 'mother, daughter and wife, and pretty much the instigator of all heated discussions'. The families have progressively planted 1.2 hectares each of chenin blanc, sauvignon blanc and shiraz, and slightly less than 1 hectare of cabernet sauvignon. Michael Garland is making the wines, but the Trappers Gully business plan calls for an on-site winery to be erected in the near future.

Treen Ridge Estate
NR

Packer Road, Pemberton, WA 6260 **REGION** Pemberton
T (08) 9776 1131 **F** (08) 9776 0442 **OPEN** Wed–Fri 11–5, weekends 10–5
WINEMAKER Andrew Mountford (Contract) **EST.** 1992 **CASES** 600
PRODUCT RANGE ($15–25 CD) Riesling, Sauvignon Blanc, Springfield Shiraz, Reserve Vintage Shiraz, Sparkling Shiraz.
SUMMARY The 1.7-hectare Treen Ridge vineyard and three-room accommodation is set between the Treen Brook State Forest and The Warren National Park and is operated by Mollie and Barry Scotman.

Treeton Estate
NR

North Treeton Road, Cowaramup, WA 6284 **REGION** Margaret River
T (08) 9755 5481 **F** (08) 9755 5051 **OPEN** 7 days 10–6
WINEMAKER David McGowan **EST.** 1984 **CASES** 3000
PRODUCT RANGE ($15–17 R) Chardonnay, Riesling, Estate White, Petit Rouge, Shiraz, Liqueur Muscat.
SUMMARY In 1982 David McGowan and wife Corinne purchased the 30-hectare property upon which Treeton Estate is established, beginning to plant the vines 2 years later. David has done just about everything in his life, and in the early years was working in Perth, which led to various setbacks for the vineyard. The wines are light and fresh, sometimes rather too much so.

Trentham Estate

Sturt Highway, Trentham Cliffs, NSW 2738 **REGION** Murray Darling
T (03) 5024 8888 **F** (03) 5024 8800 **OPEN** 7 days 9.30–5
WINEMAKER Anthony Murphy, Shane Kerr **EST.** 1988 **CASES** 65 000
PRODUCT RANGE ($10–20 CD) Riesling, Murphy's Lore Semillon Chardonnay, Sauvignon Blanc, Viognier, Chardonnay, Noble Taminga, Sparkling Ruby, Pinot Noir, Shiraz, Cellar Reserve Shiraz,

Murphy's Lore Shiraz Cabernet, Nebbiolo, Merlot, Ruby Cabernet, Petit Verdot, Cabernet Sauvignon Merlot, Vintage Port, Burke & Wills Tawny Port.

SUMMARY Remarkably consistent tasting notes across all wine styles from all vintages since 1989 attest to the expertise of ex-Mildara winemaker Tony Murphy, now making the Trentham wines from his family vineyards. All of the wines, whether at the bottom or top end of the price range, offer great value for money. The winery restaurant is also recommended. National retail distribution; exports to the US, the UK, Belgium and New Zealand.

ŸŸŸŸ **Pinot Noir 2002** An outstanding achievement for the region; real style and varietal character; cherry, strawberry; length and balance. One of the very best value Pinots on the Australian market. **RATING** 90 **DRINK** Now $13

ŸŸŸŸ **Chardonnay 2003** Fine, elegant, fruit-driven; melon, fig and stone fruit; subtle oak influence. **RATING** 89 **DRINK** Now $14.50
Viognier 2003 Clean, light to medium-bodied; peach and pastille flavours flow well; not phenolic. **RATING** 87 **DRINK** Now $18
Merlot 2001 Typical Trentham style, with an excellent touch in winemaking; savoury edges to sweet berry fruit; fine tannins. **RATING** 87 **DRINK** 2007 $15
Cabernet Sauvignon 2002 Quite fragrant; cassis and a touch of mint; soft tannins. **RATING** 87 **DRINK** 2007 $15
Petit Verdot 2002 Deeply coloured; pungent, herbal edges to black fruit aromas; a savoury, multi-faceted palate; excellent tannin structure. **RATING** 87 **DRINK** Now $18
Noble Taminga (375 ml) 2001 Intensely fragrant fruit salad and citrus mix neatly balanced by acidity. **RATING** 87 **DRINK** Now $12.50

ŸŸŸŸ **Murphy's Lore Semillon Chardonnay 2003 RATING** 86 **DRINK** Now $10
Sauvignon Blanc 2003 RATING 84 **DRINK** Now $13
Murphy's Lore Spatlese Lexia 2003 RATING 84 **DRINK** Now $10

ŸŸŸ **Murphy's Lore Shiraz Cabernet 2001 RATING** 83 $10

Trevelen Farm ★★★★

Weir Road, Cranbrook, WA 6321 **REGION** Great Southern
T (08) 9826 1052 **F** (08) 9826 1209 **OPEN** Thurs–Mon 10–4.30, or by appointment
WINEMAKER Michael Staniford (Contract) **EST.** 1993 **CASES** 3000
PRODUCT RANGE ($16–20 CD) Riesling, Sauvignon Blanc Semillon, Chardonnay, Cabernet Sauvignon Merlot.
SUMMARY John and Katie Sprigg, together with their family, operate a 1300-hectare wool, meat and grain-producing farm, run on environmental principles with sustainable agriculture at its heart. As a minor, but highly successful, diversification they established 5 hectares of sauvignon blanc, riesling, chardonnay, cabernet sauvignon and merlot in 1993, adding 1.5 hectares of shiraz in 2000. Vines, it seems, are in the genes, for John Sprigg's great-great-grandparents established 20 hectares of vines at Happy Valley, South Australia, in the 1870s. The quality of the wines is as consistent as the prices are modest, and visitors to the cellar door have the added attraction of both garden and forest walks, the latter among 130 hectares of remnant bush which harbours many different orchids which flower from May to December. Exports to the UK, Europe, the US and Asia.

ŸŸŸŸ **Cabernet Merlot 2002** Smoky bacon oak aromas; light to medium-bodied, with fresh, bright red fruits; slight lack of structure. **RATING** 89 **DRINK** 2009 $18
Sauvignon Blanc 2001 Crisp, minerally; some underlying tropical fruit comes through on a relatively full-bodied palate. **RATING** 88 **DRINK** Now $16

Tuart Ridge

344 Stakehill Road, Baldivis, WA 6171 **REGION** Peel
T (08) 9524 3333 **F** (08) 9524 2168 **OPEN** Weekends 10–4
WINEMAKER Phil Franzone **EST.** 1996 **CASES** 2000
PRODUCT RANGE ($10–15 CD) Chenin Blanc, Verdelho, Classic White, Chardonnay, Bianchino, Shiraz, Merlot, Cabernet Sauvignon.
SUMMARY Phil Franzone has established 5 hectares of chardonnay, verdelho, shiraz, cabernet sauvignon, grenache and merlot on the coastal tuart soils. 2001 was the first vintage, and production

will peak at around 3000 cases. Phil Franzone also acts as contract winemaker for several of the many new ventures springing up in the Peel region.

ŸŸŸŸŸ **Shiraz 2002** Redolent with luscious blackberry and plum fruit; ripe tannins, subtle oak. **RATING** 91 **DRINK** 2012 $ 15

ŸŸŸŸ **Cabernet Sauvignon 2002** Attractive light to medium-bodied style, the structure similar to the Merlot, but with a touch more red fruits. **RATING** 88 **DRINK** 2009 $ 15

ŸŸŸŸ **Merlot 2002** Savoury, olive and earth notes to the core of red berry fruit; light to medium-bodied; appropriate structure for the variety. **RATING** 86 **DRINK** 2008 $ 15

Tuck's Ridge ★★★★

37 Shoreham Road, Red Hill South, Vic 3937 **REGION** Mornington Peninsula
T (03) 5989 8660 **F** (03) 5989 8579 **OPEN** 7 days 12–5
WINEMAKER Phillip Kittle **EST.** 1988 **CASES** 14 000
PRODUCT RANGE ($15–60 CD) Riesling, Chardonnay, Callanans Road Chardonnay, Callanans Road Late Harvest Pinot Grigio, Vues, Pinot Noir, Altera Pinot Noir, Callanans Road Pinot Noir, Trial Selection Pinot Noir, Callanans Road Shiraz, Merlot; under the Prentice brand Whitfield Pinot Gris, Whitlands Pinot Noir.
SUMMARY After an initial burst of frenetic activity following its launch in July 1993, Tuck's Ridge has slowed down a little. Nonetheless, plantings have been increased to a little over 25 hectares, making it one of the largest vineyards in production on the Mornington Peninsula, with wine quality to match. Rumours of a sale in early 2002 turned out to be entirely wrong. Tuck's Ridge has sold its Red Hill vineyard for $2.4 million, and used the proceeds to retire debt and acquire the Prentice wine brand, which will henceforth be available both retail and through the Tuck's Ridge cellar door. Exports to the US, Hong Kong and China.

ŸŸŸŸŸ **Buckle Vineyard Pinot Noir 2001** Excellent colour; clean, ripe mix of plum and cherry on entry augmented by some savoury complexity to the long finish. **RATING** 91 **DRINK** 2008 $ 60
Pinot Gris 2003 Fragrant apple, pear, musk and spice aromas; a Pinot Gris with attitude and flavour. Screwcap. Easily carries its 14.5 degrees alcohol. **RATING** 90 **DRINK** Now $ 27
Pinot Noir 2001 Spice, plum and black cherry; great mouthfeel, structure and length; pure Pinot; very good aftertaste. Succeeded well with its '01 Pinots. **RATING** 90 **DRINK** 2008 $ 27

ŸŸŸŸ **Callanans Road Shiraz 2002** Nice mouthfeel and balance; dark cherry, blackberry, licorice and spice on the medium-bodied palate; nice tannins. **RATING** 89 **DRINK** 2008 $ 20
Callanans Road Pinot Noir 2002 A savoury mix of forest floor and sappy cherry; long but unforced; early-drinking style. A blend of Mount Beauty and Mornington Peninsula grapes. **RATING** 87 **DRINK** Now $ 20

🍎 Tulloch ★★★☆

'Glen Elgin', De Beyers Road, Pokolbin, NSW 2321 **REGION** Lower Hunter Valley
T (02) 4998 7850 **F** (02) 4998 7682 **OPEN** 7 days 10–5
WINEMAKER Jay Tulloch **EST.** 1895 **CASES** 30 000
PRODUCT RANGE ($13.99–35 R) Semillon, Verdelho, Chardonnay, The Cuve, Hector Shiraz, Cabernet Sauvignon.
SUMMARY The revival of the near-death Tulloch brand continues apace. Angove's, the national distributors for the brand, have invested in the business, the first time the Angove family has taken a strategic holding in any business other than their own. Inglewood Vineyard (aka Two Rivers) also has a shareholding in the new venture, and will be the primary source of grapes for the brand. A lavish new cellar door and function facility has been built and opened, and Jay Tulloch is in overall control.

ŸŸŸŸ **Verdelho 2003** Has more presence and length than the vast majority of wines made from this ordinary variety, although the gold medal given to it at the Melbourne Wine Show speaks more for the show than the wine. **RATING** 87 **DRINK** Now $ 14

Tumbarumba Wine Estates ★★★

Glenroy Hills Road, Tumbarumba, NSW 2653 **REGION** Tumbarumba
T (02) 6948 8326 **F** (02) 6948 8326 **OPEN** 7 days
WINEMAKER Various contract **EST.** 1989 **CASES** 2000
PRODUCT RANGE ($14.50–19 CD) Mannus range of Sauvignon Blanc, Chardonnay, Pinot Noir
Chardonnay, Reserve Pinot Noir, Merlot, Cabernet Merlot, Cabernet Shiraz, Mannus Creek Cabernet
Merlot.
SUMMARY Having established his vineyards progressively since 1982, Frank Minutello decided to
seek to add value (and interest) to the enterprise by having a small proportion of his production
vinified, commencing with the 1995 vintage.

Tumbarumba Wine Growers NR

Sunnyside, Albury Close, Tumbarumba, NSW 2653 **REGION** Tumbarumba
T (02) 6948 3055 **F** (02) 6948 3055 **OPEN** Weekends and public holidays, or by appointment
WINEMAKER (Contract) **EST.** 1996 **CASES** 600
PRODUCT RANGE ($15–25 R) Chardonnay, Pinot Noir and Pinot Chardonnay sparkling wines under
the Black Range label, with further individual labels likely for the future.
SUMMARY Tumbarumba Wine Growers has taken over the former George Martins Winery (itself
established in 1990) to provide an outlet for wines made from Tumbarumba region grapes. It is
essentially a co-operative venture, involving local growers and businessmen, and with modest
aspirations to growth.

▼▼▼▼   **Mannus Reserve Pinot Noir 2002** Spicy, earthy, foresty aromas; tangy spice and herbs
with small red fruit flavours; brisk finish. **RATING** 87 **DRINK** Now

▼▼▼   **Mannus Creek Cabernet Merlot 2000 RATING** 83 $ 19

Turkey Flat ★★★★☆

Bethany Road, Tanunda, SA 5352 **REGION** Barossa Valley
T (08) 8563 2851 **F** (08) 8563 3610 **OPEN** 7 days 11–5
WINEMAKER Peter Schell **EST.** 1990 **CASES** 16 000
PRODUCT RANGE ($15.50–42 R) Semillon, Semillon Marsanne, Rose, Grenache, Butchers Block
(Mataro Shiraz Grenache blend), Shiraz, Cabernet Sauvignon.
SUMMARY The establishment date of Turkey Flat is given as 1990 but it might equally well have been
1870 (or thereabouts), when the Schulz family purchased the Turkey Flat vineyard, or 1847, when the
vineyard was first planted to the very shiraz which still grows today. In addition, there are 8 hectares
of very old grenache and 8 hectares of much younger semillon and cabernet sauvignon, together with
a total of 7.3 hectares of mourvedre, dolcetto and (a recent arrival) marsanne. An on-site winery
completed just prior to the 2001 vintage will give Turkey Flat even greater control over its wine
production. Retail distribution in Adelaide, Melbourne and Sydney; exports to the US, Canada, the
UK, Germany, Switzerland and New Zealand.

▼▼▼▼▽   **Shiraz 2001** Blackberry, earth, oak and tannins all coalesce; not over the top in any way;
classic style. **RATING** 93 **DRINK** 2021 $ 42
Rose 2003 As immaculately made and balanced as ever; fruit-driven strawberry and
cherry; subliminal sweetness. **RATING** 92 **DRINK** Now $ 18

🐌 Turner's Flat Vineyard NR

PO Box 104, Inglewood, Qld 4387 **REGION** Granite Belt
T (07) 4652 1179 **F** (07) 4652 1179 **OPEN** Not
WINEMAKER Contract **EST.** 1999
PRODUCT RANGE A range of varietally denominated table wines reflecting the plantings.
SUMMARY Bruce and Lynette Babington have established their vineyard at the far western outskirts of
the Granite Belt, where they have planted 16 hectares of semillon, chardonnay, cabernet sauvignon,
shiraz and ruby cabernet. The contract-made wines are at this juncture sold only by mail order.

🐌 Turner's Vineyard   NR

Mitchell Highway, Orange, NSW 2800 **REGION** Orange
T (02) 6369 1045 **F** (02) 6369 1046 **OPEN** 7 days 10–5
WINEMAKER Contract **EST.** 1996 **CASES** 8000
PRODUCT RANGE Riesling, Sauvignon Blanc, Semillon Chardonnay, Chardonnay, Pinot Noir, Shiraz.
SUMMARY Turner's Vineyard is one of the larger developments in the Orange region, with a
substantial motel with 30 suites, and 12 luxury one and two-bedroom spa villa units, and was a
finalist in the 2003 NSW Tourism Awards for Deluxe Accommodation.

Turramurra Estate   ★★★☆

RMB 4327 Wallaces Road, Dromana Vic 3926 **REGION** Mornington Peninsula
T (03) 5987 1146 **F** (03) 5987 1286 **OPEN** Wed–Sun 12–5, or by appointment
WINEMAKER David Leslie **EST.** 1989 **CASES** 6000
PRODUCT RANGE ($20–36 CD) Sauvignon Blanc, Chardonnay, Pinot Noir, Shiraz, Cabernet
Sauvignon.
SUMMARY Dr David Leslie gave up his job as a medical practitioner after completing the Bachelor of
Applied Science (Wine Science) at Charles Sturt University, to concentrate on developing the family's
10-hectare estate at Dromana; wife Paula is the viticulturist. It has also established what is descibed
as the first purpose-built cooking school in an Australian vineyard. Details at
www.turramuraestate.com.au/cookingatturra. Limited retail distribution in Melbourne and
Sydney; exports to the UK, the US and Hong Kong.

12 Acres   ★★★

Nagambie–Rushworth Road, Bailieston, Vic 3608 **REGION** Goulburn Valley
T (03) 5794 2020 **F** (03) 5794 2020 **OPEN** Thurs–Mon 10–6, July weekends only
WINEMAKER Peter Prygodicz, Jana Prygodicz **EST.** 1994 **CASES** 700
PRODUCT RANGE ($13–16 CD) Not Quite White (Cabernet Franc), Grenache Rose, Shiraz, Merlot,
Cabernet Franc, Cabernet Sauvignon.
SUMMARY The charmingly named 12 Acres is a red wine specialist, with Peter and Jana Prygodicz
making the wines on-site in a tiny winery. The wines could benefit from renewal of the oak in which
they are matured; the underlying fruit is good.

TTTT **Shiraz 2001** Medium-bodied; well-balanced and structured black cherry and blackberry;
fine tannins; subtle oak. **RATING** 87 **DRINK** 2009 $ 16

TTT **Not Quite White Cabernet Franc 2003 RATING** 82 $ 13
Grenache Rose 2001 RATING 80 $ 13

Twelve Staves Wine Company   ★★★☆

Box 620, McLaren Vale, SA 5171 **REGION** McLaren Vale
T (08) 8178 0900 **F** (08) 8178 0900 **OPEN** Not
WINEMAKER Peter Dennis, Phil Christinson, Brian Light (Consultant) **EST.** 1997 **CASES** 600
PRODUCT RANGE ($20–45 R) Grenache, Old Vine Shiraz.
SUMMARY Twelve Staves has a single vineyard block of a little under 5 hectares of 70-year-old, bush-
pruned grenache vines. The highly experienced team of Peter Dennis and Brian Light (in a
consulting role) produce an appealing Grenache in a lighter mode and a monumental Shiraz. An
eclectic range of retail outlets on the east coast, and limited exports to the US, Canada and the UK.

Twin Bays   NR

Lot 1 Martin Road, Yankalilla, SA 5203 **REGION** Southern Fleurieu
T (08) 8267 2844 **F** (08) 8239 0877 **OPEN** Weekends and holidays
WINEMAKER Bruno Giorgio, Alan Dyson **EST.** 1989 **CASES** 1000
PRODUCT RANGE ($11–23 CD) Riesling, Reserve Bin Riesling, Aged Riesling, Liqueur Riesling,
Outrageous Sparkling Late Picked Pinot Noir, Rosado, Shiraz, Wild Grenache, Cabernet Shiraz,
Cabernet Sauvignon, fortifieds.

SUMMARY Adelaide doctor and specialist Bruno Giorgio, together with wife Ginny, began the establishment of their vineyard back in 1989, but have opted to keep it small (and beautiful). The principal plantings are of cabernet sauvignon, with lesser amounts of shiraz and riesling, taking the total plantings to 2 hectares. It was the first vineyard to be established in the Yankalilla district of the Fleurieu Peninsula, and has spectacular views from the vineyard, sited on the slopes above Normanville, taking in hills, valleys, the coastal plains, and the rugged Rapid Bay and more tranquil Lady Bay as the prime focus. The cellar door features the ocean views, the wines on sale being complemented by red and white wine vinegar, Fleurieu olive oil and other local souvenirs.

🐏 Twin Oaks   NR

146 Windsor Street, Woodford, Qld 4514 **REGION** Queensland Coastal
T (07) 5496 1368 **F** (07) 5496 1076 **OPEN** 7 days 10–5
WINEMAKER Trevor Phillips **EST.** 1998
PRODUCT RANGE ($14–25 CD) Bunya Pine Verdelho, Archers Homestead Unwooded Chardonnay, Old Woodford Cottage Chardonnay, Picnic Red Chambourcin, Saddler's Rest Red Chambourcin, Blacksmith's Forge Shiraz, Timbercutter's Red Cabernet Sauvignon, Windsor Ruby Red Chambourcin Muscat; ports.
SUMMARY The Twin Oaks property was purchased by Trevor and Carlin Phillips in 1980, but it was not until 1998 that the first plantings of verdelho, chardonnay and cabernet sauvignon took place. The first vintage followed 2 years later, and the winery and restaurant were opened another 2 years later, in December 2002. The restaurant is open every day for lunch and on Friday and Saturday evenings; other nights by arrangement. Twin Oaks caters for small and large functions, including weddings.

Two Hands Wines   ★★★★★

Neldner Road, Marananga, SA 5355 **REGION** Warehouse
T (08) 8562 4566 **F** (08) 8562 4744 **OPEN** Wed–Fri 11–5, weekends and public holidays 10–5
WINEMAKER Matt Wenk **EST.** 2000 **CASES** 10 000
PRODUCT RANGE ($25–120 R) The Picture series of The Wolf Riesling, Angel's Share Shiraz, Brave Faces Shiraz Grenache, The Bad Impersonator Barossa Valley Shiraz, The Bull and the Bear Shiraz Cabernet; the Garden series of Lily's Garden McLaren Vale Shiraz, Samantha's Garden Clare Valley Shiraz, Bella's Garden Barossa Valley Shiraz; flagship wine is Ares Barossa Valley Shiraz at $120.
SUMMARY The 'Hands' in question are those of South Australian businessmen Michael Twelftree and Richard Mintz, Twelftree in particular having extensive experience in marketing Australian wine in the US (for other producers) and now turning that experience to his own benefit (and that of Richard Mintz, of course). On the principle that if big is good, bigger is better, and biggest is best, the style of the wines has been aimed fairly and squarely at the palate of Robert Parker Jnr and that of the *Wine Spectator's* Harvey Steiman. Each of the individual wines is made in microscopic quantities (down to 50 dozen) and exported to the US, Canada and the UK, the policy being (one assumes) to keep demand well in excess of supply in any given market. The 2002 vintage wines are extremely good.

ΥΥΥΥΥ **Bella's Garden Shiraz 2002** Saturated but supple plum and blackberry fruit; while not over-extracted, in the ultra full-bodied Battlestar Galactica style. **RATING** 94 **DRINK** 2022 $55
Samantha's Garden Shiraz 2002 Powerful, tightly framed dark berry fruits; elegant finish for such a big wine; considerable length. **RATING** 94 **DRINK** 2017 $55

ΥΥΥΥΫ **Lily's Garden Shiraz 2002** Medium to full-bodied; savoury, earthy, bitter chocolate, mint and blackberry flavours; fine-grained tannins. **RATING** 93 **DRINK** 2017 $55
The Bull and The Bear 2002 Rich, complex, multi-faceted aromas and flavours; medium to full-bodied; spice and black fruits; nice oak and tannin management. **RATING** 93 **DRINK** 2017 $45
Bad Impersonator Shiraz 2002 Powerful, dense herb, earth, blackberry and bitter chocolate; good use of French oak. Full-bodied. **RATING** 91 **DRINK** 2012 $45

ΥΥΥΥ **The Wolf Riesling 2003** Developed colour given the screwcap; unashamedly rich and tropical, with some sweetness; good early-drinking style. **RATING** 87 **DRINK** Now $25

🐢 Two People's Bay Wines ★★★☆

RMB 8700 Nanarup Road, Lower Kalgan, WA 6331 **REGION** Great Southern
T (08) 9846 4346 **F** (08) 9846 4346 **OPEN** 7 days 12–4, 11–5 in peak season
WINEMAKER Diane Miller (Contract) **EST.** 1998 **CASES** 2700
PRODUCT RANGE ($12.50–18 ML) Riesling, Semillon, Semillon Sauvignon Blanc, Sauvignon Blanc, Cabernet Franc, Cabernet Sauvignon.
SUMMARY The Saunders family (Phil and Wendy Saunders, with sons Warren and Mark) began the establishment of their 10-hectare vineyard, planted to sauvignon blanc, riesling, semillon, shiraz, cabernet sauvignon, cabernet franc and pinot noir, in 1998, continuing the plantings in 1999. The name comes from the Two People's Bay Nature Reserve, which can be seen from the vineyard to the east; it also has spectacular views to the Porongorups and Sterling Ranges 60 kilometres north. A cellar door looms within the next 12 months, as do exports to the UK. The quality and modest pricing of the initial releases should guarantee their success.

🍷🍷🍷🍷🍷 **Sauvignon Blanc 2002** Spotlessly clean; clear gooseberry and tropical aromas; good mouthfeel and balance. **RATING** 90 **DRINK** Now $ 12.50

🍷🍷🍷🍷 **Sauvignon Blanc 2003** Clean, delicate, minerally aromas; good balance, touches of herb and gooseberry; fine structure. **RATING** 89 **DRINK** Now $ 12.50
Shiraz 2002 Clean and fresh; medium-bodied raspberry, blackberry and spice; nicely balanced acidity; minimal oak. **RATING** 89 **DRINK** 2007 $ 18

🍷🍷🍷🍷 **Semillon 2002** **RATING** 85 **DRINK** 2007 $ 15

Two Rivers ★★★☆

Yarrawa Road, Denman, NSW 2328 (postal) **REGION** Upper Hunter Valley
T (02) 6547 2556 **F** (02) 6547 2546 **OPEN** Not
WINEMAKER Greg Silkman **EST.** 1988 **CASES** 25 000
PRODUCT RANGE ($14–25 R) Stone's Throw Semillon, Shady Bank Verdelho Chardonnay, Hidden Hive Verdelho, Wild Fire Unwooded Chardonnay, Lightning Strike Chardonnay, Winters Mist Merlot, Golfer's Folly Cabernet Franc, Thunderbolt Shiraz, Rocky Crossing Cabernet Sauvignon; Reserve Inglewood Hunter Valley Semillon, Chardonnay, Shiraz, Cabernet Sauvignon.
SUMMARY A significant addition to the viticultural scene in the Upper Hunter Valley, with almost 170 hectares of vineyards established, involving a total investment of around $7 million. Part of the fruit is sold under long-term contracts, but part is made under contract for the expanding winemaking and marketing operations of Two Rivers, the chief brand of Inglewood Vineyards. The emphasis is on Chardonnay and Semillon, and the wines have been medal winners in the wine show circuit. The labels proudly bear gold medals for Hunter Valley Vigneron of the Year and Hunter Farmer of the Year. It is also a partner in the Tulloch business, together with the Tulloch and Angove familes.

🍷🍷🍷🍷🍷 **Hidden Hive Verdelho 2003** Abundant tropical fruit flavour balanced by acidity; above-average length, and full of character. Very highly commended 2003 Hunter Valley Wine Show. **RATING** 91 **DRINK** Now $ 14
Inglewood Reserve Semillon 1998 Glowing yellow-green; a very good, bottle-developed mix of honey, toast and citrus; smooth and long. **RATING** 90 **DRINK** 2008 $ 20

🍷🍷🍷🍷 **Reserve McLaren Vale Shiraz 2001** Attractive blackberry and chocolate fruit; medium-bodied; appropriate vanilla oak. **RATING** 87 **DRINK** 2011 $ 25
Rocky Crossing Cabernet Sauvignon 2000 Has flavour and varietal character; olive and berry; good tannins. **RATING** 87 **DRINK** 2008 $ 15

🍷🍷🍷🍷 **Wild Fire Unwooded Chardonnay 2002** **RATING** 86 **DRINK** 2007 $ 14
Reserve Chardonnay 2002 **RATING** 86 **DRINK** Now $ 18.50
Lightning Strike Chardonnay 2003 **RATING** 85 **DRINK** Now $ 14
Reserve McLaren Vale Cabernet Sauvignon 2001 **RATING** 84 **DRINK** 2007 $ 25

🍷🍷🍷 **Wild Fire Unwooded Chardonnay 2003** **RATING** 83 $ 14
Winter's Mist Merlot 2002 **RATING** 83 $ 15
Golfer's Folly Cabernet Franc 2000 **RATING** 83 $ 15
Thunderbolt Shiraz 2002 **RATING** 81 $ 15

🐂 Two Tails Wines

NR

963 Orara Way, Nana Glen, NSW 2450 **REGION** Northern Rivers Zone
T (02) 6654 3633 **F** (02) 6654 3633 **OPEN** 7 days 10–5
WINEMAKER Jeff Maher **EST.** 1998
PRODUCT RANGE An interesting range of varietal table wines.
SUMMARY Four members of the Maher family have established Two Tails Wines, with an exotic mix of gewurztraminer, semillon, chardonnay, verdelho, pinot noir, shiraz, chambourcin, ruby cabernet and villard blanc on their 2-hectare vineyard. The wines are made on-site, and are sold by mail order and through the cellar door, which also has barbecue, crafts and picnic facilities.

Tyrrell's

★★★★★

Broke Road, Pokolbin, NSW 2321 **REGION** Lower Hunter Valley
T (02) 4993 7000 **F** (02) 4998 7723 **OPEN** Mon–Sat 8–5
WINEMAKER Andrew Spinaze, Mark Richardson **EST.** 1858 **CASES** 520 000
PRODUCT RANGE ($12–75 CD) The core of the business now focuses on the Old Winery varietal range; then the higher-priced Rufus Stone range from Heathcote and McLaren Vale; next up is the individual vineyard range, including Lost Block Semillon, Shee-Oak; then come Reserve Stevens Semillon and Shiraz; and at the top are the various Vat wines, most notably Vat 1 Semillon, Vat 47 Chardonnay, Vat 6 Pinot Noir, Vat 8 Shiraz Cabernet and Vat 9 Shiraz.
SUMMARY One of the most successful family wineries, this was a humble operation for the first 110 years of its life, but has grown out of all recognition over the past 35 years. In 2003 it cleared the decks by selling its Long Flat range of wines for an eight-figure sum, allowing it to focus on its premium, super-premium and ultra-premium wines, where individual vineyard semillons are one of the most dominant wines in the Australian show system, and Vat 47 Chardonnay is one of the pace-setters for this variety. It has an awesome portfolio of single-vineyard Semillons released when 5–6 years old. Exports to the US, Canada and the UK.

ΥΥΥΥΥ **Belford Semillon 1997** Great green-yellow; complex, strong herb, spice and lanolin varietal fruit; long, lingering, intense and fresh. **RATING** 95 **DRINK** 2012 $ 30
Vat 1 Semillon 2003 Complex mix of lemon, lime, mineral and talc; clean, crisp and long; touch of sherbet. **RATING** 94 **DRINK** 2018 $ 25
Stevens Reserve Semillon 1998 Six gold medals to date for a wine just starting to seriously hit its straps is testament to the quality of the Stevens vineyard. Brilliant colour, and powerful herb and lanolin aromas, herald a wine which is still remarkably fresh, owing in part to its spine of minerally acidity. **RATING** 94 **DRINK** 2017 $ 25
Lost Block Cabernet Sauvignon 2002 Abundant sweet cassis fruit; fine line and acidity. Unanimous gold 2003 National Wine Show. **RATING** 94 **DRINK** 2012 $ 16

ΥΥΥΥ° **Stevens Reserve Semillon 1999** Abundant lemon, herb and citrus aromas; still a very fine palate; long future. **RATING** 93 **DRINK** 2012 $ 25
Lost Block Semillon 2003 A clean, crisp bouquet with perfectly focused sweet citrus fruit on the palate; good balance. **RATING** 92 **DRINK** 2013 $ 16
Old Winery Semillon 2002 Punchy, powerful, positive fruit to both bouquet and palate; long finish; great value. **RATING** 90 **DRINK** 2007 $ 12
Vat 47 Chardonnay 2001 Toasty melon, citrus, honey and peach aromas and flavours offset by surprising lemony acidity. **RATING** 90 **DRINK** 2008 $ 42
Vat 6 Pinot Noir 2000 Excellent texture, structure, line and balance; varietal character is not intense, but is there. Truly, the dog talking. **RATING** 90 **DRINK** 2007 $ 48

ΥΥΥΥ **Old Winery Chardonnay Semillon 2003** Interesting wine; Chardonnay peachy richness, Semillon length; old-fashioned but works very well. **RATING** 89 **DRINK** 2007 $ 12
Rufus Stone Heathcote Shiraz 2002 Menthol and eucalypt aromas; soft, velvety palate with red berry fruit and ripe tannins. **RATING** 89 **DRINK** 2010 $ 22
McLaren Vale Cabernet Malbec 2002 Clean, soft, medium-bodied, supple mix of red fruits and a dash of chocolate. **RATING** 89 **DRINK** 2012 $ 22
Old Winery Shiraz 2002 A clean, attractive array of red cherry/raspberry fruit; minimal tannins and oak. A three-State blend. **RATING** 88 **DRINK** Now $ 12

Rufus Stone McLaren Vale Shiraz 2001 Ripe, plum, blackberry and prune; then a savoury, spicy finish. **RATING** 88 **DRINK** 2009 $ 23

Futures Semillon 2003 Abundant grass, herb and lemon aromatics and flavours, almost (but not quite) sweet. **RATING** 87 **DRINK** 2010

▼▼▼▽ **Old Winery Semillon 2003** **RATING** 86 **DRINK** 2008 $ 12
Old Winery Semillon Sauvignon Blanc 2003 **RATING** 86 **DRINK** Now $ 12
Moon Mountain Chardonnay 2003 **RATING** 86 **DRINK** Now $ 19
Old Winery Verdelho 2003 **RATING** 86 **DRINK** Now $ 12
Old Winery Pinot Noir 2002 **RATING** 86 **DRINK** Now $ 12
Rufus Stone Heathcote Shiraz 2001 **RATING** 86 **DRINK** Now $ 22
Vat 9 Shiraz 2000 **RATING** 86 **DRINK** 2011 $ 48
Vat 9 Shiraz 1998 **RATING** 86 **DRINK** 2008 $ 48
Old Winery Cabernet Merlot 2002 **RATING** 85 **DRINK** 2007 $ 12
Old Winery Cabernet Sauvignon 2002 **RATING** 85 **DRINK** 2007 $ 12
Old Winery Chardonnay 2002 **RATING** 84 **DRINK** Now $ 12
Rufus Stone McLaren Vale Merlot 2001 **RATING** 84 **DRINK** 2007 $ 23

Uleybury Wines ★★★★☆

Uley Road, Uleybury, SA 5114 **REGION** Adelaide Zone
T (08) 8280 7335 **F** (08) 8280 7925 **OPEN** 7 days 10–4
WINEMAKER Tony Pipicella **EST.** 1995 **CASES** 10 000
PRODUCT RANGE ($11.90–45 R) Semillon, Uley Chapel Shiraz, Grenache, Grenache Shiraz, Merlot, Sangiovese, Cabernet Sauvignon; AP Reserve range of Sangiovese, Merlot, Grenache, Shiraz.
SUMMARY The Pipicella family — headed by Italian-born Tony — has established nearly 45 hectares of vineyard near the township of One Tree Hill in the Mount Lofty Ranges. Ten varieties have been planted, with more planned. Daughter Natalie Pipicella, who has completed the wine marketing course at the University of South Australia, was responsible for overseeing the design of labels, the promotion and advertising, and the creation of the website <www.uleybury.com>. The wines are currently being made off-site under the direction of Tony Pipicella, who seems able to invest the wines with great texture and mouthfeel. A cellar door opened in June 2002; an on-site winery followed in 2003. Exports to Canada.

▼▼▼▼▽ **AP Reserve Grenache 2002** Spice, cedar, lush black fruits and Christmas cake; good structure and tannins. **RATING** 92 **DRINK** 2010 $ 35

Semillon 2003 Fine, elegant citrus and apple blossom; utterly belies its 13.5 degrees alcohol. **RATING** 91 **DRINK** 2009 $ 19.50

AP Reserve Sangiovese 2002 A complex array of warm, savoury aromas and flavours; good balance and structure; impressive example of a touchy variety. **RATING** 91 **DRINK** 2008 $ 35

AP Reserve Shiraz 2002 An elegant, fine, light to medium-bodied wine; black fruits; spice and pepper; fine, herbal tannins. **RATING** 90 **DRINK** 2010 $ 35

AP Reserve Merlot 2002 Medium-bodied, spicy/cedary/savoury overtones; ripe tannins on the finish; good balance. **RATING** 90 **DRINK** 2011 $ 35

🐌 Ulithorne ★★★★★

PO Box 487, McLaren Vale, SA 5171 **REGION** McLaren Vale
T (08) 8382 5528 **F** (08) 8382 5528 **OPEN** Not
WINEMAKER Brian Light (Contract) **EST.** 1971 **CASES** 1000
PRODUCT RANGE ($40 R) Frux Frugis Shiraz.
SUMMARY If ever a wine had an accidental, not to say off-putting, birth, Ulithorne is it. The vineyard was planted in 1971 to absorb the effluent from the piggery which Frank Harrison (father/father-in-law of the current-owners) wished to establish. The council was not persuaded, the piggery did not go ahead, and the vineyard was neglected. In 1997 abstract painter Sam Harrison and marketing consultant partner Rose Kentish purchased the vineyard, becoming full-time vignerons, and resurrecting it from a near-derelict state. For good measure they extended the plantings with 8 hectares of cabernet sauvignon, 3 hectares of merlot and an additional 3 hectares of shiraz.

ᵀᵀᵀᵀᵀ **McLaren Vale Frux Frugis Shiraz 2002** Strongly spicy black fruits; Côte Rôtie style, with an exotic tang; abundant fruit; great palate structure and ripe tannins. **RATING** 94 **DRINK** 2017 $40

ᵀᵀᵀᵀ♀ **McLaren Vale Frux Frugis Shiraz 2001** Rich, dark chocolate and blackberry fruit; silky but powerful palate; a ripple of sweet fruit through the back palate and long finish. Lovely wine. **RATING** 93 **DRINK** 2016 $40

Undercliff   NR

Yango Creek Road, Wollombi, NSW 2325 **REGION** Lower Hunter Valley
T (02) 4998 3322 **F** (02) 4998 3322 **OPEN** 7 days 10–5, or by appointment
WINEMAKER David Carrick **EST.** 1990 **CASES** 1800
PRODUCT RANGE ($17–35 CD) Semillon, Chardonnay, Azure Dessert Semillon, Sparkling Shiraz, Shiraz, Chambourcin, Muscat.
SUMMARY Peter and Jane Hamshere are the new owners of Undercliff, but it continues to function as both winery cellar door and art gallery. The wines, produced from 2.5 hectares of estate vineyards, have won a number of awards in recent years at the Hunter Valley Wine Show and the Hunter Valley Small Winemakers Show. All of the wine is sold through the cellar door.

Upper Murray Estate   NR

Murray River Road, Walwa, Vic 3709 **REGION** North East Victoria Zone
T (02) 6037 1456 **F** (03) 6037 1457 **OPEN** 7 days 10–6
WINEMAKER Howard Anderson (Contract) **EST.** 1998 **CASES** 300
PRODUCT RANGE ($16.50–18.50 CD) Unwooded Chardonnay, Chardonnay, Pinot Noir, Shiraz, Merlot, Cabernet Merlot Shiraz, Cabernet Sauvignon.
SUMMARY The Upper Murray Estate vineyard has been established at a height of 400 metres roughly equidistant between Tumbarumba and Corryong. It is on the banks of what is a fast-flowing Murray River as it descends from the mountains. The estate is part of a much larger business offering the largest tourism and convention facilities in northeast Victoria, based on 16 single and double-storey cottages and four motel-type rooms. There are approximately 4 hectares each of chardonnay, pinot noir, merlot, shiraz and cabernet sauvignon, with 2.3 hectares of riesling. Industry veteran Howard Anderson makes the wines at his Rutherglen winery. The first two vintages — 2000 and 2001 — were, to put it mildly, interesting. It will be fascinating to see what emerges as the vines mature and weather patterns (presumably) cease to be so extreme.

Upper Reach Vineyard   ★★★☆

77 Memorial Avenue, Baskerville, WA 6056 **REGION** Swan Valley
T (08) 9296 0078 **F** (08) 9296 0278 **OPEN** Thurs–Mon 11–5
WINEMAKER Derek Pearse, John Griffiths **EST.** 1996 **CASES** 5000
PRODUCT RANGE ($13–25 CD) Verdelho, Chenin Blanc, Semillon Sauvignon Blanc, Unwooded Chardonnay, Reserve Chardonnay, Black Bream White, Black Bream Red, Shiraz, Cabernet Sauvignon Shiraz, Cabernet Sauvignon.
SUMMARY The 10-hectare property, situated on the banks of the upper reaches of the Swan River, was purchased by Laura Rowe and Derek Pearse in 1996. Four hectares of 12-year-old chardonnay made up the original vineyard, being expanded with 1.5 hectares of shiraz and 1 hectare of cabernet sauvignon, with plans for trials of merlot, zinfandel and barbera in the pipeline. The partners also own 4 hectares of vineyard in the Margaret River region planted to shiraz, cabernet sauvignon, merlot and semillon, but the releases so far have been drawn from the Swan Valley vineyards. The fish on the label, incidentally, is black bream, which can be found in the pools of the Swan River during the summer months. Exports to the UK.

ᵀᵀᵀᵀ **Shiraz 2002** Very youthful purple; concentrated, blackberry anise, plum and chocolate; fruit-driven; ripe tannins. **RATING** 89 **DRINK** 2017 $25

Unwooded Chardonnay 2003 Attractive melon and citrus aromas and flavours; good length; inevitably, slightly simple. **RATING** 87 **DRINK** Now $15

Cabernet Sauvignon 2002 Elegant, light to medium-bodied; clean, fresh mulberry and raspberry fruit; fine tannins. Swan Valley and Margaret River blend. **RATING** 87 **DRINK** 2010 $ 23

▼▼▼▽ **Reserve Chardonnay 2002** **RATING** 86 **DRINK** Now $ 18

▼▼▼ **Verdelho 2003** **RATING** 83 $ 15

Vale View Wines   NR

5 Berrys Road, Vale View, Qld 4352 **REGION** Queensland Zone
T (07) 4696 2282 **F** (07) 4696 2039 **OPEN** Weekends and public holidays 10–5, 7 days during school holidays, or by appointment
WINEMAKER Giovanni Chersini, Hazel Chersini **EST.** 1999 **CASES** 320
PRODUCT RANGE ($15 CD) Semillon, Chardonnay, Wooded Chardonnay, Shiraz, Cabernet Sauvignon, Dolce Rosso, Muscat, fruit wines.
SUMMARY Giovanni (John) Chersini was born in Valle d'Isria (then in Italy but now part of Croatia) in a wine-growing region. Visits by John, wife Hazel and son Matthew to John's birthplace inspired the planting of a few experimental vines in 1991, and to the subsequent expansion of the vineyard to its present 2.4 hectares of cabernet sauvignon, shiraz, chardonnay, semillon and frontignac. A family affair it may be, but it is also a multicultural one in the fullest sense of the word: both Hazel and Matthew are nearing completion of the external course in wine science at Charles Sturt University, while John prefers to adhere to the philosophies and practices inherited from his forebears.

Vale Vineyard   ★★★★☆

2914 Frankston–Flinders Road, Balnarring, Vic 3926 (postal) **REGION** Mornington Peninsula
T (03) 5983 1521 **F** (03) 5983 1942 **OPEN** Not
WINEMAKER John Vale **EST.** 1991 **CASES** 1000
PRODUCT RANGE ($19.95–29.95 R) Riesling, Chardonnay, Pinot Grigio, Cabernet Sauvignon, Cabernet Sauvignon Pressings.
SUMMARY After a lifetime in the retail liquor industry, John and Susan Vale took a busman's retirement by purchasing a grazing property at Balnarring in 1991. They planted a little under 0.5 hectare of cabernet sauvignon, and John Vale undertook what he describes as 'formal winemaking training' before building a 20-tonne winery in 1997 from stone and recycled materials. In 2000 they extended the plantings with 1.4 hectares of tempranillo, riesling and durif, seeking to move outside the square with unusual varieties. Verduzzo and Arneis have been made from grapes grown nearby, and will be exclusively sold through a local restaurant. In the meantime the wine range has been extended by the purchase of chardonnay and pinot grigio from local growers.

▼▼▼▼▼ **Chardonnay 2002** Fragrant and complex; stone fruit and grapefruit have soaked up the oak; exceedingly long palate and finish. Unsurprisingly, top gold 2003 Cool Climate Wine Show. **RATING** 94 **DRINK** 2010 $ 29.95

▼▼▼▼▽ **Riesling 2003** Penetrating and powerful; lime juice, herb and nettle; tightness reminiscent of Rheingau, with steely acidity. Very, very unusual for a maritime climate. **RATING** 92 **DRINK** 2010 $ 19.95

▼▼▼▽ **Tempranillo 2003** **RATING** 86 **DRINK** 2007 $ 21

🍎 Valley Wines   NR

352 Lennard Street, Herne Hill, WA 6056 **REGION** Swan District
T (08) 9296 4416 **F** (08) 9296 4754 **OPEN** Wed–Sun
WINEMAKER Charlie Zannino **EST.** 1973
PRODUCT RANGE A range of varietal table and fortified wines.
SUMMARY Valley Wines is a long-established, traditional Swan Valley winery owned by Charlie Zannino. Primarily a grape grower, he has 16 hectares of chenin blanc, semillon, chardonnay, grenache, shiraz and pedro ximenez, making table and fortified wines from a small portion of the annual production, with sales through the cellar door.

Varrenti Wines

NR

'Glenheather', Blackwood Road, Dunkeld, Vic 3294 REGION Grampians
T (03) 5577 2368 F (03) 5577 2367 OPEN 7 days 12–5
WINEMAKER Ettore Varrenti EST. 1999 CASES 500
PRODUCT RANGE ($15 CD) Grenache, Grenache Shiraz, Cabernet Shiraz.
SUMMARY Ettore Varrenti has established 4 hectares of pinot noir, malbec, shiraz and cabernet sauvignon at the extreme southern end of the Grampians National Park. It is remote from any other winery, and appears to be on the edge of the Grampians region.

Vasse Felix

★★★★★

Cnr Caves Road and Harmans Road South, Wilyabrup, WA 6284 REGION Margaret River
T (08) 9756 5000 F (08) 9755 5425 OPEN 7 days 10–5
WINEMAKER Clive Otto, David Dowden EST. 1967 CASES 150 000
PRODUCT RANGE ($12–65 CD) Classic Dry White, Semillon, Chardonnay, Heytesbury Chardonnay, NV Brut, Noble Riesling, Classic Dry Red, Shiraz, Cabernet Merlot, Cabernet Sauvignon, Heytesbury (Cabernet blend).
SUMMARY In 1999 the production of Vasse Felix wines moved to a new 2000-tonne winery; the old winery is dedicated entirely to the restaurant and tasting rooms. A relatively new 140-hectare vineyard at Jindong in the north of the Margaret River supplies a large part of the increased fruit intake. National Australian distribution; exports to the US, the UK, Europe and Asia.

TTTTT **Cabernet Sauvignon 2001** Medium to full-bodied; rich, complex dark fruits with balanced tannins; austere but very stylish; great length. RATING 96 DRINK 2016 $ 30
Heytesbury 2001 A powerful, complex and concentrated array of black fruits and leather; integrated oak; persistent but ripe tannins. RATING 94 DRINK 2016 $ 65

TTTTY **Chardonnay 2002** Clean, gentle barrel-ferment inputs; intense stone fruit and citrus; long, clear-cut finish. RATING 92 DRINK 2012 $ 22.50
Margaret River Shiraz 2002 Elegant, medium-bodied; fine black cherry fruit; fine tannins and cedar oak; a touch of austerity. RATING 92 DRINK 2012 $ 38
Heytesbury Chardonnay 2002 Ultra-complex aromas of barrel ferment, malolactic ferment and lees contact; a long and powerful palate; slightly hot alcohol detracts.
RATING 90 DRINK 2008 $ 35
Margaret River Shiraz 2001 Ripe black cherry, raspberry and blackberry fruit; supple palate; controlled oak and extract. RATING 90 DRINK 2011 $ 38
Cabernet Merlot 2001 Substantial, medium to full-bodied, with typical touches of Margaret River gravel and savoury notes around a core of blackcurrant fruit; good length.
RATING 90 DRINK 2014 $ 22.50

TTTT **Classic Dry White 2003** Excellent herb and citrus fruit, nicely ripened; good balance and length. RATING 89 DRINK Now $ 19
Semillon 2003 Generous fruit on both bouquet and palate, then piercing acidity is a fraction over the top. RATING 88 DRINK 2009 $ 22.50
Classic Dry Red 2001 Fresh bright red fruits on the mid-palate; light to medium-bodied, and finishes well. RATING 88 DRINK 2009 $ 19

TTTY **Extra Brut NV** RATING 85 DRINK Now $ 29

Vasse River Wines

NR

Bussell Highway, Carbunup, WA 6280 REGION Margaret River
T (08) 9755 1011 F (08) 9755 1011 OPEN 7 days 10–5
WINEMAKER Robert Credaro, Bernie Stanlake, Frank Kittler EST. 1993 CASES 5000
PRODUCT RANGE ($14–20 CD) Under the Vasse River label: Semillon, Sauvignon Blanc, Chardonnay; under the Carbunup Estate label: Semillon Sauvignon Blanc, Verdelho, Chardonnay, Shiraz, Ruby Red, Cabernet Merlot.
SUMMARY This is a major and rapidly growing business owned by the Credaro Family. Ninety hectares of chardonnay, semillon, verdelho, sauvignon blanc, cabernet sauvignon, merlot and shiraz

have been established on the typical gravelly red loam soils of the region. These plantings will be in full production by 2005, and it is intended to build a new winery and cellar-door sales area prior to that time. The wines are released under two labels; Vasse River for the premium, and Carbunup Estate for the lower-priced varietals.

Veritas ★★★★

Cnr Seppeltsfield and Stelzer Roads, Tanunda, SA 5352 **REGION** Barossa Valley
T (08) 8562 3300 **F** (08) 8562 1177 **OPEN** Mon–Fri 10–4.30, weekends 11–4
WINEMAKER Rolf Binder, Christa Deans **EST.** 1955 **CASES** 22 000
PRODUCT RANGE ($11–94 CD) Tramino, Christa Rolf Semillon, Chardonnay, Shiraz, Hanisch Shiraz, Binder's Bull's Blood Shiraz, Christa Rolf Shiraz Grenache, Henrich Shiraz Mataro Grenache, Mourvedre Pressings, Cabernet Sauvignon Merlot, Tawny Port, Oom Pah Pah Port, Special Liqueur Muscadelle.
SUMMARY The Hungarian influence is obvious in the naming of some of the wines, but Australian technology is paramount in shaping the generally very good quality. Veritas has 28 hectares of estate vineyards to draw on. A near-doubling of production has coincided with the establishment of export markets to the UK, Germany, Belgium, Austria, Asia, Canada and the US. The occasional tasting here and there fully justifies the rating.

Verona Vineyard ★★★

Small Winemakers Centre, McDonalds Road, Pokolbin, NSW 2321 **REGION** Lower Hunter Valley
T (02) 4998 7668 **F** (02) 4998 7430 **OPEN** 7 days 10–5
WINEMAKER Greg Silkman, Gary Reed (Contract) **EST.** 1972
PRODUCT RANGE ($15–22.50 CD) Produces two ranges: under the Verona label are Verdelho, Semillon and Shiraz; also Tallamurra Verdelho, Chardonnay and Shiraz.
SUMMARY Verona has had a chequered history, and is still a significant business, acting, as it does, as a sales point for a number of other Hunter Valley winemakers from its premises in McDonalds Road, directly opposite Brokenwood. The Verona wines come from 22 hectares at Muswellbrook, and 5 hectares surrounding the winery.

TTTY **Shiraz 2000 RATING** 85 **DRINK** 2011 $ 22.50

Versace Wines ★★★☆

Lot 258 Heaslip Road, MacDonald Park, SA 5121 **REGION** Adelaide Plains
T (08) 8379 7132 **F** (08) 8338 0979 **OPEN** By appointment
WINEMAKER Dominic Versace, Armando Verdiglione **EST.** 2000 **CASES** 1500
PRODUCT RANGE ($20–50 R) Shiraz, Casalingo Rosso (Shiraz Sangiovese Grenache), Sangiovese Ruspantino.
SUMMARY Dominic Versace and brother-in-law Armando Verdiglione have a long association with wine, through their families in Italy, and in Australia since 1980. In that year Dominic Versace planted 4.5 hectares of shiraz, grenache and sangiovese (one of the earliest such plantings in Australia), selling the grapes to Joe Grilli of Primo Estate until 1999. Armando Verdiglione had in the meantime helped create the first commercial vineyard on Kangaroo Island, with Caj Amadio and Michael von Berg. In 2000 the pair decided to pool their experience and resources, using the near-organically grown grapes from the Versace vineyard, and using deliberately rustic winemaking techniques, including open fermenters, a basket press, no filtration, no pumping and old barrels.

TTTTY **Limited Release Adelaide Plains Shiraz 2002** Prune, plum and blackberry fruit; excellent texture, richness and weight to the mid-palate; controlled oak. **RATING** 92 **DRINK** 2015 $ 50

TTTY **Bel Moscato 2003 RATING** 86 **DRINK** Now $ 27
Casalingo Adelaide Plains Sangiovese Grenache Shiraz 2002 RATING 85 **DRINK** 2007 $ 28

Vicarys

NR

Northern Road, Luddenham, NSW 2745 **REGION** Sydney Basin
T (02) 4773 4161 **F** (02) 4773 4411 **OPEN** Mon–Fri 9–5, weekends 10–5
WINEMAKER Chris Niccol **EST.** 1923 **CASES** 3000
PRODUCT RANGE ($12–36 CD) Chardonnay, Semillon, Riesling, Gewurztraminer, Fume Blanc,
Cabernet Sauvignon, Shiraz Cabernet Merlot, sparklings, fortifieds. Also produces kosher wines.
SUMMARY Vicarys justifiably claims to be the Sydney region's oldest continuously operating winery,
having been established in a large and very attractive stone shearing shed built about 1890. Most of
the wines come from other parts of Australia, but the winery does draw upon 1 hectare of estate
traminer and 3 hectares of chardonnay for those wines, and has produced some good wines of all
styles over the years.

Vico

NR

Farm 1687 Beelbangera Road, Griffith, NSW 2680 **REGION** Riverina
T (02) 6962 2849 **OPEN** Mon–Fri 9–5
WINEMAKER Ray Vico **EST.** 1973 **CASES** 1200
PRODUCT RANGE ($5–16 CD) Semillon, Late Harvest Semillon, Barbera, Cabernet Sauvignon, Liqueur
Muscat.
SUMMARY Ray Vico has been growing grapes for many years, with 9 hectares of vines, more recently
deciding to bottle and sell part of the production under the Vico label. From $70 a dozen for the table
wines and $16 per bottle for the 1984 Liqueur Muscat, the prices are positively mouthwatering. Be
aware, however, that the message on the answer phone is in Italian.

Victor Harbor Winery

NR

Cnr Mount Rosa and Adelaide Roads, Hindmarsh Valley, SA 5211 **REGION** Southern Fleurieu
T (08) 8554 6504 **F** (08) 8554 6504 **OPEN** Wed–Sun and public holidays 10–5
WINEMAKER Alan Dyson (Contract) **EST.** 1999
PRODUCT RANGE A range of varietally denominated table wines reflecting the plantings.
SUMMARY The business is based on 4 hectares of sauvignon blanc, semillon, pinot noir, cabernet
sauvignon and shiraz, and has established exports to Japan in a relatively short space of time. The
other principal sales are by mail order and through the cellar door.

Viking Wines

★★★★☆

RSD 108 Seppeltsfield Road, Marananga, SA 5355 **REGION** Barossa Valley
T (08) 8562 3842 **F** (08) 8562 4266 **OPEN** 7 days 11–5
WINEMAKER Rolf Binder (Contract) **EST.** 1995 **CASES** 1000
PRODUCT RANGE ($45–55 CD) Grand Shiraz, Grand Shiraz Cabernet; also Odin's Honour and Odin's
Reserve.
SUMMARY Based upon 50-year-old dry-grown and near-organic vineyards with a yield of only 1–1.5
tonnes per acre, Viking Wines has been 'discovered' by Robert Parker, with inevitable consequences for
the price of its top Shiraz. There are 5 hectares of shiraz and 3 of cabernet sauvignon. The Odin's
Honour wines also come from old (20 to 100 years) dry-grown vines around Marananga and Greenoch.
The immensely experienced Rolf Binder is contract winemaker for this operation, which sells its wine
through several retailers in Sydney and Melbourne, and exports to the US, Europe and Japan.

ŸŸŸŸŸ **Grand Shiraz Cabernet 2002** Intense fruit aromas; tightly wound and concentrated black
fruits; excellent texture and structure. **RATING** 93 **DRINK** 2017 $ 45
Grand Shiraz 2002 Ultra-powerful, concentrated black fruits, licorice and earth;
demands patience. **RATING** 91 **DRINK** 2017 $ 55
Odin's Honour Cabernet Shiraz 2002 Concentrated and complex blackberry,
blackcurrant and spice; sweet oak and ripe tannins. **RATING** 90 **DRINK** 2012 $ 40

ŸŸŸŸ **Odin's Honour Reserve Shiraz 2001** Good colour; powerful structure; black/savoury
fruit dips slightly before finishing strongly. **RATING** 89 **DRINK** 2011 $ 45
Odin's Honour Shiraz Grenache 2002 Lively mint and juicy berry aromas and flavours;
fine tannins. **RATING** 88 **DRINK** 2007 $ 40

🍇 Villacoola Vineyard & Winery NR

Carnarvon Highway, Surat, Qld 4417 **REGION** Queensland Zone
T (07) 4626 5103 **F** (07) 4626 5516 **OPEN** 7 days 10–5
WINEMAKER Contract **EST.** 1992
PRODUCT RANGE A range of varietally denominated table wines reflecting the plantings.
SUMMARY Ron Ritchie has ventured far to the west to establish Villacoola Vineyard & Winery; its nearest neighbour is Romavilla (at Roma) 78 kilometres to the north. The 2.5-hectare vineyard is planted to sauvignon blanc, semillon, chardonnay, merlot, shiraz and muscat, the muscats providing the fortified wines for which Romavilla has been famous for 140 years. The cellar door offers light meals.

🍇 Villa d'Esta Vineyard NR

2884 Wallambah Road, Dyers Crossing, NSW 2429 **REGION** Northern Rivers Zone
T (02) 6550 2236 **F** (02) 6550 2236 **OPEN** 7 days 10–5
WINEMAKER Zoltan Toth **EST.** 1997
PRODUCT RANGE A range of varietally denominated table wines reflecting the plantings.
SUMMARY Zolton Toth and Maria Brizuela have 2.25 hectares of chardonnay, verdelho, chasselas dore, pinot noir, cabernet sauvignon, merlot, shiraz, muscat, hamburg and chambourcin. They make the wines on-site, and sell by mail order and through the cellar door.

Villa Primavera NR

Mornington–Flinders Road, Red Hill, Vic 3937 **REGION** Mornington Peninsula
T (03) 5989 2129 **F** (03) 5931 0045 **OPEN** Weekends, public holidays 10–5 and 7 days from Dec 26 to end January
WINEMAKER Gennaro Mazzella **EST.** 1984 **CASES** 300
PRODUCT RANGE ($18–30 CD) Chardonnay, Pinot Noir, Limoncello, Methode Champenoise.
SUMMARY A most unusual operation, which is in reality a family Italian-style restaurant at which the wine is principally sold and served, and which offers something totally different on the Mornington Peninsula. A consistent winner of tourism and food awards, it is praised by all who go there.

🍇 Villa Terlato NR

1200 Bass Highway, The Gurdies, Vic 3984 **REGION** Gippsland
T (03) 5997 6381 **OPEN** 7 days
WINEMAKER John Terlato **EST.** 1988
PRODUCT RANGE Riesling, Chardonnay, Pinot Noir, Cabernet Sauvignon.
SUMMARY John and Francis Terlato have planted 2 hectares of riesling, chardonnay, pinot noir and cabernet sauvignon, making the wine on-site. The cellar door offers barbecue and picnic facilities.

Vinden Estate ★★★★

17 Gillards Road, Pokolbin, NSW 2320 **REGION** Lower Hunter Valley
T (02) 4998 7410 **F** (02) 4998 7421 **OPEN** 7 days 10–5
WINEMAKER Guy Vinden, John Baruzzi (Consultant) **EST.** 1998 **CASES** 2500
PRODUCT RANGE ($19.50–28 CD) Semillon, Unwooded Chardonnay, Chardonnay, Shiraz.
SUMMARY Sandra and Guy Vinden have bought their dream home, with landscaped gardens in the foreground and 9 hectares of vineyard with the Brokenback mountain range in the distance. Much of the winemaking is now done on-site, and the wine is increasingly drawn from the estate vineyards. The wines are available through the cellar door and also via a wine club which offers buying advantages to members. The restaurant, Thai on Gillards Road, is open weekends and public holidays from 10.30 am to 4 pm.

ΥΥΥΥΥ **Semillon 2003** Crisp, slatey, herbal almost peppery bouquet; long, lively, crisp lemony palate. **RATING** 91 **DRINK** 2008 $19.50

ΥΥΥΥ **Merlot 2002** Assertive regional portrayal of the variety; olive, earth and forest, but with sweet fruit on back palate. **RATING** 88 **DRINK** 2008 $28

Unwooded Chardonnay 2003 Melon and stone fruit flavour; has some weight and persistence. **RATING** 87 **DRINK** Now $ 19.50

Basket Press Shiraz 2002 Medium-bodied; juicy black and red fruits; subtle oak; low tannin and lively finish. **RATING** 87 **DRINK** 2009 $ 22

Vinecrest ★★★

Cnr Barossa Valley Way and Vine Vale Road, Tanunda, SA 5352 **REGION** Barossa Valley
T (08) 8563 0111 **F** (08) 8563 0444 **OPEN** 7 days 11–4
WINEMAKER Mos Kaesler **EST.** 1999 **CASES** 2000
PRODUCT RANGE ($16–24 CD) Semillon, Semillon Sauvignon Blanc, Late Harvest, Shiraz, Connections Shiraz, Sparkling Shiraz, Merlot, Cabernet Sauvignon.
SUMMARY The Mader family has a long connection with the Barossa Valley. Ian Mader is a fifth-generation descendant of Gottfried and Maria Mader, who immigrated to the Barossa Valley in the 1840s, while his wife Suzanne is the daughter of a former long-serving vineyard manager for Penfolds. In 1969 Ian and Suzanne established their 12-hectare Sandy Ridge Vineyard, and more recently a further 12 hectares on the Turrung Vineyard a few minutes from the township of Tanunda. Having been grape growers for 30 years, in 1999 they decided to establish Vinecrest, utilising a small portion of the production from their vineyards and establishing their cellar door on the Turrung Vineyard, adjacent to the tall gum trees of Kroemer's Reserve.

ϓϓϓϓ **Merlot 2002** Clearly expressed varietal fruit; redcurrant core; good extract and structure; balanced oak. **RATING** 87 **DRINK** 2009 $ 19

ϓϓϓϓ **Shiraz 2001** **RATING** 84 **DRINK** 2008 $ 24

Vinifera Wines ★★★☆

194 Henry Lawson Drive, Mudgee, NSW 2850 **REGION** Mudgee
T (02) 6372 2461 **F** (02) 6372 6731 **OPEN** 7 days 10–5.30
WINEMAKER Phillip van Gent, Tony McKendry **EST.** 1997 **CASES** 1500
PRODUCT RANGE ($14–23 CD) Riesling, Semillon, Chardonnay, Easter Semillon (sweet), Rose, Tempranillo, Gran Tito, Cabernet Sauvignon.
SUMMARY Tony and Debbie McKendry have much in common with (the late) Dave and Leslie Robertson of Thistle Hill, the latter another Mudgee winery. Dave Robertson lost a leg in a motorcycle accident, and used the compensation proceeds to establish Thistle Hill, turning adversity into good fortune. The McKendrys tell a similar tale. Having lived in Mudgee for 15 years, Tony McKendry (a regional medical superintendent) and Debbie succumbed to the lure, and planted and tended their small (1.5-hectare) vineyard in 1995. In Debbie's words, 'Tony, in his spare 2 minutes per day, also decided to start Wine Science at Charles Sturt University in 1992.' She continues, 'His trying to live 27 hours per day (plus our four kids!) fell to pieces when he was involved in a severe car smash in 1997. Two months in hospital stopped full-time medical work, and the winery dreams became inevitable.' Here, too, financial compensation finally came through and the small winery was built. The vineyard now extends to 11 hectares, including 2 hectares of tempranillo and 1 hectare of graciano.

ϓϓϓϓ **Semillon 2003** Big, rich and powerful, with a combination of faintly charry oak, ripe peach and substantial alcohol. **RATING** 89 **DRINK** 2013 $ 16

Easter Semillon 2002 Developed gold; a massively sweet, heavily botrytised palate; so rich it needed a touch more acidity for top points. **RATING** 88 **DRINK** 2009 $ 19

Limited Release Semillon 2003 Clear-cut varietal character; as ever, very close to Hunter Valley Semillon; is, however, slightly overweight on entry, tailing off towards the finish. Should fill out with age. **RATING** 87 **DRINK** 2008 $ 16

Gran Tinto 2003 Clean, high-toned cherry/cherry pip fruit; fresh, bright acidity; entirely fruit-driven. A blend of Tempranillo, Cabernet Sauvignon and Grenache. **RATING** 87 **DRINK** 2008 $ 21

ϓϓϓϓ **Chardonnay 2003** **RATING** 86 **DRINK** 2007 $ 19

Tempranillo 2002 Light colour; clean, spicy cherry fruit and brisk acidity; has varietal integrity. **RATING** 86 **DRINK** 2007 $ 23

Semillon 2002 **RATING** 85 **DRINK** 2009 $ 16

ΥΥΥ   **Cabernet Sauvignon 2002 RATING** 83 $19
               Riesling 2003 RATING 81 $16

Vino Italia

NR

81 Campersic Road, Middle Swan, WA 6056 **REGION** Swan District
T (08) 9396 4336 **F** (08) 9296 4924 **OPEN** 7 days 10–5
WINEMAKER Eugenio Valenti, Allesandro Calabrese **EST.** 1954
PRODUCT RANGE Traditional table and fortified wines.
SUMMARY Surprising though it may seem to some, the Italian winemaking community in the Swan Valley is significantly smaller than that from Dalmatia. Nonetheless, this business is well named, for it is run by Eugenio Valenti and Alessandro Calabrese, who have 34 hectares of chenin blanc, semillon, grenache, shiraz and muscadelle. They make both table and fortified wines, which are sold to local clientele by mail order and through the cellar door.

Vintina Estate

NR

1282 Nepean Highway, Mount Eliza, Vic 3930 **REGION** Mornington Peninsula
T (03) 9787 8166 **F** (03) 9775 2035 **OPEN** 7 days 9–5
WINEMAKER Jim Filippone, Kevin McCarthy (Consultant) **EST.** 1985 **CASES** 400
PRODUCT RANGE ($12–14 CD) Chardonnay, Semillon, Pinot Gris, Pinot Noir, Cabernet Sauvignon.
SUMMARY The initial releases of Vintina from 1.6 hectares of estate plantings (the only wines tasted to date) were mediocre. With competent contract-winemaking, improvement might be expected.

Virgin Block Vineyard

NR

Caves Road, Yallingup, WA 6282 **REGION** Margaret River
T (08) 9755 2394 **F** (08) 9755 2357 **OPEN** 7 days 10–5
WINEMAKER Bruce Dukes, Anne-Coralie Fleury (Contract) **EST.** 1995 **CASES** 3000
PRODUCT RANGE ($17–23 CD) Semillon Sauvignon Blanc, Shiraz, Cabernet Merlot.
SUMMARY Virgin Block has been established on a 30-hectare property 3 kilometres from the Indian Ocean, and is surrounded by large Jarrah and Marri forest trees. The substantial, indeed ornate, buildings on-site include a cellar door and café emporium, which opened in 2004. The site has gardens, local produce for sale, picnic facilities and caters for functions.

Virgin Hills

Salisbury Road, Lauriston West via Kyneton, Vic 3444 **REGION** Macedon Ranges
T (03) 5422 7444 **F** (03) 5422 7400 **OPEN** By appointment
WINEMAKER Josh Steele **EST.** 1968 **CASES** 2500
PRODUCT RANGE ($55 R) A single Cabernet Sauvignon Shiraz Merlot Blend called Virgin Hills; occasional limited Reserve release.
SUMMARY Virgin Hills has passed through several ownership changes in a short period of time. It is now owned by Michael Hope, who presides over the fast-growing Hope Estate in the Hunter Valley. While there were one or two raised eyebrows at some of the events in the Hunter Valley several years ago, the quality of the wines currently being made at Hope Estate cannot be questioned, any more than the quality of the 1998 Virgin Hills. So, after some prevarication, the five-star rating remains in place. Exports to the UK and the US.

Voyager Estate

Lot 1 Stevens Road, Margaret River, WA 6285 **REGION** Margaret River
T (08) 9757 6354 **F** (08) 9757 6494 **OPEN** 7 days 10–5
WINEMAKER Cliff Royle **EST.** 1978 **CASES** 30 000
PRODUCT RANGE ($22–100 R) Semillon, Sauvignon Blanc Semillon, Tom Price Semillon Sauvignon Blanc, Chardonnay, Shiraz, Cabernet Sauvignon Merlot, Tom Price Cabernet Sauvignon.
SUMMARY Voyager Estate has come a long way since it was acquired by Michael Wright (of the mining family) in May 1991. It now has an important, high quality 63.5-hectare vineyard which puts Voyager Estate in the position of being able to select only the best parcels of fruit for its own label, and to

supply surplus (but high-quality) wine to others. The Cape Dutch-style tasting room and vast rose garden are a major tourist attraction, although the winery itself remains in strictly utilitarian form. Exports to the UK, The Netherlands, Switzerland, China, Malaysia, Singapore, Japan, New Zealand, Canada and the US.

ŸŸŸŸŸ **Chardonnay 2002** A complex but perfectly balanced wine; fine nectarine and grapefruit flavours; subtle oak. **RATING** 94 **DRINK** 2012 $ 38

ŸŸŸŸŸ **Cabernet Sauvignon Merlot 2001** Powerful, concentrated blackcurrant/blackberry fruit, then long, powerful tannins; infinite patience required. **RATING** 93 **DRINK** 2026 $ 45
Sauvignon Blanc Semillon 2003 Grass, herb, capsicum and more tropical notes on bouquet; intense but refined mix on the palate; clean finish. **RATING** 92 **DRINK** 2008 $ 22
Shiraz 2002 Mixed aromas of black cherry and blackberry; potent, incisive fruit on the palate; controlled extract; needs time. **RATING** 92 **DRINK** 2015 $ 29.50

ŸŸŸŸ **Semillon 2002** Complex and spicy, with plenty of palate weight. **RATING** 89 **DRINK** 2007 $ 25
Semillon Sauvignon Blanc 2003 Smooth and supple mouthfeel; gently tropical fruit warmth. **RATING** 88 **DRINK** 2008 $ 22

Wadjekanup River Estate ★★★☆

Flatrocks Road, Broomehill, WA 6318 **REGION** Great Southern
T (08) 9825 3080 **F** (08) 9825 3007 **OPEN** By appointment
WINEMAKER Michael Staniford (Alkoomi Contract) **EST.** 1995 **CASES** 400
PRODUCT RANGE ($16–18 CD) Sauvignon Blanc, Shiraz.
SUMMARY The Witham family (Scott and Sue, Jim and Ann) began the development of Wadjekanup River Estate in 1995 as a minor diversification for a 3000-hectare wool, prime lamb, beef and cereal cropping enterprise worked by the family. They began with 1.2 hectares of shiraz and sauvignon blanc, since extended to 8 hectares, including a 1-hectare block of merlot with its first production in 2001. The aims for the future include a purpose-built cellar for storage and sales, with a possibility of farm-stay accommodation also being considered. The present wine range of Sauvignon Blanc and Shiraz will be extended with a varietal Merlot, and the possibility of a Semillon or other white somewhere down the track.

ŸŸŸŸ **Shiraz 2002** Quite elegant; red berry fruits; fine, long tannin finish and aftertaste. **RATING** 87 **DRINK** 2009 $ 18

Wallington Wines NR

Nyrang Creek Vineyard, Canowindra, NSW 2904 **REGION** Cowra
T (02) 6344 7153 **F** (02) 6344 7105 **OPEN** By appointment
WINEMAKER Blair Duncan, Murray Smith (Contract) **EST.** 1992 **CASES** 1500
PRODUCT RANGE ($12–20 CD) Chardonnay, Shiraz, Cabernet Sauvignon.
SUMMARY Anthony and Margaret Wallington commenced the development of their Nyrang Creek Vineyard with 2 hectares of cabernet sauvignon in 1992, followed by 7 hectares of chardonnay in 1994, then shiraz (2 hectares) and semillon (0.75 hectare) in 1995, 0.75 hectare each of cabernet franc and pinot noir in 1998, thereafter adding a mix of grenache, mourvedre, tempranillo and viognier. Most of the production is sold, but Arrowfield makes the Wallington Chardonnay and Murray Smith of Canobolas-Smith Wines at Orange makes the Cabernet Sauvignon and Shiraz. The quality of the wines is such that exports to the US have already commenced.

Walsh Family Winery NR

90 Walnut Road, Bickley, WA 6076 **REGION** Perth Hills
T (08) 9291 7341 **F** (08) 9291 7341 **OPEN** Weekends 11–5
WINEMAKER Rob Marshall (Contract) **EST.** 1995 **CASES** 200
PRODUCT RANGE ($12–17 CD) Gewurztraminer, Mary's Request Shiraz.
SUMMARY Walsh Family Winery is aptly named: it is a partnership of the Walshes and their eight children. One of those children has established 11 hectares of vines near Bridgetown in the Great Southern; the grapes from there form part of the Walsh Family winery intake.

Wandana Estate ★★☆

113 Oakey Creek Road, Hall, NSW 2618 **REGION** Canberra District
T (02) 6230 2140 **F** (02) 6230 2151 **OPEN** Weekends 10–5
WINEMAKER Contract **EST.** 1997
PRODUCT RANGE A range of varietally denominated table wines reflecting the plantings.
SUMMARY The small Wandana Estate is managed by Colin Bates; it has 5 hectares of cabernet
sauvignon, merlot and shiraz, and the wines are sold by mail order and through the cellar door.

ΨΨΨ   **Shiraz 2001 RATING** 80 $ 18

Wandering Brook Estate NR

North Wandering Road, Wandering, WA 6308 **REGION** Peel
T (08) 9884 1084 **F** (08) 9884 1064 **OPEN** Weekends 9.30–6
WINEMAKER Steve Radojkovich **EST.** 1989 **CASES** 1400
PRODUCT RANGE Verdelho, Chardonnay, Unwooded Chardonnay, Soft Red and White, Cabernet
Sauvignon, Sparkling Verdelho, Port.
SUMMARY Laurie and Margaret White have planted 10 hectares of vines on their 130-year-old family
property in a move to diversify. Until 1994 the wines were made at Goundrey; they are currently
made at Jadran. Renamed Wandering Brook Estate late in 1994; up till then known as Red Hill
Estate. Over half the annual production of grapes is sold.

Wandin Valley Estate ★★★☆

Wilderness Road, Lovedale, NSW 2320 **REGION** Lower Hunter Valley
T (02) 4930 7317 **F** (02) 4930 7814 **OPEN** 7 days 10–5
WINEMAKER Janelle Zerk, Karl Stockhausen (Consultant) **EST.** 1973 **CASES** 10 000
PRODUCT RANGE ($17–28 CD) Reserve Semillon, Sauvignon Blanc Semillon, Estate Verdelho, Reserve
Chardonnay, Hunter Valley Rose, Estate Shiraz, Bridie's Reserve Shiraz, Estate Cabernet Merlot,
Riley's Reserve Cabernet Sauvignon, Muscat.
SUMMARY Very much part of the Hunter Valley establishment, Wandin Valley continues to produce
reliable wines notwithstanding a number of (friendly) changes in the winemaking team. Janelle
Zerk, a fifth-generation member of a Barossa Valley producer, has become winemaker after working
at St Hallett and then Brokenwood, taking over from Sarah-Kate Dineen. The estate also boasts a
Cope-Williams-type village cricket oval and extensive cottage accommodation, the Café Crocodile is
open Wednesday–Sunday for lunch, and dinner Friday and Saturday. Exports to the US, the UK,
Denmark, Malaysia, Singapore and Japan.

ΨΨΨΨ̈   **Reserve Chardonnay 2003** Complex and stylish; barrel-ferment characters integrated
with melon and white peach fruit; slightly hot alcohol. **RATING** 90 **DRINK** 2007 $ 20
Riley's Reserve Cabernet Sauvignon 2002 Lots of redcurrant, cassis and blackcurrant
fruit; smooth and supple; well crafted. **RATING** 90 **DRINK** 2012 $ 28

ΨΨΨΨ   **Hunter/Clare Shiraz 2002** Much deeper colour, flavour and length; a mix of black fruits
and dark chocolate; big Clare impact. **RATING** 89 **DRINK** 2012 $ 18
Bridie's Reserve Shiraz 2002 Light to medium-bodied; spicy, earthy undertones to sweet
red fruits; fragrant, early drinking. **RATING** 87 **DRINK** Now $ 28

ΨΨΨΨ̈   **Sauvignon Blanc Semillon 2003 RATING** 86 **DRINK** Now $ 18
Bridie's Reserve Shiraz 2001 RATING 86 **DRINK** 2009 $ 28
Pavilion Rose 2003 RATING 85 **DRINK** Now $ 17
Semillon 2002 RATING 84 **DRINK** 2012 $ 18
Verdelho 2003 RATING 84 **DRINK** Now $ 17
Riley's Reserve Cabernet Sauvignon 2001 RATING 84 **DRINK** 2007 $ 28

ΨΨΨ   **Semillon 2003 RATING** 80 $ 18

🐾 Wandoo Farm ★★☆

'Glencraig', Duranillin, WA 6393 **REGION** Central Western Australia Zone
T (08) 9863 1066 **F** (08) 9863 1067 **OPEN** By appointment
WINEMAKER Camilla Vote **EST.** 1997 **CASES** 1750
PRODUCT RANGE ($13–14 CD) Verdelho, Verdelho Viognier, Shiraz, Cabernet Shiraz, Cabernet Sauvignon.
SUMMARY Wandoo Farm lies outside any of the existing wine regions, due east of Bunbury, and also east of the Blackwood Valley, its nearest regional neighbour. Donald Cochrane owns a 650-hectare sheep, cattle and grain farm near Duranillin, with a 23-inch annual rainfall and abundant underground water. His maternal grandfather came to Australia from Kaiser Stuhl in Germany, later settling near Kojonup, where he planted a vineyard and made the community wine. Donald Cochrane has one of his original vines (malbec) growing in the present-day Wandoo Farm vineyard. Here there are 7 hectares of cabernet sauvignon, shiraz, zinfandel, verdelho, viognier and marsanne. For good measure there is an experimental block consisting of between 30 and 200 vines of another 11 varieties. When he planted the vineyard, he said he had no intention of ever having any wine made, intending simply to sell the grapes. Now he says he does not intend to build a winery, but acknowledges that intentions change. The wines are sold through 18 outlets spread across the country areas of Western Australia.

▼▼▼▽ **Cabernet Sauvignon 2002 RATING** 86 **DRINK** 2009 $ 14

▼▼▼ **Verdelho Viognier 2003 RATING** 83 $ 13
Verdelho 2002 RATING 82 $ 13

Wangolina Station ★★★★

Cnr Southern Ports Highway and Limestone Coast Road, Kingston SE, SA 5275 **REGION** Mount Benson
T (08) 8768 6187 **F** (08) 8768 6149 **OPEN** 7 days 10–5
WINEMAKER Anita Goode **EST.** 2001 **CASES** 1500
PRODUCT RANGE ($15 CD) Semillon, Sauvignon Blanc, Cabernet Sauvignon Shiraz.
SUMMARY Four generations of the Goode family have been graziers at Wangolina Station, renowned for its shorthorn cattle stud. The family now has two connections with the wine industry: it sold land to Kreglinger for its vineyard and winery, and also sold land to Ralph Fowler. The second connection is even more direct: fifth-generation Anita Goode has become a vigneron, with 3.2 hectares of shiraz and 1.6 hectares each of cabernet sauvignon, sauvignon blanc and semillon established on the family property.

▼▼▼▼▽ **Cabernet Sauvignon Shiraz 2002** Fragrant red fruits, and a splash of blackcurrant; balanced, medium-bodied but well structured; good oak handling. **RATING** 92 **DRINK** 2012 $ 15

▼▼▼▼ **Sauvignon Blanc 2003** Clean, fresh, clear light-bodied varietal flavours in a lemon/herb/apple spectrum; crisp finish. **RATING** 87 **DRINK** Now $ 15

Wansbrough Wines NR

Richards Road, Ferguson, WA 6236 **REGION** Geographe
T (08) 9728 3091 **F** (08) 9728 3091 **OPEN** Weekends 10–5
WINEMAKER Willespie Wines (Contract) **EST.** 1986 **CASES** 250
PRODUCT RANGE ($12–18 CD) Riesling, Semillon, Sauvignon Blanc, Constantia (late-picked Semillon), Shiraz Cabernet, Port.
SUMMARY Situated east of Dardanup in the picturesque Ferguson Valley, Wansbrough enjoys views of the distant Geographe Bay and the nearer State Forest with the Bibblemun Track running along its northern and eastern borders. To taste the wine you need either to order by mail or visit the Wansbrough restaurant on weekends.

Wantirna Estate

NR

Bushy Park Lane, Wantirna South, Vic 3152 (postal) **REGION** Yarra Valley
T (03) 9801 2367 **F** (03) 9887 0225 **OPEN** Not
WINEMAKER Maryann Egan, Reg Egan **EST.** 1963 **CASES** 800
PRODUCT RANGE ($55–60 ML) Isabella Chardonnay, Lily Pinot Noir, Amelia Cabernet Sauvignon Merlot.
SUMMARY Situated well within the boundaries of the Melbourne metropolitan area, Wantirna Estate is an outpost of the Yarra Valley, and one of the first established in the rebirth of the Valley. In deference to Reg Egan's very firmly held views on the subject, neither the winery nor the wines are rated.

Isabella Chardonnay 2002 Intense, aromatic penetrating grapefruit and stone fruit; long, lingering finish; best for years. **NR DRINK** 2010 $ 55
Lily Pinot Noir 2002 Elegant style, lighter than many from the vintage; lots of spice and sous bois; fine texture and tannins. **NR DRINK** 2009 $ 60
Amelia Cabernet Sauvignon Merlot 2001 Medium-bodied; very good structure and mouthfeel; abundant black and red fruits flow evenly. **NR DRINK** 2016 $ 60

Warby Range Estate

Jones Road, Taminick via Glenrowan, Vic 3675 **REGION** Glenrowan
T (03) 5765 2314 **OPEN** Thurs–Mon 10–5, or by appointment
WINEMAKER Ralph Judd **EST.** 1989 **CASES** 500
PRODUCT RANGE ($10–15 CD) Shiraz, Durif.
SUMMARY Ralph and Margaret Judd began the development of their vineyard in 1989 as contract growers for Southcorp. They have gradually expanded the plantings to 4 hectares of shiraz and 0.5 hectare of durif; they also have 100 vines each of zinfandel, ruby cabernet, cabernet sauvignon, petit verdot, nebbiolo, tempranillo and sangiovese for evaluation. Until 1995, all of the grapes were fermented and then sent by tanker to Southcorp, but in 1996 the Judds made their first barrel of wine; they have now moved to opening a small cellar-door sales facility. The wines are monumental in flavour and depth, in best Glenrowan tradition, and will richly repay extended cellaring.

Durif 2002 Densely coloured, and packed with blackberry, licorice, prune and spice fruit; the generous tannins on the finish are now beginning to soften. **RATING** 91 **DRINK** 2016 $ 15

Wards Gateway

Barossa Valley Highway, Lyndoch, SA 5351 **REGION** Barossa Valley
T (08) 8524 4138 **OPEN** 7 days 9–5.30
WINEMAKER Ray Ward, plus Contract **EST.** 1979 **CASES** 50
PRODUCT RANGE ($7.50–17 CD) Riesling, Frontignac, Chardonnay, Frontignac Spatlese, Barossa Shiraz, Cabernet Sauvignon, Port.
SUMMARY The very old vines surrounding the winery produce the best wines, which are made without frills or new oak and sold without ostentation. Ray Ward has been bravely battling illness (and old age), but as at mid-2003 was still holding on. No update available.

Warrabilla

Murray Valley Highway, Rutherglen, Vic 3685 **REGION** Rutherglen
T (02) 6035 7242 **F** (02) 6035 7298 **OPEN** 7 days 10–5
WINEMAKER Andrew Sutherland Smith **EST.** 1990 **CASES** 9000
PRODUCT RANGE ($12–46 CD) Marsanne, Chardonnay, KV Brut Rose, Reserve Shiraz, Parola's Limited Release Shiraz, Merlot, Reserve Merlot, Reserve Durif (Magnum), Parola's Limited Release Durif, Brimin Cabernet Durif, Reserve Cabernet, Vintage Port, Liqueur Muscat.
SUMMARY Former All Saints winemaker Andrew Sutherland Smith has leased a small winery at Corowa to make the Warrabilla wines from a 17-hectare vineyard developed by himself and Carol Smith in the Indigo Valley. The red wines are made in open fermenters, hand-plunged and basket-pressed, then matured in quality oak, mainly French.

ΥΥΥΥΥ **Parola's Limited Release Durif 2002** Impenetrable purple; chocolate, licorice and black morello cherry aromas precede a wine which is chewed, rather than drunk. 17.5 degrees alcohol is absolutely astonishing; keep it for 20 years and then serve it with an ox cooked over an open pit. **RATING** 94 **DRINK** 2030 $ 30

ΥΥΥΥΥ **Reserve Durif 2002** Dense, deep purple; blackberry jam, spice, earth and licorice aromas precede a mouth-coating blast of black fruits and bitter chocolate. A mere 17 degrees alcohol: drink the wine in the safety of your home. **RATING** 93 **DRINK** 2020 $ 22
Parola's Limited Release Shiraz 2002 Dense red-purple; a powerful blackberry, licorice and vanilla bouquet then a massive palate, crammed with dark fruits and bitter chocolate; 16.5 degrees alcohol, but the tannins are controlled. **RATING** 92 **DRINK** 2020 $ 30
Reserve Shiraz 2002 Full red-purple; clean, but complex, black fruits, a touch of earth, and evident vanilla oak; 16 degrees alcohol. **RATING** 90 **DRINK** 2017 $ 22
Liqueur Muscat NV Olive-brown; a rich raisin and plum pudding bouquet; raisin, toffee and plum pudding flavours; excellent value. **RATING** 90 $ 15

Warramate ★★★★

27 Maddens Lane, Gruyere, Vic 3770 **REGION** Yarra Valley
T (03) 5964 9219 **F** (03) 5964 9219 **OPEN** 7 days 10–6
WINEMAKER David Church **EST.** 1970 **CASES** 900
PRODUCT RANGE ($25–38 CD) Riesling, Shiraz, Cabernet Merlot.
SUMMARY Wine quality has been variable in recent years; it would seem that the oak in some of the older barrels is questionable. At their best, the wines reflect the distinguished site on which the vineyard sits. The 2000/2001 extension of the 30-year-old vineyard will lead to greater production in the years ahead.

ΥΥΥΥΥ **Shiraz 2002** Fragrant and fresh; a lively, medium-bodied palate with black cherry, plum and blackberry; fine, lingering tannins. Screwcap. **RATING** 91 **DRINK** 2017 $ 38
Shiraz 2001 Excellent colour; clean black cherry and plum aromas; medium-bodied, smooth and supple; bright fruit and subtle oak. Excellent outcome. **RATING** 90 **DRINK** 2014 $ 38

ΥΥΥΥ **Riesling 2003** Clean slate and mineral; well balanced, with good acidity; subliminal, with sweetness, perhaps simply the fruit. Impressive. **RATING** 89 **DRINK** 2013 $ 25

ΥΥΥΥ **Cabernet Merlot 2001 RATING** 86 **DRINK** 2011 $ 35

Warraroong Estate ★★★☆

Wilderness Road, Lovedale, NSW 2321 **REGION** Lower Hunter Valley
T (02) 4930 7594 **F** (02) 4930 7199 **OPEN** Thurs–Mon 10–5
WINEMAKER Andrew Thomas, Adam Rees **EST.** 1978 **CASES** 2500
PRODUCT RANGE ($10–25 CD) Semillon, Sauvignon Blanc, Chenin Blanc, Verdelho, Chardonnay, Semillon Methode Champenoise, Ruby Cabernet Methode Champenoise, Malbec Rose, Shiraz, Malbec.
SUMMARY Warraroong Estate was formerly Fraser Vineyard; it adopted its new name after it changed hands in 1997. The name 'Warraroong' is an Aboriginal word for hillside, reflecting the southwesterly aspect of the property, which looks back towards the Brokenback Range and Watagan Mountains. The label design is from a painting by local Aboriginal artist Kia Kiro who, while coming from the Northern Territory, is living and working in the Hunter Valley.

ΥΥΥΥΥ **Chardonnay 2003** Melon and some citrus with well-integrated oak; good structure and length; lingering finish. **RATING** 90 **DRINK** Now $ 20

ΥΥΥΥ **Shiraz 2002** Clean, light to medium-bodied; pleasantly sweet fruit and nicely made, but needs more depth. **RATING** 86 **DRINK** 2007 $ 20
Sauvignon Blanc Semillon 2003 RATING 84 **DRINK** 2007 $ 16

ΥΥΥ **Chenin Blanc 2003 RATING** 83 $ 10
Verdelho 2003 RATING 82 $ 15.25

Warrego Wines ★★★

9 Seminary Road, Marburg, Qld 4306 **REGION** Queensland Coastal
T (07) 5464 4400 **F** (07) 5464 4800 **OPEN** 7 days 10–4
WINEMAKER Kevin Watson **EST.** 2000 **CASES** 24 000
PRODUCT RANGE ($9.95–28.95 CD) Cane Cutter's Riesling, Sawmill Sauvignon Blanc, Voyage Verdelho, Coalface Chardonnay, Sirois Chardonnay, Dance's Delight (sweet), Cane Cutter's Cuvee, The Ranges Red, Cane Cutter's Pinot Noir, Pioneer's Pinot Noir, Brigalow Shiraz, Seminary Shiraz, Cunningham's Coonawarra Cabernet Sauvignon, Rum Distillery Tawny Port.
SUMMARY Cathy and Kevin Watson have established their small winery in the historic Dances Bakery at Marburg, which is halfway between Toowoomba and Brisbane, attracted — like so many others — by the lifestyle opportunities and the tourism potential of southern Queensland. Kevin Watson has completed his wine science degree at Charles Sturt University, and the primary purpose of his business is custom winemaking for the many small growers in the region. In 2001 a company, Marburg Custom Crush, developed a state-of-the-art winery (as the cliché goes), cellar door and restaurant. $500 000 in government funding, local business investment and significant investment from China provided the funds, and the complex opened in April 2002. (In 2004 Warrego crushed over 400 tonnes, 95 per cent of which was contract winemaking for others.)

ŸŸŸŸŸ **Pioneer's Pinot Noir 2000** Fine, spicy, tangy flavours; long and lingering, with great varietal character; skilfully made and a bargain. From Tasmanian Tamar Valley and Victorian Strathbogie Ranges grapes. **RATING** 92 **DRINK** Now $18.95

ŸŸŸŸ **Voyage Verdelho 2003** Good aroma and entry; nice fruit salad flavour, dipping slightly on the finish. **RATING** 86 **DRINK** Now $16.95
Marburg Merlot 2002 RATING 85 **DRINK** Now $19.95
The Bacchae 2001 RATING 85 **DRINK** Now $34.95

ŸŸŸ **Half Way White White 2003 RATING** 83 $11.95
Rum Distillery Tawny Port NV RATING 83 $15.95
The Ranges Red 2002 RATING 82 $9.95
Dance's Delight 2003 RATING 82 $9.95
Cunningham's Coonawarra Cabernet Sauvignon 2001 RATING 81 $19.95

Warrenmang Vineyard & Resort ★★★★

Mountain Creek Road, Moonambel, Vic 3478 **REGION** Pyrenees
T (03) 5467 2233 **F** (03) 5467 2309 **OPEN** 7 days 10–5
WINEMAKER Luigi Bazzani, Paul Smart **EST.** 1974 **CASES** 8500
PRODUCT RANGE ($13–80 R) A quartet of wines under the Bazzani label; then varietals under the Warrenmang Estate label; and finally the ultra-premium Black Puma Avoca Shiraz.
SUMMARY At the time of going to print, the future direction for Warrenmang was uncertain. An ambitious plan to raise funds through an IPO, taking in Massoni as part of the expanded business, had stalled. It's a case of 'watch this space'.

Warrina Wines NR

Back Road, Kootingal, NSW 2352 **REGION** Northern Slopes Zone
T (02) 6760 3985 **F** (02) 6765 5746 **OPEN** Weekends 10–4
WINEMAKER David Nicholls **EST.** 1989 **CASES** 100
PRODUCT RANGE ($5–12 CD) Sauvignon Blanc, Chardonnay, Shiraz, Cabernet Sauvignon.
SUMMARY David and Susan Nicholls began the establishment of their 2.5-hectare vineyard all the way back in 1989, and were content to sell the grapes to other producers, making occasional forays into winemaking, until deciding to commence winemaking on a commercial basis in 2001.

Watchbox Wines ★★★

Indigo Creek Road, Barnawartha, Vic 3688 **REGION** Rutherglen
T (03) 6026 9299 **F** (03) 6026 9299 **OPEN** Fri–Sun and public holidays 10–5
WINEMAKER Alan Clark **EST.** 2001
PRODUCT RANGE Riesing, Sauvignon Blanc, Chardonnay, Shiraz, Merlot, Cabernet Sauvignon.

SUMMARY Alan and Lisa Clark have established their 5-hectare vineyard in the Indigo Valley; it is planted to riesling, sauvignon blanc, chardonnay, cabernet sauvignon, merlot, shiraz, durif and muscat. They make the wine on-site. It is sold by mail order and through the cellar door, which offers light meals and a wide range of facilities, including barbecue and picnic areas.

ᵀᵀᵀᵞ **Shiraz 2002** RATING 84 DRINK 2009 $18

Watershed Wines ★★★★★

Cnr Bussell Highway and Darch Road, Margaret River, WA 6285 **REGION** Margaret River
T (08) 9758 8633 **F** (08) 9757 3999 **OPEN** 7 days 10–5
WINEMAKER Cathy Spratt, John Wade (Consultant) **EST.** 1999 **CASES** 40 000
PRODUCT RANGE ($19.95–32 R) Sauvignon Blanc, Chardonnay, Shiraz, Cabernet Merlot.
SUMMARY Watershed Premium Wines has been established by a syndicate of investors, and no expense has been spared in establishing the vineyard and building a striking cellar-door sales area, with a 200-seat café and restaurant recently completed. Situated towards the southern end of the Margaret River region, its neighbours include Voyager Estate and Leeuwin Estate. Its 2001 wines (the first vintage) have had significant show success.

ᵀᵀᵀᵀᵀ **Shiraz 2002** Elegant, light to medium bodied; spice, pepper and black fruits, fine tannins, good length, subtle oak. **RATING** 94 **DRINK** 2012 $28.95

ᵀᵀᵀᵀᵞ **Cabernet Merlot 2002** Complex, ripe black fruits; nicely rounded tannins; plenty of oak suport. **RATING** 93 **DRINK** 2012 $26.95
Sauvignon Blanc 2003 Spotlessly clean; gentle tropical/gooseberry fruit; good mouthfeel and length. **RATING** 91 **DRINK** 2006 $19.95
Chardonnay 2003 Complex, tangy barrel ferment/malolactic inputs; stone fruit and citrus come through on the palate with excellent length and finish. **RATING** 90 **DRINK** 2008 $17.95
Shiraz 2001 Deep colour; very rich and complex with strong French oak influences throughout; fleshy texture and fine tannins. Typical John Wade style. **RATING** 90 **DRINK** 2016 $28.95

Waterton Estate NR

Rowella, Tas 7270 **REGION** Northern Tasmania
T (03) 6327 4170 **F** (03) 6331 9982 **OPEN** Not
WINEMAKER Julian Alcorso, Nick Butler (Contract) **EST.** 1995 **CASES** 400
PRODUCT RANGE ($11 ML) Riesling, Chardonnay, Cabernet Sauvignon.
SUMMARY The near-invisible Waterton Estate is owned by a seven-member syndicate who doubtless consume much of the annual production themselves, selling the remainder by word of mouth to friends and acquaintances. Contract winemaking by Julian Alcorso and Nick Butler does the rest.

Water Wheel ★★★☆

Bridgewater-on-Loddon, Bridgewater, Vic 3516 **REGION** Bendigo
T (03) 5437 3060 **F** (03) 5437 3082 **OPEN** Oct–Apr 7 days 11–5, May–Sept Mon–Fri 11–5, weekends and public holidays 1–4
WINEMAKER Peter Cumming, Bill Trevaskis **EST.** 1972 **CASES** 35 000
PRODUCT RANGE ($14–18 R) Bendigo Sauvignon Blanc, Bendigo Chardonnay, Bendigo Shiraz, Bendigo Cabernet Sauvignon.
SUMMARY Peter Cumming gained great respect as a winemaker during his 4-year stint with Hickinbotham Winemakers, and his 1989 purchase of Water Wheel was greeted with enthusiasm by followers of his work. The wines are of remarkably consistent quality and modest price. They are distributed throughout Australia and exported to New Zealand, the Phillipines, the UK, Switzerland, Belgium, the US and Canada.

ᵀᵀᵀᵀᵀ **Bendigo Shiraz 2002** Greater concentration, depth and complexity than usual; driven by plum and blackberry fruit, supported by fine tannins. Exceptional bargain. **RATING** 94 **DRINK** 2015 $18

▼▼▼▼ **Bendigo Sauvignon Blanc 2003** Clean, good length, passionfruit and citrus; builds towards the finish and aftertaste. Impressive. **RATING** 87 **DRINK** Now $ 15
Bendigo Cabernet Sauvignon 2001 As reliable as ever; light to medium-bodied, soft and supple, with juicy blackberry and mint; good value. **RATING** 87 **DRINK** Now $ 18
Memsie Shiraz Cabernet Malbec 2002 Fresh red berry and mint aromas, then surprising depth and power to the ripe plummy fruit on the palate. 14.5 degrees alcohol. Screwcap. **RATING** 87 **DRINK** 2012 $ 15

▼▼▼▽ **Chardonnay 2003** **RATING** 84 **DRINK** Now $ 15

Wattagan Estate Winery   NR

'Wattagan', Oxley Highway, Coonabarabran, NSW 2357 **REGION** Western Plains Zone
T (02) 6842 2456 **F** (02) 6842 2656 **OPEN** 7 days 10–5
WINEMAKER Contract **EST.** 1996
PRODUCT RANGE ($10.50–18 CD) Sauvignon Blanc, Chardonnay, Shiraz, Cabernet Merlot.
SUMMARY Coonabarabran is known for its sheep grazing, but most emphatically not for viticulture. As far north of Sydney as Port Macquarie, it is 440 kilometres west of that town, with the striking Warrumbungle Range on one side, and the National Park on the other. The modest production is sold through three outlets in Coonabarabran, and 'exported' to Gunnedah and Boggabri.

Wattlebrook Vineyard   ★★★☆

Fordwich Road, Broke, NSW 2330 **REGION** Lower Hunter Valley
T (02) 9929 5668 **F** (02) 9929 5668 **OPEN** First Saturday of each month, or by appointment
WINEMAKER Andrew Margan (Contract) **EST.** 1994 **CASES** 1000
PRODUCT RANGE ($13.75–19 ML) Semillon Verdelho, Chardonnay, Shiraz Gulgong Reserve Shiraz, Cabernet, Gulgong Reserve Cabernet Sauvignon Shiraz.
SUMMARY Wattlebrook Vineyard was founded by NSW Supreme Court Justice Peter McClellan and family in 1994, with its substantial vineyard lying between the Wollemi National Park and Wollombi Brook. The family's viticultural investment was extended by the commencement of another major vineyard in 1998 on Henry Lawson Drive at Mudgee, planted to shiraz, merlot and cabernet sauvignon. The Wollombi Vineyard is planted to chardonnay, semillon, verdelho, cabernet sauvignon and shiraz. The wines, contract-made by Andrew Margan, have been consistent medal winners at New South Wales and Hunter Valley Wine Shows, the high point coming with the trophy and gold medal awarded to the 1999 Wattlebrook Chardonnay at the Hunter Valley Wine Show of the same year.

▼▼▼▼ **Semillon 2003** Slightly smoky overtones to the bouquet, then a tight herb and grass-accented palate; promising debut. **RATING** 87 **DRINK** 2010 $ 14.50
Shiraz 2002 Complex leather, mint and berry aromas and flavours; ripe tannins and controlled oak. **RATING** 87 **DRINK** 2010 $ 15

▼▼▼ **Chardonnay 2001** **RATING** 81 $ 14.50

Wattle Ridge Vineyard   ★★★☆

Lot 11950 Boyup–Greenbushes Road, Greenbushes, WA 6254 **REGION** Blackwood Valley
T (08) 9764 3594 **F** (08) 9764 3594 **OPEN** 7 days 10–5
WINEMAKER Contract **EST.** 1997 **CASES** 1000
PRODUCT RANGE ($12–18 CD) Semillon, Sauvignon Blanc, Cabernet Merlot, Cabernet Sauvignon, Cabernet Sauvignon Blackwood Reserve.
SUMMARY James and Vicky Henderson have established 6.5 hectares of vines at their Nelson vineyard, planted to riesling, verdelho, merlot and cabernet sauvignon. The contract-made wines are sold by mail order and through the cellar door, which offers light meals, crafts and local produce.

▼▼▼▼ **Two Tinsmith Series Cabernet Sauvignon 2002** Spicy, scented blackberry aromas; tangy and lively, soft tannins. **RATING** 87 **DRINK** 2009

Waugoola Wines

NR

Cultowa Road, Canowindra, NSW 2804 **REGION** Cowra
T (02) 6342 1435 **OPEN** Weekends 10–6, or by appointment
WINEMAKER Rodney Hooper (Contract) **EST.** 1996 **CASES** 1300
PRODUCT RANGE Carro Park Chardonnay, Cultowa Shiraz, Shiraz.
SUMMARY Casey and Laura Proctor have established two vineyards, Cultowa Road of 4 hectares, and Carro Park of 2.5 hectares. Part of the production is sold, and part contract-made by the talented Rodney Hooper.

Waverley Estate

Waverley-Honour, Palmers Lane, Pokolbin, NSW 2320 **REGION** Lower Hunter Valley
T (02) 4998 7953 **F** (02) 4998 7952 **OPEN** 7 days 10–5
WINEMAKER Gary Reed (Contract) **EST.** 1989 **CASES** 4500
PRODUCT RANGE ($35–72 CD) Waverley Estate Semillon, Chardonnay, Lady of the Lake Sparkling, Hermitage, Cabernet Sauvignon, Gallant Grey Vintage Port.
SUMMARY Waverley Estate Aged Wines (to give it its full name) is the new name for the Maling Family Estate; as its name suggests, it specialises in offering a range of fully mature wines. As at March 2004, Semillon dating back to 1989, Chardonnay to 1991 and Shiraz to 1991 were all available. The wines are chiefly made from the 21.5 hectares of estate plantings (shiraz, semillon, chardonnay, cabernet sauvignon).

ȲȲȲȲ **Semillon 1996** Excellent colour, bright and tinged green; still delicate and evolving, but has length and intensity; slate, mineral, citrus. **RATING** 88 **DRINK** Now $40

ȲȲȲȲ **Semillon 1995** **RATING** 85 **DRINK** Now $40

ȲȲȲ **Semillon 2003** **RATING** 80 $40

ȲȲȲ **Chardonnay 1996** **RATING** 79 $38

Waybourne

NR

60 Lemins Road, Waurn Ponds, Vic 3221 **REGION** Geelong
T (03) 5241 8477 **F** (03) 5241 8477 **OPEN** By appointment
WINEMAKER David Cowburn (Contract) **EST.** 1980 **CASES** 730
PRODUCT RANGE ($12–16 ML) Riesling, Trebbiano, Pinot Gris, Cabernet Sauvignon.
SUMMARY Owned by Tony and Kay Volpato, who have relied upon external consultants to assist with the winemaking.

Wayne Thomas Wines

26 Kangarilla Road, McLaren Vale, SA 5171 **REGION** McLaren Vale
T (08) 8323 9737 **F** (08) 8323 9737 **OPEN** Not
WINEMAKER Wayne Thomas, Tim Geddes **EST.** 1994 **CASES** 5000
PRODUCT RANGE ($15–25 R) Riesling, Unwooded Chardonnay, Patricia Sparkling Chardonnay, Shiraz, Cabernet Sauvignon, Old Tawny Port.
SUMMARY Wayne Thomas is a McLaren Vale veteran, having commenced his winemaking career in 1961, working for Stonyfell, Ryecroft and Saltram before establishing Fern Hill with his late wife Pat in 1975. When they sold Fern Hill in April 1994 they started again, launching the Wayne Thomas Wines label, using grapes sourced from ten growers throughout McLaren Vale. The wines are exported to the US, as well as enjoying limited retail distribution through all Australian States except Western Australia.

Wedgetail Estate

40 Hildebrand Road, Cottles Bridge, Vic 3099 **REGION** Yarra Valley
T (03) 9714 8661 **F** (03) 9714 8676 **OPEN** Weekends and public holidays 12–5, or by appointment, closed from 25 Dec, reopens Australia Day weekend
WINEMAKER Guy Lamothe **EST.** 1994 **CASES** 1500

PRODUCT RANGE ($17–65 CD) Sauvignon Blanc, Semillon Sauvignon Blanc, Old Barrique Chardonnay, Chardonnay, Par 3 Pinot, Pinot Noir, Reserve Pinot Noir, Merlot, Cabernet.

SUMMARY Canadian-born photographer Guy Lamothe and partner Dena Ashbolt started making wine in the basement of their Carlton home in the 1980s. Insidiously, the idea of their own vineyard started to take hold, and the search for a property began. Then, in their words, 'one Sunday, when we were "just out for a drive", we drove past our current home. The slopes are amazing, true goat terrain, and it is on these steep slopes that in 1994 we planted our first block of pinot noir.' While the vines were growing — they now have 5.5 hectares in total — Lamothe enrolled in the wine-growing course at Charles Sturt University, having already gained practical experience working at Tarrawarra in the Yarra Valley, Mornington Peninsula and Meursault. The net result is truly excellent wine. Exports to the UK.

TTTTT **Chardonnay 2002** Long, intense, fruit-driven palate; strong citrussy overtones to stone fruit and melon; subtle oak. **RATING** 94 **DRINK** 2010 $ 32

TTTT **Pinot Noir 2002** Complex, savoury, foresty; has finesse but not the flavour one expects. **RATING** 89 **DRINK** 2008 $ 38
Par 3 Sauvignon Blanc 2003 Clean, crisp mineral and herb aromas; fills out on the palate with tropical notes. **RATING** 87 **DRINK** Now $ 22

🦅 Wedgetail Ridge Estate   NR

656 Kingsthorpe-Haden Road, Kingsthorpe, Qld 4400 **REGION** Granite Belt
T (07) 4699 3029 **F** (07) 4699 3029 **OPEN** 7 days 10–5
WINEMAKER Brian Wilson (Contract) **EST.** 1999
PRODUCT RANGE A range of varietally denominated table wines reflecting the plantings.
SUMMARY Suzanne Nation has established an 8-hectare vineyard 30 kilometres northeast of Toowoomba. It is planted to chardonnay, viognier, merlot, shiraz, cabernet sauvignon and durif, and the wine is made on the premises. Light meals are available at the cellar door, but the primary focus of the business is on contract winemaking for others.

Wehl's Mount Benson Vineyards   ★★★★★

Wrights Bay Road, Mount Benson, SA 5275 **REGION** Mount Benson
T (08) 8768 6251 **F** (08) 8678 6251 **OPEN** 7 days 10–4
WINEMAKER Contract **EST.** 1989 **CASES** 1000
PRODUCT RANGE ($25 R) Shiraz, Cabernet Sauvignon.
SUMMARY Peter and Leah Wehl were the first to plant vines in the Mount Benson area, beginning the establishment of their 24-hectare vineyard, two-thirds shiraz and one-third cabernet sauvignon, in 1989. While primarily grape growers, they have moved into winemaking via contract makers, and plan to increase the range of wines available by grafting 1 hectare of merlot and 1.5 hectares of sauvignon blanc onto part of the existing plantings. They also intend to upgrade their cellar-door facilities in the future.

TTTTT **Shiraz 2002** Excellent colour; a fragrant and sweet fusion of blackberry, licorice and spice; very well balanced; fine, ripe tannins. **RATING** 94 **DRINK** 2012 $ 26

TTTTY **Cabernet Sauvignon 2002** Powerful, rich and concentrated blackcurrant and a dash of bitter chocolate; again pronounced tannins; again, for cellaring. **RATING** 92 **DRINK** 2017 $ 26
Cabernet Sauvignon 2000 Cedar, olive, earth and blackcurrant; good balance and length; fine tannins and overall elegance. **RATING** 92 **DRINK** 2012 $ 26
Cabernet Sauvignon Merlot 2002 Very ripe, luscious, full-bodied blackcurrant and blackberry fruit, then pronounced tannins. For cellaring. **RATING** 91 **DRINK** 2017 $ 22.50

TTTY **Rose 2003** Fresh, lively strawberry flavours; good balance, sweetness and acidity. **RATING** 86 **DRINK** Now $ 18

Wellington   ★★★★★

Cnr Richmond and Denholms Roads, Cambridge, Tas 7170 **REGION** Southern Tasmania
T (03) 6248 5844 **F** (03) 6248 5855 **OPEN** First Sunday of every month 12–4, or by appointment
WINEMAKER Andrew Hood, Jeremy Dineen **EST.** 1990 **CASES** 5000

PRODUCT RANGE ($18–28 CD) Riesling, FGR Riesling, Iced Riesling, Sauvignon Blanc, Pinot Gris, Chardonnay, Pinot Noir, Ruby Port.

SUMMARY In late 2003 Wellington was acquired by Tony Scherer and Jack Kidwiler of Frogmore Creek. The Wellington winery will continue to operate as previously, making both its own label wines and wines for its other contract customers, while a new winery is constructed on the Frogmore Creek property. The latter will be exclusively devoted to organically grown wines; Andrew Hood will remain in charge of winemaking both at Wellington and at the new Frogmore Creek operation.

ŸŸŸŸŸ **Riesling 2003** Great green-gold colour; ultra-fragrant lime and mineral aromas; the palate rich in mouthfeel and flavour, yet retaining finesse. RATING 95 DRINK 2013 $ 19
Chardonnay 2001 Glowing yellow-green, this wine has developed slowly over the past 3 years, and now has super-elegant stone fruit, citrus, the barest touch of oak, and crunchy acidity. RATING 94 DRINK 2008 $ 24

ŸŸŸŸŸ **Pinot Noir 2002** Deeply coloured; potent, rich, plummy fruit with a touch of smoky bacon oak; particularly good length. RATING 93 DRINK 2009 $ 28
Sauvignon Blanc 2003 Clean; gently ripe, slightly tropical fruit; good length and balance; flawlessly crafted. RATING 92 DRINK 2007 $ 22
Iced Riesling 375 ml 2003 Clean, fresh, crisp and lively, with zesty minerality. RATING 92 DRINK 2007 $ 22
Roaring 40s Chardonnay 2003 Light-bodied but perfectly balanced melon/nectarine fruit and subtle oak in support. RATING 90 DRINK Now $ 18
Chardonnay 2002 Very youthful and still quite estery; blossom and citrus aromas and flavours show the very cool vintage. Definitely needs time. RATING 90 DRINK 2008 $ 24
Reserve Chardonnay 2002 Extremely tight, fine, elegant and focused; perfectly balanced and integrated oak; prickly acidity needs to fold back into the wine. RATING 90 DRINK 2010

ŸŸŸŸ **Roaring 40s Pinot Noir 2003** RATING 86 DRINK 2007 $ 18
Roaring 40s Pinot Noir 2002 RATING 86 DRINK 2007 $ 18
Pinot Gris 2003 RATING 85 DRINK 2007 $ 22

Wells Parish Wines ★★★★

Benerin Estate, Sydney Road, Kandos, NSW 2848 REGION Mudgee
T (02) 6379 4168 F (02) 6379 4996 OPEN By appointment
WINEMAKER Pieter Van Gent, Philip Van Gent EST. 1995 CASES 1000
PRODUCT RANGE ($11–16.50 CD) Verdelho, Chardonnay, Merlot, Shiraz, Cabernet Sauvignon, Strayleaves Vintage Port.
SUMMARY Richard and Rachel Trounson, with help from father Barry Trounson, have established 18 hectares of vineyards at Benerin Estate since 1995. Most of the grapes are sold to Southcorp, but small quantities of wine are made for sale under the Wells Parish label. The vineyards are situated at the eastern extremity of the Mudgee region, near Rylstone, and both the soils and climate are distinctly different from those of the traditional Mudgee area.

ŸŸŸŸŸ **Cabernet Sauvignon 2002** Deeply coloured; big, fleshy mint and blackcurrant; good balance, flavour and length. RATING 90 DRINK 2015 $ 16.50

ŸŸŸ **Verdelho 2003** RATING 83 $ 16.50

Welshmans Reef Vineyard NR

Maldon–Newstead Road, Welshmans Reef, Vic 3462 REGION Bendigo
T (03) 5476 2733 F (03) 5476 2537 OPEN Weekends and public holidays 10–5
WINEMAKER Ronald Snep EST. 1994 CASES 1200
PRODUCT RANGE ($16–22 CD) Welshman's Reef Semillon, Barrel Fermented Semillon, Unwooded Chardonnay, Cabernet Sauvignon; Burnt Acre Riesling, Shiraz.
SUMMARY The Snep family (Ronald, Jackson and Alexandra) began the development of Welshmans Reef Vineyard in 1986 with the planting of cabernet sauvignon, shiraz and semillon. Chardonnay and merlot were added in the early 1990s, with more recent plantings of sauvignon blanc and tempranillo. For some years the grapes were sold to other wineries, but in the early 1990s the Sneps decided to share winemaking facilities established in the Old Newstead Co-operative Butter Factory with several other small vineyards. When the Butter Factory facility was closed down, the Sneps built

their own winery and purpose-built mudbrick tasting room on-site, 6 kilometres north of Newstead and just before the hamlet which gave the vineyard its name. An Italian-style domed pizza oven has been completed, and the winery stages concerts ranging from Baroque to jazz. Details available either by email or via <www.welshmansreef.com>.

Wendouree ★★★★★

Wendouree Road, Clare, SA 5453 **REGION** Clare Valley
T (08) 8842 2896 **OPEN** By appointment
WINEMAKER Tony Brady **EST.** 1895 **CASES** 2500
PRODUCT RANGE ($18–40 ML) Shiraz, Shiraz Malbec, Shiraz Mataro, Cabernet Malbec, Cabernet Sauvignon, Muscat of Alexandria.
SUMMARY The iron fist in a velvet glove best describes these extraordinary wines. They are fashioned with passion and yet precision from the very old vineyard with its unique terroir by Tony and Lita Brady, who rightly see themselves as custodians of a priceless treasure. The 100-year-old stone winery is virtually unchanged from the day it was built; this is in every sense a treasure beyond price. For two reasons, neither Tony Brady nor I see any point in providing tasting notes for the most recently released vintage. First, the wines will have sold out, and there is no room for newcomers on the mailing list for the next release. Second, all I will ever be able to say is wait for 20 years before drinking the wine.

We're Wines ★★★★★

Cnr Wildberry and Johnson Roads, Wilyabrup, WA 6280 **REGION** Margaret River
T (08) 9755 6273 **F** (08) 9389 9166 **OPEN** Wed–Sun and public holidays 10.30–5
WINEMAKER Jan Davies (Contract) **EST.** 1998 **CASES** 3600
PRODUCT RANGE ($14–28 CD) Semillon Sauvignon Blanc, Sauvignon Blanc Semillon, Shiraz, Cabernet Sauvignon.
SUMMARY Owners Diane and Gordon Davies say, 'We are different. We're original, we're bold, we're innovative and we want to be.' This is all reflected in the bold, graphic design of the front labels; the even more unusual back labels, incorporating pictures of the innumerable pairs of braces which real estate agent Gordon Davies wears on his Perth job; in the early move to screwcaps for both white and red wines; and, for that matter, to the underground trickle irrigation system installed in their Margaret River vineyard, which can be controlled from Perth. The wines, made by Jan Davies, are excellent.

 Cabernet Sauvignon 2001 Elegant, cedary blackcurrant aromas; a long and silky palate with classic cool-grown savoury tannins. **RATING** 94 **DRINK** 2011 $ 27.95

 Semillon Sauvignon Blanc 2003 Excellent varietal expression; gooseberry, passionfruit and herb; has length. **RATING** 92 **DRINK** 2008 $16

West Cape Howe Wines ★★★★★

Lot 42 South Coast Highway, Denmark, WA 6333 **REGION** Denmark
T (08) 9848 2959 **F** (08) 9848 2903 **OPEN** 7 days 10–5
WINEMAKER Brenden Smith, Dave Cleary, Coby Ladwig **EST.** 1997 **CASES** 42 000
PRODUCT RANGE ($13–25 CD) Riesling, Semillon Sauvignon Blanc, Sauvignon Blanc, Viognier, Unwooded Chardonnay, Chardonnay, Late Picked Riesling, Shiraz, Cabernet Merlot, Cabernet Sauvignon, Muscat.
SUMMARY Brenden Smith was senior winemaker at Goundrey Wines for many years and has branched into business on his own with a contract winemaking facility for growers throughout the Great Southern region. The overall quality and consistency of the wines is wholly admirable, doubtless the reason why production has more than doubled. West Cape Howe wines are exported to Hong Kong, Singapore, Japan and The Netherlands.

 Sauvignon Blanc 2003 A mix of passionfruit, gooseberry and tropical fruits; good length and balance; particularly appealing finish and aftertaste. **RATING** 94 **DRINK** Now $15.50

 Unwooded Chardonnay 2003 Aromatic and lively, with cool-grown grapefruit and stone fruit aromas and flavours, finishing with cleansing acidity. Fully deserved its gold medal at the Qantas Wine Show of Western Australia. **RATING** 92 **DRINK** Now $16

Landsdale Shiraz Cabernet Sauvignon 2001 Fresh red and blackcurrant fruit aromas and flavours; elegant, medium-bodied; judicious oak. **RATING** 92 **DRINK** 2012 $ 13

Cabernet Sauvignon 2002 Intense, powerful, focused blackcurrant, herb and olive; classic cool-grown Cabernet; great length. **RATING** 92 **DRINK** 2012 $ 21.50

Riesling 2003 Rich and full; plenty of weight to citrus and lime fruit; quicker-developing style. **RATING** 90 **DRINK** 2008 $ 15.50

Viognier 2002 Aromas of honeysuckle and a hint of French oak; mouthfilling and rich, with plenty of varietal flavour; phenolics well handled. Impressive. **RATING** 90 **DRINK** Now $ 25

ΥΥΥΥ **Viognier 2003** Nice flavour; shows some soft pastille varietal character; on the light side, but not forced, and well balanced. **RATING** 88 **DRINK** 2007 $ 25

Semillon Sauvignon Blanc 2003 Crisp, clean and fresh; lingering citrus, herb and mineral flavours. Screwcap. **RATING** 87 **DRINK** Now $ 16

Westend Estate Wines ★★★☆

1283 Brayne Road, Griffith, NSW 2680 **REGION** Riverina
T (02) 6964 1506 **F** (02) 6962 1673 **OPEN** Mon–Fri 8.30–5, weekends 9.30–4
WINEMAKER William Calabria, Bryan Currie **EST.** 1945 **CASES** 140 000
PRODUCT RANGE ($8.95–21.95 CD) Sauvignon Blanc, Chardonnay, Shiraz, Cabernet Sauvignon; Outback Traminer Riesling, Semillon Sauvignon Blanc, Unwooded Chardonnay, Shiraz; Richland Sauvignon Blanc, Chardonnay, Shiraz, Merlot, Cabernet Merlot, Cabernet Sauvignon; Port and Liqueur Muscat; 3 Bridges range of Chardonnay, Shiraz, Durif, Cabernet Sauvignon; Golden Mist Botrytis Semillon.
SUMMARY Along with a number of Riverina producers, Westend is making a concerted move to lift both the quality and the packaging of its wines, spearheaded by the 3 Bridges range, which has an impressive array of gold medals to its credit since being first released in April 1997; this range is anchored in part on 20 hectares of estate vineyards. It has also ventured into the export market, with distribution in the UK, Germany, the US, New Zealand, South Korea, Hong Kong and Malyasia.

ΥΥΥΥΥ **3 Bridges Golden Mist Botrytis Semillon 2003** Deliciously complex and balanced botrytis style, the luscious sweetness perfectly offset by acidity; has it down pat. **RATING** 94 **DRINK** 2008 $ 19.95

ΥΥΥΥ **3 Bridges Durif 2002** An aggressive, slightly edgy bouquet, but a big, multi-flavoured palate with abundant dark berry, licorice and chocolate flavours. **RATING** 89 **DRINK** 2010 $ 19.95

3 Bridges Adelaide Hills Pinot Noir 2002 Big, solid, plummy fruit; plenty of weight; not complex, but may well develop in bottle. **RATING** 88 **DRINK** 2007 $ 21.95

3 Bridges Cabernet Sauvignon 2001 A solid mix of blackcurrant, blackberry and a splash of spice; savoury tannins, good length. **RATING** 87 **DRINK** 2010 $ 21.95

ΥΥΥ♀ **3 Bridges Chardonnay 2003** Plenty of mid-palate weight and flavour; peachy fruit and subtle oak; slightly short finish. **RATING** 86 **DRINK** Now $ 15.95

Richland Chardonnay 2003 **RATING** 86 **DRINK** Now $ 10.95

3 Bridges Merlot 2002 **RATING** 86 **DRINK** 2007 $ 21.95

Richland Cabernet Sauvignon 2003 Fresh, gently sweet red and blackcurrant fruit; good drink-now style. Screwcap. **RATING** 86 **DRINK** Now $ 11.90

Richland Shiraz 2003 **RATING** 85 **DRINK** 2007 $ 11.90

Richlands Sauvignon Blanc 2003 **RATING** 84 **DRINK** Now $ 10.95

3 Bridges Shiraz 2001 **RATING** 84 **DRINK** Now $ 19.95

ΥΥΥ **Outback Semillon Sauvignon Blanc 2003** **RATING** 83 $ 8.95

Outback Shiraz 2002 **RATING** 83 $ 8.95

Richland Merlot 2003 **RATING** 83 $ 11.90

Outback Traminer Riesling 2003 **RATING** 82 $ 8.95

Western Range Wines

★★★☆

Lot 88 Chittering Road, Lower Chittering, WA 6084 **REGION** Perth Hills
T (08) 9571 8800 **F** (08) 9571 8844 **OPEN** Wed–Sun 10–5
WINEMAKER Steve Hagan **EST.** 2001 **CASES** 42 000
PRODUCT RANGE ($11–25 CD) The wines are released in four disciplined price levels: Lot 88 varietals at the bottom; Goyamin Pool varietals; Julimar Viognier, Shiraz Viognier, Carnelian Shiraz; and organic wines (Chenin Chardonnay and Shiraz) at the top.
SUMMARY Between the mid-1990s and 2001 several prominent West Australians, including Marilyn Corderory, Malcolm McCusker, Terry and Kevin Prindiville and Tony Rechner, have established approximately 125 hectares of vines (under separate ownerships) in the Perth Hills, with a kaleidoscopic range of varietals. The next step was to join forces to build a substantial winery. This is a separate venture from the growers' individual vineyards, but it takes the grapes and then markets the wine under the Western Range brand. All in all, an impressive combination. Distribution through all mainland States, primarily by Australian Liquor Merchants. Exports to the UK, the US, Canada and Sweden.

 ▼▼▼▼ **Old Vine Grenache 2002** Closed with a screwcap, the bouquet is fragrant, the palate lively and fresh, with ripe raspberry, cherry and spice flavours, uncomplicated by oak or tannins. **RATING** 89 **DRINK** Now $ 14.30
Carnelian Shiraz 2001 A fragrant and piquant bouquet; fresh, zippy, lively style; slight dip on the finish. **RATING** 87 **DRINK** 2008 $ 18.35

 ▼▼▼▽ **8 Vineyard Chenin Blanc Verdelho 2002 RATING** 85 **DRINK** Now $ 12
Accord Shiraz 2002 RATING 84 **DRINK** 2007 $ 19

 ▼▼▼ **Lot 99 Frisky Rose 2003 RATING** 83 $ 12

Westgate Vineyard

NR

'Westgate', RMB 1124, Ararat, Vic 3377 **REGION** Grampians
T (03) 5356 2394 **F** (03) 5356 2594 **OPEN** By appointment
WINEMAKER Bruce Dalkin **EST.** 1999 **CASES** 200
PRODUCT RANGE ($17–19 CD) Riesling, Cabernet Shiraz.
SUMMARY Westgate has been in the Dalkin family ownership since the 1860s, and the present owners, Bruce and Robyn Dalkin, are the sixth generation owners. The property today focuses on grape production, a small winery, four and a half star accommodation, and wool production. Over 12 hectares of vineyards have been established since 1969, including a key holding of 10 hectares of shiraz; most of the grapes are sold to Mount Langi Ghiran and Seppelt Great Western, but a vigneron's licence was obtained in 1999 and a small amount of wine is made under the Westgate Vineyard label.

Wharncliffe

★★★

Summerleas Road, Kingston, Tas 7050 **REGION** Southern Tasmania
T (03) 6229 7147 **F** (03) 6229 2298 **OPEN** Weekends by appointment, **T** 0438 297 147
WINEMAKER Andrew Hood (Contract) **EST.** 1990 **CASES** 125
PRODUCT RANGE ($18 ML) Chardonnay.
SUMMARY With total plantings of 0.75 hectare, Wharncliffe could not exist without the type of contract winemaking service offered by Andrew Hood, which would be a pity, because the vineyard is beautifully situated on the doorstep of Mount Wellington, the Huon Valley and the Channel regions of southern Tasmania.

 ▼▼▼▽ **Chardonnay 2001 RATING** 85 **DRINK** Now $ 18

Whiskey Gully Wines

NR

Beverley Road, Severnlea, Qld 4352 **REGION** Granite Belt
T (07) 4683 5100 **F** (07) 4683 5155 **OPEN** 7 days 9–5
WINEMAKER Philippa Hambleton, Rod MacPherson **EST.** 1997 **CASES** 500
PRODUCT RANGE ($12–30 CD) Leaping Lizard Colombard, Hitching Rail Colombard Chardonnay, Opera House Unwooded Chardonnay, Beverley Chardonnay, Republic Red, Shiraz, Upper House Cabernet Sauvignon.

SUMMARY Close inspection of the winery letterhead discloses that The Media Mill Pty Ltd trades as Whiskey Gully Wines. It is no surprise, then, to find proprietor John Arlidge saying, 'Wine and politics are a heady mix; I have already registered the 2000 Republic Red as a voter in 26 marginal electorates and we are considering nominating it for Liberal Party pre-selection in Bennelong.' Wit to one side, John Arlidge has big long-range plans for Whiskey Gully Wines: to establish 40 hectares of vineyards, extending the varietal range with petit verdot, malbec, merlot, semillon and sauvignon blanc. At present the wines are made off-site, but if production and sales increase significantly, on-site winemaking will be progressively introduced.

Whispering Brook ★★★

165 Hill Street, Broke, NSW 2330 **REGION** Lower Hunter Valley
T (02) 9818 4126 **F** (02) 9818 4156 **OPEN** By appointment
WINEMAKER Stephen Dodd (Contract), Susan Frazier, Adam Bell **EST.** 2000 **CASES** 900
PRODUCT RANGE ($19–24 ML) Semillon, Chardonnay, Merlot, Shiraz.
SUMMARY Susan Frazier and Adam Bell say the choice of Whispering Brook was a result a of a 5-year search to find the ideal viticultural site whilst studying for wine science degrees at Charles Sturt University. Some may question whether the Broke subregion of the Hunter Valley needed such a persistent effort to locate, but the property does in fact have a combination of terra rossa loam soils on which the reds are planted, and sandy flats for the white wines. The partners have also established an olive grove of three different varieties and accommodation for between 6–14 guests in the large house set in the vineyard.

ＹＹＹＹ　**Semillon 2003** RATING 85 DRINK 2010 $19
　　　　Shiraz 2002 RATING 84 DRINK 2007 $24

Whispering Hills NR

580 Warburton Highway, Seville, Vic 3139 **REGION** Yarra Valley
T (03) 5964 2822 **F** (03) 5964 2064 **OPEN** Thurs–Mon 10–6, or by appointment
WINEMAKER Murray Lyons, MasterWineMakers (Contract) **EST.** 1985 **CASES** 1200
PRODUCT RANGE ($22–42 CD) Chardonnay, Pinot Noir, Shiraz, Cabernet Sauvignon.
SUMMARY The minuscule production of Whispering Hills from its 3.5-hectare vineyard is limited to four wines, which are sold by mail order and word of mouth, as well as at 20 or so local restaurants. While no tastings, Whispering Hills starred at the 2002 Concours des Vins du Victoria.

Whisson Lake ★★★☆

Lot 2 Gully Road, Carey Gully, SA 5144 **REGION** Adelaide Hills
T (08) 8390 1303 **F** (08) 8390 3822 **OPEN** By appointment
WINEMAKER Torbreck (Contract) **EST.** 1985 **CASES** 300
PRODUCT RANGE ($27.50–31.50 CD) Pinot Noir.
SUMMARY Mark Whisson (a plant biochemist) is primarily a grape grower, with 4.5 hectares of close-planted, steep-sloped north-facing vineyard on Mount Carey in the Piccadilly Valley. A small quantity of the production is made for the Whisson Lake label by Dave Powell of Torbreck fame. The wine has a consistent style — distinctly savoury — and ages well. His partner in the venture is Bruce Lake, an engineer living in Perth. Tiny quantities are exported to the US and the UK.

ＹＹＹＹ　**Pinot Noir 1999** Very much in the style of Whisson Lake, with foresty/savoury accents driving a long, though not particularly generous, palate. **RATING** 88 **DRINK** 2007

Whistler Wines ★★★★☆

Seppeltsfield Road, Marananga, SA 5355 **REGION** Barossa Valley
T (08) 8562 4942 **F** (08) 8562 4943 **OPEN** 7 days 10.30–5
WINEMAKER Rolf Binder, Christa Deans (Contract) **EST.** 1999 **CASES** 3000
PRODUCT RANGE ($12–35 CD) Unwooded Semillon, Late Harvest Semillon, Black Piper Sparkling Shiraz, Black Piper Sparkling Merlot, Shiraz, Merlot, Cabernet Merlot, Cabernet Sauvignon.
SUMMARY Whistler Wines had a dream start to its life at the 2000 Barossa Valley Wine Show, when its 2000 Semillon won trophies for the Best Dry White Semillon and for the Most Outstanding Barossa White Table Wine. Add to that the distinguished US importer Weygandt-Metzler, and it is

no surprise to find the sold out sign going up on the extremely attractive (modern) galvanised iron cellar-door building. The operation is presently based on 5 hectares of shiraz and 2 hectares each of semillon and merlot and 1 hectare of cabernet sauvignon, with an additional 4 hectares of grenache, mourvedre and riesling planted in 2001. The hope is to gradually increase production to match already existing market demands. Exports to the US and Canada.

ŸŸŸŸŸ **Cabernet Merlot 2002** Luscious cassis and blackcurrant; smooth and rich; ripe tannins, nice oak. Gold medal Barossa Valley Wine Show 2003. **RATING** 92 **DRINK** 2015 $ 19
Cabernet Sauvignon 2002 Rich, focused blackcurrant/blackberry aromas; similarly luscious and intense palate, oozing fruit. **RATING** 92 **DRINK** 2017 $ 21
Shiraz 2002 Rich blackberry, dark chocolate, plum and prune; supple, ripe tannins; good balance. **RATING** 90 **DRINK** 2012 $ 26
Merlot 2002 Powerful, savoury fruit and varietal character; dark berries, chocolate and olive; another tribute to the vintage. **RATING** 90 **DRINK** 2011 $ 23

ŸŸŸŸ **Semillon 2003** Glowing yellow-green, lit from within; round, fleshy, gentle tropical flavours; good acidity. Screwcap. **RATING** 88 **DRINK** Now $ 19
The Black Piper Sparkling Merlot NV Tangy, juicy, lemony; lingering finish. Only 400 bottles made. Spent 14 months in American oak, but how long in bottle? **RATING** 87 **DRINK** Now $ 35
The Black Piper Sparkling Shiraz NV Complex, very ripe plum pudding, blackberry and vanilla fruit, slightly sweet finish. 800 bottles made. Same non-vital statistics. **RATING** 87 **DRINK** 2007 $ 35

ŸŸŸŸ **Late Harvest Golden Semillon 2002** **RATING** 86 **DRINK** Now $ 12

Whitehorse Wines

NR

4 Reid Park Road, Mount Clear, Vic 3350 **REGION** Ballarat
T (03) 5330 1719 **F** (03) 5330 1288 **OPEN** Weekends 11–5
WINEMAKER Noel Myers **EST.** 1981 **CASES** 900
PRODUCT RANGE ($10–18 CD) Riesling, Riesling Muller Thurgau, Chardonnay, Pinot Noir, Cabernet Shiraz.
SUMMARY The Myers family has moved from grape growing to winemaking, utilising the attractive site on its sloping hillside south of Ballarat. Four hectares of vines are in production, with pinot noir and chardonnay the principal varieties.

Whitsend Estate

★★★

52 Boundary Road, Coldstream, Vic 3770 **REGION** Yarra Valley
T (03) 9739 1917 **F** (03) 9739 0217 **OPEN** By appointment
WINEMAKER Paul Evans **EST.** 1998 **CASES** 500
PRODUCT RANGE ($21–22 CD) Chardonnay, Merlot, Cabernet Sauvignon.
SUMMARY The Baldwin family, headed by Ross and Simone, but with Trish, Tim and Jenny Baldwin all involved in one way or another, have established a 13-hectare vineyard planted to pinot noir, shiraz, merlot and cabernet sauvignon. The lion's share of the production is sold to local wineries, but a small amount is retained and made for the Baldwins by Paul Evans.

ŸŸŸŸ **Chardonnay 2002** Complex cashew, melon and oak mix; the sweetness is a fraction distracting. **RATING** 87 **DRINK** 2007 $ 21

ŸŸŸ **Cabernet Sauvignon 2002** **RATING** 83 $ 22

ŸŸŸ **Merlot 2002** **RATING** 78 $ 22

Wignalls Wines

Chester Pass Road (Highway 1), Albany, WA 6330 **REGION** Albany
T (08) 9841 2848 **F** (08) 9842 9003 **OPEN** 7 days 12–4
WINEMAKER Rob Wignall **EST.** 1982 **CASES** 7000
PRODUCT RANGE ($16–30 CD) Sauvignon Blanc, Chardonnay, Late Harvest Frontignac, Pinot Noir, Shiraz, Cabernet Sauvignon, Tawny Port.

SUMMARY A noted producer of Pinot Noir which has extended the map for the variety in Australia. The Pinots have shown style and flair, but do age fairly quickly. The white wines are elegant, and show the cool climate to good advantage. A new winery was constructed and opened for the 1998 vintage, utilising the production from the 16 hectares of estate plantings. Exports to Japan, Singapore and Indonesia.

ΥΥΥΥΥ **Shiraz 2002** Very complex, compelling, cool-grown style; spicy blackberry and damson plum fruit; good texture, line and length; fine tannins. **RATING** 94 **DRINK** 2012 $ 21

ΥΥΥΥ **Sauvignon Blanc 2003** Fragrant gooseberry and herb aromas; lively, tangy, lemony gooseberry fruit. **RATING** 89 **DRINK** Now $ 16
Cabernet Sauvignon 2001 Olive, leaf, cedar, mint and blackcurrant in Bordeaux style; tannins OK. **RATING** 87 **DRINK** 2010 $ 25

ΥΥΥΥ **Chardonnay 2003 RATING** 86 **DRINK** 2007 $ 19.50
Pinot Noir 2002 Elegant, spicy and fragrant, with red strawberry flavours; lacks intensity. **RATING** 86 **DRINK** Now $ 27

Wild Broke Wines   NR

Milbrodale Road, Broke, NSW 2330 **REGION** Lower Hunter Valley
T (02) 6579 1065 **OPEN** Not
WINEMAKER Monarch Winemaking Services (Contract) **EST.** 1999 **CASES** 600
PRODUCT RANGE ($40 R) The Idlewild range of Wild Yeast Chardonnay, Succo Del Sol (dessert wine), Cabernet Shiraz, Barbera and Cabernet Franc.
SUMMARY Wild Broke Wines is a spin-off from Ryan Family Wines; it is a partnership between Matthew Ryan, who continues as viticulturist for Ryan Family Wines on Broke Estate and Minimbah Vineyards, and wife Tina Ryan, who continues to run Wild Rhino PR Marketing and Events in Sydney. At the present time it draws on 2 hectares of shiraz and cabernet sauvignon, and 1 hectare each of merlot, barbera, chardonnay and tempranillo.

ΥΥΥΥΥ **Idlewild Succo del Sol NV** A very interesting wine, blending 2001 and 2002. Liquid brandysnap, spice, glazed apricot and marmalade flavours from sun-dried grapes; French oak fermentation. Bold but successful. **RATING** 94 **DRINK** 2007

ΥΥΥΥ **Idlewild Cabernet Shiraz 1999** Light to medium-bodied; red and black fruits sweetened by well-integrated oak and its 14.4 degrees alcohol; comes together well. **RATING** 88 **DRINK** 2010
Idlewild Yeast Chardonnay 2001 Has the complexity the '02 doesn't have; pleasantly funky barrel ferment/bottle-developed aromas; plenty of sweet stone fruit to carry the funk. **RATING** 87 **DRINK** Now

ΥΥΥΥ **Idlewild Cabernet Franc 2002 RATING** 86 **DRINK** 2009
Idlewild Barbera 2001 RATING 86 **DRINK** 2008
Idlewild Wild Yeast Chardonnay 2002 RATING 85 **DRINK** Now

Wildcroft Estate   ★★★☆

98 Stanleys Road, Red Hill South, Vic 3937 **REGION** Mornington Peninsula
T (03) 5989 2646 **F** (03) 9783 9469 **OPEN** 7 days 10–5
WINEMAKER Phillip Jones (Contract) **EST.** 1988 **CASES** 650
PRODUCT RANGE ($26–59 CD) Black Sheep is the premium range of Shiraz and Cabernet Sauvignon; the second range is Wildcroft Chardonnay, Pinot Noir and Cabernet Sauvignon.
SUMMARY Wildcroft Estate is the brainchild of Devendra Singh, best known as the owner of Siddhartha, established in 1984 and one of Victoria's oldest Indian restaurants. In 1988 he purchased the land upon which 4 hectares of pinot noir, chardonnay, shiraz and cabernet sauvignon have been established, with the management and much of the physical work carried out by Devendra's wife Shashi Singh, who is currently undertaking a viticulture course. The vineyard is one of the few unirrigated vineyards on the peninsula, and the wines are made by the renowned Phillip Jones (of Bass Phillip). The mudbrick cellar door also has a restaurant — Café 98 — allowing Devendra Singh to explore the novel matching of Indian food with wine. Chef Lindsey Perry serves modern cuisine with Indian and Middle Eastern influences, using local produce wherever possible.

Wild Dog   NR

South Road, Warragul, Vic 3820 **REGION** Gippsland
T (03) 5623 1117 **F** (03) 5623 6402 **OPEN** 7 days 9–5
WINEMAKER John Farrington **EST.** 1982 **CASES** 3000
PRODUCT RANGE ($12–22 CD) Riesling, Unwooded Chardonnay, Chardonnay, Wild Dog Sparkling,
Rose, Pinot Noir, Shiraz, Cabernets.
SUMMARY An aptly named winery which produces somewhat rustic wines from its 12 hectares of
estate vineyards; even the Farringtons say that the Shiraz comes 'with a bite', also pointing out that
there is minimal handling, fining and filtration.

Wild Duck Creek Estate   NR

Spring Flat Road, Heathcote, Vic 3523 **REGION** Heathcote
T (03) 5433 3133 **F** (03) 5433 3133 **OPEN** By appointment
WINEMAKER David Anderson **EST.** 1980 **CASES** 4000
PRODUCT RANGE ($25–75 CD) Springflat Shiraz, Alan's Cabernets, Alan's Cabernets Pressings, The
Blend, Duck Muck, Cabernet Sauvignon Reserve, Sparkling Duck 2.
SUMMARY The first release of Wild Duck Creek Estate from the 1991 vintage marked the end of 12
years of effort by David and Diana Anderson. They commenced planting the 4.5-hectare vineyard in
1980, made their first tiny quantities of wine in 1986, the first commercial quantities of wine in 1991,
and built their winery and cellar-door facility in 1993. Exports to the US (where Duck Muck has
become a cult wine), Canada, the UK, Singapore, Belgium and New Zealand.

Wild Soul   ★★★

Horans Gorge Road, Glen Aplin, Qld 4381 **REGION** Granite Belt
T (07) 4683 4201 **F** (07) 4683 4201 **OPEN** Weekends and public holidays 10–4
WINEMAKER Andy Boullier **EST.** 1995 **CASES** 25
PRODUCT RANGE ($13–16 CD) Shiraz, Cabernet Sauvignon.
SUMMARY Andy and Beth Boullier have been on the land their whole lives, working in various
capacities, before buying their small property at Glen Aplin. They have established a little over 1
hectare of vines, more or less equally split between cabernet sauvignon and shiraz, with a little
merlot. They use organic principles in growing the fruit, which provides challenges of themselves,
challenges compounded by birds, drought, kangaroos and finally bushfires in 2003 which killed 20
per cent of the vines and decimated the crop. A small winery enables Andy Boullier to make the wine
on-site.

▼▼▼▼ **Cabernet Sauvignon 2002** Dense blackcurrant/blackberry/anise fruit; powerful and
completely unevolved; patience will repay. **RATING** 87 **DRINK** 2015 $16

▼▼▼▽ **Shiraz 2002 RATING** 84 **DRINK** 2009 $15

Wildwood   ★★★★

St John's Lane, Wildwood, Bulla, Vic 3428 **REGION** Sunbury
T (03) 9307 1118 **F** (03) 9331 1590 **OPEN** 7 days 10–6
WINEMAKER Dr Wayne Stott, Kirk Macdonald **EST.** 1983 **CASES** 2000
PRODUCT RANGE ($20–30 CD) Chardonnay, Pinot Noir, Shiraz, Cabernets.
SUMMARY Wildwood is situated just 4 kilometres past Melbourne airport, at an altitude of 130
metres, in the Oaklands Valley, which provides unexpected views back to Port Phillip Bay and the
Melbourne skyline. Plastic surgeon Wayne Stott has taken what is very much a part-time activity
rather more seriously than most by undertaking (and completing) the Wine Science degree at
Charles Sturt University. Four years of drought has cut production and forced the early release of the
red wines.

▼▼▼▼▽ **Pinot Noir 2002** Fragrant, stylish spice, plum and black cherry fruits; long, lingering
finish; not forced. **RATING** 91 **DRINK** 2007 $25

▼▼▼▼ **Chardonnay 2003** Subtle melon, fig and cashew barrel-ferment/malolactic-ferment
inputs; lacks intensity, but is well balanced. **RATING** 87 **DRINK** Now $20

Wildwood of Yallingup ★★★★

Caves Road, Yallingup, WA 6282 **REGION** Margaret River
T (08) 9755 2066 **F** (08) 9754 1389 **OPEN** 7 days 10–5
WINEMAKER James Pennington **EST.** 1984 **CASES** 3000
PRODUCT RANGE ($14–28 CD) Hotham Valley Semillon, Semillon Sauvignon Blanc, Sunrise White, Pennington Chardonnay, Sparkling Dawn, Sparkling Dusk, Pinot Noir, Sunset Red, Shiraz Cabernet, Pennington Cabernet Merlot, Tawny Port.
SUMMARY In the wake of the demise of the Hotham Valley wine group, and its subsequent restructuring and renaming, James Pennington acquired the 5.5-hectare Wildwood vineyard; it was planted in the mid-1980s, having been first cleared in the late 1940s. The vineyard was established without irrigation and remains dry-grown. All of the future releases will be released either under the Wildwood of Yallingup label or Pennington, but small stocks of previously bottled and labelled Hotham Valley Semillon were being sold in 2003.

ŶŶŶŶŶ **Pennington Chardonnay 2002** Considerable richness and depth; complex peach and butterscotch; fruit has eaten the oak. **RATING** 92 **DRINK** 2010 $28
Pennington Cabernet Merlot 2002 Complex array of blackberry, blackcurrant, cedar and spice flavours; fine tannins to close. **RATING** 90 **DRINK** 2011 $28

ŶŶŶŶ **Semillon 2003** Full-flavoured mix of citrus, herbs and grass; smooth and supple, well balanced. **RATING** 89 **DRINK** 2010 $18
Pinot Noir 2002 Spice, cedar and oak over plummy fruit; good mouthfeel and length. **RATING** 87 **DRINK** Now $20

ŶŶŶŶ **Semillon Sauvignon Blanc 2003** **RATING** 86 **DRINK** 2007 $16

Wilkie Estate NR

Lot 1 Heaslip Road, Penfield, SA 5121 **REGION** Adelaide Plains
T (08) 8284 7655 **F** (08) 8284 7618 **OPEN** 7 days 10–5
WINEMAKER Trevor Spurr **EST.** 1990
PRODUCT RANGE A range of varietally denominated table wines reflecting the plantings.
SUMMARY Trevor and Bill Spurr have 17.5 hectares of organic-certified vineyards planted to verdelho, cabernet sauvignon, merlot and ruby cabernet. They make the wine on-site, and, in addition to cellar-door and mail order sales, have established exports to the UK and Japan.

Willespie ★★★☆

Harmans Mill Road, Wilyabrup via Cowaramup, WA 6284 **REGION** Margaret River
T (08) 9755 6248 **F** (08) 9755 6210 **OPEN** 7 days 10.30–5
WINEMAKER Kevin Squance **EST.** 1976 **CASES** 10 000
PRODUCT RANGE ($16–60 R) Riesling, Semillon Sauvignon Blanc, Verdelho, Chardonnay, Shiraz, Cabernets, Cabernet Sauvignon, Cabernet Sauvignon Reserve; Harmans Mill White and Harmans Mill Red are cheaper second-label wines.
SUMMARY Willespie has produced many attractive white wines over the years, typically in brisk, herbaceous Margaret River style. All are fruit rather than oak-driven; the newer Merlot also shows promise. The wines have had such success that the Squance family (which founded and owns Willespie) has substantially increased winery capacity, drawing upon an additional 26 hectares of estate vineyards now in bearing. Exports to Europe, the US, Singapore and Hong Kong.

ŶŶŶŶ **Semillon Sauvignon Blanc 2000** Nice bottle-developed aromas and flavours; good texture. Food style. **RATING** 87 **DRINK** Now $20

Williams Springs Road NR

76 Dauncey Street, Kingscote, Kangaroo Island, SA 5223 **REGION** Kangaroo Island
T (08) 8553 2053 **F** (08) 8553 3042 **OPEN** By appointment
WINEMAKER Contract **EST.** 1995 **CASES** 200
PRODUCT RANGE Chardonnay, Shiraz.

SUMMARY Roger and Kate Williams have established 11 hectares of chardonnay, cabernet sauvignon, shiraz and petit verdot. Most of the grapes are sold to Kangaroo Island Trading Co, with a small amount of chardonnay and shiraz made under the Williams Springs Road label. Cellar-door sales through the head office at Dauncey Street.

Willow Bridge Estate ★★★★☆

Gardin Court Drive, Dardanup, WA 6236 **REGION** Geographe
T (08) 9728 0055 **F** (08) 9728 0066 **OPEN** 7 days 11–5
WINEMAKER David Crawford **EST.** 1997 **CASES** 25 000
PRODUCT RANGE ($13.50–60 CD) Sauvignon Blanc Semillon, Chenin Blanc, Shiraz, Merlot, Cabernet Sauvignon; Winemaker's Reserve range of Sauvignon Blanc, Semillon Sauvignon Blanc, Chardonnay, Cabernet Rose, Black Dog Shiraz, Shiraz, Cabernet Sauvignon Merlot.
SUMMARY The Dewar family has followed a fast track in developing Willow Bridge Estate since acquiring their spectacular 180-hectare hillside property in the Ferguson Valley in 1996. Sixty hectares of chardonnay, semillon, sauvignon blanc, shiraz and cabernet sauvignon have already been planted, with tempranillo added in the spring of 2000, and another 10 hectares due to be planted over the next year or two. A state-of-the-art winery which is capable of handling the 1200 to 1500 tonnes from the estate plantings has been constructed. Exports to the US, Canada, the UK, France, Germany and Hong Kong.

ŦŦŦŦŦ **Winemaker's Reserve Semillon Sauvignon Blanc 2003** A clean, rich, smooth tropical and lemon mix; lingering finish. **RATING** 93 **DRINK** 2008 $18
Sauvignon Blanc Semillon 2003 A very intense, highly focused and long mix of lemon and tropical fruit; no phenolics. **RATING** 92 **DRINK** 2007 $16.50
Winemaker's Reserve Shiraz 2002 Medium-bodied but complex; spicy savoury black fruits, persistent but fine tannins; good length and aftertaste. **RATING** 90 **DRINK** 2013 $28
Winemaker's Reserve Shiraz 2001 Massive wine, with strong dark chocolate and blackberry fruit; powerful tannins; needs lots of time. **RATING** 90 **DRINK** 2015 $28

ŦŦŦŦ **Winemaker's Reserve Sauvignon Blanc 2003** Powerful, intense, faintly funky bouquet; concentrated tropical/gooseberry palate; good length. Cork. **RATING** 89 **DRINK** Now $18
Chenin Blanc 2003 Full, rich, tropical and pineapple aromas and flavours; solid, but not sweet. **RATING** 87 **DRINK** 2007 $13.50

ŦŦŦŦ **Winemaker's Reserve Cabernet Sauvignon Rose 2003** **RATING** 86 **DRINK** Now $17
Shiraz 2002 **RATING** 86 **DRINK** 2009 $17
Cabernet Sauvignon 2002 **RATING** 85 **DRINK** 2008 $17
Cabernet Sauvignon Merlot 2002 **RATING** 84 **DRINK** 2007 $15

Willow Creek ★★★★☆

166 Balnarring Road, Merricks North, Vic 3926 **REGION** Mornington Peninsula
T (03) 5989 7448 **F** (03) 5989 7584 **OPEN** 7 days 10–5
WINEMAKER Phil Kerney **EST.** 1989 **CASES** 10 000
PRODUCT RANGE ($15–45 CD) In two varietal ranges, the top under the Tulum label, the other under the Willow Creek label.
SUMMARY Yet another significant player in the Mornington Peninsula area, with 9 hectares of vines planted to cabernet sauvignon, chardonnay and pinot noir. Expansion of the cellar door was completed by January 1998, with a winery constructed for the 1998 vintage. The restaurant is open for lunch 7 days and Friday and Saturday nights for dinner. The wines are exported to the US and the UK.

ŦŦŦŦ **Pinot Noir 2001** Excellent youthful hue; aromatic strawberry and cherry fruit offset by gently savoury, ultra-fine tannins; great mouthfeel and a long finish. **RATING** 92 **DRINK** 2008 $25
Unoaked Chardonnay 2001 One of the most complex unoaked Chardonnays I have encountered; exotically smoky, tangy and long; quite striking and special bottle-developed characters. **RATING** 91 **DRINK** 2007 $15
Tulum Cabernet Sauvignon 2001 Medium-bodied, savoury blackberry fruit; avoids minty/leafy notes. Good texture and oak handling. Has developed well. **RATING** 90 **DRINK** 2011 $35

Ꭲ Ꭲ Ꭲ Ꭲ **Pinot Noir 2000** Light to medium-bodied; quite sweet and gentle overall impact; good balance. **RATING** 89 **DRINK** Now $ 25
Pinot Saignee 2003 Fragrant strawberry and cherry aromas; light, crisp and clean. **RATING** 87 **DRINK** Now $ 20
Cabernet Sauvignon 2000 Obvious cool-grown style; cassis, berry, leaf and mint; light tannins. **RATING** 87 **DRINK** 2008 $ 25

Ꭲ Ꭲ Ꭲ Ꭲ **Cabernet Sauvignon 1999** **RATING** 85 **DRINK** Now $ 25
Unoaked Chardonnay 2003 **RATING** 84 **DRINK** Now $ 15

Willowvale Wines

NR

Black Swamp Road, Tenterfield, NSW 2372 **REGION** Northern Slopes Zone
T (02) 6736 3589 **F** (02) 6736 3753 **OPEN** 7 days 9–5
WINEMAKER John Morley **EST.** 1994 **CASES** 1200
PRODUCT RANGE ($14–25 CD) Federation Classic White, Ambrosia, London Bridge Chardonnay, Late Harvest Riesling, London Bridge Dry Red, London Bridge Soft Red, London Bridge Merlot, Bushranger Musket, Centenary of Federation Port.
SUMMARY John and Lyn Morley commenced establishing 1.8 hectares of vineyard of equal portions of chardonnay, merlot and cabernet sauvignon in 1994, with further planting in 1999 and 2000. The vineyard is at an altitude of 940 metres and was the first in the growing Tenterfield region. Advanced vineyard climatic monitoring systems have been installed, and a new winery building was constructed and equipped in time for the 2000 vintage.

🐛 Wills Domain Vineyard

35 Ash Grove, Duncraig, WA 6023 (postal) **REGION** Margaret River
T (08) 9755 2172 **F** (08) 9755 2172 **OPEN** Not
WINEMAKER Bruce Dukes (Contract) **EST.** 2000 **CASES** 5200
PRODUCT RANGE ($15–28 ML) Semillon Reserve, Classic Dry White, Chardonnay, Shiraz, Cabernet Sauvignon.
SUMMARY Another newcomer to the Margaret River, with a little over 10 hectares of semillon, chardonnay, viognier, cabernet sauvignon, merlot, malbec, shiraz, cabernet franc and petit verdot under the control of Darren Haunold. The wines are contract-made, and sold by mail order and through limited retail outlets.

Ꭲ Ꭲ Ꭲ Ꭲ Ꭲ **Semillon 2002** Elegant and lingering; a beautifully sculpted wine; subtle oak, superb aftertaste. **RATING** 96 **DRINK** 2014 $ 19.80

Ꭲ Ꭲ Ꭲ Ꭲ **Cabernet Sauvignon 2002** **RATING** 84 **DRINK** Now $ 28

Will Taylor Wines

1B Victoria Avenue, Unley Park, SA 5061 **REGION** Warehouse
T (08) 8271 6122 **F** (08) 8271 6122 **OPEN** By appointment
WINEMAKER Various contract **EST.** 1997 **CASES** 1500
PRODUCT RANGE ($21–40 R) Clare Valley Riesling, Hunter Valley Semillon, Adelaide Hills Sauvignon Blanc, Yarra Valley/Geelong Pinot Noir, Coonawarra Cabernet Sauvignon.
SUMMARY Will Taylor is a partner in the leading Adelaide law firm Finlaysons and specialises in wine law. Together with Suzanne Taylor, he has established a classic negociant wine business, having wines contract-made to his specification. Moreover, he chooses what he considers to be the best regions for each variety; he added a Geelong/Yarra Valley Pinot Noir in 2000. Most of the wine is sold to restaurants, with small volumes sold to a select group of fine wine stores and mail order. Exports to the US.

Ꭲ Ꭲ Ꭲ Ꭲ **Clare Valley Riesling 2003** A very firm, tight wine with slate, mineral and a hint of lime; died-in-the-wool stayer. **RATING** 91 **DRINK** 2013 $ 21
Coonawarra Cabernet Sauvignon 2002 Attractive cassis and blackcurrant; medium-bodied, long and supple. **RATING** 91 **DRINK** 2012 $ 40
Adelaide Hills Sauvignon Blanc 2003 Spotlessly clean; attractive mix of herb, gooseberry and passionfruit; crisp finish. **RATING** 90 **DRINK** Now $ 21

Yarra Valley/Geelong Pinot Noir 2002 Elegant, unforced style; seamless plum and cherry fruit; needs a few years. **RATING** 90 **DRINK** 2008 $ 40

ŸŸŸŸ **Hunter Valley Semillon 2003** Plenty of citrus, lemon and herb fruit; should develop into a White Burgundy style sooner rather than later. **RATING** 89 **DRINK** 2008 $ 25

Hunter Valley Semillon 1999 Attractive, quite rich bottle-developed flavours; soft, moderate length; tails off on the finish. **RATING** 88 **DRINK** Now $ 25

Wilmot Hills Vineyard   NR

407 Back Road, Wilmot, Tas 7310 **REGION** Northern Tasmania
T (03) 6492 1193 **F** (03) 6492 1193 **OPEN** 7 days 9–7
WINEMAKER John Cole, Ruth Cole **EST.** 1991
PRODUCT RANGE ($12–35 CD) Muller Thurgau Gewurztraminer, Gamay, Pinot Noir, El Niño Pinot Noir, fruit wines and ciders.
SUMMARY The beautiful Wilmot Hills Vineyard is situated on the western side of Lake Barrington, not far from the Cradle Mountain road, with marvellous views to Mount Roland and the adjacent peaks. It is very much a family affair, established by John and Ruth Cole, and produces both wine and cider. John Cole spent 18 years in Melbourne participating in engineering design and some graphic art; Ruth worked in the hospitality industry for 10 years and has made fruit wines for 20 years. The neat on-site winery was both designed and built by the Coles, as was much of the wine and cider-making equipment.

Wilson's Legana Vineyard   NR

24 Vale Street, Prospect Vale, Tas 7250 **REGION** Northern Tasmania
T (03) 6344 8030 **F** (03) 6343 2937 **OPEN** By appointment
WINEMAKER Michael Wilson **EST.** 1966 **CASES** 150
PRODUCT RANGE Pinot Noir, Cabernet Sauvignon.
SUMMARY After several changes in ownership, what was the original Legana Vineyard of Heemskerk is now owned by Michael and Mary Wilson, who have appended their names to the brand. Michael Wilson, with a viticulture course under his belt and a little home winemaking experience, has now taken on full responsibility for all aspects of the business.

Wilson Vineyard   ★★★★☆

Polish Hill River, Sevenhill via Clare, SA 5453 **REGION** Clare Valley
T (08) 8843 4310 **OPEN** Weekends 10–4
WINEMAKER John Wilson, Daniel Wilson **EST.** 1974 **CASES** 4000
PRODUCT RANGE ($12.50–26.50 CD) Gallery Series Riesling, DJW Riesling, Chardonnay, Leucothea (sweet), Shiraz, Hippocrene Sparkling Burgundy, Zinfandel, Cabernet Sauvignon.
SUMMARY Dr John Wilson is a tireless ambassador for the Clare Valley and for wine (and its beneficial effect on health) in general. His wines are made using techniques and philosophies garnered early in his wine career and can occasionally be idiosyncratic, but in recent years have been most impressive. The wines are sold through the cellar door and by retail outlets in Sydney, Melbourne, Brisbane and Adelaide; no mailing list. Exports to the US.

ŸŸŸŸŸ **DJW Riesling 2003** Bursting with intense, sweet lime fruit; tropical nuances; clean as a whistle. **RATING** 95 **DRINK** 2018 $ 19.50

ŸŸŸŸŸ **Gallery Series Riesling 2003** Aromatic and flowery bouquet; remarkably intense, flavour-packed and long. **RATING** 93 **DRINK** 2015 $ 19.50

Polish Hill River Shiraz 2001 Rich, ripe blackberry, prune and dark chocolate fruit; mouthfilling and fleshy; a thoroughly sexy wine. Screwcapped. **RATING** 92 **DRINK** 2021 $ 26

ŸŸŸŸ **Cabernet Sauvignon 2001 RATING** 86 **DRINK** 2010 $ 23

🐟 Wily Trout ★★★★

Marakei–Nanima Road, via Hall, NSW 2618 **REGION** Canberra District
T (02) 6230 2487 **F** (02) 6230 2211 **OPEN** 7 days 10–5
WINEMAKER Dr Roger Harris, Andrew McEwen (Contract) **EST.** 1998 **CASES** 750
PRODUCT RANGE ($18–30 CD) Sauvignon Blanc, Chardonnay, Pinot Noir, Shiraz, Merlot, Cabernet Sauvignon, Sparkling Brut Reserve.
SUMMARY The 20-hectare Wily Trout Vineyard shares its home with the Poachers Pantry, a renowned gourmet smokehouse. Thus the Smokehouse Café doubles as a tasting room and cellar door. The quality of the wines is very good, and a testimonial to the skills of the contract winemakers. The northeast-facing slopes, at an elevation of 720 metres, provide some air drainage and hence protection against spring frosts.

🍷🍷🍷🍷 **Shiraz 2002** Fragrant, bright and fresh fruit-driven style; an array of red and black fruits; soft, lingering tannins. **RATING** 90 **DRINK** 2012 $ 24

🍷🍷🍷🍷 **Sauvignon Blanc 2003** Powerful, punchy style; herb, grass, lemon and some stone fruit. **RATING** 88 **DRINK** Now $ 18
Chardonnay 2003 Clean, light-bodied; citrus, stone fruit and mineral; clean finish. **RATING** 87 **DRINK** Now $ 18

🍷🍷🍷🍷 **Pinot Noir 2002** **RATING** 86 **DRINK** Now $ 24
Merlot 2002 **RATING** 86 **DRINK** 2008 $ 30

Wimbaliri Wines ★★★☆

Barton Highway, Murrumbateman, NSW 2582 **REGION** Canberra District
T (02) 6227 5921 **F** (02) 6227 5921 **OPEN** Weekends 10–5, or by appointment
WINEMAKER John Andersen **EST.** 1988 **CASES** 700
PRODUCT RANGE ($19–24 CD) Chardonnay, Pinot Noir, Shiraz, Cabernet Merlot.
SUMMARY John and Margaret Andersen moved to the Canberra district in 1987 and commenced the establishment of their vineyard at Murrumbateman in 1988; the property borders two highly regarded Canberra producers, Doonkuna and Clonakilla. The vineyard is close-planted with a vertical trellis system, and has a total of 2.2 hectares planted to chardonnay, pinot noir, shiraz, cabernet sauvignon and merlot (plus a few vines of cabernet franc).

🍷🍷🍷🍷 **Pinot Noir 2002** Quite rich; plum and black cherry at the fully ripe end of the varietal spectrum; lots of overall flavour; tannins evident but balanced. Worth cellaring. Grown at 620 metres. **RATING** 89 **DRINK** 2007 $ 24
Chardonnay 2002 Full-bodied rich and ripe yellow peach and tropical fruit aromas and flavours; oak in the background. **RATING** 88 **DRINK** 2007 $ 19

🍷🍷🍷🍷 **Cabernet Merlot 2001** **RATING** 85 **DRINK** 2009 $ 22

Winbirra Vineyard ★★★★

173 Point Leo Road, Red Hill South, Vic 3937 **REGION** Mornington Peninsula
T (03) 5989 2109 **F** (03) 5989 2109 **OPEN** By appointment
WINEMAKER Sandro Moselle (Contract) **EST.** 1990 **CASES** 450
PRODUCT RANGE ($15–25 ML) Pinot Noir, Pinot Meunier, White Pinot.
SUMMARY Winbirra is a small, family-owned and run vineyard which has been producing grapes since 1990, between then and 1997 selling the grapes to local winemakers. Since 1997 the wine has been contract-made and sold under the Winbirra label. There are 1.5 hectares of pinot noir (with three clones) and a 0.5 hectare of pinot meunier sourced from Best's vineyard at Great Western.

🍷🍷🍷🍷 **Pinot Noir 2001** Very powerful and intense; laden with ripe plummy fruit; strongly varietal; developing slowly. **RATING** 90 **DRINK** Now $ 25

🍷🍷🍷🍷 **Pinot Meunier 2001** **RATING** 84 **DRINK** Now $ 18

Winbourne Wines

Bunnan Road, Scone, NSW 2337 **REGION** Upper Hunter Valley
T 0417 650 0834 **F** (02) 6545 1636 **OPEN** By appointment
WINEMAKER John Hordern, Stephen Hagan, Michael De Iuliis **EST.** 1996 **CASES** 3000
PRODUCT RANGE ($11–21 ML) Semillon, Verdelho, Chardonnay, Shiraz, Merlot.
SUMMARY David White, a legal contemporary of mine, whom I have known for 40 years, is one of the faces behind Winbourne Wines. He still practises law at his law firm in Muswellbrook, but has also established a little under 50 hectares of vineyards planted to semillon, chardonnay, verdelho, shiraz, merlot and cabernet sauvignon. The lion's share of the production is sold as grapes, a little made into wine by several Hunter Valley winemakers. Says David, 'it could well be wondered why we are doing — have done — this'. I guess it simply proves that old lawyers are not necessarily wise lawyers.

▼▼▼▼♈ **Hunter Valley Estate Chardonnay 2002** A complex trace of funky reduction on the bouquet, but redeemed by the palate, with ripe citrus stone fruit, good depth and length; minimal oak. **RATING** 90 **DRINK** Now $ 21

▼▼▼▼ **Semillon 2001** Clean and fresh; lively herb and citrus flavours; good balance and length; zesty finish. **RATING** 89 **DRINK** 2010 $ 16
Hunter Valley Estate Shiraz 2001 Medium red; impressive, savoury black fruit aromas; sweet fruit on finish; good oak and tannins. **RATING** 89 **DRINK** 2011 $ 21

▼▼▼♈ **Dart Brook Hunter Valley Verdelho Single Vineyard 2002** Well above average, with attractive citrus tones and a long, zesty, lingering palate. **RATING** 86 **DRINK** Now $ 11
Dart Brook Hunter Valley Merlot 2002 RATING 84 **DRINK** Now $ 11
Merlot 2001 RATING 84 **DRINK** 2007 $ 12

▼▼▼ **Verdelho 2001 RATING** 83 $ 12
Melness Hunter Valley Chardonnay 2002 RATING 82 $ 11
Chardonnay 2001 RATING 82 $ 16

▼▼♈ **Melness Merlot Single Vineyard 2002 RATING** 79 $ 11

🐌 Winburndale

NR

116 Saint Anthony's Creek Road, Bathurst, NSW 2795 **REGION** Central Ranges Zone
T (02) 6337 3134 **F** (02) 6337 3134 **OPEN** Not
WINEMAKER David Lowe (Contract) **EST.** 1998
PRODUCT RANGE A range of varietally denominated table wines reflecting the plantings.
SUMMARY Michael Burleigh and family acquired the 200-hectare Winburndale property in September 1998: 160 hectares is forest, to be kept as a nature reserve; three separate vineyards, each with its own site characteristics, have been planted, under the direction of viticulturist Mark Renzaglia. The winery paddock has 2.5 hectares of shiraz facing due west at an altitude of 800–820 metres; the south paddock, with north and northwest aspects, and altitudes of 790–810 metres, is planted to chardonnay (1.2 hectares), shiraz (1 hectare) and cabernet sauvignon (3.5 hectares). The home paddock is the most level, with a slight north aspect, and has 1.2 hectares each of merlot and cabernet franc. The name, incidentally, derives from Lachlan Macquarie's exploration of the Blue Mountains in 1815.

🐌 Windance Wines

Lot 12, Loc 589, Caves Road, Yallingup, WA 6282 **REGION** Margaret River
T (08) 9755 2293 **F** (08) 9755 2293 **OPEN** Sep–May 7 days 10–5, June–Aug Fri–Mon 10–5
WINEMAKER Dave Watson, Mark Lane, Janice McDonald **EST.** 1998 **CASES** 3000
PRODUCT RANGE ($14–35 CD) Sauvignon Blanc, Semillon Sauvignon Blanc, Chenin Blanc, Rose, Shiraz, Reserve Shiraz, Cabernet Merlot, Reserve Cabernet Merlot.
SUMMARY Drew and Rosemary Brent-White own this family business, situated 5 kilometres south of Yallingup. A little over 6.5 hectares of sauvignon blanc, shiraz, merlot and cabernet sauvignon have been established, incorporating sustainable land management and organic farming practices where possible. The wines are exclusively estate-grown, and are sold through the cellar door and Perth CBD outlets serviced directly from the winery.

ΨΨΨΨ̈ **Shiraz 2002** An elegant array of red and black fruits; medium-bodied; touch of vanilla oak and fine tannins. Screwcap. Trophy for Best Shiraz 2003 Margaret River Wine Show. **RATING** 92 **DRINK** 2015 $ 35

ΨΨΨΨ **Cabernet Merlot 2002** Spicy and olive overtones to blackcurrant fruit; light to medium-bodied, slippery tannins; controlled oak. Screwcap. **RATING** 89 **DRINK** 2012 $ 16.20

Windarra
NR

De Beyers Road, Pokolbin, NSW 2321 **REGION** Lower Hunter Valley
T (02) 4998 7648 **F** (02) 4998 7648 **OPEN** Tues–Sun 10–5
WINEMAKER Tom Andresen-Jung **EST.** 1985 **CASES** 2500
PRODUCT RANGE ($10–26.50 CD) Semillon, Chardonnay, Rose, Shiraz, White Liqueur Port, Old Tawny Port, Fair Dinkum Herbal Port, Honey Meade, Gold Wine (mead, with 22-carat gold flakes), White Liqueur Port, Egg Wine Liqueur, Chocolate Liqueur.
SUMMARY The Andresen family has 6 hectares of semillon, chardonnay and shiraz; the wines are contract-made. The exotic array of fortified wines are likely to come from further afield, and are all aimed at the tourist market.

Windermere Wines
NR

Lot 3 Watters Road, Ballandean, Qld 4382 **REGION** Granite Belt
T (07) 4684 1353 **F** (07) 4684 1353 **OPEN** 7 days 9.30–5
WINEMAKER Wayne Beecham, Kate Beecham **EST.** 1995 **CASES** 500
PRODUCT RANGE ($11–17 CD) Chardonnay, Lilybrook DW Chardonnay Semillon, Sangiovese Merlot Cabernet, Millroad DR Cabernet Merlot, Shiraz, Liqueur Muscat; a selection of liqueurs and fruit wines.
SUMMARY After spending 3 years travelling in Europe (1983–86), Wayne Beecham returned to Australia to take up a position with what was then Thomas Hardy Wines, and specifically to establish the RhineCastle wine distribution in Queensland. During the next 7.5 years he studied wine marketing at Roseworthy while working for Hardys, but in 1993 he, wife Julie and daughter Kate decided to move to the Granite Belt to establish Windermere Wines from the ground up. His long service with Hardys stood him in good stead, landing him a cellar position at Hardys Tintara in the 1994 vintage, working with winemaker David O'Leary. In typical Australian fashion, Wayne Beecham says they decided on the Granite Belt because 'if we were to succeed, we might as well do it in the toughest new region in the industry'.

Windowrie Estate
★★★

Windowrie, Canowindra, NSW 2804 **REGION** Cowra
T (02) 6344 3234 **F** (02) 6344 3227 **OPEN** 7 days 10–6 at the Mill, Vaux Street, Cowra
WINEMAKER John Holmes **EST.** 1988 **CASES** 32 000
PRODUCT RANGE ($14–26 CD) Cowra Chardonnay, Cowra Cabernet Shiraz; The Mill range of Traminer, Sauvignon Blanc, Verdelho, Chardonnay, Shiraz, Merlot, Sangiovese, Petit Verdot, Cabernet Merlot; Family Reserve Chardonnay, Family Reserve Shiraz.
SUMMARY Windowrie Estate was established in 1988 on a substantial grazing property at Canowindra, 30 kilometres north of Cowra and in the same viticultural region. A portion of the grapes from the 116-hectare vineyard is sold to other makers, with increasing quantities being made for the Windowrie Estate and The Mill labels, the Chardonnays enjoying show success. The cellar door is situated in a flour mill built in 1861 from local granite. It ceased operations in 1905 and lay unoccupied for 91 years until restored by the O'Dea family. Exports to the UK, Europe and the US.

ΨΨΨΨ **The Mill Chardonnay 2003** Clean and fresh; nicely balanced nectarine, peach and subliminal oak. **RATING** 87 **DRINK** Now $ 14

ΨΨΨΨ̈ **The Mill Verdelho 2003 RATING** 85 **DRINK** Now $ 15
The Mill Petit Verdot 2002 RATING 85 **DRINK** 2008 $ 14
Sangiovese 2002 RATING 84 **DRINK** 2007 $ 14

ΨΨΨ **Family Reserve Chardonnay 2000 RATING** 82 $ 22

Windsors Edge

NR

McDonalds Road, Pokolbin, NSW 2320 **REGION** Lower Hunter Valley
T (02) 4998 7737 **F** (02) 4998 7737 **OPEN** Fri–Mon 10–5, or by appointment
WINEMAKER Tim Windsor, Jessie Windsor **EST.** 1996 **CASES** 1500
PRODUCT RANGE ($14–30 CD) Semillon, Semillon Chardonnay, Verdelho, Chardonnay, Rose, Shiraz,
Sparkling Shiraz, Shiraz, Coonawarra Cabernet Sauvignon, Port.
SUMMARY In 1995 Tim Windsor (a Charles Sturt graduate in winemaking) and wife Jessie (an
industrial chemist) purchased the old Black Creek picnic racetrack at the northern end of
McDonalds Road in Pokolbin. The first vines were planted in 1996, and planting has continued: to
date 17 hectares of shiraz, semillon, chardonnay, tempranillo, tinta cao and touriga are in the ground.
Three luxury cottages have been built, followed by a restaurant and cellar door, with a small winery
beneath.

Windy Creek Estate

NR

Stock Road, Herne Hill, WA 6056 **REGION** Swan Valley
T (08) 9296 4210 **OPEN** Tues–Sun 11–5
WINEMAKER Tony Cobanov, Tony Roe **EST.** 1960 **CASES** 10 000
PRODUCT RANGE ($6–10 CD) Chenin Blanc, Chardonnay, Sauvignon Blanc, Verdelho, Shiraz,
Grenache, Cabernet Sauvignon.
SUMMARY A substantial family-owned operation (previously known as Cobanov Wines) producing a
mix of bulk and bottled wine from 21 hectares of estate grapes. Part of the annual production is sold
as grapes to other producers, including Houghton; part is sold in bulk; part is sold in 2-litre flagons,
and part in modestly priced bottles.

Windy Ridge Vineyard

Foster–Fish Creek Road, Foster, Vic 3960 **REGION** Gippsland
T (03) 5682 2035 **OPEN** Holiday weekends 10–5
WINEMAKER Graeme Wilson **EST.** 1978 **CASES** 300
PRODUCT RANGE ($25–39.50 CD) Traminer, Pinot Noir, Cellar Reserve Pinot Noir, Cabernet
Sauvignon Malbec.
SUMMARY The 2.8-hectare Windy Ridge Vineyard was planted between 1978 and 1986, with the first
vintage not taking place until 1988. Winemaker Graeme Wilson favours prolonged maturation, part
in stainless steel and part in oak, before bottling his wines, typically giving the Pinot Noir 3 years and
the Cabernet 2 years before bottling.

🐌 Wine & Truffle Company

PO Box 611, Mount Hawthorn, WA 6915 **REGION** Pemberton
T (08) 9228 0328 **OPEN** Not
WINEMAKER Mark Aitken (Contract) **EST.** 1996
PRODUCT RANGE ($17–28 R) Riesling, Merlot.
SUMMARY The name precisely describes this unusual venture. It is owned by a group of investors from
various parts of Australia who share the common vision of producing fine wines and black truffles.
The winemaking side is under the care of Mark Aitken, who, having graduated as dux of his class in
applied science at Curtin University in 2000, joined Chestnut Grove as assistant winemaker in
February 2002. Here he performs a dual role: he is contract winemaker for the Wine & Truffle
Company, as well as working for Chestnut Grove. The truffle side of the business is under the care of
former CSIRO scientist Dr Nicholas Malajcsuk. He has overseen the planting of 13 000 truffle
inoculated hazelnut and oak trees on the property. As a sign of faith, he is actively involved in the day-
to-day monitoring of the trees as well as in the management of the dog-training and truffle-hunting
program.

♥♥♥♥♥ Riesling 2002 Ultra-fragrant; lovely apple, lime and citrus fruit; good length, and a crisp,
clean finish. **RATING** 94 **DRINK** 2010 $17

🍷 Wine By Brad

NR

PO Box 475, Margaret River, WA 6285 **REGION** Margaret River
T (08) 9757 2957 **F** (08) 9757 2790 **OPEN** Not
WINEMAKER Various (Contract) **EST.** 2003 **CASES** 1000
PRODUCT RANGE ($17 ML) Semillon Sauvignon Blanc, Shiraz, Cabernet Merlot.
SUMMARY Brad Wehr says that wine by brad 'is the result of a couple of influential winemakers and shadowy ruffians deciding that there was something to be gained by putting together some pretty neat parcels of wine from the region, creating their own label, releasing it with minimal fuss, and then remaining anonymous for fear of reprisals'. This, therefore, is another version of the virtual winery, with sales by email and through the website <www.winebybrad.com.au>.

Winewood

NR

Sundown Road, Ballandean, Qld 4382 **REGION** Granite Belt
T (07) 4684 1187 **F** (07) 4684 1187 **OPEN** Weekends and public holidays 9–5
WINEMAKER Ian Davis **EST.** 1984 **CASES** 1000
PRODUCT RANGE ($15–20 CD) Chardonnay, Chardonnay Marsanne, Shiraz Marsanne, MacKenzies Run (Cabernet blend), Muscat.
SUMMARY A weekend and holiday activity for schoolteacher Ian Davis and town-planner wife Jeanette; the tiny winery is a model of neatness and precision planning. The use of marsanne with chardonnay and semillon shows an interesting change in direction. Has 4.5 hectares of estate plantings, having added shiraz and viognier. All wine is sold through the cellar door; tutored tastings available.

Winstead

★★★★

75 Winstead Road, Bagdad, Tas 7030 **REGION** Southern Tasmania
T (03) 6268 6417 **F** (03) 6268 6417 **OPEN** By appointment
WINEMAKER Neil Snare **EST.** 1989 **CASES** 350
PRODUCT RANGE ($18–30 CD) Riesling, Pinot Noir, Reserve Pinot Noir.
SUMMARY The good news about Winstead is the outstanding quality of its extremely generous and rich Pinot Noirs, rivalling those of Freycinet for the abundance of their fruit flavour without any sacrifice of varietal character. The bad news is that production is so limited, with only 0.8 hectare of pinot noir and 0.4 hectare of riesling being tended by fly-fishing devotee Neil Snare and wife Julieanne. Retail distribution in Melbourne.

▼▼▼▼▽ **Pinot Noir 2002** Reflects the vintage character in spades; impenetrable, brooding, River Styx; anise, black fruits and shoe polish. For the long haul. **RATING** 90 **DRINK** 2012 $30

Wirilda Creek

★★★

RSD 91 McMurtrie Road, McLaren Vale, SA 5171 **REGION** McLaren Vale
T (08) 8323 9688 **F** (08) 8323 9260 **OPEN** 7 days 10–5
WINEMAKER Kerry Flanagan **EST.** 1993 **CASES** 1500
PRODUCT RANGE ($15–25 CD) Grape Pickers Verdelho, Evening Shadows (Sparkling Shiraz), Shiraz Trad, Shiraz Rare, Vine Pruners Blend, Cabernet Sauvignon Merlot, Old Sweet White Fortified Verdelho, Liqueur Port.
SUMMARY Wirilda Creek may be one of the newer arrivals in McLaren Vale but it offers the lot: wine, lunch every day (Pickers Platters reflecting local produce) and accommodation (four rooms opening onto a private garden courtyard). Co-owner Kerry Flanagan (with partner Karen Shertock) has had great experience in the wine and hospitality industries: a Roseworthy graduate (1980), he has inter alia worked at Penfolds, Coriole and Wirra Wirra and also owned the famous Old Salopian Inn for a period of time. A little under 4 hectares of McLaren Vale estate vineyards have now been joined by a little over 3 hectares of vineyards planted at Antechamber Bay, Kangaroo Island. Limited retail distribution in New South Wales and South Australia; exports to the US, Canada and Germany.

Wirra Wirra ★★★★★

McMurtrie Road, McLaren Vale, SA 5171 **REGION** McLaren Vale
T (08) 8323 8414 **F** (08) 8323 8596 **OPEN** Mon–Sat 10–5, Sun 11–5
WINEMAKER Samantha Connew, Paul Carpenter **EST.** 1969 **CASES** 110 000
PRODUCT RANGE ($15–72 R) Hand Picked Riesling, Sauvignon Blanc, Scrubby Rise (white and red) blends), Chardonnay, Sexton's Acre Unwooded Chardonnay, The Cousins (Pinot Noir Chardonnay), Mrs Wigley Rose, The Anthem (Sparkling Shiraz), Late Picked Riesling, McLaren Vale Shiraz, Chook Block Shiraz, McLaren Vale Grenache Shiraz, Church Block (Cabernet Shiraz Merlot); The Angelus Cabernet Sauvignon and RSW Shiraz are the icons.
SUMMARY Long respected for the consistency of its white wines, Wirra Wirra has now established an equally formidable reputation for its reds. Right across the board, the wines are of exemplary character, quality and style, The Angelus Cabernet Sauvignon and RSW Shiraz battling with each other for supremacy. Long may the battle continue under the direction of the highly respected Tim James, lured from his senior position at BRL Hardy late in 2000. The wines are exported to the US, the UK, Europe and Asia.

TTTTT **RSW Shiraz 2001** Intense, concentrated and very complex aromas; crammed with black fruits, spice and dark chocolate; great fruit and oak handling. **RATING** 95 **DRINK** 2016 **$** 48
McLaren Vale Shiraz 2001 A seamlessly integrated blackberry, plum and oak bouquet, the supple, medium-bodied palate following suit, with the fruit offset by fine, ripe tannins. **RATING** 94 **DRINK** 2015 **$** 30
The Angelus Cabernet Sauvignon 2001 Rich, deep cassis aromas; round, sweet cassis/blackberry fruit; immaculate tannins and oak. **RATING** 94 **DRINK** 2015 **$** 49

TTTTY **McLaren Vale Grenache 2002** Very fragrant spice and plum aromas; chocolate joins in on the plush, luscious palate. **RATING** 92 **DRINK** 2008 **$** 30
Church Block 2002 Multi-faceted aromas and flavours of cassis, blackcurrant and spice; good texture and structure. **RATING** 91 **DRINK** 2012 **$** 23

TTTT **Watervale Riesling 2003** Reserved, flinty/minerally bouquet; very delicate, flinty, crisp lemony palate. **RATING** 89 **DRINK** 2013 **$** 24
Adelaide Hills Chardonnay 2002 A complex and potent full-on style, with barrel-ferment oak (French) and peachy fruit. **RATING** 89 **DRINK** Now **$** 24
Scrubby Rise Red 2001 Sweet, sensual black fruit, mocha and chocolate fruit; appealing mouthfeel. Screwcap. A blend of Shiraz, Cabernet Sauvignon and Petit Verdot. **RATING** 89 **DRINK** 2008 **$** 17
The Anthem NV Full-flavoured plum, blackberry and spice; solid; well-balanced finish. **RATING** 89 **DRINK** 2009 **$** 30
Mrs Wigley Rose 2003 Bright colour; abundant, positive flavour with plum, cherry and strawberry. A mongrel blend of Malbec, Grenache and Petit Verdot, appropriately named after the winery cat. **RATING** 88 **DRINK** Now **$** 16.50

TTTY **Hand Picked Riesling 2003** **RATING** 86 **DRINK** 2010 **$** 18
Adelaide Hills Sauvignon Blanc 2003 **RATING** 86 **DRINK** Now **$** 23
Scrubby Rise 2003 **RATING** 86 **DRINK** Now **$** 17

Wise Wine ★★★★

Lot 4 Eagle Bay Road, Dunsborough, WA 6281 **REGION** Margaret River
T (08) 9756 8627 **F** (08) 9756 8770 **OPEN** 7 days 10–5
WINEMAKER Amanda Kramer, Bruce Dukes (Consultant) **EST.** 1986 **CASES** 40 000
PRODUCT RANGE ($14–45 CD) Eagle Bay Semillon Sauvignon Blanc, Single Vineyard Verdelho, Classic White, Unwooded Chardonnay, Donnybrook Chardonnay, Cane Cut Semillon, Eagle Bay Pinot Noir, Classic Red, Eagle Bay Shiraz, Cabernet Sauvignon Cabernet Franc, Lot 80 Cabernet Sauvignon, Primitivo, Sangiovese Cabernet, Tokay.
SUMMARY Wise Vineyards, headed by Perth entrepreneur Ron Wise, is going from strength to strength, with 18 hectares at the Meelup Vineyard in Margaret River, 10 hectares at the Donnybrook Vineyard in Geographe, and leases over the Bramley and Bunkers Bay vineyards, with a total of almost 40 hectares. Wine quality, too, has taken a leap forward, with a number of excellent wines.

ŸŸŸŸŸ **Single Vineyard Verdelho 2003** Complex citrus and melon fruit; intense, long and lingering; fully deserves Sheraton gold medal; one of the two best Verdelhos in Australia. **RATING** 94 **DRINK** 2007 $ 24

ŸŸŸŸ **Margaret River and Pemberton Classic Dry White 2003** Lively, pure, tangy fruit; good length, line and balance. **RATING** 88 **DRINK** 2007 $ 16
The Donnybrook 2002 Clean, suave, light to medium-bodied; good length; just a little light on. **RATING** 88 **DRINK** 2009 $ 24
Pemberton Unwooded Chardonnay 2003 Tangy, lively grapefruit and melon; well above average. **RATING** 87 **DRINK** 2007 $ 18
The Donnybrook 2001 Light to medium-bodied; cedar, spice, earth, chocolate and berry flavours; light tannins. **RATING** 87 **DRINK** 2008 $ 24

ŸŸŸŸ **Margaret River Lot 80 Cabernet Sauvignon 2001** **RATING** 86 **DRINK** 2007 $ 28

ŸŸŸ **Pemberton Pinot Noir 2002** **RATING** 83 $ 30
Margaret River Lot 80 Cabernet Sauvignon 2002 **RATING** 83 **DRINK** 2007 $ 28

Witchmount Estate ★★★★

557 Leakes Road, Rockbank, Vic 3335 **REGION** Sunbury
T (03) 9747 1088 **F** (03) 9747 1066 **OPEN** Wed–Sun 10–5
WINEMAKER Tony Ramunno, Steve Goodwin **EST.** 1991 **CASES** 8000
PRODUCT RANGE ($10.90–39 CD) Summer White, Estate Chardonnay, Olivia's Paddock Chardonnay, Rose, Estate Shiraz, Lowan Park Shiraz, Nebbiolo, Estate Cabernet Sauvignon, Lowan Park Cabernet Sauvignon; Mount Cottrell range of Sauvignon Blanc Semillon, Shiraz.
SUMMARY Gaye and Matt Ramunno operate Witchmount Estate in conjunction with its on-site Italian restaurant and function rooms, which are open from Wednesday to Sunday inclusive for lunch and dinner. Over 20 hectares of vines have been established since 1991; varieties include nebbiolo, barbera, tempranillo and the rare northern Italian white grape picolit. The quality of the wines is consistently good, the prices very modest.

WJ Walker Wines ★★★★★

Burns Road, Lake Grace, WA 6353 **REGION** South West Australia Zone
T (08) 9865 1969 **OPEN** Not
WINEMAKER Porongurup Winery (Contract) **CASES** 1000
PRODUCT RANGE ($10–15 R) Lake Grace Chardonnay, Shiraz, Cabernet Sauvignon, Port.
SUMMARY Lake Grace is 300 kilometres due east of Bunbury, one of those isolated viticultural outposts which are appearing in many parts of Australia these days. There are 1.5 hectares of shiraz and 0.5 hectare of chardonnay, and the wines are sold through local outlets.

ŸŸŸŸŸ **Lake Grace Shiraz 2002** Fragrant pepper, spice and cedar; tightly focused, medium-bodied; clever oak use, and slippery, fine tannins. **RATING** 95 **DRINK** 2015

Wolf Blass ★★★★★

Bilyara Vineyards, Sturt Highway, Nuriootpa, SA 5355 **REGION** Barossa Valley
T (08) 8562 1955 **F** (08) 8562 2156 **OPEN** Mon–Fri 9.15–4.30, weekends 10–4.30
WINEMAKER Chris Hatcher (Chief), Wendy Stuckey (White), John Glaetzer and Caroline Dunn (Red) **EST.** 1966
PRODUCT RANGE ($9.99–175 R) Revamped in 2004 on six-tier colour range; in ascending order they are Red Label, Gold Label, Grey Label and Platinum Label. Within each label there are a varying number of regional/varietal wines. Off to one side is the budget-priced Eaglehawk range.
SUMMARY Although merged with Mildara and now under the giant umbrella of Beringer Blass, the brands (as expected) have been left largely intact. The white wines (made by Wendy Stuckey) are particularly impressive, none more so than the Gold Label Riesling. After a short pause, the red wines have improved out of all recognition, thanks to the sure touch (and top palate) of Caroline Dunn. All of this has occurred under the leadership of Chris Hatcher, who has harnessed the talents of the team and encouraged the changes in style. Worldwide distribution.

ΨΨΨΨΨ **Platinum Label Adelaide Hills Shiraz 2001** Deeply coloured; rich and plush, perfectly ripened blackberry fruit; exemplary oak handling and tannin management; great length. Screwcap. **RATING** 95 **DRINK** 2021 $ 175

Black Label Cabernet Sauvignon Shiraz 2000 An ultra-complex blend of all red wine components, all perfectly balanced. A style honed to perfection. **RATING** 95 **DRINK** 2015 $ 120

Gold Label Riesling 2003 Very pure citrus and spice aromas; excellent mouthfeel; gently sweet lime juice; nice balance. **RATING** 94 **DRINK** 2010 $ 23

Gold Label Adelaide Hills Shiraz Viognier 2002 Dense, complex, very rich, opulent and luscious fruit-driven style. Multiple trophies 2003 National Wine Show under Stelvin closure. This sample under cork. Why? **RATING** 94 **DRINK** 2017 $ 21

Grey Label Shiraz 2002 Complex and concentrated; seamless fusion of fruit and scented oak. A panoply of black fruits and spice; impeccable balance. Barossa/Clare/McLaren Vale. **RATING** 94 **DRINK** 2012 $ 38

ΨΨΨΨ♈ **Grey Label Cabernet Sauvignon 2002** Complex, medium-bodied; typical marriage of fruit and barrel-ferment oak; blackcurrant and chocolate in equal amounts; good length and balance. **RATING** 93 **DRINK** 2012 $ 38

Gold Label Cabernet Sauvignon Cabernet Franc 2001 A sophisticated, elegant and seamless marriage of fresh red and black fruits, oak and fine, supple tannins. Delicious now or in 10 years. **RATING** 93 **DRINK** 2011 $ 23

Gold Label Adelaide Hills Shiraz Viognier 2000 Complex, high-toned spicy fruit and oak, the flavours building along the length of the palate; fresh finish. **RATING** 92 **DRINK** 2010 $ 21

Gold Label Adelaide Hills Chardonnay 2003 Elegant and very smooth barrel-ferment and malolactic-ferment inputs; stylish, sotto voce. **RATING** 91 **DRINK** 2008 $ 23

Gold Label Shiraz 2001 Bright colour; fresh, firm red and black fruits; sensitive use of French oak; elegant style. Barossa and Eden Valleys. Screwcap. **RATING** 90 **DRINK** 2011 $ 22

Gold Label Coonawarra Cabernet Sauvignon 2000 Typical regional earthy overtones to sweet blackcurrant core; oak in restraint. **RATING** 90 **DRINK** 2010 $ 23

ΨΨΨΨ **Grey Label Cabernet Sauvignon 2001** Soft, sweet, juicy fruit and vanilla oak in traditional Blass style; soft, ripe tannins. **RATING** 89 **DRINK** 2009 $ 38

Yellow Label Riesling 2003 Quite delicate and gentle aromatics; passionfruit and lime; good length. Screwcap. **RATING** 88 **DRINK** 2007 $ 15

Yellow Label Chardonnay 2003 Finer version of the Red Label, but also ready to roll. **RATING** 88 **DRINK** Now $ 15

Red Label Chardonnay 2003 Bright yellow; stone fruit and peach; subtle oak. Ready to roll, back to the origins of the original Red Label. Composite cork. **RATING** 87 **DRINK** Now $ 11

Yellow Label Cabernet Sauvignon 2002 Attractive sweet blackcurrant fruit aromas; supple, light to medium-bodied; fruit-driven, restrained oak. **RATING** 87 **DRINK** 2008 $ 15

ΨΨΨ♈ **Semillon Sauvignon Blanc 2003** **RATING** 86 **DRINK** Now $ 14
South Australian Chardonnay 2002 **RATING** 86 **DRINK** Now $ 17
Eaglehawk Riesling 2003 **RATING** 85 **DRINK** Now $ 9.99
Red Label Semillon Sauvignon Blanc 2003 **RATING** 85 **DRINK** Now $ 11
Yellow Label Shiraz 2001 **RATING** 85 **DRINK** Now $ 15
Red Label Cabernet Merlot 2002 **RATING** 85 **DRINK** Now $ 11
Eaglehawk Shiraz Blend 2003 **RATING** 84 **DRINK** Now $ 9.99

ΨΨΨ **Red Label Shiraz Cabernet 2002** **RATING** 83 $ 12
Blue Label Merlot 2002 **RATING** 81 $ 14

🍇 Wonbah Estate
NR

302 Wonbah Road, Wonbah via Gin Gin, Qld 4671 **REGION** Queensland Coastal
T (07) 4156 3029 **F** (07) 4156 3035 **OPEN** 7 days 9.30–4
WINEMAKER Bruce Humphery-Smith (Contract) **EST.** 1997 **CASES** 1500

PRODUCT RANGE ($13–20 CD) Agnes, Verdelho, Unwooded Chardonnay, Chardonnay, Ruby, Thomas, Reserve Shiraz, Liqueurs.
SUMMARY The 5-hectare vineyard, planted to shiraz, chardonnay, cabernet sauvignon, ruby cabernet, muscat and verdelho, is located near Mount Perry, one hour's drive west of Bundaberg at the extreme northern end of the Burnett Valley, extending the viticultural map of Queensland yet further. The 100-tonne on-site winery is under the direction of the omnipresent Bruce Humphery-Smith, and the tasting room is in a restored slab hut dating from the turn of the 20th century. There are numerous tourist attractions around nearby Mount Perry, not the least being the Boolboonda Tunnel, the largest self-supporting tunnel in the southern hemisphere, which is hand-hewn, and home to a colony of fairy bats.

Woodlands

Cnr Caves and Metricup Roads, Wilyabrup via Cowaramup, WA 6284 **REGION** Margaret River
T (08) 9755 6226 **F** (08) 9481 1700 **OPEN** Weekends by appointment
WINEMAKER Stuart Watson, David Watson **EST.** 1973 **CASES** 2500
PRODUCT RANGE ($15–75 R) Unwooded Chardonnay, Reserve Chloe Chardonnay, Cabernet Merlot, Margaret Cabernet Merlot, Reserve St Peter Cabernet Merlot, Reserve du Cave in micro-quantities.
SUMMARY The production (and visibility) of Woodlands have varied over the years, the core of the business lying with 6.8 hectares of cabernet sauvignon, more recently joined by merlot (1.2 hectares), malbec (0.8 hectare), cabernet franc (0.2 hectare), pinot noir (0.2 hectare) and chardonnay (0.8 hectare), all now in bearing. Currently enjoying a purple patch with its wines. Exports to the US.

ŸŸŸŸŸ **Margaret Reserve Cabernet Merlot 2002** Clean; very rich and concentrated panoply of black fruits, ripe tannins and controlled oak. Woodlands at its best. **RATING** 93 **DRINK** 2017 $ 35
Kevin Cabernet Sauvignon 2001 Ripe, flooded with cassis/blackcurrant fruit; excellent management of tannin and oak; very good length. **RATING** 92 **DRINK** 2016 $ 75
Malbec Reserve du Cave 2002 Great varietal character; dense, ripe blackberry jam, but not over the top or gluggy. Freakish wine. **RATING** 92 **DRINK** 2017 $ 60
Cabernet Franc Reserve du Cave 2002 Underscores the synergy between cabernet franc and Margaret River; is it the clone or the region or both? Great colour, depth and ripeness. **RATING** 91 **DRINK** 2015 $ 60

ŸŸŸŸ **Cabernet Sauvignon Merlot 2002** A rich mix of cassis, blackberry and raspberry; well-handled tannins and oak. **RATING** 89 **DRINK** 2012 $ 20
Chardonnay 2003 Entirely fruit-driven; fine stone fruit, melon and fig; some sweetness helps unwooded style. Screwcap. **RATING** 87 **DRINK** 2008 $ 15
Reserve Chloe Chardonnay 2002 Complex but massive barrel-ferment oak completely over the top on the bouquet, but fruit makes a partial recovery in the mouth. **RATING** 87 **DRINK** 2008 $ 40

ŸŸŸ **Reserve du Cave Pinot Noir 2002 RATING** 83 $ 60

Woodonga Hill   NR

Cowra Road, Young, NSW 2594 **REGION** Hilltops
T (02) 6382 2972 **F** (02) 6382 2972 **OPEN** 7 days 9–5
WINEMAKER Jill Lindsay **EST.** 1986 **CASES** 4000
PRODUCT RANGE ($12.50–21 CD) Dry Rhine Riesling, Sauvignon, Chardonnay, Botrytis Semillon, Auslese Gewurztraminer, Meunier, Shiraz, Vintage Port, Cherry Liqueur Port.
SUMMARY Early problems with white wine quality appear to have been surmounted. The wines have won bronze or silver medals at regional wine shows in New South Wales and Canberra, and Jill Lindsay is also a successful contract winemaker for other small producers.

Wood Park

RMB 1139 Bobinawarrah–Whorouly Road, Milawa, Vic 3678 **REGION** King Valley
T (03) 5727 3367 **F** (03) 5727 3682 **OPEN** Wed–Mon 10–5 at Milawa Cheese Factory
WINEMAKER John Stokes **EST.** 1989 **CASES** 4000
PRODUCT RANGE ($14–35 CD) Meadow Creek Chardonnay, Whitlands Pinot Gris, Late Picked Verdelho, Rose, Whitlands Pinot Noir, Myrrhee Merlot, Kneebone's Gap Shiraz, Cabernet Sauvignon Shiraz.

SUMMARY The first vines were planted at Wood Park in 1989 by John Stokes as part of a diversification program for his property at Bobinawarrah, in the hills of the Lower King Valley to the east of Milawa. The bulk of the 8-hectare production is sold to Brown Brothers. In an unusual twist, Stokes acquires his chardonnay from cousin John Leviny, one of the King Valley pioneers, who has his vineyard at Meadow Creek. Exports to the US and Europe.

ΥΥΥΥ **Pinot Gris 2003** Flowery and fragrant; a delicate palate, with good balance and finish. **RATING** 90 **DRINK** Now $18

ΥΥΥΥ **Kneebones Gap Shiraz 2002** Elegant, pure black cherry, spice and blackberry fruit; light to medium-bodied, unforced; subtle oak. **RATING** 87 **DRINK** 2010 $26

ΥΥΥΥ **Whitlands Pinot Noir 2002** **RATING** 86 **DRINK** 2007 $25
Meadow Creek Chardonnay 2002 **RATING** 85 **DRINK** 2008 $22
Cabernet Shiraz 2001 **RATING** 85 **DRINK** 2014 $20

Woodside Valley Estate ★★★★

PO Box 332, Greenwood, WA 6924 **REGION** Margaret River
T (08) 9345 4065 **F** (08) 9345 4541 **OPEN** Not
WINEMAKER Kevin McKay **EST.** 1998 **CASES** 500
PRODUCT RANGE ($35–60 ML) The Bailly Chardonnay, The Le Bas Chardonnay, The Bonneyfoy Shiraz, The Baptiste Shiraz, The Bissy Merlot, The Baudin Cabernet Merlot, The Baudin Cabernet Sauvignon.
SUMMARY Woodside Valley has been developed by a small syndicate of investors headed by Peter Woods. In 1998 they acquired 67 hectares of land at Yallingup, and they have now established 19 hectares of chardonnay, sauvignon blanc, cabernet sauvignon, shiraz, malbec and merlot. The experienced Albert Haak is consultant viticulturist, and together with Peter Woods, took the unusual step of planting south-facing in preference to north-facing slopes. In doing so they indirectly followed in the footsteps of the French explorer Thomas Nicholas Baudin, who mounted a major scientific expedition to Australia on his ship *The Geographe*, and defied established views and tradition of the time in (correctly) asserting that the best passage for sailing ships travelling between Cape Leeuwin and Bass Strait was from west to east. It's a long bow, but it's a story for a winery which managed to produce some excellent wines from very young vines. Exports to the US and Japan.

ΥΥΥΥ **The Le Bas Chardonnay 2003** Clean, lively and fresh grapefruit-accented aromas; subtle infusion of French oak; very stylish. **RATING** 93 **DRINK** 2008 $35
The Bonnefoy Shiraz 2001 Smooth black cherry and blackberry fruit is interwoven with fruit and a touch of spicy French oak; excellent balance, structure and length, the fruit perfectly ripe. **RATING** 93 **DRINK** 2011 $48
The Baudin Cabernet Sauvignon 2001 The clean, sweet bouquet focuses on cassis/blackcurrant varietal fruit, the palate likewise; very fine tannins and neatly integrated oak underwrite the length, rather than the weight, of the wine. **RATING** 93 **DRINK** 2013 $48
The Baudin Cabernet Sauvignon 2002 Very much in the family style; reserved and tight; needing persuasion (and time) to fully exhibit its wares. **RATING** 91 **DRINK** 2017 $48
The Le Bas Chardonnay 2002 The bouquet offers a subtle but complex interplay between oak and fruit; there is considerable presence and mouthfeel to the citrus and stone fruit flavours, supported by balanced oak. **RATING** 90 **DRINK** 2007 $35
The Bissy Merlot 2001 A fragrant bouquet has touches of mint and leaf, the lively palate showing red and blackcurrant fruit complemented by good oak management; combines elegance and flavour. **RATING** 90 **DRINK** 2011 $45

ΥΥΥΥ **The Bissy Merlot 2002** Subdued bouquet, but very long and stylish in the mouth; olive, cedar, blackcurrant; fine tannins. **RATING** 89 **DRINK** 2012 $45
The Bonnefoy Shiraz 2002 Complex aromas and flavours, with some red fruits, but in the end, the mint and leaf prevail. **RATING** 87 **DRINK** 2010 $48

WoodSmoke Estate ★★★

Lot 2 Kemp Road, Pemberton, WA 6260 **REGION** Pemberton
T (08) 9776 0225 **F** (08) 9776 0225 **OPEN** By appointment
WINEMAKER Julie White **EST.** 1992 **CASES** 1500
PRODUCT RANGE ($18–25 CD) Sauvignon Blanc, Semillon, Cabernet blend.
SUMMARY The former Jimlee Estate was acquired by the Liebeck family in July 1998 and renamed WoodSmoke Estate. The original plantings of a little over 2 hectares of semillon, sauvignon blanc, cabernet franc and cabernet sauvignon were expanded with a further 2.5 hectares of cabernet franc and merlot in 2000.

TTTY **Semillon 2003** Quite ripe and fleshy; clean; light to medium-bodied; early-developing style, enjoyable now. **RATING** 86 **DRINK** 2007
Sauvignon Blanc 2003 Clean; full tropical, citrus; slightly sweet; plenty of flavour.
RATING 86 **DRINK** Now

Woodstock ★★★☆

Douglas Gully Road, McLaren Flat, SA 5171 **REGION** McLaren Vale
T (08) 8383 0156 **F** (08) 8383 0437 **OPEN** Mon–Fri 9–5, weekends, holidays 12–5
WINEMAKER Scott Collett **EST.** 1974 **CASES** 30 000
PRODUCT RANGE ($9.95–40 CD) Riesling, Semillon, Douglas Gully Semillon Sauvignon Blanc, Verdelho, Chardonnay, Botrytis Sweet White, Five Feet (dry red), Shiraz, Grenache, Douglas Gully Malbec Cabernet Sauvignon Petit Verdot, Cabernet Sauvignon, Vintage Port, Very Old Tawny Port and Muscat. The Stocks Shiraz is a recently introduced flagship.
SUMMARY One of the stalwarts of McLaren Vale, producing archetypal, invariably reliable full-bodied red wines and showing versatility with spectacular botrytis sweet whites and high-quality (14-year-old) Tawny Port. Also offers a totally charming reception-cum-restaurant, which understandably does a roaring trade with wedding receptions. Has supplemented its 22 hectares of McLaren Vale vineyards with 10 hectares at its Wirrega Vineyard near Bordertown in the Limestone Coast Zone. The wines are exported to the UK, Switzerland, the US, Canada, New Zealand, the Philippines, Malaysia and Singapore.

TTTTY **The Stocks McLaren Vale Shiraz 2001** Ultra-regional bitter chocolate and blackberry aromas and flavours; excellent supple, silky texture and structure. **RATING** 90 **DRINK** 2016
$ 40

TTT **Verdelho 2003** **RATING** 83 $ 14
Verdelho Riesling 2003 **RATING** 81 $ 14.99

Woody Nook ★★★☆

Metricup Road, Busselton, WA 6280 **REGION** Margaret River
T (08) 9755 7547 **F** (08) 9755 7007 **OPEN** 7 days 10–4.30
WINEMAKER Neil Gallagher **EST.** 1982 **CASES** 5000
PRODUCT RANGE ($15–28 CD) Sauvignon Blanc, Kelly's Farewell (Sauvignon Blanc Semillon), Classique (Semillon Sauvignon Blanc Chardonnay), Chenin Blanc, Late Harvest, Shiraz, Merlot, Killdog Creek Cabernet Merlot, Cabernet Sauvignon, Nooky Delight; Gallagher's Choice Cabernet Sauvignon is top of the range.
SUMMARY This improbably named and not terribly fashionable winery has produced some truly excellent wines over the years, featuring in such diverse competitions as Winewise, the Sheraton Wine Awards and the Qantas West Australian Wines Show. Cabernet Sauvignon has always been its strong point, but it has the habit of bobbing up with excellent white wines in various guises. Since 2000, owned by Peter and Jane Baily, but Neil Gallagher continues as viticulturist, winemaker and minority shareholder. Exports to the UK and Hong Kong.

TTTT **Sauvignon Blanc 2003** Very complex and powerful; loaded with flavour and big in the mouth. **RATING** 88 **DRINK** Now $ 19.95
Chenin Blanc 2003 Crisp yet gentle fruit salad; well balanced, medium length; dry finish.
RATING 87 **DRINK** Now $ 17

Woolshed Wines ★★★

380 Horseflat Lane, Mullamuddy via Mudgee, NSW 2850 **REGION** Mudgee
T (02) 6373 1299 **F** (02) 6373 1299 **OPEN** 7 days 10–5
WINEMAKER David Lowe (Contract) **EST.** 1999
PRODUCT RANGE A range of varietally denominated table wines reflecting the plantings.
SUMMARY Kay and Mick Burgoyne own and run the 8-hectare vineyard formerly known as Valley View Estates. It is planted to chardonnay, cabernet, merlot, shiraz and muscat hamburg. The wines are primarily sold through the cellar door and by mail order; the cellar door offers barbecues in a garden setting, and can cater for functions, concerts or festivals by arrangement.

ŸŸŸŸ **Shiraz 2002** Very ripe fruit ranging through plum, prune and blackberry; ripe tannins; pushes the envelope. **RATING** 87 **DRINK** 2010

ŸŸŸ♀ **Merlot 2002** **RATING** 84 **DRINK** 2007

Woongarra Estate ★★★

95 Hayseys Road, Narre Warren East, Vic 3804 **REGION** Port Phillip Zone
T (03) 9796 8886 **F** (03) 9796 8580 **OPEN** Thurs–Sun 9–5 by appointment
WINEMAKER Graeme Leith, Mal Stewart **EST.** 1992 **CASES** 2000
PRODUCT RANGE ($12–15 CD) Sauvignon Blanc Semillon; Three Wise Men range of Pinot Noir and Shiraz also available.
SUMMARY Dr Bruce Jones and wife Mary purchased their Narre Warren East 16-hectare property many years ago; it falls within the Yarra Ranges Shire Council's jurisdiction and is zoned 'Landscape', but because nearby Cardinia Creek does not flow into the Yarra River, it is not within the Yarra Valley wine region. In 1992 they planted 1 hectare of sauvignon blanc, a small patch of shiraz and a few rows of semillon. Over 1 hectare of sauvignon blanc and pinot noir followed in 1996 (mostly MV6, some French clone 114 and 115), with yet more 114 and 115 pinot noir in 2000, lifting total plantings to 3.2 hectares of pinot noir, 1.4 hectares of sauvignon blanc and a splash of the other two varieties. The white grapes have had various purchasers and contract makers; the spectacular success has come with the Three Wise Men Pinot Noir, which is jointly owned by Woongarra and is available from Woongarra direct.

ŸŸŸ♀ **Sauvignon Blanc 2003** **RATING** 84 **DRINK** Now $ 15

Woongooroo Estate NR

35 Doyles Road, Mount Archer, Kilcoy, Qld 4515 (postal) **REGION** Queensland Coastal
T (07) 5496 3529 **F** (07) 5496 3529 **OPEN** Not
WINEMAKER Sam Costanzo, Ray Costanzo **EST.** 1997
PRODUCT RANGE ($12–13 ML) Semillon, Semillon Chardonnay, Chardonnay, Somerset White, Somerset Red, Shiraz, Shiraz Cabernet Franc, Cabernet Franc.
SUMMARY Woongooroo Estate was established by primary schoolteachers Phil and Gail Close when they planted a little over 3 hectares of chardonnay, semillon, shiraz, cabernet franc, merlot and verdelho, together with a commercial olive grove. They chose the Costanzo brothers of Golden Grove Estate in the Granite Belt as their contract winemakers, with a cellar door/vineyard café planned. It is part of yet another new Queensland wine region known as the Somerset Valleys Grape and Wine Producers Association, more generically falling within the Queensland Coastal Hinterland.

Word of Mouth Wines ★★★☆

Campbell's Corner, Pinnacle Road, Orange, NSW 2800 **REGION** Orange
T (02) 6362 3509 **F** (02) 6365 3517 **OPEN** Fri–Sun and public holidays 11–5
WINEMAKER David Lowe, Jane Wilson (Contract) **EST.** 1991 **CASES** 1500
PRODUCT RANGE ($18–22 CD) Sauvignon Blanc, Pinot Gris, Late Harvest Riesling; Pinot Noir, Merlot and Cabernet to come.
SUMMARY Word of Mouth Wines acquired the former Donnington Vineyard in 2003, inheriting 10 hectares of mature vineyards, planted (in descending order of size) to sauvignon blanc, chardonnay, merlot, cabernet sauvignon, pinot noir, riesling and pinot gris between 1991 and 1996. Word of Mouth Wines Pty Limited has four shareholders, two based in Sydney and two in Orange, and David

Lowe and Jane Wilson have been appointed winemakers. The vineyard and cellar door, established at an altitude of over 950 metres, have panoramic views over the surrounding countryside.

ŶŶŶŶ **Orange Late Harvest Riesling 2003** Fine, tangy, citrussy, showing varietal fruit through the climatic vicissitudes it faced; good balance and length. **RATING** 88 **DRINK** Now $ 18
Orange Sauvignon Blanc 2003 Well made; moderately intense, gentle tropical/gooseberry fruit; no phenolics. **RATING** 87 **DRINK** Now $ 20

ŶŶŶŶ **Pinot Noir 2003** Strongly savoury/briary/foresty style but well made; just needed a touch more sweet fruit. Screwcap. **RATING** 86 **DRINK** 2007 $ 22
Merlot Cabernet 2003 RATING 85 **DRINK** 2008 $ 18

Wordsworth Wines

NR

Cnr South Western Highway and Thompson Road, Harvey, WA 6220 **REGION** Geographe
T (08) 9773 4576 **F** (08) 9733 4269 **OPEN** 7 days 10–5
WINEMAKER Tim Mortimer **EST.** 1997 **CASES** 2500
PRODUCT RANGE ($16–22 CD) Verdelho, Chardonnay, Daffodil Medium Dry White, Shiraz, Cabernet Merlot.
SUMMARY David Wordsworth has established a substantial business in a relatively short space of time. Thirty-three hectares of vines have been planted, with cabernet sauvignon (12 hectares) and shiraz (5 hectares) predominant, and lesser amounts of merlot, zinfandel, petit verdot, chardonnay, chenin blanc and verdelho. The winery features massive jarrah beams, and the tasting room is built to size, with seating for 40 people. The wines have had show success in the limited period of time the winery has been operating.

Wyanga Park

 ★★☆

Baades Road, Lakes Entrance, Vic 3909 **REGION** Gippsland
T (03) 5155 1508 **F** (03) 5155 1443 **OPEN** 7 days 9–5
WINEMAKER Damien Twigg **EST.** 1970 **CASES** 3000
PRODUCT RANGE ($12–18 CD) Sauvignon Blanc, Chardonnay, Ensay Chardonnay, Miriam's Fancy Chardonnay, Rose, Boobialla (medium-sweet white), Pinot Noir, Shiraz Cabernet Sauvignon, fortifieds.
SUMMARY Offers a broad range of wines of diverse provenance directed at the tourist trade; one of the Chardonnays and the Cabernet Sauvignon are estate-grown. Winery cruises up the north arm of the Gippsland Lake to Wyanga Park are scheduled 4 days a week throughout the year.

ŶŶŶ **Estate Grown Chardonnay 2002 RATING** 83 $ 17

Wyndham Estate

 ★★★★

Dalwood Road, Dalwood, NSW 2335 **REGION** Lower Hunter Valley
T (02) 4938 3444 **F** (02) 4938 3422 **OPEN** Mon–Fri 9.30–5, weekends 10–4
WINEMAKER Brett McKinnon **EST.** 1828 **CASES** 1 million
PRODUCT RANGE ($6.95–25 R) In ascending order: Bin TR2 Select White and Select Red; 1828 varietal range; Bin 777 Semillon, Bin 111 Verdelho, Bin 222 Chardonnay, Bin 333 Pinot Noir, Bin 555 Shiraz, Bin 999 Merlot, Bin 888 Cabernet Merlot, Bin 444 Cabernet Sauvignon; Show Reserve range of Semillon, Chardonnay, Shiraz, Cabernet Merlot; Vintage Chardonnay Brut Cuvee.
SUMMARY Has risen to the challenge in recent years, even if it's all rather like the curate's egg, making an all-inclusive rating very difficult.

ŶŶŶŶ **Show Reserve Semillon 1999** Citrus, mineral and a whiff of toast; still delicate and fresh. Great value. **RATING** 92 **DRINK** 2009 $ 22
Bin 222 Chardonnay 2002 Combines complexity and elegance; stone fruit flavours; excellent line and length; subtle oak. **RATING** 92 **DRINK** Now $ 12.99
Bin 777 Semillon 2003 Clean and fresh; long, quite intense; lingering, lemony acidity. **RATING** 91 **DRINK** 2013 $ 13.99

ŶŶŶ **Show Reserve Shiraz 1999 RATING** 83 $ 25
Bin 444 Cabernet Sauvignon 2001 RATING 83 $ 13.99

Wynns Coonawarra Estate ★★★★

Memorial Drive, Coonawarra, SA 5263 **REGION** Coonawarra
T (08) 8736 2225 **F** (08) 8736 2228 **OPEN** 7 days 10–5
WINEMAKER Sue Hodder, Sarah Pidgeon **EST.** 1891
PRODUCT RANGE ($13.50–145 CD) Wynns Coonawarra Estate Riesling, Chardonnay, Shiraz, Cabernet
Shiraz Merlot, Cabernet Sauvignon and Black Label Cabernet Sauvignon; Michael Shiraz, John
Riddoch Cabernet Sauvignon.
SUMMARY The large-scale production has in no way prevented Wynns from producing excellent
wines covering the full price spectrum from the bargain basement Riesling and Shiraz through to the
deluxe John Riddoch Cabernet Sauvignon and Michael Shiraz. Even with steady price increases,
Wynns offers extraordinary value for money. Good though that may be, there is even greater promise
for the future; the vineyards are being rejuvenated by new trellising or replanting, and a regime
directed to quality rather than quantity has been introduced, all under the direction of Allen Jenkins.
He, in turn, is receiving enthusiastic support from the winemaking team headed by Sue Hodder, who
is actively seeking more refinement and length to already fine wines. The release of the 2002 vintage
wines will see the winery rating leap.

ΨΨΨΨ **Black Label Cabernet Sauvignon 2001** A complex interaction of blackberry fruit and
French oak; rich but supple fruit and ripe tannins; complete, well balanced. **RATING** 93
DRINK 2016 $ 32

ΨΨΨΨ **Riesling 2003** A mix of mineral, talc, apple and lime aromas and flavours; good length,
although a slightly hard finish. **RATING** 88 **DRINK** 2008 $ 13.50
Cabernet Shiraz Merlot 2001 A fragrant mix of berry, mint, leaf and earth; medium-
bodied, well balanced. **RATING** 88 **DRINK** 2011 $ 19.95

Xanadu Normans Wines ★★★★★

Boodjidup Road, Margaret River, WA 6285 **REGION** Margaret River
T (08) 9757 2581 **F** (08) 9757 3389 **OPEN** 7 days 10–5
WINEMAKER Jurg Muggli, Glenn Goodall, Jodie Opie **EST.** 1977 **CASES** 100 000
PRODUCT RANGE ($14–70 R) A range of varietals under the Margaret River banner, the Secession
banner, and specials under the Frankland River Show Reserve and Lagan Estate labels.
SUMMARY Xanadu, once a somewhat quirky, small family winery has reinvented itself with the arrival
of substantial outside investment capital and the acquisition of the key brands of Normans Wines of
South Australia. One hundred and thirty hectares of vineyard estate and much expanded
winemaking facilities have been complemented by a large, open courtyard, a bar area, a new cellar
door and a café-style restaurant. Wine quality, led by outstanding Merlot, has also risen. Late in 2003
the decision was taken to name the group Xanadu Normans. Exports to all major markets.

ΨΨΨΨΨ **Sauvignon Blanc Semillon 2003** Strong varietal fruit aromas and flavours; depth and
length; partial barrel ferment supports gentle tropical fruit. **RATING** 94 **DRINK** 2007 $ 19
Semillon Sauvignon Blanc 2003 Fine, elegant and perfumed; beautiful passionfruit and
herb flavours; clean finish. **RATING** 94 **DRINK** 2008 $ 19
Cabernet Sauvignon 2001 Excellent purple-red; the clean, smooth bouquet marries
blackcurrant/cassis fruit with attractively balanced and integrated French oak; the palate
has lovely depth, texture and structure. **RATING** 94 **DRINK** 2011 $ 29.50

ΨΨΨΨ **Chardonnay 2003** Fine, elegant, tight and long; almost crunchy stone fruit/kernel; subtle
barrel ferment; will grow. **RATING** 93 **DRINK** 2010 $ 28
Semillon 2002 Clever and sophisticated winemaking; good length and focus; fruit at the
centre, stylish oak on the perimeter. **RATING** 92 **DRINK** 2010 $ 24
Lagan Estate Cabernet Merlot Cabernet Franc 1999 Complex array of spice, leaf, earthy
blackcurrant and redcurrant flavours; fine, savoury tannins. **RATING** 91 **DRINK** 2009 $ 70

ΨΨΨΨ **Chardonnay 2002** A complex, slightly funky bouquet; long and citrussy palate; slightly
edgy. **RATING** 89 **DRINK** 2008 $ 28
Cabernet Merlot 2002 Supple red fruits with nice varietal cross-cut of olive and bramble;
light to medium-bodied. **RATING** 89 **DRINK** 2010 $ 19

🍷🍷🍷🍷 **Secession Chardonnay 2003** RATING 85 DRINK Now $14
Secession Semillon Sauvignon Blanc 2003 RATING 84 DRINK Now $14
Secession Shiraz Cabernet 2002 RATING 84 DRINK Now $14

Yaldara Wines   NR

Gomersal Road, Lyndoch, SA 5351 REGION Barossa Valley
T (08) 8524 4200 F (08) 8524 4678 OPEN 7 days 9–5
WINEMAKER Matt Tydeman EST. 1947 CASES 500 000
PRODUCT RANGE ($10–45 R) A full range of wines under (in ascending order) the Lakewood, Earth's
Portrait, Julians, and super-premium The Farms label.
SUMMARY At the very end of 1999 Yaldara became part of the publicly listed Simeon Wines, the
intention being that it (Yaldara) should become the quality flagship of the group. Despite much
expenditure and the short-lived stay of at least one well-known winemaker, the plan failed to deliver
the expected benefits. In February 2002 McGuigan Wines made a reverse takeover for Simeon, and
the various McGuigan brands will (presumably) fill the role intended for Yaldara.

Yalumba   ★★★★☆

Eden Valley Road, Angaston, SA 5353 REGION Barossa Valley
T (08) 8561 3200 F (08) 8561 3393 OPEN Mon–Fri 8.30–5, Sat 10–5, Sun 12–5
WINEMAKER Brian Walsh, Alan Hoey, Louisa Rose, Peter Gambetta, Kevin Glastonbury, Natalie
Fryar, Philip Lehmann EST. 1849 CASES 900 000
PRODUCT RANGE ($6.50–115 CD) A clearly structured portfolio arranged by price point, commencing
at the bottom with Oxford Landing, then the Y series; next the Yalumba Barossa wines; then
premium regional wines from the Eden Valley, Adelaide Hills, Clare Valley; Vinnovations Nebbiolo
and Cienna; then at the top of the dry table wines are The Octavius Barossa Shiraz, The Signature
Cabernet Sauvignon Shiraz and The Reserve Cabernet Sauvignon Shiraz; a trio of Noble Pick sweet
wines are rounded off with the Yalumba D sparkling wines and fortifieds.
SUMMARY Family-owned and run by Robert Hill-Smith; much of its prosperity in the late 1980s and
early 1990s turned on the great success of Angas Brut in export markets, but the company has always
had a commitment to quality and shown great vision in its selection of vineyard sites, new varieties
and brands. It has always been a serious player at the top end of full-bodied (and full-blooded)
Australian reds, and was the pioneer in the use of Stelvin screwcaps (for Pewsey Vale Riesling). While
its 940 hectares of estate vineyards are largely planted to mainstream varieties, it has taken
marketing ownership of Viognier. Exports to all major markets.

🍷🍷🍷🍷🍷 **Signature Cabernet Shiraz 1999** Cassis, chocolate and raspberry fruit aromas and
flavours fill a wine with excellent structure, weight, texture and balance; a long, lingering,
fruit-driven finish shows the deft use of oak. RATING 95 DRINK 2020 $39.95
The Virgilius 2002 Intense, complex aromas; excellent mouthfeel and length; lemony
overtones to honeysuckle fruit; no alcohol heat. RATING 94 DRINK 2007 $49.95
Octavius Shiraz 1999 Highly scented, rich, oaky style but with abundant blackberry fruit
to carry the oak. RATING 94 DRINK 2018 $89.95

🍷🍷🍷🍷 **Wild Ferment Eden Valley Chardonnay 2003** Powerful, long and intense;
citrus/nectarine married with cashew and oak; lingering finish; great value. Strangely,
cork-finished. RATING 92 DRINK 2007 $16.95
Y Series Riesling 2003 Zesty, limey palate; concentrated and powerful but not coarse;
passionfruit and grapefruit. Screwcap. RATING 91 DRINK 2010 $23.95
MGS Grenache Shiraz Mourvedre 2002 An aromatic, tangy bouquet, then an
unexpectedly muscular and masculine palate, with black fruits and built-in tannins.
RATING 91 DRINK 2027 $28.95
Octavius Shiraz 2000 Supple, smooth and round raspberry, plum and blackberry; much
less dense and oaky than usual; clever response to the vintage. RATING 90 DRINK 2010
$89.95
Barossa Valley Shiraz Viognier 2000 Spicy, savoury blackberry aromas; a strongly
accented, unusually oaky, palate, the viognier adding yet another dimension. A Guigal
super-cuvee lookalike. RATING 90 DRINK 2010 $28.95

Growers Bush Vine Grenache 2002 Sweet plum and spice; good length and structure; much the best so far under this label. **RATING** 90 **DRINK** 2008 $ 16.95

Tri-Centenary Grenache 2002 Elegant, fresh, juicy berry fruit flavours; silky texture and nice balance. **RATING** 90 **DRINK** 2007 $ 29.95

Ringbolt Cabernet Sauvignon 2001 Powerful black fruits; hints of earth and chocolate; very fine, gently savoury tannins. A new Margaret River brand. **RATING** 90 **DRINK** 2011 $ 19.95

ΨΨΨΨ **Eden Valley Viognier 2002** Light to medium-bodied; well balanced; some honeysuckle and apricot; not intense. **RATING** 89 **DRINK** Now $ 22.95

Christobels Dry White 2003 Strikingly fragrant and aromatic; tropical, gooseberry, with good balancing acidity; fresh and clean. Excellent value. **RATING** 89 **DRINK** Now $ 11.95

Signature Cabernet Shiraz 2000 Blackberry, blackcurrant and earth; overall quite savoury and slightly boney. **RATING** 89 **DRINK** 2010 $ 39.95

Single Spur Chardonnay 2002 Tangy, intense, aromatic nectarine and citrus aromas and flavours; entirely fruit-driven; good length. From the Adelaide Hills; an odd explanation of the name on the back label, incidentally. **RATING** 88 **DRINK** 2008 $ 22.95

Barossa Growers Shiraz 2001 Quite complex; traditional black fruits and vanilla oak flavours; medium-bodied and honest. **RATING** 88 **DRINK** 2011 $ 16.95

Oxford Landing Shiraz 2002 A vintage when all Christmases came at once in the Riverland; very good colour; a smooth basket of red fruits; good balance and length; sensational value. **RATING** 87 **DRINK** Now $ 6.50

The Menzies Cabernet Sauvignon 2000 Clean, fragrant blackcurrant aromas; long, slightly mouth-puckering tannins to close. **RATING** 87 **DRINK** 2009 $ 35.95

ΨΨΨΨ **Oxford Landing Sauvignon Blanc 2003** Good flavour; not too sweet or phenolic; tropical/gooseberry fruit; excellent value. **RATING** 86 **DRINK** Now $ 7.95

Oxford Landing Chardonnay 2003 Supremely honest; not forced, phenolic nor sweet; generous stone fruit and the barest hint of oak. **RATING** 86 **DRINK** Now $ 7.95

Antipodean Sangiovese Rose 2003 That distinctive lemony, citrussy tang of the variety as grown in Australia; interesting wine. Screwcap. **RATING** 86 **DRINK** Now $ 16.50

Galway Vintage Shiraz 2002 **RATING** 86 **DRINK** 2007 $ 12.95

Y Series Shiraz 2002 **RATING** 86 **DRINK** Now $ 12.95

Y Series Cabernet Sauvignon 2002 **RATING** 85 **DRINK** 2009 $ 11.95

Oxford Landing Cabernet Sauvignon Shiraz 2002 Nice wine; berry, leaf and mint; low tannins; very good value. **RATING** 85 **DRINK** Now $ 6.50

Y Series Unwooded Chardonnay 2003 **RATING** 84 **DRINK** Now $ 9.10

ΨΨΨ **Barossa Semillon Sauvignon Blanc 2003** **RATING** 83 $ 16.95

Yalumba The Menzies (Coonawarra) ★★★☆

Riddoch Highway, Coonawarra, SA 5263 **REGION** Coonawarra
T (08) 8737 3603 **F** (08) 8737 3604 **OPEN** 7 days 10–4.30
WINEMAKER Louisa Rose, Peter Gambetta **EST.** 2002 **CASES** 5000
PRODUCT RANGE ($17.50–37.95 CD) The Menzies Cabernet Sauvignon; Mawson's range of Coonawarra Shiraz, Coonawarra Cabernet Franc, Coonawarra Cabernet Sauvignon Shiraz Merlot; and Smith & Hooper Wrattonbully range of Merlot, Cabernet Sauvignon Merlot.
SUMMARY Like many South Australian companies, Yalumba had been buying grapes from Coonawarra and elsewhere in the Limestone Coast Zone long before it became a landowner there. In 1993 it purchased the 20-hectare vineyard which had provided the grapes previously purchased, and a year later added a nearby 16-hectare block. Together, these vineyards now have 22 hectares of cabernet sauvignon and 4 hectares each of merlot and shiraz. The next step was the establishment of 82 hectares of vineyard in the Wrattonbully region, led by 34 hectares of cabernet sauvignon, the remainder equally split between shiraz and merlot. The third step was to build The Menzies Wine Room and Vineyard on the first property acquired — named Menzies Vineyard — and to offer the full range of Limestone Coast wines through this striking rammed-earth tasting and function centre.

ΨΨΨΨ **Smith & Hooper Limited Edition Merlot 2001** Positive varietal character with small red and black berry fruits; still with a relatively simple, straight-line texture and structure. **RATING** 87 **DRINK** 2008 $ 36.95

ᵀᵀᵀ **Smith & Hooper Cabernet Sauvignon Merlot 2001** RATING 86 DRINK 2011 $16.95
Coonawarra Shiraz 2001 RATING 85 DRINK 2008 $24.95
Cabernet Sauvignon 2001 RATING 85 DRINK 2007 $35.95

Yandoit Hill Vineyard ★★★

Nevens Road, Yandoit Creek, Vic 3461 REGION Bendigo
T (03) 9379 1763 F (03) 9379 1763 OPEN By appointment (special open days for mailing list customers)
WINEMAKER Colin Mitchell EST. 1988 CASES 300
PRODUCT RANGE ($19–25 CD) Arneis, Merlot, Cabernets, Barbera, Tromba d'Aria, Nebbiolo Cabernet Sauvignon.
SUMMARY Colin and Rosa Mitchell commenced the development of Yandoit Hill with the first plantings in 1988 of merlot, and a little under a hectare each of cabernet franc and cabernet sauvignon, followed by 0.5 hectare each of arneis (the first planting in Australia), and nebbiolo in 1995. The vineyard is situated 20 kilometres north of Daylesford, roughly halfway between Ballarat and Bendigo and, although situated on the north-facing slope of Yandoit Hill, is in an uncompromisingly cool climate.

ᵀᵀᵀ **Tromba d'Aria Barbera 2002** RATING 84 DRINK 2008 $19

Yangarra Estate ★★★★☆

Kangarilla Road, McLaren Vale, SA 5171 REGION McLaren Vale
T (08) 8383 7459 F (08) 8383 7518 OPEN By appointment
WINEMAKER Peter Fraser EST. 2000 CASES 100 000
PRODUCT RANGE ($28–30 R) McLaren Vale Shiraz, McLaren Vale Old Vine Grenache, McLaren Vale Grenache Shiraz Mourvedre.
SUMMARY This is the Australian operation of Kendall-Jackson, one of the leading premium wine producers in California. In December 2000 Kendall-Jackson acquired the 172-hectare Eringa Park vineyard from Normans Wines; 97 hectares are under vine, the oldest dating back to 1923. The name change to Yangarra Park provides the key estate base for the operation, and from the 2003 vintage, wines will be virtually 100 per cent estate-grown. The 2002 wines have moved in this direction, and are a significant improvement on prior releases. Exports to the US, the UK and Europe.

ᵀᵀᵀᵀ **McLaren Vale Shiraz 2002** A rich, classic mix of blackberry and dark chocolate seamlessly fused with oak; nice, ripe tannins. Screwcap. RATING 93 DRINK 2017 $30
McLaren Vale Grenache Shiraz Mourvedre 2002 Impenetrable colour; dark berries and oak in profusion; depth and structure; appropriate oak. RATING 93 DRINK 2012 $28
McLaren Vale Old Vine Grenache 2002 Quite aromatic; a firm, lingering spicy aftertaste which gives the wine personality and lift. RATING 90 DRINK 2010 $28

Yanmah Ridge NR

Yanmah Road, Manjimup, WA 6258 REGION Manjimup
T (08) 9772 1301 F (08) 9772 1501 OPEN By appointment
WINEMAKER Peter Nicholas, John Wade (Consultant) EST. 1987 CASES 3500
PRODUCT RANGE ($12.99–28 ML) Sauvignon Blanc, Chardonnay, Karrimont (sparkling), Merlot, Reserve Merlot, Cabernet Merlot; Fishermans second label includes White, Fizz and Red.
SUMMARY Peter and Sallyann Nicholas have established 26 hectares of vineyards planted on elevated, north-facing slopes, with semillon, sauvignon blanc, chardonnay, pinot noir, sangiovese, merlot, cabernet franc and cabernet sauvignon. The property on which the vineyard is planted was identified by Peter Nicholas in 1986 as 'the perfect location'; this was the outcome of a study of grape-growing regions in Western Australia. The project was the last requirement for Nicholas to complete his winemaking degree at Roseworthy Agricultural College. Their viticulture is environmentally friendly, with no residual herbicides or chemical pesticides. Although a new winery was built on-site in time for the 2001 vintage, the lion's share of the annual production is still sold (as grapes or wine) to other producers. Wholesale distribution through Working Wine, Victoria, Lionel Samson, Western Australia and Simsed Agencies, New South Wales and Queensland. Exports to England, Canada and Hong Kong.

Yarrabank ★★★★★

38 Melba Highway, Yarra Glen, Vic 3775 **REGION** Yarra Valley
T (03) 9730 0100 **F** (03) 9739 0135 **OPEN** 7 days 10–5
WINEMAKER Michel Parisot, Tom Carson, Darren Rathbone **EST.** 1993 **CASES** 5000
PRODUCT RANGE ($30–35 CD) Cuvee, Creme de Cuvee, Brut Cuvee.
SUMMARY The 1997 vintage saw the opening of the majestic new winery, established as part of a joint venture between the French Champagne house Devaux and Yering Station, and which has added another major dimension to the Yarra Valley. Until 1997 the Yarrabank Cuvee Brut was made under Claude Thibaut's direction at Domaine Chandon, but thereafter the entire operation has been conducted at Yarrabank. Four hectares of dedicated 'estate' vineyards have been established at Yering Station; the balance of the intake comes from other growers in the Yarra Valley and southern Victoria. Wine quality has been quite outstanding, the wines having a delicacy unmatched by any other Australian sparkling wines. Exports to all major markets.

YYYYY **Cuvee 1999** Light, bright straw-green; finely structured; apple, stone fruit and citrus intermingling with creamy/toasty notes. **RATING** 96 **DRINK** Now $ 35

Yarra Brook Estate ★★☆

Yarraview Road, Yarra Glen, Vic 3775 **REGION** Yarra Valley
T (03) 9763 7066 **F** (03) 9763 8757 **OPEN** By appointment
WINEMAKER MasterWineMakers (Contract) **EST.** 1997 **CASES** 2000
PRODUCT RANGE ($15 CD) Chardonnay, Pinot Noir, Shiraz, Cabernet Sauvignon.
SUMMARY Beginning in 1997, Chris Dhar has established 26 hectares of vines, the lion's share being pinot noir (10.4 hectares) and chardonnay (6.8 hectares), the remainder shared equally between sauvignon blanc, merlot, shiraz and cabernet sauvignon. Most of the grapes are sold, but part of the production is made by MasterWineMakers. The prices ex the mail list are very reasonable, thanks to the exemption from WET for small wineries selling direct.

YYY **Chardonnay 2002** **RATING** 83

Yarra Burn ★★★★☆

Settlement Road, Yarra Junction, Vic 3797 **REGION** Yarra Valley
T (03) 5967 1428 **F** (03) 5967 1146 **OPEN** 7 days 10–5
WINEMAKER Ed Carr, Tom Newton **EST.** 1975 **CASES** 15 000
PRODUCT RANGE ($17.99–47.99 R) Sauvignon Blanc Semillon, Chardonnay, Pinot Noir, Chardonnay Pinot Noir, Shiraz, Cabernet Sauvignon, Sparkling Pinot, Chardonnay Pinot; Bastard Hill Chardonnay, Bastard Hill Pinot Noir.
SUMMARY Acquired by BRL Hardy in 1995 and, for the time being, the headquarters of Hardys' very substantial Yarra Valley operations, the latter centring on the large production from its Hoddles Creek vineyards. The new brand direction has largely taken shape. Care needs to be taken in reading the back labels of the wines other the Bastard Hill duo, for the majority are regional blends, albeit with a substantial Yarra Valley component. Exports to the UK and the US.

YYYYY **Bastard Hill Chardonnay 1999** Utterly striking wine; in super-opulent White Burgundy style; complex and potent mix of barrel ferment and intense fruit; excellent length, depth and structure. Four trophies. **RATING** 95 **DRINK** 2009 $ 45

YYYYY **Pinot Noir 2002** Massive wine; a cocktail of fruit, oak and alcohol, yet retains varietal character. **RATING** 90 **DRINK** 2009 $ 23.99

YYYY **Pinot Gris 2003** Quite intense and perfumed pear and apple aromas; good texture and mouthfeel; apple, spice and mineral; real length. **RATING** 89 **DRINK** Now $ 21.50
Shiraz Viognier 2002 Fragrant blackberry, raspberry and spice aromas and flavours; light to medium-bodied; good balance and length. **RATING** 88 **DRINK** 2008 $ 19

Yarra Edge ★★★☆

PO Box 390, Yarra Glen, Vic 3775 **REGION** Yarra Valley
T (03) 9730 0100 **F** (03) 9739 0135 **OPEN** At Yering Station, 7 days 10–5
WINEMAKER Tom Carson, Darren Rathbone **EST.** 1984 **CASES** 2000
PRODUCT RANGE ($25–30 CD) Chardonnay, Pinot Noir, Single Vineyard Red (Bordeaux blend).
SUMMARY Now leased to Yering Station, which makes the wines but continues to use the Yarra Edge brand for grapes from this estate. Tom Carson, Yering Station winemaker, was briefly winemaker/manager at Yarra Edge and knows the property intimately, so the rich style can be expected to continue. Exports to Hong Kong.

ŶŶŶŶ **Single Vineyard 1999** Quite complex, savoury bottle-developed characters; touches of chocolate and briar; struggles in competition with younger and better vintages. **RATING** 87 **DRINK** Now $ 30

Yarraman Estate ★★★☆

Yarraman Road, Wybong, NSW 2333 **REGION** Upper Hunter Valley
T (02) 6547 8118 **F** (02) 6547 8039 **OPEN** 7 days 10–5
WINEMAKER Angus Campbell **EST.** 1958 **CASES** 25 000
PRODUCT RANGE ($14.95–24.95 R) Classic Hunter Series of Semillon, Chardonnay, Shiraz, Merlot; Black Cypress Series of Gewurztraminer, Semillon, Chardonnay, Shiraz, Chambourcin, Cabernet Shiraz; Sensus white and red.
SUMMARY This is the oldest winery and vineyard in the Upper Hunter, established in 1958 as Penfolds Wybong Estate; it was acquired by Rosemount in 1974, and retained until 1994. During 1999–2001 a new winery and storage area was built; after hitting financial turbulence, it was acquired by a small group of Sydney businessmen. The appointments of Angus Campbell as winemaker/general manager and Richard Winchester as sales and marketing manager have stabilised the business.

ŶŶŶŶŶ **Black Cypress Semillon 2002** Very positive lemon, herb and lanolin varietal fruit; lots of character and flavour. Screwcap. **RATING** 90 **DRINK** 2008 $ 14.95
Merlot 2001 Good texture and weight; a nice mix of berry fruit, olive and bramble; good tannin and oak management; a surprise packet. **RATING** 90 **DRINK** 2009 $ 24.95

ŶŶŶŶ **Black Cypress Cabernet Shiraz 2001** Sourced from the Frankland River; elegant, medium-bodied, bright juicy berry fruit; subtle oak. **RATING** 88 $ 14.95
Black Cypress Chambourcin 2003 Ripe, full-on entry to the mouth; supple black fruits; as ever, tails off on the finish. **RATING** 87 **DRINK** Now $ 14.95

ŶŶŶŶ **Black Cypress Chardonnay 2002** **RATING** 86 **DRINK** Now $ 14.95
Black Cypress Shiraz 2001 **RATING** 86 **DRINK** 2009 $ 14.95
Black Cypress Chambourcin 2002 **RATING** 86 **DRINK** 2010 $ 14.95
Black Cypress Shiraz 2002 **RATING** 85 **DRINK** 2008 $ 14.95

ŶŶŶ **Black Cypress Gewurztraminer 2002** **RATING** 83 $ 14.95
Shiraz 2001 **RATING** 83 $ 24.95
Chardonnay 2002 **RATING** 82 $ 22.95

Yarrambat Estate ★★★★☆

45 Laurie Street, Yarrambat, Vic 3091 (postal) **REGION** Yarra Valley
T (03) 9717 3710 **F** (03) 9717 3712 **OPEN** Not
WINEMAKER John Ellis (Contract) **EST.** 1995 **CASES** 1500
PRODUCT RANGE ($25–35 ML) Chardonnay, Pinot Noir, Merlot Cabernet, Cabernet Sauvignon.
SUMMARY Ivan McQuilkin has a little over 2.6 hectares of chardonnay, pinot noir, cabernet sauvignon and merlot on his vineyard in the northwestern corner of the Yarra Valley, not far from the Plenty River, which joins the Yarra River near Melbourne. The vineyard has been planted on an easterly slope, with north–south row orientation. In the first 2 years of production (1998 and 1999) the grapes were sold to Yering Station, but since that time the grapes have been vinified under the Yarrambat Estate label. It is very much an alternative occupation for McQuilkin, whose principal activity is as an

international taxation consultant to expatriate employees. While the decision to make the wine was at least in part triggered by falling grape prices, hindsight proves it to have been a good one, because the red wines, in particular, are outstanding. There are no cellar-door sales; the conditions of the licence are that wine sales can only take place by mail order or via the internet <www.yarrambat-estate.com>, in the same fashion as Studley Park.

ᵀᵀᵀᵀᵠ **Merlot Cabernet 2001** Good colour; spicy edges to blackcurrant fruit; supple, light to medium-bodied, stylish palate. **RATING** 90 **DRINK** 2011 $ 35

Cabernet Sauvignon 2001 Well balanced and poised; cedar, spice and blackcurrant; good oak handling; like the Merlot Cabernet, light to medium-bodied. **RATING** 90 **DRINK** 2011 $ 35

Yarra Ridge ★★★★

Glenview Road, Yarra Glen, Vic 3755 **REGION** Yarra Valley
T (03) 9730 1022 **F** (03) 9730 1131 **OPEN** 7 days 10–5
WINEMAKER Matt Steel **EST.** 1983 **CASES** 45 000
PRODUCT RANGE ($16–42 R) Sauvignon Blanc, Chardonnay, Pinot Noir, Reserve Pinot Noir, Achilles Heel Pinot Noir, Shiraz, Reserve Shiraz, Merlot, Cabernet Sauvignon, Reserve Cabernet Sauvignon; Mount Tanglefoot has been introduced as a second range, made from grapes grown in regions other than the Yarra Valley.
SUMMARY Under the sole ownership and control of Beringer Blass, with a winery which is strained to its limits. Recent vineyard plantings in the Yarra Valley, and continued purchasing of Yarra Valley grapes, mean that the majority of the wines will continue to be Yarra Valley-sourced. That said, they have a commercial veneer, and are reliable rather than exciting.

ᵀᵀᵀᵀᵀ **Pinot Noir 2002** Great return to form; intense, fine, long and elegant; great finish. **RATING** 94 **DRINK** 2009 $ 22

ᵀᵀᵀᵀᵠ **Merlot 2001** Appealing wine; ripe, soft blackcurrant fruit; supple texture; good oak handling. Screwcap. **RATING** 91 **DRINK** 2011 $ 22

ᵀᵀᵀᵀ **Pinot Grigio 2003** Pale blush pink; perfumed spice, apple and strawberry aromas; delicate, light and fresh in the mouth; ideal brasserie wine. **RATING** 89 **DRINK** Now $ 24

Sauvignon Blanc 2003 Abundant varietal gooseberry and passionfruit aroma and flavour; a ghost of reduction, but its best for years. Sourced predominantly from the Upper Yarra. **RATING** 88 **DRINK** Now $ 19

Cabernet Sauvignon 2001 Smooth, light to medium-bodied; clear cassis/blackcurrant fruit; not a great deal of structure. **RATING** 88 **DRINK** 2011 $ 22

Unwooded Chardonnay 2003 Fresh and light, the fruit part citrus, part melon; clean finish. Screwcap. **RATING** 87 **DRINK** Now $ 22

ᵀᵀᵀᵠ **Rose 2003 RATING** 86 **DRINK** Now $ 24

Yarra Track Wines ★★★☆

518 Old Healesville Road, Yarra Glen, Vic 3775 **REGION** Yarra Valley
T (03) 9730 1349 **F** (03) 9730 1910 **OPEN** 7 days 10–5.30
WINEMAKER MasterWineMakers (Contract) **EST.** 1989 **CASES** 800
PRODUCT RANGE ($25–28 CD) Chardonnay, Nina's Chardonnay, Lucy's Chardonnay, Pinot Noir.
SUMMARY Jim and Diana Viggers began the establishment of their vineyard back in 1989; it now has 3.1 hectares of chardonnay and 3.4 hectares of pinot noir. The Viggers have chosen very competent winemakers and intend to increase wine production progressively while selling part of the grape production in the meantime. The wine is sold only through the cellar door and at local restaurants.

ᵀᵀᵀᵀᵠ **Pinot Noir 2003** Deeply coloured; intense plum and black cherry fruit; powerful finish. **RATING** 91 **DRINK** 2010 $ 28

ᵀᵀᵀᵀ **Lucy's Chardonnay 2003** Complex tangy, smoky aromas; a more direct, well-balanced palate. **RATING** 89 **DRINK** 2008 $ 25

Yarra Vale

NR

Paynes Road, Seville, Vic 3139 **REGION** Yarra Valley
T (03) 9735 1819 **F** (03) 9737 6565 **OPEN** Not
WINEMAKER Domenic Bucci **EST.** 1982 **CASES** 1500
PRODUCT RANGE ($13–26 R) Chardonnay, Rose, Merlot, Cabernet Sauvignon.
SUMMARY This is the second time around for Domenic Bucci, who built the first stage of what is now Eyton-on-Yarra before being compelled to sell the business in the hard times of the early 1990s. He has established 2 hectares of cabernet sauvignon and 0.5 hectare of merlot, supplemented by chardonnay which is supplied in return for his winemaking services to the grower. The wines have retail distribution in Melbourne through Sullivan Wine Agencies, and exports via Rubins Productions.

Yarra Valley Gateway Estate

★★★☆

669 Maroondah Highway, Coldstream, Vic 3770 **REGION** Yarra Valley
T (03) 9739 0568 **F** (03) 9739 0568 **OPEN** 7 days 9–5
WINEMAKER Matt Aldridge (Contract) **EST.** 1993 **CASES** 1200
PRODUCT RANGE ($19–22 R) Sauvignon Blanc, Chardonnay, Pinot Noir.
SUMMARY Rod Spurling extended his successful hydroponic tomato-growing business by the planting of 5 hectares of sauvignon blanc, chardonnay and pinot noir in 1993. It is part of a new grouping of so-called Micro Masters which have begun business in the Yarra Valley over the past few years.

ŸŸŸŸ **Spurling Hill Vineyard Sauvignon Blanc 2003** Clean, crisp; citrussy fruit; good finish and length. **RATING** 87 **DRINK** Now $19
Spurling Hill Vineyard Chardonnay 2003 Light, clean melon, peach and nectarine; easy-access style. **RATING** 87 **DRINK** 2007 $22
Spurling Hill Vineyard Pinot Noir 2003 Light to medium-bodied; cherry, plum and spice; another well-made wine. **RATING** 87 **DRINK** 2008 $22

Yarra Valley Hills

★★★

c/- Dromana Estate, Harrison's Road and Bittern–Dromana Road, Dromana, Vic 3936
REGION Yarra Valley
T (03) 5987 3177 **F** (03) 5987 3977 **OPEN** Not
WINEMAKER Rollo Crittenden **EST.** 1989 **CASES** 10 000
PRODUCT RANGE ($17–21 CD) Sauvignon Blanc, Chardonnay, Pinot Noir, Cabernet Sauvignon.
SUMMARY The business of Yarra Valley Hills was acquired by Dromana Estate in 2000. Dromana has kept the Yarra Valley Hills brand, but sold the winery to MasterWineMakers, who uses it to provide custom crush and make facilities for other Yarra Valley wineries and for Martin Williams to make his own Metier brand.

ŸŸŸŸ **Semillon Sauvignon Blanc 2003** **RATING** 86 **DRINK** Now $17

🐚 Yarra Valley Vineyards

NR

159 Lilydale–Monbulk Road, Silvan, Vic 3795 **REGION** Yarra Valley
T (03) 9737 9630 **OPEN** By appointment
WINEMAKER Contract **EST.** 1993
SUMMARY Don Smarrelli has an 8-hectare vineyard at Silvan, in one of the cooler parts of the Yarra Valley; it has the red volcanic soils generally encountered on this southern edge. The wines are exported to the US, China and elsewhere in Asia.

🐚 Yarrawalla Wines

★★★☆

Maddens Lane, Coldstream, Vic 3770 **REGION** Yarra Valley
T (03) 5964 9363 **F** (03) 5964 9363 **OPEN** By appointment
WINEMAKER Dominique Portet (Contract) **EST.** 1994
PRODUCT RANGE ($16–17.50 CD) Sauvignon Blanc, Chardonnay, Pinot Noir.

SUMMARY A very prominent vineyard on Maddens Lane, with 24 hectares of chardonnay, 12.7 hectares of pinot noir and 6.5 hectares of sauvignon blanc. Most of the grape production has been sold, with significant amounts going to Coldstream Hills over the years. With the arrival of Dominique Portet (also on Maddens Lane), Yarrawalla has ventured into winemaking under its own label, although the major part of the production continues to be sold as grapes.

ŸŸŸŸ **Sauvignon Blanc 2003** Abundant fruit on both bouquet and palate, in full-bodied, ripe-fruit style. **RATING** 88 **DRINK** Now $16
Chardonnay 2002 Clean; subtle fruit and oak; nectarine and citrus flavours; well made, with considerable length. **RATING** 87 **DRINK** Now $17.50

ŸŸŸŸ **Sauvignon Blanc 2002** **RATING** 85 **DRINK** Now $16

ŸŸŸ **Pinot Noir 2001** **RATING** 83 $17.50

Yarra Yarra ★★★★★

239 Hunts Lane, Steels Creek, Vic 3775 **REGION** Yarra Valley
T (03) 5965 2380 **F** (03) 5965 2086 **OPEN** By appointment
WINEMAKER Ian Maclean **EST.** 1979
PRODUCT RANGE ($30–60 CD) Semillon Sauvignon Blanc, Merlot, Syrah, Cabernets, The Yarra Yarra (previously Reserve Cabernet Sauvignon).
SUMMARY Despite its small production, the wines of Yarra Yarra have found their way onto a veritable who's who listing of Melbourne's best restaurants. This has encouraged Ian Maclean to increase the estate plantings from 2 hectares to over 7 hectares during the 1996 and 1997 seasons. The demand for the beautifully crafted wines continued to exceed supply, so the Macleans have planted yet more vines and increased winery capacity. Exports to the UK and Singapore.

Yarra Yering ★★★★★

Briarty Road, Coldstream, Vic 3770 (postal) **REGION** Yarra Valley
T (03) 5964 9267 **F** (03) 5964 9239 **OPEN** Usually first Saturday in May
WINEMAKER Bailey Carrodus, Mark Haisma **EST.** 1969
PRODUCT RANGE Dry White No. 1 (Sauvignon Blanc Semillon), Chardonnay, Pinot Noir, Dry Red No. 1 (Bordeaux blend), Dry Red No. 2 (Rhône blend), Merlot (tiny quantities at $100 a bottle), Underhill Shiraz, Underhill 3 Year Cask Shiraz, Portsorts. The portfolio continues to expand, with Dry Red No. 3, Sangiovese and Viognier.
SUMMARY Dr Bailey Carrodus makes extremely powerful, occasionally idiosyncratic wines from his 30-year-old, low-yielding, unirrigated vineyards. Both red and white wines have an exceptional depth of flavour and richness, although my preference for what I believe to be his great red wines is well known. As he has expanded the size of his vineyards, so has the range of wines become ever more eclectic, none more so than the only Vintage Port being produced in the Yarra Valley. The wines are exported to the UK, the US, Switzerland, Germany, Hong Kong, Japan, Malaysia and Singapore.

Yass Valley Wines NR

5 Crisps Lane, Murrumbateman, NSW 2582 **REGION** Canberra District
T (02) 6227 5592 **F** (02) 6227 5592 **OPEN** Wed–Sun and public holidays 11–5, or by appointment
WINEMAKER Michael Withers **EST.** 1978 **CASES** 500
PRODUCT RANGE ($16–18 CD) Traminer, Dry White, Rieselle (semi-sweet), Shiraz, Barbera, Merlot.
SUMMARY Michael Withers and Anne Hillier purchased Yass Valley in January 1991 and have subsequently rehabilitated the existing run-down vineyards and extended the plantings. Mick Withers is a chemist by profession and has completed a wine science degree at Charles Sturt University; Anne is a registered psychologist and has completed a viticulture diploma at Charles Sturt. Crisps Lane Café is open weekends and public holidays from 11 am to 5 pm, and has an emphasis on local produce.

Yaxley Estate ★★★★

31 Dransfield Road, Copping, Tas 7174 **REGION** Southern Tasmania
T (03) 6253 5222 **F** (03) 6253 5222 **OPEN** 7 days 10–6.30
WINEMAKER Andrew Hood (Contract) **EST.** 1991 **CASES** 330
PRODUCT RANGE ($22–25 CD) Sauvignon Blanc, Pinot Gris, Chardonnay, Pinot Noir.
SUMMARY While Yaxley Estate was established back in 1991, it was not until 1998 that it offered each of the four wines from its vineyard plantings, which total just under 2 hectares. Once again, the small-batch handling skills (and patience) of contract winemaker Andrew Hood have made the venture possible.

Yellowglen ★★★☆

Whites Road, Smythesdale, Vic 3351 **REGION** Ballarat
T (03) 5342 8617 **F** (03) 5333 7102 **OPEN** Mon–Fri 10–5, weekends 11–5
WINEMAKER Charles Hargrave **EST.** 1975 **CASES** 420 000
PRODUCT RANGE ($11–35 R) Grand Cuvee range of Pinot Noir Chardonnay, Brut Cremant, Brut Rose, Pinot Noir; Premium range of Vintage Brut, Y Premium, Y Sparkling Burgundy, Cuvee Victoria; also Yellow and Red.
SUMMARY Just as the overall quality of Australian sparkling wine has improved out of all recognition over the past 15 years, so has that of Yellowglen. Initially the quality lift was apparent only at the top end of the range; it now extends right to the non-vintage commercial releases.

ΨΨΨΨΨ **Vintage Cuvee Victoria 1999** Excellent mousse; the bouquet a cornucopia of baker's shop bready/yeasty aromas, the palate refocusing on punchy, crisp fruit. **RATING** 95 **DRINK** Now $35

ΨΨΨΨ **Vintage Pinot Chardonnay 2001** Bronze tints; fresh; touches of spice and bread; strawberry fruit on the palate; good length, crisp finish; clever dosage. **RATING** 88 **DRINK** Now $18

Y NV Crisp, clean and lingering; citrus and a touch of strawberry; fresh finish. **RATING** 87 **DRINK** Now $20

ΨΨΨΫ **Cremant Sparkling 2001 RATING** 85 **DRINK** Now $18

ΨΨΨ **Pink NV RATING** 81 $11

Yellymong ★★★

Moulamein Road, Swan Hill, Vic 3585 **REGION** Swan Hill
T (03) 5032 2160 **F** (03) 5032 2160 **OPEN** By appointment
WINEMAKER Allan Cooper **EST.** 2000 **CASES** 300
PRODUCT RANGE ($18–25 CD) Pinot Gris.
SUMMARY Gary and Jo Jeans have a tiny planting of 0.4 hectare of pinot gris, supplemented by purchases of other varieties from local growers, all of which are hand-picked. The Pinot Gris is remarkably good given the (theoretically) unsuitable (ie too-warm) climate.

ΨΨΨΫ **Pinot Gris 2003** Well made; remarkable flavour and style from this region; good balance. Screwcap. **RATING** 86 **DRINK** Now $22

Yengari Wine Company NR

La Trobe University, Beechworth, Vic 3747 **REGION** Beechworth
T (03) 5728 1438 **F** (03) 5833 9201 **OPEN** By appointment
WINEMAKER Tony Lacy **EST.** 2000 **CASES** 500
PRODUCT RANGE ($12–35 CD) Chardonnay, Shiraz, Merlot, Cabernet Sauvignon.
SUMMARY Tony Lacy and partner Trish Flores run an interesting grape and olive produce business, wines from the 2.4 hectares of shiraz, 1.2 hectares of chardonnay and 0.5 hectare of viognier forming but part of the range of products. Painted candles coloured with wine lees, stationery tinted using the same colour bases, wine soap (shiraz, chardonnay and cabernet sauvignon) and watercolour paints (shiraz from 100 per cent sun-dried wine lees and chardonnay from sun-dried wine lees plus traces of natural water colour) are all produced and sold.

Yeringberg ★★★★☆

Maroondah Highway, Coldstream, Vic 3770 **REGION** Yarra Valley
T (03) 9739 1453 **F** (03) 9739 0048 **OPEN** By appointment
WINEMAKER Guill de Pury **EST.** 1863 **CASES** 1000
PRODUCT RANGE ($30–45 CD) Chardonnay, Marsanne/Roussanne, Pinot Noir, Yeringberg (Cabernet blend).
SUMMARY Makes wines for the new millennium from the low-yielding vines re-established on the heart of what was one of the most famous (and originally much larger) vineyards of the 19th century. In the riper years, the red wines have a velvety generosity of flavour which is rarely encountered, yet never lose varietal character, while the Yeringberg White takes students of history back to Yeringberg's fame in the 19th century. The wines are exported to the UK, the US, Switzerland, Malaysia, Hong Kong and Singapore.

TTTTY **Dry Red 2002** Elegant, medium-bodied, highly polished amalgam of Cabernet Sauvignon, Cabernet Franc, Merlot and Malbec; lingering red fruits on the finish. **RATING** 93 **DRINK** 2015 **$** 45
Pinot Noir 2002 Elegant and fine; a seamless fruit and oak marriage; light to medium-bodied plum and savoury fruit; very long finish. **RATING** 92 **DRINK** 2012 **$** 45
Chardonnay 2003 Fine, elegant, very tight and youthful; latent complexity will flower with time in bottle; cashew, melon and mineral; great length. **RATING** 91 **DRINK** 2010 **$** 30
Marsanne Roussanne 2003 Spiced apple and pear aromas; a powerful palate, slightly hot, but also very long. **RATING** 90 **DRINK** 2013 **$** 30

Yering Farm ★★★☆

St Huberts Road, Yering, Vic 3770 **REGION** Yarra Valley
T (03) 9739 0461 **F** (03) 9739 0467 **OPEN** 7 days 10–5
WINEMAKER Alan Johns **EST.** 1988 **CASES** 7000
PRODUCT RANGE ($20–45 CD) Sauvignon Blanc, Chardonnay, Pinot Noir, Shiraz, Merlot, Cabernet Merlot, Cabernet Sauvignon, Reserve Cabernet.
SUMMARY Former East Doncaster orchardists Alan and Louis Johns acquired the 40-hectare Yeringa Vineyard property in 1980; the property had originally been planted by the Deschamps family in the mid-19th century, and was then known as Yeringa Cellars. The plantings now extend to 12 hectares, the first wines being made by Alan Johns in 1992. Since that time all of the wines have been made on-site. They have enjoyed consistent show success over the years, none greater, however, than the trophy at the 2002 Victorian Wines Show for Best Pinot Noir, awarded to the 2000 Yering Farm Pinot Noir.

TTTTY **Chardonnay 2002** Clean; driven by melon, citrus and nectarine fruit; subtle oak, good length. **RATING** 90 **DRINK** 2010 **$** 23

TTTT **Cabernet Sauvignon 2000** Medium-bodied; supple blackcurrant and blackberry fruit; balanced oak and tannins. **RATING** 89 **DRINK** 2010 **$** 25
Chardonnay 2001 Tangy melon and citrus; some bottle development but in very similar fruit-driven style to the 2002. **RATING** 88 **DRINK** 2007 **$** 23
Pinot Noir 2002 Cherry, strawberry and earth; light-bodied; good length, not especially complex. **RATING** 88 **DRINK** 2008 **$** 23
Shiraz 2001 Savoury/earthy/leafy/spicy varietal fruit; light to medium-bodied; soft tannins. **RATING** 87 **DRINK** Now **$** 25
The Emerson Merlot 2002 Very earthy, leathery, savoury aromas, but sweetens up somewhat on the palate without losing varietal definition. **RATING** 87 **DRINK** 2009 **$** 30
Reserve Cabernet Sauvignon 2002 Light to medium-bodied; a clean but fairly tight frame and straight-line mouthfeel. Needs to flesh out with more bottle age. **RATING** 87 **DRINK** 2010 **$** 45

TTTY **Cabernet Merlot 2002** **RATING** 86 **DRINK** 2009 **$** 30
Wild Ferment Pinot Rose 2003 **RATING** 85 **DRINK** Now **$** 20
Cabernet Merlot 2001 **RATING** 85 **DRINK** Now **$** 30
The George Cabernet Sauvignon 2002 **RATING** 85 **DRINK** 2007
Cabernet Sauvignon 2001 **RATING** 85 **DRINK** Now **$** 25

Yering Range Vineyard

NR

14 McIntyre Lane, Coldstream, Vic 3770 **REGION** Yarra Valley
T (03) 9739 1172 **F** (03) 9739 1172 **OPEN** By appointment
WINEMAKER John Ellis (Contract) **EST.** 1989 **CASES** 200
PRODUCT RANGE ($25 CD) Cabernet Sauvignon.
SUMMARY Yering Range has 2 hectares of cabernet sauvignon under vine; part is sold and part is made under the Yering Range label by John Ellis at Hanging Rock. The tiny production is sold through a mailing list.

Yering Station

★★★★★

38 Melba Highway, Yarra Glen, Vic 3775 **REGION** Yarra Valley
T (03) 9730 0100 **F** (03) 9730 0135 **OPEN** 7 days 10–5
WINEMAKER Tom Carson, Darren Rathbone, Caroline Mooney **EST.** 1988 **CASES** 50 000
PRODUCT RANGE ($15.50–58 CD) Barak's Bridge Semillon Sauvignon Blanc, Chardonnay, Botrytis Semillon, Pinot Noir, Shiraz, Cabernet Blend; Yering Station Sauvignon Blanc, Marsanne Viognier Roussanne, Pinot Gris, Chardonnay, Reserve Chardonnay, Pinot Gris Botrytis, Pinot Noir Rose ED, Pinot Noir, Shiraz Viognier, Merlot, Sangiovese, Cabernet Sauvignon, Fortified Shiraz; Laura Barnes Single Vineyard Chardonnay, Pinot Noir and Cabernet Sauvignon Merlot.
SUMMARY The historic Yering Station (or at least the portion of the property on which the cellar-door sales and vineyard are established) was purchased by the Rathbone family in January 1996 and is now the site of a joint venture with the French Champagne house Devaux. A spectacular and very large winery which handles the Yarrabank sparkling wines and the Yering Station and Yarra Edge table wines has been erected. Has immediately become one of the focal points of the Yarra Valley, particularly with the historic Chateau Yering, where luxury accommodation and fine dining are available, next door. Yering Station's own restaurant is open every day for lunch, providing the best cuisine in the valley. Since 2002, a sister company of Mount Langi Ghiran, now also owned by the Rathbone family. Exports to all major markets.

ŶŶŶŶŶ **Reserve Shiraz Viognier 2002** A very complex array of French oak and a multiplicity of fruit aromas and flavours, centred on black cherry and blackberry; supple, rich and textured. Multi-trophy winner. **RATING** 96 **DRINK** 2017 $ 58
Reserve Shiraz Viognier 2001 Bright purple-red; the fragrance leaps from the glass, red and black cherries intermingling with a suite of spices; the palate is superbly balanced and impressively long. **RATING** 96 **DRINK** 2016 $ 58
Reserve Chardonnay 2002 The bouquet is subtle and still developing, but the wine drives through to a crescendo on the finish and a lingering aftertaste. Its whole life is in front of it. **RATING** 95 **DRINK** 2012 $ 58
Reserve Pinot Noir 2002 Complex and intense; plum, sous bois and French oak; a powerful palate, paradoxically without the same length as the varietal. **RATING** 94 **DRINK** 2011 $ 58
Shiraz Viognier 2001 Fragrant, lively and fresh; a brilliant array of red and black fruits accentuated by the Viognier; good length. **RATING** 94 **DRINK** 2017 $ 23

ŶŶŶŶ♈ **Chardonnay 2002** Lovely nectarine, stone fruit and melon; fused oak; long, fine and supple finish. **RATING** 92 **DRINK** 2009 $ 20.50
Chardonnay 2001 Ultra-complex, funky barrel-ferment aromas and flavours offset by regional acidity sustaining the finish. **RATING** 91 **DRINK** 2009 $ 20.50
Pinot Noir 2002 Elegant, aromatic, cherry, strawberry and plum; at the lighter end of the spectrum for the 2002 vintage, but has length and a lingering finish. **RATING** 90 **DRINK** 2007 $ 23
Cabernet Sauvignon 2001 Sweet blackcurrant/blackberry fruit; some chocolate and mocha; fine, ripe tannins; subtle oak. **RATING** 90 **DRINK** 2011 $ 23
Sangiovese 2002 Scented, spicy cherry/cherry pip and touches of cedar; a lively, expressive light to medium-bodied palate; well above the average for this variety in Australia. **RATING** 90 **DRINK** 2009 $ 23

ŶŶŶŶ **Cabernet Sauvignon 2000** Toasty, smoky oak aromas; light to medium-bodied palate with cassis/currant fruit and fine tannins. **RATING** 89 **DRINK** 2010 $ 23

Pinot Noir 2001 Light to medium-bodied; still clean and fresh, but has not developed overmuch complexity. **RATING** 88 **DRINK** Now $ 23

Wild River Chardonnay 2003 Ultra-fragrant grapefruit and stone fruit aromas; the palate comes back a little, but is still vibrant and zesty. Restaurants only; exclusive distribution by Nelson Wine Company. **RATING** 87 **DRINK** 2007 $ 20

MVR 2003 Fresh apple and pear; some mineral; pleasant flavours but lacks punch. A blend of Marsanne, Viognier and Roussanne. **RATING** 87 **DRINK** 2007 $ 23

ΨΨΨΨ **Barak's Bridge Chardonnay 2002 RATING** 86 **DRINK** Now $ 15.50

ΨΨΨ **Laura Barnes Pinot Noir 2000 RATING** 83 $ 33

🐾 Yerong Creek Estate NR

'Barwon', Yerong Creek, NSW 2642 **REGION** Riverina
T (02) 6920 3569 **F** (02) 6920 3503 **OPEN** 7 days 10–5
WINEMAKER Damien Cofield (Contract) **EST.** 1996
PRODUCT RANGE A range of varietally denominated table wines reflecting the plantings.
SUMMARY Robert and Julie Yates have 5 hectares planted to chardonnay and shiraz, with the winemaking taking place under the direction of Damien Cofield at his family's winery at Rutherglen. The wines are chiefly sold by mail order and through the cellar door.

🐾 Yilgarnia

6634 Redmond West Road, Redmond, WA 6327 **REGION** Albany
T (08) 9845 3031 **F** (08) 9845 3031 **OPEN** Not
WINEMAKER Contract **EST.** 1997 **CASES** 1500
PRODUCT RANGE ($14.95–20.95 ML) Sauvignon Blanc, Unwooded Chardonnay, Shiraz, Merlot, Cabernet Sauvignon.
SUMMARY Melbourne-educated (Scotch College and then Longerenong Agricultural College) Peter Buxton travelled across the Nullarbor to settle on a bush block of 405 acres on the Hay River, 6 kilometres north of Wilson Inlet, home to the town of Denmark. That was 40 years ago, and for the first 10 years Buxton built on his brief time with the Soil Conservation Authority in Victoria by joining the West Australian Department of Agriculture in Albany. In this role he surveyed several of the early vineyards in Western Australia, and recognised the potential of his family's property to produce high-quality wine. However, the initial activity of Yilgarnia Wines and Wildflowers was the growing of Australian native wildflowers, planted on south-facing slopes, complementing grazing activities. Adjoining parcels of land were added to the original block, and today there are 10 hectares of vines in bearing, with another 6 hectares planted in 2002 and 2003. All the vineyard plantings (eight varieties in all) are on north-facing blocks. Needless to say, Peter Buxton has an immensely detailed knowledge of the soil structure of each of the blocks, the geological history of which stretches back two billion years.

ΨΨΨΨΨ **Shiraz 2001** Excellent hue; potent blackberry, blackcurrant and spice aromas; velvety mouthfeel and fine, ripe tannins; great finish. **RATING** 91 **DRINK** 2016 $ 20.95

Cabernet Sauvignon 2001 Dense colour; cassis, blackcurrant and plum pudding aromas; very ripe and fleshy, rich fruit; fine tannins and controlled oak. **RATING** 91 **DRINK** 2015 $ 20.95

Merlot 2001 Fine and fragrant; excellent varietal flavour and structure; raspberry and plum offset by olive; fine, savoury tannins. **RATING** 90 **DRINK** 2011 $ 20.95

ΨΨΨΨ **Unwooded Chardonnay 2002** Well above average varietal character and body; citrus, melon and stone fruit provide real personality. **RATING** 87 **DRINK** Now $ 15.95

ΨΨΨ **Sauvignon Blanc 2002 RATING** 83 $ 14.95

Yokain Vineyard Estate

Worsley Back Road, Allanson, WA 6225 (postal) **REGION** Geographe
T (08) 9725 3397 **F** (08) 9725 3397 **OPEN** Not
WINEMAKER Camilla Vote **EST.** 1998 **CASES** 1000

PRODUCT RANGE ($8–12 ML) Riesling, Verdelho, Chardonnay, Simply Red Shiraz Cabernet Sauvignon, Oaked Shiraz Merlot Cabernet Franc, Simply Red Cabernet Sauvignon Shiraz, Oaked Cabernet Sauvignon Merlot Cabernet Franc.

SUMMARY David and Julie Gardiner began the establishment of their 17-hectare vineyard in 1998, with all but 2 hectares planted in that year. Verdelho, chardonnay, semillon, shiraz, cabernet sauvignon, merlot and cabernet franc are in production; the 2000 plantings of riesling and zinfandel produced their first grapes in 2003. Although they do not have a cellar door, they are in the process of establishing a wine bar at Dunsborough, and in the meantime are selling the wine by mail order for between $8 and $12 a bottle.

Yrsa's Vineyard ★★★☆

105 Tucks Road, Main Ridge, Vic 3928 **REGION** Mornington Peninsula
T (03) 5989 6500 **F** (03) 5989 6501 **OPEN** By appointment
WINEMAKER Craig McLeod, Judy Gifford (Contract) **EST.** 1994 **CASES** 200
PRODUCT RANGE ($22–38 R) Chardonnay, Pinot Noir, Hurdy Gurdy Creek Pinot Noir.
SUMMARY Yrsa's Vineyard is named after the lady from whom Steven and Marianne Stern acquired the property. She, in turn, was named after Yrsa, Queen of Sweden, born in 565, whose story is told in the Norse sagas. Well-known patent and trademark attorney Steven Stern (whose particular area of expertise is in the wine and liquor business) and wife Marianne have established around 2.5 hectares each of pinot noir and chardonnay, and initially marketed the wines only in the UK. The tiny production has been further circumscribed by the loss of the 2002 vintage due to weather conditions. However, the wines are to be found on some icon Melbourne restaurant wine lists, including Lynch's, Sud and Bistro 1. A wine-tasting studio available for small wine tastings (up to 10 people) is available by prior arrangement. Exports to the UK.

Zanella Estate NR

Burnets Road, Traralgon, Vic 3844 **REGION** Gippsland
T (03) 5174 0557 **F** (03) 5174 0557 **OPEN** 7 days
WINEMAKER Ettore Zanella **EST.** 1996
PRODUCT RANGE Chardonnay, Shiraz, Cabernet Merlot.
SUMMARY Ettorre Zanella has established 1.5 hectares of chardonnay, cabernet sauvignon, merlot and shiraz and makes the wine on-site; it is sold through the cellar door.

Zappacosta Estate Wines NR

301 Kidman Way, Hanwood, NSW 2680 **REGION** Riverina
T (02) 6963 0278 **F** (02) 6963 0278 **OPEN** 7 days 10–5
WINEMAKER Dino Zappacosta **EST.** 1956 **CASES** 50 000
PRODUCT RANGE ($12 CD) Riesling, Semillon, Dry White, Shiraz.
SUMMARY Zappacosta Estate, briefly known as Hanwood Village Wines, is a relatively new business, with the first release from the 1996 vintage, although the vineyard dates back to 1956.

Zarephath Wines ★★★☆

Moorialup Road, East Porongurup, WA 6324 **REGION** Porongurup
T (08) 9853 1152 **F** (08) 9841 8124 **OPEN** Mon–Sat 10–5, Sun 12–4
WINEMAKER Robert Diletti **EST.** 1994 **CASES** 3000
PRODUCT RANGE ($17–25 CD) Riesling, Unwooded Chardonnay, Chardonnay, Pinot Noir, Shiraz, Cabernet Sauvignon.
SUMMARY The 9-hectare Zarephath vineyard is owned and operated by Brothers and Sisters of The Christ Circle, a Benedictine community. They say the most outstanding feature of the location is the feeling of peace and tranquility which permeates the site, something I can well believe on the basis of numerous visits to the Porongurups. Exports to the US and the UK.

♥♥♥♥♡ **Chardonnay 2002** Abundant depth and richness; stone fruit, fig, cashew and citrus; gentle oak. **RATING** 90 **DRINK** 2007 $22

ŸŸŸŸ **Shiraz 2002** Elegant, medium-bodied fruit-driven style; briar/spice/blackberry and cherry fruit; fine tannins. **RATING** 89 **DRINK** 2009 $ 25
Cabernet Sauvignon 2002 Still very youthful and angular; mint, cassis, leaf and berry; will evolve slowly. **RATING** 87 **DRINK** 2012 $ 25

ŸŸŸŸ **Riesling 2003 RATING** 86 **DRINK** 2007 $ 18

ŸŸŸ **Pinot Noir 2002 RATING** 83 $ 22

Zema Estate ★★★★★

Riddoch Highway, Coonawarra, SA 5263 **REGION** Coonawarra
T (08) 8736 3219 **F** (08) 8736 3280 **OPEN** 7 days 9–5
WINEMAKER Tom Simons **EST.** 1982 **CASES** 10 000
PRODUCT RANGE ($20–45 CD) Shiraz, Family Selection Shiraz, Merlot, Cluny (Cabernet blend), Cabernet Sauvignon, Family Selection Cabernet Sauvignon.
SUMMARY Zema is one of the last outposts of hand-pruning in Coonawarra, the various members of the Zema family tending a 60-hectare vineyard progressively planted since 1982 in the heart of Coonawarra's terra rossa soil. Winemaking practices are straightforward; if ever there was an example of great wines being made in the vineyard, this is it. Exports to the UK, France, Germany, Malaysia, Thailand, Hong Kong and New Zealand.

ŸŸŸŸŸ **Family Selection Shiraz 2001** Beautifully controlled and modulated plum, black cherry and blackberry; satiny texture; good length. **RATING** 94 **DRINK** 2016 $ 40
Cabernet Sauvignon 2001 Good colour; quite complex, medium-bodied; good balance and texture; a complete wine. **RATING** 94 **DRINK** 2011 $ 22

ŸŸŸŸ **Merlot 2001** Dense, deep purple-red; opulent mulberry and blackcurrant fruit-driven style; silky tannins; right out of left field. **RATING** 93 **DRINK** 2015 $ 25

ŸŸŸŸ **Family Selection Cabernet Sauvignon 2001** Sweet, slightly minty fruit; a touch of chocolate; soft tannins and balanced oak. **RATING** 87 **DRINK** 2009 $ 40

Ziebarth Wines NR

Foleys Road, Goodger, Qld 4610 **REGION** South Burnett
T (07) 4162 3089 **F** (07) 4162 3084 **OPEN** 7 days 10–5
WINEMAKER John Crane (Contract) **EST.** 1998 **CASES** 420
PRODUCT RANGE ($13.50–14.50 CD) Semillon, Fairview White, Rose, Shiraz Cabernet Franc.
SUMMARY The 4-hectare vineyard (with 1 hectare each of semillon, cabernet sauvignon, merlot and chardonnay, together with 0.25 hectare of chambourcin) is a minor diversification on a beef cattle property set on the edge of the Stuart Range, and which enjoys superb views. It is a small family operation whose aim is to provide a wine experience for visitors; the wines are made for Ziebarth by John Crane at Crane Winery.

Zig Zag Road

201 Zig Zag Road, Drummond, Vic 3461 **REGION** Macedon Ranges
T (03) 5423 9390 **F** (03) 5423 9390 **OPEN** Weekends and public holidays 10–6, or by appointment
WINEMAKER Alan Stevens, Eric Bellchambers **EST.** 1972 **CASES** 300
PRODUCT RANGE ($18–25 ML) Riesling, Pinot Noir, Shiraz, Cabernet Merlot, Cabernet Sauvignon.
SUMMARY Alan Stevens and Deb Orton purchased the vineyard in 1988; it was then 16 years old, having been established way back in 1972 by Roger Aldridge. The dry-grown vines produce relatively low yields, and until 1996 the grapes were sold to Hanging Rock Winery. In 1996 the decision was taken to manage the property on a full-time basis, and to make the wine on-site, utilising 0.25 hectare each of riesling, merlot and pinot noir, and 1 hectare each of shiraz and cabernet sauvignon.

ŸŸŸŸ **Cabernet Merlot 2001 RATING** 85 **DRINK** 2007 $ 22
Cabernet Sauvignon 2001 RATING 84 **DRINK** 2007 $ 22

Zilzie Wines ★★★☆

Lot 66 Kulkyne Way, Karadoc via Red Cliffs, Vic 3496 **REGION** Murray Darling
T (03) 5025 8100 **F** (03) 5025 8116 **OPEN** Not
WINEMAKER Bob Shields, Leigh Sparrow **EST.** 1999
PRODUCT RANGE ($9.99–20 R) The varietal wines are offered under three banners: Buloke Reserve
($9.99), Zilzie Estate ($13–15) and Zilzie Show Reserve ($20), a model of clarity and simplicity.
SUMMARY The Forbes family has been farming Zilzie Estate since 1911; it is currently run by Ian and
Ros Forbes, together with their sons Steven and Andrew. A diverse range of farming activities now
include grape growing, with 250 hectares of vineyards. Having established a position as a dominant
supplier of grapes to Southcorp, Zilzie took the next step of forming a wine company in 1999 and
built a winery in 2000; it has a capacity of 16 000 tonnes at the moment, but is so designed that
modules can be added to take it to 50 000 tonnes. The winery business includes contract storage,
contract processing, contract winemaking, bulk wine production and bottled and branded wines.
The wines are distributed nationally through Rutherglen Wine and Spirit Company Limited; exports
to the UK, the US, Canada, New Zealand, Singapore and Thailand.

ΨΨΨΨ **Show Reserve Shiraz 2002** Medium-bodied, combines complexity and elegance;
blackberry and black plum, spice and vanilla; good tannins. **RATING** 90 **DRINK** 2009 $ 20

ΨΨΨΨ **Viognier 2003** Good varietal aromas; solid, rich pastille fruit, likewise strongly varietal.
Slightly phenolic. **RATING** 89 **DRINK** Now $ 15
Shiraz 2003 Medium-bodied, driven by abundant black cherry and blackberry fruit;
minimal oak; soft tannins, supple mouthfeel. **RATING** 89 **DRINK** 2009 $ 15
Cabernet Sauvignon 2002 Good colour; medium to full-bodied; well-balanced black
fruits and integrated oak. **RATING** 89 **DRINK** 2010 $ 15
Cabernet Sauvignon 2003 Abundant red and blackcurrant fruit in a fresh, light to
medium-bodied mode; ready to go, but has length. **RATING** 88 **DRINK** Now $ 15
Show Reserve Cabernet Merlot Petit Verdot 2002 Attractive suite of red and black
fruits; driven by fruit rather than oak. **RATING** 88 **DRINK** 2007 $ 18.99
Buloke Reserve Alternative Tempranillo 2003 Good colour; black cherry plus touches of
herb and mint; altogether interesting and worthwhile. **RATING** 88 **DRINK** 2008 $ 9.99
Buloke Reserve Chardonnay 2003 More elegant and restrained than the heavily sweet
Show Reserve version; still a powerful wine. **RATING** 87 **DRINK** Now $ 9.99
Chardonnay 2003 Lightest of the 2003 releases, but the best balanced; tangy melon fruit;
oak not evident. **RATING** 87 **DRINK** Now $ 15
Buloke Reserve Shiraz 2003 Intense purple-red colour; oozing lush blackberry fruit; no
aspirations to complexity. **RATING** 87 **DRINK** Now $ 9.99
Buloke Reserve Merlot 2003 Clean, direct red fruits; raspberry and redcurrant; fruit-
driven. **RATING** 87 **DRINK** Now $ 9.99
Buloke Reserve Alternative Petit Verdot 2003 Similar dark fruits/blackberry/mulberry;
simple but satisfying; a very good-value trio. **RATING** 87 **DRINK** Now $ 9.99

ΨΨΨ **Buloke Reserve Alternative Rose 2003** Full flavoured, quite complex; drop-dead, off-
dry, cellar-door style. **RATING** 86 **DRINK** Now $ 9.99
Merlot 2003 RATING 86 **DRINK** Now $ 15
Buloke Reserve Alternative Sangiovese 2003 RATING 86 **DRINK** 2007 $ 9.99
Buloke Reserve Sauvignon Blanc 2003 RATING 84 **DRINK** Now $ 9.99
Buloke Reserve Classic Dry White 2003 RATING 84 **DRINK** Now $ 9.99

ΨΨΨ **Show Reserve Chardonnay 2003 RATING** 82 $ 20

Index

Adelaide Hills

Aldgate Ridge 6
Annvers Wines 15
Arranmore Vineyard 18
Ashton Hills 20
Barratt 32
Basket Range Wines 35
Battunga Vineyards 36
Bird in Hand 49
Birdwood Estate 50
Bridgewater Mill 65
Cawdor Wines 96
Chain of Ponds 99
Christmas Hill 110
Cobb's Hill 117
Galah 184
Geoff Hardy Wines 190
Geoff Weaver 191
Grove Hill 211
Hahndorf Hill Winery 212
Harris Estate 218
Hillstowe 234
Johnston Oakbank 259
Jupiter Creek Winery 261
Knappstein Lenswood Vineyards 275
Leabrook Estate 288
Leland Estate 290
Llangibby Estate 301
Longview Vineyard 303
Malcolm Creek Vineyard 315
Mawson Ridge 322
Maximilian's Vineyard 322
Millers Samphire 332
Morialta Vineyard 344
Mt Lofty Ranges Vineyard 354
Mount Torrens Vineyards 357
Murdoch Hill 360
Nepenthe Vineyards 365
New Era Vineyard 366
Next Generation Wines 366
Normans 369
Paracombe Wines 383
Parish Hill Wines 385
Perrini Estate 398
Petaluma 399
Pfitzner 403

Piccadilly Fields 406
Pike & Joyce 407
Salem Bridge Wines 455
Setanta Wines 468
Shaw & Smith 474
Spoehr Creek Wines 483
Talunga 504
Teakles Hill Wines 511
The Deanery Vineyards 514
The Lane 517
Whisson Lake 565

Adelaide Plains

Ceravolo Wines 98
Diloreto Wines 144
Farosa Estate 171
Gawler River Grove 188
Hazyblur Wines 222
Primo Estate 419
Thornborough Estate 522
Versace Wines 546
Wilkie Estate 569

Adelaide Zone

Patritti Wines 388
Penfolds Magill Estate 394
Rumball Sparkling Wines 450
Uleybury Wines 542

Albany

Jinnunger Vineyard 258
Montgomery's Hill 339
Phillips Brook Estate 404
Wignalls Wines 566
Yilgarnia 598

Alpine Valleys

Annapurna Wines 15
Bogong Estate 56
Boynton's 59
Ceccanti Kiewa Valley Wines 96
Gapsted Wines 186
Kancoona Valley Wines 264

Michelini Wines 329
Park Wines 386
Tawonga Vineyard 510

Ballarat

Captains Creek Organic Wines 88
Chepstowe Vineyard 107
Dulcinea 155
Eastern Peake 158
Mount Beckworth 349
Mount Buninyong Winery 350
Mount Coghill Vineyard 351
Tomboy Hill Vineyard 529
Whitehorse Wines 566
Yellowglen 595

Barossa Valley

Balthazar of the Barossa 27
Barossa Ridge Wine Estate 30
Barossa Settlers 31
Barossa Valley Estate 31
Basedow 34
Beer Brothers 40
Bethany Wines 45
Burge Family Winemakers 75
Cellarmasters 97
Charles Cimicky 103
Charles Melton 103
Chateau Dorrien 105
Chateau Tanunda 106
Craneford 126
Domain Day 147
Dutschke Wines 156
Elderton 159
Gibson's Barossa Vale Wines 193
Glaetzer Wines 195
Glen Eldon Wines 197
Gnadenfrei Estate 200
Gordon Sunter Wines 202
Grant Burge 207
Greenock Creek Wines 208
Haan Wines 211
Hamilton's Ewell Vineyards 214
Harbord Wines 216
Hare's Chase 218
Heritage Wines 228
Jenke Vineyards 255
Kabminye Wines 262
Kaesler Wines 262
Kalleske Wines 263
Kellermeister/Trevor Jones 267
Kies Family Wines 269
Killawarra 271
Kurtz Family Vineyards 280
Langmeil Winery 286
Leo Buring 292
Liebich Wein 294
Limb Vineyards 296
McLean's Farm Wines 310
Marschall Groom Cellars 320

Massena Vineyards 321
Mengler View Wines 326
Orlando 378
Penfolds 393
Peter Lehmann 400
Queen Adelaide 424
Richmond Grove 435
Rockford 442
Rocland Wines 443
Roehr 443
Rosenvale Wines 446
Ross Estate Wines 447
Rusden Wines 450
St Hallett 453
Saltram 457
Schild Estate Wines 462
Schubert Estate 463
Seppelt 466
Sheep's Back 475
Shiralee Wines 476
Small Gully Wines 481
Stanley Brothers 485
Stone Chimney Creek 490
Tait Wines 501
The Willows Vineyard 520
Thorn-Clarke Wines 522
Tim Smith Wines 525
Tollana 529
Torbreck Vintners 531
Turkey Flat 537
Veritas 546
Viking Wines 547
Vinecrest 549
Wards Gateway 554
Whistler Wines 565
Wolf Blass 579
Yaldara Wines 587
Yalumba 587

Beechworth

Amulet Vineyard 11
Battely Wines 36
Castagna Vineyard 94
Cow Hill 124
Fighting Gully Road 174
Flamsteed 176
Giaconda 192
Pennyweight Winery 396
Savaterre 461
Sorrenberg 482
Star Lane 486
Yengari Wine Company 595

Bendigo

Avonmore Estate 23
Balgownie Estate 25
Bendigo Wine Estate 43
Big Hill Vineyard 47
BlackJack Vineyards 51
Blanche Barkly Wines 52

Charlotte Plains 104
Chateau Dore 105
Chateau Leamon 106
Connor Park Winery 120
Cooperage Estate 121
Glenalbyn 196
Harcourt Valley Vineyards 216
Kangderaar Vineyard 264
Laanecoorie 281
Langanook Wines 285
Mandurang Valley Wines 315
Minto Wines 333
Mount Alexander Vineyard 348
Mount Moliagul 355
Munari Wines 359
Nuggetty Vineyard 371
Old Loddon Wines 374
Passing Clouds 386
Pondalowie Vineyards 414
Sandhurst Ridge 459
Sutton Grange Winery 498
Tannery Lane Vineyard 506
Tipperary Hill Estate 528
Water Wheel 557
Welshmans Reef Vineyard 561
Yandoit Hill Vineyard 589

Blackwood Valley

Blackwood Crest Wines 51
Blackwood Wines 52
Hillbillé 232
Lauren Brook 287
Scotts Brook 465
Seashell Wines 465
Tanglewood Vines 506
Wattle Ridge Vineyard 558

Canberra District

Affleck 5
Brindabella Hills 65
Clonakilla 114
Dionysus Winery 145
Doonkuna Estate 150
England's Creek 164
Gallagher Estate 185
Gidgee Estate Wines 193
Helm 225
Hillbrook 233
Jeir Creek 255
Kamberra 263
Kyeema Estate 280
Lake George Winery 283
Lark Hill 286
Lerida Estate 292
Little Bridge 299
McKellar Ridge Wines 310
Madew Wines 313
Milimani Estate 331
Mount Majura Vineyard 354
Mundoonen 360

Murrumbateman Winery 362
Pankhurst 383
Pialligo Estate 405
Shaw Vineyard Estate 474
Surveyor's Hill Winery 497
Wandana Estate 552
Wily Trout 573
Wimbaliri Wines 573
Yass Valley Wines 594

Central Ranges Zone

Bell River Estate 41
Bunnamagoo Estate 75
Chateau Champsaur 105
Glenfinlass 198
Hermes Morrison Wines 229
Hoppers Hill Vineyards 238
Monument Vineyard 340
Sand Hills Vineyard 459
Winburndale 574

Central Victorian Zone

Akrasi Wines/New Mediterranean Winery 5
Gentle Annie 190
Norton Estate 370
Pretty Sally Estate 418
Tallis Wines 503

Central Western Australia Zone

Avonbrook Wines 23
Chapman Valley Wines 102
Rex Vineyard 433
Stratherne Vale Estate 493
Wandoo Farm 553

Clare Valley

Annie's Lane 15
Australian Domaine Wines 21
Brian Barry Wines 63
Cardinham Estate 89
Claymore Wines 112
Clos Clare 115
Crabtree of Watervale 125
Eldredge 159
Eyre Creek 169
Grosset 210
Inchiquin Wines 247
Inghams Skilly Ridge Wines 247
Jeanneret Wines 255
Jim Barry Wines 256
Kilikanoon 270
Kirrihill Estates 274
Knappstein Wines 276
Leasingham 289
Little Brampton Wines 299
Mintaro Wines 333
Mitchell 335
Mount Horrocks 353

Mt Surmon Wines 357
Neagles Rock Vineyards 364
Old Station Vineyard 374
O'Leary Walker Wines 375
Olssens of Watervale 376
Paulett 389
Pearson Vineyards 391
Penna Lane Wines 395
Pikes 408
Pycnantha Hill Estate 423
Reilly's Wines 431
Sevenhill Cellars 470
Skillogalee 480
Stephen John Wines 488
Stringy Brae 494
Tatehams Wines 509
Taylors 510
Tim Adams 524
Tim Gramp 525
Wendouree 562
Wilson Vineyard 572

Coonawarra

Balnaves of Coonawarra 26
Banks Thargo Wines 27
Bowen Estate 58
Brand's of Coonawarra 61
DiGiorgio Family Wines 144
Ey Estate 168
Flint's of Coonawarra 177
Gartner Family Vineyards 188
Highbank 231
Hollick 236
Jamiesons Run 252
Katnook Estate 266
Koonara 277
Ladbroke Grove 281
Lawrence Victor Estate 288
Leconfield 289
Lindemans (Coonawarra) 297
Majella 314
Murdock 361
Parker Coonawarra Estate 385
Patrick T Winemaking Services 388
Penley Estate 394
Punters Corner 421
Redman 429
Reschke Wines 432
Rymill Coonawarra 451
S Kidman Wines 480
The Blok Estate 514
Wynns Coonawarra Estate 586
Yalumba The Menzies 588
Zema Estate 600

Cowra

Bindaree Estate 49
Catherine's Ridge 95
Chiverton 109
Cowra Estate 124

Danbury Estate 133
Falls Wines 170
Hamiltons Bluff 213
Kalari Wines 263
Mulligan Wongara Vineyard 359
Mulyan 359
Nassau Estate 364
River Park 438
Rosnay Organic Wines 447
Spring Ridge Wines 484
Tom's Waterhole Wines 530
Wallington Wines 551
Waugoola Wines 559
Windowrie Estate 575

Currency Creek

Ballast Stone Estate Wines 26
Currency Creek Estate 130
Middleton Wines 330

Darling Downs

Gowrie Mountain Estate 204

Denmark

Due South 155
Harewood Estate 218
Howard Park (Denmark) 240
John Wade Wines 260
Karriview 265
Mariners Rest 318
Matilda's Estate 322
Nelson Touch 365
Rickety Gate 436
Somerset Hill Wines 482
Tingle-Wood 526
West Cape Howe Wines 562

Eden Valley

Barossa Cottage Wines 30
Eden Springs 158
Glen Eldon Wines 197
Hartz Barn Wines 219
Heathvale 224
Heggies Vineyard 225
Henschke 227
Hill Smith Estate 234
Hutton Vale Vineyard 245
Irvine 250
Karl Seppelt 265
Mountadam 347
Pewsey Vale 402
Tin Shed Wines 527
Tobias Wines 528

Fleurieu Zone

The Islander Estate Vineyards 516
Marquis Phillips 319

Frankland

Alkoomi 7
Ferngrove Vineyards 173
Frankland Estate 181
Garlands 187

Frankland River

Old Kent River 374

Geelong

Amietta Vineyard and Winery 11
Austin's Barrabool 21
Bannockburn Vineyards 28
Bellarine Estate 42
by Farr 78
Clyde Park Vineyard 116
Curlewis Winery 129
del Rios 141
Farr Rising 171
Gralaine Vineyard 204
Heytesbury Ridge 230
Innisfail Vineyards 248
Jindalee Estate 257
Kilgour Estate 270
Le 'Mins Winery 291
Lethbridge Wines 292
Leura Park Estate 293
McGlashan's Wallington Estate 308
Mermerus Vineyard 326
Mount Anakie Wines 348
Mount Duneed 351
Otway Estate 380
Pettavel 401
Prince Albert 419
Provenance Wines 420
Scotchmans Hill 464
Shadowfax Vineyard and Winery 472
Staughton Vale Vineyard 487
The Minya Winery 518
Waybourne 559

Geographe

Barrecas 32
Brookhampton Estate 69
Byramgou Park 79
Capel Vale 86
Donnybrook Estate 150
Ferguson Falls Estate 172
Hackersley 212
Harvey River Bridge Estate 219
Henty Brook Estate 227
Idlewild Wines 246
Kingtree Wines 274
Mandalay Estate 315
St Aidan 452
Thomson Brook Wines 521
Wansbrough Wines 553
Willow Bridge Estate 570

Wordsworth Wines 585
Yokain Vineyard Estate 598

Gippsland

Ada River 4
Bass Phillip 35
Bass Valley Estate Wines 35
Briagolong Estate 63
Caledonia Australis 80
Cannibal Creek Vineyard 83
Chestnut Hill Vineyard 108
Coalville Vineyard 116
Dargo Valley Winery 134
Djinta Djinta Winery 147
Drummonds Corrina Vineyard 154
Ensay Winery 165
Holley Hill 235
Jinks Creek Winery 258
Kongwak Hills Winery 277
Kouark Vineyard 279
Lochmoore 301
Lyre Bird Hill 307
McAlister Vineyards 307
Moondarra 340
Mount Markey 355
Narkoojee 363
Nicholson River 367
Paradise Enough 384
Phillip Island Vineyard 404
Ramsay's Vin Rose 425
Sarsfield Estate 460
Steler Estate Wines 488
Tanjil Wines 506
Tarwin Ridge 508
The Gurdies 516
Toms Cap Vineyard 529
Villa Terlato 548
Wild Dog 568
Windy Ridge Vineyard 576
Wyanga Park 585
Zanella Estate 599

Glenrowan

Auldstone 21
Baileys of Glenrowan 24
Goorambath 201
Taminick Cellars 505
Warby Range Estate 554

Goulburn Valley

Avenel Park/Hart Wines 22
Beckingham Wines 39
Beechwood Wines 39
Cape Horn Vineyard 85
Fyffe Field 184
Goulburn Terrace 202
Goulburn Valley Estate Wines 202
Hankin Estate 215
Hayward's Whitehead Creek 222

Heritage Farm Wines 228
Longleat Estate 303
Monichino Wines 338
Mt Samaria Vineyard 356
New Glory 366
Nillahcootie Estate 368
Strathkellar 493
The Carriages Vineyard 514
12 Acres 538

Grampians

Armstrong Vineyards 18
Best's Wines 44
Cathcart Ridge Estate 95
Clayfield Wines 112
Donovan Wines 150
Garden Gully Vineyards 187
Grampians Estate 205
Kimbarra Wines 271
Michael Unwin Wines 329
Montara 339
Mount Langi Ghiran Vineyards 354
Seppelt Great Western 467
The Gap Vineyard 515
Varrenti Wines 545
Westgate Vineyard 564

Granite Belt

Aventine Wines 22
Bald Mountain 25
Ballandean Estate 26
Boireann 56
Bungawarra 75
Casley Mount Hutton Winery 93
Castle Glen Vineyard 94
Catspaw Farm 96
Cody's 118
Felsberg Winery 171
Golden Grove Estate 200
Granite Ridge Wines 206
Heritage Estate 228
Hidden Creek 230
Jester Hill Wines 256
Kominos Wines 277
Lilyvale Wines 296
Lucas Estate 306
Mary Byrnes Wine 321
Mountview Wines 358
Old Caves 374
Preston Peak 418
Pyramids Road Wines 423
Raven Wines 426
Robert Channon Wines 439
Robinsons Family Vineyards 440
Rumbalara 450
Severn Brae Estate 471
Stone Ridge 492
Summit Estate 497
Symphony Hill Wines 500
Tobin Wines 528

Turner's Flat Vineyard 537
Wedgetail Ridge Estate 560
Whiskey Gully Wines 564
Wild Soul 568
Windermere Wines 575
Winewood 577

Great Southern

Abbey Creek Vineyard 3
Oranje Tractor Wine/Lincoln & Gomm
    Wines 377
The Lily Stirling Range 517
3 Drops 523
Trevelen Farm 535
Two People's Bay Wines 540
Wadjekanup River Estate 551

Greater Perth Zone

Coorinja 122
Paul Conti Wines 389

Gundagai

Borambola Wines 57
Paterson's Tumblong Vineyard 387

Hastings River

Bago Vineyards 24
Cassegrain 93
Inneslake Vineyards 248
Long Point Vineyard 303
Sherwood Estate 476

Heathcote

Barfold Estate 30
Barnadown Run 30
Burke and Wills Winery 76
Coliban Valley Wines 119
Domaines Tatiarra 149
Downing Estate Vineyard 151
Eppalock Ridge 165
Grace Devlin Wines 204
Heathcote Winery 223
Huntleigh Vineyards 244
Jasper Hill 254
Knots Wines 276
Lake Cooper Estate 283
McIvor Creek 309
McIvor Estate 309
Mount Burrumboot Estate 350
Mount Ida 353
Occam's Razor 373
Paul Osicka 389
Red Edge 428
Redesdale Estate Wines 428
St Michael's Vineyard 455
Sanguine Estate 460
Toolleen Vineyard 530
Wild Duck Creek Estate 568

Henty

Barretts Wines 32
Bochara Wines 55
Crawford River Wines 126
Hochkirch Wines 235
Kelso 268
Kingsley 272
St Gregory's 453
Tarrington Vineyards 508

Hilltops

Barwang Vineyard 34
Chalkers Crossing 100
Demondrille Vineyards 142
Grove Estate 210
Hansen Hilltops 215
Woodonga Hill 581

Kangaroo Island

Bay of Shoals 37
Cape d'Estaing 84
Dudley Partners 154
Kangaroo Island Vines 264
Williams Springs Road 569

King Valley

Avalon Vineyard 22
Bettio Wines 46
Boggy Creek Vineyards 55
Brown Brothers 70
Chrismont Wines 109
Ciavarella 111
Dal Zotto Estate 132
Darling Estate 134
Henderson Hardie 226
John Gehrig Wines 259
King River Estate 272
La Cantina King Valley 281
Markwood Estate 319
Pizzini 410
Politini Wines 413
Reads 427
Station Creek 487
Symphonia Wines 500
Wood Park 581

Langhorne Creek

Angas Plains Estate 13
Angas Vineyards 13
Bleasdale Vineyards 52
Bremerton Wines 62
Brothers in Arms 70
Casa Freschi 91
Cleggett Wines 113
Heartland Wines 223
Lake Breeze Wines 282
Lindrum 298

Marandoo Estate 317
Oddfellows Wines 373
Raydon Estate 426
Salomon Estates 456
Step Road Winery 489
Temple Bruer 511

Limestone Coast Zone

Frog Island 182
Governor Robe Selection 203
Heartland Wines 223
Heathfield Ridge Wines 224
Marquis Phillips 319
St Mary's 454

Lower Hunter Valley

Allandale 7
Apthorpe Estate 16
Audrey Wilkinson 20
Bainton Family Wines 25
Ballabourneen Wines 25
Batchelor's Terrace Vale 35
Beaumont Estate 38
Belgenny Vineyard 40
Ben's Run 43
Beyond Broke Vineyard 46
Bimbadgen Estate 48
Bishop Grove Wines 50
Blueberry Hill Vineyard 53
Bluebush Estate 54
Boatshed Vineyard 55
Briar Ridge 63
Broke Estate/Ryan Family Wines 67
Brokenwood 68
Broke's Promise Wines 68
Brush Box Vineyard 73
Calais Estate 79
Capercaillie 87
Carindale Wines 90
Catherine Vale Vineyard 95
Chateau Francois 105
Chateau Pâto 106
Chatto Wines 107
Cockfighter's Ghost 118
Colvin Wines 119
Constable & Hershon 120
Cooper Wines 121
Crisford Winery 127
De Bortoli (Hunter Valley) 137
De Iuliis 141
Drayton's Family Wines 152
Drews Creek Wines 152
Elsmore's Caprera Grove 163
Elysium Vineyard 163
Emma's Cottage Vineyard 164
Evans Family Wines 167
Fairview Wines 169
Farrell's Limestone Creek 171
First Creek Wines 174
Foate's Ridge 178

Fordwich Estate 179
Gabriel's Paddocks Vineyard 184
Gartelmann Hunter Estate 187
Glenguin 199
Golden Grape Estate 200
Hanging Tree Wines 215
Heartland Vineyard 222
Hillside Estate Wines 233
Hollyclare 236
Honeytree Estate 237
Hope Estate 238
House of Certain Views 240
Hudson's Peak Wines 241
Hungerford Hill 243
Iron Gate Estate 249
Ivanhoe Wines 251
Jackson's Hill Vineyard 251
JYT Wines 261
Keith Tulloch Wine 267
Kelman Vineyards 268
Kevin Sobels Wines 269
Krinklewood 279
Kulkunbulla 280
Lake's Folly 283
Latara 287
Lindemans (Hunter Valley) 297
Little Wine Company 300
Louis-Laval Wines 305
Lowe Family Wines (Hunter Valley) 306
Lucy's Run 306
Mabrook Estate 307
McGuigan Wines 308
McLeish Estate 310
Macquariedale Estate 311
McWilliam's Mount Pleasant 312
Madigan Vineyard 313
Margan Family 317
Marsh Estate 320
Meerea Park 324
Millbrook Estate 331
Millfield 332
Mistletoe Wines 335
Molly Morgan Vineyard 337
Monahan Estate 338
Moorebank Vineyard 341
Mount Broke Wines 349
Mount Eyre Vineyard 352
Mount View Estate 358
Nightingale Wines 367
Oakvale 373
Outram Estate 380
Palmers Wines 382
Peacock Hill Vineyard 390
Pendarves Estate 392
Pepper Tree Wines 397
Peschar's 398
Peterson Champagne House 401
Petersons 401
Piggs Peake 407
Pokolbin Estate 413
Poole's Rock 415
Pothana 417

Racecourse Lane Wines 424
Reg Drayton Wines 431
Roche Wines 440
Rocklea Vineyard 443
Rosebrook Estate 444
Rothbury Ridge 448
Rothvale Vineyard 449
Saddlers Creek 452
St Petrox 455
Sandalyn Wilderness Estate 458
Scarborough 461
Serenella 468
Sevenoaks Wines 471
SmithLeigh Vineyard 481
Stonehurst Wines Cedar Creek 491
Taliondal 502
Tallavera Grove Vineyard and Winery 502
Tamburlaine 505
Tatler Wines 510
Tempus Two Wines 512
Thalgara Estate 513
The Rothbury Estate 518
The Vineyards Estate 519
Thomas Wines 521
Tinklers Vineyard 526
Tinonee Vineyard 527
Tintilla Wines 527
Tower Estate 532
Tranquil Vale 533
Tulloch 536
Tyrrell's 541
Undercliff 543
Verona Vineyard 546
Vinden Estate 548
Wandin Valley Estate 552
Warraroong Estate 555
Wattlebrook Vineyard 558
Waverley Estate 559
Whispering Brook 565
Wild Broke Wines 567
Windarra 575
Windsors Edge 576
Wyndham Estate 585

Macedon Ranges

Ashworths Hill 20
Big Shed Wines 48
Bindi Wine Growers 49
Blackgum Estate 51
Braewattie 60
Candlebark Hill 82
Chanters Ridge 101
Cleveland 114
Cobaw Ridge 117
Cope-Williams 122
Curly Flat 130
Ellender Estate 161
Epis/Epis & Williams 165
Farrawell Wines 170
Gisborne Peak Wines 195
Glen Erin Vineyard Retreat 198

Index | 611

Granite Hills 206
Hanging Rock Winery 214
Kyneton Ridge Estate 281
Lancefield Winery 284
Langleyvale Vineyard 285
Loxley Vineyard 306
Metcalfe Valley 327
Mount Charlie Winery 351
Mount Gisborne Wines 352
Mount William Winery 358
O'Shea & Murphy Rosebery Hill Vineyard 380
Patrick's Vineyard 387
Pegeric Vineyard 391
Portree 416
Rock House 443
Sandy Farm Vineyard 460
Snowdon Wines 481
Stonemont 491
Straws Lane 494
Tarrangower Estate 507
Virgin Hills 550
Zig Zag Road 600

Manjimup

Batista 36
Black George 51
Chestnut Grove 107
Middlesex 31 330
Peos Estate 397
Piano Gully 405
Sinclair Wines 479
Smithbrook 481
Stone Bridge Estate 490
Yanmah Ridge 589

Margaret River

AbbeyVale 3
Adinfern 4
Alexandra Bridge Wines 6
Allison Valley Wines 9
Amarok Estate 10
Amberley Estate 10
Arlewood Estate 17
Artamus 18
Ashbrook Estate 19
Beckett's Flat 39
Bettenay's 46
Bramley Wood 60
Briarose Estate 64
Brookland Valley 69
Brookwood Estate 70
Broomstick Estate 70
Brown Hill Estate 72
Calem Blue/Shelton Wines 80
Cape Grace 85
Cape Mentelle 87
Carbunup Crest Vineyard 88
Casas Wines 92
Chalice Bridge Estate 99

Chapman's Creek Vineyard 102
Churchview Estate 110
Clairault 111
Cullen Wines 129
Deep Woods Estate 139
Devil's Lair 143
Driftwood Estate 152
Eagle Vale 157
Edwards Vineyard 158
Etain 166
Evans & Tate 166
Fermoy Estate 172
Fire Gully 174
Flinders Bay 177
Flying Fish Cove 178
Forester Estate 179
Frazer Woods Wines 182
Gralyn Estate 205
Green Valley Vineyard 208
Hamelin Bay 213
Happs 216
Harmans Ridge Estate 218
Hay Shed Hill Wines 221
Hesperos Wines 229
Higher Plane Wines 231
Howard Park (Margaret River) 240
Hunt's Foxhaven Estate 245
Injidup Point 248
Island Brook Estate 250
Jarvis Estate 254
Juniper Estate 261
Karri Grove Estate 265
Killerby 271
Laurance of Margaret River 287
Leeuwin Estate 290
Lenton Brae Wines 291
Maiolo Wines 314
Marybrook Vineyards 320
Maslin Old Dunsborough Wines 321
Minot Vineyard 333
Moss Brothers 346
Moss Wood 347
Olsen 376
Oscar's Leap 379
Palandri Wines 381
Palmer Wines 382
Peacetree Estate 390
Pierro 406
Preveli Wines 418
Random Valley Organic Wines 426
Redgate 428
Rivendell 437
Rockfield Estate 442
Rosabrook Estate 444
Rosily Vineyard 447
Sandalford 458
Sandstone 459
Saracen Estates 460
Serventy Organic Wines 468
Settlers Ridge 469
Sewards 472
Stellar Ridge Estate 488

Suckfizzle & Stella Bella 496
Swallows Welcome 498
Tassell Park Wines 508
The Grove Vineyard 516
Thompson Estate 521
Thornhill/The Berry Farm 523
Tintagel Wines 527
Treeton Estate 534
Vasse Felix 545
Vasse River Wines 545
Virgin Block Vineyard 550
Voyager Estate 550
Watershed Wines 557
We're Wines 562
Wildwood of Yallingup 569
Willespie 569
Wills Domain Vineyard 571
Windance Wines 574
Wine By Brad 577
Wise Wine 578
Woodlands 581
Woodside Valley Estate 582
Woody Nook 583
Xanadu Normans Wines 586

McLaren Vale

Aldinga Bay Winery 6
Andrew Garrett 12
Arakoon 17
Bent Creek Vineyards 43
Beresford Wines 44
Blown Away 53
Bosworth 58
Brewery Hill Estates 63
Cape Barren Wines 84
Cascabel 92
Chalk Hill 100
Chapel Hill 102
Clarence Hill 111
Clarendon Hills 112
Classic McLaren Wines 112
Coriole 123
d'Arenberg 133
Dennis 142
DogRidge Vineyard 147
Dowie Doole 151
Dyson Wines 156
Edwards & Chaffey 158
Fern Hill Estate 174
Five Geese/Hillgrove Wines 175
Fox Creek Wines 180
Gemtree Vineyards 189
Geoff Merrill Wines 191
Grancari Estate Wines 205
Hardys Reynella 217
Hardys Tintara 217
Haselgrove 220
Hastwell & Lightfoot 221
Hawkers Gate 221
Hills View Vineyards 234
Hoffmann's 235

Horndale 238
Hugh Hamilton 242
Hugo 242
Ingoldby 247
Kangarilla Road Vineyard & Winery 264
Kay Bros Amery 266
Kimber Wines 272
Koltz 277
McLaren Vale III Associates 310
Maglieri of McLaren Vale 314
Marienberg 317
Marius Wines 319
Maxwell Wines 323
Middlebrook Estate 330
Mr Riggs Wine Company 334
Mitolo Wines 337
Morgan Simpson 343
Needham Estate Wines 365
Neighbours Vineyards 365
Nick Haselgrove Wines 367
Noon Winery 368
Oliverhill 375
Olivers Taranga Vineyards 376
Paxton Wines 390
Penny's Hill 396
Pertaringa 398
Pirramimma 410
Possums Vineyard 417
Potters Clay Vineyards 417
Reynell 433
Richard Hamilton 434
RockBare Wines 442
Rogues Gallery 443
Rosemount Estate (McLaren Vale) 445
Sabella Vineyards 451
Scarpantoni Estate 461
Serafino Wines 467
Shingleback 476
Shirvington 476
Shottesbrooke 477
Simon Hackett 478
Sylvan Springs Estates 499
Tapestry 507
Tatachilla 509
The Fleurieu 515
The Settlement Wine Co. 519
Tinlins 526
Twelve Staves Wine Company 538
Ulithorne 542
Wayne Thomas Wines 559
Wirilda Creek 577
Wirra Wirra 578
Woodstock 583
Yangarra Estate 589

Mornington Peninsula

Barak Estate 29
Barrymore Estate 33
Bayview Estate 38
B'darra Estate 38
Beckingham Wines 39

Boneo Plains 56
Box Stallion 59
Bristol Farm 66
Charlotte's Vineyard 104
Craig Avon Vineyard 125
Crittenden at Dromana 127
Darling Park 134
Dromana Estate 153
Dromana Valley Wines 154
Elan Vineyard 159
Eldridge Estate 160
Elgee Park 160
Ermes Estate 165
Five Sons Estate 176
Foxeys Hangout 181
Frogspond 184
Hickinbotham 230
HPR Wines 241
Hurley Vineyard 245
Karina Vineyard 265
Kooyong 278
Lindenderry at Red Hill 298
Little Valley 300
Main Ridge Estate 314
Mantons Creek Vineyard 316
Marinda Park Vineyard 318
Maritime Estate 318
Massoni 321
Mcrli 326
Merricks Creek Wines 326
Merricks Estate 327
Miceli 328
Montalto Vineyards 338
Moorooduc Estate 342
Morning Star Estate 344
Morning Sun Vineyard 345
Mornington Estate 345
Mount Eliza Estate 351
Myrtaceae 362
Nazaaray 364
Osborns 379
Paradigm Hill 384
Paringa Estate 385
Phaedrus Estate 403
Pier 10 406
Poplar Bend 416
Port Phillip Estate 416
Red Hill Estate 429
Rigel Wines 436
Ryland River 451
Schindler Northway Downs 463
Scorpo Wines 463
Sea Winds Vineyard 465
Silverwood Wines 478
Stonier Wines 492
Stumpy Gully 495
Summerhill Wines 497
Tanglewood Downs 506
Ten Minutes by Tractor Wine Co 512
T'Gallant 513
The Duke Vineyard 514
The Garden Vineyard 516

Tuck's Ridge 536
Turramurra Estate 538
Vale Vineyard 544
Villa Primavera 548
Vintina Estate 550
Wildcroft Estate 567
Willow Creek 570
Winbirra Vineyard 573
Yrsa's Vineyard 599

Mount Barker

Bowmans Wines 59
Chatsfield 107
Deep Water Estate 139
Forest Hill Vineyard 180
Galafrey 184
Gilberts 194
Goundrey 202
Marribrook 319
Merrebee Estate 326
Pattersons 388
Plantagenet 411
Towerhill Estate 532
Trappers Gully 534

Mount Benson

Anthony Dale 16
Baudin Rock Wines 37
Cape Jaffa Wines 85
Dawson Estate 135
Guichen Bay Vineyards 211
Kreglinger Estate 279
M. Chapoutier Australia 323
Murdup Wines 361
Ralph Fowler Wines 425
Stoney Rise 492
Wangolina Station 553
Wehl's Mount Benson Vineyards 560

Mount Gambier

Benarra Vineyards 43
Haig 213

Mount Lofty Ranges Zone

Macaw Creek Wines 307

Mudgee

Abercorn 3
Andrew Harris Vineyards 12
Blue Wren 54
Botobolar 58
Burnbrae 77
Burrundulla 78
Clearview Estate Mudgee 113
Cooyal Grove 122
di Lusso Wines 144
Eljamar 161

Elliot Rocke Estate 162
Farmer's Daughter Wines 170
5 Corners Wines 175
Frog Rock 183
High Valley Wines 232
Huntington Estate 244
Knights Vines 276
Knowland Estate 277
Lawson's Hill 288
Lowe Family Wines 305
Mansfield Wines 316
Martins Hill Wines 320
Miramar 333
Mountilford 353
Mudgee Wines 358
Pieter van Gent 407
Poet's Corner 412
Red Clay Estate 427
Robert Stein Vineyard 439
Seldom Seen Vineyard 465
Shawwood Estate 474
Simon Gilbert Wines 478
Thistle Hill 520
Vinifera Wines 549
Wells Parish Wines 561
Woolshed Wines 584

Murray Darling

Abbey Rock 3
Brockville Wines 66
Callipari Wine 80
Capogreco Winery Estate 88
Carn Estate 91
Deakin Estate 136
Evans & Tate Salisbury 167
Irymple Estate Winery 250
Lindemans (Karadoc) 297
Mildara (Murray Darling) 331
Mulcra Estate Wines 359
Murray Estate 361
Nursery Ridge Estate 371
Pasut Family Wines 386
Purple Patch Wines 422
Ribarits Estate Wines 434
Roberts Estate 439
Robinvale 440
Tall Poppy Wines 503
Trentham Estate 534
Zilzie Wines 601

Nagambie Lakes

Baptista 29
Burramurra 77
Dalfarras 131
David Traeger 135
Kirwan's Bridge Wines 275
McGee Wines 308
McPherson Wines 311
Mitchelton 336
Tahbilk 501

North East Victoria Zone

Upper Murray Estate 543

Northern Rivers Zone

Divers Luck Wines 146
Great Lakes Wines 208
Ilnam Estate 246
Port Stephens Winery 416
Raleigh Winery 425
Red Tail Wines 430
Two Tails Wines 541
Villa d'Esta Vineyard 548

Northern Slopes Zone

Gilgai Winery 194
Kurrajong Downs 280
New England Estate 366
Reedy Creek Vineyard 430
Richfield Estate 434
Tangaratta Estate 505
Warrina Wines 556
Willowvale Wines 571

Northern Tasmania

Andrew Pirie 13
Barringwood Park 33
Bass Fine Wines 35
Bay of Fires 37
Brook Eden Vineyard 68
Bundaleera Vineyard 75
Chartley Estate 104
Cliff House 114
Clover Hill 115
Dalrymple 131
Delamere 140
East Arm Vineyard 157
Elmslie 162
Ghost Rock Vineyard 192
Golders Vineyard 201
Grey Sands 209
Hawley Vineyard 221
Hillwood Vineyard 235
Holm Oak 237
Iron Pot Bay Wines 249
Jansz 253
Jinglers Creek Vineyard 258
Kelly's Creek 268
Lake Barrington Estate 282
Leven Valley Vineyard 293
Moores Hill Estate 341
Pipers Brook Vineyard 409
Providence Vineyards 421
Rosevears Estate 446
Rotherhythe 448
St Matthias 455
Sharmans 473
Silk Hill 477
Sterling Heights 489

Tamar Ridge 504
The Mews 517
Waterton Estate 557
Wilmot Hills Vineyard 572
Wilson's Legana Vineyard 572

Orange

Belgravia Vineyards 41
Belubula Valley Vineyards 42
Bloodwood 53
Brangayne of Orange 61
Burke & Hills 76
Bush Piper Vineyard 78
Canobolas-Smith 83
Cargo Road Wines 89
Dindima Wines 145
Faisan Estate 169
Gold Dust Wines 200
Golden Gully Wines 200
Highland Heritage Estate 232
Ibis Wines 245
Indigo Ridge 247
Jarretts of Orange 254
Logan Wines 302
Mortimers of Orange 346
Nashdale Wines 363
Orange Country Wines 376
Orange Mountain Wines 377
Pinnacle Wines 408
Prince of Orange 420
Printhie Wines 420
Reynolds Vineyards 433
Ross Hill Vineyard 448
Sharpe Wines of Orange 474
Templer's Mill 511
Turner's Vineyard 538
Word of Mouth Wines 584

Padthaway

Browns of Padthaway 72
Henry's Drive 226
Lindemans (Padthaway) 298
Morambro Creek Wines 343
Padthaway Estate 381
Stonehaven 491

Peel

Amarillo Vines 10
Cape Bouvard 84
Drakesbrook Wines 151
Peel Estate 391
Tuart Ridge 535
Wandering Brook Estate 552

Pemberton

Channybearup Vineyard 101
Donnelly River Wines 150
Fonty's Pool Vineyards 179
Gloucester Ridge Vineyard 199

Hidden River Estate 231
Hillbrook Wines 233
Lillian 295
Lost Lake 304
Merum 327
Mountford 352
Petrene Estate 401
Phillips Estate 405
Picardy 405
Salitage 456
Silkwood Wines 477
Southern Dreams 482
Tantemaggie 506
The Warren Vineyard 520
Treen Ridge Estate 534
Wine & Truffle Company 576
WoodSmoke Estate 583

Perricoota

Morrisons Riverview Winery 346
St Anne's Vineyards 452
Stevens Brook Estate 489

Perth Hills

Ashley Estate 19
Avalon Wines 22
Briery Estate 65
Brookside Vineyard 69
Carosa 91
Chidlow's Well Estate 109
Chittering Valley Winery/
    Nesci Estate Wines 109
Cosham 124
Darlington Estate 135
Deep Dene Vineyard 139
François Jacquard 181
Glen Isla Estate 199
Hainault 213
Hartley Estate 219
Jadran 251
Jarrah Ridge Winery 253
Lake Charlotte Wines 282
Millbrook Winery 331
Piesse Brook 407
Scarp Valley Vineyard 462
Stringybark 494
Walsh Family Winery 551
Western Range Wines 564

Porongurup

Castle Rock Estate 94
Duke's Vineyard 155
Fernbrook Estate Wines 173
Gibraltar Rock 193
Ironwood Estate 249
Jingalla 257
Millinup Estate 332
Mount Trio Vineyard 357
Springviews Wine 485
Zarephath Wines 599

Port Phillip Zone

Brunswick Hill Wines 73
Patterson Lakes Estate 388
Rojo Wines 444
Studley Park Vineyard 495
Three Wise Men 524
Toomah Wines 531
Woongarra Estate 584

Pyrenees

Amherst Winery 11
Berrys Bridge 44
Blue Pyrenees Estate 54
Dalwhinnie 132
Horvat Estate 239
Hundred Tree Hill 242
Kara Kara Vineyard 265
Landsborough Valley Estate 284
Massoni 321
Moonbark Estate Vineyard 340
Mount Avoca Winery 348
Peerick Vineyard 391
Polleters 414
Pyrenees Ridge Vineyard 424
Redbank Winery 427
St Ignatius Vineyard 454
Scotts Hill Vineyard 465
Summerfield 496
Taltarni 503
Warrenmang Vineyard & Resort 556

Queensland Coastal

Albert River Wines 6
Archer Falls Vineyard & Winery 17
Big Barrel Vineyard and Winery 47
Brischetto Wines 66
Canungra Valley Vineyards 84
Cedar Creek Estate 96
Delaney's Creek Winery 140
Dingo Creek Vineyard 145
Eumundi Winery 166
Gecko Valley 188
Gin Gin Wines 194
Glastonbury Estate Wines 195
Glengariff Estate Winery 198
Ironbark Ridge Vineyard 248
Kenilworth Bluff Wines 269
Maroochy Springs 319
Nirvana Estate 368
Noosa Valley Winery 369
Norse Wines 370
O'Regan Creek Vineyard and Winery 378
Settlers Rise Montville 469
7 Acres Winery 470
Sirromet Wines 479
Springbrook Mountain Vineyard 483
Tamborine Estate Wines 505
Thumm Estate Wines 524
Twin Oaks 539

Warrego Wines 556
Wonbah Estate 580
Woongooroo Estate 584

Queensland Zone

Governor's Choice Winery 203
Jimbour Wines 256
Kooroomba Vineyards 278
Normanby Wines 369
Rimfire Vineyards 437
Riversands Vineyards 438
Romavilla 444
Stanton Estate 486
Sweet Water Hill Wines 499
Three Moon Creek 523
Vale View Wines 544
Villacoola Vineyard & Winery 548

Riverina

Baratto's 30
Barramundi Wines 32
Beelgara Estate 40
Casella Estate 92
Clancy's of Conargo 111
De Bortoli 136
Lillypilly Estate 296
McWilliam's 312
Melange Wines 325
Miranda Wines 334
Murrin Bridge Wines 361
Nugan Estate 370
Piromit Wines 410
Riverina Estate 438
Terrel Estate Wines 513
Toorak Estate 531
Vico 547
Westend Estate Wines 563
Yerong Creek Estate 598
Zappacosta Estate Wines 599

Riverland

Angove's 14
Banrock Station 28
Berri Estates 44
Bonneyview 57
Broken Earth 67
Cockatoo Ridge 117
Golden Mile Wines 201
Kingston Estate 273
Loch Luna 301
Pennyfield Wines 395
Red Mud 430
Salena Estate 456
Thomson Vintners 522

Rutherglen

All Saints Estate 8
Anderson 11

Bullers Calliopes 74
Campbells 81
Chambers Rosewood 100
Cofield Wines 118
Drinkmoor Wines 153
Gehrig Estate 189
Jones Winery & Vineyard 260
Lake Moodemere Vineyard 283
Lilliput Wines 295
Morris 345
Mount Prior Vineyard 356
Pfeiffer 402
Platt's 411
Rutherglen Estates 450
St Leonards 454
Stanton & Killeen Wines 485
Sutherland Smith Wines 498
Warrabilla 554
Watchbox Wines 556

Shoalhaven Coast

Cambewarra Estate 81
Coolangatta Estate 120
Crooked River Wines 127
Fern Gully Winery 174
Jasper Valley 255
Seven Mile Vineyard 470
The Silos Estate 519

South Burnett

Barambah Ridge 29
Bridgeman Downs 65
Captain's Paddock 88
Clovely Estate 115
Copper Country 123
Crane Winery 126
Dusty Hill Estate 156
Hunting Lodge Estate 243
Kingsley Grove 272
Rodericks 443
Stuart Range 494
Ziebarth Wines 600

South Coast Zone

Cobbitty Wines 117
Grevillea Estate 209
Remo & Son's Vineyard 432
Tilba Valley 524

South West Australia Zone

Barwick Wines 34
WJ Walker Wines 579

Southern Eyre Peninsula

Boston Bay Wines 57
Delacolline Estate 140

Southern Fleurieu

Allusion Wines 9
Angus Wines 14
Duerden's Wines 155
Mt Billy 349
Mt Jagged Wines 353
Parri Estate 386
Trafford Hill Vineyard 533
Twin Bays 538
Victor Harbor Winery 547

Southern Flinders Ranges

Bundaleer Wines 74
Springton Cellars 484

Southern Highlands

Centennial Vineyards 98
Cuttaway Hill Estate 131
Howards Lane Vineyard 241
Joadja Vineyards 259
McVitty Grove 311
Saint Derycke's Wood Winery 453
Southern Highland Wines 483
Statford Park 486

Southern New South Wales Zone

Bidgeebong Wines 47
Charles Sturt University Winery 103
Eling Forest Winery 161
Kells Creek Vineyards 267
Lambert Vineyards 283
Mount Panorama Winery 356
Mundrakoona Estate 360
Snowy River Winery 482
Transylvania Winery 534

Southern Tasmania

Apsley Gorge Vineyard 16
Bamajura 27
Bellendena 42
Bracken Hill 60
Bream Creek 62
Broadview Estate 66
Casa Fontana 91
Charles Reuben Estate 103
Clemens Hill 113
Coal Valley Vineyard 116
Colmaur 119
Coombend Estate 121
Craigie Knowe 125
Craigow 126
Cross Rivulet 128
Crosswinds Vineyard 128
Darlington Vineyard 135
Derwent Estate 142
Domaine A 147
Elsewhere Vineyard 163
ese Vineyards 165

572 Richmond Road 176
Fluted Cape Vineyard 178
Freycinet 182
Frogmore Creek 183
Geebin Wines 188
GlenAyr 196
Grandview Vineyard 206
Hartzview Wine Centre 219
Herons Rise Vineyard 229
Home Hill 237
Jollymont 260
Kelvedon 269
Kinvarra Estate 274
Kraanwood 279
Laurel Bank 287
Meadowbank Estate 324
Meure's Wines 328
Milford Vineyard 331
Moorilla Estate 341
Morningside Wines 344
Nandroya Estate 363
No Regrets Vineyard 369
Observatory Hill Vineyard 373
Orani Vineyard 377
Oyster Cove Vineyard 381
Palmara 382
Panorama 383
Pembroke 392
Pontville Station 414
Pooley Wines 415
Puddleduck Vineyard 421
Richmond Park Vineyard 435
Spring Vale Vineyards 484
Stefano Lubiana 487
Tinderbox Vineyard 526
Touchwood Wines 532
Wellington 560
Wharncliffe 564
Winstead 577
Yaxley Estate 595

Southwest Australia Zone

Dalyup River Estate 132

Strathbogie Ranges

Antcliff's Chase 16
Baarrooka Vineyard 23
Dominion Wines 149
Elgo Estate 160
Maygars Hill Winery 323
Plunkett 412
The Falls Vineyard 515

Sunbury

Andraos Bros 12
Arundel 19
Bacchanalia Estate 23
Bacchus Hill 24
Craiglee 125

Diggers Rest 143
Fenton Views Winery 172
Galli Estate 185
Goona Warra Vineyard 201
Kennedys Keilor Valley 269
Ray-Monde 426
Wildwood 568
Witchmount Estate 579

Swan District

Aquila Estate 17
Carabooda Estate 88
Faranda Wines 170
Gilead Estate 194
Platypus Lane Wines 411
Susannah Brook Wines 497
Valley Wines 544
Vino Italia 550

Swan Hill

Andrew Peace Wines 13
Brumby Wines 72
Bulga Wine Estates 73
Bullers Beverford 73
Carpinteri Vineyards 91
Oak Dale Wines 372
Renewan Murray Gold Wines 432
Yellymong 595

Swan Valley

Ambrook Wines 10
Baxter Stokes Wines 37
Carilley Estate 90
Faber Vineyard 169
Garbin Estate 186
Henley Park Wines 226
Highway Wines 232
Holly Folly 237
Houghton 239
Jane Brook Estate 252
John Kosovich Wines 259
Lamont Wines 284
LedaSwan 290
Lilac Hill Estate 294
Little River Wines 300
Mann 316
Moondah Brook 340
Oakover Estate 372
Olive Farm 375
Pinelli 408
RiverBank Estate 437
Sandalford 458
Sittella Wines 480
Swanbrook Estate Wines 499
Swan Valley Wines 499
Talijancich 501
The Natural Wine Company 518
Upper Reach Vineyard 543
Windy Creek Estate 576

Sydney Basin

Camden Estate Vineyards 81
Gledswood Homestead and Winery 196
Kirkham Estate 274
Richmond Estate 435
Tizzana Winery 528
Vicarys 547

The Peninsulas Zone

Gregory's Wines 209

Tumbarumba

Excelsior Peak 168
Glenburnie Vineyard 197
Lighthouse Peak 294
Tumbarumba Wine Estates 537
Tumbarumba Wine Growers 537

Upper Goulburn

Beattie Wines 38
Cathedral Lane Wines 95
Cheviot Bridge/Long Flat 108
Delatite 141
Glen Creek Wines 197
Growlers Gully 211
Henke 226
Kinloch Wines 274
Little River Estate 300
Lost Valley Winery 304
Louee 305
Melaleuca Grove 325
Mount Cathedral Vineyards 350
Murrindindi 362
Penbro Estate 392
Peppin Ridge 397
Rees Miller Estate 431
Scrubby Creek Wines 465
Strath Valley Vineyard 493
Tallarook 502

Upper Hunter Valley

Allyn River Wines 9
Arrowfield 18
Bell's Lane Wines 41
Birnam Wood Wines 50
Camyr Allyn Wines 82
Cruickshank Callatoota Estate 128
Glendonbrook 197
Horseshoe Vineyard 238
Hunter Park 243
James Estate 251
London Lodge Estate 302
Penmara 394
Polin & Polin Wines 413
Pyramid Hill Wines 423
Rosemount Estate (Hunter Valley) 445
Southern Grand Estate 482

Two Rivers 540
Winbourne Wines 574
Yarraman Estate 591

Warehouse

Bress 62
Broken Gate Wines 67
Burton Premium Wines 78
Calyla Vines Estate 80
Celtic Farm 97
Hewitson 229
Journeys End Vineyards 260
Lashmar 286
Lengs & Cooter 291
Paperbark Vines 383
Peter Howland Wines 399
Timmins Wines 525
Two Hands Wines 539
Will Taylor Wines 571

Western Plains Zone

Boora Estate 57
Canonbah Bridge 83
Lazy River Estate 288
Red Earth Estate Vineyard 427
Tombstone Estate 529
Wattagan Estate Winery 558

Western Victoria Zone

Empress Vineyard 164
Red Rock Winery 430

Wrattonbully

Kopparossa Wines 278
Russet Ridge 450
Stone Coast 490
Tapanappa 507

Yarra Valley

Ainsworth Estate 5
Allinda 8
Arthurs Creek Estate 19
Badger's Brook 24
Bianchet 46
Brahams Creek Winery 60
Britannia Creek Wines 66
Bulong Estate 74
Burgi Hill Vineyard 76
Cahillton 79
Carlei Estate & Green Vineyards 90
Coldstream Hills 118
Coombe Farm Vineyard 121
Copper Bull Wines 123
Dawson's Patch Valley 136
De Bortoli (Victoria) 138
Diamond Valley Vineyards 143
Di Stasio 146

Dixons Run 146
Domaine Chandon 148
Dominique Portet 149
Elmswood Estate 162
Eltham Vineyards 163
Evelyn County Estate 168
Fergusson 172
Five Oaks Vineyard 176
Gembrook Hill 189
Giant Steps 192
Gracedale Hills Estate 204
Hanson-Tarrahill Vineyard 215
Healesville Ridge 222
Helen's Hill Estate 225
Henkell Wines 226
Hillcrest Vineyards 233
Hills of Plenty 234
Immerse 246
International Vintners Australia 248
Kellybrook 268
Killara Park Estate 271
Kings of Kangaroo Ground 272
Labyrinth 281
Langbrook Estate Vineyard 285
Lillydale Estate 295
Lirralirra Estate 299
Long Gully Estate 302
Lovegrove Vineyard and Winery 305
Metier Wines 328
Monbulk Winery 338
Morgan Vineyards 343
Mount Delancey Winery 351
Mount Mary 355
Naked Range Wines 362
Oakridge 372
Panton Hill Winery 383
Paternoster 387
Punt Road 422
Ridgeback Wines 436
Ridgeline 436
RiverStone Wines 438
Rochford's Eyton 441

Roundstone Winery & Vineyard 449
St Huberts 454
Samson Hill Estate 457
Seville Estate 471
Seville Hill 472
Shantell 473
Shelmerdine Vineyards 475
SpringLane 484
Steels Creek Estate 487
Sticks 490
Strathewen Hills 493
Sutherland Estate 498
Tarrawarra Estate 508
The Oaks Vineyard and Winery 518
Tin Cows 526
Tokar Estate 529
Toolangi Vineyards 530
Train Trak 533
Wantirna Estate 554
Warramate 555
Wedgetail Estate 559
Whispering Hills 565
Whitsend Estate 566
Yarrabank 590
Yarra Brook Estate 590
Yarra Burn 590
Yarra Edge 591
Yarrambat Estate 591
Yarra Ridge 592
Yarra Track Wines 592
Yarra Vale 593
Yarra Valley Gateway Estate 593
Yarra Valley Hills 593
Yarra Valley Vineyards 593
Yarrawalla Wines 593
Yarra Yarra 594
Yarra Yering 594
Yeringberg 596
Yering Farm 596
Yering Range Vineyard 597
Yering Station 597